THE LIBRARY OF CHRISTIAN
CLASSICS

VOLUME XX

CALVIN:
INSTITUTES OF THE CHRISTIAN
RELIGION

THE LIBRARY OF CHRISTIAN CLASSICS

Volume XX

CALVIN:

INSTITUTES OF THE CHRISTIAN RELIGION

IN TWO VOLUMES

(VOL. XX: BOOKS I.i TO III.xix)

Edited by

JOHN T. McNEILL

Auburn Professor Emeritus of Church History
Union Theological Seminary
New York

Translated and Indexed by

FORD LEWIS BATTLES

Philip Schaff Professor of Church History
The Hartford Theological Seminary
Hartford, Connecticut

in collaboration with the editor
and a committee of advisers

Philadelphia

THE WESTMINSTER PRESS

Published simultaneously in the United States of America and in Great Britain by The Westminster Press, Philadelphia, and the S. C. M. Press, Ltd., London.

Library of Congress Catalog Card No. 60-5379

ISBN 0-664-22020-7 (Vol. 1)

Printed in the United States of America

18   19   20   21   22   23

GENERAL EDITORS' PREFACE

The Christian Church possesses in its literature an abundant and incomparable treasure. But it is an inheritance that must be reclaimed by each generation. THE LIBRARY OF CHRISTIAN CLASSICS is designed to present in the English language, and in twenty-six volumes of convenient size, a selection of the most indispensable Christian treatises written prior to the end of the sixteenth century.

The practice of giving circulation to writings selected for superior worth or special interest was adopted at the beginning of Christian history. The canonical Scriptures were themselves a selection from a much wider literature. In the patristic era there began to appear a class of works of compilation (often designed for ready reference in controversy) of the opinions of well-reputed predecessors, and in the Middle Ages many such works were produced. These medieval anthologies actually preserve some noteworthy materials from works otherwise lost.

In modern times, with the increasing inability even of those trained in universities and theological colleges to read Latin and Greek texts with ease and familiarity, the translation of selected portions of earlier Christian literature into modern languages has become more necessary than ever; while the wide range of distinguished books written in vernaculars such as English makes selection there also needful. The efforts that have been made to meet this need are too numerous to be noted here, but none of these collections serves the purpose of the reader who desires a library of representative treatises spanning the Christian centuries as a whole. Most of them embrace only the age of the church fathers, and some of them have long been out of print. A fresh translation of a work already translated may shed much new light upon its meaning. This is true even of Bible translations despite the work of many experts through the centuries. In some instances old translations have been adopted in this series, but wherever necessary or desirable, new ones have been made. Notes have been supplied where these were needed to explain the author's meaning. The introductions provided for the several treatises and extracts will, we believe, furnish welcome guidance.

JOHN BAILLIE
JOHN T. McNEILL
HENRY P. VAN DUSEN

CONTENTS

xi

page

page

CONTENTS xvii

EDITOR'S PREFACE

To bring to English readers this work of magnitude and importance, unimpaired in its energy and power, was a task to be approached with fear and trembling. It was felt that, to assure a satisfactory result, more than a translator and an editor were needed. Accordingly a corps of expert Latinists and Calvin scholars was enlisted to read and criticize the translation as it was being prepared. Those who have been associated with the work in this way are: Dr. Albert Billheimer, Professor Emeritus of Classics, New York University; Dr. John S. Burleigh, Principal of New College, Edinburgh; Dr. Allen Cabaniss, Professor of History, University of Mississippi; Dr. Edward A. Dowey, Jr., Professor of the History of Christian Doctrine, Princeton Theological Seminary; Dr. George E. McCracken, Professor of Classics, Drake University; Dr. M. Eugene Osterhaven, Professor of Systematic Theology, Western Theological Seminary; Dr. Matthew Spinka, Professor Emeritus of Church History, Hartford Theological Seminary, and Dr. Leonard J. Trinterud, Professor of Church History, McCormick Theological Seminary. With a generous expenditure of time and thought, these scholars have compared, in whole or in part, the draft of the translation with the Latin text, and have offered specific criticisms which have been gratefully utilized in the subsequent process of revision. None of these valued associates is in any degree responsible for the wording finally adopted. As editor I have been closely in touch with the work of translation at all stages.

The translation is furnished with headings of two sorts. (*a*) The chapters, excepting only a few very short ones, are subdivided into several parts with headings (here original) supplied. (*b*) Subordinate to these are headings for each of the sections separately numbered in the 1559 edition. Most of these section headings are translated from those provided in the German edition of Otto Weber. They are here employed by kind permission of Professor Weber and his publishers, Verlag der Buchhandlung des Erziehungsvereins, Neukirchen Kreis Moers. Where, as is not infrequently the case, Dr. Weber has not given a heading for a numbered section, one is supplied. In rare cases, a heading given by him has been shortened or otherwise altered, and in a few instances, the editor has substituted a heading of his own. The section headings here marked with an asterisk (*) are freshly inserted; those marked with a dagger (†) are Weber's with some variation; those unmarked are taken over simply from him, mainly in Dr. Battles' translation.

With regard to the footnotes, indebtedness is gratefully acknowledged to Professor Dowey, who, following an early arrangement, provided materials that have been incorporated in numerous theological notes in Books I and II, and to the translator, who has spotted a number of hitherto unnoticed classical and patristic references, and supplied other data. Valued, if incidental, contributions have also been made by a number of scholars in conversation and correspondence. All such contributed materials have of necessity been so merged with my own comments that I alone must take responsibility for the form and content of the notes as they now appear, and be charged with all their errors and defects.

The work of European editors of the *Institutes* has been freely utilized. Among these there is a primary indebtedness to the *Institutio Christianae religionis, 1559,* edited by Peter Barth and Wilhelm Niesel, which comprises Volumes III, IV, and V of their five-volume series *Joannis Calvini Opera Selecta.* These editors furnish copious notes in Latin, which are arranged in two classes, cited, respectively, by the use of letters and Arabic numerals. The former record variations in the texts published in Calvin's lifetime; the latter consist in part of the annotations found in the earlier successive Latin editions with many needed corrections, and in part of citations, never previously made, of passages to which Calvin alludes without identification. To identify accurately the vast number of such hidden references is perhaps not humanly possible, but Barth and Niesel have made an impressive attempt to do this. They provide, however, in general, citations only, bearing no explicit information on the content, or the context, of the passage referred to. The present editor has in nearly all instances gone to the original passage, and where it seemed useful toward the explanation of Calvin's argument, has offered a word of interpretation, or a short quotation or paraphrase. Detailed recognition of the debt to Barth and Niesel would have been absurdly cumbrous: it can be discovered on almost every page by anyone who cares to make a comparison. But there has been no hesitation in disregarding some of their citations where the matter concerned seemed possibly unoriginal in the source given, or of a trivial nature, or where the identification seemed questionable. In a very few instances comparison will disclose the correction of an inaccurate citation. For the convenience of the reader, English translations of the sources noted have been cited wherever possible, along with editions of the original texts.

In the case of the notes supplied by the editors of French editions of the work, dependence has not been so constant, and in general has been acknowledged in detail except when quite secondary. The edition of the 1541 French text by J. Pannier and others has yielded a good deal of needed material. J.-D. Benoit's critical edition of the French text of 1560, so far as published (Books I–III), has also been an indispensable aid. Frequent use has been made also of notes in J. Cadier's modernized version of the 1560 text. While the notes in these editions are naturally concerned primarily with matters of text and language, they also furnish a good deal of direction in the historical and theological interpretation of the work.

Many of the footnotes will be found to be independent of the work of previous editors. This is generally the case in references to historical events and historical studies, and to theological writings of the centuries between Calvin's and our own. The citations of Calvin's predecessors, classical and ecclesiastical, extend somewhat beyond those previously given. New also are a few relevant allusions in the field of *belles lettres*. In a work of such range as the *Institutes* the possibility of annotation is limitless. The purpose held in view has been simply to clarify the work for the modern reader, and, by a selected minimum of serviceable information and interpretative comment, to give an impression of its theological and historical depth and range.

It would be tedious to name all the libraries in which materials for the notes have been obtained. Most of the labor was done in the Harvard Andover and Widener Libraries, the Folger Shakespeare Library, the Library of Congress, the Library of Union Theological Seminary, and the New York Public Library. Books and films have been made available through these libraries from many others. The courteous and efficient help of many librarians has been highly appreciated. The difficult task of typing the notes has been done by Mrs. Robert C. Douglas; and the consistency and accuracy of the citations have been greatly enhanced through the patient labor of the staff of The Westminster Press, especially by Mrs. Mildred G. Lehr, Mrs. Marian Noecker, and Miss Lucille Wolfe.

The editor is extremely grateful to the Trustees of the Folger Shakespeare Library for having appointed him to a fellowship to pursue the work. He is also deeply indebted to the Simon Guggenheim Foundation for the award of a fellowship which at a later stage relieved the financial burden of research. The interest and encouragement of Dr. Paul L. Meacham of The Westminster Press have been a constant support. Special thanks are also due to Dr. Baillie and Dr. Van Dusen, editors of the series, and to Professor Osterhaven, for their critical reading of the Introduction in draft form; the two last named have also helpfully examined a draft of most of the footnotes.

J. T. M.

TRANSLATOR'S NOTE

The translation of John Calvin's *Institutes of the Christian Religion* here offered has been newly made from the 1559 Latin Text [VL] as edited by Barth and Niesel, collated, however, with the earlier editions of that text and also with the 1536, 1539, 1543, 1545, 1550, 1553, and 1554 versions. The French versions [VG] of 1560 (CR and Benoit) and of 1541 (Pannier) have been consulted: where a rendering has been adopted from the French, the fact is duly noted. Occasional recourse has been had to the Dutch of A. Sizoo and the German of O. Weber.

Behind the present English version lie extensive studies of Calvin's vocabulary and investigations of his Scriptural usage. These have been entered on thousands of slips which have also served as the basis of full indexes published in this edition. Particular attention has been paid to the nuances of Calvin's synonyms: e.g., *amor/charitas/dilectio, deitas/divinitas/numen, foedus/pactio/pactum/testamentum, tessera/symbolum/signum, constringere/obdurare/obfirmare/indurare/roborare/aggravare,* etc. The aim has been to achieve a reasonably consistent rendering of Calvin's meaning in modern English.

In attempting to transmit something of the directness and color of Calvin's Latin, the translator has broken up many long sentences, so foreign to current English prose, and has avoided wherever possible the aridities of a heavily Latinate theological language—while at the same time honoring the precise distinctions of Calvin's thought. And he has not softened the vivid and sometimes harsh language of the text. In recasting an ancient work in modern idiom there is always a dilemma: how to balance faithfulness to the original over against due attention to the current ways of English speech.

A word of explanation needs to be said about the handling of Calvin's Scriptural usage in the present translation. At the outset, it became obvious that Calvin more often quotes Scripture *ad sensum* than *ad litteram* and that even when he is quoting directly very often no known Scriptural version is followed verbatim. As a consequence, there has been frequent collation of Scriptural passages with Calvin's Commentaries [Comm.], with the Vulgate [Vg.], the Septuagint [LXX], and the Hebrew. Erasmus has also been consulted, and in a few instances (in Proverbs, where no commentary of Calvin exists) parallels with the Geneva Bible have been noted. Even in the same section two different renderings of a verse may be found. When Scripture has been cast in *oratio obliqua,* pronouns shifted, or other slight alteration made by Calvin, the citation has been marked with a "p" and carried in quotation marks. While no attempt has been made to exhaust Calvin's Scriptural usage, many new citations have been added, and previous inaccuracies have been silently corrected. Where comparative studies of the *Institutes,* Commentaries, and Biblical text have shed light (as in the instance of the hardening of Pharaoh's heart, I.xviii.2; II.iv.4; etc.), Calvin's citations of Scripture have been closely inspected and altered wherever necessary.

The reader will observe certain superscript letters in the text of the translation. These indicate five main editorial strata and three lesser ones, as follows: a-1536, b-1539, c-1543, d-1550, e-1559. The editions of 1545, 1553, and 1554 are signaled by "x" with a footnote indicating which edition is involved. Of necessity, this device cannot indicate the more minute textual alterations (for these the reader is referred to Barth and Niesel's *Opera Selecta*), but the primary editorial blocs are indicated. Capitalization conforms to the practice of The Westminster Press; pronouns referring to the Deity are capitalized only to avoid necessary ambiguity.

The translator wishes here to acknowledge the aid of the board of critics mentioned and a personal debt to Professor Goodwin Beach of Trinity College, Hartford, Connecticut. He is indebted to the libraries of the Hartford Seminary Foundation, of McCormick Seminary, and of the Library of the Seminary of the Église Libre du Canton de Vaud (Lausanne, Switzerland) for their assistance. Lastly, he acknowledges the help of many students, of his typist, Mrs. C. Freeman Reynolds, and of his wife, who read the whole work in its various drafts.

F. L. B.

ABBREVIATIONS AND SYMBOLS

ABBREVIATIONS

ACW—*Ancient Christian Writers.*

ANF—*The Ante-Nicene Fathers.*

Aquinas, *Summa Theol.*—Thomas Aquinas, *Summa Theologica.*

Augustine, *Psalms*—Augustine, *Enarrationes in Psalmos.*

Augustine, *John's Gospel*—Augustine, *In Joannis evangelium tractatus.*

Ayer, *Source Book*—Ayer, J. C., *A Source Book of Ancient Church History.*

Benoit, *Institution*—Benoit, J.-D., *Jean Calvin: Institution de la Religion Chrestienne,* livres I–III.

Cadier, *Institution*—Cadier, J. and Marcel, P., *Jean Calvin: Institution de la Religion Chrétienne.*

Calvin, *Letters*—*Letters of John Calvin,* ed. J. Bonnet.

Calvin, *Tracts*—*Calvin's Tracts.*

CC—*Corpus Catholicorum. Werke catholischer Schriftsteller im Zeitalter der Glaubens-spaltung.*

CCL—*Corpus Christianorum, series Latina.*

Comm.—Commentary, in the text designates a Scripture passage conforming to translation given, in the notes indicates a statement made in the appropriate commentary of Calvin.

CR—*Corpus Reformatorum: Johannis Calvini Opera quae supersunt omnia.*

CR Melanchthon—*Corpus Reformatorum: Philippi Melanchthonis Opera quae supersunt omnia.*

CR Zwingli—*Corpus Reformatorum: Huldreich Zwinglis sämmtliche Werke.*

CSEL—*Corpus Scriptorum Ecclesiasticorum Latinorum.*

Doumergue, *Calvin*—Doumergue, É., *Jean Calvin—Les hommes et les choses de son temps.*

Du Cange, *Glossarium*—C. du F. Du Cange, *Glossarium ad scriptores mediae et infimae latinitatis.*

FC—*Fathers of the Church.*

Friedberg—Friedberg, E. (ed.), *Corpus iuris canonici.*

HDRE—Hastings, J. (ed.), *Dictionary of Religion and Ethics.*

Hefele-Leclercq—Hefele, C. J., ed. Leclercq, H., *Histoire des conciles d'après les documents originaux.*

Heppe RD—Heppe, H., *Reformed Dogmatics.* Tr. G. T. Thomson.

Herminjard, *Correspondance*—Herminjard, A.-L., *Correspondance des Réformateurs dans les pays de langue française.*

GCS—*Die griechischen Christlichen Schriftsteller der ersten drei Jahrhunderte.*

LCC—*The Library of Christian Classics.*

LCL—*The Loeb Classical Library.*

LF—*A Library of the Fathers of the Holy Catholic Church.*

Lombard, *Sentences*—Peter Lombard, *Libri quatuor sententiarum.*

Luther, *Werke* WA—*Martin Luthers Werke.* Kritische Gesammtausgabe. Weimar.

LXX—The Septuagint: Greek version of the Old Testament.

Mansi—Mansi, J. D., *Sacrorum conciliorum nova et amplissima collectio.*

MGH—*Monumenta Germaniae Historica.*

MPG—Migne, J. P., *Patrologiae cursus completus, series Graeca.*

MPL—Migne, J. P., *Patrologiae cursus completus, series Latina.*

NPNF—*A Select Library of the Nicene and Post-Nicene Fathers,* first series.

NPNF—2 ser.—Second series of the above.

OS—Barth, P. and Niesel, W., *Calvini Opera Selecta.*

p.—paraphrase, designates a Scripture quotation or near-quotation, not conforming fully to any as yet ascertainable source; many of these are in *oratio obliqua.*

Pannier, *Institution*—Pannier, J., and others, *Oeuvres complètes de Calvin: Institution de la Religion Chrestienne.*

par.—paragraph.

Schaff, *Creeds*—Schaff, P., *The Creeds of Christendom.*

sec.—section, especially one of the numbered sections of chapters in the *Institutes.*

Smits—Smits, L., *Saint Augustine dans l'oeuvre de Jean Calvin.*

Vg.—Vulgate version of the Bible.

VG—*Versio Gallica.* French text of the *Institutes.*

Wendel, *Calvin*—Wendel, F., *Calvin: Sources et évolution de sa pensée religieuse.*

SYMBOLS

a—edition of 1536
b—edition of 1539
c—edition of 1543
d—edition of 1550
e—edition of 1559
e(b)—edition of 1539 as altered in 1559
e/b—of mixed origin
x—with a footnote indicates editions of 1545, 1553, 1554
*—following a section title indicates that the title has been supplied by the present editor.
†—indicates that the section title is taken from the German translation of the *Institutes* by Otto Weber, but with modification.

Introduction

THE CELEBRATED TREATISE HERE PRESENTED IN A NEW ENGLISH translation holds a place in the short list of books that have notably affected the course of history, molding the beliefs and behavior of generations of mankind. Perhaps no other theological work has so consistently retained for four centuries a place on the reading list of studious Christians. In a wider circle, its title has been familiar, and vague ideas of its content have been in circulation. It has, from time to time, called forth an extensive literature of controversy. It has been assailed as presenting a harsh, austere, intolerant Christianity and so perverting the gospel of Christ, and it has been admired and defended as an incomparable exposition of Scriptural truth and a bulwark of evangelical faith. Even in times when it was least esteemed, its influence remained potent in the life of active churches and in the habits of men. To many Christians whose worship was proscribed under hostile governments, this book has supplied the courage to endure. Wherever in the crises of history social foundations are shaken and men's hearts quail, the pages of this classic are searched with fresh respect. In our generation, when most theological writers are schooled in the use of methods, and of a terminology, widely differing from those employed by Calvin, this masterpiece continues to challenge intensive study, and contributes a reviving impulse to thinking in the areas of Christian doctrine and social duty.

I

The *Christianae religionis institutio* (to cite the first form of Calvin's title) sprang from the vivid experience of a gifted young man amid the revival of Scriptural Christianity that marked the Protestant Reformation. We have every reason to believe that Calvin's convictions were born of struggle and anguish, though we cannot be certain of the stages through which he came or of the date of what he calls his "sudden conversion." From a boyhood in the cathedral city of Noyon he went early to the University of Paris and later studied law in Orléans and Bourges, but turned from the legal profession to give his attention to classical literature. During the decade of these activities (1523–1533) he must have been increasingly aware of the religious crisis of the age that was now manifesting itself in France in Biblical studies, evangelical fervor, persecution, and martyrdom.

When his friend Nicolas Cop[1] became rector of the University, Calvin was in some way implicated in the rectorial address he delivered, November 1, 1533. This discourse has been too hastily regarded as a definitely Protestant utterance. Rather, it reflects the Biblical humanism of the party of Marguerite d'Angoulême, inspired by the influential but now very aged scholar, Jacques Lefèvre of Étaples (Faber Stapulensis), who had translated the Bible into French. Some acquaintance with Luther is also evident in the address, but it does not bear proof of having been written by one who had espoused Reformation doctrines. Nevertheless, its boldness alarmed the authorities, and because of his association with it Calvin was in flight and hiding through most of the following year. In the spring, after a visit to Lefèvre at Nérac, he went to Noyon to act on a new decision. There May 4, 1534, he resigned the clerical benefices that had been provided for him during his childhood, and thus broke off relations with the unreformed church and clergy.[2] It is possible that the talks with Lefèvre, the spent leader of the non-Protestant Biblical movement, formed the occasion of his "conversion," which set him definitely within the Protestant ranks.

A new stage now began. He would never cease thereafter from tireless activity in the cause of evangelical faith. Later in that year he wrote two ardent prefaces that were to appear at the beginning of the Old Testament and of the new Testament in the French Bible prepared by his cousin, Pierre Robert Olivétan,

---

[1] Nicolas Cop was the son of Guillaume Cop, distinguished Paris physician and scholar. In the weeks preceding the address, Nicolas Cop had strongly defended at the University the cause of Marguerite d'Angoulême, sister of the king, whose *Mirror of a Sinful Soul* had been condemned by the Sorbonne. Cop's address (*Concio academica*) is printed in the works of Calvin, CR X. ii. 30–36; OS I. iv–x.

[2] Discussions of these events, and of the conversion of Calvin, include the following: P. Imbart de la Tour, *Les Origines de la Réforme* I. 478–568; J. Viénot, *Histoire de la Réforme française des origines a l'Édit de Nantes,* Pt. ii, ch. 1; F. Wendel, *Calvin: Sources et évolution de sa pensée religieuse,* pp. 20–26; J. T. McNeill, *The History and Character of Calvinism,* ch. vii.

for the Waldenses of Piedmont. When this book was published, in June, 1535, Calvin was in Basel and his manuscript of the *Institutes of the Christian Religion*[3] was undoubtedly at an advanced stage. A beginning of the work may have been made in 1534 while he was still in France. The Du Tillet family had then given him shelter and "a quiet nest" at Claix in Angoulême. To say the least, the extensive library to which he there had access may have furnished materials later to be incorporated in the book.

In France, the situation became more and more precarious for all marked leaders of the new movement. For this reason, and because he was surrounded by inquirers wherever he went, Calvin decided to seek abroad a safe retreat for study. About the beginning of January, 1535, he left France and made his way to Basel. Many Protestants were at that time taking flight from the growingly intense persecution. The king, Francis I,[4] had been incensed by the incident of the Placards, October 18, 1534, when copies of a handbill containing crude attacks on the Mass were in the night attached to public buildings and even thrust into the royal bedchamber. Many suspects were imprisoned and burnings took place from day to day.

[3] The word *institutio,* sometimes in the plural, *institutiones,* appears often in the titles of Latin works on law and is employed by Christian writers in titles of compendia on various topics, e.g., by Lactantius, Ambrose, Isidore, Paul the Deacon, Hinkmar, and Bernard. In his choice of the word, however, Calvin may have recalled its use by Erasmus in *Institutio principis Christiani* (1516), or by Guillaume Budé in *L'Institution du prince* (1516), which, though unpublished (until 1547), may easily have been available to Calvin, who was well acquainted with Budé's family. Erasmus' title has been rendered, in L. W. Born's translation, "The Education of a Christian Prince." A common rendering of *institutio* in this sense is "instruction." Thus German versions have rendered the word *Unterweisung* or *Unterricht;* the Dutch have used *onderwijsinghe,* modern *onderwijzing.* See also Q. Breen, *John Calvin: A Study in French Humanism,* pp. 119 ff., and J. T. McNeill, *Christian Hope for World Society,* pp. 90–95. The plural form does not appear in the title of the whole work prior to 1654, when it was used in the Elzevir edition. In English, "Institution" was, until 1813, the word commonly used in references and uniformly in the title of the work when published in its entirety. But in 1580, Edward May, the translator of Edmund Bunney's abridgment, has *Institutions,* and this form was followed by Henry Holland in his English version of John Piscator's *Aphorisms* in 1596. John Allen, in his translation of the entire treatise, employed the word *Institutes,* 1813, and this form has since prevailed. (See below, p. xlv.)

[4] King of France, 1515–1547. Francis was a patron of the Renaissance. His policy toward the church was designed to secure his control of it. This involved some conception of its reform, but his attitude toward the Protestants within his kingdom was increasingly hostile.

It is principally in the Preface to his Commentary on the Psalms,[5] published in 1558, that Calvin informs us of this crucial period in his life. With simple eloquence he tells how, after he left his native land to seek "a quiet hiding place" for his studies, reports reached him of the many burnings taking place in France and the perverse explanations given for these. While Calvin "was hidden unknown at Basel," false statements emanating from the French court were being circulated in German circles to allay the severe anti-French reaction to which the persecutions had given rise. These statements, as Calvin says, represented the sufferers as consisting of "Anabaptists and seditious men." Such a manifesto, supposedly from the hand of Guillaume du Bellay, brother of the bishop of Paris and negotiator for the king with the German governments and theologians, is known to have been issued at the beginning of February.[6] Convinced that such declarations were intended to excuse greater bloodshed to come, Calvin decided that silence on his part would entail a just charge of cowardice and treachery. He could not be silent while those who had suffered death for their faith, and whom he regarded as faithful and "holy martyrs," were so grossly misrepresented, and while many still living were similarly imperiled. Some of the sufferers were his personal friends, notably the Paris merchant, Étienne de la Forge, a Waldensian from Piedmont, who was burned February 15, 1535. He felt bound, as he says, to "vindicate from undeserved insult my brethren whose death was precious in the sight of the Lord," and, by moving foreign peoples, to help the cause of others exposed to the same sufferings. Under the impact of these events the book took shape. Whatever his previous intentions regarding his work may have been, he now made speed to prepare it for publication.

While he labored at his book from January to August, 1535, he continued to learn of grave events in France. The attempt of the king to suppress all printing failed, but the persecution was intensified at the end of January and was little abated until July, when the death of the aged Cardinal Duprat, credited with the direction of the king's religious policy, brought a lull. Negotiations with the German Lutherans, begun by the French court two years earlier but interrupted, were now resumed. A pressing invitation was conveyed to Melanchthon and Bucer to come to Paris for consultation on church reform, and this project was not abandoned until August 28, a few days after Calvin completed

---

[5] CR XXXI. 23–27; tr. Comm. Psalms I. xli ff.; LCC XXIII. 51 ff.
[6] J. Viénot, *op. cit.*, p. 129.

his manuscript of the *Institutio*.[7] The fact that the king seemed inconsistent and irresolute in all this probably led many Protestants to hope for a favorable change. In the same period, Calvin had reason to fear that the Protestant cause in Europe would be discredited by the revolutionary Anabaptist movement centering in Münster, whose adherents were after a long siege ruthlessly crushed at the end of June, 1535. Calvin may have hoped to have his book appear at the Frankfurt autumn fair in 1535, but the manuscript was not completed until August 23 of that year, the date that he appends with his name to the Prefatory Address to Francis I, which precedes the treatise. The Basel printers, Thomas Platter and Balthasar Lasius, with the editorial co-operation of Jean Oporin, proceeding without haste, issued it in March, 1536. The Latin title of this first edition may be translated as follows:

The Institute of the Christian Religion, Containing almost the Whole Sum of Piety and Whatever It is Necessary to Know in the Doctrine of Salvation. A Work Very Well Worth Reading by All Persons Zealous for Piety, and Lately Published. A Preface to the Most Christian King of France, in Which this Book is Presented to Him as a Confession of Faith. Author, John Calvin, of Noyon. Basel, MDXXXVI.

II

Both parts of the title have significance. The word *institutio* itself was familiar in the sense of "instruction" or "education." The work was designed both as a compendium of the doctrines of the Christian religion and as a confession offered to a persecuting king in behalf of the author's fellow believers. Not only the Prefatory Address, a powerful and direct plea to the king, but at many points the work itself is alive with realization of the historic crisis amid which it was written. Themes of fundamental concern for the religious mind, grandly conceived and luminously expounded, are freely linked with the issues of Calvin's age and the struggle of the Reformed church for existence and survival. It is characteristic of his method that the Address to King Francis was retained by Calvin in his later editions of the *Institutio* both before and after the death of the king. Though written with intense realization of contemporary affairs, it is in fact a perpetually cogent defense of persecuted adherents of Scriptural faith.

The body of the treatise of 1536 consists of six chapters. Four

[7] See *A History of the Ecumenical Movement, 1517–1948,* ed. Ruth Rouse and Stephen Neill, p. 40.

are on topics familiar in the history of Christian instruction and then recently employed in Luther's Catechisms: the Law, the Creed, the Lord's Prayer, and the sacraments of Baptism and the Lord's Supper. The fifth consists of a denunciatory argument against recognition as sacraments of five rites so regarded in the medieval church (confirmation, penance, extreme unction, priestly orders, and matrimony), and the sixth is a challenging discussion of Christian liberty, involving some elements of political and social teaching. The volume contains (including the short index) 520 octavo pages of about 6⅛ by 4 inches, and is about the length of the New Testament to the end of Ephesians. It was to be subjected to repeated expansions by the author until it reached its final form in 1559,[8] when it was about equal in size to the Old Testament plus the Synoptic Gospels. Half a year after the book's appearance, Calvin began his work in Geneva. Within a year from its publication the edition was exhausted and he was asked to furnish a revised text. Amid trying labors he undertook this, but completed the revision only in 1538 during his stay in Basel. After some delay, involving a change of printers, it was published in Strasbourg by Wendelin Rihel in August, 1539.

The title was now altered to read: *Institutio Christianae Religionis,* perhaps to differentiate the edition as much as possible from the former one. The curious phrase that follows, "at length truly corresponding to its title," seems to disparage the large assumptions of the former full title, and certainly conveys a sense of the superiority of the new edition. Calvin had reason to congratulate himself on the changes embodied in it. Instead of six chapters there are now seventeen of similar length. The academic weight of the work is much enhanced by the inclusion of many references to Augustine, Origen, and other church fathers, to Plato, Aristotle, Cicero, and Seneca, and to some then recent scholarly works. The citations of Scripture are also multiplied. Among the added chapters several are on themes of recognized importance in the structure of Calvin's thought, such as the knowledge of God, the similarities and differences of the Old and

---

[8] There is no complete study in English of the early editions of the *Institutio.* The best is that of Benjamin B. Warfield, an article published in *The Presbyterian and Reformed Review* X (1899), 193–219, and inserted with some changes in the 1909 edition of Allen's translation. D. Clement, in *Bibliothèque curieuse historique et critique, ou Catalogue raisonné de livres difficiles à trouver* VI. 64–102, provides much convenient information on special features of numerous early editions known to him, but this excellent work is now rare. There is an extensive account in the *Corpus Reformatorum* edition of Calvin's works (CR XXIII–XLVI), but this is superseded by that given in the *Opera Selecta* (OS), edited by P. Barth and W. Niesel, III. vi–l.

New Testaments, predestination and providence, and the Christian life. A brief epistle to the reader, dated August 1, 1539, speaks of the author's surprise at the favorable response to the first edition, defective though it was, and states the purpose of his revision. He now sees it as a textbook to be used in "the preparation of candidates in theology for the reading of the divine Word." In accordance with this idea, the format of the volume is one adapted for desk use. The pages, allowing for errors in their numbering, 346 in all, are 13 by 8 inches and have wide margins for student's notes. In a part of the edition to be circulated in France the letters of Calvin's name were transposed to read "Alcuinus."

The question has been raised whether a French rendering of the first edition was, shortly after its appearance, prepared and published by Calvin. In a letter to Francis Daniel, written October 13, 1536, reporting his settlement in Geneva and subsequent illness, Calvin says he has been continually occupied on the French version of his "little book" (*libellus*). The assumption that the "little book" was the *Institutio* is plausible but not conclusive. It may be questioned whether at this stage Calvin would speak of the treatise as a *"libellus"*; the word he uses for the 1536 edition in the 1539 preface is *opus*. About the time of his letter to Daniel, written just after the Disputation of Lausanne, Calvin apparently busied himself with the preparation of his *Instruction and Confession of Faith*[9] for the use of the Geneva church. The French edition of this appeared early in 1537, the Latin at Basel a year later. But the editors of the *Corpus Reformatorum* edition of Calvin's works have shown reason to think that the French is mainly a translation of a Latin original virtually identical with that of 1538.[10] This is a simply and vigorously written summary of essential arguments of the *Institutio*. It is truly a "little book," yet its composition in Latin and translation into French would for a few weeks fully occupy the hours Calvin could spare from his new work of church reorganization. Calvin's pressing tasks that autumn can hardly have permitted him to translate a work of the length of the *Institutio*. At any rate, no trace has survived of a French edition of 1536 or 1537. The first of which we have knowledge is the celebrated edition of 1541, Calvin's own translation from the Latin of 1539.

[9] The *Instruction et confession de foy* has been translated with explanatory notes by P. T. Fuhrmann, *Instruction in Faith (1537)*.

[10] CR XXII. 7.

III

This French edition was from the press of Jean Girard (or Gérard) in Geneva, and forms a compact volume of 822 pages, 7¼ by 4½ inches, rather inexpertly printed in small type. The book was readily portable and was designed for the lay reader who could not use the Latin work. Since there was little hope of its being permitted in France, the number of copies made was apparently restricted, with a French-speaking Swiss public chiefly in view. In the "Argument" prefaced to it, no reference is made to its academic use. Its purpose is described in the phrase: "to help those who desire to be instructed in the doctrines of salvation." Nevertheless, save for one change in the order of chapters, it is simply the 1539 edition in French dress. By students of the evolution of French prose, including many quite out of accord with Calvin's opinions, it has been very warmly praised for its style.[11] It is also undeniably the earliest work in which the French language is used as a medium for the expression of sustained and serious thought. It is remarkable that a book so creative in giving character to the language of the French nation should have been itself a translation made by an author who had from boyhood habitually thought in Latin. Every effort was made to prevent its circulation in France and, amid other measures of repression, in July, 1542, and again in February, 1544, copies were piled and burned in front of Notre Dame, Paris.

All the apologetic elements of the first edition were of course retained as the work grew, but the new prefaces and the added materials indicate that instruction, whether of theological students or of a lay public, is increasingly the author's conscious aim. In the third Latin edition, 1543 (the second printed by Rihel in Strasbourg), four new chapters are inserted, bringing the number to twenty-one. This edition was reissued in 1545, and in that year the expanded work appeared in French from Girard's press in Geneva. The Latin edition of 1550, also by Girard, shows only minor changes from that of 1543. A notable improvement introduced in the 1550 edition is the numbering of the paragraph divisions. In the twenty-one chapters are found, in all, 1,217 of these. Two indexes are appended, the first of the topics treated, the second of Scripture passages and works cited by the author.

One of the greatest of Renaissance printers came to Geneva

---

[11] Laudatory comments on Calvin's French style from competent literary critics are very abundant. See below, pp. lxviii ff. E. Doumergue, in *Jean Calvin— Les hommes et les choses de son temps* IV. 5–8, has quoted some of these. See also J. Pannier, *Jean Calvin: Institution de la Religion Chrestienne* I. xxii–xxiv.

from Paris in 1550 and resumed there, in close association with the Geneva ministers, his lifework in the production of Bibles and religious texts that he had found it impossible to continue in France. This was Robert Estienne (Robertus Stephanus), a distinguished member of the great Estienne family of scholar printers to whom the New Learning and the Reformation owed a measureless debt.[12] In February, 1553, he brought out the finest edition of the *Institutio* that Calvin had yet seen, a folio volume 13½ by 8¾ inches, almost faultlessly printed in handsome type. It contains 441 pages, exclusive of the Address to the King and the indexes. In content, however, it makes no advance from the edition of 1550. The brothers Adam and Jean Rivery printed the work again in Geneva in 1554, in small octavo format, without change of text but with an improved index.

There are modern readers who would be well content with the first edition, and many who express a preference for that of 1539 or its French version of 1541 over the more expanded work of 1559 that is translated in these volumes. At the earlier stage, they say, the book was less laborious, less controversial, sufficiently comprehensive, and more pleasing to read. It is not necessary, and may not be possible, to refute these opinions. Without question, republication of the earlier editions is legitimate and desirable. But it would be inept to ignore the author's own evaluation of the editions, and to obliterate the fruits of the labor undertaken and pursued through trying days, in which he remade the work to match his own long-cherished ideal. The Latin edition of 1559 must always be held to bear Calvin's most indisputable imprint of authority. Here, in his opening address to the reader, he speaks of the previous revisions by which the work has been enriched, and adds: "Although I did not regret the labor spent, I was never satisfied until the work had been arranged in the order now set forth." He claims that in laboring at the revision through a time of illness with a quartan fever he has furnished clear evidence of the zeal that moved him "to carry out this task for the God's church." The sense of achievement reflected in these words was so far respected by later editors that for the Latin text it was this final edition which, until 1863, was exclusively reprinted, and from which translations and abridgments were made.

There is another reason why we cannot escape this definitive

---

[12] Robert was the son of Henri Estienne (d. 1520), founder of the printing house, and was himself a front-rank classical scholar and the author of valuable reference works. In Paris, he had editorial assistance from Mathurin Cordier, who had awakened the young Calvin's enthusiasm for Latin at Paris, and who too ended his days in Geneva.

edition. Recent decades have witnessed a rising interest in, and respect for, Calvin's theology, and the effort to understand and interpret his teachings has become a marked feature of theological writing. Naturally it is to the *Institutio* that inquiry has been primarily directed, and in modern studies normally the citations of passages from the work are to the 1559 edition. The numerals that mark out its sections and facilitate reference are to be regarded (like those of the *Summa* of Thomas Aquinas) as almost a part of the common language of theological discussion. The work is about 80 per cent larger than the edition it superseded. It has been so long habitually in use in all countries that there is now no practical possibility of returning to an earlier edition for purposes of scholarly intercourse.

It was printed in Geneva and came from the press of Robert Estienne, August 16, 1559. Calvin's signature to the address to the reader (quoted above) is dated August 1. The eminent printer and productive scholar, Estienne, died three weeks later, and thus the *Institutio* in its final form is the last product of his technical skill. It bears the title:

Institutio Christianae religionis, in libris quatuor nunc primum digesta, certisque distincta capitibus, ad aptissimam methodum: aucta etiam tam magna accessione ut propemodum opus novum haberi possit.

Institute of the Christian Religion, now first arranged in four books and divided by definite headings in a very convenient way: also enlarged by so much added matter that it can almost be regarded as a new work.

The name of the author follows, below it the name of the printer with his well-known emblem of the olive branch, and at the foot: GENEVAE/M.D.LIX.

IV

Calvin made no further revision of the Latin *Institutio*. A French translation of the enlarged work from the press of Jean Crespin in Geneva appeared in 1560. It is the opinion of most recent scholars that Calvin himself prepared or closely supervised this translation.[13] Both in Latin and in French the work was at

[13] The editors of the CR edition were convinced that the 1560 French version, with the exception of the first seven chapters of Book I, was not by Calvin, but was carelessly made without his oversight. (CR III. xxv–xxvii and XXI. 56. 87 f.) This view was adopted by Doumergue (*Jean Calvin* IV. 10 f.) and

once in wide demand and was frequently reprinted, even before Calvin's death (1564). There were two new printings of the Latin in 1561, one an attractive folio volume apparently by Calvin's Strasbourg printer Rihel, the other a 980-page octavo by Antoine Reboul (Antonius Rebulius) in Geneva. Reboul explains that he is responding to the request of many readers when he inserts at the end an alphabetic index of topics, with citations to book, chapter, and section. This rather ample index, extending to 59 (unnumbered) pages, was printed with many later editions in French and Latin, in some instances along with the two indexes of Marlorat mentioned below. Reboul's volume is in a readable small type, with the Scripture references neatly set in the margins. Of the later Latin editions, two are especially important for their editorial matter. These are the celebrated folio volume printed by the Elzevir house, renowned printers of Leiden, in 1654, and the one that constitutes Volume IX of the *Opera Calvini* published by J. J. Schipper of Amsterdam in 1667.

The French text of 1560 was reprinted in Geneva twice in 1561. In 1562 there were four printings of this text, one at Geneva, one at Caen, and two without indication of place or printer. There were printings at Lyons in 1563 and at Geneva in 1564. The octavo edition issued by the Geneva printer Jaques Bourgeois in 1562 was the first to incorporate the two indexes prepared by Augustin Marlorat,[14] a scholarly minister and minor theological

was first seriously challenged by J. W. Marmelstein in *Étude comparative des textes latins et français de l'Institution de la Religion Chrétienne de Calvin*. Marmelstein answers the argument from defects of style by citing similar lapses in the 1541 edition, and argues from explicit statements of Nicolas Colladon and Theodore Beza that Calvin was directly responsible for the translation. This view has been adopted by P. Barth and W. Niesel in OS III. xxxviii–xlviii; by J. Cadier in his preface to the modernized edition, *Jean Calvin: Institution de la Religion Chrétienne* I. x–xiii; and by J.-D. Benoit in the Introduction to his edition of the French version: *Jean Calvin: Institution de la Religion Chrestienne* I. 9 ff. The weight of argument compels us to adopt Marmelstein's main contention. English translators have differed in their recognition of the French edition. Norton (1561) calls the Latin of 1559 "the author's last edition"; but Allen (1813) uses this expression for the 1560 French. Those who are convinced that the translation passed through Calvin's hands or was his work tend to date his labor on it largely before the publication of the 1559 Latin. Yet nobody denies that it is definitely a translation from the Latin, with only a few intentional variations. It is noteworthy that changes made in the French version were never transferred to the Latin, though in later printings Calvin had ample opportunity to do this. This may be partially explained on the ground that the French edition was specifically intended for popular use and some of its variations from the original would have been unsuitable in a Latin text. But in any case, the 1559 Latin edition remains Calvin's final redaction of the work for international circulation, and as such retains its authority.

writer whose life ended at the hands of persecutors in Rouen in the same year. The first of these is an index of the principal matters contained in the work; the second is of the Bible passages quoted or referred to in it. Marlorat has an interesting preface in which he indicates that he had found the Bible references of earlier editions seriously inaccurate. He gives the verses of Scripture in full, even where Calvin uses only an identifying phrase. A Latin version of these serviceable indexes appeared with the next subsequent printing of the Latin *Institutes,* that of Francis Perrin, Geneva, 1568, and numerous later editions in Latin, French, English, and Dutch made use of them.

Translations into other languages than French had already begun. The 1536 text probably was rendered into Spanish in 1540 by Francisco Enzinas (Dryander) of Burgos, friend of Melanchthon, protégé of Cranmer, correspondent of Calvin, and eminent New Testament scholar and translator.[14a] If the first Spanish version actually preceded Calvin's own French rendering, the first Italian version depended on a later French edition. It was in 1557 that Giulio Cesare Pascali, a young Italian poet and religious refugee in Geneva, produced there his Italian translation. Pascali made primary use of the French text, which had been revised in 1551 and reprinted in 1553 and 1554. It was dedicated to the most eminent member of the Italian refugee church in Geneva, Galleazzo Caraccioli, Marquis of Vico, to whom Calvin a year earlier had dedicated his Commentary on First Corinthians.

The numerous translations that followed were from the completed work. As early as December 5, 1560, a Dutch version was issued, apparently at Emden and Dort simultaneously. The translator reveals his name only by the initials "I. D." The initials stand for Johannes Dyrkinus (d. 1592), a minister and writer of some distinction, then at Emden.[15] In 1572, the first German translation was brought out at Heidelberg, prepared by members

[14] Marlorat (1506–1562) was a former Augustinian monk who became a Reformed minister, held parishes in the Vaud, attended the Colloquy at Poissy (1561), and met a cruel death with great resolution at Rouen. His numerous writings include an Exposition of the New Testament (1561) (Eugene Haag and Émile Haag, *La France Protestante* VII. 256–259; CR I. xiv).

[14a] Enzinas Hebraized his name to "Elao," and apparently the place of publication, given as "Topeia," was Ghent. B. F. Stockwell, "Historia literaria de la Institucion," prefaced to the Buenos Aires facsimile reproduction of Valera's translation of 1597, pp. xx. f.

[15] Among works translated by Dyrkinus are the New Testament, the *Hausbuch* of Heinrich Bullinger, and Calvin's Commentaries on the Epistles of Paul. The main facts of his life are in the article "Johannes Dyrkinus," by A. A. van Schelven, in *Nieuw Nederlandsch Biographisch Woordenboek,* ed. P. O.

of the theological faculty there and with an expository introduction.[16] This version was republished in 1582 at Heidelberg, and at Hanau in 1597. In that year also the work appeared in a Spanish translation. This was the work of a Spanish refugee, Cipriano de Valera, who, after a stay in Geneva, had spent many years in England and held a master's degree from Cambridge.[17] A Czech version by Jiřík Strejc (Georg Vetter), who died in 1599, remained only partially published: Books I and II appeared in 1617. The Hungarian translation by Albert Molnár (d. 1634), eminent minister, scholar, and poet of the Hungarian Reformed Church, was published at Hanau in 1624.[18] It has been supposed by qualified scholars, but never verified, that an Arabic version was made by the Zurich Orientalist, John Henry Hottinger (d. 1667).

The editions of the *Institutes* by A. Tholuck (Latin, 1834, 1846, 1872), by F. Baumgartner (1560 French, 1888), and by A. Sizoo (Dutch translation from the Latin, 1931, 1949) have

Molhuysen, *et al.*, IV. 547 ff., and in W. Hollweg, *Heinrich Bullinger's Hausbuch*, pp. 92 ff. (Spellings of his name are numerous.) There are copies of this translation (*Institutie ofte onderwijsinghe der Christlicken religie*) in the University Library, Leiden, and in the Library of the Dutch Church of London. It was reprinted in 1566 and in 1578 at Dort, and in 1596 at Leiden, but the version by Charles Agricola, 1602, superseded it, and this in turn gave place to the superior work of William Corsman, 1650.

[16] "*Institutio Christianae religionis. Das ist underweisung inn Christlicher Religion in Vier Bücher verfasset. Durch Herrn Johannem Calvinum. Aus Lateinischer und Frantzöschischer Sprach treulich verteutscht Gedruckt in der Churfürstlichen Statt Heydelberg durch Johannem Meyer. M.D.LXXII.*" (There is a copy in the Library of Colby College, Waterville, Maine.) It opens with a 3½ page address to the Christian reader by the theologians and church officers (*Kirchendiener*) of Heidelberg, commending the work as an unrivaled "*summa Christlicher Religion*" and declaring that the German text is a translation and not a paraphrase of the Latin. No names of translators are given: we know that in 1572 the theological Faculty of Heidelberg included the eminent Reformed scholars, Caspar Olevianus (1536–1585), Zacharius Ursinus (1534–1583), Hieronymus Zanchius (1516–1590), and Pierre Boquin (ca. 1500–1582).

[17] Valera spent most of the period of Elizabeth's reign in England. His preface to the *Institutes* contains a passage in warm praise of the queen's policy in harboring Protestant refugees. He helped to revise the earlier Spanish translation of the Bible. In 1637, the celebrated Giovanni Deodati of Geneva stated that three thousand copies of Valera's *Institucion* had been circulated throughout Spain. (T. McCrie, *History of the Reformation in Spain*, p. 374.) On Valera's early life, see the article "A Spanish Heretic: Cipriano de Valera," by L. J. Hutton, *Church History* XXVII (1958), 23–31.

[18] For notes on early editions in Czech and Hungarian, see G. Loesche, *Luther, Melanthon, und Calvin in Österreich-Ungarn*, pp. 356 ff. See also the entries in R. Pitcairn's "Catalogue Raisonné of the Earlier Editions of Calvin's Institutes" in H. Beveridge, *Institutes of the Christian Religion* (Edinburgh, 1845) I. lxvi.

value as texts only. O. Weber's German translation from the Latin (one-volume edition, 1955) and J. Cadier's modernization of the 1560 French (four volumes, 1955–1958) are provided with analytical headings and classified indexes. A Japanese translation from the Latin, by Masaki Nakayama, was published in Tokyo in 1934 and was reprinted in 1949.

V

Readers of the present translation will welcome somewhat fuller reference to the first English form of the *Institutes*. The Latin editions prior to that of 1559 had been circulated in England and Scotland, but only the chapters on the Christian life (Book III, chapters vi–x, in the final order of the work) had been put into English.[19] The whole work now appeared in a handsome black-letter folio edition under the following title:

> *The Institution of Christian Religion, wrytten in Latine by maister Jhon Calvin, and translated into Englysh according to the authors last edition. Seen and allowed according to the order appointed in the Quenes Maiesties instructions.*

The printer's emblem, a brazen serpent coiled on a wooden cross upheld by clasped hands, is followed by the colophon: "Imprinted at London by Reinolde Wolfe & Richarde Harison, anno 1561."

On the final page of the book the place is given more exactly as "in Paules Churcheyard," and the date as "1561. The 6 day of Maye." Thus the translation was printed in London less than twenty-one months after the Latin edition left the press of Stephanus in Geneva. Yet the printers insert on the back of the title page a somewhat cryptic paragraph bearing their excuse for the delay in its appearance. The task had been assigned to "John Dawes," and he had presented a manuscript "more than a twelve-month past," but for "diuerse necessarie causes" they had been "constrayned to entreat another frende to translate it whole agayn."[20] The initials "T. N." are set at the end of the text, after

---

[19] *The Life and Communicacion of a Christen Man*, translated by Thomas Broke, 1549. Broke was at the time an official of the ports of Dover and Calais. In his preface he indicates a desire to translate the whole work. As a translator he is not distinguished, and certainly inferior to Norton. Cf. note 65, below.

[20] In some copies of this edition the printer's note is omitted. One of these is in the Harvard Andover Library. John Dawes is probably the Cambridge graduate (M.A., 1540) of that name who was rector of Sutton, Suffolk, 1570–1602; see *Alumni Cantabrigenses*, Part I, Vol. I (1922), 19. We need hardly hesitate to identify him also with the John Daus of Ipswich who translated

which six pages are devoted to the list of chapter headings and a short index. In the second edition, 1562, the translator inserts a short preface to which he appends his initials. Only in the improved third edition is the name "Thomas Norton" spelled out on the title page.

Thomas Norton (1532–1584) was about twenty-nine years old when the work appeared. He had already attained some fame as a writer. On Twelfth-night, 1561, *The Tragedy of Gorboduc,* the joint work of Norton and his fellow student at law, Thomas Sackville, had its first performance, and two weeks later it was played by command before the queen. This gory but still impressive drama in blank verse stands at the beginning of the modern development of English tragedy and is the work by which Norton is best known. But his earlier poems in Latin and English, and his less successful versifications of some of the psalms, were familiar to his contemporaries, together with a variety of translations of religious works and other prose pieces dealing controversially with ecclesiastical issues. He had been a very precocious amanuensis to the Duke of Somerset at a time when the Duke was in correspondence with Calvin. When, after Somerset's death, Calvin wrote to inquire about his children, it was Norton who was deputed to reply. In 1555, he married a daughter of Thomas Cranmer, and he later gave publicity to important manuscripts left by the archbishop. A convinced Calvinist, he was also an advocate of Puritan measures of reform in the church and was at one time imprisoned for criticism of the bishops. Norton became a member of Parliament in 1558 and was frequently thereafter prominent in parliamentary debates and committees. He participated in trials of Roman Catholics, especially those implicated in the Rebellion of 1569, and exhibited in that connection a harsh and blameworthy zeal. Though scholarly, talented, and versatile, Norton never played a major role either in literature or in affairs; but his gifts were such that Calvin was fortunate in his English translator.[21]

John Sleidan's *Reign of Charles V, A Fameuse Cronicle of oure time called Sleidanes Commentaries* . . . published September 1560, and *A Hundred Sermons upon the Apocalips,* by Henry Bullinger, March, 1561. The dates of these substantial books may help to excuse Dawes if he failed to deliver a satisfactory manuscript of the *Institutes* as expected. From what is said it is quite possible, however, that the manuscript had been accidentally lost or destroyed.

[21] There is a good article on Norton by Sidney Lee in the *Dictionary of National Biography.* Eighteen metrical psalms by him appeared in T. Sternhold and J. Hopkins, *The Whole Book of Psalms collected into English Metre* (London, 1562).

In the third edition of Norton's version, 1574, the original preface, "The Translator to the Reader," is revised and expanded so as to indicate precisely the circumstances in which his work of translation was done. Norton had been asked to undertake it by two well-known printers to the queen. One of these was Edward Whitchurch, who, with Richard Grafton, had published the Great Bible, 1539, and *The Book of Common Prayer*, 1549. The other was Reginald (or Reinolde) Wolfe, a native of Strasbourg who had become an important figure in the English book trade. It was in the house of Whitchurch in Greyfriars that the translator's task was done. Norton does not mention the fact that the wife of Whitchurch was Cranmer's widow and his own wife's mother.[22] Writing after Whitchurch's death, which took place late in 1561, Norton refers to him as "an ancient zealous Gospeller, as plaine and true a frend as euer I knew living." He also expresses gratitude for the critical advice of numerous "learned men," naming especially David Whitehead who, he states, compared every sentence with the Latin text. Whitehead was a former Marian exile who had been associated with the party favoring the Edwardian *Prayer Book* in the strife at Frankfurt, 1555. An eminent clergyman of recognized (though privately acquired) learning, he had declined the see of Armagh and possibly also the see of Canterbury.

In 1845, Henry Beveridge, while admitting that "Norton on the whole executed his task with great fidelity," criticized him sharply for an "overscrupulous" preservation of the Latin forms of speech to the serious injury of the English style. Norton himself explains that because of the "great hardness" of the book from its being "interlaced with Schoolmen's controversies," fearing to miss Calvin's meaning, he had decided "to follow the words so neare as the phrase of the Englysh tongue would suffer." It is true that this method sometimes produces a strained effect; but to say with Beveridge that Norton gives us only "English words in a Latin idiom" is surely misleading. The translation is not far from typical, plain, early Elizabethan prose, which was then still, as one authority has remarked, "largely the work of churchmen and translators" and had none of the affectations and embellishments that mark the writing of the next generation.[23]

---

[22] Norton married Margery Cranmer, third daughter of the archbishop, in 1555. Her mother, as is well known, was a niece of Andreas Osiander, leader of the Reformation in Nuremberg, who is sharply criticized by Calvin: I. xv. 3, 5; II. xii. 5–7; III. xi. 5–12.

[23] Alexander Nowell, dean of St. Paul's, London, one of whose three catechisms Norton translated from Latin in 1570, was highly pleased with Norton's ver-

In his third edition, Norton was happy to be able to rid the book of its many printer's errors. These he attributes to "the evill manner of my scribbling hand, the enterlining of my Copies, and some other causes well-knowen" to printers. He indicates that some three hundred errors had been corrected in the second edition, and believes the third to be virtually free from such faults. The translation is now for the first time provided not only with a version of the index of A. Reboul ("Table of Matters Entreated Of") but also with the two indexes of Marlorat, preceded by the latter's preface. After this revision of .1574, Norton's book was reprinted with slight alterations in 1578, 1582, 1587, 1599, 1611, and 1634. These editions, especially the last mentioned, show an effort to keep abreast of language changes. Thus, in 1634, "Jhon Calvin" has become "John Calvin," "truthe" is written "truth," "glorie" becomes "glory," "geuen" is changed to "given," and the abbreviations used in the first edition have disappeared. The attempt to modernize the work was carried further in the Glasgow edition of 1762, which not only uses the then current spelling but freely alters many Latinized or archaic phrases.

VI

From that date Norton's version was not republished. The next English translation of the entire work was that of John Allen (1771–1839):

> *Institutes of the Christian Religion by John Calvin, trans-
> lated from the Latin and collated with the author's last edi-
> tion in French. London: J. Walker, 1813.*

Allen was a layman who had become head of a Dissenting Academy at Hackney. His other writings included an earlier controversial work entitled *The Fathers, the Reformers, and the Public Formularies of England in Harmony with Calvin . . .* (1811), and a treatise on modern Judaism (1816). The greater part of Allen's translation was made from the Latin and revised with consultation of the French version; for the remainder he used both versions alike. Although he dismisses Norton's translation as "long antiquated, uncouth, and obscure," his principle of translation differs little from that of Norton. He states that he has

---

sion, regarding it as a model of good English. In this connection, however, Anthony à Wood remarks that Norton "tied himself" to the Latin words (R. Churton, *Life of Alexander Nowell*, p. 176). For this work, in Norton's translation with the spelling modernized, see *The Fathers of the English Church* VIII. 1–141.

"aimed at a medium between servility and looseness and endeavored to follow the style of the original as far as the respective idioms of the Latin and English would admit." The result is a conscientious though not a distinguished translation, marked by a reserved rendering of Calvin's vehement passages and vivid metaphors, but with very few errors seriously affecting the sense of the original. Allen's version has had a continuous circulation especially in America, where it was thirty times republished to 1936. In the edition of 1909, commemorating the four hundredth anniversary of Calvin's birth, B. B. Warfield's valuable essay, "On the Literary History of Calvin's *Institutes*,"[24] was inserted; and in the 1936 edition (timed with reference to the four hundred years since Calvin's first edition), Thomas C. Pears, Jr., added "An account of the American Editions." Allen's text has undergone several minor revisions at the hands of American editors, notably that of Joseph Paterson Engles in 1841.

Allen's version was not long without competition. In 1845 appeared

> *The Institutes of the Christian Religion by John Calvin.*
> *A New Translation by Henry Beveridge.*

The work was published in Edinburgh under the auspices of the Calvin Translation Society.[25] Beveridge (1799–1863) had intended to enter the ministry; he later trained for the law, but made writing his chief employment. His translations for the Calvin Society included a collection of Calvin's *Tracts Relating to the Reformation*, three volumes, 1844. He later turned to other studies and produced *A Comprehensive History of India*. His edition of the *Institutes* came out in three volumes, and contained in the introductory matter items that have been, not without loss, dropped out of later printings in both America and Britain. One is the "Catalogue Raisonné of the Earlier Editions," prepared by Robert Pitcairn, secretary of the Society. This was a useful description of most of the editions we have referred to above, a good number of which Pitcairn had carefully examined; but certain omissions and other defects make his catalog an unsafe guide. In his list three abridgments of the work are included, one of which is mistaken for a full text, and his information on the early Dutch and German translations is far from comprehensive. Another feature of Beveridge's introduction is the well-chosen series of facsimiles of title pages from early editions available

[24] Referred to in note 8, above.
[25] This society, founded in May, 1843, published (1845–1855) translations of the *Institutes, Commentaries, Tracts,* and *Letters* of Calvin.

to him and his collaborators. These are from the Latin editions
of 1536, 1539 (the Alcuin variant), 1545, 1559, 1561, the French
of 1545, the Italian of 1557, and the Spanish of 1597. In the last
two instances the translator's prefaces as originally printed are also
reproduced.[26]

Beveridge's low opinion of the work of Norton has been noted.
Strangely enough, he does not even mention Allen. His own translation is of uneven quality. In parts his early Victorian vocabulary
seems more distant from our present usage than does that of
Allen's earlier work. There are passages that may well prompt
the criticism he himself hurls at Norton: "English words in
Latin idiom." He is rather less accurate than either of his predecessors, and is chargeable with numerous minor omissions and a
few clearly erroneous renderings. Yet many sections are admirably
done, and in the finer passages Beveridge manifestly feels Calvin's

---

[26] Beveridge appends to his translation as a summary of the work, "One Hundred Aphorisms, containing, within a narrow compass, the substance and
order of the four books of the *Institutes*." In a note he states that this material has been "furnished by the Reverend William Pringle of Auchter-
arder." No other source is mentioned. The "Aphorisms" consist, however,
of a translation of the *"Centum Aphorismi"* found in the Geneva Latin
editions by J. Le Preux, 1590 and 1607, the Elzevir Leiden edition of 1654,
and the Amsterdam edition by J. J. Schipper, 1667. Le Preux, in his preface,
tells us that they are *"ex tabulis Gulielmi Launaei in Anglia excusis col-
lecti"*—gathered from the tables of Guillaume Delaune printed in England—and the ascription to this source is repeated in the Elzevir and Schipper
editions. The reference is to the elaborate tabular exhibit of Calvin's doctrines in Delaune's *Epitome* (1583), to which attention is called below. A
comparison of the documents at once confirms Le Preux's statement. Delaune's phrases have been edited into a sequence of one hundred propositions, and his chapter references are omitted. The quotation by D. Clement
(*op. cit.*, VI. 85) of Le Preux's preface first led the present editor to this
identification. The One Hundred Aphorisms first appeared in English translation in 1596, in somewhat amplified phraseology. They are included in
The Contents of Scripture by Robert Hill, published with two separately
paged appendixes: *The Consent of the Foure Evangelists*, by "C. I.," and
our Aphorisms under the title, *An Hundredth Aphorismes, Short sentences
sumarily containing the matter and Method of Maister Calvines Institutions,
in far other order than that set out by Piscator: taken out of the last and best
edition*. The "edition" referred to is not that of Piscator, but that of the
Institutio, not improbably Le Preux's of 1590. Piscator's far more numerous
"Aphorismi" actually bear no resemblance to this series derived from Delaune. The book by Hill and "C. I." was printed in London by Adam Islip
for Richard Jackson in 1596. The Hundred Aphorisms appeared also in
French editions. Pitcairn, in his essay (cf. note 18, above), mentions the series
in passing as a feature of Charles Icard's edition of the French text, 1713, but
this is overlooked in Beveridge's note. A. Tholuck, in his Latin edition
(Berlin, 1834, 1846), which Beveridge used, simply appends the *Centum
Aphorismi* without explanation.

rhetorical power and succeeds in conveying much of it to the reader.

VII

The cumbrous bulk of the *Institutes,* and the interest aroused in it, led to the early appearance of numerous abridgments. These, like the work itself, were generally first published in Latin and later in vernacular translations. One of the earliest was that compiled by Edmund Bunney (Bunnie) (1540–1619), a popular itinerant preacher of Calvinist doctrines in England, with the title *Institutionis Christianae Religionis . . . Compendium* (London, 1576). It was translated by Edward May as *The Institutions of Christian Religion . . . compendiously abridged by Edmund Bunnie, bachelor of divinity . . .* (London, 1580). The book is not a set of extracts but a condensed abridgment mainly in Bunney's words. It was soon surpassed by the painstaking volume of William Delaune (Laneus, Launeus, Lawne): *Institutionis Christianae Religionis . . . Epitome* (London, 1583). Delaune (d. 1610) was a Huguenot refugee, and his printer was his fellow religionist Thomas Vautrollier (d. 1587)[27] who, in 1576, had produced the only Latin edition of the *Institutes* to appear in England.[28] The *Epitome* is an excellent example of the digest that retains as far as possible the author's language. It contains 371 octavo pages of material from the *Institutes,* following closely and proportionately the arrangement of 1559. Where Calvin reports and confutes the views of his opponents, the text takes the form of objection and reply in the manner of a dialogue. At the beginning, twenty-one unnumbered

[27] Vautrollier's activities in Edinburgh and London are described in the article on him in the *Dictionary of National Biography*. A daughter of Vautrollier became the wife of Richard Field, printer of Valera's Spanish edition of the *Institutes* and of many religious works in translation. After Vautrollier's death, Field carried on his printing establishment in Blackfriars. His father's connection with the Shakespeare family in Stratford and London is well known, and he himself printed several early works of Shakespeare.

[28] In the preparation of Vautrollier's edition of the Latin *Institutes* he had the editorial assistance of Edmund Bunney. A special feature of this excellent edition is the elaborate set of marginal references to the *Loci communes* and other works of Peter Martyr Vermigli. The *Loci communes* is a work put together in 1575 from notes left by Peter Martyr (d. 1562) and "arranged according to Calvin's system" by Robert Masson, a French minister in London. It appeared in London in 1576; it was reprinted in 1580 and (by Vautrollier) in 1583. See Vautrollier's preface (*Typographus Lectori*) to the 1576 *Institutio,* and C. Schmidt, *Peter Martyr Vermigli, Leben und ausgewählte Schriften,* p. 295.

pages are filled with a "General Table" of the course of argument in the work, presented in an elaborate structure of bracketed divisions and subdivisions.[29] In his *Epistola Nuncupatoria*, or address of dedication to Richard Martin, Master of the Mint, Delaune speaks of his book as "a nosegay from the pleasant garden of divinity." The margins are utilized for carefully prepared analytical notes. The text is followed by a twenty-five page index. The book appeared in a translation, complete in all details, by Christopher Fetherstone (Edinburgh, 1585), whose admirable translation of Calvin's Commentary on Acts appeared in the same year. As a presentation of the *Institutes* in brief, it must have been a godsend to the hard-pressed student or the eager reader with limited time. There was a Dutch edition of Delaune in 1650, and the English version was reprinted in 1837.

Another widely circulated Latin abridgment was made by John Piscator (Fischer) (1546–1625), a prominent Reformed theologian and Biblical scholar of the Academy of Herborn in Nassau. Piscator was the associate and successor of Caspar Olevianus,[30] and he utilized an "epitome" arranged by the latter (1586) for classroom use. His *Aphorismi doctrinae Christianae maximam partem ex Institutione Calvini excerpti sive loci communes theologici* (Herborn, 1589) was also compiled for convenience in student discussions, and was soon in such demand that by 1615 it was in its eighth edition. It appeared also in English in a translation by Henry Holland made from the third edition: *Aphorismes of Christian Religion in a verie compendious abridgment of M. J. Calvin's Institutions*, printed by Richard Field, London, 1596. In accordance with Piscator's subtitle, the text is divided into twenty-eight *loci*. Each of these main sections contains a numbered series of "aphorisms," the numbers varying from eight to thirty-four. The length of the aphorisms ranges from a sentence to several pages. Piscator explains that he has chosen the word *aphorismi* in preference to *theses* since the latter term would suggest debatable uncertainties, and the statements given are not open to doubt or debate.

There soon followed another abridgment of the *Institutes*, the

[29] This section is referred to in note 26, above, as the source of the "One Hundred Aphorisms" appended to the work by some modern editors.

[30] Caspar Olevianus had studied under Calvin. He was associated with Zacharias Ursinus in the authorship of the Heidelberg Catechism (1563). From 1576 to 1584 he taught at Berleberg, later at Herborn, where he died in 1585. On his *Institutionis Christianae religionis epitome* (Herborn, 1586), see P. Henry, *Das Leben Johann Calvins* III. 188. Henry also refers to an anonymous German abridgment published in Herborn, 1586, and to the *Theatrum Sapientiae*, an analysis of the *Institutes* by Theodor Zwinger (Basel, 1652).

Analysis paraphrastica Institutionum theologicarum Johannis Calvini (Leiden, 1628) by Daniel Colonius (Van Ceulen), regent of the Walloon College at Leiden. Colonius was a son-in-law of the head of the Elzevir printing firm, and a year after the compiler's death a duodecimo edition very neatly printed in minute type was issued by Elzevir (Leiden, 1636). Colonius divides his book into forty-one "disputations," but keeps references to the sections of the original and in the main uses Calvin's language. The *Analysis paraphrastica* is rated highly as a student's manual by Dr. Warfield, but, unlike Delaune's book, it is without marginal headings and index. The 950 small pages contain approximately one third of the *Institutes*—rather too much for a handy abridgment.[31]

VIII

The great treatise of Calvin is justly regarded as a classical statement of Protestant theology. The work expanded under his hand until the range of its subject matter amounted to the whole field of Christian theology. If in its comprehensiveness it surpasses other theological treatises of its century, its superiority is still greater with respect to the order and symmetry with which it is composed, and the substantial consistency of its detailed judgments. The completed work bears few traces of the fact that it had been subjected to repeated enlargements and much rearrange-

[31] Apparently, the eighteenth century saw no new abridgments of the *Institutes*. The series is resumed with the appearance of H. P. Kalthoff's *Christliche Unterweisung in einem kernhaften Auszug*, published at Elberfeld, 1828. Samuel Dunn's *Christian Theology Selected and Systematically Arranged* is a book of the same class; it was published in a Welsh translation in 1840. A Dutch abridgment by G. Elzenga, *Calvijn's Institutie of onderwijzing in den Christlijken Godsdienst,* was published at Kampen in 1903 and B. Wielenga later used the same title (subtitles differ) for a larger book. More ample still is the admirable abridgment by E. F. K. Müller, *Unterricht in der Christlichen Religion.* H. T. Kerr's *A Compend of the Institutes of the Christian Religion by John Calvin* contains about one tenth of the material of the work, and consists of thoughtfully chosen selections from Allen's translation. Another, prepared in very free translation and excluding Book IV, by J. P. Wiles, *John Calvin's Instruction in Christianity, an Abbreviated Edition of the Institutes,* has been further abridged by D. O. Fuller. Allen's text is again used for a brief selection of extracts with connective comments in *John Calvin on the Christian Faith; Selections from the Institutes and Other Writings* (Library of Liberal Arts, No. 93), by J. T. McNeill. A larger set of extracts from the *Institutes*, with an introduction by J. T. McNeill, translated into Chinese by Ching Yu Hsu, has appeared in Hong Kong (2 vols.) (Christian Classics Library, published by the Board of Founders of Nanking Theological Seminary; General Editor, Francis P. Jones; 2d series, Nos. 4 and 5).

ment of its parts. Orderliness is not, however, gained at the expense of persuasiveness and force. It is a living, challenging book that makes personal claims upon the reader. This is because it presents, with eloquent insistence, that which has laid hold upon the author himself. Looking back at his conversion, Calvin wrote, "God subdued my heart to teachableness."[32] As a consequence of that profound and lasting inward change, he lived and wrote as a man constantly aware of God. At the beginning of the *Institutes* he deals impressively with the theme: How God is known. The whole work is suffused with an awed sense of God's ineffable majesty, sovereign power, and immediate presence with us men.

This awareness of God is for him neither a product of speculative thinking nor an incentive to it. He rejects the intellectual indulgence of detached speculation. If he had any talent for this, it was deliberately checked. He never adopts the attitude of the impersonal inquirer. It is not what God is in Himself—a theme in his view beyond human capacity—that concerns his mind, but what God is in relation to His world and to us.[33] God is not known by those who propose to search him out by their proud but feeble reason; rather, he makes himself known to those who in worship, love, and obedience consent to learn his will from his Holy Word.

One who takes up Calvin's masterpiece with the preconception that its author's mind is a kind of efficient factory turning out and assembling the parts of a neatly jointed structure of dogmatic logic will quickly find this assumption challenged and shattered. The discerning reader soon realizes that not the author's intellect alone but his whole spiritual and emotional being is enlisted in his work. Calvin might well have used the phrase later finely composed by Sir Philip Sidney, "Look in thy heart, and write." He well exemplifies the ancient adage, "The heart makes the theologian." He was not, we may say, a theologian by profession, but a deeply religious man who possessed a genius for orderly thinking and obeyed the impulse to write out the implications of his faith. He calls his book not a *summa theologiae* but a *summa pietatis*. The secret of his mental energy lies in his piety; its product is his theology, which is his piety described at length. His task is to expound (in the language of his original title) "the whole sum of piety and whatever it is necessary to know in the doctrine of salvation." Quite naturally, in the preface to his last Latin edition he affirms that in the labor of preparing it

[32] Preface to the Commentary on the Psalms, CR XXXI. 21. Cf. LCC XXIII. 52.

[33] *"Non quis sit apud se, sed qualis erga nos."* I. x. 2. Cf. I. ii. 2; III. ii. 6.

his sole object has been "to benefit the church by maintaining the pure doctrine of godliness."

For him, piety is unavoidably associated with doctrine, and all experience a challenge to thought. But he knows experiences that lie beyond his powers of thought, and sometimes brings us to the frontier where thinking fails and the mystery is impenetrable to his mental powers. At this point he can only bid us go reverently on if we are able. He would not, he says, have the sublime mystery of the Eucharist measured by his insufficiency—"by the little measure of my childishness";[34] but he exhorts his readers not to confine their comprehension of it by his limitations, but to strive upward far higher than he can lead them.[35] Within that recognized frontier, however, he writes with great clarity and conviction.

To the modern mind the word "piety" has lost its historic implications and status. It has become suspect, as bearing suggestions of ineffectual religious sentimentality or canting pretense. For Calvin and his contemporaries, as for ancient pagan and Christian writers, *pietas* was an honest word, free from any unsavory connotation. It was a praiseworthy dutifulness or faithful devotion to one's family, country, or God. Calvin insistently affirms that piety is a prerequisite for any sound knowledge of God. At the first mention of this principle he briefly describes piety as "that reverence joined with love of God which the knowledge of his benefits induces." It exists when men "recognize that they owe everything to God, that they are nourished by his fatherly care, that he is the Author of their every good."[36] The word *pietas* occurs with great frequency in Calvin's writings, and in the *Institutes* it keeps recurring like the ringing of a bell to call us back from the allurements of a secular intellectualism. "For Calvin," says Émile Doumergue, "religion and piety are one and the same thing."[37] "Piety," says A. Mitchell Hunter, "was the keynote of his character. He was a God-possessed soul. Theology was no concern to him as a study in itself; he devoted himself to it as a framework for the support of all that religion meant to him."[38] Gratitude, love, and obedience are involved in this religious attitude which is the indispensable condition of a sound theology. Since we "owe everything to God," in Calvin's pages we are everywhere confronting God, not toying with ideas or balancing opinions about him. As a result of this,

[34] *"Infantiae meae modulo."* IV. xvii. 7.
[35] *"Multo altius assurgere contendant quam meo ductu possint,"* ibid.
[36] I. ii. 1.
[37] *Jean Calvin,* IV. 29.
[38] *The Teaching of Calvin,* 2d revised edition, p. 296.

regardless of detailed agreement with the author, the reader finds him the companion of his own religious struggles. He is indeed a peculiarly articulate and intelligible reporter of religious insights and spiritual promptings that come at least vaguely to consciousness whenever men strive to frame thoughts of the God with whom they have to do.

Calvin's clarity of expression may at first lead the reader to suppose that his thought is easy to grasp. Actually, he lays heavy demands upon the mind, and some of those best versed in his writings have confessed the difficulty of explaining some elements of his thought. Interpretations of his theology have often clashed, and in our day a persistent debate over important aspects of his teaching in the *Institutes* has been a salient feature of Protestant theological discussion. This is the common fate of a classic treatise. It is an arsenal for later thinkers, and when it has become a means of bringing to expression their nascent ideas the temptation is strong to think of it as a testimonial to the new formulation rather than to allow it to make its own fresh impression. Calvin's treatment of the natural in relation to his doctrine of grace has been much controverted.[39] Unquestionably, he earnestly affirmed on the one hand that a sense of deity is so indelibly engraved on the human heart that even the worst of men cannot rid themselves of it, and on the other, stressed the evidence of God's handiwork that meets our senses in the beauty and order of the world and in the marvels of man's thought and skill. He does not doubt that the objective world bears ample intimation that God exists, and that he is almighty, just, and wise and exercises a "fatherly kindness" toward his creatures. Yet men are so damaged by the heritage of sin entailed by Adam's fall that they miss this testimony of creation to the Creator, and grope blindfold in this bright theater of the universe with only erroneous and unworthy notions of the God who made it.[40]

IX

But God has not abandoned man in this plight. Since we fail to find Him in his works, he has revealed himself in his Word. Usually when Calvin speaks of God's Word, he does not differen-

[39] P. Barth, *Das Problem der natürlichen Theologie bei Calvin,"* in the series Theologische Existenz Heute, No. 18; G. Gloede, *Theologia naturalis bei Calvin;* E. A. Dowey, Jr., *The Knowledge of God in Calvin's Theology,* ch. III and appendix 3; W. M. Horton, *Contemporary Continental Theology: An Interpretation for Anglo-Saxons;* W. Niesel, *The Theology of Calvin,* translated by H. Knight, pp. 39–53.

[40] I. iii. 3; I. v. 3–5, 8. Calvin's stress on the point that man's sin has impaired not only his will but his intellect should be remembered here: cf. II. ii. 12–25.

tiate it from the canonical Scriptures. Yet if forced to define it, he would not simply point to the words spelled out on the sacred page. It is "the everlasting Wisdom, residing with God, from which both all oracles and all prophecies go forth." By "the everlasting Wisdom" in this context, he intends a reference to Christ, by whose Spirit, he says, the ancient prophets spoke.[41] Thus Christ, the Word, by whom all things were created (John 1:1), is the Author of the written Word, by which the eternal Word is known. Holy Scripture, thus understood, assumes for Calvin unquestionable and infallible authority and is made his constant reliance and resource. His readiness in bringing Scripture passages to bear upon each point of argument is astonishing, and has perhaps never been surpassed. But in his case, familiarity with the text rarely if ever results in a disorderly excess of quotations. Where his quotations seem unduly abundant, it will usually be found that he is meeting an opponent's use of the same texts. With rare exceptions, he does not attempt to force the passages used to yield more of doctrine than they actually contain. Nor does he adduce texts that from the standpoint of Biblical science in his time are alien to his argument, and then (as others do) try to justify their use by capricious allegorical exegesis. He is always alert to expose such "trifling with the Scriptures." In general, he holds faithfully to his principle of simple and literal interpretation. He disdains the use of allegory to confirm dogmas and cites Scripture only as authenticating what it directly says.[42] The authority of the Bible as God's Word and the source of indisputable truth is never called in question by Calvin, and he assumes that his readers share this assurance. Yet he is not concerned to assert what in later controversy has been spoken of as "verbal inerrancy." His whole emphasis is thrown on the message or content of Scripture rather than on the words. It began in the oracles and visions that God imparted to the patriarchs, whose minds were so impressed with their truth that they passed them down orally to their descendants, until at length God brought it about that the revelations were recorded for the use of later generations.[43]

The human writers are not automatons but persons whose minds and hearts have embraced the truth of what they write. Even when he is stressing the point of the authority of the sacred writings, he usually appears to have in mind the writer, and he seeks to expound the message itself, not merely the words that convey it. Thus in the oft-quoted description of the apostolic

[41] I. xiii. 7.
[42] III. iv. 4–6.
[43] I. vi. 2.

writers as "sure and genuine scribes" (in the French text, "sworn notaries") of the Holy Spirit,[44] the context does not bear upon the Scripture words as such but refers rather to the inspired teaching they express. He has, in fact, no systematic treatment of the manner of inspiration. If there are passages in his writings in which he seems to associate the inspiration with the words themselves, his prevailing concern is nevertheless to carry the reader beyond the words to the message. To evaluate his position on this, we should need to search the Commentaries as well as the *Institutes*. It was less a problem to him than to some moderns. Doubtless he would have liked to assert without qualification the complete accuracy of Scripture, but he is frank to recognize that some passages do not admit of the claim of inerrancy on the verbal level. Thus he discusses an inaccuracy in Paul's quotation of Ps. 51:4 in Rom. 3:4, and is led to generalize thus: "For we know that in repeating the words of Scripture the apostles were often pretty free [*liberiores*], since they held it sufficient if they cited them in accordance with the matter; for this reason, they did not make the words a point of conscience [*quare non tantum illis fuit verborum religio*]."[45] The expression here used, *verborum religio*, occurs in the *Institutes*[46] in a scornful characterization of opponents who wrangle on the basis of an artificially scrupulous insistence on each several word of a passage under interpretation. Calvin's keen sense of style is freely applied to the Bible writers. "John, thundering from the heights" is contrasted with the other Evangelists who use "a humble and lowly style," but this involves no divergence in the message.[47] The "elegance" of Isaiah and the "rudeness" of Amos are alike employed to express the "majesty" of the Holy Spirit.[48]

The divine authority of Holy Scripture is not derived from any declaration by the church; rather, it is upon Scripture that the church is built.[49] That God is the Author of Scripture is capable of rational demonstration, but this would be wholly ineffectual to build up a sound faith. Its authority is self-authenticating to those who yield to the guidance of the Holy Spirit. The testimony of the Holy Spirit is more excellent than all reason. Certainty of its divine truth such as piety requires is ours only when

[44] IV. viii. 9.
[45] CR XLIX. 49. Similarly, Calvin's own quotations of Scripture, while true to the sense, are often verbally free. Cf. J. A. Cramer, *De Heilige Schrift bij Calvijn*, pp. 116–141; J. Haroutunian in LCC XXXIII. 31–35.
[46] IV. xvii. 20. Another phrase here is *"literae exactores,"* exactors of the letter.
[47] I. viii. 11.
[48] I. viii. 2.
[49] I. vii. 1–2.

the Spirit who spoke by the prophets enters our hearts. Then we realize that the Scripture has come to us "from the very mouth of God by the ministry of men."[50] The Spirit too is its interpreter, and seals its teaching upon the reader's heart. Thus for Calvin the Bible is the believer's infallible book of truth when it is read under the direction of the Spirit. Furthermore, Holy Scripture has its organizing principle in the revelation of Christ, and has its chief office in enabling us to appropriate the life-giving grace of Christ. "The Scriptures are to be read," says Calvin in his Commentary on John's Gospel, "with the purpose of finding Christ there."[51] It is important to realize that the focal point of the *Institutes* is not found in God's sovereignty, or in predestination, or in insistence on obedience to God's Word itself, apart from constant reference to Jesus Christ, whom the written Word makes known.[52]

In the Bible he identifies the principles that should guide the organization and discipline of the church and govern its public worship. This means that all innovations in these matters since the apostles are subjected to the judgment of Scripture. The Scriptures amply supplied Calvin with munitions by which to assail the superstition that he saw prevalent in the pre-Reformation decline of the church. He also castigates those of his contemporaries who present what he regards as hasty, irresponsible, and slanted interpretations of Scripture passages. In this connection, the treatment of Matt. 26:26 ("This is my body") in his discussion of the Lord's Supper offers a brief description of his own method:

"But as for us, we study with no less obedience than care to obtain a sound understanding of this passage, as we do in the whole of Scripture. And we do not with perverted ardor and without discrimination rashly seize upon what first springs to our minds. Rather, after diligently meditating upon it, we embrace the meaning which the Spirit of God offers. Relying upon it, we look down from a height at whatever of earthly wisdom is set against it. Indeed, we hold our minds captive, that they dare not

---

[50] I. vii. 5; I. viii. 13.

[51] On John 5:39; CR XLVIII. 125.

[52] Cf. Luther's Preface to the Epistles of James and Jude: "And in this all genuine holy books agree, that they all together preach and stress Christ [*Christum predigen und treiben*]. Moreover, the true touchstone of criticism [*tadeln*] is when we see whether they stress Christ or not. What does not teach Christ is not apostolic, even if Peter or Paul teach it. Again, what preaches Christ would be apostolic even if Judas, Annas, Pilate, or Herod were to do it." (*Dr. Martin Luther's sämmtliche Werke* LXIII. 156 f.) Cf. the translation in *Works of Martin Luther* VI. 478. See also I. ix. 3

raise even one little word of protest; and humble them that they
dare not rebel against it."[53]

X

Throughout the *Institutes* Calvin's self-confessed debt to Augustine is constantly apparent. Amid the general adoption by the
Scholastics of a semi-Pelagian view of man's powers, the age
before Calvin had seen the rise of a new affirmation of the teaching of Augustine that man is morally helpless in himself and
wholly dependent on divine grace. After Gottschalk of Orbais,
who was condemned for heresy in 849, the first eminent representative of an unqualified Augustinianism was the scholarly
theologian and ecclesiastic, Thomas Bradwardine, called Doctor
Profundus, who died immediately after his consecration as archbishop of Canterbury in 1349. In his long treatise *De causa Dei
contra Pelagium,* Bradwardine tells us that in his early foolishness and vanity he had imbibed the Pelagian notions that prevailed about him, but that he had been "visited" by the conviction of God's initiative "as by a beam of grace." Habitually citing
Augustine and the Bible, he argues that "grace is given *gratis,*"
not on condition of previous works, and that predestination is
"according to the free [*gratuitam*] will of God," without reference to works.[54] Similar views were held by Gregory of Rimini,[55]

---

[53] IV. xvii. 25.

[54] *Thomae Braduardini archiepiscopi olim Cantuariensis De causa Dei contra
Pelagium et de virtute causarum, libri tres,* edited by Henry Saville (London,
1618). The work is analyzed in Joseph and Isaac Milner's *History of the
Church* IV. 79–106. In the *Nun's Priest's Tale* of Chaucer, Bradwardine is
ranked with Augustine and Boethius, in course of a passage in which the
poet facetiously brings to notice, but declines to discuss, the issues involved
in predestination:

> But I ne kan nat bulte it to the bren
> As kan the hooly doctour Augustyn,
> Or Boece, or bisshop Bradwardyn, . . .
> I wil nat han to do of swich mateere.

Bradwardine was distinguished as a mathematician, and his treatise remarkably combines mathematical logic with an eager personal faith. See Saville's
edition, pp. 327, 420, and H. A. Oberman, *Archbishop Thomas Bradwardine, a Fourteenth-Century Augustinian,* chs. i, v, vii. Cf. G. Leff, *Bradwardine and the Pelagians: A Study of His De causa Dei and Its Opponents.*

[55] Gregory of Rimini asserts that God has predestinated the elect gratis and
in compassion, but he also affirms reprobation as without reference to divine
foreknowledge of the individual's bad use of free will or resistance to grace.
See P. Vigneau, *Justification et prédestination au xive siècle: Duns Scot,
Pierre d'Auriole, Guillaume d'Occam, Grégoire de Rimini,* ch. iv; Oberman, *op. cit.,* pp. 211–223.

who died as general of the Augustinian Hermits in 1358. In this area of doctrine, Wycliffe was a disciple of Augustine, and John Hus, though less a Wycliffite than his accusers supposed, was hardly less than Wycliffe an Augustinian.[56]

It has been said that "the Reformation, inwardly considered, was just the ultimate triumph of Augustine's doctrine of grace over Augustine's doctrine of the church."[57] The measure of dependence of Luther and Calvin upon Augustine cannot easily be stated, but certainly both Reformers were frank to recognize their debt to him, without in the least exempting his opinions from the test of Scripture. Calvin may be said to stand at the culmination of the later Augustinianism.[58] He actually incorporates in his treatment of man and of salvation so many typical passages from Augustine that his doctrine seems here entirely continuous with that of his great African predecessor. Yet his occasional dissent from Augustine on minor points marks him as a not uncritical disciple.[59] Calvin goes beyond Augustine in his explicit assertion of double predestination, in which the reprobation of those not elected is a specific determination of God's inscrutable will. Apparently, the statement of this became a constituent element in Calvin's theology through his never relaxed conviction, borne out by his reading of Scripture and reflection on his own experience, of the unconditioned sovereignty of God. He feels under obligation to close the door to the notion that anything happens otherwise than under the control of the divine will. Man is

[56] M. Spinka, *John Hus and the Czech Reform; Advocates of Reform: From Wyclif to Erasmus* (LCC XIV), pp. 196 f., 249, 261 f.

[57] Article, "Augustine," by B. B. Warfield, HDRE II. 224.

[58] It should be remembered, however, that nearly a century later Cornelius Jansen was to inaugurate a vehement controversy within Roman Catholicism by a fresh appropriation of Augustine's doctrines of sin and grace.

[59] H. Barnikol, in *Die Lehre Calvins vom unfreien Willens und ihr Verhältnis zur Lehre der übrigen Reformatoren, und Augustins,* views Calvin as "the reimpristinator of Augustinian theology." J. B. Mozley, in an old work that is still helpful, *A Treatise on the Augustinian Doctrine of Predestination,* acutely marks similarities and distinctions among numerous writers in the field of his title, with chief attention to Augustine, Aquinas, and Calvin. Cf. A. D. R. Polman, *De praedestinatieleer van Augustinus, Th. van Aquino, en Calvijn.* The references to Augustine are very abundant in the *Institutes.* In general, Calvin uses Augustine's opinions only as corroboration of Scripture, but at some points, such as III. xxiii. 1, 5, 11, 13, 14; IV. vi. 4, he seems to rely on Augustine for the substance of an argument. His debt to Augustine can best be realized from the evidence presented by L. Smits in *Saint Augustine dans l'oeuvre de Jean Calvin:* see esp. I. 254–271. Smits has labored through the works of both theologians. The second of his two volumes consists of elaborate statistical tables. Other notable studies are J. Cadier, "Calvin et Saint Augustine," in *Augustinus Magister* (Communications du Congrès International Augustinien) II. 1033–1056; D. Nauta, *Augustinus en de Reformatie.*

wholly unable to contribute to his own salvation; nor is election conditioned by divine foreknowledge of a man's faith or goodness.

That some men are eternally damned was a traditionally orthodox and almost uncontested belief. Like some Augustinians before him, but with greater insistence and exactness, Calvin linked this damnation of some with the operation of God's sovereign will. What is to become of every man in the hereafter has been determined by God's eternal decree; and some are ordained to everlasting woe. In this he may be said to have welded together two theological commonplaces. The result, however, was shocking even to his own mind and has proved unacceptable or distressing to many of his readers. Dreadful (*horribile*) to contemplate though this decree is with respect to the damned, it is not to be denied or evaded.[60] Calvin states and reiterates this doctrine of reprobation with the greatest precision. He is not content to confine the function of God's will to his having "passed by" the nonelect in bestowing his saving grace: the action of his will is not "preterition" but "reprobation." If Paul says, "Whom he will he hardens" (Rom. 9:18), Calvin makes the similarly laconic assertion, "Whom God passes by, he reprobates."[61]

Calvin shudders at this conclusion even while expounding and defending it, and he knows well the moral difficulty it involves. He is very impatient with those who hold it to imply that God is the author of sin. God is always both loving and just, though here in ways that escape our feeble understanding. Calvin's prolonged attention to predestination is partly explicable by the fact that he is appalled before the mystery of it. Accordingly, he asks for great caution in the mention of the topic.[62] Anxiety about our own election he regarded as "a temptation of Satan." Yet he would have mature minds reflect upon "this high and incomprehensible mystery" in thinking of which "we should be sober and humble." The fruits of election are in no respect visible in any outward advantage or prosperity enjoyed in this life, where impiety prospers and the pious are forced to bear a cross. The blessing of the elect lies rather in their assurance of God's sufficiency and unfailing protection amid their afflictions, and in the happy anticipation of the life to come.

XI

Calvin stresses that transformation of the soul which is called regeneration. It is attended by sincere repentance which involves

---

[60] III. xxiii. 7.
[61] *"Quos Deus praeterit, reprobat."* III. xxiii. 1.
[62] III. xxiii. 14.

"mortification of the flesh and vivification of the spirit." As we participate in Christ's death our old nature is crucified, and as we share in his resurrection we are renewed in the image of God.[63] We enlist, so to speak, in a new spiritual enterprise, the progressive approach to a perfection that in this life is never fully attained. This incompleteness is not in the least a counsel of despair; it is associated rather with a glowing sense of the reality of the life to come, toward which our thoughts aspire.[64]

While this world is not our home, it is to be taken seriously as our place of pilgrimage and probation, and Calvin will have no morose rejection either of its duties or of its boons. In five chapters,[65] he gives a brief directory for the Christian life that is balanced, penetrating, and practical. God is our Father, and his image is being restored in us. He adopts us as his children on the implied condition that we "represent Christ" in our lives. This involves self-denial and charitable service of others, in whom, however intractable they seem, we must recognize the image of God inviting us to love them.[66] Very impressive in the light of current discussion of eschatology is the treatment of "meditation on the future life," and not less so the discussion of our use and enjoyment of God's gifts as aids in the present life.[67]

Sanctification is for Calvin the process of our advance in piety through the course of our life and in the pursuit of our vocation. In his treatment of faith,[68] repentance, and justification he deals in his distinctive way with these doctrines so much discussed in the Reformation. Faith is more than an assurance of God's veracity in the Scripture; it is also a full persuasion of God's mercy and of his favor toward us. It stands clear of works and of the law, since it has for its primary object Christ and is imparted to us by the Holy Spirit. Calvin denounces certain Scholastic treatments of faith in which it is severed from piety and love.[69] Although with Luther he uses the phrase "justified by faith alone,"[70] he is careful to say too that faith does not of itself effect justification, but embraces Christ by whose grace we are justified.

[63] III. iii. 8–10.
[64] III. vi. 5.
[65] III. vi–x, sometimes separately published and known as *The Golden Booklet of the Christian Life*. A separate printing of this material as it stood in the 1550 Latin edition was made in Geneva, 1550. Cf. note 19, above.
[66] III. vii. 6.
[67] III. ix, x.
[68] III. ii. 7. E. A. Dowey, Jr., in *The Knowledge of God in Calvin's Theology*, ch. iv, presents an acute discussion of Calvin's doctrine of faith especially as this is related to the knowledge of God.
[69] III. ii. 9.
[70] III. iii. 1; III. xi. 7.

XII

Book IV contains a large amount of new material ingeniously integrated with sections drawn from various parts of the previous edition, so as virtually to constitute a well-ordered treatise in itself. Calvin's title for this book is: "The External Means or Aids by Which God Invites Us Into the Society of Christ and Holds Us Therein." The *Christi societas* is the Holy Catholic Church. This great theme, highly congenial to Calvin's mind, engages all his power and skill.

He follows Luther in the view that in the Creed, "catholic church" and "communion of saints" are terms that refer to the same entity, in which all Christians are members. The invisible church of the elect, whose membership is known to God alone, is differentiated but not dissevered from the organized church visible on earth, whose members are known to each other. Calvin warmly accepts Cyprian's figure of the church as the mother of believers: as such, she conceives, bears, nourishes, and instructs her children, who, indeed, may never leave her school.[71] Though we know that there are "many hypocrites" in the visible church, it is our duty by a "charitable judgment" to recognize as members "those who, by confession of faith, by example of life, and by partaking of the sacraments, profess the same God and Christ."

A true church is recognizable by the marks of the true preaching and faithful hearing of the Word, the right administration of the sacraments, and, subordinate to these yet essential, a functioning discipline to guard the sanctity of communion. The peril of departing from such a church is viewed with the utmost gravity. Since all of us have faults and suffer from "the mists of ignorance," we should not renounce communion with others on slight grounds. Much is made here of the fact that the church is the one society in which it is recognized that forgiveness of sins is constantly required. The visible church is holy, in the sense not of its attainment but of its progress and its goal.[72] Only when the ministry of the Word and sacraments has been perverted and discipline has failed are Christians justified in leaving the organization. This condition Calvin finds in the church adhering to the papacy, although some vestiges of a true church remain within it.[73] A high doctrine of the ministry, its offices and functions, is amply set forth on the basis of New Testament evidence;

[71] IV. i. 4.
[72] IV. i. 7–18.
[73] IV. ii. 1–2, 9, 11–12.

and the development and deterioration of the ministry are traced through the patristic age.[74] Calvin's very considerable knowledge of church history is used in an animated polemic against Roman assertions of Peter's authority in Rome and the rising claim and exercise of papal power in the Middle Ages. If the too abundant invective were removed from these chapters, there would remain a rather impressive body of historical data germane to the issue; but he views historical changes with too little sense of the complexity of the forces involved.

Since his doctrine of the ministry does not allow a separate order of bishops distinct from presbyters, it is notable that he shows much respect for the ancient hierarchy in their functions of government and discipline. For Calvin, the great defection sets in with the proud claims put forth in the era after Gregory the Great, when Boniface III was allowed to assert the papal headship over all churches, and especially after the pact formed between Pope Zachary and the Frankish ruler Pippin, which he regards as an alliance to seize and divide power. Although he wrote these pages before the appearance of the *Magdeburg Centuries* (1559–1574),[75] in which the ninth-century Pseudo-Isidorian Decretals were first effectively exposed, Calvin scoffs at those fraudulent documents. He has read Lorenzo Valla's exposure of the Donation of Constantine[76] and hence regards that eighth-century document also as a forgery. He charges Hildebrand with the unwarranted assertion of a papal imperial authority, which is one of the marks of Antichrist, and he brings Bernard to testify to the growing corruption that ensued. This has continued through the later centuries until the condition under the papacy is one "directly contrary to church order."[77] Authority, which ought to reside in the Word of God, has been assumed by the decadent church and its councils without respect to the Word. He vehemently attacks the many abuses of jurisdiction that have arisen while the papacy, armed with forged documents, pursues its secular ends.[78]

---

[74] IV. v.

[75] A voluminous history of the church to A.D. 1400, prepared by Lutheran theologians under the direction of Matthias Flacius and published at Basel (1559–1574).

[76] This document, forged apparently at Rome between 753 and 775, represents Constantine the Great (306–337) as transferring the rule of a great part of the West to Pope Silvester I. Valla's *De falso credita et ementita Constantini donatione declamatio* was written in 1439 and printed at Basel in 1540. Cf. IV. xi. 12.

[77] IV. vii. 26.

[78] IV. xii. 6, 7.

Calvin employs historical data also in his constructive treatment of discipline and the sacraments. The modern reader, whose experience of church discipline has little in common with that of early Reformed practice, may be startled by the degree of church and pastoral authority assumed here. He will also be impressed by the careful discrimination, moderation, and hopeful patience expected of those charged with the exercise of discipline. Discipline is a very real and a very necessary thing: it is for the church as the ligaments that hold the body together, or as a bridle for restraint, or as a father's chastising rod.[79] No rank or station exempts anyone from its procedures, and these are conducted with such religious gravity as to leave no doubt that "Christ presides in his tribunal." The ends in view in the discipline are three: that the church be not dishonored, the good not corrupted, and offenders brought to repentance.[80] Discipline, then, should be firm and yet kindly. Calvin dwells upon examples of the brotherly considerateness of Paul, Cyprian, Augustine, and Chrysostom in dealing with offenders. We are not to despair of those whose stubbornness necessitates their excommunication, nor to cease to pray for such persons or "consign them to destruction."[81]

XIII

These topics are so treated by Calvin as to exhibit very convincingly his sense of the corporate nature of the church. Five ample chapters are devoted to the sacraments of Baptism and the Lord's Supper, and another to the five rites, "falsely termed sacraments," confirmation, penance, extreme unction, priestly orders, and marriage.[82] Augustine's characterization of a sacrament as "a visible form of an invisible grace" is approved, but for greater clarity Calvin prefers to say that it is "a testimony of divine grace toward us, confirmed by an outward sign, with mutual attestation of our piety toward him." By various metaphors he creates a clear impression of the relation of Word and sacraments, in which the latter are seals of the divine promises, pledges exchanged between God and the believer, and tokens before men of our discipleship. But these are void and fruitless without faith and the invisible grace ministered by the Holy Spirit. The treatment of baptism is remarkable as a defense of the baptism of infants. In this connection stress is laid on the role of circumcision as a valid

[79] IV. xii. 1.
[80] IV. xii. 5.
[81] IV. xii. 8–11.
[82] IV. xiv–xix.

Old Testament sacrament of initiation. Calvin also makes the most possible of the New Testament evidence. Since Christ called the little ones to his embrace and said, "Of such is the Kingdom of Heaven" (Matt. 19:13–14), it is very sinful to deny to the children of believers access to Christ.[83] This is especially objectionable in those who teach, as do the Anabaptists, that there is no salvation for the unbaptized. This erroneous opinion is held also by the Romanists. The latter authorize the baptism by lay men and women of those about to die, and in these circumstances allow it to be hastily and crudely administered. This, Calvin regards as a travesty of the sacrament, arising from the false assumption that those who have missed the opportunity of baptism are therefore damned. "God," he says, "declares that he adopts our babies as his own before they are born." Thus baptism, profoundly important as it is in the economy of salvation, is not a saving rite. He does not say, as Zwingli does, that all who die in infancy are saved, but he points out that Christ is not said to have condemned anyone who was not yet baptized. While discarding the traditional doctrine of baptismal regeneration, Calvin holds that in the covenantal relationship a secret influence operates in the mind of the child as he progressively learns the implications of his acceptance by, and initiation into, the church and comes under its care and teaching. Thus "infants are baptized into future repentance and faith."[84]

In the discussion of the Lord's Supper he labors to show the real presence of Christ's body and blood, but rejects the localization of these in the elements, along with the related doctrine, developed in Lutheranism, of the ubiquity of Christ's resurrected body. On the analogy of other passages, the words "This is my body" must be taken not literally but as a metonymy. The body of Christ was seen taken up to heaven: it remains in heaven and cannot be enclosed in bread and wine.[85] Instead, the communicant is spiritually lifted up to heaven to partake of the body. This doctrine of a spiritual partaking of Christ's true body and blood is distinctive of the Calvinist churches.[86] The mere expression "spiritual presence" is inadequate as an index to Calvin's Eucharistic doctrine. His position is difficult for the modern mind to grasp in its entirety. He has to confess here, as in predestination,

---

[83] IV. xvi. 7.
[84] IV. xv. 20; xvi. 20, 26.
[85] IV. xvii. 22, 30.
[86] A typical confessional statement of this is that of the Belgic Confession, art. xxxv: "We . . . truly receive by faith . . . the true body and blood of Christ, our only Savior, in our souls for our spiritual life."

that he is confronted by a mystery which he has no words to explain. He can only say, "I rather experience than understand it."[87] In some way incomprehensible to reason, our communion in Christ's body is made possible through the secret operation of the Holy Spirit. No writer has gone beyond Calvin in his estimate of the importance of this sacrament in the corporate life of the church. He urges its frequent use, fervently depicts the religious experience of the devout communicant, and stresses "the bond of love" created by participation, with its implications of social duty.[88] The Roman doctrine of the Mass is assailed, especially with respect to the claim that it is an act of satisfaction for sin. This he regards as a negation of Christ's all-sufficient atonement and of the very institution of the Supper. Calvin similarly, with unnecessary vituperation, attacks the arguments used in support of the other five alleged sacraments, rejecting claims that they have the authority of Scripture and of usage in the early church.[89]

XIV

The final chapter, "Civil Government,"[90] is one of the most impressive parts of the work. Like the Prefatory Address to Francis I at the outset, this chapter illustrates the vital contact of Calvin's thought with the world of political action. In the Address, the young scholar ventures to admonish a proud monarch against the evil advice of those who have suggested his policy of persecuting good Christians. Francis is asked to acknowledge the rule of Christ, to whom all earthly kings should bow. In a passage that reflects Augustine's celebrated "mirror of princes," in which those emperors are called happy who "make their power the handmaid of God's majesty,"[91] Calvin declares that it is "true royalty" in a king to acknowledge himself "the minister of God," and that it is his duty to rule according to God's Holy Word. We may here recall also the chapter on "Christian Freedom" (III.xix) at the close of which the topic of political government is introduced, only to be postponed. From the point of view of high theology it might have been expected that the *Institutes* would close on another note than this. In the editions of 1539 to 1554 this section was given the third, and then the second, position from the end; but in 1559 it returned to the place it held in the

---

[87] *"Experior magis quam intelligam."* IV. xvii. 32.
[88] IV. xvii. 38, 42, 44.
[89] IV. xviii. 1–14; xix.
[90] IV. xx.
[91] *City of God* V. xxiv.

1536 edition, at the conclusion of the work. Why did Calvin choose to accord this position of emphasis to the theme of the political society? The answer is found in the chapter itself and in Calvin's other writings bearing on political affairs.[92] His treatment of politics, like that of Thomas Aquinas and of other Scholastics, makes that topic a province of theology. The chapter abounds in quotations from the Bible, which here as elsewhere is his primary guide. But the subject has pressing importance for Calvin from the fact that he is always deeply aware of the way in which the fluctuating policies of rulers affect the reform of the church and the lot of those who commit themselves to the Reformation. The final chapter is indeed only slightly expanded from that of the first edition. It was mainly written during the excitements of the Münster episode, when the Reformation was being characterized by its opponents as a movement of political subversion. Calvin undoubtedly continued to feel the importance of stating a positive conception of politics as a part of his apologetic for the Reformation, and as a practical defense of the doctrines asserted throughout the treatise. As is well known, his correspondence is replete with evidence of his interest in those political issues which could affect the course of evangelical religion.

Although it is true that for Calvin the chief issue involved is the service of the political society to the church of Christ, it is nevertheless a little misleading to say, with Wilhelm Niesel, that "he is not concerned about the state as such, nor even about the Christian state."[93] He vehemently rejects the view of those "fanatics" who in their espousal of a spiritual Christianity loftily withdraw from political interests and obligations. The thought of the extermination of the political state is both repulsive and absurd to him. "Its function among men is no less than that of bread, water, sun, and air; indeed, its place of honor is far more excellent."[94] It serves the purpose of maintaining man's corporate life, and this has an importance far from negligible. But the state renders its highest service in the assertion of a moral order in the affairs of men, and in the protection of a public form of the Christian religion. The church, for Calvin, is free from the control of the state, but should be able to rely on its favor and support.

Calvin is interested not only in the duties of those who govern

[92] A selection of other politically significant passages from Calvin's writings will be found in *John Calvin on God and Political Duty,* edited with an introduction by J. T. McNeill (Library of Liberal Arts, No. 23).
[93] *The Theology of Calvin,* p. 230.
[94] IV. xx. 3.

but also in the forms of government. In his Commentaries he has praise for the few pious kings of the Old Testament, but his references to kings, ancient and modern, are prevailingly unfavorable; and this cannot be dissociated from the implication of a disapproval of kingship itself. Yet he broadly accepts the contemporary variety of governments and asks for co-operation with them where they obey God, and patience where they are oppressive. No one is more anxious than he to discountenance violent revolution. He would like to avoid disputation about the forms of government, but quietly declares his decided preference for "aristocracy, or a system compounded of aristocracy and democracy." This well-known statement was first made in the edition of 1543, and in 1559 he inserted after it a characteristic explanation. Kings are very rarely good and competent, and the defects of men render it best that a number (*plures*) hold sway so that they may help and admonish each other and restrain anyone who wants to domineer.[95] These principles of plural government and mutual fraternal correction run through the units of organization of church and state. They are illustrated in routine practice in the meetings both of ministers and of magistrates in Calvin's Geneva.[96]

The eloquent paragraphs with which the work is ended stand unchanged, except for a reinforcing insertion, from the 1536 edition. They include the brief, startling passage which became a commonplace of political treatises, in which Calvin with a delusive gentleness proposes that the "three estates" of contemporary nations take up the functions of the ancient ephors, tribunes, and demarchs as constitutional defenders of the people's liberty against the oppression of kings. This is not presented as an incitement to revolt but as an appeal to an existing magistracy to fulfill its legitimate functions. It would have been superfluous to refer to the fact that the ancient magistrates mentioned were elected by the people. Calvin's closing sections are charged with power, and reflection on them will help to make possible an appreciation of the impact of his teaching on world history. But at the end he banishes any suggestion of reliance upon political action or advantage. Though we are menaced by the wrath of kings, we whom

[95] IV. xx. 8.
[96] J. Mackinnon, *Calvin and the Reformation*, pp. 163 f.; J. T. McNeill, *The History and Character of Calvinism*, pp. 162, 187. For the Ecclesiastical Ordinances of Geneva, *Project d'Ordonnances ecclésiastiques* (1541), see the edition in OS II. 325–245, where it is followed by the revised Ordinances of 1561 and the laws of the Academy of Geneva, 1559; see tr. in LCC XXII. 58–71. Cf. CR X. i. 15–30 and B. J. Kidd, *Documents of the Continental Reformation*, pp. 588–603.

Christ has redeemed at priceless cost must obey God and endure all things rather than compromise piety or become slaves to the depraved desires of men.

XV

The wide circulation and acceptance of Calvin's *Institutes*, as of his other writings, cannot be dissociated from the qualities of his style.[97] When this is discussed it is often his style in French that is held chiefly in view,[98] but many scholars in his own time and later have also celebrated his success as a writer of Latin.[99] Calvin's Strasbourg friend, John Sturm, in a commendation that appears on the title page of the 1543 Latin edition of the *Institutes*, aptly characterized the work and its author when he said: "John Calvin has been endowed with a most acute judgment, the highest gift of teaching, and an exceptional memory. As a writer he is diversified, copious, and pure." The prodigiously learned Joseph Scaliger (d. 1609) wrote shrewdly that "his style has greater purity and elegance than is suitable to [*deceat*] a theologian." It is unquestionable that few theologians have wielded so felicitous a pen.

His mastery of Latin grew out of the advantage of his education. In mature years he paid a handsome tribute to Mathurin Cordier, his first Latin teacher at the University of Paris, for having so opened to him the gates of learning as to make possible all that he had later achieved.[1] Thus in his fourteenth year he had been initiated into the beauties of Latin and had begun to realize its resources for communication and persuasion. His later

[97] Numerous writers, favorable and unfavorable to Calvin's theology, have paid glowing tributes to his style. Many of these are quoted along with general comments on his personality in the translation of the Commentary on Joshua, published by the Calvin Translation Society (Edinburgh, 1854), pp. 376–464. There is a comparable collection of such appreciations in P. Schaff, *History of the Christian Church* VII. 270–295. A number of these with some others are recited by J. Pannier in *Calvin écrivain, sa place et sa rôle dans l'histoire de la langue et da la littérature française*. See also L. Wencelius, *L'Esthétique de Calvin*, pp. 344–373.

[98] F. Brunetière, "L'Oeuvre littéraire de Calvin," *Revue des Deux Mondes* 161 (Paris, 1900), 898–923; Pannier, *op. cit.*; Pannier, *Introduction to the Institution of 1541* I. xxii ff.; A. Lefranc, *Calvin et l'éloquence française*.

[99] Both Étienne Pasquier (d. 1615), French author and jurist, and the celebrated Bishop Bossuet (d. 1704) are among the many opposing writers who yet praised Calvin's Latin; they are quoted in the works cited in note 97, above. Cf. W. Leon, "Le Classicisme de Calvin," *Humanisme et Renaissance* V (1938). 231–246.

[1] Dedicatory Epistle to Comm. I Thess. (1550); J. Lecoultre, *Maturin Cordier et les origines de la pédagogique protestante dans les pays de langue française*.

classical studies provided him with a Latin vocabulary of exceptional range. Q. Breen speaks of "the precipitate of humanism" carried over into his theology,[2] and F. Wendel observes that "he remained always more or less the humanist he was in 1532."[3] These writers are thinking of more than style, but they are aware that the stylistic influence of the Latin classics was never shaken off. "A certain elegance," says Breen, "lies upon all that he wrote, the light of classical clearness."[4] One has an impression in reading him that when he is unusually eloquent, or sarcastic, he is apt to show a reminiscence of Cicero. Yet Calvin never "played the sedulous ape" to any preceding writer. Cicero and Quintilian would have been pained by the freedom of his divergence from classic models. Attention has been called by A. Veerman to the pronounced influence on his style from postclassical Christian Latin, especially in the extensive use of abstract terms and of vulgarisms, or elements from common speech, by which his vocabulary was extended. Veerman also shows that his sequence of words is shifted at will for emphasis, and that the verb tends to fall in the middle of the sentence rather than at the end. In the *Institutes* he habitually uses long periodic sentences, but these differ from Cicero's in that they lack the latter's artificial, rhythmical structure. Calvin, however, obtains a rhythmical effect by the use of parallel and triple constructions, paired synonyms, and more complicated devices. A concern for the effect upon the ear is further shown in a limited and judicious use of alliteration, assonance, verbal repetition, punning, and similar endings in adjacent clauses.[5] Calvin clearly discerns the variations of style among the Scripture writers. While he takes delight in Scripture passages of marked elegance and beauty, he insists on the point that a divine quality no less inheres in those portions of Scripture which use rude and unadorned language. The Scripture, indeed, has a "force of truth" independent of rhetoric, while it shows, in parts, a surpassing eloquence.[6] That his admiration for the Bible as written discourse was an influence balancing the classical tradition in the shaping of Calvin's style cannot be denied; but this appears more in his popular sermons than in his treatises, where the influence of the patristic writers is more in evidence. Very frequently, however, he commends the Biblical writers in general

---

[2] Q. Breen, *John Calvin: A Study in French Humanism*, p. 146.

[3] F. Wendel, *Calvin: Sources et évolution de sa pensée religieuse*, p. 21.

[4] Breen, *op. cit.*, p. 148. In the Geneva Academy, Calvin required of the highest class that they *"exercent diligement leur style"* (CR X. 1. 79; OS II. 370).

[5] A. Veerman, *De Stijl van Calvijn in de Institutio Christianae Religionis*, pp. 26 ff., 60 ff., 72 ff., 76 f., 92–110, 121 ff.

[6] I. viii. 1, 2.

for their clarity, simplicity, and brevity, qualities that he especially prized and sought to attain. He is not in fact concerned for style as such, but only to write in such a way as to communicate his whole thought clearly and with no waste of words.

Brevity is a quality often praised by him, and in many instances he indicates how this principle excludes some elaboration that he is tempted to practice. He has no patience with prolix writers, especially where the urgent issues of religion are discussed. He even criticizes on this ground his admired friends and associates, Bucer[7] and Farel. In a letter to Farel he gently but firmly disapproves of the latter's "involved and elaborate" style, points to the difference between it and his own, and involves Augustine himself in the same censure. "You know," Calvin remarks, "how reverently I feel toward Augustine, yet I do not conceal the fact that his prolixity is displeasing to me. Still, it may be that my brevity is too concise."[8]

His claim to have achieved brevity will not escape question. Can we credit with brevity the author of so long a treatise? There are, in fact, many passages in the *Institutes* that must seem to us tediously extended. Something should be allowed here for certain theological interests of his time to which little emphasis is given today. The real test of brevity as a quality of style has no direct bearing upon the length of a work planned with such a vastness and variety of subject matter as the *Institutes*. It is well remarked by Émile Faguet that although the claim of brevity may seem laughable to modern readers, it is justified in the fact that his phrases are "not overloaded" and that "though he has his wearisome passages, he has no verbiage."[9] With few exceptions his sentences and paragraphs are packed with thought and have all the condensation possible without sacrifice of constituent matter. Calvin's deep convictions bring to his writing a quality of urgency which in some passages takes on an oratorical character. It is much less by formal logic than by enlisting the emotions that he has power to persuade. Habitually, as Breen

---

[7] See his Epistle to Simon Grynaeus, introducing Comm. Rom. (CR X. ii. 406; tr. LCC XXIII. 75).

[8] Letter to Farel, Sept. 1, 1549 (CR XIII. 374). The remark is incidental to his criticism of a book of Farel's, apparently *La Glaive de la parole véritable*, then about to be published. His comparable judgment of Seneca's style in the preface to the Seneca Commentary (1532) is also noteworthy: with all his elegance Seneca has "rather too much verbosity." Cf. Pannier, *Calvin écrivain*, p. 10; A. M. Hugo, *Calvijn en Seneca*, pp. 177 ff., and Hugo's English translation of the preface, *ibid.*, p. 231.

[9] É. Faguet, *Seizième siècle, études littéraires*, p. 190. In this work on sixteenth-century French writers, Faguet has an acute study of Calvin, pp. 127–197.

has pointed out, his arguments are not formally syllogistic. It is perhaps due to his desire for brevity that where logical sequence is featured he prefers the clipped syllogism, or enthymeme, which leaves one premise to be supplied by the reader;[10] but this tends to lessen the importance of logic, while the reader is the more rapidly carried on to the point of persuasion.

If there is any habitual violation of the principle of brevity, it consists in the abundance of adjectives and adverbs of emotional content often employed in commendation or condemnation of a position discussed. On occasion, Calvin shows a typically humanist mastery of the language of disparagement and vituperation. His horror of abuses led him at times to use epithets of abuse, and he sometimes resorts to this in assailing the legitimate views of an opponent. This is a deplorable feature by which in parts Calvin's work is marred for the sensitive reader, but it is not so prevalent as some critics have charged; and in his case invective is not a substitute for argument but a misconceived attempt to enhance its force.

It is not upon his antagonisms and negations that Calvin's power and persuasiveness depend, but upon the intensity of his positive convictions and the rich resources of his mind. This work is his greatest legacy to later ages; and even the new interests that captivate our generation do not lessen the relevance and worth of its message. "Today," Calvin once wrote, "all sorts of subjects are eagerly pursued; but the knowledge of God is neglected. . . . Yet to know God is man's chief end, and justifies his existence. Even if a hundred lives were ours, this one aim would be sufficient for them all."[11]

10 Q. Breen, "John Calvin and the Rhetorical Tradition," *Church History* XXVI (1957). 14 f.
11 Comm. Jer. 9:24 (tr. LCC XXIII. 125).

INSTITUTES OF THE CHRISTIAN RELIGION

John Calvin to the Reader

1559

ᵇIn the first edition of this work of ours I did not in the least expect that success which, out of his infinite goodness, the Lord has given. Thus, for the most part I treated the subject summarily, as is usually done in small works. But when I realized that it was received by almost all godly men with a favor for which I never would have ventured to wish, much less to hope, I deeply felt that I was much more favored than I deserved. Consequently I thought that I should be showing extreme ingratitude not to try at least, to the best of my slender ability, to respond to this warm appreciation for me, an appreciation that demanded my further diligence. ᵉ⁽ᵇ⁾Not only did I attempt this in the second edition, but each time the work has been reprinted since then, it has been enriched with some additions. Although I did not regret the labor spent, I was never satisfied until the work had been arranged in the order now set forth. Now I trust that I have provided something that all of you will approve.

In any event, I can furnish a very clear testimony of my great zeal and effort to carry out this task for God's church. Last winter when I thought the quartan fever[1] was summoning me to my death, the more the disease pressed upon me the less I spared myself, until I could leave a book behind me that might, in some measure, repay the generous invitation of godly men. Indeed I should have preferred to do it sooner, ᵇbut it is done soon enough

---

[1] During his illness with this disease, a form of malaria, from October, 1558, to May, 1559, Calvin made the final major revision of the *Institutes* and of the Commentary on Isaiah. Beza, *Vita Calvini,* CR XXI. 156 (tr. H. Beveridge, *Life of John Calvin by Theodore Beza,* pp. 82 f.).

3

if it is done well enough.[2] Moreover, I shall think my work has appeared at an opportune time as soon as I perceive that it has borne some richer fruit for the church of God than heretofore. ᶜThis is my only prayer. Unless I remained content with the approbation of God alone and despised both the foolish and perverse judgments of ignorant men and the wrong and malicious ones of the wicked, things would go ill with me. God has filled my mind with zeal to spread his Kingdom and to further the public good. I am also duly clear in my own conscience, and have God and the angels to witness, that since I undertook the office of teacher in the church, I have had no other purpose than to benefit the church by maintaining the pure doctrine of godliness. Yet I think that there is no one who is assailed, bitten, and wounded by more false accusations than I.

When this epistle was in press, I ascertained that at Augsburg, where the assembly of the Estates of the Empire was meeting, a rumor had been spread abroad of my defection to the papacy and that it was more eagerly received in the courts of the princes than was fitting.[3] Such indeed is the gratitude of those to whom the very many evidences of my constancy are certainly not hidden! These evidences repel so base a calumny, and should also have protected me from it before all fair and humane judges. But the devil with his whole troop is deceived if, in overwhelming me with foul lies, he thinks that this indignity will make me more feeble or more pliant. For I trust that God out of his infinite goodness will permit me to persevere with unwavering patience in the path of his holy calling. In this edition I set forth new proof of this fact for godly readers.

ᵇMoreover, it has been my purpose in this labor to prepare and instruct candidates in sacred theology for the reading of the divine Word, in order that they may be able both to have easy access to it and to advance in it without stumbling. For I believe I have so embraced the sum of religion in all its parts, and have arranged it in such an order, that if anyone rightly grasps it, it will not be difficult for him to determine what he ought especially to seek in Scripture, and to what end he ought to relate its contents. If, after

---

[2] *"Verum sat cito si sat bene."* Apparently a memory of Suetonius, *Lives of the Caesars, Augustus* II. xxv: *"Sat celeriter fieri quidquid fiat satis bene"* (LCL Suetonius I. 158). Petrarch repeats the sentence in *Epistolae rerum senilium* xvi. 2 (*Opera*, Basel, 1581, II. 965). It has been wrongly attributed to the Huguenot poet Guillaume du Bartas. May it not have suggested Shakespeare's "If it were done when 'tis done, then 'twere well it were done quickly" (*Macbeth* I. vii)?

[3] The reference is to the Diet held at Augsburg, February 25 to March 28, 1558.

this road has, as it were, been paved, I shall publish any interpretations of Scripture,[4] I shall always condense them, because I shall have no need to undertake long doctrinal discussions, and to digress into commonplaces. In this way the godly reader will be spared great annoyance and boredom, provided he approach Scripture armed with a knowledge of the present work, as a necessary tool. But because the program of this instruction is clearly mirrored in all my commentaries,[5] I prefer to let the book itself declare its purpose rather than to describe it in words.

Farewell, kindly reader, and if you benefit at all from my labors, help me with your prayers before God our Father.

Geneva, 1st August 1559

> e'Tis those whose cause my former booklet pled
> Whose zeal to learn has wrought this tome instead.[6]

cAugustine, Epistle 7

"I count myself one of the number of those who write as they learn and learn as they write."[7]

[4] These words appeared in the second edition of the *Institutes*, published in August, 1539, and thus before Calvin's first Scripture commentary (Romans), which was dedicated October 18, 1539, and published in 1540.
[5] Editions 1539–1554 insert here: "The Commentaries on the Letter to the Romans will furnish an example."
[6] This sentence in the text is a Latin distich, evidently original with Calvin. No rendering of it is given in the French version (VG) of 1560, but it reappears as a quatrain in French in the edition of 1561, and its Latin form is there ascribed to "the author." Cf. Benoit, *Institution* I. 24.
[7] This quotation is really from Augustine, *Letters* cxliii. 2 (MPL 33. 585; tr. NPNF I. 490 and FC 20. 150).

Subject Matter of the Present Work

FROM THE FRENCH EDITION OF 1560

In order that my readers may better profit from this present work, I should like to indicate briefly the benefit they may derive from it. For, in doing this, I shall show them the purpose to which they ought to bend and direct their intention while reading it. Although Holy Scripture contains a perfect doctrine, to which one can add nothing, since in it our Lord has meant to display the infinite treasures of his wisdom, yet a person who has not much practice in it has good reason for some guidance and direction, to know what he ought to look for in it, in order not to wander hither and thither, but to hold to a sure path, that he may always be pressing toward the end to which the Holy Spirit calls him. Perhaps the duty of those who have received from God fuller light than others is to help simple folk at this point, and as it were to lend them a hand, in order to guide them and help them to find the sum of what God meant to teach us in his Word. Now, that cannot be better done through the Scriptures than to treat the chief and weightiest matters comprised in the Christian philosophy.[8] For he who knows these things will be prepared to

---

[8] The concept of a "Christian philosophy" is seen in the Greek and Latin fathers and in numerous medieval and Renaissance writers. It was given prominence by Erasmus. For instances in Byzantine writers, see F. Dölger, *Byzanz und die Europäischer Staatenwelt,* pp. 197 ff. Fourth-century writers often speak of Christian asceticism as the life of "philosophy," e.g., Eusebius, *Ecclesiastical History* II. 17; III. 38. But the expression usually takes the wider meaning of the wisdom of true Christian piety. A study of the Christian philosophy as understood in ninth-century Byzantine theology is made on the basis of an utterance of Saint Constantine-Cyril (d. 869) by Thor Sevecenko, "The Definition of Philosophy in the Life of Saint Con-

profit more in God's school in one day than another in three months—particularly as he knows fairly well to what he must refer each sentence, and has this rule to embrace all that is presented to him.

It is very necessary to help in this way those who desire to be instructed in the doctrine of salvation. Consequently, I was constrained, according to the ability that the Lord gave me, to undertake this task. Such was my purpose in composing the present book. First of all I put it into Latin so as to serve all men of learning, to whatever nation they belonged; then afterward, desiring to communicate what could bear fruit for our French nation, I have also translated it into our tongue. I dare not render too favorable testimony concerning it, nor yet declare how profitable the reading of it could be, for I would shrink from seeming to appraise my work too highly. Nevertheless, I can at least promise that it can be a key to open a way for all children of God into a good and right understanding of Holy Scripture. Thus, if henceforth our Lord gives me the means and opportunity of writing some commentaries,[9] I shall use the greatest possible brevity, because there will be no need for long digressions, seeing that I have here treated at length almost all the articles pertaining to Christianity. Since we must recognize that all truth and sound doctrine proceed from God, I shall in all simplicity dare fearlessly to protest what I think of this work; I shall recognize that

stantine," in the volume *For Roman Jakobson*, pp. 448–457. For Western writers on this theme, É. Gilson has an extended analytical bibliography at the conclusion of his Gifford Lectures, *L'Esprit de la philosophie médiévale*, pp. 413–440. (This is omitted from the English edition.) Augustine speaks of "our Christian philosophy" in the treatise *Against Julian the Pelagian* IV. xiv. 72 (MPL 44. 774; tr. FC 35. 228), and in *City of God* XXII. xxii (MPL 41. 784 ff.; tr. NPNF II. 499) makes true philosophy dependent on the grace of God. John Scotus Erigena holds that "true philosophy is true religion and true religion is true philosophy," *De divina praedestinatione* i. 1 (MPL 122. 357). Cf. H. Leclercq, "Pour l'histoire de l'expression Philosophie Chrétienne," *Mélanges de sciences religieuses* IX. 221–226, and J. Bohatec, *Budé und Calvin*, pp. 33 ff. Erasmus, in his *Paracelsis, id est adhortatio ad Christianae philosophiae studium* (*Opera* [Leyden, 1704] V. 141 f.), thinks the Christian philosophy adopted only by a few, and "seated in emotions rather than in syllogisms, a life rather than an argument, inspiration (*afflatus*) rather than erudition, a transformation rather than a system of reason." Calvin, in III. vii. 1, sharply distinguishes the "Christian philosophy" from that of "the philosophers" as a life not ordered according to reason alone but renewed in Christ and directed by the Holy Spirit. Cf. III. vi. 4; I. xi. 7; I. xii. 1; III. xx. 1, note 1; Comm. I Cor. 13:8. W. Niesel points out that Calvin in "Christian philosophy" had in mind chiefly the exposition of Scripture: *The Theology of Calvin*, tr. H. Knight, pp. 23 ff.

[9] Cf. note 4, above.

it is God's more than mine. And, in truth, any praise for it must be rendered to him.

Thus, I exhort all those who have reverence for the Lord's Word, to read it, and to impress it diligently upon their memory, if they wish to have, first, a sum of Christian doctrine, and, secondly, a way to benefit greatly from reading the Old as well as the New Testament. When they will have done this they will recognize, by experience, that I have not at all meant to misuse words. If anyone cannot understand all the contents, he must not therefore despair, but must ever press onward, hoping that one passage will give him a more familiar explanation of another. Above all, I must urge him to have recourse to Scripture in order to weigh the testimonies that I adduce from it.[10]

[10] Cf. III. iv. 29, note 62.

Prefatory Address to King Francis I of France

[a]For the Most Mighty and Illustrious Monarch, Francis, Most Christian King of the French, His Sovereign, John Calvin Craves Peace and Salvation in Christ.

1. CIRCUMSTANCES IN WHICH THE BOOK WAS FIRST WRITTEN

When I first set my hand to this work, nothing was farther from my mind, most glorious King, than to write something that might afterward be offered to Your Majesty. My purpose was solely to transmit certain rudiments by which those who are touched with any zeal for religion might be shaped to true godliness. And I undertook this labor especially for our French countrymen, very many of whom I knew to be hungering and thirsting for Christ; but I saw very few who had been duly imbued with even a slight knowledge of him. The book itself witnesses that this was my intention, adapted as it is to a simple and, you may say, elementary form of teaching.

But I perceived that the fury of certain wicked persons has prevailed so far in your realm that there is no place in it for sound doctrine. Consequently, it seemed to me that I should be doing something worth-while if I both gave instruction to them and made confession before you with the same work. From this you may learn the nature of the doctrine against which those madmen burn with rage who today disturb your realm with fire and sword. And indeed I shall not fear to confess that here is contained almost the sum of that very doctrine which they shout must be punished by prison, exile, proscription, and fire, and be exterminated on land and sea. Indeed, I know with what horrible reports they have filled your ears and mind, to render our cause

9

as hateful as possible to you.[1] But, as fits your clemency, you ought to weigh the fact that if it is sufficient merely to make accusation, then no innocence will remain either in words or in deeds.

Suppose anyone, to arouse hatred, pretends that this doctrine, an account of which I am trying to render to you, has long since been condemned both by the verdict of all estates and by many judgments of the courts. This will surely be saying nothing other than that it has in part been violently rejected by the partisanship and power of its opponents, and in part insidiously and fraudulently oppressed by their falsehoods, subtleties, and slanders. It is sheer violence that bloody sentences are meted out against this doctrine without a hearing; it is fraud that it is undeservedly charged with treason and villainy. So that no one may think we are wrongly complaining of these things, you can be our witness, most noble King, with how many lying slanders it is daily traduced in your presence. It is as if this doctrine looked to no other end than to wrest the scepters from the hands of kings, to cast down all courts and judgments, to subvert all orders and civil governments, to disrupt the peace and quiet of the people, to abolish all laws, to scatter all lordships and possessions—in short, to turn everything upside down! And yet you hear only a very small part of the accusation, for dreadful reports are being spread abroad among the people. If these were true, the whole world would rightly judge this doctrine and its authors worthy of a thousand fires and crosses. Who now can wonder that public hatred is aroused against it, when these most wicked accusations are believed? This is why all classes with one accord conspire to condemn us and our doctrine. Those who sit in judgment, seized with this feeling, pronounce as sentences the prejudices which they have brought from home. And they think they have duly discharged their office if they order to be brought to punishment no one not convicted either by his own confession or by sure testimony. But of what crime? Of this condemned doctrine, they say.

[1] The reference is to the persecutions in France following the incident of the Placards, October 18, 1534). See Introduction, p. xxxi, above. The charge that the Protestant reform party in France consisted of seditious extremists is illustrated in documents given by A.-L. Herminjard, *Correspondance* III. A letter of Francis I to the Estates of the Empire, February 1, 1535, is especially pertinent (Herminjard, *Correspondance* III. 249 ff.). The rumor had been circulated that the evangelicals plotted armed attacks on worshiping assemblies. The distressed condition of the French Waldenses was also in Calvin's mind. On August 4, 1535, Farel and Viret wrote to the evangelicals of Switzerland and Germany describing the "cruel and savage persecution" that the Waldenses were suffering. The reply of Capito from Strasbourg is of the same date as that of Calvin's Address to the King, August 23, 1535 (Herminjard, *Correspondance* III. 335 ff.).

But with what right has it been condemned? Now, the very stronghold of their defense was not to disavow this very doctrine but to uphold it as true. Here even the right to whisper is cut off.

2. PLEA FOR THE PERSECUTED EVANGELICALS

^aFor this reason, most invincible King, I not unjustly ask you to undertake a full inquiry into this case, which until now has been handled—we may even say, tossed about—with no order of law and with violent heat rather than judicial gravity. And do not think that I am here preparing my own personal defense, thereby to return safely to my native land. Even though I regard my country with as much natural affection as becomes me, as things now stand I do not much regret being excluded. Rather, I embrace the common cause of all believers, that of Christ himself—a cause completely torn and trampled in your realm today, lying, as it were, utterly forlorn, more through the tyranny of certain Pharisees than with your approval.

But here is not the place to tell how it has come about: certainly our cause lies afflicted. For ungodly men have so far prevailed that Christ's truth, even if it is not driven away scattered and destroyed, still lies hidden, buried and inglorious. The poor little church has either been wasted with cruel slaughter or banished into exile, or so overwhelmed by threats and fears that it dare not even open its mouth. And yet, with their usual rage and madness, the ungodly continue to batter a wall already toppling and to complete the ruin toward which they have been striving. Meanwhile no one comes forward to defend the church against such furies. But any who wish to appear as greatly favoring truth feel that they should pardon the error and imprudence of ignorant men. For so speak moderate men, calling error and imprudence what they know is the most certain truth of God; calling untutored men those whose intelligence was not so despicable to Christ as to prevent him for bestowing upon them the mysteries of his heavenly wisdom! So ashamed are they all of the gospel!

It will then be for you, most serene King, not to close your ears or your mind to such just defense, especially when a very great question is at stake: how God's glory may be kept safe on earth, how God's truth may retain its place of honor, how Christ's Kingdom may be kept in good repair among us.[2] Worthy indeed is this matter of your hearing, worthy of your cognizance, worthy

---

[2] For similar statements see IV. xx. 29, 31 and Comm. Rom. 13:1-7. Cf. Augustine's passage on the good emperor, traditionally called the "mirror of princes," *City of God* V. xxiv (MPL 41. 170; tr. NPNF II. 104 f.). The last sentence of this statement shows a recollection of Plautus, *Trinummus* 317: *"sarta tecta tua praecepta"* (LCL Plautus V. 126).

of your royal throne! Indeed, this consideration makes a true king: to recognize himself a minister of God in governing his kingdom. Now, that king who in ruling over his realm does not serve God's glory exercises not kingly rule but brigandage.[3] Furthermore, he is deceived who looks for enduring prosperity in his kingdom when it is not ruled by God's scepter, that is, his Holy Word; for the heavenly oracle that proclaims that "where prophecy fails the people are scattered" [Prov. 29:18] cannot lie. And contempt for our lowliness ought not to dissuade you from this endeavor. Indeed, we are quite aware of what mean and lowly little men we are. Before God, of course, we are miserable sinners; in men's eyes most despised—if you will, the offscouring and refuse [cf. I Cor. 4:13] of the world, or anything viler that can be named. Thus, before God nothing remains for us to boast of, save his mercy [cf. II Cor. 10:17–18], whereby we have been received into hope of eternal salvation through no merit of our own [cf. Titus 3:5]; and before men nothing but our weakness [cf. II Cor. 11:30; 12:5, 9], which even to admit by a nod is to them the greatest dishonor. But our doctrine must tower unvanquished above all the glory and above all the might of the world, for it is not of us, but of the living God and his Christ whom the Father has appointed King to "rule from sea to sea, and from the rivers even to the ends of the earth" [Ps. 72:8; 72:7, Vg.]. And he is so to rule as to smite the whole earth with its iron and brazen strength, with its gold and silver brilliance, shattering it with the rod of his mouth as an earthen vessel, just as the prophets have prophesied concerning the magnificence of his reign [Dan. 2:32–35; Isa. 11:4; Ps. 2:9, conflated]. Indeed, our adversaries cry out that we falsely make the Word of God our pretext, and wickedly corrupt it.[4] By reading our confession you can judge according to your prudence not only how malicious a calumny but also what utter effrontery this is.

Yet we must say something here to arouse your zeal and attention, or at least to prepare the way for you to read our confession. When Paul wished all prophecy to be made to accord with the analogy of faith [Rom. 12:6],[5] he set forth a very clear rule to test

---

[3] *"Nec iam regnum ille sed latrocinium exercet."* An echo of Augustine's famous phrase: "When justice is taken away, what are kingdoms [*regna*] but a vast banditry [*magna latrocinia*]?" *City of God* IV. iv (MPL 41. 115; tr. NPNF II. 66).

[4] Alfonsus de Castro (d. 1558), *Adversus omnes haereses* I. iv (1543 edition, fo. 7, 8). The heresies are arranged alphabetically. This author, an able controversialist, was a Spanish Franciscan who attended Philip II in England and the Netherlands.

[5] *"Fidei analogia."* Cf. IV. xvii. 32. See also Comm. Rom. 12:6, and the edi-

all interpretation of Scripture. Now, if our interpretation be measured by this rule of faith, victory is in our hands. For what is more consonant with faith than to recognize that we are naked of all virtue, in order to be clothed by God? That we are empty of all good, to be filled by him? That we are slaves of sin, to be freed by him? Blind, to be illumined by him? Lame, to be made straight by him? Weak, to be sustained by him? To take away from us all occasion for glorying, that he alone may stand forth gloriously and we glory in him [cf. I Cor. 1:31; II Cor. 10:17]? When we say these and like things our adversaries interrupt and complain that in this way we shall subvert some blind light of nature, imaginary preparations, free will, and works that merit eternal salvation, even with their supererogations.[6] For they cannot bear that the whole praise and glory of all goodness, virtue, righteousness, and wisdom should rest with God. But we do not read of anyone being blamed for drinking too deeply of the fountain of living water [John 4:14]. On the contrary, those have been harshly rebuked who "have dug for themselves cisterns, broken cisterns that can hold no water" [Jer. 2:13]. Besides, what is better and closer to faith than to feel assured that God will be a propitious Father where Christ is recognized as brother and propitiator? Than confidently to look for all happy and prosperous things from Him whose unspeakable love toward us went so far that "he . . . did not spare his own Son but gave him up for us all" [Rom. 8:32]? Than to repose in certain expectation of salvation and eternal life, when we meditate upon Christ, given by the Father, in whom such treasures are hidden? Here they seize upon us, and cry out that such certainty of trust is not free from arrogance and presumption. But as we ought to presume nothing of ourselves, so ought we to presume all things of God; nor are we stripped of vainglory for any other reason than to learn to glory in the Lord [cf. II Cor. 10:17; I Cor. 1:31; Jer. 9:23–24].

What further? Examine briefly, most mighty King, all the parts of our case, and think us the most wicked of wicked men, unless you clearly find that "we toil and suffer reproach because

tor's note in John Owen's English edition, p. 461. William Bucanus, professor of theology at Lausanne, in his elaborate catechism, *Institutiones Theologicae* (Geneva, 1605), defines the analogy of faith as "the constant and perpetual sense of Scripture expounded in the manifest places of Scripture and agreeable to the Apostles' Creed, the Ten Commandments, and the general sentences and axioms of every main point of divinity." (Tr. Robert Hill [1606], p. 44.) Cf. Heppe RD, pp. 34–36.

[6] The authoritative doctrine of the treasury of merits and supererogatory works is well illustrated in the decretal of Clement VI, *Unigenitus* (1343) (*Extravagantes communes* IX. ii; Friedberg II. 1304 ff.). Cf. III. v. 2–5.

we have our hope set on the living God" [I Tim. 4:10]; because we believe that "this is eternal life: to know the only true God, and Jesus Christ whom he has sent" [John 17:3 p.]. For the sake of this hope some of us are shackled with irons, some beaten with rods, some led about as laughingstocks, some proscribed, some most savagely tortured, some forced to flee. All of us are oppressed by poverty, cursed with dire execrations, wounded by slanders, and treated in most shameful ways.

Now look at our adversaries (I speak of the order of priests, at whose nod and will the others are hostile toward us), and consider with me for a moment what zeal motivates them. They readily allow themselves and others to ignore, neglect, and despise the true religion, which has been handed down in the Scriptures, and which ought to have had a recognized place among all men. They think it of no concern what belief anyone holds or does not hold regarding God and Christ, if only he submit his mind with implicit faith[7] (as they call it) to the judgment of the church. The sight of God's glory defiled with manifest blasphemies does not much trouble them, bprovided no one raises a finger against the primacy of the Apostolic See and against the authority of Holy Mother Church. aWhy, therefore, do they fight with such ferocity and bitterness for the Mass, purgatory, pilgrimages, and trifles of that sort, denying that there can be true godliness without a most explicit faith, so to speak, in such things, even though they prove nothing of them from God's Word? Why? unless for them "their God is the belly" [Phil. 3:19]; their kitchen their religion! If these are taken away, they believe that they will not be Christians, not even men! For, even though some glut themselves sumptuously while others gnaw upon meager crusts, still all live out of the same pot, a pot that without this fuel would not only grow cold but freeze through and through. Consequently, the one most concerned about his belly proves the sharpest contender for his faith. In fine, all men strive to one goal: to keep either their rule intact or their belly full. No one gives the slightest indication of sincere zeal.

3. Charges of Antagonists Refuted: Newness, Uncertainty; the Value of Miracles

aDespite this, they do not cease to assail our doctrine and to reproach and defame it with names that render it hated or

---

[7] The question of explicit and implicit faith is discussed in III. ii. 2–5, and by Thomas Aquinas in *Summa Theol.* II IIae. ii. 5–8. Aquinas rejects (art. 6) the view that all are bound to believe everything explicitly, but holds that those of higher degree, whose duty it is to teach others, "are bound to believe explicitly more things than others are."

suspect. They call it "new" and "of recent birth." They reproach it as "doubtful and uncertain." They ask what miracles have confirmed it. They inquire whether it is right for it to prevail against the agreement of so many holy fathers and against most ancient custom. They urge us to acknowledge that it is schismatic because it wages war against the church, or that the church was lifeless during the many centuries in which no such thing was heard. Finally, they say that there is no need of many arguments, for one can judge by its fruits what it is, seeing that it has engendered such a heap of sects, so many seditious tumults, such great licentiousness.[8] Indeed, it is very easy for them to revile a forsaken cause before the credulous and ignorant multitude. But if we too might speak in our turn, this bitterness which they licentiously and with impunity spew at us from swollen cheeks would subside.

First, by calling it "new" they do great wrong to God, whose Sacred Word does not deserve to be accused of novelty. Indeed, I

[8] These were staple arguments against Luther and the other Reformers from the beginning. Numerous specific references to works against Luther are given in the notes in OS III. 13–15. Characteristic is John Eck's *Enchiridion locorum communium adversus Lutheranos* (1526; enlarged edition, *Enchiridion locorum communium adversus Martinum Lutherum et asseclas eius*, 1532), dedicated to Henry VIII and Thomas More. This work was printed ninety-one times to 1600. Eck made use of writings against the Lutherans by John Fisher of Rochester, John Faber, Kaspar Schatzgeyer, Jerome Emser, Augustin Alveld, and others. In the first edition he deals with twenty-nine of the Lutheran positions, of which the first five are especially vital: the church and its authority; church councils; the primacy of the apostolic see; the Scriptures; faith and works. The other topics include a broad series of controverted points such as the Mass and other sacraments, excommunication, indulgences, purgatory, the burning of heretics, the baptism of infants. Prominent also in this class of writers were Alfonsus de Castro (cf. note 4, above) and Josse Clichtove (Judocus Clichtoveus, d. 1543), a Netherlander, professor in the Collège de Navarre, Paris, who, having earlier supported Lefèvre, strongly opposed the Reformation in *Antilutherus*, 1525. This is an extended treatise in three books, presenting many arguments in defense of the medieval papacy, hierarchy, and theology. A more voluminous writer was John Cochlaeus (d. 1552), of Wendelstein (near Nuremberg), whose *De authoritate ecclesiae et scripture, adversus Lutheranos* (1524) was one of the earliest of weighty anti-Lutheran writings. His *De sacris reliquiis Christi et sanctorum eius* (1549) is a reply to Calvin's *Treatise on Relics* (1543). He also wrote against Melanchthon and Bullinger. For a short account of recent literature and editions for the study of this class of writers, see "The Catholic Reform in the Sixteenth Century," by G. H. Tavard, *Church History* XXVI (1957), 275–288. Cf. J. Bohatec, *Budé und Calvin*, pp. 128 ff., where it is charged that the weightiest opponents whom Calvin had in mind have been missed by Barth and Niesel. These include Budé, who exchanged writings with Cochlaeus. Bohatec shows that Budé, with Robert Cenau, bishop of Avranches, and Cardinal Sadoleto, had aroused the king against the evangelicals after the Placard incident, October 18, 1534.

do not at all doubt that it is new to them, since to them both Christ himself and his gospel are new. But he who knows that this preaching of Paul is ancient, that "Jesus Christ died for our sins and rose again for our justification" [Rom. 4:25 p.], will find nothing new among us.

That it has lain long unknown and buried is the fault of man's impiety. Now when it is restored to us by God's goodness, its claim to antiquity ought to be admitted at least by right of recovery.[9]

The same ignorance leads them to regard it as doubtful and uncertain. This is precisely what the Lord complains of through his prophet, that "the ox knew its owner, and the ass its master's crib; but his own people did not know him" [Isa. 1:3 p.]. But however they may jest about its uncertainty, if they had to seal their doctrine in their own blood, and at the expense of their own life, one could see how much it would mean to them. Quite the opposite is our assurance, which fears neither the terrors of death nor even God's judgment seat.

In demanding miracles of us, they act dishonestly. For we are not forging some new gospel, but are retaining that very gospel whose truth all the miracles that Jesus Christ and his disciples ever wrought serve to confirm. But, compared with us, they have a strange power: even to this day they can confirm their faith by continual miracles! Instead they allege miracles which can disturb a mind otherwise at rest—they are so foolish and ridiculous, so vain and false! And yet, even if these were marvelous prodigies, they ought not to be of any moment against God's truth, for God's name ought to be always and everywhere hallowed, whether by miracles or by the natural order of things.

ᵇPerhaps this false hue could have been more dazzling if Scripture had not warned us concerning the legitimate purpose and use of miracles. For Mark teaches that those signs which attended the apostles' preaching were set forth to confirm it [Mark 16:20]. In like manner, Luke relates that our "Lord . . . bore witness to the word of his grace," when these signs and wonders were done by the apostles' hands [Acts 14:3 p.]. Very much like this is that word of the apostle: that the salvation proclaimed by the gospel has been confirmed in the fact that "the Lord has attested it by signs and wonders and various mighty works [Heb. 2:4 p.; cf. Rom. 15:18–19]. When we hear that these are the seals of the gospel, shall we turn them to the destruction of faith in the gospel?

---

[9] "Postliminii iure." A legal term for the recovery of property or privilege so as to have secure possession. Postliminium means literally "behind the threshold," hence, in safekeeping.

When we hear that they were appointed only to seal the truth, shall we employ them to confirm falsehoods? In the first place, it is right to investigate and examine that doctrine which, as the Evangelist says, is superior to miracles. Then, if it is approved, it may rightly be confirmed from miracles. Yet, if one does not tend to seek men's glory but God's [John 7:18; 8:50], this is a mark of true doctrine, as Christ says. Since Christ affirms this test of doctrine, miracles are wrongly valued that are applied to any other purpose than to glorify the name of the one God [Deut. 13:2 ff.]. aAnd we may also fitly remember that Satan has his miracles, which, though they are deceitful tricks rather than true powers, are of such sort as to mislead the simple-minded and untutored [cf. II Thess. 2:9–10]. Magicians and enchanters have always been noted for miracles. Idolatry has been nourished by wonderful miracles, yet these are not sufficient to sanction for us the superstition either of magicians or of idolaters.

The Donatists of old overwhelmed the simplicity of the multitude with this battering-ram: that they were mighty in miracles. We, therefore, now answer our adversaries as Augustine then answered the Donatists: the Lord made us wary of these miracle workers when he predicted that false prophets with lying signs and prodigies would come to draw even the elect (if possible) into error [Matt. 24:24].[10] And Paul warned that the reign of Antichrist would be "with all power, and signs and lying wonders" [II Thess. 2:9]. But these miracles, they say, are done neither by idols, nor by magicians, nor by false prophets, but by the saints. As if we did not understand that to "disguise himself as an angel of light" [II Cor. 11:14] is the craft of Satan! The Egyptians of old worshiped Jeremiah, who was buried in their land, rendering to him sacrifices and divine honors.[11] Did they not misuse the holy prophet of God for idolatrous purposes? And yet, they thought that the curing of snake bite was a just reward for such veneration of his tomb. What shall we say except that it has always been, and ever will be, a very just punishment of God to "send to those" who have not received the love of truth "a strong delusion to make them believe a lie" [II Thess. 2:11]?

Well, we are not entirely lacking in miracles, and these very certain and not subject to mockery. On the contrary, those "miracles" which our adversaries point to in their own support are

---

[10] Augustine, *John's Gospel* xiii. 17 (MPL 35. 1501; tr. NPNF VII. 93). Augustine cites the magicians of Pharaoh, Ex. 7:12.
[11] Not found in Jerome, as indicated in the original annotation, but in Isidore of Seville (d. 636), *De ortu et obitu patrum* xxxiii. 74 (MPL 83. 143).

sheer delusions of Satan, for they draw the people away from the true worship of their God to vanity [cf. Deut. 13:2 ff.].

4. MISLEADING CLAIM THAT THE CHURCH FATHERS OPPOSE THE REFORMATION TEACHING

aMoreover, they unjustly set the ancient fathers against us[12] (I mean the ancient writers of a better age of the church) as if in them they had supporters of their own impiety. If the contest were to be determined by patristic authority, the tide of victory —to put it very modestly—would turn to our side. Now, these fathers have written many wise and excellent things. Still, what commonly happens to men has befallen them too, in some instances. For these so-called pious children of theirs, with all their sharpness of wit and judgment and spirit, worship only the faults and errors of the fathers. The good things that these fathers have written they either do not notice, or misrepresent or pervert. You might say that their only care is to gather dung amid gold.[13] Then, with a frightful to-do, they overwhelm us as despisers and adversaries of the fathers! But we do not despise them; in fact, if it were to our present purpose, I could with no trouble at all prove that the greater part of what we are saying today meets their approval. Yet we are so versed in their writings as to remember always that all things are ours [I Cor. 3:21-22], to serve us, not to lord it over us [Luke 22:24-25], and that we all belong to the

---

[12] Calvin's command of the patristic literature was already well developed in 1535 when he wrote this passage, which contains references even to works not generally familiar. At the Lausanne Disputation, on October 5, 1536, Calvin effectively replied to the charge that he and his associates rejected "the holy doctors of antiquity," claiming for their doctrine of the Eucharist the support of Tertullian, Cyprian, Chrysostom, and Augustine. (Cf. LCC XXII. 38 ff.) While he recognizes in general the authoritative position of the fathers in Christian thought, this is always under the limitation of their fallibility and mutual divergences, and of the superior authority of Scripture. These paragraphs invite comparison with the celebrated *Sic et Non* of Peter Abailard (d. 1142) (V. Cousin, *Ouvrages inédits d'Abélard*, pp. 1–169), in which are recited discordant opinions of the fathers on 157 topics. It does not appear that Calvin is indebted to Abailard. While he too points to individual judgments made by the ancient writers, his aim is to show their differences not from each other but from contemporary defenders of the medieval system. Alfonsus de Castro cites Cyprian, Ambrose, Chrysostom, Jerome, Augustine, Gelasius, Gregory, and Bede in opposition to Luther's opinions, and says rhetorically: *"Nam si Lutherus ait, Cyprianus negat; Lutherus ait, Hieronymus abnuit; Lutherus ait, Augustinus contradicit; Lutherus ait, Ambrosius obstat." Adversus omnes haereses* I. vii (1543 edition, fo. 13 F, G). Calvin here, as usual, does not name either Luther or his assailants, but shows familiarity with the controversy.

[13] Cassiodorus, *De institutione divinarum literarum* i (MPL 70. 1112).

one Christ [I Cor. 3:23], whom we must obey in all things without exception [cf. Col. 3:20]. He who does not observe this distinction will have nothing certain in religion, inasmuch as these holy men were ignorant of many things, often disagreed among themselves, and sometimes even contradicted themselves. It is not without cause, they say, that Solomon bids us not to transgress the limits set by our fathers [Prov. 22:28]. But the same rule does not apply to boundaries of fields, and to obedience of faith, which must be so disposed that "it forgets its people and its father's house" [Ps. 45:10 p.]. But if they love to allegorize so much, why do they not accept the apostles (rather than anyone else) as the "fathers" who have set the landmarks that it is unlawful to remove [Prov. 22:28]? Thus has Jerome interpreted this verse, and they have written his words into their canons.[14] But if our opponents want to preserve the limits set by the fathers according to their understanding of them, why do they themselves transgress them so willfully as often as it suits them?

It was one of the fathers who said that our God neither drinks nor eats, and therefore has no need of plates or cups.[15] Another, that sacred rites do not require gold, and those things not bought with gold do not please with gold.[16] They therefore transgress this limit when in their ceremonies they take so much delight in gold, silver, ivory, marble, precious stones, and silks; and think that God is not rightly worshiped unless everything swims with untoward splendor, or, rather, mad excess.

It was a father who said that he freely ate meat on the day others abstained from it, because he was a Christian.[17] They transgress the limits, therefore, when they execrate any person who has tasted of meat in Lent.

There were two fathers, one of whom said that a monk who does not labor with his hands must be considered equal to a thug,

14 Gratian, *Decretum* II. xxiv. 3. 33 (Friedberg I. 999; MPL 187. 1508).

15 Acacius, bishop of Amida, addressing his clergy as he was about to melt the gold and silver vessels of the church to obtain food for captive Persians. Socrates, *Ecclesiastical History* vii. 21 (MPG 67. 781–784; tr. NPNF 2 ser. II. 164). Calvin derived his materials at this point from the *Tripartite History* compiled by Cassiodorus (d. 583), a mosaic in Latin of the three ecclesiastical histories of Socrates (for 305–409), Sozomen (for 323–425), and Theodoret (for 325–429). The passage in the *Historia tripartita* (XI. 16) is in MPL 69. 1198; CSEL 71. 651 f.

16 Ambrose, *De officiis clericorum* ii. 28 (MPL 16. 140; tr. [*On the Duties of the Clergy*] NPNF 2 ser. X. 64).

17 From Sozomen's description of Spyridion, bishop of Trimithus in Cyprus, *Ecclesiastical History* i. 11; Cassiodorus, *Historia tripartita* I. 10 (MPL 69. 895; tr. NPNF 2 ser. II. 247).

or (if you prefer) a brigand;[18] the second, that it is not lawful for monks to live off the goods of others, even though they be assiduous in contemplation, in prayer, and in study.[19] They have also transgressed this limit when they have put the lazy, wine-cask bellies of monks in these stews and brothels to be crammed with substance of others.

It was a father who termed it a dreadful abomination to see an image either of Christ or of some saint painted in the churches of Christians.[20] c"What is reverenced is not to be depicted upon walls" was not the mere declaration of one man but the decree of an ecclesiastical council.[21] aThey are far from remaining within these limits when they leave not a corner free of images. Another father counseled that, after having exercised in burial the office of humanity toward the dead, we should let them rest.[22] They break these limits when they stir up perpetual solicitude for the dead.

It was one of the fathers c(a)who testified that in the Eucharist the substance of bread and wine remained and did not cease to be, just as in Christ the Lord the substance and nature of man remained, joined to the divine nature.[23] Therefore, they overstep the bounds in pretending that when the Lord's words are repeated the substance of bread and wine ceases and is transubstantiated into body and blood.[24]

cThey were fathers who, as they set forth only one Eucharist for the whole church and consequently excluded wicked and

[18] Referring apparently to Serapion, head of a monastery near Arsinoë in Egypt, who required his monks to earn their food by labor. Sozomen, op. cit., vi. 28; Cassiodorus, Historia tripartita VIII. i (MPL 69. 1103; tr. NPNF 2 ser. II. 365).

[19] Augustine, On the Work of Monks xiv–xvii (MPL 40. 560–564; tr. NPNF III. 511–513).

[20] "Epistle of Epiphanius to John of Jerusalem," translated by Jerome, in his Letters li. 9 (CSEL 54. 411; tr. NPNF 2 ser. VI. 89). Epiphanius, bishop of Salamis in Cyprus, tells how in a church at Anablatha he tore up a curtain bearing an image and replaced it by a plain curtain. He declares images in churches "contrary to our religion" (A.D. 394). Cf. I. xi. 11, 16; I. xii. 2.

[21] Council of Elvira (Illiberitanum) in Spain, ca. A.D. 305, canon xxxvi: "That there ought not to be images [picturas] in a church, that what is worshiped and adored should not be depicted on the walls." Hefele-Leclercq I. 240; Mansi II. 264.

[22] Ambrose, De Abraham I. ix. 80 (MPL 14. 472).

[23] "Et tamen esse non desinit substantia vel natura panis et vini." Gelasius, De duabus naturis in Christo adversus Eutychem et Nestorium, Tract. iii. 14 (Epistolae Romanorum pontificum, ed. A. Thiel, I. 541).

[24] Canon i of the Fourth Lateran Council, A.D. 1215, declares that in the sacrament of the altar the bread is by divine power transubstantiated into the body and the wine into the blood of Christ. (Mansi XXII. 954; Hefele-Leclercq V. 1325; tr. H. J. Schroeder, Disciplinary Decrees of the General Councils, p. 338.)

criminal persons, most gravely condemned all those who though present did not receive it.[25] How far have they removed the boundaries when they fill not only churches but also private houses with their Masses, admitting anyone at all to observe them, each one the more willingly the more he pays, however impure and wicked he may be! They invite no one to faith in Christ and believing communion of the sacraments; rather, they put their work on sale, as the grace and merit of Christ.

[a]There were two fathers, one of whom decreed that those content with participation in one kind, but abstaining from the other, were to be excluded entirely from participation in the Sacred Supper of Christ;[26] the other strongly contends that one must not deny the blood of their Lord to Christian folk, who, in confessing him, are bidden to shed their own blood.[27] They have removed these landmarks when they have commanded by an inviolable law the very thing that the former father punished by excommunication and the latter reproved with a valid reason.[28]

It was a father who affirmed it rashness, when judging of some obscure matter, to take one side or another without clear and evident witness of Scripture.[29] They forgot this limit when they established so many constitutions, canons, and doctrinal decisions, without any word of God. It was a father who reproached Montanus for, among other heresies, being the first to impose laws of fasting.[30] They also passed far beyond those limits when they ordained fasts by very strict law.[31]

[25] Chrysostom, *Commentary on Ephesians*, ch. 1, hom. iii. 4, 5 (MPG 62. 28–30; tr. NPNF XIII. 63–65), and Calixtus as quoted by Gratian, *Decretum (De consecratione)* III. ii. 18 (Friedberg I. 1320; MPL 187. 1759).

[26] In a passage dubiously attributed to Pope Gelasius and found in Gratian (*Decretum* III. ii. 12; Friedberg I. 1318; MPL 59. 141; 187. 1736), communicants are required to take the wine with the bread or abstain from both: "*aut integra sacramenta percipiant, aut ad integris arceantur.*" The withdrawal of the wine from the laity called forth the protests of Scriptural sects, especially the Hussites. Luther treats the subject in his *Babylonish Captivity* (1520), section "On the Sacrament of the Bread" (*Werke* WA VI. 502 ff.; tr. *Works of Martin Luther* II. 179 ff.).

[27] Cyprian, *Letters* lvii. 2 (CSEL 3. ii. 651 f.; tr. ANF [letter liii. 2] V. 337).

[28] Council of Constance, session 13 (1415), definition on communion in both kinds. This was confirmed by Martin V's bull *In eminentis* (1418) (Texts in Mansi XXVII. 727 f., 1215, 1219).

[29] Augustine, *De peccatorum meritis et remissione et de baptismo parvulorum* II. xxxvi. 59 (MPL 44. 186; CSEL 60. 128; tr. NPNF V. 67 f.): "In obscure matters where the Scriptures do not give guidance, rash judgment is to be avoided." Cf. Augustine, *Letters* cxl. 37. 85 (MPL 33. 576; tr. FC 20. 135).

[30] Apollonius, cited in Eusebius, *Ecclesiastical History* V. 18 (MPG 1. 472; tr. NPNF 2 ser. I. 235 ff.).

[31] Gratian, *Decretum* III. iii. 9 (MPL 187. 1734; Friedberg I. 1354 f.).

It was a father who denied that marriage should be forbidden to the ministers of the church, and declared cohabitation with one's wife to be chastity. And other fathers agreed with his opinion.[32] By severely enjoining celibacy for their priests, they have gone beyond this limit.[33] It was a father who deemed that one must listen to Christ alone, for Scripture says, "Hear him" [Matt. 17:5]; and that we need not be concerned about what others before us either said or did, but only about what Christ, who is the first of all, commanded.[34] When they set over themselves and others any masters but Christ, they neither abode by this boundary nor permitted others to keep it. cIt was a father who contended that the church ought not to set itself above Christ, for he always judges truthfully, but ecclesiastical judges, like other men, are often mistaken.[35] When this boundary is also broken through, they do not hesitate to declare that the whole authority of Scripture depends entirely upon the judgment of the church.[36]

aAll the fathers with one heart have abhorred and with one voice have detested the fact that God's Holy Word has been contaminated by the subtleties of sophists and involved in the squabbles of dialecticians.[37] When they attempt nothing in life but to enshroud and obscure the simplicity of Scripture with endless contentions and worse than sophistic brawls, do they keep themselves within these borders? Why, if the fathers were now brought back to life, and heard such brawling art as these persons call speculative theology, there is nothing they would less suppose than that these folk were disputing about God! But my discourse would overflow its proper limit if I chose to review how wantonly they reject the yoke of the fathers, whose obedient children they

---

[32] Sozomen *(Ecclesiastical History* i. 23) records that Paphnutius the Confessor, an ardent ascetic, swayed the decision of the Council of Nicaea (325) against requiring clerical celibacy by the declaration here reported. Calvin probably used Cassiodorus' text, *op. cit.,* II. xiv (MPL 69. 933; tr. NPNF 2 ser. II. 256).

[33] On the development of the law of clerical celibacy, see H. Leclercq's excursus, "La Législation conciliaire relatif au célibat ecclésiastique," *Histoire des conciles* II. 1321–1348; Schroeder, *op. cit.,* pp. 105, 107, 192 f.; H. C. Lea, *History of Sacerdotal Celibacy.*

[34] Cyprian, *Letters* lxiii. 14 (CSEL 3. ii. 712; tr. ANF [letter lxii. 14] V. 362).

[35] *"Non igitur debet ecclesia se Christo praeponere."* Augustine, *Contra Cresconium Grammaticum Donatistam* ii. 21 (MPL 43. 482; CSEL 52. 385).

[36] This view, asserted by John Eck, *Enchiridion* (1526), ch. i. (1541, fo. 76), and others, was repeatedly rejected by Zwingli and his associates. The opposing thesis that "the church is born of the Word of God" was affirmed at the Disputation of Ilanz, 1526, and at the Disputation of Bern, 1528. Cf. I. vii. 2, note 4.

[37] Tertullian, *De praescriptione haereticorum* vii (CCL Tertullianus I. 192; tr. LCC V. 35 f.); Augustine, *On Christian Doctrine* II. xxxi (MPL 34. 57; tr. NPNF II. 550; also FC 4. 102–103).

wish to seem. Indeed, months and even years would not suffice
me! Nevertheless they are of such craven and depraved impudence
as to dare reproach us for not hesitating to pass beyond the ancient
boundaries.

5. THE APPEAL TO "CUSTOM" AGAINST TRUTH

aEven in their appeal to "custom" they accomplish nothing. To
constrain us to yield to custom would be to treat us most unjustly. Indeed, if men's judgments were right, custom should have
been sought of good men. But it often happens far otherwise:
what is seen being done by the many soon obtains the force of
custom; while the affairs of men have scarcely ever been so well
regulated that the better things pleased the majority. Therefore,
the private vices of the many have often caused public error, or
rather a general agreement on vices, which these good men now
want to make law. Those with eyes can perceive it is not one sea
of evils that has flooded the earth, but many dangerous plagues
have invaded it, and everything is rushing headlong. Hence, one
must either completely despair of human affairs or grapple with
these great evils—or rather, forcibly quell them. And this remedy
is rejected for no other reason save that we have long been accustomed to such evils. But, granting public error a place in the
society of men, still in the Kingdom of God his eternal truth must
alone be listened to and observed, a truth that cannot be dictated
to by length of time, by long-standing custom, or by the conspiracy of men. In such manner Isaiah of old instructed God's
elect not to "call conspiracy all that this people call conspiracy,"
"not" to "fear what they fear, nor be in dread" thereof, but rather
to "hallow the Lord of Hosts and let him be their fear and dread"
[Isa. 8:12–13].

Now, then, let our adversaries throw at us as many examples as
they wish, both of past and present ages. If we hallow the Lord of
Hosts, we shall not be greatly afraid. Even though many ages may
have agreed in like impiety, the Lord is strong to wreak vengeance,
even to the third and fourth generation [Num. 14:18; cf. Ex. 20:4].
Even though the whole world may conspire in the same wickedness, he has taught us by experience what is the end of those who
sin with the multitude. This he did when he destroyed all mankind by the Flood, but kept Noah with his little family; and Noah
by his faith, the faith of one man, condemned the whole world
[Gen. 7:1; Heb. 11:7]. To sum up, evil custom is nothing but a
kind of public pestilence in which men do not perish the less
though they fall with the multitude. cMoreover, our opponents
ought to have pondered what Cyprian somewhere says: that those

who sin out of ignorance, even though they cannot clear themselves of all blame, may still seem somehow excusable; but they
who stubbornly reject the truth offered them by God's goodness
have nothing to plead as an excuse.[38]

6. Errors About the Nature of the Church

ᵃBy their double-horned argument they do not press us so hard
that we are forced to admit either that the church has been lifeless for some time or that we are now in conflict with it. Surely
the church of Christ has lived and will live so long as Christ
reigns at the right hand of his Father. It is sustained by his hand;
defended by his protection; and is kept safe through his power.
For he will surely accomplish what he once promised: that he
will be present with his own even to the end of the world [Matt.
28:20].[39] Against this church we now have no quarrel. For, of one
accord with all believing folk, we worship and adore one God,
and Christ the Lord [I Cor. 8:6], as he has always been adored by
all godly men. But they stray very far from the truth when they do
not recognize the church unless they see it with their very eyes, and
try to keep it within limits to which it cannot at all be confined.

Our controversy turns on these hinges: first, they contend that
the form of the church is always apparent and observable. Secondly, they set this form in the see of the Roman Church and its
hierarchy.[40] We, on the contrary, affirm that the church can exist
without any visible appearance, and that its appearance is not contained within that outward magnificence which they foolishly
admire. Rather, it has quite another mark: namely, the pure
preaching of God's Word and the lawful administration of the

---

[38] Cyprian, *Letters* lxiii. 17 (CSEL 3. ii. 715; tr. ANF [letter lxii] V. 363)
and lxxiii. 13 (CSEL 3. ii. 787; tr. ANF [letter lxxii] V. 382).

[39] Cf. IV. i. 17. Reformed theology has strongly affirmed the doctrine that the
Holy Catholic Church is imperishable and perpetual in the world. Thus
Bullinger (*Fifth Decade* [1551], sermon 1) states: "But . . . the catholic
church of God has continued with us from age to age . . . and . . . shall
remain upon the earth to the world's end" (LCC XXIV. 293). Cf. Second
Helvetic Confession XVII. 1: "*Semper fuisse, nunc esse, et ad finem usque
seculi futuram esse ecclesiam*" (Schaff, *Creeds* III. 271); J. H. Heidegger:
"Christ's church is of necessity in possession of constant existence in the
world" (*Medulla theologiae Christianae* [1696] XXVI. 11); Westminster
Confession XXV. 5: "Nevertheless, there shall always be a church on earth
to worship God according to his will." See also Heppe RD, p. 664; J. T.
McNeill, "The Church in Sixteenth-Century Reformed Theology," *Journal
of Religion* XXII (1942), 256 f.

[40] Eck (*Enchiridion* [1526], ch. i) answers the Lutheran charge that the church,
which is the congregation of all believers, does not decide what the pope,
cardinals, and bishops decide. Cf. De Castro, *Adversus omnes haereses*
I. vi (1543 edition, fo. 9K-10E).

sacraments.[41] They rage if the church cannot always be pointed to with the finger. But among the Jewish people how often was it so deformed that no semblance of it remained? What form do we think it displayed when Elijah complained that he alone was left [I Kings 19:10, or 14]? How long after Christ's coming was it hidden without form? How often has it since that time been so oppressed by wars, seditions, and heresies that it did not shine forth at all? If they had lived at that time, would they have believed that any church existed? But Elijah heard that there still remained seven thousand men who had not bowed the knee before Baal.[42] And we must not doubt that Christ has reigned on earth ever since he ascended into heaven. But if believers had then required some visible form, would they not have straightway lost courage? [b]Indeed, Hilary considered it a great vice in his day that, being occupied with foolish reverence for the episcopal dignity, men did not realize what a deadly hydra lurked under such a mask. For he speaks in this way: "One thing I admonish you, beware of Antichrist. It is wrong that a love of walls has seized you; wrong that you venerate the church of God in roofs and buildings; wrong that beneath these you introduce the name of peace. Is there any doubt that Antichrist will have his seat in them? To my mind, mountains, woods, lakes, prisons, and chasms are safer. For, either abiding in or cast into them, the prophets prophesied."[43]

Yet what does the world today venerate in its horned bishops[44] but to imagine those whom it sees presiding over renowned cities to be holy prelates of religion? Away, therefore, with such a foolish appraisement! Rather, [a]since the Lord alone "knows who are his" [II Tim. 2:19], let us leave to him the fact that he sometimes removes from men's sight the external signs by which the church is known. That is, I confess, a dreadful visitation of God upon the earth. But if men's impiety deserves it, why do we strive to oppose God's just vengeance? In such a way the Lord of old punished men's ingratitude. For, because they had refused to obey his truth and had extinguished his light, he allowed their blinded senses to be both deluded by foolish lies and plunged into profound darkness, so that no form of the true church remained. Meanwhile, he preserved his own children from extinction,

41 Cf. Augsburg Confession II. vii (Schaff, *Creeds* III. 60) and IV. i. 7, below.
42 Cf. IV. i. 2 and Second Helvetic Confession XVII. 15 (Schaff, *Creeds* III. 276).
43 "*Male enim vos parietum amor cepit.*" Hilary of Poitiers, *Against the Arians or Auxentius of Milan* xii (MPL 10. 616).
44 The protruding points of the miter worn by a bishop were called *cornua*, horns.

though they are scattered and hidden in the midst of these errors and darkness. And this is no marvel: for he knew how to preserve them in the confusion of Babylon, and in the flame of the fiery furnace [Dan., ch. 3].

Now I shall point out how dangerous is their desire to have the form of the church judged by some sort of vain pomp. This I shall sketch rather than explain at length lest I endlessly prolong my discourse. The pontiff of Rome, they say, who occupies the Apostolic See, and those who have been anointed and consecrated bishops by him, provided they are distinguished by miters and crosiers, represent the church, and must be taken for the church; therefore they cannot err. Why so? Because, they reply, they are pastors of the church and have been consecrated by the Lord. Were not Aaron and the other leaders of the people of Israel also pastors? Indeed, Aaron and his sons, though designated priests, still erred when they fashioned the calf [Ex. 32:4]. Why, according to this reasoning, would not those four hundred prophets who deceived Ahab [I Kings 22:12] have represented the church? But the church was on the side of Micaiah, a single contemptible man, yet one who spoke the truth. Did not the prophets who rose up against Jeremiah, boasting that "the law could not perish from the priest, nor counsel from the wise, nor the word from the prophet" [Jer. 18:18 p.], bear the name and face of the church? Against the whole tribe of the prophets, Jeremiah alone is sent from the Lord to announce that "the law was going to perish from the priest, counsel from the wise, the word from the prophet" [Jer. 18:18; cf. ch. 4:9]. Was not such pomp manifested in that council where the priests, scribes, and Pharisees assembled to deliberate concerning the execution of Christ [John 11:47 ff.]? Now let them go and cling to this outward mask—making Christ and all the prophets of God schismatics; Satan's ministers, conversely, the organs of the Holy Spirit!

But if they speak from the heart, let them answer me in good faith: in what region or among what people do they think the church resided after Eugenius, by decree of the Council of Basel, was deposed from the pontificate and replaced by Amadeus? If they were to burst, they could not deny that the council was lawful as to its outward arrangements, and was summoned not only by one pope but by two. Eugenius was there condemned for schism, rebellion, and obstinacy, with the whole company of cardinals and bishops who had plotted the dissolution of the council with him. Nevertheless, subsequently supported by the favor of princes, he recovered his papal office unscathed. That election of Amadeus, duly solemnized by the authority of a general and holy council, went up in smoke, except that the aforesaid Amadeus was appeased by a cardinal's hat, as a barking dog by a morsel.[45] From these rebellious and obstinate heretics have come forth all future popes, cardinals, bishops, abbots, and priests. Here they must be stopped and held fast. For on which side will they bestow the name of church? Will they deny that the council was general, which lacked nothing of outward majesty, was solemnly convoked by two bulls, consecrated by the presiding legate of the Roman see, well ordered in every respect, and preserving the same dignity to the end? Will they admit that Eugenius and all his company, by whom they were consecrated, were schismatic? Let them, therefore, either define the form of the church in other terms, or we will adjudge them—however numerous they are—who knowingly and willingly have been ordained by heretics, to be schismatic. But if it had never been discovered before, they who under that fine title "church" have for so long superciliously hawked themselves to the world, even though they have been deadly plagues upon the church, can furnish us with abundant proof that the church is not bound up with outward pomp. I speak not concerning their morals and tragic misdeeds, with which their whole life swarms, since they speak of themselves as the Pharisees, who are to be heard but not imitated [Matt. 23:3].[46] If you will devote a little of your leisure to the reading of our words, you will unmistakably recognize that this, this very doctrine itself whereby they claim to be the church, is a deadly butchery of souls, a firebrand, a ruin, and a destruction of the church.

7. TUMULTS ALLEGED TO RESULT FROM REFORMATION PREACHING

Lastly, they do not act with sufficient candor when they invidiously recount how many disturbances, tumults, and contentions the preaching of our doctrine has drawn along with it, and what fruits it now produces among many. The blame for these evils is unjustly laid upon it, when this ought to have been imputed to Satan's malice. Here is, as it were, a certain characteristic

[45] The facts referred to here include the following: Pope Eugenius IV was deposed by the Council of Basel June 25, 1439. On November 5, Amadeus VIII, Duke of Savoy, who had previously adopted a life of asceticism, was elected, and on January 1, following, he took office as Felix V. Eugenius, however, won the support of the new emperor, Frederick III (1440–1493), and, April 7, 1449, Felix abdicated, becoming cardinal-bishop of Sabina and vicar-apostolic for Savoy: L. Pastor, *History of the Popes from the End of the Middle Ages* (tr. F. J. Antrobus) I. 328 f.; M. Creighton, *History of the Popes from the Great Schism to the Sack of Rome* III. 20 ff., 109 f.; *Cambridge Medieval History* VIII. 40 f.

[46] Eck, *Enchiridion* (1526), ch. ii, *ad finem*, quoting Matt. 23:3 to urge reverence for the clergy.

of the divine Word, that it never comes forth while Satan is at rest and sleeping. This is the surest and most trustworthy mark to distinguish it from lying doctrines, which readily present themselves, are received with attentive ears by all, and are listened to by an applauding world. Thus for some centuries during which everything was submerged in deep darkness, almost all mortals were the sport and jest of this lord of the world, and, not unlike some Sardanapalus,[47] Satan lay idle and luxuriated in deep repose. For what else had he to do but jest and sport, in tranquil and peaceable possession of his kingdom? Yet when the light shining from on high in a measure shattered his darkness, when that "strong man" had troubled and assailed his kingdom [cf. Luke 11:22], he began to shake off his accustomed drowsiness and to take up arms. And first, indeed, he stirred up men to action that thereby he might violently oppress the dawning truth.[48] And when this profited him nothing, he turned to stratagems: he aroused disagreements and dogmatic contentions through his catabaptists[49] and other monstrous rascals in order to obscure and at last extinguish the truth. And now he persists in besieging it with both engines. With the violent hands of men he tries to uproot that true seed, and seeks (as much as lies in his power) to choke it with his weeds, to prevent it from growing and bearing fruit. But all that is in vain, if we heed the Lord our monitor, who long since laid open Satan's wiles before us, that he might not catch us unawares; and armed us with defenses firm enough against all his devices. Furthermore, how great is the malice that would ascribe to the very word of God itself the odium either of seditions, which wicked and rebellious men stir up against it, or of sects, which impostors excite, both of them in opposition to its teaching! Yet this is no new example. Elijah was asked if it was not he who was troubling Israel [I Kings 18:17]. To the Jews, Christ was seditious [Luke 23:5; John 19:7 ff.]. The charge of stirring up the people was laid against the apostles [Acts 24:5 ff.]. What else are they doing who blame us today for all the disturbances, tumults, and contentions that boil up against us? Elijah taught us what we ought to reply to such charges: it is not we who

---

[47] Greek form of the name of Ashurbanipal, king of Assyria (668–626 B.C.). Legend (in contrast with fact) makes him spend years in indolence and indulgence and finally, in desperation, burn himself to death in his house.

[48] Cf. Comm. Isa. 6:10 and the discussion of Calvin's view of this "satanic reaction to the inevitable advance of the Kingdom of Christ through the preaching of the word," by R. S. Wallace, *Calvin's Doctrine of the Word and Sacrament*, pp. 92 ff.

[49] A term in common use for the Anabaptists, as the adversaries of traditional baptism.

either spread errors abroad or incite tumults; but it is they who contend against God's power [I Kings 18:18].

But as that one answer is enough to check their rashness, it is also sufficient to meet the foolishness of others who often happen to be moved by such scandals and, thus perturbed, to waver. In order not to give way under this perturbation and be driven from their ground, let them, however, know that the apostles in their day experienced the same things that are now happening to us. There were unlearned and unstable men who, to their own destruction, distorted things that had been divinely written by Paul, as Peter says [II Peter 3:16]. They were despisers of God who, when they heard that sin abounded that grace might more abound, immediately concluded: "We shall remain in sin, that grace may abound" [cf. Rom. 6:1]. When they heard that believers were not under the law, straightway they chirped: "We shall sin because we are not under the law, but under grace" [cf. Rom. 6:15]. There were people who accused Paul of being a persuader to evil. Many false apostles were intruding themselves to destroy the churches that he had built [I Cor. 1:10 ff.; II Cor. 11:3 ff.; Gal. 1:6 ff.]. "Some preached the gospel out of envy and strife" [Phil. 1:15 p.], "not sincerely," even maliciously, "thinking thereby to lay further weight upon his bonds" [Phil. 1:17 p.]. Elsewhere the gospel made little headway. "They all sought their own interests, not those of Jesus Christ" [Phil. 2:21]. Others returned to themselves, as "dogs . . . to their vomit, and swine . . . to their wallowing in the mire" [II Peter 2:22 p.]. Many degraded the freedom of the Spirit to the license of the flesh [II Peter 2:18–19]. Many brethren crept in by whom the godly were exposed to dangers [II Cor. 11:3 ff.]. Among these very brethren various contentions broke out [Acts, chs. 6; 11; 15]. What were the apostles to do here? Ought they not to have dissembled for a time, or, rather, laid aside that gospel and deserted it because they saw that it was the seedbed of so many quarrels, the source of so many dangers, the occasion of so many scandals? Yet in tribulations of this sort they were helped by the thought that Christ is "a rock of offense, a stone of stumbling" [Rom. 9:33; cf. I Peter 2:8; Isa. 8:14], "set for the fall and rising of many . . . and for a sign that is spoken against" [Luke 2:34]. Armed with this assurance, they boldly advanced through all the dangers of tumults and offenses. It is fitting that we too be sustained by the same consideration, inasmuch as Paul testifies to this eternal character of the gospel, that "it may be a fragrance of death unto death" [II Cor. 2:15] for those who perish; yet for us it was destined to this use: "to be a fragrance from life to life" [II Cor. 2:16], "and the power of

God unto the salvation of believers" [Rom. 1:16]. cThis very thing we should certainly experience, if by our ungratefulness we did not corrupt this singular blessing of God and pervert to our ruin what ought for us to have been a unique assurance of salvation.

8. LET THE KING BEWARE OF ACTING ON FALSE CHARGES: THE INNOCENT AWAIT DIVINE VINDICATION

aBut I return to you, O King. May you be not at all moved by those vain accusations with which our adversaries are trying to inspire terror in you: that by this new gospel (for so they call it) men strive and seek only after the opportunity for seditions and impunity for all crimes. "For our God is not author of division, but of peace" [I Cor. 14:33 p.]; and the Son of God is not "the minister of sin" [Gal. 2:17], for he has come to "destroy the devil's works" [I John 3:8].

And we are unjustly charged, too, with intentions of such a sort that we have never given the least suspicion of them. We are, I suppose, contriving the overthrow of kingdoms—we, from whom not one seditious word was ever heard; we, whose life when we lived under you was always acknowledged to be quiet and simple; we, who do not cease to pray for the full prosperity of yourself and your kingdom, although we are now fugitives from home! We are, I suppose, wildly chasing after wanton vices! Even though in our moral actions many things are blameworthy, nothing deserves such great reproach as this. And we have not, by God's grace, profited so little by the gospel that our life may not be for these disparagers an example of chastity, generosity, mercy, continence, patience, modesty, and all other virtues. It is perfectly clear that we fear and worship God in very truth since we seek, not only in our life but in our death, that his name be hallowed [cf. Phil. 1:20]. And hatred itself has been compelled to bear witness to the innocence and civic uprightness of some of us upon whom the punishment of death was inflicted for that one thing which ought to have occasioned extraordinary praise. But if any persons raise a tumult under the pretext of the gospel[50]—hitherto no such persons have been found in your realm—if any deck out the license of their own vices as the liberty of God's grace—I have known very many of this sort—there are laws and legal penalties by which they may be severely restrained according to their deserts. Only let not the gospel of God be blasphemed in the meantime because of the wickedness of infamous men.

The wicked poison of our calumniators has, O King, in its

[50] The reference is to the Münster incident, 1534–1535.

many details, been sufficiently disclosed that you may not incline an ear credulous beyond measure to their slanders. I fear even that too many details have been included, since this preface has already grown almost to the size of a full-scale apology. In it I have not tried to formulate a defense, but merely to dispose your mind to give a hearing to the actual presentation of our case. Your mind is now indeed turned away and estranged from us, even inflamed, I may add, against us; but we trust that we can regain your favor, if in a quiet, composed mood you will once read this our confession, which we intend in lieu of a defense before Your Majesty. Suppose, however, the whisperings of the malevolent so fill your ears that the accused have no chance to speak for themselves, but those savage furies, while you connive at them, ever rage against us with imprisonings, scourgings, rackings, maimings, and burnings [cf. Heb. 11:36–37]. Then we will be reduced to the last extremity even as sheep destined for the slaughter [Isa. 53:7–8; Acts 8:33]. Yet this will so happen that "in our patience we may possess our souls" [Luke 21:19 p.]; and may await the strong hand of the Lord, which will surely appear in due season, coming forth armed to deliver the poor from their affliction and also to punish their despisers, who now exult with such great assurance.

May the Lord, the King of Kings, establish your throne in righteousness [cf. Prov. 25:5], and your dominion in equity, most illustrious King.

At Basel, on the 1st August, in the year 1536.[51]

51 The date here given is doubly erroneous. As first shown by A. Lefranc, it should be August 23, 1535. Beveridge was aware of the problem: see his edition of 1845, I. xi f. Calvin's first edition, published March, 1536, gives at the end of the Address to the King the date, "X. Calendas Septembres" (i.e., August 23), without year. Obviously, the preceding August is meant, and indeed the French editions of 1541 and 1545 have "vingttroysiesme D'aoust mil cinq cent trente cinq." But August 1 was the date of the Preface (not the Address) in the 1539 Latin edition, and thereafter the Latin editions shifted this date to the Address itself. At the same time the year date 1536 was carelessly inserted, obviously from the publication date given at the end of the 1536 volume. A. Lefranc, *Jean Calvin: Institution de la religion Chrestienne . . . 1541*, Introduction, p. 4; OS I. 283; III. 30; Benoit, *Institution* I. 49.

BOOK ONE

THE KNOWLEDGE OF GOD THE CREATOR

The Knowledge[1] of God the Creator

^cCHAPTER I

THE KNOWLEDGE OF GOD AND THAT OF OURSELVES ARE CONNECTED. HOW THEY ARE INTERRELATED[2]

1. Without knowledge of self there is no knowledge of God

^{b(a)}Nearly all the wisdom we possess, that is to say, true and sound wisdom, consists of two parts: the knowledge of God and of ourselves.[3] ^cBut, while joined by many bonds, ^bwhich one precedes and brings forth the other is not easy to discern. ^cIn the first place, no one can look upon himself without immediately turning his thoughts to the contemplation of God, in whom he "lives and moves" [Acts 17:28]. For, quite clearly, the mighty gifts with which we are endowed are hardly from ourselves; indeed, our very being is nothing but subsistence in the one God.

---

[1] The word "knowledge" in the title, chosen rather than "being" or "existence" of God, emphasizes the centrality of revelation in both the structure and the content of Calvin's theology. Similarly, the term "Creator," subsuming the doctrines of Trinity, Creation, and Providence, stresses God's revealing work or acts rather than God in himself. The latter is more prominent in Scholastic doctrines of God, both medieval and later "Calvinist." Despite the titles of Books I and II, Calvin's epistemology is not fully developed in the *Institutes* until Book III, "The Way in Which We Receive the Grace of Christ." Cf. especially the meaning of knowledge in faith, III. ii, *passim.*

The Latin for "knowledge" is here *cognitio,* while in the title of ch. i following it is *notitia.* The words are used interchangeably by Calvin, and both are by him here translated into French (1541) as *cognoissance.* Knowledge, whatever the word employed, is for Calvin never "mere" or "simple" or purely objective knowledge. Cf. III. ii. 14, which is his most definitive,

Then, by these benefits shed like dew from heaven upon us, we are led as by rivulets to the spring itself. Indeed, our very poverty better discloses the infinitude of benefits reposing in God. The miserable ruin, into which the rebellion of the first man cast us, especially compels us to look upward. Thus, not only will we, in fasting and hungering, seek thence what we lack; but, in being aroused by fear, we shall learn humility.[4] [b]For, as a veritable world of miseries is to be found in mankind, [c(b)]and we are thereby despoiled of divine raiment, our shameful nakedness exposes a teeming horde of infamies. Each of us must, then, be so stung by the consciousness of his own unhappiness as to attain at least some knowledge of God. [b]Thus, from the feeling of our own ignorance, vanity, poverty, infirmity, and—what is more—depravity and corruption, we recognize that the true light of wisdom, sound virtue, full abundance of every good, and purity of righteousness rest in the Lord alone. To this extent we are prompted

brief statement on the meaning of knowledge in a religious context. Probably "existential apprehension" is the nearest equivalent in contemporary parlance. Among other closely related words used by Calvin are *agnitio,* recognition or acknowledgment; *intelligentia,* primarily meaning perception; and *scientia,* primarily expert knowledge.

The knowledge of God is dealt with by B. B. Warfield in *Calvin and Calvinism,* pp. 29–130, and by P. Lobstein, "La Connaissance religieuse d'après Calvin," *Revue de théologie et de philosophie religieuses* XLII (1909), 53–110. The most important recent analyses stress the problem of relating the knowledge of the Creator and of the Redeemer (see title, *Institutes,* Book II). T. H. L. Parker does this briefly in *The Doctrine of the Knowledge of God: A Study in Calvin's Theology,* and E. A. Dowey, Jr., more elaborately in *The Knowledge of God in Calvin's Theology.* See also W. Niesel, *The Theology of Calvin,* ch. 2.

[2] Throughout editions 1539–1554, Calvin entitled the opening chapters, "Of the Knowledge of God," and "Of the Knowledge of Man." But in 1559, he shows more clearly the close interrelation of these by creating a separate ch. i, and emphasizing, both in title and content, "how they are interrelated." The former ch. ii, much expanded, becomes finally the series of opening chapters of Book II. Note the revealing echoes of the opening words in I. xv. 1; II. i. 1; and II. viii. 1.

[3] This statement, thrice revised, stands at the beginning of every edition of the *Institutes.* The French version of 1560 expresses even more strongly the association of the two aspects of sound knowledge: "In knowing God, each of us also knows himself." These decisive words set the limits of Calvin's theology and condition every subsequent statement. They are echoed in the introductory words of Book II and at such important junctures as I. xv. 1 and II. viii. 1. Cf. Doumergue, *Calvin* IV. 245 ff.; J. Köstlin, "Calvins Institutio nach Form und Inhalt," *Theologische Studien und Kritiken* (1868), p. 55; Lobstein, *op. cit.,* p. 63. Calvin's basic concept here is discoverable in Clement of Alexandria's *Instructor* iii. 1 (MPG 8. 555 f.; tr. ANF II. 271: "If one knows himself, he will know God"), and finds frequent expression in Augustine. In his *Soliloquies* I. ii. 7, Augustine has this dialogue: "I desire to know God and the soul." "Nothing more?" "Nothing whatever"; and in II. i. 1 occurs the prayer, "Let me know myself,

by our own ills to contemplate the good things of God; and we cannot seriously aspire to him before we begin to become displeased with ourselves. For what man in all the world would not gladly remain as he is—what man does not remain as he is—so long as he does not know himself, that is, while content with his own gifts, and either ignorant or unmindful of his own misery? Accordingly, the knowledge of ourselves not only arouses us to seek God, but also, as it were, leads us by the hand to find him.

2. *Without knowledge of God there is no knowledge of self*

[b]Again, it is certain that man never achieves a clear knowledge of himself[5] unless he has first looked upon God's face, and then descends from contemplating him to scrutinize himself.[6] For we always seem to ourselves righteous and upright and wise and holy —this pride is innate in all of us—unless by clear proofs we stand convinced of our own unrighteousness, foulness, folly, and impurity. Moreover, we are not thus convinced if we look merely to ourselves and not also to the Lord, who is the sole standard by which this judgment must be measured. For, because all of us are inclined by nature to hypocrisy,[7] a kind of empty image of

---

let me know thee" (MPL 32. 872, 886; tr. LCC VI. 26, 41). Cf. Aquinas: "Sacred doctrine is not concerned with God and the creatures equally. It is concerned with God fundamentally, and with the creatures in so far as they relate to God as their beginning or end." *Summa Theol.* I. i. 3 (tr. LCC XI. 38 f.). Calvin makes explicit the same order of importance between knowledge of God and of the creatures in the "Argument" preceding his Commentary on Genesis, English tr., p. 60. The passage may also be compared with William Farel's *Sommaire de la foi* (1525), chs. i and ii, and with Calvin's own *Instruction et confession de foy* (1537), i–iv (OS I. 378–381; tr., with notes, P. T. Fuhrmann, *Instruction in Faith* (*1537*), pp. 17–21). It is worth noting that Descartes, in an important letter to Father Marin Mersenne, April 15, 1630, parallels Calvin's language here. Having referred to "human reason," Descartes continues: "I hold that all those to whom God has given the use of this reason are bound to employ it in the effort to know him and to know themselves." (*Oeuvres de Descartes,* edited by C. Adam and P. Tannery, I. 144.) In his *Discourse on Method* (1637), he aims, unlike Calvin, to "demonstrate the existence of God and the soul," and he is concerned with the same issue in his *Meditations in Prime Philosophy* (1641); see especially Meditations iii, v, and vi. George Berkeley, in his *Treatise on the Principles of Human Knowledge* (1710), holds that existence can be predicated of God and the soul only.

[4] The close relation of humility and self-knowledge constitutes an often repeated theme for Calvin. Cf. II. ii. 10–11; II. xvi. 1; III. ii. 23; III. xii. 5, 6; IV. xvii. 40 (end). Without humility, self-knowledge serves pride and is the root of all error in philosophy: I. v. 4; II. i. 1–3.

[5] *"Sui notitiam."* Our knowledge of ourselves may be construed to include both all mankind and all creation (of which man is a microcosm, I. v. 3). Hence, I. xiv and xv may be subsumed here along with II. i–v.

[6] Cf. I. v. 3, note 11.

righteousness in place of righteousness itself abundantly satisfies us. And because nothing appears within or around us that has not been contaminated by great immorality, what is a little less vile pleases us as a thing most pure—so long as we confine our minds within the limits of human corruption. Just so, an eye to which nothing is shown but black objects judges something dirty white or even rather darkly mottled to be whiteness itself. Indeed, we can discern still more clearly from the bodily senses how much we are deluded in estimating the powers of the soul. For if in broad daylight we either look down upon the ground or survey whatever meets our view round about, we seem to ourselves endowed with the strongest and keenest sight; yet when we look up to the sun and gaze straight at it, that power of sight which was particularly strong on earth is at once blunted and confused by a great brilliance, and thus we are compelled to admit that our keenness in looking upon things earthly is sheer dullness when it comes to the sun. So it happens in estimating our spiritual goods. As long as we do not look beyond the earth, being quite content with our own righteousness, wisdom, and virtue, we flatter ourselves most sweetly, and fancy ourselves all but demigods. Suppose we but once begin to raise our thoughts to God, and to ponder his nature, and how completely perfect are his righteousness, wisdom, and power—the straightedge to which we must be shaped. Then, what masquerading earlier as righteousness was pleasing in us will soon grow filthy in its consummate wickedness. What wonderfully impressed us under the name of wisdom will stink in its very foolishness. What wore the face of power will prove itself the most miserable weakness. That is, what in us seems perfection itself corresponds ill to the purity of God.

3. Man before God's majesty

ᵇHence that dread and wonder[8] with which Scripture commonly

---

[7] Calvin uses the words "nature," "natural," and "by nature" in two very different senses: (1) "Nature" may mean created perfection in which there is no evil (including even the created perfection of the devil), e.g., I. xiv. 3, 16; or (2) "nature" may mean the state of man and angels after having fallen from perfection, as here used, and clearly distinguished from the former in II. i. 10, 11. The opening sentence of II. i. 11 places the two uses side by side. This distinction is indispensable for understanding the relation of God to creation and to sin as well as the precise sense in which a doctrine of "total" depravity may be attributed to Calvin. Once this double use of "nature" is understood, Calvin's meaning at a given place is easily determined by context.

[8] "Horror ille et stupor." This basic component of the "saints'" knowledge of God appears close to what Rudolf Otto calls mysterium tremendum in Das Heilige (tr. J. W. Harvey, The Idea of the Holy). Cf., below, I. ii. 2; I. iii. 2, where this inescapable apprehension is sheer terror to the wicked.

represents the saints as stricken and overcome whenever they felt the presence of God. Thus it comes about that we see men who in his absence normally remained firm and constant, but who, when he manifests his glory, are so shaken and struck dumb as to be laid low by the dread of death—are in fact overwhelmed by it and almost annihilated. As a consequence, we must infer that man is never sufficiently touched and affected by the awareness of his lowly state until he has compared himself with God's majesty. Moreover, we have numerous examples of this consternation both in The Book of Judges and in the Prophets. So frequent was it that this expression was common among God's people: "We shall die, for the Lord has appeared to us" [Judg. 13:22; Isa. 6:5; Ezek. 2:1; 1:28; Judg. 6:22–23; and elsewhere]. The story of Job, in its description of God's wisdom, power, and purity, always expresses a powerful argument that overwhelms men with the realization of their own stupidity, impotence, and corruption [cf. Job 38:1 ff.]. And not without cause: for we see how Abraham recognizes more clearly that he is earth and dust [Gen. 18:27] when once he had come nearer to beholding God's glory; and how Elijah, with uncovered face, cannot bear to await his approach, such is the awesomeness of his appearance [I Kings 19:13]. And what can man do, who is rottenness itself [Job 13:28] and a worm [Job 7:5; Ps. 22:6], when even the very cherubim must veil their faces out of fear [Isa. 6:2]? It is this indeed of which the prophet Isaiah speaks: "The sun will blush and the moon be confounded when the Lord of Hosts shall reign" [Isa. 24:23]; that is, when he shall bring forth his splendor and cause it to draw nearer, the brightest thing will become darkness before it [Isa. 2:10, 19 p.].

Yet, however the knowledge of God and of ourselves may be mutually connected, the order of right teaching requires that we discuss the former first, then proceed afterward to treat the latter.

eCHAPTER II

WHAT IT IS TO KNOW GOD, AND TO WHAT PURPOSE THE KNOWLEDGE OF HIM TENDS

*1. Piety is requisite for the knowledge of God**

e(b/a)Now, the knowledge of God, as I understand it, is that by which we not only conceive that there is a God ebut also grasp what befits us and is proper to his glory, in fine, what is to our advantage to know of him. Indeed, we shall not say that, properly speaking, God is known where there is no religion or piety.[1] Here

---

[1] It is a favorite emphasis in Calvin that *pietas*, piety, in which reverence and love of God are joined, is prerequisite to any true knowledge of God.

I do not yet touch upon the sort of knowledge with which men, in themselves lost and accursed, apprehend God the Redeemer in Christ the Mediator; but I speak only of the primal and simple knowledge to which the very order of nature would have led us if Adam had remained upright.[2] In this ruin of mankind no one now experiences God either as Father or as Author of salvation, or favorable in any way, until Christ the Mediator comes forward to reconcile him to us. Nevertheless, it is one thing to feel that God as our Maker supports us by his power, governs us by his providence, nourishes us by his goodness, and attends us with all sorts of blessings—and another thing to embrace the grace of reconciliation offered to us in Christ. First, as much in the fashioning of the universe as in the general teaching of Scripture the Lord shows himself to be simply the Creator. Then in the face of Christ [cf. II Cor. 4:6] he shows himself the Redeemer. Of the resulting twofold knowledge of God[3] we shall now discuss the first aspect; the second will be dealt with in its proper place.[4]

Moreover, although our mind cannot apprehend God without rendering some honor to him, it will not suffice simply to hold e(b/a)that there is One whom all ought to honor and adore, unless we are also persuaded that he is the fountain of every good, and that we must seek nothing elsewhere than in him. This I take to mean that not only does he sustain this universe (as he once founded it) by his boundless might, regulate it by his wisdom, pre-

Cf. I. iv. 4. The brief characterization of *pietas* that follows here may be compared with his words written in 1537: "The gist of true piety does not consist in a fear which would gladly flee the judgment of God, but . . . rather in a pure and true zeal which loves God altogether as Father, and reveres him truly as Lord, embraces his justice and dreads to offend him more than to die"; *Instruction in Faith (1537)*, tr. P. T. Fuhrmann, pp. 18 f. (original in OS I. 379). For an examination of *"pietas literata"* with reference to Erasmus, John Sturm, Melanchthon, and Cordier, see P. R. Bolgar, *The Classical Heritage and Its Beneficiaries,* pp. 329–356. (In many contexts *pietas* is translated "godliness" in the present work.)

[2] *"Si integer stetisset Adam."* The controlling thought of I. ii–v, which is the *locus classicus* for a discussion of "natural theology" in Calvin, is contained in this phrase. The revelation of God in creation, for Calvin, would have been the basis of a sound natural theology only *"if* Adam had remained upright." Because of sin no sound theology of this type is possible. Scripture is the only medium of knowing the Creator, and of apprehending his revelation in creation (I. vi ff.). Cf. Introduction, pp. liii ff., above. Calvin expressed himself similarly at the beginning of his Preface to the New Testament, written in 1534 and published in Olivétan's French Bible (1535) (CR IX. 791; tr. LCC XXIII. 58).

[3] *"Duplex . . . cognitio."* The distinction, "twofold" knowledge, added to the *Institutes* in 1559, is basic to the structure of the completed work. Calvin calls attention to this repeatedly in a striking series of methodological statements, all added in 1559 to clarify the course of the argument.

serve it by his goodness, and especially rule mankind by his right-eousness and judgment, bear with it in his mercy, watch over it by his protection; but also that no drop will be found either of wisdom and light, or of righteousness or power or rectitude, or of genuine truth, which does not flow from him, and of which he is not the cause. e(b)'Thus we may learn to await and seek all these things from him, and thankfully to ascribe them, once received, to him. eFor this sense of the powers of God[5] is for us a fit teacher of piety, from which religion is born. I call "piety" that reverence joined with love of God which the knowledge of his benefits induces. For until men recognize that they owe everything to God, that they are nourished by his fatherly care, that he is the Author of their every good, that they should seek nothing beyond him—they will never yield him willing service. Nay, unless they establish their complete happiness in him, they will never give themselves truly and sincerely to him.

*2. Knowledge of God involves trust and reverence**

eWhat is God? Men who pose this question are merely toying with idle speculations. It is more important for us to know of what sort he is and what is consistent with his nature.[6] What good is it to profess with Epicurus some sort of God who has cast aside the care of the world only to amuse himself in idleness?[7] What help is it, in short, to know a God with whom we have nothing to do? e(b)Rather, our knowledge should serve first to teach us fear and reverence; secondly, with it as our guide and teacher, we should learn to seek every good from him, and, having received it, to credit

Cf. I. vi 1, 2; x. 1; xiii. 9, 11, 23, 24; xiv. 20, 21, and II. vi. 1. Hence, noth-ing in Book I belongs to the knowledge of the Redeemer, although every-thing after ch. v is based in the *special* revelation of Scripture.

4 What is called "the first" makes up the entire remainder of Book I. "The second" broadly corresponds to the whole material of Books II–IV. Strictly speaking, the subject is taken up in II. vi, which is a chapter entirely new in 1559, added to make the transition to the second element of twofold knowledge. The doctrine of sin, II. iv, thus falls between the two books in subject matter, preceding redemption in such a way as to show the occa-sion for it.

5 *"Virtutum Dei sensus."*

6 Cf. I. x. 2; III. ii. 6, "knowing what is his will toward us." *In Praelectiones in Ezechielem*, on Ezek. 1:26 (CR XL. 57), and often elsewhere, Calvin criti-cizes speculative refinements in the treatment of aspects of the doctrine of God. The reference here is to Scholastic writers, but in a letter sent *"familiariter inter nos"* to Bullinger, January, 1552, he finds Zwingli at fault for his "knotted paradoxes" in the work *De Providentia* (CR XIV. 253).

it to his account. ᵇFor how can the thought of God penetrate your mind without your realizing immediately that, since you are his handiwork, you have been made over and bound to his command by right of creation, that you owe your life to him?—that whatever you undertake, whatever you do, ought to be ascribed to him? If this be so, it now assuredly follows that your life is wickedly corrupt unless it be disposed to his service, seeing that his will ought for us to be the law by which we live. Again, you cannot behold him clearly unless you acknowledge him to be the fountainhead and source of every good. From this too would arise the desire to cleave to him and trust in him, but for the fact that man's depravity seduces his mind from rightly seeking him.

For, to begin with, the pious mind does not dream up for itself any god it pleases, but contemplates the one and only true God. And it does not attach to him whatever it pleases, but is content to hold him to be as he manifests himself; furthermore, the mind always exercises the utmost diligence and care not to wander astray, or rashly and boldly to go beyond his will. It thus recognizes God because it knows that he governs all things; and trusts that he is its guide and protector, therefore giving itself over completely to trust in him. ᵉ⁽ᵇ⁾Because it understands him to be the Author of every good, if anything oppresses, if anything is lacking, immediately it betakes itself to his protection, waiting for help from him. Because it is persuaded that he is good and merciful, it reposes in him with perfect trust, and doubts not that in his loving-kindness a remedy will be provided for all its ills. Because it acknowledges him as Lord and Father, the pious mind also deems it meet and right to observe his authority in all things, reverence his majesty, take care to advance his glory, and obey his commandments. Because it sees him to be a righteous judge, armed with severity to punish wickedness, it ever holds his judgment seat before its gaze, and through fear of him restrains itself

[7] Epicurus (342–270 B.C.), whose extensive writings are extant in fragments only, seems to have been known to Calvin chiefly through Cicero's *De finibus* and *De natura deorum*. Book I of the latter work is devoted mainly to an exposition and an animated criticism of the Epicurean conception of deity. This sentence of Calvin sums up the impression of Cicero's dialogue. Cotta, the Academician, pours scorn upon the Epicurean notion of remote, idle, unloving gods, asserting that Epicurus has in effect abolished the gods. Calvin as a Scriptural theologian could not fail to share this adverse judgment. Cicero, *Nature of the Gods* I. xlii. 117; I. xliii. 120 ff. (LCL edition, pp. 112 ff.); Calvin, *Instruction et confession de foy* (1537) i, ii (OS I. 378 f.; tr. Fuhrmann, *Instruction in Faith*, pp. 17–19). Cf., below, I. iv. 2; I. v. 4; I. v. 12. For the opinion, similarly reflecting Cicero, of William Budé, Paris Greek scholar well known to Calvin, see J. Bohatec, *Budé und Calvin*, p. 74.

from provoking his anger. ᵇAnd yet it is not so terrified by the awareness of his judgment as to wish to withdraw, even if some way of escape were open. But it embraces him no less as punisher of the wicked than as benefactor of the pious. For the pious mind realizes that the punishment of the impious and wicked and the reward of life eternal for the righteous equally pertain to God's glory. Besides, this mind restrains itself from sinning, not out of dread of punishment alone; but, because it loves and reveres God as Father, it worships and adores him as Lord. Even if there were no hell, it would still shudder at offending him alone.

Here indeed is pure and real religion: faith so joined with an earnest fear of God[8] ᵉ⁽ᵇ⁾that this fear also embraces willing reverence, and carries with it such legitimate worship as is prescribed in the law. ᵉAnd we ought to note this fact even more diligently: all men have a vague general veneration for God, but very few really reverence him; and wherever there is great ostentation in ceremonies, sincerity of heart is rare indeed.

ᵉCHAPTER III

THE KNOWLEDGE OF GOD HAS BEEN NATURALLY IMPLANTED IN THE MINDS OF MEN[1]

1. The character of this natural endowment
ᵇThere is within the human mind, and indeed by natural instinct, an awareness of divinity.[2] This we take to be beyond controversy. To prevent anyone from taking refuge in the pretense of ignorance, God himself ᶜhas implanted ᵇin all men a certain understanding of his divine majesty. ᵉEver renewing its memory, he

---

[8] On faith joined with fear, see Melanchthon, *Loci communes* (1521), ed. H. Engelland, in the series *Melanchthons Werke in Auswahl*, ed. R. Stupperich, II. i. 119 ff.; tr. C. L. Hill (from Th. Kolde's 1910 edition), *The Loci Communes of Philip Melanchthon*, pp. 211 ff.

[1] "*Hominum mentibus naturaliter . . . inditam.*" The revelation of God "within" man (ch. iii) is extinguished by human sin (ch. iv). The same is true of that which comes to man "from without" through God's signs and tokens (*insignia, specimina*) in external nature (v. 14). Thus these chapters, iii–v, require for full understanding Calvin's entire doctrine of man: as created, I. xv; and as ravaged by sin, II. i–v.

[2] "*Divinitatis sensum.*" This term and "seed of religion," used immediately below (cf. I. iv. 1), refer generally to a numinous awareness of God, and are closely related to conscience, which is a moral response to God. Cf. I. i. 3 and Comm. John 1:5, 9. On verse 5, Calvin writes: "There are two principal parts of the light which still remains in corrupt nature: first, the seed of religion is planted in all men; next, the distinction between good and evil is engraved on their consciences."

repeatedly [b]sheds [c]fresh drops.[3] [b]Since, therefore, men one and all perceive that there is a God and that he is their Maker, they are condemned by their own testimony because they have failed to honor him and to consecrate their lives to his will. If ignorance of God is to be looked for anywhere, surely one is most likely to find an example of it among the more backward folk and those more remote from civilization. Yet there is, as the eminent pagan says, no nation so barbarous, no people so savage, that they have not a deep-seated conviction that there is a God.[4] And they who in other aspects of life seem least to differ from brutes still continue to retain some seed of religion. So deeply does the common conception occupy the minds of all, so tenaciously does it inhere in the hearts of all! Therefore, since from the beginning of the world there has been no region, no city, in short, no household, that could do without religion, there lies in this a tacit confession of a sense of deity inscribed in the hearts of all.

Indeed, even idolatry is ample proof of this conception. We know how man does not willingly humble himself so as to place other creatures over himself. Since, then, he prefers to worship wood and stone rather than to be thought of as having no God, clearly this is a most vivid impression of a divine being. So impossible is it to blot this from man's mind that natural disposition would be more easily altered, as altered indeed it is when man voluntarily sinks from his natural haughtiness to the very depths in order to honor God!

2. Religion is no arbitrary invention

[b]Therefore it is utterly vain for some men to say that religion was invented by the subtlety and craft of a few to hold the simple folk in thrall by this device and that those very persons who originated the worship of God for others did not in the least believe that any God existed.[5] I confess, indeed, that in order to hold

---

[3] Cf. Cicero, *Tusculan Disputations* II. x (LCL edition, pp. 172 ff.).

[4] The pagan (*ethnicus*) is Cicero. Calvin's view that all men have a natural sense or intimation of deity is in accord with the presupposition of all the characters of Cicero's dialogue *On the Nature of the Gods*, including the Epicurean, Velleius, who asks: "Where is there to be found a race or tribe of men which does not hold, without instruction, some preconception of the gods?" *Nature of the Gods* I. xvi. 43 (A. S. Pease, *M. Tulii Ciceronis De natura deorum*, pp. 294 f.; LCL edition, pp. 44 f.).

[5] This and the following section continue to reflect Cicero's *Nature of the Gods* in which the Epicureans' belief in gods is discounted by their critics. They are linked with those who escape superstition by denial and regard religion as an invention designed to subject men to government. Calvin, in *De scandalis* (1550), charges some of his contemporaries by name with atheism (CR VIII. 44 ff., with footnote 5; OS II. 200 f.). J. Bohatec, in *Budé*

men's minds in greater subjection, clever men have devised very many things in religion by which to inspire the common folk with reverence and to strike them with terror. But they would never have achieved this if men's minds had not already been imbued with a firm conviction about God, from which the inclination toward religion springs as from a seed. And indeed it is not credible that those who craftily imposed upon the ruder folk under pretense of religion were entirely devoid of the knowledge of God. If, indeed, there were some in the past, and today not a few appear, who deny that God exists, yet willy-nilly they from time to time feel an inkling of what they desire not to believe. One reads of no one who burst forth into bolder or more unbridled contempt of deity than Gaius Caligula;[6] yet no one trembled more miserably when any sign of God's wrath manifested itself; thus—albeit unwillingly—he shuddered at the God whom he professedly sought to despise. You may see now and again how this also happens to those like him; how he who is the boldest despiser of God is of all men the most startled at the rustle of a falling leaf [cf. Lev. 26:36]. Whence does this arise but from the vengeance of divine majesty, which strikes their consciences all the more violently the more they try to flee from it? Indeed, they seek out every subterfuge to hide themselves from the Lord's presence, and to efface it again from their minds. But in spite of themselves they are always entrapped. Although it may sometimes seem to vanish for a moment, it returns at once and rushes in with new force. If for these there is any respite from anxiety of conscience, it is not much different from the sleep of drunken or frenzied persons, who do not rest peacefully even while sleeping because they are continually troubled with dire and dreadful dreams. The impious themselves therefore exemplify the fact that some conception of God is ever alive in all men's minds.

3. Actual godlessness is impossible

eMen of sound judgment will always be sure that a sense of divinity which can never be effaced is engraved upon men's minds.

und Calvin, pp. 149–240, examines this topic at length with specific references to Pierre Brunel, Agrippa von Nettesheim, Étienne Dolet, Simon Villanovanus, Bonaventure des Périers, François Rabelais, Antonius Goveanus, and Jacques Gruet.

[6] Roman emperor, A.D. 37-41; grandnephew and successor of Tiberius Caesar. Suetonius says of this depraved emperor that he despised the gods but was so terrified when it thundered that he would leap from his bed and hide under it. (Lives of the Caesars IV. li; LCL Suetonius I. 482.) Cf. Comm. Harmony of the Evangelists, Matt. 26:69-75 (tr. LCC XXIII. 322).

Indeed, the perversity of the impious, who though they struggle furiously are unable to extricate themselves from the fear of God, is abundant testimony that this conviction, namely, that there is some God, is naturally inborn in all, and is fixed deep within, as it were in the very marrow. Although Diagoras[7] and his like may jest at whatever has been believed in every age concerning religion, and Dionysius[8] may mock the heavenly judgment, this is sardonic laughter,[9] for the worm of conscience, sharper than any cauterizing iron, gnaws away within. I do not say, as Cicero did, that errors disappear with the lapse of time, and that religion grows and becomes better each day.[10] For the world (something will have to be said of this a little later)[11] tries as far as it is able to cast away all knowledge of God, and by every means to corrupt the worship of him. I only say that though the stupid hardness in their minds, which the impious eagerly conjure up to reject God, wastes away, yet the sense of divinity, which they greatly wished to have extinguished, thrives and presently burgeons. From this we conclude that it is not a doctrine that must first be learned in school, but one of which each of us is master from his mother's womb and which nature itself permits no one to forget, although many strive with every nerve to this end.

[b]Besides, if all men are born and live to the end that they may know God, and yet if knowledge of God is unstable and fleeting unless it progresses to this degree, it is clear that all those who do not direct every thought and action in their lives to this goal degenerate from the law of their creation. This was not unknown to the philosophers. Plato meant nothing but this when he often taught that the highest good of the soul is likeness to

[7] Diagoras of Melos, called "the atheist" (a contemporary of Socrates), Theodore of Cyrene, and Protagoras the Sophist are taken by Cicero as examples of atheistic impiety. (All three were for this obliged to leave Athens.) (*Nature of the Gods* I. i. 2; I. xxiii. 63; LCL edition, pp. 4 f., 61 f.)

[8] Dionysius, tyrant of Syracuse, 405–367 B.C. His reputed acts of sacrilege and pillage are related by Cicero in *Nature of the Gods* III. xxxiv. 83 (LCL edition, pp. 368 f.). Cf. Calvin's reference in *Comm. Seneca On Clemency* I. xii (CR V. 92).

[9] "*Sardonius risus.*" Calvin uses the expression probably with a recollection of Vergil's proverbial allusion, "*Sardonius amarior . . . herbis,*" more bitter than Sardonian (Sardinian) herbs. (*Eclogues* vii. 41; LCL Vergil I. 51.)

[10] Calvin dissents from the opinion expressed by Cotta, the Academician in Cicero's *Nature of the Gods,* who refers to man's belief in God "which is only strengthened with ongoing time and more firmly rooted with the ages and the generations of men." (*Nature of the Gods* II. ii. 5; LCL edition, pp. 126 f.)

[11] Cf. I. iv. 1.

God, where, when the soul has grasped the knowledge of God, it is wholly transformed into his likeness.[12] In the same manner also Gryllus, in the writings of Plutarch, reasons very skillfully, affirming that, if once religion is absent from their life, men are in no wise superior to brute beasts, but are in many respects far more miserable. Subject, then, to so many forms of wickedness, they drag out their lives in ceaseless tumult and disquiet.[13] Therefore, it is worship of God alone that renders men higher than the brutes, and through it alone they aspire to immortality.[14]

cCHAPTER IV

This Knowledge Is Either Smothered or Corrupted, Partly by Ignorance, Partly by Malice

1. Superstition

   eAs experience shows, God has sown a seed of religion in all men. But scarcely one man in a hundred is met with who fosters it, once received, in his heart, and none in whom it ripens—much less shows fruit in season [cf. Ps. 1:3]. Besides while some may evaporate in their own superstitions and others deliberately and wickedly desert God, yet all degenerate from the true knowledge of him. And so it happens that no real piety remains in the world. But as to my statement that some erroneously slip into superstition, I do not mean by this that their ingenuousness should free them from blame. For the blindness under which they labor is almost always mixed with proud vanity and obstinacy. Indeed, vanity joined with pride can be detected in the fact e(b)that, in seeking God, miserable men do not rise above themselves as they should, but measure him by the yardstick of their own carnal stupidity, and neglect sound investigation; thus out of curiosity they fly off into empty speculations. They do not therefore apprehend God as he offers himself, bbut imagine him as they have fashioned him in their own presumption. When this gulf opens, in whatever direction they move their

---

12 Plato, *Theaetetus* 176. To escape evil and attain true wisdom, men must "become like God . . . righteous, holy, and wise" (LCL Plato II. 128 f.). Cf. *Phaedo* 107 C (LCL Plato I. 368–371).
13 Apparently a reference to Plutarch's dialogue, *Bruta animalia ratione uti,* in which Gryllus, whom Circe has transformed into a beast, indicates examples of the superiority of animal behavior to that of perverted humans (ch. 7) (LCL Plutarch, *Moralia* XII. 516 ff.).
14 Cf. II. ii. 12, 17, where "reason" is said to be that which distinguishes men from the brutes.
1 Cf. I. iii. 1, note 2.

feet, they cannot but plunge headlong into ruin. Indeed, whatever they afterward attempt by way of worship or service of God, they cannot bring as tribute to him, for they are worshiping not God but a figment and a dream of their own heart.[2] ᵉPaul eloquently notes this wickedness: "Striving to be wise, they make fools of themselves" [Rom. 1:22 p.]. He had said before that "they became futile in their thinking" [Rom. 1:21]. In order, however, that no one might excuse their guilt, he adds that they are justly blinded. For not content with sobriety but claiming for themselves more than is right, they wantonly bring darkness upon themselves—in fact, they become fools in their empty and perverse haughtiness. From this it follows that their stupidity is not excusable, since it is caused not only by vain curiosity but by an inordinate desire to know more than is fitting, joined with a false confidence.

2. Conscious turning away from God

ᵉDavid's statement that ungodly men and fools feel in their hearts that there is no God [Ps. 14:1; 53:1] must first, as we shall see again a little later, be limited to those who, by extinguishing the light of nature, deliberately befuddle themselves. Accordingly, we see that many, after they have become hardened in insolent and habitual sinning, furiously repel all remembrance of God, although this is freely suggested to them inwardly from the feeling of nature. But to render their madness more detestable, David represents them as flatly denying God's existence; not that they deprive him of his being, but because, in despoiling him of his judgment and providence, they shut him up idle in heaven.[3] Now there is nothing less in accord with God's nature than for him to cast off the government of the universe and abandon it to fortune, and to be blind to the wicked deeds of men, so that they may lust unpunished. Accordingly, whoever heedlessly indulges himself, his fear of heavenly judgment extinguished, denies that there is a God.[4] And it is God's just punishment of the wicked that fatness envelops their hearts, so that after they have closed their eyes, in seeing they see not [Matt. 13:14–15; cf. Isa. 6:9–10 and Ps. 17:10]. And David is the best interpreter of his thought when in another place he says that "the fear of God is not before the eyes of the ungodly" [Ps. 36:1 p.]. Likewise, because they

---

[2] Calvin uses similar expressions in the Latin Catechism published in 1538 (CR V. 323–324).

[3] Cf. I. ii. 2, note 7.

[4] Cicero, Nature of the Gods I. xx. 54; I. xxx. 85 f.; I. xliv. 123 (LCL edition, pp. 52 ff., 82 f., 118 f.).

persuade themselves that God does not see, they proudly applaud their own wrongdoing [Ps. 10:11].

Even though they are compelled to recognize some god, they strip him of glory by taking away his power. For, as Paul affirms, just as "God cannot deny himself," because "he remains" forever like himself [II Tim. 2:13], so they, by fashioning a dead and empty idol, are truly said to deny God. At this point we ought to note that, however much they struggle against their own senses, and wish not only to drive God thence but also to destroy him in heaven, their stupidity never increases to the point where God does not at times bring them back to his judgment seat. But because no fear restrains them from rushing violently against God, it is certain that so long as this blind urge grips them, their own oafish forgetfulness of God will hold sway over them.

3. We are not to fashion God according to our own whim[†]

ᵇThus is overthrown that vain defense with which many are wont to gloss over their superstition. For they think that any zeal for religion, however preposterous, is sufficient. But they do not realize that true religion ought to be conformed to God's will as to a universal rule; that God ever remains like himself, and is not a specter or phantasm to be transformed according to anyone's whim. One can clearly see, too, how superstition mocks God with pretenses while it tries to please him. For, seizing almost solely upon what God has testified to be of no concern to himself, superstition either holds in contempt or else openly rejects that which he prescribes and enjoins as pleasing to himself. Thus all who set up their own false rites to God worship and adore their own ravings. Unless they had first fashioned a God to match the absurdity of their trifling,[5] they would by no means have dared trifle with God in this way. The apostle accordingly characterizes that vague and erroneous opinon of the divine as ignorance of God. "When you did not know God," he says, "you were in bondage to beings that by nature were no gods" [Gal. 4: 8 p.]. And elsewhere he teaches that the Ephesians were "without God" at the time they were straying away from the right knowledge of the one God [Eph. 2:12]. Nor is it of much concern, at least in this circumstance, whether you conceive of one God or several; for you continually depart from the true God and forsake him, and, having left him, you have nothing left except an accursed idol. Therefore it remains for us to assert with

[5] Cf. I. xi–xii; IV. viii. 3, 4, 8, 9, 11, 13; IV. ix. 8; IV. x. 8, 16–18. The rejection of human invention in worship is a consistent theme of Calvin against both paganism and the Roman Church.

Lactantius that no religion is genuine unless it be joined with truth.[6]

4. Hypocrisy

[e(b)]A second sin arises, that they never consider God at all unless compelled to; and they do not come nigh until they are dragged there despite their resistance. And not even then are they impressed with the voluntary fear that arises out of reverence for the divine majesty, but merely with a slavish, forced fear, which God's judgment extorts from them. [b]This, since they cannot escape it, they dread even to the point of loathing. That saying of Statius' that fear first made gods in the world[7] corresponds well to this kind of irreligion, and to this alone. Those who are of a mind alien to God's righteousness know that his judgment seat stands ready to punish transgressions against him, yet they greatly desire its overthrow. Feeling so, they wage war against the Lord, who cannot be without judgment. But while they know that his inescapable power hangs over them because they can neither do away with it nor flee from it, they recoil from it in dread. And so, lest they should everywhere seem to despise him whose majesty weighs upon them, they perform some semblance of religion. Meanwhile they do not desist from polluting themselves with every sort of vice, and from joining wickedness to wickedness, until in every respect they violate the holy law of the Lord and dissipate all his righteousness. Or at least they are not so restrained by that pretended fear of God from wallowing blithely in their own sins and flattering themselves, and preferring to indulge their fleshly intemperance rather than restrain it by the bridle of the Holy Spirit.

This, however, is but a vain and false shadow of religion, scarcely even worth being called a shadow. [e(b)]From it one may easily grasp anew how much this confused knowledge of God differs from the piety from which religion takes its source,[8] which is instilled in the breasts of believers only. [e]And yet hypocrites

[6] Calvin does not here quote the words of Lactantius but summarizes much of his teaching in *Divine Institutes* I. ii, v, vi, xx and IV. v, where the test of "truth" is persistently applied to pagan beliefs (MPL 6. 120 f., 129 ff., 456 ff.; tr. ANF VII. 11, 13 ff., 32 ff., 104 f.).

[7] *"Timorem primum, fecisse in orbe deos."* Cf. Statius, *Thebaid* III. 661: *"Primus in orbe deos fecit timor"* (LCL Statius I. 500 f.).

[8] *"Pietas, ex qua demum religio nascitur."* See Introduction, pp. li f., above. Calvin has numerous emphatic statements of this view; cf. I. ii. 1; I. iv. 1; I. ix, title; II. vi. 4; III. iii. 16; IV. i. 5; IV. 1. 9; IV. i. 12; IV. xx. 9, 10, 13, 15; Comm. Jer. 10:25; *Instruction in Faith* (tr. Fuhrmann, p. 19). Cf. Cicero, *Pro Plancio* xii. 29: *"Pietas fundamentum est omnium virtutum"* (LCL edition, p. 442).

would tread these twisting paths so as to seem to approach the God from whom they flee. ᵇFor where they ought to have remained consistently obedient throughout life, they boldly rebel against him in almost all their deeds, and are zealous to placate him merely with a few paltry sacrifices. Where they ought to serve him in sanctity of life and integrity of heart, they trump up frivolous trifles and worthless little observances with which to win his favor. ᶜNay, more, with greater license they sluggishly lie in their own filth, because they are confident that they can perform their duty toward him by ridiculous acts of expiation. ᵉ⁽ᵇ⁾Then while their trust ought to have been placed in him, they neglect him and rely upon themselves, his creatures though they be. Finally, they entangle themselves in such a huge mass of errors that blind wickedness stifles and finally extinguishes those sparks which once flashed forth to show them God's glory. ᵇYet that seed remains which can in no wise be uprooted: that there is some sort of divinity; but this seed is so corrupted that by itself it produces only the worst fruits.

ᵉFrom this, my present contention is brought out with greater certainty, that a sense of divinity is by nature engraven on human hearts. For necessity forces from the reprobate themselves a confession of it. In tranquil times they wittily joke about God, indeed are facetious and garrulous in belittling his power. If any occasion for despair presses upon them, it goads them to seek him and impels their perfunctory prayers. From this it is clear that they have not been utterly ignorant of God, but that what should have come forth sooner was held back by stubbornness.

ᵉCHAPTER V

The Knowledge of God Shines Forth in the Fashioning of the Universe and the Continuing Government of It

(God manifested in his created works, 1–10)
1. The clarity of God's self-disclosure strips us of every excuse
ᵉ⁽ᵇ⁾The final goal of the blessed life, moreover, rests in the knowledge of God [cf. John 17:3].[1] Lest anyone, then, be excluded from access to happiness,[2] he not only sowed in men's minds that

---

[1] Cf. the oft-quoted words of Aquinas: "The final felicity of man consists only in the contemplation of God" (*Contra gentes* iii. 37 [tr. A. C. Pegis, *Basic Writings of St. Thomas Aquinas* ii. 60]); Augustine, *Confessions* X. xx. 29: "When I seek thee, I seek a happy life" (MPL 32. 791; tr. LCC X. 219).
[2] Calvin holds God's purpose in all revelation to be blessedness (cf. I. x. 2),

seed of religion of which we have spoken but revealed himself and daily discloses himself in the whole workmanship of the universe. As a consequence, men cannot open their eyes without being compelled to see him. Indeed, his essence is incomprehensible;[3] hence, his divineness far escapes all human perception. But upon his individual works he has engraved unmistakable marks of his glory, so clear and so prominent that even unlettered and stupid folk cannot plead the excuse of ignorance. ᵉTherefore the prophet very aptly exclaims that he is "clad with light as with a garment" [Ps. 104:2 p.]. It is as if he said: Thereafter the Lord began to show himself in the visible splendor of his apparel, ever since in the creation of the universe he brought forth those insignia whereby he shows his glory to us, whenever and wherever we cast our gaze. Likewise, the same prophet skillfully compares the heavens, as they are stretched out, to his royal tent and says that he has laid the beams of his chambers on the waters, has made the clouds his chariot, rides on the wings of the wind, and that the winds and lightning bolts are his swift messengers. [Ps. 104:2–4.] And since the glory of his power and wisdom shine more brightly above, heaven is often called his palace [Ps. 11:4]. ᵇYet, in the first place, wherever you cast your eyes, there is no spot in the universe wherein you cannot discern at least some sparks of his glory. You cannot in one glance survey this most vast and beautiful system of the universe, in its wide expanse, without being completely overwhelmed by the boundless force of its brightness.[4] The reason why the author of The Letter to the Hebrews elegantly calls the universe the appearance of things invisible [Heb. 11:3] is that this skillful ordering of the universe is for us a sort of mirror in which we can contem-

but because of human sin, the effect of this revelation in creation is to deepen man's guilt. See I. vi. 1 and cf. I. v. 14–15; II. ii. 23.

[3] See I. iii. 1, and cf. I. xiii. 21. Similarly, in the Catechism of 1538, it is said that God's "nature is incomprehensible, and remotely hidden from human understanding" (CR V. 324); and in that of 1542: "Our understanding is not capable of comprehending his essence" (CR VI. 16). He "accommodates" himself to our understanding in revelation; cf. Comm. Gen. 3:8; Comm. I Cor. 2:7.

[4] For a passage of lyrical delight in the manifestation of God in creation, see Calvin's Preface to the New Testament, written in 1534 and published in Olivétan's French Bible in June, 1535 (CR IX. 793; tr. LCC XXIII. 59 f.). Cf. J. T. McNeill, The History and Character of Calvinism, p. 232. Such passages have basic significance for Calvin's aesthetics, and they are also integral to his theology. Although the natural man derives from nature's evidence no true knowledge of God, being "blind in this glorious theater," yet Christians are enjoined to contemplate God in his works, on the pattern of Ps. 145 (I. v. 8, 9; I. vi. 2; II. vi. 1). Many similar passages in Calvin are cited by L. Wencelius, L'Esthétique de Calvin, chs. 1 and 2.

plate God, who is otherwise invisible. The reason why the prophet attributes to the heavenly creatures a language known to every nation [Ps. 19:2 ff.] is that therein lies an attestation of divinity so apparent that it ought not to escape the gaze of even the most stupid tribe. The apostle declares this more clearly: "What men need to know concerning God has been disclosed to them, . . . for one and all gaze upon his invisible nature, known from the creation of the world, even unto his eternal power and divinity" [Rom. 1:19–20 p.].

2. The divine wisdom displayed for all to see[t]

ᵇThere are innumerable evidences both in heaven and on earth that declare his wonderful wisdom; not only those more recondite matters for the closer observation of which astronomy, medicine, and all natural science are intended, but also those which thrust themselves upon the sight of even the most untutored and ignorant persons, so that they cannot open their eyes without being compelled to witness them.[5] Indeed, men who have either quaffed or even tasted the liberal arts penetrate with their aid far more deeply into the secrets of the divine wisdom.[6] Yet ignorance of them prevents no one from seeing more than enough of God's workmanship in his creation to lead him to break forth in admiration of the Artificer. To be sure, there is need of art and of more exacting toil in order to investigate the motion of the stars, to determine their assigned stations, to measure their intervals, to note their properties. As God's providence shows itself more explicitly when one observes these, so the mind must rise to a somewhat higher level to look upon his glory. Even the common folk and the most untutored, who have been taught only by the aid of the eyes, cannot be unaware of the excellence of divine art, for it reveals itself in this innumerable and yet distinct and well-ordered variety of the heavenly host. It is, accordingly, clear that there is no one to whom the Lord does not abundantly show his wisdom. Likewise, in regard to the structure of the human

---

[5] Cf. Cicero, Nature of the Gods II. ii. 4, where the view that contemplation of the heavens proves them to be governed by a supreme intelligence is taken as hardly requiring argument. (LCL edition, pp. 124 f.) In Comm. Ps. 19:4, Calvin refers to "the splendor of the heavens preaching the glory of God like a teacher in a seminary of learning."

[6] "Divinae sapientiae arcana." Possibly a recollection of Seneca's words in a letter of urgent exhortation to Lucilius, assuring him that devotion to noble studies will bring him knowledge of the secrets of nature (naturae arcana) (Epistulae morales cii. 28; LCL Seneca III. 184). To Calvin, liberal studies were an aid to comprehension of the divine wisdom conveyed in the Scriptures.

body[7] one must have the greatest keenness in order to weigh, with Galen's skill,[8] its articulation, symmetry, beauty, and use. But yet, as all acknowledge, the human body shows itself to be a composition so ingenious that its Artificer is rightly judged a wonder-worker.

3. Man as the loftiest proof of divine wisdom

ᵉCertain philosophers, accordingly, long ago not ineptly called man a microcosm[9] because he is a rare example of God's power, goodness, and wisdom, and contains within himself enough miracles to occupy our minds, if only we are not irked at paying attention to them. Paul, having stated that the blind can find God by feeling after him, immediately adds that he ought not to be sought afar off [Acts 17:27].[10] For each one undoubtedly feels within the heavenly grace that quickens him. Indeed, if there is no need to go outside ourselves to comprehend God, what pardon will the indolence of that man deserve who is loath to descend within himself[11] to find God? For the same reason, David, when he has briefly praised the admirable name and glory of God,

---

[7] Calvin has numerous references to the wisdom of God as exhibited in the human body. Cf. Comm. Ps. 139:15: "The inconceivable skill which appears in the formation of the human body," in which nothing can be altered without inconvenience, "even to the nails on our fingers." Calvin reverts to this topic in his argument for the resurrection, III. xxv. 7. Cf. also I. xv. 3; Wencelius, op. cit., pp. 37 f.; Cicero, Nature of the Gods II. lvi. 140 (LCL edition, pp. 256 ff.).

[8] Claudius Galenus of Pergamos (ca. 131–200), in whom ancient Greek medical learning reached its peak, was philosopher as well as physician and anatomist. The reference is to his περὶ χρείας μορίων (De usu partium) on the functions of the parts of the human body. An account of Galen's work is contained in L. Thorndike's A History of Magic and Experimental Science I. 117–181.

[9] "μικρόκοσμον." Aristotle's thought of man as microcosmos over against, and analogous to, the macrocosmos, or universe as a whole, is expressed in his Physics viii. 2: "Now if this can occur in an animal, why should not the same be true of the universe as a whole? If it can occur in a small world (ἐν μικρῷ κόσμῳ), it can also occur in a great one." (Tr. R. McKeon, Basic Works of Aristotle, p. 359; cf. LCL Aristotle, Physics II. 286 f.) This notion recurs in many later writers. It was frequently utilized in the Renaissance and became a literary commonplace. See G. P. Conger, Theories of Macrocosms and Microcosms in the History of Philosophy, pp. 59–72.

[10] With this and the following section, cf. Comm. Acts 17:26-29.

[11] "In se descendere," an expression frequently used by Calvin for the intense self-examination in which we are confronted by God and, at the same time, by our sinfulness. See I. i. 2; I. v. 10; II. viii. 3; III. xx. 6; IV. xvii. 40; Reply to Sadoleto (tr. LCC XXIII. 251). Cf. Augustine, Confessions VII. x: "I entered into my inmost soul, guided by thee" (MPL 32. 786; tr. LCC VII. 146).

which shine everywhere, immediately exclaims: "What is man that thou art mindful of him?" [Ps. 8:4]. Likewise, "Out of the mouths of babes and sucklings thou hast established strength." [Ps. 8:2.] Indeed, he not only declares that a clear mirror of God's works is in humankind, but that infants, while they nurse at their mothers' breasts, have tongues so eloquent to preach his glory that there is no need at all of other orators. Consequently, also, he does not hesitate to bring their infant speech into the debate, as if they were thoroughly instructed, to refute the madness of those who might desire to extinguish God's name in favor of their own devilish pride. Consequently, too, there comes in that which Paul quotes from Aratus, that we are God's offspring [Acts 17:28], because by adorning us with such great excellence he testifies that he is our Father. In the same way the secular poets, out of a common feeling and, as it were, at the dictation of experience, called him "the Father of men."[12] Indeed, no one gives himself freely and willingly to God's service unless, having tasted his fatherly love, he is drawn to love and worship him in return.

4. But man turns ungratefully against God

  eHere, however, the foul ungratefulness of men is disclosed. They have within themselves a workshop graced with God's unnumbered works and, at the same time, a storehouse overflowing with inestimable riches. They ought, then, to break forth into praises of him but are actually puffed up and swollen with all the more pride. They feel in many wonderful ways that God works in them; they are also taught, by the very use of these things, what a great variety of gifts they possess from his liberality. They are compelled to know—whether they will or not—that these are the signs of divinity; yet they conceal them within. Indeed, there is no need to go outside themselves, provided they do not, by claiming for themselves what has been given them from heaven, bury in the earth that which enlightens their minds to see God clearly.

  Even today the earth sustains many monstrous spirits who, to destroy God's name, do not hesitate to misdirect all the seed of divinity spread abroad in human nature. How detestable, I ask you, is this madness: that man, finding God in his body and

---

12 Aratus of Soli in Cilicia was a Greek poet and writer on astronomy who flourished about 270 B.C. It is from his poem *Phaenomena* that Paul quotes in Acts 17:28. This work was translated into Latin by Cicero. Cf. Cicero, *Nature of the Gods* II. xli. 104 f.; II. lxiii. 159 (LCL edition, pp. 222 f., 276 f.). See also I. xv. 5.

soul a hundred times, on this very pretense of excellence denies that there is a God? They will not say it is by chance that they are distinct from brute creatures. Yet they set God aside, the while using "nature," which for them is the artificer of all things, as a cloak. They see such exquisite workmanship in their individual members, from mouth and eyes even to their very toenails. Here also they substitute nature for God.[13] But such agile motions of the soul, such excellent faculties, such rare gifts, especially bear upon the face of them a divinity that does not allow itself readily to be hidden—unless the Epicureans, like the Cyclopes,[14] should from this height all the more shamelessly wage war against God. Do all the treasures of heavenly wisdom concur in ruling a five-foot worm while the whole universe lacks this privilege? First, to establish that there is something organic in the soul that should correspond to its several parts in no way obscures God's glory, but rather illumines it. Let Epicurus answer what concourse of atoms cooks food and drink, turns part of it into excrement, part into blood, and begets such industry in the several members to carry out their tasks, as if so many souls ruled one body by common counsel!

5. The confusion of creature with Creator

eBut now I have no concern with that pigsty;[15] rather, I take to task those given to fanciful subtleties who willingly drag forth in oblique fashion that frigid statement of Aristotle[16] both to destroy the immortality of the soul and to deprive God of his right. For, since the soul has organic faculties, they by this pretext bind the soul to the body so that it may not subsist without it, and by praising nature they suppress God's name as far as they can.[17] Yet the powers of the soul are far from being confined

[13] Cicero, *Nature of the Gods* II. ii. 4, quoting the phrase of Ennius: "Father of gods and men" (LCL edition, pp. 124–125).

[14] The French text substitutes for "*Cyclopes,*" "*des geans ou hommes sauvages.*" In Greek mythology Zeus was aided in his war on the Titans by arms furnished by the Cyclopes, the malformed giants whom he had liberated.

[15] Cf. Horace, *Epistles* I. iv. 15: "a hog from Epicurus' herd" (LCL edition, *Satires, Epistles, and Ars Poetica,* pp. 276 f.).

[16] Cf. Aristotle, *De anima* II. 1. Having discussed the intimate co-ordination of soul and body, so that the soul is "the first grade of actuality of a natural body having life potentially in it," Aristotle goes on to assert that "the soul is inseparable from the body" (R. McKeon, *Basic Works of Aristotle,* pp. 555 f.; LCL Aristotle, *On the Soul,* pp. 68–73). Calvin here expressly denies the latter statement.

[17] This paragraph on Aristotelian unbelief may have reference to Pietro Pomponazzi's *De immortalitate animae* (1516), in which it is argued that im-

to functions that serve the body. Of what concern is it to the body that you measure the heavens, gather the number of the stars, determine the magnitude of each, know what space lies between them, with what swiftness or slowness they complete their courses, how many degrees this way or that they decline? I confess, indeed, that astronomy has some use; but I am only showing that in this deepest investigation of heavenly things there is no organic symmetry, but here is an activity of the soul distinct from the body. I have put forth one example, from which it will be easy for my readers to derive the rest. Manifold indeed is the nimbleness of the soul with which it surveys heaven and earth, joins past to future, retains in memory something heard long before, nay, pictures to itself whatever it pleases. Manifold also is the skill with which it devises things incredible, and which is the mother of so many marvelous devices. These are unfailing signs of divinity in man.[18] Why is it that the soul not only vaguely roves about but conceives many useful things, ponders concerning many, even divines the future—all while man sleeps? What ought we to say here except that the signs of immortality which have been implanted in man cannot be effaced? Now what reason would there be to believe that man is divine and not to recognize his Creator? Shall we, indeed, distinguish between right and wrong by that judgment which has been imparted to us, yet will there be no judge in heaven? Will there remain for us even in sleep some remnant of intelligence, yet will no God keep watch in governing the world? Shall we think ourselves the inventors of so many arts and useful things that God may be defrauded of his praise even though experience sufficiently teaches that what we have has been unequally distributed among us from another source?

Some persons, moreover, babble about a secret inspiration that gives life to the whole universe, but what they say is not only weak but completely profane. Vergil's famous saying pleases them:

"First of all, an inner spirit feeds
Sky, earth, and watery fields, the shining orb
Of moon, and Titan's star; and mind pervades
Its members, sways all the mass, unites

mortality is philosophically indefensible and is to be accepted only on grounds of revelation. The work is translated with an introduction by J. H. Randall in *The Renaissance Philosophy of Man,* ed. E. Cassirer, P. O. Kristeller, and J. H. Randall, pp. 257–381. Cf. OS III. 48 f.

[18] This whole passage reflects Cicero's *Tusculan Disputations* I. xxiv–xxvii (LCL edition, pp. 64–79), though Calvin has changed the argument.

With its great frame. Thence come the race of man
And beast, the life of winged things, strange shapes
That ocean bears beneath his glassy floor.
Of fire the vigor, and divine the source
Of those life-seeds."[19]

As if the universe, which was founded as a spectacle of God's glory, were its own creator! For thus the same author has elsewhere followed the view common to Greeks and Latins alike:

"The bees, some teach, received a share of mind,
Divine, ethereal draught. For God, men say,
Pervades all things, the earth, expanse of seas
And heaven's depth. From him the flocks and herds,
Men and beasts of every sort, at birth
Draw slender life; yea, unto him all things
Do then return; unmade, are then restored;
Death has no place; but still alive they fly
Unto the starry ranks, to heaven's height."[20]

See, of what value to beget and nourish godliness in men's hearts is that jejune speculation about the universal mind which animates and quickens the world! This shows itself even more clearly in the sacrilegious words of the filthy dog Lucretius which have been deduced from that principle.[21] This is indeed making a shadow deity to drive away the true God, whom we should fear and adore. I confess, of course, that it can be said reverently, provided that it proceeds from a reverent mind, that nature is God; but because it is a harsh and improper saying, since nature is rather the order prescribed by God, it is harmful in such weighty matters, in which special devotion is due, to involve God confusedly in the inferior course of his works.[22]

6. The Creator reveals his lordship over the creation

ᵉLet us therefore remember, whenever each of us contemplates his own nature, that there is one God who so governs all natures that he would have us look unto him, direct our faith to him, and worship and call upon him. For nothing is more preposterous

---

[19] Vergil, *Aeneid* VI. 724–730 (translation adapted from H. R. Fairclough in LCL Vergil I. 556 f.).

[20] Vergil, *Georgics* IV. 219–227 (translation adapted from H. R. Fairclough in LCL Vergil I. 210 ff.).

[21] Lucretius, *De rerum natura* i. 54–79 (LCL edition, pp. 6 f.).

[22] These sentences reflect statements of Lactantius, who credits Seneca with being the best of the Stoics, since he "saw nature to be nothing else than God." *Divine Institutes* II. ix (CSEL 19. 134; MPL 6. 299; tr. ANF VII. 53). But Lactantius also points to the confusion arising from this identification; *op. cit.*, III. xxviii (CSEL 19. 264; MPL 6. 438; tr. ANF VII. 97).

than to enjoy the very remarkable gifts that attest the divine nature within us, yet to overlook the Author who gives them to us at our asking. ᵇWith what clear manifestations his might draws us to contemplate him! Unless perchance it be unknown to us in whose power it lies to sustain this infinite mass of heaven and earth by his Word: by his nod alone sometimes to shake heaven with thunderbolts, to burn everything with lightnings, to kindle the air with flashes; sometimes to disturb it with various sorts of storms, and then at his pleasure to clear them away in a moment; to compel the sea, which by its height seems to threaten the earth with continual destruction, to hang as if in mid-air;²³ sometimes to arouse it in a dreadful way with the tumultuous force of winds; sometimes, with waves quieted, to make it calm again! ᶜBelonging to this theme are the praises of God's power from the testimonies of nature which one meets here and there especially indeed in The Book of Job and in Isaiah. These I now intentionally pass over, for they will find a more appropriate place where I shall discuss from the Scriptures the creation of the universe.²⁴ Now I have only wanted to touch upon the fact that this way of seeking God is common both to strangers and to those of his household,²⁵ if they trace the outlines that above and below sketch a living likeness of him. ᵇThis very might leads us to ponder his eternity; for he from whom all things draw their origin must be eternal and have beginning from himself. Furthermore, if the cause is sought by which he was led once to create all these things, and is now moved to preserve them, we shall find that it is his goodness alone. But this being the sole cause, it ought still to be more than sufficient to draw us to his love, inasmuch as there is no creature, as the prophet declares, upon whom God's mercy has not been poured out [Ps. 145:9; cf. Ecclus. 18:11; 18:9, Vg.].

7. God's government and judgment

ᵇIn the second kind of works, which are outside the ordinary

---

²³ Calvin's traditional cosmology requires that water, "being an element, must be circular, and being the element heavier than air but lighter than earth, it ought to cover the latter in its entire circumference." Comm. Gen. 1:6–9. God, who separated the waters at creation, so that dry land appeared, now restrains them by a "perpetual ordinance" beyond barriers of mere sand. "Whence we learn that there is nothing to hinder the sea from overflowing the whole earth but the command of God, which it obeys." Comm. Jer. 5:22; cf. Comm. Ps. 33:7.

²⁴ Cf. I. xiv. 1–2, 20–22.

²⁵ This comment by Calvin on his method, which was added to the *Institutes* in 1559, makes clear that he is here arguing solely on the basis of human reason, and that such Biblical allusions as he makes are comparative and confirmatory (cf. I. x. 2), not constitutive of his argument

course of nature also, proofs of his powers just as clear are set forth. For in administering human society he so tempers his providence[26] that, although kindly and beneficent toward all in numberless ways, he still by open and daily indications declares his clemency to the godly and his severity to the wicked and criminal. For there are no doubts about what sort of vengeance he takes on wicked deeds. Thus he clearly shows himself the protector and vindicator of innocence, while he prospers the life of good men with his blessing, relieves their need, soothes and mitigates their pain, and alleviates their calamities; and in all these things he provides for their salvation. And indeed the unfailing rule of his righteousness ought not to be obscured by the fact that he frequently allows the wicked and malefactors to exult unpunished for some time, while he permits the upright and deserving to be tossed about by many adversities, and even to be oppressed by the malice and iniquity of the impious. But a far different consideration ought, rather, to enter our minds: that, when with a manifest show of his anger he punishes one sin, he hates all sins; that, when he leaves many sins unpunished, there will be another judgment to which have been deferred the sins yet to be punished. Similarly, what great occasion he gives us to contemplate his mercy when he often pursues miserable sinners with unwearied kindness, until he shatters their wickedness by imparting benefits and by recalling them to him with more than fatherly kindness!

8. God's sovereign sway over the life of men

ᵉTo this end, the prophet is mindful that in their desperate straits God suddenly and wonderfully and beyond all hope succors the poor and almost lost; those wandering through the desert he protects from wild beasts and at last guides them back to the way [Ps. 107:4–7]; to the needy and hungry he supplies food [v. 9]; the prisoners he frees from loathsome dungeons and iron bands [vs. 10–16]; the shipwrecked he leads back to port unharmed [vs. 23–30]; the half dead he cures of disease [vs. 17–20]; he burns the earth with heat and dryness, or makes it fertile with the secret watering of grace [vs. 33–38]; he raises up the humblest from the crowd, or casts down the lofty from the high level of their dignity [vs. 39–41]. By setting forth examples of this sort, the prophet shows that what are thought to be chance occurrences are just so many proofs of heavenly providence, especially of fatherly kindness. And hence ground for rejoicing is

---

[26] Cf. I. xvi–xviii, where the providence of God in the events of human life is discussed at large.

given to the godly, while as for the wicked and the reprobate, their mouths are stopped [v. 42]. But because most people, immersed in their own errors, are struck blind in such a dazzling theater,[27] he exclaims that to weigh these works of God wisely is a matter of rare and singular wisdom [v. 43], in viewing which they who otherwise seem to be extremely acute profit nothing. And certainly however much the glory of God shines forth, scarcely one man in a hundred[28] is a true spectator of it!

bIn no greater degree is his power or his wisdom hidden in darkness. His power shows itself clearly when the ferocity of the impious, in everyone's opinion unconquerable, is overcome in a moment, their arrogance vanquished, their strongest defenses destroyed, their javelins and armor shattered, their strength broken, their machinations overturned, and themselves fallen of their own weight; and when their audacity, which exalted them above heaven, lays them low even to the center of the earth; when, conversely the humble are raised up from the dust, and the needy are lifted up from the dung heap [Ps. 113:7]; the oppressed and afflicted are rescued from their extreme tribulation; the despairing are restored to good hope; the unarmed, few and weak, snatch victory from the armed, many and strong. Indeed, his wisdom manifests his excellence when he dispenses everything at the best opportunity; when he confounds all wisdom of the world [cf. I Cor. 1:20]; when "he catches the crafty in their own craftiness" [I Cor. 3:19 p.; cf. Job 5:13]. In short, there is nothing that he does not temper in the best way.

9. We ought not to rack our brains about God; but rather, we should contemplate him in his works

bWe see that no long or toilsome proof is needed to elicit evidences that serve to illuminate and affirm the divine majesty; since from the few we have sampled at random, whithersoever you turn, it is clear that they are so very manifest and obvious that they can easily be observed with the eyes and pointed out with the finger. And here again we ought to observe that we are called to a knowledge of God: not that knowledge which, content with empty speculation, merely flits in the brain, but that which will be sound and fruitful if we duly perceive it, and if it takes

----

27 Calvin has similar references to the heavens and the earth as a theater (*theatrum*) in which we may behold the Creator's glory in I. vi. 2; I. xiv. 20; II. vi. 1; III. ix. 2; Comm. Gen. 1:6; Comm. Ps. 138:1; and frequently elsewhere.
28 Cf. I. iv. 1.

root in the heart.[29] For the Lord manifests himself by his powers, the force of which we feel within ourselves and the benefits of which we enjoy. We must therefore be much more profoundly affected by this knowledge than if we were to imagine a God of whom no perception came through to us. Consequently, we know the most perfect way of seeking God, and the most suitable order, is not for us to attempt with bold curiosity to penetrate to the investigation of his essence, which we ought more to adore than meticulously to search out, but for us to contemplate him in his works whereby he renders himself near and familiar to us, and in some manner communicates himself. The apostle was referring to this when he said that we need not seek him far away, seeing that he dwells by his very present power in each of us [Acts 17:27–28]. For this reason, David, having first confessed his unspeakable greatness [Ps. 145:3], afterward proceeds to mention his works and professes that he will declare his greatness [Ps. 145:5–6; cf. Ps. 40:5]. It is also fitting, therefore, for us to pursue this particular search for God, which may so hold our mental powers suspended in wonderment as at the same time to stir us deeply. cAnd as Augustine teaches elsewhere, because, disheartened by his greatness, we cannot grasp him, we ought to gaze upon his works, that we may be restored by his goodness.[30]

10. The purpose of this knowledge of God

bKnowledge of this sort, then, ought not only to arouse us to the worship of God but also to awaken and encourage us to the hope of the future life.[31] For since we notice that the examples that the Lord shows us both of his clemency and of his severity are inchoate and incomplete, doubtless we must consider this to presage even greater things, the manifestation and full exhibition of which are deferred to another life. On the other hand— since we see the pious laden with afflictions by the impious, stricken with unjust acts, overwhelmed with slanders, wounded with abuses and reproaches; while the wicked on the contrary flourish, are prosperous, obtain repose with dignity and that without punishment—we must straightway conclude that there will be another life in which iniquity is to have its punishment,

[29] Calvin here distinguishes between *cerebrum* and *cor*, brain and heart, in relation to the knowledge of God, characteristically giving the importance to the latter. Cf. I. ii. 1; III. ii. 36; III. vi. 4. On the existential character of his doctrine, see E. A. Dowey, *The Knowledge of God in Calvin's Theology*, pp. 24–28.
[30] Augustine, *Psalms*, Ps. 144. 6 (MPL 37. 1872; tr. LF *Psalms* VI. 319).
[31] Cf. III. ix.

and righteousness is to be given its reward. Furthermore, since we observe that believers are often chastised by the Lord's rods, we may with full assurance believe that one day the wicked must no less suffer his lash. ᶜIndeed, Augustine's remark is well known: "If now every sin were to suffer open punishment, it would seem that nothing is reserved for the final judgment. Again, if God were now to punish no sin openly, one would believe that there is no providence."[32]

ᵇWe must therefore admit in God's individual works—but especially in them as a whole—that God's powers are actually represented as in a painting. Thereby the whole of mankind is invited and attracted to recognition of him, and from this to true and complete happiness. Now those powers appear most clearly in his works. Yet we comprehend their chief purpose, their value, and the reason why we should ponder them, only when we descend into ourselves and contemplate by what means the Lord shows in us his life, wisdom, and power; and exercises in our behalf his righteousness, goodness, and mercy. ᶜFor even though David justly complains that unbelievers are foolish because they do not ponder the deep designs of God in the governance of mankind [Ps. 92:5–6], yet what he says elsewhere is very true: that God's wonderful wisdom here abounds more than the hairs of our head [cf. Ps. 40:12]. But because this argument is to be treated more amply below,[33] I now pass over it.

(Man nevertheless, failing to know and worship him, falls into superstition and confusion, 11–12)

*11. The evidence of God in creation does not profit us** *

ᵇBut although the Lord represents both himself and his everlasting Kingdom in the mirror of his works with very great clarity, such is our stupidity that we grow increasingly dull toward so manifest testimonies, and they flow away without profiting us. For with regard to the most beautiful structure and order of the universe, how many of us are there who, when we lift up our eyes to heaven or cast them about through the various regions of earth, recall our minds to a remembrance of the Creator, and do not rather, disregarding their Author, sit idly in contemplation of his works? In fact, with regard to those events which daily take place outside the ordinary course of nature, how many of us do not reckon that men are whirled and twisted about by blindly indiscriminate fortune,[34] rather than governed by God's

---

[32] Augustine, *City of God* I. viii (MPL 41. 20; tr. NPNF II. 5).
[33] Cf. I. xvi. 6–9.
[34] "*Caeca fortunae temeritate.*" Cf. below in this section "*temeraria fortunae*

providence? Sometimes we are driven by the leading and direction of these things to contemplate God; this of necessity happens to all men. Yet after we rashly grasp a conception of some sort of divinity, straightway we fall back into the ravings or evil imaginings of our flesh, and corrupt by our vanity the pure truth of God. In one respect we are indeed unalike, because each one of us privately forges his own particular error; yet we are very much alike in that, one and all, we forsake the one true God for prodigious trifles. Not only the common folk and dull-witted men, but also the most excellent and those otherwise endowed with keen discernment, are infected with this disease.

In this regard how volubly has the whole tribe of philosophers shown their stupidity and silliness! For even though we may excuse the others (who act like utter fools), Plato, the most religious of all and the most circumspect, also vanishes in his round globe.[35] And what might not happen to others when the leading minds, whose task it is to light the pathway for the rest, wander and stumble! It is the same where the governance of human affairs shows providence so manifestly that we cannot deny it; yet we profit no more by it than if we believed that all things were turned topsy-turvy by the heedless will of fortune —so great is our inclination toward vanity and error! I always speak of the most excellent, not of those vulgar folk whose madness in profaning God's truth is beyond measure.

12. The manifestation of God is choked by human superstition and the error of the philosophers

ᵉHence arises that boundless filthy mire of error wherewith the whole earth was filled and covered. For each man's mind is like a labyrinth,[36] so that it is no wonder that individual nations

---

voluntate" and similar language in I. xvi. 2; I. xvi. 8; I. xvii. 1. Personified and deified in the ancient world, Fortuna retained a fascination for the Western mind and was a common term of discourse in the Renaissance, when ideas of chance and fate versus the divine ordering of events had a wide vogue. Here and in the other passages cited Calvin is probably thinking of the rejection of this notion by Lactantius in the *Divine Institutes* III. xxviii. 45 (CSEL 19. 264; tr. ANF VII. 97); and by Augustine, e.g., in *City of God* V. ix–xi (MPL 41. 447–450; tr. NPNF II. 90–93); *Retractations* I. i. 2 (MPL 32. 585). See also C. N. Cochrane, *Christianity and Classical Culture*, pp. 478 ff.; H. R. Patch, "The Tradition of the Goddess Fortuna," *Smith College Studies in Modern Languages* III, pp. 204–230; A. Doren, *Fortuna im Mittelalter und in der Renaissance*, pp. 71–144.

[35] Plato, *Timaeus* 33 B (LCL Plato VII. 62 f.) Cf. Cicero, *Nature of the Gods* I. x. 24, where Velleius sarcastically prefers four other geometric figures to Plato's sphere (LCL edition, pp. 26 f.).

[36] The pictorial figure of the labyrinth is in Calvin's writings frequently em-

were drawn aside into various falsehoods; and not only this—but individual men, almost, had their own gods. For as rashness and superficiality are joined to ignorance and darkness, scarcely a single person has ever been found who did not fashion for himself an idol or specter in place of God. Surely, just as waters boil up from a vast, full spring, so does an immense crowd of gods flow forth from the human mind, while each one, in wandering about with too much license, wrongly invents this or that about God himself. However, it is not necessary here to draw up a list of the superstitions with which the world has been entangled, because there would be no end to it, and so without a word of them it is sufficiently clear from so many corruptions how horrible is the blindness of the human mind. I pass over the rude and untutored crowd. But among the philosophers who have tried with reason and learning to penetrate into heaven, how shameful is the diversity![37] As each was furnished with higher wit, graced with art and knowledge, so did he seem to camouflage his utterances; yet if you look more closely upon all these, you will find them all to be fleeting unrealities. The Stoics thought themselves very clear when they said that one could elicit from all parts of nature various names for God, yet without on this account destroying the unity of God—as if, indeed, we were not already more than prone to vanity, without being drawn farther and more violently into error by the multiplicity of gods foisted upon us! Even the mystic theology of the Egyptians[38] shows all have sedulously brooded upon this so as not to appear to rave without reason. And perchance even at first glance something that seemed probable would deceive the simple and careless; but no mortal ever contrived anything that did not basely corrupt religion.

And this very confused diversity emboldened the Epicureans and other cross despisers of piety[39] to cast out all awareness of God. For when they saw the wisest persons contending with

ployed as a symbol of human frustration and confusion. Cf. I. vi. 1; I. vi. 3; I. xiii. 21; III. ii. 2–3; III. vi. 2; III. viii. 1; III. xix. 7; III. xxi. 1; III. xxv. 11; IV. vii. 22. In religious literature the conception is most impressively elaborated in J. A. Comenius, *The Labyrinth of the World and the Paradise of the Heart* (1623) (tr. M. Spinka).

[37] The disagreement among the learned about the gods was one of Cicero's reasons for writing his *Nature of the Gods* (see I. vi. 14; LCL edition, pp. 16 f.).

[38] Eusebius, *Praeparatio evangelica* III. iv (MPG 21. 171 f.); Augustine, *City of God* VIII. xxiii, xxvii (MPL 41. 247 ff., 256; tr. NPNF II. 159 f., 165); Plutarch, *De Iside et Osiride* 11 (LCL Plutarch, *Moralia* V. 28–29).

[39] No doubt the numerous passages in Cicero's *Nature of the Gods* (e.g., I. ii. 3; I. xxiii. 63; I. xxx. 85; I. xlii. 117; I. xliii. 121) charging the Epicureans

contrary opinions, from the disagreements of these—and even from their frivolous or absurd teaching—they did not hesitate to gather that men vainly and foolishly bring torments upon themselves when they seek for a god that is not. And this they thought to do with impunity because it would be preferable to deny outright God's existence than to fashion uncertain gods, and then stir up endless quarrels. But these folk pass a purely foolish judgment, or, rather, they conjure up a cloud out of men's ignorance to conceal their own impiety; in such ignorance there is not the least justification for departing from God. But since all confess that there is nothing concerning which the learned and the unlearned at the same time disagree so much, hence one may conclude that the minds of men which thus wander in their search after God are more than stupid and blind in the heavenly mysteries. Some praise the reply of Simonides,[40] who, asked by the tyrant Hiero what God was, begged to be given a day to ponder. When on the following day the tyrant asked the same question, he asked for two days more, and after having frequently doubled the number of days, finally answered, "The longer I consider this, the more obscure it seems to me." He wisely indeed suspended judgment on a subject so obscure to himself. Yet hence it appears that if men were taught only by nature, they would hold to nothing certain or solid or clear-cut, but would be so tied to confused principles as to worship an unknown god [cf. Acts 17:23].[41]

(Persistent in error, we are without excuse, 13–15)
13. The Holy Spirit rejects all cults contrived by men
    eNow we must also hold that all who corrupt pure religion—and this is sure to happen when each is given to his own opinion—separate themselves from the one and only God. Indeed, they

with practical atheism are here in mind; but there is an implied censure of contemporaries such as Rabelais. Cf. J. Bohatec, *Budé und Calvin*, pp. 226 ff.
[40] The anecdote is in Cicero, *Nature of the Gods* I. xxii. 60 (LCL edition, pp. 58–59).
[41] Natural theology (human reasoning about God, under the conditions of sin, unaided by special revelation) has been the subject of this chapter through section 12. All scholars agree that the above words present Calvin's verdict upon it, held consistently in all his writings. There is a sharp divergence of opinion, however, among interpreters as to Calvin's view of the usefulness of such natural theology to the Christian, especially its role in the Christian's observation of nature. Cf. I. x. 2–3. See also K. Barth and E. Brunner, tr. P. Fraenkel, *Natural Theology*; W. Niesel, *The Theology of Calvin*, pp. 39 ff.; E. A. Dowey, *The Knowledge of God in Calvin's Theology*, pp. 64 ff. Barth again, in his Gifford Lectures, *The Knowledge of God and the Service of God According to the Teaching of the*

will boast that they have something else in mind; but what they intend, or what they have persuaded themselves of, has not much bearing on the matter, seeing that the Holy Spirit pronounces them all to be apostates who in the blindness of their own minds substitute demons in place of God [cf. I Cor. 10:20]. For this reason, Paul declares that the Ephesians were without God until they learned from the gospel what it was to worship the true God [Eph. 2:12–13]. And this must not be restricted to one people, since elsewhere he states generally that all mortals "became vain in their reasonings" [Rom. 1:21] after the majesty of the Creator had been disclosed to them in the fashioning of the universe. For this reason, Scripture, to make place for the true and only God, condemned as falsehood and lying whatever of divinity had formerly been celebrated among the heathen; nor did any divine presence remain except on Mt. Zion, where the proper knowledge of God continued to flourish [Hab. 2:18, 20]. Certainly among the pagans in Christ's lifetime the Samaritans seemed to come closest to true piety; yet we hear from Christ's mouth that they knew not what they worshiped [John 4:22]. From this it follows that they were deluded by vain error.

In short, even if not all suffered under crass vices, or fell into open idolatries, yet there was no pure and approved religion, founded upon common understanding alone. For even though few persons did not share in the madness of the common herd, there remains the firm teaching of Paul that the wisdom of God is not understood by the princes of this world [I Cor. 2:8]. But if even the most illustrious wander in darkness, what can we say of the dregs? It is therefore no wonder that the Holy Spirit rejects as base all cults contrived through the will of men; for in the heavenly mysteries, opinion humanly conceived, even if it does not always give birth to a great heap of errors, is nevertheless the mother of error. And though nothing more harmful may result, yet to worship an unknown god [cf. Acts 17:23] by chance is no light fault. Nevertheless, by Christ's own statement all who have not been taught from the law what god they ought to worship are guilty in this matter [John 4:22]. And surely they who were the best legislators did not progress farther than to hold that religion was founded upon public agreement. Nay, according to Xenophon, Socrates praises the oracle of Apollo, which commanded that every man worship the gods after the manner of his forefathers and according to the custom of his own city.[42] But whence comes this law to mortals that they may by their own

Reformation, holds all natural theology alien to Reformed theology, e.g., lectures i, xx.
[42] Xenophon, *Memorabilia* IV. iii. 16 (LCL edition, pp. 306 f.).

authority define what far surpasses the world? Or who could so acquiesce in decrees of his ancestors, or enactments of the people, as to receive without hesitation a god humanly taught him? Each man will stand upon his own judgment rather than subject himself to another's decision.[43] Therefore, since either the custom of the city or the agreement of tradition is too weak and frail a bond of piety to follow in worshiping God, it remains for God himself to give witness of himself from heaven.

*14. The manifestation of God in nature speaks to us in vain**
ᵇIt is therefore in vain that so many burning lamps shine for us in the workmanship of the universe to show forth the glory of its Author. Although they bathe us wholly in their radiance, yet they can of themselves in no way lead us into the right path. Surely they strike some sparks, but before their fuller light shines forth these are smothered. For this reason, the apostle, in that very passage where he calls the worlds the images of things invisible, adds that through faith we understand that they have been fashioned by God's word [Heb. 11:3]. He means by this that the invisible divinity is made manifest in such spectacles, but that we have not the eyes to see this unless they be illumined by the inner revelation of God through faith. And where Paul teaches that what is to be known of God is made plain from the creation of the universe [Rom. 1:19], he does not signify such a manifestation as men's discernment can comprehend; but, rather, shows it not to go farther than to render them inexcusable. The same apostle also, even if he somewhere denies that God is to be sought far off, inasmuch as he dwells within us [Acts 17:27], in another place teaches of what avail that sort of nearness is, saying: "In past generations the Lord let the nations follow their own ways. Yet God did not leave himself without witness, sending benefits from heaven, giving rain and fruitful seasons, filling men's hearts with food and gladness" [Acts 14:16–17; vs. 15–16, Vg.]. Therefore, although the Lord does not want for testimony while he sweetly attracts men to the knowledge of himself with many and varied kindnesses, they do not cease on this account to follow their own ways, that is, their fatal errors.

*15. We have no excuse**
ᵇBut although we lack the natural ability to mount up unto the pure and clear knowledge of God, all excuse is cut off because the fault of dullness is within us. And, indeed, we are not allowed

---

[43] Cicero has Cotta say that it would be enough for him to accept the view that gods exist, merely because it is an opinion "handed down from our

thus to pretend ignorance without our conscience itself always convicting us of both baseness and ingratitude. As if this defense may properly be admitted: for a man to pretend that he lacks ears to hear the truth when there are mute creatures with more than melodious voices to declare it; or for a man to claim that he cannot see with his eyes what eyeless creatures point out to him; or for him to plead feebleness of mind when even irrational creatures give instruction![44] Therefore we are justly denied every excuse when we stray off as wanderers and vagrants even though everything points out the right way. But, however that may be, yet the fact that men soon corrupt the seed of the knowledge of God, sown in their minds out of the wonderful workmanship of nature (thus preventing it from coming to a good and perfect fruit), must be imputed to their own failing; nevertheless, it is very true that we are not at all sufficiently instructed by this bare and simple testimony which the creatures render splendidly to the glory of God. For at the same time as we have enjoyed a slight taste of the divine from contemplation of the universe, having neglected the true God, we raise up in his stead dreams and specters of our own brains, and attribute to anything else than the true source the praise of righteousness, wisdom, goodness, and power. Moreover, we so obscure or overturn his daily acts by wickedly judging them that we snatch away from them their glory and from their Author his due praise.

ᵉCHAPTER VI

Scripture Is Needed as Guide and Teacher for Anyone Who Would Come to God the Creator

1. God bestows the actual knowledge of himself upon us only in the Scriptures

ᵉ⁽ᵇ⁾That brightness which is borne in upon the eyes of all men both in heaven and on earth is more than enough to withdraw all support from men's ingratitude—just as God, to involve the human race in the same guilt, sets forth to all without exception his presence portrayed in his creatures. Despite this, it is needful that another and better help be added to direct us aright to the very Creator of the universe. ᵉIt was not in vain, then, that he

forefathers"; *Nature of the Gods* III. iv. 9 (LCL edition, pp. 294–295). This is cited by Lactantius, *Divine Institutes* II. vii (CSEL 19. 124; MPL 6. 285; tr. ANF VII. 50).

[44] It is a favorite thought of Calvin that the creatures of God declare His glory. Cf. I. v. 1, 2.

added the light of his Word by which to become known unto salvation; and he regarded as worthy of this privilege those whom he pleased to gather more closely and intimately to himself. For because he saw the minds of all men tossed and agitated, after he chose the Jews as his very own flock, he fenced them about that they might not sink into oblivion as others had. With good reason he holds us by the same means in the pure knowledge of himself, since otherwise even those who seem to stand firm before all others would soon melt away. Just as old or bleary-eyed men and those with weak vision, if you thrust before them a most beautiful volume, even if they recognize it to be some sort of writing, yet can scarcely construe two words, but with the aid of spectacles[1] will begin to read distinctly; so Scripture, gathering up the otherwise confused knowledge of God in our minds, having dispersed our dullness, clearly shows us the true God. This, therefore, is a special gift, [b]where God, to instruct the church, not merely uses mute teachers but also opens his own most hallowed lips. Not only does he teach the elect to look upon a god, but also shows himself as the God upon whom they are to look. He has from the beginning maintained this plan for his church, so that besides these common proofs he also put forth his Word, which is a more direct and more certain mark whereby he is to be recognized.[2]

(Two sorts of knowledge of God in Scripture)
[e(b)]There is no doubt that Adam, Noah, Abraham, and the rest of the patriarchs with this assistance penetrated to the intimate knowledge of him [e]that in a way distinguished them from unbelievers. I am not yet speaking of the proper doctrine of faith whereby they had been illumined unto the hope of eternal life. For, that they might pass from death to life, it was necessary to recognize God not only as Creator but also as Redeemer, for undoubtedly they arrived at both from the Word. First in order came that kind of knowledge by which one is permitted to grasp who that God is who founded and governs the universe. Then that other inner knowledge was added, which alone quickens dead

---

[1] This simile, repeated in I. xiv. 1, in Comm. Gen. "Argument," and elsewhere, is probably Calvin's decisive utterance on the role of Scripture as related to the revelation of the Creator in creation. In modern Calvin study there has been much diversity in discussions of this expression and its implications. Cf. B. B. Warfield, *Calvin and Calvinism,* pp. 260 f.; P. Barth, *Das Problem der natürlichen Theologie bei Calvin;* G. Gloede, *Theologia naturalis bei Calvin;* T. H. L. Parker, *The Doctrine of the Knowledge of God: A Study in Calvin's Theology;* and the titles in note 41 on I. v. 12.

[2] Cf. II. i–v.

souls, whereby God is known not only as the Founder of the universe and the sole Author and Ruler of all that is made, but also in the person of the Mediator as the Redeemer. But because we have not yet come to the fall of the world and the corruption of nature, I shall now forego discussion of the remedy.[3] My readers therefore should remember that I am not yet going to discuss that covenant by which God adopted to himself the sons of Abraham, or that part of doctrine which has always separated believers from unbelieving folk, for it was founded in Christ. But here I shall discuss only how we should learn from Scripture that God, the Creator of the universe, can by sure marks be distinguished from all the throng of feigned gods. Then, in due order, that series will lead us to the redemption.[4] We shall derive many testimonies from the New Testament, and other testimonies also from the Law and the Prophets, where express mention is made of Christ. Nevertheless, all things will tend to this end, that God, the Artificer of the universe, is made manifest to us in Scripture, and that what we ought to think of him is set forth there, lest we seek some uncertain deity by devious paths.

2. *The Word of God as Holy Scripture*

ᵉ⁽ᵇ⁾But whether God became known to the patriarchs through oracles and visions or by the work and ministry of men, he put into their minds what they should then hand down to their posterity. At any rate, there is no doubt that firm certainty of doctrine was engraved in their hearts, so that they were convinced and understood that what they had learned proceeded from God.[5] For by his Word, God rendered faith unambiguous forever, a faith that should be superior to all opinion. Finally, in order that truth might abide forever in the world with a continuing succession of teaching and survive through all ages, the same oracles he had given to the patriarchs it was his pleasure to have recorded, as it were, on public tablets. ᵉWith this intent the law was published, and the prophets afterward added as its interpreters. For even though the use of the law was manifold, as will be seen

---

[3] Cf. II. vi, vii, and III, passim. On the covenant, see also II. viii. 21; II. x. 1–5, 8; II. xi. 4, 11; III. xvii. 6; III. xxi. 5–7; IV. xiv. 6; IV. xv. 22; IV. xvi. 5, 6, 14; IV. xvii. 20.

[4] Cf. II. v. 7; II. xvi. 5–12.

[5] Calvin does not here offer an explanation of the manner of inspiration in the origin of the Scriptures. However, the suggestion his language conveys is not of a mechanical verbal dictation, but of an impartation of divine truth that enters the hearts of the Scripture writers. See also J. T. McNeill, "The Significance of the Word of God for Calvin," *Church History* XXVIII (1959), 131–146.

more clearly in its place,[6] it was especially committed to Moses and all the prophets to teach the way of reconciliation between God and men, whence also Paul calls "Christ the end of the law" [Rom. 10:4]. Yet I repeat once more: besides the specific doctrine of faith and repentance that sets forth Christ as Mediator, Scripture adorns with unmistakable marks and tokens the one true God, in that he has created and governs the universe, in order that he may not be mixed up with the throng of false gods. Therefore, however fitting it may be for man seriously to turn his eyes to contemplate God's works, since he has been placed in this most glorious theater to be a spectator of them, it is fitting that he prick up his ears to the Word, the better to profit. And it is therefore no wonder that those who were born in darkness become more and more hardened in their insensibility; for there are very few who, to contain themselves within bounds, apply themselves teachably to God's Word, but they rather exult in their own vanity. Now, in order that true religion may shine upon us, we ought to hold that it must take its beginning from heavenly doctrine and that no one can get even the slightest taste of right and sound doctrine unless he be a pupil of Scripture. Hence, there also emerges the beginning of true understanding when we reverently embrace what it pleases God there to witness of himself. But not only faith, perfect and in every way complete, but all right knowledge of God is born of obedience.[7] [e(b)]And surely in this respect God has, by his singular providence, taken thought for mortals through all ages.

3. Without Scripture we fall into error

[b]Suppose we ponder how slippery is the fall of the human mind into forgetfulness of God, how great the tendency to every kind of error, how great the lust to fashion constantly new and artificial religions. Then we may perceive how necessary was such written proof of the heavenly doctrine, that it should neither perish through forgetfulness nor vanish through error nor be corrupted by the audacity of men. It is therefore clear that God has provided the assistance of the Word for the sake of all those to whom he has been pleased to give useful instruction because he foresaw that his likeness imprinted upon the most beautiful form of the universe would be insufficiently effective. Hence, we must strive

[6] Cf. II. vii and viii.
[7] This sentence, "Omnis recta cognitio Dei ab obedientia nascitur," is quoted by K. Barth in affirming that dogmatics must presuppose Christian faith (Kirchliche Dogmatik I. i. 17; tr. G. T. Thomson. The Doctrine of the Word of God I. 19).

onward by this straight path if we seriously aspire to the pure contemplation of God. We must come, I say, to the Word, where God
is truly and vividly described to us from his works, while these
very works are appraised not by our depraved judgment but by
the rule of eternal truth. If we turn aside from the Word, as I
have just now said, though we may strive with strenuous haste,
yet, since we have got off the track, we shall never reach the goal.
For we should so reason that the splendor of the divine countenance, which even the apostle calls "unapproachable" [I Tim.
6:16], is for us like an inexplicable labyrinth unless we are conducted into it by the thread of the Word; so that it is better to
limp along this path than to dash with all speed outside it.[8] ᶜDavid
very often, therefore, teaching that we ought to banish superstitions from the earth so that pure religion may flourish, represented God as regnant [Ps. 93:1; 96:10; 97:1; 99:1; and the like].
Now he means by the word "regnant" not the power with which
he is endowed, and which he exercises in governing the whole
of nature, but the doctrine by which he asserts his lawful
sovereignty. For errors can never be uprooted from human hearts
until true knowledge of God is planted therein.

*4. Scripture can communicate to us what the revelation in the
creation cannot*

ᵇAccordingly, the same prophet, after he states, "The heavens
declare the glory of God, the firmament shows forth the works of
his hands, the ordered succession of days and nights proclaims his
majesty" [Ps. 19:1-2 p.], then proceeds to mention his Word:
"The law of the Lord is spotless, converting souls; the testimony of the Lord is faithful, giving wisdom to little ones; the
righteous acts of the Lord are right, rejoicing hearts; the precept
of the Lord is clear, enlightening eyes" [Ps. 18:8-9, Vg.; 19:7-8,
EV]. ᵉ⁽ᵇ⁾For although he also includes other uses of the law, he
means in general that, since God in vain calls all peoples to himself by the contemplation of heaven and earth, this is the very
school of God's children. ᶜPsalm 29 looks to this same end, where
the prophet—speaking forth concerning God's awesome voice,
which strikes the earth in thunder [v. 3], winds, rains, whirlwinds
and tempests, causes mountains to tremble [v. 6], shatters the
cedars [v. 5]—finally adds at the end that his praises are sung in
the sanctuary because the unbelievers are deaf to all the voices

[8] Augustine, *Psalms*, Ps. 31. ii. 4 (MPL 36. 260; tr. LF *Psalms* I. 253); *Sermons*
cxli. 4: *"Melius est in via claudicare quam praeter viam fortiter ambulare"*
(MPL 38. 778; tr. LF *Sermons* II. 656 f.). Cf. *Sermons* clxix. 15 (MPL 38.
926; tr. LF *Sermons* II. 870 f.).

of God that resound in the air [vs. 9–11]. Similarly, he thus ends another psalm where he has described the awesome waves of the sea: "Thy testimonies have been verified, the beauty and holiness of thy temple shall endure forevermore" [Ps. 93:5 p.]. ᶜHence, also, arises that which Christ said to the Samaritan woman, that her people and all other peoples worshiped they knew not what; that the Jews alone offered worship to the true God [John 4:22]. For, since the human mind because of its feebleness can in no way attain to God unless it be aided and assisted by his Sacred Word, all mortals at that time—except for the Jews—because they were seeking God without the Word, had of necessity to stagger about in vanity and error.

ᶜCHAPTER VII

Scripture Must Be Confirmed by the Witness of the Spirit. Thus May Its Authority[1] Be Established as Certain; and It Is a Wicked Falsehood that Its Credibility Depends on the Judgment of the Church

1. Scripture has its authority from God, not from the church

ᶜBefore I go any farther, it is worth-while to say something about the authority of Scripture,[2] not only to prepare our hearts to reverence it, but to banish all doubt. ᵇWhen that which is set forth is acknowledged to be the Word of God, there is no one so deplorably insolent—unless devoid also both of common sense and of humanity itself—as to dare impugn the credibility of Him who speaks. Now daily oracles are not sent from heaven, for it pleased the Lord to hallow his truth to everlasting remembrance in the Scriptures alone [cf. John 5:39]. ᵉ⁽ᵇ⁾Hence the Scriptures obtain full authority among believers only when men regard them as having sprung from heaven, ᵇas if there the living words of God were heard. This matter is very well worth treating more fully and weighing more carefully. But my readers will pardon me if I

---

[1] Cf. IV. viii for a related treatment of the authority and inspiration of Scripture.

[2] Chapters vii–ix form an excursus on Biblical authority. Both the doctrines of the deity of the Spirit (I. xiii. 14–15) and the redemptive work of the Spirit (Book III, throughout, especially chs. i–ii) form the immediate theological context of the doctrine of the "inner testimony." Calvin refers the reader "elsewhere" (I. vii. 5), but this has often been overlooked. It is crucial for the interpretation of Calvin whether this doctrine of Scripture is seen as complete in itself or in the larger epistemological context of III. ii. Cf. Warfield, *Calvin and Calvinism*, p. 71, *et passim*; Doumergue, *Calvin* IV. 68, 247; Dowey, *The Knowledge of God in Calvin's Theology*, pp. 87, 157–164, 174.

regard more what the plan of the present work demands than what the greatness of this matter requires.

But a most pernicious error widely prevails that Scripture has only so much weight as is conceded to it by the consent of the church. As if the eternal and inviolable truth of God depended upon the decision of men! For they mock the Holy Spirit when they ask: Who can convince us that these writings came from God? Who can assure us that Scripture has come down whole and intact even to our very day? Who can persuade us to receive one book in reverence but to exclude another, unless the church prescribe a sure rule for all these matters? What reverence is due Scripture and what books ought to be reckoned within its canon depend, they say, upon the determination of the church.[3] Thus these sacrilegious men, wishing to impose an unbridled tyranny under the cover of the church, do not care with what absurdities they ensnare themselves and others, provided they can force this one idea upon the simple-minded: that the church has authority in all things. Yet, if this is so, what will happen to miserable consciences seeking firm assurance of eternal life if all promises of it consist in and depend solely upon the judgment of men? Will they cease to vacillate and tremble when they receive such an answer? Again, to what mockeries of the impious is our faith subjected, into what suspicion has it fallen among all men, if we believe that it has a precarious authority dependent solely upon the good pleasure of men!

2. The church is itself grounded upon Scripture

[b]But such wranglers are neatly refuted by just one word of the apostle. He testifies that the church is "built upon the foundation of the prophets and apostles" [Eph. 2:20]. If the teaching of the prophets and apostles is the foundation, this must have had authority before the church began to exist. Groundless, too, is their subtle objection that, although the church took its beginning here, the writings to be attributed to the prophets and apostles nevertheless remain in doubt until decided by the church. For if the Christian church was from the beginning founded upon the writings of the prophets and the preaching of the apostles,

---

[3] Cf. Bullinger, De scripturae sacrae authoritate (1538), fo. 4a. The claim of church authority in the interpretation of Scripture is defended by Cochlaeus in De authoritate ecclesiae et scripture (1524), and in De canonicae scripture et catholicae ecclesiae authoritate, ad Henricum Bullingerium (1543). In the latter work (ch. iii), he states that no claim is made for the superior authority of the church over the Scripture, but holds (ch. iv) that the church has authority circa scripturas, and that such authority is most necessary. Cf. also John Eck, Enchiridion (1533), ch. i, fo. 4a–6b.

wherever this doctrine is found, the acceptance of it—without which the church itself would never have existed—must certainly have preceded the church.[4] It is utterly vain, then, to pretend that the power of judging Scripture so lies with the church that its certainty depends upon churchly assent. Thus, while the church receives and gives its seal of approval to the Scriptures, it does not thereby render authentic what is otherwise doubtful or controversial. But because the church recognizes Scripture to be the truth of its own God, as a pious duty it unhesitatingly venerates Scripture. As to their question—How can we be assured that this has sprung from God unless we have recourse to the decree of the church?—it is as if someone asked: Whence will we learn to distinguish light from darkness, white from black, sweet from bitter? Indeed, Scripture exhibits fully as clear evidence of its own truth[5] as white and black things do of their color, or sweet and bitter things do of their taste.

3. Augustine cannot be cited as counterevidence

ᵈIndeed, I know that statement of Augustine is commonly referred to, that he would not believe the gospel if the authority of the church did not move him to do so.[6] But it is easy to grasp from the context how wrongly and deceptively they interpret this passage. Augustine was there concerned with the Manichees, who wished to be believed without controversy when they claimed, but did not demonstrate, that they themselves possessed the truth. Because in fact they used the gospel as a cloak to promote faith in their Mani, Augustine asks: "What would they do if they were to light upon a man who does not even believe in the gospel? By what kind of persuasion would they bring him around to their opinion?" Then he adds, "Indeed, I would not believe the gospel," etc., meaning that if he were alien to the faith, he could not be led to embrace the gospel as the certain truth of God

---

[4] Cf. Introduction, pp. lxi ff. This view of the antecedence of Scripture to the church was common to the Reformers. It appears in Luther's *Lectures on the Psalms* (*Werke* WA III. 454), where he says, "The Scripture is the womb from which are born the divine truth and the church." Cf. K. Holl, *Gesammelte Aufsätze zur Kirchengeschichte* I. *Luther*, 288 ff.; R. E. Davies, *The Problem of Authority in the Continental Reformers*, pp. 41 f.; McNeill, *The History and Character of Calvinism*, pp. 73 ff.

[5] Cf. I. vii. 5.

[6] Augustine, *Contra epistolam Manichaei quam vocant fundamenti* v (MPL 42. 176; tr. NPNF IV. 131): "For my part, I should not believe the gospel except as moved by the authority of the catholic church." Luther, in his tract *That the Doctrines of Men Are to Be Rejected* (1522), had largely anticipated Calvin's interpretation of Augustine's meaning in this passage (*Werke* WA X. ii. 89; tr. *Works of Martin Luther* II. 451 ff.).

unless constrained by the authority of the church. And what wonder if someone, not yet having known Christ, should have respect for men! Augustine is not, therefore, teaching that the faith of godly men is founded on the authority of the church; nor does he hold the view that the certainty of the gospel depends upon it. He is simply teaching that there would be no certainty of the gospel for unbelievers to win them to Christ if the consensus of the church did not impel them. And this he clearly confirms a little later, saying: "When I praise what I believe, and laugh at what you believe, how do you think we are to judge, or what are we to do? Should we not forsake those who invite us to a knowledge of things certain and then bid us believe things uncertain? Must we follow those who invite us first to believe what we are not yet strong enough to see, that, strengthened by this very faith, we may become worthy to comprehend what we believe [Col. 1:4–11, 23]—with God himself, not men, now inwardly strengthening and illumining our mind?"[7]

These are Augustine's very words. From them it is easy for anyone to infer that the holy man's intention was not to make the faith that we hold in the Scriptures depend upon the assent or judgment of the church. He only meant to indicate what we also confess as true: those who have not yet been illumined by the Spirit of God are rendered teachable by reverence for the church, so that they may persevere in learning faith in Christ from the gospel. Thus, he avers, the authority of the church is an introduction through which we are prepared for faith in the gospel. For, as we see, he wants the certainty of the godly to rest upon a far different foundation. I do not deny that elsewhere, when he wishes to defend Scripture, which they repudiate, he often presses the Manichees with the consensus of the whole church. Hence, he reproaches Faustus[8] for not submitting to the gospel truth—so firm, so stable, celebrated with such glory, and handed down from the time of the apostles through a sure succession. But it never occurs to him to teach that the authority which we ascribe to Scripture depends upon the definition or decree of men. He puts forward only the universal judgment of the church, in which he was superior to his adversaries, because of its very great value in this case. If anyone desires a fuller proof of this,

---

[7] Augustine, *Contra epistolam Manichaei quam vocant fundamenti* xiv (MPL 42. 183; tr. NPNF IV. 136).
[8] Augustine, *De ordine* II. ix. 27–x. 28 (MPL 32.1007 f.; tr. R. P. Russell, *Divine Providence and the Problem of Evil: A Translation of Augustine's De ordine*, pp. 122–127); *Against Faustus the Manichee* xxxii. 19 (MPL 42. 509; tr. NPNF IV. 339).

let him read Augustine's little book *The Usefulness of Belief*.[9]
There he will find that the author recommends no other induce-
ment to believe except what may provide us with an approach
and be a suitable beginning for inquiry, as he himself says; yet
we should not acquiesce in mere opinion, but should rely on sure
and firm truth.

4. *The witness of the Holy Spirit: this is stronger than all proof*

ᵉWe ought to remember what I said a bit ago:[10] credibility of
doctrine is not established until we are persuaded beyond doubt
that God is its Author.[11] Thus, the highest proof of Scripture
derives in general from the fact that God in person speaks in it.
The prophets and apostles do not boast either of their keenness or
of anything that obtains credit for them as they speak; nor do
they dwell upon rational proofs. Rather, they bring forward God's
holy name, that by it the whole world may be brought into obedience to him. Now we ought to see how apparent it is not only by
plausible opinion but by clear truth that they do not call upon
God's name heedlessly or falsely. ᵇIf we desire to provide in the
best way for our consciences—that they may not be perpetually
beset by the instability of doubt or vacillation, and that they may
not also boggle at the smallest quibbles—we ought to seek our conviction in a higher place than human reasons, judgments, or conjectures, that is, in the secret testimony of the Spirit.[12] ᵉTrue, if
we wished to proceed by arguments, we might advance many
things that would easily prove—if there is any god in heaven—
that the law, the prophets, and the gospel come from him. Indeed,
ever so learned men, endowed with the highest judgment, rise up
in opposition and bring to bear and display all their mental
powers in this debate. Yet, unless they become hardened to the
point of hopeless impudence, this confession will be wrested from
them: that they see manifest signs of God speaking in Scripture.
From this it is clear that the teaching of Scripture is from heaven.
And a little later we shall see that all the books of Sacred Scripture
far surpass all other writings. Yes, if we turn pure eyes and upright

---

[9] Augustine, *The Usefulness of Belief* i. 2, 3 (MPL 42. 65 ff.; tr. LCC VI. 292 ff.).
[10] Referring to I. vii. 1.
[11] Cf. Aquinas, *Summa Theol.* I. i. 10: "The author of Holy Scripture is God."
[12] On Calvin's doctrine of the inner witness of the Holy Spirit to the truth
   of Scripture, see I. vii. 4; III. i. 1; III. i. 3 f.; III. ii. 15, 33–36; Geneva
   Catechism (1545) xiv. 91; xviii. 113 (OS II. 88, 92; tr. LCC XXII. 102, 105);
   Comm. II Tim. 3:16; Doumergue, *Calvin* IV. 54–69; Dowey, *op. cit.,* pp.
   106 ff.; Niesel, *The Theology of Calvin*, pp. 30–39; G. S. Hendry, *The
   Holy Spirit in Christian Theology*, pp. 72–95. The Westminster Confession
   I. 5 succinctly states the Reformed doctrine.

senses toward it, the majesty of God will immediately come to view, subdue our bold rejection, and compel us to obey.

Yet they who strive to build up firm faith in Scripture through disputation are doing things backwards.[13] For my part, although I do not excel either in great dexterity or eloquence, if I were struggling against the most crafty sort of despisers of God, who seek to appear shrewd and witty in disparaging Scripture, I am confident it would not be difficult for me to silence their clamorous voices. And if it were a useful labor to refute their cavils, I would with no great trouble shatter the boasts they mutter in their lurking places. But even if anyone clears God's Sacred Word from man's evil speaking, he will not at once imprint upon their hearts that certainty which piety requires. Since for unbelieving men religion seems to stand by opinion alone, they, in order not to believe anything foolishly or lightly, both wish and demand rational proof that Moses and the prophets spoke divinely.[14] But I reply: the testimony of the Spirit is more excellent than all reason. For as God alone is a fit witness of himself in his Word,[15] so also the Word will not find acceptance in men's hearts before it is sealed by the inward testimony of the Spirit. The same Spirit, therefore, who has spoken through the mouths of the prophets must penetrate into our hearts to persuade us that they faithfully proclaimed what had been divinely commanded. Isaiah very aptly expresses this connection in these words: "My Spirit which is in you, and the words that I have put in your mouth, and the mouths of your offspring, shall never fail" [Isa. 59:21 p.]. Some good folk

[13] Cf. Lactantius, *Divine Institutes* III. i (CSEL 19. 178; tr. ANF VII. 69).

[14] This passage is associated by Barth and Niesel with a letter sent by "Capnio" (Antoine Fumée) to Calvin from Paris, late 1542 or early 1543 (OS III. 70, note 1). The letter may be read in Herminjard, *Correspondance* VIII. 228 ff., and in CR XI. 490 ff. The writer, a counselor of the Parlement, expresses alarm over the dangerously negative opinions of a group in Paris who ridicule the doctrine of eternal punishment and other received teachings of Christianity. They have taken as their motto, "Live, drink, and be merry." To gain adherents, "they stroke complacent ears with their blandishments," and thus "entice many incautious persons." J. Bohatec regards Rabelais as the leader of the group referred to, mentioning also Des Périers and Dolet. He shows that numerous phrases in the letter are reflected in Calvin's *De scandalis* (1550). The views of Jacques Gruet, expressed in a manuscript hidden by him and found in April, 1550, resemble those reported by Fumée. (*Budé und Calvin*, pp. 221 f.; OS III. 70, note 1; CR XIII. 567–571.) Cf. I. viii. 5, note 6.

[15] Cf. Hilary of Poitiers, *On the Trinity* I. xviii: "For He whom we can know only through his own utterances is a fitting witness concerning himself" (MPL 10. 38; tr. NPNF 2 ser. IX. 45).

are annoyed that a clear proof is not ready at hand when the impious, unpunished, murmur against God's Word. As if the Spirit
were not called both "seal" and "guarantee" [II Cor. 1:22] for
confirming the faith of the godly; because until he illumines their
minds, they ever waver among many doubts!

5. Scripture bears its own authentication

ᵉLet this point therefore stand: that those whom the Holy Spirit
has inwardly taught truly rest upon Scripture, and that Scripture
indeed is self-authenticated;[16] hence, it is not right to subject it to
proof and reasoning. And the certainty it deserves with us, it
attains by the testimony of the Spirit.[17] ᵇFor even if it wins reverence for itself by its own majesty, it seriously affects us only when
it is sealed upon our hearts through the Spirit. Therefore, illumined by his power, we believe neither by our own nor by anyone else's judgment that Scripture is from God; but above human
judgment we affirm with utter certainty (just as if we were gazing
upon the majesty of God himself) that it has flowed to us from
the very mouth of God by the ministry of men. We seek no proofs,
no marks of genuineness upon which our judgment may lean; but
we subject our judgment and wit to it as to a thing far beyond
any guesswork! This we do, not as persons accustomed to seize
upon some unknown thing, which, under closer scrutiny, displeases them, but fully conscious that we hold the unassailable
truth! Nor do we do this as those miserable men who habitually
bind over their minds to the thralldom of superstition; but we
feel that the undoubted power of his divine majesty lives and
breathes there. By this power we are drawn and inflamed, knowingly and willingly, to obey him, yet also more vitally and more
effectively than by mere human willing or knowing!

ᵉGod, therefore, very rightly proclaims through Isaiah that the
prophets together with the whole people are witnesses to him;
for they, instructed by prophecies, unhesitatingly held that God
has spoken without deceit or ambiguity [Isa. 43:10]. ᵇSuch, then,
is a conviction that requires no reasons; such, a knowledge with
which the best reason agrees—in which the mind truly reposes
more securely and constantly than in any reasons; such, finally,
a feeling that can be born only of heavenly revelation. I speak
of nothing other than what each believer experiences within him-

---

[16] "αὐτόπιστον." Cf. I. vii. 2 (end) and Hendry, op. cit., pp. 76 ff.
[17] Cf. Summary of Doctrine Concerning the Ministry of the Word and Sacraments, doubtfully attributed to Calvin (CR IX. 773–778; tr. LCC XXII.
171–177), esp. paragraphs v, vi.

self—though my words fall far beneath a just explanation of the matter.

dI now refrain from saying more, since I shall have opportunity to discuss this matter elsewhere.[18] Let us, then, know that the only true faith is that which the Spirit of God seals in our hearts. eIndeed, the modest and teachable reader will be content with this one reason: Isaiah promised all the children of the renewed church that "they would be God's disciples" [Isa. 54:13 p.]. God deems worthy of singular privilege only his elect, whom he distinguishes from the human race as a whole. Indeed, what is the beginning of true doctrine but a prompt eagerness to hearken to God's voice? But God asks to be heard through the mouth of Moses, as it is written: "Say not in your heart, who will ascend into heaven, or who will descend into the abyss: behold, the word is in your mouth" [conflation of Deut. 30:12, 14 and Ps. 107:26; 106:26, Vg.]. If God has willed this treasure of understanding to be hidden from his children, it is no wonder or absurdity that the multitude of men are so ignorant and stupid! Among the "multitude" I include even certain distinguished folk, until they become engrafted into the body of the church. Besides, Isaiah, warning that the prophetic teaching would be beyond belief, not only to foreigners but also to the Jews who wanted to be reckoned as members of the Lord's household, at the same time adds the reason: "The arm of God will not be revealed" to all [Isa. 53:1 p.]. Whenever, then, the fewness of believers disturbs us, let the converse come to mind, that only those to whom it is given can comprehend the mysteries of God [cf. Matt. 13:11].

eCHAPTER VIII

So Far as Human Reason Goes, Sufficiently Firm Proofs Are at Hand to Establish the Credibility of Scripture

(The unique majesty and impressiveness, and the high antiquity, of Scripture, 1–4)
1. Scripture is superior to all human wisdom
bUnless this certainty, higher and stronger than any human judgment, be present, it will be vain to fortify the authority of Scripture by arguments, to establish it by common agreement of the church, or to confirm it with other helps. For unless this

---

[18] The topic of the secret operation and testimony of the Spirit is resumed in III. i. 1, introducing the treatment of "the way in which we receive the grace of Christ," which is the subject of Book III. See also note 12, above.

foundation is laid, its authority will always remain in doubt. Conversely, once we have embraced it devoutly as its dignity deserves, and have recognized it to be above the common sort of things, those arguments—not strong enough before to engraft and fix the certainty of Scripture in our minds—become very useful aids. What wonderful confirmation ensues when, with keener study, we ponder the economy of the divine wisdom, so well ordered and disposed; the completely heavenly character of its doctrine, savoring of nothing earthly; the beautiful agreement of all the parts with one another—as well as such other qualities as can gain majesty for the writings. But our hearts are more firmly grounded when we reflect that we are captivated with admiration for Scripture more by grandeur of subjects than by grace of language. For it was also not without God's extraordinary providence that the sublime mysteries of the Kingdom of Heaven came to be expressed largely in mean and lowly words, lest, if they had been adorned with more shining eloquence, the impious would scoffingly have claimed that its power is in the realm of eloquence alone. Now since such uncultivated and almost rude simplicity inspires greater reverence for itself than any eloquence, what ought one to conclude except that the force of the truth of Sacred Scripture is manifestly too powerful to need the art of words? Therefore the apostle rightly contends that the faith of the Corinthians was founded "upon God's power, not upon human wisdom" [I Cor. 2:5 p.] because his own preaching among them commended itself "not in persuasive words of human wisdom but in demonstration of the Spirit and of might" [ch. 2:4 p.]. For truth is cleared of all doubt when, not sustained by external props, it serves as its own support.

Now this power which is peculiar to Scripture is clear from the fact that of human writings, however artfully polished, there is none capable of affecting us at all comparably. Read Demosthenes or Cicero; read Plato, Aristotle, and others of that tribe. They will, I admit, allure you, delight you, move you, enrapture you in wonderful measure. But betake yourself from them to this sacred reading. Then, in spite of yourself, so deeply will it affect you, so penetrate your heart, so fix itself in your very marrow, that, compared with its deep impression, such vigor as the orators and philosophers have will nearly vanish. Consequently, it is easy to see that the Sacred Scriptures, which so far surpass all gifts and graces of human endeavor, breathe something divine.[1]

[1] Calvin's language here reflects his experience when, after absorption in the classics, he entered upon the devout study of Scripture, and literary delight gave place to heartfelt conviction. Quoting this passage, H. Strohl

2. Not style but content is decisive

[c]Indeed, I admit that some of the prophets had an elegant and clear, even brilliant, manner of speaking, so that their eloquence yields nothing to secular writers;[2] and by such examples the Holy Spirit wished to show that he did not lack eloquence while he elsewhere used a rude and unrefined style. But whether you read David, Isaiah, and the like, whose speech flows sweet and pleasing, or Amos the herdsman, Jeremiah, and Zechariah, whose harsher style savors of rusticity, that majesty of the Spirit of which I have spoken will be evident everywhere. And I am not unaware that Satan is in many ways an imitator of God, in order by a false likeness to insinuate himself into the minds of simple folk. He has thus cleverly sowed, by uncultivated and even barbarous language, impious errors and by them has deceived miserable men. He has often made use of obsolete forms of speech, that under this mask he may cloak his impostures.[3] But all men endowed with moderate sense see how empty and loathsome is this affectation. As far as Sacred Scripture is concerned, however much froward men try to gnaw at it, nevertheless it clearly is crammed with thoughts that could not be humanly conceived. Let each of the prophets be looked into: none will be found who does not far exceed human measure. Consequently, those for whom prophetic doctrine is tasteless ought to be thought of as lacking taste buds.

3. The great antiquity of Scripture

[d]Others have dealt with this argument at length; it will therefore be enough to select for the present only a few main details that summarize the whole matter. Besides those points which I have already touched upon, the very antiquity of Scripture has no slight weight. For however much Greek writers may talk about the Egyptian theology, no monument of any religion is

---

refers to John Sturm's Strasbourg Academy and notes that the designation *divus* was applied by Sturm to Cicero, by Bucer to Plato, and to Seneca by Zwingli. (*La Pensée de la Réforme*, pp. 78 f.) On the same passage in the 1541 French edition, J. Pannier cites Lefèvre's reference to a comparable experience (*Psalterium quintuplex*, 1509): "A light so brilliant met my gaze that human teachings seemed dark shadows in comparison with divine studies." (Pannier, *Institution* I. 310, note *b* on p. 69.)

[2] On the peculiar eloquence of the Bible writers, see Augustine, *On Christian Doctrine* IV. vi. 9–vii. 21 (MPL 34. 92–98; tr. NPNF II. 577–581).

[3] Justin Martyr, *First Apology* liv–lx, holds that demons produced imitations of matters given in Scripture, such as are found in pagan tales, and that Plato borrowed from Moses. (MPG 6. 107–118; tr. LCC I. 277–281.)

extant that is not far later than the age of Moses.[4] And Moses devised no new god, but rather set forth what the Israelites had accepted concerning the eternal God handed down by the patriarchs age after age. For what else does he do but call them back to the covenant begun with Abraham [Gen. 17:7]? Had he, however, brought forward something unheard of, it would not have been approved. But their liberation from the slavery in which they were held must have been a matter of such common knowledge that the very mention of it would immediately arouse the minds of all. Indeed, it is likely that they had been taught concerning the four-hundred-year period [Gen. 15:13; Ex. 12:40; Gal. 3:17]. Now, if Moses (who nevertheless is so much earlier in time than all other writers) traced the transmission of his doctrine back to such a remote source, we must ponder how much Sacred Scripture outstrips all other writings in antiquity.

4. The truthfulness of Scripture shown by Moses' example

[e]Unless, perhaps, one chooses to believe the Egyptians, who extend their antiquity to six thousand years before the creation of the world! But since their garrulity was always held in derision, even by every secular writer, there is no reason for me to toil in refuting it. Moreover, Josephus cites, in his *Against Apion*, testimonies out of very ancient writers worth recalling, from which one may conclude that by the agreement of all nations the doctrine set forth in the law was renowned from the remotest ages, even though it was neither read nor truly known.[5]

Now to prevent any suspicion from persisting among the malicious, and to remove any occasion for the wicked to quibble, God meets both dangers with the best of remedies. While Moses recalls what Jacob almost three hundred years before had declared under heavenly inspiration concerning his posterity, does he in any way ennoble his tribe? No—he brands it with eternal

---

[4] Tatian, in his *Address to the Greeks* (ca. 170) xxxi, xxxvi–xli, argues that Moses was earlier than Homer and all known writers. Clement of Alexandria (*Stromata* I. xv), Theophilus of Antioch (*To Autolychus* III. xxiii), Eusebius (*Ecclesiastical History* IV. 30 and *Praeparatio evangelica* II. i), Augustine (*City of God* XVIII. xxxvii and *On Christian Doctrine* IV. vi), and other representative Christian writers follow this view. For the passage in Tatian, the earliest of these, see the edition by E. Schwartz in O. Gebhardt and A. Harnack, Texte und Untersuchungen zur Geschichte der altchristlichen Literatur IV. i. 31 f., 37–43 (tr. ANF II. 77 f., 80 f.).

[5] Augustine, *City of God* XVIII. xl (MPL 41. 599; tr. NPNF II. 384). Flavius Josephus, the Jewish historian, in his two books against Apion concerning the antiquity of the Jews, argues that the law of Moses is earlier, as well as more just and humane, than those of pagan lawgivers. For the points referred to, see *Contra Apionem* I. xxii; II. xxxvi; II. xxxix (CSEL 37. 36, 132, 137 ff.; LCL Josephus I. 226 ff., 394 ff., 405 f.).

infamy in the person of Levi! "Simeon and Levi," says he, "are vessels of iniquity: may my soul not enter into their counsel, nor my tongue into their secret place." [Gen. 49:5–6 p.] Surely he could have remained silent about that shame, not only to spare his father, but also not to besmirch himself and his whole family with part of the same ignominy. How could Moses be suspected, who first preached to the family from which he had sprung that their progenitor was utterly detestable to the oracle of the Holy Spirit, and who did not think of his own personal interests or refuse to suffer the odium of his relations for whom this was doubtless an annoyance? Also, when he recalls the wicked murmuring of his brother Aaron and his sister Miriam [Num. 12:1], shall we say that he speaks from the feeling of his flesh, or that he is obedient to the command of the Holy Spirit? Moreover, since his was the highest authority, why did he not at least leave the right of the high priest to his sons, but instead relegate them to the lowest place? I select only a few instances out of many; but in the law itself, here and there, we will meet many proofs that vindicate the full assurance that Moses undoubtedly came forth like an angel of God from heaven.

(*Refutation of objections regarding miracles and prophecy, 5–10*)
5. *Miracles strengthen the authority of God's messengers*
    ᵈNow these very numerous and remarkable miracles which he relates are so many confirmations of the law that he has delivered, and of the doctrine that he has published. For—that he was borne up into the mountain in a cloud; that there he was without human fellowship for forty days [Ex. 24:18]; that in the very promulgation of the law his face shone like the rays of the sun [Ex. 34:29]; that lightnings flashed round about, thunders and crashes were heard throughout the heavens, and a trumpet blown by no human mouth resounded [Ex. 19:16]; that the entrance to the Tabernacle, covered by a cloud, was hidden from the people's view [Ex. 40:34]; that by the dreadful death of Korah, Dathan, and Abiram, and their whole wicked faction,[6] his authority was most marvelously vindicated [Num. 16:24]; that

---

[6] In his *Harmony of the Four Last Books of Moses*, Calvin treats the passages here referred to and presents an animated discussion of the revolt against Moses (Num., ch. 16). From the miraculous vindication of Moses he argues that to harm God's servants is to war against God. The disposition of some of his contemporaries to question the authority of the Pentateuch was associated by Calvin with the spirit of the ancient detractors of Moses. Cf. the passages in *De scandalis*, found in OS II. 186, 201 f., with the notes 1–5 on p. 201. For Bohatec's identifications of the contemporary opponents, see note 14 on I. vii. 4.

the rock struck by his rod straightway brought forth a river
[Num. 20:10–11; Ex. 17:6; cf. I Cor. 10:4]; that manna rained
from heaven at his prayer [Num. 11:9; Ex. 16:13; cf. I Cor. 10:3]
—by these was not God, from heaven, commending Moses as his
undoubted prophet? If anyone should object that I am taking
as fact what is controversial, this subtle objection is easy to answer.
Inasmuch as Moses published all these things before the congregation, among eyewitnesses of the events what opportunity
was there for fraud? Moses would, of course, have appeared before the people, rebuked them for their unfaithfulness, obstinacy,
ungratefulness, and other offenses, and then would have boasted
that under their very eyes his doctrine had been authenticated
by miracles that they had never seen!

6. Moses' miracles are incontestable

^eFor this is also worth noting: every time he tells of miracles, at
the same time there are disagreeably conjoined things that could
stir up the whole people to contradict loudly if the slightest
occasion had presented itself. From this it is clear that they
have been led to assent solely because they were quite enough
convinced by their own experience. But since the matter was
too manifest for secular writers to be free to deny that Moses
performed miracles, the father of lies slanderously attributed
them to magic arts [cf. Ex. 7:11 or 9:11]. Moses shrank so much
from this superstition as to order that anyone who merely consulted magicians and soothsayers should be stoned to death [Lev.
20:6]. By what conjecture then do they make him out to have
been a magician? Surely any impostor plies his legerdemain in an
effort to overwhelm the minds of the multitude to snatch renown.
But what about Moses? Proclaiming that he and his brother
Aaron are nothing but only following what God has laid down
[Ex. 16:7], he sufficiently wipes away every mark of reproach.
Now if the events themselves be considered, what sort of incantation could cause manna daily raining from heaven to provide
sufficient food for the people: if anyone had more than his due
measure stored up, to teach him from its very putrefaction that
his unbelief was divinely punished [Ex. 16:19–20]? Besides, God
allows his servant so to be tested by many severe proofs that
the wicked may now have no success in clamoring against him.
Sometimes the whole people rose up in their pride and insolence;
sometimes certain ones among them conspired in an attempt
to overthrow God's holy servant. How, then, could Moses by
legerdemain have escaped this fury of theirs? And the outcome
plainly bears out that in this way his doctrine was sanctioned
for all time.

7. Prophecies that are fulfilled contrary to all human expectation

dIn addition, who can deny that the prophetic spirit, in the person of the patriarch Jacob, caused the primacy to be assigned to the tribe of Judah [Gen. 49:10]—especially if we take the act itself into account, as its outcome has proved? Picture Moses as the first author of this prophecy. Yet from the time that this writing was recorded, four hundred years passed during which there was no mention of a scepter in the tribe of Judah. After the consecration of Saul [I Sam. 11:15], the royal power seems to have resided in the tribe of Benjamin. When David was anointed by Samuel [I Sam. 16:13], what visible reason was there for the transference of the kingly power? Who would have anticipated that a king was to come forth from the lowly house of a herdsman? And since there were seven brothers in the family, who would have marked the youngest for the honor? How could he have any hope of the Kingdom? Who would say that his anointing had been determined by human art or effort or prudence, and was not rather the fulfillment of heavenly prophecy? Similarly, Moses foretells things, albeit obscurely, concerning the election of the Gentiles into God's covenant [Gen. 49:10], which actually took place almost two thousand years later. Is this not plain proof that he spoke by divine inspiration? I omit other predictions, which so clearly breathe the divine revelation as to convince sane men that it is God who speaks. In brief, Moses' one song [Deut., ch. 32] is a bright mirror in which God is manifest.

8. God has confirmed the prophetic words

dBut in the remaining prophets it is now discerned even more clearly. I will select only a few examples, for to gather all of them together would be too toilsome. Although in the time of Isaiah the Kingdom of Judah was at peace, and perhaps even regarded itself as somewhat under the Chaldeans' protection, Isaiah spoke publicly of the fall of the city and the exile of the people [Isa. 39:6–7]. Let us grant that to predict, long before, what at the time seemed incredible but at last actually came to pass was not yet a clear enough token of divine inspiration. Yet from what source but God shall we say have come those prophecies which Isaiah at the same time utters concerning release? He names Cyrus [Isa. 45:1] through whom the Chaldeans had to be conquered and the people set free. More than a hundred years elapsed from the time the prophet so prophesied and the time Cyrus was born;[7] for the latter was born about a hundred years after the prophet's

---

[7] The modern view of the late date of Isa., ch. 45, does not of course enter Calvin's mind in this argument.

death. No one could have divined then that there was to be a man named Cyrus who would wage war with the Babylonians, would subdue such a powerful monarchy, and terminate the exile of the people of Israel. Does not this bare narrative, without any verbal embellishment, plainly show the things Isaiah recounts to be undoubted oracles of God, not the conjectures of a man? Again, when Jeremiah, some time before the people were led away into exile, set the duration of the captivity at seventy years and indicated the return and liberation [Jer. 25:11–12; 29:10], must not his tongue have been under the guidance of the Spirit of God? How shameless will it be to say that the authority of the prophets has not been confirmed by such proofs, and that what they boast, to claim credibility for their own words, has not so far been fulfilled! "Behold, the former things have come to pass, . . . new things I declare; before they spring forth I point them out to you." [Isa. 42:9, Comm.] I pass over the fact that Jeremiah and Ezekiel, far apart yet prophesying at the same time, in all their statements commonly agreed as if each had dictated the other's words. What of Daniel? Did he not so clothe his prophecies of future events almost to the six hundredth year as if he were writing a history of past events generally known? If godly men take these things to heart, they will be abundantly equipped to restrain the barking of ungodly men; for this is a proof too clear to be open to any subtle objections.

9. The transmission of the law is to be trusted

dI know what certain rascals bawl out in corners in order to display the keenness of their wit in assailing God's truth. For they ask, Who assures us that the books that we read under the names of Moses and the prophets were written by them?[8] They even dare question whether there ever was a Moses. Yet if anyone were to call in doubt whether there ever was a Plato, an Aristotle, or a Cicero, who would not say that such folly ought to be chastised with the fist or the lash? The law of Moses was wonderfully preserved by heavenly providence rather than by human effort. And although by priests' negligence the law lay buried for a short time, after godly King Josiah found it [II Kings 22:8; cf. II Chron. 34:15], it continued to be read age after age.[9] Indeed, Josiah did not put it forward as something unknown or new, but as something that had always been of common

---

[8] Cf. I. vii. 4, note 14; I. viii. 3, note 4; Bohatec, *op. cit.,* pp. 164, 178, 216–228, 239.

[9] Cf. Justinian, *Digest* I. ii. 2. *Corpus iuris civilis,* ed. P. Krueger, *Digesta,* p. 34; tr. C. H. Monro, *The Digest of Justinian* I, p. 23.

knowledge, the memory of which was then famous. The archetypal roll was committed to the Temple; a copy was made from it and designated for the royal archives [Deut. 17:18–19]. What had happened was merely this: the priests had ceased to publish the law itself according to the solemn custom, and the people themselves also had neglected the habit of reading it. Why is it that almost no age goes by in which its sanction is not confirmed and renewed? Was Moses unknown to those who were versed in David? But, to generalize concerning all sacred authors, it is absolutely certain that their writings passed down to posterity in but one way: from hand to hand. Some had heard their actual words; others learned that they had so spoken from hearers whose memories were still fresh.

10. God has marvelously preserved the Law and the Prophets

dIndeed, the passage in the history of the Maccabees that they put forth in order to detract from the authenticity of Scripture is such that nothing more appropriate could be thought of to establish it. Yet first let us wipe away their pretenses; then we shall turn back upon them the siege engine they are erecting against us. Since Antiochus (they say) ordered all books to be burned [I Macc. 1:56–57], where did the copies that we now have come from?[10] But I, in turn, ask, In what workshop could they have been fabricated so quickly? For it is well known that directly after the persecutions had ceased, the books were extant, and were acknowledged without controversy by all the godly, who were brought up on their doctrine and knew them intimately. But even though all wicked men, as if conspiring together, have so shamelessly insulted the Jews, no one has ever dared charge them with substituting false books. For whatever, in their opinion, the Jewish religion may be, they confess Moses to be its author. What but their own more than canine shamelessness do these babblers betray when they utter the lie that these books (whose sacred antiquity is confirmed by the agreement of all histories) are spurious? But not to expend further effort uselessly in refuting such filthy calumnies, let us rather ponder here how much care the Lord has taken to preserve his Word, when, contrary to everybody's expectation, he snatched it away from a most cruel and savage tyrant, as from a raging fire. Let us consider how he armed godly priests and others with so great constancy that they did not hesitate to transmit to their posterity this treasure redeemed, if necessary, at the expense of

[10] Antiochus IV, Epiphanes, of Syria (176–164 B.C.), oppressor of the Jews, whose tyranny led to the Maccabean revolt.

their own lives; and how he frustrated the whole fierce book hunt of rulers and their minions. Who does not recognize as a remarkable and wonderful work of God the fact that those sacred monuments, which the wicked had persuaded themselves had utterly perished, soon returned and took their former place once more, and even with enhanced dignity? For the Greek translation followed, which published them abroad throughout the world.[11]

The miracle appeared not only in that God delivered the Tables of his covenant from the bloody edicts of Antiochus, but also in that the Jewish people, ground down and wasted by such manifold misfortunes, were soon almost exterminated, yet the writings remained safe and intact. The Hebrew language lay not only unesteemed, but almost unknown; and to be sure, if God had not been pleased to care for their religion, it would have perished completely. ᵉFor after the Jews were brought back from exile, how much they departed from the true use of the mother tongue appears from the prophets of that age, a fact worth noting because from this comparison one more clearly perceives the antiquity of the Law and the Prophets. ᵈAnd through whom did God preserve for us the doctrine of salvation embraced in the Law and the Prophets, that Christ in his own time might be made manifest [Matt. 22:37–40]? Through the Jews, Christ's most violent enemies, whom Augustine justly calls the "bookmen" of the Christian church,[12] because they have furnished us with reading matter of which they themselves do not make use.

(Simplicity and heavenly character and authority of the New Testament, 11)

11. ᵉNext, if one comes to the New Testament, with what solid props its truth is supported! Three Evangelists recount their history in a humble and lowly style; for many proud folk this simplicity[13] arouses contempt. This is because they do not pay attention to the chief divisions of doctrine from which it would be easy to infer that the Evangelists are discussing heavenly mysteries above human capacity. Surely all who are endowed with a drop of sincere modesty, on reading the first chapter of Luke,

---

[11] The Septuagint version, completed about 150 B.C.

[12] *"Ecclesiae Christianae librarios . . . appellat."* Cf. Augustine, *Psalms*, Ps. 56. 9: *"Librarii nostri facti sunt"* (MPL 36. 366). For the variant uses of the word *librarius* in medieval Latin, see Du Cange, *Glossarium, s.v.* Norton here translates: "keepers of the librarie."

[13] In this section there is a continued reference to the matter of I. viii. 5. Cf. also I. vii. 4 and OS II. 201.

will be made ashamed. Now Christ's discourses, briefly summarized by those three Evangelists, readily clear their writings of all contempt. But John, thundering from the heights, lays low more mightily than any thunderbolt the obstinacy of those whom he does not impel to the obedience of faith. Let all those sharp-nosed faultfinders—whose highest desire is to drive the reverence for Scripture from their own and others' hearts—come into the open. Let them read John's Gospel: whether they want to or not, there they shall find a thousand sayings to arouse, at least, their dull minds—nay, I should rather say, to burn a dreadful brand upon their consciences for the restraint of their mockery. The same thing applies to Paul and Peter. Although most men are blind to their writings, yet the very heavenly majesty therein holds all men closely attached and as it were bound to itself.[14] But this one fact raises their doctrine more than enough above the world: Matthew, previously tied to the gain of his table, Peter and John going about in their boats—all of them rude, uneducated men— had learned nothing in the school of men that they could pass on to others. Paul, not only a sworn but fierce and murderous enemy, was converted into a new man; this sudden and unhoped-for change shows that he was compelled by heavenly authority to affirm a doctrine that he had assailed. Let these dogs deny that the Holy Spirit came down upon the apostles; or even let them discredit history. Yet the truth cries out openly that these men who, previously contemptible among common folk, suddenly began to discourse so gloriously of the heavenly mysteries must have been instructed by the Spirit.

(Consent of the church, and fidelity of the martyrs, 12–13)
12. Unvarying testimony of the church to the Scripture*

[d(b)]Besides this, there are other very good reasons why the consent of the church should not be denied its due weight. [b]Since the publication of Scripture, age after age agreed to obey it steadfastly and harmoniously. By countless wondrous means Satan with the whole world has tried either to oppress it or overturn it, to obscure and obliterate it utterly from the memory of men—yet, like the palm, it has risen ever higher and has remained unassailable. Indeed, there has scarcely ever been either a sophist or rhetorician of superior ability who did not try his power against it; yet all were unsuccessful. Such facts as these should be accounted of no slight importance. The whole power of earth has armed itself to destroy it, yet all these efforts have gone up in smoke. How could it, assailed so strongly from every side, have resisted if it had relied upon human protection alone? Rather, by this very fact it is proved to be from God, because, with all human efforts striving against it, still it has of its own power thus far prevailed. Besides this, it is not one state, not one people, that has agreed to receive and embrace it; but, as far and as wide as the earth extends, it has obtained its authority by the holy concord of divers peoples, who otherwise had nothing in common among themselves. Such agreement of minds, so disparate and otherwise disagreeing in everything among themselves, ought to move us greatly, since it is clear that this agreement is brought about by nothing else than the divine will. Yet no little weight is added thereto when we observe the godliness of those who so agree, not of all, indeed, but of those whom the Lord has made to shine as lamps in his church.

13. Martyrs died firmly for Scripture doctrine*

ᵇNow with what assurance ought we to enlist under that doctrine which we see confirmed and attested by the blood of so many holy men! They, having once received it, did not hesitate, courageously and intrepidly, and even with great eagerness, to suffer death for it. Should we not accept with sure and unshaken conviction what has been handed on to us with such a pledge? It is no moderate approbation of Scripture that it has been sealed by the blood of so many witnesses, especially when we reflect that they died to render testimony to the faith; not with fanatic excess (as erring spirits are sometimes accustomed to do), but with a firm and constant, yet sober, zeal toward God.

ᵇThere are other reasons, neither few nor weak, for which the dignity and majesty of Scripture are not only affirmed in godly hearts, but brilliantly vindicated against the wiles of its disparagers; yet of themselves these are not strong enough to provide a firm faith, until our Heavenly Father, revealing his majesty there, lifts reverence for Scripture beyond the realm of controversy. Therefore Scripture will ultimately suffice for a saving knowledge of God only when its certainty is founded upon the inward persuasion of the Holy Spirit. Indeed, these human testimonies which exist to confirm it will not be vain if, as secondary aids to our feebleness, they follow that chief and highest testimony. ᵈBut those who wish to prove to unbelievers that Scripture is the Word of God are acting foolishly, for only by faith can this be known. Augustine therefore justly warns that godliness and peace of mind ought to come first if a man is to understand anything of such great matters.[15]

[14] Cf. I. vii. 5; I. viii. 1.
[15] Augustine, *The Usefulness of Belief* xviii. 36 (MPL 42. 92; tr. LCC VI. 322).

^cCHAPTER IX

FANATICS, ABANDONING SCRIPTURE AND FLYING OVER TO REVELATION, CAST DOWN ALL THE PRINCIPLES OF GODLINESS

1. The fanatics wrongly appeal to the Holy Spirit

^bFurthermore, those who, having forsaken Scripture, imagine some way or other of reaching God, ought to be thought of as not so much gripped by error as carried away with frenzy. For of late, certain giddy men have arisen who, with great haughtiness exalting the teaching office of the Spirit, despise all reading and laugh at the simplicity of those who, as they express it, still follow the dead and killing letter.[1] But I should like to know from them what this spirit is by whose inspiration they are borne up so high that they dare despise the Scriptural doctrine as childish and mean. For if they answer that it is the Spirit of Christ, such assurance is utterly ridiculous. Indeed, they will, I think, agree that the apostles of Christ and other believers of the primitive church were illumined by no other Spirit. Yet no one of them thence learned contempt for God's Word; rather, each was imbued with greater reverence as their writings most splendidly attest. ^eAnd indeed it had thus been foretold through the mouth of Isaiah. For where he says, "My Spirit which is in you, and the words that I have put in your mouth, will not depart from your mouth, nor from the mouth of your seed . . . forever" [Isa. 59:21 p., cf. Vg.], he does not bind the ancient folk to outward doctrine as if they were learning their ABC's; rather, he teaches that under the reign of Christ the new church will have this true and complete happiness: to be ruled no less by the voice of God than by the Spirit. Hence we conclude that by a heinous sacrilege these rascals tear apart those things which the prophet joined together with an inviolable bond. Besides this, Paul, "caught up even to the third heaven" [II Cor. 12:2], yet did not fail to become proficient in the doctrine of the Law and the Prophets, just as also he urges Timothy, a teacher of singular excellence, to give heed to reading [I Tim. 4:13]. And worth remembering is that praise with which he adorns Scripture, that it "is useful for teaching, admonishing, and reproving in order that the servants of God may be made perfect" [II Tim. 3:16–17 p.]. What devilish madness is it to pretend that the use of Scripture, which leads the children of God even to the final goal, is fleeting or temporal?

[1] These opinions of the Libertines were assailed by Calvin in his tract *Contre la secte phantastique et furieuse des Libertins* (1545) (CR VII. 147–248), especially chs. ix–xi (173–181).

ᵇThen, too, I should like them to answer me whether they have drunk of another spirit than that which the Lord promised his disciples. Even if they are completely demented, yet I do not think that they have been seized with such great dizziness as to make this boast. But in promising it, of what sort did he declare his Spirit would be? One that would speak not from himself but would suggest to and instill into their minds what he had handed on through the Word [John 16:13]. Therefore the Spirit, promised to us, has not the task of inventing new and unheard-of revelations, or of forging a new kind of doctrine, to lead us away from the received doctrine of the gospel, but of sealing our minds with that very doctrine which is commended by the gospel.

2. *The Holy Spirit is recognized in his agreement with Scripture*
ᵇFrom this we readily understand that we ought zealously to apply ourselves both to read and to hearken to Scripture if indeed we want to receive any gain and benefit from the Spirit of God —ᶜeven as Peter praises the zeal of those who were attentive to the prophetic teaching, which nevertheless could be seen to have given up its place after the light of the gospel dawned [II Peter 1:19]. ᵇBut on the contrary, if any spirit, passing over the wisdom of God's Word, foists another doctrine upon us, he justly deserves to be suspected of vanity and lying [Gal. 1:6–9]. What then? Since "Satan disguises himself as an angel of light" [II Cor. 11:14], what authority will the Spirit have among us, unless he be discerned by a most certain mark? And he is very clearly pointed out to us by the voice of the Lord: except that these miserable folk willingly prefer to wander to their doom, while they seek the Spirit from themselves rather than from him. Yet, indeed, they contend that it is not worthy of the Spirit of God, to whom all things ought to be subject, himself to be subject to Scripture. As if, indeed, this were ignominy for the Holy Spirit to be everywhere equal and in conformity with himself, to agree with himself in all things, and to vary in nothing! To be sure, if the Spirit were judged by the rule of men, or of angels, or of anything else, then one would have to regard him as degraded, or if you like, reduced to bondage; but when he is compared with himself, when he is considered in himself, who will on this account say that injustice is done him? Nevertheless, he is thus put to a test, I confess, but a test by which it pleased him to establish his majesty among us. He ought to be sufficient for us as soon as he penetrates into us. But lest under his sign the spirit of Satan should creep in, he would have us recognize him in his own image, which he has stamped upon the Scriptures. He is the Author of the Scrip-

tures: he cannot vary and differ from himself. Hence he must ever remain just as he once revealed himself there. This is no affront to him, unless perchance we consider it honorable for him to decline or degenerate from himself.

3. Word and Spirit belong inseparably together

[b]They censure us for insisting upon the letter that kills,[2] but in this matter they pay the penalty for despising Scripture. For it is clear enough that Paul there [II Cor. 3:6] contends against the false apostles, who indeed, in commending the law apart from Christ, were calling the people away from the benefits of the New Testament, in which the Lord covenants "to engrave his law in the inward parts of believers, and to write it in their hearts" [Jer. 31:33 p.]. The letter, therefore, is dead, and the law of the Lord slays its readers where it both is cut off from Christ's grace [II Cor. 3:6] and, leaving the heart untouched, sounds in the ears alone. But if through the Spirit it is really branded upon hearts, if it shows forth Christ,[3] it is the word of life [cf. Phil. 2:16] "converting souls, . . . giving wisdom to little ones," etc. [Ps. 18:8, Vg.; 19:7, EV]. What is more, in the very same place the apostle calls his preaching "the ministration of the Spirit" [II Cor. 3:8], meaning, doubtless, that the Holy Spirit so inheres in His truth, which He expresses in Scripture, that only when its proper reverence and dignity are given to the Word does the Holy Spirit show forth His power. And what has lately been said[4]—that the Word itself is not quite certain for us unless it be confirmed by the testimony of the Spirit—is not out of accord with these things. For by a kind of mutual bond the Lord has joined together the certainty of his Word and of his Spirit so that the perfect religion of the Word may abide in our minds when the Spirit, who causes us to contemplate God's face, shines; and that we in turn may embrace the Spirit with no fear of being deceived when we recognize him in his own image, namely, in the Word. So indeed it is. God did not bring forth his Word among men for the sake of a momentary display, intending at the coming of his Spirit to abolish it. Rather, he sent down the same Spirit by whose power he had dispensed the Word, to complete his work by the efficacious confirmation of the Word.

[2] *Ibid.,* col. 174.
[3] Calvin here comes close to the well-known dictum of Luther regarding Scripture books in his Preface to James and Jude, where the test of genuineness is whether they lay emphasis on Christ or not (*"ob sie Christum treiben, oder nicht"*). See Introduction, p. lvi, note 52.
[4] I. vii. 4–5.

In this manner Christ opened the minds of two of his disciples [Luke 24:27, 45], not that they should cast away the Scriptures and become wise of themselves, but that they should know the Scriptures. Similarly Paul, while he urges the Thessalonians not to "quench the Spirit" [I Thess. 5:19–20], does not loftily catch them up to empty speculations without the Word, but immediately adds that prophecies are not to be despised. By this, no doubt, he intimates that the light of the Spirit is put out as soon as prophecies fall into contempt. What say these fanatics, swollen with pride,[5] who consider this the one excellent illumination when, carelessly forsaking and bidding farewell to God's Word, they, no less confidently than boldly, seize upon whatever they may have conceived while snoring? Certainly a far different sobriety befits the children of God, who just as they see themselves, without the Spirit of God, bereft of the whole light of truth, so are not unaware that the Word is the instrument by which the Lord dispenses the illumination of his Spirit to believers. For they know no other Spirit than him who dwelt and spoke in the apostles, and by whose oracles they are continually recalled to the hearing of the Word.

ᶜCHAPTER X

Scripture, to Correct All Superstition, Has Set the True God Alone Over Against All the Gods of the Heathen[1]

1. The Scriptural doctrine of God the Creator
ᵇWe have taught that the knowledge of God, otherwise quite clearly set forth in the system of the universe[2] and in all creatures, is nonetheless more intimately and also more vividly revealed in his Word. But now it is worth-while to ponder whether the Lord represents himself to us in Scripture as we previously saw him delineate himself in his works. This would indeed be a long

---

5 "*Tumidi isti ἐνθουσιασταί.*"

1 This title applies strictly only to sec. 3. In secs. 1 and 2, Calvin is summing up, comparing, and signifying agreement between what Scripture and creation teach about God. In the remaining chapters of Book I, he deals with that part of the knowledge of the Creator which cannot be derived from creation, or seen in creation even with the "spectacles" of Scripture, but is found solely in Scripture.

2 "*Mundi machina.*" Cf. Lucretius: "*Ruet moles et machina mundi,*" *De rerum natura* v. 96 (LCL edition, p. 346). Similar expressions are not infrequent, e.g., "*mundi fabrica,*" I. v. title; II. vi. 1; "*orbis machinam,*" I. xvi. 1; I. xvi. 4; I. xvii. 2; "*caelestis machinae,*" I. xiv. 21. Cf. Comm. Harmony of the Evangelists, Matt., ch. 25: "*tota mundi machina resonabit*" (CR XXVIII. 685). Cf. Comm. Ps. 68: 32-35 (CR XXXI. 636).

matter, if anyone wished to pause and treat it more thoroughly. Yet I shall be content to have provided godly minds with a sort of index to what they should particularly look for in Scripture concerning God, and to direct their search to a sure goal. ᵉI do not yet touch upon the special covenant by which he distinguished the race of Abraham from the rest of the nations [cf. Gen. 17:4]. For, even then in receiving by free adoption as sons those who were enemies, he showed himself to be their Redeemer. We, however, are still concerned with that knowledge which stops at the creation of the world, and does not mount up to Christ the Mediator. But even if it shall be worth-while a little later[3] to cite certain passages from the New Testament, in which the power of God the Creator and of his providence in the preservation of the primal nature are proved, yet I wish to warn my readers what I now intend to do, lest they overleap the limits set for them. Finally, at present let it be enough to grasp how God, the Maker of heaven and earth, governs the universe founded by him. Indeed, both his fatherly goodness and his beneficently inclined will are repeatedly extolled; and examples of his severity are given, which show him to be the righteous avenger of evil deeds, especially where his forbearance toward the obstinate is of no effect.

2. The attributes of God according to Scripture agree with those known in his creatures

ᵇIndeed, in certain passages clearer descriptions are set forth for us, wherein his true appearance is exhibited, to be seen as in an image.[4] For when Moses described the image, he obviously meant to tell briefly whatever was right for men to know about him. "Jehovah," he says, "Jehovah, a merciful and gracious God, patient and of much compassion, and true, who keepest mercy for thousands, who takest away iniquity and transgression, . . . in whose presence the innocent will not be innocent, who visitest the iniquity of the fathers upon the children and the children's children." [Ex. 34:6–7, cf. Vg.] Here let us observe that his eternity and his self-existence[5] are announced by that wonderful name twice repeated. Thereupon his powers are mentioned, by which he is shown to us not as he is in himself, but as he is toward us:[6] so that this recognition of him consists more in living experience than in vain and high-flown speculation. Now we hear the same

---

[3] Cf. I. xiv–xviii.
[4] "εἰκονικῶς."
[5] "καὶ αὐτουσίαν." Cf. I. xiv. 3.
[6] Cf. I. ii. 2; III. ii. 6.

powers enumerated there that we have noted as shining in heaven and earth: kindness, goodness, mercy, justice, judgment, and truth. For power and might are contained under the title *Elohim*.

By the same epithets also the prophets designate him when they wish to display his holy name to the full. That we may not be compelled to assemble many instances, at present let one psalm [Ps. 145] suffice for us, in which the sum of all his powers is so precisely reckoned up that nothing would seem to have been omitted [esp. Ps. 145:5]. And yet nothing is set down there that cannot be beheld in his creatures. Indeed, with experience as our teacher we find God just as he declares himself in his Word. In Jeremiah, where God declares in what character he would have us know him, he puts forward a less full description but one plainly amounting to the same thing. "Let him who glories, glory in this," he says, "that he knows that I am the Lord who exercise mercy, judgment, and justice in the earth." [Jer. 9:24; I Cor. 1:31.] Certainly these three things are especially necessary for us to know: mercy, on which alone the salvation of us all rests; judgment, which is daily exercised against wrongdoers, and in even greater severity awaits them to their everlasting ruin; justice, whereby believers are preserved, and are most tenderly nourished. When these are understood, the prophecy witnesses that you have abundant reason to glory in God. Yet neither his truth, nor power, nor holiness, nor goodness is thus overlooked. For how could we have the requisite knowledge of his justice, mercy, and judgment unless that knowledge rested upon his unbending truth? And without understanding his power, how could we believe that he rules the earth in judgment and justice? But whence comes his mercy save from his goodness? If, finally, "all his paths are mercy" [Ps. 25:10], judgment, justice [cf. Ps. 25:8–9], in these also is his holiness visible.

Indeed, the knowledge of God set forth for us in Scripture is destined for the very same goal as the knowledge whose imprint shines in his creatures, in that it invites us first to fear God, then to trust in him. By this we can learn to worship him both with perfect innocence of life and with unfeigned obedience, then to depend wholly upon his goodness.

3. Because the unity of God was also not unknown to the heathen, the worshipers of idols are the more inexcusable

^eBut here I propose to summarize the general doctrine. And first, indeed, let readers observe that Scripture, to direct us to the true God, distinctly excludes and rejects all the gods of the heathen, for religion was commonly adulterated throughout al-

most all ages. Indeed, it is true that the name of one God was everywhere known and renowned. For men who worshiped a swarm of gods, whenever speaking from a real feeling of nature, as if content with a single God, simply used the name "God"; and Justin Martyr, wisely noting this, composed a book, *God's Monarchy*, in which he showed by very many testimonies that the unity of God has been engraved upon the hearts of all.[7] Tertullian likewise proves the same point by phrases in common use.[8] But all the heathen, to a man, by their own vanity either were dragged or slipped back into false inventions, and thus their perceptions so vanished that whatever they had naturally sensed concerning the sole God had no value beyond making them inexcusable.[9] For even the wisest of them openly display the vague wanderings of their minds when they long for some god or other to be present among them, and so invoke dubious gods in their prayers. Besides this, in imagining a god of many natures—although they held a view less absurd than the ignorant multitude with its Jupiter, Mercury, Venus, Minerva, and the rest—they, too, were not free of Satan's deceptions. As we have already said elsewhere,[10] all the evasions the philosophers have skillfully contrived do not refute the charge of defection; rather, the truth of God has been corrupted by them all. For this reason, Habakkuk, when he condemned all idols, bade men seek God "in his temple" [Hab. 2:20] lest believers admit someone other than him who revealed himself by his Word.

ᵉCHAPTER XI

IT IS UNLAWFUL TO ATTRIBUTE A VISIBLE FORM TO GOD, AND GENERALLY WHOEVER SETS UP IDOLS REVOLTS AGAINST THE TRUE GOD[1]

(Scriptural argument for rejecting images in worship, 1–4)
1. We are forbidden every pictorial representation of God
ᵉBut as Scripture, having regard for men's rude and stupid wit, customarily speaks in the manner of the common folk, where it

---

[7] Justin, *De monarchia* i. 2 (MPG 6. 314 ff.; tr. ANF I. 290 f.).
[8] Tertullian, *The Testimony of the Soul* ii (MPL 1. 611; CCL Tertullianus I. 176; tr. ANF III. 176).
[9] Augustine, *Letters* xvi, xvii (alias xliii, xliv) (MPL 33. 81–85; tr. FC 12. 37–43).
[10] I. v. 11.
[1] Chapters xi and xii, on the worship of God, form a significant prologue to the doctrines of Trinity, Creation, and Providence. Some of this material is taken verbatim from the analysis of the Second Commandment in earlier

would distinguish the true God from the false it particularly contrasts him with idols. It does this, not to approve what is more subtly and elegantly taught by the philosophers, but the better to expose the world's folly, nay, madness, in searching for God when all the while each one clings to his own speculations. Therefore, that exclusive definition, encountered everywhere, annihilates all the divinity that men fashion for themselves out of their own opinion: for God himself is the sole and proper witness of himself.[2]

Meanwhile, since this brute stupidity gripped the whole world —to pant after visible figures of God, and thus to form gods of wood, stone, gold, silver, or other dead and corruptible matter— we must cling to this principle: God's glory is corrupted by an impious falsehood whenever any form is attached to him. Therefore in the law, after having claimed for himself alone the glory of deity, when he would teach what worship he approves or repudiates, God soon adds, "You shall not make for yourself a graven image, nor any likeness" [Ex. 20:4]. By these words he restrains our waywardness from trying to represent him by any visible image, and briefly enumerates all those forms by which superstition long ago began to turn his truth into falsehood. For we know that the Persians worshiped the sun; all the stars they saw in the heavens the stupid pagans also fashioned into gods for themselves. There was almost no animal that for the Egyptians was not the figure of a god. Indeed, the Greeks seemed to be wise above the rest, because they worshiped God in human form.[3] But God does not compare these images with one another, as if one were more suitable, another less so; but without exception he repudiates all likenesses, pictures, and other signs by which the superstitious have thought he will be near them.

2. *Every figurative representation of God contradicts his being*

[c]One readily infers this from the reasons that he adds to the prohibition. [b]First, according to Moses: Remember "what Jehovah spoke to you in the valley of Horeb" [Deut. 4:15]; you

editions. Cf. II. viii. 17, where Calvin refers to this passage. True and acceptable worship thus is a basic ingredient of the "knowledge" of the Creator. "Frigid" speculation is precluded.

[2] "For He whom we can know only through His own utterances is a fitting witness concerning Himself." Hilary of Poitiers, *On the Trinity* I. xviii (MPL 10. 38; tr. NPNF 2 ser. IX. 45).

[3] Maximus of Tyre (ca. A.D. 150), *Philosophoumena* ii (ed. H. Hobein, pp. 18 ff.; tr. T. Taylor, *The Dissertations of Maximus Tyrius* II. 188 ff.). (Taylor's Dissertation xxxviii = No. ii in Hobein.)

heard a voice, "you did not see a body" [ch. 4:12, cf. Comm.].
"Therefore take heed to yourself" [ch. 4:15] "lest perchance,
deceived, you make for yourself any likeness," etc. [ch. 4:16].
eWe see how openly God speaks against all images, that we may
know that all who seek visible forms of God depart from him.
Of the prophets it is enough to cite only bIsaiah, who is most
emphatic in presenting this. He teaches that God's majesty is
sullied by an unfitting and absurd fiction, when the incorporeal is
made to resemble corporeal matter, the invisible a visible likeness,
the spirit an inanimate object, the immeasurable a puny bit of
wood, stone, or gold [Isa. 40:18–20 and 41:7, 29; 45:9; 46:5–7].
Paul also reasons in the same way: "Since we are the offspring of
God, we ought not to judge the Deity to be like gold, and silver,
or a stone, carved by the art or devising of man" [Acts 17:29 p.].
From this it is clear that e(b)every statue man erects, or every
image he paints to represent God, bsimply displeases God as something dishonorable to his majesty. dAnd what wonder if the Holy
Spirit thunders these oracles from heaven, since he compels poor
and blind idolaters on earth to bring forth a like confession?
Well known is that complaint of Seneca, which we read in Augustine: "They establish the holy immortal and inviolable gods in
the most vile and ignoble matter, and invest them with the appearance of men and wild beasts; esome fashion them with sexes
confused and with incongruous bodies, and call them divinities;
if these received breath, and confronted us, they would be considered monsters."4 From this again it is quite evident that the
supporters of images fall back upon a worthless dodge when they
allege that images were forbidden to the Jews because they were
inclined toward superstition. As if, indeed, what God brings
forth from his eternal essence and from the continuing order of
nature belonged to but one people! Actually, Paul was addressing, not the Jews, but the Athenians, when he refuted their error
of making a representation of God.

4 *City of God* VI. x (MPL 41. 190; tr. NPNF II. 119). In opposing the use
of images in Christian worship, Augustine here quotes a work of Seneca
against superstitions that is not extant. It is noteworthy that, amid Western
reverberations of the Iconoclastic Controversy, Bishop Agobard of Lyons
wrote (ca. 826) his treatise *Against the Superstition of Those Who Think
that Worship Ought to Be Offered to Pictures and Images of the Saints*
(MPL 104. 199–228). For a brief description of this work, which relies on
Augustine and other fathers, see A. Cabaniss, *Agobard of Lyons, Church-
man and Critic*, pp. 54 f. Agobard's opinions (which are related to the
Libri Carolini: cf. sec. 14, note 28) bear a certain resemblance to Calvin's:
he would like to see the offending images "ground to powder" (MPL 104. 208).

3. Even direct signs of the divine Presence give no justification for images

ᵇGod, indeed, from time to time showed the presence of his divine majesty by definite signs, so that he might be said to be looked upon face to face. But all the signs that he ever gave forth ᵉ⁽ᵇ⁾aptly conformed to his plan of teaching and at the same time clearly told men of his incomprehensible essence. For clouds and smoke and flame [Deut. 4:11], although they were symbols of heavenly glory, restrained the minds of all, like a bridle placed on them, from attempting to penetrate too deeply. ᵇTherefore Moses, to whom, nevertheless, God revealed himself more intimately than to the others [Ex. 33:11], did not succeed by prayers in beholding that face; but he received the answer that man is not able to bear such great brightness [Ex. 33:20]. ᵉThe Holy Spirit appeared under the likeness of a dove [Matt. 3:16]. Since, however, he vanished at once, who does not see that by one moment's symbol the faithful were admonished to believe the Spirit to be invisible in order that, content with his power and grace, they might seek no outward representation for themselves? For the fact that God from time to time appeared in the form of a man was the prelude to his future revelation in Christ. Therefore the Jews were absolutely forbidden so to abuse this pretext as to set up for themselves a symbol of deity in human form.

ᵇThe mercy seat from which God manifested the presence of his power under the law was so constructed as to suggest that the best way to contemplate the divine is where minds are lifted above themselves with admiration. Indeed, the cherubim with wings outspread covered it; the veil shrouded it; the place itself deeply enough hidden concealed it [Ex. 25:17–21]. Hence it is perfectly clear that those who try to defend images of God and the saints with the example of those cherubim are raving madmen. What, indeed, I beg you, did those paltry little images mean? Solely that images are not suited to represent God's mysteries. For they had been formed to this end, that veiling the mercy seat with their wings ᵉ⁽ᵇ⁾they might bar not only human eyes but all the senses from beholding God, and thus correct men's rashness. ᵈIn addition to this, the prophets depict the seraphim as appearing in their visions with face veiled toward us [Isa. 6:2]. By this they signify that the splendor of divine glory is so great that the very angels also are restrained from direct gaze, and the tiny sparks of it that glow in the angels are withdrawn from our eyes. All who judge rightly recognize that the cherubim with which we are now concerned belonged to the antiquated tutelage[5] of the law. Thus it is absurd to drag them in as an example to serve our own age. For that childish age, so to speak, for which rudiments of this sort were intended [Gal. 4:3], is gone by. ^eAnd it is quite shameful that profane writers are more proficient interpreters of God's law than the papists. Juvenal upbraided the Jews for worshiping mere clouds and the deity of the sky.[6] When he denies that any effigy of God existed among them, he speaks perversely indeed and impiously, yet more truly than the papists, who prate that there was some visible likeness of God.[7] This people with fervid swiftness repeatedly rushed forth to seek out idols for themselves as waters from a great wellspring gush out with violent force. From this fact let us learn how greatly our nature inclines toward idolatry, rather than, by charging the Jews with being guilty of the common failing, we, under vain enticements to sin, sleep the sleep of death.

4. Images and pictures are contrary to Scripture

^eThe saying, "The idols of the heathen are silver and gold, the works of men's hands" [Ps. 135:15; cf. Ps. 115:4], has the same purpose. For from the material of which they are made, the prophet infers that they are not gods whose images are of gold or silver; and he takes it for granted that all we conceive concerning God in our own minds is an insipid fiction. He mentions gold and silver rather than clay or stone, that neither the splendor nor the price may win reverence for the idols. Yet he concludes in general that nothing is less commendable than for gods to be fashioned from any dead matter. Meanwhile he insists no less on the other point: that mortals are carried away by too much folly and rashness who, precariously drawing a fleeting breath from moment to moment, dare to confer God's honor upon idols. Man will be compelled to confess[8] that he is a transient being, and yet he will want to be counted as God a piece of metal,

---

[5] Cf. II. xi. 2.

[6] The phrase is from Juvenal, *Satires* V. xiv. 97: *"Nubes et caeli numen adorant"* (Calvin: *adorent*) (LCL edition, pp. 270 f., and note 3).

[7] Eck, *Enchiridion* (1526), ch. xv (1541, ch. xvi). With Eck's defense of images may be compared the treatment of the subject by the Paris theologian Josse Clichtove (see Prefatory Address to the King, note 8) in his *Propugnaculum ecclesiae adversus Lutheranos* I. x (Paris, 1526) and in his *Compendium veritatum ad fidem pertinentium contra erroneas Lutheranorum assertiones* (Paris, 1529), ch. xxii, fo. 122b–127a. The latter work is an interpretation of the anti-Lutheran decisions of the Synod of Paris, 1528, and is prefaced by an address to Francis I, which shows alarm over the activities of "the Lutheran sect" in France.

[8] Cf. III. ix. 2.

to whose deity he himself gave origin. For whence came the beginning of idols but from the opinion of men? Most just is that profane poet's mockery: "Once I was a little fig tree trunk, a useless bit of wood, when the workman, in doubt whether he should make a stool, preferred that I be a god,"[9] etc. So then the earthly manikin, who almost every moment breathes out his life, by his own cleverness would transfer God's name and honor to a dead trunk! But because that Epicurean in witty jest had no regard for religion, let us pass over his witticisms and those of men like him. Rather, let the prophet's reproof sting us, indeed transfix us, that they are utterly foolish who from the same wood warm themselves, kindle a fire to bake bread, roast or boil meat, and fashion a god before whom they prostrate themselves as suppliants to pray [Isa. 44:12–17]. Therefore he elsewhere not only accuses them as guilty before the law, but reproaches them for not learning from the foundations of the earth [Isa. 40:21]. For surely there is nothing less fitting than to wish to reduce God, who is immeasurable and incomprehensible, to a five-foot measure! And yet custom shows this monstrous thing, which is openly hostile to the order of nature, to be natural to men.

Now we ought to bear in mind that Scripture repeatedly describes superstitions in this language: they are the "works of men's hands," which lack God's authority [Isa. 2:8; 31:7; 37:19; Hos. 14:3; Micah 5:13]; this is done to establish the fact that all the cults men devise of themselves are detestable. The prophet heaps up fury in a psalm because men endowed with the intelligence to know that all things are moved solely by God's power call upon dead and insensible things for help. But because corruption of nature drives all peoples as well as each one individually to such great madness, finally the Spirit fulminates with a dire threat: "Let those who make them and those who trust in them become like them" [Ps. 115:8; cf. Ps. 113b:8, Vg.]. bBut we must note that a "likeness" no less than a "graven image" is forbidden. Thus is the foolish scruple of the Greek Christians refuted. For they consider that they have acquitted themselves beautifully if they do not make sculptures of God, while they wantonly indulge in pictures more than any other nation.[10] But the Lord forbids not only that a likeness be erected to him by a maker of statues but

---

[9] Horace, *Satires* I. viii. 1–3 (LCL edition, pp. 96 f.). Cf. Lactantius, *Divine Institutes* II. iv. 1 (CSEL 19. 107; tr. ANF VII. 44).

[10] The reference is to the fact that the Eastern Orthodox Churches, unlike those of the West, use no solid statues of deity in worship. (HDRE VII. 81. Cf. L. Bréhier, *La Sculpture et les arts mineurs byzantins*, pp. 7, 16.) •

that one be fashioned by any craftsman whatever, because he is thus represented falsely and with an insult to his majesty.

(Pope Gregory's error in this refuted from Scripture and the fathers, 5–7)

5. *Scripture judges otherwise*

ᵈI know that it is pretty much an old saw that images are the books of the uneducated. Gregory said this;[11] yet the Spirit of God declares far otherwise; if Gregory had been taught in His school with regard to this, he never would have spoken thus. For when Jeremiah declares that "the wood is a doctrine of vanity" [Jer. 10:8, cf. Vg., order changed]; when Habakkuk teaches that "a molten image is a teacher of falsehood" [Hab. 2:18 p.], from such statements we must surely infer this general doctrine, that whatever men learn of God from images is futile, indeed false. If anyone takes exception that it was those who were misusing images for impious superstition who were rebuked by the prophets, I admit it is so. But I add, what is clear to all, that the prophets totally condemn the notion, taken as axiomatic by the papists, that images stand in place of books. For the prophets set images over against the true God as contraries that can never agree. This comparison, I say, is set forth in the passages that I have just now cited. Since there is one true God whom the Jews were wont to worship, visible figures are wickedly and falsely fashioned to represent God; and all who seek the knowledge of God from these are miserably deluded. In short, if it were not true that whatever knowledge of God is sought from images is fallacious and counterfeit, the prophets would not so generally have condemned it. At least I hold this: when we teach that it is vanity and falsehood for men to try to fashion God in images, we are doing nothing else but repeating word for word what the prophets have taught.

6. *The doctors of the church, too, partly judged otherwise*

ᵇOne ought, besides, to read what Lactantius and Eusebius have written concerning this matter, who do not hesitate to take as a fact that all whose images are seen were once mortals.[12] Likewise, Augustine clearly declares that it is wrong not only to worship

---

11 Gregory the Great, *Letters* IX. 105; XI. 13, both addressed to Serenus, bishop of Marseilles (MGH *Epistolae* II. 112, 273 f.; MPL 77. 1027 f., 1128); Eck, *Enchiridion* (1526), ch. xvi; Clichtove, *Compendium*, fo. 124a.

12 Lactantius, *Divine Institutes* I. viii, xv, xviii (CSEL 19. 29 f., 55 f., 63–67; tr. ANF VII. 18, 26–30); Eusebius, *Praeparatio evangelica* II. iv; III. ii (MPG 21. 163, 175); Augustine, *City of God* VI. vii. 1; VI. viii. 1; VIII. v, xxvi (MPL 41. 184, 186, 229 f., 253 f.; tr. NPNF II. 115 f., 147, 163).

images but to set them up to God.[13] cYet he says nothing else but what had been decreed many years before in the Council of Elvira, of which the thirty-sixth canon reads: "It is decreed that there shall be no pictures in churches, that what is reverenced or adored be not depicted on the walls."[14] dBut especially memorable is what the same Augustine elsewhere cites from Varro, and confirms by his own subscription, that the first men to introduce statues of the gods "removed fear and added error."[15] If Varro alone had said this, perhaps it would have had little authority, yet it deservedly ought to strike shame in us that a pagan man, groping so to speak in the dark, arrived at this light, that bodily images are unworthy of God's majesty because they diminish the fear of him in men and increase error. Facts themselves certainly testify that this was said no less truly than wisely; but Augustine, having borrowed from Varro, as it were, brings it forth from his own thought. And at the outset, indeed, he points out that the first errors concerning God in which men were entangled did not begin from images, but once this new element was added, errors multiplied. Next, he explains that the fear of God was diminished or even destroyed, because in the folly of images and in stupid and absurd invention his divinity could easily be despised. On the second of these points, would that we might not have experienced it to be so true! Whoever, therefore, desires to be rightly taught must learn what he should know of God from some other source than images.

7. *The images of the papists are entirely inappropriate*

d(a)Therefore, if the papists have any shame, let them henceforward not use this evasion, that pictures are the books of the uneducated, because it is plainly refuted by very many testimonies of Scripture. Even if I were to grant them this, yet they would not thus gain much to defend their idols. It is well known that they set monstrosities of this kind in place of God. aThe pictures or statues that they dedicate to saints—what are they but examples of the most abandoned lust and obscenity? If anyone wished to model himself after them, he would be fit for the lash. Indeed, brothels show harlots clad more virtuously and modestly than

---

[13] "It is sinful to set up an image of God in a Christian temple": Augustine, *Faith and the Creed* vii. 14 (MPL 40. 188; tr. LCC VI. 360); cf. *De diversis quaestionibus*, qu. 78 (MPL 40. 90).

[14] Council of Elvira (ca. 305). See Prefatory Address, above, note 21.

[15] Augustine, *City of God* IV. ix, xxxi (MPL 41. 119, 138; tr. NPNF II. 69, 74 f.). The work of Varro, here referred to by Augustine, is not extant.

the churches show those objects which they wish to be thought images of virgins. ᵇFor martyrs they fashion a habit not a whit more decent. ᵃTherefore let them compose their idols at least to a moderate decency, that they may with a little more modesty falsely claim that these are books of some holiness!

(There would be no "uneducated" at all if the church had done its duty)

But then we shall also answer that this is not the method of teaching within the sacred precincts believing folk, whom God wills to be instructed there with a far different doctrine than this trash. In the preaching of his Word and sacred mysteries he has bidden that a common doctrine be there set forth for all. ᵇBut those whose eyes rove about in contemplating idols betray that their minds are not diligently intent upon this doctrine.

ᵃTherefore, whom, then, do the papists call uneducated whose ignorance allows them to be taught by images alone? Those, indeed, whom the Lord recognizes as his disciples, ᶜwhom he honors by the revelation of his heavenly philosophy, whom he wills to be instructed in the saving mysteries of his Kingdom. I confess, as the matter stands, that today there are not a few who are unable to do without such "books." But whence, I pray you, this stupidity if not because they are defrauded of that doctrine which alone was fit to instruct them? ᵈIndeed, those in authority in the church turned over to idols the office of teaching for no other reason than that they themselves were mute. ᵉPaul testifies that by the true preaching of the gospel "Christ is depicted before our eyes as crucified" [Gal. 3:1 p.]. ᵃWhat purpose did it serve for so many crosses—of wood, stone, silver, and gold—to be erected here and there in churches, if this fact had been duly and faithfully taught: that Christ died on the cross to bear our curse [Gal. 3:13], to expiate our sins by the sacrifice of his body [Heb. 10:10], to wash them by his blood [Rev. 1:5], ᵈin short, to reconcile us to God the Father [Rom. 5:10]? ᵃFrom this one fact they could have learned more than from a thousand crosses of wood or stone. For perhaps the covetous fix their minds and eyes more tenaciously upon gold and silver than upon any word of God.

(Origin of the use of images, and consequent corruption of worship, although sculpture and painting are gifts of God, 8–16)
8. The origin of images: man's desire for a tangible deity
ᵈNext, what is held in the book of Wisdom concerning the origin of idols is received virtually by public consent: that the

originators of idols were those who conferred this honor on the dead, and thus superstitiously worshiped their memory.[16] Of course, I admit that this perverse custom was very ancient, nor do I deny that it was a torch with which to fire men's mad dash into idolatry all the more; yet I do not concede that this was the original source of the evil. For it appears from Moses that idols were in use before this eagerness to consecrate images of the dead prevailed, which is frequently mentioned by secular writers. When he relates that Rachel stole her father's idols [Gen. 31:19], he is speaking of a vice that was common. From this we may gather that man's nature, so to speak, is a perpetual factory of idols. After the Flood there was a sort of rebirth of the world, but not many years passed by before men were fashioning gods according to their pleasure. eAnd it is believable that while the holy patriarch was still living his descendants were giving themselves over to idolatry, so that he discerned with his eyes (not without the bitterest pain) that the earth, whose corruptions God had recently purged by a most dreadful judgment, was polluted with idols. For as Joshua testifies [Josh. 24:2], Terah and Nahor were worshipers of false gods before the birth of Abraham. If Shem's offspring degenerated very rapidly, what are we to judge of Ham's descendants who had already been cursed in their father? dSo it goes. e(a)Man's mind, full as it is of pride and boldness, dares to imagine a god according to its own capacity; as it sluggishly plods, indeed is overwhelmed with the crassest ignorance, it conceives an unreality and an empty appearance as God.

To these evils a new wickedness joins itself, that man tries to express in his work the sort of God he has inwardly conceived. Therefore the mind begets an idol; the hand gives it birth. The example of the Israelites shows the origin of idolatry to be that men do not believe God is with them unless he shows himself physically present. b"We know not," they said, "what has become of this Moses; make us gods who may go before us." [Ex. 32:1.] They knew, indeed, that this was God whose power they had experienced in very many miracles; but they did not trust that he was near them unless they could discern with their eyes a physical symbol of his countenance, which for them would be a testimony of the ruling God. Therefore they wished to recognize from an image going before them that God was the leader of their march. Daily experience teaches that flesh is always uneasy until it has obtained some figment like itself in which it may fondly find solace as in an image of God. In almost every age

16 Wisdom of Solomon 14:15-16.

since the beginning of the world, men, [a]in order that they might obey this blind desire, have set up symbols in which they believed God appeared before their bodily eyes.

9. Any use of images leads to idolatry*

[d]Adoration promptly follows upon this sort of fancy: [a]for when men thought they gazed upon God in images, they also worshiped him in them. Finally, all men, having fixed their minds and eyes upon them, began to grow more brutish and to be overwhelmed with admiration for them, as if something of divinity inhered there. [b]Now it appears that men do not rush forth into the cult of images before they have been imbued with some opinion too crass—not indeed that they regard them as gods, but because they imagine that some power of divinity dwells there. Therefore, when you prostrate yourself in veneration, representing to yourself in an image either a god or a creature, you are already ensnared in some superstition. For this reason, the Lord forbade not only the erection of statues constructed to represent himself but also the consecration of any inscriptions and stones that would invite adoration [Ex. 20:25]. [d]For the same reason, also, in the precept of the law a second part is subjoined concerning adoration. For just as soon as a visible form has been fashioned for God, his power is also bound to it. Men are so stupid that they fasten God wherever they fashion him;[17] and hence they cannot but adore. And there is no difference whether they simply worship an idol, or God in the idol. It is always idolatry when divine honors are bestowed upon an idol, under whatever pretext this is done. And because it does not please God to be worshiped superstitiously, whatever is conferred upon the idol is snatched away from Him.

[a]Let those persons take note of this who are looking for miserable excuses to defend the execrable idolatry by which true religion for many past ages has been overwhelmed and subverted. Images, they assert, are not regarded as gods. The Jews, too, were not so thoughtless as to forget that it was God by whose hand they had been led out of Egypt [Lev. 26:13] before they fashioned the calf [Ex. 32:4]. [b]But when Aaron said that those were the gods by whom they had been set free from the land of Egypt, they boldly assented [Ex. 32:4, 8], obviously meaning that they wished to retain that liberating God, provided they could see him going before them in the calf. [a]And we must not think the heathen so stupid that they did not understand God to be something other than stocks and stones. For while they changed

17 Calvin uses a pun: *"Deum affigant ubicunque affingunt."*

images at pleasure, they always kept the same gods in mind. There
were many images for one god; yet they did not devise for themselves as many gods as the multitude of images. Moreover, they
daily consecrated new images, yet did not believe themselves to
be making new gods. cRead the excuses that Augustine refers to
as having been pretended by the idolaters of his own age: when
they were accused, the vulgar sort replied that they were not
worshiping that visible object but a presence that dwelt there in-
visibly. Those who were of what he called "purer religion" stated
that they were worshiping neither the likeness nor the spirit;
but that through the physical image they gazed upon the sign of
the thing that they ought to worship.[18] aWhat then? All idolaters,
whether Jews or pagans, bwere motivated just as has been said.
Not content with spiritual understanding, they thought that
through the images a surer and closer understanding would be
impressed upon them. Once this perverse imitation of God
pleased them, they never stopped until, deluded by new tricks,
they presently supposed that God manifested his power in images.
aIn these images, nevertheless, the Jews were convinced that they
were worshiping the eternal God, the one true Lord of heaven
and earth; the pagans, that they were worshiping their gods
whom, though false, they imagined as dwelling in heaven.

10. Image worship in the church

aThose who assert that this was not done heretofore, and within
our memory is still not being done, lie shamelessly. For why do
they prostrate themselves before these things? Why do they, when
about to pray, turn to them as if to God's ears? cIndeed, what
Augustine says is true, that no one thus gazing upon an image
prays or worships without being so affected that he thinks he is
heard by it, or hopes that whatever he desires will be bestowed
upon him.[19] bWhy is there so much difference among the images
of the same God, that one is passed over or honored in a common
manner, but upon another is bestowed every solemn honor? Why
do they tire themselves out with votive pilgrimages to see images
whose like they have at home? aWhy do they take up the sword to
defend these images today as if they were altars and hearth fires,
even to the point of butchery and carnage, and more easily bear
being deprived of the one God than of their idols? Nevertheless, I
do not yet enumerate the crass errors of the multitude, which are
well-nigh infinite, and which occupy the hearts of almost all men;

[18] Augustine, *Psalms*, Ps. 113. ii. 4-6 (on v. 5) (MPL 37. 1483 f.; tr. NPNF
    [Ps. 115] VIII. 552).
[19] Augustine, *Psalms*, Ps. 113. ii. 4-6.

I am only indicating what they profess when they especially wish to exculpate themselves of idolatry. We do not call them "our gods," they say. Neither did Jews nor pagans of old so speak of them, and yet the prophets did not hesitate repeatedly to accuse them of fornications with wood and stone [Jer. 2:27; Ezek. 6:4 ff.; cf. Isa. 40:19–20; Hab. 2:18–19; Deut. 32:37] only for doing the very things that are daily done by those who wish to be counted Christians, namely, that they carnally venerated God in wood and stone.

11. Foolish evasions of the papists

dYet I am not unaware, nor ought I to conceal the fact, that they escape by a wily distinction, of which fuller mention will be made a little later.[20] For the honor that they pay to their images they allege to be idol service, denying it to be idol worship.[21] For they speak thus when they teach that the honor which they call dulia can be given to statues and pictures without wronging God. Therefore they deem themselves innocent if they are only servants of idols, not worshipers of them too. As if, indeed, it were not something slighter to worship than to serve! And yet while they take refuge in a Greek word, they childishly contradict themselves. For since λατρεύειν means nothing else among the Greeks than "to worship," what they say signifies the same thing as confessing that they "worship the images but without worship." And there is no reason for them to object that I am trying to trip them in words; but they themselves display their own ignorance while they try to spread darkness over the eyes of the simple folk. Yet however eloquent they may be, never will they succeed by their eloquence in proving to us that one and the same thing is really two things. Let them show, I say, the real difference that makes them unlike the ancient idolaters. For just as an adulterer or a homicide cannot escape guilt by dubbing his crime with some other name, so it is absurd for them to be absolved by the subtle device of a name if they differ in no respect from idolaters whom they themselves are compelled to condemn. Yet so far are they from separating their own cause from the cause of these idolaters that the source of the whole evil is rather a preposterous emulation in which they vie with the latter while they

[20] I. xi. 16; I. xii. 2.
[21] Calvin uses the Greek words "εἰδωλοδουλεία," "εἰδωλολατρεία." The distinction discussed in earlier centuries between dulia, the respectful service of a slave, and latria, the worship due to a deity, was used by John Cochlaeus in his reply to Calvin's *Inventory of Relics*, entitled *De sacris reliquiis Christi et sanctorum eius* (1549), chs. 2 and 3. Cf. note 27 and I. xii. 2–3.

both contrive by their own wit, and fashion with their own hands, the symbols to represent God for themselves.

12. The functions and limits of art

cAnd yet I am not gripped by the superstition of thinking absolutely no images permissible. But because sculpture and painting are gifts of God, I seek a pure and legitimate use of each, lest those things which the Lord has conferred upon us for his glory and our good be not only polluted by perverse misuse but also turned to our destruction. We believe it wrong that God should be represented by a visible appearance, because he himself has forbidden it [Ex. 20:4] and it cannot be done without some defacing of his glory. And lest they think us alone in this opinion, those who concern themselves with their writings will find that all well-balanced writers have always disapproved of it. If it is not right to represent God by a physical likeness, much less will we be allowed to worship it as God, or God in it. Therefore it remains that only those things are to be sculptured or painted which the eyes are capable of seeing: let not God's majesty, which is far above the perception of the eyes, be debased through unseemly representations. Within this class some are histories and events, some are images and forms of bodies without any depicting of past events. The former have some use in teaching or admonition; as for the latter, I do not see what they can afford other than pleasure. And yet it is clear that almost all the images that until now have stood in churches were of this sort. From this, one may judge that these images had been called forth not out of judgment or selection but of foolish and thoughtless craving. I am not saying how wickedly and indecently the greater part of them have been fashioned, how licentiously the painters and sculptors have played the wanton here—a matter that I touched upon a little earlier.[22] I only say that even if the use of images contained nothing evil, it still has no value for teaching.

13. As long as doctrine was pure and strong, the church rejected images

cBut setting aside this distinction, let us in passing examine if it is expedient to have in Christian churches any images at all, whether they represent past events or the bodies of men. First, if the authority of the ancient church moves us in any way, we will recall that for about five hundred years, during which religion was still flourishing, and a purer doctrine thriving, Christian churches were commonly empty of images.[23] Thus, it was

[22] I. xi. 7.

when the purity of the ministry had somewhat degenerated that they were first introduced for the adornment of churches. I shall not discuss what reason impelled those who were the first authors of this thing; but if you compare age with age, you will see that these innovations had much declined from the integrity of those who had done without images. Why? Are we to think that those holy fathers would have allowed the church to go for so long without something they adjudged useful and salutary? Of course it was because they saw in it either no usefulness or very little, but very much danger, that they repudiated it out of deliberation and reason, rather than overlooked it out of ignorance or negligence. Augustine even states this in clear words: "When they are established in these seats," he says, "in honorable loftiness, so that they are attended by those who pray and those who sacrifice, by the very likeness of living members and senses—although they lack both sense and life—they affect infirm minds, so that they seem to live and breathe," etc.[24] And elsewhere, "For the shape of the idol's bodily members makes and in a sense compels the mind dwelling in a body to suppose that the idol's body too has feeling, because it looks very like its own body," etc. A little later, "Images have more power to bend the unhappy soul, because they have mouth, eyes, ears, feet, than to straighten it, because they do not speak, or see, or hear, or walk."[25]

This seems likely to be the reason why John wished to warn us not only against the worship of idols but also against idols themselves [I John 5:21]. And by the dreadful madness that has heretofore occupied the world almost to the total destruction of godliness, we have experienced too much how the ensign of idolatry is, as it were, set up, as soon as images are put together in churches. For men's folly cannot restrain itself from falling headlong into superstitious rites. But even if so much danger were not threatening, when I ponder the intended use of churches, somehow or other it seems to me unworthy of their holiness for them to take on images other than those living and symbolical ones which the Lord has consecrated by his Word. I mean Baptism

[23] Calvin here would seem to give countenance to the teaching of those "syncretists" who later, returning to the teaching of Vincent of Lérins, advocated "the consensus of the first five centuries" as a basis of Christian unity and reform. See J. T. McNeill, *Unitive Protestantism*, pp. 271 ff.; W. K. Ferguson, *The Renaissance in Historical Thought*, pp. 41 f., 49 f. In his Latin Catechism of 1538, Calvin, advocating unity and peace among Christians, exclaims that the devil's darts ought to move us to seek a syncretism— *"ad syncretismum agendum admovere debet"* (OS I. 431).

[24] Augustine, *Letters* cii (MPL 33. 377; tr. FC 18. 161); *City of God* IV. xxxi (MPL 41. 137 f.; tr. NPNF II. 81).

[25] Augustine, *Psalms*, Ps. 113. ii. 5 f. (MPL 37. 1483 f.; tr. NPNF [Ps. 115] VIII. 552 f.).

and the Lord's Supper, together with other rites by which our eyes must be too intensely gripped and too sharply affected to seek other images forged by human ingenuity.

aBehold! The incomparable boon of images, for which there is no substitute, dif we are to believe the papists!

14. Childish arguments for images at the Council of Nicaea (787)*

dNow, I believe, I should have said quite enough of this matter but for the fact that the Nicene Council commands my attention —not that most celebrated council called by Constantine the Great, but the one held eight hundred years ago at the command and under the auspices of the Empress Irene.[26] For it decreed not only that there were to be images in churches but also that they were to be worshiped.[27] For whatever I say, the authority of the Council will occasion a great prejudice in favor of the opposite side. Yet, to speak the truth, this does not move me so much as does the desire to inform my readers how far the madness went of those who were more attached to images than was becoming to Christians. But let us dispose of this first. Those who today defend the use of images allege the support of that Council of Nicaea. However, there exists a book in refutation under the name of Charlemagne, the style of which leads me to conclude that it was composed at the same time.[28] In it are set forth the opinions of the bishops who participated in the Council and the proofs which they employed. John, the legate of the Easterns, said: "God created man in his image" [Gen. 1:27], and from this

[26] Irene ruled as empress in the Eastern Empire, 780–802. In the French version, Calvin here calls her "a wicked Proserpine named Irene."

[27] Second Council of Nicaea, 787, session 7. (Mansi XIII. 377 f.; tr. H. Bettenson, Documents of the Christian Church, p. 132.) Bowing in veneration (προσκύνησις) before the images is enjoined, but actual worship (λατρεία) is forbidden as "proper only to the divine nature." Cf. I. xii. 3; Hefele-Leclercq III. 2. 772 f. For a summary of the discussions in the the Council, see E. J. Martin, A History of the Iconoclastic Movement, ch. vi.

[28] In secs. 14–16, written in 1550, Calvin derives his data from the Libri Carolini, the four books prepared at Charlemagne's direction in response to the action of the Second Council of Nicaea, 787, and adopted by the Synod of Frankfort, 794. An edition of the Libri Carolini by Jean du Tillet had appeared in 1549. The passages referred to are: Libri Carolini I. 7, 9, 10, 13, 23, 24, 28, 30; II. 5, 6, 10; III. 7, 15, 17, 26, 31; IV. 6, 18. The work may be consulted in MPL 98, where these passages are in cols. 1022 f., 1027 ff., 1034 f., 1053 f., 1057 f., 1061 f., 1065 f., 1071 ff., 1075 f., 1127 ff., 1142 f., 1148 f., 1170 ff., 1180 ff., 1197 ff., 1221 ff. The notes in OS III. 103 f. provide the references to the text in Monumenta Germaniae Historica, Leges III. Concilia II. The editors here indicate two instances in which Calvin has erroneously ascribed to "John, the Eastern legate" (who spoke frequently at the council) words that should be attributed to others present. Calvin's quotations are otherwise in accord with the text.

he therefore concluded that we must have images. The same man thought that images were commended to us by this sentence: "Show me thy face, for it is beautiful" [Cant. 2:14]. Another, to prove that images ought to be set upon altars, cited this testimony: "No one lights a lantern and puts it under a bushel" [Matt. 5:15]. Still another, to show us that looking upon them is useful to us, adduced a verse from The Psalms: "O Lord, the light of thy countenance has been sealed upon us" [Ps. 4:7, Vg.; 4:6, EV]. Another seized upon this comparison: just as the patriarchs have used the sacrifices of the heathen, so ought saints' images for Christians to take the place of the heathens' idols. To the same end they twisted that verse: "O Lord, I love the beauty of thy house" [Ps. 25:5, Vg.; 26:8, EV]. But pre-eminently ingenious is this interpretation: "As we have heard, so also have we seen" [I John 1:1 p.]. Therefore he implies that men know God not only by hearing his Word but also by looking upon images. Bishop Theodore speaks with similar penetration: "Wonderful is God in his saints" [Ps. 67:36, Vg.]; and elsewhere it is said, "To the saints who are on earth" [Ps. 15:3, Vg.; 16:3, EV]. Therefore this ought to refer to images. In short, so disgusting are their absurdities that I am ashamed even to mention them.

15. Ridiculous misuse of Scripture texts*

dWhen they are discussing adoration, they bring forward the adoration of Pharaoh [Gen. 47:10], of Joseph's rod [Gen. 47:31; Heb. 11:21], and of the pillar set up by Jacob [Gen. 28:18].

Notwithstanding, in this last allegation they not only corrupt the meaning of Scripture, but seize upon something that is nowhere to be read. Then, "Worship his footstool" [Ps. 98:5, Vg.; 99:5, EV]; likewise, "Worship on his holy mountain" [Ps. 98:9, Vg.; 99:9, EV]; again, "All the rich men of the people shall entreat thy countenance" [Ps. 44:13, Vg.; 45:13, EV]. These appear to be absolutely firm and apposite proofs for them. If anyone in mockery wished to attribute a ridiculous character to the patrons of images, could he enumerate greater and grosser follies? To remove any remaining doubt, Theodosius, Bishop of Mira, confirms the adoration of images from the dreams of his archdeacon as gravely as if a heavenly oracle had been present. Now let the promoters of images go and urge upon us the decree of that synod. As if those venerable fathers do not abrogate all trust in themselves either by treating Scripture so childishly or by rending it so impiously and foully!

16. Blasphemous and shocking claims for images*

dI come now to the terrible blasphemies, which it is a marvel that they have dared to spew forth, and a double marvel that everybody did not cry out against them with greatest loathing. But it is expedient that this wicked madness be publicly exposed, that the pretense of antiquity which the papists allege may at least be torn away from the worship of images. Theodosius, Bishop of Amorium, pronounces anathema against all who are unwilling that images be adored. Another imputes all the misfortunes of Greece and the East to the crime that images had not been adored. What punishments do the prophets, apostles, martyrs, deserve, in whose day no images existed? Thereafter they add: if the image of the emperor be approached with perfume and incense, much more do we owe this honor to the images of saints. Constantius, Bishop of Constance in Cyprus, professes to embrace images reverently, and affirms that he is going to show toward them the same worship and honor that is owed to the life-giving Trinity. Anyone who refuses to do the same he anathematizes and relegates among the Manichees and Marcionites. And lest you think this the private opinion of one man, the rest agree. Indeed, John, the legate of the Easterns, moved by even greater heat, warned that it would be better to admit all brothels into the city than to deny the worship of images. Finally, it was determined by the consent of all that the Samaritans are worse than all heretics, yet image fighters[29] are worse than the Samaritans. Besides, lest the play should go unapplauded,[30] a clause is added: let those who, having an image of Christ, offer sacrifice to it rejoice and exult.[31] Where now is the distinction between latria and dulia, by which they are wont to hoodwink God and men? For the Council accords, without exception, as much to images as to the living God.

eCHAPTER XII

How God Is to Be So Distinguished from Idols that Perfect Honor May Be Given to Him Alone

1. True religion binds us to God as the one and only God
eMoreover, we said at the beginning[1] that the knowledge of God does not rest in cold speculation, but carries with it the

---

[29] "εἰκονομάχοι."

[30] Referring to the customary formal applause following the close of a play in the Roman theater. Cf. Horace, *Ars Poetica* V. 154 f. (LCL edition, pp. 462 f. and note *e*).

[31] Cf. sec. 11, note 21, above, and Calvin, *On the Necessity of Reforming the Church* (1549) (CR VI. 463; tr. *Tracts* I. 131).

[1] Cf. I. ii. 2; I. v. 6, 9, 10.

honoring of him. In passing, we also touched upon how he is to be rightly worshiped, a point that will have to be dealt with at greater length in other places.[2] Now I only briefly repeat: as often as Scripture asserts that there is one God, it is not contending over the bare name, but also prescribing that nothing belonging to his divinity is to be transferred to another. From this it is also clear in what respect pure religion differs from superstition. Undoubtedly, for the Greeks the word εὐσέβεια, meaning "religion," also connotes befitting reverence. For even the blind themselves, groping in darkness, felt the need of adhering to a definite rule, to avoid the perverted honoring of God. Even though Cicero truly and learnedly derives the word "religion" from the word *relegere*,[3] the reason that he assigns is forced and farfetched: that upright worshipers often reread and diligently weighed what was true. Rather, I believe that this word is opposed to giddy license; for the greater part of the world thoughtlessly seizes upon whatever is at hand, nay, even flits hither and thither. But godliness, to stand on a firm footing, keeps itself within its proper limits. Likewise, it seems to me that superstition is so called because, not content with the prescribed manner and order, it heaps up a needless mass of inanities.

But discussion aside, all ages have always agreed that religion was vitiated and perverted by falseness and error. From this we conclude that when we allow ourselves anything out of heedless zeal the excuse that the superstitious pretend is silly. Yet even though this confession cries out from all men's lips, a foul ignorance appears; for, as we have already taught,[4] they neither cleave to the one God nor manifest any delight in honoring him. But God, to claim his own right, declares himself a jealous God, and a severe avenger if he be confused with any fictitious god [cf. Ex. 20:5]. Then he defines lawful worship in order to hold mankind in obedience. He combines both under his law, first when he binds believers to himself to be their sole lawgiver, and then when he prescribes a rule whereby he is to be duly honored according to his own will. As for the law, since its use and purpose are manifold, I will discuss it in its own place.[5] I now touch merely on this point, that by it a bridle has been imposed upon men, to prevent their sinking into vicious rites. But what

[2] II. viii. 17–19; IV. x. 8–31.

[3] *Nature of the Gods* II. xxviii. 72 (LCL edition, pp. 192 f. and note a). Lactantius adopts this derivation, while criticizing Cicero's way of distinguishing religion from the superstitious fear (*Divine Institutes* IV. xxviii; CSEL 19. 389; tr. ANF VII. 131).

[4] In I. iv. 1; I. v. 8.

[5] See esp. II. viii.

I have set down in an earlier section is to be kept in mind, that unless everything proper to his divinity resides in the one God, he is despoiled of his honor, and the reverencing of him profaned.

ᵇHere we must more carefully attend to those subtleties with which superstition disports itself. Indeed, it does not so decline to other gods as seemingly to desert the highest God, or to reduce him to the level of the rest. But while it concedes to him the supreme place, it surrounds him with a throng of lesser gods, among whom it parcels out his functions. The glory of his divinity is so rent asunder (although stealthily and craftily) that his whole glory does not remain with him alone.⁶ Thus, in the past, men, Jews as well as heathen, put a vast throng of gods under the father and ruler of the gods. Each of these gods according to his rank held in common with the highest god the government of heaven and earth. Thus a few centuries ago the saints who had departed this life were elevated into copartnership with God, to be honored, and also to be invoked and praised in his stead. Indeed, we suppose that by such an abomination God's majesty is not even obscured, while it is in great part suppressed and extinguished, except that we retain some sterile notion of his supreme power; ᶜmeanwhile, deceived by the trappings, we are drawn to various gods.

2. *A distinction without a difference**

ᵈIn fact, the distinction between latria and dulia, as they called them, was invented in order that divine honors might seem to be transferred with impunity to angels and the dead.⁷ For it is obvious that the honor the papists give to the saints really does not differ from the honoring of God. Indeed, they worship both God and the saints indiscriminately, except that, when they are pressed, they wriggle out with the excuse that they keep unimpaired for God what is due him because they leave latria to him. But since the thing itself, not the word, is in question, who can permit them to make light of this most important of all matters? But—to pass over this also—their distinction in the end boils down to this: they render honor [*cultus*] to God alone, but undergo servitude [*servitium*] for the others. For λατρεία among the Greeks means the same thing as *cultus* among the Latins; δουλεία properly signifies *servitus*; and yet in Scripture this distinction is sometimes blurred. But suppose we concede it to be unvarying. Then we must inquire what both words mean: δουλεία is servitude; λατρεία, honor. Now no one doubts that it is

⁶ Augustine, *City of God* IV. ix (MPL 41. 119; tr. NPNF II. 69).
⁷ Cf. I. xi. 11, 16.

greater to be enslaved than to honor. For it would very often be hard for you to be enslaved to one whom you were not unwilling to honor. Thus it would be unequal dealing to assign to the saints what is greater and leave to God what is lesser. Yet many of the old writers used this distinction. What, then, if all perceive that it is not only inept but entirely worthless?

3. Honoring images is dishonor to God*

ᵈLet us drop fine distinctions and examine the thing itself. When Paul reminds the Galatians what they were like before they were illumined in the knowledge of God, he says that "they exhibited dulia toward beings that by nature were no gods" [Gal. 4:8 p.]. When he does not call it latria, is their superstition for this reason excusable? Assuredly, by labeling that perverse superstition dulia, he condemns it no less than if he had used the word "latria." And when Christ fends off Satan's insult with this shield, "It is written, 'You shall worship the Lord your God' " [Matt. 4:10], it is not a question of the word "latria."[8] For Satan demanded of him only a reverent kneeling.[9] Likewise, when John was rebuked by the angel because he fell down on his knees before him [Rev. 19:10; 22:8–9], we ought not to suppose John to be so senseless as to wish to transfer to an angel the honor due God alone. But because any reverential act that has been joined with religion cannot but savor of something divine, he could not have "knelt" to the angel without detracting from God's glory. Indeed, we often read that men were worshiped: but such an act was, so to speak, a civil honor. Religion, however, has another concern; as soon as it has been joined with. an act of reverence, it carries the profanation of divine honor along with it.

We can see this in Cornelius [Acts 10:25]. He had not advanced so ill in godliness as not to pay God alone the highest reverence. Therefore, when he prostrated himself before Peter, undoubtedly he did not intend to worship Peter in place of God, yet Peter earnestly forbade him to do it. Why, unless because men never so articulately discern between the honoring of God and of creatures without indiscriminately transferring to the creature what belonged to God? ᵇThus, if we wish to have one God, we should remember that we must not pluck away even a particle of his

[8] Cf. I. xi. 11, note 21; P. Lombard, *Sentences* III. ix. 1 (MPL 192. 775 f.). Aquinas distinguishes latria, worship that is paid to God, from dulia, which is paid to excellent creatures, but also notes different kinds of dulia, including hyperdulia, which is accorded to the Blessed Virgin (*Summa Theol.* II IIae. lxxxiv. 1; ciii. 4). Cf. also Eck, *Enchiridion* (1526, 1533), ch. xv (1541, ch. xvi): *"De imaginibus Crucifixi et sanctorum."*

[9] *"προσκύνησις."*

glory and that he must retain what is his own. ᵉTherefore Zechariah, when he speaks of the restoration of the church, eloquently asserts not only that "God will be one" but also that "his name will be one" [Zech. 14:9 p.], in order no doubt that he may have nothing in common with idols. What sort of reverence God requires will be seen elsewhere in its proper place.[10] For by his law it pleases him to prescribe for men what is good and right, and thus to hold them to a sure standard that no one may take leave to contrive any sort of worship he pleases.

But because it is not expedient to burden my readers by mingling many things, I do not yet touch on that matter. It is enough to recognize that, whenever any observances of piety are transferred to some one other than the sole God, sacrilege occurs. And first, indeed, superstition contrived divine honors either for the sun and the stars or for idols. Then followed ambition, which, by adorning mortals with the spoils of God, dared profane everything sacred. And although there remained the principle of worshiping a supreme Being, it was a common custom to offer sacrifices indiscriminately to tutelary divinities, lesser gods, or dead heroes. So inclined are we to lapse into this error that what God rigorously reserves for himself alone we distribute among a great throng.

ᵉCHAPTER XIII

IN SCRIPTURE, FROM THE CREATION ONWARD, WE ARE TAUGHT ONE ESSENCE OF GOD, WHICH CONTAINS THREE PERSONS[1]

(Terms used in the doctrine of the Trinity by the orthodox fathers, 1–6)

1. God's nature is immeasurable and spiritual

The Scriptural teaching concerning God's infinite and spiritual essence ought to be enough, not only to banish popular delusions,

---

[10] II. vii, viii.

[1] Throughout all editions the doctrine of the Trinity stands prior to the analysis of the first article of the Apostles' Creed (the Creator), but up to 1559 it followed immediately the discussion of Christ as the sole object (*scopus*) of faith. Here, with faith deferred to III. ii, under the redeeming work of the Spirit, the doctrine is presented without full epistemological preparation. Otherwise, and with many expansions, the sequence remains the same: Father, I. xiv ff.; Son, II. vi ff.; and Spirit, III. i ff. A systematically presented list of divine attributes (*"virtutes,"* here ordinarily rendered "powers"), characteristic of both medieval theologians and Reformed orthodoxy, is notably absent from Calvin. The nearest approach is I. x. 2, above, but it receives no systematic development. References to the *virtutes Dei* are found also in I. v. 10; I. xiv. 21; III. xx. 40–41; Comm. Rom.

but also to refute the subtleties of secular philosophy. One of the ancients seems aptly to have remarked, "Whatever we see, and whatever we do not see, is God."[2] According to this, he fancied that divinity was poured out into the various parts of the world. But even if God to keep us sober speaks sparingly of his essence, yet by those two titles that I have used he both banishes stupid imaginings and restrains the boldness of the human mind. Surely, his infinity ought to make us afraid to try to measure him by our own senses. Indeed, his spiritual nature forbids our imagining anything earthly or carnal of him. For the same reason, he quite often assigns to himself a dwelling place in heaven. And yet as he is incomprehensible he also fills the earth itself. But because he sees that our slow minds sink down upon the earth, and rightly, in order to shake off our sluggishness and inertia he raises us above the world. [e(b)]And hence falls to the ground the error of the Manichees, who by postulating two principles [e]made the devil almost equal to God.[3] Undoubtedly this was to wreck God's unity and restrict his infinity. [e(b)]Indeed, that they dared abuse certain testimonies of Scripture was due to base ignorance; just as the error itself sprang from execrable madness. [b]The Anthropomorphites, also, who imagined a corporeal God from the fact that Scripture often ascribes to him a mouth, ears, eyes, hands, and feet,[4] are easily refuted. For who even of slight intelligence does not understand that, as nurses commonly do with infants, God is wont in a measure to "lisp" in speaking to us? Thus such forms of speaking do not so much express clearly what God is like as accommodate the knowledge of him to our slight capacity. To do this he must descend far beneath his loftiness.

1:21. The reader will probably look in vain for the noun "sovereignty" applied to God in Calvin's writings (G. B. Beyerhaus, *Studien zur Staatsanschauung Calvins*, ch. iii, "Calvins Souveränitätslehre," esp. p. 58), although the subject matter usually designated thereby appears in the doctrine of Providence, which makes frequent use of the traditional term "omnipotence" (cf. I. xvi. 3). The Beveridge and Allen translations of the *Institutes* sometimes have introduced the terms "sovereign," "sovereignty," and even inserted the term "decree" in accord with orthodox usage, where Calvin's text does not contain it.

[2] Seneca, *Natural Questions*, Prologue, I. 13 (tr. J. Clarke, *Physical Science in the Time of Nero*, p. 7).

[3] The dualistic sect founded by the Persian Manichaeus (or Mani) (d. 277). Cf. Augustine, *On Genesis in the Literal Sense* XI. xiii. 17 (MPL 34. 436); *De haeresibus* xlvi (MPL 42. 34–38); *Contra Julianum, opus imperfectum* I. cxv–cxxiii (MPL 45. 1125–1127).

[4] This sect, founded by Audius (d. 372) in Mesopotamia, taught that since man was made in God's image (Gen. 1:26), God has human form. Cf. Augustine, *De haeresibus* l–50 (MPL 42. 39).

2. The three "Persons" in God

ᵉBut God also designates himself by another special mark to distinguish himself more precisely from idols. For he so proclaims himself the sole God as to offer himself to be contemplated clearly in three persons. Unless we grasp these, only the bare and empty name of God flits about in our brains, to the exclusion of the true God. Again, lest anyone imagine that God is threefold, or think God's simple essence to be torn into three persons,[5] we must here seek a short and easy definition to free us from all error.

But because some hatefully inveigh against the word "person,"[6] as if humanly devised, we ought first to see with what justice they do this. ᵉ⁽ᵇ⁾The apostle, calling the Son of God "the stamp of the Father's hypostasis" [Heb. 1:3], doubtless assigns some subsistence[7] to the Father wherein he differs from the Son. For to consider hypostasis equivalent to *essence* (as certain interpreters have done, as if Christ, like wax imprinted with a seal, represented in himself the substance of the Father) would be not only uncouth but also absurd. For since the essence of God is simple and undivided, and he contains all in himself, without portion or derivation, but in integral perfection, the Son will be improperly, even foolishly, called his "stamp." But because the Father, although

---

[5] Calvin here and in sec. 3 alludes to numerous opinions found in the works of anti-Trinitarian writers of his time. Barth and Niesel have supplied detailed references to writings of Michael Servetus (d. 1553), Matthaeus Gribaldi (d. 1564), George Blandrata (d. 1585), Valentine Gentile (d. 1566), Gianpaulo Alciati (d. ca. 1573). (OS III. 109 ff.) For the ideas and activities of these men, see E. M. Wilbur, *A History of Unitarianism: Socinianism and Its Antecedents.* The charge that traditional orthodoxy affirmed "a threefold God," or "three gods," appears in Servetus, *De Trinitatis erroribus,* 1531, I, fo. 21 (tr. E. M. Wilbur, *On the Errors of the Trinity* I. 30, 31, pp. 33 f.; Harvard Theological Studies 16). The later literature of research in this field has been examined by G. H. Williams in LCC XXV. 285 ff. and in "Studies in the Radical Reformation: A Bibliographical Survey of Research Since 1939," *Church History* XXVII (1958), 46–69.

[6] Servetus, *op. cit.,* I, fo. 35, 36 (tr. Wilbur, *op. cit.,* I. 50, 51, pp. 55 f.).

[7] In these sentences Calvin has in mind the words of Heb. 1:3: " χαρακτὴρ τῆς ὑποστάσεως αὐτοῦ," rendered in the Vulgate, *figura substantiae eius,* in KJV "the express image of his person," and in RSV "the very stamp of his nature." *Subsistentia* as against *substantia* in the Latin rendering of ὑπόστασις was adopted by the sixth-century writers Boethius and Cassiodorus, and was familiar in the Middle Ages. By this language Calvin affirms the distinctiveness of the Persons of the Trinity. Cf. Aquinas, *Summa Theol.* I. xxix. 2. For this section consult also Origen, *De principiis* I. ii. 2 (GCS 22. 28; tr. G. W. Butterworth, *Origen On First Principles,* p. 16; Augustine, *On the Trinity* V. viii. 10; VII. iv. 7 (MPL 42. 917, 939; tr. NPNF III. 92, note 7; 109 f.); A. Blaise, *Dictionnaire Latin-Français des auteurs chrétiens,* and Du Cange, *Glossarium, s.v.* "subsistentia."

distinct in his proper nature, expresses himself wholly in the Son, for a very good reason is it said that he has made his hypostasis visible in the latter. [e]In close agreement with this are the words immediately following, that the Son is "the splendor of his glory" [Heb. 1:3, cf. Vg.]. Surely we infer from the apostle's words that the very hypostasis that shines forth in the Son is in the Father. From this we also easily ascertain the Son's hypostasis, which distinguishes him from the Father.

The same reasoning applies to the Holy Spirit: for we shall presently prove that he is God, and yet it is necessary for him to be thought of as other than the Father. Indeed, this is not a distinction of essence, which it is unlawful to make manifold. Therefore, if the testimony of the apostle obtains any credence, it follows that there are in God three hypostases. Since the Latins can express the same concept by the word "person," to wrangle over this clear matter is undue squeamishness and even obstinacy. If anyone longs to translate word for word, let him use "subsistence." Many have used "substance" in the same sense. Nor was the word "person" in use only among the Latins, for the Greeks, perhaps to testify their agreement, taught that there are three *prosōpa*[7a] in God. Although they, whether Greek or Latin, differ among themselves over the word, yet they quite agree in the essential matter.

3. The expressions "Trinity" and "Person" aid the interpretation of Scripture and are therefore admissible

[e(a)]Now, although the heretics[8] rail at the word "person," or certain squeamish men[9] cry out against admitting a term fashioned by the human mind, they cannot shake our conviction that three are spoken of, each of which is entirely God, yet that there is not more than one God. What wickedness, then, it is [a]to disapprove of words that explain nothing else than what is attested and sealed by Scripture!

[7a] "πρόσωπα," sing. "πρόσωπον," equivalent of Latin *persona*, with a range of meaning from "face," "countenance," or "mask" to "person"; used especially of the three manifestations, or Persons, of the Trinity. Cf. sec. 4, note 11.

[8] Cf. sec. 2, note 6.

[9] "*Morosi.*" If, as suggested in OS III. 111, Calvin had in mind here Bullinger's discussion of the two natures of Christ (*Utriusque in Christo naturae tam divinae quam humanae . . . assertio orthodoxa*, 1534), it is remarkable that no edition of the *Institutes* prior to 1559 bears this allusion. The 1536 edition associates *morositas* with the *heretici*, and in his *Response to the Questions of George Blandrata*, 1557, Calvin applies to this anti-Trinitarian the adjective *morosus*, CR IX. 329. Cf. IV. i. 16, 20. It is certain, however, that Bullinger withheld approval from Calvin in the latter's dispute with Pierre Caroli, 1537. See Bullinger's letter to Oswald Myconius, July 23, 1537 (Herminjard, *Correspondance* IV. 264 f.; CR X. 2. 116 f.; OS III. iii, note 4).

It would be enough, they say, to confine within the limits of Scripture not only our thoughts but also our words, rather than scatter foreign terms about, which would become seedbeds of dissension and strife. For thus are we wearied with quarreling over words, thus by bickering do we lose the truth, thus by hateful wrangling do we destroy love.

If they call a foreign word one that cannot be shown to stand written syllable by syllable in Scripture, they are indeed imposing upon us an unjust law which condemns all interpretation not patched together out of the fabric of Scripture. But if that is "foreign" which has been curiously devised and is superstitiously defended, which conduces more to contention than to edification, which is made use of either unseasonably or fruitlessly, which by its harshness offends pious ears, which detracts from the simplicity of God's Word—I wholeheartedly embrace their soberness. For I do not feel that concerning God we should speak with less conscientiousness than we should think, since whatever by ourselves we think concerning him is foolish, and whatever we speak, absurd. Yet some measure ought to be preserved: we ought to seek from Scripture a sure rule for both thinking and speaking, to which both the thoughts of our minds and the words of our mouths should be conformed. But what prevents us from explaining in clearer words those matters in Scripture which perplex and hinder our understanding, yet which conscientiously and faithfully serve the truth of Scripture itself, and are made use of sparingly and modestly and on due occasion? There are quite enough examples of this sort of thing. ᵇWhat is to be said, moreover, when it has been proved that the church is utterly compelled to make use of the words "Trinity" and "Persons"? ᵃIf anyone, then, finds fault with the novelty of the words, does he not deserve to be judged as bearing the light of truth unworthily, since he is finding fault only with what renders the truth plain and clear?

4. The church has regarded expressions like "Trinity," "Person," etc., as necessary to unmask false teachers

ᵃHowever, the novelty of words of this sort (if such it must be called) becomes especially useful when the truth is to be asserted against false accusers, who evade it by their shifts. Of this today we have abundant experience in our great efforts to rout the enemies of pure and wholesome doctrine. With such crooked and sinuous twisting these slippery snakes glide away unless they are boldly pursued, caught, and crushed. Thus men of old, stirred up by various struggles over depraved dogmas, were compelled to set forth with consummate clarity what they felt, lest they leave any devious shift to the impious, who cloaked their errors in layers of verbiage. Because he could not oppose manifest oracles, Arius confessed that Christ was God and the Son of God, and, as if he had done what was right, pretended some agreement with the other men. Yet in the meantime he did not cease to prate that Christ was created and had a beginning, as other creatures. The ancients, to drag the man's versatile craftiness out of its hiding places, went farther, declaring Christ the eternal Son of the Father, consubstantial with the Father. Here impiety boiled over when the Arians began most wickedly to hate and curse the word *homoousios*.[10] But if at first they had sincerely and wholeheartedly confessed Christ to be God, they would not have denied him to be consubstantial with the Father. Who would dare inveigh against those upright men as wranglers and contentious persons because they became aroused to such heated discussion through one little word, and disturbed the peace of the church? Yet that mere word marked the distinction between Christians of pure faith and sacrilegious Arians. Afterward Sabellius[11] arose, who counted the names of Father, Son, and Holy Spirit as almost of no importance, arguing that it was not because of any distinction that they were put forward, but that they were diverse attributes of God, of which sort there are very many. If it came to a debate, he was accustomed to confess that he recognized the Father as God, the Son as God, and the Spirit as God; but afterward a way out was found, contending that he had said nothing else than if he had spoken of God as strong, and just, and wise. And so he re-echoed another old song, that the Father is the Son, and the Holy Spirit the Father, without rank, without distinction. To shatter the man's wickedness the upright doctors, who then had piety at heart, loudly responded that three properties must truly be recognized in the one God. And that they might fortify themselves against his tortuous cunning with the open and simple truth, they truly affirmed that a trinity of persons subsists in the one God, or, what was the same thing, subsists in the unity of God.

5. Limits and necessity of theological terms

ªIf, therefore, these terms were not rashly invented, we ought to beware lest by repudiating them we be accused of overweening

---

[10] ὁμοουσίου, consubstantial, the word of emphasis in the Creed of Nicaea, 325, by which Arianism was rejected.
[11] The chronological order is here inverted: Arius died in 337; Sabellius flourished about 250. His doctrine of the πρόσωπα has been compared with the view of the Trinity held by Schleiermacher: C. C. Richardson, *The Doctrine of the Trinity*, ch. vii.

rashness. Indeed, I could wish they were buried, if only among all men this faith were agreed on: that Father and Son and Spirit are one God, yet the Son is not the Father, nor the Spirit the Son, but that they are differentiated by a peculiar quality.

ᵇReally, I am not, indeed, such a stickler as to battle doggedly over mere words. For I note that the ancients, who otherwise speak very reverently concerning these matters, agree neither among themselves nor even at all times individually with themselves. What, now, are the formulas employed by the councils and excused by Hilary?[12] With what great freedom does Augustine sometimes burst forth?[13] How unlike are the Greeks and the Latins? But one example of the difference will suffice. When the Latins wished to translate the word *homoousios* they said "consubstantial," indicating that the substance of Father and Son is one, thus employing "substance" instead of "essence." ᶜHence, likewise, Jerome in a letter to Damasus calls it a sacrilege to predicate three substances in God. ᵇYet you will find more than a hundred times in Hilary that there are three "substances" in God.[14] ᶜBut how confused is Jerome by the word "hypostasis"! For he suspects poison lurking when three hypostases in one God are mentioned! Even if one uses this word in a pious sense, he does not, nevertheless, hide the fact that it is an improper expression. ᵉThis would be true even if he spoke sincerely, rather than tried willingly and knowingly to charge the Eastern bishops, whom he hates, with unjust calumnies! Surely he shows little candor in asserting that in all profane schools *ousia* is nothing else but hypostasis,[15] an opinion repeatedly refuted by common and well-worn usage. Augustine is more moderate and courteous, since even though he says that the word *hypostasis* in this sense is new to Latin ears, yet he leaves to the Greeks their manner of speaking so much that he gently bears with the Latins who had imitated the Greek phrase.[16] ᶜAnd what Socrates writes concerning *hypostasis* in Book 6 of the *Tripartite History* suggests that it was wrongly applied to this matter by unlearned men.[17] ᵇBut the same Hilary accuses the heretics of a great crime, that by their wickedness he is forced to submit to the peril of human speech what

[12] Hilary of Poitiers, *On the Councils* xii ff. (MPL 10. 489 f.; tr. NPNF 2 ser. IX. 7 f.).

[13] Augustine, *On the Trinity* VII. vi. 11 (MPL 42. 945; tr. NPNF III. 111 ff.).

[14] Hilary, *On the Councils* xxvii. 67–71 (MPL 10. 525 ff.; tr. NPNF 2 ser. IX. 22).

[15] Jerome, *Letters* xv. 3, 4 (CSEL 54. 64 f.; tr. NPNF 2 ser. VI. 19).

[16] Augustine, *On the Trinity* V. viii–x (MPL 42. 916 f.; tr. NPNF III. 91 f.).

[17] Cassiodorus, *Historia tripartita* VI. 21 (MPL 69. 1042), from Socrates, *Ecclesiastical History* iii. 7 (tr. NPNF 2 ser. II. 81).

ought to have been locked within the sanctity of men's minds; and he does not hide the fact that this is to do things unlawful, to speak things inexpressible, to presume things not conceded. A little later he excuses himself at length for daring to put forward new terms; for when he has set forth the natural names— Father, Son, and Spirit—he adds that whatever is sought besides these is beyond the meaning of language, above the reach of sense, above the capacity of understanding.[18] And elsewhere he pronounces the bishops of Gaul happy because they had neither wrought out, nor received, nor known, any other confession at all than the ancient and very simple one that had been received among all churches from the apostolic age.[19] eAnd Augustine's excuse is similar: on account of the poverty of human speech in so great a matter, the word "hypostasis" had been forced upon us by necessity, not to express what it is, but only not to be silent on how Father, Son, and Spirit are three.[20]

And bthis modesty of saintly men ought to warn us against forthwith so severely taking to task, like censors, those who do not wish to swear to the words conceived by us, eprovided they are not doing it out of either arrogance or frowardness or malicious craft. e(b)But let these very persons, in turn, weigh the necessity that compels us to speak thus, that gradually they may at length become accustomed to a useful manner of speaking. Also let them learn to beware, alest, when they have to resist Arians on the one hand and Sabellians on the other, while indignant that the opportunity to evade the issue is cut off, they arouse some suspicion that they are disciples either of Arius or of Sabellius.[21] Arius says that Christ is God, but mutters that he was made and had a beginning. He says that Christ is one with the Father, but secretly whispers in the ears of his own partisans that He is united to the Father like other believers, although by a singular privilege. Say "consubstantial" and you will tear off the mask of this turncoat, and yet you add nothing to Scripture. Sabellius says that Father, Son, and Spirit signify no distinctions in God.

[18] "The error of others compels us to err in daring to express in human terms truths which ought to be hidden in the silent veneration of the heart." Hilary, On the Trinity II. ii (MPL 10. 51; tr. NPNF 2 ser. IX. 52).
[19] Hilary, On the Councils xxvii. 63 (MPL 10. 522 f.; tr. NPNF 2 ser. IX. 21).
[20] Augustine, On the Trinity VII. iv. 7, 9 (MPL 42. 939; tr. NPNF III. 109 ff.). Admitting the insufficiency of language to express the Trinity, Augustine resorts to homely illustrations from species of animals and trees.
[21] Barth and Niesel point out that Calvin's language here seems to have reference not only to Arius and Sabellius but also to Servetus. See OS III. 115; De Trinitatis erroribus I, fo. 21ab, 22b, 23b; III. 80ab (tr. Wilbur, op. cit., I, pp. 33 ff., 123 f., 131 f.; Harvard Theological Studies 16).

Say they are three, and he will scream that you are naming three Gods. Say that in the one essence of God there is a trinity of persons; you will say in one word what Scripture states, and cut short empty talkativeness. b(a)Indeed, if anxious superstition so constrains anyone that he cannot bear these terms, yet no one could now deny, even if he were to burst, that awhen we hear "one" we ought to understand "unity of substance"; when we hear "three in one essence," the persons in this trinity are meant. When this is confessed without guile, we need not dally over words. cBut I have long since and repeatedly been experiencing that all who persistently quarrel over words nurse a secret poison. As a consequence, it is more expedient to challenge them deliberately than speak more obscurely to please them.

6. The meaning of the most important conception

cBut laying aside disputation over terms, I shall proceed to speak of the thing itself: "Person," therefore, I call a "subsistence" in God's essence, which, while related to the others, is distinguished by an incommunicable quality. By the term "subsistence" we would understand something different from "essence."[22] For if the Word were simply God, and yet possessed no other characteristic mark, John would wrongly have said that the Word was always with God [John 1:1]. When immediately after he adds that the Word was also God himself, he recalls us to the essence as a unity. But because he could not be with God without residing in the Father, hence emerges the idea of a subsistence, which, even though it has been joined with the essence by a common bond and cannot be separated from it, yet has a special mark whereby it is distinguished from it. Now, of the three subsistences I say that each one, while related to the others, is distinguished by a special quality. This "relation" is here distinctly expressed: because where simple and indefinite mention is made of God, this name pertains no less to the Son and the Spirit than to the Father. But as soon as the Father is compared with the Son, the character of each distinguishes the one from the other. Thirdly, whatever is proper to each individually, I maintain to be incommunicable because whatever is attributed to the Father as a distinguishing mark cannot agree with, or be transferred to, the Son. Nor am I displeased with Tertullian's definition, provided it be taken in the right sense, that there is a kind of distribution or economy in God which has no effect on the unity of essence.[23]

22 Cf. sec. 2, note 6.
23 Tertullian, *Against Praxeas* ii, ix (CCL Tertullianus II. 1160, 1168 f.; tr. ANF III. 598, 603 f.). E. Evans, *Tertullian's Treatise Against Praxeas,* has

(The eternal deity of the Son, 7–13)

7. The deity of the Word

e(b)Yet before I proceed farther, I must demonstrate the deity of the Son and of the Holy Spirit. Thereafter we shall see how they differ from each other.

Certainly, bwhen God's word is set before us in Scripture it would be the height of absurdity to imagine a merely fleeting and vanishing utterance, which, cast forth into the air, projects itself outside of God; and that both the oracles announced to the patriarchs and all prophecies were of this sort.[24] Rather, "Word" means the everlasting Wisdom, residing with God, from which both all oracles and all prophecies go forth. For, as Peter testifies, the ancient prophets spoke by the Spirit of Christ just as much as the apostles did [I Peter 1:10–11; cf. II Peter 1:21], and all who thereafter ministered the heavenly doctrine. eIndeed, because Christ had not yet been manifested, it is necessary to understand the Word as begotten of the Father before time [cf. Ecclus. 24:14, Vg.]. But if that Spirit, whose organs were the prophets, was the Spirit of the Word, we infer without any doubt that he was truly God. And Moses clearly teaches this in the creation of the universe, setting forth this Word as intermediary. For why does he expressly tell us that God in his individual acts of creation spoke, Let this or that be done [Gen., ch. 1] unless so that the unsearchable glory of God may shine forth in his image? It would be easy for censorious babblers to get around this, saying that the Word is to be understood as a bidding and command. But the apostles are better interpreters, who teach that the world was made through the Son, and that he upholds all things by his powerful word [Heb. 1:2–3]. For here we see the Word understood as the order or mandate of the Son, who is himself the eternal and essential Word of the Father. bAnd indeed, sane and modest men do not find obscure Solomon's statement, where he introduces wisdom as having been begotten of God before time [Ecclus. 24:14, Vg.], and presiding over the creation of things

critical text, pp. 90, 97 f., translation pp. 131, 140. Praxeas was an extreme representative of the Monarchian heresy, who held that God the Father suffered in the crucifixion (Patripassianism). K. Barth, discussing Calvin's doctrine of the eternal Son, treats theologically the suspicion cast upon the Reformer's orthodoxy on the Trinity at the time of his contention with Pierre Caroli, 1537 and 1540 (*Kirchliche Dogmatik* I. i. 438 f.; tr. G. T. Thomson, *The Doctrine of the Word of God* I. 477 ff.). During this dispute, Calvin, challenged by Caroli, refused, though with no heretical intent, to declare his acceptance of the Athanasian, and even of the Nicene, Creed. Cf. CR VII. 294 f.; Herminjard, *Correspondance* IV. 185 ff., 239 f.

[24] The opinions censured in sections 7 and 8 are found in Servetus, *De Trinitatis erroribus* II, fo. 47a (tr. Wilbur, *op. cit.*, II. 4, p. 75).

and all God's works [Prov. 8:22 ff.]. e(b)For it would be foolish and silly to fancy a certain temporary volition of God; when God willed to set forth his fixed and eternal plan, and also something more secret. eThat saying of Christ's also applies here: "My Father and I have worked even to this day" [John 5:17 p.]. For, affirming that he was constantly at work with the Father from the very beginning of the world, he explains more explicitly what Moses had briefly touched upon. Therefore we conclude that God has so spoken that the Word might have his share in the work and that in this way the work might be common to both. bBut John spoke most clearly of all when he declared that that Word, God from the beginning with God, was at the same time the cause of all things, together with God the Father [John 1:1-3]. For John at once attributes to the Word a solid and abiding essence, eand ascribes something uniquely His own, and clearly shows how God, by speaking, was Creator of the universe. bTherefore, inasmuch as all divinely uttered revelations are correctly designated by the term "word of God," so this substantial Word is properly placed at the highest level, as the wellspring of all oracles. Unchangeable, the Word abides everlastingly one and the same with God, and is God himself.

8. The eternity of the Word

bHere some dogs bark out, who, while they dare not openly deprive him of his divinity, secretly filch away his eternity. For they say the Word for the first time began to be when God opened his holy mouth in the creation of the universe.[25] But they are too reckless in inventing a sort of innovation in God's substance. For as the names of God that have respect to his outward activity began to be attributed to him after the existence of his work (as when he is called Creator of heaven and earth), so piety recognizes or allows no name which intimates that anything new has happened to God in himself. eFor if there had been anything adventitious, the passage of James would fall to the ground: that "every perfect gift comes from above, and descends from the Father of lights, with whom there is no variation or shadow of change" [James 1:17 p.]. Therefore nothing should be more intolerable to us than to fancy a beginning of that Word who both was always God and afterward was the artificer of the universe. bBut they think they are reasoning shrewdly when they aver that Moses, by narrating that God then spoke for the first time, hints thereby that there

[25] Servetus, op. cit. Cf. I. xiii. 22; Comm. John 1:1; also Bucer's treatment of this passage in his In sacra quatuor Evangelia enarrationes, 1553 edition, fo. 221ab.

had been in him no Word before. Nothing is more trifling than this! For because something begins to be manifested at a certain time, we ought not therefore to gather that it never existed before. Indeed, I conclude far otherwise: the Word had existed long before God said, "Let there be light" [Gen. 1:3] and the power of the Word emerged and stood forth. Yet if anyone should inquire how long before, he will find no beginning. Nor does He delimit a certain space of time when he says, "Father, glorify thy Son with the glory which I had with thee before the foundations of the universe were laid" [John 17:5 p.]. ᵉNor did John overlook this: because, before he passes on to the creation of the universe [John 1:3], he says that "in the beginning the Word was with God" [John 1:1 p.]. ᵇTherefore we again state that the Word, conceived beyond the beginning of time by God, has perpetually resided with him. By this, his eternity, his true essence, and his divinity are proved.

9. The deity of Christ in the Old Testament

ᵉFurther, I do not yet touch upon the person of the Mediator, but postpone it until we reach the treatment of redemption.[26] Despite this, because it ought to be agreed among all that Christ is that Word endued with flesh, the testimonies affirming Christ's deity are suitably included here. ᵉ⁽ᵇ⁾Though it is said in Ps. 45, "O God, thy throne is everlasting and forever and ever" [Ps. 45:6; 44:7, Vg.], the Jews[27] turned their backs and made the name Elohim fit also the angels and the highest powers. Yet nowhere in Scripture do we find a like passage, which raises up an eternal throne for a creature; ᵇnor, indeed, is he called simply "God," but also the eternal ruler. Furthermore, this title is bestowed on no one without an addition, as when Moses is said to become "as God to Pharaoh" [Ex. 7:1]. ᵉOthers read "of Pharaoh" in the genitive case, which is exceedingly silly. Indeed, I confess that what is remarkable for its singular excellence is often called "divine," but from the context it is clear enough that such an interpretation here is hard and forced, and really does not make sense.

But if their stubbornness does not yield, quite evidently ᵉ⁽ᵇ⁾Christ is brought forward by Isaiah both as God and as adorned with the highest power, which is the characteristic mark of the one God. ᵇ"This is," he says, "the name by which they will call him, Mighty

---

[26] The topic is discussed in II. xii–xvii.

[27] The references are to opinions expressed by the medieval Jewish commentators, Rashi (d. 1105), Abraham Ibn Ezra (d. 1167), and David Kimchi (d. 1235). Cf. L. I. Newman, *Jewish Influences in Christian Reform Movements*, 325 f., 350 f.

God, Father of the coming age," etc. [Isa. 9:6 p.] The Jews also rail here, and thus invert the reading, "This is the name by which the Mighty God, Father of the coming age, shall call him," etc., e(b)leaving to the Son only the title "Prince of Peace." But to what purpose would so many titles be heaped up in this place to God the Father, since the intention of the prophet is to adorn Christ with clear marks to build up our faith in him? eTherefore there is no doubt that for the same reason he is now called "Mighty God" as a little before he was called "Immanuel." b(a)Yet nothing clearer can be found than the passage of Jeremiah, that "this will be the name by which the branch of David will be called, 'Jehovah our Righteousness'" [Jer. 23:5–6 p.; cf. ch. 33:15–16]. For, since the Jews further teach that other names of God are nothing but titles, but that this one alone [Jehovah], which they speak of as ineffable, is a substantive to express his essence, we infer that the only Son is the eternal God who elsewhere declares that he will not give his glory to another [Isa. 42: 8].

bThe Jews, indeed, take refuge here, pointing out that Moses imposed this name upon the altar erected by him, and Ezekiel did so upon the new city of Jerusalem. But who does not see that the altar was built as a reminder that God was "the exaltation of Moses," and that Jerusalem was not marked with God's name simply to testify to God's presence? For so does the prophet speak: "The name of the city from that day shall be 'Jehovah is there'" [Ezek. 48:35]. Indeed, Moses expresses himself in this way: "He built an altar and called its name 'Jehovah my exaltation'" [Ex. 17:15, cf. Vg.]. But more debate remains over another passage of Jeremiah, where this very formula is referred to Jerusalem in these words: "This is the name by which they will call it, 'Jehovah our righteousness'" [Jer. 33:16, cf. Vg. and Comm.]. However, this testimony is so very far from obscuring the truth that we are defending as rather to lend support to it. For whereas before he had witnessed that Christ was the true Jehovah, from whom righteousness comes, now he declares that the church of God will be so clearly aware of this that it is able to glory in the very name. eTherefore in the former passage the source and cause of righteousness is set forth; in the latter, the effect is added.

10. The "Angel of the Eternal God"*

eBut if this evidence does not satisfy the Jews, I do not see by what subtleties they can elude the fact that Jehovah is so frequently set forth in the person of an angel. To the holy patriarchs an angel is said to have appeared, claiming for himself the name of the Eternal God [Judg. 6:11, 12, 20, 21, 22; 7:5, 9]. If someone takes exception that this is said in regard to the role that he plays, the difficulty is by no means thus resolved. For as a servant he would not permit a sacrifice to be offered to himself and thus deprive God of His honor. Yet the angel, refusing to eat bread, commands that a sacrifice be offered to Jehovah [Judg. 13:16]. Indeed, the fact itself proves that he is Jehovah himself [ch. 13: 20]. Therefore Manoah and his wife infer from this sign that they have seen not only an angel but God himself. Hence that exclamation: "We shall . . . die because we have seen God" [ch. 13:22]. And when the wife answers, "If Jehovah had willed us to die, he would not have received the offering from our hand" [ch. 13: 23], she confesses that he who was previously called an angel is truly God. Besides, the angel's reply removes all doubt: "Why do you ask concerning my name, which is wonderful?" [ch. 13:18].

The impiety of Servetus[28] was even more detestable, when he asserted that God was never revealed to Abraham and the other patriarchs, but that in his place an angel was worshiped. But the orthodox doctors of the church have rightly and prudently interpreted that chief angel to be God's Word, who already at that time, as a sort of foretaste, began to fulfill the office of Mediator.[29] For even though he was not yet clothed with flesh, he came down, so to speak, as an intermediary, in order to approach believers more intimately. Therefore this closer intercourse gave him the name of angel. Meanwhile, what was his he retained, that as God he might be of ineffable glory. The same thing is meant by Hosea, who, after recounting Jacob's struggle with the angel, says, "Jehovah, the God of Hosts, Jehovah, his name is a remembrance" [Hos. 12:5, Vg.]. Again, Servetus yelps that God took on the person of an angel. As if the prophet does not indeed confirm what had been said by Moses, "Why do you ask my name?" [Gen. 32:29 p.]! And the confession of the holy patriarch sufficiently declares that he was not a created angel, but one in whom full deity dwelt, when Jacob says, "I have seen God face to face" [v. 30]. Hence, also, that saying of Paul's that Christ was the leader of the people in the wilderness [I Cor. 10:4];[30] because even though the time of humbling had not yet arrived, that eternal Word nevertheless set forth a figure of the office to which he had been destined. Now if we review objectively the second chapter of

[28] Servetus is here first named in the *Institutes*.
[29] Justin, *Dialogue with Trypho* lvi, lviii, cxxvii (MPG 6. 595 ff., 607 ff., 771 ff.; tr. ANF I. 223, 225, 263); Tertullian, *Against Marcion* III. ix (MPL 3. 333; CCL Tertullianus I. 519 f.; tr. ANF III. 328).
[30] Cf. I. xiv. 9; Comm. Acts 7:30.

Zechariah, the angel who sends the other angel [Zech. 2:3] is immediately declared to be the God of Hosts, and to him is ascribed the highest power [v. 9]. I pass over innumerable testimonies on which our faith safely agrees, even though they move the Jews not a whit. For when it is said in Isaiah, "Behold, this is our God; . . . he is Jehovah; we shall wait upon him, and he will preserve us" [Isa. 25:9, cf. Vg.], anyone with eyes can see that this refers to God, who rises up anew to save his people. And the emphatic demonstrations twice repeated permit a reference here to no one else but Christ. Even clearer and fuller is a passage in Malachi, where he promises that the ruler then awaited will come to his temple [Mal. 3:1]. Certainly that temple was sacred to no other than to the one supreme God, yet the prophet claims it for Christ. From this it follows that he is the same God who had always been worshiped among the Jews.

*11. The divinity of Christ in the New Testament: witness of the apostles**

ᵇMoreover, the New Testament abounds with innumerable testimonies. We must therefore take the trouble to make a brief selection rather than to heap up all. ᶜBut although the apostles spoke of him after he had already appeared in the flesh as the Mediator, still all I bring forward will be a suitable proof of his eternal deity.

ᵇFirst of all, a point worth especial attention is the apostles' teaching that what had been foretold concerning the eternal God had already been revealed in Christ or was someday to be manifested in him. For when Isaiah prophesies that the Lord of Hosts is to be "a stone of stumbling and a rock of offense for the Judeans and Israelites" [Isa. 8:14 p.], Paul declares this prophecy fulfilled in Christ [Rom. 9:32–33]. Therefore he proclaims Christ to be Lord of Hosts. Similarly, elsewhere he says, "We must all stand once before the judgment seat of Christ" [Rom. 14:10 p.]. "For it is written, . . . To me every knee shall bow [Rom. 14:11, Vg.], to me . . . every tongue shall swear" [Isa. 45:23, order changed]. Since in Isaiah, God foretells this concerning himself, and Christ, indeed, shows it forth in himself, it follows that he is that very God whose glory cannot be transferred to another. It is evident that what Paul cites to the Ephesians from The Psalms applies to God alone: "Ascending on high, he led the captivity" [Eph. 4:8; Ps. 68:18; 67:19, Vg.]. Understanding that an ascension of this sort had been prefigured when in a notable victory God put forth his power against the foreign nations, Paul indicates that it was manifested more fully in Christ. Thus John testifies that it was the glory of the Son which had been revealed through Isaiah's vision [John 12:41; Isa. 6:1], even though the prophet himself writes that he saw the majesty of God. Obviously the titles of God that the apostle in The Letter to the Hebrews confers upon the Son are the most glorious of all: "In the beginning, thou, O Lord, didst found heaven and earth" [Heb. 1:10 p.; Ps. 101:26 p., Vg.; 102:25, EV], etc. Likewise, "Adore him, all ye his angels" [Ps. 96:7, Vg.; 97:7, EV; cf. Heb. 1:6]. And still he does not misuse them when he applies them to Christ. Indeed, whatever they sing in The Psalms, He alone fulfills. For he it was who, rising up, was merciful to Zion [Ps. 101:14, Vg.; 102:13, EV]; he who asserted for himself the rule over all nations and islands [Ps. 96:1, Vg.; 97:1, EV]. And why should John have hesitated to refer the majesty of God to Christ, when he had declared that the Word was ever God [John 1:1, 14]? Why should Paul have feared to place Christ on God's judgment seat [II Cor. 5:10], when he had previously proclaimed his divinity so openly, saying that he was "God . . . blessed forever" [Rom. 9:5]? And to make clear how consistent he is in this respect, in another passage he writes that "God has been manifested in the flesh" [I Tim. 3:16 p.]. If God is to be praised forever, he, then, it is to whom alone all glory and honor are due, as Paul affirms in another place [I Tim. 1:17]. And he does not conceal this, but openly proclaims: "Though he was in the form of God, he would not have counted it robbery if he had shown himself equal with God, yet he voluntarily emptied himself" [Phil. 2:6–7 p.]. And lest the impious carp about some feigned god, John went farther, saying: "He is the true God, and eternal life" [I John 5:20 p.]. However, it ought to be more than enough for us that he is called God, especially by that witness who aptly declares to us that there are not many gods, but one [Deut. 6:4]. Moreover, it is that Paul who said, "Though many are called gods, whether in heaven or on earth, . . . yet for us there is one God, from whom are all things." [I Cor. 8:5–6 p.] When we hear from the same mouth that "God was manifested in the flesh" [I Tim. 3:16 p.], that "God has purchased the church by his blood" [Acts 20:28 p.], why do we imagine a second god, whom Paul acknowledges not at all? And no doubt the same was the opinion of all godly men. In like manner Thomas openly proclaims him his Lord and God [John 20:28], and thus professes him to be that sole God whom he had always worshiped.

12. The divinity of Christ is demonstrated in his works
   ᵇNow if we weigh his divinity by the works that are ascribed

to him in the Scriptures, it will thereby shine forth more clearly.
Indeed, when he said that he had been working hitherto from
the beginning with the Father [John 5:17], the Jews, utterly
stupid to all his other sayings, still sensed that he made use of
divine power. And therefore, as John states, "the Jews sought
all the more to kill him, because he not only broke the Sabbath,
but also called God his Father, making himself equal with God"
[John 5:18]. How great will our stupidity then be if we do not
feel that his divinity is here plainly affirmed? And verily, to govern the universe with providence and power, and to regulate all
things by the command of his own power [Heb. 1:3], deeds that
the apostle ascribes to Christ, is the function of the Creator alone.
And he not only participates in the task of governing the world
with the Father; but he carries out also other individual offices,
which cannot be communicated to the creatures. The Lord proclaims through the prophet, "I, even I, am the one who blots out
your transgressions for my own sake" [Isa. 43:25 p.]. According
to this saying, when the Jews thought that wrong was done to
God in that Christ was remitting sins, Christ not only asserted in
words, but also proved by miracle, that this power belonged to
him [Matt. 9:6]. We therefore perceive that he possesses not the
administration merely but the actual power of remission of sins,
which the Lord says will never pass from him to another. What?
Does not the searching and penetrating of the silent thoughts
of hearts belong to God alone? Yet Christ also had this power
[Matt. 9:4; cf. John 2:25]. From this we infer his divinity.

13. The divinity of Christ is demonstrated by his miracles

bHow plainly and clearly is his deity shown in miracles! Even
though I confess that both the prophets and the apostles performed miracles equal to and similar to his, yet in this respect
there is the greatest of differences: they distributed the gifts of
God by their ministry, but he showed forth his own power. Indeed, he sometimes used prayer to render glory to the Father
[John 11:41]. But for the most part we see his own power shown
to us. And why would he not be the real author of miracles, who
by his own authority commits the dispensation of them to others?
For the Evangelist relates that he gave to the apostles the power
of raising the dead, curing lepers, casting out demons, etc. [Matt.
10:8; cf. Mark 3:15; 6:7]. Moreover, they so used that sort of
ministry as to show sufficiently that the power came from none
other than Christ. "In the name of Jesus Christ," says Peter,
" . . . arise and walk." [Acts 3:6.] No wonder, then, if Christ
offered his miracles to confound the unbelief of the Jews, inas-

much as these were done by his power and thus rendered the fullest testimony of his divinity [John 5:36; 10:37; 14:11].

Moreover, if apart from God there is no salvation, no righteousness, no life, yet Christ contains all these in himself, God is certainly revealed. And let no one object to me that life and salvation have been infused into Christ by God,[31] for Christ is not said to have received salvation, but to be salvation itself. And if no one but God is good [Matt. 19:17], how could a mere man be— I do not say good and just—but goodness and justice itself? Why is it that, by the testimony of the Evangelist, life was in him from the beginning of Creation, and even then existing as life he was the light of men [John 1:4]? Accordingly, relying upon such proofs, we dare put our faith and hope in him, although we know it to be a sacrilegious impiety for anyone to place his trust in creatures. "Do you believe in God?" he asks. "Believe also in me." [John 14:1 p.] And thus does Paul interpret two passages of Isaiah: "Whoever hopes in him will not be put to shame" [Rom. 10:11; Isa. 28:16]. Also, "There will come from the root of Jesse one who will arise to rule over peoples; in him will the nations hope." [Rom. 15:12 p.; Isa. 11:10.] And why should we search out more testimonies of Scripture concerning this matter, when we come so often upon this sentence: "He who believes in me has eternal life" [e.g., John 6:47]? Now the prayer that depends upon faith is also due Christ, yet it specially belongs to the divine majesty, if anything else does belong to it. For the prophet says: "Whoever will call upon the name of Jehovah will be saved." [Joel 2:32, Vg.] Another: "The name of Jehovah is a very strong tower: the righteous will flee to it and be saved." [Prov. 18:10 p.] But the name of Christ is invoked for salvation; therefore it follows that he is Jehovah. Moreover, we have an example of such invocation in Stephen, where he says, "Lord Jesus, receive my spirit" [Acts 7:59]. Later in the whole church, as Ananias testifies in the same book, saying, "Lord, thou knowest how many evils this man has inflicted upon all the saints who call upon thy name" [Acts 9:13–14 p.]. And to have it more plainly understood that "the whole fullness of divinity dwells bodily" in Christ [Col. 2:9], the apostle confesses that he introduced no other doctrine among the Corinthians than knowledge of him, and that he has preached nothing but this [I Cor. 2:2].

What wondrous and great thing is this, I ask, that the name of the Son alone is announced to us, when God bade us glory in the knowledge of him alone? [Jer. 9:24]. Who has dared talk of him as a mere creature, when the knowledge of him is our only

31 Servetus, *op. cit.*, III, fo. 77 f. (tr. Wilbur, *op. cit.*, III. 12 f., pp. 119 ff.).

reason for glorying? Besides this, e(b)the salutations prefixed to the letters of Paul pray for the same benefits from the Son as from the Father [Rom. 1:7; I Cor. 1:3; II Cor. 1:2; Gal. 1:3; etc.]. By this we are taught not only that by the Son's intercession do those things which the Heavenly Father bestows come to us but that by mutual participation in power the Son himself is the author of them. bThis practical knowledge is doubtless more certain and firmer than any idle speculation.[32] There, indeed, does the pious mind perceive the very presence of God, and almost touches him, when it feels itself quickened, illumined, preserved, justified, and sanctified.

(The eternal deity of the Spirit, 14–15)
14. The divinity of the Spirit is demonstrated in his work
bAccordingly, we ought to seek from the same source proof of the deity of the Spirit. eIndeed, that testimony of Moses in the history of the Creation is very clear, that "the Spirit of God was spread over the deeps" [Gen. 1:2, cf. Vg.], or formless matter; for it shows not only that the beauty of the universe (which we now perceive) owes its strength and preservation to the power of the Spirit but that before this adornment was added, even then the Spirit was occupied with tending that confused mass. And men cannot subtly explain away Isaiah's utterance, "And now Jehovah has sent me, and his Spirit" [Isa. 48:16, cf. Comm.], for in sending the prophets he shares the highest power with the Holy Spirit.[33] From this his divine majesty shines forth. But the best confirmation for us, as I have said, will be from familiar use. bFor what Scripture attributes to him and we ourselves learn by the sure experience of godliness is far removed from the creatures. For it is the Spirit who, everywhere diffused, sustains all things, causes them to grow, and quickens them in heaven and in earth. Because he is circumscribed by no limits, he is excepted from the category of creatures; but in transfusing into all things his energy, and breathing into them essence, life, and movement, he is indeed plainly divine.

Again, if regeneration into incorruptible life is higher and much more excellent than any present growth, what ought we to think of him from whose power it proceeds? Now, Scripture teaches in many places that he is the author of regeneration not

---

[32] Cf. Melanchthon, *Loci communes* (1521), ed. H. Engelland, p. 6: "*Mysteria divinitatis rectius adoraverimus quam vestigaverimus*" (tr. C. L. Hill, *The Loci Communes of Philip Melanchthon*, p. 67).

[33] Cf. Comm. Acts 20:28. For comment on the topics of sections 14–20, see B. B. Warfield, *Biblical and Theological Studies* (ed. S. G. Craig), ch. v.

by borrowing but by his very own energy; and not of this only, but of future immortality as well. In short, upon him, as upon the Son, are conferred functions that especially belong to divinity. "For the Spirit searches . . . even the depths of God" [I Cor. 2:10], who has no counselor among the creatures [Rom. 11:34]; he bestows wisdom and the faculty of speaking [I Cor. 12:10], although the Lord declares to Moses that it is his work alone [Ex. 4:11]. Thus through him we come into communion with God, so that we in a way feel his life-giving power toward us. Our justification is his work; from him is power, sanctification [cf. I Cor. 6:11], truth, grace, and every good thing that can be conceived, since there is but one Spirit from whom flows every sort of gift [I Cor. 12:11]. ᵉEspecially worth noting is this saying of Paul's: "Although there are divers gifts" [I Cor. 12:4] and manifold and varied distribution [cf. Heb. 2:4], "but the same Spirit" [I Cor. 12:4 p.]; because this makes him not only the beginning or source, but also the author. This Paul also more clearly expresses a little later in these words: "One and the same Spirit apportions all things as he will" [I Cor. 12:11 p.]. For if the Spirit were not an entity subsisting in God, choice and will would by no means be conceded to him. Paul, therefore, very clearly attributes to the Spirit divine power, and shows that He resides hypostatically in God.

15. Express testimonies for the deity of the Spirit

ᵇNor, indeed, does Scripture in speaking of him refrain from the designation "God." For Paul concludes that we are the temple of God from the fact that his Spirit dwells in us [I Cor. 3:16–17; 6:19; II Cor. 6:16]. We are not lightly to pass over this fact. For, while God indeed frequently promises that he will choose us as a temple for himself, this promise is not otherwise fulfilled than by his Spirit dwelling in us. ᶜCertainly, as Augustine very clearly states: "If we are bidden to make a temple for the Spirit out of wood and stone, because this honor is due to God alone, such a command would be a clear proof of the Spirit's divinity. Now, then, how much clearer is it that we ought not to make a temple for him, but ought ourselves to be that temple?"[34] ᵇAnd the apostle himself sometimes writes that "we are God's temple" [I Cor. 3:16–17; II Cor. 6:16], at other times, in the same sense, "the temple of the Holy Spirit" [I Cor. 6:19]. Indeed, Peter, rebuking Ananias for lying to the Holy Spirit, says that he has lied not to men but to God [Acts 5:3–4]. And where Isaiah introduces the Lord of Hosts speaking, Paul teaches that it is the Holy Spirit

[34] Augustine, *Letters* clxx. 2 (MPL 33. 749; tr. FC 30. 62).

who speaks [Isa. 6:9; Acts 28:25–26]. ᵉIndeed, where the prophets usually say that the words they utter are those of the Lord of Hosts, Christ and the apostles refer them to the Holy Spirit [cf. II Peter 1:21]. It therefore follows that he who is pre-eminently the author of prophecies is truly Jehovah. Again, ᵇwhere God complains that he was provoked to anger by the stubbornness of his people, Isaiah writes that "his Holy Spirit was grieved" [Isa. 63:10 p.]. ᵉFinally, if blasphemy against the Spirit is remitted neither in this age nor in the age to come, although he who has blasphemed against the Son may obtain pardon [Matt. 12:31; Mark 3:29; Luke 12:10], by this his divine majesty, to injure or diminish which is an inexpiable crime, is openly declared. I deliberately omit many testimonies that the church fathers used. They thought it justifiable to cite from David, "By the word of the Lord the heavens were established, and all their power by the spirit of his mouth" [Ps. 33:6 p.], to prove that the universe was no less the work of the Holy Spirit than of the Son. But since it is common practice in The Psalms to repeat the same thing twice, and since in Isaiah "spirit of the mouth" means the same thing as "the word" [Isa. 11:4], that was a weak reason. Thus I have chosen to touch only a few things upon which godly minds may securely rest.

(Distinction and unity of the three Persons, 16–20)
16. Oneness

ᵉMoreover, because God more clearly disclosed himself in the coming of Christ, thus he also became known more familiarly in three persons. ᵉ⁽ᵇ/ᵃ⁾But of the many testimonies this one will suffice for us.³⁵ ᵃFor Paul so connects these three—God, faith, and baptism [Eph. 4:5]—as to reason from one to the other: namely, because faith is one, that he may thereby show God to be one; because baptism is one, that he may thence show faith also to be one. ᵇTherefore, if through baptism we are initiated into the faith and religion of one God, we must consider him into whose name we are baptized to be the true God. ᵉ⁽ᵇ⁾Indeed, there is no doubt that Christ willed by this solemn pronouncement to testify that the perfect light of faith was manifested when he said, "Baptize them into the name of the Father, and of the Son, and of the Holy Ghost" [Matt. 28:19 p.]. For this means precisely to be baptized into the name of the one God who has shown himself with complete clarity in the Father, the Son, and the Spirit. Hence it is quite clear that in God's essence reside three persons in whom one God is known.

³⁵ Cf. Luther, *Enchiridion piarum precationum* (1529) (*Werke* WA X. ii. 389).

e(a)Indeed, faith ought not to gaze hither and thither, nor to discourse of various matters, abut to look upon the one God, to unite with him, to cleave to him. From this, then, it is easily established that if there are various kinds of faith, there must also be many gods. Now because Baptism is the sacrament of faith, it confirms for us the unity of God from the fact that it is one. b(a)Hence it also follows that we are not permitted to be baptized except into the one God, because we embrace the faith of him into whose name we are baptized. What, then, did Christ mean when he commanded that Baptism should be in the name of the Father, and of the Son, and of the Holy Spirit, except that we ought with one faith to believe in the Father, the Son, and the Spirit? aWhat else is this than to testify clearly that Father, Son, and Spirit are one God? bTherefore, since that there is one God, not more, is regarded as a settled principle, we conclude that Word and Spirit are nothing else than the very essence of God. The Arians used to prate most foolishly when, in confessing the divinity of the Son, they took away the substance of God from him. A like madness tormented the Macedonians,[36] who by "Spirit" wanted to understand only those gifts of grace poured out upon men. For, as wisdom, understanding, prudence, fortitude, and fear of the Lord proceed from him, so is he the one Spirit of wisdom, prudence, fortitude, and godliness [cf. Isa. 11:2]. And he is not divided according to the distribution of gifts, but however diversely they may be divided; yet, says the apostle, he remains "one and the same" [I Cor. 12:11].

17. Threeness

bAgain, Scripture sets forth a distinction of the Father from the Word, and of the Word from the Spirit. Yet the greatness of the mystery warns us how much reverence and sobriety we ought to use in investigating this. And that passage in Gregory of Nazianzus vastly delights me:

"I cannot think on the one without quickly being encircled by the splendor of the three; nor can I discern the three without being straightway carried back to the one."[37] Let us not, then, be led to imagine a trinity of persons that keeps our thoughts distracted and does not at once lead them back to that unity. Indeed, the words "Father," "Son," and "Spirit" imply a real distinction

---

[36] Supporters of Macedonius (d. ca. 360), Semi-Arian bishop of Constantinople, who rejected the doctrine of the deity of the Holy Spirit.

[37] Gregory of Nazianzus, On Holy Baptism, oration xl. 41 (MPG 36. 418; tr. NPNF 2 ser. VII. 375). Calvin quotes the sentence in Greek and renders it into Latin.

—let no one think that these titles, whereby God is variously designated from his works, are empty—but a distinction, not a division. $^{c(b)}$The passages ^{e}that we have already cited [e.g., Zech. 13:7] $^{c(b)}$show that the Son has a character distinct from the Father, ^{e}because the Word would not have been with God unless he were another than the Father, nor would he have had his glory with the Father were he not distinct from the Father. ^{b}In like manner he distinguishes the Father from himself when he says that there is another who bears witness to him [John 5:32; 8:16; and elsewhere]. $^{b(a)}$And with this agrees what is said elsewhere: that the Father created all things through the Word [John 1:3; Heb. 11:3]. This he could not have done without being somehow distinct from the Word. Furthermore, it was not the Father who descended upon the earth, but he who went forth from the Father; the Father did not die, nor did he arise again, but rather he who had been sent by the Father. Nor did this distinction have its beginning from the time that he assumed flesh,[38] but before this also it is manifest that he was the only-begotten "in the bosom of the Father" [John 1:18]. For who would take upon himself to assert that the Son did not enter into the bosom of the Father until he descended from heaven to assume humanity? Therefore he was in the bosom of the Father before, and held his own glory in the presence of the Father [John 17:5]. Christ implies the distinction of the Holy Spirit from the Father when he says that the Holy Spirit proceeds from the Father [John 15:26; cf. ch. 14:26]. He implies the distinction of the Holy Spirit from himself as often as he calls the Spirit "another," as when he announces that he will send another Comforter [John 14:16], and often elsewhere.

18. Difference of Father, Son, and Spirit

^{b}I really do not know whether it is expedient to borrow comparisons from human affairs to express the force of this distinction. Men of old were indeed accustomed sometimes to do so, but at the same time they confessed that the analogies they advanced were quite inadequate.[39] Thus it is that I shrink from all rashness here: lest if anything should be inopportunely expressed, it may give occasion either of calumny to the malicious, or of delusion to the ignorant. Nevertheless, it is not fitting to suppress the distinction that we observe to be expressed in Scripture. It is this: to the Father is attributed the beginning of activity,[40] and the

---

[38] Servetus, De Trinitatis erroribus, fo. 7ab (tr. Wilbur, op. cit., pp. 13 f.).
[39] Cf. Augustine, Faith and the Creed ix. 17 (MPL 40. 189; tr. LCC VI. 362); On the Trinity I. i. 2, 3 (MPL 42. 820 f.; tr. NPNF III. 18).
[40] Cf. I. xiii. 25; I. xvi. 3; I. xvi. 5.

fountain and wellspring of all things; to the Son, wisdom, counsel, and the ordered disposition of all things; but to the Spirit is
assigned the power and efficacy of that activity. Indeed, although
the eternity of the Father is also the eternity of the Son and the
Spirit, since God could never exist apart from his wisdom and
power, and we must not seek in eternity a *before* or an *after*,
nevertheless the observance of an order is not meaningless or
superfluous, when the Father is thought of as first, then from him
the Son, and finally from both the Spirit. For the mind of each
human being is naturally inclined to contemplate God first, then
the wisdom coming forth from him, and lastly the power whereby
he executes the decrees of his plan. For this reason, the Son is
said to come forth from the Father alone; the Spirit, from the
Father and the Son[41] at the same time. This appears in many
passages, [b(a)]but nowhere more clearly than in chapter 8 of
Romans, where the same Spirit is indifferently called sometimes
the Spirit of Christ [v. 9], sometimes the Spirit of him "who
raised up Christ . . . from the dead" [v. 11]—[b]and not without
justification. For Peter also testifies that it was by the Spirit of
Christ that the prophets prophesied [II Peter 1:21; cf. I Peter
1:11], even though Scripture often teaches that it was the Spirit
of God the Father.

19. The relationship of Father, Son, and Spirit

[b]Furthermore, this distinction is so far from contravening the
utterly simple unity of God as to [b(a)]permit us to prove from it
that the Son is one God with the Father because he shares with
the Father one and the same Spirit; and that the Spirit is not
something other than the Father and different from the Son,
because he is the Spirit of the Father and the Son. [b]For in each
hypostasis the whole divine nature is understood, with this qualification—that to each belongs his own peculiar quality. The
Father is wholly in the Son, the Son wholly in the Father, even as
he himself declares: "I am in the Father, and the Father in me"
[John 14:10]. And ecclesiastical writers do not concede that the
one is separated from the other by any difference of essence. [c]By
these appellations which set forth the distinction (says Augustine)
is signified their mutual relationships and not the very substance
by which they are one. [b]In this sense the opinions of the ancients
are to be harmonized, which otherwise would seem somewhat to
clash. Sometimes, indeed, they teach that the Father is the beginning of the Son; sometimes they declare that the Son has both

41 *"Et Filio,"* corresponding to *"Filioque"* in the Western form of the Nicene
Creed.

divinity and essence from himself, ᶜand thus has one beginning
with the Father. Augustine well and clearly expresses the cause
of this diversity in another place, when he speaks as follows:
"Christ with respect to himself is called God; with respect to the
Father, Son. Again, the Father with respect to himself is called
God; with respect to the Son, Father. In so far as he is called
Father with respect to the Son, he is not the Son; in so far as he is
called the Son with respect to the Father, he is not the Father; in
so far as he is called both Father with respect to himself, and Son
with respect to himself, he is the same God."⁴² Therefore, when
we speak simply of the Son without regard to the Father, we well
and properly declare him to be of himself; and for this reason
we call him the sole beginning. But when we mark the relation
that he has with the Father, we rightly make the Father the beginning of the Son. ᵉThe whole fifth book of Augustine *On the
Trinity* is concerned with explaining this matter. Indeed, it is far
safer to stop with that relation which Augustine sets forth than
by too subtly penetrating into the sublime mystery to wander
through many evanescent speculations.

20. The triune God

ᵉTherefore, let those who dearly love soberness, and who will
be content with the measure of faith, receive in brief form what
is useful to know:⁴³ namely, that, when we profess to believe in
one God, under the name of God is understood a single, simple
essence, in which we comprehend three persons, or hypostases.
Therefore, whenever the name of God is mentioned without particularization, there are designated no less the Son and the Spirit
than the Father; but where the Son is joined to the Father, then
the relation of the two enters in; and so we distinguish among the
persons. But because the peculiar qualities in the persons carry
an order within them, e.g., in the Father is the beginning and
the source, so often as mention is made of the Father and the
Son together, or the Spirit, the name of *God* is peculiarly applied to the Father. In this way, unity of essence is retained, and
a reasoned order is kept, which yet takes nothing away from the
deity of the Son and the Spirit. Certainly, since we have already

⁴² Augustine, *Psalms*, Ps. 109. 13 (MPL 37. 1457; tr. NPNF [Ps. 110] VIII. 542
f.); *John's Gospel* i–v (MPL 35. 1682 f.; tr. NPNF VII. 222); *Psalms*, Ps. 68.
5 (MPL 36. 895; tr. NPNF [Ps. 69] VIII. 301).
⁴³ That the subsequent sentences in this section bear reference to the anti-
Trinitarians is evident from their resemblance to a passage in Calvin's
Response to the Questions of George Blandrata (CR IX. 325 ff.; cf. CR
XVII. 169 ff.). Cf. OS I. 134, note 1, where the date of this document is
indicated as summer, 1557.

seen that the apostles declared him to be the Son of God whom
Moses and the prophets testified to be Jehovah, it is always
necessary to come to the unity of essence. Thus we regard it a de-
testable sacrilege for the Son to be called another God than the
Father, for the simple name of God admits no relation, nor can
God be said to be this or that with respect to himself.[44]

Now, that the name of Jehovah taken without specification
corresponds to Christ is also clear from Paul's words: "Three
times I besought the Lord about this" [II Cor. 12:8]. When he
received Christ's answer, "My grace is sufficient for you," he
added a little later, "That the power of Christ may dwell in me"
[II Cor. 12:9]. For it is certain that the name "Lord" was put
there in place of "Jehovah," and thus it would be foolish and
childish so to restrict it to the person of the Mediator, seeing that
in his prayer he uses an absolute expression which introduces no
reference to the relationship of Father and Son. And we know
from the common custom of the Greeks that the apostles usually
substitute the name κύριος [Lord] for Jehovah. And to take a
ready example, Paul prayed to the Lord in no other sense than
that in which Peter cites the passage from Joel, "Whoever calls
upon the name of the Lord shall be saved" [Acts 2:21; Joel 2:32].
Where this name is expressly applied to the Son, we shall see in its
proper place that the reason is different. For the present, it is
enough to grasp that when Paul calls upon God in an absolute
sense he immediately adds the name of Christ. [e(b/a)]Even so, Christ
himself calls God in his entirety "Spirit" [John 4:24]. [b(a)]For
nothing excludes the view that the whole essence of God is spiritual, in which are comprehended Father, Son, and Spirit. This
is made plain from Scripture. For as we there hear God called
Spirit, so also do we hear the Holy Spirit, seeing that the Spirit is a
hypostasis of the whole essence, spoken of as of God and from
God.

(*Refutation of anti-Trinitarian heresies, 21–29*)
21. The ground of all heresy: a warning to all
[b(a)]Moreover, Satan, in order to tear our faith from its very
roots, has always been instigating great battles, partly concerning
the divine essence of the Son and the Spirit, partly concerning
the distinction of the persons. He has during nearly all ages stirred
up ungodly spirits to harry orthodox teachers over this matter
[e]and today also is trying to kindle a new fire from the old embers.
For these reasons, it is important here to resist the perverse ravings
of certain persons. [e(b/a)]Hitherto it has been my particular intention

[44] CR XVII. 169 ff.

to lead by the hand those who are teachable, but not to strive hand to hand with the inflexible and the contentious. But now the truth which has been peaceably shown must be maintained against all the calumnies of the wicked. b(a)And yet I will exert especial effort to the end that they who lend ready and open ears to God's Word may have a firm standing ground. bHere, indeed, if anywhere in the secret mysteries of Scripture, we ought to play the philosopher soberly and with great moderation; let us use great caution that neither our thoughts nor our speech go beyond the limits to which the Word of God itself extends. For how can the human mind measure off the measureless essence of God according to its own little measure,[45] a mind as yet unable to establish for certain the nature of the sun's body, though men's eyes daily gaze upon it? Indeed, how can the mind by its own leading come to search out God's essence when it cannot even get to its own? Let us then willingly leave to God the knowledge of himself. For, as Hilary says, he is the one fit witness to himself, and is not known except through himself.[46] But we shall be "leaving it to him" if we conceive him to be as he reveals himself to us, without inquiring about him elsewhere than from his Word. On this question there are extant five homilies of Chrysostom *Against the Anomoeans;*[47] yet not even these could restrain the presumptuous Sophists from giving their stuttering tongues free rein. For in this matter they have behaved no more modestly than they usually do everywhere. We ought to be warned by the unhappy outcome of this presumption so that we may take care to apply ourselves to this question with teachableness rather than with subtlety. And let us not take it into our heads either to seek out God anywhere else than in his Sacred Word, or to think anything about him that is not prompted by his Word, or to speak anything that is not taken from that Word. c(b)But if some distinction does exist in the one divinity of Father, Son, and Spirit—something hard to grasp—and occasions to certain minds more difficulty and trouble than is expedient, elet it be remembered that men's minds, when they indulge their curiosity, enter into a labyrinth.[48] And so let them yield themselves to be

---

[45] Cf. I. v. 7.

[46] Hilary, *On the Trinity* I. xviii (MPL 10. 38; tr. NPNF 2 ser. IX. 45). The sentences, "For how . . . his Word" are quoted by K. Barth (*Kirchliche Dogmatik* I. i. 317; tr. G. T. Thomson, *The Doctrine of the Word of God* I. 345).

[47] Chrysostom, *Homiliae de incomprehensibili Dei natura, contra Anomoeos* v. 7 (MPG 48. 745 ff.). The Anomoeans taught, as the name suggests, the *unlikeness* of the Father and the Son.

[48] Cf. I. v. 12, note 36.

ruled by the heavenly oracles, even though they may fail to capture the height of the mystery.

22. *Servetus' contention against the Trinity*

ᶜTo frame a catalogue of the errors with which the sincerity of the faith was once assailed on this head of doctrine would be too long and needlessly irksome. And very many of the heretics with brutish ravings, seeking to overthrow the whole glory of God, have thought it enough to alarm and confuse the uninstructed. Presently, indeed, from a few men there have boiled up several sects, which partly tore asunder God's essence, partly confused the distinction that exists between the persons. Indeed, if we hold fast to what has been sufficiently shown above from Scripture —that the essence of the one God is simple and undivided, and that it belongs to the Father, the Son, and the Spirit; and on the other hand that by a certain characteristic the Father differs from the Son, and the Son from the Spirit—the gate will be closed not only to Arius and Sabellius but to other ancient authors of errors.

But because in our own day there have arisen certain frenzied persons, such as Servetus and his like, who have entangled everything with new deceptions, it is of importance to discuss their fallacies in a few words. For Servetus the name "Trinity" was so utterly hateful and detestable that he commonly labeled all those whom he called Trinitarians as atheists.[49] I pass over the senseless words that he thought up to rail at them. This, indeed, was the sum of his speculations: God is assumed to be tripartite when three persons are said to reside in his essence; this is an imaginary triad, because it clashes with God's unity. Meanwhile, he would hold the persons to be certain external ideas which do not truly subsist in God's essence, but represent God to us in one manifestation or another. In the beginning there was no distinction in God, because the Word and the Spirit were formerly one and the same: but when Christ came forth as God from God, the Spirit pro-

---

[49] Calvin seems to have been surprised by Servetus' application of the word "Trinitarian" to him and to other defenders of the received doctrine of the Trinity. This occurs frequently in *Christianismi restitutio, De Trinitate* I. For Servetus' statement, *"Athei vere sunt trinitarii omnes,"* see p. 31 of that work. I am indebted to Mr. Chalmers McCormick for the information that in his studies of John Campanus (ca. 1500–1575) he finds evidence of the use of the word *trinitarii* for *opponents* of the orthodox doctrine. This is indicated, for instance, in J. G. Schelhorn's quotations from George Witzel of a text not later than 1537 (*Amoenitates literaria* XI [1729]. 32–42). Cf. G. Richter, *Die Schriften Georg Witzels*, p. 183. Thus Servetus was reversing the meaning of *trinitarius* as it had been bandied in recent disputation. Perhaps its older use in the title of a monastic order (1197) was not forgotten.

ceeded from him as another God. But even though he sometimes colors his absurdities with allegories, as when he says that the eternal Word of God was the Spirit of Christ with God and the refulgence of his idea, and that the Spirit was the shadow of deity, yet afterward he annihilates the deity of both, declaring that as God metes out according to his dispensation there is a part of God both in the Son and in the Spirit, just as the same Spirit, being substantially in us and also in wood and stone, is a portion of God. We will see in its proper place what he babbles concerning the person of the Mediator. Indeed, this monstrous fabrication, that "person" is nothing else than a visible manifestation of the glory of God, needs no long refutation. For although John affirms that the Word[50] was God when the universe was as yet not created, he utterly distinguishes Word from idea [John 1:1]. If then, also, that Word who was God from farthest eternity both was with the Father and had his own glory with the Father [John 17:5], surely he could not have been an outward or figurative splendor, but of necessity it follows that he was a hypostasis that resided in God himself.

Moreover, although no mention is made of the Spirit except in the history of the creation of the universe, nevertheless the Spirit is introduced here, not as a shadow, but as the essential power of God, when Moses tells that the as yet formless mass was itself sustained in him [Gen. 1:2]. Therefore it then has become clear that the eternal Spirit had always been in God, while with tender care he supported the confused matter of heaven and earth, until beauty and order were added. Surely there could not yet be a likeness or representation of God, as Servetus dreams. Elsewhere, indeed, he is forced to disclose more openly his impious notion that God, by decreeing through his eternal reason a Son visible to himself, in this way showed himself visibly. For if this be true, no other divinity is left to Christ, except in so far as the Son has been ordained by God's eternal decree. Besides this, he so transforms those specters which he posits in place of hypostases that he does not hesitate falsely to attach new accidental qualities to God. Indeed, to be execrated far beyond all else is the fact that he indiscriminately mingles both the Son of God and the Spirit with created beings generally. For he publicly declares that in the essence of God there are parts and divisions, each portion of which is God: indeed, he particularly states that the spirits of believers are coeternal and consubstantial with God, although he elsewhere assigns a substantial deity not only to the soul of man but to other created things.

50 "λόγος."

23. *The Son is God even as the Father*

eFrom this morass another similar monster has come forth.[51] For certain rascals, to escape the invidiousness and shame of Servetus' impiety, indeed confessed that there are three persons; but they added the provision that the Father, who is truly and properly the sole God, in forming the Son and the Spirit, infused into them his own deity. Indeed, they do not refrain from this dreadful manner of speaking: the Father is distinguished from the Son and the Spirit by this mark, that he is the only "essence giver."[52] First they allege the specious argument that Christ is commonly called the Son of God and infer from this that no other than the Father is, properly speaking, God. Yet they do not observe that, even though the name "God" is also common to the Son, it is sometimes applied to the Father par excellence[53] because he is the fountainhead and beginning of deity—and this is done to denote the simple unity of essence.

They object: if he is truly the Son of God, it is absurd to think of him as the Son of a person. I reply that both are true: that is, he is the Son of God, because the Word was begotten by the Father before all ages [cf. I Cor. 2:7] (for we do not yet have occasion to mention the person of the Mediator); and yet for the sake of clarification we must have regard to the person, so as not to take the name of God here without qualification, but as used of the Father. For if we consider no one but the Father to be God, we definitely cast the Son down from this rank. Therefore whenever mention is made of deity, we ought by no means to admit any antithesis between Son and Father, as if the name of the true God applied to the latter alone. For of course the God who manifested himself to Isaiah [Isa. 6:1] was the true and only God, the God whom nevertheless John affirms to have been Christ [John 12:41]. He who also through the mouth of Isaiah testified that he would be as a stone of stumbling for the Jews [Isa. 8:14] was the only God, whom Paul declared to have been Christ [Rom. 9:33]. When through Isaiah he proclaims, "I live" [Isa. 49:18]: "to me every knee shall bow" [Rom. 14:11, Vg.; cf. Isa. 45:24, Vg.], he is the sole God; yet Paul interprets the same to be Christ [Rom. 14:11]. To this are added the testimonies that the apostle puts forward: "Thou, O God, hast founded heaven and earth" [Heb. 1:10; Ps.

51 Valentine Gentile is meant. The documents for Gentile's trial in Geneva have been edited by H. Fazy: *Procès de Valentin Gentilis et de Nicolas Gallo (1555)*. The essential materials are in CR IX.
52 "*Essentiator*." Cf. Gentile's second confession, August, 1558, CR IX. 393 f. For a brief account of the circumstances, see J. Mackinnon, *Calvin and the Reformation*, pp. 166 f.
53 "κατ᾽ ἐξοχήν."

102:25–26]. Likewise: "Let all the angels of God adore him." [Heb. 1:6; Ps. 97:7.] These things are appropriate only to the sole God: nevertheless, he contends that they are proper titles of Christ. And there is no value in the subtle distinction that what is proper to God is transferred to Christ, because he is the splendor of his glory [Heb. 1:3]. For, since the name of Jehovah is set forth everywhere, it follows that with respect to his deity his being is from himself. For if he is Jehovah, it cannot be denied that he is that same God who elsewhere proclaims through Isaiah, "I, I am, and apart from me there is no God" [Isa. 44:6 p.]. Jeremiah's utterance also bears considering: "The gods who did not make heaven and earth shall perish from the earth which is under heaven" [Jer. 10: 11 p.].

On the other hand, it will be necessary to admit that the Son of God is he whose deity is quite often proved in Isaiah from the creation of the universe. But how will the Creator, who gives being to all, not have being from himself, but borrow his essence from elsewhere? For whoever says that the Son has been given his essence from the Father denies that he has being from himself. But the Holy Spirit gives the lie to this, naming him "Jehovah." Now if we concede that all essence is in the Father alone, either it will become divisible or be taken away from the Son. And thus deprived of his essence, he will be God in name only. The essence of God, if these babblers are to be believed, belongs to the Father only, inasmuch as he alone is, and is the essence giver of the Son. Thus the divinity of the Son will be something abstracted from God's essence, or a part derived from the whole.

Now they are compelled from their own presupposition to concede that the Spirit is of the Father alone, because if he is a derivation from the primal essence, which is proper only to the Father, he will not rightly be considered the Spirit of the Son. Yet this is disproved by Paul's testimony, where he makes the Spirit common to Christ and the Father [Rom. 8:9]. Furthermore, if the person of the Father is expunged from the Trinity, in what respect would he differ from the Son and the Spirit except that only he is God himself? They confess Christ to be God, and yet to differ from the Father. Conversely, there must be some mark of differentiation in order that the Father may not be the Son. Those who locate that mark in the essence clearly annihilate Christ's true deity, which without essence, and indeed the whole essence, cannot exist. Certainly the Father would not differ from the Son unless he had in himself something unique, which was not shared with the Son. Now what can they find to distinguish him? If the distinction is in the essence, let them answer whether or not he has shared it with the Son. Indeed, this could not be done in part because it would be wicked to fashion a half-God. Besides, in this way they would basely tear apart the essence of God. It remains that the essence is wholly and perfectly common to Father and Son. If this is true, then there is indeed with respect to the essence no distinction of one from the other. If they make rejoinder that the Father in bestowing essence nonetheless remains the sole God, in whom the essence is, Christ then will be a figurative God, a God in appearance and name only, not in reality itself. For there is nothing more proper to God than to be, according to that saying, "He who is has sent me to you" [Ex. 3:14, Vg.].

24. The name "God" in Scripture does not refer to the Father alone

ᵉFrom many passages one can readily refute as false their assumption that any unqualified reference to God in Scripture applies to the Father alone. In the very passages that they cite on their own side they shamelessly disclose their thoughtlessness, for the name of the Son is in these set beside that of the Father. From this it appears that the name of God is understood in a relative sense, and is therefore to be restricted to the person of the Father. Thus their objection, "Unless the Father alone were truly God, he would be his own Father," is removed with one word. Nor, indeed, is it absurd for him who not only has begotten his own wisdom from himself but is also the God of the Mediator, as I shall treat more fully in its proper place,[54] to be specially called God on account of degree and rank. For from the time that Christ was manifested in the flesh, he has been called the Son of God, not only in that he was the eternal Word begotten before all ages from the Father, but because he took upon himself the person and office of the Mediator, that he might join us to God. And since they so brazenly exclude the Son from the honor of God, I should like to know, when he declares that no one is good except the one God [Matt 19:17], whether he deprives himself of goodness. I am not speaking of his human nature, lest they counter that whatever good there was in it flowed from a free gift. I ask whether the eternal Word of God is good or not. If they deny it, their impiety stands sufficiently convicted; by admitting it, they cut their own throats. But the fact that at first glance Christ seems to put away from himself the name of "good" all the more confirms our contention. Surely, since it is the singular title of the one God, when as he was greeted as "good" in the common manner of speaking, Christ repudiated

[54] II. xii ff.

the false honor, and so admonished them that the goodness with which he was endowed was divine.

I also ask, when Paul affirmed that God alone is immortal [I Tim. 1:17], wise [Rom. 16:27], and true [Rom. 3:4], whether by these words Christ is reduced to the level of stupid and false mortals. Will he not therefore be immortal who from the beginning was life to confer immortality upon the angels? Will he not be wise who is God's eternal wisdom? Will he not be true who is truth itself? Furthermore, I ask whether they think Christ ought to be worshiped or not. For if he rightly claimed for himself that every knee should bow before him [Phil. 2:10], it follows that he is the God who in the law forbade anyone else than himself to be worshiped [Ex. 20:3]. If they mean to be understood of the Father alone what is said in Isaiah, "I am, and there is none beside me" [Isa. 44:6 p.], I turn this testimony back upon them, when we see that whatever is of God is attributed to Christ. Nor is there any place for their subtle distinction that Christ was exalted in the flesh in which he had been humbled, and in respect to the flesh all power has been given to him in heaven and on earth. For even though the majesty of King and Judge is extended to the whole person of the Mediator, yet unless he had been God manifested in the flesh he could not have been raised to such a height without God himself striving against himself. And Paul best settles this controversy, teaching that he was equal to God before he humbled himself under the form of a servant [Phil. 2:6–7]. Indeed, how would this equality stand had he not been the God whose name is Jah and Jehovah, who rides above the cherubim [cf. Ps. 17:10; 79:2; 98:1, all Vg.], who is King of the whole earth [Ps. 46:8, Vg.], and King of the ages? Now no matter how they grumble they cannot take away from Christ what Isaiah says elsewhere: "He, he is our God; we have waited for him" [Isa. 25:9 p.]. With these words he describes the coming of God the Redeemer who not only led the people back from the Babylonian exile but fully restored the church to all its numbers.

And they will not benefit at all by another evasion, that Christ was God in his Father. For even though we admit that in respect to order and degree the beginning of divinity is in the Father, yet we say that it is a detestable invention that essence is proper to the Father alone, as if he were the deifier of the Son. For in this way either essence would be manifold or they call Christ "God" in title and imagination only. If they grant that the Son is God, but second to the Father, then in him will be begotten and formed the essence that is in the Father unbegotten and unformed. e(b/a)I know that many censorious persons laugh at us for deriving the distinction of the persons from Moses' words, where he introduces God as speaking thus: "Let us make man in our own image" [Gen. 1: 26]; yet pious readers see how uselessly and absurdly Moses would have introduced this conversation, so to speak, if not more than one person subsisted in the one God. It is certain that those whom the Father is addressing were uncreated; but there is nothing uncreated except God himself, and he is one. Now therefore unless they grant that the power of creating was common to the Father, the Son, and the Spirit, common also the authority to command, it will follow that God did not speak thus within himself, but addressed other outside artificers. ᵉFinally, one passage easily rids us at once of two of their objections. For what Christ himself declared, that "God is Spirit" [John 4:24], would not be appropriately restricted to the Father alone, as if the Word were not himself of a spiritual nature. But if the name "Spirit" fits the Son equally with the Father, I conclude that the Son is to be comprehended under the unparticularized name "God." Nevertheless he adds immediately after[55] that no one else but those who worship the Father in spirit and in truth prove themselves to be worshipers of the Father [John 4:23]. From this follows the other point: since Christ exercises the office of Teacher under the Head [the Father], he ascribes to the Father the name of God, not to abolish his own deity, but to raise us up to it by degrees.   *athanasius*

25. *The divine nature is common to all three Persons*

ᵉBut they are obviously deceived in this connection, for they dream of individuals, each having its own separate part of the essence. Yet we teach from the Scriptures that God is one in essence, and hence that the essence both of the Son and of the Spirit is unbegotten; but inasmuch as the Father is first in order, and from himself begot his wisdom, as has just been said,[56] he is rightly deemed the beginning and fountainhead of the whole of divinity. Thus God without particularization is unbegotten; and the Father also in respect to his person is unbegotten. They also foolishly think they may conclude from our statement that we have set up a quaternity, for they falsely and calumniously ascribe this fiction of their own brain to us, as if we pretended that three persons came forth by derivation from one essence. On the contrary, it is clear from our writings that we do not separate the persons from the essence, but we distinguish among them while they remain

---

[55] By an inadvertence, the order of John 4:23 and 24 is reversed.
[56] Cf. I. xiii. 18, note 40; I. xiii. 28, note 65; I. xvi. 3, note 6; I. xvi. 5, note 12. In a critical discussion of the orthodox doctrine, C. C. Richardson uses for illustration secs. 24 and 25 here: *The Doctrine of the Trinity*, pp. 58 f.

within it. If the persons had been separate from the essence, the reasoning of these men might have been probable; but in this way there would have been a trinity of gods, not of persons whom the one God contains in himself.

Thus is their useless question answered: whether or not the essence co-operates in producing the Trinity, as if we imagined that three gods descend from it.[57] Their rejoinder that if not, the Trinity would therefore be without God, is born of the same foolishness. For although the essence does not enter into the distinction as a part or a member of the Trinity, nevertheless the persons are not without it, or outside it; because the Father, unless he were God, could not have been the Father; and the Son could not have been the Son, unless he were God. Therefore we say that deity in an absolute sense exists of itself; whence likewise we confess that the Son since he is God, exists of himself, but not in respect of his Person; indeed, since he is the Son, we say that he exists from the Father. Thus his essence is without beginning; while the beginning of his person is God himself. Those orthodox writers who formerly spoke concerning the Trinity applied this name only to the persons, since it would have been not only an absurd error but even the sheerest impiety to embrace the essence in this distinction. For those who want to make a Trinity of these three— Essence, Son, and Spirit—are plainly annihilating the essence of the Son and the Spirit; otherwise the parts joined together would fall apart, and this is faulty in any distinction. Finally, if Father and God were synonymous, thus would the Father be the deifier; nothing would be left in the Son but a shadow; and the Trinity would be nothing else but the conjunction of the one God with two created things.

26. *The subordination of the incarnate Word to the Father is no counterevidence*

eThey object that Christ, if he be properly God, is wrongly called Son. To this I have replied[58] that when a comparison of one person is made with another, the name of God is not to be taken without particularization, but restricted to the Father, seeing that he is the beginning of deity, not in the bestowing of essence, as fanatics babble, but by reason of order. In this sense is to be understood that saying of Christ to the Father, "This is eternal life, that they believe thee to be the one true God, and Jesus Christ whom thou

---

[57] Gentile, in *Epistola* 5 (CR IX. 390 f.; Fazy, *op. cit.*, pp. 65 f.). Vincent of Lérins charges Nestorius with teaching a "quaternity": *Commonitory* xvi (MPL 50. 659; tr. LCC IX. 59).

[58] I. xiii. 20, 23.

hast sent" [John 17:3 p.]. For speaking in the person of the Mediator, he holds a middle rank between God and man; yet his majesty is not on this account diminished. For even though he emptied himself [Phil. 2:7], he lost not his glory with the Father which was hidden to the world. Thus the apostle in Heb., ch. 2, although he admits that Christ was for a short time abased beneath the angels [vs. 7, 9], does not hesitate at the same time to declare him to be the everlasting God who founded the earth [ch. 1:10].

Therefore we must hold that, as often as Christ in this person of Mediator addresses God, under this name of God is included his deity, which is also Christ's. Thus when he said to the apostles, "It is expedient that I go up to the Father" [John 16:7; cf. ch. 20:17] "because the Father is greater than I" [ch. 14:28, Vg.], he does not attribute to himself merely a secondary deity so that he is inferior to the Father with respect to eternal essence; but because endowed with heavenly glory he gathers believers into participation in the Father. He places the Father in the higher rank, seeing that the bright perfection of splendor that appears in heaven differs from that measure of glory which was seen in him when he was clothed with flesh. With the same intent, Paul elsewhere says that Christ "shall deliver up the Kingdom to the God and Father" [I Cor. 15: 24], "that God may be all in all" [I Cor. 15:28]. Nothing is more absurd than to deny that Christ's deity is everlasting. But if he will never cease to be the Son of God, but will ever remain the same as he was from the beginning, it follows that there is comprehended under the name of "Father" the unique essence of God which is common to both. And certainly for this reason Christ descended to us, to bear us up to the Father, and at the same time to bear us up to himself, inasmuch as he is one with the Father. Therefore to restrict the name "God" to the Father, to the exclusion of the Son, is neither lawful nor right. On this account, also, John indeed declares him to be the true God [John 1:1; I John 5:20] lest anyone think of placing him in a second rank of deity beneath the Father. Moreover, I wonder what these makers of new gods mean when, having confessed Christ as true God, they immediately exclude him from the deity of the Father. As if he could be true God and not be one God, and as if a divinity transfused were anything but a newfangled fiction!

27. Our adversaries falsely appeal to Irenaeus

ᵉThey pile up many passages from Irenaeus,[59] where he declares the Father of Christ to be the sole and eternal God of Israel. This is either shameful ignorance or consummate depravity. For they

59 Irenaeus, *Against Heresies* III. vi. 4 (MPG 7. 863; tr. ANF I. 419).

ought to have considered that that saintly man was dealing and contending with fanatics who denied that the Father of Christ was that same God who had of old spoken through Moses and the prophets, but fancied a sort of specter produced from the corruption of the world. Therefore he is wholly concerned with this point: to make it plain that no other God is proclaimed in Scripture than the Father of Christ, and that it is wrong to imagine another. Hence it is no wonder he so often concludes that there was no other God of Israel than he who is celebrated by Christ and the apostles. So also now, when we must resist another sort of error, we shall truly say: the God who of old appeared to the patriarchs was no other than Christ. Indeed, if anyone objects that it was in fact the Father, our reply will be ready: while we contend for the divinity of the Son, we do not at all exclude the Father. If the readers were to pay attention to this advice of Irenaeus, all contention would cease. In Chapter 6 of Book 3 all strife is easily brought to naught, where the godly man insists on this one thing, "that he who in Scripture is called God in an absolute and undifferentiated sense is in truth the only God, and that Christ indeed is called God in an absolute sense." Let us remember that this was the basis of his argument, as is clear from the whole drift, and especially in Book 2, Chapter 46: that he is not called Father enigmatically and parabolically.

Besides this, he elsewhere contends that both the Son and the Father were jointly declared to be God by the prophets and the apostles [Book 3, Chapter 9]. Afterward he defines how Christ, who is Lord over all things, and King, and God, and Judge, received power from him who is God of all things, namely, in respect to subjection in that he was humbled even to death on the cross [Book 3, Chapter 12]. Moreover, a little later he affirms that the Son was the Maker of heaven and earth, who gave the law through the hand of Moses, and appeared to the patriarchs. Now if anyone prates that for Irenaeus the Father alone was the God of Israel, I shall turn back upon him what the same writer openly teaches, that Christ is one and the same, just as the prophecy of Habakkuk also refers to him: "God will come from the south" [Hab. 3:3, Vg.] [Book 3, Chapters 18 and 23]. To the same end pertains what is read in Book 4, Chapter 9. Christ himself, therefore, is God with the Father of the living. And in Chapter 12 of the same book he explains that Abraham believed in God, because the Maker of heaven and earth, and the sole God, is Christ.[60]

[60] Irenaeus, *op. cit.* (in order of reference), III. vi. 1; II. xxvii. 2; III. ix. 1; III. xii. 13; III. xv. 3; III. xx. 4; IV. v. 2–3 (MPG 7. 860, 803, 868 f., 907, 919, 945, 984 f.; tr. ANF I. 418, 398, 422, 435, 440, 451, 467).

28. The appeal to Tertullian also is of no avail

ᵉNot a whit more truthfully do they adopt Tertullian as their advocate; for even if he is sometimes rough and thorny in his mode of speech, yet he not ambiguously hands on the sum of the doctrine that we defend. In his view, although God is one, his Word exists by dispensation or economy; God is one in unity of substance, and nonetheless the unity is disposed into a trinity by the mystery of dispensation. There are thus three, not in status, but in degree; not in substance, but in form; not in power, but in its manifestation. He says, indeed, that he retains the Son as second to the Father, but he understands him to be not different except by way of distinction. Elsewhere he speaks of the Son as visible; but after he has argued both sides of the question, he decides that he is invisible in so far as he is the Word. Finally, affirming that the Father is determined by his own person, Tertullian proves himself far removed from that fabrication which we are refuting. And although he recognizes no other God than the Father, nevertheless, explaining himself in the next passage, he shows that he is not speaking exclusively with respect to the Son, because he denies that there is another God than the Father, and thus his monarchy is not broken by distinction of person. And from his unwavering purpose one can readily gather the meaning of his words. For he contends against Praxeas that although God is distinguished into three persons, yet this does not make more than one God, nor is his unity sundered. And because according to Praxeas' fabrication Christ could not be God without being the same as the Father, he therefore toils mightily over this distinction. That he, indeed, calls the Word and the Spirit a portion of the whole, even though it is a hard saying, is yet excusable, seeing that it is not applied to substance, but merely marks the disposition and economy that has to do with the persons alone, as Tertullian himself testifies. Upon this also hangs his statement: "How many persons, O most wicked Praxeas, do you think there are, unless there be as many as there are names?" Thus, also, a little later: "That they may believe the Father and the Son each in their names and persons."[61] By these references I think I have been able sufficiently to refute the impudence of those who try from Tertullian's authority to deceive the simple.

[61] Tertullian, *Against Praxeas* (in order of reference), ii, vii, ix, xiv, xviii, xx, iii, i, ii, xi, ix, xxvi (MPL 2. 157, 162 ff., 174, 177, 179, 154 ff., 166 f., 164, 189 f.; also in CCL Tertullianus II. 1159–1196; tr. ANF III. 598, 601 f., 603 f., 609, 613, 610 f., 599, 597, 598, 608 f., 603 f., 622). E. Evans, *Tertullian's Treatise Against Praxeas*, has critical text of these sections, pp. 89–123, translation, pp. 130–172.

*29. All acknowledged doctors of the church confirm the doctrine
of the Trinity*

eAnd certainly anyone who diligently compares the writings of
the ancients among themselves will find in Irenaeus nothing else
than what his successors set forth. Justin is one of the earliest, yet
he supports us at every point.[62] They will object that both by him
and by the rest the Father of Christ is called the one God. Hilary
also teaches the same thing, indeed speaks more sharply, that
eternity is in the Father.[63] Is that to deprive the Son of the divine
essence? Yet he is wholly concerned with the defense of the very
faith to which we adhere. Our enemies, however, are not ashamed
to pluck out any kind of mutilated utterances, from which they
would have us believe that Hilary is the patron of their error!

With regard to their citation of Ignatius, if they want it to have
any weight, let them prove that the apostles made a law concerning
Lent and like corruptions. Nothing is more disgusting than those
vile absurdities which have been put forth under the name of
Ignatius.[64] Even less tolerable is the shamelessness of those who
cover themselves with such masks in order to deceive. Indeed, the
agreement of the ancients is clearly seen here, that in the Council
of Nicaea, Arius dared not make a pretense on the basis of the
authority of any proved writer; and no one of the Greeks or the
Latins excuses himself for disagreeing with those before him. We
need say nothing of how carefully Augustine (toward whom these
rascals are most hostile) searched the writings of all, and how
reverently he embraced them. To be sure, in some small details
he was accustomed to show why he was compelled to depart from
them. Even in this argument, if he read anything ambiguous or
obscure among other writers, he does not hide it. Nevertheless,
he takes for granted the doctrine these men are attacking, as received without controversy from the earliest times.[65] Yet from a
single word it is clear that what others had taught before was not

---

[62] Justin, *Apology* I. vi, xiii; tr. ANF I. 164, 166 f.; cited by Servetus, *Christianismi restitutio, De Trinitate* I, p. 33.

[63] Hilary, *On the Trinity* I. v; II. vi (MPL 10. 28, 55; tr. NPNF 2 ser. IX.
41, 53).

[64] The canon of Ignatius' letters was not determined until the nineteenth
century. Numerous spurious epistles were ascribed to him by Jacques
Lefèvre in an edition of 1498. These are translated from W. Cureton's
Corpus Ignatianum (1849) in ANF I. The spurious letter to the Philippians
contains (ch. xiii) the injunction, "Despise not the period of forty days"
(Cureton, p. 155; tr. ANF I. 119; cf. LCC I. 81 ff.; OS III. 150, notes 6, 7).

[65] Augustine, *On the Trinity* I. iv. 7; VI (MPL 42. 824, 923–932; tr. NPNF
III. 20, 97–103); *On Nature and Grace* lxi. 71–lxvi. 79 (MPL 44. 282–286;
tr. NPNF V. 146–149); *Against Julian* II. i.1–II. ix. 32 (MPL 44. 671–696;
tr. FC 35. 55–96).

unknown to him, when in Book 1, *Christian Doctrine,* he says that unity is in the Father. Will they chatter about his then forgetting himself? Yet elsewhere he clears himself of this calumny, where he calls the Father the beginning of all deity because he is from no one; and wisely considers that the name of God is especially ascribed to the Father because if the beginning comes not from him, the simple unity of God cannot be conceived.[66]

Now, the godly reader will, I hope, recognize that these words refute all the chicaneries by which Satan has heretofore tried to pervert or darken the pure faith of doctrine. Finally, I trust that the whole sum of this doctrine has been faithfully explained, if my readers will impose a limit upon their curiosity, and not seek out for themselves more eagerly than is proper troublesome and perplexed disputations. For I suspect that those who intemperately delight in speculation will not be at all satisfied. Certainly I have not shrewdly omitted anything that I might think to be against me: but while I am zealous for the edification of the church, I felt that I would be better advised not to touch upon many things that would profit but little, and would burden my readers with useless trouble. For what is the point in disputing whether the Father always begets? Indeed, it is foolish to imagine a continuous act of begetting, since it is clear that three persons have subsisted in God from eternity.[67]

ᶜCHAPTER XIV

EVEN IN THE CREATION OF THE UNIVERSE AND OF ALL THINGS, SCRIPTURE BY UNMISTAKABLE MARKS DISTINGUISHES THE TRUE GOD FROM FALSE GODS

(Creation of the world and of man, 1–2)
1. We cannot and should not go behind God's act of creation in our speculation
ᵉIsaiah rightly charges the worshipers of false gods with obtuse-

---

[66] "To all three belong the same eternity . . . the same power. In the Father is unity, in the Son equality, in the Holy Spirit the harmony of unity and equality." Augustine, *On Christian Doctrine* I. v (MPL 34. 21; tr. NPNF II. 524). Again, noting that Christ said, not "whom the Father will send" but "whom I shall send to you from the Father" (John 15:26), Augustine states that while the Persons of the Trinity are equal, the Father is the *principium totius deitatis,* the beginning of the whole deity. *On the Trinity* IV. xx. 29 (MPL 42. 908; tr. NPNF III. 85 [see there note 6]).

[67] Lombard discusses the question "Whether the Son is always begotten" in *Sentences* I. ix. 10–15, citing the opinions of Gregory, Origen, and Hilary (MPL 192. 547 ff.).

ness, because they have not learned from the foundations of the earth and the circle of the heavens who is the true God [Isa. 40: 21; cf. v. 22; see Comm.]. Despite this, such is the slowness and dullness of our wit that, to prevent believers from deserting to the fabrications of the heathen, we must depict the true God more distinctly than they do. Since the notion of God as the mind of the universe[1] (in the philosophers' eyes, a most acceptable description) is ephemeral, it is important for us to know him more intimately, lest we always waver in doubt. Therefore it was his will that the history of Creation be made manifest, in order that the faith of the church, resting upon this, might seek no other God but him who was put forth by Moses as the Maker and Founder of the universe.

Therein time was first marked so that by a continuing succession of years believers might arrive at the primal source of the human race and of all things. This knowledge is especially useful not only to resist the monstrous fables that formerly were in vogue in Egypt and in other regions of the earth, but also that, once the beginning of the universe is known, God's eternity may shine forth more clearly, and we may be more rapt in wonder at it. And indeed, that impious scoff ought not to move us: that it is a wonder how it did not enter God's mind sooner to found heaven and earth, but that he idly permitted an immeasurable time to pass away, since he could have made it very many millenniums earlier, albeit the duration of the world, now declining to its ultimate end, has not yet attained six thousand years. For it is neither lawful nor expedient for us to inquire why God delayed so long, because if the human mind strives to penetrate thus far, it will fail a hundred times on the way. And it would not even be useful for us to know what God himself, to test our moderation of faith, on purpose willed to be hidden. When a certain shameless fellow mockingly asked a pious old man what God had done before the creation of the world, the latter aptly countered that he had been building hell for the curious.[2]

Let this admonition, no less grave than severe, restrain the wantonness that tickles many and even drives them to wicked and hurtful speculations. In short, let us remember that that invisible God, whose wisdom, power, and righteousness are incomprehensible, sets before us Moses' history as a mirror in which his living likeness glows. For just as eyes, when dimmed with age or weakness or by some other defect, unless aided by spectacles, discern nothing

---

[1] Cf. I. v. 5 and Cicero, *Nature of the Gods* I. xiii. 33 (LCL edition, pp. 34–35).

[2] Augustine, *Confessions* XI. xii (MPL 32. 815; tr. LCC VII. 253).

distinctly; so, such is our feebleness, unless Scripture guides us in seeking God, we are immediately confused.[3] They who, indeed, indulge their own wantonness, since they are now warned in vain, will feel too late by a dreadful ruin how much better it would have been for them reverently to accept God's secret purposes than to belch forth blasphemies by which to obscure heaven. And Augustine rightly complains that wrong is done to God when a higher cause of things than his will is demanded.[4] Elsewhere the same man wisely warns that it is no less wrong to raise questions concerning immeasurable stretches of time than of space.[5] Indeed, however widely the circuit of the heavens extends, it still has some limit. Now if anyone should expostulate with God that the void exceeds the heavens a hundredfold, would not this impudence be detestable to all the godly? Into such madness leap those who carp at God's idleness because he did not in accord with their judgment establish the universe innumerable ages before. To gratify their curiosity, they strive to go forth outside the world. As if in the vast circle of heaven and earth enough things do not present themselves to engross all our senses with their incomprehensible brightness! As if within six thousand years God has not shown evidences enough on which to exercise our minds in earnest meditation! Therefore let us willingly remain enclosed within these bounds to which God has willed to confine us, and as it were, to pen up our minds that they may not, through their very freedom to wander, go astray.

2. *The work of the six days shows God's goodness toward men*

ᶜWith the same intent Moses relates that God's work was completed not in a moment but in six days [Gen. 2:2]. For by this circumstance we are drawn away from all fictions to the one God who distributed his work into six days that we might not find it irksome to occupy our whole life in contemplating it. For even though our eyes, in whatever direction they may turn, are compelled to gaze upon God's works, yet we see how changeable is our attention, and how swiftly are dissipated any godly thoughts that may touch us. Here also, until human reason is subjected to the obedience of faith and learns to cultivate that quiet to which the sanctification of the seventh day invites us, it grumbles, as if such proceedings were foreign to God's power. But we ought in the very order of things diligently to contemplate God's fatherly

---

[3] Cf. I. v. 12, 15 and the "spectacles" illustration in I. vi. 1.
[4] Augustine, *On Genesis, Against the Manichees* I. ii. 4 (MPL 34. 175).
[5] Augustine, *City of God* XI. v (MPL 41. 320; tr. NPNF II. 207).

love toward mankind,[6] in that he did not create Adam until he had lavished upon the universe all manner of good things. For if he had put him in an earth as yet sterile and empty, if he had given him life before light, he would have seemed to provide insufficiently for his welfare. Now when he disposed the movements of the sun and stars to human uses, filled the earth, waters, and air with living things, and brought forth an abundance of fruits to suffice as foods, in thus assuming the responsibility of a foreseeing and diligent father of the family he shows his wonderful goodness toward us. If anyone should more attentively ponder what I only briefly touch upon, it will be clear that Moses was a sure witness and herald of the one God, the Creator. I pass over what I have already explained,[7] that he there not only speaks of the bare essence of God, but also sets forth for us His eternal Wisdom and Spirit; that we may not conjure up some other god than him who would have himself recognized in that clear image.

(The angels, 3–12)
3. God is Lord over all!

e(c)But before I begin more fully to discuss man's nature,[8] I ought to insert something concerning angels. To be sure, Moses, accommodating himself to the rudeness of the common folk, mentions in the history of the Creation no other works of God than those which show themselves to our own eyes. Yet afterward when he introduces angels as ministers of God, one may easily infer that he, to whom they devote their effort and functions, is their Creator. eAlthough Moses, speaking after the manner of the common people, did not in laying down basic principles immediately reckon the angels among God's creatures, yet nothing prevents us from conveying plainly and explicitly what Scripture elsewhere repeatedly teaches concerning them. For if we desire to recognize God from his works, we ought by no means to overlook such an illustrious and noble example. Besides, this part of doctrine is very necessary to refute many errors. The pre-eminence of the angelic nature has so overwhelmed the minds of many that they think the angels wronged if, subjected to the authority of the one God, they are, as it were, forced into their own rank. For this reason, divinity was falsely attributed to them.

Also, Mani,[9] with his sect, arose, cfashioning for himself two principles: God and the devil. To God he attributed the origin of

6 Cf. I. xiv. 22.
7 I. xiii. 22–24.
8 I. xv and II. i.
9 Cf. I. xiii. 1, note 3.

good things, but evil natures he referred to the devil as their author. ᵉ⁽ᶜ⁾If this madness held our minds ensnared, God's glory in the creation of the universe would not abide with him. ᶜFor, since nothing is more characteristic of God than eternity and self-existence[10]—that is, existence of himself, so to speak—do not those who attribute this to the devil in a sense adorn him with the title of divinity? Now where is God's omnipotence, if such sovereignty is conceded to the devil that he carries out whatever he wishes, against God's will and resistance? The Manichees have only one foundation: that it is wrong to ascribe to the good God the creation of any evil thing. This does not in the slightest degree harm the orthodox faith, which does not admit that any evil nature exists in the whole universe. For the depravity and malice both of man and of the devil, or the sins that arise therefrom, do not spring from nature, but rather from the corruption of nature.[11] And from the beginning nothing at all has existed in which God has not put forth an example both of his wisdom and of his righteousness. ᵉTherefore, in order to meet these perverse falsehoods it is necessary to lift up our minds higher than our eyes can reach. ᵉ⁽ᶜ⁾It is probably for this purpose that in the Nicene Creed, where God is called the Creator of all things, invisible things are expressly mentioned. Nevertheless, we will take care to keep to the measure which the rule of godliness prescribes, that our readers may not, by speculating more deeply than is expedient, wander away from simplicity of faith. And in fact, while the Spirit ever teaches us to our profit, he either remains absolutely silent upon those things of little value for edification, or only lightly and cursorily touches them. It is also our duty willingly to renounce those things which are unprofitable.

(Creation and functions of angels, 4–12)
4. Also we should not indulge in speculations concerning the angels, but search out the witness of Scripture

ᶜSince the angels are God's ministers, ordained to carry out his commands, there should be no question that they are also his creatures [Ps. 103:20–21]. Is it not evidence of stubbornness rather than of diligence to raise strife over the time and order in which

---

[10] "αὐτουσία."

[11] Augustine asserts against the Manichees that *"natura, in qua nullum bonum est, non potest,"* City of God XIX. xiii (MPL 41. 641; tr. NPNF II. 409), and that the evil in man is not from nature but from its corruption, *Against Julian* I. v. 16, 17 (MPL 44. 650 f.; tr. FC 35. 18 ff.); cf. also his *Contra Julianum, opus imperfectum* I. cxiv (MPL 45. 1124 f.).

they were created?[12] Moses tells that the earth was finished and that the heavens with all their host were finished [Gen. 2:1]. What point, then, is there in anxiously investigating on what day, apart from the stars and planets, the other more remote heavenly hosts began also to exist? Not to take too long, let us remember here, as in all religious doctrine, that we ought to hold to one rule of modesty and sobriety: not to speak, or guess, or even to seek to know, concerning obscure matters anything except what has been imparted to us by God's Word. Furthermore, in the reading of Scripture we ought ceaselessly to endeavor to seek out and meditate upon those things which make for edification. Let us not indulge in curiosity or in the investigation of unprofitable things. And because the Lord willed to instruct us, not in fruitless questions, but in sound godliness, in the fear of his name, in true trust, and in the duties of holiness, let us be satisfied with this knowledge. For this reason, if we would be duly wise, we must leave those empty speculations[13] which idle men have taught apart from God's Word concerning the nature, orders, and number of angels. I know that many persons more greedily seize upon and take more delight in them than in such things as have been put to daily use. But, if we are not ashamed of being Christ's disciples, let us not be ashamed to follow that method which he has prescribed. Thus it will come to pass that, content with his teaching, we shall not only abandon but also abhor those utterly empty speculations from which he calls us back.

No one will deny that Dionysius, whoever he was,[14] subtly and skillfully discussed many matters in his *Celestial Hierarchy*. But if anyone examine it more closely, he will find it for the most part nothing but talk. The theologian's task is not to divert the ears with chatter, but to strengthen consciences by teaching things true, sure, and profitable. If you read that book, you would think

---

[12] Augustine, *City of God* XI. ix (MPL 41. 323–325; tr. NPNF II. 209 f.); Lombard, *Sentences* II. ii. 1 (MPL 192. 655).

[13] "ματαιώματα."

[14] "*Dionysium illum, quicunque fuerit.*" The reference is to Pseudo-Dionysius, *De coelesti hierarchia* (MPG 3. 119–368; tr. J. Parker, *The Celestial and Ecclesiastical Hierarchy of Dionysius Areopagitica*). Calvin probably had in mind Luther, *Babylonish Captivity*, section on Ordination: "But for my part . . . to accord so much credit to this Dionysius, whoever he was (*quisquis fuerit*), altogether displeases me, for there is virtually no sound learning in him" (Luther, *Werke* WA VI. 562, present editor's translation; cf. *Works of Martin Luther* II. 275). Luther's condemnation by the Sorbonne, April 15, 1521, was partly based on this passage. The pseudonymous character of the various (late fifth-century) works attributed to the Dionysius Areopagitica of Acts 17:34 was not universally recognized until the seventeenth century.

a man fallen from heaven recounted, not what he had learned, but what he had seen with his own eyes. Yet Paul, who had been caught up beyond the third heaven [II Cor. 12:2], not only said nothing about it, but also testified that it is unlawful for any man to speak of the secret things that he has seen [II Cor. 12:4]. Therefore, bidding farewell to that foolish wisdom, let us examine in the simple teaching of Scripture what the Lord would have us know of his angels.

5. The designation of the angels in Scripture

cOne reads here and there in Scripture that angels are celestial spirits whose ministry and service God uses to carry out all things he has decreed [e.g., Ps. 103:20–21]. Hence, likewise, this name has been applied to them because God employs them as intermediary messengers to manifest himself to men. The other names by which they are called have also been taken for a like reason. They are called "hosts" [Luke 2:13] because, as bodyguards surround their prince, they adorn his majesty and render it conspicuous; like soldiers they are ever intent upon their leader's standard, and thus are ready and able to carry out his commands. As soon as he beckons, they gird themselves for the work, or rather are already at work. The other prophets describe the image of God's throne so as to declare his magnificence, but Daniel especially does this where he says that a thousand thousands and ten thousand times ten thousand stood when God ascended his tribunal [Dan. 7:10]. Indeed, since the Lord through them wonderfully sets forth and declares the power and strength of his hand, for this reason they are called virtues [Eph. 1:21; I Cor. 15:24]. Because he exercises and administers his authority in the world through them, they are sometimes called principalities, sometimes powers, sometimes dominions [Col. 1:16; Eph. 1:21; I Cor. 15:24]. Finally, because in a sense the glory of God resides in them, they are for this reason also called thrones [Col. 1:16]. dStill, of this last I would rather say nothing; because a different interpretation fits equally well or even better.[15] But, to pass over this name, cthe Holy Spirit often uses those dprevious names cto commend the dignity of the angelic ministry. And is he not reasonable to pass over without honor those instruments through which God particularly shows forth the presence of his divine majesty? Likewise, on this account they are more than once called gods [e.g., Ps. 138:1], because in their ministry as in a mirror they in some respect exhibit his divinity to us.

---

[15] Cf. CR LII. 85; Dante, *Divine Comedy*, Paradise xxviii. 97–139 (following Pseudo-Dionysius) and Milton's line (*Paradise Lost* V. 601, repeated 769): "Thrones, Dominations, Princedoms, Virtues, Powers."

For even though I am not displeased that the ancient writers, when Scripture relates that the angel of God appeared to Abraham [Gen. 18:1], Jacob [Gen. 32:2, 28], Moses, and others [Josh. 5:14; Judg. 6:14; 13:10, 22], interpret that angel to have been Christ, yet more often when mention is made of all angels, the designation "gods" is applied to them [cf. Vg.; e.g., Gen. 22:11–12]. That ought not to seem anything marvelous; for if the honor is given to princes and governors [Ps. 82:6] because they are vicegerents of God, who is the highest King and Judge, there is far greater reason why it should be conferred upon the angels, in whom the brightness of the divine glory shines forth much more richly.

6. The angels as protectors and helpers of believers

ᶜBut Scripture strongly insists upon teaching us what could most effectively make for our consolation and the strengthening of our faith: namely, that angels are dispensers and administrators of God's beneficence toward us. For this reason, Scripture recalls that they keep vigil for our safety, take upon themselves our defense, direct our ways, and take care that some harm may not befall us. Universal are the statements that apply first of all to Christ, the Head of the church, then to all believers. "He has commanded his angels to guard you in all your ways. They shall bear you in their hands, that you may not stumble upon a stone." [Ps. 90:11–12, Vg.; 91:11–12, EV.] Likewise: "The angel of the Lord abides round about those who fear him, and rescues them." [Ps. 34:7 p.] God hereby shows that he delegates to the angels the protection of those whom he has undertaken to guard. According to this reckoning, the angel of the Lord consoles the fleeing Hagar and commands her to be reconciled to her mistress [Gen. 16:9]. He promises to Abraham, his servant, an angel to be his guide for the journey. [Gen. 24:7.] Jacob in blessing Ephraim and Manasses prays that the angel of the Lord, through whom he has been delivered from all evil, will cause them to prosper. [Gen. 48:16.] Thus an angel was appointed to protect the camps of the Israelites [Ex. 14:19; 23:20]; and as often as God would have Israel rescued from the hand of the enemy, he raised up avengers by the ministry of angels [Judg. 2:1; 6:11; 13:3–20]. In short (there is no need to recite other instances), the angels ministered to Christ [Matt. 4:11] and were present with him in all his tribulations [Luke 22:43]. They announced his resurrection to the women [Matt. 28:5, 7; Luke 24:5], his glorious coming to the disciples [Acts 1:10]. Thus, to fulfill the task of protecting us the angels fight against the devil and all our enemies, and carry out God's vengeance against those who harm us. As we read, the angel of God, to lift the siege of Jerusalem, slew 185,000 in the camp of the King of Assyria in a single night [II Kings 19:35; Isa. 37:36].

7. Guardian angels?

^cBut whether individual angels have been assigned to individual believers for their protection, I dare not affirm with confidence. Certainly, when Daniel introduces the angel of the Persians and the angel of the Greeks [Dan. 10:13, 20; 12:1] he signifies that specific angels have been appointed as guardians over kingdoms and provinces. Christ also, when he says that the children's angels always behold the Father's face [Matt. 18:10], hints that there are certain angels to whom their safety has been committed. But from this I do not know whether one ought to infer that each individual has the protection of his own angel. ^dWe ought to hold as a fact that the care of each one of us is not the task of one angel only, but all with one consent watch over our salvation. ^cFor it is said of all the angels together that they rejoice more over the turning of one sinner to repentance than over ninety-nine righteous men who have stood fast in righteousness [Luke 15:7]. Also, it is said of a number of angels that "they bore Lazarus' soul to Abraham's bosom" [Luke 16:22 p.]. ^dAnd Elisha does not in vain show to his servant so many fiery chariots which had been destined especially for him [II Kings 6:17].

^cThere is one passage that seems to confirm this a little more clearly than the rest. For when Peter, led out of the prison, knocked at the gates of the house in which the brethren were gathered, since they could not imagine it was he, "they said, 'It is his angel'" [Acts 12:15]. This seems to have entered their minds from the common notion that each believer has been assigned his own guardian angel. Although here, also, it can be answered that nothing prevents us from understanding this of any angel at all to whom the Lord had then given over the care of Peter; yet he would not on that account be Peter's perpetual guardian. Similarly the common folk imagine two angels, good and bad—as it were different geniuses—attached to each person.[16] Yet it is not worth-while anxiously to investigate what it does not much concern us to know. For if the fact that all the heavenly host are keeping watch for his safety will not satisfy a man, I do not see what benefit he could derive from knowing that one angel has been given to him as his especial guardian. ^eIndeed, those who confine to one angel the care that God takes of each one of us

[16] Cf. Comm. Harmony of the Evangelists, Mark 5:9: "Every man has many angels to act as his guardians."

are doing a great injustice both to themselves and to all the members of the church; as if it were an idle promise that we should fight more valiantly with these hosts supporting and protecting us round about!

8. The hierarchy, number, and form of the angels

cLet those who dare determine the number and orders of angels[17] see what sort of foundation they have. Michael, I admit, is called "the great prince" in The Book of Daniel [ch. 12:1], and "the archangel" in Jude [v. 9]. And Paul teaches that it will be the archangel who will call men to judgment with a trumpet [I Thess. 4:16; cf. Ezek. 10:5]. But who could on this basis determine the degrees of honor among the angels, distinguish each by his insignia, assign to each his place and station? For the two names that exist in Scripture, Michael [Dan. 10:21] and Gabriel [Dan. 8:16; Luke 1:19, 26], and a third [Raphael] if you wish to add the one from the history of Tobit [Tobit 12:15], could seem from their meaning to have been applied to angels on account of the feebleness of our capacity, although I prefer to leave that an open question.

As to number, we hear from Christ's mouth "many legions" [Matt. 26:53], from Daniel "many myriads" [Dan. 7:10]; eElisha's servant saw full chariots [II Kings 6:17]; and that the angels are said to "camp round about those who fear God" indicates a huge multitude [Ps. 34:7 p.].[18]

It is certain that spirits lack bodily form, and yet Scripture, matching the measure of our comprehension, usefully depicts for us winged angels under the names of cherubim and seraphim, that we may not doubt that they are ever ready to bring help to us with incredible swiftness, should circumstance require it, even as lightning sent forth from heaven flies to us with its usual speed.

---

[17] Origen ascribes certain special offices to the archangels Raphael, Gabriel, and Michael: De principiis I. viii. 1 (GCS 22. 228; MPG 11. 176; tr. ANF IV. 264 f.; Butterworth, Origen On First Principles, pp. 193 f.). In describing the ranks of angels and their various functions, medieval theology was under the influence of Pseudo-Dionysius, an authority rejected by Calvin. See Lombard, Sentences II. ix (MPL 192. 669), and the extended discussion in Aquinas, Summa Theol. I. cvi–cxiv. In the opening and closing sentences of this section, as in sec. 4 above, Calvin characteristically repudiates the elaborately speculative treatment of angels represented by Aquinas. Allusions to the latter can be readily identified on consulting Summa Theol. I, questions cviii, cxiii, on the hierarchy of angels and on guardian angels, respectively.

[18] See Comm. Ps. 34:7, where Calvin affirms that many angels are appointed to care for each of God's people.

ᶜWhatever besides can be sought of both their number and order, let us hold it among those mysteries whose full revelation is delayed until the Last Day. Therefore let us remember not to probe too curiously or talk too confidently.

9. The angels are not mere ideas, but actuality

ᶜYet this point, which some restless men call in question,[19] ought to be held certain: that angels are "ministering spirits" [Heb. 1:14], whose service God uses for the protection of his own, and through whom he both dispenses his benefits among men and also carries out his remaining works. Indeed, it was the opinion of the Sadducees of old [Acts 23:8] that by angels nothing was meant but either the impulses that God inspires in men or those examples of his power which he puts forth. But so many testimonies of Scripture cry out against this nonsense that it is a wonder such crass ignorance could be borne with in that people. For, to omit those passages which I have referred to above, where thousands [Rev. 5:11] and legions [Matt. 26:53] of angels are mentioned, where joy is attributed to them [Luke 15:10], where they are said to lift up believers by their hands [Ps. 91:11; Matt. 4:6; Luke 4:10–11], and to carry their souls to rest [Luke 16:22], to see the face of the Father [Matt. 18:10], and the like—there are other passages from which it is clearly demonstrated that they are, indeed, spirits having a real existence.[20] For we must so understand, however much it may be twisted, what Stephen and Paul say, that the law was given by the hand of the angels [Acts 7:53; Gal. 3:19]. We must in like manner understand Christ's statement that after the resurrection the elect will be like the angels [Matt. 22:30], that the Day of Judgment is not known even to the angels [Matt. 24:36], and that then he will come with the holy angels [Matt. 25:31; Luke 9:26]. Similarly, when Paul charged Timothy before Christ and his chosen angels to keep his commandments [I Tim. 5:21], he meant not qualities or inspirations without substance, but true spirits. And what one reads in The Letter to the Hebrews does not otherwise make sense: that Christ was made more excellent than the angels [Heb. 1:4], that the world was not subjected to them [Heb. 2:5], and that Christ assumed the nature not of them but of men [Heb. 2:16], unless we

---

[19] See I. ix. 1, note 1. In Contre la secte phantastique des Libertins xi (CR VII. 179 f.), Calvin recites the "pagan" notions of the Libertines about angels.

[20] "Spiritus naturae subsistentis."

mean that they are blessed spirits, to whom these comparisons may apply. And the author of the letter makes himself clear when he assembles the souls of believers and the holy angels at the same time in the Kingdom of God [Heb. 12:22].

eLet us add what we have already referred to, that the angels of children ever see God's face [Matt. 18:10], that we are defended by their guard [Luke 4:10–11], that they rejoice over our salvation [Luke 15:10], that they marvel at the manifold grace of God in the church, and that they are under Christ the Head.[21] This is related to their numerous appearances to the holy patriarchs under the form of men, their speaking and receiving hospitality [Gen. 18:2]. And Christ himself, because of the primacy that he holds in the person of the Mediator, is called an angel [Mal. 3:1]. eIt seemed good to me to touch on this by the way, to fortify the simple against those foolish and absurd opinions which, raised by Satan many ages ago, from time to time break out afresh.

10. The divine glory does not belong to the angels

eIt remains for us to cope with that superstition which frequently creeps in, to the effect that angels are the ministers and dispensers of all good things to us. For at once, man's reason so lapses that he thinks that no honor ought to be withheld from them. Thus it happens that what belongs to God and Christ alone is transferred to them. Thus we see that Christ's glory was for some ages past obscured in many ways, when contrary to God's Word unmeasured honors were lavished upon angels. And among those vices which we are today combating, there is hardly any more ancient. For it appears that Paul had a great struggle with certain persons who so elevated angels that they well-nigh degraded Christ to the same level. Hence he urges with very great solicitude in the letter to the Colossians that not only is Christ to be preferred before all angels but that he is the author of all good things that they have [Col. 1:16, 20]. This he does that we may not depart from Christ and go over to those who are not self-sufficient but draw from the same well as we. Surely, since the splendor of the divine majesty shines in them, nothing is easier for us than to fall down, stupefied, in adoration of them, and then to attribute to them everything that is owed to God alone. Even John in Revelation confesses that this happened to him, but at the same time he adds that this answer came to him [chs. 19:10; 22:8–9]: "You must not do that! I am a fellow servant with you. . . . Worship God."

[21] Cf. secs. 6 and 7, above.

11. God makes use of the angels, not for his own sake, but for ours

ᶜYet we shall well avoid this peril if we inquire why it is through them rather than through himself without their service that God is wont to declare his power, to provide for the safety of believers, and to communicate the gifts of his beneficence to them. Surely he does not do this out of necessity as if he could not do without them, for as often as he pleases, he disregards them and carries out his work through his will alone, so far are they from being to him a means of lightening difficulty. Therefore he makes use of angels to comfort our weakness, that we may lack nothing at all that can raise up our minds to good hope, or confirm them in security. One thing, indeed, ought to be quite enough for us: that the Lord declares himself to be our protector. But when we see ourselves beset by so many perils, so many harmful things, so many kinds of enemies—such is our softness and frailty—we would sometimes be filled with trepidation or yield to despair if the Lord did not make us realize the presence of his grace according to our capacity. For this reason, he not only promises to take care of us, but tells us he has innumerable guardians whom he has bidden to look after our safety; that so long as we are hedged about by their defense and keeping, whatever perils may threaten, we have been placed beyond all chance of evil. I confess that we act wrongly when, after that simple promise of the protection of the one God, we still seek whence our help may come [cf. Ps. 121:1; 120:1, Vg.]. But because the Lord, out of his immeasurable kindness and gentleness, wishes to remedy this fault of ours, we have no reason to disregard his great benefit. We have an example of this thing in Elisha's servant, who, when he saw the mountain besieged by the Syrian army and that there was no escape, was overwhelmed with fear, as if all was over for himself and his master. Here Elisha prayed to God that He might open his servant's eyes. Straightway the servant saw the mountain filled with fiery horses and chariots, that is, with a host of angels, who were to protect him as well as the prophet [II Kings 6:17]. Strengthened by this vision, he recovered himself and was able with undaunted courage to look down upon his enemies, at sight of whom he had almost expired.

12. The angels must not divert us from directing our gaze to the Lord alone

ᶜSo, then, whatever is said concerning the ministry of angels, let us direct it to the end that, having banished all lack of trust, our hope in God may be more firmly established. Indeed, these helps have been prepared for us by the Lord that we may not be frightened by the multitude of the enemy, as if they might prevail against His assistance, but that we may take refuge in that utterance of Elisha that "there are more for us than against us" [II Kings 6:16 p.]. How preposterous, then, it is for us to be led away from God by the angels, who have been established to testify that his help is all the closer to us! But they do lead us away unless they lead us by the hand straight to him, that we may look upon him, call upon him, and proclaim him as our sole helper; unless we regard them as his hands that are moved to no work without his direction; unless they keep us in the one Mediator, Christ, that we may wholly depend upon him, lean upon him, be brought to him, and rest in him. For what is described in the vision of Jacob ought to stick and be deeply fixed within our minds: that angels descend to the earth, to men, and ascend from men to heaven by a ladder upon which the Lord of Hosts stands [Gen. 28:12]. This indicates that only through Christ's intercession is it brought about that the angels' ministrations come to us, ᵉas he himself affirms: "Hereafter you will see the heavens opened and angels . . . descending upon the Son of Man" [John 1:51]. ᶜTherefore the servant of Abraham, though entrusted to the angel's charge [Gen. 24:7], does not for that reason call upon him to help him, but, relying on that commitment, pours out his prayers unto the Lord, and beseeches him to show his mercy to Abraham [Gen. 24:12]. For as God does not make them ministers of his power and goodness to share his glory with them, so he does not promise us his help through their ministry in order that we should divide our trust between them and him. Farewell, then, to that Platonic philosophy of seeking access to God through angels, and of worshiping them with intent to render God more approachable to us.²² This is what superstitious and curious men have tried to drag into our religion from the beginning and persevere in trying even to this day.

(The devils in the purposes of God, 13–19)
13. Scripture forearms us against the adversary
ᶜAll that Scripture teaches concerning devils aims at arousing us to take precaution against their stratagems and contrivances, and also to make us equip ourselves with those weapons which are strong and powerful enough to vanquish these most powerful

---

²² Plato, *Epinomis* E 984 (LCL Plato VIII. 462 f.), where the daemons are to be honored with prayers as intermediaries. Cf. *Symposium* 202 (LCL Plato V. 178 f.). Calvin's citation of Cratylus here appears to Benoit to be in error (*Institution* I. 196): "*Cratylus* 398" is cited in OS III. 164, but the passage is hardly relevant.

foes. For when Satan is called the god [II Cor. 4:4] and prince [John 12:31] of this world, when he is spoken of as a strong armed man [Luke 11:21; cf. Matt. 12:29], the spirit who holds power over the air [Eph. 2:2], a roaring lion [I Peter 5:8], these descriptions serve only to make us more cautious and watchful, and thus more prepared to take up the struggle. This also sometimes is noted explicitly: for Peter, after he has said that the devil "prowls around like a roaring lion seeking someone to devour" [I Peter 5:8], immediately subjoins the exhortation that with faith we steadfastly resist him [I Peter 5:9]. And Paul, after he has warned us that our struggle is not with flesh and blood, but with the princes of the air, with the powers of darkness, and spiritual wickedness [Eph. 6:12], forthwith bids us put on that armor capable of sustaining so great and dangerous a contest [Eph. 6:13 ff.]. We have been forewarned that an enemy relentlessly threatens us, an enemy who is the very embodiment of rash boldness, of military prowess, of crafty wiles, of untiring zeal and haste, of every conceivable weapon and of skill in the science of warfare.[23] We must, then, bend our every effort to this goal: that we should not let ourselves be overwhelmed by carelessness or faintheartedness,[24] but on the contrary, with courage rekindled stand our ground in combat. Since this military service ends only at death, let us urge ourselves to perseverance. Indeed, conscious of our weakness and ignorance, let us especially call upon God's help, relying upon him alone in whatever we attempt, since it is he alone who can supply us with counsel and strength, courage and armor.

14. The realm of wickedness

cMoreover, in order that we may be aroused and exhorted all the more to carry this out, Scripture makes known that there are not one, not two, nor a few foes, but great armies, which wage war against us. For Mary Magdalene is said to have been freed from seven demons by which she was possessed [Mark 16:9; Luke 8:2], and Christ bears witness that usually after a demon has once been cast out, if you make room for him again, he will take with him seven spirits more wicked than he and return to his empty possession [Matt. 12:43–45]. Indeed, a whole legion

23 The warfare of the Kingdom of God against the kingdom of Satan is a theme frequently present to Calvin's mind. Cf. K. Fröhlich, *Gottesreich, Welt und Kirche bei Calvin*, pp. 19 ff.

24 "*Socordia vel ignavia*," probably suggested by Sallust's phrase found in his *War with Catiline* lii. 29 and lviii. 4, and *Letter to Caesar* x. 9: "*Quorum animos socordia atque ignavia invasit*" (LCL edition, pp. 106, 118, 482).

is said to have assailed one man [Luke 8:30]. We are therefore taught by these examples that we have to wage war against an infinite number of enemies, lest, despising their fewness, we should be too remiss to give battle, or, thinking that we are sometimes afforded some respite, we should yield to idleness.

But the frequent mention of Satan or the devil in the singular denotes the empire of wickedness opposed to the Kingdom of Righteousness. For as the church and fellowship of the saints has Christ as Head, so the faction of the impious and impiety itself are depicted for us together with their prince who holds supreme sway over them. For this reason, it was said: "Depart, . . . you cursed, into the eternal fire, prepared for the devil and his angels" [Matt. 25:41].

15. An irreconcilable struggle

ᶜThe fact that the devil is everywhere called God's adversary and ours also ought to fire us to an unceasing struggle against him. For if we have God's glory at heart, as we should have, we ought with all our strength to contend against him who is trying to extinguish it. If we are minded to affirm Christ's Kingdom as we ought, we must wage irreconcilable war with him who is plotting its ruin. Again, if we care about our salvation at all, we ought to have neither peace nor truce with him who continually lays traps to destroy it. So, indeed, is he described in Gen., ch. 3, where he seduces man from the obedience owed to God, that he may simultaneously deprive God of his due honor and hurl man himself into ruin [vs. 1–5]. So, also, in the Evangelists, where he is called "an enemy" [Matt. 13:28, 39], and is said to sow weeds in order to corrupt the seed of eternal life [Matt. 13:25]. In sum, we experience in all of Satan's deeds what Christ testifies concerning him, that "from the beginning he was a murderer . . . and a liar" [John 8:44]. For he opposes the truth of God with falsehoods, he obscures the light with darkness, he entangles men's minds in errors, he stirs up hatred, he kindles contentions and combats, everything to the end that he may overturn God's Kingdom and plunge men with himself into eternal death. From this it appears that he is in nature depraved, evil, and malicious. For there must be consummate depravity in that disposition which devotes itself to assailing God's glory and man's salvation. This, also, is what John means in his letter, when he writes that "the devil has sinned from the beginning" [I John 3:8]. Indeed, he considers him as the author, leader, and architect of all malice and iniquity.

16. The devil is a degenerate creation of God

cYet, since the devil was created by God, let us remember that this malice, which we attribute to his nature, came not from his creation but from his perversion. For, whatever he has that is to be condemned he has derived from his revolt and fall. For this reason, Scripture warns us lest, believing that he has come forth in his present condition from God, we should ascribe to God himself what is utterly alien to him. For this reason, Christ declares that "when Satan lies, he speaks according to his own nature" and states the reason, because "he abode not in the truth" [John 8:44 p.]. Indeed, when Christ states that Satan "abode not in the truth," he hints that he was once in it, and when he makes him "the father of lies," he deprives him of imputing to God the fault which he brought upon himself.

But although these things are briefly and not very clearly stated, they are more than enough to clear God's majesty of all slander. And what concern is it to us to know anything more about devils or to know it for another purpose? Some persons grumble that Scripture does not in numerous passages set forth systematically and clearly that fall of the devils, its cause, manner, time, and character. But because this has nothing to do with us, it was better not to say anything, or at least to touch upon it lightly, because it did not befit the Holy Spirit to feed our curiosity with empty histories to no effect. And we see that the Lord's purpose was to teach nothing in his sacred oracles except what we should learn to our edification. Therefore, lest we ourselves linger over superfluous matters, let us be content with this brief summary of the nature of devils: they were when first created angels of God, but by degeneration they ruined themselves. and became the instruments of ruin for others. Because this is profitable to know, it is plainly taught in Peter and Jude. God did not spare those angels who sinned [II Peter 2:4] and kept not their original nature, but left their abode [Jude 6]. eAnd Paul, in speaking of the "elect angels" [I Tim. 5:21], is no doubt tacitly contrasting them with the reprobate angels.

17. The devil stands under God's power

cAs for the discord and strife that we say exists between Satan and God, we ought to accept as a fixed certainty the fact that he can do nothing unless God wills and assents to it. For we read in the history of Job that he presented himself before God to receive his commands [Job 1:6; 2:1], and did not dare undertake any evil act without first having obtained permission [chs. 1:12;

2:6]. Thus, also, when Ahab was to be deceived, Satan took upon himself to become a spirit of falsehood in the mouths of all the prophets; and commissioned by God, he carried out his task [I Kings 22:20–22]. For this reason, too, the spirit of the Lord that troubled Saul is called "evil" because the sins of the impious king were punished by it as by a lash [I Sam. 16:14; 18:10]. And elsewhere it is written that the plagues were inflicted upon the Egyptians by God "through evil angels" [Ps. 78:49]. According to these particular examples Paul generally testifies that the blinding of unbelievers is God's work [II Thess. 2:11], although he had before called it the activity of Satan [II Thess. 2:9; cf. II Cor. 4:4; Eph. 2:2]. Therefore Satan is clearly under God's power, and is so ruled by his bidding as to be compelled to render him service. Indeed, when we say that Satan resists God, and that Satan's works disagree with God's works, we at the same time assert that this resistance and this opposition are dependent upon God's sufferance. I am not now speaking of Satan's will, nor even of his effort, but only of his effect. For inasmuch as the devil is by nature wicked, he is not at all inclined to obedience to the divine will, but utterly intent upon contumacy and rebellion. From himself and his own wickedness, therefore, arises his passionate and deliberate opposition to God. By this wickedness he is urged on to attempt courses of action which he believes to be most hostile to God. But because with the bridle of his power God holds him bound and restrained, he carries out only those things which have been divinely permitted to him; and so he obeys his Creator, whether he will or not, because he is compelled to yield him service wherever God impels him.

18. Assurance of victory!

ᶜNow, because God bends the unclean spirits hither and thither at will, he so governs their activity that they exercise believers in combat, ambush them, invade their peace, beset them in combat, and also often weary them, rout them, terrify them, and sometimes wound them; yet they never vanquish or crush them. But the wicked they subdue and drag away; they exercise power over their minds and bodies, and misuse them as if they were slaves for every shameful act. As far as believers are concerned, because they are disquieted by enemies of this sort, they heed these exhortations: "Give no place to the devil" [Eph. 4:27, Vg.]. "The devil your enemy goes about as a roaring lion, seeking someone to devour; resist him, be firm in your faith" [I Peter 5:8–9 p.], and the like. Paul admits that he was not free from this sort of strife when he writes that, as a remedy to tame his pride, he was given an angel of Satan to humble him [II Cor. 12:7]. Therefore this exercise is common to all the children of God. But because that promise to crush Satan's head [Gen. 3:15] pertains to Christ and all his members in common, I deny that believers can ever be conquered or overwhelmed by him. Often, indeed, are they distressed, but not so deprived of life as not to recover; they fall under violent blows, but afterward they are raised up; they are wounded, but not fatally; in short, they so toil throughout life that at the last they obtain the victory.

ᵉYet I do not confine this to individual acts. For we know that by God's just vengeance David was for a time given over to Satan, that at his prompting he should take a census of the people [II Sam. 24:1]. And Paul does not abandon hope of pardon as impossible, even if men are ensnared in the devil's net [II Tim. 2:25–26]. ᶜIn another passage Paul shows that the promise mentioned above begins to have effect in this life, wherein we must struggle; and that after the struggle it is fulfilled. As he puts it, "The God of peace will soon crush Satan under your feet." [Rom. 16:20.] In our Head, indeed, this victory always fully existed, for the prince of the world had nothing in him [John 14:30]. Moreover, it now appears in part in us, who are his members; it will be completed when we shall have put off our flesh, in respect to which we are as yet subject to infirmity, and will be filled with the power of the Holy Spirit.

To the extent that Christ's Kingdom is upbuilt, Satan with his power falls; as the Lord himself says, "I saw Satan fall like lightning from heaven" [Luke 10:18]. For, by this answer he confirms what the apostles had related concerning the power of their preaching. ᵉLikewise: "When a prince occupies his own palace, all his possessions are undisturbed. But when one stronger than he overcomes him, he is cast out," etc. [Luke 11:21–22 p.]. And Christ, by dying, conquered Satan, who had "the power of death" [Heb. 2:14], and triumphed over all his forces, to the end that they might not harm the church. Otherwise, at every moment they would do away with it a hundred times over. For, such is our weakness and such is the power of his fury, how could we stand even in the slightest against his manifold and continuous attacks, unless we relied upon the victory of our leader? ᶜTherefore God does not allow Satan to rule over the souls of believers, but gives over only the impious and unbelievers, whom he deigns not to regard as members of his own flock, to be governed by him. For the devil is said to occupy this world unchallenged until he is cast out by Christ [cf. Luke 11:21]. Likewise, he is said to blind all those who do not believe in the gospel [II Cor. 4:4]. Again, to carry out his "work in the sons of disobedience" [Eph. 2:2], and rightly, for all the impious are vessels of wrath. Hence, to whom would they be subjected but to the minister of divine vengeance? Finally, they are said to be of their father the devil [John 8:44]; for, as believers are recognized as the children of God because they bear his image, so are those rightly recognized to be the children of Satan from his image, into which they have degenerated [I John 3:8–10].

19. Devils are not thoughts, but actualities

ᶜInasmuch as we have before refuted[25] that trifling philosophy about the holy angels which teaches that they are nothing but good inspirations or impulses which God arouses in men's minds, so also in this place ought those men to be refuted who babble of devils as nothing else than evil emotions or perturbations which come upon us from our flesh.[26] We shall be able to do this briefly because there are not a few testimonies of Scripture clear enough on this matter. First, when those who have degenerated from their original state [Jude 6] are called unclean spirits and apostate angels [Matt. 12:43], the names themselves sufficiently express, not impulses or affections of minds, but rather what are called minds or spirits endowed with sense perception and understanding. Likewise, when the children of God are compared with the children of the devil both by Christ and by John [John 8:44; I John 3:10], would this comparison not be pointless if the name "devil" signified nothing but evil inspirations? And John adds something even clearer, that "the devil has sinned from the beginning" [I John 3:8]. So, also, when Jude introduces "the archangel Michael, as contending with the devil" [Jude 9], he surely sets against the good angel an evil and rebellious one. What we read in the history of Job agrees with this, that Satan appeared with the holy angels in God's presence [Job 1:6; 2:1]. Moreover, clearest of all are those passages which make mention of the punishment, which the devils have begun to feel from God's judgment, and will especially feel at the resurrection. "O Son" of David, why "have you come to torment us before the time?" [Matt. 8:29.] Likewise: "Depart, you cursed ones, into the eternal fire prepared for the devil and his angels." [Matt. 25:41.] Also: "If he spared not his own angels, but cast them bound with chains into darkness to be kept for eternal damnation," etc. [II Peter 2:4.]

How meaningless would these expressions be, that the devils

---

[25] I. xiv. 9.

[26] Contre la secte phantastique des Libertins xii, xxii, xxiii (CR VII. 181, 228, 239).

are destined for eternal judgment, that fire has been prepared for them, that they are now tormented and tortured by Christ's glory, if devils were nonexistent! But this matter does not require discussion among those who have faith in the Lord's Word, while among these empty speculators, indeed, to whom nothing is pleasing unless it be new, there is little profit in the testimonies of Scripture. It seems to me, therefore, that I have accomplished what I meant to do, namely, to equip godly minds against such delusions, with which uneasy men confound themselves and others more simple-minded than they. But it was worth-while to touch upon this point, also, lest any persons, entangled in that error, while thinking themselves without an enemy, become more slack and heedless about resisting.

(*The spiritual lessons of Creation, 20–22*)
20. Greatness and abundance of Creation

e(c)Meanwhile let us not be ashamed to take pious delight in the works of God open and manifest in this most beautiful theater.[27] cFor, as I have elsewhere said,[28] although it is not the chief evidence for faith, yet it is the first evidence in the order of nature, to be mindful that wherever we cast our eyes, all things they meet are works of God, and at the same time to ponder with pious meditation to what end God created them. Therefore, that we may apprehend with true faith what it profits us to know of God, it is important for us to grasp first the history of the creation of the universe, as it has been set forth briefly by Moses [Gen., chs. 1 and 2], and then has been more fully illustrated by saintly men, especially by Basil and Ambrose.[29] From this history we shall learn that God by the power of his

---

[27] Cf. I. v. 8, note 27; I. vi. 2; II. vi. 1; III. ix. 2.
[28] I. v. 1–5.
[29] Basil, *Hexaemeron* (homilies on the six days of Creation) (MPG 29. 3–207; tr. NPNF 2 ser. VIII. 52–107); Ambrose, *Hexameron* (CSEL 32 i. 1–261; MPL 14. 133–288). The prevailing Christian view of creation is that God created the world out of nothing (*ex nihilo*). Cf. I. xv. 5. In antiquity the possibility of this was denied by the Epicureans: "*Nil posse creari de nilo*," wrote Lucretius (*De rerum natura* i. 155; LCL edition, p. 12). Augustine (apart from the doctrine of the origin of individual souls, on which his position is indeterminate) asserts *creatio ex nihilo*, e.g., in *Faith and the Creed* ii. 2 (MPL 40. 182; tr. LCC VI. 354 f.). It is thus stated in the Westminster Confession IV. 1: "It pleased God . . . to create, or make of nothing, the world, and all things therein." Cf. E. Brunner, *The Christian Doctrine of Creation* (tr. O. Wyon) II. 9 ff.; L. B. Gilkey, *Maker of Heaven and Earth*, pp. 46 f., 88; H. A. Wolfson, "The Meaning of *ex nihilo* in the Church Fathers, Arabic and Hebrew Philosophy, and St. Thomas": *Medieval Studies in Honor of J. D. M. Ford*, pp. 355–367.

Word and Spirit created heaven and earth out of nothing; that thereupon he brought forth living beings and inanimate things of every kind, that in a wonderful series he distinguished an innumerable variety of things, that he endowed each kind with its own nature, assigned functions, appointed places and stations; and that, although all were subject to corruption, he nevertheless provided for the preservation of each species until the Last Day. We shall likewise learn that he nourishes some in secret ways, and, as it were, from time to time instills new vigor into them; on others he has conferred the power of propagating, lest by their death the entire species perish; that he has so wonderfully adorned heaven and earth with as unlimited abundance, variety, and beauty of all things as could possibly be, quite like a spacious and splendid house, provided and filled with the most exquisite and at the same time most abundant furnishings. Finally, we shall learn that in forming man and in adorning him with such goodly beauty, and with such great and numerous gifts, he put him forth as the most excellent example of his works. But since it is not my purpose to recount the creation of the universe, let it be enough for me to have touched upon these few matters again in passing. For it is better, as I have already warned my readers, to seek a fuller understanding of this passage from Moses and from those others who have faithfully and diligently recorded the narrative of Creation [Gen., chs. 1 and 2].

21. How should we view God's works?

e(c)Nothing is to be gained by further discussing what direction the contemplation of God's works should take and to what goal such contemplation ought to be applied, inasmuch as the greater part of this topic has been disposed of in another place,[30] cand it is possible to accomplish in a few words whatever concerns our present purpose. Indeed, if we chose to explain in a fitting manner how God's inestimable wisdom, power, justice, and goodness shine forth in the fashioning of the universe, no splendor, no ornament of speech, would be equal to an act of such great magnitude. There is no doubt that the Lord would have us uninterruptedly occupied in this holy meditation; that, while we contemplate in all creatures, as in mirrors, those immense riches of his wisdom, justice, goodness, and power, we should not merely run over them cursorily, and, so to speak, with a fleeting glance; but we should ponder them at length, turn them over in our minds seriously and faithfully, and recollect them repeatedly. But because our purpose here is to teach, it is proper for us to omit

[30] I. v. 1–4.

those matters which require long harangue. Therefore, to be brief, let all readers know that they have with true faith apprehended what it is for God to be Creator of heaven and earth, if they first of all follow the universal rule, not to pass over in ungrateful thoughtlessness or forgetfulness those conspicuous powers which God shows forth in his creatures, and then learn so to apply it to themselves that their very hearts are touched. The first part of the rule is exemplified when we reflect upon the greatness of the Artificer who stationed, arranged, and fitted together the starry host of heaven in such wonderful order that nothing more beautiful in appearance can be imagined; who so set and fixed some in their stations that they cannot move; who granted to others a freer course, but so as not to wander outside their appointed course; who so adjusted the motion of all that days and nights, months, years, and seasons of the year are measured off; who so proportioned the inequality of days, which we daily observe, that no confusion occurs. It is so too when we observe his power in sustaining so great a mass, in governing the swiftly revolving heavenly system,[31] and the like. For these few examples make sufficiently clear what it is to recognize God's powers in the creation of the universe. Otherwise, as I have said, if I decide to set forth the whole matter in my discourse, there will be no end. For there are as many miracles of divine power, as many tokens of goodness, and as many proofs of wisdom, as there are kinds of things in the universe, indeed, as there are things either great or small.

22. *The contemplation of God's goodness in his creation will lead us to thankfulness and trust*
    ^cThere remains the second part of the rule, more closely related to faith. It is to recognize that God has destined all things for our good and salvation but at the same time to feel his power and grace in ourselves and in the great benefits he has conferred upon us, and so bestir ourselves to trust, invoke, praise, and love him.[32] Indeed, as I pointed out a little before,[33] God himself has

---

[31] "*Caelestis machinae.*" Cf. I. x. 1, note 2. Joseph Addison's stately hymn "The Spacious Firmament on High" has affinities with this and similar passages in Calvin.

[32] This statement is substantially repeated in CR XXVI. 255; XXVIII. 22, 232; XXXII. 89, 428; XXXIII. 572; XXXVI. 589; XLI. 67; XLIII. 254; XLIV. 5. The belief that the material universe was made for the sake of man was espoused by the Stoics in opposition to the Epicureans. For its flat denial by Lucretius, see his *De rerum natura* v. 156 f. (LCL edition, pp. 350 f.). Cicero's Stoic speaker Balbus, in *Nature of the Gods* II. lxii. 154–lxvi. 167 (LCL edition, pp. 273–283), discourses at some length on the

shown by the order of Creation that he created all things for man's sake. For it is not without significance that he divided the making of the universe into six days [Gen. 1:31], even though it would have been no more difficult for him to have completed in one moment the whole work together in all its details than to arrive at its completion gradually by a progression of this sort. But he willed to commend his providence and fatherly solicitude toward us in that, before he fashioned man, he prepared everything he foresaw would be useful and salutary for him. How great ingratitude would it be now to doubt whether this most gracious Father has us in his care, who we see was concerned for us even before we were born! How impious would it be to tremble for fear that his kindness might at any time fail us in our need, when we see that it was shown, with the greatest abundance of every good thing, when we were yet unborn! Besides, from Moses we hear that, through His liberality, all things on earth are subject to us [Gen. 1:28; 9:2]. It is certain that He did not do this to mock us with the empty title to a gift. Therefore nothing that is needful for our welfare will ever be lacking to us.

To conclude once for all, whenever we call God the Creator of heaven and earth, let us at the same time bear in mind that the dispensation of all those things which he has made is in his own hand and power and that we are indeed his children, whom he has received into his faithful protection to nourish and educate. We are therefore to await the fullness of all good things from him alone and to trust completely that he will never leave us destitute of what we need for salvation, and to hang our hopes on none but him! We are therefore, also, to petition him for whatever we desire; and we are to recognize as a blessing from him, and thankfully to acknowledge, every benefit that falls to our share. So, invited by the great sweetness of his beneficence and goodness, let us study to love and serve him with all our heart.

theme that "the world was created for the sake of gods and men, and the things that it contains were provided and contrived for the enjoyment of men." In approval of this, Lactantius remarks: "God must have made the world for some use. The Stoics say that it was made for man, and rightly so." *Epitome of the Divine Institutes* lxviii (CSEL 19. 752; tr. ANF VII. 252).

[33] I. xiv. 2.

CHAPTER XV

^eDISCUSSION OF HUMAN NATURE AS CREATED, OF THE FACULTIES OF THE SOUL, OF THE IMAGE OF GOD, OF FREE WILL, AND OF THE ORIGINAL INTEGRITY OF MAN'S NATURE[1]

(Man's nature deformed; yet his soul bears, though almost obliterated, the image of God, 1–4)

1. Man proceeded spotless from God's hand; therefore he may not shift the blame for his sins to the Creator

We must now speak of the creation of man: not only because among all God's works here is the noblest and most remarkable example of his justice, wisdom, and goodness; but because, as we said at the beginning,[2] we cannot have a clear and complete knowledge of God unless it is accompanied by a corresponding knowledge of ourselves. This knowledge of ourselves is twofold: namely, to know what we were like when we were first created and what our condition became after the fall of Adam. While it would be of little benefit to understand our creation unless we recognized in this sad ruin what our nature in its corruption and deformity is like, we shall nevertheless be content for the moment with the description of our originally upright nature. ^{e(b)}And to be sure, before we come to the miserable condition of man to which he is now subjected, it is worth-while to know what he was like when first created. ^bNow we must guard against singling out only those natural evils of man, lest we seem to attribute them to the Author of nature. For in this excuse, impiety thinks it has sufficient defense, if it is able to claim that whatever defects it possesses have in some way proceeded from God. It does not hesitate, if it is reproved, to contend with God himself, and to impute to him the fault of which it is deservedly accused. And those who wish to seem to speak more reverently of the Godhead still willingly blame their depravity on nature, not realizing that they also, although more obscurely, insult God. For if any defect were proved to inhere in nature, this would bring reproach upon him.

Since, then, we see the flesh panting for every subterfuge by which it thinks that the blame for its own evils may in any way be diverted from itself to another, we must diligently oppose this evil intent. Therefore we must so deal with the calamity of mankind that we may cut off every shift, and may vindicate God's

---

[1] Calvin's teaching about man is mainly in two separate parts of the *Institutes*. Here he is dealing with man as he was created. In II. i–iv, he discusses man in his fallen state.

[2] Cf. I. i. 1; I. v. 2–3; I. xv. 1; II. viii. 1.

justice from every accusation. ᵉAfterward, in the proper place, we shall see how far away men are from the purity that was bestowed upon Adam.³ And first we must realize that when he was taken from earth and clay [Gen. 2:7; 18:27], his pride was bridled. For nothing is more absurd than for those who not only "dwell in houses of clay" [Job 4:19], but who are themselves in part earth and dust, to boast of their own excellence. But since God not only deigned to give life to an earthen vessel, but also willed it to be the abode of an immortal spirit, Adam could rightly glory in the great liberality of his Maker.

2. Diversity of body and soul

ᵉFurthermore, that man consists of a soul and a body ought to be beyond controversy. Now I understand by the term "soul" an immortal yet created essence, which is his nobler part. Sometimes it is called "spirit." For even when these terms are joined together, they differ from one another in meaning; yet when the word "spirit" is used by itself, it means the same thing as soul; as when Solomon, speaking of death, says that then "the spirit returns to God who gave it" [Eccl. 12:7]. And when Christ commended his spirit to the Father [Luke 23:46] and Stephen his to Christ [Acts 7:59] they meant only that when the soul is freed from the prison house of the body, God is its perpetual guardian. Some imagine the soul to be called "spirit" for the reason that it is breath, or a force divinely infused into bodies, but that it nevertheless is without essence; both the thing itself and all Scripture show them to be stupidly blundering in this opinion. It is of course true that while men are tied to earth more than they should be they grow dull; indeed, because they have been estranged from the Father of Lights [James 1:17], they become blinded by darkness, so that they do not think they will survive death; yet in the meantime the light has not been so extinguished in the darkness that they remain untouched by a sense of their own immortality. Surely the conscience, which, discerning between good and evil, responds to God's judgment, is an undoubted sign of the immortal spirit. For how could a motion without essence penetrate to God's judgment seat, and inflict itself with dread at its own guilt? For the body is not affected by the fear of spiritual punishment, which falls upon the soul only; from this it follows that the soul is endowed with essence. Now the very knowledge of God sufficiently proves that souls, which transcend the world, are immortal, for no transient energy could penetrate to the fountain of life.

In short, the many pre-eminent gifts with which the human

³ II. i. 3.

mind is endowed proclaim that something divine has been engraved upon it; all these are testimonies of an immortal essence. For the sense perception inhering in brute animals does not go beyond the body, or at least extends no farther than to material things presented to it. But the nimbleness of the human mind in searching out heaven and earth and the secrets of nature, and when all ages have been compassed by its understanding and memory, in arranging each thing in its proper order, and in inferring future events from past, clearly shows that there lies hidden in man something separate from the body.[4] With our intelligence we conceive the invisible God and the angels, something the body can by no means do. We grasp things that are right, just, and honorable, which are hidden to the bodily senses. Therefore the spirit must be the seat of this intelligence. Indeed, sleep itself, which benumbs man, seeming even to deprive him of life, is no obscure witness of immortality, since it suggests not only thoughts of things that have never happened, but also presentiments of the future. I have briefly touched upon these things which secular writers grandly extol and depict in more brilliant language;[5] but among godly readers this simple reminder will be enough.

Now, unless the soul were something essential, separate from the body, Scripture would not teach that we dwell in houses of clay [Job 4:19] and at death leave the tabernacle of the flesh, putting off what is corruptible so that at the Last Day we may finally receive our reward, according as each of us has done in the body. For surely these passages and similar ones that occur repeatedly not only clearly distinguish the soul from the body, but by transferring to it the name "man" indicate it to be the principal part. Now when Paul urges believers to cleanse themselves of every defilement of flesh and spirit [II Cor. 7:1], he points out the two parts in which the filth of sin resides. Peter, also, calling Christ "shepherd and bishop of . . . souls" [I Peter 2:25], would have spoken wrongly if there had not been souls on whose behalf he might fulfill this office. If souls did not have their own proper essence, there would be no point in Peter's statement about the eternal "salvation of . . . souls" [I Peter 1:9], or in his injunction

---

[4] Cf. Tertullian, *Against Marcion* II. ix (CSEL 47. 346; CCL Tertullianus I. 484 f.; tr. ANF III. 304); Augustine, *Retractations* I. x. 3 (MPL 32. 600).
[5] Cf. Cicero, *Tusculan Disputations* I. xxvii (LCL edition, pp. 78 f.); *Nature of the Gods* II. liv. 133–lxi. 153 (LCL edition, pp. 251–271); Aristotle, *De partibus animalium* 686. 25–35 (tr. *Aristotle, Selections,* ed. W. D. Ross, pp. 181 ff.). On the topic of sleep Tertullian recites and criticizes a variety of pagan opinions: *On the Soul* xlii–xlix (CCL Tertullianus II. 845–855; Tertullian, *De anima,* ed., with commentary by J. H. Waszink, pp. 58–67, 461; tr. ANF III. 221–227).

to purify our souls and ascertain that "wicked lusts . . . war against the soul" [I Peter 2:11 p.]. The same applies to the statement of the author of Hebrews, that the pastors "stand watch . . . to render account for our souls" [Heb. 13:17 p.]. The fact that Paul, upon his soul, calls God to witness [II Cor. 1:23, Vg.] points to the same conclusion, because it would not become guilty before God unless it were liable for punishment. This is expressed even more clearly in Christ's words, when he bids us be afraid of him who, after he has killed the body, can send the soul into the Gehenna of fire [Matt. 10:28; Luke 12:5]. Now when the author of The Letter to the Hebrews distinguishes the fathers of our flesh from God, who is the one "Father of spirits" [Heb. 12:9], he could not assert more clearly the essence of souls. Besides, unless souls survive when freed from the prison houses of their bodies, it would be absurd for Christ to induce the soul of Lazarus as enjoying bliss in Abraham's bosom, and again, the soul of the rich man sentenced to terrible torments [Luke 16:22–23]. Paul confirms this same thing, teaching us that we journey away from God so long as we dwell in the flesh, but that we enjoy his presence outside the flesh [II Cor. 5:6, 8]. Lest I go any farther in a topic of no great difficulty, I shall add only this word from Luke, that among the errors of the Sadducees it is mentioned that they did not believe in spirits and angels [Acts 23:8].

3. God's image and likeness in man[t]

ᵉAlso, a reliable proof of this matter may be gathered from the fact that man was created in God's image [Gen. 1:27].[6] For although God's glory shines forth in the outer man, yet there is no doubt that the proper seat of his image is in the soul. I do not deny, indeed, that our outward form, in so far as it distinguishes and separates us from brute animals, at the same time more closely joins us to God. And if anyone wishes to include under "image of God" the fact that, "while all other living things being bent over look earthward, man has been given a face uplifted, bidden to gaze heavenward and to raise his countenance to the stars,"[7] I shall not contend too strongly—provided it be regarded as a settled principle that the image of God, which is seen or glows in these outward marks, is spiritual. For Osiander,[8] whose writings

---

[6] Peter Martyr Vermigli (d. 1562) has a parallel statement, *Loci communes* I. xii. 27–28 (1576 edition, pp. 101 f.).

[7] Ovid, *Metamorphoses* I. 84 ff. (LCL edition, p. 8); cf. Cicero, *Nature of the Gods* II. lvi. 140 (LCL edition, pp. 256 ff.).

[8] Andreas Osiander (1498–1552) was a prominent Lutheran pastor at Nuremberg and from 1549 professor at Königsberg. In 1550 he introduced an

prove him to have been perversely ingenious in futile inventions, indiscriminately extending God's image both to the body and to the soul, mingles heaven and earth. He says that Father, Son, and Holy Spirit place their image in man, because however upright Adam might have remained, yet Christ would have to become man. Thus, according to them,[9] the body that was destined for Christ was the exemplar and type of that corporeal figure which was then formed. But where will he find that Christ is the image of the Spirit? I admit that in the person of the Mediator the glory of the whole divinity surely shines, but how will the Eternal Word be called the image of the Spirit, whom he precedes in order? In short, the distinction between Son and Spirit is overthrown if the latter calls the former the image of himself. Furthermore, I should like to know from him how in the flesh that he took upon himself Christ resembles the Holy Spirit, and by what marks or lineaments he expresses his likeness. And since that saying, "Let us make man," etc. [Gen. 1:26], is common also to the person of the Son, it would follow that he is the image of himself. This is repugnant to all reason. Besides this, if Osiander's fabrication is accepted, man was formed only after the type and exemplar of Christ as man; and thus the pattern from which Adam was taken was Christ in so far as he was to be clothed with flesh. But Scripture teaches in a far other sense that he was created in God's image. There is more color to the cleverness of those who explain that Adam was created in God's image because he conformed to Christ, who is the sole image of God[10]; but in that, also, there is nothing sound.

Also, there is no slight quarrel over "image" and "likeness" when interpreters seek a nonexistent difference between these two words, except that "likeness" has been added by way of explanation. First, we know that repetitions were common among the Hebrews, in which they express one thing twice; then in the thing itself there is no ambiguity, simply man is called God's

independent and startling doctrine of justification. Cf. III. xi. 5, 6 and notes appended. In the same year he published a short treatise, *An filius Dei fuerit incarnandus . . . (Whether the Son of God Would Have Had to Be Incarnated if Sin Had Not Entered the World)*, to which was appended an essay on the image of God, *De imagine Dei quid sit*. Calvin states here, and rejects, Osiander's doctrine in *An filius Dei* of the necessity of the incarnation regardless of Adam's sin. See Niesel, *The Theology of Calvin*, pp. 126, 133 ff., and the titles there cited (p. 126, note 1). It is noteworthy that Osiander contributed to the advance of science by his cautious preface introducing the epochal work of Copernicus, *De revolutionibus orbium coelestium*, 1543.

[9] Text has plural *"eos"*; cf. VG, *"selon leur reverie."*

[10] Servetus, *Christianismi restitutio* (1553), dial. iii *On the Trinity*, p. 102.

image because he is like God. Accordingly, those who thus philosophize more subtly over these terms appear to be ridiculous: they either apply *zelem*, that is, image, to the substance of the soul, and *demuth*, that is, likeness, to its qualities; or they adduce something different.[11] For, when God determined to create man in his image, which was a rather obscure expression, he for explanation repeats it in this phrase, "According to his likeness," as if he were saying that he was going to make man, in whom he would represent himself as in an image, by means of engraved marks of likeness. Therefore Moses, a little after, reciting the same thing, repeats "image of God" twice, without mentioning "likeness." Osiander's objection is trivial, that not a part of man— say, the soul with its endowments—is called God's image, but the whole Adam, whose name was given him from the earth whence he was taken. Trivial, I say, all readers of sound mind will deem it. For, while the whole man is called mortal, the soul is not thereby subjected to death; nor does reason or intelligence belong to the body merely because man is called a "rational animal."[12] Therefore, although the soul is not man, yet it is not absurd for man, in respect to his soul, to be called God's image; even though I retain the principle I just now set forward, that the likeness of God extends to the whole excellence by which man's nature towers over all the kinds of living creatures. Accordingly, the integrity with which Adam was endowed is expressed by this word, when he had full possession of right understanding, when he had his affections kept within the bounds of reason, all his senses tempered in right order, and he truly referred his excellence to exceptional gifts bestowed upon him by his Maker. And although the primary seat of the divine image was in the mind and heart, or in the soul and its powers, yet there was no part of man, not even the body itself, in which some sparks did not glow. It is sure that even in the several parts of the world some traces of God's glory shine. From this we may gather that when his image is placed in man a tacit antithesis is introduced which raises man above all other creatures and, as it were, separates him from the common mass. And indeed, we ought not to deny that angels were created according to God's likeness, inasmuch as our highest perfection, as Christ testifies, will be to become like them [Matt. 22:30]. But by this particular title Moses rightly commends

11 Cf. Bernard, *Concerning Grace and Free Will* ix. 28 (MPL 182. 1016).
12 Repeated I. xv. 8. Cf. Seneca, *Moral Epistles* lxi. 8: *"Rationale enim animal est homo"* (LCL Seneca, *Moral Epistles* I. 276). In its Greek form this expression is attributed to Chrysippus (d. 206 B.C.). Liddell and Scott, *Greek-English Lexicon, s.v.* "λογικός."

God's grace toward us, especially when he compares only the visible creatures with man.

4. The true nature of the image of God is to be derived from what Scripture says of its renewal through Christ

ᵉNevertheless, it seems that we do not have a full definition of "image" if we do not see more plainly those faculties in which man excels, and in which he ought to be thought the reflection of God's glory. That, indeed, can be nowhere better recognized than from the restoration of his corrupted nature. There is no doubt that Adam, when he fell from his state, was by this defection alienated from God. Therefore, even though we grant that God's image was not totally annihilated and destroyed in him, yet it was so corrupted that whatever remains is frightful deformity. Consequently, the beginning of our recovery of salvation is in that restoration which we obtain through Christ, who also is called the Second Adam for the reason that he restores us to true and complete integrity. For even though Paul, contrasting the life-giving spirit that the believers receive from Christ with the living soul in which Adam was created [I Cor. 15:45], commends the richer measure of grace in regeneration, yet he does not remove that other principal point, that the end of regeneration is that Christ should reform us to God's image. ᵉ⁽ᵇ⁾Therefore elsewhere he teaches that "the new man is renewed . . . according to the image of his Creator" [Col. 3:10 p.]. With this agrees the saying, "Put on the new man, who has been created according to God" [Eph. 4:24, Vg.].

Now we are to see what Paul chiefly comprehends under this renewal. In the first place he posits knowledge, then pure righteousness and holiness. From this we infer that, to begin with, God's image was visible in the light of the mind, in the uprightness of the heart, and in the soundness of all the parts. For although I confess that these forms of speaking are synecdoches, yet this principle cannot be overthrown, that what was primary in the renewing of God's image[13] also held the highest place in the creation itself. ᵉ⁽ᶜ⁾To the same pertains what he teaches elsewhere, that "we . . . with unveiled face beholding the glory of Christ are being transformed into his very image" [II Cor. 3:18].

---

[13] "*In renovatione imaginis Dei.*" The use of words like *renovatio* and *reparatio* in this section (which was revised and expanded in 1559) has a methodological significance. Much of the picture of man at creation is derived from the account of the image of God as restored in redemption. Cf. II. ii. 12; Comm. I Cor. 15:44–50; Niesel, *The Theology of Calvin*, pp. 67 ff., 129 f.

Now we see how Christ is the most perfect image of God; if we are conformed to it, we are so restored that with true piety, righteousness, purity, and intelligence we bear God's image.

ᵉWhen this has been established, Osiander's fancy concerning the shape of the body readily vanishes of itself. But the statement in which man alone is called by Paul "the image and glory of God" [I Cor. 11:7, Vg.] and woman excluded from this place of honor is clearly to be restricted, as the context shows, to the political order. Yet I now consider it sufficiently proved that whatever has to do with spiritual and eternal life is included under "image," mention of which has been made. John confirms this same point in other words, declaring that "the life" which was from the beginning in God's Eternal Word "was the light of men" [John 1:4]. It was his intent to praise God's singular grace, wherein man excels the remaining living creatures, in order to separate him from the multitude because he attained no common life, but one joined with the light of understanding. Accordingly, he shows at the same time how man was created in God's image. Now God's image is the perfect excellence of human nature which shone in Adam before his defection, but was subsequently so vitiated and almost blotted out that nothing remains after the ruin except what is confused, mutilated, and disease-ridden. Therefore in some part it now is manifest in the elect, in so far as they have been reborn in the spirit; but it will attain its full splendor in heaven.

Yet in order that we may know of what parts this image consists, it is of value to discuss the faculties of the soul. For that speculation of Augustine, that the soul is the reflection of the Trinity because in it reside the understanding, will, and memory,[14] is by no means sound. ᵉ⁽ᵇ⁾Nor is there any probability in the opinion of those who locate God's likeness in the dominion given to man, as if in this mark alone he resembled God, that he was established as heir and possessor of all things; ᵉwhereas God's image is properly to be sought within him, not outside him, indeed, it ᶜis an inner good of the soul.

5. Manichaean error of the soul's emanation

ᵉBut before we go farther, we must confront the delusion of the Manichees, which Servetus has tried to introduce once more in this age. Because it is said that God breathed the breath of life

---

[14] Augustine, *On the Trinity* X. xi, xii; XIV. iv, vi, viii; XV. xxi (MPL 42. 982–984, 1040–1042, 1044 f., 1088 f.; tr. NPNF III. 142 f., 186 ff., 194; LCC VIII. 88 f., 103 f., 168 f.); *City of God* XI. xxvi, xxviii (MPL 41. 339, 342; tr. NPNF II. 220 f.).

upon man's face [Gen. 2:7], they thought the soul to be a derivative of God's substance, as if some portion of immeasurable divinity had flowed into man. Yet it is easy to point out quickly what crass and foul absurdities this devilish error drags in its train. For if man's soul be from the essence of God through derivation,[15] it will follow that God's nature is subject not only to change and passions, but also to ignorance, wicked desires, infirmity, and all manner of vices. Nothing is more inconstant than man. Contrary motions stir up and variously distract his soul. Repeatedly he is led astray by ignorance. He yields, overcome by the slightest temptation. We know his mind to be a sink and lurking place for every sort of filth. All these things one must attribute to God's nature, if we understand the soul to be from God's essence, or to be a secret inflowing of divinity. Who would not shudder at this monstrous thing? Indeed, Paul truly quotes Aratus[16] that we are God's offspring [Acts 17:28], but in quality, not in essence, inasmuch as he, indeed, adorned us with divine gifts. Meanwhile, to tear apart the essence of the Creator so that everyone may possess a part of it is utter folly. Therefore we must take it to be a fact that souls, although the image of God be engraved upon them, are just as much created as angels are. But creation is not inpouring, but the beginning of essence out of nothing. Indeed, if the spirit has been given by God, and in departing from the flesh returns to him [cf. Eccl. 12:7], we must not forthwith say that it was plucked from his substance. And Osiander, while carried away with his own delusions, as in this matter entangled himself in an impious error; he does not recognize the image of God in man apart from essential righteousness, as if God were unable to make us conform to himself by the inestimable power of his Spirit, apart from Christ's pouring his own substance into us! However some persons may try to camouflage these deceptions, they will never prevent well-balanced readers from seeing that such savor of the error of the Manichaeans. And when Paul discusses the restoration of the image, it is clear that we should infer from his words that man is made to conform to

[15] "*Si ex Dei essentia per traducem sit anima hominis.*" Cf. I. xiv. 20, note 29; II. i. 7, note 10; II. xiv. 8. Calvin takes his position unequivocally against traducianism, the doctrine that all human souls are derived from an original transmission (*tradux*) to Adam from the divine essence. He asserts the opposing doctrine of creationism, that an act of divine creation out of nothing (*ex nihilo*) takes place each time a child is given life. Numerous passages from Augustine related to Calvin's argument here are cited in Smits II. 29. See esp. *City of God* XI. xxii (MPL 41. 336; tr. NPNF II. 217).

[16] Cf. I. v. 3, note 12.

God, not by an inflowing of substance, but by the grace and power of the Spirit. For he says that by "beholding Christ's glory, we are being transformed into his very image . . . as through the Spirit of the Lord" [II Cor. 3:18], who surely works in us without rendering us consubstantial with God.

(Opinions of the philosophers on the soul criticized in view of the fall of Adam, 6–8)
6. *The soul and its faculties*
ᵉIt would be foolish to seek a definition of "soul" from the philosophers. Of them hardly one, except Plato, has rightly affirmed its immortal substance. Indeed, other Socratics also touch upon it, but in a way that shows how nobody teaches clearly a thing of which he has not been persuaded. Hence Plato's opinion is more correct, because he considers the image of God in the soul.[17] Others so attach the soul's powers and faculties to the present life that they leave nothing to it outside the body.[18]

Indeed, from Scripture we have already taught that the soul is an incorporeal substance;[19] now we must add that, although properly it is not spatially limited, still, set in the body, it dwells there as in a house; not only that it may animate all its parts and render its organs fit and useful for their actions, but also that it may hold the first place in ruling man's life, not alone with respect to the duties of his earthly life, but at the same time to arouse him to honor God. Even though in man's corruption this last point is not clearly perceived, yet some vestige remains imprinted in his very vices. For whence comes such concern to men about their good name but from shame? And whence comes shame but from regard for what is honorable? The beginning and cause of this is that they understand themselves to have been born to cultivate righteousness, in which the seed of religion is enclosed. But, without controversy, just as man was made for meditation upon the heavenly life,[20] so it is certain that the knowledge of it was engraved upon his soul. And if human happiness, whose perfection it is to be united with God, were hidden from man, he would in fact be bereft of the principal use of his understanding. Thus, also, the chief activity of the soul is to aspire thither. Hence the more

[17] Plato, *Phaedo* 105–107; *Phaedrus* 205–209; *Alcibiades* I. 133 (LCL Plato I. 364–373; I. 468–481; VIII. 210 f.); Cicero, *Tusculan Disputations* I. xxvii. 66 (LCL edition, pp. 76 f.).
[18] Pietro Pomponazzi, *De immortalitate animae* (1516) iv (tr. W. H. Hay in E. Cassirer, P. O. Kristeller, and J. H. Randall, *The Renaissance Philosophy of Man*, pp. 286–297). Cf. I. v. 4, note 17.
[19] Sec. 2, above.
[20] Cf. III. ix.

anyone endeavors to approach to God, the more he proves himself endowed with reason.

We ought to repudiate those persons who would affirm more than one soul in man, that is, a sensitive and a rational soul,[21] because there is nothing firm in their reasonings, even though they seem to be asserting something probable, unless we want to torture ourselves in trivial and useless matters. They say that there is great disagreement between organic motions and the soul's rational part. As if reason itself did not also disagree with itself and were not at cross-purposes with itself, just like armies at war. But since this disturbance arises out of depravity of nature, it is wrong to conclude from this that there are two souls, just because the faculties do not agree among themselves in befitting proportion.

e(b)But I leave it to the philosophers to discuss these faculties in their subtle way. For the upbuilding of godliness a simple definition will be enough for us. eI, indeed, agree that the things they teach are true, not only enjoyable, but also profitable to learn, and skillfully assembled by them. And I do not forbid those who are desirous of learning to study them. Therefore bI admit in the first place that there are five senses, which Plato preferred to call organs, by which all objects are presented to common sense, as a sort of receptacle.[22] There follows fantasy, which distinguishes those things which have been apprehended by common sense; then reason, which embraces universal judgment; finally understanding, which in intent and quiet study contemplates what reason discursively ponders. Similarly, to understanding, reason, and fantasy (the three cognitive faculties of the soul) correspond three appetitive faculties: will, whose functions consist in striving after what understanding and reason present; the capacity for anger, which seizes upon what is offered to it by reason and fantasy; the capacity to desire inordinately, which apprehends what is set before it by fantasy and sense.[23]

Although these things are true, or at least are probable, yet since I fear that they may involve us in their own obscurity rather than help us, I think they ought to be passed over. I shall not strongly oppose anyone who wants to classify the powers of the soul in some other way: to call one appetitive, which, even though without reason, if directed elsewhere, yet obeys reason; to call the other intellective, which is through itself participant in reason.

---

[21] Cf. Plato, *Republic* IV. 439 CD (LCL Plato, *Republic* I. 396 f.).
[22] Plato, *Theaetetus* 184 D (LCL Plato II. 156 f.).
[23] Themistius, *In libros Aristotelis de anima paraphrasis* II, VII (ed. R. Heinze, pp. 36, 120–122).

Nor would I refute the view that there are three principles of action: sense, understanding, appetite.

But let us rather choose a division within the capacity of all, which cannot be successfully sought from the philosophers. For they, while they want to speak with utter simplicity, divide the soul into appetite and understanding, but make both double. They say the latter is sometimes contemplative because, content with knowledge alone, it has no active motion (a thing that Cicero thought to be designated by the term "genius");[24] sometimes practical because by the apprehension of good or evil it variously moves the will. In this division is included the knowledge of how to live well and justly. The former part (I mean the appetitive) they also divide, into will and concupiscence; and as often as appetite, which they call βούλησις, obeys reason, it is ὁρμή; but it becomes πάθος when the appetite, having thrown off the yoke of reason, rushes off to intemperance.[25] Thus they always imagine reason in man as that faculty whereby he may govern himself aright.

7. Understanding and will as the truly fundamental faculties

e(b)We are forced to part somewhat from this way of teaching because the philosophers, ignorant of the corruption of nature that originated from the penalty for man's defection, mistakenly confuse two very diverse states of man. bThus let us, therefore, hold—as indeed is suitable to our present purpose—that the human soul consists of two faculties, understanding and will. Let the office, moreover, of understanding be to distinguish between objects, as each seems worthy of approval or disapproval; while that of the will, to choose and follow what the understanding pronounces good, but to reject and flee what it disapproves.[26] Let not those minutiae of Aristotle delay us here, that the mind has no motion in itself, but is moved by choice.[27] This choice he calls the appetitive understanding. Not to entangle ourselves in useless questions, let it be enough for us that the understanding is, as it were, the leader and governor of the soul; and that the will is always mindful of the bidding of the understanding, and in its own desires awaits the judgment of the understanding. For this reason, Aristotle himself truly teaches the same: that shunning or

---

24 Aristotle, Nicomachean Ethics VI. 2 (LCL edition, pp. 328 f.); Cicero, De finibus II. xi. 33 f.; V. vi. 17; V. xiii. 36 (LCL edition, pp. 118 ff., 408 f., 432 f.).
25 Themistius, op. cit., VII (ed. Heinze, pp. 113 f.).
26 Plato, Phaedrus 253 D (LCL Plato I. 492 f.).
27 Aristotle, Nicomachean Ethics, loc. cit.

seeking out in the appetite corresponds to affirming or denying in the mind. Indeed, in another place[28] we shall see how firmly the understanding now governs the direction of the will; here we wish to say only this, that no power can be found in the soul that does not duly have reference to one or the other of these members. And in this way we include sense under understanding. The philosophers, on the other hand, make this distinction: that sense inclines to pleasure, while understanding follows the good; thence it comes about that sensual appetite becomes inordinate desire and lust; the inclination of the understanding, will. Again, for the term "appetite," which they prefer, I substitute the word "will," which is more common.

8. Free choice and Adam's responsibility[t]

[e]Therefore God provided man's soul with a mind, by which to distinguish good from evil, right from wrong; and, with the light of reason as guide, to distinguish what should be followed from what should be avoided. For this reason, the philosophers called this directing part τὸ ἡγεμονικόν.[29] To this he joined the will, under whose control is choice. Man in his first condition excelled in these pre-eminent endowments, so that his reason, understanding, prudence, and judgment not only sufficed for the direction of his earthly life, but by them men mounted up even to God and eternal bliss. Then was choice added, to direct the appetites and control all the organic motions, and thus make the will completely amenable to the guidance of the reason.

In this integrity man by free will had the power, if he so willed, to attain eternal life. Here it would be out of place to raise the question of God's secret predestination because our present subject is not what can happen or not, but what man's nature was like. Therefore Adam could have stood if he wished, seeing that he fell solely by his own will. But it was because his will was capable of being bent to one side or the other, and was not given the constancy to persevere, that he fell so easily. Yet his choice of good and evil was free, and not that alone, but the highest rectitude was in his mind and will, and all the organic parts were rightly composed to obedience, until in destroying himself he corrupted his own blessings.

Hence the great obscurity faced by the philosophers, for they

---

[28] Cf. II. ii. 12–26.

[29] "ἡγεμονικόν." Cf. Plato, Protagoras 352 B (LCL Plato IV. 224); Plutarch, De virtute morali 441 C 3 (LCL Plutarch, Moralia VI. 22); Tertullian, On the Soul xiv (Waszink, op. cit., pp. 17 ff.; CCL Tertullianus II. 800; tr. ANF III. 193).

were seeking in a ruin for a building, and in scattered fragments for a well-knit structure. They held this principle, that man would not be a rational animal unless he possessed free choice of good and evil;[30] also it entered their minds that the distinction between virtues and vices would be obliterated if man did not order his life by his own planning. Well reasoned so far—if there had been no change in man. But since this was hidden from them, it is no wonder they mix up heaven and earth! They, as professed disciples of Christ, are obviously playing the fool when, by compromising between the opinions of the philosophers and heavenly doctrine, so that these touch neither heaven nor earth, in man—who is lost and sunk down into spiritual destruction—they still seek after free choice. But these matters will be better dealt with in their proper place.[31] Now we need bear only this in mind: man was far different at the first creation from his whole posterity, who, deriving their origin from him in his corrupted state, have contracted from him a hereditary taint. For, the individual parts of his soul were formed to uprightness, the soundness of his mind stood firm, and his will was free to choose the good.[32] If anyone objects that his will was placed in an insecure position because its power was weak, his status should have availed to remove any excuse; nor was it reasonable for God to be constrained by the necessity of making a man who either could not or would not sin at all. Such a nature would, indeed, have been more excellent. But to quarrel with God on this precise point, as if he ought to have conferred this upon man, is more than iniquitous, inasmuch as it was in his own choice to give whatever he pleased. But the reason he did not sustain man by the virtue of perseverance lies hidden in his plan; sobriety is for us the part of wisdom. Man, indeed, received the ability provided he exercised the will; but he did not have the will to use his ability, for this exercising of the will would have been followed by perseverance.[33] Yet he is not excusable, for he received so much that he voluntarily brought about his own destruction; indeed, no necessity was imposed upon God of giving man other than a mediocre and even transitory will, that from man's Fall he might gather occasion for his own glory.

[30] Aristotle, *Nicomachean Ethics*, loc. cit.
[31] II. ii. 2–4.
[32] Augustine, *On Genesis, Against the Manichees* II. vii. 9 (MPL 34. 200 f.).
[33] Augustine, *On Rebuke and Grace* xi. 32 (MPL 44. 936; tr. NPNF V. 484 f.).

^cCHAPTER XVI

GOD BY HIS POWER NOURISHES AND MAINTAINS THE WORLD CREATED BY HIM, AND RULES ITS SEVERAL PARTS BY HIS PROVIDENCE[1]

(God's special providence asserted, against the opinions of philosophers, 1–4)

1. Creation and providence inseparably joined

^cMoreover, to make God a momentary Creator, who once for all finished his work, would be cold and barren, and we must differ from profane men especially in that we see the presence of divine power shining as much in the continuing state of the universe as in its inception. ^bFor even though the minds of the impious too are compelled by merely looking upon earth and heaven to rise up to the Creator, yet faith has its own peculiar way of assigning the whole credit for Creation to God. To this pertains that saying of the apostle's to which we have referred before,[2] that only "by faith we understand that the universe was created by the word of God" [Heb. 11:3]. For unless we pass on to his providence—however we may seem both to comprehend with the mind and to confess with the tongue—we do not yet properly grasp what it means to say: "God is Creator." Carnal sense, once confronted with the power of God in the very Creation, stops there, and at most weighs and contemplates only the wisdom, power, and goodness of the author in accomplishing such handiwork. (These matters are self-evident, and even force themselves upon the unwilling.) It contemplates, moreover, some general preserving and governing activity, from which the force of motion derives. ^cIn short, carnal sense thinks there is an energy divinely bestowed from the beginning, sufficient to sustain all things.

^bBut faith ought to penetrate more deeply, namely, having found him Creator of all, forthwith to conclude he is also everlasting Governor and Preserver—not only in that he drives the celestial frame[3] as well as its several parts by a universal motion, but also in that he sustains, nourishes, and cares for, everything

---

[1] In editions 1539–1554, Calvin treated the topics of providence and predestination in the same chapter. In the final edition they are widely separated, providence being set here in the context of the knowledge of God the Creator, while predestination is postponed to III. xxi–xxiv, where it comes within the general treatment of the redemptive work of the Holy Spirit. See Benoit, *Institution* I. 221, note 2; P. Jacobs, *Prädestination und Verantwortlichkeit bei Calvin,* pp. 64–66, 71, *et passim.*

[2] In I. v. 14.

[3] *"Orbis machinam."* Cf. I. x. 1, note 2.

he has made, even to the least sparrow [cf. Matt. 10:29]. ᵉThus David, having briefly stated that the universe was created by God, immediately descends to the uninterrupted course of His providence, "By the word of Jehovah the heavens were made, and all their host by the breath of his mouth" [Ps. 33:6; cf. Ps. 32:6, Vg.]. Soon thereafter he adds, "Jehovah has looked down upon the sons of men" [Ps. 33:13; cf. Ps. 32:13–14, Vg.], and what follows is in the same vein. For although all men do not reason so clearly, yet, because it would not be believable that human affairs are cared for by God unless he were the Maker of the universe, and nobody seriously believes the universe was made by God without being persuaded that he takes care of his works, David not inappropriately leads us in the best order from the one to the other. In general, philosophers teach and human minds conceive that all parts of the universe are quickened by God's secret inspiration. ᵉ⁽ᵇ⁾Yet they do not reach as far as David is carried, bearing with him all the godly, when he says: ᵇ"These all look to thee, to give them their food in due season; when thou givest to them, they gather it up; when thou openest thy hand, they are filled with good things; when thou hidest thy face, they are dismayed; when thou takest away their breath, they die and return to the earth. If thou sendest forth thy spirit again, they are created, and thou renewest the face of the earth" [Ps. 104:27–30 p.]. ᵉIndeed, although they subscribe to Paul's statement that we have our being and move and live in God [Acts 17:28], yet they are far from that earnest feeling of grace which he commends, because they do not at all taste God's special care, by which alone his fatherly favor is known.

2. There is no such thing as fortune or chance

ᵉThat this difference may better appear, we must know that God's providence, as it is taught in Scripture, is opposed to fortune and fortuitous happenings.[4] Now it has been commonly accepted in all ages, and almost all mortals hold the same opinion today, that all things come about through chance. What we ought to believe concerning providence is by this depraved opinion most certainly not only beclouded, but almost buried. Suppose a man falls among thieves, or wild beasts; is shipwrecked at sea by a sudden gale; is killed by a falling house or tree. Suppose another man wandering through the desert finds help in his straits; hav-

---

[4] "Fortunae et casibus fortuitis." Cf. I. v. 11; I. xvi. 8, and accompanying notes.

ing been tossed by the waves, reaches harbor; miraculously escapes death by a finger's breadth. Carnal reason ascribes all such happenings, whether prosperous or adverse, to fortune. But anyone who has been taught by Christ's lips that all the hairs of his head are numbered [Matt. 10:30] will look farther afield for a cause, and will consider that all events are governed by God's secret plan. e(c)And concerning inanimate objects we ought to hold that, although each one has by nature been endowed with its own property, yet it does not exercise its own power except in so far as it is directed by God's ever-present hand. cThese are, thus, nothing but instruments to which God e(c)continually imparts as much effectiveness as he wills, and according to his own purpose bends and turns them to either one action or another.

cNo creature has a force more wondrous or glorious than that of the sun. For besides lighting the whole earth with its brightness, how great a thing is it that by its heat it nourishes and quickens all living things! That with its rays it breathes fruitfulness into the earth! That it warms the seeds in the bosom of the earth, draws them forth with budding greenness, increases and strengthens them, nourishes them anew, until they rise up into stalks! That it feeds the plant with continual warmth, until it grows into flower, and from flower into fruit! That then, also, with baking heat it brings the fruit to maturity! That in like manner trees and vines warmed by the sun first put forth buds and leaves, then put forth a flower, and from the flower produce fruit! Yet the Lord, to claim the whole credit for all these things, willed that, before he created the sun, light should come to be and earth be filled with all manner of herbs and fruits [Gen. 1:3, 11, 14]. Therefore a godly man will not make the sun either the principal or the necessary cause of these things which existed before the creation of the sun, but merely the instrument that God uses because he so wills; for with no more difficulty he might abandon it, and act through himself. eThen when we read that at Joshua's prayers the sun stood still in one degree for two days [Josh. 10:13], and that its shadow went back ten degrees for the sake of King Hezekiah [II Kings 20:11 or Isa. 38:8], God has witnessed by those few miracles that the sun does not daily rise and set by a blind instinct of nature but that he himself, to renew our remembrance of his fatherly favor toward us, governs its course. Nothing is more natural than for spring to follow winter; summer, spring; and fall, summer—each in turn. Yet in this series one sees such great and uneven diversity that it readily appears each year, month, and day is governed by a new, a special, providence of God.

3. God's providence governs all

[b(a)]And truly God claims, and would have us grant him, omnipotence—not the empty, idle, and almost unconscious sort that the Sophists[5] imagine, but a watchful, effective, active sort, [c]engaged in ceaseless activity. Not, indeed, an omnipotence that is only a general principle of confused motion, as if he were to command a river to flow through its once-appointed channels, but one that is directed toward individual and particular motions. [b]For he is deemed omnipotent, not because he can indeed act, yet sometimes ceases and sits in idleness, [c(b)]or continues by a general impulse that order of nature which he previously appointed; but because, governing heaven and earth by his providence, he so regulates all things that nothing takes place without his deliberation. For when, in The Psalms, it is said that "he does whatever he wills" [Ps. 115:3; cf. Ps. 113(b): 3, Vg.], a certain and deliberate will is meant. [c]For it would be senseless to interpret the words of the prophet after the manner of the philosophers, that God is the first agent because he is the beginning and cause of all motion;[6] for in times of adversity believers comfort themselves with the solace that they suffer nothing except by God's ordinance and command, for they are under his hand.

But if God's governance is so extended to all his works, it is a childish cavil to enclose it within the stream of nature. Indeed, those as much defraud God of his glory as themselves of a most profitable doctrine who confine God's providence to such narrow limits as though he allowed all things by a free course to be borne along according to a universal law of nature.[7] For nothing would be more miserable than man if he were exposed to every movement of the sky, air, earth, and waters. Besides, in this way God's particular goodness toward each one would be too unworthily reduced. David exclaims that infants still nursing at their mothers' breasts are eloquent enough to celebrate God's glory [Ps. 8:2], for immediately on coming forth from the womb, they find food prepared for them by his heavenly care. Indeed, this is in general true, provided what experience plainly demonstrates does not escape our eyes and senses, that some mothers have full and

---

[5] "Sophistae." The word is used by Calvin, in common with the other Reformers and with many Humanists, to designate the Scholastic writers when these are treated adversely.

[6] Cf. I. xiii. 18, note 39, and Aquinas, Summa Theol I. xix. 6: "An effect cannot possibly escape the order of the universal cause."

[7] Andreas Hyperius discusses this opinion adversely in his posthumously published *Methodus Theologiae* (Basel, 1568), pp. 232 ff., 252. Hyperius (1511–1564) was a Reformed scholar, and professor in Marburg.

abundant breasts, but others' are almost dry, as God wills to feed one more liberally, but another more meagerly.

e(b)Those who ascribe just praise to God's omnipotence doubly benefit thereby. First, power ample enough to do good there is in him in whose possession are heaven and earth, and to whose beck all creatures are so attentive as to put themselves in obedience to him. Secondly, they may safely rest in the protection of him to whose will are subject all the harmful things which, whatever their source, we may fear; whose authority curbs Satan with all his furies and his whole equipage; and upon whose nod depends whatever opposes our welfare. e(c)And we cannot otherwise correct or allay these uncontrolled and superstitious fears, which we repeatedly conceive at the onset of dangers. We are superstitiously timid, I say, if whenever creatures threaten us or forcibly terrorize us we become as fearful as if they had some intrinsic power to harm us, cor might wound us inadvertently and accidentally, or there were not enough help in God against their harmful acts.

For example, the prophet forbids God's children "to fear the stars and signs of heaven, as disbelievers commonly do" [Jer. 10:2 p.]. Surely he does not condemn every sort of fear. But when unbelievers transfer the government of the universe from God to the stars, they fancy that their bliss or their misery depends upon the decrees and indications of the stars, not upon God's will; so it comes about that their fear is transferred from him, toward whom alone they ought to direct it, to stars and comets. Let him, therefore, who would beware of this infidelity ever remember that there is no erratic power, or action, or motion in creatures, e(c)but that they are governed by God's secret plan in such a way that nothing happens except what is knowingly and willingly decreed by him.[8]

4. The nature of providence

eAt the outset, then, let my readers grasp that providence means

---

[8] This subject is treated by Calvin in relation to judicial astrology in *Avertissment contre l'astrologie judiciare* (1549). (CR VII. 509–544, especially cols. 523, 525–533.) Cf. J. Bohatec, *Budé und Calvin*, pp. 270–280, where Calvin's opinions on the religious bearings of judicial astrology are seen to be in agreement with those of Pico della Mirandola, the celebrated Christian Neoplatonist of Florence (d. 1494). On Pico's opinion, see also L. Thorndike, *A History of Magic and Experimental Science* IV. 534 ff. Cf. the first sentence of this section, and the similar language in I. ii. 2 and I. iv. 2.

not that by which God idly observes from heaven[9] what takes place on earth, but that by which, as keeper of the keys, he governs all events. Thus it pertains no less to his hands than to his eyes. And indeed, when Abraham said to his son, "God will provide" [Gen. 22:8], he meant not only to assert God's foreknowledge of a future event, but to cast the care of a matter unknown to him upon the will of Him who is wont to give a way out of things perplexed and confused. Whence it follows that providence is lodged in the act; [e(b)]for many babble too ignorantly of bare foreknowledge. Not so crass is the error of those who attribute a governance to God, [b]but of a confused and mixed sort, as I have said, namely, one that by a general motion revolves and drives the system of the universe, with its several parts, but which does not specifically direct the action of individual creatures. [e]Yet this error, also, is not tolerable; [b]for by this providence which they call universal, they teach that nothing hinders all creatures from being contingently moved, or man from turning himself hither and thither by the free choice of his will. And they so apportion things between God and man that God by His power inspires in man a movement by which he can act in accordance with the nature implanted in him, but He regulates His own actions by the plan of His will. Briefly, they mean that the universe, men's affairs, and men themselves are governed by God's might but not by His determination. I say nothing of the Epicureans (a pestilence that has always filled the world) who imagine that God is idle and indolent; and others just as foolish, who of old fancied that God so ruled above the middle region of the air that he left the lower regions to fortune.[10] As if the dumb creatures themselves do not sufficiently cry out against such patent madness!

("General" and "special" providence)

[e(b)]For now I propose to refute the opinion (which almost universally obtains) that concedes to God some kind of blind and ambiguous motion, while taking from him the chief thing: that he directs everything by his incomprehensible wisdom and disposes it to his own end. [b]And so in name only, not in fact, it makes God the Ruler of the universe because it deprives him of his control. What, I pray you, is it to have control but so to be in

---

[9] Cf. I. ii. 2, note 7; I. iv. 2, Cicero, *Nature of the Gods* I. ii. 3; I. xvii. 45; I. xix. 51; I. xl. 111 (LCL edition, pp. 4 f., 46 f., 50 f., 106 f.).

[10] Pietro Pomponazzi's opinions may be alluded to here: cf. his *De fato, de libero arbitrio, et de praedestinatione* (1520) II. i, iv, v, cited by Barth and Niesel (OS III. 193) along with references to the thirteenth-century Averroists, Siger de Brabant and Boethius of Dacia, who denied the doctrine of providence.

authority that you rule in a determined order those things over which you are placed? ᵉYet I do not wholly repudiate what is said concerning universal providence, provided they in turn grant me that the universe is ruled by God, not only because he watches over the order of nature set by himself, but because he exercises especial care over each of his works. It is, indeed, true that the several kinds of things are moved by a secret impulse of nature, as if they obeyed God's eternal command, and what God has once determined flows on by itself.

ᵉ⁽ᵇ⁾At this point we may refer to Christ's statement that from the very beginning he and the Father were always at work [John 5:17]; and to Paul's teaching that "in him we live, move, and have our being" [Acts 17:28]; also, what the author of The Letter to the Hebrews[11] says, meaning to prove the divinity of Christ, that all things are sustained by his mighty command [Heb. 1:3]. But they wrongly conceal and obscure by this excuse that special providence which is so declared by sure and clear testimonies of Scripture that it is a wonder anyone can have doubts about it. ᵉAnd surely they who cast over it the veil of which I spoke are themselves compelled to add, by way of correction, that many things take place under God's especial care. But they wrongly restrict this to particular acts alone. Therefore we must prove God so attends to the regulation of individual events, and they all so proceed from his set plan, that nothing takes place by chance.

(Doctrine of special providence supported by the evidence of Scripture, 5–7)

5. God's providence also directs the individual

ᵉSuppose we grant that the beginning of motion[12] is with God, but that all things, either of themselves or by chance, are borne whither inclination of nature impels. Then the alternation of days and nights, of winter and summer, will be God's work, inasmuch as he, assigning to each one his part, has set before them a certain law; that is, if with even tenor they uninterruptedly maintain the same way, days following after nights, months after months, and years after years. But that sometimes immoderate heat joined with dryness burns whatever crops there are, that at other times unseasonable rains damage the grain, that sudden calamity strikes from hail and storms—this will not be God's work, unless, perhaps because clouds or fair weather, cold or heat, take their origin

---

[11] Note that Calvin distinguishes the author of Hebrews from Paul. Cf. Comm. Heb., "Argument," where he says, "The manner of teaching and the style sufficiently show that Paul was not the author."

[12] Cf. I. xiii. 18, note 40.

from the conjunction of the stars and other natural causes. Yet in this way no place is left for God's fatherly favor, nor for his judgments. If they say that God is beneficent enough to mankind because he sheds upon heaven and earth an ordinary power, by which they are supplied with food, this is too weak and profane a fiction. As if the fruitfulness of one year were not a singular blessing of God, and scarcity and famine were not his curse and vengeance! But because it would take too long to collect all the reasons, let the authority of God himself suffice. e(b)In the Law and in the Prophets he often declares that as often as he waters the earth with dews and rain [Lev. 26:3–4; Deut. 11:13–14; 28:12] he testifies to his favor; but when the heaven is hardened like iron at his command [Lev. 26:19], the grainfields consumed by a blight and other harmful things [Deut. 28:22], as often as the fields are struck with hail and storms [cf. Isa. 28:2; Hag. 2:18, Vg.; 2:17, EV, etc.], these are a sign of his certain and special vengeance. If we accept these things, it is certain that not one drop of rain falls without God's sure command.

Indeed, David praises God's general providence, that he gives food to the young of the ravens which call upon him [Ps. 147:9; cf. Ps. 146:9, Vg.]; but when God himself threatens the animals with famine, does he not sufficiently declare that he feeds all living things sometimes with a meager, at other times with a fuller, portion as seems best? It is childish, as I have already said, to restrict this to particular acts, since Christ says, without exception, that not even a tiny and insignificant sparrow falls to the ground without the Father's will [Matt. 10:29]. eSurely if the flight of birds is governed by God's definite plan, we must confess with the prophet that he so dwells on high as to humble himself to behold whatever happens in heaven and on earth [Ps. 113:5–6].

6. God's providence especially relates to men

eBut because we know that the universe was established especially for the sake of mankind,[13] we ought to look for this purpose in his governance also. bThe prophet Jeremiah exclaims, "I know, O Lord, that the way of man is not his own, nor is it given to man to direct his own steps" [Jer. 10:23, cf. Vg.]. Moreover, Solomon says, "Man's steps are from the Lord [Prov. 20:24 p.] and how may man dispose his way?" [Prov. 16:9 p., cf. Vg.]. Let them now say that man is moved by God according to the inclination of his nature, but that he himself turns that motion whither he pleases. Nay, if that were truly said, the free choice of his ways would be in man's control. Perhaps they will deny this because he can do

[13] Cf. I. xiv. 22, note 32.

nothing without God's power. Yet they cannot really get by with that, since it is clear that the prophet and Solomon ascribe to God not only might but also choice and determination. Elsewhere Solomon elegantly rebukes this rashness of men, who set up for themselves a goal without regard to God, as if they were not led by his hand. "The disposition of the heart is man's, but the preparation of the tongue is the Lord's." [Prov. 16:1, 9, conflated.] It is an absurd folly that miserable men take it upon themselves to act without God, when they cannot even speak except as he wills!

Indeed, Scripture, to express more plainly that nothing at all in the world is undertaken without his determination, shows that things seemingly most fortuitous are subject to him. For what can you attribute more to chance than when a branch breaking off from a tree kills a passing traveler? But the Lord speaks far differently, acknowledging that he has delivered him to the hand of the slayer [Ex. 21:13]. Likewise, who does not attribute lots to the blindness of fortune? But the Lord does not allow this, claiming for himself the determining of them. He teaches that it is not by their own power that pebbles are cast into the lap and drawn out, but the one thing that could have been attributed to chance he testifies to come from himself [Prov. 16:33]. ᵉIn the same vein is that saying of Solomon, "The poor man and the usurer meet together; God illumines the eyes of both" [Prov. 29:13; cf. ch. 22:2]. He points out that, even though the rich are mingled with the poor in the world, while to each his condition is divinely assigned, God, who lights all men, is not at all blind. And so he urges the poor to patience; because those who are not content with their own lot try to shake off the burden laid upon them by God. Thus, also, another prophet rebukes the impious who ascribe to men's toil, or to fortune, the fact that some lie in squalor and others rise up to honors. "For not from the east, nor from the west, nor from the wilderness comes lifting up; because God is judge, he humbles one and lifts up another." [Ps. 75:6–7.] Because God cannot put off the office of judge, hence he reasons that it is by His secret plan that some distinguish themselves, while others remain contemptible.

7. God's providence also regulates "natural" occurrences

ᵉAlso, I say that particular events are generally testimonies of the character of God's singular providence. In the desert God stirred up the south wind, which brought to the people an abundance of birds. [Ex. 16:13; Num. 11: 31.] When he would have Jonah cast into the sea, God sent a wind by stirring up a whirlwind [Jonah 1:4]. Those who do not think that God controls the government of the universe will say that this was outside the common course. Yet from it I infer that no wind ever arises or increases except by God's express command. Otherwise it would not be true that he makes the winds his messengers and the flaming fire his ministers, that he makes the clouds his chariots and rides upon the wings of the wind [Ps. 104:3–4; cf. Ps. 103:3–4, Vg.], unless by his decision he drove both clouds and winds about, and showed in them the singular presence of his power. So, also, we are elsewhere taught that whenever the sea boils up with the blast of winds those forces witness to the singular presence of God. "He commands and raises the stormy wind which lifts on high the waves of the sea" [Ps. 107:25; cf. Ps. 106:25, Vg.]; "then he causes the storm to become calm, so that the waves cease for the sailors" [Ps. 107:29]; just as elsewhere he declares that he "has scourged the people with burning winds" [Amos 4:9, cf. Vg.].

So too, although the power to procreate is naturally implanted in men, yet God would have it accounted to his special favor that he leaves some in barrenness, but graces others with offspring [cf. Ps. 113:9]; "for the fruit of the womb is his gift" [Ps. 127: 3 p.]. For this reason, Jacob said to his wife, "Am I God that I can give you children?" [Gen. 30:2 p.]. To end this at once: there is nothing more ordinary in nature than for us to be nourished by bread. e(b)Yet the Spirit declares not only that the produce of the earth is God's special gift but that "men do not live by bread alone" [Deut. 8:3; Matt. 4:4]; because it is not plenty itself that nourishes men, but God's secret blessing;[14] ejust as conversely he threatens that he is going to "take away the stay of bread" [Isa. 3:1]. And indeed, that earnest prayer for daily bread [Matt. 6:11] could be understood only in the sense that God furnishes us with food by his fatherly hand. For this reason, the prophet, to persuade believers that God in feeding them fulfills the office of the best of all fathers of families, states that he gives food to all flesh [Ps. 136:25; cf. Ps. 135:25, Vg.]. Finally, when we hear on the one side, "The eyes of the Lord are upon the righteous and his ears toward their prayers" [Ps. 34: 15], but on the other, "The eye of the Lord is upon the impious, to destroy their memory from the earth" [Ps. 34:16 p.], let us know that all creatures above and below are ready to obey, that he may apply them to any use he pleases. From this we gather that his general providence not only flourishes among creatures so

---

[14] Cf. III. xx. 44.

as to continue the order of nature, but is by his wonderful plan adapted to a definite and proper end.

(Discussion of fortune, chance, and seeming contingency in events, 8–9)
8. *The doctrine of providence is no Stoic belief in fate!*
ᵇThose who wish to cast odium upon this doctrine defame it as the Stoics' dogma of fate. This charge was once hurled at Augustine.[15] Even though we are unwilling to quarrel over words, yet we do not admit the word "fate," both because it is one of those words whose profane novelties Paul teaches us to avoid [I Tim. 6:20], and because men try by the odium it incurs to oppress God's truth. Indeed, we are falsely and maliciously charged with this very dogma. We do not, with the Stoics, contrive a necessity out of the perpetual connection and intimately related series of causes, which is contained in nature; but we make God the ruler and governor of all things, who in accordance with his wisdom has from the farthest limit of eternity decreed what he was going to do, and now by his might carries out what he has decreed. From this we declare that not only heaven and earth and the inanimate creatures, but also the plans and intentions of men, are so governed by his providence that they are borne by it straight to their appointed end.

What then? you will ask. Does nothing happen by chance, nothing by contingency? I reply: Basil the Great has truly said that "fortune" and "chance" are pagan terms, with whose significance the minds of the godly ought not to be occupied.[16] For if every success is God's blessing, and calamity and adversity his curse, no place now remains in human affairs for fortune or chance. ᶜAnd that saying of Augustine also ought to impress us: "It grieves me that in my books *Against the Academics* I have so often mentioned Fortune; although I did not mean some goddess or other to be understood by this name, but only a fortuitous outcome of things in outward good or evil.[17] From *fortuna* also come those words which we should have no scruple about using: *forte, forsan, forsitan, fortasse, fortuito* [haply, perchance, mayhap, perhaps, fortuitously]; which nevertheless must be wholly referred to divine providence. And I did not pass over this in silence but said it, for perhaps what is commonly called 'fortune'

[15] Augustine, *Against Two Letters of the Pelagians* II. v. 10–vi. 12 (MPL 44. 577 ff.; tr. NPNF V. 395 f.).
[16] Basil, *Homilies on the Psalms*, Ps. 32:4 (MPG 29. 329 f.).
[17] Augustine, *Retractations* I. i. 2 (MPL 32. 585); *Against the Academics* I. i; III. ii. 2–4 (MPL 32. 905, 935 f.; tr. ACW XII. 35 f., 98–101).

is also ruled by a secret order, and we call a 'chance occurrence' only that of which the reason and cause are secret. Indeed, I said this: but I regret having thus mentioned 'fortune' here, since I see that men have a very bad custom, that where one ought to say 'God willed this,' they say, 'fortune willed this.' " ᵉIn fine, Augustine commonly teaches that if anything is left to fortune, the world is aimlessly whirled about. And although in another place he lays down that all things are carried on partly by man's free choice, partly by God's providence, yet a little after this he sufficiently demonstrates that men are under, and ruled by, providence; taking as his principle that nothing is more absurd than that anything should happen without God's ordaining it, because it would then happen without any cause. For this reason he excludes, also, the contingency that depends upon men's will; soon thereafter he does so more clearly, denying that we ought to seek the cause of God's will. How the term "permission," so frequently mentioned by him, ought to be understood will best appear from one passage, where he proves that God's will is the highest and first cause of all things because nothing happens except from his command or permission.[18] Surely he does not conjure up a God who reposes idly in a watchtower, willing the while to permit something or other, when an actual will not his own, so to speak, intervenes, which otherwise could not be deemed a cause.

9. The true causes of events are hidden to us

ᵉ⁽ᵇ⁾Yet since the sluggishness of our mind lies far beneath the height of God's providence, we must employ a distinction to lift it up. ᵇTherefore I shall put it this way: however all things may be ordained by God's plan, according to a sure dispensation, for us they are fortuitous. Not that we think that fortune rules the world and men, tumbling all things at random up and down, for it is fitting that this folly be absent from the Christian's breast! But since the order, reason, end, and necessity of those things which happen for the most part lie hidden in God's purpose, and are not apprehended by human opinon, those things, which it is certain take place by God's will, are in a sense fortuitous. For they bear on the face of them no other appearance, whether they are considered in their own nature or weighed according to our knowledge and judgment. Let us imagine, for example, a merchant who, entering a wood with a company of faithful men, unwisely wanders away from his companions, and in

[18] Augustine, *De diversis quaestionibus*, qu. 24, 27, 28 (MPL 40. 17 f.); *On the Trinity* III. iv. 9 (MPL 42. 873; tr. NPNF III. 58 f.).

his wandering comes upon a robber's den, falls among thieves, and is slain. His death was not only foreseen by God's eye, but also determined by his decree. For it is not said that he foresaw how long the life of each man would extend, but that he determined and fixed the bounds that men cannot pass [Job 14:5]. Yet as far as the capacity of our mind is concerned, all things therein seem fortuitous. What will a Christian think at this point? Just this: whatever happened in a death of this sort he will regard as fortuitous by nature, as it is; yet he will not doubt that God's providence exercised authority over fortune in directing its end. The same reckoning applies to the contingency of future events.[19] As all future events are uncertain to us, so we hold them in suspense, as if they might incline to one side or the other. Yet in our hearts it nonetheless remains fixed that nothing will take place that the Lord has not previously foreseen.

eIn this sense the term "fate" is often repeated in Ecclesiastes [chs. 2:14–15; 3:19; 9:2–3, 11],[20] because at first glance men do not penetrate to the first cause, which is deeply hidden. And yet what is set forth in Scripture concerning God's secret providence was never so extinguished from men's hearts without some sparks always glowing in the darkness. Thus the soothsayers of the Philistines, although they wavered in doubt, yet attributed their adverse fate partly to God, partly to fortune. If the Ark, they say, shall pass through that way, we shall know that it is God who has struck us; but if it passes through another way, then it has happened to us by chance [I Sam. 6:9]. Foolishly indeed, where their divination deceived them, they took refuge in fortune. Meanwhile we see them constrained from daring to think simply fortuitous what had happened unfavorably to them. But how God by the bridle of his providence turns every event whatever way he wills, will be clear from this remarkable example. At the very moment of time in which David was trapped in the wilderness of Maon, the Philistines invaded the land, and Saul was compelled to depart [I Sam. 23:26–27]. If God, intending to provide for his servant's safety, cast this hindrance in Saul's way, surely, although the Philistines took up arms suddenly and above all human expectation, yet we will not say that this took place by

19 Cf. Comm. Harmony of the Evangelists, Matt. 10:29. Calvin holds all contingency within the operation of God's providence. So also Westminster Confession V. 2: ". . . by the same providence, he ordereth . . . [all things] to fall out according to the nature of second causes, either necessarily, freely, or contingently." See the quoted statements on contingent events by Reformed theologians in Heppe RD, ch. xii, pp. 265 ff.

20 "Eventus."

chance; but what for us seems a contingency, faith recognizes to have been a secret impulse from God.

Not always does a like reason appear, but we ought undoubtedly to hold that whatever changes are discerned in the world are produced from the secret stirring of God's hand. But what God has determined must necessarily so take place, even though it is neither unconditionally, nor of its own peculiar nature, necessary. A familiar example presents itself in the bones of Christ. When he took upon himself a body like our own, no sane man will deny that his bones were fragile; yet it was impossible to break them [John 19:33, 36]. Whence again we see that distinctions concerning relative necessity and absolute necessity, likewise of consequent and consequence,[21] were not recklessly invented in schools, when God subjected to fragility the bones of his Son, which he had exempted from being broken, and thus restricted to the necessity of his own plan what could have happened naturally.

ᶜCHAPTER XVII

How We May Apply This Doctrine to Our Greatest Benefit

(Interpretation of divine providence with reference to the past and the future, 1–5)
1. The meaning of God's ways
ᶜMoreover, as men's dispositions are inclined to vain subtleties, any who do not hold fast to a good and right use of this doctrine can hardly avoid entangling themselves in inscrutable difficulties. Therefore it is expedient here to discuss briefly to what end Scripture teaches that all things are divinely ordained.

Three things, indeed, are to be noted. First, God's providence must be considered with regard to the future as well as the past. Secondly, it is the determinative principle of all things in such a way that sometimes it works through an intermediary, sometimes without an intermediary, sometimes contrary to every intermediary. Finally, it strives to the end that God may reveal his concern for the whole human race, but especially his vigilance in ruling the church, which he deigns to watch more closely. Now this, also, ought to be added, that although either fatherly favor

---

[21] Aquinas, *Summa Theol.* I. xix. 3. Barth and Niesel, citing Bonaventura, Duns Scotus, Erasmus, and Eck in agreement, point out Luther's rejection of this view in his *De servo arbitrio* (*Werke* WA XVIII. 615 ff.). Melanchthon's position is not different from that of Aquinas and of Calvin: *Loci communes*, 1543 (CR Melanchthon XXI. 649 f.); *Loci theologici*, 1559 (ed. Engelland, *op. cit.*, pp. 229 f., 233).

and beneficence or severity of judgment often shine forth in the whole course of providence, nevertheless sometimes the causes of the events are hidden. So the thought creeps in that human affairs turn and whirl at the blind urge of fortune;[1] or the flesh incites us to contradiction, as if God were making sport of men by throwing them about like balls. It is, indeed, true that if we had quiet and composed minds ready to learn, the final outcome would show that God always has the best reason for his plan: either to instruct his own people in patience, or to correct their wicked affections and tame their lust, or to subjugate them to self-denial, or to arouse them from sluggishness; again, to bring low the proud, to shatter the cunning of the impious and to overthrow their devices. Yet however hidden and fugitive from our point of view the causes may be, we must hold that they are surely laid up with him, and hence we must exclaim with David: "Great, O God, are the wondrous deeds that thou hast done, and thy thoughts toward us cannot be reckoned; if I try to speak, they would be more than can be told" [Ps. 40:5]. For even though in our miseries our sins ought always to come to mind, that punishment itself may incite us to repentance, yet we see how Christ claims for the Father's secret plan a broader justice than simply punishing each one as he deserves. For concerning the man born blind he says: "Neither he nor his parents sinned, but that God's glory may be manifested in him" [John 9:3 p.]. For here our nature cries out, when calamity comes before birth itself, as if God with so little mercy thus punished the undeserving. Yet Christ testifies that in this miracle the glory of his Father shines, provided our eyes be pure.

But we must so cherish moderation that we do not try to make God render account to us, but so reverence his secret judgments as to consider his will the truly just cause of all things. When dense clouds darken the sky, and a violent tempest arises, because a gloomy mist is cast over our eyes, thunder strikes our ears and all our senses are benumbed with fright, everything seems to us to be confused and mixed up; but all the while a constant quiet and serenity ever remain in heaven. So must we infer that, while the disturbances in the world deprive us of judgment, God out of the pure light of his justice and wisdom tempers and directs these very movements in the best-conceived order to a right end. And surely on this point it is sheer folly that many dare with

---

[1] Cf. I. v. 11, note 34; Comm. Ps. 36:6; 73:1. C. Trinkhaus uses this passage to illustrate Calvin's stand "against the chaotic character of historical events and personal destinies": "Renaissance Problems in Calvin's Theology," *Studies in the Renaissance* III, ed. W. Peery, p. 65.

greater license to call God's works to account, and to examine his secret plans, and to pass as rash a sentence on matters unknown as they would on the deeds of mortal men. For what is more absurd than to use this moderation toward our equals, that we prefer to suspend judgment rather than be charged with rashness; yet haughtily revile the hidden judgments of God, which we ought to hold in reverence?

2. God's rule will be observed with respect!

ᵉTherefore no one will weigh God's providence properly and profitably but him who considers that his business is with his Maker[2] and the Framer of the universe, and with becoming humility submits himself to fear and reverence. Hence it happens that today so many dogs assail this doctrine with their venomous bitings, or at least with barking: for they wish nothing to be lawful for God beyond what their own reason prescribes for themselves. Also they rail at us with as much wantonness as they can; because we, not content with the precepts of the law, which comprise God's will, say also that the universe is ruled by his secret plans.[3] As if what we teach were a figment of our brain, and the Holy Spirit did not everywhere expressly declare the same thing and repeat it in innumerable forms of expression. But, because some shame restrains them from daring to vomit forth these blasphemies against heaven, they feign it is with us they are contending, that they may rave more freely.

But if they do not admit that whatever happens in the universe is governed by God's incomprehensible plans, let them answer to what end Scripture says that his judgments are a deep abyss [Ps. 36:6]. For since Moses proclaims that the will of God is to be sought not far off in the clouds or in abysses, because it has been set forth familiarly in the law [Deut. 30:11–14], it follows that he has another hidden will[4] which may be compared to a

---

[2] For Calvin, every man in all circumstances has dealings with God (*negotium cum Deo*). Cf. III. iii. 6; III. iii. 16; III. vii. 2. This conviction was held by him in a very personal sense. For example, in his letter to Farel when in the stress of decision regarding his return to Geneva: "I am well aware that it is with God that I have to do [*mihi esse negotium cum Deo*]." The date of this letter is October 24, 1540, not as conjectured by Bonnet, August, 1541 (CR XI. 100; tr. Calvin, *Letters* I. 281).

[3] The reference is apparently to a criticism raised by Sebastian Castellio, or some advocate of his cause, against Calvin. Cf. Calvin's *Calumniae nebulonis cuiusdam . . . ad easdem responsio*, 1558 (CR IX. 269, 279). Cf. I. xviii. 1, note 3.

[4] "*Aliam voluntatem absconditam.*" Calvin does not delineate two wills in God, but thinks of the inaccessible abyss of God's inner being (cf. I. xiii. 1–2) and the mysteries of revelation itself. Cf. I. xviii. 2–3: "But even

deep abyss; concerning which Paul also says: "O depth of the riches and wisdom and knowledge of God! How unsearchable are his judgments, and how inscrutable his ways! 'For who has known the mind of the Lord, or who has been his counselor?' " [Rom. 11:33–34; cf. Isa. 40:13–14]. And it is, indeed, true that in the law and the gospel are comprehended mysteries which tower far above the reach of our senses. But since God illumines the minds of his own with the spirit of discernment [Job 20:3 or Isa. 11:2][5] for the understanding of these mysteries which he has deigned to reveal by his Word, now no abyss is here; rather, a way in which we ought to walk in safety, and a lamp to guide our feet [Ps. 118:105, Vg.; 119:105, EV], the light of life [cf. John 1:4; 8:12], and the school of sure and clear truth. Yet his wonderful method of governing the universe is rightly called an abyss, because while it is hidden from us, we ought reverently to adore it.

Moses has beautifully expressed both ideas in a few words: "The secret things," he says, "belong to the Lord our God, but what is here written, to you and your children" [Deut. 29:29 p.]. For we see how he bids us not only direct our study to meditation upon the law, but to look up to God's secret providence with awe. Also, in The Book of Job is set forth a declaration of such sublimity as to humble our minds. For after the author, in surveying above and below the frame of the universe, has magnificently discoursed concerning God's works, he finally adds: "Behold! These are but the outskirts of his ways, and how small a thing is heard therein!" [Job 26:14]. In this way he distinguishes in another place between the wisdom that resides with God and the portion of wisdom God has prescribed for men. For when he has discoursed on the secrets of nature, he says that wisdom is known to God alone, but "eludes the eyes of all the living" [Job 28:21]. But he adds a little later that His wisdom has been published to be searched out, because it is said to man: "Behold, the fear of the Lord is wisdom" [Job 28:28]. To this point the saying of Augustine applies: "Because we do not know all the things which God in the best possible order does concerning us, we act solely in good will according to the law, but in other things we are acted upon according to the law, because his providence is an unchangeable law."[6] Therefore, since God assumes to himself

---

though his will is one and simple in him, it appears manifold to us" (sec. 3). Note also I. xviii. 1, 4 (the distinction between will and precept); III. xx. 43; III. xxiv. 17, note 31.

[5] Cf. I. xvi. 1; III. ii. 14.

[6] Augustine, *On Diverse Questions*, qu. 27 (MPL 40. 18).

the right (unknown to us) to rule the universe, let our law of soberness and moderation be to assent to his supreme authority, that his will may be for us the sole rule of righteousness, and the truly just cause of all things. Not, indeed, that absolute will of which the Sophists babble, by an impious and profane distinction separating his justice from his power[7]—but providence, that determinative principle of all things, from which flows nothing but right, although the reasons have been hidden from us.

3. God's providence does not relieve us from responsibility

 ^eAll who will compose themselves to this moderation will not murmur against God on account of their adversities in time past, nor lay the blame for their own wickedness upon him as did the Homeric Agamemnon, saying: "I am not the cause, but Zeus and fate."[8] And they will not, as if carried off by the fates, out of desperation cast themselves to destruction like that youth of Plautus: "Unstable is the lot of things, the fates drive men according to their own pleasure. I will betake myself to the precipice, that there I may lose my goods with my life." And they will not follow the example of another, and cover up their own evil deeds with the name "God." For thus Lyconides says in another comedy: "God was the instigator; I believe the gods willed it. For I know if they had not so willed, it would not have happened."[9] But rather let them inquire and learn from Scripture what is pleasing to God so that they may strive toward this

---

[7] Cf. Calvin, *De aeterna Dei praedestinatione*, where he assails the "Sorbonnist dogma that ascribes to God absolute power" dissociated from justice. "One might more readily take the sun's light from its heat or its heat from its fire, than separate God's power from his justice. . . . He who severs God from law [*Deum exlegem qui facit*] despoils him of a part of his glory." (CR VIII. 361.) Similarly, in *Sermons on Job* lxxxviii, on Job 23:1–7: "What the Sorbonne doctors say, that God has an absolute power, is a diabolical blasphemy which has been invented in hell" (CR XXXIV. 339 f.). Cf. McNeill, *The History and Character of Calvinism*, p. 212. The opinion here censured was affirmed by Ockham: *Super quatuor libros sententiarum subtilissimae quaestiones* I. xvii. 2; cf. Gabriel Biel, *Epythoma et collectorium circa quatuor sententiarum libros* I. xvii. 2. Wendel indicates that Duns Scotus, usually cited as its originator, should be understood in a somewhat different sense (Wendel, *Calvin*, pp. 92 f.).

[8] From Agamemnon's address to the assembly of warriors in Homer, *Iliad* xix. 86 f. (LCL Homer, *Iliad* II. 342 f.). (Calvin quotes the line in Greek without a translation.)

[9] "*Deus impulsor fuit,*" etc. From a speech of Lyconides in Plautus, *Aulularia* 737, 742: "*Deus impulsor mihi fuit . . . deos credo voluisse; nam nisi vellent, non fieret, scio*" (LCL Plautus I. 310). The previous reference to the "youth" is to Pistoclerus in the *Bacchides* of Plautus.

under the Spirit's guidance. At the same time, being ready to follow God wherever he calls, they will show in very truth that nothing is more profitable than the knowledge of this doctrine.

ᶜ⁽ᵇ⁾Profane men[10] with their absurdities foolishly raise an uproar, ᵇso that they almost, as the saying is, mingle heaven and earth. If the Lord has indicated the point of our death, they say, we cannot escape it. Therefore it is vain for anyone to busy himself in taking precautions. One man does not dare take a road that he hears is dangerous, lest he be murdered by thieves; another summons physicians, and wears himself out with medicines to keep himself alive; another abstains from coarser foods, lest he impair his weak health; another is afraid of living in tumble-down houses. In short, all devise ways and forge them with great purpose of mind, to attain what they desired. Now either all these remedies which attempt to correct God's will are vain; or else there is no fixed decree of God that determines life and death, health and disease, peace and war, and other things that men, as they desire or hate them, so earnestly try by their own toil either to obtain or to avoid. Also they conclude that believers' prayers, by which the Lord is asked to provide for things that he has already decreed from eternity, are perverse, not to say superfluous. To sum up, they cancel all those plans which have to do with the future, as militating against God's providence, which, without their being consulted, has decreed what he would have happen. Then whatever does happen now, they so impute to God's providence that they close their eyes to the man who clearly has done it. Does an assassin murder an upright citizen? He has carried out, they say, God's plan. Has someone stolen, or committed adultery? Because he has done what was foreseen and ordained by the Lord, he is the minister of God's providence. Has a son, neglecting remedies, with never a care awaited the death of a parent? He could not resist God, who had so appointed from eternity. Thus all crimes, because subject to God's ordinance, they call virtues.

4. God's providence does not excuse us from due prudence

ᵇBut with respect to future events, Solomon easily brings human deliberations into agreement with God's providence. For just as he laughs at the dullness of those who boldly undertake something or other without the Lord, as though they were not

---

[10] The "profane men" are those of the Libertine sect. Cf. *Contre la secte phantastique des Libertins* xiii–xvi (CR VII. 183–198). Sections 3, 4, 7, 8 here employ a number of expressions found in this part of the tract.

ruled by his hand, so elsewhere he says: "Man's heart plans his way, but the Lord will direct his steps" [Prov. 16:9 p.]. This means that we are not at all hindered by God's eternal decrees either from looking ahead for ourselves or from putting all our affairs in order, but always in submission to his will. The reason is obvious. For he who has set the limits to our life has at the same time entrusted to us its care; he has provided means and helps to preserve it; he has also made us able to foresee dangers; that they may not overwhelm us unaware, he has offered precautions and remedies. Now it is very clear what our duty is: thus, if the Lord has committed to us the protection of our life, our duty is to protect it; if he offers helps, to use them; if he forewarns us of dangers, not to plunge headlong; if he makes remedies available, not to neglect them. But no danger will hurt us, say they, unless it is fatal, and in this case it is beyond remedies. But what if the dangers are not fatal, because the Lord has provided you with remedies for repulsing and overcoming them? See how your reckoning fits in with the order of divine dispensation. You conclude that we ought not to beware of any peril because, since it is not fatal, we shall escape it even without taking any precaution. But the Lord enjoins you to beware, because he would not have it fatal for you. These fools do not consider what is under their very eyes, that the Lord has inspired in men the arts of taking counsel and caution, by which to comply with his providence in the preservation of life itself. Just as, on the contrary, by neglect and slothfulness they bring upon themselves the ills that he has laid upon them. How does it happen that a provident man, while he takes care of himself, also disentangles himself from threatening evils, but a foolish man perishes from his own unconsidered rashness, unless folly and prudence are instruments of the divine dispensation in both cases? For this reason, God pleased to hide all future events from us, in order that we should resist them as doubtful, and not cease to oppose them with ready remedies, until they are either overcome or pass beyond all care. ᵉI have therefore already remarked that God's providence does not always meet us in its naked form, but God in a sense clothes it with the means employed.

5. God's providence does not exculpate our wickedness

ᵉ⁽ᵇ⁾The same men wrongly and rashly lay the happenings of past time to the naked providence of God. For since on it depends everything that happens, ᵇtherefore, say they, neither thefts, nor adulteries, nor murders take place without God's will intervening. Why therefore, they ask, should a thief be punished, who has plundered someone whom the Lord would punish with poverty? Why shall a murderer be punished, who has killed one whose life the Lord had ended? If all such men are serving God's will, why shall they be punished? On the contrary, I deny that they are serving God's will. For we shall not say that one who is motivated by an evil inclination, by only obeying his own wicked desire, renders service to God at His bidding. A man, having learned of His will, obeys God in striving toward the goal to which he is called by that same will. From what source do we learn but from his Word? In such fashion we must in our deeds search out God's will which he declares through his Word. God requires of us only what he commands. If we contrive anything against his commandment, it is not obedience but obstinacy and transgression. Yet, unless he willed it, we would not do it. I agree. But do we do evil things to the end that we may serve him? Yet he by no means commands us to do them; rather we rush headlong, without thinking what he requires, but so raging in our unbridled lust that we deliberately strive against him. And in this way we serve his just ordinance by doing evil, for so great and boundless is his wisdom that he knows right well how to use evil instruments to do good. And see how absurd their argument is: they would have transgressors go unpunished, on the ground that their misdeeds are committed solely by God's dispensation.

I grant more: thieves and murderers and other evildoers are the instruments of divine providence, and the Lord himself uses these to carry out the judgments that he has determined with himself. Yet I deny that they can derive from this any excuse for their evil deeds. Why? Will they either involve God in the same iniquity with themselves, or will they cloak their own depravity with his justice? They can do neither. In their own conscience they are so convicted as to be unable to clear themselves; in themselves they so discover all evil, but in him only the lawful use of their evil intent, as to preclude laying the charge against God. Well and good, for he works through them. And whence, I ask you, comes the stench of a corpse, which is both putrefied and laid open by the heat of the sun? All men see that it is stirred up by the sun's rays; yet no one for this reason says that the rays stink.[11] Thus, since the matter and guilt of evil repose in a wicked man, what reason is there to think that God contracts any defilement, if he uses his service for his own purpose? Away, therefore, with this doglike impudence, which can indeed bark at God's justice afar off but cannot touch it.

[11] Augustine, *Faith and the Creed* iv. 10 (MPL 40. 187; tr. LCC VI. 359).

(Meditating on the ways of God in providence: the happiness of recognizing acts of providence, 6–11)

6. God's providence as solace of believers

ᵉ⁽ᵇ⁾But these calumnies, or rather ravings of distracted men, will be easily dispersed by pious and holy meditation on providence, which the rule of piety dictates to us, so that from this we may receive the best and sweetest fruit. ᵇTherefore the Christian heart, since it has been thoroughly persuaded that all things happen by God's plan, and that nothing takes place by chance, will ever look to him as the principal cause of things, yet will give attention to the secondary causes in their proper place. Then the heart will not doubt that God's singular providence keeps watch to preserve it, and will not suffer anything to happen but what may turn out to its good and salvation. But since God's dealings are first with man, then with the remaining creatures, the heart will have assurance that God's providence rules over both. As far as men are concerned, whether they are good or evil, the heart of the Christian will know that their plans, wills, efforts, and abilities are under God's hand; that it is within his choice to bend them whither he pleases and to constrain them whenever he pleases.

There are very many and very clear promises that testify that God's singular providence watches over the welfare of believers: "Cast your care upon the Lord, and he will nourish you, and will never permit the righteous man to flounder" [Ps. 55:22 p.; cf. Ps. 54:23, Vg.]. For he takes care of us. [I Peter 5:7 p.] "He who dwells in the help of the Most High will abide in the protection of the God of heaven." [Ps. 91:1; 90:1, Vg.] "He who touches you touches the pupil of mine eye." [Zech. 2:8 p.] "I will be your shield" [Gen. 15:1 p.], "a brazen wall" [Jer. 1:18; 15:20]; "I will contend with those who contend with you" [Isa. 49:25]. "Even though a mother may forget her children, yet will I not forget you." [Isa. 49:15 p.] Indeed, the principal purpose of Biblical history is to teach that the Lord watches over the ways of the saints with such great diligence that they do not even stumble over a stone [cf. Ps. 91:12].

ᵉ⁽ᵇ⁾Therefore, as we rightly rejected a little above[12] the opinion of those ᵇwho imagine a universal providence of God, which does not stoop to the especial care of any particular creature, yet first of all it is important that we recognize this special care toward us.[13] Whence Christ, when he declared that not even a tiny spar-

[12] I. xvi. 4.
[13] Luther, in *Tesseradecas consolatoria* (*The Fourteen Comforts*), 1520, speaks impressively of God's providential care of us even when we are unaware

row of little worth falls to earth without the Father's will [Matt. 10:29], immediately applies it in this way: that since we are of greater value than sparrows, we ought to realize that God watches over us with all the closer care [Matt. 10:31]; and he extends it so far that we may trust that the hairs of our head are numbered [Matt. 10:30]. What else can we wish for ourselves, if not even one hair can fall from our head without his will? ᵉI speak not only concerning mankind; but, because God has chosen the church to be his dwelling place, there is no doubt that he shows by singular proofs his fatherly care in ruling it.

7. God's providence in prosperity*

ᵇThe servant of God, strengthened both by these promises and by examples, will join thereto the testimonies which teach that all men are under his power, whether their minds are to be conciliated, or their malice to be restrained that it may not do harm. For it is the Lord who gives us favor, not alone among those who wish us well, but even "in the eyes of the Egyptians" [Ex. 3:21]; indeed, he knows how to shatter the wickedness of our enemies in various ways. For sometimes he takes away their understanding so that they are unable to comprehend anything sane or sober, as when he sends forth Satan to fill the mouths of all the prophets with falsehood in order to deceive Ahab [I Kings 22:22]. He drives Rehoboam mad by the young men's advice that through his own folly he may be despoiled of the kingdom [I Kings 12:10, 15]. Sometimes when he grants them understanding, he so frightens and dispirits them that they do not wish, or plan, to carry out what they have conceived. Sometimes, also, when he permits them to attempt what their lust and madness has prompted, he at the right moment breaks off their violence, and does not allow their purpose to be completed. Thus Ahitophel's advice, which would have been fatal for David, he destroyed before its time [II Sam. 17:7, 14]. Thus, also, it is his care to govern all creatures for their own good and safety; and even the devil himself, who, we see, dared not attempt anything against Job without His permission and command [Job 1:12].

Gratitude of mind for the favorable outcome of things, patience in adversity, and also incredible freedom from worry about the future all necessarily follow upon this knowledge. Therefore whatever shall happen prosperously and according to the desire

of it. *Werke* WA VI. 110 f., 125 f.; tr. B. Woolf, *Reformation Writings of Martin Luther* II. 28 ff., 55 ff. Calvin's Commentaries on the Psalms abound in expressions of this sort.

of his heart, God's servant will attribute wholly to God, whether he feels God's beneficence through the ministry of men, or has been helped by inanimate creatures. For thus he will reason in his mind: surely it is the Lord who has inclined their hearts to me, who has so bound them to me that they should become the instruments of his kindness toward me. In abundance of fruits he will think: "It is the Lord who 'hears' the heaven, that the heaven may 'hear' the earth, that the earth also may 'hear' its offspring" [cf. Hos. 2:21–22, Vg.; 2:22–23, EV]. In other things he will not doubt that it is the Lord's blessing alone by which all things prosper. Admonished by so many evidences, he will not continue to be ungrateful.

8. Certainty about God's providence helps us in all adversities

ᵇIf anything adverse happens, straightway he will raise up his heart here also unto God, whose hand can best impress patience and peaceful moderation of mind upon us. If Joseph had stopped to dwell upon his brothers' treachery, he would never have been able to show a brotherly attitude toward them. But since he turned his thoughts to the Lord, forgetting the injustice, he inclined to gentleness and kindness, even to the point of comforting his brothers and saying: "It is not you who sold me into Egypt, but I was sent before you by God's will, that I might save your life" [Gen. 45:5, 7–8 p.]. "Indeed you intended evil against me, but the Lord turned it into good." [Gen. 50:20, cf. Vg.] If Job had turned his attention to the Chaldeans, by whom he was troubled, he would immediately have been aroused to revenge; but because he at once recognized it as the Lord's work, he comforts himself with this most beautiful thought: "The Lord gave, the Lord has taken away; blessed be the name of the Lord" [Job 1:21]. Thus David, assailed with threats and stones by Shimei, if he had fixed his eyes upon the man, would have encouraged his men to repay the injury; but because he knows that Shimei does not act without the Lord's prompting, he rather appeases them: "Let him alone," he says, "because the Lord has ordered him to curse" [II Sam. 16:11]. ᵉBy this same bridle he elsewhere curbs his inordinate sorrow: "I have kept silence and remained mute," says he, "because thou hast done it, O Jehovah" [Ps. 39:9 p.]. ᵇIf there is no more effective remedy for anger and impatience, he has surely benefited greatly who has so learned to meditate upon God's providence that he can always recall his mind to this point: the Lord has willed it; therefore it must be borne, not only because one may not contend against it, but also because he wills nothing but what is just and expedient. ᵉ⁽ᵇ⁾To sum this up: when we are unjustly wounded by men, let us overlook their wickedness (which would but worsen our pain and sharpen our minds to revenge), remember to mount up to God, and learn to believe for certain that whatever our enemy has wickedly committed against us was permitted and sent by God's just dispensation.

ᵉPaul, to restrain us from retaliation for injuries, wisely points out that our struggle "is not with flesh and blood" [Eph. 6:12], but with our spiritual enemy the devil [Eph. 6:11], in order that we may prepare ourselves for the combat. Yet a most useful admonition to still all impulses to wrath is that God arms both the devil and all the wicked for the conflict, and sits as a judge of the games to exercise our patience.

ᵉ⁽ᵇ⁾But if the destruction and misery that press upon us happen without human agency, let us recall the teaching of the law: "Whatever is prosperous flows from the fountain of God's blessing, and all adversities are his curses" [Deut. 28:2 ff., 15 ff. p.]. ᵉLet this dreadful warning terrify us: "If you happen to walk contrary to me, I will also happen to walk contrary to you" [Lev. 26:23–24, cf. Comm.]. In these words our sluggishness is rebuked as a crime; for after the common sense of the flesh we regard as fortuitous whatever happens either way, whether good or evil, and so are neither aroused by God's benefits to worship him, nor stimulated by lashes to repentance. ᵉ⁽ᵇ⁾It is for this same reason that Jeremiah and Amos bitterly expostulated with the Jews, for they thought both good and evil happened without God's command [Lam. 3:38; Amos 3:6]. ᵉIn the same vein is Isaiah's declaration: "I, God, creating light and forming darkness, making peace and creating evil: I, God, do all these things" [Isa. 45:7, cf. Vg.].

9. No disregard of intermediate causes!

ᵇMeanwhile, nevertheless, a godly man will not overlook the secondary causes. And indeed, he will not, just because he thinks those from whom he has received benefit are ministers of the divine goodness, pass them over, as if they had deserved no thanks for their human kindness; but from the bottom of his heart will feel himself beholden to them, willingly confess his obligation, and earnestly try as best he can to render thanks and as occasion presents itself. In short, for benefits received he will reverence and praise the Lord as their principal author, but will honor men as his ministers; and will know what is in fact true: it is by God's will that he is beholden to those through whose hand God willed to be beneficent. If this godly man suffers any loss because of negligence or imprudence, he will conclude that it came about by the Lord's will, but also impute it to himself. Suppose a disease should carry off anyone whom he treated negligently, although it was his duty to take care of him. Even though he knows that this person had come to an impassable boundary, he will not on this account deem his misdeed less serious; rather, because he did not faithfully discharge his duty toward him, he will take it that through the fault of his negligence the latter had perished. Where fraud or premeditated malice enters into the committing of either murder or theft, he will even less excuse such a crime on the pretext of divine providence; but in this same evil deed he will clearly contemplate God's righteousness and man's wickedness, as each clearly shows itself.

But especially with reference to future events he will take into consideration inferior causes of this sort. For he will count it among the blessings of the Lord, if he is not destitute of human helps which he may use for his safety. Therefore he will neither cease to take counsel, nor be sluggish in beseeching the assistance of those whom he sees to have the means to help him; but, considering that whatever creatures are capable of furnishing anything to him are offered by the Lord into his hand, he will put them to use as lawful instruments of divine providence. And since it is uncertain what will be the outcome of the business he is undertaking (except that he knows that in all things the Lord will provide for his benefit), he will aspire with zeal to that which he deems expedient for himself, as far as it can be attained by intelligence and understanding. Yet in taking counsel he will not follow his own opinion, but will entrust and submit himself to God's wisdom, to be directed by his leading to the right goal. But his confidence will not so rely upon outward supports as to repose with assurance in them if they are present, or, if they are lacking, to tremble as if left destitute. For he will always hold his mind fixed upon God's providence alone, and not let preoccupation with present matters draw him away from steadfast contemplation of it. eThus Joab, though recognizing the outcome of the battle to be in God's hand, has yielded not to idleness, but diligently carries out the duties of his calling. To the Lord, moreover, he commits the determination of the outcome: "We will stand fast," says he, "for our people and the cities of our God; but let the Lord do what is good in his eyes" [II Sam. 10:12 p.]. This same knowledge will drive us to put off rashness and overconfidence, and will impel us continually to call upon God. Then also he will buttress our minds with good hope, that, with confidence and courage, we may not hesitate to despise those dangers which surround us.

10. Without certainty about God's providence life would be unbearable

ᵇHence appears the immeasurable felicity of the godly mind.[14] Innumerable are the evils that beset human life; innumerable, too, the deaths that threaten it. We need not go beyond ourselves: since our body is the receptacle of a thousand diseases—in fact holds within itself and fosters the causes of diseases—a man cannot go about unburdened by many forms of his own destruction, and without drawing out a life enveloped, as it were, with death. For what else would you call it, when he neither freezes nor sweats without danger? Now, wherever you turn, all things around you not only are hardly to be trusted but almost openly menace, and seem to threaten immediate death. Embark upon a ship, you are one step away from death. Mount a horse, if one foot slips, your life is imperiled. Go through the city streets, you are subject to as many dangers as there are tiles on the roofs. If there is a weapon in your hand or a friend's, harm awaits. All the fierce animals you see are armed for your destruction. But if you try to shut yourself up in a walled garden, seemingly delightful, there a serpent sometimes lies hidden. Your house, continually in danger of fire, threatens in the daytime to impoverish you, at night even to collapse upon you. Your field, since it is exposed to hail, frost, drought, and other calamities, threatens you with barrenness, and hence, famine. I pass over poisonings, ambushes, robberies, open violence, which in part besiege us at home, in part dog us abroad. Amid these tribulations must not man be most miserable, since, but half alive in life, he weakly draws his anxious and languid breath, as if he had a sword perpetually hanging over his neck?

You will say: these events rarely happen, or at least not all the time, nor to all men, and never all at once. I agree; but since we are warned by the examples of others that these can also happen to ourselves, and that our life ought not to be excepted any more than theirs, we cannot but be frightened and terrified as if such events were about to happen to us. What, therefore, more calamitous can you imagine than such trepidation? Besides that, if we say that God has exposed man, the noblest of creatures, to all sorts of blind and heedless blows of fortune, we are not guiltless of reproaching God. But here I propose to speak only of that misery which man will feel if he is brought under the sway of fortune.

[14] *"Inaestimabilis piae mentis foelicitas."* Cf. I. v. 1, note 2.

*11. Certainty about God's providence puts joyous trust toward
God in our hearts*

ᵇYet, when that light of divine providence has once shone upon
a godly man, he is then relieved and set free not only from the
extreme anxiety and fear that were pressing him before, but
from every care. For as he justly dreads fortune, so he fearlessly
dares commit himself to God. His solace, I say, is to know that his
Heavenly Father so holds all things in his power, so rules by his
authority and will, so governs by his wisdom, that nothing can
befall except he determine it. Moreover, it comforts him to know
that he has been received into God's safekeeping and entrusted to
the care of his angels, and that neither water, nor fire, nor iron
can harm him, except in so far as it pleases God as governor to
give them occasion. Thus indeed the psalm sings: "For he will
deliver you from the snare of the fowler and from the deadly
pestilence. Under his wings will he protect you, and in his pinions
you will have assurance; his truth will be your shield. You will
not fear the terror of night, nor the flying arrow by day, nor
the pestilence that stalks in darkness, nor the destruction that
wastes at midday" [Ps. 91:3–6; cf. Ps. 90:3–6, Vg.; cf. Comm.].

From this, also, arises in the saints the assurance that they may
glory. "The Lord is my helper" [Ps. 118:6; 117:6, Vg.]; "I will
not fear what flesh can do against me" [Ps. 56:4; 55:5, Vg.]. "The
Lord is my protector; what shall I fear?" [Ps. 27:1; cf. Ps. 26:1,
Vg.] "If armies should stand together against me" [Ps. 27:3; cf.
Ps. 26:3, Vg.], "if I should walk in the midst of the shadow of
death" [Ps. 22:4, Vg.; 23:4, EV], "I will not cease to have good
hope" [Ps. 56:5; 55:4, Vg.; 71:14; 70:14, Vg.]. Whence, I pray
you, do they have this never-failing assurance but from knowing
that, when the world appears to be aimlessly tumbled about, the
Lord is everywhere at work, and from trusting that his work will
be for their welfare? Now if their welfare is assailed either by the
devil or by wicked men, then indeed, unless strengthened through
remembering and meditating upon providence, they must needs
quickly faint away. But let them recall that the devil and the
whole cohort of the wicked are completely restrained by God's
hand as by a bridle, so that they are unable either to hatch any
plot against us or, having hatched it, to make preparations or, if
they have fully planned it, to stir a finger toward carrying it out,
except so far as he has permitted, indeed commanded. ᵉLet them,
also, recall that the devil and his crew are not only fettered, but
also curbed and compelled to do service. ᵇSuch thoughts will provide them abundant comfort. For as it belongs to the Lord to

arouse their fury and turn and direct it whither he pleases; so, also, is it his to set a measure and limit, lest they licentiously exult in their own lust.

ePaul, supported by this conviction, after saying in one passage that his journey had been hindered by Satan [I Thess. 2:18], states elsewhere that with God's permission he determined to set out [I Cor. 16:7]. If he had said only that the obstacle was from Satan, he would have seemed to give too much power to him, as if it were in his power to overthrow even the very plans of God; but now when he declares God the Ruler upon whose permission all his journeys depend, he at the same time shows that Satan cannot carry out anything that he may contrive except with God's assent. For the same reason, David, on account of the various changes by which the life of men is continually turned, and as it were, whirled about, betakes himself to this refuge: that his "times are in God's hand" [Ps. 31:15]. He could have put here either "course of life" or "time" in the singular, but he chose to express by using the plural "times" that however unstable the condition of men may be, whatever changes take place from time to time, they are governed by God. bFor this reason, although Rezin and the King of Israel, having joined forces to destroy Judah, seemed firebrands kindled to destroy and consume the land, they are called by the prophet "smoking firebrands," that can do nothing but breathe out a little smoke [Isa. 7:4]. cThus Pharaoh, although to all he was fearsome both on account of his riches and strength, and the size of his armies, is himself compared to a sea monster, and his troops to fish [Ezek. 29:4]. God therefore announces that he is going to seize the leader and the army with his hook and drag them where He pleases. bIn short, not to tarry any longer over this, if you pay attention, you will easily perceive that ignorance of providence is the ultimate of all miseries; the highest blessedness lies in the knowledge of it.

(Answer to objections, 12–14)
12. On God's "repentance"
bWe should have said enough concerning God's providence to achieve the perfect instruction and comfort of believers (for nothing whatsoever can be sufficient to satisfy the curiosity of vain men, nor ought we to wish to satisfy it) if certain passages did not stand in the way. These seem to suggest, contrary to the above exposition, that the plan of God does not stand firm and sure, but is subject to change in response to the disposition of things below. First, God's repenting is several times mentioned, as when he re-

pented of having created man [Gen. 6:6]; of having put Saul over the kingdom [I Sam. 15:11]; and of his going to repent of the evil that he had determined to inflict upon his people, as soon as he sensed any change of heart in them [Jer. 18:8]. Next, some abrogations of his decrees are referred to. He made known through Jonah to the Ninevites that after forty days had passed Nineveh would be destroyed, yet he was immediately persuaded by their repentance to give a more kindly sentence. [Jonah 3:4, 10.] He proclaimed the death of Hezekiah through the mouth of Isaiah; but he was moved by the king's tears and prayers to defer this [Isa. 38:1, 5; II Kings 20:1, 5; cf. II Chron. 32:24]. Hence many contend that God has not determined the affairs of men by an eternal decree, but that, according to each man's deserts or according as he deems him fair and just, he decrees this or that each year, each day, and each hour.[15]

Concerning repentance, we ought so to hold that it is no more chargeable against God than is ignorance, or error, or powerlessness. For if no one wittingly and willingly puts himself under the necessity of repentance, we shall not attribute repentance to God without saying either that he is ignorant of what is going to happen, or cannot escape it, or hastily and rashly rushes into a decision of which he immediately has to repent. But that is far removed from the intention of the Holy Spirit, who in the very reference to repentance says that God is not moved by compunction because he is not a man so that he can repent [I Sam. 15:29]. ᵉAnd we must note that in the same chapter both are so joined together that the comparison well harmonizes the apparent disagreement. When God repents of having made Saul king, the change of mind is to be taken figuratively. A little later there is added: "The strength of Israel will not lie, nor be turned aside by repentance; for he is not a man, that he may repent" [I Sam. 15:29 p.]. By these words openly and unfiguratively God's unchangeableness is declared. ᵇTherefore it is certain that God's ordinance in the managing of human affairs is both everlasting and above all repentance. And lest there be doubt as to his constancy, even his adversaries are compelled to render testimony to this. For Balaam, even against his will, had to break forth into these words: "God is not like man that he should lie, nor as the son of man that he should change. It cannot be that he will not do what he has said or not fulfill what he has spoken" [Num. 23: 19 p., cf. Vg.].

---

[15] Origen, *De principiis* III. i. 17 (GCS 22. 228; MPG 11. 283 ff.; tr. ANF IV. 322; G. W. Butterworth, *Origen On First Principles*, pp. 193 f.).

13. Scripture speaks of God's "repentance" to make allowance for our understanding

ᵇWhat, therefore, does the word "repentance" mean? Surely its meaning is like that of all other modes of speaking that describe God for us in human terms. For because our weakness does not attain to his exalted state, the description of him that is given to us must be accommodated to our capacity so that we may understand it. Now the mode of accommodation is for him to represent himself to us not as he is in himself, but as he seems to us. Although he is beyond all disturbance of mind, yet he testifies that he is angry toward sinners. Therefore whenever we hear that God is angered, we ought not to imagine any emotion in him, but rather to consider that this expression has been taken from our own human experience; because God, whenever he is exercising judgment, exhibits the appearance of one kindled and angered. So we ought not to understand anything else under the word "repentance" than change of action, because men are wont by changing their action to testify that they are displeased with themselves. Therefore, since every change among men is a correction of what displeases them, but that correction arises out of repentance, then by the word "repentance" is meant the fact that God changes with respect to his actions. Meanwhile neither God's plan nor his will is reversed, nor his volition altered; but what he had from eternity foreseen, approved, and decreed, he pursues in uninterrupted tenor, however sudden the variation may appear in men's eyes.

14. God firmly executes his plan

ᵇThe sacred history does not show that God's decrees were abrogated when it relates that the destruction which had once been pronounced upon the Ninevites was remitted [Jonah 3:10]; and that Hezekiah's life, after his death had been intimated, had been prolonged [Isa. 38:5].[16] Those who think so are deceived in these intimations. Even though the latter make a simple affirmation, it is to be understood from the outcome that these nonetheless contain a tacit condition. For why did the Lord send Jonah to the Ninevites to foretell the ruin of the city? Why did he through Isaiah indicate death to Hezekiah? For he could have destroyed both the Ninevites and Hezekiah without any messenger of destruction. Therefore he had in view something other than that, forewarned of their death, they might discern it coming from a

---

[16] Cf. Erasmus, *De libero arbitrio*, ed. J. von Walter (*Quellenschriften zur Geschichte des Protestantismus* 8), pp. 38, 79; Calvin, *Sermons sur le cantique du roi Ezekias* (on Isa. 38:9–20) (CR XXV. 252–579).

distance. Indeed, he did not wish them to perish, but to be changed lest they perish. Therefore Jonah's prophecy that after forty days Nineveh would be destroyed was made so it might not fall. Hezekiah's hope for longer life was cut off in order that it might come to pass that he would obtain longer life. Who now does not see that it pleased the Lord by such threats to arouse to repentance those whom he was terrifying, that they might escape the judgment they deserved for their sins? If that is true, the nature of the circumstances leads us to recognize a tacit condition in the simple intimation.

This is also confirmed by like examples. The Lord, rebuking King Abimelech because he had deprived Abraham of his wife, uses these words: "Behold, you will die on account of the woman whom you have taken, for she has a husband" [Gen. 20:3, Vg.]. But after Abimelech excused himself, God spoke in this manner: "Restore the woman to her husband, for he is a prophet, and will pray for you that you may live. If not, know that you shall surely die, and all that you have" [Gen. 20:7, Vg.]. Do you see how in the first utterance, he strikes Abimelech's mind more violently in order to render him intent upon satisfaction, but in the second sentence he clearly explains his will? Inasmuch as there is a similar meaning in other passages, do not infer from them that there was any derogation from the Lord's first purpose because he had made void what he had proclaimed. For the Lord, when by warning of punishment he admonishes to repentance those whom he wills to spare, paves the way for his eternal ordinance, rather than varies anything of his will, or even of his Word, although he does not express syllable by syllable what is nevertheless easy to understand. That saying of Isaiah must indeed remain true: "The Lord of Hosts has purposed, and who will annul it? His hand is stretched out, and who will turn it back?" [Isa. 14:27].

ᶜCHAPTER XVIII

GOD SO USES THE WORKS OF THE UNGODLY, AND SO BENDS THEIR MINDS TO CARRY OUT HIS JUDGMENTS, THAT HE REMAINS PURE FROM EVERY STAIN[1]

1. No mere "permission"!

ᶜFrom other passages, where God is said to bend or draw Satan himself and all the wicked to his will, there emerges a more difficult question. For carnal sense can hardly comprehend how in

---

[1] This chapter, new in 1559, treats many issues that appear incidentally in other contexts, e.g., II. iv, v; III. xxiii, xxiv.

acting through them he does not contract some defilement from their transgression, and even in a common undertaking can be free of all blame, and indeed can justly condemn his ministers. Hence the distinction was devised between doing and permitting[2] because to many this difficulty seemed inexplicable, that Satan and all the impious are so under God's hand and power that he directs their malice to whatever end seems good to him, and uses their wicked deeds to carry out his judgments. And perhaps the moderation of those whom the appearance of absurdity alarms would be excusable, except that they wrongly try to clear God's justice of every sinister mark by upholding a falsehood. It seems absurd to them for man, who will soon be punished for his blindness, to be blinded by God's will and command. Therefore they escape by the shift that this is done only with God's permission, not also by his will;[3] but he, openly declaring that he is the doer, repudiates that evasion. However, that men can accomplish nothing except by God's secret command, that they cannot by deliberating accomplish anything except what he has already decreed with himself and determines by his secret direction, is proved by innumerable and clear testimonies. What we have cited before from the psalm, that God does whatever he wills [Ps. 115:3], certainly pertains to all the actions of men. If, as is here said, God is the true Arbiter of wars and of peace, and this without any exception, who, then, will dare say that men are borne headlong by blind motion unbeknown to God or with his acquiescence?

But particular examples will shed more light. From the first chapter of Job we know that Satan, no less than the angels who willingly obey, presents himself before God [Job 1:6; 2:1] to receive his commands. He does so, indeed, in a different way and with a different end; but he still cannot undertake anything unless God so wills. However, even though a bare permission to afflict the holy man seems then to be added, yet we gather that God was the author of that trial of which Satan and his wicked thieves were the ministers, because this statement is true: "The

---

[2] Lombard, *Sentences* I. xlv. 11 (MPL 192. 643). Cf. Augustine, *De ordine* I. i–iii (MPL 32. 977 ff.; tr. R. P. Russell, *Divine Providence and the Problem of Evil,* pp. 6–11); *Enchiridion* xxiv. 95 f. (MPL 40. 276; tr. LCC VII. 394 f.).

[3] Cf. I. xvii. 2, note 3. See also the tract *Calumniae nebulonis cuiusdam de occulta providentia Dei . . . ad easdem responsio* (1558). In the work, attributed to Sebastian Castellio, quoted and answered in this tract, Calvin is charged (sec. vii) with teaching that God has two contrary wills and is taunted with having two wills of his own, so that when he says one thing he thinks and wishes another. To this Calvin replies with some warmth (CR IX. 278 f., 302 ff.).

Lord gave, the Lord has taken away; as it has pleased God, so is it done" [Job 1:21, Vg. (p.)]. Satan desperately tries to drive the holy man insane; the Sabaeans cruelly and impiously pillage and make off with another's possessions. Job recognizes that he was divinely stripped of all his property, and made a poor man, because it so pleased God. Therefore, whatever men or Satan himself may instigate, God nevertheless holds the key, so that he turns their efforts to carry out his judgments. God wills that the false King Ahab be deceived; the devil offers his services to this end; he is sent, with a definite command, to be a lying spirit in the mouth of all the prophets [I Kings 22:20, 22]. If the blinding and insanity of Ahab be God's judgment, the figment of bare permission vanishes: because it would be ridiculous for the Judge only to permit what he wills to be done, and not also to decree it and to command its execution by his ministers.

ᵉ⁽ᵇ⁾The Jews intended to destroy Christ; Pilate and his soldiers complied with their mad desire; yet in solemn prayer the disciples confess that all the impious ones had done nothing except what "the hand and plan" of God had decreed [Acts 4:28, cf. Vg.]. So Peter had already preached that "by the definite plan and foreknowledge of God, Christ had been given over" to be killed [Acts 2:23, cf. Vg.]. It is as if he were to say that God, to whom from the beginning nothing was hidden, wittingly and willingly determined what the Jews carried out. As he elsewhere states: "God, who has foretold through all his prophets that Christ is going to suffer, has thus fulfilled it" [Acts 3:18, cf. Vg.]. ᵉAbsalom, polluting his father's bed by an incestuous union, commits a detestable crime [II Sam. 16:22]; yet God declares this work to be his own; for the words are: "You did it secretly; but I will do this thing openly, and in broad daylight" [II Sam. 12:12 p.]. Jeremiah declared that every cruelty the Chaldeans exercised against Judah was God's work [Jer. 1:15; 7:14; 50:25, and *passim*]. For this reason Nebuchadnezzar is called God's servant [Jer. 25:9; cf. ch. 27:6]. God proclaims in many places that by his hissing [Isa. 7:18 or 5:26], by the sound of his trumpet [Hos. 8:1], by his authority and command, the impious are aroused to war [cf. Zeph. 2:1]. The Assyrian he calls the rod of his anger [Isa. 10:5 p.], and the ax that he wields with his hand [cf. Matt. 3:10]. The destruction of the Holy City and the ruin of the Temple he calls his own work [Isa. 28:21]. David, not murmuring against God, but recognizing him as the just judge, yet confesses that the curses of Shimei proceeded from His command [II Sam. 16:10]. "The Lord," he says, "commanded him to curse." [II Sam. 16:11.] We very often find in the Sacred History that whatever happens proceeds from the

Lord, as for instance the defection of the ten tribes [I Kings 11:31], the death of Eli's sons [I Sam. 2:34], and very many examples of this sort. Those who are moderately versed in the Scriptures see that for the sake of brevity I have put forward only a few of many testimonies. Yet from these it is more than evident that they babble and talk absurdly who, in place of God's providence, substitute bare permission—as if God sat in a watchtower awaiting chance events, and his judgments thus depended upon human will.

2. How does God's impulse come to pass in men?

ᵉAs far as pertains to those secret promptings we are discussing, Solomon's statement that the heart of a king is turned about hither and thither at God's pleasure [Prov. 21:1] certainly extends to all the human race, and carries as much weight as if he had said: "Whatever we conceive of in our minds is directed to his own end by God's secret inspiration." And surely unless he worked inwardly in men's minds, it would not rightly have been said that he removes speech from the truthful, and prudence from the old men [Ezek. 7:26]; that he takes away the heart of the princes of the earth so they may wander in trackless wastes [Job 12:24; cf. Ps. 107:40; 106:40, Vg.]. To this pertains what one often reads: that men are fearful according as dread of him takes possession of their minds [Lev. 26:36]. So David went forth from Saul's camp without anyone's knowing it, because the sleep of God had overtaken them all. [I Sam. 26:12.] But one can desire nothing clearer than where he so often declares that he blinds men's minds [Isa. 29:14], smites them with dizziness [cf. Deut. 28:28; Zech. 12:4], makes them drunk with the spirit of drowsiness [Isa. 29:10], casts madness upon them [Rom. 1:28], hardens their hearts [Ex. 14:17 and *passim*]. These instances may refer, also, to divine permission, as if by forsaking the wicked he allowed them to be blinded by Satan. But since the Spirit clearly expresses the fact that blindness and insanity are inflicted by God's just judgment [Rom. 1:20–24], such a solution is too absurd. It is said that he hardened Pharaoh's heart [Ex. 9:12], also that he made it heavy [ch. 10:1] and stiffened it [chs. 10:20, 27; 11:10; 14:8]. By this foolish cavil certain ones get around these expressions, for while it is said elsewhere that Pharaoh himself made heavy his own heart [Ex. 8:15, 32; 9:34], God's will is posited as the cause of hardening. As if these two statements did not perfectly agree, although in divers ways, that man, while he is acted upon by God, yet at the same time himself acts! Moreover, I throw their objection back upon them: for if "to harden" denotes bare permission, the very prompting to obstinacy will not properly exist in Pharaoh. Indeed, how weak and foolish would it be to interpret this as if Pharaoh only suffered himself to be hardened! Besides, Scripture cuts off any occasion for such cavils. "I will restrain," says God, "his heart." [Ex. 4:21.] Thus, also, concerning the dwellers in the Land of Canaan, Moses said they had come forth to battle because God stiffened their hearts [Josh. 11:20; cf. Deut. 2:30]. The same thing is repeated by another prophet, "He turns their hearts to hate his people" [Ps. 105:25]. Likewise in Isaiah, He declares that he will send the Assyrians against the deceitful nation and will command them "to take spoil and seize plunder" [Isa. 10:6]—not because he would teach impious and obstinate men to obey him willingly, but because he will bend them to execute his judgments, as if they bore his commandments graven upon their hearts; from this it appears that they had been impelled by God's sure determination.

I confess, indeed, that it is often by means of Satan's intervention that God acts in the wicked, but in such a way that Satan performs his part by God's impulsion and advances as far as he is allowed. An evil spirit troubles Saul; but it is said to have come from God [I Sam. 16:14], that we may know that Saul's madness proceeds from God's just vengeance. Also, it is said that the same Satan "blinds the minds of unbelievers" [II Cor. 4:4]; but whence does this come, unless the working of error flows from God himself [II Thess. 2:11], to make those believe lies who refuse to obey the truth? According to the former reason it is said, "If any prophet should speak in lies, I, God, have deceived him" [Ezek. 14:9]. According to the second reason, he himself is indeed said to "give men up to an evil mind" [Rom. 1:28, cf. Vg.] and cast them into base desires [cf. Rom. 1:29]; because he is the chief author of his own just vengeance, while Satan is but the minister of it. But because we must discuss this matter again when we discourse in the Second Book concerning man's free or unfree choice,[4] it seems to me that I have now briefly said as much as the occasion calls for. To sum up, since God's will is said to be the cause of all things, I have made his providence the determinative principle for all human plans and works, not only in order to display its force in the elect, who are ruled by the Holy Spirit, but also to compel the reprobate to obedience.

3. God's will is a unity

eWhile hitherto I have recounted only those things which are openly and unambiguously related in Scripture, let those who do

4 II. iv. 1–4.

not hesitate to brand the heavenly oracles with sinister marks of ignominy see what kind of censure they use. For if they seek from pretending ignorance to be praised for moderation, what haughtier thing can be imagined than to oppose God's authority with one little word such as "To me it seems otherwise," or, "I do not want to touch upon this"? But if they openly curse, what will they gain by spitting at the sky? Indeed, an example of such petulance is not new, for in every age there have been impious and profane men, who have frothed and snarled against this portion of doctrine. But they shall surely feel to be true what the Spirit declared of old through David's mouth, that God may overcome when he is judged [Ps. 50:6, Vg.; 51:4, EV]. David indirectly reproves the madness of men in the very unbridled license with which, out of their own filthiness, they not only argue against God, but claim for themselves the power to condemn him. Meanwhile, he briefly warns that the blasphemies they spew out against heaven do not reach God, but that he, dispelling their clouds of calumnies, makes his own righteousness shine forth. Even our faith (because, founded upon God's Sacred Word, it is above the whole world [cf. I John 5:4]) from its lofty height despises these clouds.

For it is easy to dispose of their first objection, that if nothing happens apart from God's will, there are in him two contrary wills, because by his secret plan he decrees what he has openly forbidden by his law. Yet before I answer, I should like my readers again to be warned that this cavil is not hurled against me but against the Holy Spirit, who surely put this confession in the mouth of the holy man Job, "As it pleased God, so was it done" [Job 1:21, cf. Vg.]. When he had been robbed by thieves, in their unjust acts and evil-doing toward him he recognized God's just scourge. What does Scripture say elsewhere? Eli's sons did not obey their father because God willed to slay them [I Sam. 2:25]. Another prophet also proclaims that "God, who resides in heaven, does whatever he pleases" [Ps. 115:3]. And now I have already shown plainly enough that God is called the Author of all the things that these faultfinders would have happen only by his indolent permission. He declares that he creates light and darkness, that he forms good and bad [Isa. 45:7 p.]; that nothing evil happens that he himself has not done [Amos 3:6]. Let them tell me, I pray, whether he exercises his judgments willingly or unwillingly. Yet, as Moses teaches, he who is killed by a chance slip of the ax has been divinely given over to the striker's hand. [Deut. 19:5; cf. Ex. 21:13.]

Thus, according to Luke, the whole church says that Herod

and Pilate conspired to do what God's hand and plan had decreed. [Acts 4:28.] And indeed, unless Christ had been crucified according to God's will, whence would we have redemption? Yet God's will is not therefore at war with itself, nor does it change, nor does it pretend not to will what he wills. But even though his will is one and simple in him, it appears manifold to us because, on account of our mental incapacity, we do not grasp how in divers ways it wills and does not will something to take place. When Paul said that the calling of the Gentiles was "a mystery hidden" [Eph. 3:9], he added shortly thereafter that in it was shown forth "God's manifold wisdom" [Eph. 3:10].[5] Because God's wisdom appears manifold (or "multiform" as the old translator renders it), ought we therefore, on account of the sluggishness[6] of our understanding, to dream that there is any variation in God himself, as if he either may change his plan or disagree with himself? Rather, when we do not grasp how God wills to take place what he forbids to be done, let us recall our mental incapacity, and at the same time consider that the light in which God dwells is not without reason called unapproachable [I Tim. 6:16], because it is overspread with darkness. Therefore all godly and modest folk readily agree with this saying of Augustine: "Sometimes with a good will a man wills something which God does not will. . . . For example, a good son wills that his father live, whom God wills to die. Again, it can happen that the same man wills with a bad will what God wills with a good will. For example, a bad son wills that his father die; God also wills this. That is, the former wills what God does not will; but the latter wills what God also wills. And yet the filial piety of the former, even though he wills something other than God wills, is more consonant with God's good will than the impiety of the latter, who wills the same thing as God does. There is a great difference between what is fitting for man to will and what is fitting for God, and to what end the will of each is directed, so that it be either approved or disapproved. For through the bad wills of evil men God fulfills what he righteously wills." A little before he had said that by their defection the apostate angels and all the

---

[5] "πολυποίκιλον."

[6] The two motifs of faith and human incapacity (*imbecillitas*) or sluggishness (*hebetudo*) are the basis on which Calvin, in secs. 3 and 4, consciously makes self-contradictory statements about God "willing" what he "forbids," yet with a will that remains "one and simple." Logic is thus subordinated to Scripture, and, characteristically for Calvin, is rejected as a device for understanding what is beyond the limits of the revealed mysteries. Cf. I. xiii. 1–3; III. ii. 14; III. xxiv. 17; and the rejection of a logical conclusion on the same grounds in III. xviii. 10.

wicked, from their point of view, had done what God did not will, but from the point of view of God's omnipotence they could in no way have done this, because while they act against God's will, his will is done upon them. Whence he exclaims: "Great are God's works, sought out in all his wills" [Ps. 111:2; cf. Ps. 110:2, Vg.]; so that in a wonderful and ineffable manner nothing is done without God's will, not even that which is against his will. For it would not be done if he did not permit it; yet he does not unwillingly permit it, but willingly; nor would he, being good, allow evil to be done, unless being also almighty he could make good even out of evil."[7]

4. Even when God uses the deeds of the godless for his purposes, he does not suffer reproach

ᵉIn this way, also, the other objection is solved, or rather vanishes by itself: if God not only uses the work of the ungodly, but also governs their plans and intentions, he is the author of all wickednesses; and therefore men are undeservedly damned if they carry out what God has decreed because they obey his will. His will is wrongly confused with his precept: innumerable examples clearly show how utterly different these two are. For even though, when Absalom committed adultery with his father's wives [II Sam. 16:22], God willed to punish David's adultery with this shameful act, yet he did not for this reason bid the wicked son commit incest, unless perhaps with regard to David, as he speaks concerning Shimei's railings. For when he confesses that Shimei curses him at God's command [II Sam. 16:10–11], he does not at all commend his obedience, as if that impudent dog were obeying God's authority. But recognizing his tongue to be a scourge of God, he patiently bears the chastisement. We ought, indeed, to hold fast by this: while God accomplishes through the wicked what he has decreed by his secret judgment, they are not excusable, as if they had obeyed his precept which out of their own lust they deliberately break.

Now the choice of King Jeroboam [I Kings 12:20] shows clearly that what men do perversely is of God, and ruled by his hidden providence. In this choice the rashness and insanity of the people is condemned for having perverted the order sanctioned by God, and having faithlessly fallen away from the house of David. And yet we know that he willed him to be anointed. Accordingly in Hosea's statements there likewise occurs a certain appearance

---

[7] Augustine, *Enchiridion* xxvi. 100 f. (MPL 40. 279; tr. LCC VII. 399 f.); Augustine, *Psalms*, Ps. 111. 2 (Latin, Ps. 110. 2) (MPL 37. 1464; Calvin, Comm. Ps. 111:2).

of contradiction: for God complained in one place that that kingdom had been established without his knowledge and against his will [Hos. 8:4]; yet elsewhere he proclaims that in his anger he had given King Jeroboam [Hos. 13:11]. How will these statements agree: that Jeroboam did not reign by God's will and yet was appointed king by the same God? The answer is obviously that the people could neither revolt from the house of David without shaking off the divinely imposed yoke, nor was God himself deprived of the freedom to punish Solomon thus for his ungratefulness. Therefore we see how God does not will a breach of faith, yet with another end in view, justly wills defection. Hence likewise, contrary to expectation, he compelled Jeroboam with sacred anointing to become king. In this way the Sacred History says that an enemy was raised up by God [I Kings 11:23] to divest Solomon's son of part of his kingdom.

Let my readers weigh both these things with care. Because it had pleased God that his people be governed under the hand of one king, when the nation is split into two parts, it is done against his will. And yet the beginning of the separation came from the will of the same God. For surely when the prophet both by word of mouth and by the token of anointing stirred Jeroboam, who was thinking of no such thing, to the expectation of the kingdom, this was not done without the knowledge or against the will of God, who so commanded it to be done. And yet the rebellion of the people is rightly condemned because against God's will they revolted from David's descendants. For this reason, also, it is afterward added that Rehoboam haughtily despised the petitions of the people and that this was done by God to establish the Word which he had proclaimed through the hand of Ahijah his servant [I Kings 12:15]. Note how it is against God's will that the sacred unity is broken, and yet how by his same will the ten tribes are estranged from Solomon's son. Besides this, there is another similar example, where with the people's consent—indeed, with them lending a hand—the sons of King Ahab are murdered, and all his posterity exterminated [II Kings 10:7]. Indeed, Jehu rightly reports that "nothing of God's words has fallen to the ground, but he has done what he said by the hand of his servant Elijah" [II Kings 10:10 p.]. And yet not without cause did he rebuke the citizens of Samaria because they had given assistance. "Are you righteous?" he asks; "if I conspired against my master, who killed all these?" [II Kings 10:9; IV Kings 10:9, Vg.] I have, unless I am mistaken, already clearly explained how in the same act as man's evil deed shows itself, so God's justice shines forth.

And for modest minds this answer of Augustine will always be enough: "Since the Father delivered up the Son, and Christ, his body, and Judas, his Lord, why in this delivering up is God just and man guilty, unless because in the one thing they have done, the cause of their doing it is not one?"[8] But if some people find difficulty in what we are now saying—namely, that there is no agreement between God and man, where man does by God's just impulsion what he ought not to do—let them recall what the same Augustine points out in another passage: "Who does not tremble at these judgments, where God works even in evil men's hearts whatever he wills, yet renders to them according to their deserts?"[9] And surely in Judas' betrayal it will be no more right, because God himself both willed that his Son be delivered up and delivered him up to death, to ascribe the guilt of the crime to God than to transfer the credit for redemption to Judas. Therefore the same writer correctly points out, elsewhere, that in this examination God does not inquire into what men have been able to do, or what they have done, but what they have willed to do,[10] so that purpose and will may be taken into account.

Let those for whom this seems harsh consider for a little while how bearable their squeamishness is in refusing a thing attested by clear Scriptural proofs because it exceeds their mental capacity, and find fault that things are put forth publicly, which if God had not judged useful for men to know, he would never have bidden his prophets and apostles to teach. For our wisdom ought to be nothing else than to embrace with humble teachableness, and at least without finding fault, whatever is taught in Sacred Scripture. Those who too insolently scoff, even though it is clear enough that they are prating against God, are not worthy of a longer refutation.

[8] Augustine, *Letters* xciii. 2 (MPL 33. 324; tr. FC 18. 63).

[9] Augustine, *On Grace and Free Will* xxi. 42 (MPL 44. 907; tr. NPNF V. 462).

[10] Augustine, *Psalms*, Ps. 61. 22: "*Discutit Deus quid quisque voluerit; non quid potuerit*" (MPL 36. 746; tr. LF [Ps. 62] *Psalms* III. 208); Augustine, *John's Gospel* vii (on John 4:7): "*Non quid faciat homo, sed quo animo et voluntate faciat*" (MPL 35. 2033; tr. NPNF VII. 503 f.).

BOOK TWO

THE KNOWLEDGE OF GOD THE REDEEMER IN CHRIST,
FIRST DISCLOSED TO THE FATHERS UNDER THE LAW,
AND THEN TO US IN THE GOSPEL

BOOK TWO

The Knowledge of God the Redeemer in Christ, First Disclosed to the Fathers Under the Law, and Then to Us in the Gospel

ᶜCHAPTER I

BY THE FALL AND REVOLT OF ADAM THE WHOLE HUMAN RACE
WAS DELIVERED TO THE CURSE, AND DEGENERATED FROM ITS
ORIGINAL CONDITION; THE DOCTRINE OF ORIGINAL SIN

(A true knowledge of ourselves destroys self-confidence, 1–3)
1. Wrong and right knowledge of self
ᵇWith good reason the ancient proverb strongly recommended knowledge of self to man.[1] For if it is considered disgraceful for us not to know all that pertains to the business of human life, even more detestable is our ignorance of ourselves, by which, when making decisions in necessary matters, we miserably deceive and even blind ourselves!

But since this precept is so valuable, we ought more diligently

---

[1] Calvin is here recalling the opening words of the *Institutes* on the knowledge of God and of ourselves. Cf. I. i. 1, and secs. 1 and 4, below. See also Erasmus, *Enchiridion* 3 (tr. LCC XIV. 308 ff.). The inscription "Γνῶθι σαυτόν" (or "σεαυτόν"), "Know thyself," on the temple at Delphi, supplies the text for a lesson taught by Socrates in Xenophon's *Memorabilia* IV. ii. 24–29 (LCL edition, pp. 286 f.). Cf. Aristotle, *Rhetoric* II. xxi. 1395a (LCL edition, pp. 282 ff.). Cicero several times quotes and comments on this expression, e.g.: When Apollo says, 'Know thyself,' he is saying, 'Know thy soul,' " *Tusculan Disputations* I. xxii. 52 (LCL edition, pp. 62 f.). With this, Calvin's meaning accords.

to avoid applying it perversely. This, we observe, has happened to certain philosophers, who, while urging man to know himself, propose the goal of recognizing his own worth and excellence. And they would have him contemplate in himself nothing but what swells him with empty assurance and puffs him up with pride [Gen. 1:27].

ᵉBut knowledge of ourselves lies first in considering what we were given at creation and how generously God continues his favor toward us, in order to know how great our natural excellence would be if only it had remained unblemished; yet at the same time to bear in mind that there is in us nothing of our own, but that we hold on sufferance whatever God has bestowed upon us. Hence we are ever dependent on him. Secondly, to call to mind our miserable condition after Adam's fall; the awareness of which, when all our boasting and self-assurance are laid low, should truly humble us and overwhelm us with shame. In the beginning God fashioned us after his image [Gen. 1:27] that he might arouse our minds both to zeal for virtue and to meditation upon eternal life. Thus, in order that the great nobility of our race (which distinguishes us from brute beasts) may not be buried beneath our own dullness of wit, it behooves us to recognize that we have been endowed with reason and understanding so that, by leading a holy and upright life, we may press on to the appointed goal of blessed immortality.

ᵉ⁽ᵇ⁾But that primal worthiness cannot come to mind without the sorry spectacle of our foulness and dishonor presenting itself by way of contrast, since in the person of the first man we have fallen from our original condition. From this source arise abhorrence and displeasure with ourselves, as well as true humility; and thence is kindled a new zeal to seek God, in whom each of us may recover those good things which we have utterly and completely lost.

2. Man by nature inclines to deluded self-admiration

ᵇHere, then, is what God's truth requires us to seek in examining ourselves: it requires the kind of knowledge that will strip us of all confidence in our own ability, deprive us of all occasion for boasting, and lead us to submission. We ought to keep this rule if we wish to reach the true goal of both wisdom and action. I am quite aware how much more pleasing is that principle which invites us to weigh our good traits rather than to ᵉ⁽ᵇ⁾look upon our miserable want and dishonor, which ought to overwhelm us with shame. ᵇThere is, indeed, nothing that man's nature seeks more eagerly than to be flattered. Accordingly, when his nature

becomes aware that its gifts are highly esteemed, it tends to be
unduly credulous about them. It is thus no wonder that the
majority of men have erred so perniciously in this respect. For,
since blind self-love is innate in all mortals, they are most freely
persuaded that nothing inheres in themselves that deserves to
be considered hateful. Thus even with no outside support the
utterly vain opinion generally obtains credence that man is
abundantly sufficient of himself to lead a good and blessed life.[2]
But if any take a more modest attitude and concede something
to God, so as not to appear to claim everything for themselves,
they so divide the credit that the chief basis for boasting and confidence remains in themselves.

Nothing pleases man more than the sort of alluring talk that
tickles the pride that itches in his very marrow. Therefore, in
nearly every age, when anyone publicly extolled human nature
in most favorable terms, he was listened to with applause. But
however great such commendation of human excellence is that
teaches man to be satisfied with himself, it does nothing but delight in its own sweetness; indeed, it so deceives as to drive those
who assent to it into utter ruin. For what do we accomplish
when, relying upon every vain assurance, we consider, plan, try,
and undertake what we think is fitting; then—while in our very
first efforts we are actually forsaken by and destitute of sane understanding as well as true virtue—we nonetheless rashly press
on until we hurtle to destruction? Yet for those confident they can
do anything by their own power, things cannot happen otherwise.
Whoever, then, heeds such teachers as hold us back with thought
only of our good traits will not advance in self-knowledge, but
will be plunged into the worst ignorance.

3. The two chief problems of self-knowledge

ᵇGod's truth, therefore, agrees with the common judgment of
all mortals, that the second part of wisdom consists in the knowledge of ourselves; yet there is much disagreement as to how we
acquire that knowledge. According to carnal judgment, man
seems to know himself very well, when, confident in his understanding and uprightness, he becomes bold and urges himself
to the duties of virtue and, declaring war on vices, endeavors to
exert himself with all his ardor toward the excellent and the
honorable. But he who scrutinizes and examines himself accord-

---

[2] Cicero, Nature of the Gods III. xxxv. 87, 88, where the Academician Cotta
says that while intellect, virtue, and faith are within ourselves, safety,
wealth, and victory are to be sought from the gods. (Tr. LCL edition, pp.
372–375.)

ing to the standard of divine judgment finds nothing to lift his heart to self-confidence. And the more deeply he examines himself, the more dejected he becomes, until, utterly deprived of all such assurance, he leaves nothing to himself with which to direct his life aright.

e(b)Yet God would not have us forget our original nobility, which he had bestowed upon our father Adam, band which ought truly to arouse in us a zeal for righteousness and goodness. For we cannot think upon either our first condition or to what purpose we were formed without being prompted to meditate upon immortality, and to yearn after the Kingdom of God. That recognition, however, far from encouraging pride in us, discourages us and casts us into humility. For what is that origin? It is that from which we have fallen. What is that end of our creation? It is that from which we have been completely estranged, so that sick of our miserable lot we groan, and in groaning we sigh for that lost worthiness.[3] But when we say that man ought to see nothing in himself to cause elation, we mean that he has nothing to rely on to make him proud.

Therefore, if it is agreeable, let us divide the knowledge that man ought to have of himself. First, he should consider for what purpose he was created and endowed with no mean gifts.[4] By this knowledge he should arouse himself to meditation upon divine worship and the future life.[5] Secondly, he should weigh his own abilities—or rather, lack of abilities. When he perceives this lack, he should lie prostrate in extreme confusion, so to speak, reduced to nought. The first consideration tends to make him recognize the nature of his duty; the second, the extent of his ability to carry it out. We shall discuss each as the order of teaching demands.

(Adam's sin entailed loss of man's original endowment and ruin of the whole human race, 4–7)
4. The history of the Fall shows us what sin is [Gen., ch. 3]: unfaithfulness

eBecause what God so severely punished must have been no light sin but a detestable crime, we must consider what kind of sin there was in Adam's desertion that enkindled God's fearful

---

[3] Pannier notes that Calvin here reveals the dynamism of the doctrine of the unfree will: when we realize the end for which we have been created, together with our actual moral impotence, we are led to seek power and deliverance from God. (Pannier, *Institution* I. 311, note *a* on p. 84.)
[4] Cf. I. xv. 1–4.
[5] "*Vitaeque futurae meditationem.*" Cf. III. ix.

vengeance against the whole of mankind. To regard Adam's sin as gluttonous intemperance (a common notion) is childish. As if the sum and head of all virtues lay in abstaining solely from one fruit, when all sorts of desirable delights abounded everywhere; and not only abundance but also magnificent variety was at hand in that blessed fruitfulness of earth!

We ought therefore to look more deeply. Adam was denied the tree of the knowledge of good and evil to test his obedience and prove that he was willingly under God's command. The very name of the tree shows the sole purpose of the precept was to keep him content with his lot and to prevent him from becoming puffed up with wicked lust. But the promise by which he was bidden to hope for eternal life so long as he ate from the tree of life, and, conversely, the terrible threat of death once he tasted of the tree of the knowledge of good and evil, served to prove and exercise his faith. Hence it is not hard to deduce by what means Adam provoked God's wrath upon himself. Indeed, Augustine speaks rightly when he declares that pride was the beginning of all evils.[6] For if ambition had not raised man higher than was meet and right, he could have remained in his original state.

But we must take a fuller definition from the nature of the temptation which Moses describes. Since the woman through unfaithfulness was led away from God's Word by the serpent's deceit, it is already clear that disobedience was the beginning of the Fall. This Paul also confirms, teaching that all were lost through the disobedience of one man. [Rom. 5:19.] Yet it is at the same time to be noted that the first man revolted from God's authority, not only because he was seized by Satan's blandishments, but also because, contemptuous of truth, he turned aside to falsehood. And surely, once we hold God's Word in contempt, we shake off all reverence for him. For, unless we listen attentively to him, his majesty will not dwell among us, nor his worship remain perfect. Unfaithfulness, then, was the root of the Fall. But thereafter ambition and pride, together with ungratefulness, arose, because Adam by seeking more than was granted him shamefully spurned God's great bounty, which had been lavished upon him. To have been made in the likeness of God seemed a small matter to a son of earth unless he also attained equality with God —a monstrous wickedness! If apostasy, by which man withdraws from the authority of his Maker—indeed insolently shakes off his yoke—is a foul and detestable offense, it is vain to extenuate Adam's sin. Yet it was not simple apostasy, but was joined with vile reproaches against God. These assented to

[6] Augustine, *Psalms*, Ps. 18. ii. 15 (MPL 36. 163; tr. LF *Psalms* I. 138 f.).

Satan's slanders, which accused God of falsehood and envy and ill will. Lastly, faithlessness opened the door to ambition, and ambition was indeed the mother of obstinate disobedience; as a result, men, having cast off the fear of God, threw themselves wherever lust carried them. Hence Bernard rightly teaches that the door of salvation is opened to us when we receive the gospel today with our ears, even as death was then admitted by those same windows when they were opened to Satan [cf. Jer. 9:21].[7] For Adam would never have dared oppose God's authority unless he had disbelieved in God's Word. Here, indeed, was the best bridle to control all passions: the thought that nothing is better than to practice righteousness by obeying God's commandments; then, that the ultimate goal of the happy life is to be loved by him. Therefore Adam, carried away by the devil's blasphemies, as far as he was able extinguished the whole glory of God.

5. The first sin as original sin

eAs it was the spiritual life of Adam to remain united and bound to his Maker, so estrangement from him was the death of his soul. Nor is it any wonder that he consigned his race to ruin by his rebellion when he perverted the whole order of nature in heaven and on earth. "All creatures," says Paul, "are groaning" [Rom. 8:22], "subject to corruption, not of their own will" [Rom. 8:20]. If the cause is sought, there is no doubt that they are bearing part of the punishment deserved by man, for whose use they were created. Since, therefore, the curse, which goes about through all the regions of the world, flowed hither and yon from Adam's guilt, it is not unreasonable if it is spread to all his off-spring. e(b/a)Therefore, after the heavenly image was obliterated in him, he was not the only one to suffer this punishment—b(a)that, in place of wisdom, virtue, holiness, truth, and justice, with which adornments he had been clad, there came forth the most filthy plagues, blindness, impotence, impurity, vanity, and injustice—e(b/a)but he also entangled and immersed his offspring in the same miseries.

bThis is the inherited corruption, which the church fathers termed "original sin," meaning by the word "sin" the depravation of a nature previously good and pure. e(b)There was much contention over this matter, einasmuch as nothing is farther from the usual view than for all to be made guilty by the guilt of one, and thus for sin to be made common. This seems to be the reason why the most ancient doctors of the church touched upon this

---

[7] Bernard, Sermons on the Song of Songs xxviii (MPL 183. 923; tr. S. J. Eales, Life and Works of St. Bernard IV. 179).

subject so obscurely. At least they explained it less clearly than was fitting. Yet this timidity could not prevent Pelagius from rising up with the profane fiction that Adam sinned only to his own loss without harming his posterity.[8] Through this subtlety Satan attempted to cover up the disease and thus to render it incurable. [b]But when it was shown by the clear testimony of Scripture that sin was transmitted from the first man to all his posterity [Rom. 5:12], Pelagius quibbled that it was transmitted through imitation, not propagation. Therefore, good men (and Augustine above the rest) labored to show us that we are corrupted not by derived wickedness, but that we bear inborn defect from our mother's womb.[9] To deny this was the height of shamelessness. But no man will wonder at the temerity of the Pelagians and Coelestians when he perceived from that holy man's warnings what shameless beasts they were in all other respects. Surely there is no doubt that David confesses himself to have been "begotten in iniquities, and conceived by his mother in sin" [Ps. 51:5 p.]. There he does not reprove his father and mother for their sins; but, that he may better commend God's goodness toward himself, from his very conception he carries the confession of his own perversity. Since it is clear that this was not peculiar to David, it follows that the common lot of mankind is exemplified in him.

[8] Pelagius (ca. 354–420), a British monk who combated Augustine's doctrine of man's innate depravity resulting from Adam's sin, thus calling forth a body of treatises and letters by Augustine in exposition and defense of this doctrine. Cf. Augustine, *Retractations* I. xiii. 5 (MPL 32. 604); *Against Julian* III. xxvi. 59 (MPL 44. 732 f.; tr. FC 35. 159 f.). With his more aggressive associate, Coelestius, an Irishman, Pelagius emerged from Rome, visited North Africa, Palestine, and Asia Minor, and won numerous adherents. Pelagianism was condemned in Councils of Carthage, 412 and 418, and in an imperial edict, 418, after which Pope Zosimus withdrew the favor in which he had held Coelestius and joined in his condemnation. But elements of this heresy were perpetuated. It is essentially an assertion of the natural moral ability of man. For a useful brief selection of documents on the controversy, see H. Bettenson, *Documents of the Christian Church*, pp. 74–87. The work of Pelagius has been edited by A. Souter, *Pelagius's Expositions of the Thirteen Epistles of St. Paul*, Texts and Studies IX (Part I, Introduction; Part II, Text).

[9] Cf. Augustine, *City of God* XVI. xxvii: "Infants, . . . according to the common origin of the human race, have all broken God's covenant in that one in whom all have sinned. . . . Infants are . . . born in sin not actual but original" (MPL 41. 506; tr. NPNF II. 326). Other passages from Augustine of similar import are cited in Smits II. 30 and in OS III. 233 f. The first opposition of Pelagius to Augustine had been called forth against the implications of man's helplessness in the well-known sentence in the *Confessions* (X. xxix. 40; X. xxxi. 45): *"Da quod iubes et iube quod vis"* ("Give what thou commandest and command what thou wilt"). (MPL 32. 796, 798; tr. LCC VII. 225, 228.) Cf. II. v. 7, note 17; II. viii. 57, note 67.

Therefore all of us, who have descended from impure seed, are born infected with the contagion of sin. In fact, before we saw the light of this life we were soiled and spotted in God's sight. "For who can bring a clean thing from an unclean? There is not one"—as The Book of Job says [Job 14:4, cf. Vg.].

6. Original sin does not rest upon imitation

cWe hear that the uncleanness of the parents is so transmitted to the children that all without any exception are defiled at their begetting. But we will not find the beginning of this pollution unless we go back to the first parent of all, as its source. bWe must surely hold that Adam was not only the progenitor but, as it were, the root of human nature; and that therefore in his corruption mankind deserved to be vitiated. This the apostle makes clear from a comparison of Adam with Christ. "As through one man sin came into the world and through sin death, which spread among all men when all sinned" [Rom. 5:12], thus through Christ's grace righteousness and life are restored to us [Rom. 5:17]. What nonsense will the Pelagians chatter here? That Adam's sin was propagated by imitation? Then does Christ's righteousness benefit us only as an example set before us to imitate? Who can bear such sacrilege! But if it is beyond controversy that Christ's righteousness, and thereby life, are ours by communication, it immediately follows that both were lost in Adam, only to be recovered in Christ; and that sin and death crept in through Adam, only to be abolished through Christ. cThese are no obscure words: "Many are made righteous by Christ's obedience as by Adam's disobedience they had been made sinners" [Rom. 5:19 p.]. Here, then, is the relationship between the two: Adam, implicating us in his ruin, destroyed us with himself; but Christ restores us to salvation by his grace.

In such clear light of truth, I think that there is no need for longer or more laborious proof. In the first letter to the Corinthians, Paul wishes to strengthen the faith of the godly in the resurrection. Here he accordingly shows that the life lost in Adam is recovered in Christ [I Cor. 15:22]. Declaring that all of us died in Adam, Paul at the same time plainly testifies that we are infected with the disease of sin. For condemnation could not reach those untouched by the guilt of iniquity. The clearest explanation of his meaning lies in the other part of the statement, in which he declares that the hope of life is restored in Christ. But it is well known that this occurs in no other way than that wonderful communication whereby Christ transfuses into us the power of his righteousness. As it is written elsewhere, "The Spirit is life to us because of righteousness" [Rom. 8:10 p.]. There is consequently but one way for us to interpret the statement, "We have died in Adam": Adam, by sinning, not only took upon himself misfortune and ruin but also plunged our nature into like destruction. This was not due to the guilt of himself alone, which would not pertain to us at all, but was because he infected all his posterity with that corruption into which he had fallen.

ᵉPaul's statement that "by nature all are children of wrath" [Eph. 2:3] could not stand, unless they had already been cursed in the womb itself. Obviously, Paul does not mean "nature" as it was established by God, but as it was vitiated in Adam. For it would be most unfitting for God to be made the author of death. Therefore, Adam so corrupted himself that infection spread from him to all his descendants. Christ himself, our heavenly judge, clearly enough proclaims that all men are born wicked and depraved when he says that "whatever is born of flesh is flesh" [John 3:6], and therefore the door of life is closed to all until they have been reborn [John 3:5].

7. The transmission of sin from one generation to another

ᵇNo anxious discussion is needed to understand this question, which troubled the fathers not a little—whether the son's soul proceeds by derivation[10] from the father's soul—because the contagion chiefly lies in it. With this we ought to be content: that the Lord entrusted to Adam those gifts which he willed to be conferred upon human nature. Hence Adam, when he lost the gifts received, lost them not only for himself but for us all. Who should worry about the derivation of the soul when he hears

---

[10] Calvin here uses the debated word *tradux* and has in mind the arguments among the fathers on the origin of the individual soul. Cf. I. xv. 5, note 15. Though both Augustine and Calvin hold strongly the unity of mankind in creation, neither commits himself to traducianism, by which Adam's soul is regarded as bearing an element transmitted from the divine essence and as the source of all human souls. Calvin, indeed, completely rejects this teaching. But Augustine opposed the alternate view of creationism as it was somewhat crudely presented by Vincentius Victor. See Augustine, *On the Soul and Its Origin* I. iv; II. xiv (MPL 44. 477; 507 f.; tr. NPNF V. 316; 340 f.). For the prevailing medieval view, cf. E. R. Fairweather's note on a passage from Anselm of Laon (LCC X. 261, note 2). On the whole controversy, see C. Hodge, *Systematic Theology* II. iii, and J. F. Bethune-Baker, *An Introduction to the Early History of Christian Doctrine,* pp. 302 ff. Calvinist theology has favored creationism, the doctrine that each soul is a new creation of God. Says Hodge, p. 64: "Calvin, Beza, Turretin, and the great majority of Reformed theologians were creationists." This view was also voiced by certain opponents of the Reformation: cf. Alfonso de Castro, *Adversus omnes haereses* II, *s.v.* "anima" (1543, fo. 34 C–35 A).

that Adam had received for us no less than for himself those gifts which he lost, and that they had not been given to one man but had been assigned to the whole human race? There is nothing absurd, then, in supposing that, when Adam was despoiled, human nature was left naked and destitute, or that when he was infected with sin, contagion crept into human nature. Hence, rotten branches came forth from a rotten root, which transmitted their rottenness to the other twigs sprouting from them. For thus were the children corrupted in the parent, so that they brought disease upon their children's children. That is, the beginning of corruption in Adam was such that it was conveyed in a perpetual stream from the ancestors into their descendants. ᵈFor the contagion does not take its origin from the substance of the flesh or soul, but because it had been so ordained by God that the first man should at one and the same time have and lose, both for himself and for his descendants, the gifts that God had bestowed upon him.[11]

ᵇBut it is easy to refute the quibble of the Pelagians, who hold it unlikely that children should derive corruption from godly parents, inasmuch as the offspring ought rather to be sanctified by their parents' purity [cf. I Cor. 7:14]. For they descend not from their parents' spiritual regeneration but from their carnal generation. ᶜHence, as Augustine says, whether a man is a guilty unbeliever or an innocent believer, he begets not innocent but guilty children, for he begets them from a corrupted nature.[12] ᵇNow, it is a special blessing of God's people that they partake in some degree of their parents' holiness. This does not gainsay the fact that the universal curse of the human race preceded. ᵈFor guilt is of nature, but sanctification, of supernatural grace.

(Original sin defined as a depravity of nature, which deserves punishment, but which is not from nature as created, 8–11)
8. The nature of original sin
ᵇSo that these remarks may not be made concerning an uncertain and unknown matter, let us define original sin.[13] It is not my intention to investigate the several definitions proposed by various

[11] Benoit here cites Calvin, Comm. John 3:6, where it is said that original sin is not transmitted from parents by physical generation, but that by divine ordinance all are corrupted in Adam, being despoiled of the gifts with which in him we were adorned.

[12] Cf. Augustine: "*Regeneratus non regenerat filios carnis, sed generat.*" *On the Grace of Christ and on Original Sin* II. xl. 45 (MPL 44. 407; tr. NPNF V. 253).

[13] *Acts of the Synod of Trent with the Antidote* I, session 5, decree 1 (CR VII. 425 f.; tr. Calvin, *Tracts* III. 86 ff.).

writers, but simply to bring forward the one that appears to me most in accordance with truth. Original sin, therefore, seems to be a hereditary depravity and corruption of our nature, diffused into all parts of the soul, which first makes us liable to God's wrath, then also brings forth in us those works which Scripture calls "works of the flesh" [Gal. 5:19]. And that is properly what Paul often calls sin. ^aThe works that come forth from it—such as adulteries, fornications, thefts, hatreds, murders, carousings—he accordingly calls "fruits of sin" [Gal. 5:19–21], although they are also commonly called "sins" in Scripture, and even by Paul himself.

^bWe must, therefore, distinctly note these two things. First, we are so vitiated and perverted in every part of our nature that by this great corruption we stand justly condemned and convicted before God, to whom nothing is acceptable but righteousness, innocence, and purity. And this is not liability for another's transgression. For, since it is said that we became subject to God's judgment through Adam's sin, we are to understand it not as if we, guiltless and undeserving, bore the guilt of his offense but in the sense that, since we through his transgression have become entangled in the curse, he is said to have made us guilty. Yet not only has punishment fallen upon us from Adam, but a contagion imparted by him resides in us, which justly deserves punishment. For this reason, Augustine, though he often calls sin "another's" to show more clearly that it is distributed among us through propagation, nevertheless declares at the same time that it is peculiar to each.[14] And the apostle himself most eloquently testifies that "death has spread to all because all have sinned" [Rom. 5:12]. That is, they have been enveloped in original sin and defiled by its stains. For that reason, even infants themselves, while they carry their condemnation along with them from the mother's womb, are guilty not of another's fault but of their own. For, even though the fruits of their iniquity have not yet come forth, they have the seed enclosed within them. Indeed, their whole nature is a seed of sin; hence it can be only hateful and abhorrent to God. ^eFrom this it follows that it is rightly considered sin in God's sight, for without guilt there would be no accusation.

^bThen comes the second consideration: that this perversity never ceases in us, but continually bears new fruits—the works of the flesh that we have already described—just as a burning furnace gives forth flame and sparks, or water ceaselessly bubbles up from a spring. ^aThus those who have defined original sin as "the lack

14 Augustine, *On the Grace of Christ and on Original Sin* loc. cit.

of the original righteousness, which ought to reside in us," ᵇalthough they comprehend in this definition the whole meaning of the term, ᵃhave still not expressed effectively enough its power and energy.[15] For our nature is not only destitute and empty of good, but so fertile and fruitful of every evil that it cannot be idle. Those who have said that original sin is "concupiscence"[16] have used an appropriate word, if only it be added—something that most will by no means concede—that whatever is in man, from the understanding to the will, from the soul even to the flesh, has been defiled and crammed with this concupiscence. Or, to put it more briefly, the whole man is of himself nothing but concupiscence.

9. Sin overturns the whole man

ᵉFor this reason, I have said that all parts of the soul were possessed by sin after Adam deserted the fountain of righteousness. For not only did a lower appetite seduce him, but unspeakable impiety occupied the very citadel of his mind, and pride penetrated to the depths of his heart. Thus it is pointless and foolish to restrict the corruption that arises thence only to what are called the impulses of the senses; or to call it the "kindling wood" that attracts, arouses, and drags into sin only that part which they term "sensuality." In this matter Peter Lombard has betrayed his complete ignorance. For, in seeking and searching out its seat, he says that it lies in the flesh, as Paul testifies; yet not intrinsically, but because it appears more in the flesh.[17] As if

[15] Melanchthon describes original sin as "a native propensity and a certain genial impulse and energy [genialis impetus et energia] by which we are drawn toward sinning." He illustrates it by the upward direction of flames and by the attraction of a magnet. It is thus wrong to differentiate, in the Scholastic manner, between original and actual sin. While he approves the Scholastic description of it as "the lack of original righteousness," he emphatically points to the insufficiency of this as a definition, since the sin is an active impiety springing from a primary self-love. Loci communes (1521), ed. H. Engelland, in the series Melanchthons Werke in Auswahl, ed. R. Stupperich, II. i. 17 ff.; tr. from Kolde's 1910 edition, C. L. Hill, The Loci Communes of Philip Melanchthon, pp. 81 ff.

[16] The term "concupiscence" is much used by Augustine, e.g., in his treatise On Marriage and Concupiscence, where in its broadest sense the word means "the law of sin in our sinful flesh" (I. xxxiv) (MPL 44. 435; tr. NPNF V. 277). Peter Lombard, in discussing the transmission of Adam's sin to his posterity, describes original sin as "fomes peccati, id est, concupiscentia," and also calls it "a vice of nature vitiating all men, who through Adam are born in concupiscence." Sentences, II. xxx. 7 f. (MPL 192. 722). Cf. the interesting and typically Scholastic argument of Stephen Langton on original sin in LCC X. 352 ff.

[17] Lombard, Sentences, II. xxx. 7 f. and xxxi. 2-4 (MPL 192. 722, 724).

Paul were indicating that only a part of the soul, and not its entire nature, is opposed to supernatural grace! Paul removes all doubt when he teaches that corruption subsists not in one part only, but that none of the soul remains pure or untouched by that mortal disease. For in his discussion of a corrupt nature Paul not only condemns the inordinate impulses of the appetites that are seen, but especially contends the mind is given over to blindness and the heart to depravity.[18]

The whole third chapter of Romans is nothing but a description of original sin [vs. 1–20]. From the "renewal" that fact appears more clearly. For the Spirit, who is opposed to the old man and to the flesh, not only marks the grace whereby the lower or sensual part of the soul is corrected, but embraces the full reformation of all the parts. Consequently, Paul not only enjoins that brute appetites be brought to nought but bids us "be renewed in the spirit of our mind" [Eph. 4:23]; in another passage he similarly urges us to "be transformed in newness of mind" [Rom. 12: 2]. From this it follows that that part in which the excellence and nobility of the soul especially shine has not only been wounded, but so corrupted that it needs to be healed and to put on a new nature as well. We shall soon see to what extent sin occupies both mind and heart. Here I only want to suggest briefly that the whole man is overwhelmed—as by a deluge—from head to foot, so that no part is immune from sin and all that proceeds from him is to be imputed to sin. As Paul says, all turnings of the thoughts to the flesh are enmities against God [Rom. 8:7], and are therefore death [Rom. 8:6].

10. Sin is not our nature, but its derangement

[b]Now away with those persons who dare write God's name upon their faults, because we declare that men are vicious by nature![19] They perversely search out God's handiwork in their own pollution, when they ought rather to have sought it in that unimpaired and uncorrupted nature of Adam. Our destruction, therefore, comes from the guilt of our flesh, not from God, inasmuch as we have perished solely because we have degenerated from our original condition.

Let no one grumble here that God could have provided better for our salvation if he had forestalled Adam's fall.[20] Pious minds

---

[18] Cf. II. ii. 15, *ad finem;* II. iii. 2.

[19] This is one of the charges brought against the Libertines in Calvin's *Contre la secte phantastique des Libertins* (1545) (CR VII. 184 f.), and in his *Epistre contre un certain Cordelier* (1547) (CR VII. 347, 350 ff.).

[20] Cf. Augustine, *On Genesis in the Literal Sense* XI. iv, vi, x, xiii (MPL 34. 431–434).

ought to loathe this objection, because it manifests inordinate curiosity. Furthermore, the matter has to do with the secret of predestination, which will be discussed later in its proper place.[21] Let us accordingly remember to impute our ruin to depravity of nature, in order that we may not accuse God himself, the Author of nature. True, this deadly wound clings to nature, but it is a very important question whether the wound has been inflicted from outside or has been present from the beginning. Yet it is evident that the wound was inflicted through sin. We have, therefore, no reason to complain except against ourselves. Scripture has diligently noted this fact. For Ecclesiastes says: "This I know, that God made man upright, but they have sought out many devices." [Ch. 7:29.] Obviously, man's ruin is to be ascribed to man alone; for he, having acquired righteousness by God's kindness, has by his own folly sunk into vanity.

11. "Natural" corruption of the "nature" created by God

[b]Therefore we declare that man is corrupted through natural vitiation, but a vitiation that did not flow from nature.[22] We deny that it has flowed from nature in order to indicate that it is an adventitious quality which comes upon man rather than a substantial property which has been implanted from the beginning. Yet we call it "natural" in order that no man may think that anyone obtains it through bad conduct, since it holds all men fast by hereditary right. Our usage of the term is not without authority. The apostle states: "We are all by nature children of wrath." [Eph. 2:3.] How could God, who is pleased by the least of his works, have been hostile to the noblest of all his creatures? But he is hostile toward the corruption of his work rather than toward the work itself. Therefore if it is right to declare that man, because of his vitiated nature, is naturally abominable to God, it is also proper to say that man is naturally depraved and faulty. Hence Augustine, in view of man's corrupted nature, is not afraid to call "natural" those sins which necessarily reign in our flesh wherever God's grace is absent.[23] Thus vanishes the foolish trifling of the Manichees, who, when they imagined wickedness of substance in man, dared fashion another creator for him in

---

[21] III. xxi–xxiv; cf. I. xv. 8. In the corresponding passage in the editions of 1539 and 1541, Pannier finds the first occurrence of the word "predestination" in Calvin's writings. (Pannier, *Institution* I. 312.) However, the verbal form appears in the *Instruction et confession de foy* (1537) (OS I. 390; tr. P. T. Fuhrmann, *Instruction in Faith*, p. 36).

[22] Cf. I. i. 2, note 7; I. xiv. 3, note 11.

[23] Augustine, *On Genesis in the Literal Sense* I. i. 3 (MPL 34. 221); *Contra Julianum, opus imperfectum* V. xl (MPL 45. 1477).

order that they might not seem to assign the cause and beginning of evil to the righteous God.[24]

ᶜCHAPTER II

MAN HAS NOW BEEN DEPRIVED OF FREEDOM OF CHOICE AND BOUND OVER TO MISERABLE SERVITUDE

(Perils of this topic: point of view established, 1)

1. ᵇWe have now seen that the dominion of sin, from the time it held the first man bound to itself, not only ranges among all mankind, ᶜbut also completely occupies individual souls. ᵇIt remains for us to investigate ᶜmore closely ᵇwhether we have been deprived of all freedom since we have been reduced to this servitude; and, if any particle of it still survives, how far its power extends. But in order that the truth of this question may be more readily apparent to us, I shall presently set a goal to which the whole argument should be directed. The best way to avoid error will be to consider the perils that threaten man on both sides. (1) When man is denied all uprightness, he immediately takes occasion for complacency from that fact; and, because he is said to have no ability to pursue righteousness on his own, he holds all such pursuit to be of no consequence, as if it did not pertain to him at all. (2) Nothing, however slight, can be credited to man without depriving God of his honor, and without man himself falling into ruin through brazen confidence. Augustine points out both these precipices.[1]

Here, then, is the course that we must follow if we are to avoid crashing upon these rocks: when man has been taught that no good thing remains in his power, and that he is hedged about on all sides by most miserable necessity, in spite of this he should nevertheless be instructed to aspire to a good of which he is empty, to a freedom of which he has been deprived. In fact, he may thus be more sharply aroused from inactivity than if it were supposed that he was endowed with the highest virtues. Everyone sees how necessary this second point is. I observe that too many persons have doubts about the first point. For since this is an undoubted fact, that nothing of his own ought to be taken away from man, it ought to be clearly evident how important it is for him to be barred from false boasting. At the time when man was distinguished with the noblest marks of honor through God's benef-

---

[24] Cf. I. xiii. 1.
[1] Augustine, *Letters* ccxv, interpreting Prov. 4:26 (MPL 33. 971 ff.; tr. FC 32. 65 ff.); *John's Gospel* liii. 8 (MPL 35. 1778; tr. NPNF VII. 293 f.).

icence, not even then was he permitted to boast about himself. How much more ought he now to humble himself, cast down as he has been—due to his own ungratefulness—from the loftiest glory into extreme disgrace! At that time, I say, when he had been advanced to the highest degree of honor, Scripture attributed nothing else to him than that he had been created in the image of God [Gen. 1:27], thus suggesting that man was blessed, not because of his own good actions, but by participation in God. What, therefore, now remains for man, bare and destitute of all glory, but to recognize God for whose beneficence he could not be grateful when he abounded with the riches of his grace; and at least, by confessing his own poverty, to glorify him in whom he did not previously glory in recognition of his own blessings?[2]

Also, it is no less to our advantage than pertinent to God's glory that we be deprived of all credit for our wisdom and virtue. Thus those who bestow upon us anything beyond the truth add sacrilege to our ruin. When we are taught to wage our own war, we are but borne aloft on a reed stick, only to fall as soon as it breaks! Yet we flatter our strength unduly when we compare it even to a reed stick! For whatever vain men devise and babble concerning these matters is but smoke. Therefore Augustine with good reason often repeats the famous statement that free will is by its defenders more trampled down than strengthened.[3] It has been necessary to say this by way of preface because some, while they hear that man's power is rooted out from its very foundations that God's power may be built up in man, bitterly loathe this whole disputation as dangerous, not to say superfluous.[4] Nonetheless, it appears both fundamental in religion and most profitable for us.

(Critical discussion of opinions on free will given by philosophers and theologians, 2–9)
2. *The philosophers trust in the power of the understanding*
    eSince we said just above that the faculties of the soul are situ-

---

[2] Similar language is used in Calvin's *Instruction et confession de foy* (1537) (OS I. 382; tr. Fuhrmann, *Instruction in Faith*, p. 23). Cf. Pannier, *Institution* I. 95, note a on p. 312.

[3] Augustine, *John's Gospel* lxxxi. 2 (MPL 35. 1841; tr. NPNF VII. 345; *Letters* ccxvii. 3 (MPL 33. 981; tr. FC 32. 80 f.).

[4] The position of Erasmus in his treatise against Luther on free will, *De libero arbitrio* διατριβή (ed. J. von Walter, *Quellenschriften zur Geschichte des Protestantismus* 8, pp. 1, 5 ff.). Extensive portions of this treatise are translated in *The Portable Renaissance Reader*, ed. J. B. Ross and M. M. McLaughlin, pp. 677–693. The entire treatise is in LCC XVII.

ated in the mind and the heart,[5] [b]now let us examine what both parts can do. The philosophers (obviously with substantial agreement) imagine that the reason is located in the mind, which like a lamp illumines all counsels, and like a queen governs the will. For they suppose that it is suffused with divine light to take the most effective counsel; and that it excels in power to wield the most effective command. On the other hand, they imagine that sense perception is gripped by torpor and dimness of sight; so that it always creeps along the ground, is entangled in baser things, and never rises up to true discernment. They hold that the appetite, if it undertakes to obey the reason and does not permit itself to be subjected to the senses, is borne along to the pursuit of virtues, holds the right way, and is molded into will. But if it subjects itself to the bondage of the senses, it is so corrupted and perverted by the latter as to degenerate into lust.[6] In their opinion those faculties of which I have spoken above[7]—understanding, sense, appetite, or will (which last designation is now accepted in more common usage)—have their seat in the soul. These philosophers consequently declare that the understanding is endowed with reason, the best ruling principle for the leading of a good and blessed life, provided it sustains itself within its own excellence and displays the strength bestowed upon it by nature. But they state that the lower impulse, called "sense," by which man is drawn off into error and delusion is such that it can be tamed and gradually overcome by reason's rod. Further, they locate the will midway between reason and sense. That is, it possesses right and freedom of itself either to obey reason or to prostitute itself to be ravished by sense—whichever it pleases.

3. Thus, in spite of all, the philosophers assert freedom of the will

[b]Sometimes, convinced by experience itself, they do not deny the great difficulty with which man establishes the rule of reason a kingdom within himself. At one time he is tickled by the enticements of pleasures; at another is tricked by a false image of good things; and again is violently struck by immoderate inclinations, and as by cords and strings is pulled in divers directions, as Plato says.[8]

Accordingly, Cicero says that the faint glimmer given us by

[5] I. xv. 7.

[6] Plato, *Republic* IV. 14 ff., 439 ff. (LCL Plato, *Republic* I. 394 ff.); Aristotle, *De anima* III. x. 433 (LCL edition, pp. 186–191).

[7] I. xv. 6.

[8] Plato, *Laws* I. 644 E (LCL Plato, *Laws* I. 68 f.).

nature is soon quenched by our wicked opinions and evil customs.[9] The philosophers concede that such diseases, once they have occupied men's minds, rage so violently that no one can easily restrain them. Nor do these writers hesitate to compare them to wild horses, which when reason is overthrown, as a charioteer tossed from his chariot, intemperately and without restraint play the wanton.[10]

Nevertheless, the philosophers hold as certain that virtues and vices are in our power. They say: If to do this or that depends upon our choice, so also does not to do it. Again, if not to do it, so also to do it. Now we seem to do what we do, and to shun what we shun, by free choice. Therefore, if we do any good thing when we please, we can also not do it; if we do any evil, we can also shun it.[11] Indeed, certain of them have broken forth into such license as to boast that the fact that we live is a gift of the gods, but if we live well and holily, it is our own doing. ͨThence, also, comes that saying of Cicero in the person of Cotta, that "because every man acquires virtue for himself, no wise man ever has thanked God for it. For we are praised for our virtue, and glory in our virtue. This would not happen if the gift were of God and not from ourselves." A little later he says: "This is the judgment of all mortals, that fortune is to be sought from God but that wisdom is to be acquired from oneself."[12] ᵇThis is the sum of the opinion of all philosophers: reason which abides in human understanding is a sufficient guide for right conduct; the will, being subject to it, is indeed incited by the senses to evil things; but since the will has free choice, it cannot be hindered from following reason as its leader in all things.

4. The church fathers generally show less clarity but a tendency to accept freedom of the will. What is free will?

ᵇAll ecclesiastical writers have recognized both that the soundness of reason in man is gravely wounded through sin, and that the will has been very much enslaved by evil desires. Despite this, many of them have come far too close to the philosophers.[13] Of

---

[9] Cicero, *Tusculan Disputations* III. i. 2 (LCL edition, pp. 226 f.).

[10] Cf. Plato, *Phaedrus* 74 ff., 253 D–254 E (LCL Plato I. 494–497).

[11] Aristotle, *Nicomachean Ethics* III. 5. 1113b: "For virtue is in our power and so too is vice. For where it is in our power to act, it is also in our power not to act" (tr. R. McKeon, *Basic Works of Aristotle*, p. 972; cf. LCL edition, pp. 142 f.); Seneca, *Moral Epistles* xc. 1 (LCL Seneca, II. 394 f.).

[12] Cicero, *Nature of the Gods* III. xxxvi. 86 f. (LCL edition, pp. 372 f.).

[13] In the *De scandalis* (1550), Calvin similarly charges certain of the fathers with undue deference to the philosophers in ascribing free will to man. (CR VIII. 19; cf. Benoit, *Institution* II. 25.)

these, the early ones seem to me to have, with a twofold intent, elevated human powers for the following reasons. First, a frank confession of man's powerlessness would have brought upon them the jeers of the philosophers with whom they were in conflict. Second, they wished to avoid giving fresh occasion for slothfulness to a flesh already indifferent toward good.[14] Therefore, that they might teach nothing absurd to the common judgment of men, they strove to harmonize the doctrine of Scripture halfway with the beliefs of the philosophers. Yet they paid especial attention to the second point, not to give occasion for slothfulness. This appears from their words. Chrysostom somewhere expresses it: "Since God has placed good and evil in our power, he has granted free decision of choice, and does not restrain the unwilling, but embraces the willing." Again: "He who is evil, if he should wish, is often changed into a good man; and he who is good falls through sloth and becomes evil. For the Lord has made our nature free to choose. Nor does he impose necessity upon us, but furnishes suitable remedies and allows everything to hinge on the sick man's own judgment." Again: "Just as we can never do anything rightly unless we are aided by God's grace, so we cannot acquire heavenly favor unless we bring our portion." But he had said before: "In order that not everything may depend on divine help, we must at the same time bring something ourselves." One of his common expressions is: "Let us bring what is ours; God will furnish the rest."[15] What Jerome says agrees with this: "Ours is to begin, God's to fulfill; ours to offer what we can, his to supply what we cannot."[16]

Surely you see by these statements that they credited man with more zeal for virtue than he deserved because they thought that they could not rouse our inborn sluggishness unless they argued that we sinned by it alone. But how skillfully they did this we shall subsequently see. A little later it will be quite evident that these opinions to which we have referred are utterly false.

Further, even though the Greeks above the rest—and Chrysostom especially among them—extol the ability of the human will, yet all the ancients, save Augustine, so differ, waver, or speak confusedly on this subject, that almost nothing certain can be derived from their writings. Therefore, we shall not stop to

[14] While his references are to the fathers, Calvin nevertheless slants his argument against contemporary Humanists, including Erasmus. See Pannier, *Institution* I. 313, note *a* on p. 101.

[15] Chrysostom, *De proditione Judaeorum*, hom. i (MPG 49. 377); *Homilies on Genesis:* hom. xix. 1; hom. liii. 2; hom. xxv. 7 (MPG 53. 158; 54. 466; 53. 228).

[16] Jerome, *Dialogus contra Pelagianos* III. 1 (MPL 23. 569).

list more exactly the opinions of individual writers; but we shall only select at random from one or another, as the explanation of the argument would seem to demand.

The other writers who came after them, while each sought praise for his own cleverness in his defense of human nature, one after another gradually fell from bad to worse, until it came to the point that man was commonly thought to be corrupted only in his sensual part and to have a perfectly unblemished reason and a will also largely unimpaired.[17] ᵉMeanwhile the well-known statement flitted from mouth to mouth: that the natural gifts in man were corrupted, but the supernatural taken away.[18] But scarcely one man in a hundred had an inkling of its significance. For my part, if I wanted clearly to teach what the corruption of nature is like, I would readily be content with these words. But it is more important to weigh carefully what man can do, vitiated as he is in every part of his nature and shorn of supernatural gifts. Those, then, who boasted that they were Christ's disciples spoke of this matter too much like philosophers. ᵇThe term "free will" has always been used among the Latins, ᵉas if man still remained upright. ᵇThe Greeks were not ashamed to use a much more presumptuous word. They called it "self-power,"[19] as if each man had power in his own hands. All—even the common folk—were imbued with this principle, that man is endowed with free will. Yet some of them who wish to seem distinguished do not know how far it extends. Let us, therefore, first investigate the force of this term; then let us determine from the simple testimony of Scripture what promise man, of his own nature, has for good or ill.

[17] Duns Scotus, *In sententias* II. xxix. 1 (*Opera omnia* XIII. 267 f.).

[18] This sentence, much in Augustine's style and based upon his thought, is of medieval formulation. Lombard has *"alia sunt corrupta per peccatum, id est naturalia . . . alia subtracta"* (*Sentences* II. xxv. 8; MPL 192. 207). See also Augustine, *Questions on the Gospels* ii. 19, on the good Samaritan, Luke, ch. 10. Man is alive, says Augustine, in that by which he has understanding and knowledge of God, but as oppressed by sin he is dead; hence he is said to be half alive (*semivivus,* Luke 10:30) (MPL 35. 1340). Other related passages are *On Nature and Grace* iii. 3; xix. 21; xx. 22 (MPL 44. 249 f.–256 f.; tr. NPNF V. 122; 127 f.); Pseudo-Augustine, *Hypomnesticon* [commonly called *Hypognosticon*] *contra pelagianos et caelestinos* III. viii. 11 (MPL 45. 1628). See also II. v. 19, note 38; note 21, below; sec. 12, note 53; sec. 16, note 62; Comm. Ezek. 11:19–20; T. F. Torrance, *Calvin's Doctrine of Man,* ch. vii.

[19] "αὐτεξούσιος." Among the church fathers this word is apparently first used by Clement of Alexandria, who interprets Paul's "When I became a man" (I Cor. 13:11) as applying "to us who are obedient to the Word and masters of ourselves [αὐτεξουσίους]." *Instructor* I. vi. 33 (GCS Clemens Alexandrinus I. 110; MPG 8. 289 f.; tr. ANF II. 217).

Few have defined what free will is, although it repeatedly occurs in the writings of all. Origen seems to have put forward a definition generally agreed upon among ecclesiastical writers when he said that it is a faculty of the reason to distinguish between good and evil, a faculty of the will to choose one or the other.[20] Augustine does not disagree with this when he teaches that it is a faculty of the reason and the will to choose good with the assistance of grace; evil, when grace is absent.[21] Bernard, wishing to speak subtly, "on account of the imperishable freedom of the will, and of the unfailing judgment of the reason," more obscurely says it is "consent."[22] And Anselm's well-known definition is not plain enough: that it is the power of maintaining rectitude for its own sake.[23] As a consequence, Peter Lombard and the Scholastics preferred to accept Augustine's definition because it was clearer and did not exclude God's grace. They realized that without grace the will could not be sufficient unto itself. Nevertheless, they bring forward their own ideas, which they consider either to be better or to make for a fuller explanation. First, they agree that the noun *arbitrium* ought rather to refer to reason, whose task it is to distinguish between good and evil; that the adjective *liberum* pertains properly to the will, which can be turned to one side or the other.[24] Hence, Thomas says that, since freedom properly belongs to the will, it would be most suitable to call free will a "power of selection," which, derived from a mingling of understanding and appetite, yet inclines more to appetite.[25] We now find wherein they teach that the power of free decision resides, that is, in the reason and the will. ᵉ⁽ᵇ⁾It remains for us to see briefly how much they attribute to each.

5. *Different kinds of "will" and of "freedom" in the church fathers*

ᵇUnder man's free counsel they commonly class those intermediate things[26] which obviously do not pertain to God's Kingdom; but they refer true righteousness to God's special grace and

---

[20] Origen, *De principiis* III. i. 3 (GCS 22. 197; MPG 11. 252; tr. ANF IV. 303; Butterworth, *Origen On First Principles*, p. 159).

[21] Cf. Augustine, *Sermons* clvi. 9–13 (MPL 38. 855–857; tr. LF *Sermons* II. 767–770); Pseudo-Augustine (school of Hugh of St. Victor), *Summa sententiarum* iii. 8 (MPL 176. 101); Lombard, *Sentences* II. xxiv. 5 (MPL 192. 702) and note 18, above. See also OS III. 246, note 3; Smits II. 31.

[22] Bernard, *De gratia et libero arbitrio* ii. 4 (MPL 182. 1004; tr. W. W. Williams, *Concerning Grace and Free Will*, p. 10).

[23] Anselm, *Dialogus de libero arbitrio* iii (MPL 158. 494): "*Potestas servandi rectitudinem propter ipsam rectitudinem.*"

[24] Lombard, *Sentences* II. xxiv. 5 (MPL 192. 702).

[25] Aquinas, *Summa Theol.* I. lxxxiii. 3.

[26] "*Res medias,*" things intermediate, or indifferent, a rendering of the Greek

spiritual regeneration. To show this, the author of the work *The Calling of the Gentiles* enumerates three kinds of will: first, the sensual; second, the psychic; third, the spiritual. With the first two, he teaches, man is freely endowed; the last is the work of the Holy Spirit in man.[27] We shall discuss in its proper place whether this is true. Now I intend briefly to weigh, not to refute, the statements of others. Hence, it happens that when the church fathers are discussing free will, they first inquire, not into its importance for civil or external actions, but into what promotes obedience to the divine law. Although I grant this latter question is the main one, I do not think the former ought to be completely neglected. I hope I shall render a very good account of my own opinion.[28]

Now in the schools three kinds of freedom are distinguished: first from necessity, second from sin, third from misery. The first of these so inheres in man by nature that it cannot possibly be taken away, but the two others have been lost through sin.[29] I willingly accept this distinction, except in so far as necessity is falsely confused with compulsion. The extent of the difference between them and the need to bear it in mind will appear elsewhere.[30]

6. "Operating" and "co-operating" grace?

ᵇIf this be admitted, it will be indisputable that free will is not sufficient to enable man to do good works, unless he be helped by grace, indeed by special grace, which only the elect receive through regeneration. ᶜFor I do not tarry over those fanatics who babble that grace is equally and indiscriminately distributed.[31]

ἀδιάφορα (cf. German, *Mitteldinge*). See the discussion under "Christian Freedom" III. xix. 7–9; also II. ii. 12–14; II. iii. 5.

[27] Prosper of Aquitaine, *De vocatione omnium gentium* (ca. 450) I. ii. This treatise was published with the works of Ambrose (Basel, 1492) and appears with the spurious works formerly attributed to him in MPL 17; also, in variant form, with the works of Prosper, MPL 51. For this passage, see MPL 17. 1075; 51. 649 f., and the translation by P. de Letter, *St. Prosper of Aquitaine, The Call of All Nations* (tr. ACW XIV), p. 27. Cf. M. Cappuyns, "L'Auteur du *De vocatione omnium gentium*," *Revue Bénédictine* XXXIX (1927), 198–226.

[28] II. xii–xviii.

[29] Lombard, *Sentences* II. xxv. 9 (MPL 192. 708); Bernard, *De gratia et libero arbitrio* iii. 7 (MPL 182. 1005; tr. W. W. Williams, *Concerning Grace and Free Will*, pp. 15 f.).

[30] II. iii. 5.

[31] In his response (June 5, 1555) to questions addressed to him by Laelius Socinus (to whom he may be alluding here), Calvin distinguishes between

ᵇBut it has not yet been demonstrated whether man has been wholly deprived of all power to do good, or still has some power, though meager and weak; a power, indeed, that can do nothing of itself, but with the help of grace also does its part. The Master of the Sentences meant to settle this point when he taught: "We need two kinds of grace to render us capable of good works." He calls the first kind "operating," which ensures that we effectively will to do good. The second he calls "co-operating," which follows the good will as a help.[32] The thing that displeases me about this division is that, while he attributes the effective desire for good to the grace of God, yet he hints that man by his very own nature somehow seeks after the good—though ineffectively. Thus Bernard declares the good will is God's work, yet concedes to man that of his own impulse he seeks this sort of good will. But this is far from Augustine's thought, from whom Peter Lombard pretended to have taken this distinction.[33] The ambiguity in the second part offends me, for it has given rise to a perverted interpretation. They thought we co-operate with the assisting grace of God, because it is our right either to render it ineffectual by spurning the first grace, or to confirm it by obediently following it. This the author of the work *The Calling of the Gentiles* expresses as follows: "Those who employ the judgment of reason are free to forsake grace, so that not to have forsaken it is a meritorious act; and what could not be done without the co-operation of the Spirit is counted meritorious for those whose own will could not have accomplished it."[34] I chose to note these two points in passing that you, my reader, may see how far I disagree with the sounder Schoolmen. I differ with the more recent Sophists[35] to an even greater extent, as they are farther removed from antiquity. However, we at least understand from this division in what way they grant free will to man. For Lombard finally declares that we have free will, not in that we are equally capable of doing or thinking

the effective giving of grace to the elect and the "inferior operation of the Spirit" in the reprobate. *Responsio ad aliquot Laelii Socini quaestiones*, 2–4 (CR X. 163 ff.).

[32] Lombard, *Sentences* II. xxvi. 1 (MPL 192. 710).

[33] Bernard, *De gratia et libero arbitrio* xiv. 46 (MPL 182, 1026; tr. W. W. Williams, *Concerning Grace and Free Will*, p. 48); Augustine, *On Grace and Free Will* xvii. 33 (MPL 44. 901; tr. NPNF V. 457).

[34] Prosper of Aquitaine, *The Call of All Nations* II. iv (MPL 51. 96; tr. ACW XIV. 96).

[35] Note the distinction between the earlier and "sounder" Schoolmen and the *recentiores sophistae*. In the latter expression Calvin apparently has in mind Ockham, his later interpreters such as Gabriel Biel (d. 1495), and the Sorbonne theologians of his own day.

good and evil, but merely that we are freed from compulsion. According to Lombard, this freedom is not hindered, even if we be wicked and slaves of sin, and can do nothing but sin.[36]

7. That man is necessarily, but without compulsion, a sinner establishes no doctrine of free will

[b]Man will then be spoken of as having this sort of free decision, not because he has free choice equally of good and evil, but because he acts wickedly by will, not by compulsion. Well put, indeed, but what purpose is served by labeling with a proud name such a slight thing? A noble freedom, indeed—for man not to be forced to serve sin, yet to be such a willing slave[37] that his will is bound by the fetters of sin! Indeed, I abhor contentions about words,[38] with which the church is harassed to no purpose. But I have scrupulously resolved to avoid those words which signify something absurd, especially where pernicious error is involved. But how few men are there, I ask, who when they hear free will attributed to man do not immediately conceive him to be master of both his own mind and will, able of his own power to turn himself toward either good or evil? Yet (someone will say) this sort of danger will be removed if the common folk are diligently warned of its meaning. Man's disposition voluntarily so inclines to falsehood that he more quickly derives error from one word than truth from a wordy discourse. In this very word we have more certain experience of this matter than we should like. For, overlooking that interpretation of the ancient writers, almost all their successors, while they have clung to the etymological meaning of the word, have been carried into a ruinous self-assurance.

---

[36] Lombard, *Sentences* II. xxv. 8 (MPL 192. 708). Cf. II. ii. 15, which describes the continuing good in sinful man, and II. iii. 2 (especially the last sentence), which denies him all good. Such comparison will show both the hyperbole of Calvin's expression and the underlying theological position on the basis of which he can say that "many good qualities" remain in man and yet that he is "totally destitute of all good." Cf. *Instruction et confession de foy* (1537) (OS I. 381; CR XXII. 36 f.; tr. Fuhrmann, *Instruction in Faith* 5, p. 22): "The Scripture testifies often that man is a slave of sin. . . . Because the heart, totally imbued with the poison of sin, can emit nothing but the fruits of sin." Note also the "gift" quality of the heathen virtues, II. iii. 3–4, and the relative degrees of goodness within the state of human depravity. T. F. Torrance has shed much light on this aspect of Calvin's thought in *Calvin's Doctrine of Man*, chs. vii, viii.

[37] "ἐθελόδουλος." Pannier points out that Étienne de Boétie (the friend of Montaigne) had written his famous political treatise *La servitude volontaire* in 1548.

[38] "λογομαχίας."

8. Augustine's doctrine of "free will"

ᵇNow, if the authority of the fathers has weight with us, they indeed have the word constantly on their lips, yet at the same time they declare what it connotes to them. First of all, there is Augustine, who does not hesitate to call it "unfree."[39] Elsewhere he is angry toward those who deny that the will is free; but he states his main reason in these words: "Only let no one so dare to deny the decision of the will as to wish to excuse sin."[40] Yet elsewhere he plainly confesses that "without the Spirit man's will is not free, since it has been laid under by shackling and conquering desires."[41] Likewise, when the will was conquered by the vice into which it had fallen, human nature began to lose its freedom.[42] Again, man, using free will badly, has lost both himself and his will. Again, the free will has been so enslaved that it can have no power for righteousness. ᶜAgain, what God's grace has not freed will not be free. Again, the justice of God is not fulfilled when the law so commands, and man acts as if by his own strength; but when the Spirit helps, and man's will, not free, but freed by God, obeys. And he gives a brief account of all these matters when he writes elsewhere: man, when he was created, received great powers of free will, but lost them by sinning.[43] Therefore in another passage, after showing that free will is established through grace, he bitterly inveighs against those who claim it for themselves without grace. "Why then," he says, "do miserable men either dare to boast of free will before they have been freed, or of their powers, if they have already been freed? And they do not heed the fact that in the term 'free will' freedom seems to be implied. 'Now where the Spirit of the Lord is, there is freedom.' [II Cor. 3:17.] If, therefore, they are slaves of sin, why do they boast of free will? For a man becomes the slave of him who has overcome him. Now, if they have been freed, why do they boast as if it had come about through their own effort? Or are they so free as not to wish

---

[39] Augustine, *Against Julian* II. viii. 23 (MPL 44. 689; tr. FC 35. 83 f.). Cf. Calvin, *Instruction in Faith (1537),* 5 (OS I. 381; CR XXII. 36; tr. Fuhrmann, p. 22).

[40] Augustine, *John's Gospel* liii. 8 (MPL 35. 1778; tr. NPNF VII. 293).

[41] Augustine, *Letters* cxlv. 2 (MPL 33. 593; tr. FC 20. 163 f.).

[42] Augustine, *On Man's Perfection in Righteousness* iv. 9 (MPL 44. 296; tr. NPNF V. 161).

[43] The additional passages from Augustine quoted in the above sentences are: *Enchiridion* ix. 30 (MPL 40. 246; tr. LCC VII. 356 f.); *Against Two Letters of the Pelagians* III. viii. 24 (MPL 44. 607; tr. NPNF V. 414); I. iii. 6 (MPL 44. 553; tr. NPNF V. 379); III. vii. 20: "*Hominis libera, sed Dei gratia liberata, voluntas*" (MPL 44. 603; tr. NPNF V. 412); *Sermons* cxxxi. 6 (MPL 38. 732).

to be the slaves of him who says: 'Without me you can do nothing' " [John 15:5]?

ᵇWhy, elsewhere he seems to ridicule the use of this word when he says that the will is indeed free but not freed: free of righteousness but enslaved to sin! ᶜHe also repeats and explains this statement in another place, where he teaches that man is not free from righteousness except by decision of the will; moreover, he does not become free from sin except by the grace of the Savior.⁴⁴ ᵇWhen he asserts that man's freedom is nothing but emancipation or manumission from righteousness he seems aptly to mock its empty name. If anyone, then, can use this word without understanding it in a bad sense, I shall not trouble him on this account. But I hold that because it cannot be retained without great peril, it will, on the contrary, be a great boon for the church if it be abolished. I prefer not to use it myself, and I should like others, if they seek my advice, to avoid it.

9. Voices of truth among the church fathers

ᵇPerhaps I may seem to have brought a great prejudice upon myself when I confess that all ecclesiastical writers, except Augustine, have spoken so ambiguously or variously on this matter that nothing certain can be gained from their writings. Some will interpret this as if I wanted to deprive them of any voice in the matter because they all are my opponents. But I meant nothing else than that I wanted simply and sincerely to advise godly folk; for if they were to depend upon those men's opinions in this matter, they would always flounder in uncertainty. At one time these writers teach that man, despoiled of the powers of free will, takes refuge in grace alone. At another time they provide, or seem to provide, him with his own armor.

Nevertheless, it is not difficult to demonstrate that they, in the ambiguity of their teaching, held human virtue in no or very slight esteem, but ascribed all credit for every good thing to the Holy Spirit. For this purpose I shall introduce certain of their expressions that clearly teach this. For what else does that statement of Cyprian mean which Augustine so often repeats: "We ought to glory in nothing, because nothing is ours,"⁴⁵ except

---

⁴⁴ Augustine, *On the Spirit and the Letter* xxx. 52 (MPL 44. 234; CSEL 60. 208 f.; tr. LCC VIII. 236 f.); *On Rebuke and Grace* xiii. 42 (MPL 44. 942; tr. NPNF V. 489); *Against Two Letters of the Pelagians* I. ii. 5 (MPL 44. 552; tr. NPNF V. 378).

⁴⁵ Augustine, *On the Predestination of the Saints* iii. 7; iv. 8 (MPL 44. 964, 966; tr. NPNF V. 500). Here Augustine quotes Cyprian, *Testimonies Against the Jews, to Quirinus* III. iv: "We should boast in nothing, since nothing is ours" (MPL 4. 764; tr. ANF V. 528). The same quotation occurs

that man, rendered utterly destitute in his own right, should learn to depend wholly upon God? What do Augustine and Eucherius mean when they interpret the tree of life as Christ and say that whoever extends his hand to it will live; while they interpret the tree of the knowledge of good and evil as the decision of the will, and say that he who, bereft of God's grace, tastes of it will die?[46] What does Chrysostom mean when he says that every man is not only a sinner by nature, but wholly sin?[47] If there is no good in us, if man is wholly sin from head to foot, if he is not even allowed to test how far the power of the will can be effective—how could anyone possibly parcel out the credit for good works between God and man? I could refer to very many statements of this sort from other authors. Lest, however, anyone should charge that I am choosing only what serves my purpose while I craftily suppress what disagrees with it, I shall refrain from such testimony. Yet I dare affirm this: however excessive they sometimes are in extolling free will, they have had this end in view—to teach man utterly to forsake confidence in his own virtue and to hold that all his strength rests in God alone. Now I come to a simple explanation of the truth concerning the nature of man.

(*We must abandon all self-approbation, 10–11*)
10. The doctrine of free will is always in danger of robbing God of his honor
ᵇNevertheless, what I mentioned at the beginning of this chapter I am compelled here to repeat once more: that whoever is utterly cast down and overwhelmed by the awareness of his calamity, poverty, nakedness, and disgrace has thus advanced farthest in knowledge of himself.[48] For there is no danger of man's depriving himself of too much so long as he learns that in God must be recouped what he himself lacks. Yet he cannot claim for himself ever so little beyond what is rightfully his without losing himself in vain confidence and without usurping God's honor, and thus becoming guilty of monstrous sacrilege. And truly, whenever this lust invades our mind to compel us to seek out some-

in *Against Two Letters of the Pelagians* IV. ix. 25–26 (MPL 44. 627 f.; tr. NPNF V. 428).
[46] Augustine, *On Genesis in the Literal Sense* VIII. iv–vi (MPL 34. 375 ff.); Eucherius (bishop of Lyons, 434–450), *Commentarii in Genesim* I, on Gen. 2:9 (MPL 50. 907).
[47] In the edition of Chrysostom's works by Erasmus (Basel, 1530), these words occur in a homily for the first Sunday in Advent, but the homily is not contained or mentioned in later editions (OS III. 252, note 2).
[48] II. ii. 1; cf. II. i. 1–3.

thing of our own that reposes in ourselves rather than in God, let us know that this thought is suggested to us by no other counselor than him who induced our first parents to want to become "like gods, knowing good and evil" [Gen. 3:5]. If it is the devil's word that exalts man in himself, let us give no place to it unless we want to take advice from our enemy. Sweet, indeed, it is for you to have so much power of your own that you are able to rely on yourself! But, not to be deluded by this empty confidence, let us be deterred by numerous weighty passages of Scripture that utterly humiliate us. Such are these: "Cursed is the man who trusts in man and makes flesh his arm." [Jer. 17:5.] Again, "God's delight is not in the strength of the horse, nor his pleasure in the legs of a man, but he takes pleasure in those who fear him, relying upon his goodness." [Ps. 147:10–11.] Again, "He gives power to the faint, and to him who has no might he increases strength. He causes youths to faint and be weary, and young men to fall exhausted; but they who trust in him alone shall be strengthened." [Isa. 40:29–31.] All these passages have this purpose: that we should not rely on any opinion of our own strength, however small it is, if we want God to be favorable toward us, Who "opposes the proud, but gives grace to the meek" [James 4:6 and I Peter 5:5, Vg.; cf. Prov. 3:34]. Then let these promises come to mind: "I will pour water on the thirsty land, and streams on the dry ground" [Isa. 44:3]. Again, "All ye who thirst come to the waters." [Isa. 55:1.] These testify that no one is permitted to receive God's blessings unless he is consumed with the awareness of his own poverty. And we must not pass over other statements like these, such as this one of Isaiah: "The sun shall be no more your light by day, nor for brightness shall the moon give light to you by night; but the Lord will be your everlasting light" [Isa. 60:19]. Surely the Lord does not take away the brightness of the sun or moon from his servants; but because he wills alone to appear glorious in them, he calls them far away from trust even in those things which they deem most excellent.

11. True humility gives God alone the honor
  ᵇA saying of Chrysostom's has always pleased me very much, that the foundation of our philosophy is humility.[49] But that of Augustine pleases me even more: "When a certain rhetorician was asked what was the chief rule in eloquence, he replied, 'Delivery'; what was the second rule, 'Delivery'; what was the third rule, 'Delivery';[50] so if you ask me concerning the precepts of the

---

[49] Chrysostom, *De profectu evangelii* 2 (MPG 51. 312).
[50] The French text names Demosthenes. The anecdote is told of Demos-

Christian religion, first, second, third, and always I would answer, 'Humility.' "

But, as he elsewhere declares, Augustine does not consider it humility when a man, aware that he has some virtues, abstains from pride and arrogance; but when man truly feels that he has no refuge except in humility. "Let no man," he says, "flatter himself; of himself he is Satan. His blessing comes from God alone. For what do you have of your own but sin? Remove from yourself sin which is your own; for righteousness is of God." Again: "Why do we presume so much on ability of human nature? It is wounded, battered, troubled, lost. What we need is true confession, not false defense." ᶜAgain: "When anyone realizes that in himself he is nothing and from himself he has no help, the weapons within him are broken, the wars are over. But all the weapons of impiety must be shattered, broken, and burned; you must remain unarmed, you must have no help in yourself. The weaker you are in yourself, the more readily the Lord will receive you." Thus in his interpretation of the Seventieth Psalm he forbids us to remember our own righteousness, that we may know God's righteousness; and he shows that God so commends his grace to us that we know that we are nothing. By God's mercy alone we stand, since by ourselves we are nothing but evil.[51] ᵇAt this point, then, let us not contend against God concerning our right, as if what is attributed to him were withdrawn from our well-being. As our humility is his loftiness, so the confession of our humility has a ready remedy in his mercy. Now I do not claim that man, unconvinced, should yield himself voluntarily, and that, if he has any powers, he should turn his mind from them in order that he may be subjected to true humility. But I require only that, laying aside the disease of self-love and ambition,[52] by

thenes by Quintilian, *Institutio oratoria* XI. iii. 6 (LCL Quintilian IV. 244 f.). For its use by Augustine, see his *Letters* cxiii. 3. 22 (MPL 33. 442; tr. FC 18. 282). Calvin, like the monastic and Scholastic moralists, regards pride as the chief of vices, and humility as the pre-eminent virtue. Cf. *Sermons on Job* lxxx, where humility is the "sovereign virtue . . . the mother and root of all virtue" (CR XXXIV. 234; tr. A. Golding (1580 edition, p. 376). The classic passage in Benedict of Nursia's *Rule of Monks* vii, "the twelve steps of humility," cannot have been unfamiliar to Calvin (J. McCann, *The Rule of St. Benedict in Latin and English,* pp. 36–49; tr. LCC XII. 301–304). Cf. Bernard's devotional treatise *De gradibus humilitatis et superbiae* (annotated Latin text by B. R. V. Mills in *Select Treatises of St. Bernard;* tr. by B. R. V. Mills, *The Twelve Degrees of Humility and Pride*).

[51] Augustine, *John's Gospel* xlix. 8 (MPL 35. 1750; tr. NPNF VII. 273); *On Nature and Grace* liii. 62 (MPL 44. 277; tr. NPNF V. 142); *Psalms,* Ps. 45. 13 (MPL 36. 523); *Psalms,* Ps. 70. 1, 2 (MPL 36. 876; tr. NPNF [Ps. 46 and 71] VIII. 160. 315).

[52] "φιλαυτίας καὶ φιλονεικίας *morbo.*"

which he is blinded and thinks more highly of himself than he ought [cf. Gal. 6:3], he rightly recognize himself in the faithful mirror of Scripture [cf. James 1:22–25].

(Man's natural endowments not wholly extinguished: the understanding, 12–17)

12. Supernatural gifts destroyed; natural gifts corrupted; but enough of reason remains to distinguish man from brute beasts*

ᵉAnd, indeed, that common opinion which they have taken from Augustine pleases me: that the natural gifts were corrupted in man through sin, but that his supernatural gifts were stripped from him.[53] For by the latter clause they understand the light of faith as well as righteousness, which would be sufficient to attain heavenly life and eternal bliss. Therefore, withdrawing from the Kingdom of God, he is at the same time deprived of spiritual gifts, with which he had been furnished for the hope of eternal salvation. From this it follows that he is so banished from the Kingdom of God that all qualities belonging to the blessed life of the soul have been extinguished in him, until he recovers them through the grace of regeneration. Among these are faith, love of God, charity toward neighbor, zeal for holiness and for righteousness. All these, since Christ restores them in us, are considered adventitious, and beyond nature: and for this reason we infer that they were taken away. On the other hand, soundness of mind and uprightness of heart were withdrawn at the same time. This is the corruption of the natural gifts. For even though something of understanding and judgment remains as a residue along with the will, yet we shall not call a mind whole and sound that is both weak and plunged into deep darkness. And depravity of the will is all too well known.

Since reason, therefore, by which man distinguishes between good and evil, and by which he understands and judges, is a natural gift, it could not be completely wiped out; but it was partly weakened and partly corrupted, so that its misshapen ruins appear. John speaks in this sense: "The light still shines in the darkness, but the darkness comprehends it not" [John 1:5]. In these words both facts are clearly expressed. First, in man's perverted and degenerate nature some sparks still gleam. These show him to be a rational being, differing from brute beasts, because he is endowed with understanding. Yet, secondly, they show this light choked with dense ignorance, so that it cannot come forth effectively.

[53] See, above, sec. 4, notes 17, 18, 21; Augustine, *On Nature and Grace* iii. 3; xix. 21; xx. 22 (MPL 44. 249, 256 f.; tr. NPNF V. 122, 127 f.).

Similarly the will, because it is inseparable from man's nature, did not perish, but was so bound to wicked desires that it cannot strive after the right. This is, indeed, a complete definition, but one needing a fuller explanation.

Therefore, ᵇso that the order of discussion may proceed according to our original division of man's soul into understanding and will,[54] let us first of all examine the power of the understanding.

ᵇWhen we so condemn human understanding for its perpetual blindness as to leave it no perception of any object whatever, we not only go against God's Word, but also run counter to the experience of common sense. For we see implanted in human nature some sort of desire to search out the truth to which man would not at all aspire if he had not already savored it. Human understanding then possesses some power of perception, since it is by nature captivated by love of truth. The lack of this endowment in brute animals proves their nature gross and irrational. Yet this longing for truth, such as it is, languishes before it enters upon its race because it soon falls into vanity. Indeed, man's mind, because of its dullness, cannot hold to the right path, but wanders through various errors and stumbles repeatedly, as if it were groping in darkness, until it strays away and finally disappears. Thus it betrays how incapable it is of seeking and finding truth.

Then it grievously labors under another sort of vanity: often it cannot discern those things which it ought to exert itself to know. For this reason, in investigating empty and worthless things, it torments itself in its absurd curiosity, while it carelessly pays little or no attention to matters that it should particularly understand. Indeed, it scarcely ever seriously applies itself to the study of them. Secular writers habitually complain of this perversity, yet they are almost all found to have entangled themselves in it. For this reason, Solomon, through the whole of his Ecclesiastes, after recounting all those studies in which men seem to themselves to be very wise, declares them to be vain and trifling [chs. 1:2, 14; 2:11; etc.].

13. The power of the understanding with respect to earthly things and the form of the human community

ᵇYet its efforts do not always become so worthless[55] as to have no effect, especially when it turns its attention to things below. On

[54] I. xv. 7, 8.
[55] In the following account Calvin fails to mention the fine arts, which, however, are admired by him. Cf. I. xi. 12; Comm. Gen. 4:20; Comm. Harmony Books of Moses, Ex. 20:4; 34:17. The subject is treated by L.

the contrary, it is intelligent enough to taste something of things above, although it is more careless about investigating these. Nor does it carry on this latter activity with equal skill. For when the mind is borne above the level of the present life, it is especially convinced of its own frailty. Therefore, to perceive more clearly how far the mind can proceed in any matter according to the degree of its ability, we must here set forth a distinction. This, then, is the distinction: that there is one kind of understanding of earthly things; another of heavenly. I call "earthly things" those which do not pertain to God or his Kingdom, to true justice, or to the blessedness of the future life; but which have their significance and relationship with regard to the present life and are, in a sense, confined within its bounds. I call "heavenly things" the pure knowledge of God, the nature of true righteousness, and the mysteries of the Heavenly Kingdom. The first class includes government, household management, all mechanical skills, and the liberal arts. In the second are the knowledge of God and of his will, and the rule by which we conform our lives to it.

Of the first class the following ought to be said: since man is by nature a social animal,[56] he tends through natural instinct to foster and preserve society. Consequently, we observe that there exist in all men's minds universal impressions of a certain civic fair dealing and order. Hence no man is to be found who does not understand that every sort of human organization must be regulated by laws, and who does not comprehend the principles of those laws. Hence arises that unvarying consent of all nations and of individual mortals with regard to laws. For their seeds have, without teacher or lawgiver, been implanted in all men.

I do not dwell upon the dissension and conflicts that immediately spring up. Some, like thieves and robbers, desire to overturn all law and right, to break all legal restraints, to let their lust alone masquerade as law. Others think unjust what some have sanctioned as just (an even commoner fault), and contend that what some have forbidden is praiseworthy. Such persons hate laws not because they do not know them to be good and holy; but raging with headlong lust, they fight against manifest reason. What they approve of in their understanding they hate on account of their lust. Quarrels of this latter sort do not nullify the orig-

Wencelius, *L'Esthétique de Calvin* II. v, vi, and by J. Bohatec, *Budé und Calvin,* pp. 467–471.

[56] Seneca, *On Clemency* I. iii. 2; *On Benefits* VIII. i. 7 (LCL Seneca, *Moral Essays* I. 364 f.; III. 458 f.); Lactantius, *Divine Institutes* VI. x, xvii (CSEL 19. 515, 545; MPL 6. 668, 696; tr. ANF VII. 173, 182). In Comm. Gen. 2:18, Calvin speaks of the "general principle that man was created to be a social animal." Cf. *Comm. Seneca On Clemency* I. iii (CR V. 40).

inal conception of equity. For, while men dispute among themselves about individual sections of the law, they agree on the general conception of equity. In this respect the frailty of the human mind is surely proved: even when it seems to follow the way, it limps and staggers. Yet the fact remains that some seed of political order has been implanted in all men. And this is ample proof that in the arrangement of this life no man is without the light of reason.

14. Understanding as regards art and science

ᵇThen follow the arts, both liberal and manual. The power of human acuteness also appears in learning these because all of us have a certain aptitude. But although not all the arts are suitable for everyone to learn, yet it is a certain enough indication of the common energy that hardly anyone is to be found who does not manifest talent in some art. There are at hand energy and ability not only to learn but also to devise something new in each art or to perfect and polish what one has learned from a predecessor. This prompted Plato to teach wrongly that such apprehension is nothing but recollection.[57] Hence, with good reason we are compelled to confess that its beginning is inborn in human nature. Therefore this evidence clearly testifies to a universal apprehension of reason and understanding by nature implanted in men. Yet so universal is this good that every man ought to recognize for himself in it the peculiar grace of God. The Creator of nature himself abundantly arouses this gratitude in us when he creates imbeciles. Through them he shows the endowments that the human soul would enjoy unpervaded by his light, a light so natural to all that it is certainly a free gift of his beneficence to each! Now the discovery or systematic transmission of the arts, or the inner and more excellent knowledge of them, which is characteristic of few, is not a sufficient proof of common discernment. Yet because it is bestowed indiscriminately upon pious and impious, it is rightly counted among natural gifts.

15. Science as God's gift

ᵇWhenever we come upon these matters in secular writers, let that admirable light of truth shining in them teach us that the mind of man, though fallen and perverted from its wholeness, is nevertheless clothed and ornamented with God's excellent gifts. If we regard the Spirit of God as the sole fountain of truth, we shall neither reject the truth itself, nor despise it wherever it shall

[57] Plato, *Meno* 81 f., 84 (*Dialogues of Plato*, tr. Jowett I. 361 ff.).

appear, unless we wish to dishonor the Spirit of God.[58] For by holding the gifts of the Spirit in slight esteem, we contemn and reproach the Spirit himself. What then? Shall we deny that the truth shone upon the ancient jurists who established civic order and discipline with such great equity? Shall we say that the philosophers were blind in their fine observation and artful description of nature? Shall we say that those men were devoid of understanding who conceived the art of disputation and taught us to speak reasonably? Shall we say that they are insane who developed medicine, devoting their labor to our benefit? What shall we say of all the mathematical sciences? Shall we consider them the ravings of madmen? No, we cannot read the writings of the ancients on these subjects without great admiration. We marvel at them because we are compelled to recognize how preeminent they are. But shall we count anything praiseworthy or noble without recognizing at the same time that it comes from God? Let us be ashamed of such ingratitude, into which not even the pagan poets fell, for they confessed that the gods had invented philosophy, laws, and all useful arts.[59] Those men whom Scripture [I Cor. 2:14] calls "natural men"[60] were, indeed, sharp and penetrating in their investigation of inferior things. Let us, accord-

---

[58] Cf. I. iv. 3, note 6. This assertion of the divine origin and authentication of "truth wherever it appears" could hardly be more emphatic. While the natural capacities of the human mind are here chiefly associated with temporal and "inferior" concerns, elsewhere Calvin frequently recognizes the discernment by pagan philosophers of elements of religious truth. Cf. I. iii. 1; I. v. 3. It is to be noted that, in his welcome to truth found in nonscriptural sources and in the natural man, we have no thought of the concept (best represented by Duns Scotus) of two kinds of truth that are not mutually harmonious. Rather, his view is of one God-given truth manifested on two levels, one of which is of value for temporal and mundane concerns only. He is on common ground with Lactantius, who says that though the philosophers missed "the sum of things," viz., that the world was created by God so that man might worship him, yet each of them saw something of the truth. Lactantius, *Divine Institutes* VII. vi–vii (CSEL 19. 605 f.; MPL 6. 757, 759; tr. ANF VII. 203 f.). The statement of Clement of Alexandria that the truth of philosophy as it investigates the nature of things "is the truth of which the Lord himself said: I am the truth" (*Stromata* I. v. 32; GCS II. 21; tr. ANF II. 307), startling as it appears, can be read in a similar sense. Calvin may here be indebted to Augustine, *Against Julian* IV. xii. 60: "*In ipsis* [i.e., in pagan writers] *reperiuntur nonnulla vestigia veritatis*" (MPL 44. 767; tr. FC 35. 218). In Comm. Titus 1:12, Calvin says that anything true, though said by wicked men, is from God. Cf. Comm. John 4:36.

[59] Cicero, *Tusculan Disputations* I. xxvi. 64 (LCL edition, pp. 74 f.). (Cicero's reference is to Plato, *Timaeus* 47.)

[60] "ψυχικούς."

ingly, learn by their example how many gifts the Lord left to human nature even after it was despoiled of its true good.[61]

16. Human competence in art and science also derives from the Spirit of God

[b]Meanwhile, we ought not to forget those most excellent benefits of the divine Spirit, which he distributes to whomever he wills, for the common good of mankind. The understanding and knowledge of Bezalel and Oholiab, needed to construct the Tabernacle, had to be instilled in them by the Spirit of God [Ex. 31:2–11; 35:30–35]. It is no wonder, then, that the knowledge of all that is most excellent in human life is said to be communicated to us through the Spirit of God. Nor is there reason for anyone to ask, What have the impious, who are utterly estranged from God, to do with his Spirit? We ought to understand the statement that the Spirit of God dwells only in believers [Rom. 8:9] as referring to the Spirit of sanctification through whom we are consecrated as temples to God [I Cor. 3:16]. Nonetheless he fills, moves, and quickens all things by the power of the same Spirit, and does so according to the character that he bestowed upon each kind by the law of creation. But if the Lord has willed that we be helped in physics, dialectic, mathematics, and other like disciplines, by the work and ministry of the ungodly, let us use this assistance. For if we neglect God's gift freely offered in these arts, we ought to suffer just punishment for our sloths. But lest anyone think a man truly blessed when he is credited with possessing great power to comprehend truth under the elements of this world [cf. Col. 2:8], we should at once add that all this capacity to understand, with the understanding that follows upon it, is an unstable and transitory thing in God's sight, when a solid foundation of truth does not underlie it. For with the greatest truth Augustine teaches that as the free gifts were withdrawn from man after the Fall, so the natural ones remaining were corrupted. On this, the Master of the Sentences and the Schoolmen,[62] as we have said, are compelled to agree with him. Not that the gifts could become defiled by themselves, seeing that they came from God. But to defiled man these gifts were no longer pure, and from them he could derive no praise at all.

---

[61] Cf. II. iii. 2, *ad finem*.
[62] Lombard, *Sentences* II. xxv. 8 (MPL 192. 707). In adding *"et scholastici"* here, Calvin has reference to the numerous commentaries on Lombard's *Sentences* written by the Schoolmen. See, above, sec. 4, notes 17, 18; sec. 12, note 53.

17. Summary of 12–16

ᵉTo sum up: We see among all mankind that reason is proper to our nature; it distinguishes us from brute beasts, just as they by possessing feeling differ from inanimate things. Now, because some are born fools or stupid, that defect does not obscure the general grace of God.[63] Rather, we are warned by that spectacle that we ought to ascribe what is left in us to God's kindness. For if he had not spared us, our fall would have entailed the destruction of our whole nature. Some men excel in keenness; others are superior in judgment; still others have a readier wit to learn this or that art. In this variety God commends his grace to us, lest anyone should claim as his own what flowed from the sheer bounty of God. For why is one person more excellent than another? Is it not to display in common nature God's special grace,[64] which, in passing many by, declares itself bound to none? Besides this, God inspires special activities, in accordance with each man's calling. Many examples of this occur in The Book of Judges, where it is said that "the Spirit of the Lord took possession" of those men whom he had called to rule the people [ch. 6:34]. In short, in every extraordinary event there is some particular impulsion. For this reason, Saul was followed by the brave men "whose hearts God had touched" [I Sam. 10:26]. And when Saul's consecration as king was foretold, Samuel said: "Then the Spirit of the Lord will come mightily upon you, and you shall be another man" [I Sam. 10:6]. And this was extended to the whole course of government,

---

[63] *"Generalem Dei gratiam."* Calvin's conception of "common grace" has been intensively studied by H. Kuiper, *Calvin on Common Grace,* following discussions by A. Kuyper and H. Bavinck, and has since been variously treated by other scholars. Numerous passages in the *Institutes* illustrate the thought here expressed, e.g.: I. iii. 1–3; I. iv. 2 ("light of nature"); I. v. 3–4; I. v. 7–8; I. xi. 12; I. xiii. 14; I. xvii. 1; II. ii. 12–27; II. iii. 3; II. vii. 1; III. ii. 32; III. vii. 6; III. ix. 3; III. xiv. 2; III. xx. 15; IV. x. 5; IV. xx. 1–4; IV. xx. 9–11. H. Kuiper treats these and many other references throughout the entire corpus of Calvin's writings. Cf. Benoit, *Institution* II. 42, note 1. The difficulty of stating Calvin's doctrine is illustrated in C. Van Til's *Common Grace.* Kuiper and his predecessors employ the term to designate Calvin's recognition that the good in mankind, including religious aspiration, decent behavior, social brotherliness, artistic and scientific achievement, is bestowed by God. See Pannier's notes on the 1541 French text, the passages corresponding to II. ii. 13–15 (*Institution* I. 117, note *a;* I. 119, notes *b, c,* given on pp. 314 f.).

[64] Neither common grace nor the special grace here mentioned has any relation to the salvation of its possessor. Special grace is a special endowment of capacity, virtue, or heroism by which a man is fitted to serve the divine purpose in this world, while he himself may remain in the common state of human depravity. Cf. II. iii. 4, where Calvin views in this light Camillus, Saul, and the Homeric heroes referred to by Plato.

as is said afterward of David: "The Spirit of the Lord came upon him from that day forward" [I Sam. 16:13]. The same thing is taught elsewhere with respect to particular actions. Even in Homer, men are said to excel in natural ability not only as Jupiter has bestowed it upon each, but "as he leads them day by day."[65] And surely experience shows that, when those who were once especially ingenious and skilled are struck dumb, men's minds are in God's hand and under his will, so that he rules them at every moment. For this reason it is said: "He takes understanding away from the prudent [cf. Job 12:20] and makes them wander in trackless wastes" [Job 12:24; cf. Ps. 107:40]. Still, we see in this diversity some remaining traces of the image of God, which distinguish the entire human race from the other creatures.

(But spiritual discernment is wholly lost until we are regenerated, 18–21)

18. The limits of our understanding

ᵇWe must now analyze what human reason can discern with regard to God's Kingdom and to spiritual insight. This spiritual insight consists chiefly in three things: (1) knowing God; (2) knowing his fatherly favor in our behalf, in which our salvation consists; (3) knowing how to frame our life according to the rule of his law. In the first two points—and especially in the second— the greatest geniuses are blinder than moles! Certainly I do not deny that one can read competent and apt statements about God here and there in the philosophers, but these always show a certain giddy imagination. As was stated above, the Lord indeed gave them a slight taste of his divinity that they might not hide their impiety under a cloak of ignorance.[66] And sometimes he impelled them to make certain utterances by the confession of which they would themselves be corrected. But they saw things in such a way that their seeing did not direct them to the truth, much less enable them to attain it! They are like a traveler passing through a field at night who in a momentary lightning flash sees far and wide, but the sight vanishes so swiftly that he is plunged again into the darkness of the night before he can take even a step— let alone be directed on his way by its help. Besides, although they may chance to sprinkle their books with droplets of truth, how many monstrous lies defile them! In short, they never even sensed that assurance of God's benevolence toward us (without which man's understanding can only be filled with boundless confusion).

---

[65] "οῖον ἐπ' ἦμαρ ἄγησι." Homer, *Odyssey* xviii. 137 (LCL Homer, *Odyssey* II 206 f.).

[66] I. iii. 1, 3.

Human reason, therefore, neither approaches, nor strives toward, nor even takes a straight aim at, this truth: to understand who the true God is or what sort of God he wishes to be toward us.[67]

19. Man's spiritual blindness shown from John 1:4–5*

ᵇBut we are drunk with the false opinion of our own insight and are thus extremely reluctant to admit that it is utterly blind and stupid in divine matters. Hence, it will be more effective, I believe, to prove this fact by Scriptural testimonies than by reasons. John very beautifully teaches it in a passage that I have previously quoted;[68] he writes that: "Life was in God from the beginning and that life was the light of men; this light shines in the darkness, but the darkness comprehends it not" [John 1:4–5]. He shows that man's soul is so illumined by the brightness of God's light as never to be without some slight flame or at least a spark of it; but that even with this illumination it does not comprehend God. Why is this? Because man's keenness of mind is mere blindness as far as the knowledge of God is concerned. For when the Spirit calls men "darkness," he at once denies them any ability of spiritual understanding. Therefore he declares that those believers who embrace Christ are "born not of blood nor of the will of the flesh nor of the will of man, but of God" [John 1:13]. This means: Flesh is not capable of such lofty wisdom as to conceive God and what is God's, unless it be illumined by the Spirit of God. As Christ testified, the fact that Peter recognized him was a special revelation of the Father [Matt. 16:17].

20. Man's knowledge of God is God's own work

ᵇIf we were convinced that our nature lacks everything that our Heavenly Father bestows upon his elect through the Spirit of regeneration [cf. Titus 3:5]—a fact that should be beyond controversy—we would have here no occasion for doubt! For so speak the faithful people according to the prophet: "For with thee is the fountain of life; in thy light shall we see light" [Ps. 36:9]. The apostle testifies the same when he says that "no one can say 'Jesus is Lord' except by the Holy Spirit" [I Cor. 12:3]. And John the Baptist, seeing his disciples' wonderment, exclaimed: "No one can receive anything except what is given him from above" [John 3:27]. That he understands by "gift" a special illumination,[69] not a common endowment of nature, is evident

---

[67] Cf. I. i. 2; I. x. 2; III. ii. 16.

[68] Calvin says "recently [*nuper*] quoted," but the reference is to I. xvii. 2. See also Comm. John 1:5.

[69] Cf. sec. 16, note 62, above.

from his complaint that the very words with which he commended Christ to his disciples availed him not. "I see," he says, "that my words have no power to imbue men's minds with divine matters, unless the Lord through his Spirit gives understanding." Even Moses, reproaching the people for their forgetfulness, nevertheless notes at the same time that one cannot become wise in God's mysteries except by his gift. He says: "Your eyes saw those signs and great wonders; but the Lord has not given you a heart to understand, or ears to hear, or eyes to see." [Deut. 29:3–4, cf. Vg.] What more could he express if he called us "blocks" in our contemplation of God's works? For this reason, the Lord as a singular grace promises through the prophet he will give the Israelites a heart to know him [Jer. 24:7]. This doubtless means man's mind can become spiritually wise only in so far as God illumines it.

ᶜChrist also confirmed this most clearly in his own words when he said: "No one can come to me unless it be granted by my Father" [John 6:44 p.]. Why? Is he not himself the living image of the Father [cf. Col. 1:15], wherein the whole splendor of his glory is revealed [cf. Heb. 1:3a]? Therefore, he could characterize our capacity to know God in no better way than by denying that we have eyes to see his image even when it is openly exhibited before us. Why? Did not Christ descend to earth in order to reveal the Father's will to men [cf. John 1:18]? And did he not faithfully carry out his mission? This is obviously so. But nothing is accomplished by preaching him if the Spirit, as our inner teacher, does not show our minds the way. Only those men, therefore, who have heard and have been taught by the Father come to him. What kind of learning and hearing is this? Surely, where the Spirit by a wonderful and singular power forms our ears to hear and our minds to understand. And Christ cites the prophecy of Isaiah to show that this is nothing new. When He promises the renewal of the church, he teaches that those who will be gathered unto salvation [Isa. 54:7] "shall be God's disciples" [John 6:45; Isa. 54:13]. If God is there foretelling some particular things concerning his elect, it is evident that he is not speaking of that sort of instruction which the impious and profane also share.

It therefore remains for us to understand that the way to the Kingdom of God is open only to him whose mind has been made new by the illumination of the Holy Spirit.[70] ᵇPaul, however, having expressly entered this discussion, speaks more clearly than all [I Cor. 1:18 ff.]. ᶜAfter condemning the stupidity and vanity of all human wisdom and utterly reducing it to nothing [cf. I Cor. 1:13 ff.], ᵇhe concludes: "The natural man cannot receive the

[70] Cf. I. vii. 4–5; II. v. 5 (latter part); III. xi. 19; III. xxiv. 2.

things of the Spirit of God, for they are folly to him, and he is not able to understand them because they are spiritually discerned" [I Cor. 2:14]. Whom does he call "natural"? The man who depends upon the light of nature. He, I say, comprehends nothing of God's spiritual mysteries. Why is this? Is it because he neglects them out of laziness? No, even though he try, he can do nothing, for "they are spiritually discerned." What does this mean? Because these mysteries are deeply hidden from human insight, they are disclosed solely by the revelation of the Spirit. Hence, where the Spirit of God does not illumine them, they are considered folly. Previously, however, Paul had extolled above the capacity of eye, ear, and mind "what God has prepared for those who love him" [I Cor. 2:9]. Indeed, he had likened human wisdom to a veil that hinders the mind from seeing God. What then? The apostle declares, "God has made foolish the wisdom of this world." [I Cor. 1:20.] Shall we then attribute to it the keen insight by which man can penetrate to God and to the secret places of the Kingdom of Heaven? Away with such madness!

*21. Without the light of the Spirit, all is darkness**

cAccordingly, what Paul here denies to men, elsewhere, in prayer, he ascribes to God alone. "May God," he says, " . . . and the Father of Glory give to you the Spirit of wisdom and revelation." [Eph. 1:17, Vg. and Comm.] Now you hear that all wisdom and revelation are God's gift. What else does he say? "Having the eyes of your mind enlightened." [Eph. 1:18a, Vg. and Comm.] Surely, if they have need of new revelation, they are blinded of themselves. There follows: "That you may know the hope to which he has called you," etc. [Eph. 1:18b, cf. Vg. and Comm.]. He admits that men's minds are incapable of sufficient understanding [70x]to know their own calling.

cLet no Pelagian[71] babble here that God remedies this stupidity or, if you will, ignorance, when he directs man's understanding by the teaching of his Word to that which it could not have reached without guidance. For David had the Law in which was comprised all wisdom that can be desired; yet not content with it, he asks that his eyes be opened to "contemplate the mysteries of His law" [Ps. 119:18 p.]. By this expression he evidently means that the sun rises upon the earth when God's Word shines upon men; but they do not have its benefit until he who is called the

---

[70x] The following words are from the 1545 edition.
[71] Cf. II. i. 5, note 9. Numerous passages from Augustine are cited in Smits in II. 32 f., and in OS III. 264.

"Father of lights" [James 1:17] either gives eyes or opens them. For wherever the Spirit does not cast his light, all is darkness. In this same way the apostles were properly and fully taught by the best of teachers. Yet if they had not needed the Spirit of truth to instruct their minds in this very doctrine which they had heard before [John 14:26], he would not have bidden them to wait for him [Acts 1:4]. If we confess that we lack what we seek of God, and he by promising it proves our lack of it, no one should now hesitate to confess that he is able to understand God's mysteries only in so far as he is illumined by God's grace. He who attributes any more understanding to himself is all the more blind because he does not recognize his own blindness.

(*Sin is distinct from ignorance* [*vs. Plato*], *but may be occasioned by delusion, 22–25*)

22. *The evidence of God's will that man possesses makes him inexcusable but procures for him no right knowledge*

ᵇThere remains the third aspect of spiritual insight,[72] that of knowing the rule for the right conduct of life. This we correctly call the "knowledge of the works of righteousness." The human mind sometimes seems more acute in this than in higher things. For the apostle testifies: "When Gentiles, who do not have the law, do the works of the law, they are a law to themselves . . . and show that the work of the law is written on their hearts, while their conscience also bears witness, and their thoughts accuse them among themselves or excuse them before God's judgment" [Rom. 2:14–15 p.]. If the Gentiles by nature have law righteousness engraved upon their minds, we surely cannot say they are utterly blind as to the conduct of life.

There is nothing more common than for a man to be sufficiently instructed in a right standard of conduct by natural law[73] (of which the apostle is here speaking). Let us consider, however, for what purpose men have been endowed with this knowledge of the law. How far it can lead them toward the goal of reason and truth will then immediately appear. This is also clear from Paul's words, if we note their context. He had just before said that those who sinned in the law are judged through the law; they who sinned without the law perish without the law. Because it

---

[72] Cf. the enumeration in II. ii. 18.
[73] Cf. II. viii. 1–2, 51, and Comm. Rom. 2:14–16; G. Gloede, *Theologia naturalis bei Calvin*, pp. 178 ff.; cf. J. Bohatec, *Calvins Lehre von Staat und Kirche*, pp. 20–35; E. Brunner, *Justice and the Social Order* (tr. M. Hottinger, p. 233); J. T. McNeill, "Natural Law in the Teaching of the Reformers," *Journal of Religion* XXVI (1946), 168–182.

might seem absurd that the Gentiles perish without any preceding judgment, Paul immediately adds that for them conscience stands in place of law; this is sufficient reason for their just condemnation. The purpose of natural law, therefore, is to render man inexcusable. This would not be a bad definition: natural law is that apprehension of the conscience which distinguishes sufficiently between just and unjust, and which deprives men of the excuse of ignorance, while it proves them guilty by their own testimony. Man is so indulgent toward himself that when he commits evil he readily averts his mind, as much as he can, from the feeling of sin. This is why Plato seems to have been compelled to consider (in his *Protagoras*) that we sin only out of ignorance.[74] This might have been an appropriate statement if only human hypocrisy had covered up vices with sufficient skill to prevent the mind from being recognized as evil in God's sight. The sinner tries to evade his innate power to judge between good and evil. Still, he is continually drawn back to it, and is not so much as permitted to wink at it without being forced, whether he will or not, at times to open his eyes. It is falsely said, therefore, that man sins out of ignorance alone.

23. *Judgment of good and evil is unclear, so long as it takes place arbitrarily*
    [b]Themistius more correctly teaches that the intellect is very rarely deceived in general definition or in the essence of the thing; but that it is illusory when it goes farther, that is, applies the principle to particular cases.[75] In reply to the general question, every man will affirm that murder is evil. But he who is plotting the death of an enemy contemplates murder as something good. The adulterer will condemn adultery in general, but will privately flatter himself in his own adultery. Herein is man's ignorance: when he comes to a particular case, he forgets the general principle that he has just laid down. On this point Augustine has expressed himself beautifully in his exposition of the first verse of Ps. 57.
    Themistius' rule, however, is not without exception. Sometimes the shamefulness of evil-doing presses upon the conscience so that one, imposing upon himself no false image of the good, knowingly and willingly rushes headlong into wickedness. Out of such a disposition of mind come statements like this: "I see

---

[74] Plato, *Protagoras* 357 (LCL Plato IV. 240 f.).
[75] Themistius, *In libros Aristotelis de anima paraphrasis* VI (ed. R. Heinze, p. 112).

what is better and approve it, but I follow the worse."[76] To my mind Aristotle has made a very shrewd distinction between incontinence and intemperance: "Where incontinence reigns," he says, "the disturbed mental state or passion so deprives the mind of particular knowledge that it cannot mark the evil in its own misdeed which it generally discerns in like instances; when the perturbation subsides, repentance straightway returns. Intemperance, however, is not extinguished or shattered by the awareness of sin, but on the contrary, stubbornly persists in choosing its habitual evil."[77]

24. Human knowledge wholly fails as regards the First Table of the Law; as regards the Second, fails in a critical situation

[b]Now when you hear of a universal judgment discriminating between good and evil, do not consider it to be sound and whole in every respect. For if men's hearts have been imbued with the ability to distinguish just from unjust, solely that they should not pretend ignorance as an excuse, it is not at all a necessary consequence that truth should be discerned in individual instances. It is more than enough if their understanding extends so far that evasion becomes impossible for them, and they, convicted by the witness of their own conscience, begin even now to tremble before God's judgment seat. And if we want to measure our reason by God's law, the pattern of perfect righteousness, we shall find in how many respects it is blind! Surely it does not at all comply with the principal points of the First Table;[78] such as putting our faith in God, giving due praise for his excellence and righteousness, calling upon his name, and truly keeping the Sabbath [Ex. 20:3–17]. What soul, relying upon natural perception, ever had an inkling that the lawful worship of God consists in these and like matters? For when profane men desire to worship God, even if they be called away a hundred times from their empty trifles, they always slip back into them once more. [e]They admit, of course, that God is not pleased with sacrifices unless sincerity of intention accompany them.[79] [e(b)]By this they testify that

---

[76] "*Video meliora proboque, deteriora sequor*," from Medea's speech in Ovid, *Metamorphoses* VII. 20 (LCL edition, *Metamorphoses* I. 342).

[77] Aristotle, *Nicomachean Ethics* VII. 1–3. 1145–1147 (LCL edition, pp. 374–377; tr. McKeon, *Basic Works of Aristotle*, pp. 1036–1042). Aristotle here contends against Plato's view of the equation between virtue and knowledge.

[78] Cf. II. viii. 12, note 16.

[79] "They shall approach the gods in purity, bringing piety and leaving riches behind." Cicero, *De legibus* II. viii. 19, 24 (LCL edition, pp. 392 f., 400 f.).

they have some notion of the spiritual worship of God, yet they at once pervert it with false devisings. For they could never be persuaded that what the law prescribes concerning worship is the truth. ᵇShall I then say that the mind that can neither be wise of itself nor heed warnings excels in discernment?

Men have somewhat more understanding of the precepts of the Second Table [Ex. 20:12 ff.] because these are more closely concerned with the preservation of civil society among them. Yet even here one sometimes detects a failure to endure. A man of most excellent disposition finds it utterly senseless to bear an unjust and excessively imperious domination, if only he can in some way throw it off. And this is the common judgment of human reason: the mark of a servile and abject person is to bear it with patience; that of an honorable and freeborn man to shake it off. ᶜNor do the philosophers consider the avenging of injuries to be a vice. ᵇBut the Lord condemns this excessive haughtiness and enjoins upon his own people a patience disgraceful in men's eyes. But in all our keeping of the law we quite fail to take our concupiscence into account. For the natural man refuses to be led to recognize the diseases of his lusts. The light of nature is extinguished before he even enters upon this abyss. While the philosophers label the immoderate incitements of the mind as "vices," they have reference to those which are outward and manifested by grosser signs. They take no account of the evil desires that gently tickle the mind.

25. Every day we need the Holy Spirit that we may not mistake our way

ᵇJust as we deservedly censured Plato above because he imputed all sins to ignorance,[80] so also ought we to repudiate the opinion of those who suppose that there is deliberate malice and depravity in all sins. For we know all too well by experience how often we fall despite our good intention. Our reason is overwhelmed by so many forms of deceptions, is subject to so many errors, dashes against so many obstacles, is caught in so many difficulties, that it is far from directing us aright. Indeed, Paul shows us in every part of life how empty reason is in the Lord's sight when he denies "that we are sufficient of ourselves to claim something as coming from us as if it really did" [II Cor. 3:5]. He is not speaking of the will or the emotions; but he even takes from us the ability to think how the right doing of anything can enter our minds. Is our diligence, insight, understanding, and carefulness so completely corrupted that we can devise or prepare

[80] II. ii. 22, and note 74, above.

nothing right in God's eyes? No wonder that it seems too hard for us who grudgingly suffer ourselves to be deprived of keenness of reason, which we count the most precious gift of all! But to the Holy Spirit who "knows that all the thoughts of the wise are futile" [I Cor. 3:20; cf. Ps. 94:11] and who clearly declares that "every imagination of the human heart is solely evil" [Gen. 6:5; 8:21 p.] it seems most fitting. If whatever our nature conceives, instigates, undertakes, and attempts is always evil, how can that which is pleasing to God, to whom holiness and righteousness alone are acceptable, even enter our minds?

Thus we can see that the reason of our mind, wherever it may turn, is miserably subject to vanity. David was aware of this feebleness when he prayed to be given understanding to learn the Lord's commandments rightly [Ps. 119:34]. In desiring to obtain a new understanding he intimates that his own nature is insufficient. cAnd not once, but almost ten times in a single psalm he repeats the same prayer [Ps. 119:12, 18, 19, 26, 33, 64, 68, 73, 124, 125, 135, 169]. By this repetition he suggests how great is the necessity that compels him to pray thus. And what David seeks for himself alone, Paul is accustomed to implore for the churches in common. "We ceased not to pray for you and to ask that you may be filled with the knowledge of God in all spiritual wisdom and understanding in order that you may walk worthily before God," etc. [Col. 1:9–10 p.; cf. Phil. 1:9.] We should remember, however, that whenever he represents this thing as a benefit from God he bears witness at the same time that it has not been placed within man's ability. bBut Augustine so recognizes this inability of the reason to understand the things of God that he deems the grace of illumination no less necessary for our minds than the light of the sun for our eyes. Not content with this, he adds the correction that we ourselves open our eyes to behold the light, but the eyes of the mind, unless the Lord open them, remain closed.[81] cNor does Scripture teach that our minds are illumined only on one day and that they may thereafter see of themselves. For what I have just quoted from Paul has reference to continuing progress and increase. David has aptly expressed it in these words: "With my whole heart I have sought thee; let me not wander from thy commandments!" [Ps. 119:10]. Although he had been reborn and had advanced to no mean extent in true godliness, he still confesses that he needs continual direction at every moment, lest he decline from the knowledge with which he has been endowed. Therefore he prays elsewhere

[81] Augustine, *On the Merits and Remission of Sins* II. v. 5 (MPL 44. 153 f.; tr. NPNF V. 45 f.).

that a right spirit, lost by his own fault, be restored [Ps. 51:10]. For it is the part of the same God to restore that which he had given at the beginning, but which had been taken away from us for a time.

(Man's inability to will the good, 26–27)
26. The natural instinct that treats the "good" and the "acceptable" alike has nothing to do with freedom
ᵇNow we must examine the will,[82] upon which freedom of decision especially depends; for we have already seen that choice belongs to the sphere of the will rather than to that of the understanding.[83] To begin with, the philosophers teach that all things seek good through a natural instinct, and this view is received with general consent. But that we may not suppose this doctrine to have anything to do with the uprightness of the human will, let us observe that the power of free choice is not to be sought in such an appetite, which arises from inclination of nature rather than from deliberation of mind. Even the Schoolmen admit that free will is active only when the reason considers alternative possibilities.[84] By this they mean that the object of the appetite must be amenable to choice, and deliberation must go before to open the way to choice. And actually, if you consider the character of this natural desire of good in man, you will find that he has it in common with animals. For they also desire their own well-being; and when some sort of good that can move their sense appears, they follow it. But man does not choose by reason and pursue with zeal what is truly good for himself according to the excellence of his immortal nature; nor does he use his reason in deliberation or bend his mind to it. Rather, like an animal he follows the inclination of his nature, without reason, without deliberation. Therefore whether or not man is impelled to seek after good by an impulse of nature has no bearing upon freedom of the will. This instead is required: that he discern good by right reason; that knowing it he choose it; that having chosen it he follow it.

That no reader may remain in doubt, we must be warned of a double misinterpretation. For "appetite" here signifies not an impulse of the will itself but rather an inclination of nature; and "good" refers not to virtue or justice but to condition, as when things go well with man. ᵉTo sum up, much as man desires to follow what is good, still he does not follow it. There is no

[82] The "examination" of the will begun here is continued through chs. ii–v following.
[83] II. ii. 4.
[84] Aquinas, *Summa Theol.* I. lxxxiii. 3.

man to whom eternal blessedness is not pleasing, yet no man aspires to it except by the impulsion of the Holy Spirit. ᵇThe desire for well-being natural to men no more proves freedom of the will than the tendency of metals and stones toward perfection of their essence proves it in them. This being so, we must now examine whether in other respects the will is so deeply vitiated and corrupted in its every part that it can beget nothing but evil; or whether it retains any portion unimpaired, from which good desires may be born.

27. Our will cannot long for the good without the Holy Spirit

ᵇThose who attribute to God's first grace the fact that we effectually will, seem to imply, on the other hand, that there is a faculty in the soul voluntarily to aspire to good, but one too feeble to be able to come forth into firm intention, or to arouse effort. There is no doubt that this opinion, taken from Origen and certain other ancient writers, was commonly held by the Schoolmen: they usually consider man in "mere nature," as they phrase it.[85] As such, man is described in the apostle's words: "For I do not do the good I will, but the evil I do not will is what I do. It lies in my power to will, but I find myself unable to accomplish" [Rom. 7:19, 18, cf. Vg.]. But they wrongly pervert the whole argument that Paul is pursuing here. For he is discussing the Christian struggle (more briefly touched in Galatians [ch. 5:17]), which believers constantly feel in themselves in the conflict between flesh and spirit. But the Spirit comes, not from nature, but from regeneration. Moreover, it is clear that the apostle is speaking of these regenerated, because when he had said that no good dwelt in him, he adds the explanation that he is referring to his flesh [Rom. 7:18]. Accordingly, he declares that it is not he who does evil, but sin dwelling in him. [Rom. 7:20.] What does he mean by this correction: "In me, that is, in my flesh" [Rom. 7:18]? It is as if he were speaking in this way: "Good does not dwell in me of myself, for nothing good is to be found in my flesh." Hence follows that form of an excuse: "I myself do not do evil, but sin that dwells in me" [Rom. 7:20]. This excuse applies only to the regenerate who tend toward good with the chief part of their soul. Now the conclusion appended clearly explains this whole matter: "For I delight in the law . . . accord-

---

[85] Origen, De principiis III. i. 20 (GCS 22. 234 f.; MPG 11. 294 ff.; tr. ANF IV. 324; Butterworth, Origen On First Principles, p. 157); Chrysostom, Homilies on Hebrews, hom. xii. 3 (MPG 63. 99; tr. LF 44. 155); Lombard, Sentences II. xxiv. 5 (MPL 192. 702); Duns Scotus, In sententias I. xvii. 2. 12 and 3. 19 (Opera omnia X. 51b, 74a).

ing to the inner man, but I see in my members another law at war with the law of my mind" [Rom. 7:22–23]. Who would have such strife in himself but a man who, regenerated by the Spirit of God, bears the remains of his flesh about with him? Therefore, Augustine, although at one time he had thought that passage to be concerned with man's nature, later retracted his interpretation as false and inappropriate.[86] Yet if we hold the view that men have, apart from grace, some impulses (however puny) toward good, what shall we reply to the apostle who even denies that we are capable of conceiving anything [II Cor. 3:5]? What shall we reply to the Lord, who through Moses declares that every imagination of man's heart is only evil [Gen. 8:21]? Since they have stumbled in their false interpretation of a single passage, there is no reason for us to tarry over their view. Rather let us value Christ's saying: "Every one who commits sin is a slave to sin" [John 8:34]. We are all sinners by nature; therefore we are held under the yoke of sin. But if the whole man lies under the power of sin, surely it is necessary that the will, which is its chief seat, be restrained by the stoutest bonds. ᵉPaul's saying would not make sense, that "it is God who is at work to will in us" [Phil. 2:13 p.], if any will preceded the grace of the Spirit. Away then with all that "preparation" which many babble about![87] For even if believers sometimes ask that their hearts be conformed to obedience to God's law, as David in a number of passages does, yet we must also note that this desire to pray comes from God. This we may infer from David's words. When he desires that a clean heart be created in himself [Ps. 51:10], surely he does not credit himself with the beginning of its creation. For this reason we ought rather to value Augustine's saying: "God has anticipated you in all things; now do you yourself—while you may—anticipate his wrath. How? Confess that you have all these things from God:

---

[86] Augustine, *Against Two Letters of the Pelagians* I. x. 22 (MPL 44. 561; tr. NPNF V. 384). Where Calvin writes "natural man," Augustine has "man under the law." The point was discussed with animation in the Arminian controversy, Arminius taking the view at first adopted by Augustine and, as Calvin states, finally rejected by him in the passage cited. See Arminius, *Dissertation on the Seventh Chapter of Romans (Works of James Arminius)*, tr. J. Nichols, II. 287–322: "The man about whom the apostle treats in this passage is an unregenerate man, and not placed under grace but under the law" (p. 322). Luther, in his *Lectures on Romans* (1515–1516), marvels that the words of Rom. 7:24, "O wretched man that I am," could be thought of as the utterance of "an old carnal man": only a spiritual man could say this (*Werke* WA LVI. 346).

[87] J. Fisher (John Fisher, bishop of Rochester, 1504–1535), *Assertionis Lutheranae confutatio* (1523), pp. 548 f.; J. Cochlaeus, *De libero arbitrio hominis* II, fo. L 6b; A. de Castro, *Adversus omnes haereses* IX (1543 ed., fo. 125 D–F).

whatever good you have is from him; whatever evil, from yourself." And a little later, "Nothing is ours but sin."[88]

CHAPTER III

ONLY DAMNABLE THINGS COME FORTH FROM MAN'S CORRUPT NATURE

*(Corruption of man's nature is such as to require total renewal
of his mind and will, 1–5)*

1. The whole man is flesh

But man cannot be better known in both faculties of his soul
than if he makes his appearance with those titles whereby Scripture marks him. If the whole man is depicted by these words of
Christ, "What is born of flesh, is flesh" [John 3:6] (as is easy to
prove), man is very clearly shown to be a miserable creature.
"For to set the mind on the flesh," as the apostle testifies, "is
death. Because there is enmity against God, it does not submit to
God's law, indeed it cannot." [Rom. 8:6–7 p.] Is the flesh so perverse that it is wholly disposed to bear a grudge against God, cannot agree with the justice of divine law, can, in short, beget
nothing but the occasion of death? Now suppose that in man's
nature there is nothing but flesh: extract something good from
it if you can. But, you will say, the word "flesh" pertains only
to the sensual part of the soul, not to the higher part.[1] This is
thoroughly refuted from the words of Christ and of the apostle.
The Lord's reasoning is: Man must be reborn [John 3:3], for
he "is flesh" [John 3:6]. He is not teaching a rebirth as regards
the body. Now the soul is not reborn if merely a part of it is
reformed, but only when it is wholly renewed. The antithesis
set forth in both passages confirms this. The Spirit is so contrasted with flesh that no intermediate thing is left. Accordingly,
whatever is not spiritual in man is by this reckoning called
"carnal." We have nothing of the Spirit, however, except through
regeneration. Whatever we have from nature, therefore, is flesh.

But Paul relieves us of any possible doubt on this matter. Hav-

---

[88] Augustine, *Sermons* clxxvi. 5–6 (MPL 38. 952 f.).

[1] Fisher, *Assertionis Lutheranae confutatio* (1523), pp. 560 ff., 568 f.; Erasmus, *De libero arbitrio*, ed. J. von Walter, pp. 61 ff.; J. Cochlaeus, *De
libero arbitrio* I, fo. E 2b ff. According to these writings, the proclivity toward evil that many show does not wholly take away freedom of the choice
of good, though it cannot be wholly overcome without the "aid" of divine
grace.

ing described the old man who, he had said, was "corrupted by deceptive desires" [Eph. 4:22 p.], he bids us "be renewed in the spirit of our mind" [Eph. 4:23 p.]. You see that he lodges unlawful and wicked desires not solely in the sensual part of the soul, but even in the mind itself, and for this reason he requires its renewal. To be sure, a little while before he had painted a picture of human nature that showed us corrupt and perverted in every part. He writes that "all the Gentiles walk in the vanity of their minds, being darkened in their understanding, alienated from the life of God, because of the ignorance which is in them, and their blindness of heart." [Eph. 4:17–18.] There is not the least doubt that this statement applies to all those whom the Lord has not yet formed again to the uprightness of his wisdom and justice. This also becomes clearer from the comparison immediately added wherein he admonishes believers that they "did not so learn Christ" [Eph. 4:20]. We, indeed, infer from these words that the grace of Christ is the sole remedy to free us from that blindness and from the evils consequent upon it. Isaiah also had so prophesied concerning Christ's Kingdom when he promised: "The Lord will be an everlasting light" for his church [Isa. 60: 19 p.], while "shadows will shroud the earth and darkness will cover the peoples" [ch. 60:2]. He there testifies that the light of God will arise in the church alone; and leaves only shadows and blindness outside the church.[2] ᵇI shall not individually recount the statements made everywhere concerning men's vanity, especially in The Psalms and the Prophets. Great is the utterance of David: "If a man be weighed with vanity, he shall be vainer than vanity itself" [Ps. 61:10, Vg.; Ps. 62:9, EV]. Man's understanding is pierced by a heavy spear when all the thoughts that proceed from him are mocked as stupid, frivolous, insane, and perverse.

2. *Romans, ch. 3, as witness for man's corruption*

ᵇThat condemnation of the heart when it is called "deceitful and corrupt above all else" [Jer. 17:9 p.] is no less severe. But because I am striving for brevity, I shall be content with but one passage; yet it will be like the clearest of mirrors in which we may contemplate the whole image of our nature. For the apostle, when he wishes to cast down the arrogance of humankind, does so by these testimonies: " 'No one is righteous, no one understands, no one seeks God. All have turned aside, together they have become unprofitable; no one does good, not even one' [[Ps. 14:1–3; 53:1–3]]. 'Their throat is an open grave, they use their

2 Cf. Cyprian: *"Salus extra ecclesiam non est"*: *Letters* lxxiii. 21 (CSEL 3. ii. 795; tr. ANF V. 384).

tongues deceitfully' [[Ps. 5:9]]. 'The venom of asps is under their lips' [[Ps. 140:3]]. 'Their mouth is full of cursing and bitterness' [[Ps. 10:7]]. 'Their feet are swift to shed blood; in their paths are ruin and misery' [[Isa. 59:7 p.]]. There is no fear of God before their eyes" [Rom. 3:10–16, 18 p.]. With these thunderbolts he inveighs not against particular men but against the whole race of Adam's children. Nor is he decrying the depraved morals of one age or another, but indicting the unvarying corruption of our nature.[3] Now his intention in this passage is not simply to rebuke men that they may repent, but rather to teach them that they have all been overwhelmed by an unavoidable calamity from which only God's mercy can deliver them. Because this could not be proved unless it rested upon the ruin and destruction of our nature, he put forward these testimonies which prove our nature utterly lost.

Let this then be agreed: that men are as they are here described not merely by the defect of depraved custom, but also by depravity of nature. The reasoning of the apostle cannot otherwise stand: Except out of the Lord's mercy there is no salvation for man, for in himself he is lost and forsaken [Rom. 3:23 ff.]. I shall not toil in proving the applicability of these passages, in order that they may not seem to have been inappropriately seized upon by the apostle. I shall proceed as if these statements had first been made by Paul, not drawn from the Prophets. First of all, he strips man of righteousness, that is, integrity and purity; then, of understanding [Rom. 3:10–11]. Indeed, apostasy from God proves defect of understanding, for to seek him is the first degree of wisdom. This defect, therefore, is necessarily found in all who have forsaken God. He adds that all have fallen away and have, as it were, become corrupt, that there is no one who does good. Then he adds the shameful acts with which they—once they have been let loose in wickedness—defile their several members. Finally, he declares them devoid of the fear of God, to whose rule our steps ought to have been directed. If these are the hereditary endowments of the human race, it is futile to seek anything good in our nature. Indeed, I grant that not all these wicked traits appear in every man; yet one cannot deny that this hydra lurks in the breast of each. For as the body, so long as it nourishes in itself the cause and matter of disease (even though pain does not yet rage), will not be called healthy, so also will the soul not be considered healthy while it abounds with so many fevers of vice. This comparison, however, does not fit in every detail. For in the diseased body some vigor of life yet remains; although the soul,

[3] Cf. II. i. 6.

plunged into this deadly abyss, is not only burdened with vices, but is utterly devoid of all good.

3. God's grace sometimes restrains where it does not cleanse*

ᵇAlmost the same question that was previously answered now confronts us anew. In every age there have been persons who, guided by nature, have striven toward virtue throughout life.⁴ I have nothing to say against them even if many lapses can be noted in their moral conduct. For they have by the very zeal of their honesty given proof that there was some purity in their nature. Although in discussing merit of works we shall deal more fully with what value such virtues have in God's sight, we must nevertheless speak of it also at this point, inasmuch as it is necessary for the unfolding of the present argument. These examples, accordingly, seem to warn us against adjudging man's nature wholly corrupted, because some men have by its prompting not only excelled in remarkable deeds, but conducted themselves most honorably throughout life. But here it ought to occur to us that amid this corruption of nature there is some place for God's grace; not such grace as to cleanse it, but to restrain it inwardly. For if the Lord gave loose rein to the mind of each man to run riot in his lusts, there would doubtless be no one who would not show that, in fact, every evil thing for which Paul condemns all nature is most truly to be met in himself [Ps. 14:3; Rom. 3:12].

What then? Do you count yourself exempt from the number of those whose "feet are swift to shed blood" [Rom. 3:15], whose hands are fouled with robberies and murders, "whose throats are like open graves, whose tongues deceive, whose lips are envenomed" [Rom. 3:13]; whose works are useless, wicked, rotten, deadly; whose hearts are without God; whose inmost parts, depravities; whose eyes are set upon stratagems; whose minds are eager to revile—to sum up, whose every part stands ready to commit infinite wickedness [Rom. 3:10–18]? If every soul is subject to such abominations as the apostle boldly declares, we surely see what would happen if the Lord were to permit human lust to wander according to its own inclination. No mad beast would rage as unrestrainedly; no river, however swift and violent, burst so madly into flood. In his elect the Lord cures these diseases in a way that we shall soon explain. Others he merely restrains by throwing a bridle over them only that they may not break loose, inasmuch as he foresees their control to be expedient to preserve all that is. Hence some are restrained by shame from breaking out into many kinds of foulness, others by the fear of

⁴ II. ii. 12.

the law—even though they do not, for the most part, hide their impurity. Still others, because they consider an honest manner of life profitable, in some measure aspire to it. Others rise above the common lot, in order by their excellence to keep the rest obedient to them. Thus God by his providence bridles perversity of nature, that it may not break forth into action; but he does not purge it within.

4. Uprightness is God's gift; but man's nature remains corrupted
ᵇNevertheless the problem has not yet been resolved. For either we must make Camillus equal to Catiline, or we shall have in Camillus an example proving that nature, if carefully cultivated, is not utterly devoid of goodness.⁵ Indeed, I admit that the endowments resplendent in Camillus were gifts of God and seem rightly commendable if judged in themselves. But how will these serve as proofs of natural goodness in him? Must we not hark back to his mind and reason thus:⁶ if a natural man excelled in such moral integrity, undoubtedly human nature did not lack the ability to cultivate virtue? Yet what if the mind had been wicked and crooked, and had followed anything but uprightness? And there is no doubt that it was such, if you grant that Camillus was a natural man. What power for good will you attribute to human nature in this respect, if in the loftiest appearance of integrity, it is always found to be impelled toward corruption? Therefore as you will not commend a man for virtue when his vices impress you under the appearance of virtues, so you will not attribute to the human will the capability of seeking after the right so long as the will remains set in its own perversity.

Here, however, is the surest and easiest solution to this question: these are not common gifts of nature, but special graces of God, which he bestows variously and in a certain measure upon men otherwise wicked. For this reason, we are not afraid, in common parlance, to call this man wellborn, that one depraved in nature. Yet we do not hesitate to include both under the universal condition of human depravity; but we point out what special grace⁷ the Lord has bestowed upon the one, while not

---

⁵ Catiline's evil nature is described by Sallust, *The War with Catiline* iii. 5; LCL edition, pp. 8 ff. He was assailed by Cicero, and was held up to reproach, while Camillus, the noble but unrewarded patriot, was celebrated with praise by Horace, Vergil, and Juvenal. Cf. Augustine, *City of God* II. xvii, xxiii; III. xvii (MPL 41. 61 f., 96 f.; tr. NPNF II. 32, 37, 54).
⁶ Augustine, *Against Julian* IV. iii. 16 ff. (MPL 44. 774 ff.; tr. FC 35. 179 f.).
⁷ On the expressions *"speciales Dei gratias"* . . . *"specialis gratiae,"* cf. II. ii. 17, notes 63, 64; II. iv. 7, note 13; and above, on Camillus, in this sec. 4.

deigning to bestow it upon the other. ᵉWhen he wished to put Saul over the kingdom he "formed him as a new man" [I Sam. 10:6 p.]. This is the reason why Plato, alluding to the Homeric legend, says that kings' sons are born with some distinguishing mark.[8] For God, in providing for the human race, often endows with a heroic nature those destined to command. From this workshop have come forth the qualities of great leaders celebrated in histories. Private individuals are to be judged in the same way. But because, however excellent anyone has been, his own ambition always pushes him on—a blemish with which all virtues are so sullied that before God they lose all favor—anything in profane men that appears praiseworthy must be considered worthless. Besides, where there is no zeal to glorify God, the chief part of uprightness is absent; a zeal of which all those whom he has not regenerated by his Spirit are devoid. There is good reason for the statement in Isaiah, that "the spirit of the fear of God rests" upon Christ [Isa. 11:2 p.]. By this we are taught that all estranged from Christ lack "the fear of God," which "is the beginning of wisdom" [Ps. 111:10 p.]. As for the virtues that deceive us with their vain show, they shall have their praise in the political assembly and in common renown among men; but before the heavenly judgment seat they shall be of no value to acquire righteousness.

5. *Man sins of necessity, but without compulsion*

ᵇBecause of the bondage of sin by which the will is held bound, it cannot move toward good, much less apply itself thereto; for a movement of this sort is the beginning of conversion to God, which in Scripture is ascribed entirely to God's grace. So Jeremiah prayed to the Lord to be "converted" if it were his will to "convert him" [Jer. 31:18, cf. Vg.]. Hence the prophet in the same chapter, describing the spiritual redemption of the believing folk, speaks of them as "redeemed from the hand of one stronger than they" [v. 11 p.]. By this he surely means the tight fetters with which the sinner is bound so long as, forsaken by the Lord, he lives under the devil's yoke. Nonetheless the will remains, with the most eager inclination disposed and hastening to sin. For man, when he gave himself over to this necessity, was not deprived of will, but of soundness of will. Not inappropriately Bernard teaches that to will is in us all: but to will good is gain;

Those special endowments that make possible admirable and heroic actions by nonelect persons are by Calvin referred to God's special grace.

[8] Plato, *Cratylus* 393 f. (LCL Plato VI. 38–45).

to will evil, loss. Therefore simply to will is of man; to will ill, of a corrupt nature; to will well, of grace.[9]

Now, when I say that the will bereft of freedom is of necessity either drawn or led into evil, it is a wonder if this seems a hard saying to anyone, since it has nothing incongruous or alien to the usage of holy men. But it offends those who know not how to distinguish between necessity and compulsion.[10] Suppose someone asks them: Is not God of necessity good? Is not the devil of necessity evil? What will they reply? God's goodness is so connected with his divinity that it is no more necessary for him to be God than for him to be good. But the devil by his fall was so cut off from participation in good that he can do nothing but evil. But suppose some blasphemer sneers that God deserves little praise for His own goodness, constrained as He is to preserve it.[11] Will this not be a ready answer to him: not from violent impulsion, but from His boundless goodness comes God's inability to do evil? Therefore, if the fact that he must do good does not hinder God's free will in doing good; if the devil, who can do only evil, yet sins with his will—who shall say that man therefore sins less willingly because he is subject to the necessity of sinning? Augustine everywhere speaks of this necessity; and even though Caelestius caviled against him invidiously, he did not hesitate to affirm it in these words: "Through freedom man came to be in sin, but the corruption which followed as punishment turned freedom into necessity."[12] cAnd whenever he makes mention of the matter, he does not hesitate to speak in this manner of the necessary bondage of sin.

bThe chief point of this distinction, then, must be that man, as he was corrupted by the Fall, sinned willingly, not unwillingly

[9] Bernard, *Concerning Grace and Free Will* vi. 16 (MPL 182. 1040; tr. W. W. Williams, p. 32).

[10] Luther had made this distinction in his dispute with Erasmus: "By necessity I do not mean compulsion, but the necessity of immutability"; he explains that an evil man does evil spontaneously but that he cannot of himself leave off doing evil. *De servo arbitrio* (*Werke* WA XVIII. 634; tr. H. Cole, *The Bondage of the Will*, p. 72). De Castro virtually identifies the two. *Adversus omnes haereses* IX (1543, fo. 123 D).

[11] In *Defensio doctrinae de servitute humani arbitrii contra A. Pighium* (1543), Calvin assails Pighius for this opinion (CR VI. 333 f.). Albert Pighius was a Louvain scholar who served Adrian VI and succeeding popes in Rome and who published various anti-Reformation books. Calvin's treatise is a reply to his *De libero hominis arbitrio et divina gratia* (Cologne, 1542). Cf. also Augustine, *On Nature and Grace* xlvi. 54 (MPL 44. 273; tr. NPNF V. 139).

[12] Augustine, *On Man's Perfection in Righteousness* iv. 9 (MPL 44. 295; tr. NPNF V. 161); *On Nature and Grace* lxvi. 79, quoting Ps. 25:17 (Vg. Ps. 24:17): "*de miserationibus meis*" (MPL 44. 286; tr. NPNF V. 149).

or by compulsion; by the most eager inclination of his heart, not by forced compulsion; by the prompting of his own lust, not by compulsion from without. Yet so depraved is his nature that he can be moved or impelled only to evil. But if this is true, then it is clearly expressed that man is surely subject to the necessity of sinning.[13]

ᵉBernard, agreeing with Augustine, so writes: "Among all living beings man alone is free; and yet because sin has intervened he also undergoes a kind of violence, but of will, not of nature, so that not even thus is he deprived of his innate freedom. For what is voluntary is also free." And a little later: "In some base and strange way the will itself, changed for the worse by sin, makes a necessity for itself. Hence, neither does necessity, although it is of the will, avail to excuse the will, nor does the will, although it is led astray, avail to exclude necessity. For this necessity is as it were voluntary." Afterward he says that we are oppressed by no other yoke than that of a kind of voluntary servitude. Therefore we are miserable as to servitude and inexcusable as to will because the will, when it was free, made itself the slave of sin. Yet he concludes: "Thus the soul, in some strange and evil way, under a certain voluntary and wrongly free necessity is at the same time enslaved and free: enslaved because of necessity; free because of will. And what is at once stranger and more deplorable, it is guilty because it is free, and enslaved because it is guilty, and as a consequence enslaved because it is free."[14] Surely my readers will recognize that I am bringing forth nothing new, for it is something that Augustine taught of old with the agreement of all the godly, and it was still retained almost a thousand years later in monastic cloisters. But Lombard, since he did not know how to distinguish necessity from compulsion, gave occasion for a pernicious error.

(Conversion of the will is the effect of divine grace inwardly bestowed, 6–14)
6. Men's inability to do good manifests itself above all in the work of redemption, which God does quite alone
ᵉ⁽ᵇ⁾On the other hand, it behooves us to consider the sort of remedy by which divine grace corrects and cures the corruption

---

[13] This distinction is similarly made, but with different terminology, in Reinhold Niebuhr's view that man sins "inevitably" but "responsibly." *The Nature and Destiny of Man*, first series, pp. 251–264.
[14] Bernard, *Sermons on the Song of Songs* lxxxi. 7, 9 (MPL 183. 1174 f.; tr. S. J. Eales, *Life and Works of St. Bernard* IV. 498 f.); Lombard, *Sentences* II. xxv. 5, 9 (MPL 192. 707).

of nature. ᵇSince the Lord in coming to our aid bestows upon us what we lack, when the nature of his work in us appears, our destitution will, on the other hand, at once be manifest. When the apostle tells the Philippians he is confident "that he who began a good work in you will bring it to completion at the day of Jesus Christ" [Phil. 1:6], there is no doubt that through "the beginning of a good work" he denotes the very origin of conversion itself, which is in the will. God begins his good work in us, therefore, by arousing love and desire and zeal for righteousness in our hearts; or, to speak more correctly, by bending, forming, and directing, our hearts to righteousness. He completes his work, moreover, by confirming us to perseverance. In order that no one should make an excuse that good is initiated by the Lord to help the will which by itself is weak, the Spirit elsewhere declares what the will, left to itself, is capable of doing: "A new heart shall I give you, and will put a new spirit within you; and I will remove the heart of stone from your flesh, and give you a heart of flesh. And I shall put my spirit within you, and cause you to walk in my statutes" [Ezek. 36:26–27].¹⁵ Who shall say that the infirmity of the human will is strengthened by his help in order that it may aspire effectively to the choice of good, when it must rather be wholly transformed and renewed?

If in a stone there is such plasticity that, made softer by some means, it becomes somewhat bent, I will not deny that man's heart can be molded to obey the right, provided what is imperfect in him be supplied by God's grace. But if by this comparison the Lord wished to show that nothing good can ever be wrung from our heart, unless it become wholly other, let us not divide between him and us what he claims for himself alone. If, therefore, a stone is transformed into flesh when God converts us to zeal for the right, whatever is of our own will is effaced. What takes its place is wholly from God. ᵉI say that the will is effaced; not in so far as it is will,¹⁶ for in man's conversion what belongs to his primal nature remains entire. I also say that it is created anew; not meaning that the will now begins to exist, but that it is changed from an evil to a good will. I affirm that this is wholly God's doing, for according to the testimony of the same apostle, "we are not even capable of thinking" [II Cor. 3:5 p.]. Therefore he states in another place that God not only assists the weak

---

¹⁵ Lombard, *Sentences* II. xxiv. 5; II. xxv. 16 (MPL 192. 702, 709); Erasmus, *De libero arbitrio*, ed. J. von Walter, p. 6.

¹⁶ Cf. secs. 7, 10, 12, 13, 14, below, on Calvin's terminology of will: whether the will is removed and replaced, or whether the same "natural gift" is renovated.

will or corrects the depraved will, but also works in us to will
[Phil. 2.13]. From this, one may easily infer, as I have said, that
everything good in the will is the work of grace alone. In this
sense he says elsewhere: "It is God who works all things in all"
[I Cor. 12:6 p.]. There he is not discussing universal governance,
but is uttering praise to the one God for all good things in which
believers excel. Now by saying "all" he surely makes God the
author of spiritual life from beginning to end. Previously he had
taught the same thing in other words: that believers are from
God in Christ [Eph. 1:1; I Cor. 8:6]. Here he clearly commends
the new creation, which sweeps away everything of our common
nature. We ought to understand here an antithesis between Adam
and Christ, which he explains more clearly in another place,
where he teaches that "we are his workmanship, created in Christ
for good works, which God prepared beforehand, that we should
walk in them" [Eph. 2:10, cf. Vg.]. For he would prove our salvation a free gift [cf. Eph. 2:5], because the beginning of every
good is from the second creation, which we attain in Christ. And
yet if even the least ability came from ourselves, we would also
have some share of the merit. But Paul, to strip us, argues that we
deserve nothing because "we have been created in Christ . . . for
good works which God prepared beforehand" [Eph. 2:10, cf. Vg.].
He means by these words that all parts of good works from their
first impulse belong to God. In this way the prophet, after saying
in the psalm that we are God's handiwork, so that we may not
share it with him, immediately adds: "And we ourselves have not
done it" [Ps. 100:3 p.]. It is clear from the context that he is
speaking of regeneration, which is the beginning of the spiritual
life; for he goes on to say that "we are his people, and the sheep
of his pasture" [Ps. 100:3]. Moreover, we see how, not simply content to have given God due praise for our salvation, he expressly
excludes us from all participation in it. It is as if he were saying
that not a whit remains to man to glory in, for the whole of salvation comes from God.

*7. It is not a case of the believer's "co-operation" with grace; the
will is first actuated through grace*[†]
ᵇBut perhaps some will concede that the will is turned away
from the good by its own nature and is converted by the Lord's
power alone, yet in such a way that, having been prepared, it
then has its own part in the action. As Augustine teaches, grace
precedes every good work; while will does not go before as its
leader but follows after as its attendant.[17] ᵉThis statement, which

---

[17] Augustine, *Letters* clxxxvi. 3. 10 (MPL 33. 819; tr. FC 30. 196).

the holy man made with no evil intention, has by Lombard been preposterously twisted to that way of thinking.[18] e(b)But I contend that in the words of the prophet that I have cited, as well as in other passages, two things are clearly signified: b(1) the Lord corrects our evil will, or rather extinguishes it; (2) he substitutes for it a good one from himself. In so far as it is anticipated by grace, to that degree I concede that you may call your will an "attendant." But because the will reformed is the Lord's work, it is wrongly attributed to man that he obeys prevenient grace with his will as attendant. Therefore Chrysostom erroneously wrote: "Neither grace without will nor will without grace can do anything."[19] As if grace did not also actuate the will itself, as we have just seen from Paul [cf. Phil. 2:13]! Nor was it Augustine's intent, in calling the human will the attendant of grace, to assign to the will in good works a function second to that of grace. His only purpose was, rather, to refute that very evil doctrine of Pelagius which lodged the first cause of salvation in man's merit.

Enough for the argument at hand, Augustine contends, was the fact that grace is prior to all merit. In the meantime he passes over the other question, that of the perpetual effect of grace, which he nevertheless brilliantly discusses elsewhere. For while Augustine on several occasions says that the Lord anticipates an unwilling man that he may will, and follows a willing man that he may not will in vain, yet he makes God himself wholly the Author of good works. cHowever, his statements on this matter are clear enough not to require a long review. "Men labor," he says, "to find in our will something that is our own and not of God; and I know not how it can be found." Moreover, in *Against Pelagius and Caelestius,* Book I, he thus interprets Christ's saying "Every one who has heard from my Father comes to me" [John 6:45 p.]: "Man's choice is so assisted that it not only knows what it ought to do, but also does because it has known. And thus when God teaches not through the letter of the law but through the grace of the Spirit, He so teaches that whatever anyone has learned he not only sees by knowing, but also seeks by willing, and achieves by doing."[20]

---

[18] Lombard, *Sentences* II. xxvi. 3 (MPL 192. 711). Cf. John Fisher, *Assertio Lutheranae confutatio,* p. 604: *"Auxilium Dei paratum est omnibus."*

[19] Chrysostom, *Homilies on Matthew,* hom. lxxxiv. 4 (MPG 58. 756; tr. NPNF X. 494 f.).

[20] Calvin has here condensed the teachings of the following passages from treatises of Augustine: *Enchiridion* ix. 32 (MPL 40. 248; tr. LCC VII. 358); *On the Merits and Remission of Sins* II. xviii. 28 (MPL 44. 168; tr. NPNF V. 56); *On the Grace of Christ and on Original Sin* I. xiv. 15 (MPL 44. 368; tr. NPNF V. 223).

8. Scripture imputes to God all that is for our benefit

[b]Well, then, since we are now at the principal point, let us undertake to summarize the matter for our readers by but a few, and very clear, testimonies of Scripture. Then, lest anyone accuse us of distorting Scripture, let us show that the truth, which we assert has been drawn from Scripture, lacks not the attestation of this holy man—I mean Augustine. I do not account it necessary to recount[21] item by item what can be adduced from Scripture in support of our opinion, but only from very select passages to pave the way to understanding all the rest, which we read here and there. On the other hand, it will not be untimely for me to make plain that I pretty much agree with that man whom the godly by common consent justly invest with the greatest authority.

[e]Surely there is ready and sufficient reason to believe that good takes its origin from God alone. And only in the elect does one find a will inclined to good. Yet we must seek the cause of election outside men. It follows, thence, that man has a right will not from himself, but that it flows from the same good pleasure by which we were chosen before the creation of the world [Eph. 1:4]. Further, there is another similar reason: for since willing and doing well take their origin from faith, we ought to see what is the source of faith itself.

But since the whole of Scripture proclaims that faith is a free gift of God, it follows that when we, who are by nature inclined to evil with our whole heart, begin to will good, we do so out of mere grace. [b]Therefore, the Lord when he lays down these two principles in the conversion of his people—that he will take from them their "heart of stone" and give them "a heart of flesh" [Ezek. 36:26]—openly testifies that what is of ourselves ought to be blotted out to convert us to righteousness; but that whatever takes its place is from him. And he does not declare this in one place only, for he says in Jeremiah: "I will give them one heart and one way, that they may fear me all their days" [Jer. 32:39]. A little later: "I will put the fear of my name in their heart, that they may not turn from me" [Jer. 32:40]. Again, in Ezekiel: "I will give them one heart and will give a new spirit in their inward parts. I will take the stony heart out of their flesh and give them a heart of flesh" [Ezek. 11:19]. He testifies that our conversion is the creation of a new spirit and a new heart. What other fact could more clearly claim for him, and take away from us, every vestige of good and right in our will? For it always follows that nothing good can arise out of our will until it has been reformed;

[21] "Account . . . recount," following Calvin's play on words: *"Censeo . . . recenseantur."*

and after its reformation, in so far as it is good, it is so from God, not from ourselves.

9. The prayers in Scripture especially show how the beginning, continuation, and end of our blessedness come from God alone
ᵇSo, also, do we read the prayers composed by holy men. "May the Lord incline our heart to him," said Solomon, "that we may keep his commandments." [I Kings 8:58 p.] He shows the stubbornness of our hearts: by nature they glory in rebelling against God's law, unless they be bent. ᵉThe same view is also held in The Psalms: "Incline my heart to thy testimonies [Ps. 119:36]. We ought always to note the antithesis between the perverse motion of the heart, by which it is drawn away to obstinate disobedience, and this correction, by which it is compelled to obedience. ᵇWhen David feels himself bereft, for a time, of directing grace, and prays God to "create in" him "a clean heart," "to renew a right Spirit in his inward parts" [Ps. 51:10; cf. Ps. 50:12, Vg.], does he not then recognize that all parts of his heart are crammed with uncleanness, and his spirit warped in depravity? Moreover, does he not, by calling the cleanness he implores "creation of God," attribute it once received wholly to God? ᵉIf anyone objects that this very prayer is a sign of a godly and holy disposition,[22] the refutation is ready: although David had in part already repented, yet he compared his previous condition with that sad ruin which he had experienced. Therefore, taking on the role of a man estranged from God, he justly prays that whatever God bestows on his elect in regeneration be given to himself. Therefore, he desired himself to be created anew, as if from the dead, that, freed from Satan's ownership, he may become an instrument of the Holy Spirit.

ᵇStrange and monstrous indeed is the license of our pride! The Lord demands nothing stricter than for us to observe his Sabbath most scrupulously [Ex. 20:8 ff.; Deut. 5:12 ff.], that is, by resting from our labors. Yet there is nothing that we are more unwilling to do than to bid farewell to our own labors and to give God's works their rightful place. If our unreason did not stand in the way, Christ has given a testimony of his benefits clear enough so that they cannot be spitefully suppressed. "I am," he says, "the vine, you the branches [John 15:5]; my Father is the cultivator [ch. 15:1]. Just as branches cannot bear fruit of themselves unless they abide in the vine, so can you not unless you abide in me [ch. 15:4]. For apart from me you can do nothing" [ch. 15:5].[22a]

[22] John Fisher, *Assertionis Lutheranae confutatio*, pp. 565 f.
[22a] The passages from John are quoted from Vg.

If we no more bear fruit of ourselves than a branch buds out when it is plucked from the earth and deprived of moisture, we ought not to seek any further the potentiality of our nature for good. Nor is this conclusion doubtful: "Apart from me you can do nothing" [John 15:5]. He does not say that we are too weak to be sufficient unto ourselves, but in reducing us to nothing he excludes all estimation of even the slightest little ability. If grafted in Christ we bear fruit like a vine—which derives the energy for its growth from the moisture of the earth, from the dew of heaven, and from the quickening warmth of the sun—I see no share in good works remaining to us if we keep unimpaired what is God's. ᵉIn vain this silly subtlety is alleged: there is already sap enclosed in the branch, and the power of bearing fruit; and it does not take everything from the earth or from its primal root, because it furnishes something of its own.²³ Now Christ simply means that we are dry and worthless wood when we are separated from him, for apart from him we have no ability to do good, as elsewhere he also says: "Every tree which my Father has not planted will be uprooted" [Matt. 15:13, cf. Vg.]. ᵇFor this reason, in the passage already cited the apostle ascribes the sum total to him. "It is God," says he, "who is at work in you, both to will and to work." [Phil. 2:13.]

The first part of a good work is will; the other, a strong effort to accomplish it; the author of both is God. Therefore we are robbing the Lord if we claim for ourselves anything either in will or in accomplishment. If God were said to help our weak will, then something would be left to us. But when it is said that he makes the will, whatever of good is in it is now placed outside us. But since even a good will is weighed down by the burden of our flesh so that it cannot rise up, he added that to surmount the difficulties of that struggle we are provided with constancy of effort sufficient to achieve this. Indeed, what he teaches in another passage could not otherwise be true: "It is God alone who works all things in all" [I Cor. 12:6]. ᵉIn this statement, as we have previously noted, the whole course of the spiritual life is comprehended.²⁴ So, too, David, after he has prayed the ways of God be made known to him so that he may walk in his truth, immediately adds, "Unite my heart to fear thy name" [Ps. 86:11; cf. Ps. 119:33]. By these words he means that even well-disposed persons have been subject to so many distractions that they readily

---

²³ As argued by A. Pighius, *De libero hominis arbitrio et divina gratia* (1542), fo. 97.
²⁴ II. iii. 6.

vanish or fall away unless they are strengthened to persevere. In this way elsewhere, after he has prayed that his steps be directed to keep God's word, he begs also to be given the strength to fight: "Let no iniquity," he says, "get dominion over me" [Ps. 119:133]. ᵇTherefore the Lord in this way both begins and completes the good work in us. It is the Lord's doing that the will conceives the love of what is right, is zealously inclined toward it, is aroused and moved to pursue it. Then it is the Lord's doing that the choice, zeal, and effort do not falter, but proceed even to accomplishment; lastly, that man goes forward in these things with constancy, and perseveres to the very end.

10. God's activity does not produce a possibility that we can exhaust, but an actuality to which we cannot add

ᵇHe does not move the will in such a manner as has been taught and believed for many ages—that it is afterward in our choice either to obey or resist the motion—but by disposing it efficaciously. Therefore one must deny that oft-repeated statement of Chrysostom: "Whom he draws he draws willing."²⁵ By this he signifies that the Lord is only extending his hand to await whether we will be pleased to receive his aid. We admit that man's condition while he still remained upright was such that he could incline to either side. But inasmuch as he has made clear by his example how miserable free will is unless God both wills and is able to work in us, what will happen to us if he imparts his grace to us in this small measure? But we ourselves obscure it and weaken it by our unthankfulness. For the apostle does not teach that the grace of a good will is bestowed upon us if we accept it, but that He wills to work in us. This means nothing else than that the Lord by his Spirit directs, bends, and governs, our heart and reigns in it as in his own possession. ᵉIndeed, he does not promise through Ezekiel that he will give a new Spirit to his elect only in order that they may be able to walk according to his precepts, but also that they may actually so walk [Ezek. 11:19–20; 36:27].

ᵇNow can Christ's saying ("Every one who has heard . . . from the Father comes to me" [John 6:45, cf. Vg.]) be understood in any other way than that the grace of God is efficacious of itself. This Augustine also maintains.²⁶ The Lord does not indiscrim-

---

²⁵ *"Quem trahit, volentem trahit"*: Chrysostom, *De ferendis reprehensionibus* 6 (MPG 51. 143); *Homilies on the Gospel of John*, hom. x. 1 (MPG 59. 73; tr. NPNF XIV. 35; FC 33. 95). In Comm. John 6:44, Calvin calls the sentence "a false, profane assertion."

²⁶ Augustine, *On the Predestination of the Saints* viii. 13 (MPL 44. 970; tr. NPNF V. 504 f.).

inately deem everyone worthy of this grace, as that common saying of Ockham (unless I am mistaken) boasts: grace is denied to no one who does what is in him.[27] Men indeed ought to be taught that God's loving-kindness is set forth to all who seek it, without exception. But since it is those on whom heavenly grace has breathed who at length begin to seek after it, they should not claim for themselves the slightest part of his praise. It is obviously the privilege of the elect that, regenerated through the Spirit of God, they are moved and governed by his leading. ᵉFor this reason, Augustine justly derides those who claim for themselves any part of the act of willing, just as he reprehends others who think that what is the special testimony of free election is indiscriminately given to all. "Nature," he says, "is common to all, not grace." The view that what God bestows upon whomever he wills is generally extended to all, Augustine calls a brittle glasslike subtlety of wit, which glitters with mere vanity. Elsewhere he says: "How have you come? By believing. Fear lest while you are claiming for yourself that you have found the just way, you perish from the just way. I have come, you say, of my own free choice; I have come of my own will. Why are you puffed up? Do you wish to know that this also has been given you? Hear Him calling, 'No one comes to me unless my Father draws him' [John 6:44 p.]."[28] And one may incontrovertibly conclude from John's words that the hearts of the pious are so effectively governed by God that they follow Him with unwavering intention. "No one begotten of God can sin," he says, "for God's seed abides in him." [I John 3:9.] For the intermediate movement the Sophists dream up, which men are free either to accept or refuse, we see obviously excluded when it is asserted that constancy is efficacious for perseverance.

11. Perseverance is exclusively God's work; it is neither a reward nor a complement of our individual act

ᵇPerseverance would, without any doubt, be accounted God's free gift if a most wicked error did not prevail that it is distributed according to men's merit, in so far as each man shows

---

[27] Calvin doubtfully ascribes to Ockham a phrase from Gabriel Biel's commentary on Lombard's *Sentences: Epythoma pariter et collectorium circa quatuor sententiarum libros* II. xxvii. 2. Cf. Nicholas (Ferber of) Herborn's statement that if a man fulfills that which is in him (*quod in se est*), he would appear to have done enough and that co-operating grace will aid him: *Locorum communium adversus huius temporis haereses enchiridion* xxxviii (ed. P. Schlager, from the 1529 edition, CC 12. 132).

[28] Augustine, *Sermons* xxvi. 3, 12, 4, 7 (MPL 38. 172, 177, 172 f., 174); xxx. 8, 10 (MPL 38. 192).

himself receptive to the first grace. But since this error arose from the fact that men thought it in their power to spurn or to accept the proffered grace of God, when the latter opinion is swept away the former idea also falls of itself. However, there is here a twofold error. For besides teaching that our gratefulness for the first grace and our lawful use of it are rewarded by subsequent gifts, they add also that grace does not work in us by itself, but is only a co-worker with us.[29]

As for the first point: we ought to believe that—while the Lord enriches his servants daily and heaps new gifts of his grace upon them—because he holds pleasing and acceptable the work that he has begun in them, he finds in them something he may follow up by greater graces. This is the meaning of the statement, "To him who has shall be given" [Matt. 25:29; Luke 19:26]. Likewise: "Well done, good servant; you have been faithful in a few matters, I will set you over much" [Matt. 25:21, 23; Luke 19:17; all Vg., conflated]. But here we ought to guard against two things: (1) not to say that lawful use of the first grace is rewarded by later graces, as if man by his own effort rendered God's grace effective; or (2) so to think of the reward as to cease to consider it of God's free grace. I grant that believers are to expect this blessing of God: that the better use they have made of the prior graces, the more may the following graces be thereafter increased. But I say this use is also from the Lord and this reward arises from his free benevolence. ᵉAnd they perversely as well as infelicitously utilize that worn distinction between operating and co-operating grace. Augustine indeed uses it, but moderates it with a suitable definition: God by co-operating perfects that which by operating he has begun. It is the same grace but with its name changed to fit the different mode of its effect.[30] Hence it follows that he is not dividing it between God and us as if from the individual movement of each a mutual convergence occurred, but he is rather making note of the multiplying of grace. What he says elsewhere bears on this: many gifts of God precede man's good will, which is itself among his gifts. From this it follows that the will is left nothing to claim for itself. ᵇThis Paul has expressly declared. For after he had said, "It is God who works in us to will and to accomplish," he went on to say that he does both "for his good pleasure" [Phil. 2:13 p.]. By this expression he means that God's loving-kindness is freely given. To this, our adversaries usually say

---

[29] Lombard, *Sentences* II. xxvi. 8, 9; xxvii. 5 (MPL 192. 713, 715).
[30] Augustine, *On Grace and Free Will* xvii. 33 (MPL 44. 901; tr. NPNF V. 457 f.); *Enchiridion* ix. 32 (MPL 40. 248; tr. LCC VII. 358 f.).

that after we have accepted the first grace, then our own efforts co-operate with subsequent grace.[31] To this I reply: If they mean that after we have by the Lord's power once for all been brought to obey righteousness, we go forward by our own power and are inclined to follow the action of grace, I do not gainsay it. For it is very certain that where God's grace reigns, there is readiness to obey it. Yet whence does this readiness come? Does not the Spirit of God, everywhere self-consistent, nourish the very inclination to obedience that he first engendered, and strengthen its constancy to persevere? Yet if they mean that man has in himself the power to work in partnership with God's grace, they are most wretchedly deluding themselves.

12. Man cannot ascribe to himself even one single good work apart from God's grace

e(b)Through ignorance they falsely twist to this purport that saying of the apostle: b"I labored more than they all—yet not I but the grace of God which was with me" [I Cor. 15:10]. Here is how they understand it: because it could have seemed a little too arrogant for Paul to say he preferred himself to all, he therefore corrected his statement by paying the credit to God's grace; yet he did this in such a way as to call himself a fellow laborer in grace. It is amazing that so many otherwise good men have stumbled on this straw. For the apostle does not write that the grace of the Lord labored with him to make him a partner in the labor. Rather, by this correction he transfers all credit for labor to grace alone. "It is not I," he says, "who labored, but the grace of God which was present with me." [I Cor. 15:10 p.] Now, the ambiguity of the expression deceived them, but more particularly the absurd Latin translation in which the force of the Greek article had been missed.[32] cFor if you render it word for word, he does not say that grace was a fellow worker with him; but that the grace that was present with him was the cause of everything. Augustine teaches this clearly, though briefly, when he speaks as follows: "Man's good will precedes many of God's gifts, but not all. The very will that precedes is itself among these gifts. The reason then follows: for it was written, 'His mercy anticipates me'

---

[31] Erasmus, *De libero arbitrio* (ed. J. von Walter), pp. 75 f., based on his interpretation of Luke 15:11–24, I Cor. 5:10, Rom. 8:26; Eck, *Enchiridion* (1532) L 7b.

[32] Cf. Comm. I Cor. 15:10. The reference here is apparently to the interpretation given by Erasmus, *De libero arbitrio* (ed. J. von Walter), p. 72. Modern editors read: "ἡ χάρις αὐτοῦ ἡ εἰς ἐμὲ": the second ἡ is the article referred to.

[Ps. 59:10; cf. Ps. 58:11 Vg.].[33] And 'His mercy will follow me' [Ps. 23:6]. Grace anticipates unwilling man that he may will; it follows him willing that he may not will in vain." [e]Bernard agrees with Augustine when he makes the church speak thus: "Draw me, however unwilling, to make me willing; draw me, slow-footed, to make me run."[34]

13. Augustine also recognizes no independent activity of the human will

[b]Now let us hear Augustine speaking in his own words, lest the Pelagians of our own age, that is, the Sophists of the Sorbonne, according to their custom, charge that all antiquity is against us.[35] In this they are obviously imitating their father Pelagius, by whom Augustine himself was once drawn into the same arena. In his treatise *On Rebuke and Grace to Valentinus,* Augustine treats more fully what I shall refer to here briefly, yet in his own words. The grace of persisting in good would have been given to Adam if he had so willed. It is given to us in order that we may will, and by will may overcome concupiscence. Therefore, he had the ability if he had so willed, but he did not will that he should be able. To us it is given both to will and to be able. The original freedom was to be able not to sin; but ours is much greater, not to be able to sin. And that no one may think that he is speaking of a perfection to come after immortality, as Lombard falsely interprets it, Augustine shortly thereafter removes this doubt. He says: "Surely the will of the saints is so much aroused by the Holy Spirit that they are able because they so will, and that they will because God brings it about that they so will. Now suppose that in such great weakness in which, nevertheless, God's power must be made perfect to repress elation [II Cor. 12:9], their own will were left to them in order, with God's aid, to be able, if they will, and that God does not work in them that they will: amid so many temptations the will itself would then succumb through weakness, and for that reason they could not persevere. Therefore assistance is given to the weakness of the human will to move it unwaveringly and inseparably by divine grace, and hence, however great its weakness, not to let it fail." He then discusses more fully how our hearts of necessity respond to God as he works upon them. Indeed, he says that the Lord draws men by their

---

[33] Based on the Vulgate text, where the number is Ps. 59:10.
[34] Bernard, *Sermons on the Song of Songs* xxi. 9 (MPL 183. 876; tr. S. J. Eales, *Life and Works of St. Bernard* IV. 121).
[35] Cf. Prefatory Address to the King of France, above, pp. 18 ff.

own wills, wills that he himself has wrought.[36] Now we have from
Augustine's own lips the testimony that we especially wish to
obtain: not only is grace offered by the Lord, which by anyone's
free choice may be accepted or rejected; but it is this very grace
which forms both choice and will in the heart, so that whatever
good works then follow are the fruit and effect of grace; and it
has no other will obeying it except the will that it has made.
There are also Augustine's words from another place: "Grace
alone brings about every good work in us."[37]

14. Augustine does not eliminate man's will, but makes it wholly dependent upon grace

[b]Elsewhere he says that will is not taken away by grace, but is
changed from evil into good, and helped when it is good. By this
he means only that man is not borne along without any motion
of the heart, as if by an outside force; rather, he is so affected
within that he obeys from the heart. Augustine writes to Boniface
that grace is specially and freely given to the elect in this manner:
"We know that God's grace is not given to all men. To those to
whom it is given it is given neither according to the merits of
works, nor according to the merits of the will, but by free grace.
To those to whom it is not given we know that it is because of
God's righteous judgment that it is not given." And in the same
epistle he strongly challenges the view that subsequent grace is
given for men's merits because by not rejecting the first grace they
render themselves worthy. For he would have Pelagius admit that
grace is necessary for our every action and is not in payment for
our works, in order that it may truly be grace. But the matter
cannot be summed up in briefer form than in the eighth chapter
of the book *On Rebuke and Grace to Valentinus*. There Augustine first teaches: the human will does not obtain grace by freedom, but obtains freedom by grace; when the feeling of delight
has been imparted through the same grace, the human will is
formed to endure; it is strengthened with unconquerable fortitude; controlled by grace, it never will perish, but, if grace forsake it, it will straightway fall; by the Lord's free mercy it is converted to good, and once converted it perseveres in good; the direction of the human will toward good, and after direction its
continuation in good, depend solely upon God's will, not upon

---

[36] Augustine, *On Rebuke and Grace* xi. 31 f.; xii. 33, 38; xiv. 45 (MPL 44.
935 f., 939 f., 943; tr. NPNF V. 484 f., 487, 489 f.); Lombard, *Sentences* II.
xxv. 3 (MPL 192. 707).

[37] Augustine, *Letters* cxciv. 5: "*Omne bonum meritum nostrum non in nobis
faciat nisi gratia*" (MPL 33. 880; tr. FC 30. 313).

any merit of man. Thus there is left to man such free will, if we please so to call it, as he elsewhere describes: that except through grace the will can neither be converted to God nor abide in God; and whatever it can do it is able to do only through grace.[38]

^cCHAPTER IV

How God Works in Men's Hearts[1]

(Man under Satan's control: but Scripture shows God making use of Satan in hardening the heart of the reprobate, 1–5)
1. Man stands under the devil's power, and indeed willingly

^bUnless I am mistaken, we have sufficiently proved that man is so held captive by the yoke of sin that he can of his own nature neither aspire to good through resolve nor struggle after it through effort. Besides, we posited a distinction between compulsion and necessity from which it appears that man, while he sins of necessity, yet sins no less voluntarily.[2] But, while he is bound in servitude to the devil, he seems to be actuated more by the devil's will than by his own. It consequently remains for us to determine the part of the devil and the part of man in the action. Then we must answer the question whether we ought to ascribe to God any part of the evil works in which Scripture signifies that some action of his intervenes.

Somewhere Augustine compares man's will to a horse awaiting its rider's command, and God and the devil to its riders. "If God sits astride it," he says, "then as a moderate and skilled rider, he guides it properly, spurs it if it is too slow, checks it if it is too swift, restrains it if it is too rough or too wild, subdues it if it balks, and leads it into the right path. But if the devil saddles it, he violently drives it far from the trail like a foolish and wanton rider, forces it into ditches, tumbles it over cliffs, and goads it into obstinacy and fierceness."[3] Since a better comparison does not

---

[38] Passages from Augustine quoted or alluded to in sec. 14 are: *On Grace and Free Will* xx. 41 (MPL 44. 905; tr. NPNF V. 461); *On the Spirit and the Letter* xxx. 52 (MPL 44. 233; tr. NPNF V. 106); *Letters* ccxvii. 5. 16 (MPL 33. 984 f.; tr. FC 32. 86); *Sermons* clxxvi. 5, 6 (MPL 38. 952 f.; tr. LF *Sermons* II. 907 f.); *On Rebuke and Grace* viii. 17 (MPL 44. 926; tr. NPNF V. 478); *Letters* ccxiv. 7 (MPL 33. 970; tr. FC 32. 61 f.).

[1] Cf. III. i. 3.

[2] Cf. II. iii. 5.

[3] Apparently a variation on Pseudo-Augustine, *Hypomnesticon* (commonly *Hypognosticon*) II. xi. 20 (MPL 45. 1632). Luther uses the metaphor in his *Bondage of the Will* (*Werke* WA XVIII. 635; tr. J. L. Parker and D. R. Johnston, *The Bondage of the Will*, pp. 103 f.). Cf. *Martin Luther, Ausgewählte Werke*, ed. H. H. Borcherdt, Erganzungsband, pp. 46 f.; E. G. Schwie-

come to mind, we shall be satisfied with this one for the present. It is said that the will of the natural man is subject to the devil's power and is stirred up by it. This does not mean that, like unwilling slaves rightly compelled by their masters to obey, our will, although reluctant and resisting, is constrained to take orders from the devil. It means rather that the will, captivated by Satan's wiles, of necessity obediently submits to all his leading. For those whom the Lord does not make worthy to be guided by his Spirit he abandons, with just judgment, to Satan's action. For this reason the apostle says that "the god of this world has blinded the minds of the unbelievers," who are destined to destruction, that they may not see the light of the gospel [II Cor. 4:4]; and in another place that he "is . . . at work in the disobedient sons" [Eph. 2:2]. The blinding of the impious and all iniquities following from it are called "the works of Satan." Yet their cause is not to be sought outside man's will, from which the root of evil springs up, and on which rests the foundation of Satan's kingdom, that is, sin.

2. God, Satan, and man active in the same event

bFar different is the manner of God's action in such matters. To make this clearer to us, we may take as an example the calamity inflicted by the Chaldeans upon the holy man Job, when they killed his shepherds and in enmity ravaged his flock [Job 1:17]. Now their wicked act is perfectly obvious; nor does Satan do nothing in that work, for the history states that the whole thing stems from him [Job 1:12].

But Job himself recognizes the Lord's work in it, saying that He has taken away what had been seized through the Chaldeans [Job 1:21]. How may we attribute this same work to God, to Satan, and to man as author, without either excusing Satan as associated with God, or making God the author of evil? Easily, if we consider first the end, and then the manner, of acting. The Lord's purpose is to exercise the patience of His servant by calamity; Satan endeavors to drive him to desperation; the Chaldeans strive to acquire gain from another's property contrary to law and right. So great is the diversity of purpose that already strongly marks the deed. There is no less difference in the manner. The Lord permits Satan to afflict His servant; He hands the Chaldeans over to be impelled by Satan, having chosen them as His ministers for this task. Satan with his poison darts arouses the wicked minds of the Chaldeans to execute that evil deed. They dash madly into injustice, and they render all their members guilty

bert, *Luther and His Times*, pp. 691 f. See also Augustine, *Psalms*, Ps. 33:5; 148:2 (MPL 36. 310; 37. 1938; tr. NPNF VIII. 74, 673).

and befoul them by the crime. Satan is properly said, therefore, to act in the reprobate over whom he exercises his reign, that is, the reign of wickedness. God is also said to act in His own manner, in that Satan himself, since he is the instrument of God's wrath, bends himself hither and thither at His beck and command to execute His just judgments. I pass over here the universal activity of God whereby all creatures, as they are sustained, thus derive the energy to do anything at all.[4] I am speaking only of that special action which appears in every particular deed. Therefore we see no inconsistency in assigning the same deed to God, Satan, and man; but the distinction in purpose and manner causes God's righteousness to shine forth blameless there, while the wickedness of Satan and of man betrays itself by its own disgrace.

3. What does "hardness" mean?

[b]The church fathers sometimes scrupulously shrink from a simple confession of the truth because they are afraid that they may open the way for the impious to speak irreverently of God's works. As I heartily approve of this soberness, so do I deem it in no way dangerous if we simply adhere to what Scripture teaches. At times not even Augustine was free of that superstition; for example, he says that hardening and blinding refer not to God's activity but to his foreknowledge.[5] Yet very many expressions of Scripture do not admit these subtleties, but clearly show that something more than God's mere foreknowledge is involved. [c]And Augustine himself in the *Against Julian*, Book V, argues at great length that sins happen not only by God's permission and forbearance, but by his might, as a kind of punishment for sins previously committed.[6] [b]Likewise what they report concerning permission is too weak to stand. Very often God is said to blind and harden the reprobate, to turn, incline, and impel, their hearts [e.g.. Isa. 6:10], as I have taught more fully elsewhere.[7] The nature of this activity is by no means explained if we take

---

[4] Cf. I. xvi. 4.

[5] In the work *De praedestinatione et gratia*, erroneously attributed to Augustine but showing semi-Pelagian features, the statement is made: "Before he had made us, he foreknew us and in the very foreknowledge [*ipsa praescientia*], although he had not yet made us, he elected us"; *De praedestinatione et gratia*, chs. vi, vii (MPL 45. 1668). Calvin apparently does not doubt Augustine's authorship, which had been accepted in two Basel editions of Augustine (the second by Erasmus) and was first discarded in the Louvain edition of 1577. See the *admonitio* in MPL 45. 1665 and H. Pope, *St. Augustine of Hippo*, p. 387. See also Smits I. 191 f.

[6] Augustine, *Against Julian* V. iii (MPL 44. 786 ff.; tr. FC 35. 247–250).

[7] I. xviii.

refuge in foreknowledge or permission. We therefore reply that it takes place in two ways. For after his light is removed, nothing but darkness and blindness remains. When his Spirit is taken away, our hearts harden into stones. When his guidance ceases, they are wrenched into crookedness. Thus it is properly said that he blinds, hardens, and bends those whom he has deprived of the power of seeing, obeying, and rightly following.

The second way, which comes much closer to the proper meaning of the words, is that to carry out his judgments through Satan as minister of his wrath, God destines men's purposes as he pleases, arouses their wills, and strengthens their endeavors. eThus Moses, when he relates that King Sihon did not give passage to the people because God had hardened his spirit and made his heart obstinate, immediately adds the purpose of His plan· that, as he says, "He might give him into our hands" [Deut. 2:30, cf. Comm.]. Therefore, because God willed that Sihon be destroyed, He prepared his ruin through obstinacy of heart.

4. Scriptural examples of how God treats the godless

bAccording to the first way this seems to have been said: "He takes away speech from the truthful, and deprives the elders of reason" [Job 12:20; cf. Ezek. 7:26]. "He takes the heart from those who are in authority over the people of the land, and makes them wander in trackless wastes." [Job 12:24 p.; cf. Ps. 107:40.] Likewise, "O Lord, why hast thou driven us mad and hardened our heart, that we may not fear thee?" [Isa. 63:17, cf. Vg.] These passages indicate what sort of men God makes by deserting them rather than how he carries out his work in them.

Yet there are other testimonies that go beyond these. Such, for example, are those of the hardening of Pharaoh: "I will harden his heart, . . . so that he may not hear you [Ex. 7:3-4] and let the people go" [Ex. 4:21]. Afterward he said that he had made Pharaoh's heart "heavy" [Ex. 10:1] and "stiffened" it [Ex. 10:20, 27; 11:10; 14:8]. Did he harden it by not softening it? This is indeed true, but he did something more. He turned Pharaoh over to Satan to be confirmed in the obstinacy of his breast. This is why he had previously said, "I will restrain his heart" [Ex. 4:21]. The people go forth from Egypt; as enemies the inhabitants of the region come to meet them. What has stirred them up? Moses, indeed, declared to the people that it was the Lord who stiffened their hearts [Deut. 2:30]. The prophet, indeed, recounting the same history, says: "He turned their hearts to hate his people" [Ps. 105:25]. Now you cannot say that they stumbled from being deprived of God's counsel. For if they were "stiffened" and "turned," they were deliberately bent to that very thing. Moreover, whenever it pleased him to punish the transgressions of the people, how did he carry out his work through the reprobate? So that anyone may see that the power of execution was with him while they merely provided service. Accordingly he threatens to call them forth by his whistle [Isa. 5:26; 7:18], then to use them as a snare to catch [Ezek. 12:13; 17:20], then as a hammer to shatter, the Israelites [Jer. 50:23]. But he expressly declared that he did not idly stand by when he called Sennacherib an ax [Isa. 10:15] that was aimed and impelled by His own hand to cut them down. In another place Augustine rather well defines the matter as follows: "The fact that men sin is their own doing; that they by sinning do this or that comes from the power of God, who divides the darkness as he pleases."[8]

5. Satan also must serve God

[b]One passage will however be enough to show that Satan intervenes to stir up the reprobate whenever the Lord by his providence destines them to one end or another. For in Samuel it is often said that "an evil spirit of the Lord" and "an evil spirit from the Lord" has either "seized" or "departed from" Saul [I Sam. 16:14; 18:10; 19:9]. It is unlawful to refer this to the Holy Spirit. Therefore, the impure spirit is called "spirit of God" because it responds to his will and power, and acts rather as God's instrument than by itself as the author. [e(b)]At the same time we ought to add what Paul teaches: the working of error and seduction is divinely sent "that those who have not obeyed the truth may believe a lie" [II Thess. 2:10–11, cf. Vg.]. [b]Yet in the same work there is always a great difference between what the Lord does and what Satan and the wicked try to do. God makes these evil instruments, which he holds under his hand and can turn wherever he pleases, to serve his justice. They, as they are evil, by their action give birth to a wickedness conceived in their depraved nature. The other considerations that are concerned with vindicating God's majesty from blame, or cutting off any excuses of the wicked, have already been discussed in the chapter on providence.[9] Here my sole intention was briefly to indicate how Satan reigns in a reprobate man, and how the Lord acts in both.

[8] Augustine, *On the Predestination of the Saints* xvi. 33 (MPL 44. 984; tr. NPNF V. 514).
[9] I. xvi–xviii.

(God's providence overrules men's wills in external matters, 6–8)

6. In actions of themselves neither good nor bad, we are not thrown on our own

ᵇEven though we have touched upon the matter above,¹⁰ we have not yet explained what freedom man may possess in actions that are of themselves neither righteous nor corrupt, and look toward the physical rather than the spiritual life. In such things some have conceded him free choice,¹¹ more (I suspect) because they would not argue about a matter of no great importance than because they wanted to assert positively the very thing they grant. I admit that those who think they have no power to justify themselves hold to the main point necessary to know for salvation. Yet I do not think this part ought to be neglected: to recognize that whenever we are prompted to choose something to our advantage, whenever the will inclines to this, or conversely whenever our mind and heart shun anything that would otherwise be harmful—this is of the Lord's special grace.

The force of God's providence extends to this point: not only that things occur as he foresees to be expedient, but that men's wills also incline to the same end. Indeed, if we ponder the direction of external things, we shall not doubt that to this extent they are left to human judgment. But if we lend our ears to the many testimonies which proclaim that the Lord also rules men's minds in external things, these will compel us to subordinate decision itself to the special impulse of God. Who inclined the wills of the Egyptians toward the Israelites so that they should lend them all their most precious vessels [Ex. 11:2–3]? They would never voluntarily have been so inclined. Therefore, their minds were more subject to the Lord than ruled by themselves.

ᶜIndeed, if Jacob had not been persuaded that God according to his pleasure variously disposes men, he would not have said of his son Joseph, whom he thought to be some heathen Egyptian,

---

¹⁰ II. ii. 13–17.

¹¹ The reference is to Lutheran statements represented by the Augsburg Confession I. xviii: "Man's will has some liberty to work a civil righteousness . . . no power to work the righteousness of God." Cf. Melanchthon, *Loci communes*, 1535, where it is stated that man retains a certain power of choice respecting "outward civil works." Thus "the human will is able of its own force without renewal [*suis viribus sine renovatione*] to do some outward works of the law. This is the freedom of will which philosophers rightly attribute to man." (CR Melanchthon XXI. 374.) Calvin would have us view all such human choice and action as within the operation of divine providence.

"May God grant you to find mercy in this man's sight" [Gen. 43: 14]. Also, as the whole church confesses in the psalm, when God would have mercy upon his people, he tamed the hearts of the cruel nations to gentleness [cf. Ps. 106:46]. On the other hand, when Saul so broke out into anger as to gird himself for war, the cause is stated: the Spirit of God impelled him [I Sam. 11:6]. ᵇWho turned Absalom's mind from embracing Ahithophel's counsel, which was usually regarded as an oracle [II Sam. 17:14]? Who inclined Rehoboam to be persuaded by the young men's counsel [I Kings 12:10, 14]? ᶜWho caused the nations previously very bold to tremble at the coming of Israel? Even the harlot Rahab confessed that this was done by God [Josh. 2:9 ff.]. Again, who cast down the hearts of Israel with fear and dread, but he who threatened in the Law to give them "a trembling heart" [Deut. 28:65; cf. Lev. 26:36]?

7. In each case God's dominion stands above our freedom

ᵇSomeone will object that these are particular examples to whose rule by no means all instances ought to be applied.¹² But I say that they sufficiently prove what I contend: God, whenever he wills to make way for his providence, bends and turns men's wills even in external things; nor are they so free to choose that God's will does not rule over their freedom. Whether you will or not, daily experience compels you to realize that your mind is guided by God's prompting rather than by your own freedom to choose. That is, in the simplest matters judgment and understanding often fail you, while in things easy to do the courage droops. On the contrary, in the obscurest matters, ready counsel is immediately offered; in great and critical matters there is courage to master every difficulty.

In this way I understand Solomon's words, "God made both the ear to hear and the eye to see" [Prov. 20:12 p.]. For he seems to me not to be speaking of their creation, but of the peculiar gift of their function.¹³ When he writes, "In his hand the Lord holds the king's heart as streams of water, and turns it wherever he will" [Prov. 21:1], Solomon actually comprehends the whole genus under a single species. If any man's will has been released from all subjection, this privilege belongs above all to the kingly will, which in a measure exercises rule over others' wills. But if the king's will is bent by God's hand, our wills are not exempt from that condition. On this point there is a notable saying of

¹² Erasmus, De libero arbitrio, ed. J. von Walter, p. 66.
¹³ A different turn of thought is found in VG: "Mais de la grace speciale que Dieu fait aux hommes de jour en jour."

Augustine: "Scripture, if diligently searched, shows that not only the good wills which he has made out of evil ones and directs, once so made by him, to good actions and to eternal life are in God's power; but so also are those wills which preserve the creatures of this world. And they are so in his power that he causes them to be inclined where and when he will, either to bestow benefits, or to inflict punishments—indeed by his most secret but most righteous judgment."[14]

8. The question of "free will' does not depend on whether we can accomplish what we will, but whether we can will freely[t]

[b]Here let my readers remember that man's ability to choose freely is not to be judged by the outcome of things, as some ignorant folk absurdly have it. For they seem to themselves neatly and cleverly to prove the bondage of men's will from the fact that not even for the highest monarchs do all things go according to their liking. Anyhow, this ability of which we are speaking we must consider within man, and not measure it by outward success. In discussing free will we are not asking whether a man is permitted to carry out and complete, despite external hindrances, whatever he has decided to do; but whether he has, in any respect whatever, both choice of judgment and inclination of will that are free. If men have sufficient of both, Atilius Regulus, confined in a nail-studded wine cask, has no less of free will than Augustus Caesar, governing at his command a great part of the world.[15]

[e]CHAPTER V

REFUTATION OF THE OBJECTIONS COMMONLY PUT FORWARD IN DEFENSE OF FREE WILL

(Answers to arguments for free will alleged on grounds of common sense, 1–5)

1. First argument: necessary sin is not sin; voluntary sin is avoidable[t]

[b]It would seem that enough had been said concerning the bondage of man's will, were it not for those who by a false notion of freedom try to cast down this conception and allege in opposi-

---

[14] Augustine, *On Grace and Free Will* xx. 41 (MPL 44. 906; tr. NPNF V. 461).

[15] The virtues of Regulus, who met a cruel death at the hands of the Carthaginians rather than break his promise, were celebrated by Cicero, Horace, Seneca, and other Roman writers. Augustine, to meet pagan charges against Christianity, presents the story of Regulus as an instance in which the Roman gods could not avail to save a faithful man (*City of God* I. xv; MPL 41. 28; LCL Augustine, I. 68 ff.; tr. NPNF II. 11).

tion some reasons of their own to assail our opinion. First, they heap up various absurdities to cast odium upon it, as something abhorrent also to common sense; afterward with Scriptural testimonies they contend against it. We shall beat back both siege engines in turn. If sin, they say, is a matter of necessity, it now ceases to be sin; if it is voluntary, then it can be avoided.[1] These were also the weapons with which Pelagius assailed Augustine. Yet we do not intend to crush them by the weight of Augustine's name until we have satisfactorily treated the matter itself. I therefore deny that sin ought less to be reckoned as sin merely because it is necessary. I deny conversely the inference they draw, that because sin is voluntary it is avoidable. For if anyone may wish to dispute with God and escape judgment by pretending that he could not do otherwise, he has a ready reply, e(b)which we have brought forward elsewhere:[2] it is not from creation but from corruption of nature that men are bound to sin and can will nothing but evil. For whence comes that inability which the wicked would freely use as an excuse, but from the fact that Adam willingly bound himself over to the devil's tyranny? Hence, therefore, the corruption that enchains us: the first bman fell away from his Maker. If all men are deservedly held guilty of this rebellion, let them not think themselves excused by the very necessity in which they have the most evident cause of their condemnation. eI explained this clearly above, and gave the devil himself as an example; from which it is clear that he who sins of necessity sins no less voluntarily. This is, conversely, true of the elect angels: although their will cannot turn away from good, yet it does not cease to be will. Bernard also aptly teaches the same thing: that we are the more miserable because the necessity is voluntary, a necessity which nevertheless having bound us to it, so constrains us that we are slaves of sin, as we have mentioned before.[3] bThe second part of their syllogism is defective because it erroneously leaps from "voluntary" to "free." For we

---

[1] Erasmus, *De libero arbitrio*, ed. von Walter, p. 25. Augustine repeats and answers formulations of the same argument in his unfinished treatise against the Pelagian, Julian of Eclanum; *Contra secundam Juliani responsionem, imperfectum opus* I. xlvi–xlviii, lx, lxxxii, lxxxiv, cvi (MPL 45. 1067–1071, 1081, 1103 f., 1119 f.); *On Man's Perfection in Righteousness* ii. 2 (MPL 44. 293; tr. NPNF V. 160); *On Nature and Grace* lxvii. 80 (MPL 44. 286; tr. NPNF V. 49).

[2] II. iii. 5. The references to previous statements that follow in this paragraph are to the same passage.

[3] Bernard, *Sermons on the Song of Songs* lxxxi. 7, 9 (MPL 183. 1174 f.; tr. S. J. Eales, *Life and Works of St. Bernard* IV. 498 f.).

proved above that something not subject to free choice is never-theless voluntarily done.

2. *Second argument: reward and punishment lose their meaning*[t]
ᵇThey submit that, unless both virtues and vices proceed from the free choice of the will, it is not consistent that man be either punished or rewarded. I admit that this argument, even though it is Aristotle's, is somewhere used by Chrysostom and Jerome. Yet Jerome himself does not hide the fact that it was a common argument of the Pelagians, and he even quotes their own words: "If it is the grace of God working in us, then grace, not we who do not labor, will be crowned."[4]

Concerning punishments, I reply that they are justly inflicted upon us, from whom the guilt of sin takes its source. What dif-ference does it make whether we sin out of free or servile judg-ment, provided it is by voluntary desire—especially since man is proved a sinner because he is under the bondage of sin? As for the rewards of righteousness, it is a great absurdity for us to admit that they depend upon God's kindness rather than our own merits.

How often does this thought recur in Augustine: "God does not crown our merits but his own gifts"; "we call 'rewards' not what are due our merits, but what are rendered for graces already be-stowed"![5] To be sure, they sharply note this: that no place is now left for merits if they do not have free will as their source.[6] But in regarding this so much a matter for disagreement they err greatly. ᶜAugustine does not hesitate habitually to teach as an unavoidable fact what they think unlawful so to confess. For ex-ample, he says: "What are the merits of any men? When he comes not with a payment due but with free grace, he, alone free of sin and the liberator from it, finds all men sinners." Also: "If you shall be paid what you deserve, you must be punished. What then happens? God has not rendered you the punishment you deserve,

---

[4] Aristotle, *Nicomachean Ethics* III. 5. 1113b (LCL edition, pp. 142 f.); Chrysostom, *Homily on the Passage "The way of man is not in himself"* (Jer. 10:23) (MPL 56. 153–162); Jerome, *Letters* cxxxiii. 5 (CSEL 56. 249; tr. NPNF 2 ser. VI. 231); *Dialogue Against the Pelagians* I. 6 (MPL 23. 501).
[5] Augustine, *Letters* cxciv. 5. 19 (MPL 33. 880): *"Cum Deus coronat merita nostra nihil aliud coronat quam munera sua"* (tr. FC 30. 313); *On Grace and Free Will* vi. 15 (MPL 44. 890; tr. NPNF V. 450).
[6] The references to contemporary opinions in this paragraph are to passages in Cochlaeus, *De libero arbitrio,* and in Erasmus, *De libero arbitrio.* See J. von Walter's edition of the latter, pp. 50, 53, 59, and the citations in OS III. 299.

but bestows undeserved grace. If you would be estranged from grace, boast of your own merits." Again: "Of yourself you are nothing. Sins are your own, but merits are God's. You deserve punishment, and when the reward comes he will crown his own gifts, not your merits." ᵉIn the same vein he teaches elsewhere that grace does not arise from merit, but merit from grace! And a little later Augustine concludes that God precedes all merits with his gifts, that from them he may bring forth his own merits; he gives them altogether free because he finds no reason to save man.[7]

ᶜWhy, then, is it necessary to list more proofs when such sentences recur again and again in Augustine's writings? ᵇYet the apostle will even better free our adversaries from this error if they will hear from what principle he derives the glory of the saints. "Those whom he chose, he called; those whom he called, he justified; those whom he justified, he glorified." [Rom. 8:30 p.] Why, then, according to the apostle, are believers crowned [II Tim. 4:8]? Because they have been chosen and called and justified by the Lord's mercy, not by their own effort. Away, then, with this empty fear that there will be merit no longer if free will is not to stand! It is the height of foolishness to be frightened away and to flee from the very thing to which Scripture calls us. "If you received all things," he says, "why do you boast as if it were not a gift?" [I Cor. 4:7 p.] You see that Paul has taken everything away from free will in order not to leave any place for merits. But ᵉ⁽ᵇ⁾nevertheless, inexhaustible and manifold as God's beneficence and liberality are, ᵇhe rewards, as if they were our own virtues, those graces which he bestows upon us, because he makes them ours.

3. Third argument: all distinction between good and evil would be obliterated

ᵇOur opponents add an objection, which seems to have been drawn from Chrysostom: if to choose good or evil is not a faculty of our will, those who share in the same nature must be either all bad or all good.[8] Close to this point of view is the writer (whoever he was) of that work, *The Calling of the Gentiles*, which has been circulated under Ambrose's name. He reasons: no one would ever have departed from the faith if God's grace had not left us

---

[7] Augustine, *Psalms,* Ps. 70. ii. 5 (MPL 36. 895; tr. NPNF [Ps. 71] VIII. 324). In *Sermons* clxix. 2, Augustine has the sentence: *"Nihil in eis invenis unde salves, et tamen salvas"* (MPL 38. 917).

[8] Chrysostom, *Homilies on Genesis,* hom. xxiii. 5 (MPG 53. 204).

in a mutable condition.[9] Strange that such great men should have been so forgetful! For how did it not occur to Chrysostom that it is God's election which so distinguishes among men? Now we are not in the least afraid to admit what Paul asserts with great earnestness: all men are both depraved and given over to wickedness [cf. Rom. 3:10]. But we add with him that it is through God's mercy that not all remain in wickedness. Therefore, though all of us are by nature suffering from the same disease, only those whom it pleases the Lord to touch with his healing hand will get well. The others, whom he, in his righteous judgment, passes over,[10] waste away in their own rottenness until they are consumed. There is no other reason why some persevere to the end, while others fall at the beginning of the course. For perseverance itself is indeed also a gift of God, which he does not bestow on all indiscriminately, but imparts to whom he pleases. If one seeks the reason for the difference—why some steadfastly persevere, and others fail out of instability—none occurs to us other than that the Lord upholds the former, strengthening them by his own power, that they may not perish; while to the latter, that they may be examples of inconstancy, he does not impart the same power.

4. Fourth argument: all exhortation would be meaningless

ᵇFurthermore, they insist that it is vain to undertake exhortations, pointless to make use of admonitions, foolish to reprove, unless it be within the sinner's power to obey.[11] When Augustine long ago was met by similar objections, he was constrained to write his treatise *On Rebuke and Grace*. Even though in it he amply refutes those charges, he recalls his adversaries to this chief point: "O man! Learn by precept what you ought to do; learn by rebuke that it is by your own fault that you have it not; learn by prayer whence you may receive what you desire to have." ᵉIn the book *On the Spirit and the Letter* he uses almost the same argument: God does not measure the precepts of his law according to human powers, but where he has commanded what is right, he freely gives to his elect the capacity to fulfill it.[12] And this matter does not require long discussion. ᵇFirst, we are not alone in this cause, but Christ and all the apostles are with us.

---

[9] Prosper of Aquitaine, *The Call of All Nations* II. iv (MPL 17. 1112; 51. 689 f.; tr. ACW XIV. 96 f.). Cf. II. ii. 5, note 27.

[10] "*Praetermittit.*"

[11] Erasmus, *De libero arbitrio,* ed. von Walter, pp. 40 f.; Herborn, *Locorum communium enchiridion* xxxviii (CC 12. 132).

[12] Augustine, *On Rebuke and Grace* iii. 5 (MPL 44. 918; tr. NPNF V. 473); *On the Spirit and the Letter* (MPL 44. 199; tr. NPNF V. 83–114).

Let these men look to it how they may gain the upper hand in the struggle they are waging against such antagonists. Christ declares: "Without me you can do nothing." [John 15:5.] Does he for this reason any less reprove and chastise those who apart from him have been doing evil? Or does he for this reason any less urge everyone to devote himself to good works? How severely Paul inveighs against the Corinthians for their neglect of love [I Cor. 3:3; 16:14]! Yet he indeed prays that the Lord may give them love. Paul says in the letter to the Romans: "It depends not upon him who wills or upon him who runs, but upon God who shows mercy" [Rom. 9:16]. Still, he does not cease afterward to admonish as well as to urge and rebuke. Why do they not therefore importune the Lord not to labor in vain in requiring of men what he alone can give and in chastising what is committed out of lack of his grace? Why do they not warn Paul to spare those who do not have the power to will or to run, unless God's mercy, which has now forsaken them, goes before? As if the best reason of his teaching, which readily offers itself to those who more fervently seek it, did not rest in the Lord himself! Paul writes, "Neither he who plants nor he who waters is anything, but God who gives the growth alone acts effectively." [I Cor. 3:7.] In this he indicates how much teaching, exhortation, and reproof do to change the mind! ᵉThus we see how Moses placed the commandments of the law under severe sanctions [Deut. 30:19], and how the prophets bitterly menaced and threatened the transgressors. Yet they then confess that men become wise only when an understanding heart is given them [e.g., Isa. 5:24; 24:5; Jer. 9:13 ff.; 16:11 ff.; 44:10 ff.; Dan. 9:11; Amos 2:4], and that it is God's own work to circumcise hearts [cf. Deut. 10:16; Jer. 4:4] and to give hearts of flesh for hearts of stone [cf. Ezek. 11:19]; his to inscribe his law on our inward parts [cf. Jer. 31:33]; in fine, by renewing our souls [cf. Ezek. 36:26], to make his teaching effective.

5. The meaning of exhortation

ᵇTo what purpose then are exhortations? If rejected by the ungodly out of an obstinate heart, these shall be a testimony against them when they come to the Lord's judgment seat. Even now these are striking and beating their consciences. For, however much the most insolent person scoffs at them, he cannot condemn them. But, you ask, what will miserable little man do when softness of heart, which is necessary for obedience, is denied him? Indeed, what excuse will he have, seeing that he can credit hardness of heart to no one but himself? Therefore the impious, freely prepared to make sport of God's exhortations if they can, are, in spite of themselves, dumfounded by the power of them.

But we must consider their especial value for believers, in whom (as the Lord does all things through his Spirit) he does not neglect the instrument of his Word but makes effective use of it. Let this, then, be held true: all the righteousness of the pious rests upon God's grace. ᵉAs the prophet said: "I will give them a new heart . . . that they may walk in my statutes" [Ezek. 11:19–20]. Yet you will object, ᵇwhy are they now admonished about their duty, rather than left to the guidance of the Spirit? Why are they plied with exhortations, when they can hasten no more than the Spirit impels them? Why are they chastised whenever they stray from the path, when they have lapsed through the unavoidable weakness of the flesh?

O man, who are you to impose law upon God? If he wills to prepare us through exhortation to receive this very grace, by which we are made ready to obey the exhortation, what in this dispensation have you to carp or scoff at? If exhortations and reproofs profit the godly nothing except to convict them of sin, these ought not for this reason to be accounted utterly useless. Now, who would dare mock these exhortations as superfluous, since, with the Spirit acting within, they are perfectly able to kindle in us the desire for the good, to shake off sluggishness, to remove the lust for iniquity and its envenomed sweetness—on the contrary to engender hatred and loathing toward it?

If anyone wants a clearer answer, here it is: God works in his elect in two ways: within, through his Spirit; without, through his Word.[13] By his Spirit, illuminating their minds and forming their hearts to the love and cultivation of righteousness, he makes them a new creation. By his Word, he arouses them to desire, to seek after, and to attain that same renewal. In both he reveals the working of his hand according to the mode of dispensation. When he addresses the same Word to the reprobate, though not to correct them, he makes it serve another use: today to press them with the witness of conscience, and in the Day of Judgment to render them the more inexcusable. ᵉThus, although Christ declares that no one except him whom the Father draws can come to him, and the elect come after they have "heard and learned from the Father" [John 6:44–45], still Christ does not neglect the teacher's office, but with his own voice unremittingly summons those who need to be taught within by the Holy Spirit

[13] Calvin here characteristically affirms the necessity of a conjunction of the Word of Scripture with the operation of the Holy Spirit. Cf. I. vii. 4; III. i, *passim,* and notes appended.

in order to make any progress. Paul points out that teaching is not useless among the reprobate, because it is to them "a fragrance from death to death" [II Cor. 2:16], yet "a sweet fragrance to God" [II Cor. 2:15].

(Answers to arguments for free will based on interpretation of the law, promises and rebukes of Scripture, 6–11)
6. Are God's precepts "the measure of our strength"?

ᵇOur opponents take great pains to heap up Scriptural passages: and they do this so unremittingly that, although they cannot prevail, in the numbers at least they can bear us down. But as in battle, when it comes to a hand-to-hand encounter an unwarlike multitude, however much pomp and ostentation it may display, is at once routed by a few blows and compelled to flee, so for us it will be very easy to disperse these adversaries with their host. All the passages that they misuse against us, when they have been sorted out into their classes, group themselves under a very few main headings. Hence one answer will suffice for several; it will not be necessary to dispose of each one individually.

They set chief stock by God's precepts. These they consider to be so accommodated to our capacities that we are of necessity able to fulfill all their demonstrable requirements. Consequently, they run through the individual precepts, and from them take the measure of our strength. Either God is mocking us (they say) when he enjoins holiness, piety, obedience, chastity, love, gentleness; when he forbids uncleanness, idolatry, immodesty, anger, robbery, pride, and the like; or he requires only what is within our power.

Now we can divide into three classes almost all the precepts that they heap up. Some require man first to turn toward God; others simply speak of observing the law; others bid man to persevere in God's grace once it has been received. We shall discuss them all in general, then we shall get down to the three classes themselves.

A long time ago it became the common practice to measure man's capacities by the precepts of God's law, and this has some pretense of truth. But it arose out of the crassest ignorance of the law. For, those who deem it a terrible crime to say that it is impossible to observe the law press upon us as what is evidently their strongest reason that otherwise the law was given without purpose.¹⁴ Indeed, they speak as if Paul had nowhere spoken of the law. What then, I ask, do these assertions mean: "The law was put forward because of transgressions" [Gal. 3:19, cf. Vg.]; "Through the law comes knowledge of sin" [Rom. 3:20]; the

¹⁴ Cf. II. vii. 5; Eck, *Enchiridion* (1541), fo. 188a.

law engenders sin [cf. Rom. 7:7–8]; "Law slipped in to increase the trespass" [Rom. 5:20, cf. Vg.]? Was the law to be limited to our powers so as not to be given in vain? Rather, it was put far above us, to show clearly our own weakness! ᵉSurely, according to Paul's definition of the law, its purpose and fulfillment is love [cf. I Tim. 1:5]. And yet when Paul prays for the hearts of the Thessalonians to abound with it [I Thess. 3:12] he fully admits that the law sounds in our ears without effect unless God inspires in our hearts the whole sum of the law [cf. Matt. 22:37–40].

7. The law itself points our way to grace
    ᵇOf course, if Scripture taught nothing else than that the law is a rule of life to which we ought to direct our efforts, I, too, would yield to their opinion without delay. But since it faithfully and clearly explains to us the manifold use of the law,[15] it behooves us rather to consider from that interpretation what the law can do in man. With reference to the present question, as soon as the law prescribes what we are to do, it teaches that the power to obey comes from God's goodness. It thus summons us to prayers by which we may implore that this power be given us. If there were only a command and no promise, our strength would have to be tested whether it is sufficient to respond to the command. But since with the command are at once connected promises that proclaim not only that our support, but our whole virtue as well, rests in the help of divine grace, they more than sufficiently demonstrate how utterly inept, not to say unequal, we are to observe the law. For this reason, let us no longer press this proportion between our strength and the precepts of the law, as if the Lord had applied the rule of righteousness, which he was to give in the law, according to the measure of our feebleness. We who in every respect so greatly need his grace must all the more reckon from the promises how ill-prepared we are.

    But who will believe it plausible (they say) that the Lord intended his law for stocks and stones?[16] No one is trying to argue thus. For the wicked are not rocks or stumps when they are taught through the law that their lusts are opposed to God and they become guilty on their own admission; nor are believers stocks and stones when they are warned of their own weakness and take refuge in grace. On this point these profound statements of Augustine are pertinent: "God bids us do what we cannot, that

---

¹⁵ Cf. I. vi. 2; II. vii. 6, 10–12.
¹⁶ Cf. Origen, *De principiis* III. i. 5 (GCS 22. 200; MPG 11. 254; tr. G. W. Butterworth, *Origen On First Principles*, p. 162; ANF IV. 304); Augustine, *Sermons* clvi. 12. 13 (MPL 38. 857; tr. LF *Sermons* II. 769 f.).

we may know what we ought to seek from him." "The usefulness of the precepts is great if free will is so esteemed that God's grace may be the more honored." "Faith achieves what the law commands." ᶜ"Indeed, it is for this reason the law commands, that faith may achieve what had been commanded through the law. ᵇIndeed, God requires faith itself of us; yet he does not find something to require unless he has given something to find." Again, "Let God give what he commands, and command what he will."[17]

8. The several kinds of the commandments clearly show that without grace we can do nothing

ᵇThis will be more clearly seen in reviewing the three classes of precepts that we have touched on above.[18]

(1) Oftentimes both in the Law and in the Prophets the Lord commands us to be converted to him [Joel 2:12; Ezek. 18:30–32; Hos. 14:2 f.]. On the other hand, the prophet answers: "Convert me, O Lord, and I will be converted, . . . for after thou didst convert me I repented," etc. [Jer. 31:18–19, Vg.]. He bids us circumcise the foreskin of our heart [Deut. 10:16; cf. Jer. 4:4]. But through Moses he declares that this circumcision is done by His own hand [Deut. 30:6]. In some places he requires newness of heart [Ezek. 18:31], but elsewhere he testifies that it is given by him [Ezek. 11:19; 36:26]. ᶜ"But what God promises," as Augustine says, "we ourselves do not do through choice or nature; but he himself does through grace." This observation he lists in fifth place among the rules of Tychonius: we must distinguish carefully between the law and the promises, or between the commandments and grace.[19] ᵇNow away with those who infer from the precepts that man is perhaps capable of obedience, in order to destroy God's grace through which the commandments themselves are fulfilled.

(2) The precepts of the second kind are simple: by them we are bidden to honor God, to serve his will and cleave to it, to

---

[17] Augustine, *On Grace and Free Will* xvi. 32 (MPL 44. 900; tr. NPNF V. 457); *Letters* clxvii. 4. 15 (MPL 33. 739; tr. FC 30. 45); *Enchiridion* xxxi. 117 (MPL 40. 287; tr. LCL VII. 409); *Confessions* X. xxix. 40; xxxi. 45 (MPL 32. 796, 798; tr. LCC VII. 225, 228); *Psalms,* Ps. 118. xvi. 2 (MPL 37. 1545; tr. LF *Psalms* V. 381); *On the Gift of Perseverance* xx. 53 (MPL 45. 1026; tr. NPNF V. 547).

[18] Sec. 6, above.

[19] Augustine, *On the Grace of Christ and on Original Sin* I. xxx f. (MPL 44. 375; tr. NPNF V. 228); *On Christian Doctrine* III. xxxiii (MPL 34. 83; tr. NPNF II. 569). Augustine is here calling attention to the third of the seven rules for understanding Scripture, put forth about 390 by Tychonius, a Donatist who was condemned by the leaders of the sect.

observe his decrees, and to follow his teaching. But there are countless passages that bear witness that whatever righteousness, holiness, piety, and purity we can have are gifts of God.

(3) Of the third type is the exhortation of Paul and Barnabas to believers "to remain under God's grace," referred to by Luke [Acts 13:43]. But Paul also in another place teaches the source from which that virtue of constancy is to be sought. "It remains, brethren," he says, "for you to be strong in the Lord." [Eph. 6:10 p.] Elsewhere he forbids us to "grieve the Spirit of God in whom we were sealed for the day of our redemption" [Eph. 4: 30 p.]. Since men cannot fulfill what is there required, Paul asks of the Lord in behalf of the Thessalonians to "render them worthy of his holy calling and to fulfill every good resolve of his goodness and work of faith in them" [II Thess. 1:11 p.]. ᵉIn the same way Paul, dealing in the second letter to the Corinthians with alms, often commends their good and devout will [cf. II Cor. 8:11]. Yet a little later he gives thanks to God, "who has put in the heart of Titus to receive exhortation" [II Cor. 8:16 p.]. If Titus could not even make use of his mouth to exhort others except in so far as God prompted it, how could others be willing to act unless God himself directed their hearts?

*9. The work of conversion is not divided between God and man**

ᵇThe craftier of our opponents quibble over all these testimonies, holding that nothing hinders us from bringing all our strength to bear while God supports our weak efforts. They also bring forward passages from the Prophets in which the carrying out of our conversion seems to be divided equally between God and ourselves. "Be converted to me and I shall be converted to you." [Zech. 1:3.] What assistance the Lord provides us has been demonstrated above,[20] and there is no need to repeat it here. I wish this one thing at least to be conceded to me: it is pointless to require in us the capacity to fulfill the law, just because the Lord demands our obedience to it, when it is clear that for the fulfillment of all God's commands the grace of the Lawgiver is both necessary and is promised to us.

ᵉHence it is evident that at least more is required of us than we can pay. And that statement of Jeremiah cannot be refuted by any cavils: that the covenant of God made with the ancient people was invalid because it was only of the letter; moreover, that it is not otherwise established than when the Spirit enters into it to dispose their hearts to obedience [Jer. 31:32–33]. ᵇNor does this sentence lend support to their error: "Be converted to me

[20] Secs. 7, 8, above.

and I shall be converted to you" [Zech. 1:3]. For God's conversion there signifies not that by which he renews our hearts to repentance, but that by which he testifies through our material prosperity that he is kindly and well disposed toward us, just as by adverse circumstances he sometimes indicates his displeasure toward us. Since, therefore, the people, harassed by many sorts of miseries and calamities, complain that God is turned away from them, he replies that they will not lack his loving-kindness if they return to an upright life and to himself, who is the pattern of righteousness. Therefore they wrongly twist this passage when they infer from it that the work of conversion seems to be shared between God and men. We have touched this matter the more briefly because its proper place will be under the discussion of the law.[21]

10. The Biblical promises suppose (according to our opponents' view) the freedom of the will

ᵇThe second class of arguments is very closely related to the first. They cite the promises in which the Lord makes a covenant with our will. Such are: "Seek good and not evil, and you will live." [Amos 5:14 p.] "If you will and hearken, you will eat of the good things of the earth; but if you will not, . . . a sword will devour you, for the mouth of the Lord has spoken." [Isa. 1:19–20, Vg.] Again, "If you remove your abominations from my presence, you will not be cast out." [Jer. 4:1, cf. Comm.] "If you obey the voice of Jehovah your God, being careful to do all his commandments, . . . the Lord will set you high above all the nations of the earth" [Deut. 28:1, cf. Vg.]; and other like passages [Lev. 26:3 ff.].

These blessings which the Lord offers us in his promises they think to be referred to our will unsuitably and in mockery, unless it is in our power either to realize them or make them void. And it is quite easy to amplify this matter with such eloquent complaints as: "We are cruelly deluded by the Lord, when he declares that his loving-kindness depends upon our will, if the will itself is not under our control. This liberality of God would be remarkable if he so unfolded his blessings to us that we had no capacity to enjoy them! Wonderfully certain promises these—dependent upon an impossible thing, never to be fulfilled!"[22]

We shall speak elsewhere concerning such promises, which

---

21 II. vii. 8, 9.
22 Most of these passages and arguments had been used by opponents of Luther, including Schatzgeyer, Erasmus, Cochlaeus, De Castro, and Faber. For citations, see OS III. 308.

have a condition adjoined,[23] so that it will become clear that there is nothing absurd in the impossibility of their fulfillment. In so far as this point is concerned, I deny that God cruelly deludes us when, though knowing us to be utterly powerless, he invites us to merit his blessings. Now since promises are offered to believers and impious alike, they have their usefulness for both groups.

As God by his precepts pricks the consciences of the impious in order that they, oblivious to his judgments, may not too sweetly delight in their sins, so in his promises he in a sense calls them to witness how unworthy they are of his loving-kindness. For who would deny that it is entirely fair and fitting that the Lord bless those who honor him, but punish according to his severity those who despise his majesty? God therefore acts duly and in order when in his promises he lays down this law for the impious fettered by sin: only if they depart from wickedness will they at last receive his blessings, even for the simple purpose of having them understand that they are justly excluded from those blessings due the true worshipers of God.

On the other hand, since he strives in every way to spur believers to implore his grace, it will be not at all incongruous for him to attempt through his promises the same thing that, as we have shown, he has through his precepts already accomplished for their sake. When God by his precepts teaches us concerning his will, he apprizes us of our misery and how wholeheartedly we disagree with his will. At the same time he prompts us to call upon his Spirit to direct us into the right path. But because our sluggishness is not sufficiently aroused by precepts, promises are added in order, by a certain sweetness, to entice us to love the precepts. The greater our desire for righteousness, the more fervent we become to seek God's grace. That is how by these entreaties, "If you are willing," "If you hearken," the Lord neither attributes to us the free capacity to will or to hearken, nor yet does he mock us for our impotence.

11. The reproofs in Scripture, they further object, lose their meaning if the will be not free

ᵇThe third class of their arguments bears a close resemblance to the two preceding. For our opponents bring forward passages wherein God reproaches his ungrateful people that it was their own fault that they did not receive every sort of good thing from his tender mercy. Of this sort are the following passages: "Amalekites and Canaanites are before you, and you shall fall

[23] II. vii. 4; II. viii. 4; III. xvii. 1–3, 6, 7.

by their sword because you will not obey the Lord" [Num. 14:43, Vg.]. "Because . . . I called to you and you did not answer, I shall do to this house . . . as I did to Shiloh." [Jer. 7:13–14, Vg.] Again, "This . . . nation . . . did not obey the voice of the Lord their God, and did not accept discipline" [Jer. 7:28, Vg.]; for this reason it is rejected by the Lord [Jer. 7:29]. Again, Because you have hardened your heart and have not been willing to obey the Lord, all these evils have come upon you [cf. Jer. 19:15].

How, they say, could such reproaches apply against those who may at once reply: We cherished prosperity, we feared adversity. If we have not obeyed the Lord, nor heeded his voice, to obtain prosperity and avoid adversity, this came about because we were not free from bondage to the domination of sin. We are therefore without reason reproached for evils that it was not in our power to escape.

But disregarding the pretext of necessity, a weak and futile defense, I ask whether they can excuse the fault. For if they are held guilty of any fault, the Lord with reason reproaches them for not feeling, because of their perversity, the benefit of his kindness. Let them therefore answer whether they can deny that the cause of their obstinacy was their own perverse will. If they find the source of evil within themselves, why do they strain after external causes so as not to seem the authors of their own destruction? But if it is true that sinners are through their own fault both deprived of divine blessings and chastened by punishments, there is good reason why they should hearken to these reproaches from God's mouth. It is that if they obstinately persist in vices, they may learn in calamities to accuse and loathe their own worthlessness rather than to charge God with unjust cruelty; that if they have not cast off teachableness and if they are wearied with their own sins (because of which they see themselves miserable and lost), they may return to the path and acknowledge with earnest confession this very thing, namely, that the Lord reminds them by reproof.

What use the reproofs of the prophets serve among the godly is clear from the magnificent prayer of Daniel, given in the ninth chapter [Dan. 9:4–19]. We observe an example of the first use among the Jews, to whom God commanded Jeremiah to explain the cause of their miseries. Yet these things could not have happened in any other way than as the Lord had foretold: "You shall speak all these words to them, and they will not listen to you. You shall call to them, and they will not answer you" [Jer. 7:27, Vg.]. To what purpose then did they sing to the deaf? That even against their will they might understand what they were hearing to be true: that it is wicked sacrilege to transfer to God the blame for their own misfortunes, which lay in themselves.

The enemies of God's grace customarily pile up these innumerable proofs, derived from his commandments and from his protestations against the transgressors of the law, to give the delusion of free will. But by these few explanations you can very easily free yourself from them. ᵉIn a psalm the Jews are reproached as "a wicked generation . . . that kept not its heart straight" [Ps. 78:8; 77:8, Vg.]. Also, in another psalm, the prophet urges the men of his age not to "harden their hearts" [Ps. 95:8]. Surely this is because the blame for all stubbornness rests in the wickedness of men; but from this fact it is foolishly inferred that the heart, since the Lord has prepared it [cf. Prov. 16:1], can be bent alike to either side. The prophet says: "I have inclined my heart to perform thy statutes" [Ps. 119:112], namely, because he had pledged himself willingly and with cheerful attitude of mind to God. And yet he does not boast of himself as the author of his inclination, which he confesses in the same psalm to be the gift of God [Ps. 119:36]. We ought therefore to heed Paul's warning, when he bids believers, "Work out your own salvation with fear and trembling, for God is at work . . . , both to will and to accomplish" [Phil. 2:12–13 p.]. Indeed, he assigns tasks to them to do so that they may not indulge the sluggishness of the flesh. But enjoining fear and carefulness, he so humbles them that they remember what they are bidden to do is God's own work. By it he clearly intimates that believers act passively, so to speak, seeing that the capacity is supplied from heaven, that they may claim nothing at all for themselves. Then, while Peter urges us "to supplement our faith with virtue" [II Peter 1:5], he does not assign us secondary tasks as if we could do anything independently, but he is only arousing the indolence of the flesh, by which faith itself is very often choked. Paul's statement, "Do not quench the Spirit" [I Thess. 5:19], means the same thing, because sloth continually steals upon believers unless it be corrected. Yet if anyone should conclude from this that it is in their choice to nourish the light given them, such stupidity will be easily refuted, for this very earnestness which Paul enjoins comes from God alone [II Cor. 7:1].

We are in fact often bidden to purge ourselves of all filthiness, even though the Spirit claims for himself alone the office of sanctifying. In fine, it is clear from John's words that what belongs to God is transferred by concession to us: "Whoever is born of God keeps himself" [I John 5:18]. The proclaimers of free will seize upon this verse, as if we were preserved partly by God's power, partly by our own. As if we did not have from heaven this very preservation of which the apostle reminds us! Hence also Christ asks the Father to keep us from evil [John 17:15, cf. Vg.]. And we know that the pious, while they are fighting against Satan, attain victory by God's weapons alone [cf. Eph. 6:13 ff.]. For this reason, Peter, when he enjoined us to purify our souls in obedience to truth, soon added by way of correction "through the Spirit" [I Peter 1:22]. In short, John briefly shows how all human powers are of no avail in spiritual combat when he teaches that "they who are born of God cannot sin, for a seed of God abides in them" [I John 3:9 p.]. And in another passage he gives the reason: "This is the victory that overcomes the world, our faith" [I John 5:4].

(Answers to arguments based on special passages and incidents in Scripture, 12–19)

12. Deuteronomy 30:11 ff.

ᵇYet our opponents cite a passage from the law of Moses that seems to be strongly opposed to our explanation. For, after promulgating the law, Moses calls the people to witness in this manner: "For this commandment which I command you this day is not obscure, nor is it far off, nor is it in heaven. . . . But it is near you . . . in your mouth and in your heart, so that you can do it" [Deut. 30:11–12, 14 p.].[24]

Now if these words be understood as spoken concerning the bare precepts, I admit that they are of no slight importance for the present case. For even though it would be an easy matter to dodge the issue by contending that this has to do with man's capacity and disposition to understand the commandments, not with his ability to observe them, nevertheless perhaps some scruple would thus also remain. But the apostle, our sure interpreter, removes our every doubt when he declares that Moses here spoke of the teaching of the gospel [Rom. 10:8]. But suppose some obstinate person contends that Paul violently twisted these words to make them refer to the gospel. Although such a man's boldness will not be lacking in impiety, yet we have a means of refuting him apart from the apostle's authority. For if Moses was speaking of the precepts only, he inspired in the people the vainest confidence. For what else would they have done but dash into ruin, if they had set out to keep the law by their own strength, as if it were easy for them? Where is that ready capacity to keep the

---

24 Cited by Erasmus, *De libero arbitrio* (ed. von Walter, pp. 36 f.); Eck, *Enchiridion* (1541), fo. 185a; Herborn, *Locorum communium enchiridion* xxxviii (CC 12. 129).

law, when the only access to it lies over a fatal precipice? It is perfectly clear then that by these words Moses meant the covenant of mercy that he had promulgated along with the requirements of the law. ᶜFor a few verses before he had also taught that our hearts must needs be circumcised by God's hand for us to love him [Deut. 30:6]. He therefore lodged that ability, of which he immediately thereafter speaks, not in the power of man, but in the help and protection of the Holy Spirit, who mightily carries out his work in our weakness. Nevertheless, we are not to understand this passage as referring simply to the precepts, but rather to the promises of the gospel; and they, far from establishing in us the capacity to obtain righteousness, utterly destroy it.

ᵇPaul confirms this testimony that in the gospel salvation is not offered under that hard, harsh, and impossible condition laid down for us by the law—that only those who have fulfilled all the commandments will finally attain it—but under an easy, ready, and openly accessible condition. Therefore this Scripture [Rom., ch. 10] has no value in establishing the freedom of the human will.

13. God's "waiting" upon men's action is held to suppose freedom of the will

ᵇBy way of objection they commonly raise certain other passages, which show that God sometimes, having withdrawn the assistance of his grace, tries men and waits to see to what purpose they will turn their efforts. So Hosea says: "I shall go to my place, until they lay it upon their hearts to seek my face" [Hos. 5:15 p.]. It would be a ridiculous thing, they say, for the Lord to consider whether Israel would seek his face, if their minds were not capable of inclining either way through their own natural ability. As if it were not extremely common for God through his prophets to appear as one despising and rejecting his people until they should change their lives for the better! But what finally will our opponents deduce from such threats? If they mean that this people, forsaken by God, can of themselves set their minds on a conversion, they are doing so in the teeth of all Scripture. If they admit that God's grace is necessary for conversion, what quarrel do they have with us? Yet they concede grace to be necessary in such a way as to reserve to man his own ability.[25] On what basis do they prove it? Surely not from that passage or like passages. For it is one thing to withdraw from man, and to consider what he may do when left to his own devices. It is something else

---

[25] Herborn, *op. cit., loc. cit.; Acts of the Conference of Ratisbon, 1541* (in the document presented by the emperor) (CR V. 518).

to aid his powers, such as they are, in proportion to their weakness.

What, then, someone will ask, do these expressions signify? I reply that their significance is as if God were to say: "Inasmuch as warning, urging, and rebuking have no effect upon this stubborn people, I shall withdraw for a little while and quietly permit them to be afflicted. I shall see whether at any time after long calamities the remembrance of me lays hold on them so that they seek my face." The Lord's going far away signifies his withdrawal of prophecy from them. His considering what men then might do means that for a time he quietly and as it were secretly tries them with various afflictions. He does both to make us more humble. For we would sooner be beaten down by the lashes of adversity than be corrected, if he did not by his Spirit render us teachable. Now, when the Lord, offended and even wearied by our obstinate stubbornness, leaves us for a short time—that is, removes his Word, in which he habitually reveals something of his presence—and makes trial of what we might do in his absence, from this we falsely gather that we have some power of free will for him to observe and test. For he does it for no other purpose than to compel us to recognize our own nothingness.[26]

14. Are these works then not "our" works?

[b]They also argue from the manner of speaking customary both in the Scripture and in the words of men: good works are indeed called "ours"; and we are credited just as much with doing what is holy and pleasing to the Lord, as with committing sins. But if sins are rightly imputed to us as coming from ourselves, surely for the same reason some part in righteous acts ought to be assigned to us. And it would not be consonant with reason to say that we do those things which we are incapable of carrying out by our own effort and are moved like stones by God to do. Therefore, although we give the primary part to God's grace, yet those expressions indicate that our effort holds second place.

If our opponents simply urge that good works are called "ours," I will object in turn that the bread that we petition God to give us is also called "ours" [cf. Matt. 6:11]. What does the possessive pronoun "ours" signify to them but that what is otherwise by no means due us becomes ours by God's loving-kindness and free gift? Therefore they must either ridicule the same absurdity in the Lord's Prayer, or recognize that good works, in which we have nothing of our own save by God's bounty, are not foolishly called "ours."

[26] "οὐδενίαν"

Yet the second objection is a little stronger: Scripture often affirms that we ourselves worship God, preserve righteousness, obey the law, and are zealous in good works. Since these are the proper functions of the mind and will, how can one refer them to the Spirit and at the same time attribute them to ourselves, unless our zeal shares something of the divine power? We can easily dispose of these trifling objections if we duly reflect upon the way in which the Spirit of the Lord acts upon the saints.

That comparison which they spitefully throw at us does not apply. For who is such a fool as to assert that God moves man just as we throw a stone?[27] And nothing like this follows from our teaching. To man's natural faculties we refer the acts of approving and rejecting, willing and not willing, striving and resisting. That is, approving vanity and rejecting perfect good; willing evil and not willing good; striving toward wickedness and resisting righteousness. What does the Lord do in this? If he wills to utilize such depravity as the instrument of his wrath, he directs and disposes it as he pleases to carry out his good works through man's corrupt hand. Shall we then compare a wicked man, who thus serves God's might while he strives to obey only his own lust, to a stone set in motion by an outside force, and borne along by no motion, sensation, or will of its own? We see how great the difference is.

But what about good men, concerning whom there is particular question here? When the Lord establishes his Kingdom in them, he restrains their will by his Spirit that it may not according to its natural inclination be dragged to and fro by wandering lusts. That the will may be disposed to holiness and righteousness, He bends, shapes, forms, and directs, it to the rule of his righteousness. That it may not totter and fall, he steadies and strengthens it by the power of his Spirit. eIn this vein Augustine says: "You will say to me, 'Therefore we are acted upon and do not act ourselves.' Yes, you act and are acted upon. And if you are acted upon by one who is good, then you act well. The Spirit of God who acts upon you is the helper of those who act. The name 'helper' indicates that you also do something."[28] In the first part of the statement he indicates that man's action is not taken away by the movement of the Holy Spirit, because the will, which is directed to aspire to good, is of nature. But when he directly adds that from the word "help" it can be inferred that we also do something, we

[27] Cf. Cochlaeus, *De libero arbitrio* (1525) I, fo. B 1a; C 8b f.
[28] Augustine, *Sermons* clvi. 11. 11 (MPL 38. 855 f.; tr. LF *Sermons* II. 769). This is the passage referred to in the last sentence of this section. See also *On Rebuke and Grace* ii. 4 (MPL 44. 918; tr. NPNF V. 473).

must not so understand it as if something were to be attributed to each of us separately. But in order not to encourage indolence in us, he connects God's action with our own in these words: "To will is of nature, but to will aright is of grace."[29] Therefore he had said a little earlier, "Unless God helps, we shall be able neither to conquer nor even to fight."

*15. The "works" are ours by God's gift, but God's by his prompting**

ᵇHence it appears that God's grace, as this word is understood in discussing regeneration, is the rule of the Spirit to direct and regulate man's will. The Spirit cannot regulate without correcting, without reforming, without renewing. For this reason we say that the beginning of our regeneration is to wipe out what is ours. Likewise, he cannot carry out these functions without moving, acting, impelling, bearing, keeping. Hence we are right in saying that all the actions that arise from grace are wholly his. Meanwhile, we do not deny that what Augustine teaches is very true: "Grace does not destroy the will but rather restores it."[30] The two ideas are in substantial agreement: the will of man is said to be restored when, with its corruption and depravity corrected, it is directed to the true rule of righteousness. At the same time a new will is said to be created in man, because the natural will has become so vitiated and corrupted that he considers it necessary to put a new nature within.

Nothing now prevents us from saying that we ourselves are fitly doing what God's Spirit is doing in us, ᵉ⁽ᵇ⁾even if our will contributes nothing of itself distinct from his grace. ᵉTherefore we must keep in mind what we have elsewhere cited from Augustine:[31] in vain, people busy themselves with finding any good of man's own in his will. For any mixture of the power of free will that men strive to mingle with God's grace is nothing but a corruption of grace. It is just as if one were to dilute wine with muddy, bitter water. But even if there is something good in the will, it comes from the pure prompting of the Spirit. Yet because we are by nature endowed with will, we are with good reason said to do those things the praise for which God rightly claims for himself: ᵇfirst, because whatever God out of his loving-kindness does in us is ours, provided we understand that it is not of our

[29] Augustine, *Sermons* clvi. 9. 9; 11. 11–12 (MPL 38. 855 f.; tr. LF *Sermons* II. 769). Cf. Bernard, *Concerning Grace and Free Will* vi. 16 (MPL 182. 1010; tr. W. W. Williams, pp. 32 ff.).

[30] Augustine, *On Grace and Free Will* xx. 41 (MPL 44. 905; tr. NPNF V. 461).

[31] Cf. II. ii. 11 and the references in note 51, p. 269.

doing; secondly, because ours is the mind, ours the will, ours the striving, which he directs toward the good.

16. Genesis 4:7

ᵇThe other evidence that they rake together from here and there will not much bother even those of moderate understanding who have duly absorbed the refutations just given. Our opponents cite this statement from Genesis: "Its appetite will be under you, and you shall master it" [Gen. 4:7 p., cf. Vg.]. This they apply to sin, as if the Lord had promised Cain that the power of sin would not have the upper hand in his mind, if he willed to work toward conquering it![32] But we maintain that it is more in keeping with the order of the words that this verse should be applied to Abel. For there it is God's intention to reprove the wicked envy that Cain had conceived against his brother. God does this in two ways. First, Cain vainly planned a crime whereby he might excel his brother in the sight of God, before whom there is no honor except that of righteousness. Secondly, he was too ungrateful for the blessing that he had received of God, and could not bear his brother even though he was under his authority.

But lest we seem to espouse this interpretation because the other one is contrary to our view, well, let us concede to them that God was speaking here of sin. If this is so, then the Lord is either promising or commanding what he here declares. If he is commanding, we have already demonstrated that no proof of human capacity follows. If he is promising, where is the fulfillment of the promise when Cain yields to sin, which he ought to master? Will they say that there is a tacit condition included in the promise, as if it were said: "If you fight, you will achieve victory"? But who can stomach such evasions? For if this mastery refers to sin, no one can doubt that form of speech is imperative, defining not what we can do, but what we ought to do—even if it is beyond our power. ᵉHowever, both the matter itself and the principles of grammar require that Cain and Abel be compared, for the first-born brother would not have been subordinate to the younger had he not been worse through his own crime.

17. Romans 9:16; I Cor. 3:9

ᵇThey also use the testimony of the apostle: "So it depends not upon him who wills or upon him who runs but upon God who shows mercy" [Rom. 9:16]. From this they derive the notion that

[32] Herborn, op. cit., xxxviii (CC 12. 130); De Castro, Adversus omnes haereses IX (1543, fo. 123 E).

there is something in man's will and effort which, although feeble in itself, when aided by God's mercy does not fail to yield a favorable outcome.[33]

Now if they were soberly to weigh what matter Paul is discussing here, they would not misinterpret this statement so rashly. I know that they can cite Origen and Jerome in support of their exposition. ^dI could in turn oppose Augustine[34] to these. ^bBut what these hold makes no difference to us, provided we understand what Paul means. There he teaches that salvation has been prepared only for those whom the Lord deems worthy of his mercy, while ruin and death remain for all those whom He has not chosen. Paul had pointed out the destiny of the wicked by the example of Pharaoh [Rom. 9:17]. He had also confirmed by the testimony of Moses the certainty of free election: "I shall have mercy on whom I shall have mercy" [Rom. 9:15; Ex. 33:19]. He concludes, "It depends not upon him who wills or him who runs, but upon God who shows mercy." [Rom. 9:16.] But if it were understood in this way—that will and effort are not sufficient because they are unequal to such a load—what Paul said would have been inappropriate. Away then with these subtleties! It depends not upon him who wills or him who runs; therefore there is some will, there is some running.

Paul's meaning is simpler: it is not the will; it is not the running that prepares the way to salvation for us. Only the mercy of the Lord is here. Paul speaks in this very way to Titus when he writes: "When the goodness and loving-kindness of God . . . appeared . . . not because of deeds done by us in righteousness, but in virtue of his own infinite mercy" [Titus 3:4–5 p.]. Some persons prattle that Paul hinted there was some will and some running because he denied that "it depends on him who wills or upon him who runs" [Rom. 9:16 p.]. Yet not even they would grant me the right to reason along the same lines: that we do some good works, because Paul denies that we attain to God's goodness by virtue of the works that we have done. But if they detect a flaw in this argument, let them open their eyes and they will perceive that their own suffers from a like fallacy. ^dIt is a firm reason that Augustine relies on: "If therefore it were said that, 'It depends not upon him who wills or upon him who runs' [Rom. 9:16] because willing or running alone is not sufficient, then one can turn the argument around: that it does not depend upon God's mercy,

[33] Erasmus, *De libero arbitrio* (ed. von Walter), p. 49.
[34] Origen, *Commentary on Romans* vii. 16 (on Rom. 9:16) (MPG 14. 1145); Jerome, *Dialogue Against the Pelagians* I. 5 (MPL 23. 500 f.); Augustine, *Enchiridion* ix. 32 (MPL 40. 248; tr. LCC VII. 358 f.).

because it would not act alone." Since this second argument is absurd, Augustine rightly concludes: therefore this is said because man has no good will unless it be prepared by the Lord. Not that we ought not to will and to run; but because God accomplishes both in us.[35]

^eCertain persons just as ignorantly twist that saying of Paul's: "We are God's co-workers" [I Cor. 3:9].[36] This is without a doubt restricted to ministers alone. Moreover they are called "co-workers" not because they bring anything of themselves, but because God uses their work after he has rendered them capable of it and has furnished them with the necessary gifts.

18. Ecclesiasticus 15:14–17

^bThey bring forth Ecclesiasticus, a writer whose authority is known to be in doubt. Granting that we do not reject this author —although we have a perfect right to do so—what does Ecclesiasticus testify on behalf of free will? He says: "Immediately after man was created, God left him in the power of his own counsel. Commandments were given to him. If he kept the commandments, they would keep him as well. God has set . . . life and death, good and evil, . . . before man. And whichever he chooses will be given him" [Ecclus. 15:14, 15, 16, 17 p.; 15:14–18, Vg.].[37] Granted that man received at his creation the capacity to obtain life or death. What if we reply on the other side that he has lost this capacity? Surely it is not my intention to contradict Solomon, who declares "that God made man upright, but he has sought out many devices for himself" [Eccl. 7:29 p.]. But because man, in his degeneration, caused the shipwreck both of himself and of all his possessions, whatever is attributed to the original creation does not necessarily apply forthwith to his corrupt and degenerate nature. Therefore I am answering not only my opponents but also Ecclesiasticus himself, whoever he may be: If you wish to teach man to seek in himself the capacity to acquire salvation, we do not esteem your authority so highly that it may in the slightest degree raise any prejudice against the undoubted Word of God. But suppose you strive simply to repress the evil inclination of the flesh, which tries vainly to defend itself by transferring its vices to God, and for this reason you answer that uprightness

---

[35] Augustine, Letters ccxvii. 4. 12 (MPL 33. 983; tr. FC 32. 84).

[36] Eck, Enchiridion (1532) xxxi. L 5a; De Castro, Adversus omnes haereses IX (1543, fo. 124 D).

[37] Cited by Erasmus, with the remark that he does not know why Ecclesiasticus was excluded from the canon of Scripture; De libero arbitrio (ed. von Walter, p. 19).

was implanted in man that thereby it might be clear that he is the cause of his own ruin. I willingly assent to this, provided you and I agree that man has now been deprived through his own fault of those adornments with which the Lord in the beginning arrayed him. ᵉThus let us alike confess that man now needs a physician, not an advocate.

19. Luke 10:30

ᵇThey have nothing more constantly on their lips than Christ's parable of the traveler, whom thieves cast down half alive on the road [Luke 10:30]. I know that almost all writers commonly teach that the calamity of the human race is represented in the person of the traveler. From this our opponents take the argument that man is not so disfigured by the robbery of sin and the devil as not to retain some vestiges of his former good, inasmuch as he is said to have been left "half alive." For unless some portion of right reason and will remained, how could there be a "half life"?[38]

First, suppose I do not want to accept their allegory. What, pray, will they do? For no doubt the fathers devised this interpretation without regard to the true meaning of the Lord's words. Allegories[39] ought not to go beyond the limits set by the rule of Scripture, let alone suffice as the foundation for any doctrines. And I do not lack reasons, if I so please, to uproot this falsehood. The Word of God does not leave a "half life" to man, but it teaches that he has utterly died as far as the blessed life is concerned. Paul does not call the saints "half alive" when he speaks of our redemption, "Even when we were dead, . . . he made us alive" [Eph. 2:5]. He does not call upon the half alive to receive the illumination of Christ, but those who are asleep and buried [Eph. 5:14]. In the same way the Lord himself says, "The hour

[38] In the parable of the good Samaritan, the word ἡμιθανῆ, in English versions, "half dead," is rendered in the Vulgate, semivivus, "half alive." This word was allegorized in a semi-Pelagian sense in the fifth-century Pseudo-Augustine, Hypomnesticon III. viii. 11 f.: fallen man has remaining a liberum arbitrium vulneratum, a wounded free will (MPL 45. 1628 f.). Cf. Augustine, Questions on the Gospels ii. 19 (MPL 35. 240). In a variation on the allegories, the Venerable Bede says, "They left him half alive in that they despoiled him of the life immortal, but they were unable to destroy the sense of reason." In Lucae evangelium expositio III. x (MPL 92. 469). This passage was employed by opponents of Luther. Cf. Herborn, Locorum communium enchiridion xxxviii (CC 12. 129).

[39] For Calvin's repudiation of the allegorical method in the use of Scripture, see also III. iv. 4, 5 and his Comm. Gal. 4:22–26, where he requires "the natural and obvious meaning." Cf. also Comm. Gen. 2:8; Isa. 33:18; Jer. 31:24; Dan. 8: 20–25; 10:6.

has come when the dead rise again at his voice" [John 5:25 p.].
How shameless of them to oppose a slight allusion to so many
clear statements!

Yet, suppose this allegory of theirs serves as a sure testimony,
what can they nevertheless wrest from us? Man is half alive, they
say; therefore he has something safe. Of course he has a mind
capable of understanding, even if it may not penetrate to heavenly
and spiritual wisdom. He has some judgment of honesty. He has
some awareness of divinity, even though he may not attain a true
knowledge of God. But what do these qualities amount to? Surely
they cannot make out that we are to abandon Augustine's view,
approved by the common consent of the schools: the free goods
upon which salvation depends were taken away from man after
the Fall, while the natural endowments were corrupted and defiled.[40] Therefore let us hold this as an undoubted truth which no
siege engines can shake: the mind of man has been so completely
estranged from God's righteousness that it conceives, desires, and
undertakes, only that which is impious, perverted, foul, impure,
and infamous. The heart is so steeped in the poison of sin, that it
can breathe out nothing but a loathsome stench. But if some men
occasionally make a show of good, their minds nevertheless ever
remain enveloped in hypocrisy and deceitful craft, and their
hearts bound by inner perversity.

ᶜCHAPTER VI

FALLEN MAN OUGHT TO SEEK REDEMPTION[1] IN CHRIST

(*Through the Mediator, God is seen as a gracious Father, 1–2*)
1. Only the Mediator helps fallen man

ᶜThe whole human race perished in the person of Adam. Consequently that original excellence and nobility[2] which we have

---

[40] Cf. II. ii. 4, 12.

[1] This entire chapter and secs. 1 and 2 of ch. vii are completely new material in the 1559 edition. They clarify Calvin's new organization according
to the "twofold" knowledge (cf. I. ii. 1, notes 3, 4). In this chapter he enters for the first time on the knowledge of the Redeemer, the ostensible
theme of Book II. It is of decisive importance that soteriology is introduced, not by law, but by this radical *in Christo* passage, which brings
the law within the context of the promise of the gospel. Note especially
the titles of chs. vi, vii, and ix. The phrase "gospel and law," rather than
the more common "law and gospel," is appropriate to Calvin. Typical
of many sections added in 1559, the opening sentences are reminders of
the architectonics of the work and of the principal topics previously
treated. Cf. II. vii. 1, note 1.

[2] I. xv. 1–3, 8.

recounted would be of no profit to us but would rather redound to our greater shame, until God, who does not recognize as his handiwork men defiled and corrupted by sin, appeared as Redeemer in the person of his only-begotten Son. Therefore, since we have fallen from life into death, the whole knowledge of God the Creator that we have discussed[3] would be useless unless faith also followed, setting forth for us God our Father in Christ. The natural order was that the frame of the universe[4] should be the school in which we were to learn piety, and from it pass over to eternal life and perfect felicity. But after man's rebellion, our eyes—wherever they turn—encounter God's curse. This curse, while it seizes and envelops innocent creatures through our fault, must overwhelm our souls with despair. For even if God wills to manifest his fatherly favor to us in many ways, yet we cannot by contemplating the universe infer that he is Father.[5] Rather, conscience presses us within and shows in our sin just cause for his disowning us and not regarding or recognizing us as his sons. Dullness and ingratitude follow, for our minds, as they have been blinded, do not perceive what is true. And as all our senses have become perverted, we wickedly defraud God of his glory.

We must, for this reason, come to Paul's statement: "Since in the wisdom of God the world did not know God through wisdom, it pleased God through the folly of preaching to save those who believe" [I Cor. 1:21]. This magnificent theater[6] of heaven and earth, crammed with innumerable miracles, Paul calls the "wisdom of God." Contemplating it, we ought in wisdom to have known God. But because we have profited so little by it, he calls us to the faith of Christ, which, because it appears foolish, the unbelievers despise.

Therefore, although the preaching of the cross does not agree with our human inclination, if we desire to return to God our Author and Maker, from whom we have been estranged, in order that he may again begin to be our Father, we ought nevertheless to embrace it humbly. Surely, after the fall of the first man no knowledge of God apart from the Mediator[7] has had power unto salvation [cf. Rom. 1:16; I Cor. 1:24]. For Christ not only speaks of his own age, but comprehends all ages when he says: "This is eternal life, to know the Father to be the one true God, and Jesus Christ whom he has sent" [John 17:3 p.]. Thus, all the more vile

---

[3] Book I, *passim.*
[4] *"Mundi fabrica"*: cf. I. x. 1, note 2.
[5] Cf. II. vi. 4; II. ix. 1.
[6] Cf. I. v. 8; I. vi. 2; I. xiv. 20.
[7] Cf. next section and II. xii, xiv.

is the stupidity of those persons who open heaven to all the impious and unbelieving without the grace[8] of him whom Scripture commonly teaches to be the only door whereby we enter into salvation [John 10:9]. But if anyone would like to restrict this statement of Christ to the publishing of the gospel, there is a ready refutation: it was the common understanding of all ages and all nations that men who have become estranged from God [cf. Eph. 4:18] and have been declared accursed [cf. Gal. 3:10] and children of wrath [cf. Eph. 2:3] without reconciliation cannot please God.

Besides this, Christ answered the Samaritan woman: "You worship what you do not know; we worship what we know; for salvation is from the Jews" [John 4:22]. In these words he both condemns all pagan religions as false and gives the reason that under the law the Redeemer was promised to the chosen people alone. From this it follows that no worship has ever pleased God except that which looked to Christ. On this basis, also, Paul declares that all heathen were "without God and bereft of hope of life" [Eph. 2:12 p.]. Now since John teaches that life was in Christ from the beginning [John 1:4], and all the world fell away from it [cf. John 1:10], it is necessary to return to that source. So also, Christ, inasmuch as he is the propitiator, declares himself to be "life" [John 11:25; 14:6]. To be sure, the inheritance of heaven belongs only to the children of God [cf. Matt. 5:9–10]. Moreover, it is quite unfitting that those not engrafted into the body of the only-begotten Son are considered to have the place and rank of children. And John clearly declares: "Those who believe in his name become children of God" [John 1:12 p.]. But because it is not yet my purpose exhaustively to discuss faith in Christ, it will be sufficient to touch upon it in passing.

2. *Even the Old Covenant declared that there is no faith in the gracious God apart from the Mediator*
[e]Accordingly, apart from the Mediator, God never showed favor toward the ancient people, nor ever gave hope of grace to them. I pass over the sacrifices of the law, which plainly and openly

---

[8] Erasmus, *Colloquies*, "*Convivium religiosum*," which contains, with much praise of piety and virtue of the ancients, the well-known utterance, "*Sancte Socrates, ora pro nobis.*" Cf. Coelius Secundus Curio's *De amplitudine beati regni Dei* (1554) (Gouda, 1614) II. 136 ff., 147 ff., and Zwingli's *Exposition of the Faith* (1530), ch. xii. Zwingli lists certain virtuous pagans with Old Testament heroes and "the Virgin Mother of God" as among the companions of the faithful in the life to come: the pagan names are Theseus, Socrates, Aristides, Antigonus, Numa, Camillus, the Catos, and the Scipios (Zwingli, *Opera*, ed. M. Schuler and J. Schulthess, IV. 65; tr. LCC XXIV. 275). Calvin alludes adversely to these opinions.

taught believers to seek salvation nowhere else than in the atonement that Christ alone carries out. I am only saying that the blessed and happy state of the church always had its foundation in the person of Christ. For even if God included all of Abraham's offspring in his covenant [cf. Gen. 17:4], Paul nevertheless wisely reasons that Christ was properly that seed in whom all the nations were to be blessed [Gal. 3:14], since we know that not all who sprang from Abraham according to the flesh were reckoned among his offspring [Gal. 3:16]. For, to say nothing of Ishmael and others, how did it come about that of the two sons of Isaac, the twin brothers Esau and Jacob, while they were yet in their mother's womb, one was chosen, the other rejected [Rom. 9:11]? Indeed, how did it happen that the firstborn was set aside while the younger alone kept his status? How, also, did it come about that the majority was disinherited? It is therefore clear that Abraham's seed is to be accounted chiefly in one Head, and that the promised salvation was not realized until Christ appeared, whose task is to gather up what has been scattered. So, then, the original adoption of the chosen people depended upon the Mediator's grace. Even if in Moses' writings this was not yet expressed in clear words, still it sufficiently appears that it was commonly known to all the godly. For before a king had been established over the people, Hannah, the mother of Samuel, describing the happiness of the godly, already says in her song: "God will give strength to his king and exalt the horn of his Messiah" [I Sam. 2:10]. By these words she means that God will bless his church. To this corresponds the prophecy that is added a little later: "The priest whom I shall raise up . . . will walk in the presence of my Christ" [I Sam. 2:35, cf. Vg.]. And there is no doubt that our Heavenly Father willed that we perceive in David and his descendants the living image of Christ. Accordingly David, wishing to urge the pious to fear God, commands them to "kiss the Son" [Ps. 2:12, cf. RV and marg.]. To this corresponds the saying of the Gospel: "He who does not honor the Son does not honor the Father" [John 5:23]. Therefore, although the Kingdom collapsed because of the revolt of the ten tribes, yet the covenant that God made with David and his successors had to stand, just as he spoke through the prophets: "I will not tear away all the Kingdom . . . for the sake of David my servant and for the sake of Jerusalem which I have chosen . . . but to your son one tribe will remain" [I Kings 11:13, 32]. This same promise is repeated a second and a third time. It is expressly stated: "I will . . . afflict David's descendants, but not eternally" [I Kings 11:39]. Some time later it is said: "For the sake of David his servant, God gave him a lamp in

Jerusalem, to raise himself up a son and to protect Jerusalem" [I Kings 15:4, cf. Vg.]. Then, although affairs verged on ruin, it was again said: "The Lord was unwilling to destroy Judah, for the sake of David his servant, since he promised to give a lamp to him and to his sons forever" [II Kings 8:19].

To sum up: while all others were passed over, David alone was chosen, as he in whom God's good pleasure should rest, just as it is said elsewhere: "He rejected the tent of Shiloh, and the tent of Joseph; and he did not choose the tribe of Ephraim" [Ps. 78:60, 67, conflated], "but he chose the tribe of Judah, Mt. Zion, which he loved" [Ps. 78:68]. "He chose David his servant, . . . to shepherd Jacob his people, Israel his inheritance" [Ps. 78:70–71]. To conclude: God thus willed to preserve his church that its soundness and safety might depend upon that Head. Therefore David proclaims: "Jehovah is the strength of his people, the saving power of his Christ [Ps. 28:8, cf. RV marg.]. Immediately he adds the petition: "Save thy people, and bless thine inheritance" [Ps. 28:9], meaning that the condition of the church is joined by an indissoluble bond to Christ's authority. Another passage expresses the same idea: "Save us, O Jehovah; let the King hear us in the day that we shall call upon him" [Ps. 29:9].[9] By these words he clearly teaches that believers have sought refuge in God's help with no other assurance than that they were sheltered under the King's protection. This is implied in another psalm: "Save, . . . O Jehovah! . . . Blessed be he who comes in the name of Jehovah" [Ps. 118:25–26]. There, it is sufficiently clear, believers are being called back to Christ, that they may hope to be saved by God's hand. Another petition expresses the same idea, where the whole church implores God's mercy: "Let thy hand be upon the man of thy right hand, upon the son of man whom thou hast preserved (or fashioned) for thyself" [Ps. 80:17, Comm.]. For although the author of the psalm bewails the scattering of the whole people, yet he begs for their restoration in the Head alone. But when, after the people have been carried off into exile, the land laid waste, and everything seemingly destroyed, Jeremiah sorrows for the calamity of the church, he especially bewails the fact that in the ruin of the Kingdom hope has been cut off from believers. "The anointed," he says, "the breath of our mouths, has been taken captive in our sins, he to whom we said, 'Under thy shadow we shall live among the heathen.'" [Lam. 4:20, cf. Vg.] From this it is now clear enough that, since God cannot without the Mediator be propitious toward the human race, under the law Christ

[9] Comm. Ps. 20:10.

was always set before the holy fathers as the end to which they should direct their faith.

(Christ essential to the covenant and to true faith, 3–4)

3. *The faith and hope of the Old Covenant fed upon the promise*

ᵉNow, where solace is promised in affliction, especially where the deliverance of the church is described, the banner of trust and hope in Christ himself is prefigured. "God went forth for the salvation of his people with his Messiah," says Habakkuk. [Hab. 3:13 p.] And as often as the prophets mention the restoration of the church, they recall the people to the promise made to David that his kingdom would be everlasting [cf. II Kings 8:19]. And no wonder, for otherwise there would have been no stability in the covenant! To this, Isaiah's reply is especially pertinent. For inasmuch as he saw that the unbelieving King Ahaz rejected his testimony concerning the lifting of the siege of Jerusalem and its immediate safety, he rather abruptly passes on to the Messiah: "Behold, a virgin shall conceive and bear a son" [Isa. 7:14]. By this he indirectly indicates that although king and people wickedly rejected the promise offered them, as if they were purposely trying to discredit God's pledge, yet the covenant would not be invalidated, for the Redeemer would come at his appointed time.

In short, to show God merciful, all the prophets were constantly at pains to proclaim that kingdom of David upon which both redemption and eternal salvation depended. Thus Isaiah says: "I will make with you a . . . covenant, my steadfast mercies for David. Behold, I made him a witness to the peoples" [Isa. 55:3–4]. That is, under such adverse conditions believers could have no hope except when this witness was put forward that God would be compassionate to them. In the same way to lift up the despairing, Jeremiah says: "Behold, the days are coming when I will raise up for David a righteous Branch . . . and then Judah will be saved, and Israel will dwell securely" [Jer. 23:5–6]. Ezekiel, moreover, says: "I will set over my sheep one shepherd, . . . namely, my servant David. . . . I, Jehovah, will be their God, and my servant David shall be shepherd . . . and I will make with them a covenant of peace." [Ezek. 34:23–25 p.] Elsewhere, likewise, after discussing this incredible renewal, he says: "David, my servant, shall be their king, and shall be the one shepherd over all, . . . and I will make an everlasting covenant of peace with them." [Ezek. 37:24, 26 p.]

Here I am gathering a few passages of many because I merely want to remind my readers that the hope of all the godly has ever reposed in Christ alone. All the other prophets also agree. For example, in Hosea it is said: "And the children of Judah and the children of Israel shall be gathered together, and they shall appoint for themselves one head" [Hos. 1:11]. This he afterward explains more clearly: "The children of Israel shall return and seek Jehovah their God, and David their king" [Hos. 3:5]. Micah, also, referring to the people's return, clearly expresses it: "Their king will pass on before them, Jehovah at their head" [Micah 2:13]. So, too, Amos—meaning to foretell the renewal of the people—says: "In that day I will raise up the tent of David that is fallen, and repair its breaches, and raise up its ruins" [Amos 9:11]. This signifies: "I will raise up once more the royal glory in the family of David, the sole standard of salvation, now fulfilled in Christ." Hence, Zechariah, as his era was closer to the manifestation of Christ, more openly proclaims: "Rejoice, daughter of Zion! Be jubilant, daughter of Jerusalem! Lo, your king comes to you; righteous and unharmed is he" [Zech. 9:9, cf. Comm.]. This agrees with the verse of the psalm already quoted: "Jehovah is . . . the saving power of his Christ. Save, . . . O Jehovah" [Ps. 28:8–9, cf. RV marg.]. Here salvation flows from the Head to the whole body.

4. Faith in God is faith in Christ

ᵉGod willed that the Jews should be so instructed by these prophecies that they might turn their eyes directly to Christ in order to seek deliverance. Even though they had shamefully degenerated, they still could not efface the memory of that general principle: that, as had been promised to David, God would be through the hand of Christ the deliverer of the church; and that his freely given covenant, whereby God had adopted his elect, would stand fast. From this it came about that when Christ entered Jerusalem a little before his death this song was on the children's lips: "Hosanna to the son of David" [Matt. 21:9]. The hymn sung by the children apparently was commonly and widely known, and in accordance with the general notion that the sole pledge of God's mercy rested upon the coming of the Redeemer. For this reason Christ himself bade his disciples believe in him, that they might clearly and perfectly believe in God: "You believe in God; believe also in me" [John 14:1]. For even if, properly speaking, faith mounts up from Christ to the Father, yet he means this: although faith rests in God, it will gradually disappear unless he who retains it in perfect firmness intercedes as Mediator. Otherwise, God's majesty is too lofty to be attained by mortal men, who are like grubs crawling upon the earth.

For this reason I subscribe to the common saying that God

is the object of faith,[10] yet it requires qualification. For Christ is not without reason called "the image of the invisible God" [Col. 1:15]. This title warns us that, unless God confronts us in Christ, we cannot come to know that we are saved. Among the Jews the scribes obscured with false glosses what the prophets had taught concerning the Redeemer. Yet in spite of this, Christ took to be commonly known, as if received by general agreement, that there is no other remedy for a hopeless condition, no other way of freeing the church, than the appearance of the Mediator. Indeed, Paul's teaching was not commonly known—as it ought to have been—that "Christ is the end of the law" [Rom. 10:4].[11] Yet this is true and certain, as is perfectly clear from the Law itself and the Prophets. I am not yet discussing faith because there will be a more suitable place for it elsewhere.[12] Only let the readers agree on this point: let the first step toward godliness be to recognize that God is our Father to watch over us, govern and nourish us, until he gather us unto the eternal inheritance of his Kingdom. Hence, what we have recently said becomes clear,[13] that apart from Christ the saving knowledge of God does not stand. From the beginning of the world he had consequently been set before all the elect that they should look unto him and put their trust in him.

In this sense Irenaeus writes that the Father, himself infinite, becomes finite in the Son, for he has accommodated himself to our little measure lest our minds be overwhelmed by the immensity of his glory.[14] Fanatics, not reflecting upon this, twist a useful statement into an impious fantasy, as if there were in Christ only a portion of divinity, outflowing from the whole perfection of God.[15] Actually, it means nothing else than that God is comprehended in Christ alone. John's saying has always been true: "He that does not have the Son does not have the Father" [I John 2:23 p.]. For even if many men once boasted that they worshiped the Supreme Majesty, the Maker of heaven and earth, yet because they had no Mediator it was not possible for them truly to taste God's mercy, and thus be persuaded that he was their Father.

---

[10] Cf. III. ii. 1–7.

[11] Cf. II. vii. 2; II. viii. 7. The sense in which "Christ is the end of the law" (Rom. 10:4) appears in I. vi. 2; II. vii. 2; III. ii. 6: the Law and the Prophets partially anticipated Christ's work of reconciliation. Cf. Comm. Rom. 10:4: "The law in all its parts has a reference to Christ."

[12] III. ii.

[13] II. vi. 1.

[14] Irenaeus, *Adversus haereses* IV. iv. 2 (MPG 7. 982; tr. ANF I. 466).

[15] Gentile uses passages of Irenaeus to support his view that the Father is the *"essentiator"* of the Son (CR IX. 395). Cf. I. xiii. 23, note 51.

Accordingly, because they did not hold Christ as their Head, they possessed only a fleeting knowledge of God. From this it also came about that they at last lapsed into crass and foul superstitions and betrayed their own ignorance. So today the Turks, although they proclaim at the top of their lungs that the Creator of heaven and earth is God, still, while repudiating Christ, substitute an idol in place of the true God.

^eCHAPTER VII

THE LAW WAS GIVEN,[1] NOT TO RESTRAIN THE FOLK OF THE OLD COVENANT UNDER ITSELF, BUT TO FOSTER HOPE OF SALVATION IN CHRIST UNTIL HIS COMING

(The moral and ceremonial law significant as leading to Christ, 1–2)

1. The Mediator helps only fallen man

^eThe law was added about four hundred years after the death of Abraham [cf. Gal. 3:17]. From that continuing succession of witnesses which we have reviewed it may be gathered that this was not done to lead the chosen people away from Christ; but rather to hold their minds in readiness until his coming; even to kindle desire for him, and to strengthen their expectation, in order that they might not grow faint by too long delay. I understand by the word "law" not only the Ten Commandments, which set forth a godly and righteous rule of living, but the form of religion handed down by God through Moses. And Moses was not made a lawgiver to wipe out the blessing promised to the race of Abraham. Rather, we see him repeatedly reminding the Jews of that freely given covenant made with their fathers of which they were the heirs. It was as if he were sent to renew it.

---

[1] The term "law" for Calvin may mean (1) the whole religion of Moses (II. vii. 1); (2) the special revelation of the moral law to the chosen people, i.e., chiefly the Decalogue and Jesus' summary (II. viii); or (3) various bodies of civil, judicial, and ceremonial statutes (IV. xx. 14–16; Comm. *Harmony Four Books of Moses;* cf. Decalogue "supplements"). Of these, the moral law, the "true and eternal rule of righteousness" (IV. xx. 15), is most important. It appears in three contexts shown in the three "uses," below, paragraphs 6–15. For Calvin a positive evaluation of the law allows the "third use" to be the principal one, while for Luther the condemning function is the chief one: cf. Luther, Comm. Gal. 3:19. Calvin regards the condemning function as "accidental" to its true purpose: Comm. II Cor. 3:7; Comm. Rom. 7:10–11. Calvin habitually asserts that the law has validity only as it is related to Christ. Cf. Comm. John 5:38; Acts 13:39; Rom. 10:5; *Sermons on Galatians* xxvi (CR L. 603); and Benoit's note in *Institution* II. 15.

This fact was very clearly revealed in the ceremonies. For what is more vain or absurd than for men to offer a loathsome stench from the fat of cattle in order to reconcile themselves to God? Or to have recourse to the sprinkling of water and blood to cleanse away their filth? In short, the whole cultus of the law, taken literally and not as shadows and figures corresponding to the truth, will be utterly ridiculous. Therefore, with good reason, both in Stephen's speech [Acts 7:44] and in The Letter to the Hebrews [Heb. 8:5] very careful consideration is given to that passage where God orders Moses to make everything pertaining to the Tabernacle in accordance with the pattern shown to him on the mountain [Ex. 25:40]. For if something spiritual had not been set forth to which they were to direct their course, the Jews would have frittered away their effort in those matters, just as the Gentiles did in their trifles. Irreligious men, who have never exerted themselves in zeal for piety, cannot bear to hear about such complicated rites without aversion. Not only do they wonder why God wearied the ancient people with such a mass of ceremonies, but they also despise these and ridicule them as child's play. That is, they do not pay attention to the purpose of the law; if the forms of the law be separated from its end, one must condemn it as vanity.

Yet that very type[2] shows that God did not command sacrifices in order to busy his worshipers with earthly exercises. Rather, he did so that he might lift their minds higher. This also can be clearly discerned from his own nature: for, as it is spiritual, only spiritual worship delights him. Many statements of the prophets attest to this and charge the Jews with stupidity; for they think some sacrifice or other has value in God's sight. Is that because they intend to detract something from the law? Not at all. But, since they were true interpreters of it, they desired in this way to direct men's eyes to the objective from which the common people were straying. Now from the grace offered the Jews we can surely deduce that the law was not devoid of reference to Christ. For Moses proposed to them as the purpose of adoption, that they should be a priestly kingdom unto God [Ex. 19:6]. This they could not have attained if a greater and more excellent

---

[2] *"Typus ille."* The word *typus* has for its basic meaning a representative figure, or image, on a wall. In general, it is a mark or sign to indicate something not present. For Calvin, the ceremonies enjoined in the law were "types," or "foreshadowings," of the full and clear revelation of the gospel in which the ceremonies cease. Cf. II. vii. 16; II. viii. 28; II. ix. 3, 4: II. xi. 2–6; III. xx. 18. This typology became a more or less constant feature of Reformed theology. See Heppe RD, p. 403; Westminster Confession VII. 5.

reconciliation than that procured by the blood of beasts had not intervened [cf. Heb. 9:12 ff.]. Because of hereditary taint, all of Adam's children are born in bondage to sin. What, then, is less fitting than for them to be elevated to royal dignity, and in this way to become partners in God's glory, unless such pre-eminent good come to them from some other quarter? Also, how could the right of priesthood thrive among them, abominable as they were to God in the filth of their vices, were they not consecrated in the sacred Head? For this reason, Peter neatly turns that saying of Moses', teaching that the fullness of grace that the Jews had tasted under the law has been shown forth in Christ: "You are a chosen race," he says, "a royal priesthood" [I Peter 2:9]. In inverting the words, he means that those to whom Christ has appeared through the gospel have obtained more than their fathers did. For all have been endowed with priestly and kingly honor, so that, trusting in their Mediator, they may freely dare to come forth into God's presence.

2. The law contains a promise

ᵉWe must here note in passing that the kingdom finally established within the family of David is a part of the law, and contained under the administration of Moses. From this it follows that both among the whole tribe of Levi and among the posterity of David, Christ was set before the eyes of the ancient folk as in a double mirror. For, as I have just said, men enslaved by sin and death and polluted by their own corruption could not otherwise have been kings and priests before God. Hence, Paul's statement appears to be very true: that the Jews were kept under the charge of a "tutor" [Gal. 3:24] until the seed should come for whose sake the promise had been given. For, since they had not yet come to know Christ intimately, they were like children[3] whose weakness could not yet bear the full knowledge of heavenly things. How these ceremonies guided them to Christ has been stated above. This can be better understood from the many testimonies of the prophets. For even though they had to come forward daily with new sacrifices to appease God, yet Isaiah promises that all their evil deeds will be atoned for by a single sacrifice [Isa. 53:5]. Daniel agrees with this [Dan. 9:26-27]. Priests designated from the tribe of Levi customarily entered the sanctuary. But of only

[3] "Similes fuerunt pueris." Cf. the reference to Gal. 3:24, just preceding. Allied with his typology is Calvin's oft-repeated idea of the childlike stage of development of the ancient Hebrew people, a condition that rendered necessary the accommodation of revelation to an elementary mentality in the Old Testament. Cf. I. xi. 3; II. xi. 2; Comm. Gen. 1:16; 2:8.

one priest it was once said that he was divinely chosen with a solemn oath to be "a priest forever after the order of Melchizedek" [Ps. 110:4; cf. Heb. 5:6; 7:21]. There was then an anointing with visible oil; in a vision Daniel proclaimed that there would be another sort of anointing [Dan. 9:24]. Not to dwell upon too many examples, the author of The Letter to the Hebrews points out fully and clearly in chs. 4 to 11 that the ceremonies are worthless and empty until the time of Christ is reached.

With regard to the Ten Commandments we ought likewise to heed Paul's warning: "Christ is the end of the law unto salvation to every believer" [Rom. 10:4 p.]. Another: Christ is the Spirit [II Cor. 3:17] who quickens the letter that of itself is death-dealing [II Cor. 3:6]. By the former statement he means that righteousness is taught in vain by the commandments until Christ confers it by free imputation and by the Spirit of regeneration. For this reason, Paul justly calls Christ the fulfillment or end of the law. For it would be of no value to know what God demands of us if Christ did not succor those laboring and oppressed under its intolerable yoke and burden. Elsewhere he teaches that "the law was put forward because of transgressions" [Gal. 3:19]; that is, in order to humble men, having convinced them of their own condemnation. But because this is the true and only preparation for seeking Christ, all his variously expressed teachings well agree. He was disputing with perverse teachers who pretended that we merit righteousness by the works of the law. Consequently, to refute their error he was sometimes compelled to take the bare law in a narrow sense, even though it was otherwise graced with the covenant of free adoption.

(We cannot fulfill the moral law, 3–5)
3. The law renders us inexcusable and drives us into despair
ᵉBut, in order that our guilt may arouse us to seek pardon, it behooves us, briefly, to know how by our instruction in the moral law we are rendered more inexcusable. ᵇIf it is true that in the law we are taught the perfection of righteousness, this also follows: the complete observance of the law is perfect righteousness before God. By it man would evidently be deemed and reckoned righteous before the heavenly judgment seat. Therefore Moses, after he had published the law, did not hesitate to call heaven and earth to witness that he had "set before Israel life and death, good and evil" [Deut. 30:19 p.]. We cannot gainsay that the reward of eternal salvation awaits complete obedience to the law, as the Lord has promised. On the other hand, it behooves us to examine whether we fulfill that obedience, through whose merit

we ought to derive assurance of that reward. What point is there to see in the observance of the law the proffered reward of eternal life if, furthermore, it is not clear whether by this path we may attain eternal life.

At this point the feebleness of the law shows itself. Because observance of the law is found in none of us, we are excluded from the promises of life, and fall back into the mere curse. I am telling not only what happens but what must happen. For since the teaching of the law is far above human capacity, a man may indeed view from afar the proffered promises, yet he cannot derive any benefit from them. Therefore this thing alone remains: that from the goodness of the promises he should the better judge his own misery, while with the hope of salvation cut off he thinks himself threatened with certain death. On the other hand, horrible threats hang over us, constraining and entangling not a few of us only, but all of us to a man. They hang over us, I say, and pursue us with inexorable harshness, so that we discern in the law only the most immediate death.

4. *Nevertheless the promises in the law are not without meaning*
ᵃTherefore if we look only upon the law, we can only be despondent, confused, and despairing in mind, since from it all of us are condemned and accursed [Gal. 3:10]. ᵇAnd it holds us far away from the blessedness that it promises to its keepers. Is the Lord, you will ask, mocking us in this way? How little different from mockery is it to show forth the hope of happiness, to invite and attract us to it, to assure us that it is available, when all the while it is shut off and inaccessible? I reply: even if the promises of the law, in so far as they are conditional, depend upon perfect obedience to the law—which can nowhere be found —they have not been given in vain. For when we have learned that they will be fruitless and ineffectual for us unless God, out of his free goodness, shall receive us without looking at our works, and we in faith embrace that same goodness held forth to us by the gospel, the promises do not lack effectiveness even with the condition attached. For the Lord then freely bestows all things upon us so as to add to the full measure of his kindness this gift also: that not rejecting our imperfect obedience, but rather supplying what is lacking to complete it, he causes us to receive the benefit of the promises of the law as if we had fulfilled their condition. But since we will have to discuss this question more fully under the heading of justification by faith,⁴ we will not pursue it farther for the present.

⁴ III. xi. 1–7.

5. *The fulfillment of the law is impossible for us*

[b]We have said that the observance of the law is impossible. Since this is commonly looked upon as a very absurd opinion—Jerome does not hesitate to anathematize it[5]—we ought at once to explain and confirm it in a few words. I do not tarry over what Jerome thinks; let us rather inquire what is true. Here I shall not weave long circumlocutions of various kinds of possibilities. I call "impossible" what has never been, and what God's ordination and decree prevents from ever being. If we search the remotest past, I say that none of the saints, clad in the body of death [cf. Rom. 7:24], has attained to that goal of love so as to love God "with all his heart, all his mind, all his soul, and all his might" [Mark 12:30, and parallels]. I say furthermore, there was no one who was not plagued with concupiscence. Who will contradict this? Indeed, I see what sort of saints we imagine in our foolish superstition; the heavenly angels can scarcely compare with them in purity! But this goes against both Scripture and the evidence of experience. I further say that there will be no one hereafter who will reach the goal of true perfection without sloughing off the weight of the body.

For this point there are enough manifest testimonies of Scripture. "There is no righteous man upon the earth who . . . does not sin," said Solomon [Eccl. 7:21, Vg.; cf. I Kings 8:46 p.]. Moreover, David says: "Every man living will be unrighteous before thee" [Ps. 143:2]. Job affirms the same idea in many passages [cf. Job 9:2; 25:4]. Paul expresses it most clearly of all: "The flesh lusts against the Spirit, and the Spirit lusts against the flesh" [Gal. 5:17]. [b(a)]That all those under the law are accursed he proves by no other reason, [b]except that "it is written, 'Cursed be every one who will not abide by all things written in the book of the law'" [Gal. 3:10; Deut. 27:26]. Here he is obviously intimating, in fact assuming, that no one can so abide. But whatever has been declared in Scripture it is fitting to take as perpetual, even as necessary. The Pelagians plagued Augustine with such subtleties as these. [e]They claimed that it was doing an injustice to God to assume that he demanded more of believers than they were able to carry out through his grace. [b]He, to escape their slander, admitted that the Lord could indeed, if he so willed, elevate mortal man to angelic purity; but that he had never done, nor ever would do, anything contrary to what he had declared in the Scriptures.[6]

[5] Jerome, *Dialogue Against the Pelagians* I. 10; III. 3 (MPL 23. 525, 599).
[6] Augustine, *On Man's Perfection in Righteousness* iii. 8 (MPL 44. 295; tr. NPNF V. 161; *On the Spirit and the Letter* xxxvi. 66 (MPL 44. 245 f.; tr. NPNF V. 113 f.). On the argument of this section, cf. Comm. Gal. 5:17.

And I do not deny this, but yet add that it is ill-advised to pit God's might against his truth. Therefore, if someone says that what the Scriptures declare will not be, cannot be, such a statement is not to be scoffed at. But suppose they dispute about the Word itself. The Lord, when his disciples asked, "Who can be saved?" [Matt. 19:25], replied: "With men this is indeed impossible, but with God all things are possible" [Matt. 19:26]. Also, Augustine compellingly contends that in this flesh we never render to God the love we lawfully owe him. He says: "Love so follows knowledge that no one can love God perfectly who does not first fully know his goodness. While we wander upon the earth, 'we see in a mirror dimly' [I Cor. 13:12]. Therefore, it follows that our love is imperfect."[7] Let us be quite agreed, then, that the law cannot be fulfilled in this life of the flesh, if we observe the weakness of our own nature; as will, moreover, be shown from another passage of Paul [Rom. 8:3].[8]

(*The law shows the righteousness of God, and as a mirror discloses our sinfulness, leading us to implore divine help, 6–9*)
6. *The severity of the law takes away from us all self-deception*
[b(a)]But to make the whole matter clearer, let us survey briefly the function and use of what is called the "moral law."[9] Now, so far as I understand it, it consists of three parts.[10]

The first part is this: while it shows God's righteousness, that is, the righteousness alone acceptable to God, it warns, informs, convicts, and lastly condemns, every man of his own unrighteousness. For man, blinded and drunk with self-love, must be compelled to know and to confess his own feebleness and impurity.

[7] An approximation to Augustine's language in *On the Spirit and the Letter* xxxvi. 64 f. (MPL 44. 242 ff.; tr. NPNF V. 112 f.) and in *On Man's Perfection in Righteousness* viii. 17 ff. (MPL 44. 299 ff.; tr. NPNF V. 164 f.).
[8] II. xii. 4; III. iv. 27; III. xi. 23.
[9] "*Officium usumque legis.*" The "uses of the law," which in all preceding editions follow the exposition of the Decalogue, here precede it in a manner appropriate to the covenant setting, and especially to the law's "principal" use (sec. 12, below), which is that of positive guidance to the Christian. Cf. Luther's two uses in his Commentary on Galatians 3:19; 4:3 (tr. E. Middleton, pp. 281 ff., 324 f.).
[10] Melanchthon, in *Loci communes* (1521), holds that it is the proper purpose of the law to make sin manifest and confound the conscience. In the 1535 and later editions, he introduces the three uses of the law here expounded by Calvin. *Loci communes* (1521), ed. H. Engelland, in the series *Melanchthons Werke in Auswahl,* ed. R. Stupperich, II. i. 122; tr. C. L. Hill, *op. cit.,* p. 215; *Loci praecipui theologici* (1559), ed. Engelland, *op. cit.,* pp. 321–326, and note 13 on p. 321. Here emphasis is placed upon the second use, which is developed from Rom. 1:18. In the Formula of Concord, the third use is given due recognition (art. vi).

If man is not clearly convinced of his own vanity, he is puffed up with insane confidence in his own mental powers, ᵇand can never be induced to recognize their slenderness as long as he measures them by a measure of his own choice. But as soon as he begins to compare his powers with the difficulty of the law, he has something to diminish his bravado. For, however remarkable an opinion of his powers he formerly held, he soon feels that they are panting under so heavy a weight as to stagger and totter, and finally even to fall down and faint away. Thus man, schooled in the law, sloughs off the arrogance that previously blinded him.

Likewise, he needs to be cured of another disease, that of pride, with which we have said that he is sick. So long as he is permitted to stand upon his own judgment, he passes off hypocrisy as righteousness; pleased with this, he is aroused against God's grace by I know not what counterfeit acts of righteousness. But after he is compelled to weigh his life in the scales of the law, laying aside all that presumption of fictitious righteousness, he discovers that he is a long way from holiness, and is in fact teeming with a multitude of vices, with which he previously thought himself undefiled. So deep and tortuous are the recesses in which the evils of covetousness lurk that they easily deceive man's sight. The apostle has good reason to say: "I should not have known covetousness, if the law had not said, 'You shall not covet' " [Rom. 7:7]. For if by the law covetousness is not dragged from its lair, it destroys wretched man so secretly that he does not even feel its fatal stab.

7. *The punitive function of the law does not diminish its worth*

ᵇ⁽ᵃ⁾The law is like a mirror. In it we contemplate our weakness, then the iniquity arising from this, and finally the curse coming from both—just as a mirror shows us the spots on our face. ᵇFor when the capacity to follow righteousness fails him, man must be mired in sins. After the sin forthwith comes the curse. Accordingly, the greater the transgression of which the law holds us guilty, the graver the judgment to which it makes us answerable. The apostle's statement is relevant here: "Through the law comes knowledge of sin" [Rom. 3:20]. There he notes only its first function, which sinners as yet unregenerate experience. Related to this are these statements: "Law slipped in, to increase the trespass" [Rom. 5:20], and thus it is "the dispensation of death" [II Cor. 3:7] that "brings wrath" [Rom. 4:15], and slays. There is no doubt that the more clearly the conscience is struck with awareness of its sin, the more the iniquity grows. For stubborn disobedience against the Lawgiver is then added to transgression. It remains, then, to the law to arm God's wrath for the sinner's downfall, for of itself the law can only accuse, condemn, and destroy. As Augustine writes: "If the Spirit of grace is absent, the law is present only to accuse and kill us."[11]

But when we say that, we neither dishonor the law, nor detract at all from its excellence. Surely if our will were completely conformed and composed to obedience to the law, its knowledge alone would suffice to gain salvation. Yet, since our carnal and corrupted nature contends violently against God's spiritual law and is in no way corrected by its discipline, it follows that the law which had been given for salvation, provided it met with suitable hearers, turns into an occasion for sin and death.[12] For, since all of us are proved to be transgressors, the more clearly it reveals God's righteousness, conversely the more it uncovers our iniquity. The more surely it confirms the reward of life and salvation as dependent upon righteousness, the more certain it renders the destruction of the wicked.

These maxims—far from abusing the law—are of the greatest value in more clearly commending God's beneficence. Thus it is clear that by our wickedness and depravity we are prevented from enjoying the blessed life set openly before us by the law. Thereby the grace of God, which nourishes us without the support of the law, becomes sweeter, and his mercy, which bestows that grace upon us, becomes more lovely. From this we learn that he never tires in repeatedly benefiting us and in heaping new gifts upon us.

8. The punitive function of the law in its work upon believers and unbelievers

ᵇThe wickedness and condemnation of us all are sealed by the testimony of the law. Yet this is not done to cause us to fall down in despair or, completely discouraged, to rush headlong over the brink—provided we duly profit by the testimony of the law. It is true that in this way the wicked are terrified, but because of their obstinacy of heart. For the children of God the knowledge of the law should have another purpose. The apostle testifies that we are indeed condemned by the judgment of the law, "so that every mouth may be stopped, and the whole world may be held accountable to God" [Rom. 3:19]. He teaches the same idea in yet another place: "For God has shut up all men in unbelief," not that he may destroy all or suffer all to perish, but "that he may have mercy upon all" [Rom. 11:32]. This means

---

[11] Augustine. *On Rebuke and Grace* i. 2 (MPL 44. 917; tr. NPNF V. 472).
[12] Ambrose, *De Jacobo et vita beata* I. vi. 21 f. (MPL 14. 637).

that, ᵃdismissing the stupid opinion of their own strength, they come to realize that they stand and are upheld by God's hand alone; that, naked and empty-handed, they flee to his mercy, repose entirely in it, hide deep within it, and seize upon it alone for righteousness and merit. For God's mercy is revealed in Christ to all who seek and wait upon it with true faith. ᵇIn the precepts of the law, God is but the rewarder of perfect righteousness, which all of us lack, and conversely, the severe judge of evil deeds. But in Christ his face shines, full of grace and gentleness, even upon us poor and unworthy sinners.[13]

*9. The law, as Augustine states, by accusing moves us to seek grace**

ᵇAugustine often speaks of the value of calling upon the grace of His help. For example, he writes to Hilary: "The law bids us, as we try to fulfill its requirements, and become wearied in our weakness under it, to know how to ask the help of grace." He writes similarly to Asellius: "The usefulness of the law lies in convicting man of his infirmity and moving him to call upon the remedy of grace which is in Christ." Again, to Innocent of Rome: "The law commands; grace supplies the strength to act." Again, to Valentinus: "God commands what we cannot do that we may know what we ought to seek from him." ᶜAgain: "The law was given to accuse you; that accused you might fear; that fearing you might beg forgiveness; and that you might not presume on your own strength." Again: "The law was given for this purpose: to make you, being great, little; to show that you do not have in yourself the strength to attain righteousness, and for you, thus helpless, unworthy, and destitute, to flee to grace." Afterward he addresses God: "So act, O Lord; so act, O merciful Lord. Command what cannot be fulfilled. Rather, command what can be fulfilled only through thy grace so that, since men are unable to fulfill it through their own strength, every mouth may be stopped, and no one may seem great to himself. Let all be little ones, and let all the world be guilty before God."[14] But it is silly of me to amass so many testimonies, since that holy man has

---

[13] The two sentences preceding are found in Calvin's *Instruction et confession de foy* (1537); tr. Fuhrmann, *Instruction in Faith* 11, p. 35. They appear in the *Institutes* first in 1539.

[14] The following are the passages from Augustine quoted above in this paragraph: *Letters* clvii. 2. 9; cxcvi. 2. 6; clxxvii. 5 (MPL 33. 677, 893, 766; tr. FC 20. 325; 30. 336, 97); *On Grace and Free Will* xvi. 32 (MPL 44. 900; tr. NPNF V. 457); *On the Spirit and the Letter* xiii. 22 (MPL 44. 214 f.; tr. NPNF V. 92); *Psalms*, Ps. 70. i. 19; 118. xxvii. 3 (MPL 36. 889; 37. 1581; tr. LF *Psalms* V. 434). "Innocent of Rome" in the text is Pope Innocent I (402–417).

written a work specifically on this topic, entitled *On the Spirit and the Letter.*[15] ^bHe does not as expressly describe the second value of the law, either because he knew that it depended upon the first, or because he did not grasp it thoroughly, ^cor because he lacked words to express its correct meaning distinctly and plainly enough.

^bYet this first function of the law is exercised also in the reprobate. For, although they do not proceed so far with the children of God as to be renewed and bloom again in the inner man after the abasement of their flesh, but are struck dumb by the first terror and lie in despair, nevertheless, the fact that their consciences are buffeted by such waves serves to show forth the equity of the divine judgment. For the reprobate always freely desire to evade God's judgment. Now, although that judgment is not yet revealed, so routed are they by the testimony of the law and of conscience, that they betray in themselves what they have deserved.

(*The law restrains malefactors and those who are not yet believers, 10–11*)

*10. The law as protection of the community from unjust men**

^bThe second function of the law is this: ^aat least by fear of punishment to restrain certain men who are untouched by any care for what is just and right unless compelled by hearing the dire threats in the law. But they are restrained, not because their inner mind is stirred or affected, but because, being bridled, so to speak, they keep their hands from outward activity, and hold inside the depravity that otherwise they would wantonly have indulged. Consequently, they are neither better nor more righteous before God. Hindered by fright or shame, they dare neither execute what they have conceived in their minds, nor openly breathe forth the rage of their lust. Still, they do not have hearts disposed to fear and obedience toward God. Indeed, the more they restrain themselves, the more strongly are they inflamed; they burn and boil within, and are ready to do anything or burst forth anywhere—but for the fact that this dread of the law hinders them. Not only that—but so wickedly do they also hate the law itself, and curse God the Lawgiver, that if they could, they would most certainly abolish him, for they cannot bear him either when he commands them to do right, or when he takes vengeance on the despisers of his majesty. ^bAll who are still unregenerate feel—some more obscurely, some more openly—that they are not drawn

---

[15] Text in MPL 44. 201–246; tr. NPNF V. 83–114.

to obey the law voluntarily, but impelled by a violent fear do so against their will and despite their opposition to it.

ᵃBut this constrained and forced righteousness is necessary for the public community of men,[16] for whose tranquillity the Lord herein provided when he took care that everything be not tumultuously confounded. This would happen if everything were permitted to all men. ᵇNay, even for the children of God, before they are called and while they are destitute of the Spirit of sanctification [Rom. 1:4, Vg. etc.], so long as they play the wanton in the folly of the flesh, it is profitable for them to undergo this tutelage.[17] While by the dread of divine vengeance they are restrained at least from outward wantonness, with minds yet untamed they progress but slightly for the present, yet become partially broken in by bearing the yoke of righteousness. As a consequence, when they are called, they are not utterly untutored and uninitiated in discipline as if it were something unknown. The apostle seems specially to have alluded to this function of the law when he teaches "that the law is not laid down for the just but for the unjust and disobedient, for the ungodly and sinners, for the unholy and profane, for murderers of parents, for manslayers, fornicators, perverts, kidnapers, liars, perjurers, and whatever else runs counter to sound doctrine" [I Tim. 1: 9–10]. He shows in this that the law is like a halter to check the raging and otherwise limitlessly ranging lusts of the flesh.

*11. The law a deterrent to those not yet regenerate**

ᶜWhat Paul says elsewhere, that "the law was for the Jews a tutor unto Christ" [Gal. 3:24], may be applied to both functions of the law. There are two kinds of men whom the law leads by its tutelage to Christ.

Of the first kind we have already spoken: because they are too full of their own virtue or of the assurance of their own righteousness, they are not fit to receive Christ's grace unless they first be emptied. Therefore, through the recognition of their own misery, the law brings them down to humility in order thus to prepare them to seek what previously they did not realize they lacked.

Men of the second kind have need of a bridle to restrain them from so slackening the reins on the lust of the flesh as to fall clean away from all pursuit of righteousness. For where the Spirit of

---

16 Note the similar phrases in IV. xx. 3, and cf. Melanchthon: *"publicae pacis causa"* (*Loci praecipui theologici*, ed. Engelland, *op. cit.*, p. 322); cf. also IV. xx. 14–16.

17 *"Paedagogia,"* rendered *"pedagogie"* in French versions of 1545–1557, but in 1560 *"instruction puerile."*

God does not yet rule, lusts sometimes so boil that there is danger lest they plunge the soul bound over to them into forgetfulness and contempt of God. And such would happen if God did not oppose it with this remedy. Therefore, if he does not immediately regenerate those whom he has destined to inherit his Kingdom, until the time of his visitation, he keeps them safe through the works of the law under fear [cf. I Peter 2:12]. This is not that chaste and pure fear such as ought to be in his sons, but a fear useful in teaching them true godliness according to their capacity. We have so many proofs of this matter that no example is needed. For all who have at any time groped about in ignorance of God will admit that it happened to them in such a way that the bridle of the law restrained them in some fear and reverence toward God until, regenerated by the Spirit, they began wholeheartedly to love him.[18]

(*Principally it admonishes believers and urges them on in well-doing, 12–13*)

12. Even the believers have need of the law

[b]The third and principal use, which pertains more closely to the proper purpose of the law, [b(a)]finds its place among believers in whose hearts the Spirit of God already lives and reigns.[19] [a]For even though they have the law written and engraved upon their hearts by the finger of God [Jer. 31:33; Heb. 10:16], that is, have been so moved and quickened [b(a)]through the directing of the Spirit that they long to obey God, they still profit by the law in two ways.

Here is the best instrument for them to learn more thoroughly each day the nature of the Lord's will to which they aspire, and to confirm them in the understanding of it. [a]It is as if some servant, already prepared with all earnestness of heart to commend himself to his master, [b(a)]must search out and observe his master's ways more carefully in order to conform and accommodate himself to them. [b]And not one of us may escape from this necessity. For no man has heretofore attained to such wisdom as to be unable, from the daily instruction of the law, to make fresh progress toward a purer knowledge of the divine will.

Again, because we need not only teaching but also exhortation, the servant of God will also avail himself of this benefit of the law: by frequent meditation upon it to be aroused to obedience, be strengthened in it, and be drawn back from the slippery path

[18] Cf. II. viii. 51–59.
[19] Melanchthon, *Loci communes* (1521), ed. Engelland, *op. cit.*, p. 133 (tr. C. L. Hill, p. 229).

of transgression. In this way the saints must press on; for, however eagerly they may in accordance with the Spirit strive toward God's righteousness, the listless flesh always so burdens them that they do not proceed with due readiness. ªThe law is to the flesh like a whip to an idle and balky ass, to arouse it to work. ᵇEven for a spiritual man not yet free of the weight of the flesh the law remains a constant sting that will not let him stand still. Doubtless David was referring to this use when he sang the praises of the law: "The law of the Lord is spotless, converting souls; . . . the righteous acts of the Lord are right, rejoicing hearts; the precept of the Lord is clear, enlightening the eyes," etc. [Ps. 18: 8–9, Vg.; 19:7–8, EV]. Likewise: "Thy word is a lamp to my feet and a light to my path" [Ps. 119:105], and innumerable other sayings in the same psalm [e.g., Ps. 119:5]. These do not contradict Paul's statements, which show not what use the law serves for the regenerate, but what it can of itself confer upon man. But here the prophet proclaims the great usefulness of the law: the Lord instructs by their reading of it those whom he inwardly instills with a readiness to obey. ᵉHe lays hold not only of the precepts, but the accompanying promise of grace, which alone sweetens what is bitter. For what would be less lovable than the law if, with importuning and threatening alone, it troubled souls through fear, and distressed them through fright? David especially shows that in the law he apprehended the Mediator, without whom there is no delight or sweetness.

13. Whoever wants to do away with the law entirely for the faithful, understands it falsely

ᵇCertain ignorant persons,[20] not understanding this distinction, rashly cast out the whole of Moses, and bid farewell to the two Tables of the Law. For they think it obviously alien to Christians to hold to a doctrine that contains the "dispensation of death" [cf. II Cor. 3:7]. Banish this wicked thought from our minds! For Moses has admirably taught that the law, which among sinners can engender nothing but death, ought among the saints to have a better and more excellent use. When about to die, he decreed to the people as follows: "Lay to your hearts all the words which this day I enjoin upon you, that you may command them to your children, and teach them to keep, do, and fulfill all those things

[20] This is probably directed not only against the Libertine sect (cf. *Contre la secte phantastique des Libertins,* CR VII. 206 f., 220, 229, 233) but also against John Agricola, who broke from Luther and began the Antinomian Controversy, 1537, denying all Christian obligation to fulfill any part of the Old Testament law. See *Werke* WA XXXIX. i. 342 ff. and HDRE article "Antinomianism."

written in the book of this law. For they have not been commanded to you in vain, but for each to live in them" [Deut. 32: 46–47, cf. Vg.]. But if no one can deny that a perfect pattern of righteousness stands forth in the law, either we need no rule to live rightly and justly, or it is forbidden to depart from the law. There are not many rules, but one everlasting and unchangeable rule to live by. For this reason we are not to refer solely to one age David's statement that the life of a righteous man is a continual meditation upon the law [Ps. 1:2], for it is just as applicable to every age, even to the end of the world.

We ought not to be frightened away from the law or to shun its instruction merely because it requires a much stricter moral purity than we shall reach while we bear about with us the prison house of our body. For the law is not now acting toward us as a rigorous enforcement officer who is not satisfied unless the requirements are met. But in this perfection to which it exhorts us, the law points out the goal toward which throughout life we are to strive. ᵉIn this the law is no less profitable than consistent with our duty. ᵇIf we fail not in this struggle, it is well. Indeed, this whole life is a race [cf. I Cor. 9:24–26]; when its course has been run, the Lord will grant us to attain that goal to which our efforts now press forward from afar.

(Its so-called "abrogation" has reference to the liberation of the conscience, and the discontinuance of the ancient ceremonies, 14–17)

14. To what extent has the law been abrogated for believers?

ᵇ⁽ᵃ⁾Now, the law has power to exhort believers. This is not a power to bind their consciences with a curse, but one to shake off their sluggishness, by repeatedly urging them, and to pinch them awake to their imperfection. Therefore, many persons, wishing to express such liberation from that curse, say that for believers the law—I am still speaking of the moral law—has been abrogated.[21] Not that the law no longer enjoins believers to do what is right, but only that it is not for them what it formerly was: it may no longer condemn and destroy their consciences by frightening and confounding them.

ᵇPaul teaches clearly enough such an abrogation of the law [cf. Rom. 7:6]. That the Lord also preached it appears from this:

[21] Cf. Melanchthon, *Loci communes* in Engelland, *op. cit.*, pp. 120 ff., 126 f., 132 ff. (tr. Hill, *op. cit.*, pp. 214 ff., 220 f., 229 ff.); Zwingli, *Of True and False Religion* (CR Zwingli III. 710; tr. *Latin Works of Huldreich Zwingli*, ed. S. M. Jackson, III. 141: "God has put into our hearts a fire by which to kindle love of him in place of love of ourselves"

he would not have refuted the notion that he would abolish the law [Matt. 5:17] if this opinion had not been prevalent among the Jews. But since without some pretext the idea could not have arisen by chance, it may be supposed to have arisen from a false interpretation of his teaching, just as almost all errors have commonly taken their occasion from truth. But to avoid stumbling on the same stone, let us accurately distinguish what in the law has been abrogated from what still remains in force. When the Lord testifies that he "came not to abolish the law but to fulfill it" and that "until heaven and earth pass away . . . not a jot will pass away from the law until all is accomplished" [Matt. 5:17–18], he sufficiently confirms that by his coming nothing is going to be taken away from the observance of the law. And justly—inasmuch as he came rather to remedy transgressions of it. Therefore through Christ the teaching of the law remains inviolable; by teaching, admonishing, reproving, and correcting, it forms us and prepares us for every good work [cf. II Tim. 3:16–17].

15. The law is abrogated to the extent that it no longer condemns us

ᵇWhat Paul says of the curse unquestionably applies not to the ordinance itself but solely to its force to bind the conscience. The law not only teaches but forthrightly enforces what it commands. If it be not obeyed—indeed, if one in any respect fail in his duty—the law unleashes the thunderbolt of its curse. For this reason the apostle says: "All who are of the works of the law are under a curse; for it is written, 'Cursed be every one who does not fulfill all things'" [Gal. 3:10; Deut. 27:26 p.]. He describes as "under the works of the law" those who do not ground their righteousness in remission of sins, through which we are released from the rigor of the law. He therefore teaches that we must be released from the bonds of the law, unless we wish to perish miserably under them.

But from what bonds? The bonds of harsh and dangerous requirements, which remit nothing of the extreme penalty of the law, and suffer no transgression to go unpunished. To redeem us from this curse, I say, Christ was made a curse for us. "For it is written: 'Cursed be every one who hangs on a tree.'" [Gal. 3:13; Deut. 21:23.] In the following chapter Paul teaches that Christ was made subject to the law [Gal. 4:4] "that he might redeem those under the law" [Gal. 4:5a, Vg.]. This means the same thing, for he continues: "So that we might receive by adoption the right of sons" [Gal. 4:5b]. What does this mean? That we should not be borne down by an unending bondage, which would agonize our consciences with the fear of death. Meanwhile this always remains an unassailable fact: no part of the authority of the law is withdrawn without our having always to receive it with the same veneration and obedience.

16. The ceremonial law

ᵉThe ceremonies are a different matter: they have been abro gated not in effect but only in use. Christ by his coming has terminated them, but has not deprived them of anything of their sanctity; rather, he has approved and honored it. Just as the cere-monies would have provided the people of the Old Covenant with an empty show if the power of Christ's death and resurrection had not been displayed therein; so, if they had not ceased, we would be unable today to discern for what purpose they were established.

Consequently Paul, to prove their observance not only superfluous but also harmful, teaches that they are shadows whose substance exists for us in Christ [Col. 2:17]. Thus we see that in their abolition the truth shines forth better than if they, still far off and as if veiled, figured the Christ, who has already plainly revealed himself. At Christ's death "the curtain of the temple was torn in two" [Matt. 27:51] because now the living and express image of heavenly blessings was manifested, which before had been begun in indistinct outline only, as the author of The Letter to the Hebrews states [Heb. 10:1]. To this applies Christ's utterance: "The law and the prophets were until John; since then the good news of the Kingdom of God is preached" [Luke 16:16]. Not that the holy patriarchs were without the preaching that contains the hope of salvation and of eternal life, but that they only glimpsed from afar and in shadowy outline what we see today in full daylight. John the Baptist explains why the church of God had to pass quite beyond these rudiments: "The law was given through Moses; grace and truth came through Jesus Christ" [John 1:17]. For even though atonement for sins had been truly promised in the ancient sacrifices, and the Ark of the Covenant was a sure pledge of God's fatherly favor, all this would have been but shadow[22] had it not been grounded in the grace of Christ, in whom one finds perfect and everlasting stability. Let it be regarded as a fact that, although the rites of the law have ceased to be observed, by their termination one may better recognize how useful they were before the coming of Christ, who

---

[22] On the "shadowy" character and foreshadowing function of Old Testament legislation, see also II. viii. 28, 29; cf. LCC XXIII. 29 f.

in abrogating their use has by his death sealed their force and effect.

17. "The written bond against us" is blotted out
ᵇOf slightly greater difficulty is the point noted by Paul: "And you, when you were dead through sins and the uncircumcision of your flesh, God made alive together with him, having forgiven you all your sins, having canceled the written bond which was against us in the decrees, which was contrary to us. And he bore it from our midst, fixing it to the cross," etc. [Col. 2:13–14, cf. Vg.]. This statement seems to extend the abolition of the law to the point that we now have nothing to do with its decrees. They are mistaken who understand it simply of the moral law, whose inexorable severity rather than its teaching they interpret as abolished.[23] Others, more carefully weighing Paul's words, perceive that these apply properly speaking to the ceremonial law; and they point out that the word "decree" is used in Paul more than once. For he also addresses the Ephesians thus: "He is our peace, who has made us both one . . . abolishing . . . the law of commandments resting upon decrees, that he might create in himself one new man in place of the two" [Eph. 2:14–15, cf. Vg.].[24] There is no doubt that this statement concerns the ceremonies, for he speaks of them as a wall that divides the Jews from the Gentiles [Eph. 2:14]. Hence, I admit that the second group of expositors rightly criticizes the first. But the second group also still does not seem to explain the meaning of the apostle very well. For I am not at all happy about comparing the two passages in every detail. When Paul would assure the Ephesians of their adoption into the fellowship of Israel, he teaches that the hindrance which once held them back has now been removed. That was in the ceremonies. For the ritual cleansings and sacrifices, whereby the Jews were consecrated to the Lord, separated them from the Gentiles. Now who cannot see that a loftier mystery is referred to in the letter to the Colossians? The question there concerns the Mosaic observances, to which the false apostles were trying to drive the Christian people. But as in the letter to the Galatians he carries that discussion deeper—reverting, so to speak, to its starting point—so he does in this passage. For if you consider

---

[23] So Melanchthon, *Scripta exegetica*, on Col. 2:14 (CR Melanchthon XV. 1256); cf. the section *De abrogatione legis* in his *Loci communes*, 1521 (ed. Engelland, *op. cit.*, 132 ff.; tr. Hill, *op. cit.*, pp. 221 ff.).
[24] Bucer, *Metaphrases et enarrationes perpetuae epistolarum D. Pauli Apostoli* I, *ad Romanos*, Strasbourg, 1536, p. 205: "Paul here [i.e., Col. 2:14] means by 'handwriting' [*chirographum*] the law of ceremonies, that yoke which Peter said neither our fathers nor we were able to bear."

nothing else in the rites than the necessity of performing them, what is the point in calling them "the written bond[25] against us" [Col. 2:14]? Moreover, why lodge nearly the whole of our redemption in the fact that they are "blotted out"? Therefore, the thing itself cries out that we should consider it as something more inward.

But I am sure that I have come upon the true understanding of it—provided the truth be granted of what Augustine somewhere most truly writes, or rather takes from the apostle's clear words: in the Jewish ceremonies there was confession of sins rather than atonement for them [cf. Heb. 10:1 ff.; also Lev. 16:21].[26] What else did the Jews accomplish with their sacrifices than to confess themselves guilty of death, since they substituted purification in place of themselves? What else did they accomplish with their cleansings but confess themselves unclean? They thus repeatedly renewed the "written bond" of their sin and impurity. But in giving such proof there was no release from it. The apostle, for this reason, writes: "Since Christ's death has occurred, redemption from the transgressions which remained under the old covenant has been accomplished" [Heb. 9:15 p.]. The apostle rightly, therefore, calls the ceremonies "written bonds against" [Col. 2:14] those observing them, since through such rites they openly certify their own condemnation and uncleanness [cf. Heb. 10:3].

There is no contradiction in the fact that they also were partakers in the same grace with us. For they attained that in Christ; not in the ceremonies that the apostle in that passage distinguishes from Christ, inasmuch as these, then in use, obscured Christ's glory. We hold that ceremonies, considered in themselves, are very appropriately called "written bonds against" the salvation of men. For they were, so to speak, binding legal documents,[27] which attested men's obligation. When the false apostles wanted to bind the Christian church again to observe them, Paul with good reason, more profoundly restating their ultimate purpose, warned the Colossians into what danger they would slip back if they allowed themselves to be subjugated to the ceremonial law in this way [Col. 2:16 ff.]. For at the same time they were deprived of the benefit of Christ, since, when once he had carried out the eternal atonement, he abolished those daily observances, which were able only to attest sins but could do nothing to blot them out.

[25] "Chirographum," Greek: "χειρόγραφον."
[26] Augustine, On the Merits and Remission of Sins I. xxvii. 54 (MPL 44. 139; tr. NPNF V. 35).
[27] "Solennia instrumenta."

ᶜCHAPTER VIII

EXPLANATION OF THE MORAL LAW (THE TEN COMMANDMENTS)

(The written moral law a statement of the natural law, 1–2)
1. What are the Ten Commandments to us?
ᶜHere I think it will not be out of place to introduce the Ten Commandments of the law with a short explanation of them.[1] Thus, the point I have touched upon[2] will also be made clearer: that the public worship that God once prescribed is still in force. Then will come the confirmation of my second point: that the Jews not only learned from the law what the true character of godliness was; but also that, since they saw themselves incapable of observing the law, they were in dread of judgment drawn inevitably though unwillingly to the Mediator. Now ᵇin summarizing what is required for the true knowledge of God, we have taught that we cannot conceive him in his greatness without being immediately confronted ᵉ⁽ᵇ⁾by his majesty, and so compelled[3] to worship him. ᵇIn our discussion of the knowledge of ourselves we have set forth this chief point: that, empty of all opinion of our own virtue, and shorn of all assurance of our own righteousness—in fact, broken and crushed by the awareness of our own utter poverty—we may learn genuine humility and self-abasement.[4] Both of these the Lord accomplishes in his law. First, claiming for himself the lawful power to command, he calls us to reverence his divinity, and specifies wherein such reverence lies and consists. Secondly, having published the rule of his righteousness, he reproves us both for our impotence and for our unrighteousness. For our nature, wicked and deformed, is always opposing his uprightness; and our capacity, weak and feeble to do good, lies far from his perfection.

ᵇ⁽ᵃ⁾Now that inward law,[5] which we have above described as

---

[1] The Commandments, with the Creed and the Lord's Prayer, constituted a topic of lay instruction in countless medieval handbooks of religious guidance, such as the English *Lay Folk's Catechism*, attributed to John Thoresby, archbishop of York (d. 1373). Pannier cites a separate French booklet on the Commandments, *Les fleurs des commandemens* (1490, revised 1516): (*Institution* I. 322, note on p. 197). Their use in Reformation catechisms was begun by Luther (1529), and Calvin had discussed them *seriatim* in his *Instruction et confession de foy* (1537); tr. Fuhrmann, *Instruction in Faith* 8, pp. 24–32.
[2] I. vii. 1–2.
[3] I. i. 2.
[4] II. i–vi.
[5] *"Dictat lex illa interior."* Cf., below, in this section, *"in lege naturali."* References to natural law in the *Institutes* are usually, as here, associated

written, even engraved, upon the hearts of all, in a sense asserts the very same things that are to be learned from the two Tables. For our conscience does not allow us to sleep a perpetual insensible sleep without being an inner witness and monitor of what we owe God, without holding before us the difference between good and evil and thus accusing us when we fail in our duty. But man is so shrouded in the darkness of errors that he hardly begins to grasp through this natural law what worship is acceptable to God. Surely he is very far removed from a true estimate of it. Besides this, he is so puffed up with haughtiness and ambition, and so blinded by self-love, that he is as yet unable to look upon himself and, as it were, to descend within himself,[6] that he may humble and abase himself and confess his own miserable condition. Accordingly (because it is necessary both for our dullness and for our arrogance), the Lord has provided us with a written law to give us a clearer witness of what was too obscure in the natural law, shake off our listlessness, and strike more vigorously our mind and memory.

with conscience, frequently also with civil positive law and equity, and the Christian's duties to society. Cf. II. ii. 22, where the key Pauline passage for natural law, Rom. 2:14–15, is employed: see also II. vii. 3–4; II. viii. 1–2, 53; III. xix. 15–16; IV. x. 3; IV. xx. 11 ("natural equity"); IV. xx. 15 (the rule of love); IV. xx. 16 ("the moral law . . . a testimony of natural law"). Calvin's view of the Commandments as a divinely authorized text expressing and clarifying the natural law engraved on all hearts is the traditional one. Lactantius quotes in full Cicero's important paragraph, in *De republica* III. xxii, on the law of right reason agreeing with nature, which God has given to all men, and asks what Christian could have set forth so meaningfully the law of God: *Divine Institutes* VI. viii (CSEL 19. 508 f.; MPL 6. 660 f.; tr. ANF VII. 171). Cf. Augustine, *Confessions* II. iv. 9 (MPL 32. 678; tr. LCC VII. 54). Aquinas treats natural law with some fullness, e.g., in *Summa Theol.* I IIae, questions xci. 1–3; xciv; c. 1–5, where the principles of the Decalogue are identified with those of natural reason. The association of natural law with the golden rule of Matt. 7:12 is also common: see Gratian, *Decretum* I. i (Friedberg I. 2). Some references to this background are given in J. T. McNeill's article "Natural Law in the Thought of Luther" in *Church History* X (1941), 211–227; for Calvin, see also "Natural Law in the Teaching of the Reformers," *Journal of Religion* XXVI (1946), 168–182, and literature there cited. Notable references in Calvin's commentaries and sermons are: Comm. Rom. 2:14–15; *Sermons on Deuteronomy* cxix (on Deut. 19:14–15) (CR XXVII. 568); *Sermons on Job* ci, on Job 28:1–9 (CR XXXIV: 503 ff.); Comm. *Harmony Four Books of Moses*, "Praefatio in legem" (CR XXIV. 209–260). Here again the Commandments are seen as a specially accommodated restatement of the law of nature for the chosen people, and the entire body of "Mosaic" legislation is classified under the ten laws.

[6] Cf. I. i. 2, note 6. This passage succinctly presents Calvin's view of the work of the law and of conscience in conversion.

2. The inexorableness of the law

b(a)Now what is to be learned from the law can be readily understood: that God, as he is our Creator, has toward us by right the place of Father and Lord; for this reason we owe to him glory, reverence, love, and fear; bverily, that we have no right to follow the mind's caprice wherever it impels us, but, dependent upon his will, ought to stand firm in that alone which is pleasing to him; then, that righteousness and uprightness are pleasing to him, but he abominates wickedness; and that, for this reason, unless we would turn away from our Creator in impious ingratitude, we must cherish righteousness all our life. For if only when we prefer his will to our own do we render to him the reverence that is his due, it follows that the only lawful worship of him is the observance of righteousness, holiness, and purity. aAnd we cannot pretend the excuse that we lack ability and, like impoverished debtors, are unable to pay. bIt is not fitting for us to measure God's glory according to our ability; for whatever we may be, he remains always like himself: the friend of righteousness, the foe of iniquity. Whatever he requires of us (because he can require only what is right), we must obey out of natural obligation. But what we cannot do is our own fault. If our lust in which sin reigns [cf. Rom. 6:12] so holds us bound that we are not free to obey our Father, there is no reason why we should claim necessity as a defense, for the evil of that necessity is both within us and to be imputed to us.

(We learn from it that God is our Father; that he is merciful and all-holy, and in kindness requires obedience, 3–5)

3. The severity of the law has a positive goal

bWhen we have profited by the teaching of the law to this extent, we must then under its instruction descend into ourselves. From this we may at length infer two things. b(a)First, by comparing the righteousness of the law with our life, we learn how far we are from conforming to God's will. bAnd for this reason we are unworthy to hold our place among his creatures—still less to be accounted his children. Secondly, in considering our powers, we learn that they are not only too weak to fulfill the law, but utterly nonexistent. From this necessarily follows mistrust of our own virtue, then anxiety and trepidation of mind. For the conscience cannot bear the weight of iniquity without soon coming before God's judgment. Truly, God's judgment cannot be felt without evoking the dread of death. So also, constrained by the proofs of its impotence, conscience cannot but fall straightway into deep despair of its own powers. Both these emotions engender humility and self-abasement. ᵇ⁽ᵃ⁾Thus it finally comes to pass that man, thoroughly frightened by the awareness of eternal death, which he sees as justly threatening him because of his own unrighteousness, betakes himself to God's mercy alone, as the only haven of safety. Thus, realizing that he does not possess the ability to pay to the law what he owes, and despairing in himself, he is moved to seek and await help from another quarter.

4. Promises and threats

ᵇBut the Lord is not content with having obtained reverence for his righteousness. In order to imbue our hearts with love of righteousness and with hatred of wickedness, he has added promises and threats. For because the eye of our mind is too blind to be moved solely by the beauty of the good, our most merciful Father out of his great kindness has willed to attract us by sweetness of rewards to love and seek after him. He announces, therefore, that the rewards for virtues are stored up with him, and that the man who obeys his commandments does not do so in vain. Conversely, he proclaims that unrighteousness is not only hateful to him but will not escape punishment because he himself will avenge contempt of his majesty. And to urge us in every way, he promises both blessings in the present life and everlasting blessedness to those who obediently keep his commandments. He threatens the transgressors no less with present calamities than with the punishment of eternal death. For that promise ("He who does these things shall live in them" [Lev. 18:5 p.]) and its corresponding threat ("The soul that sins shall itself die" [Ezek. 18:4, 20, Vg.]) without doubt have reference to either never-ending future immortality or death. Wherever God's benevolence or wrath is mentioned, under the former is contained eternal life, under the latter eternal perdition. Nevertheless, a long list of present blessings and curses is also enumerated in the law [Lev. 26:3–39; Deut., ch. 28]. And in the penalties God's supreme purity is manifest, which cannot bear wickedness. But in the promises, besides his supreme love for righteousness, which he does not allow to be cheated of its reward, his wonderful generosity is also attested. For since we, with all that is ours, are deep in debt to his majesty, whatever he requires of us he claims with perfect right as a debt. But the payment of a debt deserves no reward. He therefore yields his own right when he offers a reward for our obedience, which we do not render voluntarily or as something not due. But what those promises of themselves bring to us has partly been stated, partly will more clearly appear in its proper place.[7] It suffices for the present if we hold and reckon that, in order to make more evident how much God is pleased by the observance of it, in the promises of the law there is no ordinary commendation of righteousness; and that the penalties are imposed in order that unrighteousness may be the more detested, lest the sinner, steeped in the blandishments of vices, forget the Lawgiver's judgment prepared for him.

5. *The sufficiency of the law*

[b]On the other hand, the Lord, in giving the rule of perfect righteousness, has referred all its parts to his will, thereby showing that nothing is more acceptable to him than obedience. The more inclined the playfulness of the human mind is to dream up various rites with which to deserve well of him, the more diligently ought we to mark this fact. In all ages this irreligious affectation of religion, because it is rooted in man's nature, has manifested itself and still manifests itself; for men always delight in contriving some way of acquiring righteousness apart from God's Word. Hence, among what are commonly considered good works the commandments of the law are accorded too narrow a place, while that innumerable throng of human precepts occupies almost the whole space. Yet what else did Moses intend but to restrain such wantonness, when after the proclamation of the law he addressed the people as follows: "Observe and heed all these words which I command you, that it may go well with you and with your children after you forever, when you do what is good and pleasing in the sight of your God" [Deut. 12:28, cf. Vg.]. "What I command you, this only you are to do . . . ; you shall not add to it or take from it." [Deut. 12:32, cf. Vg.] Previously, Moses had testified that the wisdom and understanding of Israel before all other nations was that it accepted judgments, precepts, and ceremonies from the Lord. Then he had added: "Guard yourself, then, and watch over your soul, lest you forget the words which your eyes have seen, and lest at any time they depart from your heart" [Deut. 4:9, cf. Vg.]. Surely God foresaw that the Israelites would not rest, once they had received the law, but would thereafter bring forth new precepts, unless they were severely restrained. Here, he declares, perfection of righteousness is comprehended. This ought to have been the strongest of restraints; yet they did not desist from that utterly forbidden presumption.

What about us? Surely we are constrained by the same utterance. There is no doubt that the perfect teaching of righteousness that the Lord claims for the law has a perpetual validity.

[7] II. v. 10; II. vii. 4; III. xvii. 1–3, 6, 7.

Not content with it, however, we labor mightily to contrive and forge good works upon good works. The best remedy to cure that fault will be to fix this thought firmly in mind: the law has been divinely handed down to us to teach us perfect righteousness; there no other righteousness is taught than that which conforms to the requirements of God's will; in vain therefore do we attempt new forms of works to win the favor of God, whose lawful worship consists in obedience alone; rather, any zeal for good works that wanders outside God's law is an intolerable profanation of divine and true righteousness. ᵈAugustine also very truly calls the obedience that is paid to God sometimes the mother and guardian of all virtues, sometimes their source.[8]

(It is to be spiritually understood and interpreted with reference to the purpose of the Lawgiver, 6–10)
6. Since the law is God's law, it makes a total claim upon us
ᵇBut after we have had the law of the Lord expounded more fully, then what I have already set forth concerning its function and use[9] will be more fittingly and profitably confirmed. Yet before we proceed to treat individual articles, it behooves us only to hold in view what constitutes a general knowledge of the law. First, let us agree that through the law man's life is molded not only to outward honesty but to inward and spiritual righteousness. Although no one can deny this, very few duly note it. This happens because they do not look to the Lawgiver, by whose character the nature of the law also is to be appraised. If some king by edict forbids fornication, murder, or theft, I admit that a man who merely conceives in his mind the desire to fornicate, to kill, or to steal, but does not commit such acts, will not be bound by the penalty. That is, because the mortal lawgiver's jurisdiction extends only to the outward political order, his ordinances are not violated, except when actual crimes are committed. But God, whose eye nothing escapes, and who is concerned not so much with outward appearance as with purity of heart, under the prohibition of fornication, murder, and theft, forbids lust, anger, hatred, coveting a neighbor's possessions, deceit, and the like. For since he is a spiritual lawgiver, he speaks no less to the soul than to the body. But murder that is of the soul consists in anger and hatred; theft, in evil covetousness and avarice; fornication, in lust.

---

[8] Augustine, *City of God* XIV. xii (MPL 41. 420; tr. NPNF II. 273); *On the Good of Marriage* xxiii. 30 (MPL 40. 393; tr. NPNF III. 411); *Contra adversarios legis et prophetarum* I. xiv. 19 (MPL 42. 613).
[9] II. vii. 1–12.

Human laws also, someone will say, are concerned with purposes and intentions, not chance happenings.[10] I agree, but they are intentions that come forth into the open. They determine with what intent each crime has been committed; but they do not search out secret thoughts. Human laws, then, are satisfied when a man merely keeps his hand from wrongdoing. On the contrary, because the heavenly law has been given for our souls, they must at the outset be constrained, that it may be justly observed. [a]Yet the common folk, even when they strongly conceal their contempt of the law, compose their eyes, feet, hands, and all parts of the body to some observance of the law. Meanwhile they keep the heart utterly aloof from all obedience, and think themselves well acquitted if they virtuously hide from men what they do in the sight of God. They hear: "You shall not kill; you shall not commit adultery; you shall not steal." They do not unsheathe a sword for slaughter; they do not join their bodies to prostitutes; they do not lay hands on another's goods. So far so good. But wholeheartedly they breathe out slaughter, burn with lust, look with jaundiced eye upon the goods of all others and devour them with covetousness. They are now lacking in the chief point of the law. [b]Whence, I ask, comes such gross stupidity, unless, disregarding the Lawgiver, they accommodate righteousness rather to their own predilection? [a]Against them Paul strongly protests, affirming that "the law is spiritual" [Rom. 7: 14].[11] By this he means that it not only demands obedience of soul, mind, and will, [b]but requires an angelic purity, which, cleansed of every pollution of the flesh, savors of nothing but the spirit.

7. Christ himself has restored the right understanding of the law

[a]When we say that this is the meaning of the law, we are not thrusting forward a new interpretation of our own, but we are following Christ, its best interpreter. The Pharisees had infected the people with a perverse opinion: that he who has committed nothing by way of outward works against the law fulfills the law. Christ reproves this most dangerous error, and he declares an unchaste glance at a woman to be adultery [Matt. 5:28]. He testifies that "anyone who hates his brother is a murderer" [I John 3:15]. For he makes him "liable to judgment," who even conceives anger in his heart; he makes "liable to the council" those who by muttering and grumbling have given any indication of being offended; he makes "liable to hell-fire" those who with railings

[10] Cf. Plato, *Laws* IX. 862 (LCL Plato, *Laws* II. 228 f.).
[11] Cf. Melanchthon, *Loci communes* (1521), ed. Engelland, *op. cit.*, p. 73; tr. Hill, *op. cit.*, p. 153.

and cursings burst forth into open anger [Matt. 5:21-22 p.; cf. ch. 5:43 ff.]. Those who did not comprehend these teachings fancied Christ another Moses, the giver of the law of the gospel, which supplied what was lacking in the Mosaic law. ᵇWhence that common saying about the perfection of the law of the gospel, that it far surpasses the old law[12]—in many respects a most pernicious opinion! Subsequently, when we gather together the sum of his precepts, it will be clear from Moses himself with what undeserved abuse this view brands God's law. It implies that the sanctity of the fathers was not far removed from hypocrisy, and lures us away from that sole and everlasting rule of righteousness. ᵇ⁽ᵃ⁾It is very easy to refute this error. They have thought that Christ added to the law when he only restored it to its integrity, ᵃin that he freed and cleansed it when it had been obscured by the falsehoods and defiled by the leaven of the Pharisees [cf. Matt. 16:6, 11, and parallels].

8. Ways to the right meaning

ᵇLet this be our second observation: the commandments and prohibitions always contain more than is expressed in words. But we ought so to temper this principle that it may not be for us like the Lesbian rule,[13] on which we rely to twist Scripture without restraint, thus making anything we please out of anything. By this wild, precipitate license, they degrade the authority of the law among some men; for others they dash the hope of understanding it. We must if possible, therefore, find some way to lead us with straight, firm steps to the will of God. We must, I say, inquire how far interpretation ought to overstep the limits of the words themselves so that it may be seen to be, not an appendix added to the divine law from men's glosses, but the Lawgiver's pure and authentic meaning faithfully rendered. Obviously, in almost all the commandments there are such manifest synecdoches that he who would confine his understanding of the law within the narrowness of the words deserves to be laughed at. Therefore, plainly a sober interpretation of the law goes beyond the words; but just how far remains obscure unless some measure be set. Now, I think this would be the best rule, if attention be directed to the reason of the commandment; that is, in

---

[12] Melanchthon, *Loci communes*, *loc. cit.*, and in Engelland, pp. 130 f.; tr. Hill, *op. cit.*, pp. 224 ff.; Aquinas, *Summa Theol.* I IIae. xci. 5. Cf. Comm. Ps. 19:8.

[13] A reference to Aristotle's illustration of things undetermined by law from the pliable, leaden measuring rule used in Lesbian molding. *Nicomachean Ethics* V. 10. 1137b (LCL edition, pp. 314 f.).

each commandment to ponder why it was given to us. For example, every precept either commands or forbids. The truth of each sort comes to mind at once, if we look into the reason or purpose. The purpose of the Fifth Commandment is that honor ought to be paid to those to whom God has assigned it. This, then, is the substance of the commandment: that it is right and pleasing to God for us to honor those on whom he has bestowed some excellence; and that he abhors contempt and stubbornness against them. The intent of the First Commandment is that God alone be worshiped [cf. Ex. 20:2–3; Deut. 6:4–5]. Therefore the substance of the precept will be that true piety—namely, the worship of his divinity—is pleasing to God; and that he abominates impiety. Thus in each commandment we must investigate what it is concerned with; then we must seek out its purpose, until we find what the Lawgiver testifies there to be pleasing or displeasing to himself. Finally, from this same thing we must derive an argument on the other side, in this manner: if this pleases God, the opposite displeases him; if this displeases, the opposite pleases him; if he commands this, he forbids the opposite; if he forbids this, he enjoins the opposite.

9. Commandment and prohibition

ᵇWhat we are now touching on obscurely will become clear in practice as we expound the commandments. It is sufficient, therefore, to have touched upon it, except that we must briefly confirm the last point with a separate proof. Otherwise it would not be understood, or if understood, might perchance seem at first absurd. We do not need to prove that when a good thing is commanded, the evil thing that conflicts with it is forbidden. There is no one who does not concede this. That the opposite duties are enjoined when evil things are forbidden will also be willingly admitted in common judgment. Indeed, it is a commonplace that when virtues are commended, their opposing vices are condemned. But we demand something more than what these phrases commonly signify. For by the virtue contrary to the vice, men usually mean abstinence from that vice.[14] We say that the virtue goes beyond this to contrary duties and deeds. Therefore in this commandment, "You shall not kill," men's common sense will see only that we must abstain from wronging anyone or desiring to do so. Besides this, it contains, I say, the requirement that we give our neighbor's life all the help we can. To prove that I am not speaking unreasonably: God forbids us to hurt or harm a brother unjustly, because he wills that the brother's life be dear

[14] Aquinas, Summa Theol. I IIae. xcviii. 1.

and precious to us. So at the same time he requires those duties of love which can apply to its preservation. And thus we see how the purpose of the commandment always discloses to us whatever it there enjoins or forbids us to do.

*10. By its strong language, the law shocks us into greater detestation of sin**

ᵇBut why did God, as it were by half commandments, signify through synecdoche what he willed, rather than express it? While other reasons are also commonly given, this one especially satisfies me: the flesh ever tries to wash away the foulness of sins, except when it is palpable, and to overlay it with plausible excuses. Hence, God has set forth by way of example the most frightful and wicked element in every kind of transgression, at the hearing of which our senses might shudder, in order that he might imprint upon our minds a greater detestation of every sort of sin. In appraising our vices we are quite often deceived by this into making light of those which are somewhat concealed. The Lord disabuses us of these deceptions when he accustoms us to refer the whole mass of vices to these categories which best represent how heinous each kind is. For example, when called by their own names, we do not consider anger and hatred as things to be cursed. Yet when they are forbidden under the name "murder," we better understand how abominable they are in the sight of God, by whose Word they are relegated to the level of a dreadful crime. Thus moved by his judgment, we ourselves become accustomed better to weigh the gravity of transgressions, which previously seemed light to us.

(The two Tables of the Law, and the commandments rightly assigned to each, 11–12)

11. The two Tables

ᵇIn the third place we ought to ponder what the division of the divine law into two Tables meant.[15] This is impressively mentioned at various times with good reason, as all sane men will agree. And there is a ready reason for us not to remain uncertain on this matter. God has so divided his law into two parts, which contain the whole of righteousness, ᵇ⁽ᵃ⁾as to assign the first part to those duties of religion which particularly concern the worship

---

[15] Calvin uses the traditional identification of the two "tables of stone" (Ex. 24:12; II Cor. 3:3, and elsewhere) with the two series of the commandments requiring duties to God (1–4) and duties to man (5–10). Cf. his defense of this in sec. 12, below, and Comm. Harmony of the Evangelists, on Matt. 22:37.

of his majesty; the second, to the duties of love that have to do with men.

ᵇSurely the first foundation of righteousness is the worship of God. When this is overthrown, all the remaining parts of righteousness, like the pieces of a shattered and fallen building, are mangled and scattered. What kind of righteousness will you call it not to harass men with theft and plundering, if through impious sacrilege you at the same time deprive God's majesty of its glory? Or that you do not defile your body with fornication, if with your blasphemies you profane God's most holy name? Or that you do not slay a man, if you strive to kill and to quench the remembrance of God? It is vain to cry up righteousness without religion. This is as unreasonable as to display a mutilated, decapitated body as something beautiful. Not only is religion the chief part but the very soul, whereby the whole breathes and thrives. And apart from the fear of God men do not preserve equity and love among themselves. Therefore we call the worship of God the beginning and foundation of righteousness. When it is removed, whatever equity, continence, or temperance men practice among themselves is in God's sight empty and worthless. We call it source and spirit because from it men learn to live with one another in moderation and without doing injury, if they honor God as Judge of right and wrong. Accordingly, in the First Table, God instructs us in piety and the proper duties of religion, by which we are to worship his majesty. The Second Table prescribes how in accordance with the fear of his name we ought to conduct ourselves in human society. ᵃIn this way our Lord, as the Evangelists relate, summarizes the whole law under two heads: that "we should love the Lord our God with all our heart, and with all our soul, and with all our powers"; and "that we should love our neighbor as ourselves" [Luke 10:27 p.; Matt. 22:37, 39]. ᵇYou see that of the two parts in which the law consists, one he directs to God; the other he applies to men.

12. The distribution of the commandments in the two Tables

ᵃThe whole law is contained under two heads. Yet our God, to remove all possibility of excuse, willed to set forth more fully and clearly by the Ten Commandments everything connected with the honor, fear, and love of him, and everything pertaining to the love toward men, which he for his own sake enjoins upon us. ᵇThe effort to gain familiarity with the divisions of the commandments is not ill-directed, provided you remember that it is a matter wherein each man ought to have free judgment, and ought not to strive in a contentious spirit with one who differs from him. We are of necessity obliged to touch upon this point in order that our readers may not either laugh or wonder at the division we are about to put forward as if it were new and recently devised.

That the law is divided into ten words is beyond doubt, for on the authority of God himself this has often been confirmed. Thus we are uncertain, not about the number, but about the way of dividing the Decalogue. b(a)Those who so divide them as to give three precepts to the First Table and relegate the remaining seven to the Second, erase from the number the commandment concerning images, or at least hide it under the First. There is no doubt that the Lord gave it a distinct place as a commandment, ªyet they absurdly tear in two the Tenth Commandment about not coveting the possessions of one's neighbor.[16] h(a)Besides, their division of the commandments was unknown in a purer age, as we shall soon see. bOthers, with us, count four articles in the First Table, but in place of the First Commandment they put a promise without a commandment. But I, unless convinced only by the clearest contrary evidence, take the ten words mentioned by Moses to be the Ten Commandments; and they seem to me to be arranged in quite the most beautiful order. Granting them their opinion, I shall follow what seems more probable to me, namely, that what they take as the First Commandment should occupy the place of the preface to the whole law. Then the commandments follow, four to the First Table, six to the Second. We shall take them up in this order. b(a)Origen set forth this division without controversy, as if commonly received in his day.[17] bAugustine also supports it in a letter to Boniface, and in enumerating them keeps this order: to serve the one God with religious obedience, not to worship idols, not to take the name of the Lord in vain. IIc had already separately spoken about the commandment of the Sabbath as foreshadowing the spiritual reality.[18] b(a)Elsewhere, indeed, that first division pleases him, but for a very insufficient reason: that in the number three (if the First Table consists of three commandments) the mystery of the Trinity

---

[16] The arrangement adopted by Lombard, *Sentences* III. xxxiii. 1. 2 (MPL 192. 830 f.), and followed in the Roman Catholic Church and the Lutheran Churches. (Cf. Melanchthon, *Loci communes* 1521, ed. Engelland, *op. cit.*, p. 46.) See *Catholic Encyclopedia* article, "Commandments of God," where this division is supported from Augustine, and that of Calvin (earlier stated by Bucer) is traced back to Philo Judaeus and Origen.

[17] Origen calls Ex. 20:4 the "second commandment," *Homilies on Exodus* hom. viii. 3 (MPG 12. 355).

[18] Augustine, *Against Two Letters of the Pelagians* III. iv. 10 (MPL 44. 594; tr. NPNF V. 406). On "*umbratili Sabbathi praecepto*" here, cf. II. vii. 1, note 2.

more clearly shines forth. Nevertheless, in the same place he admits that in other respects our division suits him better.[19] Besides these men, the author of the unfinished commentary on Matthew is on our side.[20] ᵇJosephus, no doubt according to the common agreement of his age, assigns five commandments to each Table.[21] This is contrary to reason in that it confuses religion and charity; furthermore, it is refuted by authority of the Lord, who according to Matthew puts the commandment to honor one's parents in the canon of the Second Table [Matt. 19:19]. Now let us hearken to God himself as he speaks in his own words.

(Detailed exposition of the individual commandments, 13–50)

ᵇ⁽ᵃ⁾First Commandment
"I am Jehovah, your God, who brought you out of the land of Egypt, out of the house of bondage. You shall have no other gods before my face." [Ex. 20:2–3, cf. Vg.]

13. The Preface ("I am Jehovah, your God. . . . ")
ᵇWhether you make the first sentence a part of the First Commandment or read it separately makes no difference to me, provided you do not deny to me that it is a sort of preface to the whole law. First, in framing laws, care must be taken that they be not abrogated out of contempt. God therefore especially provides that the majesty of the law he is about to give may not at any time fall into contempt. To secure this he uses a threefold proof. ᵇ⁽ᵃ⁾He claims for himself the power and right of authority in order to constrain the chosen people by the necessity of obeying him. ᵇHe holds out the promise of grace to draw them by its sweetness to a zeal for holiness. He recounts his benefits to the Jews that he may convict them of ingratitude should they not respond to his kindness. The name "Jehovah" signifies God's authority and lawful domination. If, then, "from him are all things and in him all things abide," it is right that all things should be referred to him, as Paul says [Rom. 11:36 p.]. With this word alone, therefore, we are sufficiently brought under the yoke of God's majesty, because it would be monstrous for us

---

[19] Augustine, *Letters* lv. 11 (MPL 33. 217; tr. FC 12. 276); *Sermons* xxxiii. 3: "*propter Trinitatem tria praecepta*" (MPL 38. 208).
[20] *Eruditi commentarii in Matthei Evangelium, opus imperfectum,* a work of unidentified authorship published with the Homilies of Chrysostom hom. xlix (MPG 56. 910).
[21] Josephus, *Antiquities of the Jews* III. v. 8. 101; III. vi. 5. 140 (LCL Josephus IV. 364 f., 380 f.). Cf LCC XXIII. 118, note 7.

to want to withdraw from his rule when we cannot exist apart
from him.

14. "I am Jehovah your God"

b(a)God first shows himself to be the one who has the right to
command and to whom obedience is due. bThen, in order not to
seem to constrain men by necessity alone, he also attracts them
with sweetness by declaring himself God of the church. For underlying this expression is a mutual correspondence contained
in the promise: "I will be their God, and they shall be my people"
[Jer. 31:33]. Hence, Christ confirms the immortality of Abraham,
Isaac, and Jacob from the fact that the Lord has declared himself
their God [Matt. 22:32]. It is as if he had spoken as follows: "I
have chosen you as my people, not only to benefit you in the
present life, but also to bestow upon you the blessedness of the
life to come."[22] The end to which this looks is attested in various
passages in the law. For since the Lord by his mercy renders us
worthy to be reckoned among the company of his people, "he has
chosen us," as Moses says, "to be his very own people, a holy people, and we are to keep all his commandments" [Deut. 7:6; 14:2;
26:18–19, conflated]. Hence that exhortation: "You shall be holy,
for I . . . am holy" [Lev. 11:44; cf. ch. 19:2]. From these two
statements is derived that protestation of the prophet: "A son
honors his father, and a servant his lord. . . . If I am a lord, where
is your fear? . . . If I am a father, where is your love?" [Mal. 1:
6 p.].

15. "Who brought you out of the land of Egypt, out of the house of bondage"

bThe recital of his benefit follows. This ought more powerfully
to move us in the same degree as the crime of ingratitude is more
despicable even among men. Indeed, he was then reminding
Israel of his recent benefit, a benefit of such marvelous and everlastingly memorable greatness as also to remain in force for posterity. Moreover, it is most appropriate to the present matter.
For the Lord means that they have been freed from miserable
bondage that they may, in obedience and readiness to serve, worship him as the author of their freedom. cHe also habitually, in
order to keep us in the true worship of him, makes himself known
by certain titles by which he distinguishes his sacred presence from
all idols and invented gods. For, as I have said before, such is our
inclination to vanity, joined with rash boldness that, as soon as

---

22 Cf. II. x. 10–18, where Calvin enlarges on the afflictions of the elect in this
life save for anticipation of future blessedness.

God's name is mentioned, our mind is unable to refrain from lapsing into some absurd invention.[23] Therefore God, willing to provide a remedy for this evil, adorns his divinity with sure titles, and so fences us in, as it were, that we may not wander hither and thither and rashly contrive for ourselves some new god—if, having abandoned the living God, we set up an idol. For this reason, the prophets, whenever they wish to designate him properly, clothe him with, and as it were, confine him to, those marks under which he had manifested himself to the people of Israel. For when he is called "the God of Abraham" or "the God of Israel" [Ex. 3:6], when he is set in the Temple of Jerusalem [Amos 1:2; Hab. 2:20] "between the cherubim" [Ps. 80:1; 99:1; Isa. 37:16], these and like expressions do not bind him to one place or people. Rather, they are put forward merely for this purpose: to keep the thoughts of the pious upon that God who by his covenant that he has made with Israel has so represented himself that it is in no wise lawful to turn aside from such a pattern.

[e]Yet let this point be agreed upon: deliverance is mentioned in order that the Jews may give themselves over more eagerly to God, who by right claims them for himself. [b(a)]But, in order that it may not seem that this has nothing to do with us, we must regard the Egyptian bondage of Israel as a type of the spiritual captivity in which all of us are held bound, until our heavenly Vindicator, having freed us by the power of his arm, leads us into the Kingdom of freedom. At a former time, God, intending to gather the scattered Israelites to worship his name, released them from the intolerable dominion of Pharaoh by which they were oppressed. So today all those to whom he professes himself their God he releases from the devil's deadly power—foreshadowed by that physical bondage. [b]For this reason there is no one whose mind ought not to be kindled to heed the law, which has come forth, he hears, from the highest King. As all things take their beginning from him, it is reasonable that they should in turn determine and direct their end to him. There is no one, I say, who ought not to be captivated to embrace the Lawgiver, in the observance of whose commandments he is taught to take especial delight; from whose kindness he expects both an abundance of all good things and the glory of immortal life; by whose marvelous power and mercy he knows himself freed from the jaws of death.

16. The First Commandment

[b]Having founded and established the authority of his law, he

[23] I. iv. 3.

sets forth the First Commandment, "Let us have no strange gods before him" [Ex. 20:3 p.]. The purpose of this commandment is that the Lord wills alone to be pre-eminent among his people, and to exercise complete authority over them. To effect this, he enjoins us to put far from us all impiety and superstition, which either diminish or obscure the glory of his divinity. For the same reason he commands us to worship and adore him with true and zealous godliness. The very simplicity of the words well-nigh expresses this. For we cannot "have" God without at the same time embracing the things that are his. Therefore, in forbidding us to have strange gods, he means that we are not to transfer to another what belongs to him. Even though there are innumerable things that we owe to God, yet they may be conveniently grouped in four headings: (1) adoration ᵈ(to which is added as an appendix, spiritual obedience of the conscience), ᵇ(2) trust, (3) invocation, (4) thanksgiving. (1) "Adoration" I call the veneration and worship that each of us, in submitting to his greatness, renders to him. ᵈFor this reason, I justly consider as a part of adoration the fact that we submit our consciences to his law. (2) ᵇ"Trust" is the assurance of reposing in him that arises from the recognition of his attributes, when—attributing to him all wisdom, righteousness, might, truth, and goodness—we judge that we are blessed only by communion with him. (3) "Invocation" is that habit of our mind, whenever necessity presses us, of resorting to his faithfulness and help as our only support. (4) "Thanksgiving" is that gratitude with which we ascribe praise to him for all good things. As the Lord suffers nothing of these to be transferred to another, so he commands that all be rendered wholly to himself.

And it will not be enough to abstain from a strange god. You must restrain yourself from doing what certain wicked despisers commonly do, who summarily dismiss all religions with derision. But true religion must come first, to direct our minds to the living God. Thus, steeped in the knowledge of him, they may aspire to contemplate, fear, and worship, his majesty; to participate in his blessings; to seek his help at all times; to recognize, and by praises[24] to celebrate, the greatness of his works—as the only goal of all the activities of this life. Then let us beware of wicked superstition, by which our minds, turning aside from the true God, are drawn away hither and thither to various gods. ᵉ⁽ᵇ⁾If we are content, therefore, with one God, let us remember ᵉwhat was said before:[25] that we are to drive away all invented

[24] *"Laudisque confessione."* Cf. III. iv. 9, where Calvin objects to the citation of *"confessio"* in Ps. 42:4 as evidence to justify sacramental confession.
[25] I. xiii. 1.

gods and are not to rend asunder the worship that the one God claims for himself. For ᵇit is unlawful to take away even a particle from his glory; rather, all things proper to him must remain with him.²⁶

ᵉ⁽ᵇ⁾The phrase that follows, "before my face," ᶜmakes the offense more heinous because God is provoked to jealousy as often as we substitute our own inventions in place of him. This is like a shameless woman who brings in an adulterer before her husband's very eyes only to vex his mind the more. ᵉ⁽ᵇ⁾Therefore, when God by his present power and grace testified that he kept watch over the people whom he had chosen, he warned them—to keep them even more from the crime of rebellion—that they could introduce no new gods without his witnessing and observing their sacrilege. To this ᵇboldness is added much impiety: man judges himself able in his desertions to pull the wool over God's eyes. On the contrary, God proclaims that whatever we undertake, whatever we attempt, whatever we make, comes into his sight. Therefore, let our conscience be clean even from the most secret thoughts of apostasy, if we wish our religion approved of the Lord. For the Lord requires that the glory of his divinity remain whole and uncorrupted not only in outward confession, but in his own eyes, which gaze upon the most secret recesses of our hearts.

ᵇ⁽ᵃ⁾Second Commandment

"You shall not make yourself a graven image, or any likeness of anything that is in heaven above, or in the earth beneath, or in the waters which are under the earth; you shall not adore or worship them." [Ex. 20:4–5, cf. Vg.]

*17. Spiritual worship of the invisible God**

ᵇ⁽ᵃ⁾In the previous commandment, he declared himself the one God, apart from whom no other gods are to be imagined or had. Now he declares more openly what sort of God he is, and with what kind of worship he should be honored, lest we dare attribute anything carnal to him. ᵇThe purpose of this commandment, then, is that he does not will that his lawful worship be profaned by superstitious rites. To sum up, he wholly calls us back and withdraws us from petty carnal observances, which our stupid minds, crassly conceiving of God, are wont to devise. And then he makes us conform to his lawful worship, that is, a spiritual worship established by himself. Moreover, he marks the grossest fault in this transgression, outward idolatry.

The commandment has two parts. The first restrains our

²⁶ I. xii. 3.

license from daring to subject God, who is incomprehensible, [a]to our sense perceptions, or to represent him by any form. [b]The second part forbids us to worship any images in the name of religion. But he briefly lists all the forms with which profane and superstitious peoples customarily represent God. By those things which are in heaven he means the sun, moon, other luminaries, and perhaps birds; as in Deut., ch. 4, expressing his mind, he mentions both birds and stars [vs. 17, 19]. I would not have noted this if I had not observed that some undiscerningly apply the expression to the angels.[27] Therefore I pass over the remaining parts because they are known of themselves. [e]We have already taught with sufficient clarity in Book I that whatever visible forms of God man devises are diametrically opposed to His nature; therefore, as soon as idols appear, true religion is corrupted and adulterated.[28]

18. Threatening words in the Second Commandment

[e(a)]The warning that is added ought to be of no little avail in shaking off our sloth. He threatens that:

[a]"I, Jehovah your God, am a God (or, 'mighty'; for this name of God is derived from 'might'),[29] [who is] jealous, visiting the iniquity of the fathers upon the children, unto the third and the fourth generation of those who hate my name, but showing mercy to thousands of those who love me and keep my commandments." [Ex. 20:5–6 p.][30]

This is as if he were saying that it was he alone to whom we ought to hold fast. [b]To bring us to that point, he makes known his power, which does not allow itself to be despised or disparaged with impunity. [d]Here we have the name EL, which means "God," but because it is derived from "might," in order better to express my meaning, [e(d)]I have not hesitated so to translate it and introduce it into the text. [b(a)]Secondly, he calls himself "jealous," being unable to bear any partner. Thirdly, he declares that he will vindicate his majesty and glory against any who may transfer it to creatures or graven images. And that is by no brief and simple revenge, but one that will extend to the children, the grandchildren, and the great-grandchildren, who obviously will become imitators of their fathers' impiety. In like manner also [a]he manifests his lasting mercy and kindness to those who love him and keep his law, [b(a)]to remote posterity.

[27] Augustine, City of God XIX. xxiii (MPL 41. 654; tr. NPNF II. 415–418).
[28] I. xi. 2, 12.
[29] "Nam hoc Dei nomen a fortitudine ductum est."
[30] Oratio obliqua, in Latin: pronouns changed in translation.

ᵇGod very commonly takes on the character of a husband to us. Indeed, the union by which he binds us to himself when he receives us into the bosom of the church is like sacred wedlock, which must rest upon mutual faithfulness [Eph. 5:29–32]. As he performs all the duties of a true and faithful husband, of us in return he demands love and conjugal chastity. That is, we are not to yield our souls to Satan, to lust, and to the filthy desires of the flesh, to be defiled by them. Hence, when he rebukes the apostasy of the Jews, he complains that they have cast away shame and become defiled with adulteries [Jer., ch. 3; Hos. 2:4 ff.; cf. Isa. 62:4–5]. The more holy and chaste a husband is, the more wrathful he becomes if he sees his wife inclining her heart to a rival. In like manner, the Lord, who has wedded us to himself in truth [cf. Hos. 2:19–20], manifests the most burning jealousy whenever we, neglecting the purity of his holy marriage, become polluted with wicked lusts. But he especially feels this when we transfer to another or stain with some superstition the worship of his divine majesty, which deserved to be utterly uncorrupted. In this way we not only violate the pledge given in marriage, but also defile the very marriage bed by bringing adulterers to it.

19. "Who visits the iniquity of the fathers upon the children . . ."
ᵇWe ought to see what he means when he threatens that he "will visit the iniquity of the fathers upon the children, to the third and fourth generation." For apart from the fact that it is foreign to divine justice and equity to punish the innocent for another's offense, God himself also declares that he will not compel the son to bear the father's iniquity [Ezek. 18:20]. Yet this sentence is often repeated about the punishments of the grandfather's sins being held over to future generations. For Moses often so addresses him: "Jehovah, Jehovah, who visitest the iniquity of the fathers upon the children unto the third and fourth generation" [Num. 14:18; Ex. 34:6–7, cf. Vg.]. Likewise Jeremiah: "Who showest mercy to thousands, but repayest the iniquity of the fathers upon the bosom of the children after them" [Jer. 32:18, Vg.]. Some, while they in their distress sweat over resolving this difficulty, think it is to be understood only of temporal punishments; these, they hold, it is not absurd for the children to bear for their parents' transgressions, since they are often inflicted for the sake of their salvation. This is indeed true. For Isaiah declared to Hezekiah that his sons would be deprived of the kingdom and be taken away into captivity because of the sin committed by him [Isa. 39:6–7]. The houses of Pharaoh and Abimelech were afflicted for the injury done to Abraham [Gen.

12:17; 20:3, 18; etc.]. But ᶜwhen this point is brought forward to solve our question, ᵇit is more an evasion than a true interpretation. For here and in like passages he proclaims a heavier punishment than one limited to the present life. So, then, it is to be understood that the Lord's righteous curse weighs not only upon the wicked man's head but also upon his whole family. Where the curse lies, what else can be expected but that the father, shorn of the Spirit of God, will live most disgracefully? Or that the son, forsaken by the Lord on account of the father's iniquity, will follow the same ruinous path? Finally, that the grandson and great-grandson, the accursed offspring of detestable men, will rush headlong after them?

20. Does not the visitation of the sins of the fathers upon the children run counter to God's justice?
ᵇFirst let us examine whether such revenge is unbecoming to divine justice. If the whole nature of men, whom the Lord does not deem worthy to share in his grace, is condemnable, we know that destruction is prepared for them. Nevertheless, they perish by their own iniquity, not by any unjust hatred on God's part. There is no basis for complaining about why they are not helped like others to salvation by God's grace. Inasmuch, then, as this punishment is inflicted upon the wicked and the infamous for their crimes, so that for many generations their houses are deprived of God's grace, who can blame God for this perfectly just revenge? Yet the Lord declares, on the other hand, that the punishment of the father's sin will not pass on to the child [Ezek. 18:20]. Observe what is being discussed here. The Israelites, troubled long and persistently by many misfortunes, began to make much of the proverb "The fathers have eaten sour grapes, and the children's teeth are set on edge" [Ezek. 18:2]. By this they meant that, even though they were otherwise righteous and did not deserve it, their fathers committed sins for which they had to suffer punishment, more on account of God's implacable wrath than his tempered severity. The prophet announces to them that this is not so; for they are punished for their own offenses. Nor does it accord with God's justice for a righteous son to pay the penalty of a wicked father, and this is not implied in the present threat; for if the visitation now under discussion is consummated when the Lord removes his grace, the light of his truth, and the other aids to salvation, from the family of the wicked—in that the children, blinded and forsaken by him, follow in their parents' footsteps—they bear God's curses for their fathers' evil deeds. But the fact that they are also subjected to

temporal miseries, and at last to eternal destruction, is the punishment inflicted by God's righteous judgment, not for another's
sins, but for their own wickedness.

21. "And shows mercy unto thousands . . ."
ᵇOn the other hand the promise is offered of extending God's
mercy unto a thousand generations.[31] This is frequently met with
in Scripture [Deut. 5:10; Jer. 32:18], and has been inserted in
the solemn covenant of the church, "I shall be your God, and the
God of your descendants after you" [Gen. 17:7, cf. Vg.]. Regarding this, Solomon writes, "Blessed are the sons of the righteous
after their fathers' death" [Prov. 20:7 p.]. This is not only because
of their holy upbringing, which is surely of no little importance;
but because of this blessing promised in the covenant, that God's
grace shall everlastingly abide in the families of the pious. Hence,
especial comfort for believers, but great terror for the wicked.
For if after death the memory both of righteousness and of wickedness has such value in God's sight that the blessing of the one
and the curse of the other redound to their posterity, much more
will it rest on the heads of the doers themselves. This is not,
however, contradicted by the fact that the offspring of the wicked
sometimes reform; those of believers sometimes degenerate. For
the Lawgiver desired here to frame no such perpetual rule as
might detract from his election. To comfort the righteous and
to frighten the sinner it is enough that this is no empty or ineffective forewarning, even though it does not always take effect.
For the temporal punishments inflicted upon a few scoundrels are
testimonies of the divine wrath against sin, and of the judgment
someday coming to all sinners, though many go unpunished
till the end of this life. Thus, when the Lord gives one example
of this blessing to show his mercy and kindness to the son for
the father's sake, he gives proof of his constant and perpetual favor
toward those who worship him. When once he pursues the in-

---

[31] *"Mille generationes."* Calvin's opinion that the Hebrew text here and
in Deut. 5:9 should be rendered "showing mercy to a thousand generations" appears in all his editions of the *Institutes,* and in his *Instruction
in Faith,* 1537 (tr. Fuhrmann, p. 26). It is repeated in II. x. 9 and appeared
four times in Comm. *Four Books of Moses,* Ex. 20:6. Many French versions
of the Bible, and some in German and English, have a corresponding
translation. Cf. J. M. P. Smith, *The Bible: An American Translation;*
L. Segond's revised French edition; Fr. Noetscher's German edition; also
the comment of A. H. McNeile, Westminster Commentaries, *Exodus,* p.
117. Calvin repeatedly uses the passage as evidence of the vastness of
God's mercy, e.g., in IV. xvi. 9. We should be unwise to stress, though we
may hardly exclude altogether, the bearing of such passages on Calvin's
expectation of the duration of the human race on earth.

iquity of the father in the son, he teaches what sort of judgment awaits all the wicked for their own offenses. In this passage he was particularly concerned with the certainty of the latter. Also, in passing he commends to us the largeness of his mercy, which he extends to a thousand generations, while he has assigned only four generations to his vengeance.

b(a)Third Commandment

"You shall not take the name of Jehovah your God in vain." [Ex. 20:7.]

22. *Interpretation of the commandment*

ᵇThe purpose of this commandment is: God wills that we hallow the majesty of his name. Therefore, it means in brief that we are not to profane his name by treating it contemptuously and irreverently. To this prohibition duly corresponds the commandment that we should be zealous and careful to honor his name with godly reverence. Therefore we ought to be so disposed in mind and speech that we neither think nor say anything concerning God and his mysteries, without reverence and much soberness; that in estimating his works we conceive nothing but what is honorable to him.

We must, in my opinion, diligently observe the three following points: First, whatever our mind conceives of God, whatever our tongue utters, should savor of his excellence, match the loftiness of his sacred name, and lastly, serve to glorify his greatness. Secondly, we should not rashly or perversely abuse his Holy Word and worshipful mysteries either for the sake of our own ambition, or greed, or amusement; but, as they bear the dignity of his name imprinted upon them, they should ever be honored and prized among us. Finally, we should not defame or detract from his works, as miserable men are wont abusively to cry out against him; but whatever we recognize as done by him we should speak of with praise of his wisdom, righteousness, and goodness. That is what it means to hallow God's name.

When we do otherwise, it is polluted with empty and wicked abuse. For, drawn away from the lawful use to which alone it had been dedicated, and though nothing else ensues, yet shorn of its dignity, it is little by little rendered contemptible. But if there is so much evil in this rash readiness violently to misuse God's name, it is a much greater sin if it be put to abominable uses, ᵃas those do who make it serve the superstitions of necromancy, frightful curses, unlawful exorcisms, and other wicked incantations. ᵇBut the commandment has particular reference to the oath, wherein the perverse abuse of the Lord's name is in the highest degree detestable, that thereby we may be better frightened away altogether from all profaning of it [cf. Deut. 5:11]. ᵉIn this commandment we are enjoined concerning the worship of God and the reverence of his name, rather than the equity that we are to keep among men. It should be useless repetition if this commandment also treated concerning the duty of love, which is reserved for the Second Table where he will condemn perjury and false witness, which harm human society. The division of the law also requires it, because, as has been said, God did not arrange his law into two tables without reason. From this we conclude that in this commandment he vindicates his own right, protects the holiness of his name, but does not here teach what men owe to men.

23. The oath as confession to God

ᵇIn the first place, we must state what an oath is. It is calling God as witness to confirm the truth of our word. Those curses which contain manifest insults to God are unfit to be regarded as oaths. Many passages of Scripture show that such an attestation, duly performed, is a sort of divine worship. For example, when Isaiah prophesies about calling the Assyrians and Egyptians into a covenant relationship with Israel, he says: "They shall speak the language of Canaan and shall swear in the name of the Lord" [Isa. 19:18]. That is, by swearing in the Lord's name they will profess his religion. Likewise, when he speaks of the extension of his Kingdom: "He who will bless himself . . . shall bless himself by the God of believers; and he who takes an oath in the land, shall swear by the God of truth" [Isa. 65:16 p.]. Jeremiah says, "If the learned will diligently teach my people to swear in my name, . . . even as they taught them to swear by Baal, then they shall be built up in the midst of my house." [Jer. 12:16 p.] And we are justly said to witness to our religion in invoking the name of the Lord as our witness. ᵇ⁽ᵃ⁾For thus we confess him to be eternal and immutable truth; and we call upon him not only the fit witness of truth above all others, but also the only affirmer of it, ᵇwho is able to bring hidden things to light; then as the knower of hearts [I Cor. 4:5]. For when men's testimonies fail, we flee to God as our witness—especially when something that lies hidden in the conscience is to be declared.

For this reason, the Lord is bitterly angry against those who swear by strange gods, and interprets that sort of swearing as a proof of open treason. "Your children have forsaken me, and swear by those who are no gods." [Jer. 5:7, Vg.] And he declares the gravity of this offense in the threat of punishment: "I will cut off . . . those who swear by the name of the Lord, and yet swear by Milcom" [Zeph. 1:4–5 p.].

24. The false oath as a desecration of God's name

bWe see how the Lord wills that worship of his name inheres in our oaths. Consequently we ought to be all the more diligent that they contain neither insolence nor contempt and low esteem instead of worship. It is no small affront to swear falsely by his name; in the law this is called "profanation" [Lev. 19:12]. What remains to the Lord when he is despoiled of his truth? He will then cease to be God. But he is indeed despoiled of it when he is made a supporter and approver of falsehood. Therefore Joshua, wishing to make Achan confess the truth, says: "My son, give glory to the Lord of Israel" [Josh. 7:19], obviously implying that the Lord is most gravely dishonored if perjury be committed in his name. And no wonder! For it is not on our account that his sacred name is not to be branded with any kind of falsehood. It is evident from the similar manner of calling God to witness used by the Pharisees in the Gospel of John [ch. 9:24] that this was the usual form among the Jews whenever anyone was called to take an oath. The modes of expression used in Scripture instruct us in this caution: "The Lord lives" [I Sam. 14:39]; "The Lord do so to me and more also" [I Sam. 14:44; cf. II Sam. 3:9; II Kings 6:31]; "God be witness upon my soul" [Rom. 1:9; II Cor. 1:23, conflated]. These sayings suggest that we cannot call God to be the witness of our words without asking him to be the avenger of our perjury if we deceive.

25. The idle oath

bGod's name is rendered cheap and common when it is used in true but needless oaths. For it is then also taken in vain. Thus it does not suffice for us to refrain from perjury, unless at the same time awe remember that oath-taking was permitted band established anot for the sake of lust or desire, but because of necessity. bHence, those who apply it to unnecessary things depart from its lawful use. Now, no other necessity can be pretended than to serve either religion or love. In this matter men today sin quite unrestrainedly, and all the more intolerably because by very custom it has ceased to be considered an offense. Surely this is deemed no slight offense before God's judgment seat! God's name is commonly and promiscuously profaned in idle talk. This is not regarded as an evil because men have come into the practice of this great depravity by long and unpunished boldness. Yet the Lord's commandment remains unalterable; the warning remains firm, and will someday have its effect. By it a peculiar vengeance is proclaimed against those who use his name in vain.

This commandment is transgressed in another respect: with manifest wickedness in oaths we substitute God's holy servants in place of him, thus transferring to them the glory of his divinity [Ex. 23:13]. With good reason, then, the Lord has, by special commandment, enjoined us to swear by his name [Deut. 6:13; 10:20]; by special prohibition he has forbidden us to be heard swearing by strange gods [Ex. 23:13]. The apostle likewise clearly testifies to this when he writes: "Men swear by a greater than themselves"; God, because he had none greater than his glory, swore by himself [Heb. 6:16–17 p.].

26. Does not the Sermon on the Mount forbid this kind of oath?

ᵇThe Anabaptists, not content with this moderation in swearing oaths, condemn all oaths without exception, since Christ's prohibition of them is general. "I say to you, Do not swear at all, . . . but let what you say be simply, 'Yes, yes' or 'No, no'; anything more than this comes from evil." [Matt. 5:34, 37; cf. James 5:12.]³² But in this way they heedlessly dash against Christ, making him the Father's enemy as if he had come down to earth to set aside God's decrees. Now the eternal God not only permits oaths as a legitimate thing under the law (which should be sufficient), but commands their use in case of necessity [Ex. 22:10–11]. But Christ declares that he is one with the Father [John 10:30]; that he brings nothing but what the Father has commanded [John 10:18]; that his teaching is not from himself [John 7:16], etc. What then? Will they make God contradict himself so that he afterward forbids and condemns what he once approved by enjoining it upon men's behavior?

But because there is some difficulty in Christ's words, let us spend a little time on them. Here, however, we shall never attain the truth unless we fix our eyes upon Christ's intention and give

---

³² Calvin had encountered this view among the Anabaptists, against whom he wrote his *Psychopannychia* in 1534 (published 1542) and with whom he was in controversy in Geneva, 1537, and in Strasbourg, 1539. Zwingli had written against this opinion in his tract *In Catabaptistas strophas elenchus*, 1527 (Zwingli, *Opera*, ed. M. Schuler and J. Schulthess III. 406 ff.; tr. S. M. Jackson, *Selected Works of Huldreich Zwingli*, "Refutation of Baptist Tricks," pp. 206 ff.). Calvin treats it also in his *Brieve instruction contre les erreurs de la secte commune des Anabaptistes* (1544), seventh article (CR VII. 92 ff.; cf. OS III. 361). Cf. W. E. Keeney, *The Development of Dutch Anabaptist Thought and Practice, 1539–1564* (Hartford Seminary dissertation, 1959), pp. 212 ff.

heed to what he is driving at in that passage. It was not his purpose either to slacken or tighten the law, but to bring back to a true and genuine understanding what had been quite corrupted by the false devisings of the scribes and Pharisees. If we understand this, we will not think that Christ condemned oaths entirely, but only those which transgress the rule of the law. From these words it is clear that the people then commonly avoided perjury only, while the law forbids not only perjuries but also empty and superfluous oaths. Therefore the Lord, the surest interpreter of the law, warns that it is evil not only to swear falsely but also to swear [Matt. 5:34]. Why "to swear"? Surely he means "to swear in vain." But the oaths that are commended in the law, he leaves untouched and free. Our opponents think that they argue more compellingly when they doggedly seize upon the expression "at all."[33] Yet this does not refer to the word "to swear," but to the forms of oaths following thereafter. For this, also, was a part of their error, that while they swore by heaven and earth they thought they did not touch the name of God. After the chief instance of transgression, therefore, the Lord also cuts off all excuses from them in order that they may not suppose they have escaped by calling on heaven and earth, while suppressing God's name. ᵉWe ought also to note this in passing: although the name of God is not expressed, yet men swear by him in indirect forms; as when they swear by the light of life, by the bread they eat, by their baptism, or by other tokens of God's generosity toward them. Christ, in that passage forbidding men to swear by heaven and earth and Jerusalem [Matt. 5:34–35], is not correcting superstition, as some falsely think. Rather, he is refuting the wily sophistry of those who see nothing wrong in idly tossing about indirect oaths—as if they spared God's sacred name, when it is actually engraved upon all his benefits. It is another matter when some mortal, or deceased person, or angel is substituted in place of God; just as among the heathen nations that loathsome form of swearing by the life or by the genius of the king was devised by way of adulation. For then such false deification obscures and lessens the glory of the one God. But when we intend only to seek confirmation of our statements from God's holy name, although it be done indirectly, injury is done to his majesty by all such trifling oaths. Christ deprives this license of vain excuse, forbidding us to "swear at all." James, repeating those words of Christ which I have cited, has the same intent [James 5:12].

[33] Zwingli, *In Catabaptistas strophas elenchus*, 1527, *loc. cit.*; Calvin, *Brieve instruction contre les erreurs de la secte commune des Anabaptistes* (1544), pp. 95 f.

For such rashness, although it is a desecration of God's name, has always been widespread in the world. If you should refer the expression "at all" to the substance, as if it were without exception unlawful to swear any oath, how would you explain what is immediately added: "Neither by heaven, nor by the earth," etc.? From these words it is sufficiently clear that Christ has met the quibbles whereby the Jews thought their fault lightened.

27. The extrajudicial oath is therefore necessarily admissible

ᵇTo men of sound judgment there can then be no doubt that the Lord in that passage disapproved only of those oaths forbidden by the law. For he, who in his life gave an example of the perfection that he taught, did not shrink from oaths whenever circumstances required. And the disciples, who, we may be sure, obeyed their Master in all things, followed the same example. Who would dare say that Paul would have sworn if the taking of oaths had been utterly forbidden? But when circumstances demanded it, he swore without any hesitation, sometimes even adding a curse [Rom. 1:9; II Cor. 1:23].

Yet the question is still not settled. For some think public oaths alone excepted from this prohibition, ᵇ⁽ᵃ⁾such as those we take which are administered and required by a magistrate; such, also, as those commonly used by princes in solemnizing treaties, or a people swearing in the name of their prince, ᵇor a soldier, when he is bound by an oath of service, and the like. ᵇ⁽ᵃ⁾In this category they also place, and justly, those statements in Paul which assert the dignity of the gospel, inasmuch as the apostles in their duties are not private citizens but public ministers of God.[34] ᵇOf course I do not deny that these are the safest oaths, because they are supported by the firmer testimonies of Scripture. In doubtful matters, the magistrate is bidden to compel the witness to swear; the latter in turn is to reply under oath; the apostle speaks of human quarrels as resolved by this means [Heb. 6:16]. In this commandment each has sound approval for what he does.

Also, one can observe among the ancient heathen that public and solemn oath-taking was held in great reverence. Common oaths, however, which were indiscriminately sworn, were considered either of very little or no importance, as if it were thought that God's majesty did not enter into them.

But it would be too dangerous to condemn private oaths undertaken soberly, with holy intent, reverently, and in necessary

---

[34] The opinions here condemned were espoused by Zwingli (*op. cit.*, p. 408) and in the 1536 *Institutio* by Calvin himself (ch. 5; *De lege, mandatum iii;* OS I. 45 f.).

circumstances, supported as they are both by reason and by examples. For if it is lawful in a grave and serious matter for private persons to call upon God as a judge between them [I Sam. 24:12], there is even greater reason to call upon him as a witness. Your brother will accuse you of breach of faith; as a duty of love you will try to clear yourself. On no terms will he admit himself satisfied. If your reputation is imperiled because of his stubborn ill will, you can without offense call upon God's judgment to make manifest your innocence in due time. If we weigh the terms "judgment" and "witness," it is a lesser matter to call God to witness. I do not, therefore, see why we should declare unlawful this calling of God to witness. We have very many examples of this. If Abraham and Isaac's oath with Abimelech is alleged as a public one [Gen. 21:24; 26:31], yet surely Jacob and Laban were private persons who confirmed their alliance by a mutual oath [Gen. 31:53–54]. Boaz was a private person who confirmed his promised marriage to Ruth in the same way [Ruth 3:13]. Obadiah was a private person, a righteous, God-fearing man, who affirmed under oath what he wished to persuade Elijah to believe [I Kings 18:10].

Thus I have no better rule than for us so to control our oaths that they may not be rash, indiscriminate, wanton, or trifling; but that they may serve a just need—either to vindicate the Lord's glory, or to further a brother's edification.[35] Such is the purpose of this commandment of the law.

b(a)Fourth Commandment
"Remember to keep holy the Sabbath Day. Six days you shall labor, and do all your work; but the seventh day is a sabbath to Jehovah your God. In it you shall not do any work," etc. [Ex. 20:8–10, cf. Vg.]

28. General interpretation
bThe purpose of this commandment is that, being dead to our own inclinations and works, we should meditate on the Kingdom of God, and that we should practice that meditation in the ways established by him. But, since this commandment has a particular consideration distinct from the others, it requires a slightly different order of exposition. b(a)The early fathers customarily called this commandment a foreshadowing because it contains the outward keeping of a day which, upon Christ's coming, was abolished

---

[35] Bucer, In sacra quatuor Evangelia, enarrationes perpetuae (Strasbourg, 1536), pp. 135 ff.

with the other figures.[36] [b]This they say truly, but they touch upon only half the matter. Hence, we must go deeper in our exposition, and ponder three conditions in which, it seems to me, the keeping of this commandment consists.

First, under the repose of the seventh day the heavenly Lawgiver meant to represent to the people of Israel spiritual rest, in which believers ought to lay aside their own works to allow God to work in them. Secondly, he meant that there was to be a stated day for them to assemble to hear the law and perform the rites, [36x]or at least to devote it particularly to meditation upon his works, and thus through this remembrance to be trained in piety. [b]Thirdly, he resolved to give a day of rest to servants and those who are under the authority of others, in order that they should have some respite from toil.

29. The Sabbath commandment as promise

[b]Nevertheless we are taught in many passages that this fore shadowing of spiritual rest[37] occupied the chief place in the Sabbath. [b(a)]The Lord enjoined obedience to almost no other commandment as severely as to this [Num. 15:32–36; cf. Ex. 31:13 ff.; 35:2]. When he wills through the prophets to indicate that all religion has been overturned, he complains that his Sabbaths have been polluted, violated, not kept, not hallowed—as if, with this homage omitted, nothing more remained in which he could be honored [Ezek. 20:12–13; 22:8; 23:38; Jer. 17:21, 22, 27; Isa. 56:2]. [b]He bestows highest approbation upon its observance. Hence, also, believers greatly esteemed the revelation of the Sabbath among the other oracles. For in The Book of Nehemiah the Levites thus spoke in public assembly: "Thou didst make known to our fathers thy holy Sabbath, and gavest them commandments and ceremonies and a law by the hand of Moses" [Neh. 9:14 p.]. You see how it is held in singular esteem among all the precepts of the law. All these precepts serve to exalt the dignity of the mystery, which Moses and Ezekiel have most beautifully ex-

---

[36] Augustine, *Against Two Letters of the Pelagians* III. iv. 10 (MPL 44. 194; tr. NPNF V. 406); *Sermons* cxxxvi. 3 (MPL 38. 752). Cf. II. vii. 16, note 22.

[36x] The words "or at least . . . piety" are from the 1545 edition.

[37] *"Spiritualis quietis adumbrationem"*; cf. *"umbratile"* in sec. 28. The spiritualizing of the Sabbath as foreshadowing the heavenly rest, seen in secs. 28 and 29, here, was anticipated by Augustine, e.g., in *Against Two Letters of the Pelagians, loc. cit.; Sermons* ix. 3. 3; xxxiii. 3. 3 (MPL 38. 77, 208); *Letters* lv. 9. 17 (MPL 33. 212; tr. FC 12. 274). Some convenient data on historical Christian discussions of Sunday will be found in *Sunday, Its Origin, History, and Present Obligation*, by J. A. Hussey (Bampton Lectures, 1860), lectures iii to vi.

pressed. Thus you have in Exodus: "See that you keep my Sabbath, for this is a sign between me and you throughout your generations, that you may know that I, the Lord, sanctify you. You shall keep the Sabbath, because it is holy for you" [ch. 31: 13–14; cf. Vg.; cf. ch. 35:2]. "Let the Children of Israel keep the Sabbath, and let them observe it throughout their generations; it is a perpetual covenant between me and the Children of Israel, and a sign forever." [Ch. 31:16–17, cf. Vg.] Ezekiel expresses it still more fully, but the sum of his statement comes to this: that the Sabbath is a sign whereby Israel may recognize that God is their sanctifier [Ezek. 20:12]. If our sanctification consists in mortifying our own will, then a very close correspondence appears between the outward sign and the inward reality. b(a)We must be wholly at rest that God may work in us; we must yield our will; we must resign our heart; we must give up all our fleshly desires. In short, we must rest from all activities of our own contriving so that, having God working in us [Heb. 13:21], we may repose in him [Heb. 4:9], as the apostle also teaches.

30. The seventh day

b(a)For the Jews the observance of one day in seven customarily represented this eternal cessation. The Lord commended it by his example that they might observe it with greater piety. To know that he is trying to imitate the Creator has no little value in arousing man's zeal.

If anyone is looking for some secret meaning in the number seven, in Scripture the number of perfection, it has been chosen with good reason to denote perpetuity. bA statement of Moses' supports this. He concludes his description of the succession of days and nights on the day when, as he relates, "the Lord rested from his works" [Gen. 2:3]. One can also interpret the number in another way: the Lord thus indicated b(a)that the Sabbath would never be perfected until the Last Day should come. For we here begin our blessed rest in him; daily we make fresh progress in it. But because there is still a continual warfare with the flesh, it will not be consummated until Isaiah's saying is fulfilled about "new moon following new moon and Sabbath following Sabbath" [Isa. 66:23]; until, that is, God shall be "all in all" [I Cor. 15:28]. It would seem, therefore, that the Lord through the seventh day has sketched for his people the coming perfection of his Sabbath in the Last Day, to make them aspire to this perfection by unceasing meditation upon the Sabbath throughout life.[38]

[38] Gregory the Great, Moralia in Job xxxv. 8. 15–17 (on Job 42:8) (MPL 76.

31. In Christ the promise of the Sabbath commandment is fulfilled.

ᵇIf anyone dislikes this interpretation of the number seven as too subtle, I have no objection to his taking it more simply, ᵇ⁽ᵃ⁾thus: the Lord ordained a certain day on which his people might, under the tutelage of the law, practice constant meditation upon the spiritual rest. ᵇAnd he assigned the seventh day, either because he foresaw that it would be sufficient; or that, by providing a model in his own example, he might better arouse the people; or at least point out to them that the Sabbath had no other purpose than to render them conformable to their Creator's example. Which interpretation we accept makes little difference, provided we retain the mystery that is principally set forth: that of perpetual repose from our labors. The prophets repeatedly recalled the Jews to the consideration of this in order that they might not think they had performed their whole duty merely by ceasing from physical labor. Besides the passages already cited, you have the following in Isaiah: "If you turn back your foot from the Sabbath, so as not to do your pleasure on my holy day, and call the Sabbath a delight and the holy day of the Lord of glory; if you glory in it, not going your own ways, and do not find your pleasure in your own talk; then you shall take delight in the Lord," etc. [Isa. 58:13–14, cf. Vg.].

ᵇ⁽ᵃ⁾But there is no doubt that by the Lord Christ's coming the ceremonial part of this commandment was abolished. ᵇFor he himself is the truth, with whose presence all figures vanish; he is the body, at whose appearance the shadows are left behind. He is, I say, the true fulfillment of the Sabbath. "We were buried with him by baptism, we were engrafted into participation in his death, that sharing in his resurrection we may walk in newness of life." [Rom. 6:4–5 p.] For this reason the apostle elsewhere writes that the Sabbath [Col. 2:16] was "a shadow of what is to come; but the body belongs to Christ" [Col. 2:17], that is, the very substance of truth, which Paul well explained in that passage. This is not confined within a single day but extends through the whole course of our life, until, completely dead to ourselves, we are filled with the life of God. Christians ought therefore to shun completely the superstitious observance of days.

32. How far does the Fourth Commandment go beyond external regulation?

ᵇThe two latter reasons for the Sabbath ought not to be rele-

757 ff.; tr. LF XXXI. 671 ff.). Cf. Bucer, *In sacra quatuor Evangelia, enarrationes perpetuae*, pp. 299 f.

gated to the ancient shadows, but are equally applicable to every age. Although the Sabbath has been abrogated, there is still occasion for us: (1) [b(a)]to assemble on stated days for the hearing of the Word, the breaking of the mystical bread, and for public prayers [cf. Acts 2:42]; (2) to give surcease from labor to servants and workmen.[39] There is no doubt that in enjoining the Sabbath the Lord was concerned with both. [b]There is ample evidence for the first, if only in the usage of the Jews. Moses in Deuteronomy pointed out the second reason, in these words: "That your manservant and your maidservant may rest as well as you, remember that you also were a servant . . . in Egypt" [ch. 5:14–15, Vg.]. Also, in Exodus: "That your ox and your ass may have rest; and the son of your bondmaid . . . may be refreshed" [ch. 23:12]. Who can deny that these two things apply as much to us as to the Jews? Meetings of the church are enjoined upon us by God's Word; and from our everyday experience we well know how we need them. But how can such meetings be held unless they have been established and have their stated days? [b(a)]According to the apostle's statement, "all things should be done decently and in order" among us [I Cor. 14:40]. [b]It is so impossible to maintain decency and order—otherwise than by this arrangement and regulation—that immediate confusion and ruin threaten the church if it be dissolved. But if we are subject to the same necessity as that to alleviate which the Lord established the Sabbath for the Jews, let no one allege that this has nothing to do with us. For our most provident and merciful Father willed to see to our needs not less than those of the Jews.

Why do we not assemble daily, you ask, so as to remove all distinction of days? If only this had been given us! Spiritual wisdom truly deserved to have some portion of time set apart for it each day. But if the weakness of many made it impossible for daily meetings to be held, and the rule of love does not allow more to be required of them, why should we not obey the order we see laid upon us by God's will?

33. Why do we celebrate Sunday?

[b]I am compelled to dwell longer on this because at present some restless spirits are stirring up tumult over the Lord's Day.[40]

[39] Bucer, In sacra quatuor Evangelia, enarrationes perpetuae, p. 300.
[40] Some of the "restless spirits" had appeared in Geneva in 1537, when a citizen named Colinaeus, or Colon, was imprisoned for unorthodox opinions on baptism and the Sabbath. The fact is referred to in a letter from Christophe Fabri, minister in Thonon, to the ministers of Geneva, July 31, 1537. Herminjard gives the letter with informing notes (Correspondance IV. 270 ff.).

They complain that the Christian people are nourished in Juda- ism because they keep some observance of days. But I reply that we transcend Judaism in observing these days because we are far different from the Jews in this respect. For we are not celebrat- ing it as a ceremony with the most rigid scrupulousness, suppos- ing a spiritual mystery to be figured thereby. Rather, we are using it as a remedy needed to keep order in the church. Yet Paul teaches that no one ought to pass judgment on Christians over the observance of this day, for it is only "a shadow of what is to come" [Col. 2:17]. For this reason, he fears that he "labored in vain" among the Galatians because they still "observed days" [Gal. 4:10–11]. And he declares to the Romans [b(a)]that it is super- stitious for anyone to distinguish one day from another [Rom. 14:5]. [b]Who but madmen cannot see what observance the apostle means? For [those whom he was addressing] did not regard the purpose to be political and ecclesiastical order; but, retaining Sabbaths as foreshadowing things spiritual, they obscured to that extent the glory of Christ and the light of the gospel. [b(a)]They therefore abstained from manual tasks not because these are a diversion from sacred studies and meditations, but with a certain scrupulousness they imagined that by celebrating the day they were honoring mysteries once commended. [b]The apostle inveighs, I say, against this absurd distinction of days, not against the lawful selection that serves the peace of the Christian fellowship. Indeed, in the churches founded by him, the Sabbath was retained for this purpose. For he prescribes that day to the Corinthians for gather- ing contributions to help the Jerusalem brethren [I Cor. 16:2]. If one fears superstition, there was more danger in the Jewish holy days than in the Lord's days that Christians now keep. For, because it was expedient to overthrow superstition, the day sacred to the Jews was set aside;[41] because it was necessary to maintain decorum, order, and peace in the church, another was appointed for that purpose.

34. Spiritual observance of the sacred day*

[c]However, the ancients did not substitute the Lord's Day (as we call it) for the Sabbath without careful discrimination. The purpose and fulfillment of that true rest, represented by the ancient Sabbath, lies in the Lord's resurrection. Hence, by the

---

[41] It is clear from this passage and from sec. 34 that for Calvin the Christian Sunday is not, as in the Westminster Confession XXI. 8, a simple continua- tion of the Jewish Sabbath "changed into the first day of the week," but a distinctively Christian institution adopted on the abrogation of the former one, as a means of church order and spiritual health.

very day that brought the shadows to an end, Christians are warned not to cling to the shadow rite. bNor do I cling to the number "seven" so as to bind the church in subjection to it. And I shall not condemn churches that have other solemn days for their meetings, provided there be no superstition. This will be so if they have regard solely to the maintenance of discipline and good order.

b(a)To sum up: as truth was delivered to the Jews under a figure, so is it set before us without shadows. First, we are to meditate throughout life upon an everlasting Sabbath rest from all our works, that the Lord may work in us through his Spirit. Secondly, [41x]each one of us privately, whenever he has leisure, is to exercise himself diligently in pious meditation upon God's works. Also, we b(a)should all observe together the lawful order set by the church for the hearing of the Word, the administration of the sacraments, and for public prayers. In the third place, we should not inhumanly oppress those subject to us.[42]

aThus vanish the trifles of the false prophets, who in former centuries infected the people with a Jewish opinion. They asserted that nothing but the ceremonial part of this commandment has been abrogated (in their phraseology the "appointing" of the seventh day), but the moral part remains—namely, the fixing of one day in seven.[43] Yet this is merely changing the day as a reproach to the Jews, while keeping in mind the same sanctity of the day. bFor we still retain the same significance in the mystery of the days as pertained among the Jews. aAnd we really see how they profit by such teaching. For those of them who cling to their constitutions surpass the Jews three times over in crass and carnal Sabbatarian superstition.[44] Hence the reproaches that we read in

---

[41x] The following words are from the 1545 edition.

[42] Calvin here refers to Cassiodorus, *Historia tripartita* IX. 38, the passage being from Socrates, *Ecclesiastical History* v. 23 (MPL 69. 1153; MPG 67. 625 f.; tr. NPNF 2 scr. II. 130). Calvin's concern to avoid the oppression of the serving class is not paralleled in this patristic source however. Luther makes much of the worker's rest day in his Larger Catechism (1529), and it is prominent in the English Reformers, John Hooper and Thomas Becon. Cf. Parker Society, Hooper, *Early Works*, pp. 337–351; Becon, *Catechism*, etc., pp. 82 f.

[43] Cf. Albertus Magnus, *Compendium veritatis theologicae* (Venice, 1485) V. 62; Aquinas, *Summa Theol.* I IIae. c. 3 ad 2; II IIae. cxxii. 4 ad 1.

[44] See *Catholic Encyclopedia* articles "Constitutions," "Constitution, papal." Calvin's position is consciously anti-Sabbatarian. A severe legalism connected with Sunday was a phenomenon of the Middle Ages, as it was of some later Protestantism. The penitential books of the early Middle Ages indicate heavy penalties for Sunday work. Cf. J. T. McNeill and H. M. Gamer, *Medieval Handbooks of Penance* (Records of Civilization XIX), index, *s.v.* "Sunday." Calvin's view is similar to that adopted in the Second

The Book of Isaiah apply to them today just as much as they did to those whom the prophet rebuked in his own time [chs. 1:13–15; 58:13]. ᵉBut we ought especially to hold to this general doctrine: that, in order to prevent religion from either perishing or declining among us, we should diligently frequent the sacred meetings, and make use of those external aids which can promote the worship of God.

ᵇ⁽ᵃ⁾Fifth Commandment

"Honor your father and your mother that you may be long-lived on the land which Jehovah your God shall give you." [Ex. 20:12, cf. Vg.]

35. The wide scope of this commandment

ᵇThe purpose is: since the maintenance of his economy[45] pleases the Lord God, the degrees of pre-eminence established by him ought to be inviolable for us. This, then, is the sum: that we should look up to those whom God has placed over us, and should treat them with honor, obedience, and gratefulness. It follows from this that we are forbidden to detract from their dignity either by contempt, by stubbornness, or by ungratefulness. For the word "honor" has a wide meaning in Scripture. Thus, when the apostle says: "Let the elders who rule well be considered worthy of double honor" [I Tim. 5:17], he refers not only to the reverence due them, but to the remuneration to which their ministry entitles them. Now this precept of subjection strongly conflicts with the depravity of human nature which, swollen with the longing for lofty position, bears subjection grudgingly. Accordingly, he has put forward as an example that kind of superiority which is by nature most amiable and least invidious, because he could thus more easily soften and bend our minds to the habit of submission. By that subjection which is easiest to tolerate, the Lord therefore gradually accustoms us to all lawful subjection, since the reason of all is the same. Indeed, he shares his name with those to whom he has given pre-eminence, so far as it is necessary to preserve this. The titles "Father," "God," and "Lord" so belong to him alone that as often as we hear any one of these our mind cannot fail to be struck with an awareness of his majesty. Those persons, therefore, with whom he shares these titles he lights up with a spark of his splendor so that each may be distinguished according to his degree. Thus, in him who is our

Helvetic Confession XXIV, which allows "no place to a Jewish observance of the day."

45 "Dispositionis." Cf. I. xiii. 6: "Dispositionem vel oeconomiam."

father we should recognize something divine because he does not bear the divine title without cause. He who is a "prince" or a "lord" has some share in God's honor.

36. The demand

ᵇFor this reason, we ought not to doubt that the Lord has here established a universal rule. That is, knowing that someone has been placed over us by the Lord's ordination, we should render to him reverence, obedience, and gratefulness, and should perform such other duties for him as we can. It makes no difference whether our superiors are worthy or unworthy of this honor, for whatever they are they have attained their position through God's providence a proof that the Lawgiver himself would have us hold them in honor. However, he has expressly bidden us to reverence our parents, who have brought us into this life. Nature itself ought in a way to teach us this. Those who abusively or stubbornly violate parental authority are monsters, not men! Hence the Lord commands that all those disobedient to their parents be put to death. For since they do not recognize those whose efforts brought them into the light of day, they are not worthy of its benefits. What we have noted is clearly true from various additions to the law, that there are three parts of the honor here spoken of: reverence, obedience, and gratefulness. The Lord confirms the first—reverence—when he enjoins that one who curses his father or mother be killed [Ex. 21:17; Lev. 20:9; Prov. 20:20]: there he punishes contempt and abuse. He confirms the second—obedience—when he decrees the penalty of death for disobedient and rebellious children [Deut. 21:18–21]. What Christ says in Matt., ch. 15, refers to the third kind of honor, gratefulness: it is of God's commandment that we do good to our parents [vs. 4–6]. And whenever Paul mentions this commandment, he interprets it as requiring obedience [Eph. 6:1–3; Col. 3:20].

37. The promise

ᵇ⁽ᵃ⁾A promise is added by way of recommendation. This is to show us better how pleasing to God is the submission that is here enjoined upon us. ᵇPaul ᵇ⁽ᵃ⁾pricks us out of our apathy with this needle ᵇwhen he says: "This is the first commandment with a promise" [Eph. 6:2]. For the promise already given in the First Table was not confined to one particular commandment, but was extended to the whole law. Now we ought to understand this as follows: the Lord particularly spoke to the Israelites of the land that he had promised them as an inheritance. If, then, the possession of the land was a guarantee of God's bounty, we ought not to wonder if the Lord willed to attest his favor by promising length of life, through which they could long enjoy his benefits. The meaning therefore is: "Honor your father and mother, that you may enjoy through a long period of life the possession of the land, which is to be yours as a testimony of my favor." Moreover, because to believers the whole earth is blessed, we rightly include the present life among God's blessings. Therefore, this promise similarly has reference to us, in so far as length of present life is indeed a proof of God's benevolence toward us. For neither is it promised to us nor was it promised to the Jews as if it contained blessedness in itself; but because for the pious it is a customary symbol of God's kindness. Therefore, if it happens that a son obedient to his parents is snatched from life before attaining maturity, a frequent occurrence, the Lord unwaveringly perseveres in the fulfillment of His promise no less than if He furnished a hundred acres of land to one to whom He had promised only one. The whole point lies here: we should reflect that we are promised long life in so far as it is a blessing of God; and that it is a blessing only in so far as it is an evidence of God's favor, which he testifies to his servants far more richly and substantially through death, and proves it in the reality.

38. The threat

ᵇBesides, while the Lord promises the blessing of the present life to those children who duly honor their parents, at the same time he implies that an inevitable curse threatens all stubborn and disobedient children. To assure that this commandment be carried out, he has, through his law, declared them subject to the sentence of death, and commanded that they undergo punishment. If they elude that judgment, he himself takes vengeance upon them in some way or other. For we see how many men of this sort perish either in battles or in quarrels; others are cast down in ways less common. Nearly all offer proof that this threatening is not in vain. Some people may escape punishment until extreme old age. Yet in this life they are bereft of God's blessing, and can only miserably pine away, being reserved for greater punishments to come. Far indeed, then, are they from sharing in the blessing promised to godly children!

But we also ought in passing to note that we are bidden to obey our parents only "in the Lord" [Eph. 6:1]. This is apparent from the principle already laid down. For they sit in that place to which they have been advanced by the Lord, who shares with them a part of his honor. Therefore, the submission paid to them ought to be a step toward honoring that highest Father. Hence, if they spur us to transgress the law, we have a perfect right to regard them not as parents, but as strangers who are trying to lead us away from obedience to our true Father. So should we act toward princes, lords, and every kind of superiors.[46] It is unworthy and absurd for their eminence so to prevail as to pull down the loftiness of God. On the contrary, their eminence depends upon God's loftiness and ought to lead us to it.

b(a)Sixth Commandment
"You shall not kill." [Ex. 20:13, Vg.]

39. The commandment

ᵇThe purpose of this commandment is: the Lord has bound mankind together by a certain unity; hence each man ought to concern himself with the safety of all. To sum up, then, all violence, injury, and any harmful thing at all that may injure our neighbor's body are forbidden to us. We are accordingly commanded, if we find anything of use to us in saving our neighbors' lives, faithfully to employ it; if there is anything that makes for their peace, to see to it; if anything harmful, to ward it off; b(a)if they are in any danger, to lend a helping hand. ᵇIf you recall that God is so speaking as Lawgiver, ponder at the same time that by this rule he wills to guide your soul. For it would be ridiculous that he who looks upon the thoughts of the heart and dwells especially upon them, should instruct only the body in true righteousness. Therefore this law also forbids murder of the heart, and enjoins the inner intent to save a brother's life. The hand, indeed, gives birth to murder, but the mind when infected with anger and hatred conceives it. See whether you can be angry against your brother without burning with desire to hurt him. If you cannot be angry with him, then you cannot hate him, for hatred is nothing but sustained anger. Although you dissimulate, and try to escape by vain shifts—where there is either anger or hatred, there is the intent to do harm. If you keep trying to evade the issue, the Spirit has already declared that "he who hates a brother in his heart is a murderer" [I John 3:15 p.]; the Lord Christ has declared that "whoever is angry with his brother is liable to judgment; whoever says 'Raca' is liable to the council; whoever says 'You fool!' is liable to the hell of fire" [Matt. 5:22 p.].

40. The reason for this commandment

ᵇScripture notes that this commandment rests upon a twofold basis: man is both the image of God, and our flesh. Now, if we do

[46] Cf. IV. xx. 32.

not wish to violate the image of God, we ought to hold our neighbor sacred. And if we do not wish to renounce all humanity, we ought to cherish his as our own flesh. We shall elsewhere discuss how this exhortation is to be derived from the redemption and grace of Christ.[47] The Lord has willed that we consider those two things which are naturally in man, and might lead us to seek his preservation: to reverence his image imprinted in man, and to embrace our own flesh in him. He who has merely refrained from shedding blood has not therefore avoided the crime of murder. If you perpetrate anything by deed, if you plot anything by attempt, if you wish or plan anything contrary to the safety of a neighbor, you are considered guilty of murder. Again, unless you endeavor to look out for his safety according to your ability and opportunity, you are violating the law with a like heinousness. But if there is so much concern for the safety of his body, from this we may infer how much zeal and effort we owe the safety of the soul, which far excels the body in the Lord's sight.

b(a)Seventh Commandment
"You shall not commit adultery." [Ex. 20:14, Vg.]

41. General interpretation
bThe purpose of this commandment is: because God loves modesty and purity, all uncleanness must be far from us. To sum up, then: we should not become defiled with any filth or lustful intemperance of the flesh. To this corresponds the affirmative commandment b(a)that we chastely and continently regulate all parts of our life. bBut he expressly forbids fornication, to which all lust tends, in order through the foulness of fornication, which is grosser and more palpable, in so far as it brands the body also with its mark, to lead us to abominate all lust.

Man has been created in this condition that he may not lead a solitary life, but may enjoy a helper joined to himself [cf. Gen. 2:18]; then by the curse of sin he has been still more subjected to this necessity. Therefore, the Lord sufficiently provided for us in this matter when he established marriage, the fellowship of which, begun on his authority, he also sanctified by his blessing. From this it is clear that any other union apart from marriage is accursed in his sight; b(a)and that the companionship of marriage has been ordained as a necessary remedy to keep us from plunging into unbridled lust. bLet us not delude ourselves, then, when

47 III. vii. 2–7; III. xx. 38, 45–46; IV. i. 11–19; IV. xiv. 9; IV. xvii. 38–40.

we hear that outside marriage man cannot cohabit with a woman without God's curse.

42. Celibacy?

ᵇNow, through the condition of our nature, and by the lust aroused after the Fall, we, ᵇ⁽ᵃ⁾except for those whom God has released through special grace, are doubly subject to women's society. Let each man, then, see what has been given to him. ᶜVirginity, I agree, is a virtue not to be despised. However, it is denied to some and granted to others only for a time. Hence, those who are troubled with incontinence and cannot prevail in the struggle should turn to matrimony to help them preserve chastity in the degree of their calling. ᵇ⁽ᵃ⁾For those who do not receive this precept [cf. Matt. 19:11], if they do not have recourse to the remedy offered and conceded them for their intemperance, are striving against God and resisting his ordinance. Let no one cry out against me—as many do today—that with God's help he can do all things.[48] ᵃFor God helps only those who walk in his ways, that is, in his calling [cf. Ps. 91:1, 14?]. ᵇ⁽ᵃ⁾All who, neglecting God's help, strive foolishly and rashly to overcome and surmount their necessities, depart from their calling. The Lord affirms that continence is a special gift of God, ᵇone of a kind that is bestowed not indiscriminately, not upon the body of the church as a whole, but upon a few of its members. For first of all, the Lord distinguishes a class of men who have castrated themselves for the sake of the Kingdom of Heaven [Matt. 19:12] —that is, to permit them to devote themselves more unreservedly and freely to the affairs of the Kingdom of Heaven. Yet lest anyone think that such castration lies in a man's power, he pointed out just before that not all men can receive this precept, but only those to whom it is especially "given" from heaven [Matt. 19:11]. From this he concludes: "He who is able to receive this, let him receive it" [Matt. 19:12]. Paul declares it even more clearly when he writes: "Each has his own special gift from God, one of one kind and one of another" [I Cor. 7:7].

43. Marriage as related to this commandment*

ᶜWe are informed by an open declaration, that it is not given to every man to keep chastity in celibacy, even if he aspires to it with great zeal and effort, and that it is a special grace which the Lord bestows only upon certain men, in order to hold them more ready for his work. Do we not, then, contend against God and the nature ordained by him, if we do not accommodate our

[48] Eck, Enchiridion, in ch. xix on clerical celibacy (1541, fo. 129b).

mode of life to the measure of our ability? Here the Lord forbids
fornication. He therefore requires purity and modesty of us.
There is but one way to preserve it: that each man measure himself by his own standard.[49] Let no man rashly despise marriage
as something unprofitable or superfluous to him; let no man long
for celibacy unless he can live without a wife. Also, let him not
provide in this state for the repose and convenience of the flesh,
but only that, freed of this marriage bond, he may be more
prompt and ready for all the duties of piety. And since this blessing is conferred on many persons only for a time, let every man
abstain from marriage only so long as he is fit to observe celibacy.
If his power to tame lust fails him, let him recognize that the
Lord has now imposed the necessity of marriage upon him. The
apostle proves this when he enjoins that to flee fornication "each
man should have his own wife, and each woman her own husband" [I Cor. 7:2]. Again: "If they cannot exercise self-control,
they should marry" in the Lord [I Cor. 7:9]. First, he means that
the greater part of men are subject to the vice of incontinence;
secondly, of those who are so subject he enjoins all without exception to take refuge in that sole remedy with which to resist un-
chastity. Therefore if those who are incontinent neglect to cure
their infirmity by this means, they sin even in not obeying this
command of the apostle. And let him who does not touch a
woman not flatter himself, as if he could not be accused of immodesty, while in the meantime his heart inwardly burns with
lust. For Paul defines modesty as "purity of heart joined with
chastity of body." "The unmarried woman," he says, "is anxious
about the affairs of the Lord, how to be holy in body and spirit."
[I Cor. 7:34.] Thus while he confirms by reason that precept
mentioned above, he says not only that it is better to take a wife
than to pollute oneself by associating with a harlot [cf. I Cor. 6:
15 ff.], but he says that "it is better to marry than to burn" [I Cor.
7:9].

44. Modesty and chastity

ᵇNow if married couples recognize that their association is
blessed by the Lord, they are thereby admonished not to pollute
it with uncontrolled and dissolute lust. For even if the honorableness of matrimony covers the baseness of incontinence, it ought
not for that reason to be a provocation thereto. ᵇ⁽ᵃ⁾Therefore let
not married persons think that all things are permitted to them,
ᵃbut let each man have his own wife soberly, and each wife her

---

[49] This reflects Horace, *Epistles* I. vii. 98 (LCL edition, Horace, *Satires, Epistles, and Ars Poetica*, pp. 302 f.).

own husband. So doing, let them not admit anything at all that is unworthy of the honorableness and temperance of marriage. ᵇ⁽ᵃ⁾For it is fitting that thus wedlock contracted in the Lord be recalled to measure and modesty so as not to wallow in extreme lewdness. ᶜAmbrose censures this wantonness with a severe but not undeserved judgment: he has called the man who has no regard for shame or honorableness in his marriage practices an adulterer toward his own wife.⁵⁰

ᵇFinally, let us consider who the Lawgiver is who here condemns fornication. It is he who, since he ought to possess us completely in his own right, requires integrity of soul, spirit, and body. Therefore, while he forbids us to commit fornication, at the same time he does not permit us to seduce the modesty of another with wanton dress and obscene gestures and foul speech. There is a good point in Archelaus' statement to a youth wearing excessively wanton and dainty clothing that it does not matter in what member he is unchaste;⁵¹ for we look to God, who loathes all uncleanness, in whatever part of our soul or body it may appear. And lest there be any doubt, remember that God is here commending modesty. If the Lord requires modesty of us, he condemns whatever opposes it. Consequently, if you aspire to obedience, let neither your heart burn with wicked lust within, nor your eyes wantonly run into corrupt desires, nor your body be decked with bawdy ornaments, nor your tongue seduce your mind to like thoughts with filthy words, nor your appetite inflame it with intemperance. For all vices of this sort are like blemishes, which besmirch the purity of chastity.

ᵇ⁽ᵃ⁾Eighth Commandment
"You shall not steal." [Ex. 20:15, Vg.]

45. General interpretation

ᵇThe purpose of this commandment is: since injustice is an abomination to God, we should render to each man what belongs to him [Rom. 13:7].⁵² To sum up: we are forbidden to pant after the possessions of others, and consequently are commanded to strive faithfully to help every man to keep his own possessions.

We must consider that what every man possesses has not come to him by mere chance but by the distribution of the supreme Lord of all. ᵇ⁽ᵃ⁾For this reason, we cannot by evil devices deprive

⁵⁰ Augustine, *Against Julian* II. vii. 20, quoting an interpretation of I Cor. 7:29 in a work of Ambrose that is not extant (MPL 44. 687; tr. FC 35. 79).
⁵¹ OS III. 383, note 2.
⁵² *"Unicuique . . . suum."*

anyone of his possessions without fraudulently setting aside God's dispensation. Now there are many kinds of thefts. One consists in violence, when another's goods are stolen by force and unrestrained brigandage. A second kind consists in malicious deceit, when they are carried off through fraud. ᵇAnother lies in a more concealed craftiness, when a man's goods are snatched from him by seemingly legal means. Still another lies in flatteries, when one is cheated of his goods under the pretense of a gift.

Let us not stop too long to recount the kinds of theft. ᵇ⁽ᵃ⁾Let us remember that all those arts whereby we acquire the possessions and money of our neighbors—when such devices depart from sincere affection to a desire to cheat or in some manner to harm—are to be considered as thefts. ᵇAlthough such possessions may be acquired in a court action, yet God does not judge otherwise. For he sees the intricate deceptions with which a crafty man sets out to snare one of simpler mind, until he at last draws him into his nets. He sees the hard and inhuman laws with which the more powerful oppresses and crushes the weaker person. He sees the lures with which the wilier man baits, so to speak, his hooks to catch the unwary. All these things elude human judgment and are not recognized. And such injustice occurs not only in matters of money or in merchandise or land, but in the right of each one; for we defraud our neighbors of their property if we repudiate the duties by which we are obligated to them.[53] If a shiftless steward or overseer devours his master's substance, and fails to attend to household business; if he either unjustly spends or wantonly wastes the properties entrusted to him; if the servant mocks his master; if he divulges his secrets; if in any way he betrays his life or goods; if the master, on the other hand, savagely harasses his household—all these are deemed theft in God's sight. For he who does not carry out what he owes to others according to the responsibility of his own calling both withholds and appropriates what is another's.

46. This commandment obligates us to care for others' good*

ᵇWe will duly obey this commandment, then, if, content with our lot, we are zealous to make only honest and lawful gain; if we do not seek to become wealthy through injustice, nor attempt to deprive our neighbor of his goods to increase our own; if we do not strive to heap up riches cruelly wrung from the blood of

[53] Both Luther and Bucer had a like emphasis. See especially Bucer's *Das ihm selbs (Traité de l'amour du prochain)* (1523); French tr. H. H. Strohl (Paris, 1949), pp. 55 f.; English, P. T. Fuhrmann, *Instruction in Christian Love*, p. 40.

others; if we do not madly scrape together from everywhere, by fair means or foul, whatever will feed our avarice or satisfy our prodigality. b(a)On the other hand, let this be our constant aim: faithfully to help all men by our counsel and aid to keep what is theirs, in so far as we can; but if we have to deal with faithless and deceitful men, let us be prepared to give up something of our own rather than to contend with them. And not this alone: but let us share the necessity of those whom we see pressed by the difficulty of affairs, assisting them in their need with our abundance.

bFinally, let each one see to what extent he is in duty bound to others, and let him pay his debt faithfully. aFor this reason let a people hold all its rulers in honor, patiently bearing their government, obeying their laws and commands, refusing nothing that can be borne without losing God's favor [Rom. 13:1 ff.; I Peter 2:13 ff.; Titus 3:1]. Again, let the rulers take care of their own common people, keep the public peace, protect the good, punish the evil. So let them manage all things as if they are about to render account of their services to God, the supreme Judge [cf. Deut. 17:19; II Chron. 19:6–7]. Let the ministers of churches faithfully attend to the ministry of the Word, not adulterating the teaching of salvation [cf. II Cor. 2:17], but delivering it pure and undefiled to God's people. And let them instruct the people not only through teaching, but also through example of life. In short, let them exercise authority as good shepherds over their sheep [cf. I Tim., ch. 3; II Tim., chs. 2; 4; Titus 1:6 ff.; I Peter, ch. 5]. Let the people in their turn receive them as messengers and apostles of God, render to them that honor of which the highest Master has deemed them worthy, and give them those things necessary for their livelihood [cf. Matt. 10:10 ff.; Rom. 10:15 and 15:15 ff.; I Cor., ch. 9; Gal. 6:6; I Thess. 5:12; I Tim. 5:17–18]. Let parents undertake to nourish, govern, and teach, their children committed to them by God, not provoking their minds with cruelty or turning them against their parents [Eph. 6:4; Col. 3:21]; but cherishing and embracing their children with such gentleness and kindness as becomes their character as parents. As we have already said, children owe obedience to their parents. Let youth reverence old age, as the Lord has willed that age to be worthy of honor. Also, let the aged guide the insufficiency of youth with their own wisdom and experience wherein they excel the younger, not railing harshly and loudly against them but tempering their severity with mildness and gentleness. Let servants show themselves diligent and eager to obey their masters—not for the eye, but from the heart, as if they were serving God. Also, let masters not conduct themselves peevishly and intractably toward their servants, oppressing them with undue rigor, or treating them abusively. Rather, let them recognize them as their brothers, their coservants under the Lord of heaven, whom they ought to love mutually and treat humanely [cf. Eph. 6:5–9; Col. 3:22–25; Titus 2:9–10; I Peter 2:18–20; Col. 4:1; Philemon 16].

In this manner, I say, let each man consider what, in his rank and station, he owes to his neighbors, and pay what he owes. ᵇMoreover, our mind must always have regard for the Lawgiver, that we may know that this rule was established for our hearts as well as for our hands, in order that men may strive to protect and promote the well-being and interests of others.

ᵇ⁽ᵃ⁾Ninth Commandment
"You shall not be a false witness against your neighbor." [Ex. 20:16.]

47. *General interpretation*
ᵇThe purpose of this commandment is: since God (who is truth) abhors a lie, we must practice truth without deceit toward one another. To sum up, then: let us not malign anyone with slanders or false charges, nor harm his substance by falsehood, in short, injure him by unbridled evilspeaking and impudence. To this prohibition the command is linked that we should faithfully help everyone as much as we can in affirming the truth, in order to protect the integrity of his name and possessions. It seems that the Lord intended to express the meaning of this commandment in Ex., ch. 23, in these words: "You shall not utter a false report. You shall not join hands [with a wicked man] to be a malicious witness" [Ex. 23:1]. Likewise, "Flee falsehood" [Ex. 23:7 p.]. Also, in another passage he warns us against lying not only in the sense of being slanderers and talebearers among the people [Lev. 19:16], but also against deceiving our brother [Lev. 19:11]. He prohibits both in specific commandments. Surely there is no doubt that, as he forbade cruelty, shamelessness, and avarice in the preceding commandments, here he bars falsehood. As we have just noted, this has two parts. For either we injure our neighbors' reputation by evil intent and vicious backbiting, or we deprive them of their goods by lying and even by defamation. But it makes no difference whether you understand here a solemn and judicial testimony, or a common one couched in private conversation. For we must always come back to this: one particular vice is singled out from various kinds as an example, and the rest are brought under the same category, the one chosen being an

especially foul vice. Yet it is more generally ^{e(b)}expedient to extend it to include slanders and perverse detraction by which our neighbors are unfairly hurt. For ^bfalsity of court testimony always involves perjury. Perjuries, in so far as they profane and violate God's name, are sufficiently dealt with in the Third Commandment. Hence this commandment is lawfully observed when our tongue, in declaring the truth, serves both the good repute and the advantage of our neighbors. The equity of this is quite evident. For if a good name is more precious than all riches [Prov. 22:1], we harm a man more by despoiling him of the integrity of his name than by taking away his possessions. In plundering his substance, however, we sometimes do as much by false testimony as by snatching with our hands.

48. The good reputation of our neighbor

^bAnd yet it is wonderful with what thoughtless unconcern we sin in this respect time and again! Those who do not markedly suffer from this disease are rare indeed. We delight in a certain poisoned sweetness experienced in ferreting out and in disclosing the evils of others. And let us not think it an adequate excuse if in many instances we are not lying. For he who does not allow a brother's name to be sullied by falsehood also wishes it to be kept unblemished as far as truth permits. Indeed, although he may guard it against lying only, he yet implies by this that it is entrusted to his care. That God is concerned about it should be enough to prompt us to keep safe our neighbor's good name. Hence, evilspeaking is without a doubt universally condemned. Now, we understand by "evilspeaking" not reproof made with intent to chastise; not accusation or judicial denunciation to remedy evil. Nor does evilspeaking mean public correction, calculated to strike other sinners with terror; nor disclosure before those who need to be forewarned lest they be endangered through ignorance. By "evilspeaking" we mean hateful accusation arising from evil intent and wanton desire to defame.

^{b(a)}Indeed, this precept even extends to forbidding us to affect a fawning politeness ^bbarbed with bitter taunts under the guise of joking. Some do this who crave praise for their witticisms, to others' shame and grief, because they sometimes grievously wound their brothers with this sort of impudence. Now if we turn our eyes to the Lawgiver, who must in his own right rule our ears and heart no less than our tongue, we shall surely see that eagerness to hear detractions, and unbecoming readiness to make unfavorable judgments, are alike forbidden. For it is absurd to think that God hates the disease of evilspeaking in the tongue, but does

not disapprove of evil intent in the heart. b(a)Therefore, if there is any true fear and love of God in us, let us take care, as far as is possible and expedient and as love requires, not to yield our tongue or our ears to evilspeaking and caustic wit, and not to give our minds without cause to sly suspicion. But as fair interpreters of the words and deeds of all, let us sincerely keep their honor safe in our judgment, our ears, and our tongue.

b(a)Tenth Commandment
"You shall not covet your neighbor's house," etc. [Ex. 20: 17, Vg.]

49. *The meaning of this commandment*
bThe purpose of this commandment is: since God wills that our whole soul be possessed with a disposition to love, we must banish from our hearts all desire contrary to love. To sum up, then: no thought should steal upon us to move our hearts to a harmful covetousness that tends to our neighbor's loss. To this corresponds the opposite precept: whatever we conceive, deliberate, will, or attempt is to be linked to our neighbor's good and advantage. But here an apparently great and perplexing difficulty confronts us. We previously said that under the terms "adultery" and "theft" are included the desire to commit adultery and the intention to harm and deceive. If this is true, it may seem superfluous that we are afterward separately forbidden to covet another's goods. But the distinction between intent and coveting will readily resolve this difficulty for us.[54] For intent, as we spoke of it under the preceding commandments, is deliberate consent of will where lust subjects the heart. But covetousness can exist without such deliberation or consent when the mind is only pricked or tickled by empty and perverse objects. The Lord has previously commanded that the rule of love govern our wills, our endeavors, and our actions. Now he enjoins that the thoughts of our mind be so controlled to the same end that none of them may become depraved or twisted and thus drive the mind in the opposite direction. As he has forbidden our minds to be inclined and led into anger, hatred, adultery, robbery, and lying, he now prohibits them from being prompted thereto.

50. *Innermost righteousness!*
bHe demands such great uprightness with good reason. For who can deny that it is right for all the powers of the soul to be

[54] Cf. II. ii. 24; III. iii. 11–13; IV. xv. 11–12.

possessed with love? But if any soul wander from the goal of love, who will not admit that it is diseased? Now how does it happen that desires hurtful to your brother enter your heart, unless it is that you disregard him and strive for yourself alone? For if your whole heart were steeped in love, not one particle of it would lie open to such imaginings. The heart, then, in so far as it harbors covetousness, must be empty of love.

Someone will object that fantasies, flitting aimlessly about the mind and then vanishing, cannot be condemned as instances of covetousness, whose seat is in the heart. I reply: here it is a question of fantasies of a kind which, while they occupy our minds, at the same time bite and strike our hearts with greed, for nothing desirable ever comes into our mind without our heart leaping with excitement. God therefore commands a wonderful ardor of love, which he does not allow one particle of covetousness to hinder. He requires a marvelously tempered heart, and does not permit the tiniest pinprick to urge it against the law of love. Do you think my view lacks authority? It was Augustine who first opened the way for me to understand this commandment.[55]

It was the Lord's plan to forbid all evil desire. Nevertheless, by way of example, he has put forward those objects whose false image of delight most frequently captivates us. Thus he leaves nothing to our desire when he deprives it of those very things which prompt it to rave and revel.

Here, then, is the Second Table of the Law, which amply teaches us what we owe men for the sake of God, upon the contemplation of whom the whole of love depends. Hence, you will fruitlessly inculcate all those duties taught in this Table, unless your teaching has fear and reverence toward God as its foundation. ᵉWithout any help from me, the wise reader will judge those who, by perversely splitting what was one commandment, would find two commandments in the prohibition of covetousness.[56] The repetition of the expression "You shall not covet" a second time does not oppose our view. For after mentioning "house," he lists its parts, beginning with "wife." From this it is quite clear that we are to read this as a whole, as the Hebrews rightly do; and that God, in short, commands us to keep the possessions of others untouched and safe, not only from injury

[55] Augustine, *On the Spirit and the Letter* xxxvi. 64–66 (MPL 44. 242 ff.; tr. NPNF V. 112 ff.). Numerous additional passages from Augustine on the Tenth Commandment are cited by Smits II. 36.
[56] Cf. II. viii. 12, note 16.

or the wish to defraud, but even from the slightest covetousness that may trouble our hearts.

(Principles of the law in the light of Christ's teaching, 51–59)
51. The sum of the law
ᵇNow it will not be difficult to decide the purpose of the whole law: the fulfillment of righteousness to form human life to the archetype of divine purity. For God has so depicted his character in the law that if any man carries out in deeds whatever is enjoined there, he will express the image of God, as it were, in his own life. For this reason, Moses, wishing to remind the Israelites of the gist of the law, said: "And now, Israel, what does the Lord your God require of you, but to fear the Lord . . . , to walk in his ways, to love him, to serve him with all your heart and with all your soul, and to keep his commandments?" [Deut. 10:12–13, cf. Vg.]. And Moses did not cease to harp on this same thought to them whenever he had to point out the aim of the law. Here is the object of the teaching of the law: to join man by holiness of life to his God, and, as Moses elsewhere says, to make him cleave to God [cf. Deut. 11:22 or 30:20].
ᵇ⁽ᵃ⁾Now the perfection of that holiness comes under the two headings already mentioned: "That we should love the Lord God with all our heart, with all our soul, and with all our strength" [Deut. 6:5 p.; cf. ch. 11:13], "and our neighbor as ourselves" [Lev. 19:18 p.; cf. Matt. 22:37, 39]. First, indeed, our soul should be entirely filled with the love of God. From this will flow directly the love of neighbor. ᵇThis is what the apostle shows when he writes that "the aim of the law is love from a pure conscience and a faith unfeigned" [I Tim. 1:5 p.]. You see how conscience and sincere faith are put at the head. In other words, here is true piety, from which love is derived.

It would, therefore, be a mistake for anyone to believe that the law teaches nothing but some rudiments and preliminaries of righteousness by which men begin their apprenticeship, and does not also guide them to the true goal, good works, since you cannot desire a greater perfection than that expressed in the statements of Moses and Paul. For whither, I submit, will any man wish to go who will not be content to be taught to fear God, to worship spiritually, to obey the commandments, to follow the Lord's upright way, and lastly, to have a pure conscience, sincere faith, and love? From this is confirmed that interpretation of the law which seeks and finds in the commandments of the law all the duties of piety and love. For those who follow only dry and bare rudiments—as if the law taught them only half of God's will—do not at all understand its purpose, as the apostle testifies.

52. Why does Scripture sometimes mention only the Second Table?

ᵇBut because, in summarizing the law, Christ and the apostles sometimes leave out the First Table, many persons are deceived into trying to apply their words to both Tables. In the Gospel of Matthew, Christ calls "mercy, judgment, and faith the weightier matters of the law" [Matt. 23:23 p.]. Under the term "faith" it is clear to me that he means truthfulness toward men. Yet some interpret the expression as piety toward God so as to extend it to the whole law.[57]

Surely this is foolish. For Christ is speaking of those works by which man ought to prove himself righteous. If we note this reason, we shall also stop wondering why in another passage to a young man asking what those commandments are by whose observance we enter into life, he replies in these words only [Matt. 19:16–17]: "You shall not kill. You shall not commit adultery. You shall not steal. You shall not bear false witness. Honor your father and your mother. . . . Love your neighbor as yourself" [Matt. 19:18–19; with some wording from Ex. 20:12–16]. For obedience to the First Table was usually either in the intention of the heart, or in ceremonies. The intention of the heart did not show itself, and the hypocrites continually busied themselves with ceremonies. Yet the works of love are such that through them we witness real righteousness.

ᵉThis occurs so often in the Prophets as to be familiar even to a reader moderately versed in them. For almost every time the prophets exhort men to repentance they omit the First Table, and urge faith, judgment, mercy, and equity. In this way they do not overlook the fear of God, but they demand through signs real evidence of it. This indeed is well known: when they discuss the observance of the law, they usually dwell upon the Second Table, for there one especially sees zeal for righteousness and integrity. There is no need to list the passages, for everyone can easily verify what I am saying [e.g., Isa. 1:18].

53. Faith and love

ᵇBut you will ask: "Does the essence of righteousness lie more in living innocently with men than in honoring God with piety?" Not at all! But because a man does not easily maintain love in all respects unless he earnestly fears God, here is proof also of

57 Melanchthon, *Annotationes in Evangelium Matthaei* (1523), fo. 46a.

his piety. Besides, since the Lord well knows, and also attests through his prophets, that no benefit can come from us to him, he does not confine our duties to himself, but he exercises us "in good works toward our neighbor" [cf. Ps. 15:2–3, Vg.; 16:2, EV]. The apostle consequently has good reason to place the whole perfection of the saints in love [Eph. 3:19; 1:5; Col. 3:14]. Elsewhere he quite rightly calls it the "fulfillment of the law," adding that "he who loves his neighbor has fulfilled the law" [Rom. 13:8]. Again, "The whole law is comprehended in one word, 'Love your neighbor as yourself.'" [Gal. 5:14 p.] Paul teaches only what Christ himself teaches when he says: "Whatever you wish that men would do to you, do so to them; for this is the law and the prophets" [Matt. 7:12]. It is certain that the Law and the Prophets give first place to faith and whatever pertains to the lawful worship of God, relegating love to a subordinate position. But the Lord means that the law only enjoins us to observe right and equity toward men, that thereby we may become practiced in witnessing to a pious fear of him, if we have any of it in us.

54. Love of neighbor

ᵇHere, therefore, let us stand fast: our life shall best conform to God's will and the prescription of the law when it is in every respect most fruitful for our brethren. ᵃIn the entire law we do not read one syllable that lays a rule upon man as regards those things which he may or may not do, for the advantage of his own flesh. And obviously, since men were born in such a state that they are all too much inclined to self-love—ᶜand, however much they deviate from truth, they still keep self-love—ᵃthere was no need of a law that would increase or rather enkindle this already excessive love.[58] Hence it is very clear that we keep the commandments not by loving ourselves but by loving God and neighbor; that he lives the best and holiest life who lives and strives for himself as little as he can, and that no one lives in a worse or more evil manner than he who lives and strives for himself alone, and thinks about and seeks only his own advantage.[59]

ᵇIndeed, to express how profoundly we must be inclined to

[58] Augustine, *On Christian Doctrine* I. xxiii–xxvi (MPL 34. 27 ff.; tr. NPNF II. 528 f.).

[59] The preceding sentences of sec. 54 show a general similarity to a passage in Luther's *Short Exposition of the Decalogue, the Apostles' Creed, and the Lord's Prayer*, 1520, the conclusion of the section on the Decalogue (*Werke* WA VII. 214; tr. B. L. Woolf, *Reformation Writings of Martin Luther* I. 82 f.). The statement is repeated word for word in the *Betbüchlein*, 1522 (*Werke* WA X. ii. 388).

love our neighbors [Lev. 19:18], the Lord measured it by the love of ourselves because he had at hand no more violent or stronger emotion than this. And we ought diligently to ponder the force of this expression. For he does not concede the first place to self-love[60] as certain Sophists stupidly imagine, and assign the second place to love.[61] Rather, he transfers to others the emotion of love that we naturally feel toward ourselves. Hence, the apostle states that "love does not seek its own" [I Cor. 13:5]. The reasoning of these Sophists is not to be considered worth a hair: that the thing ruled is always inferior to its rule. Indeed, the Lord has not established a rule regarding love of ourselves to which charity toward others should be subordinate. But he shows that the emotion of love, which out of natural depravity commonly resides within ourselves, must now be extended to another, that we may be ready to benefit our neighbor with no less eagerness, ardor, and care than ourselves.

55. Who is our neighbor?

[b(a)]Now, since Christ has shown in the parable of the Samaritan that the term "neighbor" includes even the most remote person [Luke 10:36], [b]we are not expected to limit the precept of love to those in close relationships. I do not deny that the more closely a man is linked to us, the more intimate obligation we have to assist him. It is the common habit of mankind that the more closely men are bound together by the ties of kinship, of acquaintanceship, or of neighborhood, the more responsibilities for one another they share. This does not offend God; for his providence,

---

[60] "φιλαυτία."

[61] Cf. Lombard, *Sentences* III. xxviii. 1; xxix. 1 (MPL 192. 814 f.); Aquinas, *Summa Theol.* II IIae. 26. 4. 5. In this section, Calvin employs three words corresponding to "love" and "charity" in English: *amor, dilectio, charitas.* There is no use in seeking fastidious distinctions between these words, here or elsewhere, in Calvin and other writers of his time. In a note by Ludovico Vives in his elaborate edition of Augustine's *City of God* (1522), it is stated that *amor* and *dilectio* are indifferently used in the Scriptures. Profane authors, says Vives, used the verb *diligo* for a light love and *amo* for a fervent one. He admits that *amor* is more often than *dilectio* used for obscenity. (Augustine, *Of the Citie of God, with the Learned Comments of Jo. Lod. Vives* [London, 1620], p. 478.) The detailed study of Hélène Pétré, *Caritas: étude sur le vocabulaire Latin de la charité Chrétienne,* yields a similar result. See esp. pp. 79–98, with revealing citations from Augustine, Isidore of Seville (d. 636), and other Christian Latin writers. A distinction in patristic Latin expressed by Isidore seems of general application: *amor* and *dilectio* may be used in a good or in a bad sense; *caritas,* in a good sense only. (Isidore, *Libri differentiarum* II. xxxvii. 142; MPL 83. 52.)

as it were, leads us to it. But I say: we ought to embrace the whole human race without exception in a single feeling of love; here there is no distinction between barbarian and Greek, worthy and unworthy, friend and enemy, since all should be contemplated in God, not in themselves.[62] When we turn aside from such contemplation, it is no wonder we become entangled in many errors. Therefore, if we rightly direct our love, we must first turn our eyes not to man, the sight of whom would more often engender hate than love, but to God, who bids us extend to all men the love we bear to him, that this may be an unchanging principle: whatever the character of the man, we must yet love him because we love God.

56. "Evangelical counsels"?

[a]These commandments—"Do not take vengeance; love your enemies," which were once delivered to all Jews and then to all Christians in common—have been turned by the Schoolmen into "counsels," which we are free either to obey or not to obey. What pestilential ignorance or malice is this! Moreover, they have saddled the requirement to obey these "counsels" upon the monks, even more righteous in this one respect than simple Christians because they voluntarily bound themselves to keep these "counsels," and the reason they assign for not receiving them as laws is that they seem too burdensome and heavy, especially for Christians who are under the law of grace.[63] Do they dare thus to abolish God's eternal law that we are to love our neighbor? [b(a)]Does such a distinction appear on any page of the law? Rather, do not commandments commonly occur there that very strictly require us to love our enemies? What sort of commandment is this: to feed a hungry enemy [Prov. 25:21]; to lead his stray oxen or asses back to the right path, or to assist them when they are overburdened [Ex. 23:4–5]? Shall we do good to our enemy's beasts for his sake without showing good will to the man himself? What? [a]Is not the Lord's word everlasting: "Vengeance is mine, I will repay" [Heb. 10:30; cf. Deut. 32:35]. [b]This is more plainly expressed in another place: "You shall not take vengeance or bear any grudge against . . . your own people" [Lev. 19:18]. Either let them blot out these things from the law or recognize that the Lord was Lawgiver, and let them not falsely represent him as a mere giver of counsel.

---

[62] Cf. III. vii. 6.
[63] Cf. Aquinas, *Summa Theol.* I IIae. cviii. 4; II IIae. clxxxiv. 3; clxxxvi; Melanchthon, *Loci communes,* 1521 (ed. Engelland, *op. cit.,* p. 118).

57. The commandment to love our enemy is a genuine commandment

ᵇ⁽ᵃ⁾And what, I ask you, do these statements mean, which they have dared to mock with their absurd glosses? ᵃ"Love your enemies; do good to those who hate you; pray for those who persecute you; ᵇ⁽ᵃ⁾bless those who curse you, so that you may be sons of your Father who is in heaven." [Matt. 5:44–45, conflated with Luke 6:27–28.] ᵇWho will not here conclude with Chrysostom that the obligatory character of these utterances reveals them clearly to be not exhortations but imperatives?[64] What is left for us when we are erased from the number of the sons of God? ᵇ⁽ᵃ⁾Yet in their view monks alone will be the sons of the Heavenly Father; they alone will dare call upon God the Father. ᵇIn the meantime what will become of the church? According to this same reasoning, it will be relegated to the heathen and publicans. For Christ says: "If you are kind to your friends, what favor do you expect? Do not even the heathen and publicans do the same?" [Matt. 5:46–47, conflated with Luke 6:32 and Matt. 18:17.] We shall indeed be fortunate if the mere name of Christians be left to us, though the inheritance of the Heavenly Kingdom be taken away from us! ᶜAugustine's argument is no less convincing: "When the Lord forbids us to commit adultery, he prohibits us from touching the wife of an enemy just as much as that of a friend. When he forbids theft, he allows us to steal nothing at all, whether from a friend or from an enemy."[65] Paul relates these two commandments—"Do not steal" and "Do not commit adultery"—to the rule of love. In fact, he teaches that they are included in the commandment "You shall love your neighbor as yourself" [Rom. 13: 9]. Therefore, either Paul must have been a false interpreter of the law, or it necessarily follows from the commandment that we are to love our enemies just as our friends. ᵃFor this reason, those who so wantonly shake off the common yoke of the sons of God truly betray themselves as sons of Satan. ᵇNow, you may doubt whether they spread this dogma abroad more out of stupidity or out of shamelessness. Every one of the church fathers declares as a fact that these are actual commandments. Even in Gregory's time it was not doubted, as he stoutly affirms. That these are commandments he considers indisputable.[66] ᵃAnd how

---

[64] Chrysostom, *De compunctione cordis* I. 4 (Chrysostom, *Opera*, Paris, 1834, I. 157; MPG 47. 399 f.); Chrysostom, *Adversus oppugnatores vitae monasticae* III. 14 (MPG 47. 372 ff.).

[65] Augustine, *On Christian Doctrine* I. xxx. 32 (MPL 34. 31; tr. NPNF II. 531 f.), discoursing on "Love worketh no ill to his neighbor" (Rom. 13:10), argues that "every man is to be considered our neighbor."

[66] Gregory the Great, *Homilies on the Gospels* ii. 27. 1 (MPL 76. 1206).

stupidly they argue! This would, they say, be a burden too heavy for Christians! As if we could think of anything more difficult than to love God with all our heart, all our soul, and all our strength! Compared with this law, everything ought to be considered easy—whether the requirement to love our enemy or to banish all desire for revenge from our hearts. All these are indeed hard and difficult for our feebleness, even to the least detail of the law [cf. Matt. 5:18; Luke 16:17]. It is the Lord in whom we act virtuously. "Let him give what he commands, and command what he will."[67] To be Christians under the law of grace does not mean to wander unbridled outside the law, but to be engrafted in Christ, by whose grace we are free of the curse of the law, and by whose Spirit we have the law engraved upon our hearts [Jer. 31:33]. This grace Paul called "law," not in the strict sense but alluding to the law of God, with which he was contrasting it [Rom. 8:2]. Under the term "law" these men are philosophizing about nothing.

58. Distinction of mortal and venial sins invalid![t]

[b]What they call "venial sin" is something of the same sort: either secret ungodliness, which violates the First Table, or direct transgression of the last commandment. Here is their definition: venial sin is desire without deliberate assent, which does not long remain in the heart.[68] But I say: it cannot even steal into the heart except for lack of those things which are required in the law. We are forbidden "to have other gods." When the mind, laid low by the crafty devices of unbelief, looks around elsewhere; when it is assailed by a sudden desire to transfer its blessedness to another place—where do these fleeting impulses come from but from some empty place in the soul, ready to receive such temptations? And not to prolong the argument farther, we have been commanded to "love God with all our heart, with all our mind, and with all our soul." Unless, then, all the powers of the soul are intent on loving God, we have already abandoned obedience to the law. For the enemies who rise up in our conscience against his Kingdom and hinder his decrees prove that God's throne is not firmly established therein. It has been demonstrated that the last commandment properly applies to this.[69] Has some

---

[67] Augustine, "Da quod iubes et iube quod vis," in Confessions X. xxix. 40; xxxi. 45 (MPL 32. 796, 798; tr. LCC VII. 225, 228). See also On Grace and Free Will xv. 3 (MPL 44. 899; tr. NPNF V. 456 f.); On the Perseverance of the Saints xx. 53 (MPL 45. 1026; tr. NPNF V. 347); On the Spirit and the Letter xiii. 22 (MPL 44. 214; tr. NPNF V. 92). Cf. II. v. 7, note 17.
[68] Aquinas, Summa Theol. I IIae. lxxiv. 10; cf. III. iv. 28.
[69] This chapter, secs. 49, 50.

desire pricked our heart? We are already guilty of covetousness and consequently are transgressors of the law. For the Lord forbids us not only to resolve upon and to plot something that involves another's loss, but even to be kindled and burn with covetousness. But God's curse ever presses upon the transgression of the law. There is no reason, then, for us to exempt any covetings, however light, from the judgment of death. cAugustine says: In weighing sins "let us not bring forward false balances to weigh what we please and as we please, according to our own opinion, saying, 'This is heavy'; 'This is light.' But let us bring forward the divine balance of the Holy Scriptures, as from the Lord's treasury, and in that balance let us weigh what is heavier. No—not weigh; rather, let us recognize what the Lord has already weighed."[70] cWhat does Scripture have to say on this matter? Surely when Paul calls death "the wages of sin" [Rom. 6:23], he shows that this loathsome distinction was unknown to him. Since we are unduly inclined to hypocrisy, this palliative ought by no means to be added to soothe our sluggish consciences.

59. Every sin is a deadly sin!

bWould that they might ponder what that saying of Christ means: "Whoever transgresses one of the least of these commandments, and teaches men so, will be esteemed nobody in the Kingdom of Heaven" [Matt. 5:19 p.]! Are they not of this number when they dare so to extenuate the transgression of the law as if it did not merit the death penalty? But they ought to have weighed not simply what the law commands but who it is that commands. For in every little transgression of the divinely commanded law, God's authority is set aside. Do they deem it a small matter to violate his majesty in anything? Then, if God has revealed his will in the law, whatever is contrary to the law displeases him. Do they fancy God's wrath so feeble that the death penalty will not immediately follow? And he has clearly declared this, if they could take it upon their hearts to listen to his voice rather than to becloud the clear truth with their senseless subtleties. He says: "The soul that sins shall surely die." [Ezek. 18:4, 20, Vg.] Likewise the passage just cited:[71] "The wages of sin is death" [Rom. 6:23]. What they confess to be sin because they cannot deny it they nevertheless contend is not mortal sin. But because they have heretofore indulged too much in their own folly, let them at least for once learn to become wise. But

[70] Augustine, *On Baptism, Against the Donatists* II. vi. 9 (MPL 43. 132; tr. NPNF IV. 429).
[71] In the previous section.

if they persist in their ravings, we bid them farewell. Let the children of God hold that all sin is mortal. For it is rebellion against the will of God, which of necessity provokes God's wrath, and it is a violation of the law, upon which God's judgment is pronounced without exception. The sins of the saints are pardonable, not because of their nature as saints, but because they obtain pardon from God's mercy.

ᶜCHAPTER IX

CHRIST, ALTHOUGH HE WAS KNOWN TO THE JEWS UNDER THE LAW, WAS AT LENGTH CLEARLY REVEALED ONLY IN THE GOSPEL[1]

(The grace of Christ anticipated and manifested, 1–2)
1. The advantage of the community of the New Covenant
ᵉIt was not in vain that God of old willed, through expiations and sacrifices, to attest that he was Father,[2] and to set apart for himself a chosen people. Hence, he was then surely known in the same image in which he with full splendor now appears to us. Accordingly, after Malachi has bidden the Jews heed the law of Moses, and continue in it earnestly because after his death there was to be an interruption of the prophetic office, he immediately afterward declares: "The sun of righteousness shall rise" [Mal. 4:2]. By these words he teaches that while the law serves to hold the godly in expectation of Christ's coming, at his advent they should hope for far more light. For this reason, Peter says: "The prophets . . . searched and diligently inquired about this salvation," which has now been made manifest by the gospel [I Peter 1:10]. And "it was revealed to them that they were serving not themselves," or their age, "but us, in the things which have . . . been announced" through the gospel [I Peter 1:12 p.]. Not that the teaching of these things was useless to the ancient people or without value for the prophets themselves, but because they did not come to possess that treasure which God has transmitted to us by their hand! For today the grace of which they bore witness is put before our very eyes. They had but a slight taste of it; we can more richly enjoy it. Accordingly, Christ declares that Moses bore witness to him [John 5:46], yet He extols the measure of grace in which we surpass the Jews. For he ad-

---

[1] This is an entire new chapter in edition 1559 (cf. II. vi), further emphasizing the context of law within the covenant, and the prime purpose of the law: to point to Christ. Much of the content is rehearsed again, however, in chs. x, xi, following, which date largely from 1539.
[2] Cf. I. vi. 1–4.

dresses his disciples: "Blessed are the eyes which see what you see; and blessed are the ears which hear what you hear. For many kings and prophets longed for this and did not attain it" [Luke 10:23–24; Matt. 13:16–17; conflated]. That God has preferred us to the holy patriarchs, who were men of rare piety, is no slight commendation of the gospel revelation. In close agreement with this thought is another passage, where Abraham is said to have seen Christ's day and to have rejoiced [John 8:56]. Even if the sight of something far off was rather indistinct, Abraham nevertheless had assurance of good hope. From this came that joyousness which accompanied the holy patriarch even to his death. And John the Baptist's statement—"No one has ever seen God; the only-begotten Son, who is in the bosom of the Father, has made him known" [John 1:18]—does not exclude the pious who died before Christ from the fellowship of the understanding and light that shine in the person of Christ. But, by comparing their lot with ours, he teaches that those mysteries which they but glimpsed in shadowed outline are manifest to us. The author of The Letter to the Hebrews clearly explains this: "In many and various ways God spoke of old . . . by the prophets . . . but now by his beloved Son" [Heb. 1:1–2 p.]. That only-begotten Son, who today is for us "the splendor of the glory of God the Father and the very stamp of his nature" [Heb. 1:3 p.], became known of old to the Jews. In another place we have quoted Paul's view that Christ was the leader of the former deliverance [cf. I Cor. 10:4].[3] It is, moreover, true, as Paul elsewhere teaches, that God, who "ordered light to shine out of darkness, now has shone in our hearts to give the light of the knowledge of the glory of God in the face of Jesus Christ" [II Cor. 4:6 p.]. For when he appeared in this, his image, he, as it were, made himself visible; whereas his appearance had before been indistinct and shadowed. All the more detestable and base, then, is the ungratefulness and depravity of those who are blind at midday! And Paul says their minds have been darkened by Satan that they may not see the glory of Christ shining in the gospel without an intervening veil [II Cor. 3:14–15; cf. ch. 4:4].

2. The gospel preaches the revealed Christ

ᵉNow I take the gospel to be the clear manifestation of the mystery of Christ. I recognize, of course, that since Paul calls the gospel "the doctrine of faith" [I Tim. 4:6], all those promises of free remission of sins which commonly occur in the law, whereby God reconciles men to himself, are counted as parts

[3] I. xiii. 10.

of it. For he contrasts faith with the terrors that would trouble and vex the conscience if salvation were to be sought in works. From this it follows that the word "gospel," taken in the broad sense, includes those testimonies of his mercy and fatherly favor which God gave to the patriarchs of old. In a higher sense, however, the word refers, I say, to the proclamation of the grace manifested in Christ. This is not only accepted as a matter of common usage, but rests upon the authority of Christ and the apostles [Matt. 4:17, 23; 9:35]. Hence, the fact that he preached the gospel of the Kingdom is properly attributed to him. And Mark prefaces his Gospel with: "The beginning of the gospel of Jesus Christ" [Mark 1:1]. There is no need to heap up passages to prove something so fully known. "By his advent Christ . . . has brought life and immortality to light through the gospel." [II Tim. 1: 10 p.] Paul does not mean by these words that the patriarchs were shrouded in the shadows of death until the Son of God took flesh. Rather, he claims this privilege of honor for the gospel, teaching that it is a new and unusual sort of embassy [cf. II Cor. 5:20] by which God has fulfilled what he had promised: that the truth of his promises would be realized in the person of the Son. Believers have found to be true Paul's saying that "all the promises of God find their yea and amen in Christ" [II Cor. 1: 20 p.], for these promises had been sealed in their hearts. [Cf. II Cor. 1:22.] Nevertheless, because he has in his flesh accomplished the whole of our salvation, this living manifestation of realities has justly won a new and singular commendation. From this derives Christ's saying: "Afterward you will see heaven opened, and the angels of God ascending and descending upon the Son of Man" [John 1:51 p.]. Although he seems here to allude to the ladder shown in a vision to the patriarch Jacob [Gen. 28:12], how excellent his advent is he has marked through opening by it the gate of heaven, that each one of us may enter there.

(*Refutation of errors on the relation of law and gospel: intermediate position of John the Baptist, 3–5*)
3. The promises are not abrogated for us
ᵉYet we ought to beware of the devilish imagination of Servetus, who—while he wishes to extol the greatness of Christ's grace or at least pretends to wish this—entirely abolishes the promises, as if they had ended at the same time as the law. He pretends that by faith in the gospel we share in the fulfillment of all the promises.[4] As if there were no difference between us and Christ!

---

[4] Servetus, *Christianismi restitutio* (1553), pp. 294, 324, and *Epistolae* ix (in same volume), p. 601; also in CR VIII. 667 f.

I just declared that Christ left unfinished nothing of the sum total of our salvation. But it is wrong to assume from this that we already possess the benefits imparted by him—as if that statement of Paul's, that "our salvation is hidden in hope" [Col. 3: 3 p.; cf. Rom. 8:24], were false! I admit, indeed, that in believing Christ we at once pass from death into life. But at the same time we must remember that saying of John's: although we know that "we are the children of God, it does not yet appear . . . until we shall become like him, when we shall see him as he is" [I John 3:2 p.]. Although, therefore, Christ offers us in the gospel a present fullness of spiritual benefits, the enjoyment thereof ever lies hidden under the guardianship of hope, until, having put off corruptible flesh, we be transfigured in the glory of him who goes before us. Meanwhile, the Holy Spirit bids us rely upon the promises, whose authority with us ought to silence all the barkings of that unclean dog. For, according to Paul, "Godliness . . . holds promise for the life to come as well as for the present life" [I Tim. 4:8]. For this reason, Paul boasts of himself as "an apostle of Christ . . . according to the promise of the life which is in him" [II Tim. 1:1 p.]. And in another passage he teaches that we have the same promises [II Cor. 7:1; cf. II Cor. 6:16–18] as were given to the holy men of old. Finally, he considers it the height of felicity that we are sealed with the "Holy Spirit of promise" [Eph. 1:13 p.]. We enjoy Christ only as we embrace Christ clad in his own promises. Thus it comes to pass that he indeed dwells in our hearts [cf. Eph. 3:17], and yet: "We are absent from him. For we walk by faith, not by sight" [II Cor. 5:5–7]. Now these two things agree rather well with each other: we possess in Christ all that pertains to the perfection of heavenly life, and yet faith is the vision of good things not seen [cf. Heb. 11:1]. Only, we must note a difference in the nature or quality of the promises: the gospel points out with the finger what the law foreshadowed under types.

4. The opposition between law and gospel ought not to be exaggerated

eHence, also, we refute those who always erroneously compare the law with the gospel by contrasting the merit of works with the free imputation of righteousness. This is indeed a contrast not at all to be rejected. For Paul often means by the term "law" the rule of righteous living by which God requires of us what is his own, giving us no hope of life unless we completely obey him, and adding on the other hand a curse if we deviate even in the slightest degree. This Paul does when he contends that

we are pleasing to God through grace and are accounted righteous through his pardon, because nowhere is found that observance of the law for which the reward has been promised. Paul
therefore justly makes contraries of the righteousness of the law
and of that of the gospel [Rom. 3:21 ff.; Gal. 3:10 ff.; etc.].

But the gospel did not so supplant the entire law as to bring
forward a different way of salvation. Rather, it confirmed and
satisfied whatever the law had promised, and gave substance to
the shadows.[5] When Christ says, "The Law and the Prophets
were until John" [Luke 16:16; cf. Matt. 11:13], he does not
subject the patriarchs to the curse that the slaves of the law cannot escape. He means: they had been trained in rudiments only,
thus remaining far beneath the height of the gospel teaching.
Hence Paul, calling the gospel "the power of God unto salvation
for every believer" [Rom. 1:16 p.], presently adds: "The Law and
the Prophets bear witness to it" [Rom. 3:21]. And at the end
of the same letter, although he teaches that "the preaching of
Jesus Christ is the revelation of the mystery kept in silence
through times eternal" [Rom. 16:25 p.], he qualifies this statement by adding an explanation, teaching that he was "made
known through the prophetic writings" [Rom. 16:26 p.]. From
this we infer that, where the whole law is concerned, the gospel
differs from it only in clarity of manifestation. Still, because of
the inestimable abundance of grace laid open for us in Christ,
it is said with good reason that through his advent God's Heavenly
Kingdom was erected upon earth [cf. Matt. 12:28].

5. *John the Baptist*
ᵉJohn stood between the law and the gospel, holding an intermediate office related to both. He called Christ the "Lamb of
God" and the sacrifice for the cleansing of sins [John 1:29], thus
setting forth the sum of the gospel. Yet he did not express that
incomparable power and glory which at length shone forth in
the resurrection. Hence, Christ said that he was not equal to
the apostles; this is the meaning of his words: "John excels among
the sons of women, yet he who is least in the Kingdom of
Heaven is greater than he" [Matt. 11:11 p.]. He does not commend
here the persons of men, but after setting John ahead of all the
prophets, he raises the preaching of the gospel to the highest rank.
As we have seen elsewhere, he denotes this preaching by "Kingdom
of Heaven." Now John answers that he himself is only a "voice"
[John 1:23; cf. Isa. 40:3], as if he were beneath the prophets. He
does not do this out of feigned humility, but he wishes to teach

⁵ Cf. II. vii. 16; II. viii. 28, 29, and notes there appended.

that the real ambassadorship was not entrusted to him, but that
he performed the office of harbinger, as Malachi had foretold:
"Behold, I will send you Elijah the prophet before the great
and terrible day of Jehovah comes" [Mal. 4:5]. Indeed, during
the whole course of his ministry he did nothing else than prepare
disciples for Christ. He even proves from Isaiah that this task
was enjoined upon him by God. In this sense Christ calls him
"a burning and shining lamp" [John 5:35], because full daylight
had not yet come. Yet this does not prevent him from being
numbered among the preachers of the gospel, for he actually
used the same baptism as was afterward entrusted to the apostles
[John 1:33]. But what John began the apostles carried forward
to fulfillment, with greater freedom, only after Christ was received into heaven.

ᵉCHAPTER X

THE SIMILARITY OF THE OLD AND NEW TESTAMENTS*

*(The covenant in the Old Testament really the same as that of
the New, 1–6)*

1. The question

ᵉ⁽ᵇ⁾Now we can clearly see from what has already been said
that all men adopted by God into the company of his people
since the beginning of the world were covenanted to him by the
same law and by the bond of the same doctrine as obtains among
us.[1] It is very important to make this point. Accordingly I shall

---

[1] In this chapter, especially secs. 1–5 and 8, Calvin unfolds the doctrine
of the covenant. See the passages listed in I. vi. 1, note 3. Zwingli, Oecolam-
padius, William Tyndale, Bucer, and Bullinger all made the covenant of
grace a substantive element in theology. Their conception of the covenant
was advanced by Zacharias Ursinus (d. 1583) and Caspar Olevianus (d.
1587), the Heidelberg Reformers, and by Robert Rollock (d. 1599) in
Scotland. The full development of the covenant theology came only in
the seventeenth century and was expressed in the Westminster Confession
(1647), ch. VII, and in the influential work of John Cocceius, *Summa doctrinae de foedere et testamento Dei* (1648). This amplification, in which a
covenant of works, or of nature, stands beside the covenant of grace, is
not anticipated by Calvin. Relevant information is briefly given in articles
by L. J. Trinterud, "The Origins of Puritanism," *Church History* XX
(1951), 37–57; by E. H. Emerson, "Calvin and Covenant Theology,"
Church History XXV (1956), 136–144; and with reference to Scotland, by
S. A. Burrell, "The Covenant Idea as a Revolutionary Symbol," *Church
History* XXVII (1958), 338–350. See also G. Schrenk, *Gottesreich und
Bund in älteren Protestantisimus* (Gütersloh, 1923), and the discussion by
G. D. Henderson of "The Idea of the Covenant in Scotland," *The Burning
Bush: Studies in Scottish Church History*, ch. iv.

add, by way of appendix, how far the condition of the patriarchs in this fellowship differed from ours, even though they participated in the same inheritance and hoped for a common salvation with us by the grace of the same Mediator. ᵇThe testimonies that we have gathered from the Law and the Prophets to prove this make plain that God's people have never had any other rule of reverence and piety. Nevertheless, because writers often argue at length about the difference between the Old and the New Testament, thus arousing some misgiving in the simple reader's mind, we shall rightly devote a special section to a fuller and more precise discussion of this matter. Indeed, that wonderful rascal Servetus and certain madmen of the Anabaptist sect, who regard the Israelites as nothing but a herd of swine, make necessary what would in any case have been very profitable for us. For they babble of the Israelites as fattened by the Lord on this earth without any hope of heavenly immortality.[2] So, then, to keep this pestilential error away from godly minds, and at the same time to remove all the difficulties that usually rise up immediately when mention is made of the difference between the Old and the New Testament, let us look in passing at the similarities and differences between the covenant that the Lord made of old with the Israelites before Christ's advent, and that which God has now made with us after his manifestation.

2. Chief points of agreement

ᵇBoth can be explained in one word. The covenant made with all the patriarchs is so much like ours in substance and reality that the two are actually one and the same. Yet they differ in the mode of dispensation. But because no one can gain a clear understanding from such a short statement, a fuller explanation is required if we wish to make any progress. Now, in showing their similarity—or rather, unity—it would be superfluous to examine afresh the details that have already been reviewed; ᶜand it would be inappropriate here to mingle matters to be discussed elsewhere.

ᵇHere we must take our stand on three main points. First, we hold that carnal prosperity and happiness did not constitute the goal set before the Jews to which they were to aspire. Rather, they were adopted into the hope of immortality; and assurance of this adoption was certified to them by oracles, by the law, and by the prophets. Secondly, the covenant by which they were bound

---

[2] Servetus insistently affirms the view here rejected by Calvin. "In the law," he says, "remission of sins was carnal and earthly," as also was faith. *Christianismi restitutio* (1553), pp. 322, 324; cf. pp. 233, 237 ff., 305, 314, 321–326.

to the Lord was supported, not by their own merits, but solely by the mercy of the God who called them. Thirdly, they had and knew Christ as Mediator, through whom they were joined to God and were to share in his promises. The second of these, ^{c(b)}because perhaps we do not yet sufficiently understand it, will be explained at length in its place.[3] For by numerous ^bclear testimonies of the prophets we shall confirm the truth that all those blessings which the Lord has ever given or promised to his people arose solely out of his goodness and kindness. Here and there we have also given clear proofs of the third point; and we have not left even the first point untouched.

3. The Old Testament looks to the future

^bThe first point especially refers to the present question; over it our opponents raise more controversy with us. Let us therefore give it closer attention. But we shall do this in such a way that if any gap occurs in the explanation, we can supply it as we proceed or add it at an opportune place. The apostle surely relieves us of every doubt on these three points when he says: "Long beforehand through his prophets God the Father promised in the Holy Scriptures the gospel," which he proclaimed "concerning his Son" at the appointed time [Rom. 1:2–3 p.]. Likewise, the Law and the Prophets bear witness to the righteousness of faith, which is taught through the gospel itself [Rom. 3:21]. Surely the gospel does not confine men's hearts to delight in the present life, but lifts them to the hope of immortality. It does not fasten them to earthly pleasures, but by announcing a hope that rests in heaven it, so to speak, transports them thither. Elsewhere Paul expresses it thus: "After you believed in the gospel, you were sealed with the Holy Spirit of promise, who is the guarantee of our inheritance unto the redemption of the acquired possession" [Eph. 1:13–14]. Again: "We have heard of your faith in Christ Jesus and love toward the saints, because of the hope laid up for you in heaven. Of this you have heard in the truth-telling word, the gospel" [Col. 1:4–5 p.]. Likewise, "He called us through the gospel to share in the glory of our Lord Jesus Christ." [II Thess. 2:14 p.] Hence it is called "the word of salvation" [Acts 13:26], "the power of God to save believers" [Rom. 1:16 p.], and "the Kingdom of Heaven" [Matt. 3:2; ch. 13]. But if the doctrine of the gospel is spiritual, and gives us access to the possession of incorruptible life, let us not think that those to whom it had been promised and announced omitted and neglected the care of the

---

[3] III. xv–xviii.

soul,[4] and sought after fleshly pleasures like stupid beasts. Let no one perversely say here that the promises concerning the gospel, sealed in the Law and the Prophets, were intended for the new people.[5] For the apostle, shortly after saying that the gospel was promised in the law, adds: "Whatever the law contains is without doubt intended specifically for those under the law" [Rom. 3:19 p.]. I admit that Paul said this in another context. But when he said that whatever the law teaches applies properly to the Jews, he was not so forgetful as to overlook what he had affirmed a few verses before concerning the gospel promised in the law [Rom. 1:2; cf. ch. 3:21]. When the apostle says that the promises of the gospel are contained in it, he proves with utter clarity that the Old Testament was particularly concerned with the future life.

4. Even in the Old Covenant justification derives its validity from grace alone
ᵇFor the same reason it follows that the Old Testament was established upon the free mercy of God, and was confirmed by Christ's intercession. For the gospel preaching, too, declares nothing else than that sinners are justified apart from their own merit by God's fatherly kindness; and the whole of it is summed up in Christ. Who, then, dares to separate the Jews from Christ, since with them, we hear, was made the covenant of the gospel, the sole foundation of which is Christ? Who dares to estrange from the gift of free salvation[6] those to whom we hear the doctrine of the righteousness of faith was imparted? Not to dispute too long about something obvious—we have a notable saying of the Lord: "Abraham rejoiced that he was to see my day; he saw it and was glad" [John 8:56]. And what Christ there testified concerning Abraham, the apostle shows to have been universal among the believing folk when he says: "Christ remains, yesterday and today and forever" [Heb. 13:8]. Paul is not speaking there simply of Christ's everlasting divinity but of his power, a power perpetually available to believers. Therefore, both the blessed Virgin and Zacharias in their songs called the salvation revealed in

---

[4] *"Neglectaque animae cura."* Pannier regards this as reflecting one of the grievances against the Anabaptists: Pannier, *Institution* III. 288 and note *b* on p. 10.
[5] Servetus, *Dialogorum de Trinitate libri duo: De justitia regni Christi* I. 1, 4, fo. C 7a, D 16, D 2a (tr. E. M. Wilbur, *The Two Treatises of Servetus on the Trinity*, pp. 225, 230 f.).
[6] Servetus, *De justitia regni Christi*, III. 3, fo. E 2a (tr. Wilbur, *op. cit.*, pp. 243 ff.).

Christ the manifestation of the promises that the Lord had formerly made to Abraham and the patriarchs [Luke 1:54-55, 72-73]. If the Lord, in manifesting his Christ, discharged his ancient oath, one cannot but say that the Old Testament always had its end in Christ and in eternal life.[7]

5. Similar signs of the covenant

[b]Indeed, the apostle makes the Israelites equal to us not only in the grace of the covenant but also in the signification of the sacraments. In recounting examples of the punishments with which, according to Scripture, the Israelites were chastised of old, his purpose was to deter the Corinthians from falling into similar misdeeds. So he begins with this premise: there is no reason why we should claim any privilege for ourselves, to deliver us from the vengeance of God, which they underwent, since the Lord not only provided them with the same benefits but also manifested his grace among them by the same symbols [cf. I Cor. 10:1-6, 11].[8] It is as if he said: "Suppose you trust that you are out of danger because both Baptism, with which you have been sealed, and the Supper, of which you partake daily, possess excellent promises, but at the same time you hold God's goodness in contempt and play the wanton. Know that the Jews did not lack such symbols, and yet the Lord carried out his harsh judgments against them. They were baptized in crossing the sea and in the cloud that protected them from the sun's heat." Our opponents call that crossing a carnal baptism, which corresponds in a certain measure to our spiritual baptism. But if that were accepted as true, the apostle's argument would not be effective. For Paul here means to disabuse Christians of thinking they are superior to the Jews through the privilege of baptism. Nor is what immediately follows subject to this cavil: "They ate the same spiritual food and drank the same spiritual drink" [I Cor. 10:3-4]. This he interprets as referring to Christ.[9]

---

[7] Bucer had similarly associated Christ with the ancient covenant in *Metaphrases et enarrationes perpetuae epistolarum D. Pauli Apostoli*, 1536, p. 159. Cf. Benoit, *Institution* II. 198. For patristic views of this, familiar to Calvin, see Irenaeus, *Against Heresies* IV. ix, x (MPG 7. 996–1000; tr. ANF I. 472 ff.); Augustine, *On the Morals of the Catholic Church* xxviii. 56–58 (MPL 32. 1333; tr. NPNF IV. 56 f.).

[8] Cf. Comm. I Cor. 10:1-5.

[9] Bucer, *Metaphrases et enarrationes perpetuae epistolarum D. Pauli Apostoli*, p. 158, states that the sacraments of the ancient Jews and of Christians are not different in substance. Most of the opinions condemned in this and the following section are those of Servetus.

6. Refutation of an objection based on John 6:49, 54[t]

[b]To overthrow this statement of Paul's, they make an objection
of what Christ says: "Your fathers ate the manna in the wilderness, and they died" [John 6:49]. "He who eats my flesh, shall
not die forever" [John 6:54]. These two passages can be made to
agree without any trouble. Because the Lord was then talking to
hearers who were trying only to fill their bellies with food, but
were not concerned about the true food of the soul, he accommodated his language somewhat to their capacity; especially
making the comparison of manna and their bodies in accordance
with their understanding. They demanded that, to gain authority
for himself, he prove his power by some miracle, such as Moses
performed in the wilderness when he obtained manna from
heaven. But by "manna" they understood nothing but the remedy
for the physical hunger that then afflicted the people. They did
not penetrate into that deeper mystery with which Paul was concerned. To show how much greater benefit they ought to expect
of him than what they said their fathers had received from Moses,
Christ therefore made this comparison. Suppose you consider it
a great and memorable miracle that the Lord gave heavenly food
to his people through Moses that they might not starve in the
desert, and sustained them by it for a short time. From this, then,
infer how much more excellent is the food that imparts immortality. We see why the Lord passed over the principal feature of
manna and noted only its lowest use. It is because the Jews, trying
to reproach him, had pitted Moses against him, because with
manna he had succored the people in their need. To this he
replies that he is the minister of a far higher grace, in comparison
with which the physical sustenance of the people, which alone
they highly esteemed, deserved to be despised. Paul knew that
when the Lord rained manna from heaven he did not do so
merely to feed their bellies, but also bestowed it as a spiritual
mystery, to foreshadow the spiritual quickening we have in Christ
[I Cor. 10:1–5]. Therefore he did not neglect this aspect, the
one principally worth considering. From this we can conclude
with full certainty that the Lord not only communicated to the
Jews the same promises of eternal and heavenly life as he now
deigns to give us, but also sealed them with truly spiritual sacraments. [x]Augustine debates this matter at length in his work
Against Faustus the Manichee.[10]

---

[10] Augustine, *Reply to Faustus the Manichaean* XV. 11; XIX. 16 (MPL 42. 314,
356; tr. NPNF IV. 219, 244). Last sentence is from 1553 edition.

(Argument concerning the hope of eternal life, showing that the Old Testament patriarchs looked for fulfillment of the promises in the life to come, 7–14)

7. *The fathers had the Word; with it they also had eternal life*

e(b)But my readers may prefer to have testimonies cited from the Law and the Prophets, to prove to them that, as we have heard from Christ and the apostles, the spiritual covenant was also common to the patriarchs. bWell then, I shall comply with their desire, and the more willingly because our adversaries will thus be more surely refuted; and afterward be quite unable to evade the issue.

I shall then begin with this proof—even though I know the Anabaptists will disdainfully consider it pointless and even ridiculous—yet it will be most valuable for sound and teachable folk. e(b)I take it for granted that there is such life energy in God's Word that it quickens the souls of all to whom God grants participation in it. For Peter's saying has always been valid, that it is an imperishable seed, which abides forever [I Peter 1:23], as he also infers from Isaiah's words [I Peter 1:24; Isa. 40:6]. Now since God of old bound the Jews to himself by this sacred bond, there is no doubt that he set them apart to the hope of eternal life. When I say they embraced the Word to be united more closely to God, bI do not mean that general e(b)mode of communication bwhich is diffused through heaven and earth and all the creatures of the world. For although it quickens all things—each according to the measure of its nature—it still does not free them from the exigency of corruption. Rather, I mean that special mode which both illumines the souls of the pious into the knowledge of God and, in a sense, joins them to him. Adam, Abel, Noah, Abraham, and the other patriarchs cleaved to God by such illumination of the Word. Therefore I say that without any doubt they entered into God's immortal Kingdom. For theirs was a real participation in God, which cannot be without the blessing of eternal life.

8. *In the Old Covenant, God gave his people fellowship with himself and thus eternal life*

bDoes this still seem a little unclear? Well, then, let us pass on to the very formula of the covenant. This will not only satisfy calm spirits but will also abundantly demonstrate the ignorance of those who try to contradict it. For the Lord always covenanted with his servants thus: "I will be your God, and you shall be my people" [Lev. 26:12]. The prophets also commonly explained that life and salvation and the whole of blessedness are embraced in these words. For with good reason David often declares: "Blessed the people whose God is the Lord" [Ps. 144:15]; "Blessed . . . the nation whom he has chosen as his heritage" [Ps. 33:12]. This is not for the sake of earthly happiness, but because he delivers them from death, he preserves forever and keeps in his everlasting mercy those whom he has chosen as his people. The other prophets speak similarly: "Thou art our God; we shall not die" [Hab. 1:12 p.]. "The Lord is our king, our lawgiver; he will save us" [Isa. 33:22]. "Blessed are you, O Israel, . . . for in the Lord God you are saved" [Deut. 33:29 p.].

But not to belabor superfluous matters, this admonition repeatedly occurs in the Prophets: we lack nothing for an abundance of all good things and for assurance of salvation so long as the Lord is our God. And rightly so! For if his face, the moment that it has shone forth, is a very present pledge of salvation, how can he manifest himself to a man as his God without also opening to him the treasures of His salvation? He is our God on this condition: that he dwell among us, as he has testified through Moses [Lev. 26:11]. But one cannot obtain such a presence of him without, at the same time, possessing life. And although nothing further was expressed, they had a clear enough promise of spiritual life in these words: "I am . . . your God" [Ex. 6:7]. For he did not declare that he would be a God to their bodies alone, but especially to their souls. Still, souls, unless they be joined to God through righteousness, remain estranged from him in death. On the other hand, such a union when present will bring everlasting salvation with it.

9. Even in the Old Covenant, God's goodness was stronger than death

ᵇBesides this, he not only testified that he was, but also promised that he would ever be, their God. This he did that their hope, not content with present benefits, might be extended to eternity. Many passages show that this characterization of the future life was so understood among them, when believers were comforted not only amid present misfortunes but for the future by the thought that God would never fail them. Now, in the second part of the promise, he even more clearly assured them that God's blessing would for their sake extend beyond the limits of earthly life: "I shall be the God of your seed after you" [Gen. 17:7 p.]. For if he was going to declare his benevolence toward the dead by benefiting their offspring, much less was his favor to fail toward themselves. For God is not like men, who transfer their love to their friends' children because their opportunity to perform their duties toward those to whom they wish to do well is broken off by death. God, however, whose beneficence is not hindered by death, does not withdraw the fruit of his mercy from the dead, but for their sake "conveys it to a thousand generations" [Ex. 20:6 p.]. By this splendid proof, therefore, the Lord willed to commend to them the greatness and abundance of his goodness, which they were to experience after death, when he described it as overflowing to all their posterity. The Lord then sealed the truth of this promise, bringing about its fulfillment, so to speak, when he called himself "the God of Abraham, . . . Isaac, and . . . Jacob" long after their death [Ex. 3:6]. Why? Was this not an absurd title if they had perished? Then it would have been as if he had said: "I am the God of those who do not exist." Hence, the Evangelists relate that Christ confuted the Sadducees by this one proof [Matt. 22:23–32; Luke 20:27–38]; so that they could not even deny that Moses had testified to the resurrection of the dead, that is, those who had learned from Moses himself that "all the saints are in His hand" [Deut. 33:3 p.]. From this it was easy to conclude that they whom he, who is judge of death and life, had received into his tutelage, care, and protection are not snuffed out even by death.

10. The blessedness of the ancient people was not earthly

ᵇNow let us examine the chief point in this controversy: whether or not the believers were so taught by the Lord as to perceive that they had a better life elsewhere; and, disregarding the earthly life, to meditate upon the heavenly. First, the manner of life divinely enjoined upon them was a continual exercise by which they were reminded that they were the most miserable of all men if they were happy in this life only. Adam, most unhappy from the mere remembrance of his lost happiness, meagerly sustained his need with anxious toil. And as if it were not enough to be weighed down with physical labor by God's curse [Gen. 3:17], he sustained extreme sorrow in such solace as remained to him. Of his two sons one was wickedly murdered by the other [Gen. 4:8]. Adam had good reason to detest and recoil from the sight of his surviving son. Abel, cruelly slaughtered in the flower of his age, is an example of human calamity. While the whole earth lives in carefree pleasures, Noah spends a good part of his life in great weariness building the ark [Gen. 6:22]. He escapes death by that which brings greater troubles than if he had died a hundred deaths. Besides the fact that the ark was a sort of grave for him for ten months, there can be nothing more unpleasant than to be confined so long—almost immersed in the dung of animals! Having surmounted such great difficulties, he falls into new occasions for grief. He sees himself held in derision by his own son, and is obliged to curse with his own mouth him whom by God's great benefit he had received safe from the Flood [Gen. 9:24–25].

11. The faith of Abraham

ᵉWe ought to esteem ᵇAbraham ᶜas one equal to a hundred thousand if we consider his faith, which is set before us as the best model of believing; to be children of God, we must be reckoned as members of his tribe [Gen. 12:3]. Now what could be more absurd than for Abraham to be the father of all believers [cf. Gen. 17:5] and yet not to possess even the remotest corner among them? But he cannot be removed from their number—not even from the very highest rank of honor—without wiping out the whole church. Now as for the experiences of his life—ᵇwhen he is first called by God's command [Gen. 12:1], he is taken away from his country, parents, and friends, considered by men the sweetest things in life, as if God deliberately intended to strip him of all life's delights. As soon as he has reached the land in which he has been bidden to dwell, he is driven from it by famine [Gen. 12:10]. Seeking aid, he flees to a place where he has to prostitute his wife to save his life [Gen. 12:11 ff.], an act probably more bitter than many deaths. When he has returned to the land of his abode, he is again driven from it by famine. What sort of happiness this—to dwell in a land where you often have to go hungry, even perish from hunger, unless you flee from it? He is reduced to the same straits in the land of Abimelech, so that to save his own head he has to suffer the loss of his wife [Gen. 20:1 ff.]. While in uncertainty he wanders about hither and thither for many years, he is compelled by the continual quarreling of his servants to dismiss his nephew whom he cherished as his own son [Gen. 13:5–9]. Doubtless he bore this separation as if he had undergone the amputation of a limb. Shortly thereafter, Abraham hears that his nephew has been taken captive by enemies [Gen. 14:14–16]. ᵉWherever he goes, he finds terribly barbarous neighbors who do not even let him drink water out of the wells that he had dug with great labor. For he would not have recovered the use of them from King Gerar had he not first been denied it [Gen. 21:25–31]. ᵇNow when he has reached a worn-out old age, he finds himself childless [Gen. 15:2]—the most unpleasant and bitter feature of age. Finally, beyond all hope, he begets Ishmael [Gen. 16:15], but the birth of this son costs him dear. For he is wearied by Sarah's reproaches, as if he, by encouraging the handmaid's arrogance, were himself the cause of domestic strife [Gen. 16:5]. Finally, Isaac is born [Gen. 21:2], but with this condition—Ishmael, the first-born, is to be driven out and forsaken almost like an enemy [Gen. 21:9 ff.]. When Isaac alone is left, in whom the weary old age of the good man may repose, he is shortly after ordered to sacrifice him [Gen. 22:1 ff.]. What more frightful thing can the human mind imagine than for a father to become the executioner of his own son? If Isaac had died of sickness, who would not have thought Abraham the most miserable of old men—given a son in jest—on whose account his grief of childlessness should be doubled? If he had been killed by some stranger, the calamity would have been much increased by the indignity. But for a son to be slaughtered by his own father's hand surpasses every sort of calamity. In short, throughout life he was so tossed and troubled that if anyone wished to paint a picture of a calamitous life, he could find no model more appropriate than Abraham's! Let no man object that he was not completely unhappy, because he finally came safely through so many great tempests. We will not say that he leads a happy life who struggles long and hard through infinite difficulties, but he who calmly enjoys present benefits without feeling misfortune.

12. The faith of Isaac and Jacob*

bIsaac is afflicted by lesser ills, but has scarcely even the least taste of sweetness. He also experiences such troubles as do not permit a man to be happy on earth. Famine drives him from the Land of Canaan [Gen. 26:1]. His wife is torn from his bosom [Gen. 26:7 ff.]. His neighbors repeatedly molest him and oppress him in every way, compelling him also to fight over water [Gen. 26:12 ff.]. At home his daughters-in-law cause him great annoyance [Gen. 26:34–35]. His children's strife afflicts him [Gen. 27: 41 ff.], and to remedy this great evil he has to exile the son whom he blessed [Gen. 28:1, 5].

As for Jacob, he is a notable example of nothing but extreme unhappiness.[11] He passes a most troubled boyhood at home in dread of his elder brother's threats, to which he is finally compelled to yield [Gen. 27:41–45]. When he flees from his parents

---

[11] *"Extremae infoelicitatis insigne est exemplar."* The fact that for Calvin the patriarchs, elect of God, experienced only affliction and unhappiness in the course of their lives is in accord with innumerable passages in his works that counter the unfounded notion that Calvin regarded prosperity in this life as associated with election. Cf. McNeill, *The History and Character of Calvinism,* pp. 222 f., 418 ff. On Jacob, cf. Ambrose, *On the Duties of the Clergy* ii. 5 (MPL 16. 114 ff.; tr. NPNF 2 ser. X. 46 f.).

and native soil—besides the bitterness of such banishment—he is no more kindly or gently received by his uncle Laban [Gen. 29: 15 ff.]. It is not enough for Jacob to spend seven years in the hardest and cruelest kind of servitude [Gen. 29:20]—he is also cheated of a wife by an evil trick [Gen. 29:23–26]! For his second wife he has to undergo new servitude [Gen. 29:27], scorched all day under the sun's heat, and pained all the wakeful night with frost and cold, as he himself complains [Gen. 31:40]. While enduring this very harsh life for twenty years, he is daily afflicted by the unjust acts of his father-in-law [Gen. 31:41]. And in his own household he is not quiet, for he sees it distracted and almost scattered by the hatred, quarreling, and rivalry of his wives [Gen. 30:1 ff.]. Commanded to return to his country, he has to take his departure as if in ignominious flight [Gen. 31:17 ff.]. And yet he cannot escape the wickedness of his father-in-law without being plagued in the midst of his journey by the latter's insults and abuses [Gen. 31:23]. Soon much more cruel distress overtakes him. For when he approaches his brother, he sees as many deaths before him as a cruel enemy could devise. Therefore, he is tortured beyond measure and wracked with terrible fears while waiting for Esau to come [Gen. 32:7, 11]. When Jacob sees Esau, he falls down half dead at his brother's feet, until he perceives him more favorable than he had dared hope [Gen. 33:1 ff.]. Thereupon, when first entering the land, he loses Rachel, his dearly beloved wife [Gen. 35:16–20]. Afterward he hears that the son whom he had by her, and whom for that reason he loves more than the rest, has been torn by a wild beast [Gen. 37:31–32]. He is so overcome with grief at his son's death that after long weeping he obstinately refuses all consolation, leaving no course open to himself, he declares, but to go down, sorrowing, into the grave to his son. In the meantime his daughter has been seized and raped [Gen. 34:2, 5], and his sons in their bold revenge of this [Gen. 34:25] not only make him hateful to all the inhabitants of the country but put him in ever-present peril of murder [Gen. 34:30]. What great causes for anxiety, for grief, and for loathing are these! There follows that heinous crime of Reuben, his first-born son; nothing more serious than this could happen [Gen. 35:22]. The defiling of a man's wife is considered among the greatest misfortunes—but what is to be said when that crime has been committed by his own son? Shortly thereafter the family is again polluted by incest [Gen. 38:18]. So many shameful experiences ought to break a mind otherwise very stanch and unbowed by calamities! Near the end of his life, when he seeks to allay his own hunger and that of his family, he is struck by the announcement of a new misfortune: he learns that another of his sons has been put in prison. To get him back, Jacob is compelled to commit Benjamin, his one and only joy, to the care of others [Gen. 42:34, 38]. Who can imagine that in such a flood of misfortunes he would have a single moment to breathe in peace? Accordingly, as his own best witness, he declares to Pharaoh that his days upon the earth have been short and evil [Gen. 47:9]. He asserts that he has passed his life in continual misery, and absolutely denies that he has experienced the prosperity which the Lord had promised him. Therefore, either Jacob was a hostile and ungrateful appraiser of God's favor, or he truly professed that he had been miserable on earth. If this affirmation was true, it follows that he did not have his hope set upon earthly things.

13. The patriarchs sought for everlasting life
ᵇIf these holy patriarchs looked for a blessed life, as they undoubtedly did, from God's hand, they both conceived and saw it as a blessedness other than that of earthly life. The apostle very beautifully shows this: "By faith," he says, "Abraham sojourned in the Land of Promise, as in a foreign land, living in tents with Isaac and Jacob, heirs with him of the same promise. For they looked forward to the well-founded city, whose builder and maker is God. . . . These all died in faith, not having received the promises, but having seen them and believed them from afar, and having acknowledged that they were strangers and exiles on the earth. By this they mean that they are seeking a homeland. If they had been struck with desire of that land which they had left, they would have had opportunity to return. But . . . they desire a better country, that is, a heavenly one. Therefore God is not ashamed to be called their God, for he has prepared for them a city" [Heb. 11:9–10, 13–16 p.]. For they would have been more stupid than blocks of wood to keep on pursuing the promises when no hope of these appeared on earth, unless they expected them to be fulfilled elsewhere. And Paul very rightly insists, first of all, that they call this life a "sojourn," just as Moses also speaks of it [Gen. 47:9]. For if they are strangers and sojourners in the Land of Canaan, where is the promise of the Lord that made them heirs of Abraham? Obviously, then, the Lord's promise of possession to them refers to something far different. Therefore, "they did not acquire even a foot's length" [Acts 7:5 p.] in the Land of Canaan, except for a grave. By this they testified that they hoped to receive the fruit of the promise only after death. And this is the reason why Jacob so esteemed being buried there as to bind his son Joseph by an oath to this promise [Gen. 47:29–30]; this

is why Joseph commanded that his own bones were to be transferred there at a time some centuries later, long after they had
fallen into dust [Gen. 50:25].

14. Death for the saints the entrance to life*

ᵇFinally, it is clearly established that in all their efforts in this
life they set before themselves the blessedness of the future life.
If Jacob was not intent upon a higher blessing, why did he desire
so much and seek at such great risk the right of the first-born,
which was to procure him exile and almost disinheritance, but
bring no good at all [Gen. 27:41]? With his last breath he declared
that this was his intent: "I shall wait for thy salvation, O Lord"
[Gen. 49:18, Vg.]. What salvation could he have waited for, when
he knew he was dying, unless he discerned in death the beginning of a new life? Why are we debating concerning holy men
and children of God when even one who was otherwise trying to
assail the truth had some inkling of such understanding? What
did Balaam mean when he said: "Let me die the death of the
righteous, and let my end be like theirs" [Num. 23:10 p.]—unless
he felt what David afterward declared: "Precious in the Lord's
sight is the death of the saints" [Ps. 116:15], but "the death of
the impious is very evil" [Ps. 33:22, Vg.; 34:21, EV]? If the final
boundary and goal were in death,[12] in it no difference could be
observed between just and unjust. But they differ from each
other in what awaits them after death.

(*This argument continued with references to passages from
David, Job, Ezekiel, and others, 15–22*)

15. David as proclaimer of hope

ᵇWe have not yet progressed beyond Moses. According to our
opponents, he performed no other office than to induce carnal
folk to worship God by promising them fertile fields and an
abundance of all things. Yet, unless we willfully shun the proffered light, we already possess a clear affirmation of the spiritual
covenant. If we proceed to the prophets, in them eternal life and
Christ's Kingdom are revealed in fullest splendor.

First David, as he preceded the others in time, also represented
the heavenly mysteries according to the order of divine dispensation more obscurely than the rest. Nevertheless, with what great
clearness and certainty he directs all his words to that goal! This
sentence testifies how much he values any earthly habitation:

---

[12] *"Ultima linea et meta."* Cf. Horace, *Epistles* I. xvi. 79: *"Mors ultima linea
rerum est."* (LCL edition, Horace, *Satires, Epistles, and Ars Poetica*, p.
356.)

"Here I am a stranger, a sojourner, like all my fathers" [Ps. 39:12].
"Every living man is vanity! Each one goes about as a shadow"
[Ps. 39:5–6 p.]! "And now, Lord, for what do I wait? My hope
is in thee!" [Ps. 39:7.] Surely he who has confessed that there is
nothing solid or stable on earth, yet holds fast to a firm faith in
God, contemplates his happiness as reposing elsewhere. David
habitually calls believers back to that contemplation whenever
he wishes to bring them true consolation. For in another passage,
after he has spoken of the brevity and the fleeting and transitory
image of man's life, he adds: "But the mercy of the Lord is everlasting upon those who fear him" [Ps. 103:17]. This is similar
to what he says in Ps. 102: "In the beginning, O Lord, thou didst
found the earth, and the heavens are the work of thy hands. They
will perish, but thou dost endure; they will all wear out like a
garment, and thou wilt change them like raiment. . . . But thou
art the same, and thy years will not fail. The children of thy
servants shall dwell; their posterity shall be established before
thee" [Ps. 102:25–28; cf. Ps. 101:26–29, Vg.]. If the godly do not
cease to be established before the Lord despite the destruction of
heaven and earth, it follows that their salvation is joined to God's
eternity.

Yet this hope cannot stand at all unless it rests on the promise
that is set forth in Isaiah: "The heavens," says the Lord, "will
vanish like smoke, the earth will wear out like a garment, and
they who dwell in it will die like these; but my salvation will
be forever, and my righteousness will never fail" [ch. 51:6, Vg.].
There perpetuity is attributed to righteousness and salvation, not
in so far as these reside in God, but as they are experienced by
men.

16. Additional passages applicable to the future life*

ᵇAnd what he sings in many passages in The Psalms about the
prosperity of believers may not otherwise be grasped unless it
be applied to the manifestation of heavenly glory. Such passages
are these: "The Lord . . . preserves the souls of his saints; from
the sinner's hand he will free them" [Ps. 97:10]. "Light dawns
for the righteous, and joy for the upright in heart." [Ps. 97:11.]
Likewise, "The righteousness of the godly endures forever; his
horn will be exalted in glory." [Ps. 111:9, Vg.; 112:9, EV.] "The
desire of the wicked man will come to nought." [Ps. 111:10, Vg.;
112:10, EV.] Also, "Surely the righteous shall confess thy name;
the upright shall dwell in thy presence." [Ps. 139:14, Vg.; 140:
13, EV.] Again, "The righteous . . . will be remembered forever."
[Ps. 112:6.] And another, "The Lord will redeem the souls of his

servants." [Ps. 34:22.] For the Lord often leaves his servants not only to be troubled by the lust of the wicked but to be torn and destroyed. He lets good men languish in darkness and filth, while the wicked almost shine among the stars. And he does not so cheer them with the brightness of his countenance that they enjoy lasting happiness. For this reason not even David disguises the fact that if believers keep their eyes fastened upon the present state of things, they will be smitten by very grievous temptation, as if there were for innocence neither favor nor reward with God. So very greatly does impiety prosper and flourish, while the company of the godly is oppressed by disgrace, poverty, contempt, and every kind of cross![13] "My foot," David said, "had almost stumbled, my steps had well-nigh slipped, . . . while I was envious of the prosperity of fools, while I saw the good fortune of the wicked." [Ps. 73:2–3 p.] Yet he concludes his statement: "I pondered whether I could understand this, but it is a torment to my spirit, until I shall go into the sanctuary of the Lord and perceive their end" [Ps. 73:16–17 p.].

17. The hope of the godly rises above present calamities to the future life[t]
    [b]Let us, therefore, learn from this confession of David's that the holy patriarchs under the Old Testament were aware how rarely or never God fulfills in this world what he promises to his servants; and that they therefore lifted up their hearts to God's sanctuary, in which they found hidden what does not appear in the shadows of the present life. This place was the Last Judgment of God, which, although they could not discern it with their eyes, they were content to understand by faith. Relying upon this assurance, they did not doubt that, whatever might happen in the world, the time would nevertheless come when God's promises would be fulfilled. So these statements witness: "I shall behold thy face in righteousness. . . . I shall be satisfied with thy countenance" [Ps. 17:15 p.]. Again, "I am like a green olive tree in the house of the Lord." [Ps. 52:8 p.] Again: "The righteous shall flourish like the palm tree, and grow like a cedar in Lebanon. Planted in the house of the Lord, they shall flourish in the courts of our God. They shall still bring forth fruit; in old age they shall be fat and green" [Ps. 92:12–14 p.]. [e]A little before, he had said: "How deep are thy thoughts, O Jehovah, . . . while evildoers flourish and sprout like grass, that they may perish forever" [Ps.

[13] In his emphasis on the eschatological aspect of the Old Testament promises, Calvin is disposed to minimize the element in these of hope for the present life. Cf. Pannier, *Institution* III. 290, note *d*, on p. 25.

92:5, 7 p.]. ᵇWhere does that beauty and grace of believers appear save when this world of appearances is overturned by the manifestation of God's Kingdom? When they cast their eyes upon that eternity, they despised the momentary harshness of present calamities and burst forth fearlessly in these words: "Thou wilt not allow the righteous to die. But thou . . . wilt cast the wicked down into the pit of destruction" [Ps. 55:22–23 p., cf. Comm.]. Where in this world is there a pit of eternal destruction that swallows up the wicked, in whose felicity another passage includes also the following: "They end their days in a moment without much languishing" [Job 21:13, cf. Comm.]. Where is that great stability of the saints who, as David himself everywhere laments, not only are violently shaken, but utterly oppressed and consumed? That is, he set before his eyes not what the changing course of the world brings—more unstable than the ocean tides— but what the Lord will do when he will one day sit in judgment to determine the permanent state of heaven and earth.

The psalmist aptly describes this in another passage: "Fools trust in their wealth, and boast of the abundance of their riches. And yet no one, however much he may excel in dignity, can redeem his brother from death; no one can pay to God the price of redemption. . . . Even when they see that the wise die, the wicked and the foolish alike perish and leave their wealth to others, they still think that their houses will abide forever and their dwellings will last eternally, and they sing the praises of their own names on earth. But man will not remain in honor: he will be like the beasts that perish. It is the height of folly for them to think this way, yet their posterity avidly copy them. They will be gathered in hell like a flock; death shall rule over them. When the light dawns, the righteous shall rule over them; their beauty shall perish; hell shall be their home" [Ps. 49:6–14 p., cf. Comm.].

This mockery of fools for reposing in the slippery and fleeting "blessings" of the world shows in the first place that the wise should seek a far different kind of happiness. But then David more clearly discloses the mystery of the resurrection when he raises up the Kingdom of the godly after the wicked have been lost and destroyed. What, I ask you, shall we call that "coming of the morning"[14] [cf. Ps. 30:5] but the revelation of the new life that follows the end of the present age?

*18. Their happy destiny contrasted with that of the wicked**

ᵇHence arose that aspiration which believers used as a solace

---

[14] "*Lucis exortum,*" corresponding to the phrase "*exorta luce,*" which is thrust into the quotation from Ps. 49: 6–14, above.

of misery and as a remedy for suffering: "The Lord's anger is but for a moment, but his mercy is for a lifetime" [Ps. 30:5]. How could they end their afflictions in a moment when they were afflicted almost throughout life? Where could they see such long-lasting divine generosity, when they had scarcely tasted it? If they had clung to the earth, they could have found nothing like this. But because they looked up to heaven, they acknowledged that the saints suffer the cross at the Lord's hands "only for a moment"; "the mercies" they receive "are everlasting" [Isa. 54: 7–8 p.]. On the other hand, they foresaw an eternal and never-ending ruin of the wicked who had for one day been happy as in a dream. Thus these statements: "The memory of the righteous will be a blessing, but the name of the wicked will rot" [Prov. 10:7]. "Precious in the sight of the Lord is the death of his saints" [Ps. 116:15]; "the death of the wicked is most evil" [Ps. 34:21 p.]. Likewise, in Samuel, "The Lord will guard the feet of his holy ones; but the wicked shall become silent in darkness" [I Sam. 2:9, Vg.].

These passages show the ancient fathers to have known well that, however the saints were buffeted about, their final end was to be life and salvation, while the way of the wicked is a pleasant felicity by which they gradually slip into the whirlpool of death. They therefore called the death of the wicked "the destruction of the uncircumcized" [Ezek. 28:10; cf. chs. 31:18; 32:19 ff.; etc.], meaning that they had been cut off from the hope of resurrection. David, therefore, could think of no graver curse than this: "Let them be blotted out of the book of life; let them not be enrolled among the righteous" [Ps. 69:28].

19. Job as witness of immortality

ᵇMore remarkable than the other passages is this saying of Job's: "I know that my Redeemer lives, and I shall be resurrected from the earth on the Last Day; . . . and in my flesh I shall see God my Savior. This my hope abides in my breast" [Job 19:25–27, Vg.]. They who wish to parade their cleverness, cavil that this is not to be understood as referring to the final resurrection, but to the first day on which Job hoped that God would deal more kindly with him.[15] This we concede in part. Still, we shall force them to admit, whether they are willing or not, that Job could not have attained this lofty hope if his aspiration had rested on earth. We must therefore acknowledge that he lifted up his

---

[15] Cf. III. xxv. 4. Calvin, in *Psychopannychia,* contending against the doctrine of "the sleep of the soul," expounds numerous passages of Job (CR V. 228 ff.; tr. Calvin, *Tracts* III. 486 ff.).

eyes to a future immortality, for he saw that his Redeemer would be with him even as he lay in the tomb. Indeed, for those who think only of the present life death is the final despair, but this could not cut off Job's hope. "Even if he slay me," he said, "I shall nonetheless hope in him." [Job 13:15, Vg., cf. Comm.]

Let no quibbler cry out upon me that these are the statements of a few persons, quite insufficient to prove that the Jews held such a doctrine. I will at once answer him: these few people did not manifest in such statements any secret wisdom to which only excellent spirits might individually and privately be admitted. But, as they had been appointed the teachers of the common people by the Holy Spirit, they widely published the mysteries of God that were appointed to be learned and that ought to be the principles of the religion of the people. Therefore, when we hear the public oracles of the Holy Spirit, in which he so clearly and plainly discussed spiritual life in the church of the Jews, it would be intolerable stubbornness to relegate them solely to a carnal covenant, wherein mention is made only of the earth and of earthly riches.

20. The witness of the prophets to immortality

ᵇComing down to the later prophets, we can walk freely, as it were, in our own field. For, if we proved our point without difficulty as far as David, Job, and Samuel were concerned, in the Prophets it is much easier. The Lord held to this orderly plan in administering the covenant of his mercy: as the day of full revelation approached with the passing of time, the more he increased each day the brightness of its manifestation.[16] Accordingly, at the beginning when the first promise of salvation was given to Adam [Gen. 3:15] it glowed like a feeble spark. Then, as it was added to, the light grew in fullness, breaking forth increasingly and shedding its radiance more widely. At last—when all the clouds were dispersed—Christ, the Sun of Righteousness, fully illumined the whole earth [cf. Mal., ch. 4]. We need not fear lest the prophets fail us when we seek their support to prove our point. A huge forest of material, I see, looms before us. Over this we should have to tarry much longer than the plan of this work permits; for this would require a large volume, but for the fact that I have, I believe, blazed a trail for the moderately discerning

---

[16] In this remarkable passage, and frequently elsewhere, Calvin states forcibly his view of the progressive nature of revelation. For the reference to the growing light of morning, cf. Comm. Gal. 3:23, and Benoit, *Institution* II. 213, note 3. Cf. Pannier, *Institution* III. 32, 291; Fuhrmann, *God-centered Religion*, pp. 84 f. See also "accommodation" in Index III.

reader through this forest whereby he may go forward without stumbling. Hence I shall avoid a prolixity here unnecessary.

Nevertheless, I shall warn my readers beforehand to remember to open up their way with the key that I previously put into their hands.[17] That is, whenever the prophets recount the believing people's blessedness, hardly the least trace of which is discerned in the present life,[18] let them take refuge in this distinction: the better to commend God's goodness, the prophets represented it for the people under the lineaments, so to speak, of temporal benefits. But they painted a portrait such as to lift up the minds of the people above the earth, above the elements of this world [cf. Gal. 4:3] and the perishing age, and that would of necessity arouse them to ponder the happiness of the spiritual life to come.

21. The valley of dry bones in Ezekiel*

ᵇWe shall confine ourselves to one example. When the Israelites had been carried off to Babylon they realized that their dispersion was very much like death. Accordingly, they took Ezekiel's prophecy of their restoration as a mere fable. To disabuse them of this view was difficult, for they understood his announcement literally to mean that decaying corpses were to be restored to life! The Lord, to demonstrate that even this difficulty could not prevent him from making room for his benefaction, showed the prophet a vision of a field full of dry bones to which he imparted life and growth in a moment solely by the power of his Word [Ezek. 37:1–14]. Indeed, the vision served to correct the unbelief of that time, but in the meantime it impressed upon the Jews how much the Lord's power extended beyond the restoration of the people, since at but a nod it could readily bring to life these dry and scattered bones. For this reason, you will duly compare Ezekiel's words with a passage from Isaiah: "The dead shall live, my corpse, they shall rise again. O dwellers in the dust, awake and sing for joy! For the dew of the green field is thy dew; and you shall drag the land of the giants into ruin. Come, my people, enter into your tents; shut your doors behind you; hide yourselves for a little while until the wrath is past. For behold, the Lord will come from his place to punish the inhabitants of the earth for their iniquity, and the earth will disclose her blood, and will no longer cover her slain" [Isa. 26:19–21 p., cf. Comm.].

---

[17] Cf. II. ix. 1–4.

[18] *"Vix minima vestigia."* Cf. secs. 11–14, above. Calvin keeps insisting that God's elect experience no worldly prosperity.

22. Additional passages from other prophets*

ᵇIf someone should try to reduce all the other passages to this sort of formula, he would be acting absurdly. For there are some passages that show without concealment the future immortality prepared for believers in the Kingdom of God. We have recounted some of these. Most of the rest are of the same kind, especially these two. The first is from Isaiah: "As the new heaven and the new earth, which I make to stand before me, . . . so shall your seed . . . stand. From new moon to new moon, and from Sabbath to Sabbath, all flesh shall come to worship before me, says the Lord. And they shall go forth and look on the corpses of the men that have rebelled against me; for their worm shall not die, and their fire shall not be quenched" [Isa. 66:22–24, Vg.]. The other passage is from Daniel: "At that time shall arise Michael, the great prince who stands guard over the children of God's people. And there shall be a time of trouble, such as never has been since the nations began. . . . And at that time all your people shall be delivered, every one whose name shall be found written in the book. And of those who sleep in the dust of the earth, some shall awake to everlasting life, and some to everlasting contempt" [Dan. 12:1–2, Vg., slightly altered].

23. Summary and conclusion: the agreement of the Testaments on eternal life

ᵇThere are two remaining points: that the Old Testament fathers (1) had Christ as pledge of their covenant, and (2) put in him all trust of future blessedness. These I shall not labor to prove because they are less controversial and clearer. Let us, therefore, boldly establish a principle unassailable by any stratagems of the devil: the Old Testament or Covenant that the Lord had made with the Israelites had not been limited to earthly things, but contained a promise of spiritual and eternal life. The expectation of this must have been impressed upon the hearts of all who truly consented to the covenant. But away with this insane and dangerous opinion—that the Lord promised the Jews, or that they sought for themselves, nothing but a full belly, delights of the flesh, flourishing wealth, outward power, fruitfulness of offspring, and whatever the natural man prizes! Christ the Lord promises to his followers today no other "Kingdom of Heaven" than that in which they may "sit at table with Abraham, Isaac, and Jacob" [Matt. 8:11]. Peter declared that the Jews of his day were heirs of the grace of the gospel because they were "the sons of the prophets, included in the covenant which the Lord of old made with his people" [Acts 3:25 p.]. That this might not be attested in words only, the Lord also approved it by deed. At the moment of his resurrection, he deemed many of the saints worthy of sharing in his resurrection and let them be seen in the city of Jerusalem [Matt. 27:52–53]. In this he has given a sure pledge that whatever he did or suffered in acquiring eternal salvation pertains to the believers of the Old Testament as much as to ourselves. Truly, as Peter testifies, they were endowed with the same Spirit of faith whereby we are reborn into life [Acts 15:8]. We hear that that Spirit who is like a spark of immortality in us, and for this reason is called in another place the "guarantee of our inheritance" [Eph. 1:14], dwelt in like manner in them. How, then, dare we deprive them of the inheritance of life? All the more amazing that the Sadducees of old fell into such stupidity as to deny both the resurrection [Matt. 22:23; Acts 23:8] and the existence of souls,[19] after the Scripture had sealed both doctrines with such clear testimonies!

Nor would the obtuseness of the whole Jewish nation today in awaiting the Messiah's earthly kingdom be less monstrous, had the Scriptures not foretold long before that they would receive this punishment for having rejected the gospel. For it so pleased God in righteous judgment to strike blind the minds of those who by refusing the offered light of heaven voluntarily brought darkness upon themselves. Therefore, they read Moses and continually ponder his writings, but they are hampered by a veil from seeing the light shining in his face [II Cor. 3:13–15]. Thus, Moses' face will remain covered and hidden from them until it be turned to Christ, from whom they now strive to separate and withdraw it as much as they can.

^eCHAPTER XI

The Difference Between the Two Testaments

(i. The Old Testament differs from the New in five respects: representation of spiritual blessings by temporal, 1–3)
1. Stress on earthly benefits which, however, were to lead to heavenly concerns*

^bWhat then? You will ask: will no difference remain between the Old and New Testaments? What is to become of the many passages of Scripture wherein they are contrasted as utterly different?

I freely admit the differences in Scripture, to which attention is called, but in such a way as not to detract from its established

19 *"Animarum substantiam."* VG: *"Immortalité des âmes."*

unity. This will become apparent when we have discussed them
in their order. Those chief differences, as far as I can note or
remember, are four in number. If anyone wants to add a fifth
difference, I shall not object at all. I say that all these pertain
to the manner of dispensation rather than to the substance, and
I undertake to show this. In this way there will be nothing to
hinder the promises of the Old and New Testaments from remaining the same, nor from having the same foundation of these
very promises, Christ![1]

Now this is the first difference: the Lord of old willed that
his people direct and elevate their minds to the heavenly heritage;
yet, to nourish them better in this hope, he displayed it for them
to see and, so to speak, taste, under earthly benefits. But now
that the gospel has more plainly and clearly revealed the grace
of the future life, the Lord leads our minds to meditate upon
it directly, laying aside the lower mode of training that he used
with the Israelites.

Those who do not pay attention to this plan of God think
that the ancient people did not transcend those benefits promised
to the body. They hear that the Land of Canaan is very often
characterized as the excellent and even sole reward for the
keepers of God's law. They hear that the Lord threatens the transgressors of his law with nothing harsher than expulsion from
possession of this land, and dispersion into foreign regions [cf.
Lev. 26:33; Deut 28:36]. They see herein almost the sum total
of the blessings and curses uttered by Moses. From such evidence
they unhesitatingly conclude that the Jews were set apart from
all other peoples not for their own benefit but for that of others,
in order that the Christian church might have an outward image
in which it might discern proofs of spiritual things. But Scripture
sometimes shows that God, in conferring all these earthly benefits
on them, determined to lead them by his own hand to the hope
of heavenly things. Hence it was the height of ignorance—nay,
blockishness—not to consider this sort of dispensation.

The point of our quarrel with men of this sort is this: they
teach that the Israelites deemed the possession of the Land of
Canaan their highest and ultimate blessedness, and that after
the revelation of Christ it typified for us the heavenly inheritance.[2] We contend, on the contrary, that, in the earthly posses-

---

[1] Cf. II. x. 1.

[2] Servetus had stated that the promises of the law are fulfilled spiritually to
Christians but that the Jews "obtained the Land of Canaan and were
satisfied with both milk and honey": De justitia regni Christi (1532) I,
fo. D 16; tr. E. M. Wilbur, op. cit., p. 230.

sion they enjoyed, they looked, as in a mirror, upon the future inheritance they believed to have been prepared for them in heaven.

2. *The earthly promises corresponded to the childhood of the church in the Old Covenant; but were not to chain hope to earthly things*

ᵇThis will be more apparent from the comparision that Paul made in the letter to the Galatians. He compares the Jewish nation to a child heir, not yet fit to take care of himself, under the charge of a guardian or tutor to whose care he has been entrusted [Gal. 4:1–2]. Although Paul applies this comparison chiefly to the ceremonies, nothing prevents us from applying it most appropriately here as well. Therefore the same inheritance was appointed for them and for us, but they were not yet old enough[3] to be able to enter upon it and manage it. The same church existed among them, but as yet in its childhood. Therefore, keeping them under this tutelage, the Lord gave, not spiritual promises unadorned and open, but ones foreshadowed, in a measure, by earthly promises. When, therefore, he adopted Abraham, Isaac, Jacob, and their descendants into the hope of immortality, he promised them the Land of Canaan as an inheritance. It was not to be the final goal of their hopes, but was to exercise and confirm them, as they contemplated it, in hope of their true inheritance, an inheritance not yet manifested to them. And that they might not be deceived, a higher promise was given, attesting that the land was not God's supreme benefit. Thus Abraham is not allowed to sit idly by when he receives the promise of the land, but his mind is elevated to the Lord by a greater promise. For he hears: "I am your protector, Abraham; your reward shall be very great" [Gen. 15:1 p.].

Here we see that for Abraham his final reward is put in the Lord alone—so as not to seek a fleeting and elusive reward in the elements of this world [cf. Gal. 4:3], but an imperishable one. Then he adds the promise of the land, solely as a symbol of his benevolence and as a type of the heavenly inheritance. The saints testify in their own words that they have experienced it. David thus mounts up from temporal blessings to that highest and ultimate blessing. "My heart," he says, "and my flesh fail for desire of thee. . . . God is . . . my portion forever." [Ps. 73:26 p.; cf. Ps. 84:2.] Again, "The Lord is the portion of my inheritance and of my cup; thou holdest my inheritance." [Ps. 16:5 p.] Again, "I

---

[3] Cf. I. xi. 3; II. ix. 3.

cried to thee, O Lord; I said, Thou art my hope, my portion in the land of the living." [Ps. 142:5.]

Those who dare speak thus surely profess that in their hope they transcend the world and all present benefits. Yet the prophets more often represent the blessedness of the age to come through the type that they had received from the Lord. In this sense we are to understand these sayings: "The godly will possess the land" by inheritance [Prov. 2:21 p.], but "the wicked will perish from the earth" [Job 18:17 p.; cf. Prov. 2:22; cf. Ecclus. 41:9, Vg.; cf. ch. 41:6, EV]. In many passages of Isaiah we read that Jerusalem will abound with all kinds of riches, and Zion shall overflow with plenty of all things [cf. Isa. 35:10; 52:1 ff.; 60:4 ff.; ch. 62]. We see that all these things cannot properly apply to the land of our pilgrimage, or to the earthly Jerusalem, but to the true homeland of believers, that heavenly city wherein "the Lord has ordained blessing and life forevermore" [Ps. 133:3].

3. Physical benefits and physical punishments as types

ᵇThis is why we read that the saints under the Old Testament esteemed mortal life and its blessings more than we ought today. Even though they well knew they were not to stop there as at the end of their race, yet because they recognized what the Lord had imprinted on them to be marks of divine grace to train them according to the measure of their weakness, they were attracted by its sweetness more than if they had contemplated his grace directly. But as the Lord, in testifying his benevolence toward believers by present good things, then foreshadowed spiritual happiness by such types and symbols, so on the other hand he gave, in physical punishments, proofs of his coming judgment against the wicked. Thus, as God's benefits were more conspicuous in earthly things, so also were his punishments. The ignorant, not considering this analogy and congruity, to call it that, between punishments and rewards, wonder at such great changeableness in God. He, who once was prompt to mete out stern and terrifying punishments for every human transgression, now seems to have laid aside his former wrathful mood and punishes much more gently and rarely. Why, on that account they even go so far as to imagine different Gods for the Old and New Testaments, like the Manichees![4] But we shall readily dispose of these misgivings if we turn our attention to this dispensation of God

---

[4] Servetus, *De justitia regni Christi* III, fo. D 8a–b; tr. Wilbur, *op. cit.,* pp. 240 f. On the Manichaean rejection of the God of the Old Testament, see Augustine, *On the Morals of the Catholic Church* x, 16 (MPL 32. 1317; tr. NPNF IV. 46).

which I have noted. He willed that, for the time during which he gave his covenant to the people of Israel in a veiled form, the grace of future and eternal happiness be signified and figured under earthly benefits, the gravity of spiritual death under physical punishments.

(*ii. Truth in the Old Testament conveyed by images and ceremonies, typifying Christ, 4–6*)

4. *The meaning of this difference*

ᵇThe second difference between the Old and New Testaments consists in figures: that, in the absence of the reality, it showed but an image and shadow in place of the substance; the New Testament reveals the very substance of truth as present. This difference is mentioned almost wherever the New Testament is contrasted with the Old, but a fuller discussion of it is to be found in The Letter to the Hebrews than anywhere else.[5] There the apostle argues against those who thought that the observances of the Mosaic law could not be abolished without ruining the whole religion along with them. In order to refute this error, he assumes what the prophet David foretold concerning Christ's priesthood [Ps. 110:4; Heb. 7:11]. For since Christ was given an eternal priesthood, it is certain that that priesthood, in which day after day one priest succeeded another, was abolished [Heb. 7:23]. He proves that the institution of this new priesthood will prevail because it has been established by an oath [Heb. 7:21]. Afterward he adds that in this transformation of the priesthood the covenant was also changed [Heb. 8:6–13].[6] He declares that this was necessary because the law in its weakness could not lead to perfection [Heb. 7:19]. Then he deals with the nature of this weakness: the law had outward physical acts of righteousness that could not make those who observed them perfect according to conscience. For through animal sacrifices it could neither blot out sins nor bring about true sanctification. He therefore concludes that there was in the law "the shadow of good things to come," not "the living likeness of the things themselves" [Heb. 10:1 p.]. Therefore its sole function was to be an introduction

---

[5] Cf. II. ix. 4; Comm. Heb. 7–10.

[6] *"Testamenti."* In this section and elsewhere Calvin uses the words *testamentum* and *foedus* interchangeably, as they are used in the Vulgate. The Scripture words are בְּרִית and διαθήκη. Both Latin words are here ordinarily translated "covenant" except in Scripture quotations and where *testamentum* evidently refers to one of the parts of Scripture. Cf. II. viii. 21; II. x. 7; III. xiv. 6; III. xvii. 6; III. xxi. 1, 5, 7; IV. xiv. 6. Other Latin terms are *pactio, pactum.*

to the better hope that is manifested in the gospel [Heb. 7:19; and Ps. 110:4; Heb. 7:11; 9:9; 10:1].

Here we are to observe how the covenant of the law compares with the covenant of the gospel, the ministry of Christ with that of Moses. For if the comparison had reference to the substance of the promises, then there would be great disagreement between the Testaments. But since the trend of the argument leads us in another direction, we must follow it to find the truth. Let us then set forth the covenant that he once established as eternal and never-perishing. Its fulfillment, by which it is finally confirmed and ratified, is Christ. While such confirmation was awaited, the Lord appointed, through Moses, ceremonies that were, so to speak, solemn symbols of that confirmation. A controversy arose over whether or not the ceremonies that had been ordained in the law ought to give way to Christ. Now these were only the accidental properties of the covenant, or additions and appendages, and in common parlance, accessories of it. Yet because they were means of administering it, they bear the name "covenant," just as is customary in the case of other sacraments. To sum up, then, in this passage "Old Testament" means the solemn manner of confirming the covenant, comprised in ceremonies and sacrifices.

Because nothing substantial underlies this unless we go beyond it, the apostle contends that it ought to be terminated and abrogated, to give place to Christ, the Sponsor and Mediator of a better covenant [cf. Heb. 7:22]; whereby he imparts eternal sanctifications once and for all to the elect, blotting out their transgressions, which remained under the law. Or, if you prefer, understand it thus: the Old Testament of the Lord was that covenant wrapped up in the shadowy[7] and ineffectual observance of ceremonies and delivered to the Jews; it was temporary because it remained, as it were, in suspense until it might rest upon a firm and substantial confirmation. It became new and eternal only after it was consecrated and established by the blood of Christ. Hence Christ in the Supper calls the cup that he gives to his disciples "the cup of the New Testament in my blood" [Luke 22: 20 p.]. By this he means that the Testament of God attained its truth when sealed by his blood, and thereby becomes new and eternal.

5. Childhood and manhood of the church

[b]Hence it is clear in what sense the apostle said that the Jews were led to Christ by the tutelage of the law before he appeared

[7] *"Umbratili."* Cf. II. vii. 1; II. ix. 3, 4; III. xx. 18, note 29.

in the flesh [Gal. 3:24; cf. ch. 4:1-2]. He also confesses that they were sons and heirs of God, but because of their youth they had to be under the charge of a tutor. It was fitting that, before the sun of righteousness had arisen, there should be no great and shining revelation, no clear understanding. The Lord, therefore, so meted out the light of his Word to them that they still saw it afar off and darkly. Hence Paul expresses this slenderness of understanding by the word "childhood." It was the Lord's will that this childhood be trained in the elements of this world and in little external observances, as rules for children's instruction, until Christ should shine forth, through whom the knowledge of believers was to mature [cf. Eph. 4:13].

Christ himself implied this distinction when he said: "The Law and the Prophets were until John; since then the good news of the Kingdom of God is preached" [Luke 16:16; cf. Matt. 11: 13]. What did the Law and the Prophets teach to the men of their own time? They gave a foretaste of that wisdom which was one day to be clearly disclosed, and pointed to it twinkling afar off. But when Christ could be pointed out with the finger, the Kingdom of God was opened. In him have been revealed "all the treasures of wisdom and understanding" [Col. 2:3], whereby we attain almost to the inmost sanctuary of heaven.

6. Even the great men of faith remained within the limits of the Old Covenant

ᵇThis view is not affected by the fact that almost no one can be found in the Christian church who in excellence of faith is to be compared with Abraham; and that the prophets so excelled in the power of the Spirit as to illumine the whole world through it even today. Here we are not asking what grace the Lord has bestowed upon a few, but what ordinary dispensation he has followed in teaching his people; such as is seen even in the teaching of the prophets themselves, who were endowed with a peculiar insight above the others. For even their preaching is both obscure, like something far off, and is embodied in types. Besides, however remarkable the knowledge in which they excelled, inasmuch as they had, of necessity, to submit to the common tutelage of the people, they also are to be classed as children. Finally, no one then possessed discernment so clear as to be unaffected by the obscurity of the time. For this reason, Christ said: "Many kings and prophets longed to see what you see, and did not see it, and to hear what you hear, and did not hear it" [Luke 10:24, cf. Vg. and Comm.]. Therefore, "Blessed are your eyes, for they see, . . . and your ears, for they hear." [Matt. 13:16, cf. Vg.] And it is surely right that in this privilege the presence of Christ should be pre-eminent so that from it a clearer revelation of the heavenly mysteries might come. eTo this also applies what we quoted before from The First Letter of Peter. that, as revealed to them, their labors were useful chiefly to our age [I Peter 1:12].[8]

(iii. The Old Testament is literal; the New, spiritual, 7–8)
7. Biblical origin and meaning of this difference
bI come to the third difference, taken from Jeremiah. His words are: "Behold, the days will come, says the Lord, when I will make a new covenant with the house of Israel and the house of Judah, not like the agreement which I made with your fathers, in the day when I took them by the hand to lead them out of the land of Egypt, my covenant which they broke, though I ruled over them. . . . But this will be the covenant which I will make with the house of Israel. . . . I will put my law within them, and I will write it upon their hearts . . . and I will forgive their iniquity. And each will not teach his neighbor, each man his brother. For all will know me, from the least to the greatest" [Jer. 31:31–34, Vg., with a slight change in order]. From these words the apostle took occasion to make a comparison between the law and the gospel, calling the former literal, the latter spiritual doctrine; the former he speaks of as carved on tablets of stone, the latter as written upon men's hearts; the former is the preaching of death, the latter of life; the former of condemnation, the latter of righteousness; the former to be made void, the latter to abide [II Cor. 3:6–11]. Since the apostle intended to interpret the prophet's meaning, to understand the purport of both it will be enough to examine the words of one alone. However, there is some difference between them. For the apostle speaks more opprobriously of the law than the prophet does—not simply in respect to the law itself, but, because of certain wretches who aped the law[9] and, by their perverse zeal for ceremonies, obscured the clarity of the gospel. Their error and stupid predilection prompt Paul to discuss the nature of the law. It behooves us therefore to note that particular point in Paul. But both Jeremiah and Paul, because they are contrasting the Old and New Testaments, consider nothing in the law except what properly belongs to it. For example: the law contains here and there promises of mercy, but because they have been borrowed from elsewhere, they are not counted part of the law, when only the

8 Cf. II. ix. 1.
9 "Legis κακόξηλοι."

nature of the law is under discussion. They ascribe to it only this function: to enjoin what is right, to forbid what is wicked; to promise a reward to the keepers of righteousness, and threaten transgressors with punishment; but at the same time not to change or correct the depravity of heart that by nature inheres in all men.

8. The difference in detail, according to II Cor., ch. 3

^bNow let us explain the apostle's comparison, item by item. The Old Testament is of the letter, for it was published without the working of the Spirit. The New is spiritual because the Lord has engraved it spiritually upon men's hearts [II Cor. 3:6a]. The second antithesis is by way of clarification of the first. The Old brings death, for it can but envelop the whole human race in a curse. The New is the instrument of life, for it frees men from the curse and restores them to God's favor [II Cor. 3:6b]. The Old is the ministry of condemnation, for it accuses all the sons of Adam of unrighteousness. The New is the ministry of righteousness because it reveals God's mercy, through which we are justified [II Cor. 3:9].

The final contrast is to be referred to the ceremonial law. For because the Old bore the image of things absent, it had to die and vanish with time. The gospel, because it reveals the very substance, stands fast forever [II Cor. 3:10–11]. Indeed, Jeremiah calls even the moral law a weak and fragile covenant [Jer. 31:32]. But that is for another reason: by the sudden defection of an ungrateful people it was soon broken off. However, because the people were to blame for such a violation, it cannot properly be charged against the covenant. Now the ceremonies, because by their own weakness they were abrogated at Christ's advent, had the cause of their weakness[10] within themselves. We are not to surmise from this difference between letter and spirit that the Lord had fruitlessly bestowed his law upon the Jews, and that none of them turned to him. But it was put forward by way of comparison to commend the grace abounding, wherewith the same Lawgiver—assuming, as it were, a new character—honored the preaching of the gospel. For suppose we reckon the multitude of those whom he gathers into the communion of his church from all peoples, men regenerated by his Spirit through the preaching of the gospel. Then we will say that in ancient Israel there were very few—almost none—who embraced the Lord's covenant with their whole hearts and minds. Yet, reckoned by themselves without comparison, there were many.

[10] For "*infirmitatis*" VG reads: "*de leur abrogation.*"

(iv. Bondage of the Old Testament and freedom of the New, 9–10)

9. Paul's teaching*

ᵇThe fourth difference arises out of the third. Scripture calls the Old Testament one of "bondage" because it produces fear in men's minds; but the New Testament, one of "freedom" because it lifts them to trust and assurance. So Paul states in the eighth chapter of Romans: "You did not receive the spirit of slavery again unto fear, but you have received the spirit of sonship, through which we cry, 'Abba! Father!' " [v. 15 p.]. The passage in Hebrews is also applicable here: that believers "have not come to a physical mountain, a blazing fire, whirlwind, gloom, and tempest," where nothing is heard or seen that does not strike minds with terror, so that when that terrible voice resounded, which they all begged not to hear, even Moses became terrified. "But they have come to Mt. Zion, and to the city of the living God, the heavenly Jerusalem," etc. [Heb. 12:18–22, cf. Vg.]

Paul briefly touches on this in the statement that we quoted from the letter to the Romans but explains it more fully in the letter to the Galatians, where he allegorically interprets Abraham's two sons in this way: Hagar, the bondwoman, is the type of Mt. Sinai where the Israelites received the law; Sarah, the free woman, is the figure of the heavenly Jerusalem whence flows the gospel. Hagar's offspring were born in bondage, never to arrive at the inheritance; Sarah's, free and entitled to it. In like manner, we are subjected to bondage through the law, but are restored to freedom through the gospel alone [Gal. 4:22–31]. To sum up: the Old Testament struck consciences with fear and trembling, but by the benefit of the New they are released into joy. The Old held consciences bound by the yoke of bondage; the New by its spirit of liberality emancipates them into freedom.

But suppose that our opponents object that, among the Israelites, the holy patriarchs were an exception: since they were obviously endowed with the same Spirit of faith as we, it follows that they shared the same freedom and joy. To this we reply: neither of these arose from the law. But when through the law the patriarchs felt themselves both oppressed by their enslaved condition, and wearied by anxiety of conscience, they fled for refuge to the gospel. It was therefore a particular fruit of the New Testament that, apart from the common law of the Old Testament, they were exempted from those evils. Further, we shall deny that they were so endowed with the spirit of freedom and assurance as not in some degree to experience the fear and bondage arising from the law. For, however much they enjoyed the privilege that they had received through the grace of the gospel, they were still subject to the same bonds and burdens of ceremonial observances as the common people. They were compelled to observe those ceremonies punctiliously, symbols of a tutelage resembling bondage [cf. Gal. 4:2–3]; and the written bonds [cf. Col. 2:14],[11] whereby they confessed themselves guilty of sin, did not free them from obligation. Hence, they are rightly said, in contrast to us, to have been under the testament of bondage and fear, when we consider that common dispensation by which the Lord at that time dealt with the Israelites.

10. Law and gospel[†]

[b]The three latter comparisons to which we have referred[12] are of the law and the gospel. In them the law is signified by the name "Old Testament," the gospel by "New Testament." The first[13] extends more widely, for it includes within itself also the promises published before the law. Augustine, however, said that these should not be reckoned under the name "Old Testament." This was very sensible. He meant the same thing as we are teaching: for he was referring to those statements of Jeremiah and Paul wherein the Old Testament is distinguished from the word of grace and mercy. In the same passage he very aptly adds the following: the children of the promise [Rom. 9:8], reborn of God, who have obeyed the commands by faith working through love [Gal. 5:6], have belonged to the New Covenant since the world began. This they did, not in hope of carnal, earthly, and temporal things, but in hope of spiritual, heavenly, and eternal benefits. For they believed especially in the Mediator; and they did not doubt that through him the Spirit was given to them that they might do good, and that they were pardoned whenever they sinned.[14] It is that very point which I intended to affirm: all the saints whom Scripture mentions as being peculiarly chosen of God from the beginning of the world have shared with us the same blessing unto eternal salvation. This, then, is the difference between our analysis and his: ours distinguishes between the clarity of the gospel and the obscurer dispensation of the Word that had preceded it, according to that statement of Christ, "The Law and the Prophets were until John; since then the Kingdom of God is proclaimed" [Luke 16:16, cf. Vg.]; Augustine's division

---

[11] *"Chirographa."* Cf. II. vii. 17, note 25.
[12] In secs. 4, 7, 9, above.
[13] Sec. 1, above.
[14] Augustine, *Against Two Letters of the Pelagians* III. iv. 6–12, esp. 11 (MPL 44. 591–597; tr. NPNF V. 346–351).

simply separates the weakness of the law from the firmness of the gospel.

We must also note this about the holy patriarchs: they so lived under the Old Covenant as not to remain there but ever to aspire to the New, and thus embraced a real share in it. The apostle condemns as blind and accursed those who, content with present shadows, did not stretch their minds to Christ. Not to mention the other matters—what greater blindness could be imagined than to hope for expiation of sin from a slaughtered beast? Or to seek to cleanse the soul by an outward sprinkling with water? Or to try to please God with cold ceremonies, as if he were greatly delighted by them? Those who adhere to the observances of the law without regard to Christ fall into all these absurd practices.

(v. The Old Testament has reference to one nation, the New to all nations, 11–12)

11. The wall is torn down in Christ

ᵇThe fifth difference, which may be added, lies in the fact that until the advent of Christ, the Lord set apart one nation within which to confine the covenant of his grace.[15] "When the Most High gave to the nations their inheritance, when he separated the sons of Adam," says Moses, "his people became his possession; Jacob was the cord of his inheritance." [Deut. 32:8–9 p.] Elsewhere he addresses the people as follows: "Behold, to the Lord your God belong heaven and . . . earth with all that is in it. Yet he cleaved only to your fathers, loved them so that he chose their descendants after them, namely, you out of all peoples" [Deut. 10:14, 15 p., cf. Vg.]. He, therefore, bestowed the knowledge of his name solely upon that people as if they alone of all men belonged to him. He lodged his covenant, so to speak, in their bosom; he manifested the presence of his majesty to them; he showered every privilege upon them. But—to pass over the remaining blessings—let us consider the one in question. In communicating his Word to them, he joined them to himself, that he might be called and esteemed their God. In the meantime, "he allowed all other nations to walk" in vanity [Acts 14:16], as if they had nothing whatsoever to do with him. Nor did he give them the sole remedy for their deadly disease—the preaching of his Word. Israel was then the Lord's darling son; the others were strangers. Israel was recognized and received into confidence and safekeeping; the others were left to their own darkness. Israel was hallowed by God; the others were profaned. Israel was honored with God's presence; the others were excluded from all approach

15 Cf. Melanchthon, Loci communes, 1535 (CR Melanchthon XXI. 454).

to him. "But when the fullness of time came" [Gal. 4:4] which was appointed for the restoration of all things, he was revealed as the reconciler of God and men; "the wall" that for so long had confined God's mercy within the boundaries of Israel "was broken down" [Eph. 2:14]. "Peace was announced to those who were far off, and to those who were near" [Eph. 2:17] that together they might be reconciled to God and welded into one people [Eph. 2:16]. Therefore there is now no difference between Jew and Greek [Gal. 3:28], between circumcision and uncircumcision [Gal. 6:15], but "Christ is all in all" [Col. 3:11, cf. Vg.]. "The nations have been made his inheritance, and the ends of the earth his property" [Ps. 2:8 p.], that "he may have unbroken dominion from sea to sea, and from the rivers even to the ends of the earth" [Ps. 72:8 p.; cf. Zech. 9:10].

12. The calling of the Gentiles

ᵇThe calling of the Gentiles, therefore, is a notable mark of the excellence of the New Testament over the Old.[16] Indeed, this had been attested before by many very clear utterances of the prophets, but in such a way that its fulfillment was postponed until the Kingdom of the Messiah. Even Christ at the beginning of his preaching made no immediate progress toward it. He deferred it until, having completed the work of our redemption and finished the time of his humiliation, he received from the Father "the name which is above every name . . . before which every knee should bow" [Phil. 2:9–10 p.]. For this reason, since the time was not yet ripe, he denied to the woman of Canaan that he had been sent to any but "the lost sheep of the house of Israel" [Matt. 15:24]; and he did not permit the apostles on their first mission to go beyond the boundaries of Israel. He said: "Go nowhere among the Gentiles, and enter no town of the Samaritans, but go rather to the lost sheep of the house of Israel." [Matt. 10:5.] But however many testimonies of Scripture proclaimed the calling of the Gentiles, when the apostles were about to undertake it the call seemed so new and strange to them that they shrank back from it as a monstrous thing. At last they set about it tremblingly and not without misgiving. And no wonder! For it seemed completely unreasonable that the Lord, who for so many ages had singled out Israel from all other nations, should suddenly change his plan and abandon that choice. Prophecies had indeed foretold this. But men could not heed these prophecies without being startled by the newness of the thing that met their eyes. And these evidences of the future calling of the heathen which God had given

16 *"Supra Vetus testamentum Novi excellentia."*

them of old were not sufficient to convince them. Besides the fact that he had called very few, he in a manner engrafted them into Abraham's family, thus adding them to his people. But by this public calling the Gentiles not only were made equal to the Jews, but it also was manifest that they were, so to speak, taking the place of dead Jews. ᵉBesides this, all those strangers whom God had previously received into the body of the church had never been made equal to the Jews. Paul with good reason, therefore, proclaims this a great "mystery hidden for ages and generations" [Col. 1:26; cf. Eph. 3:9], and says that it is wonderful even to the angels [cf. I Peter 1:12].

(Reply to objections regarding God's justice and consistency in these differences of administration, 13–14)
13. Why, in general, the differences?
ᶜIn these four or five points I think that I have explained faithfully and well the whole difference between the Old and the New Testament, as far as a simple statement of doctrine demands. But because some persons hold up to ridicule this variableness in governing the church, this diverse manner of teaching, these great changes of rites and ceremonies,[17] we must also answer them before we pass on to other matters. But this can be done briefly because their objections are not so firm as to require painstaking refutation. It is not fitting, they say, that God, always self-consistent, should permit such a great change, disapproving afterward what he had once commanded and commended. I reply that God ought not to be considered changeable merely because he accommodated diverse forms to different ages, as he knew would be expedient for each. If a farmer sets certain tasks for his household in the winter, other tasks for the summer, we shall not on this account accuse him of inconstancy, or think that he departs from the proper rule of agriculture, which accords with the continuous order of nature. In like manner, if a householder instructs, rules, and guides, his children one way in infancy, another way in youth, and still another in young manhood, we shall not on this account call him fickle and say that he abandons his purpose. Why, then, do we brand God with the mark of inconstancy because he has with apt and fitting marks distinguished a diversity of times? The latter comparison ought to satisfy us fully. Paul likens the Jews to children, Christians to young men

[17] Barth and Niesel point to what appears to be a reply to such statements as this in Sebastian Franck's *Paradoxa* (1535), Paradox 86 (fo. xlviib ff.), and suggest that since Franck says he had "often heard" these opinions, he drew them from Anabaptist acquaintances. (OS III. 435, note 2.)

[Gal. 4:1 ff.]. What was irregular about the fact that God confined them to rudimentary teaching commensurate with their age, but has trained us through a firmer and, so to speak, more manly discipline? Thus, God's constancy shines forth in the fact that he taught the same doctrine to all ages, and has continued to require the same worship of his name that he enjoined from the beginning. In the fact that he has changed the outward form and manner, he does not show himself subject to change. Rather, he has accommodated himself to men's capacity, which is varied and changeable.

14. God's freedom to deal with all men as he wills*

ᶜBut they reply, Whence does this diversity arise unless God willed it to be so? Could not God just as well have revealed eternal life in clear words, without any figures, at the beginning as after Christ's advent? Could he not at the outset have instructed his people by a few clear sacraments, bestowed the Holy Spirit, and diffused his grace throughout the earth? This is as if they were to quarrel with God because he created the world so late, when he could have done it from the first; or because he willed to alternate winter and summer, day and night. But let us not doubt that God has done everything wisely and justly—as all godly persons ought to believe—even if we often do not know the reason why it should have been so done. It would be claiming too much for ourselves not to concede to God that he may have reasons for his plan that are hidden from us.

But it is remarkable, they say, that he now despises and abominates animal sacrifices and all the trappings of the Levitical priesthood that of old delighted him. As if these external, fleeting things could delight God or affect him in any way! It has already been said,[18] that God did none of these things for his own sake, but arranged them all for the salvation of men. If a physician cures a young man of disease in the best way, but uses another sort of remedy on the same person when he is old, shall we then say that he has rejected the method of cure that had pleased him before? No—while he perseveres in it, he takes into account the factor of age. Thus it was necessary with one kind of sign to represent Christ absent and to proclaim him about to come; but it is fitting that, now revealed, he be represented with another. Since the advent of Christ, God's call has gone forth more widely through all peoples, and the graces of the Spirit have been more abundantly poured out than before. Who then, I pray, will say it is not meet that God should have in his own hand and will

18 Secs. 5 and 13, above.

the free disposing of his graces, and should illuminate such nations as he wills? To evoke the preaching of his Word at such places as he wills? To give progress and success to his doctrine in such way and measure as he wills? To deprive the world, because of its ungratefulness, of the knowledge of his name for such ages as he wills, and according to his mercy to restore it when he again wills? We see these, then, as too disgraceful slanders, used by impious men to trouble the simple-minded and to make them doubt either the righteousness of God or the trustworthiness of Scripture.

ᶜCHAPTER XII

CHRIST HAD TO BECOME MAN IN ORDER TO FULFILL THE OFFICE OF MEDIATOR

(Reasons why it was necessary that the Mediator should be God and should become man, 1–3)
1. Only he who was true God and true man could bridge the gulf between God and ourselves
ᵇ⁽ᵃ⁾Now it was of the greatest importance for us that he who was to be our Mediator be both true God and true man. ᶜIf someone asks why this is necessary, there has been no simple (to use the common expression) or absolute necessity. Rather, it has stemmed from a heavenly decree, on which men's salvation depended. Our most merciful Father decreed what was best for us. ᵇ⁽ᵃ⁾Since our iniquities, like a cloud cast between us and him, had completely estranged us from the Kingdom of Heaven [cf. Isa. 59:2], no man, unless he belonged to God, could serve as the intermediary to restore peace. But who might reach to him? Any one of Adam's children? ᵃNo, like their father, all of them were terrified at the sight of God [Gen. 3:8]. One of the angels? They also had need of a head,[1] through whose bond they might cleave firmly and undividedly to their God [cf. Eph. 1:22; Col. 2:10]. What then? The situation would surely have been hopeless had the very majesty of God not descended to us, since it was not in our power to ascend to him. Hence, it was necessary for the Son of God to become for us "Immanuel, that is, God with us" [Isa. 7:14; Matt. 1:23], ᵉ⁽ᵇ/ᵃ⁾and in such a way that his divinity and our human nature might by mutual connection grow together. ᵇ⁽ᵃ⁾Otherwise the nearness would not have been near enough, nor

---

[1] For Calvin's thought of Christ as Head over the angels as well as over man, see his *Responsum ad fratres Polonos* (1560), CR IX. 338: *"Primatum tenuit etiam super angelos."* Cf. Comm. Col. 1:20.

the affinity sufficiently firm, for us to hope that God might dwell with us. ᵉ⁽ᵃ⁾So great was the disagreement between our uncleanness and God's perfect purity! ᵉEven if man had remained free from all stain, his condition would have been too lowly for him to reach God without a Mediator. What, then, of man: plunged by his mortal ruin into death and hell, defiled with so many spots, befouled with his own corruption, and overwhelmed with every curse? ᵉ⁽ᵃ⁾In undertaking to describe the Mediator, Paul then, with good reason, distinctly reminds us that He is man: ᵃ"One mediator between God and men, the man Jesus Christ" [I Tim. 2:5]. He could have said "God"; or he could at least have omitted the word "man" just as he did the word "God." But because the Spirit speaking through his mouth knew our weakness, ᵉat the right moment he used a most appropriate remedy to meet it: he set the Son of God familiarly among us as one of ourselves. ᵃTherefore, lest anyone be troubled about where to seek the Mediator, or by what path we must come to him, ᵉ⁽ᵃ⁾the Spirit calls him "man," thus teaching us that he is near us, indeed touches us, since he is our flesh. Here he surely means the same thing ᵃthat is explained elsewhere at greater length: "We have not a high priest who is unable to sympathize with our weaknesses, but one who in every respect has been tempted as we are, yet without sinning" [Heb. 4:15].²

2. The Mediator must be true God and true man

ᵇ⁽ᵃ⁾This will become even clearer if we call to mind that what the Mediator was to accomplish was no common thing. His task was so to restore us to God's grace ᵃas to make of the children of men, children of God; of the heirs of Gehenna, heirs of the Heavenly Kingdom. Who could have done this had not the selfsame Son of God become the Son of man, and had not so taken what was ours as to impart what was his to us, and to make what was his by nature ours by grace? Therefore, relying on this pledge, we trust that we are sons of God, for God's natural Son fashioned for himself a body from our body, flesh from our flesh, bones from our bones, that he might be one with us [Gen. 2:23–24, mediated through Eph. 5:29–31]. Ungrudgingly he took our nature upon himself to impart to us what was his, and to become both Son of God and Son of man in common with us. ᵉHence that holy brotherhood which he commends with his own lips when he says: "I am ascending to my Father and your Father, to my God and your God" [John 20:17]. ᵉ⁽ᵇ/ᵃ⁾In this way we are assured of the inheritance of the Heavenly Kingdom; for the only

² Cf. Comm. Heb. 4:15.

Son of God, to whom it wholly belongs, [a]has adopted us as his brothers. "For if brothers, then also fellow heirs with him." [Rom. 8:17 p.]

For the same reason it was also imperative that he who was to become our Redeemer be true God and true man. It was his task to swallow up death. Who but the Life could do this? It was his task to conquer sin. Who but very Righteousness could do this? [b]It was his task to rout the powers of world and air. Who but a power higher than world and air could do this? [b(a)]Now where does life or righteousness, or lordship and authority of heaven lie but with God alone? [a]Therefore our most merciful God, when he willed that we be redeemed, made himself our Redeemer in the person of his only begotten Son [cf. Rom. 5:8].

3. Only he who was true God and true man could be obedient in our stead

[a]The second requirement of our reconciliation with God was this: that man, who by his disobedience had become lost, should by way of remedy counter it with obedience, satisfy God's judgment, and pay the penalties for sin. Accordingly, our Lord came forth as true man and took the person and the name of Adam in order to take Adam's place in obeying the Father, to present our flesh as the price of satisfaction to God's righteous judgment, and, in the same flesh, to pay the penalty that we had deserved. [b]In short, since neither as God alone could he feel death, nor as man alone could he overcome it, he coupled human nature with divine that to atone for sin he might submit the weakness of the one to death; and that, wrestling with death by the power of the other nature, he might win victory for us. [a]Those who despoil Christ of either his divinity or his humanity diminish his majesty and glory, or obscure his goodness. On the other hand, they do just as much wrong to men whose faith they thus weaken and overthrow, because it cannot stand unless it rests upon this foundation.

[e]Besides, the hoped-for Redeemer was to be that son of Abraham and David whom God had promised in the Law and the Prophets. From this, godly minds derive another benefit: on the basis of his descent from David and Abraham they are more certain that he is the Anointed One who had been hailed by so many oracles. But we should especially espouse what I have just explained: our common nature with Christ is the pledge of our fellowship with the Son of God; and clothed with our flesh he vanquished death and sin together that the victory and triumph might be ours. He offered as a sacrifice the flesh he received

from us, that he might wipe out our guilt by his act of expiation and appease the Father's righteous wrath.

(Objections to this doctrine answered, 4–7)
4. The sole purpose of Christ's incarnation was our redemption
ᵉHe who ponders these matters with the diligent attention they require will readily have done with the vague speculations that captivate the frivolous and the seekers after novelty. One such speculation is that Christ would still have become man[3] even if no means of redeeming mankind had been needed. Of course I admit that in the original order of creation and the unfallen state of nature Christ was set over angels and men as their Head. Paul for this reason calls him "the first-born of all creation" [Col. 1:15]. But since all Scripture proclaims that to become our Redeemer he was clothed with flesh, it is too presumptuous to imagine another reason or another end. We well know why Christ was promised from the beginning: to restore the fallen world and to succor lost men. Therefore, under the law, Christ's image was set forth in sacrifices to give believers the hope that God would be gracious toward them, after having been reconciled to them through atonement made for their sins. Surely, since in every age, even when the law had not yet been published, the Mediator never was promised without blood, we infer that he was appointed by God's eternal plan to purge the uncleanness of men; for shedding of blood is a sign of expiation [cf. Heb. 9:22]. Thus, the prophets in preaching about him promised that he would be the reconciler of God and man. Of all the testimonies to this, Isaiah's famous one will be enough: "He was to be smitten by God's hand . . . for the transgressions of the people, . . . that the chastisement of peace should be upon him" [Isa. 53:4–5], and he would be the high priest who would offer himself as a victim [Heb. 9:11–12]; "from his stripes there would be healing for others"; because "all . . . have gone astray" and been scattered "like sheep," it pleased God to afflict him that he might bear "the iniquities of all" [Isa. 53:5–6 p.]. Since we learn that Christ himself was divinely appointed to help miserable sinners, whoever leaps over these bounds too much indulges foolish curiosity.

When he himself appeared, he declared that the reason for his advent was by appeasing God to gather us from death unto life. The apostles testified to the same thing concerning him. So John, before he teaches that "the Word was made flesh [John 1:14],

---

[3] This is affirmed by Osiander in his treatise *An filius Dei fuerit incarnandus* (1550), K 2a, 2b, and by Servetus, *Christianismi restitutio: De regeneratione superna* I, pp. 370, 382. Calvin reverts to this point in secs. 5 and 6.

tells of man's rebellion [John 1:9–11]. But we ought especially to heed what Christ himself declares concerning his office: "God so loved the world that he gave his only-begotten Son, that whoever believes in him may not perish but have eternal life" [John 3:16]. Also, "The hour has come that the dead may hear the voice of the Son of God, and that those who hear may live." [John 5:25 p.] "I am the resurrection and the life; he who believes in me, though he has died, yet shall he live." [John 11:25.] Again, "For the Son of Man came to save what has been lost." [Matt. 18:11.] Again, "Those who are well have no need of a physician." [Matt. 9:12 p.] There would be no end of passages if we wished to refer to all of them!

The apostles with one consent call us back to this fountain. Surely, if he had not come to reconcile God and man, the honor of his priesthood would have fallen away, since a priest is appointed as an intermediary to intercede between God and men [Heb. 5:1]; he would not be our righteousness, for he became a sacrifice for us that "God might not count our trespasses against us" [II Cor. 5:19 p.]. Finally, he will be deprived of all titles that Scripture bestows upon him. Paul's statement, too, will fall: "To make satisfaction in our behalf, God has sent his own Son in the likeness of sinful flesh—something the law could not do" [Rom. 8:3–4 p., with omissions]. And what Paul teaches in another place will not stand: in this mirror "the goodness of God" and his boundless love "appeared to . . . men" when Christ was given as our Redeemer [cf. Titus 2:11]. In short, the only reason given in Scripture that the Son of God willed to take our flesh, and accepted this commandment from the Father, is that he would be a sacrifice to appease the Father on our behalf. "Thus it is written, that the Christ should suffer . . . and that repentance . . . should be preached in his name." [Luke 24:46–47.] "For this reason the Father loves me, because I lay down my life for my sheep. . . . This commandment he gave me." [John 10:17, 15, 18 p.] "As Moses lifted up the serpent in the wilderness, so must the Son of Man be lifted up." [John 3:14.] Another passage: " 'Father, save me from this hour.' . . . But for this purpose I have come to this hour. Father, glorify thy Son" [John 12:27–28, conflated with v. 23]. Here he clearly indicates why he assumed flesh: that he might become a sacrifice and expiation to abolish our sins. In the same way Zechariah declares that He came in accordance with the promise made to the patriarchs "to give light to those who sit in . . . the shadow of death" [Luke 1:79]. We remember that all these things have been said of the Son of God, "in whom"—as Paul elsewhere testifies—"are hid all the treasures

of knowledge and wisdom" [Col. 2:3], and apart from whom
Paul glories that he himself knows nothing [I Cor. 2:2].

5. Would Christ have also become man if Adam had not sinned?

ᶜSuppose someone objects that none of these things prevents
Christ—who has redeemed condemned men—from being able
also to show his love toward those who are saved and safe, by
taking on their flesh.[4] My answer is brief: Since the Spirit declares that these two were joined together by God's eternal decree,
it is not lawful to inquire further how Christ became our Redeemer and the partaker of our nature. For he who is tickled
with desire to know something more, not content with God's unchangeable ordinance, also shows that he is not even content
with this very Christ who was given to us as the price of our
redemption. Paul, indeed, not only recounts for what purpose he
was sent, but soars to the lofty mystery of predestination and
fitly restrains all the wantonness and itching curiosity of human
nature. "The Father has chosen us in Christ before the foundation
of the world" [Eph. 1:4] to adopt us as sons "according to the
purpose of his will" [Eph. 1:5, cf. Vg.]; . . . and "he has made
us accepted in his beloved Son" [Eph. 1:6, cf. KJV], "in whom
we have redemption through his blood" [Eph. 1:7, Vg.]. Here,
surely, the fall of Adam is not presupposed as preceding God's
decree in time; but it is what God determined before all ages
that is shown, when he willed to heal the misery of mankind.[5]
Suppose our adversary again objects that this plan of God depended on the ruin of man, which he foresaw. It is quite enough
for me to say that all those who propose to inquire or seek to
know more about Christ than God ordained by his secret decree
are breaking out in impious boldness to fashion some new sort of
Christ. And Paul, having so discussed the true office of Christ,
justly prays that the Ephesians be given the spirit of understanding [Eph. 3:14–17], "to comprehend . . . what is the length and
height, the breadth and depth . . . ," that is, "the love of Christ
which surpasses all knowledge" [Eph. 3:18–19 p.]. It is as if he
were purposely setting bars about our minds so that whenever
Christ is mentioned we should not in the least depart from the
grace of reconciliation. According to Paul's testimony, therefore,

---

[4] Referring to Osiander's statement, *op. cit., loc. cit.*

[5] This passage briefly shows Calvin as favoring the supralapsarian as opposed to the infralapsarian view of the decrees of God. The issue became
controversial in the Netherlands shortly after Calvin's death. Cf. McNeill,
The History and Character of Calvinism, pp. 263 f. For typical source citations on the *ordo salutis* in Reformed theology, see Heppe RD, pp.
146 ff.

since "the saying is sure, . . . that Christ . . . came . . . to save sinners" [I Tim. 1:15], I willingly agree to this. And since the same apostle elsewhere teaches that the grace that has now been revealed in the gospel was given to us "in Christ . . . before time began" [II Tim. 1:9], I resolve to abide constantly in it to the very end.

Osiander unjustly raises an outcry against this modesty. He has unhappily stirred up anew in our time this question, lightly touched on earlier by a few persons.[6] He accuses of presumption those who deny that the Son of God would have appeared in the flesh if Adam had not fallen, because no testimony of Scripture refutes this fabrication. As if Paul does not bridle perverse curiosity when, after speaking of the redemption acquired through Christ, he presently enjoins us to "avoid stupid questions" [Titus 3:9]! The madness of certain persons can riot to such an extent that, while they sought in their absurd way to appear witty, they raised the question whether the Son of God could have taken upon himself the nature of an ass.[7] Let Osiander excuse this monstrous thing—which all godly men justly abominate as detestable—with the pretext that it is nowhere specifically refuted in Scripture. As if Paul, by considering nothing precious or worth knowing "except . . . Christ . . . crucified" [I Cor. 2:2], admitted that an ass is the Author of salvation! Therefore he who elsewhere preaches that by his Father's eternal plan Christ was appointed Head to gather all things together [Eph. 1:10, cf. v. 22] will never recognize another who has not been entrusted with the task of redemption.

6. Osiander's doctrine of the image of God

ᵉBut the principle of which Osiander boasts is completely trifling. He asserts that man was created in God's image because he was fashioned according to the pattern of the Messiah to come, that man might conform to him whom the Father had already determined to clothe with flesh. From this, Osiander infers that if Adam had never fallen from his original and upright condition, Christ would still have become man. All men endowed with sound judgment understand of themselves how trivial and distorted this is. Meanwhile, Osiander thinks that he has been the

---

[6] Osiander (op. cit., fo. A 4a–B 1a) cites Alexander of Hales, Duns Scotus, and especially John Pico della Mirandola as patrons of his opinion. Cf. OS III. 443, note 2, where passages from these authors are cited.

[7] William of Ockham (d. ca. 1349), Centilogium theologicum (Lyons, 1495) (a work appended to Ockham's commentary on Lombard's Sentences), concl. 7. A.

first to see what the image of God was: that God's glory shone not only in the exceptional gifts with which Adam had been adorned, but that God dwelt essentially in him.

I admit that Adam bore God's image, in so far as he was joined to God (which is the true and highest perfection of dignity). Nevertheless, I maintain that this likeness ought to be sought only in those marks of excellence with which God had distinguished Adam over all other living creatures. All men unanimously admit that Christ was even then the image of God. Hence, whatever excellence was engraved upon Adam, derived from the fact that he approached the glory of his Creator through the only-begotten Son. "So man was created in the image of God" [Gen. 1:27 p.]; in him the Creator himself willed that his own glory be seen as in a mirror. Adam was advanced to this degree of honor, thanks to the only-begotten Son. But I add: the Son himself was the common Head over angels and men. Thus the dignity that had been conferred upon man belonged also to the angels. When we hear the angels called "children of God" [Ps. 82:6] it would be inappropriate to deny that they were endowed with some quality resembling their Father. But if he willed that his glory be represented both in angels and in men and manifested in both natures, Osiander is ignorantly babbling when he says that angels were set beneath men because they did not bear the figure of Christ. For they could not continually enjoy the direct vision of God unless they were like him. And Paul similarly teaches that "men are renewed . . . after the image of God" [Col. 3:10 p.] only if they consort with the angels so as to cleave together under one head. To sum up: if we believe in Christ, we shall take on the form of angels [Matt. 22:30] when we are received into heaven, and this will be our final happiness. But if Osiander is allowed to infer that the first pattern of God's image was in the man Christ,[8] with the same justification anyone can contend that Christ had to partake of the angelic nature because the image of God belongs to them also.

7. Point-by-point refutation of Osiander

ᵉThere is consequently no reason for Osiander to fear that unless there was in His mind a fixed and immutable decree concerning the incarnation of the Son, God can be made out a liar. For if Adam's uprightness had not failed, he along with the angels would have been like God; and it would not have been necessary for the Son of God to become either man or angel. Groundless

---

[8] Osiander, *op. cit.* The passages referred to in secs. 6 and 7 are scattered through folios C 3a to I 3a of this work.

also, and absurd, was his fear that unless, according to God's immutable plan before the creation of man, Christ was to be born not as Redeemer but as the First Man, he would have fallen from his privileged place; since he would then not have been born but for the historical contingency that he was to restore the lost human race, implying from this that he was created in the image of Adam. For why will Osiander shudder at what Scripture teaches so clearly, that Christ was made like us in all respects except sin [Heb. 4:15]? For this reason, Luke also does not hesitate to reckon him as a descendant of Adam [Luke 3:38]. I should also like to know why Paul calls Christ the "Second Adam" [I Cor. 15:47], unless the human condition was ordained for him in order that he might lift Adam's descendants out of ruin. For if Christ came before creation, then he ought to be called the "first Adam." Osiander blithely declares that because Christ as man had been foreknown in the mind of God, he was the pattern to which men were formed. But Paul, calling Christ the "Second Adam," sets the Fall, from which arose the necessity of restoring nature to its former condition, between man's first origin and the restoration that we obtain through Christ. It follows, then, that it was for this same cause that the Son of God was born to become man. Meanwhile, Osiander reasons badly and inappropriately that so long as Adam remained upright he would have been the image of himself, not of Christ. I answer, on the contrary, that even if the Son of God had never taken human flesh, the image of God would nonetheless have shone in his body and soul. For in the radiance of this image, it is always manifest that Christ is truly the Head and holds the primacy in all things. Thus we dispose of this futile subtlety, which Osiander spreads abroad, that the angels would have lacked this Head if God had not determined to clothe his Son with flesh, even apart from Adam's guilt.

Now Osiander too rashly snatches at something no sane person would admit. He asserts that except in so far as he is man Christ possesses no primacy over the angels whereby they may enjoy him as their leader. On the contrary, true inferences come readily from Paul's words. First, in so far as he is God's eternal Word he is "the first-born of all creation" [Col. 1:15]. This is not because he was created or ought to be numbered among the creatures, but because the world, in its unimpaired state—adorned as it was at the beginning with the highest beauty—had no other origin but him. Secondly, in so far as he was made man, he was "the first-born from the dead" [Col. 1:18]. The apostle in one short passage sets forth two things to be considered: (1) "through the Son all things have been created," that he may rule over the angels [Col. 1:16 p.]; (2) he was made man that he might begin to be our Redeemer [cf. Col. 1:14].

Osiander shows the same ignorance in saying that if Christ had not been man, men would have been without him as their king. As if the Kingdom of God could not stand had the eternal Son of God—though not endued with human flesh—gathered together angels and men into the fellowship of his heavenly glory and life, and himself held the primacy over all! But Osiander is always deceived—or tricks himself—in the false principle that the church would have been without a head[9] if Christ had not appeared in the flesh. As the angels enjoyed his Headship, why could Christ not rule over men also by his divine power, quicken and nourish them like his own body by the secret power of his Spirit until, gathered up into heaven, they might enjoy the same life as the angels!

Osiander considers these trivialities, which I have by now refuted, to be the firmest of oracles! Drunk with the sweetness of his own speculations, he is wont to intone his absurd paeans over nothing! He brings forth afterward what he calls a far firmer proof: the "prophecy of Adam," who when he saw his wife said, "This now is bone of my bones, and flesh of my flesh" [Gen. 2:23 p.]. But how does Osiander prove this a prophecy? Because, in Matthew, Christ attributes the same word to God. As if everything God spoke through men contained some prophecy! Let Osiander seek prophecies in the several precepts of the law that clearly have come from God as their Author! Besides, Christ would have been crude and earthly if he had confined himself to the literal sense [Matt. 19:4–6]. Here he is not discussing the mystical union with which he graced the church, but only fidelity in marriage. For this reason he teaches that God declared man and wife to be one flesh in order that no one should try to break by divorce that insoluble bond. If Osiander dislikes this simplicity, let him blame Christ for not leading his disciples into a mystery by more subtly interpreting his Father's words. Nor does Paul support Osiander's delusion. When Paul has said that we are flesh of the flesh of Christ [Eph. 5:30–31], he adds at once: "This is a mystery" [Eph. 5:32]. For Paul did not mean to tell in what sense Adam uttered the words, but to set forth under the figure and likeness of marriage the holy union that makes us one with Christ. Even the words themselves express this! For when he informs us that he is speaking of Christ and the church, by way of correction he distinguishes between the rule of marriage and

[9] "ἀκέφαλον."

the spiritual union of Christ and the church. Thus this silly contention readily vanishes. And I believe it unnecessary to deal further with such rubbish as this. For this very short refutation will expose the emptiness of it all. This sober truth is more than enough to nourish perfectly the children of God: "When the fullness of time came, God sent forth his Son, born of woman, born under the law, to redeem those who were under the law" [Gal. 4:4-5].

ᶜCHAPTER XIII

CHRIST ASSUMED THE TRUE SUBSTANCE OF HUMAN FLESH

(Referring to ancient heresies, Calvin answers Menno Simons, 1-2)

1. Proof of Christ's true manhood

ᵉ⁽ᵇ⁾The divinity of Christ has been proved elsewhere by clear and firm testimonies.[1] Hence, unless I am mistaken, it would be superfluous to discuss it again here. ᵉIt remains, then, for us to see how, clothed with our flesh, he fulfilled the office of Mediator. ᵇIndeed, the genuineness of his human nature was impugned long ago by both the Manichees and the Marcionites.[2] The Marcionites

---

[1] I. xiii. 7-13.

[2] For the Manichees, see I. xiii. 1, note 3. Marcion of Pontus taught in Rome about A.D. 150. His significance lies in his rejection of the Old Testament and in his Gnostic dualism, which expressed itself in the denial of the materiality of Christ's body and in extreme asceticism. Calvin has in mind contemporary "Marcionites," including Menno Simons (1496–1561), who refounded the Netherlands Anabaptists after the Münster incident. Calvin knew Menno's opinions, which were published only in Dutch or in the Oostersch dialect of North Germany, chiefly through Martin Micron of Norden, East Frisia. Micron several times disputed with Menno (1554, 1556) and exchanged pamphlets with him (1556, 1558), chiefly on the incarnation (*Complete Works of Menno Simons,* translated from the Dutch by L. Verduin and edited by J. C. Wenger, with a biography by Harold Bender, p. 25). An earlier tract by John à Lasco against Menno, *Defensio verae . . . doctrinae de Christi incarnatione,* was sent to Calvin by Albert Hardenberg of Bremen, 1545. This was an answer to Menno's *Brief and Clear Confession* (1544) (tr. Verduin, *op. cit.,* pp. 419–454). See also Menno's *The Incarnation of Our Lord* (1554) (tr. Verduin, *op. cit.,* pp. 783–943); *Reply to Martin Micron* (1556); *Epistle to Martin Micron* (1556). In the first mentioned of these pamphlets Menno devotes considerable space to the interpretation of the passages cited below from Heb., ch. 2 (English translation, pp. 823–832). His argument is somewhat difficult to summarize. Against John à Lasco he asserts "that there is not a letter to be found in all the Scriptures that the Word assumed our flesh . . . ; or that the divine nature miraculously united itself with our human nature" (p. 829). (The Mennonites after him have not held this

fancied Christ's body a mere appearance, while the Manichees dreamed that he was endowed with heavenly flesh. But many strong testimonies of Scripture stand against both. For the blessing is promised neither in heavenly seed nor in a phantom of a man, but in the seed of Abraham and Jacob [Gen. 12:3; 17:2, 7; 18:18; 22:18; 26:4]. Nor is an eternal throne promised to a man of air, but to the Son of David and the fruit of his loins [Ps. 45:6; 132:11]. Hence, when he was manifested in the flesh, he was called "the Son of David and of Abraham" [Matt. 1:1]. This is not only because he was born of the virgin's womb, although created in the air, but because, according to Paul's interpretation, he "was made of the seed of David according to the flesh" [Rom. 1:3 p.]. e(b)Similarly, the same apostle in another passage teaches that he descended from the Jews [Rom. 9:5]. bFor this reason the Lord himself, not content with the name "man," frequently calls himself also "Son of man," meaning thereby to explain more clearly that he is a man truly begotten of human seed. Since the Holy Spirit has often declared this plain fact by many instruments and with very great diligence and simplicity, who would have supposed that any would be so shameless as to dare besmirch it with deceptions? Yet we have other testimonies ready at hand, if we should want to amass more of them. One of these is Paul's statement: "God sent forth his Son, born of woman" [Gal. 4:4]. And there are innumerable other evidences that show him to have been subject to hunger, thirst, cold, and other infirmities of our nature. From these numerous testimonies we must choose those particular ones which serve to edify our minds in true confidence. Such are these: when it is said that he did not so concern himself with angels [Heb. 2:16] as to take their nature, but took ours, that "in flesh and blood . . . he might through death destroy him who had the power of death" [Heb. 2:14 p.]. Another: we are reckoned his brethren by the benefit of association with him [cf. Heb. 2:11]. Again: "He had to be made like his brethren . . . so that he might be a merciful and faithful intercessor." [Heb. 2:17 p.] "We have not a high priest who is unable to sympathize with our infirmities." [Heb. 4:15a.] And like passages. eWhat we touched on a little while ago pertains to this same point:[3] the sins of the world had to be expiated in our flesh, as Paul clearly declares [Rom. 8:3]. Surely, for this reason, whatever the Father bestowed upon Christ pertains to us because he is the Head "from

doctrine.) Augustine severely condemned the ancient Docetism that made Christ's flesh a phantom: *Sermons* lxxv. 7–9 (MPL 38. 477; tr. NPNF VI. 338 f.).
[3] II. xii. 3.

whom the whole body, knit together through joints," grows into one [Eph. 4:16]. Yes, otherwise this statement will not fit. "The Spirit was given to him [Christ] without measure" [John 3:34 p.] so that "we should all receive from his fullness" [John 1:16 p.]. Nothing is more absurd than that God should be enriched in his essence by some accidental gift! For this reason, also, Christ himself says in another place, "For their sake I sanctify myself" [John 17:19].

2. *Against the opponents of Christ's true manhood*

^bThey grossly distort the passages that they put forward to confirm their error. ^eAnd they accomplish nothing with the trifling subtleties by which they try to do away with what I have already adduced. ^bMarcion imagines that Christ put on a phantasm instead of a body because Paul elsewhere says that Christ was "made in the likeness of man, . . . being found in fashion as a man" [Phil. 2:7–8, KJV/RV]. But he wholly overlooks Paul's intention there: Paul does not mean to teach what sort of body Christ assumes. Rather, although Christ could justly have shown forth his divinity, he manifested himself as but a lowly and despised man. ^cFor, to exhort us to submission by his example, he showed that although he was God and could have set forth his glory directly to the world he gave up his right and voluntarily "emptied himself." ^{e(c)}He took the image of a servant, and content with such lowness, allowed his divinity to be hidden by a "veil of flesh" [cf. Phil. 2:5–7]. ^cHere Paul is really teaching not what Christ was, but how he conducted himself. ^eFrom the whole context we may easily infer that Christ emptied himself in a nature truly human. For what does "being found in fashion as a man" mean [Phil. 2:8], save that for a time the divine glory did not shine, but only human likeness was manifest in a lowly and abased condition. Peter's statement that "Christ was put to death in the flesh, but made alive in the spirit" [I Peter 3:18 p.] would not otherwise make sense unless the Son of God in human nature had been weak. Paul explains this more clearly, declaring that Christ suffered according to the infirmity of the flesh [II Cor. 13:4]. Christ is expressly said to have obtained new glory after he had humbled himself. Herein lies his exaltation. This could not very well apply except to a man endowed with human body and soul.

^bMani forged him a body of air, because Christ is called "the Second Adam of heaven, heavenly" [I Cor. 15:47]. But in this passage the apostle is introducing no heavenly essence of Christ's body, but a spiritual force that, poured out by Christ, quickens

us. ᵉNow, as we have seen, Peter and Paul separate that force from Christ's flesh. ᵇRather, the doctrine concerning Christ's flesh that flourishes among the orthodox is remarkably buttressed by this passage. For unless Christ had one bodily nature with us, the reasoning that Paul pursues with such vehemence would be meaningless: "If Christ arose, we also shall arise from the dead; if we do not arise, neither did Christ arise" [I Cor. 15:12–20 p., substance]. ᵉWhatever the subtleties with which the ancient Manichees or their modern disciples try to evade [this proof], they do not succeed.

Their nonsense, that Christ is called "Son of Man" in so far as he was promised to men,[4] is a base evasion. For it is plain that in Hebrew idiom true man is called "son of man." Now, Christ undoubtedly retained this phrase of his own language. Also, the commonly accepted understanding of "Son of Adam" ought to be beyond controversy. Not to go too far afield, the Eighth Psalm, which the apostles apply to Christ, will amply suffice: "What is man that thou art mindful of him, and the son of man that thou visitest him?" [Ps. 8:4; Heb. 2:6]. Christ's true humanity is expressed by this figure. For even though he was not immediately begotten of a mortal father, his origin derived from Adam. Otherwise the passage that I have already cited would not stand: "Christ shared in flesh and blood" that he might gather his children unto himself to obey God [Heb. 2:14 p.]. In these words Christ is clearly declared to be comrade and partner in the same nature with us. In this sense he also says that "the Author of sanctification and those who are sanctified have all one origin" [Heb. 2:11a]. The context shows that this expression refers to the fellowship of nature, for he immediately adds: "That is why he is not ashamed to call them brethren" [Heb. 2:11b]. For if he had previously said that believers are of God, in such great dignity what reason would there have been for shame? But because Christ of his boundless grace joins himself to base and ignoble men, it is said that "he is not ashamed" [Heb. 2:11b]. Moreover, baseless is their objection that in this way the impious would be Christ's brethren. For we know that the children of God are not born of flesh and blood [cf. John 1:13] but of the Spirit through faith. Hence flesh alone does not make the bond of brotherhood. Even though the apostle assigns to believers alone the honor of being one with Christ, it does not follow that unbelievers cannot be born of the same source. For example, when we say that Christ was made man that he might make us children of God, this ex-

---

[4] Cf. Augustine, *Against Faustus* ii. 4; v. 4 (MPL 42. 211, 222; tr. NPNF IV. 157, 168 f.).

pression does not extend to all men. For faith intervenes, to engraft us spiritually into the body of Christ.

They also bunglingly stir up contention over the expression "first-born." They allege that Christ should have been born of Adam at the very beginning, to "be the first-born among the brethren" [Rom. 8:29 p.]. "First-born" here refers not to age but to degree of honor and loftiness of power!

Even less plausible is their babbling that Christ assumed human, not angelic, nature [Heb. 2:16], meaning that he received humankind into grace. To enhance the honor that Christ deigned to give us, Paul compares us with the angels, to whom in this respect we were preferred. If we carefully weigh Moses' testimony —where he says that the seed of the woman will crush the serpent's head [Gen. 3:15]—the controversy will be completely resolved. For the statement there concerns not only Christ but the whole of mankind. Since we must acquire victory through Christ, God declares in general terms that the woman's offspring is to prevail over the devil. Hence it follows that Christ was begotten of mankind, for in addressing Eve it was God's intention to raise her hope that she should not be overwhelmed with despair.

(The human descent and true humanity of Christ, 3–4)
*3. Christ's descent through the Virgin Mary: an absurdity exposed**
ᶜOur opponents both foolishly and wickedly entangle in allegories those testimonies wherein Christ is called the seed of Abraham and the fruit of David's loins. For if the term "seed" had been allegorically intended, Paul surely would not have remained silent about this when he affirmed, clearly and unfiguratively, that there are not many redeemers among the children of Abraham, but only one, Christ [Gal. 3:16]. Of the same stuff is their pretense that Christ was called "son of David" only because he had been promised and at last was revealed in his own time [Rom. 1:3]. For when Paul named him "Son of David," and then immediately added "according to the flesh," he surely designates his human nature by this. Thus in the ninth chapter, after calling Christ "blessed God," he asserts separately that he descended from the Jews "according to the flesh" [Rom. 9:5]. Now, if he had not truly been begotten of the seed of David, what will be the point of this expression that he is "the fruit of her womb" [cf. Luke 1:42]? What is this promise, "From your loins will descend one who will remain upon your throne" [cf. Ps. 132: 11 p.; also, II Sam. 7:12; Acts 2:30]?

Now they sophistically disport themselves over Matthew's version of the genealogy of Christ. Matthew does not list Mary's ancestors, but Joseph's [Matt. 1:16]. Still, because he is mentioning something well known at the time, he considers it sufficient to show that Joseph sprang from the seed of David, since it was clear enough that Mary came from the same family. Luke emphasizes this even more, teaching that the salvation provided by Christ is common to all mankind. For Christ, the Author of salvation, was begotten of Adam, the common father of us all [Luke 3:38]. I admit that one can gather from the genealogy that Christ was the son of David solely in so far as he was begotten of the virgin. But in order to disguise their error—to prove that Christ took his body out of nothing—the new Marcionites too haughtily contend that women are "without seed."[5] Thus they overturn the principles of nature.

But this is not a theological issue, and such is the futility of the reasons they bring forward that these can be refuted without trouble. Accordingly, I shall not touch upon matters that belong to philosophy and medicine. It will be enough to refute the objections that they derive from Scripture, namely: Aaron and Jehoiada took wives from the tribe of Judah [Ex. 6:23; II Chron. 22:11], and so the distinction of tribes would then have been confused if women possessed the seed of generation. But it is sufficiently well known that descent is reckoned by the male line as far as the political order is concerned; yet this preferential position of the male sex does not gainsay the fact that the woman's seed must share in the act of generation.

This solution also extends to all genealogies. Often when Scripture sets out a list of human beings, it names only the males. Must we then say that women are nothing? Why, even children know that women are included under the term "men"! Women are said to bear children to their husbands because the family name always rests in the possession of the males. Now as the superiority of the male sex is conceded in the fact that children are reckoned noble or ignoble from their father's status, conversely, in slavery, "the offspring follows the womb," as lawyers say.[6] From this we shall have to infer that the offspring is en-

---

[5] "*Mulieres contendunt esse ἀσπόρους.*" This theme is developed by Menno in his *Reply to Gellius Faber* (1554) and elsewhere. (Jelle Smit, or Gellius Faber, formerly a priest, had become pastor in Emden.) Menno held the unscientific notion that in procreation woman's part is receptive only, and "the father is the real origin of his child," *Reply to Gellius Faber*, p. 768; cf. his *Reply to Martin Micron;* tr. Verduin, *op. cit.*, pp. 849 f., 886–892, 906.

[6] The phrase is found in the *Institutes* of Justinian I. 3, 4 and in his *Digest* I. v. 5, 2 (*Corpus iuris civilis: Institutiones et Digesta*, ed. P. Krueger [*Inst.,*

gendered from the mother's seed; for a long time it has been the common custom of nations to call mothers "engenderers."[7] And this agrees with God's law, which would otherwise wrongly forbid the marriage of a maternal uncle with his niece because there would then be no consanguinity. Also, it would have been right for a man to marry his maternal half sister, provided she were begotten of another father. But while I admit that a passive force is ascribed to women, I reply that the same thing is indiscriminately said of women as of men. For Christ himself is not said to have been made by woman, but from woman [Gal. 4:4]. Some of their tribe, however, casting shame aside, too wantonly ask whether we mean that Christ was engendered of the virgin's menstrual seed.[8] In return I shall ask them whether he did not unite with his mother's blood—which they will have to admit.

Therefore, it is readily inferred from Matthew's words that because Christ was begotten of Mary, he was engendered from her seed, just as when Boaz is said to have been begotten of Rahab [Matt. 1:5] a similar generation is meant. And Matthew does not here describe the virgin as a channel through which Christ flowed. Rather, he differentiates this wonderful manner of generation from the common sort in stating that through her Christ was begotten of the seed of David. In the same way that Isaac was begotten of Abraham, Solomon of David, Joseph of Jacob, Christ is said to have been begotten of his mother. For the Evangelist so arranges the order of his words. Meaning to prove that Christ took his origin from David, he was satisfied with this one thing: Christ was begotten of Mary. From this it follows that he took it as generally acknowledged that Mary was related to Joseph.[9]

4. True man—and yet sinless! True man—and yet eternal God!
ᵉThe absurdities with which they wish to weigh us down are stuffed with childish calumnies. They consider it shameful and dishonorable to Christ if he were to derive his origin from men, for he could not be exempted from the common rule, which includes under sin all of Adam's offspring without exception. But the comparison that we read in Paul readily disposes of this difficulty: "As sin came in . . . through one man, and death

p. 2; *Dig.*, p. 35]; tr. J. B. Moyle, *The Institutes of Justinian* (5th ed., pp. 6 f.); tr. C. H. Monro, *The Digest of Justinian* I, pp. 24 f.).
[7] *"Genitrices."*
[8] Cf. Menno, *Reply to Martin Micron;* tr. Verduin, *op. cit.,* pp. 896, 908. Other passages from this work are alluded to in the remainder of the chapter.
[9] VG adds: *"et par conséquent de la race de David."*

through sin . . . so through the righteousness of one man grace abounded" [Rom. 5:12, 18, 15 p.]. Another comparison of Paul's agrees with this: "The first Adam was of the earth, an earthly and natural man, the Second of the heaven, heavenly" [I Cor. 15:47 p.]. The apostle teaches the same thing in another passage, that Christ was sent "in the likeness of sinful flesh" to satisfy the law [Rom. 8:3-4]. Thus, so skillfully does he distinguish Christ from the common lot that he is true man but without fault and corruption. But they babble childishly: if Christ is free from all spot, and through the secret working of the Spirit was begotten of the seed of Mary, then woman's seed is not unclean, but only man's. For we make Christ free of all stain not just because he was begotten of his mother without copulation with man, but because he was sanctified by the Spirit that the generation might be pure and undefiled as would have been true before Adam's fall. And this remains for us an established fact: whenever Scripture calls our attention to the purity of Christ, it is to be understood of his true human nature, for it would have been superfluous to say that God is pure. Also, the sanctification of which John, ch. 17, speaks would have no place in divine nature [John 17:19]. Nor do we imagine that Adam's seed is twofold, even though no infection came to Christ. For the generation of man is not unclean and vicious of itself, but is so as an accidental quality arising from the Fall. No wonder, then, that Christ, through whom integrity was to be restored, was exempted from common corruption! They thrust upon us as something absurd the fact that if the Word of God became flesh, then he was confined within the narrow prison of an earthly body. This is mere impudence! For even if the Word in his immeasurable essence united with the nature of man into one person, we do not imagine that he was confined therein. Here is something marvelous: the Son of God descended from heaven in such a way that, without leaving heaven, he willed to be borne in the virgin's womb, to go about the earth, and to hang upon the cross; yet he continuously filled the world even as he had done from the beginning!

ᶜCHAPTER XIV

How the Two Natures of the Mediator Make One Person

(*Explanation of the human and divine natures in Christ, 1–3*)
1. Duality and unity

ᵇ⁽ᵃ⁾On the other hand, we ought not to understand the statement that "the Word was made flesh" [John 1:14] in the sense that the Word was turned into flesh or confusedly mingled with flesh. Rather, it means that, because he chose for himself the virgin's womb as a temple in which to dwell, he who was the Son of God became the Son of man—not by confusion of substance, but by unity of person. ᵇFor we affirm his divinity so joined and united with his humanity that each retains its distinctive nature unimpaired, and yet these two natures constitute one Christ.[1]

ᵇ⁽ᵃ⁾If anything like this very great mystery can be found in human affairs, the most apposite parallel seems to be that of man, whom we see to consist of two substances. ᵃYet neither is so mingled with the other as not to retain its own distinctive nature. For the soul is not the body, and the body is not the soul. Therefore, some things are said exclusively of the soul that can in no wise apply to the body; and of the body, again, that in no way fit the soul; of the whole man, that cannot refer—except inappropriately—to either soul or body separately. Finally, the characteristics of the mind[2] are [sometimes] transferred to the body, and those of the body to the soul. Yet he who consists of these parts is one man, not many. Such expressions signify both that there is one person in man composed of two elements joined together, and that there are two diverse underlying natures that make up this person.[3] Thus, also, the Scriptures speak of Christ: they sometimes attribute to him what must be referred solely to his humanity, sometimes what belongs uniquely to his divinity; and sometimes what embraces both natures but fits neither alone. ᵇ⁽ᵃ⁾And they so earnestly express this union of the

---

[1] Throughout this chapter, as in the opening sentences, Calvin adheres strictly to the line of Chalcedonian orthodoxy. On this topic the study by J. S. Witte, "Die Christologie Calvins" in *Das Konzil von Chalkedon*, ed. A. Grillmeier, III. 487–529, and W. Niesel, *The Theology of Calvin*, pp. 115 ff., should be consulted. Cf. S. Cave, *The Doctrine of the Person of Christ*, pp. 151 f.

[2] Calvin here uses *"animus"* instead of *"anima"* as in the 1536 edition.

[3] Augustine, *Sermones* clxxxvi (MPL 38. 999; *Enchiridion* xi. 36 (MPL 40. 250; tr. LCC VII. 361 f.). Augustine observes that as man is a unity of soul and flesh, so Christ is a unity of the Word and man.

two natures that is in Christ as sometimes to interchange them. This figure of speech is called by the ancient writers "the communicating of properties."[4]

2. Divinity and humanity in their relation to each other

[e(b/a)]These things would be quite unconvincing if many and oft-recurring phrases of Scripture did not prove none of them to have been humanly devised. [a]What Christ said about himself— "Before Abraham was, I am" [John 8:58]—was far removed from his humanity. [e]I am quite aware of the captious argument with which erring spirits corrupt this passage: that he was before all ages because he was already foreknown as Redeemer, both in the Father's plan and in the minds of the godly.[5] But since he clearly distinguishes the day of his manifestation from his eternal essence, and expressly commends his own authority as excelling Abraham's in antiquity, there is no doubt that he is claiming for himself what is proper to his divinity. [b]Paul declares him to be "the first-born of all creation . . . who was before all things and in whom all things hold together" [Col. 1:15, 17]. [e]Also, he says that he was "glorious in his Father's presence before the world was made" [John 17:5 p.]; and that he is working together with his Father [John 5:17]. [b]These qualities are utterly alien to man. [b(a)]Therefore they and their like apply exclusively to his divinity.

But he is called "the servant of the Father" [Isa. 42:1, and other passages]; he is said to have "increased in age and wisdom . . .

---

4 "ἰδιωμάτων κοινωνία." The doctrine of the *communicatio idiomatum,* or interchange of properties of the divine and human nature of Christ. This doctrine found occasional expression in the Nestorian controversy (ca. 428–451), having been held, though inadequately expressed, by Tertullian, Origen, Gregory of Nyssa, Ephiphanius, and other earlier writers. See the discussion in C. J. Hefele, *Conciliengeschichte* II (1856). 127 f.; Hefele-Leclercq II. i. 231 f.; tr. from the German text, *History of the Councils* III. 8, 9. Cf. Tertullian, *Of the Flesh of Christ* v (CC II. 880; tr. ANF III. 525); Cyril of Alexandria, "ἀλλήλοις ἀνακρινὰς τὰ τῶν φύσεων ἰδιώματα" (citing John 3:13), *De incarnatione Unigeniti* (MPG 75. 1244); Leo the Great, *Letters* xxviii. 5 (MPL 54. 771 f.; tr. NPNF 2 ser. XII. 41 and note 7); Athanasius, *Discourses Against the Arians* iii. 31 (tr. NPNF 2 ser. IV. 410 f.); John of Damascus, *Exposition of the Orthodox Faith* III. iii–iv (MPG 94. 993 f.; tr. NPNF 2 ser. IX. 43–49). There is a statement based on Hefele in NPNF 2 ser. XIV. 208 f. Calvin approves and explains the doctrine (sec. 2); but he rejects the use made of it by Lutheran advocates of the ubiquity of Christ's risen body. Cf. IV. xvii. 29, 30, and Luther, *Werke* WA XXV. 309. Servetus had repeatedly attacked this doctrine: see, for example, *De Trinitatis erroribus* I. 15, fo. 10b; III. 12 to 76ab; tr. Wilbur, *op. cit.,* pp. 18, 118. The doctrine is affirmed in the Second Helvetic Confession XI. 10 (Schaff, *Creeds* III. 256; tr. p. 852; Kidd, *Documents,* pp. 113 f.).

5 Cf. Servetus, *Christianismi restitutio, De Trinitate* III, p. 96.

with God and men" [Luke 2:52], and not to "seek his own glory" [John 8:50]; b"not to know the Last Day" [Mark 13:32; cf. Matt. 24:36]; not to "speak by himself" [John 14:10], and not to "do his own will" [John 6:38 p.]; he is said to have been "seen and handled" [Luke 24:39]. aAll these refer solely to Christ's humanity. In so far as he is God, he cannot increase in anything, and does all things for his own sake; bnothing is hidden from him; he does all things according to the decision of his will, and can be neither seen nor handled. cYet he does not ascribe these qualities solely to his human nature, but takes them upon himself as being in harmony with the person of the Mediator.

aBut the communicating of characteristics or properties consists in what Paul says: "God purchased the church with his blood" [Acts 20:28 p.], and "the Lord of glory was crucified" [I Cor. 2:8 p.]. cJohn says the same: "The Word of life was handled" [I John 1:1 p.]. aSurely God does not have blood, does not suffer, cannot be touched with hands. But since Christ, who was true God and also true man, was crucified and shed his blood for us, the things that he carried out in his human nature are transferred improperly, although not without reason, to his divinity. bHere is a similar example: John teaches "that God laid down his life for us" [I John 3:16 p.]. Accordingly, there also a property of humanity is shared with the other nature. aAgain, when Christ, still living on earth, said: "No one has ascended into heaven but the Son of man who was in heaven" [John 3:13 p.], surely then, as man, in the flesh that he had taken upon himself, he was not in heaven. But because the selfsame one was both God and man, for the sake of the union of both natures he gave to the one what belonged to the other.

3. The unity of the person of the Mediator

b(a)But the passages that comprehend both natures at once, very many of which are to be found in John's Gospel, set forth his true substance most clearly of all. For one reads there neither of deity nor of humanity alone, but of both at once: he received from the Father the power of remitting sins [John 1:29], of raising to life whom he will, of bestowing righteousness, holiness, salvation; he was appointed judge of the living and the dead bin order that he might be honored, even as the Father [John 5:21–23]. Lastly, he is called the "light of the world" [John 9:5; 8:12], the "good shepherd," the "only door" [John 10:11, 9], the "true vine" [John 15:1]. aFor the Son of God had been endowed with such prerogatives when he was manifested in the flesh. Even though along with the Father he held them before the creation of the world, it had not been in the same manner or respect, and they could not have been given to a man who was nothing but a man.

b(a)In the same sense we ought also to understand what we read in Paul: after the judgment "Christ will deliver the Kingdom to his God and Father" [I Cor. 15:24 p.]. Surely the Kingdom of the Son of God had no beginning and will have no end. But even as he lay concealed under the lowness of flesh and "emptied himself, taking the form of a servant" [Phil. 2:7, cf. Vg.], laying aside the splendor of majesty, he showed himself obedient to his Father [cf. Phil. 2:8]. Having completed this subjection, "he was at last crowned with glory and honor" [Heb. 2:9 p.], e(b/a)and exalted to the highest lordship that before him "every knee should bow" [Phil. 2:10]. aSo then will he yield to the Father his name and crown of glory, and whatever he has received from the Father, that "God may be all in all" [I Cor. 15:28]. eFor what purpose were power and lordship given to Christ, unless that by his hand the Father might govern us? In this sense, also, Christ is said to be seated at the right hand of the Father [cf. Mark 16:19; Rom. 8:34]. Yet this is but for a time, until we enjoy the direct vision of the Godhead. Here we cannot excuse the error of the ancient writers who pay no attention to the person of the Mediator, obscure the real meaning of almost all the teaching one reads in the Gospel of John, and entangle themselves in many snares.[6] Let this, then, be our key to right understanding: those things which apply to the office of the Mediator are not spoken simply either of the divine nature or of the human.[7] Until he comes forth as judge of the world Christ will therefore reign, joining us to the Father as the measure of our weakness permits. But when as partakers in heavenly glory we shall see God as he is, Christ, having then discharged the office of Mediator, will cease to be the ambassador of his Father, and will be satisfied with that glory which he enjoyed before the creation of the world.

And the name "Lord" exclusively belongs to the person of Christ only in so far as it represents a degree midway between

[6] Probably an allusion to ancient writers who approached Eutychean or Monophysite opinions: cf. Cyril of Alexandria, *Expositio in Evangelium Johannis*, on John 5:19; 5:30; 8:28 (MPG 73. 757 f., 386 ff., 832 ff.). See OS III. 517.

[7] The sentences following in this section reflect Calvin's clash with George Blandrata and other anti-Trinitarians of Poland, about 1558. Cf. *Responsio ad nobiles Polonos et Franciscum Stancarum Mantuarum* (CR IX. 354 ff.); *Ad quaestiones Georgii Blandratae responsum* (CR IX. 332); the second confession of Valentine Gentile (CR IX. 392).

God and us. Paul's statement accords with this: "One God . . . from whom are all things . . . and one Lord . . . through whom are all things" [I Cor. 8:6]. That is, to him was lordship committed by the Father, until such time as we should see his divine majesty face to face. Then he returns the lordship to his Father so that—far from diminishing his own majesty—it may shine all the more brightly. Then, also, God shall cease to be the Head of Christ, for Christ's own deity will shine of itself, although as yet it is covered by a veil.

(*Condemnation of the errors of Nestorius, Eutyches, and Servetus, 4–8*)

4. The two natures may not be thought of as either fused or separated

ᵇThis observation will be highly useful in solving very many difficulties, if my readers apply it intelligently. It is amazing how much ᵉ⁽ᵇ⁾untutored minds—and even some not completely uneducated—are plagued by expressions of this sort, which they see applied to Christ, yet not quite appropriate either to his divinity or to his humanity. ᵇThis is because they do not consider the expressions suitable either to his person, in which he was manifested as God and man, or to the office of the Mediator. Yet it is utterly obvious how ᵃbeautifully the various statements agree among themselves, in the hands of a sober expositor who examines such great mysteries as devoutly as they deserve.[8] But there is nothing that these mad and frantic spirits do not stir up! They seize upon the attributes of his humanity to take away his divinity, conversely upon those of his divinity to take away his humanity;[9] and upon those spoken of both natures so conjointly that they are applicable to neither, to take away both. But what else is this than to contend that Christ is not man because he is God; that he is not God because he is man; that he is neither man nor God because he is man and God at the same time?

ᵇ⁽ᵃ⁾We therefore hold that Christ, as he is God and man, ᵇconsisting ᵇ⁽ᵃ⁾of two natures united but not mingled, ᵇis our Lord and the true Son of God even according to, but not by reason of, his humanity. Away with the error of Nestorius, who in wanting to pull apart rather than distinguish the nature of Christ devised a double Christ! Yet we see that Scripture cries out against this with a clear voice: there the name "Son of God" is applied to

---

[8] Augustine, *Enchiridion* xi. 36 (MPL 40. 250; tr. LCC VII. 361 f.).

[9] Servetus, *De Trinitatis erroribus* I, fo. 2b ff.; II, fo. 58ab (tr. Wilbur, *op. cit.*, pp. 6–11, 90 ff.); *Dialogues on the Trinity* I, fo. A 6b–7b (tr. Wilbur, *op cit.*, pp. 195 ff.).

him who is born of the virgin [Luke 1:32 p.], and the virgin herself is called the "mother of our Lord" [Luke 1:43 p.]. ^cLet us beware, also, of Eutyches' madness; lest, while meaning to show the unity of the person, we destroy either nature. We have cited so many testimonies that distinguish his divinity from his humanity, and there are so many others besides, that they can stop the mouths of even the most quarrelsome persons. ^eA little later[10] I shall append some testimonies that will more effectively shatter that figment of theirs. For the present, one passage will suffice us: Christ would not have called his body a temple [John 2:19] unless divinity, as distinct from the body, dwelt therein. ^cHence, just as Nestorius had justly been condemned at the Synod of Ephesus, so Eutyches was afterward justly condemned at the Councils of Constantinople and Chalcedon.[11] For it is no more permissible to commingle the two natures in Christ than to pull them apart.

5. *Christ is the Son of God from everlasting*

^eBut in our own age too, a no less deadly monster has emerged, Michael Servetus, who has supposed the Son of God to be a figment compounded from God's essence, spirit, flesh, and three uncreated elements.[12] First of all, he denies that Christ is the Son of God for any other reason than that he was begotten of the Holy Spirit in the virgin's womb. His subtlety takes this direction: having overturned the distinction of the two natures, he regards Christ to be a mixture of some divine and some human elements, but not to be reckoned both God and man. For his whole logic bears upon the point that before Christ was revealed in the flesh there were only shadow figures in God; the truth or effect of these appeared only when the Word, who had been destined for this honor, truly began to be the Son of God.

Now we confess that the Mediator, who was born of the virgin, is properly the Son of God. And the man Christ would not be the mirror of God's inestimable grace unless this dignity had been conferred upon him, that he should both be the only-begotten

---

[10] Secs. 6–8, below.

[11] Nestorius, who sharply separated the divine and human natures of Christ, was condemned by the Synod of Ephesus, 431, through the action of Cyril of Alexandria. Eutyches, who, exaggerating Cyril's teaching, minimized so as virtually to deny Christ's human nature, was condemned by the Council of Constantinople, 448. The doctrines of both were repudiated in the creed adopted by the Ecumenical Council of Chalcedon, 451. Cf. IV. v. 6; IV. vii. 1, 9, and see the documents and references in Ayer, *Source Book*, pp. 504–521.

[12] Cf. Servetus, *Christianismi restitutio, De Trinitate, dial.* II, pp. 250 f.

Son of God and be so called. Meanwhile, the church's definition stands firm: he is believed to be the Son of God because the Word begotten of the Father before all ages[13] took human nature in a hypostatic union. Now the old writers defined "hypostatic union" as that which constitutes one person out of two natures. This expression was devised to refute the delusion of Nestorius, because he imagined that the Son of God so dwelt in the flesh that he was not man also. Servetus accuses us of making two Sons of God when we say that the eternal Word, before he was clothed with flesh, was already the Son of God[14]—as if we were saying something else than that he was manifested in the flesh. If he was God before he became man, he did not, for that reason, begin to be a new God! It is no more absurd for us to say that the Son of God was manifested in the flesh yet had by virtue of eternal generation always possessed sonship. The words of the angel to Mary hint at this: "What holy one will be born of you will be called the Son of God" [Luke 1:35 p.]; as if to say that the name "Son," which had been somewhat obscure under the law, was to be illustrious and known everywhere. Paul concurs: because we are now sons of God through Christ, we freely and confidently cry, "Abba! Father!" [Rom. 8:14–15; Gal. 4:6]. Were not the holy patriarchs of old also held to be among the sons of God? Yes—relying upon this right, they called upon God as Father. But after the only-begotten Son of God was brought into the world, the heavenly fatherhood became more clearly known. Accordingly, Paul assigns this privilege, as it were, to Christ's Kingdom. Yet this ought to be unwaveringly maintained: to neither angels nor men was God ever Father, except with regard to his only-begotten Son; and men, especially, hateful to God because of their iniquity, become God's sons by free adoption because Christ is the Son of God by nature. There is no reason why Servetus should violently object that this depends upon a filiation that God had decreed with himself. For here it is not a matter of figures, such as when atonement was set forth in the blood of beasts. Rather, they could not actually be sons of God unless their adoption was founded upon the Head. Accordingly, it is unreasonable to withdraw from the Head what the members had in common. I go farther: Scripture calls the angels "sons of God" [Ps. 82:6], whose high dignity did not depend upon the coming redemption. Yet Christ had to be above them in rank

13 *"Ante saecula."* In the Niceno-Constantinopolitan Creed the phrase is *ante omnia saecula,* "before all ages."
14 Servetus, *De Trinitatis erroribus* I. 54 ff., fo. 38a ff. (tr. Wilbur, *op. cit.,* pp. 59 ff.).

in order to reconcile them to the Father. I shall briefly repeat this statement again, applying it also to mankind. At their creation angels and men were so constituted that God was their common Father. Hence, if Paul's statement is true—that Christ was always the Head and the first-born of all creatures that he might hold primacy over all [cf. Col. 1:15 ff.]—it seems meet for me to infer that he was the Son of God also before the creation of the world.

6. Christ as Son of God and Son of man

^eBut if his filiation, so to speak, took its beginning from the time when he was made manifest in flesh, it will follow that he was Son also with respect to human nature. Servetus and frenzied men like him would have it that Christ, who was manifested in the flesh, was the Son of God because apart from the flesh he could not have been accorded this name.[15] Let them now answer me whether he is Son according to both natures and with respect to both. This is the way they prate, but Paul teaches far otherwise. ^{b(a)}We admit Christ is indeed called "son" in human flesh; not as believers are sons, by adoption and grace only, but the true and natural, and therefore the only, Son in order that by this mark he may be distinguished from all others. ^bFor God honors us who have been reborn into new life with the name "sons," but bestows the name "true and only-begotten" upon Christ alone. But how is he the "only" son among so many brothers, unless he possesses by nature what we receive as a gift?

^{e(b)}And we extend this honor to the entire person of the Mediator—so that he is truly and properly the Son of God who was both born of the virgin and offered himself as a sacrifice to the Father on the cross. ^{e(b/a)}But this is nevertheless with regard to his deity, as Paul teaches ^awhen he says that he was "set apart for the gospel of God which God had promised beforehand . . . concerning his Son, who was begotten from the seed of David according to the flesh and declared Son of God in power" [Rom. 1:1–4, cf. Vg.]. Why would Paul distinctly name him Son of David according to the flesh, yet state separately that he was designated to be Son of God, unless he meant to intimate that this depended upon something besides his flesh itself? ^eIn this sense Paul says elsewhere: "He suffered in weakness of the flesh but rose again by

---

15 Calvin has in mind both Servetus and the Italian anti-Trinitarians George Blandrata (Giorgio Blandrata), Valentine Gentile, and John Paul (Gianpaulo) Alciati. Cf. I. xiii. 20–25 and notes appended; also CR VIII. 651 f. (second letter of Servetus to Calvin from *Christianismi restitutio*, p. 580); IX. 392 f. (Gentile's second confession); XVII. 169 ff. (letter of Blandrata to Calvin). On these writers and their activities and opinions, see E. M. Wilbur, *A History of Unitarianism: Socinianism and Its Antecedents*, pp. 302 ff., 308–321.

the power of the Spirit" [II Cor. 13:4 p.]. Thus he now makes a distinction between the two natures. Surely they must admit: just as he received from his mother his reason for being called "Son of David," so from his Father he has his reason for being called "Son of God." And this is something other than and distinct from human nature.

Scripture gives him the two names: sometimes calling him Son of God, at other times Son of man. Concerning the second name, they cannot stir up a quarrel because it is common usage in the Hebrew language to speak of him as "Son of man," for he is of the posterity of Adam. On the other hand, I contend that he is called Son of God by virtue of his deity and eternal essence. For it is just as appropriate to refer the fact that he is called "Son of God" to his divine nature, as it is to refer the fact that he is called "Son of man" to his human nature.

To sum up, in this passage to which I have referred—"He who was descended from David according to the flesh and designated Son of God in power"—Paul means the same thing as he teaches in another passage: Christ who descended from the Jews "according to the flesh is . . . God . . . blessed unto the ages" [Rom. 9:5]. If both these statements note the distinction between his two natures, what right have our opponents to deny that he who is Son of man according to flesh is, with respect to his divine nature, Son of God?

7. Servetus' flimsy counterevidence

[a]They clamorously argue in defense of their error that God is said not to have spared his own Son [Rom. 8:32], that the angel enjoined that he who was to be born of the virgin be called "the Son of the Most High" [Luke 1:32].[16] [b(a)]But that they may not glory in such a futile objection, let them ponder with us for a little while how valid their reasoning is. For if it is justly concluded that he began to be the Son of God from conception because he who has been conceived is called "Son," [b]then it will follow that he began to be the Word with his manifestation in the flesh because John states that he is the Word of life, which they had touched with their hands [I John 1:1]. [a]What we read in the prophet is like John's statement: "You, Bethlehem of the land of Judah, are tiny among the thousands of Judah, from you shall come forth for me a ruler to rule my people Israel, whose origin is from the beginning, from eternal days" [Micah 5:2 and Matt. 2:6, conflated (Vg.)]. [b(a)]How will they be compelled to interpret this, if they are determined to argue in such a way?

[16] Servetus. De Trinitatis erroribus I. 9, fo. 6a; tr. Wilbur, op. cit., pp. 11 f.

ᵉI have testified that we do not agree at all with Nestorius, who imagined a double Christ, while according to our teaching, Christ made us sons of God with him by virtue of a bond of brotherhood. For in the flesh that he received from us he is the only-begotten Son of God. Augustine sagely warns us that he is the bright mirror of God's wonderful and singular grace; for he has attained an honor that, in so far as he is man, he could not have deserved.[17] Christ was therefore adorned with this excellence according to the flesh, even from the womb, to be the Son of God. Yet we must not imagine in the unity of his person a mingling that takes away what belongs to his deity. Nor is it more absurd that the eternal Word of God and Christ, since the two natures have been united into one person, is called "Son of God" in various ways than that he is called, in various respects, sometimes Son of God, at other times Son of man.[18]

Servetus' other slander also gives us no more embarrassment: before he appeared in the flesh, Christ was nowhere called "Son of God" except figuratively. For even though the description of him was then somewhat obscure, it is clearly proved that he was eternal God solely because he was the Word begotten by the eternal Father; and that this name belonged to the person of the Mediator, which he had taken upon himself, only because he was God manifest in the flesh. It is also clear that God would not have been called "Father" from the beginning unless there had already at that time been a reciprocal relationship to the Son, "from whom all kinship or fatherhood in heaven and on earth is named" [Eph. 3:15 p.]. From this evidence we may readily conclude that he was Son of God also under the Law and the Prophets, before this name became illustrious in the church. But suppose they contend over this one statement wherein Solomon tells of God's immeasurable loftiness. He declares that both God and his son are incomprehensible: "Tell me, if you can, his name or his son's name" [Prov. 30:4 p.]. I am aware that this testimony will not be sufficiently weighty for contentious persons. Hence, I do not depend very much on it, unless it shows that those who deny that Christ is the Son of God except in so far as he became man are wicked slanderers. Besides, the most ancient writers with one accord testified to this fact so clearly that the shamelessness of those who dare thrust at us Irenaeus and Tertullian is as ridiculous as it is detestable. For both of these writers confess

---

[17] Augustine, *City of God* X. xxix. 1 (MPL 41. 308; tr. NPNF II. 199).
[18] Servetus, *Christianismi restitutio,* pp. 577 ff. (first letter of Servetus to Calvin, also in CR VIII. 649 ff.), 580 (second letter; CR VIII. 580).

that the Son of God was invisible, but afterward was visibly manifested.[19]

8. Comprehensive presentation and rebuttal of Servetus' doctrine

eServetus has heaped up terrible portents, to which others would perhaps not subscribe. aYet if you press more closely e(b/a)those who recognize the Son of God only in the flesh, ayou will observe that they admit it for no other reason than that he was conceived in the virgin's womb of the Holy Spirit. The Manichees of old fancied the same thing: that man has his soul by derivation from God:[20] for they read that "God breathed upon Adam the breath of life" [Gen. 2:7 p.]. eThey so doggedly seize upon the name "Son" that they leave no distinction between the natures; rather, they confusedly babble that Christ the man is the Son of God because he was begotten of God according to his human nature. Thus the eternal begetting of wisdom of which Solomon speaks [Ecclus. 24:14, Vg.; 24:9, EV; cf. Prov. 8:22 ff.] is annihilated, and no account is taken of deity in the Mediator, or a mere appearance is put in place of true man.

It would be useful to refute Servetus' grosser deceptions, with which he has bewitched himself and certain others, that, admonished by this example, godly readers may remain sober and modest. But I believe this would be superfluous because I have already done it in a special book.[21] The sum of the matter comes to this: for Servetus, the Son of God was from the beginning an idea, and even then was preordained to be the man who would become the essential image of God. He recognizes no other Word of God than one of outward splendor. He interprets the begetting of Christ thus: the will to beget the Son was begotten in God from the beginning, and extended itself by act to the creation itself. Meanwhile, he confuses the Spirit with the Word, for God distributed the invisible Word and the Spirit into flesh and soul. In short, the figurative representation of Christ took the place

---

[19] Servetus, *De Trinitatis erroribus* II. 5, fo. 48ab; tr. Wilbur, *op. cit.,* pp. 76 ff.; Tertullian, *Against Praxeas* ii, iii, xv (MPL 2. 156–159; CCL II. 1178 ff.; E. Evans, *Tertullian's Treatise Against Praxeas,* text, p. 107; tr. p. 151; tr. ANF III. 598, 610 f.); Irenaeus, *Against Heresies* III. xvi. 6; III. xxi. 10 (MPG 7. 925, 954 f.; tr. ANF I. 442, 454). Cf. CR VIII. 507 ff., 522, 535, 574; IX. 394 ff. Augustine, *On True Religion* xvi. 30 (MPL 34. 134 f. LCC VI. 239); *John's Gospel* iii. 18 (MPL 35. 1403; tr. NPNF VII. 24); *Against the Letter of Manichaeus Called Fundamental* xxxvii. 42 (MPL 42. 202; tr. NPNF IV. 198); *On the Trinity* II. ix. 15 (MPL 42. 854 f.; tr. NPNF III. 44).

[20] *"Ex traduce Dei."* Cf. I. xv. 5; II. i. 7, note 10, and see the references given in OS III. 181, 469; Smits, II. 29, 37.

[21] The reference is to Calvin's *Defensio orthodoxae fidei de sacra Trinitate* (1554) (CR VIII. 457–644; tr. H. Cole, *Calvin's Calvinism,* pp. 25–206).

of begetting in Servetus' scheme. But he says that he who was then a shadow Son in appearance was at length begotten through the Word; thus he assigns to the Word a seminal function. From this it will follow that pigs and dogs are just as much sons of God, since they were created from the original seed of the Word of God. He compounds Christ out of three uncreated elements to make him begotten of God's essence. Nevertheless, he imagines him to be the first-born among creatures in such a way that the same essential divinity is in stones according to their degree. But lest he seem to strip Christ of his deity, he declares that His flesh was of the same substance[22] with God, and that the Word was made man by the conversion of flesh into God. Thus, while he cannot conceive of Christ as the Son of God unless his flesh came forth from God's essence, and was converted into deity, he reduces to nothing the eternal hypostasis of the Word, and he snatches from us the Son of David, who had been promised as our Redeemer. Indeed, he repeats this thought quite often: that the Son was begotten of God by knowledge and predestination, but that he was finally made man from that matter which shone at the beginning in the presence of God in three elements— elements that then appeared in the first light of the world [Gen. 1:3], in the cloud and pillar of fire [Ex. 13:21]. Furthermore, it would be too tedious to recount how shamefully Servetus sometimes disagrees with himself. Sane readers will gather from this summary that the crafty evasions of this foul dog utterly extinguished the hope of salvation. For if flesh were divinity itself, it would cease to be the temple of divinity. Only he can be our Redeemer who, begotten of the seed of Abraham and David, was truly made man according to the flesh. Servetus perversely bases his position on John's words: "The Word was made flesh" [John 1:14].[23] For, as these words resist Nestorius' error, they also give no support to that impious fabrication whose author was Eutyches, inasmuch as the sole purpose of the Evangelist was to declare unity of person in the two natures.

22 "ὁμοούσιον."
23 In the preceding sentences Calvin has in mind numerous passages in the *Christianismi restitutio* of Servetus. These are listed, with the titles of the special sections of the work, by Barth and Niesel, OS III. 470 f. The pages in the order of reference are: 578, 92 f., 679 f., 205 f., 591 f., 683, 164, 202 f., 355, 145, 159, 162, 269, 263, 590, 150, 680, 683, 205, 250, 159, 119 f., 265 f. On *homoousios* and *hypostasis*, see especially p. 269 (*De Trinitate* II).

^cCHAPTER XV

To Know the Purpose for Which Christ Was Sent by the Father, and What He Conferred Upon Us, We Must Look Above All at Three Things in Him: the Prophetic Office, Kingship, and Priesthood

(i. Christ's saving activity threefold: first the prophetic office, 1–2)

1. The need of understanding this doctrine: Scriptural passages applicable to Christ's prophetic office*

^eAs Augustine rightly states, the heretics, although they preach the name of Christ, have herein no common ground with believers, but it remains the sole possession of the church. For if we diligently consider the things that pertain to Christ, we will find Christ among the heretics in name only, not in reality.[1] So today the words "Son of God, Redeemer of the world," resound upon the lips of the papists. Yet because they are satisfied with vain pretense of the name, and strip him of his power and dignity, Paul's words apply to them: "They do not hold fast to the Head" [Col. 2:19 p.].

Therefore, in order that faith may find a firm basis for salvation in Christ, and thus rest in him, this principle must be laid down: the office enjoined upon Christ by the Father consists of three parts. For he was given to be prophet, king, and priest.[2] Yet it would be of little value to know these names without understanding their purpose and use. The papists use these names, too,[3] but coldly and rather ineffectually, since they do not know what each of these titles contains.

We have already said[4] that although God, by providing his

---

[1] Augustine, *Enchiridion* i. 5 (MPL 40. 233; tr. LCC VII. 339).

[2] On Calvin's treatment of the three offices of Christ as Prophet, Priest, and King, see J. F. Jansen, *Calvin's Doctrine of the Work of Christ.* Jansen presents some useful data on the background of this formulation (pp. 20–38). He holds that the prophetic office of Christ largely drops from Calvin's attention. In typical works of Reformed theology, however, the triple office gives structure to the doctrine of the work of Christ as Mediator. Cf. Heppe RD, pp. 452–487; C. Hodge, *Systematic Theology* II. 459–609; W. Cunningham, *Historical Theology* II. 238 ff.; E. D. Morris, *Theology of the Westminster Symbols,* pp. 322–343; Westminster Confession VIII; Larger Catechism 43–45; Shorter Catechism 24–26; T. F. Torrance, *The School of Faith,* Introduction, pp. lxxvii–xcv, ciii f.

[3] Cf. Aquinas, *Summa Theol.* III. xxii. 2: "Wherefore, as to others, one is a lawgiver, another is a priest, another is a king; but all these concur in Christ as the fount of all grace."

[4] II. vi. 2–4.

people with an unbroken line of prophets, never left them without useful doctrine sufficient for salvation, yet the minds of the pious had always been imbued with the conviction that they were to hope for the full light of understanding only at the coming of the Messiah. This expectation penetrated even to the Samaritans, though they never had known the true religion, as appears from the words of the woman: "When the Messiah comes, he will teach us all things" [John 4:25 p.]. And the Jews did not rashly presume this in their minds; but, being taught by clear oracles, they so believed. Isaiah's saying is particularly well known: "Behold, I have made him a witness to the peoples, I have given him as a leader and commander for the peoples" [Isa. 55:4]. Elsewhere, Isaiah called him "messenger or interpreter of great counsel" [Isa. 9:6, conflated with Isa. 28:29 and Jer. 32:19].[5] For this reason, the apostle commends the perfection of the gospel doctrine, first saying: "In many and various ways God spoke of old to our fathers by the prophets" [Heb. 1:1]. Then he adds, "In these last days he has spoken to us through a beloved Son." [Heb. 1:2 p.] But, because the task common to the prophets was to hold the church in expectation and at the same time to support it until the Mediator's coming, we read that in their dispersion believers complained that they were deprived of that ordinary benefit: "We do not see our signs; there is no . . . prophet among us, . . . there is no one . . . who knows how long" [Ps. 74:9]. But when Christ was no longer far off, a time was appointed for Daniel "to seal both vision and prophet"[6] [Dan. 9:24], not only that the prophetic utterance there mentioned might be authoritatively established, but also that believers might patiently go without the prophets for a time because the fullness and culmination of all revelations was at hand.

2. *The meaning of the prophetic office for us*

e(b)Now it is to be noted that the title "Christ" pertains to these three offices:[7] for we know that under the law prophets as well as priests and kings were anointed with holy oil. eHence the illustrious name of "Messiah" was also bestowed upon the

---

[5] French text: *"Ange ou ambassadeur du haut conseill."* In Comm. Isa. 9:6, Calvin does not follow this variant translation but argues for the rendering: "The Mighty God, Wonderful, Counselor, shall call," etc.

[6] *"Prophetam."* VG has *"prophetie,"* prophecy; but the Latin accords with the Hebrew.

[7] Cf. Bucer: *"Rex regum Christus est, summus sacerdos, et prophetarum caput."* *Enarrationes in Evangelia* (1536), p. 607. Benoit suggests that Calvin may have borrowed the idea from this statement of Bucer (Benoit, *Institution* II. 267, note 8).

promised Mediator. As I have elsewhere shown,[8] I recognize that Christ was called Messiah especially with respect to, and by virtue of, his kingship. Yet his anointings as prophet and as priest have their place and must not be overlooked by us. Isaiah specifically mentions the former in these words: "The Spirit of the Lord Jehovah is upon me, because Jehovah has anointed me to preach to the humble, . . . to bring healing to the brokenhearted, to proclaim liberation to the captives . . . , to proclaim the year of the Lord's good pleasure," etc. [Isa. 61:1–2; cf. Luke 4:18]. We see that he was anointed by the Spirit to be herald and witness of the Father's grace. And that not in the common way—for he is distinguished from other teachers with a similar office. On the other hand, we must note this: he received anointing, not only for himself that he might carry out the office of teaching, but for his whole body that the power of the Spirit might be present in the continuing preaching of the gospel. This, however, remains certain: the perfect doctrine he has brought has made an end to all prophecies. All those, then, who, not content with the gospel, patch it with something extraneous to it, detract from Christ's authority. The Voice that thundered from heaven, "This is my beloved Son; . . . hear him" [Matt. 17:5; cf. Matt. 3:17], exalted him by a singular privilege beyond the rank of all others. Then this anointing was diffused from the Head to the members, as Joel had foretold: "Your sons shall prophesy and your daughters . . . shall see visions," etc. [Joel 2:28 p.]. But when Paul says that He was given to us as our wisdom [I Cor. 1:30], and in another place, "In him are hid all the treasures of knowledge and understanding" [Col. 2:3 p.], he has a slightly different meaning. That is, outside Christ there is nothing worth knowing, and all who by faith perceive what he is like have grasped the whole immensity of heavenly benefits. For this reason, Paul writes in another passage: "I decided to know nothing precious . . . except Jesus Christ and him crucified" [I Cor. 2:2 p.]. This is very true, because it is not lawful to go beyond the simplicity of the gospel. And the prophetic dignity in Christ leads us to know that in the sum of doctrine as he has given it to us all parts of perfect wisdom are contained.

(ii. The kingly office—its spiritual character, 3–5)
3. The eternity of Christ's dominion
   [e]I come now to kingship. It would be pointless to speak of this without first warning my readers that it is spiritual in nature. For from this we infer its efficacy and benefit for us, as well as

[8] II. vi. 3.

its whole force and eternity. Now this eternity, which the angel in The Book of Daniel attributes to the person of Christ [Dan. 2:44], in the Gospel of Luke the angel justly applies to the salvation of the people [Luke 1:33]. But this eternity is also of two sorts or must be considered in two ways: the first pertains to the whole body of the church; the second belongs to each individual member. We must refer to the first kind the statement in The Psalms: "Once for all I have sworn by my holiness; I will not lie to David. His line shall endure forever, his throne as long as the sun before me. Like the moon, it shall be established forever; the witness of heaven is sure" [Ps. 89:35–37 p.]. God surely promises here that through the hand of his Son he will be the eternal protector and defender of his church. We find the true fulfillment of this prophecy in Christ alone, inasmuch as immediately after Solomon's death the authority over the greater part of the kingdom was destroyed, and—to the shame of the family of David—was transferred to a private person [I Kings, ch. 12].[9] Afterward it diminished more and more until it came to a sad and shameful end [II Kings, ch. 24].

Isaiah's exclamation means the same thing: "As for his generation, who will tell it?" [Isa. 53:8 p.]. For he declares that Christ will so survive death as to bind himself with his members. Therefore, whenever we hear of Christ as armed with eternal power, let us remember that the perpetuity of the church[10] is secure in this protection. Hence, amid the violent agitation with which it is continually troubled, amid the grievous and frightful storms that threaten it with unnumbered calamities, it still remains safe. David laughs at the boldness of his enemies who try to throw off the yoke of God and his Anointed, and says: "The kings and people rage in vain . . . , for he who dwells in heaven is strong enough to break their assaults" [Ps. 2:2, 4 p.]. Thus he assures the godly of the everlasting preservation of the church, and encourages them to hope, whenever it happens to be oppressed. Elsewhere, speaking in the person of God, David says: "Sit at

---

9 Calvin apparently has in mind the defection of the ten tribes to Jeroboam (I Kings, ch. 12) and the disasters recorded in II Kings, ch. 24. Cf. CR XXXVIII. 401, 409.

10 The perpetuity of the true church in the world is a constituent element in the Reformed doctrine of the church. See Heppe RD, p. 664; McNeill, "The Church in Post-Reformation Reformed Theology," *Journal of Religion* XXIV (1944), 102 f. K. Barth, in *Kirchliche Dogmatik* I. ii. 771–774, has urgently affirmed the preservation of the church as associated with the perpetual reviving power of the Word, effecting a divine *creatio continua*, so that without the Scripture the church "would dissolve at once into nothingness." (Tr. G. T. Thomson, *Doctrine of the Word of God*. I. ii. 688–691.)

my right hand, till I make your enemies your footstool" [Ps. 110: 1]. Here he asserts that, no matter how many strong enemies plot to overthrow the church, they do not have sufficient strength to prevail over God's immutable decree by which he appointed his Son eternal King. Hence it follows that the devil, with all the resources of the world, can never destroy the church, founded as it is on the eternal throne of Christ.

Now with regard to the special application of this to each one of us—the same "eternity" ought to inspire us to hope for blessed immortality. For we see that whatever is earthly is of the world and of time, and is indeed fleeting. Therefore Christ, to lift our hope to heaven, declares that his "kingship is not of this world" [John 18:36]. In short, when any one of us hears that Christ's kingship is spiritual, aroused by this word let him attain to the hope of a better life; and since it is now protected by Christ's hand, let him await the full fruit of this grace in the age to come.

4. The blessing of Christ's kingly office for us

ᵉWe have said that we can perceive the force and usefulness of Christ's kingship only when we recognize it to be spiritual. This is clear enough from the fact that, while we must figh throughout life under the cross, our condition is harsh and wretched.[11] What, then, would it profit us to be gathered under the reign of the Heavenly King, unless beyond this earthly life we were certain of enjoying its benefits? For this reason we ought to know that the happiness promised us in Christ does not consist in outward advantages—such as leading a joyous and peaceful life, having rich possessions, being safe from all harm, and abounding with delights such as the flesh commonly longs after. No, our happiness belongs to the heavenly life! In the world the prosperity and well-being of a people depend partly on an abundance of all good things and domestic peace, partly on strong defenses that protect them from outside attacks. In like manner, Christ enriches his people with all things necessary for the eternal salvation of souls and fortifies them with courage to stand unconquerable against all the assaults of spiritual enemies. ᵉ⁽ᵇ⁾From this we infer that he rules—ᵉinwardly and outwardly—ᵉ⁽ᵇ⁾more for

---

[11] A characteristic statement. Cf. Comm. Matt. 25:34: "The life of the godly is nothing but an exile full of sorrow and misery," amid which, however, the Lord gives them "a fortified and buoyant spirit that they may be able to overcome the odds against them." Similar statements abound in Calvin's works. Some examples are given in McNeill, *The History and Character of Calvinism*, pp. 222 f.

our own sake than his. ᵉHence we are furnished, as far as God knows to be expedient for us, with the gifts of the Spirit, which we lack by nature. By these first fruits we may perceive that we are truly joined to God in perfect blessedness. Then, relying upon the power of the same Spirit, let us not doubt that we shall always be victorious over the devil, the world, and every kind of harmful thing. This is the purport of Christ's reply to the Pharisees: because the Kingdom of God is within us, it will not come with observation [Luke 17:21, 20]. Probably because he professed himself King under whom God's highest blessing was to be expected, the Pharisees jestingly asked Christ to furnish his tokens. But he enjoined them to enter into their own consciences, because "the Kingdom of God . . . is righteousness and peace and joy in the Holy Spirit" [Rom. 14:17]. This he did to prevent those otherwise too much inclined to things earthly from indulging in foolish dreams of pomp. These words briefly teach us what Christ's Kingdom confers upon us. ᵉ⁽ᵇ⁾For since it is not earthly or carnal and hence subject to corruption, but spiritual, it lifts us up even to eternal life.

ᵉThus it is that we may patiently pass through this life with its misery, hunger, cold, contempt, reproaches, and other troubles —content with this one thing: that our King will never leave us destitute, but will provide for our needs until, our warfare ended, we are called to triumph. Such is the nature of his rule, that he shares with us all that he has received from the Father. ᵇNow he arms and equips us with his power, adorns us with his beauty and magnificence, enriches us with his wealth.[12] ᵉ⁽ᵇ⁾These benefits, then, give us the most fruitful occasion to glory, and also provide us with confidence to struggle fearlessly against the devil, sin, and death. Finally, clothed with his righteousness, we can valiantly rise above all the world's reproaches; and just as he himself freely lavishes his gifts upon us, so may we, in return, bring forth fruit to his glory.

5. The spiritual nature of his kingly office: the sovereignty of Christ and of the Father

ᵉ⁽ᵇ⁾Therefore the anointing of the king is not with oil or aromatic unguents. Rather, he is called "Anointed" [*Christus*] of God because "the spirit of wisdom and understanding, the spirit of counsel and might . . . and of the fear of the Lord have rested upon him" [Isa. 11:2 p.]. This is "the oil of gladness" with which the psalm proclaims he "was anointed above his fellows" [Ps. 45:7], for if such excellence were not in him, all of us

[12] Cf. *"Spirituales eius divitiae,"* sec. 5.

would be needy and hungry. As has already been said,[13] he did not enrich himself for his own sake, but that he might pour out his abundance upon the hungry and thirsty. The Father is said "not by measure to have given the Spirit to his Son" [John 3:34 p.]. The reason is expressed as follows: "That from his fullness we might all receive grace upon grace" [John 1:16 p.]. From this fountain flows that abundance of which Paul speaks: "Grace was given to each believer according to the measure of Christ's gift" [Eph. 4:7]. These statements quite sufficiently confirm what I have said: that Christ's Kingdom lies in the Spirit, not in earthly pleasures or pomp. Hence we must forsake the world if we are to share in the Kingdom.

A visible symbol of this sacred anointing was shown in Christ's baptism, when the Spirit hovered over him in the likeness of a dove [John 1:32; Luke 3:22]. e(b/a)It is nothing new, and ought not to seem absurd that the Spirit and his gifts are designated by the word "anointing" [I John 2:20, 27]. For it is only in this way that we are invigorated. Especially with regard to heavenly life, there is no drop of vigor in us save what the Holy Spirit instills. For the Spirit has chosen Christ as his seat, that from him might abundantly flow the heavenly riches of which we are in such need. The believers stand unconquered through the strength of their king, and his spiritual riches abound in them. Hence they are justly called Christians.

ePaul's statement does not detract from this eternity of which we have spoken:[14] "Then . . . he will deliver the Kingdom to his God and Father" [I Cor. 15:24]. Likewise: "The Son himself will . . . be subjected . . . that God may be all in all." [I Cor. 15:28, cf. Vg.] He means only that in that perfect glory the administration of the Kingdom will not be as it now is. e(b/a)The Father has given all power to the Son that he may by the Son's hand govern, nourish, and sustain us, keep us in his care, and help us. Thus, while for the short time we wander away from God, Christ stands in our midst, to lead us little by little to a firm union with God.

eAnd surely, to say that he sits at the right hand of the Father is equivalent to calling him the Father's deputy, who has in his possession the whole power of God's dominion. For God mediately, so to speak, wills to rule and protect the church in Christ's person. Paul explains in the first chapter of the letter to the Ephesians that Christ was placed "at the right hand of the Father" to be the "Head of the church, . . . which is Christ's body" [vs. 20–23 p.]. He means the same thing when he teaches in another

13 Sec. 2, above.
14 Sec. 3, above.

place: "God . . . has bestowed upon him the name which is above every name, that at the name of Jesus every knee should bow . . . and every tongue confess what is to the glory of God the Father" [Phil. 2:9–11 p.]. In these words Paul also commends the order in the Kingdom of Christ as necessary for our present weakness. Thus Paul rightly infers: God will then of himself become the sole Head of the church, since the duties of Christ in defending the church will have been accomplished. e(b/a)For the same reason, Scripture usually calls Christ "Lord" because the Father set Christ over us to exercise his dominion through his Son. e(b)Although there are many lordships celebrated in the world [cf. I Cor. 8:5], "for us there is one God, the Father, from whom are all things and we in him, and one Lord, Jesus Christ, through whom are all things and we through him" [I Cor. 8:6, cf. Vg.], says Paul. From this we duly infer that he is the same God who through the mouth of Isaiah declared himself to be king and lawgiver of the church [Isa. 33:22]. For even though [the Son] consistently calls all the power he holds "the benefit and gift of the Father," he merely means that he reigns by divine power. Why did he take the person of the Mediator? He descended from the bosom of the Father and from incomprehensible glory that he might draw near to us. All the more reason, then, is there that we should one and all resolve to obey, and to direct our obedience with the greatest eagerness to the divine will! Now Christ fulfills the combined duties of king and pastor for the godly who submit willingly and obediently; on the other hand, we hear that he carries a "rod of iron to break them and dash them all in pieces like a potter's vessel" [Ps. 2:9 p.]. We also hear that "he will execute judgment among the Gentiles, so that he fills the earth with corpses, and strikes down every height that opposes him" [Ps. 110:6 p.]. We see today several examples of this fact, but the full proof will appear at the Last Judgment, which may also be properly considered the last act of his reign.

(iii. The priestly office: reconciliation and intercession, 6)
6. eNow we must speak briefly concerning the purpose and use of Christ's priestly office: as a pure and stainless Mediator he is by his holiness to reconcile us to God. But God's righteous curse bars our access to him, and God in his capacity as judge is angry toward us. Hence, an expiation must intervene in order that Christ as priest may obtain God's favor for us and appease his wrath. Thus Christ to perform this office had to come forward with a sacrifice. For under the law, also, the priest was forbidden to enter the sanctuary without blood [Heb. 9:7], that believers

might know, even though the priest as their advocate stood between them and God, that they could not propitiate God unless their sins were expiated [Lev. 16:2–3]. The apostle discusses this point at length in The Letter to the Hebrews, from the seventh almost to the end of the tenth chapter. To sum up his argument: The priestly office belongs to Christ alone because by the sacrifice of his death he blotted out our own guilt and made satisfaction for our sins [Heb. 9:22]. God's solemn oath, of which he "will not repent," warns us what a weighty matter this is: "You are a priest forever after the order of Melchizedek" [Ps. 110:4; cf. Heb. 5:6; 7:15]. God undoubtedly willed in these words to ordain the principal point on which, he knew, our whole salvation turns. For, as has been said, we or our prayers have no access to God unless Christ, as our High Priest, having washed away our sins, sanctifies us and obtains for us that grace from which the uncleanness of our transgressions and vices debars us. Thus we see that we must begin from the death of Christ in order that the efficacy and benefit of his priesthood may reach us.

It follows that he is an everlasting intercessor: through his pleading we obtain favor. Hence arises not only trust in prayer, but also peace for godly consciences, while they safely lean upon God's fatherly mercy and are surely persuaded that whatever has been consecrated through the Mediator is pleasing to God. Although God under the law commanded animal sacrifices to be offered to himself, in Christ there was a new and different order, in which the same one was to be both priest and sacrifice. This was because no other satisfaction adequate for our sins, and no man worthy to offer to God the only-begotten Son, could be found. ᵉ⁽ᵇ/ᵃ⁾Now, Christ plays the priestly role, not only to render the Father favorable and propitious toward us by an eternal law of reconciliation, but also to receive us as his companions in this great office [Rev. 1:6]. For we who are defiled in ourselves, yet are priests in him,[15] offer ourselves and our all to God, and freely enter the heavenly sanctuary that the sacrifices of prayers and praise that we bring may be acceptable and sweet-smelling before God. ᵉ⁽ᵇ⁾This is the meaning of Christ's statement: "For their sake I sanctify myself" [John 17:19]. For we, imbued with his holiness in so far as he has consecrated us to the Father with himself, although we would otherwise be loathsome to him, please him as pure and clean—and even as holy. ᵉThis is why the sanctuary was anointed, as mentioned in Daniel [Dan. 9:24]. We must

---

[15] Calvin's utterances specifically on the priesthood of believers are rare and unsystematic, although in treatment of other topics he gives to that doctrine substantially the content given to it by Luther.

note the contrast between this anointing and that shadow anointing which was then in use. It is as if the angel had said, "When the shadows have been dispelled the true priesthood will shine forth in Christ." The more detestable is the fabrication of those who, not content with Christ's priesthood, have presumed to sacrifice him anew! The papists attempt this each day, considering the Mass as the sacrificing of Christ.

CHAPTER XVI

How Christ Has Fulfilled the Function of Redeemer to Acquire Salvation for Us. Here, Also, His Death and Resurrection Are Discussed, as Well as His Ascent Into Heaven

(Alienated by sin from God, who yet loved us, we are reconciled by Christ, 1–4)

1. The Redeemer

^{e(b/a)}What we have said so far concerning Christ must be referred to this one objective: condemned, dead, and lost in ourselves, we should seek righteousness, liberation, life, and salvation in him, as we are taught by that well-known saying of Peter: "There is no other name under heaven given to men in which we must be saved" [Acts 4:12]. The name "Jesus" was bestowed upon him not without reason or by chance, or by the decision of men, but it was brought from heaven by an angel, the proclaimer of the supreme decree.[1] The reason for it is added: he was sent to "save the people from their sins" [Matt. 1:21; cf. Luke 1:31]. We must note in these words what we have touched upon elsewhere:[2] the office of Redeemer was laid upon him that he might be our Savior. ^eStill, our redemption would be imperfect if he did not lead us ever onward to the final goal of salvation. Accordingly, the moment we turn away even slightly from him, our salvation, which rests firmly in him, gradually vanishes away. As a result, all those who do not repose in him voluntarily deprive themselves of all grace. Bernard's admonition is worth remembering: "The name of Jesus is not only light but also food; it is also oil, without which all food of the soul is dry; it is salt, without whose seasoning whatever is set before us is insipid; finally, it is honey in the mouth, melody in the ear, rejoicing in

[1] The "decree" of salvation proclaimed in the angel's message to Mary, Luke 1:28–33.
[2] II. vi. 1.

the heart, and at the same time medicine. Every discourse in which his name is not spoken is without savor."[3]

But here we must earnestly ponder how he accomplishes salvation for us. This we must do not only to be persuaded that he is its author, but to gain a sufficient and stable support for our faith, rejecting whatever could draw us away in one direction or another. No one can descend into himself[4] and seriously consider what he is without feeling God's wrath and hostility toward him. Accordingly, he must anxiously seek ways and means to appease God—and this demands a satisfaction. No common assurance is required, for God's wrath and curse always lie upon sinners until they are absolved of guilt. Since he is a righteous Judge, he does not allow his law to be broken without punishment, but is equipped to avenge it.

2. *The awareness of God's wrath makes us thankful for his loving act in Christ*

eBut, before we go any farther, we must see in passing how fitting it was that God, who anticipates us by his mercy, should have been our enemy until he was reconciled to us through Christ. For how could he have given in his only-begotten Son a singular pledge of his love to us if he had not already embraced us with his free favor? Since, therefore, some sort of contradiction arises here, I shall dispose of this difficulty. cThe Spirit usually speaks in this way in the Scriptures: "God was men's enemy until they were reconciled to grace by the death of Christ" [Rom. 5: 10 p.]. "They were under a curse until their iniquity was atoned for by his sacrifice." [Gal. 3:10, 13 p.] "They were estranged from God until through his body they were reconciled." [Col. 1:21–22 p.] Expressions of this sort have been accommodated to our capacity that we may better understand how miserable and ruinous our condition is apart from Christ. For if it had not been clearly stated that the wrath and vengeance of God and eternal death rested upon us, we would scarcely have recognized how miserable we would have been without God's mercy, and we would have underestimated the benefit of liberation.

For example, suppose someone is told: "If God hated you while you were still a sinner, and cast you off, as you deserved, a terrible destruction would have awaited you. But because he kept you in grace voluntarily, and of his own free favor, and did not allow you to be estranged from him, he thus delivered

---

[3] Bernard, *Sermons on the Song of Songs* xv. 6 (MPL. 183. 340 f.; tr. S. J. Eales, *Life and Work of St. Bernard* IV. 83 f.).

[4] Cf. I. i. 2; I. v. 3, and notes appended to these passages.

you from that peril." This man then will surely experience and feel something of what he owes to God's mercy. On the other hand, suppose he learns, as Scripture teaches, that he was estranged from God through sin, is an heir of wrath, subject to the curse of eternal death, excluded from all hope of salvation, beyond every blessing of God, the slave of Satan, captive under the yoke of sin, destined finally for a dreadful destruction and already involved in it; and that at this point Christ interceded as his advocate, took upon himself and suffered the punishment that, from God's righteous judgment, threatened all sinners; that he purged with his blood those evils which had rendered sinners hateful to God; that by this expiation he made satisfaction and sacrifice duly to God the Father; that as intercessor he has appeased God's wrath; that on this foundation rests the peace of God with men; that by this bond his benevolence is maintained toward them. Will the man not then be even more moved by all these things which so vividly portray the greatness of the calamity from which he has been rescued?[5]

To sum up: since our hearts cannot, in God's mercy, either seize upon life ardently enough or accept it with the gratefulness we owe, unless our minds are first struck and overwhelmed by fear of God's wrath and by dread of eternal death, we are taught by Scripture to perceive that apart from Christ, God is, so to speak, hostile to us, and his hand is armed for our destruction; to embrace his benevolence and fatherly love in Christ alone.

*3. God's wrath against unrighteousness; his love precedes our reconciliation in Christ**

cAlthough this statement is tempered to our feeble comprehension, it is not said falsely. For God, who is the highest righteousness, cannot love the unrighteousness that he sees in us all. All of us, therefore, have in ourselves something deserving of God's hatred. With regard to our corrupt nature and the wicked life that follows it, all of us surely displease God, are guilty in his sight, and are born to the damnation of hell.[6] But because the Lord wills not to lose what is his in us, out of his own kindness he still finds something to love. However much we may be

---

[5] The conception of the atonement as effectual through man's response to God's love revealed in Christ's death (a view usually associated with Abailard's name) seems momentarily suggested in this sentence. But Calvin's thought is not Abailard's. E. Brunner has justly stressed Calvin's adherence to the substitutionary doctrine of Anselm: *The Mediator* (tr. O. Wyon), pp. 438 f., 458, 507.

[6] "Gehennae."

sinners by our own fault, we nevertheless remain his creatures.
However much we have brought death upon ourselves, yet he
has created us unto life. Thus he is moved by pure and freely
given love of us to receive us into grace. Since there is a perpetual
and irreconcilable disagreement between righteousness and unrighteousness, so long as we remain sinners he cannot receive us
completely. Therefore, to take away all cause for enmity and to
reconcile us utterly to himself, he wipes out all evil in us by the
expiation set forth in the death of Christ; that we, who were
previously unclean and impure, may show ourselves righteous
and holy in his sight. Therefore, by his love God the Father goes
before and anticipates our reconciliation in Christ. Indeed, "because he first loved us" [I John 4:19], he afterward reconciles
us to himself. But until Christ succors us by his death, the unrighteousness that deserves God's indignation remains in us, and
is accursed and condemned before him. Hence, we can be fully
and firmly joined with God only when Christ joins us with him.
If, then, we would be assured that God is pleased with and
kindly disposed toward us, we must fix our eyes and minds on
Christ alone. For actually, through him alone we escape the
imputation of our sins to us—an imputation bringing with it
the wrath of God.

*4. The work of atonement derives from God's love; therefore
it has not established the latter*

cFor this reason, Paul says that the love with which God embraced us "before the creation of the world" was established
and grounded in Christ [Eph. 1:4–5]. These things are plain and
in agreement with Scripture, and beautifully harmonize those
passages in which it is said that God declared his love toward us
in giving his only-begotten Son to die [John 3:16]; and, conversely, that God was our enemy before he was again made favorable to us by Christ's death [Rom. 5:10]. But to render these
things more certain among those who require the testimony of
the ancient church, I shall quote a passage of Augustine where
the very thing is taught: "God's love," says he, "is incomprehensible and unchangeable. For it was not after we were reconciled
to him through the blood of his Son that he began to love us.
Rather, he has loved us before the world was created, that we
also might be his sons along with his only-begotten Son—before
we became anything at all. The fact that we were reconciled
through Christ's death must not be understood as if his Son
reconciled us to him that he might now begin to love those
whom he had hated. Rather, we have already been reconciled

to him who loves us, with whom we were enemies on account of sin. The apostle will testify whether I am speaking the truth: 'God shows his love for us in that while we were yet sinners Christ died for us' [Rom. 5:8]. Therefore, he loved us even when we practiced enmity toward him and committed wickedness. Thus in a marvelous and divine way he loved us even when he hated us. For he hated us for what we were that he had not made; yet because our wickedness had not entirely consumed his handiwork, he knew how, at the same time, to hate in each one of us what we had made, and to love what he had made."[7] [d]These are Augustine's words.

(The effects of the obedience and death of Christ, 5–7)
5. Christ has redeemed us through his obedience, which he practiced throughout his life
[e(b/a)]Now someone asks, How has Christ abolished sin, banished the separation between us and God, and acquired righteousness to render God favorable and kindly toward us? To this we can in general reply that he has achieved this for us by the whole course of his obedience.[8] This is proved by Paul's testimony: "As by one man's disobedience many were made sinners, so by one man's obedience we are made righteous" [Rom. 5:19 p.]. In another passage, to be sure, Paul extends the oasis of the pardon that frees us from the curse of the law to the whole life of Christ: "But when the fullness of time came, God sent forth his Son, born of woman, subject to the law, to redeem those who were under the law" [Gal. 4:4–5]. Thus in his very baptism, also, he asserted that he fulfilled a part of righteousness in obediently carrying out his Father's commandment [Matt. 3:15]. In short, from the time when he took on the form of a servant, he began to pay the price of liberation in order to redeem us.

Yet to define the way of salvation more exactly, Scripture ascribes this as peculiar and proper to Christ's death. He declares that "he gave his life to redeem many" [Matt. 20:28 p.]. Paul teaches that "Christ died for our sins" [Rom. 4:25 p.]. John the Baptist proclaimed that he came "to take away the sins of the world," for he was "the Lamb of God" [John 1:29 p.]. In another passage Paul teaches that "we are freely justified through the

---

[7] Augustine, *John's Gospel* cx. 6 (MPL 35. 1923 f.; tr. NPNF VII. 411).
[8] Pannier remarks that the clause "born of the Virgin Mary," which seems the most supernaturalist article of the Creed, serves Calvin mainly as an attestation not of the divinity, but of the humanity of Christ, of his incorporation in Adam's race. (Pannier, *Institution* II. 382, note *a* on p. 98.) See also T. F. Torrance, *The School of Faith*, Introduction, pp. lxxx f.

redemption which is in Christ, because he was put forward as a reconciler in his blood" [Rom. 3:24–25 p.]. Likewise: "We are . . . justified by his blood . . . and reconciled . . . through his death." [Rom. 5:9–10.] Again: "For our sake he who knew no sin was made sin, so that in him we might become the righteousness of God." [II Cor. 5:21.] I shall not pursue all the testimonies, for the list would be endless, and many of them will be referred to in their order. For this reason the so-called "Apostles' Creed" passes at once in the best order from the birth of Christ to his death and resurrection, wherein the whole of perfect salvation consists. Yet the remainder of the obedience that he manifested in his life is not excluded. Paul embraces it all from beginning to end: "He emptied himself, taking the form of a servant, . . . and was obedient to the Father unto death, even death on a cross" [Phil. 2:7–8 p.]. And truly, even in death itself his willing obedience is the important thing because a sacrifice not offered voluntarily would not have furthered righteousness. Therefore, when the Lord testified that he "laid down his life for his sheep" [John 10:15 p.], he aptly added, "No one takes it from me" [John 10:18]. In this sense Isaiah says, "Like a sheep that before its shearer was dumb" [Isa. 53:7; cf. Acts 8:32]. And the Gospel history relates that he went forth and met the soldiers [John 18:4], and that before Pilate he did not defend himself, but stood to submit to judgment [Matt. 27:12, 14]. Not, indeed, without a struggle; for he had taken upon himself our weaknesses, and in this way the obedience that he had shown to his Father had to be tested! And here was no common evidence of his incomparable love toward us: to wrestle with terrible fear, and amid those cruel torments to cast off all concern for himself that he might provide for us. And we must hold fast to this: that no proper sacrifice to God could have been offered unless Christ, disregarding his own feelings, subjected and yielded himself wholly to his Father's will. On this point the apostle appropriately quotes this testimony from a psalm: "It is written of me in the Book of the Law [Heb. 10:7] . . . 'that I am to do thy will, O God [Heb. 10:9]. I will it, and thy law is in the midst of my heart' [Ps. 39:9, Vg.]. Then I said, 'Lo, I come'" [Heb. 10:7]. But because trembling consciences find repose only in sacrifice and cleansing by which sins are expiated, we are duly directed thither; and for us the substance of life is set in the death of Christ.

(*The condemnation through Pilate*)

e(b/a)The curse caused by our guilt was awaiting us at God's heavenly judgment seat. Accordingly, Scripture first relates

Christ's condemnation before Pontius Pilate, governor of Judea, to teach us that the penalty to which we were subject had been imposed upon this righteous man. ᵉWe could not escape God's dreadful judgment. To deliver us from it, Christ allowed himself to be condemned before a mortal man—even a wicked and profane man. ᵉ⁽ᵇ⁾For the title "prefect"[9] is mentioned, not only to affirm the faithfulness of the history, but that we may learn what Isaiah teaches: "Upon him was the chastisement of our peace, and with his stripes we are healed" [Isa. 53:5]. To take away our condemnation, it was not enough for him to suffer any kind of death: to make satisfaction for our redemption a form of death had to be chosen in which he might free us both by transferring our condemnation to himself and by taking our guilt upon himself. ᵇIf he had been murdered by thieves or slain in an insurrection by a raging mob, in such a death there would have been no evidence of satisfaction. But when he was arraigned before the judgment seat as a criminal, accused and pressed by testimony, and condemned by the mouth of the judge to die—we know by these proofs that he took the role of a guilty man and evildoer. Here we must note two things that had been foretold by the oracles of the prophets, and which greatly comfort and confirm our faith. When we hear that Christ was led from the judge's seat to death, and hanged between thieves, we possess the fulfillment of the prophecy to which the Evangelist referred: "He was reckoned among the transgressors" [Mark 15:28, Vg.; cf. Isa. 53:12]. Why so? Surely that he might die in the place of the sinner, not of the righteous or innocent man. For he suffered death not because of innocence but because of sin. On the other hand, when we hear that he was acquitted by the same lips that condemned him (for Pilate was more than once compelled to give public testimony to his innocence [e.g., Matt. 27:23]), there should come to mind the utterance of another prophet: that he repaid what he did not steal [Ps. 69:4]. Thus we shall behold the person of a sinner and evildoer represented in Christ, yet from his shining innocence it will at the same time be obvious that he was burdened with another's sin rather than his own. He therefore suffered under Pontius Pilate, and by the governor's official sentence was reckoned among criminals. Yet not so—for he was declared righteous by his judge at the same time, when Pilate affirmed that he "found no cause for complaint in him" [John 18:38]. ᵉThis is our acquittal: the guilt that held us liable for punishment has been transferred to the head of the Son of

---

[9] "*Nomen praefecti.*" Cf. "*praeside Judaeae,*" above. Pilate's title, however, was "*procurator Judaeae*"

God [Isa. 53:12]. We must, above all, remember this substitution, lest we tremble and remain anxious throughout life—as if God's righteous vengeance, which the Son of God has taken upon himself, still hung over us.

6. "Crucified"

ᵇThe form of Christ's death also embodies a singular mystery. ᵇ⁽ᵃ⁾The cross was accursed, not only in human opinion but by decree of God's law [Deut. 21:23]. Hence, when Christ is hanged upon the cross, he makes himself subject to the curse. It had to happen in this way in order that the whole curse—which on account of our sins awaited us, or rather lay upon us—might be lifted from us, while it was transferred to him. ᵇThis was also foreshadowed in the law. Now the sacrifices and expiations offered for sins were called "Ashmoth,"[10] a Hebrew word properly signifying sin itself. By using this term figuratively the Holy Spirit intended to intimate that these were like sacrifices of purification,[11] which take upon themselves and bear the curse due for sins. What was figuratively represented in the Mosaic sacrifices is manifested in Christ, the archetype of the figures. Therefore, to perform a perfect expiation, he gave his own life as an *Asham*,[12] that is, as an expiatory offering for sin, as the prophet calls it [Isa. 53:10; cf. v. 5], upon which our stain and punishment might somehow be cast, and cease to be imputed to us. The apostle testifies this more openly when he teaches: "For our sake he who knew no sin was made sin by the Father, so that in him we might be made the righteousness of God" [II Cor. 5:21]. The Son of God, utterly clean of all fault, nevertheless took upon himself the shame and reproach of our iniquities, and in return clothed us with his purity. It seems that Paul meant the same thing when he says of sin, "He condemned sin in his flesh" [Rom. 8:3 p.]. The Father destroyed the force of sin when the curse of sin was transferred to Christ's flesh. ᶜHere, then, is the meaning of this saying: Christ was offered to the Father in death as an expiatory sacrifice that when he discharged all satisfaction through his sacrifice, we might cease to be afraid of God's wrath. ᵇNow it is clear what the prophet's utterance means: "The Lord has laid on him the iniquity of us all" [Isa. 53:6]. That is, he who was about to cleanse the filth of those iniquities was covered with them by transferred imputation. The cross, to which he was nailed, was a symbol of this, as the apostle testifies: "Christ

---

[10] "אשמות"
[11] "καθαρμάτων."
[12] "אשם"

redeemed us from the curse of the law, when he became a curse
for us. For it is written, 'Cursed be every one who hangs on a
tree,' that in Christ the blessing of Abraham might come upon
the Gentiles" [Gal. 3:13–14; Deut. 21:23]. ᵉPeter means the same
thing when he teaches: "He himself bore our sins . . . on the
tree" [I Peter 2:24], because from the very symbol of the curse
we more clearly understand that the burden with which we had
been oppressed was laid upon him. ᵇYet we must not understand
that he fell under a curse that overwhelmed him; rather—in taking the curse upon himself—he crushed, broke, and scattered its
whole force. Hence faith apprehends an acquittal in the condemnation of Christ, a blessing in his curse. ᵉPaul with good reason,
therefore, magnificently proclaims the triumph that Christ obtained for himself on the cross, as if the cross, which was full of
shame, had been changed into a triumphal chariot! For he says
that "Christ nailed to the cross the written bond which stood
against us . . . and disarmed the principalities . . . and made a
public example of them" [Col. 2:14–15 p.]. And no wonder! For
"Christ . . . through the eternal Spirit offered himself," as another
apostle testifies[13] [Heb. 9:14]. From this came that transmutation
of nature. But that these things may take root firmly and deeply
in our hearts, let us keep sacrifice and cleansing constantly in
mind. For we could not believe with assurance that Christ is
our redemption, ransom, and propitiation[14] unless he had been
a sacrificial victim. Blood is accordingly mentioned wherever
Scripture discusses the mode of redemption. Yet Christ's shed
blood served, not only as a satisfaction, but also as a laver [cf.
Eph. 5:26; Titus 3:5; Rev. 1:5] to wash away our corruption.

7. "Dead and buried"

ᵉThere follows in the Creed: "He was dead and buried."
ᵇHere again is to be seen how he in every respect took our place
to pay the price of our redemption. Death held us captive under
its yoke; Christ, in our stead, gave himself over to its power to
deliver us from it. So the apostle understands it when he writes:
"He tasted death for everyone" [Heb. 2:9 p.]. By dying, he en-
sured that we would not die, or—which is the same thing—redeemed us to life by his own death. He differed from us, however, in this respect: he let himself be swallowed up by death, as

---

[13] Using the term "the apostle," Calvin seems momentarily to accept Paul's
authorship of Hebrews, which he elsewhere repeatedly denies. Cf. Comm.
Heb., "Argument," and ch. 13:23.

[14] "ἀπολύτρωσιν καὶ ἀντίλυτρον καὶ ἱλαστήριον." Cf. Luke 21:28; Rom. 3:24; Col.
1:14; I Tim. 2:6; Heb. 9:5; Heb. 11:35.

it were, not to be engulfed in its abyss, but rather b(a)to engulf it
[cf. I Peter 3:22, Vg.] that must soon have engulfed us; he let
himself be subjected to it, not to be overwhelmed by its power,
but rather to lay it low, when it was threatening us and exulting
over our fallen state. Finally, his purpose was "that through death
he might destroy him who had the power of death, that is, the
devil, and deliver all those who through fear of death were subject to lifelong bondage" [Heb. 2:14–15]. bThis is the first fruit
that his death brought to us.

The second effect of Christ's death upon us is this: by our
participation in it, his death mortifies our earthly members so
that they may no longer perform their functions; and it kills the
old man in us that he may not flourish and bear fruit. b(a)Christ's
burial has the same effect: we ourselves as partakers in it are
buried with him to sin. bThe apostle teaches that "we have been
united with Christ in the likeness of his death" [Rom. 6:5, KJV],
and "buried with him . . . into the death" of sin [Rom. 6:4]; that
"by his cross the world has been crucified to us, and we to the
world" [Gal. 2:19; 6:14 p.]; that we have died together with him
[Col. 3:3]. By these statements Paul not only exhorts us to exhibit an example of Christ's death but declares that there inheres
in it an efficacy which ought to be manifest in all Christians, unless
they intend to render his death useless and unfruitful.

Therefore, in Christ's death and burial a twofold blessing is
set forth for us to enjoy: liberation from the death to which we
had been bound, and mortification of our flesh.

(Explanation of the doctrine of the descent into hell, 8–12)
8. *"Descended into hell"*
eBut we ought not to omit his descent into hell, a matter of
no small moment in bringing about redemption. e(b/a)Now it appears from the ancient writers that this phrase which we read in
the Creed was once not so much used in the churches.[15] Nevertheless, in setting forth a summary of doctrine a place must be
given to it, as it contains the useful and not-to-be-despised mystery
of a most important matter. bAt least some of the old writers do

---

[15] Calvin here follows Erasmus' *Explanation of the Apostles' Creed* (1533),
published with the Basel edition of his works, *Omnia Opera D. Erasmi*
(Basel, 1540) V. 967 f. On the late appearance of this doctrine and its incorporation in the Creed, see especially A. Vacant and E. Mangenot, *Dictionnaire de théologie Catholique,* article "Descent de Jesus aux enfers,"
Vol. IV. One of the earliest references to it is in the unorthodox "Dated
Creed" of the synod held at Nice in Thrace 359, as given by Socrates, *Ecclesiastical History* ii. 37 (MPG 67. 280; tr. Ayer, *Source Book,* p. 318; H. Bettenson, *Documents of the Christian Church,* p. 61).

not leave it out.[16] From this we may conjecture that it was inserted after a time, and did not become customary in the churches at once, but gradually. This much is certain: that it reflected the common belief of all the godly; for there is no one of the fathers who does not mention in his writings Christ's descent into hell, though their interpretations vary. But it matters little by whom or at what time this clause was inserted. Rather, the noteworthy point about the Creed is this: we have in it a summary of our faith, full and complete in all details; and containing nothing in it except what has been derived from the pure Word of God. ᶜIf any persons have scruples about admitting this article into the Creed,[17] ᵉ⁽ᵇ⁾it will soon be made plain how important it is to the sum of our redemption: if it is left out, much of the benefit of Christ's death will be lost. ᵇOn the other hand, there are some who think that nothing new is spoken of in this article, but that it repeats in other words what had previously been said of his burial, the word "hell" often being used in Scripture to denote a grave.[18] I grant that what they put forward concerning the meaning of the word is true: "hell" is frequently to be understood as "grave." But two reasons militate against their opinion, and readily persuade me to disagree with them. How careless it would have been, when something not at all difficult in itself has been stated with clear and easy words, to indicate it again in words that obscure rather than clarify it! Whenever two expressions for the same thing are used in the same context, the latter ought to be an explanation of the former. But what sort of explanation will it be if one says that "Christ was buried" means that "he descended into hell"? Secondly, it is not likely that a useless repetition of this sort could have crept into this summary,

---

[16] The topic is omitted by Augustine in his sermon to catechumens on the Creed (De symbolo ad catechumenos) (MPL 40. 627–656; tr. NPNF III. 369–375). The descent into hell had been called in question or rejected by some bold theologians before Calvin. Reginald Pecock presented a revision of the Creed in 1440, omitting this article. Cf. J. Lewis, Life of the Learned and Right Reverend Reynold Pecock, pp. 210, 221–225, 316, 325.

[17] The insertion of this sentence in 1559 may have been occasioned by a revival of criticism of the article. In a letter written by John à Lasco to Bullinger, June 17, 1553, it is stated that Walter Deloenus, a minister of the church of the German refugees in London, had proposed its omission as "a plant that the Lord hath not planted" (cf. Matt. 15:13). Though under rebuke he had acknowledged his fault, harmful discussion had arisen (À Lasco, Opera, ed. A. Kuyper, II. 677 f.). Cf. OS III, Addenda, p. 517, and on Deloenus (Devlin or Delvin), see Original Letters Relative to the English Reformation, edited for The Parker Society II. 575, 588.

[18] This view was held by Bucer (Enarrationes in Evangelia, 1536, pp. 511 f., 792 ff.) and apparently by Beza.

in which the chief points of our faith are aptly noted in the fewest possible words. I have no doubt that all who have weighed this matter with some care will readily agree with me.

9. Christ in the nether world?

e(b/a)Others interpret it differently: that Christ descended to the souls of the patriarchs who had died under the law, to announce redemption as accomplished and to free them from the prison where they were confined.[19] To back up this interpretation, they wrongly adduce evidence from a psalm: "He shatters the doors of bronze and . . . the bars of iron" [Ps. 107:16]. Likewise, from Zechariah: "He will redeem the captives from the waterless pit" [ch. 9:11 p.]. But the psalm foretells the liberation of those who are cast into bondage in far-off countries; Zechariah, moreover, compares the Babylonian disaster, into which the people had been cast, to a deep, dry pit or abyss, and at the same time teaches that the salvation of the whole church is a release from the nether depths. Thus, it has happened in some way or other that later generations thought it to be a place under the earth, to which they gave the name "Limbo."[20] aBut this story, although it is repeated by great authors, and even today is earnestly defended as true by many persons,[21] still is nothing but a story. eIt is childish to enclose the souls of the dead in a prison. What need, then, for Christ's soul to go down there to release them?

e(b/a)I readily admit that Christ shone upon them with the power of his Spirit, enabling them to realize that the grace which they had only tasted in hope was then manifested to the world.[22] In this way the passage in Peter can probably be explained wherein he says: "Christ came and preached to the spirits

[19] Aquinas, *Summa Theol.* III. lii. 5: "When Christ descended into hell, by the power of his Passion he delivered the saints from this penalty whereby they were excluded from the life of glory. . . ."

[20] Aquinas, in *Summa Theol.* III. Supplementum lxix. 4–7, examines questions on the *limbus patrum*, distinguishing it (Art. 6) from the *limbus puerorum*. The fathers were detained *in limbo* until delivered by Christ, and were thus in hope and in a state of rest, while the children in limbo "have no hope of the blessed life." Cf. A. Vacant and E. Mangenot, *Dictionnaire de théologie Catholique*, article "Limbes."

[21] Cf. Irenaeus, *Against Heresies* IV. ii; V. xxxi (MPG 7. 976 ff., 1068 ff.; tr. ANF I. 463 f., 504 f.). Servetus, *Christianismi restitutio*, pp. 621 f. (first letter of Servetus to Calvin, also in CR VIII. 682 f.); Peter Martyr Vermigli, *Loci communes* III. xvi. 8.

[22] Perhaps a reference to Zwingli, *Exposition of the Faith*, section on "Christ the Lord" (Zwingli, *Opera*, ed. M. Schuler and J. Schulthess, IV. 49; tr. LCC XXIV. 252). Cf. the treatment of the descent into hell by Peter Martyr, *Loci communes* III: "Simple Exposition of the Articles of the Creed" 20 and III. xvi. 8–25 (1576 edition, pp. 476, 814–825).

who were in a 'watchtower'—commonly rendered 'prison' " [I Peter 3:19, cf. Vg.]. The context leads us to suppose that believers who died before that time shared the same grace with us. For Peter extols the power of Christ's death in that it penetrated even to the dead; while godly souls enjoyed the present sight of that visitation which they had anxiously awaited. On the other hand, the wicked realized more clearly that they were excluded from all salvation. Now, while Peter does not clearly distinguish between the godly and the ungodly, we are not therefore to understand that he mixes them indiscriminately. He only means to teach that both groups have a common awareness of Christ's death.

10. The "descent into hell" as an expression of the spiritual torment that Christ underwent for us

ᶜBut ᵇwe must seek a surer explanation, apart from the Creed, ᶜof Christ's descent into hell. ᵇThe explanation given to us in God's Word is not only holy and pious, but also full of wonderful consolation. If Christ had died only a bodily death, it would have been ineffectual. ᵇ⁽ᵃ⁾No—it was expedient at the same time for him to undergo the severity of God's vengeance, to appease his wrath and satisfy his just judgment. For this reason, he must also grapple hand to hand with the armies of hell and the dread of everlasting death.[23] A little while ago[24] we referred to the prophet's statement that "the chastisement of our peace was laid upon him," "he was wounded for our transgressions" by the Father, "he was bruised for our infirmities" [Isa. 53:5 p.]. By these words he means that Christ was put in place of evildoers as surety and pledge—submitting himself even as the accused—

---

[23] Cf. secs. 8, 9, notes 17 and 20, above. Calvin first suggests this conception of the descent into hell in *Psychopannychia* (1534, published 1542: CR V. 224; tr. Calvin, *Tracts* III. 628). The prevailing interpretation of this article of the Creed was that of Aquinas, who gave some firmness to this doctrine after the rather unsystematic treatment of it by Lombard and Albertus Magnus. See *Summa Theol.* III. lii. 2, 4–6, 8. Calvin's explanation is not, as Pannier states, "entirely original" (Pannier, *Institution* II. 383, note *a* on p. 107). Nicolas of Cusa (e.g., in Sermon on Ps. 30:11), followed by Pico della Mirandola, had similarly explained the *descensus* in terms of Christ's agony. Luther adopted the view that Christ, as God and man, literally entered into hell. The Catechism of the Council of Trent, sec. 49, following Aquinas, states that Christ liberated the (Old Testament) fathers and other pious men from imprisonment in limbo. For the complicated history of discussions concerning this article, see J. A. Dietelmeier, *Historia de descensu Christi ad inferos literaria*, esp. pp. 160–191, and the sources there cited.

[24] Sec. 5, above.

to bear and suffer all the punishments that they ought to have sustained. All—with this one exception: "He could not be held by the pangs of death" [Acts 2:24 p.]. No wonder, then, if he is said to have descended into hell, for he suffered the death that God in his wrath had inflicted upon the wicked! ᵉThose who— on the ground that it is absurd to put after his burial what preceded it—say that the order is reversed in this way are making a very trifling and ridiculous objection.[25] The point is that the Creed sets forth what Christ suffered in the sight of men, and then appositely speaks of that invisible and incomprehensible judgment which he underwent in the sight of God in order that we might know not only that Christ's body was given as the price of our redemption, but that he paid a greater and more excellent price in suffering in his soul the terrible torments of a condemned and forsaken man.

11. Defense of this explanation from Scripture passages

ᵉIn this sense Peter says: "Christ arose, having loosed the pangs of death, because it was not possible for him to be held or conquered by them" [Acts 2:24 p.]. Peter does not simply name death, but expressly states that the Son of God had been laid hold of by the pangs of death that arose from God's curse and wrath—the source of death. For what a small thing it would have been to have gone forward with nothing to fear and, as if in sport, to suffer death! But this was a true proof of his boundless mercy, that he did not shun death, however much he dreaded it. There is no doubt that the apostle means the same thing when he writes in The Letter to the Hebrews: Christ "was heard for his . . . fear" [Heb. 5:7 p.]. (Others render it "reverence" or "piety,"[26] but how inappropriately is evident from the fact itself, as well as the form of speaking.) Christ, therefore, "praying with tears and loud cries, . . . is heard for his . . . fear" [Heb. 5:7 p.]; he does not pray to be spared death, but he prays not to be swallowed up by it as a sinner because he there bore our nature. ᵇAnd surely no more terrible abyss can be conceived than to feel yourself forsaken and estranged from God; and when you call upon him, not to be heard. It is as if God himself had plotted your ruin. We see that Christ was so cast down ᵃas to be compelled to cry out

---

[25] Calvin's explanation of the descent into hell as consisting of Christ's redemptive agony on the cross had been ridiculed by Sebastian Castellio, as is indicated in a letter of Calvin to Viret, March, 1544 (CR XI. 688; tr. Calvin, *Letters* I. 409). Apparently Castellio held the view here rejected. Cf. CR XI. 675; Herminjard, *Correspondance* IX. 158, 185.

[26] Vulgate: *"Exauditus est pro sua reverentia."*

in deep anguish: "My God, my God, why hast thou forsaken me?" [Ps. 22:1; Matt. 27:46]. ᵇNow some would have it that he was expressing the opinion of others rather than his own feeling.[27] This is not at all probable, for his words clearly were drawn forth from anguish deep within his heart. ᵇ⁽ᵃ⁾Yet we do not suggest that God was ever inimical or angry toward him. ᵃHow could he be angry toward his beloved Son, "in whom his heart reposed" [cf. Matt. 3:17]? How could Christ by his intercession appease the Father toward others, if he were himself hateful to God? This is what we are saying: he bore the weight of divine severity, since he was "stricken and afflicted" [cf. Isa. 53:5] by God's hand, and experienced all the signs of a wrathful and avenging God. ᵇTherefore Hilary reasons: by his descent into hell we have obtained this, that death has been overcome. In other passages he does not differ from our view, as when he says: "The cross, death, hell—these are our life." In another place: "The Son of God is in hell, but man is borne up to heaven."[28] ᵉAnd why do I quote the testimony of a private individual when the apostle, recalling this fruit of victory, asserts the same thing, that they were "delivered who through fear of death were subject to lifelong bondage"? [Heb. 2:15 p.]. He had, therefore, to conquer that fear which by nature continually torments and oppresses all mortals. This he could do only by fighting it. Now it will soon be more apparent that his was no common sorrow or one engendered by a light cause. ᵇTherefore, by his wrestling hand to hand with the devil's power, with the dread of death, with the pains of hell, he was victorious and triumphed over them, that in death we may not now fear those things which our Prince has swallowed up [cf. I Peter 3:22, Vg.].

12. Defense of the doctrine against misunderstandings and errors
ᵉHere certain untutored wretches, impelled more by malice than by ignorance, cry out that I am doing a frightful injustice to Christ. For they hold it incongruous for him to fear for the salvation of his soul. Then they stir up a harsher slander: that I attribute to the Son of God a despair contrary to faith.[29] First,

---

[27] Cyril, *De recta fide*, Oratio ii. 18 (MPG 76. 1555 ff.).
[28] Hilary, *On the Trinity* IV. xlii ("*mortem in inferno perimens*"); III. xv ("*Dei filius in inferis est; sed homo refertur ad coelum*") (MPL 10. 128, 24; tr. NPNF 2 ser. IX. 84, 66).
[29] See sec. 8, note 17; sec. 10, note. 25, above. Barth and Niesel hold it improbable that in this passage Calvin is refuting a criticism by Castellio. Although they know of no explanation in opposition to Calvin's view other than Castellio's, they would not exclude the possibility that the charges here dealt with were those of some Lutheran critic. (OS III. 497, note 1.)

these men wickedly raise a controversy over Christ's fear and dread, which the Evangelists so openly relate. For before the hour of death approached, "he was troubled in spirit" [John 13:21] and stricken with grief, and when it came upon him, he began to tremble more intensely with fear [cf. Matt. 26:37]. To say that he was pretending—as they do—is a foul evasion. We must with assurance, therefore, confess Christ's sorrow, as Ambrose rightly teaches, unless we are ashamed of the cross.[30] And surely, unless his soul shared in the punishment, he would have been the Redeemer of bodies alone. But he had to struggle to lift up those who lay prostrate. His goodness—never sufficiently praised—shines in this: he did not shrink from taking our weaknesses upon himself. Hence, it in nowise detracts from his heavenly glory. From this also arises the comfort for our anguish and sorrow that the apostle holds out to us: that this Mediator has experienced our weaknesses the better to succor us in our miseries [Heb. 4:15a].

They claim that it is unworthy to attribute to Christ something evil of itself. As if they were wiser than God's Spirit, who harmonizes these two things! "Christ in every respect has been tempted as we are, yet without sinning." [Heb. 4:15b.] There is no reason why Christ's weakness should alarm us. For he was not compelled by violence or necessity, but was induced purely by his love for us and by his mercy to submit to it. But all that he voluntarily suffered for us does not in the least detract from his power. These detractors are, moreover, deceived in this one point: they do not recognize in Christ a weakness pure and free of all vice and stain because he held himself within the bounds of obedience. Our fallen nature, whose violent and turbulent emotions know no bounds, is without moderation. Hence, our opponents wrongly measure the Son of God by that standard. But since he was uncorrupted, a moderation that restrained excess flourished in all his emotions. Hence, he could be like us [cf. Heb. 2:17] in sor-

The topic had come into discussion in England through the rejection of the article in a disputation at Cambridge by Christopher Carlisle, 1552 (Dietelmeier, *op. cit.*, pp. 205 ff.). Carlisle's discourse was published in 1582: *Touching the Descension of Our Savior Christ Into Hell*. A year later, as we have seen, the German refugee church in London was disturbed by the similar views of one of its ministers (sec. 8, note 17, above). See also Herminjard, *Correspondance* IX. 158, note 3; CR XI. 675. Later Robert Parkes resumed the attack with reference to Art. 3 of the Thirty-nine Articles, calling forth a reply by the Calvinist Andrew Willet (*Limbomastix*, 1607).

[30] Ambrose, *Exposition of Luke's Gospel* x. 56–62 (MPL 15. 1910 ff.).

row, fear, and dread, yet in such a way as to differ from us by this characteristic.

Our opponents, refuted, jump to another misrepresentation: although Christ feared death, he did not fear God's curse and wrath, from which he knew himself to be safe. But let godly readers consider how honorable it would be for Christ to have been more unmanly and cowardly than most men of the common sort! Thieves and other wrongdoers arrogantly hasten to death; many despise it with haughty courage; others bear it calmly. What sort of constancy or greatness would it have been for the Son of God to be stricken and almost stupefied with the dread of death? Something commonly considered miraculous was related about him: from the fierceness of his torment, drops of blood flowed from his face [Luke 22:44]. And he did not do this as a show for others' eyes, since he groaned to his Father in secret. This banishes all doubt: he had to have angels descend from heaven to encourage him by their unaccustomed consolation [Luke 22:43]. What shameful softness would it have been (as I have said) for Christ to be so tortured by the dread of common death as to sweat blood, and to be able to be revived only at the appearance of angels? What? Does not that prayer, coming from unbelievable bitterness of heart and repeated three times—"Father, if it be possible, let this cup pass from me" [Matt. 26:39]—show that Christ had a harsher and more difficult struggle than with common death?

From this it appears that these quibblers with whom I am contending boldly chatter about things they know nothing of. For they have never earnestly considered what it is or means that we have been redeemed from God's judgment. Yet this is our wisdom: duly to feel how much our salvation cost the Son of God.

Suppose someone should now ask whether Christ descended into hell when he prayed that death be averted.[31] I reply: this was the beginning from which we may gather what harsh and dreadful torments he suffered, when he knew that he stood accused before God's judgment seat for our sake. Although the divine power of his Spirit remained hidden for a moment to give place to weakness of flesh, we must know that the trial arising from the feeling of pain and fear was not contrary to faith. And in this way the statement in Peter's sermon was fulfilled: "He could not be held by the pangs of death" [Acts 2:24 p.]. For feeling himself, as it were, forsaken by God, he did not waver in the least from trust in his goodness. This is proved by that remarkable prayer to God in which he cried out in acute agony: "My God,

31 The reference is apparently to an opinion of Castellio's: cf. sec. 10, note 25.

my God, why hast thou forsaken me?" [Matt. 27:46]. For even though he suffered beyond measure, he did not cease to call him his God, by whom he cried out that he had been forsaken. Now this refutes the error of Apollinaris, as well as that of the so-called Monothelites. Apollinaris claimed that Christ had an eternal spirit instead of a soul, so that he was only half a man.[32] As if he could atone for our sins in any other way than by obeying the Father! But where is inclination or will to obey except in the soul? We know that it was for this reason that his soul was troubled: to drive away fear and bring peace and repose to our souls. Against the Monothelites,[33] we see that he did not will as man what he willed according to his divine nature, I pass over the fact that, with a contrary emotion, he overcame the fear of which we have spoken. This plainly appears to be a great paradox: " 'Father, save me from this hour'? No, for this purpose I have come to this hour. Father, glorify thy name" [John 12: 27–28]. Yet in his perplexity there was no extravagant behavior such as is seen in us when we strive mightily to control ourselves.

(Christ's resurrection, ascension, and heavenly session, 13–16)
13. "On the third day he rose again from the dead"
eNext comes the resurrection from the dead. Without this what we have said so far would be incomplete. bFor since only weakness appears in the cross, death, and burial of Christ, faith must leap over all these things to attain its full strength. We have in his death the complete fulfillment of salvation, for through it we are reconciled to God, his righteous judgment is satisfied, the curse is removed, and the penalty paid in full. Nevertheless, we are said to "have been born anew to a living hope" not through his death but "through his resurrection" [I Peter 1:3 p.]. For as he, in rising again, came forth victor over death, so the victory of our faith over death lies in his resurrection alone.[34] Paul's words

---

[32] Apollinaris of Laodicea taught (ca. 360) that the divine Logos "dwelt as soul in the body received from the Virgin Mary" (Lietzmann). See C. E. Raven, *Apollinarianism*, and H. Lietzmann, *From Constantine to Julian* (*A History of the Early Church*, Vol. III), pp. 209 f.

[33] The Monothelites arose in the seventh century in attempts to resolve the Monophysite schism. Whereas Monophysites taught one nature only in Christ, thus rejecting the definition of Chalcedon (451), the Monothelites, on the basis of the compromising Ecthesis of the Emperor Heraclius (638), admitted two natures but only one energy or will (θέλημα). Their doctrine was explicitly rejected in the Third Council of Constantinople, 681, session 13. (Mansi XI. 1054; Ayer, *Source Book*, pp. 671 f.; Bettenson, *Documents of the Christian Church*, p. 130.)

[34] Pannier calls attention here to the victorious note in Calvinist piety from its view of the resurrection, and quotes *Instruction et confession de foy*

better express its nature: "He was put to death for our sins, and raised for our justification" [Rom. 4:25]. This is as if he had said: "Sin was taken away by his death; righteousness was revived and restored by his resurrection." For how could he by dying have freed us from death if he had himself succumbed to death? How could he have acquired victory for us if he had failed in the struggle? Therefore, we divide the substance of our salvation between Christ's death and resurrection as follows: through his death, sin was wiped out and death extinguished; through his resurrection, righteousness was restored and life raised up, so that—thanks to his resurrection—his death manifested its power and efficacy in us. ᵉTherefore, Paul states that "Christ was declared the Son of God . . . in the resurrection itself" [Rom. 1:4 p.], because then at last he displayed his heavenly power, which is both the clear mirror of his divinity and the firm support of our faith. Elsewhere Paul similarly teaches: "He suffered in weakness of the flesh, but rose again by the power of the Spirit" [II Cor. 13:4 p.]. In the same sense Paul elsewhere discusses perfection: "That I may know him and the power of his resurrection." Yet immediately thereafter he adds, "The fellowship of his death" [Phil. 3:10 p.]. With this Peter's statement closely agrees: "God raised him from the dead and gave him glory so that our faith and hope might be in God" [I Peter 1:21 p.]. Not that faith, supported by his death, should waver, but that the power of God, which guards us under faith, is especially revealed in the resurrection itself.

So then, let us remember that whenever mention is made of his death alone, we are to understand at the same time what belongs to his resurrection. Also, the same synecdoche applies to the word "resurrection": whenever it is mentioned separately from death, we are to understand it as including what has to do especially with his death. But because by rising again he obtained the victor's prize—that there might be resurrection and life—Paul rightly contends that "faith is annulled and the gospel empty and deceiving if Christ's resurrection is not fixed in our hearts" [I Cor. 15:17 p.]. Accordingly, in another passage—after glorying in the death of Christ against the terrors of damnation—he adds by way of emphasis: surely "he who was dead has risen, and appears before God as our mediator" [Rom. 8:34 p.].

ᵇFurther, as we explained above that the mortification of our flesh depends upon participation in his cross,[35] so we must under-

(1537). See OS I. 402; Fuhrmann, *Instruction in Faith*, p. 50; Pannier, *Institution* III. 383, notes *b* and *c* on p. 108.
[35] Sec. 7, above.

stand that we obtain a corresponding benefit from his resurrection. [b(a)]The apostle says: "We were engrafted in the likeness of his death, so that sharing in his resurrection we might walk in newness of life" [Rom. 6:4 p.]. [b]Hence, in another passage, from the fact that we have died with Christ [Col. 3:3] he derives proof that we must mortify our members that are upon the earth [cf. Col. 3:5]. So he also infers from our rising up with Christ that we must seek those things above, not those on the earth [Col. 3:1–2]. By these words we are not only invited through the example of the risen Christ to strive after newness of life; but [b(a)]we are taught that we are reborn into righteousness through his power.

We also receive a third benefit from his resurrection: we are assured of our own resurrection by receiving a sort of guarantee substantiated by his. [e]Paul deals with this at greater length in I Cor. 15:12–26.

[b(a)]We must, by the way, note that he is said "to have risen from the dead." These words express the truth of his death and resurrection, as if it were said: he suffered the same death that other men naturally die; and received immortality in the same flesh that, in the mortal state, he had taken upon himself.

14. "Ascended into heaven"

[e]To the resurrection is quite appropriately joined the ascent into heaven. [b]Now having laid aside the mean and lowly state of mortal life and the shame of the cross, Christ by rising again began to show forth his glory and power more fully. Yet he truly inaugurated his Kingdom only at his ascension into heaven. The apostle shows this when he teaches that Christ "ascended . . . that he might fill all things" [Eph. 4:10, cf. Vg.]. [e]Despite the apparent contradiction, Paul shows that there is a remarkable agreement. For Christ left us in such a way that his presence might be more useful to us—a presence that had been confined in a humble abode of flesh so long as he sojourned on earth. Therefore John, after he related that notable invitation, "If any one thirst, let him come to me," etc. [John 7:37], added that "the Spirit had not yet been given" to believers, "for Jesus had not yet been glorified" [John 7:39]. The Lord himself also testified this to his disciples: "It is expedient for you that I go away; for if I do not go away, the Holy Spirit will not come" [John 16:7 p.]. He consoles them for his bodily absence, saying that he will not leave them orphans, but will come to them again in an invisible but more desirable way [cf. John 14:18–19; 16:14]. For they were then taught by a surer experience that the authority he

wielded and the power he exercised were sufficient for believers not only to live blessedly but also to die happily. ᵇIndeed, we see how much more abundantly he then poured out his Spirit, how much more wonderfully he advanced his Kingdom, how much greater power he displayed both in helping his people and in scattering his enemies. ᵇ⁽ᵃ⁾Carried up into heaven, therefore, he withdrew his bodily presence from our sight [Acts 1:9], not to cease to be present with believers still on their earthly pilgrimage, but to rule heaven and earth with a more immediate power. But by his ascension he fulfilled what he had promised: that he would be with us even to the end of the world. ᵇAs his body was raised up above all the heavens, so his power and energy were diffused and spread beyond all the bounds of heaven and earth. ᶜI prefer to explain this in Augustine's words rather than my own: "Christ was to go by death to the right hand of the Father, whence he should come to judge the living and the dead. This he would do in bodily presence, according to pure doctrine and the rule of faith. For his spiritual presence with them was to come after his ascension."[36] Elsewhere he expresses it more fully and clearly: "According to ineffable and invisible grace what he has said will be fulfilled: 'Lo, I am with you always, even to the end of the world' [Matt. 28:20]. According to the flesh that the Word took upon himself, according to the fact that he was born of the virgin, according to the fact that he was seized by the Jews, fastened to a tree, taken down from a cross, wrapped with linen, laid in a sepulcher, manifested in the resurrection, these words were fulfilled: 'You will not always have me with you' [Matt. 26:11]. Why? Because he went about in the flesh for forty days with his disciples, and while they were in his company, seeing him but not following him, he ascended into heaven [Acts 1:3, 9], and is not here: for there 'he sits at the right hand of the Father' [Mark 16:19]; yet he is here, for the presence of majesty has not withdrawn [cf. Heb. 1:3]. Therefore, we always have Christ according to the presence of majesty; but of his physical presence it was rightly said to his disciples, 'You will not always have me with you' [Matt. 26:11]. For the church had him in his bodily presence for a few days; now it holds him by faith, but does not see him with the eyes."[37]

15. "Seated at the right hand of the Father"

ᵇConsequently, these words come immediately after: "Seated

---

[36] The words quoted roughly correspond to separate sentences in Augustine, *John's Gospel* lxxviii. 1 (MPL 35. 1835; tr. NPNF VII. 340 f.).
[37] Augustine, *John's Gospel* l. 13 (MPL 35. 1763; tr. NPNF VII. 282).

at the right hand of the Father." The comparison is drawn from kings who have assessors at their side to whom they delegate the tasks of ruling and governing. ᵇ⁽ᵃ⁾So it was said that Christ, in whom the Father wills to be exalted and through whose hand he wills to reign, was received at God's right hand. This is as if it were said that Christ was invested with lordship over heaven and earth, and solemnly entered into possession of the government committed to him—ᵇand that he not only entered into possession once for all, but continues in it, until he shall come down on Judgment Day. For the apostle so expounds it when he states: "The Father made him sit at his right hand . . . far above all rule and authority and power and dominion, and above every name that is named, not only in this age, but also in that which is to come" [Eph. 1:20–21; cf. Phil. 2:9]. ᵇ⁽ᵃ⁾Also, "He has put all things in subjection under his feet" [I Cor. 15:27] and "has made him the head over all things for the church" [Eph. 1:22]. You see the purpose of that "sitting": that both heavenly and earthly creatures may look with admiration upon his majesty, be ruled by his hand, obey his nod, and submit to his power. Here is what the apostles meant to teach when they often recalled it; all things were entrusted to his decision [Acts 2:30–36; 3:21; ch. 4; Heb. 1:8]. ᵇTherefore, they are wrong who think that it designates simply his blessedness. It makes no difference that in the book of The Acts, Stephen declares that he saw him standing [Acts 7:55]. For here it is a question, not of the disposition of his body, but of the majesty of his authority. Thus "to sit" means nothing else than to preside at the heavenly judgment seat.[38]

16. Benefits imparted to our faith by Christ's ascension*

ᵇ⁽ᵃ⁾From this our faith receives many benefits. First it understands that the Lord by his ascent to heaven opened the way into the Heavenly Kingdom, which had been closed through Adam [John 14:3]. Since he entered heaven in our flesh, as if in our name, it follows, as the apostle says, that in a sense we already "sit with God in the heavenly places in him" [Eph. 2:6], so that we do not await heaven with a bare hope, but in our Head already possess it.

Secondly, as faith recognizes, it is to our great benefit that Christ resides with the Father. For, having entered a sanctuary not made with hands, he appears before the Father's face as our constant advocate and intercessor [Heb. 7:25; 9:11–12; Rom. 8:34]. Thus he turns the Father's eyes to his own righteousness to avert his gaze from our sins. He so reconciles the Father's

[38] Augustine, Faith and the Creed vii. 14 (MPL 40. 188; tr. LCC VI. 360 f.).

heart to us that by his intercession he prepares a way and access for us to the Father's throne. He fills with grace and kindness the throne that for miserable sinners would otherwise have been filled with dread.

Thirdly, faith comprehends his might, in which reposes our strength, power, wealth, and glorying against hell. "When he ascended into heaven he led a captivity captive" [Eph. 4:8, cf. Vg.; cf. Ps. 68:18], and despoiling his enemies, he enriched his own people, and daily lavishes spiritual riches upon them. He therefore sits on high, transfusing us with his power, that he may quicken us to spiritual life, sanctify us by his Spirit, adorn his church with divers gifts of his grace, keep it safe from all harm by his protection, restrain the raging enemies of his cross and of our salvation by the strength of his hand, and finally hold all power in heaven and on earth. All this he does until he shall lay low all his enemies [I Cor. 15:25; cf. Ps. 110:1] (who are our enemies too) and complete the building of his church.[39] ᵉThis is the true state of his Kingdom; this is the power that the Father has conferred upon him, until, in coming to judge the living and the dead, he accomplishes his final act.

(Christ's future return in judgment, 17)
17. "From whence he shall come to judge the living and the dead"
ᵇChrist gives to his own people clear testimonies of his very present power. Yet his Kingdom lies hidden in the earth, so to speak, under the lowness of the flesh. It is right, therefore, that faith be called to ponder that visible presence of Christ which he will manifest on the Last Day. ᵇ⁽ᵃ⁾For he will come down from heaven in the same visible form in which he was seen to ascend [Acts 1:11; Matt. 24:30]. And he will appear to all with the ineffable majesty of his Kingdom, with the glow of immortality, with the boundless power of divinity, with a guard of angels. From thence we are commanded to await him as our Redeemer on that day when he will separate the lambs from the goats, the elect from the reprobate [Matt. 25:31–33]. No one—living or dead—shall escape his judgment. The sound of the trumpet will be heard from the ends of the earth, and by it all will be summoned before his judgment seat, both those still alive at that day and those whom death had previously taken from the company of the living [I Thess. 4:16–17].

ᵇThere are some who explain the words "the living and the dead" in another way. We see, of course, that some of the old

---

[39] Calvin eagerly looks for the glorious triumph of the church, but not in its earthly existence. Cf. Pannier, *Institution* II. 384, note *a* on p. 114.

writers were in doubt over how to explain this expression.[40] But as the meaning just set forth is plain and clear, it is far closer to the Creed, which obviously was written to be understood by the common people. And this does not disagree with Paul's statement: "It is appointed to all men to die once" [Heb. 9:27]. For even though those remaining in mortal life at the Last Judgment will not die in a natural way and order, yet the change that they will undergo, because it will be like death, is not inappropriately called "death." It is certain that "not all shall sleep, but . . . all shall be changed" [I Cor. 15:51]. What does this mean? Their mortal life will perish and be swallowed up "in a moment," and be transformed directly into a new nature [I Cor. 15:52]. No one would deny that this perishing of the flesh is death; yet it still remains true that living and dead will be called to judgment. "For the dead in Christ will rise first; then those who are alive, who are left, shall be caught up together with them . . . to meet the Lord in the air." [I Thess. 4:16–17.] Now it is quite likely that this expression was taken from the sermon of Peter that Luke relates [Acts 10:42], and from Paul's solemn protestation to Timothy [II Tim. 4:1].

(*Concluding remarks on the Apostles' Creed and the sufficiency of Christ, 18–19*)

18. The Judge is the—Redeemer!

ᵇHence arises a wonderful consolation: that we perceive judgment to be in the hands of him who has already destined us to share with him the honor of judging [cf. Matt. 19:28]! Far indeed is he from mounting his judgment seat to condemn us! How could our most merciful Ruler destroy his people? How could the Head scatter his own members? How could our Advocate condemn his clients? For if the apostle dares exclaim that with Christ interceding for us there is no one who can come forth to condemn us [Rom. 8:34, 33], it is much more true, then, that Christ as Intercessor will not condemn those whom he has received into his charge and protection. No mean assurance, this—that we shall be brought before no other judgment seat than that of our Redeemer, to whom we must look for our salvation![41] Moreover, he who now promises eternal blessedness through the gospel will then fulfill his promise in judgment. Therefore, by giving all judgment to the Son [John 5:22], the Father has honored him to the end that he may care for the consciences of his people, who tremble in dread of judgment.

---

[40] Augustine, *Faith and the Creed* viii. 15 (MPL 40. 188; tr. LCC VI. 361).
[41] Ambrose, *De Jacobo et vita beata* I. vi (MPL 14. 637 f.).

 ᶜThus far I have followed the order of the Apostles' Creed because it sums up in a few words the main points of our redemption, and thus may serve as a tablet for us upon which we see distinctly and point by point the things in Christ that we ought to heed. ᵇ⁽ᵃ⁾I call it the Apostles' Creed without concerning myself in the least as to its authorship. With considerable agreement, the old writers certainly attribute it to the apostles, holding it to have been written and published by the apostles in common, or to be a summary of teaching transmitted by their hands and collected in good faith, and thus worthy of that title. I have no doubt that at the very beginning of the church, in the apostolic age, it was received as a public confession by the consent of all—ᵇwherever it originated. It seems not to have been privately written by any one person, since as far back as men can remember it was certainly held to be of sacred authority among all the godly. We consider to be beyond controversy the only point that ought to concern us: that the whole history of our faith is summed up in it succinctly and in definite order, and that it contains nothing that is not vouched for by genuine testimonies of Scripture. This being understood, it is pointless to trouble oneself or quarrel with anyone over the author. Unless, perchance, it is not enough for one to have the certain truth of the Holy Spirit, without at the same time knowing either by whose mouth it was spoken or by whose hand it was written.⁴²

19. Christ alone in all the clauses of the Creedᵗ

 ᵃWe see that our whole salvation and all its parts are comprehended in Christ [Acts 4:12]. We should therefore take care not to derive the least portion of it from anywhere else. ᵇIf we seek salvation, we are taught by the very name of Jesus that it is "of him" [I Cor. 1:30]. If we seek any other gifts of the Spirit, they will be found in his anointing. If we seek strength, it lies in his dominion; if purity, in his conception; if gentleness, it appears in his birth. For by his birth he was made like us in all respects [Heb. 2:17] that he might learn to feel our pain [cf. Heb. 5:2]. If we seek redemption, it lies in his passion; if acquittal, in his condemnation; if remission of the curse, in his cross [Gal. 3:13]; if satisfaction, in his sacrifice; if purification, in his blood; if recon-

---

⁴² Prior to the Renaissance the Apostles' Creed was believed to have been composed by the apostles themselves. But Lorenzo Valla (ca. 1440) (*Contra calumniatores . . . apologia*, *Opera* 1540, p. 800) and Erasmus (*Ratio verae theologiae*, 1518, *Opera* 1540, V. 77) rejected the traditional view. See **Schaff**, *Creeds* I. **23**; F. Kattenbusch, *Das Apostolische Symbol* I. 1–15; OS III. 506 f.

ciliation, in his descent into hell; if mortification of the flesh, in his tomb; if newness of life, in his resurrection; if immortality, in the same; if inheritance of the Heavenly Kingdom, in his entrance into heaven; if protection, if security, if abundant supply of all blessings, in his Kingdom; if untroubled expectation of judgment, in the power given to him to judge. b(a)In short, since rich store of every kind of good abounds in him, let us drink our fill from this fountain, and from no other. bSome men, not content with him alone, are borne hither and thither from one hope to another; even if they concern themselves chiefly with him, they nevertheless stray from the right way in turning some part of their thinking in another direction. Yet such distrust cannot creep in where men have once for all truly known the abundance of his blessings.

cCHAPTER XVII

CHRIST RIGHTLY AND PROPERLY SAID TO HAVE MERITED GOD'S GRACE AND SALVATION FOR US

1. Christ's merit does not exclude God's free grace, but precedes it

eBy way of addition this question also should be explained. There are certain perversely subtle men[1] who—even though they confess that we receive salvation through Christ—cannot bear to hear the word "merit," for they think that it obscures God's grace. Hence, they would have Christ as a mere instrument or minister, not as the Author or leader and prince of life, as Peter calls him [Acts 3:15]. Indeed, I admit, if anyone would simply set Christ by himself over against God's judgment, there will be no place for merit. For no worthiness will be found in man to deserve God's favor. Indeed, as Augustine very truly writes: "The clearest light of predestination and grace is the Man Christ Jesus, the Savior, who brought this to pass by the human nature that was in him, through no preceding merits of works or of faith. Answer me, I beg of you, whence did that man deserve to be the only-begotten Son of God, and to be assumed into unity of person by the Word co-eternal with the Father? We must therefore

---

[1] Presumably referring to Laelius Socinus (d. 1562). See Calvin's *Responsio ad aliquot Laelii Socini quaestiones* (1555) (CR X. i. 160–165). The questions of Socinus are not extant but can be inferred from Calvin's replies. In the first of these replies Calvin states: "It is a common rule that things subordinate are not opposed. Therefore, there is nothing to prevent the free justification of men out of the mere mercy of God from being accompanied [*et simul interveniat*] by the merit of Christ."

recognize our Head as the very foundation of grace—a grace that is diffused from him through all his members according to the measure of each. Everyone is made a Christian from the beginning of his faith by the same grace whereby that Man from his beginning became the Christ."[2] Likewise, in another passage: "There is no more illustrious example of predestination than the Mediator himself. For he who made righteous this man of the seed of David, never to be unrighteous, without any merit of his will preceding, of unrighteous makes righteous those who are members of that Head,"[3] etc. In discussing Christ's merit, we do not consider the beginning of merit to be in him, but we go back to God's ordinance, the first cause. For God solely of his own good pleasure appointed him Mediator to obtain salvation for us.

Hence it is absurd to set Christ's merit against God's mercy. For it is a common rule that a thing subordinate to another is not in conflict with it. For this reason nothing hinders us from asserting that men are freely justified by God's mercy alone, and at the same time that Christ's merit, subordinate to God's mercy, also intervenes on our behalf. Both God's free favor and Christ's obedience, each in its degree, are fitly opposed to our works. Apart from God's good pleasure Christ could not merit anything; but did so because he had been appointed to appease God's wrath with his sacrifice, and to blot out our transgressions with his obedience. To sum up: inasmuch as Christ's merit depends upon God's grace alone, which has ordained this manner of salvation for us, it is just as properly opposed to all human righteousness as God's grace is.

2. *Scripture couples God's grace and Christ's merit*

eThis distinction is inferred from very many passages of Scripture. "God so loved the world that he gave his only-begotten Son, that whoever believes in him may not perish." [John 3:16.] We see how God's love holds first place, as the highest cause or origin; how faith in Christ follows this as the second and proximate cause. Suppose someone takes exception that Christ is only a formal cause. He then diminishes Christ's power more than the words just quoted bear out. For if we attain righteousness by a faith that reposes in him, we ought to seek the matter of our salvation in him. Many passages of Scripture clearly prove this. "Not that we first loved God, but that he first loved us, and sent his Son

---

[2] Augustine, *On the Predestination of the Saints* xv. 30, 31 (MPL 44. 981 f.; tr. NPNF V. 512).

[3] Augustine, *On the Gift of Perseverance* xxiv. 67 (MPL 45. 1034; tr. NPNF V. 552).

to be the propitiation[4] for our sins." [I John 4:10.] These words clearly demonstrate this fact: that nothing might stand in the way of his love toward us, God appointed Christ as a means of reconciling us to himself. The word "appeasing"[5] is very important. For, in some ineffable way, God loved us and yet was angry toward us at the same time, until he became reconciled to us in Christ. This is the import of all the following statements: "He is the expiation for our sins" [I John 2:2]. Again, "God was pleased . . . through him to reconcile to himself all things . . . making peace in relation to himself by the blood of his cross," etc. [Col. 1:19–20.] Again, "God was in Christ reconciling the world to himself, not counting men's sins against them." [II Cor. 5:19, cf. Comm. and Vg.] Again, "He . . . bestowed his grace on us in his beloved Son." [Eph. 1:6.] Again, "That he . . . might reconcile us both . . . in one man through the cross." [Eph. 2:15–16, cf. Vg.] The explanation of this mystery is to be sought in the first chapter of the letter to the Ephesians. There, after Paul has taught us that we were chosen in Christ, he adds at the same time that we acquired favor in the same Christ [Eph. 1:4–5]. How did God begin to embrace with his favor those whom he had loved before the creation of the world? Only in that he revealed his love when he was reconciled to us by Christ's blood. God is the fountainhead of all righteousness. Hence man, so long as he remains a sinner, must consider him an enemy and a judge. Therefore, the beginning of love is righteousness, as Paul describes it: "For our sake he made him to be sin who had done no sin, so that in him we might become the righteousness of God" [II Cor. 5:21]. This means: we, who "by nature are sons of wrath" [Eph. 2:3, cf. Vg.] and estranged from him by sin, have, by Christ's sacrifice, acquired free justification in order to appease God. But this distinction is also noted whenever Christ's grace is joined to God's love. From this it follows that Christ bestows on us something of what he has acquired. For otherwise it would not be fitting for this credit to be given to him as distinct from the Father, namely, that grace is his and proceeds from him.

3. The merit of Christ in the witness of Scripture

ᵉBy his obedience, however, Christ truly acquired and merited grace for us with his Father. Many passages of Scripture surely and firmly attest this. I take it to be a commonplace that if Christ made satisfaction for our sins, if he paid the penalty owed by us, if he appeased God by his obedience—in short, if as a righteous

---

[4] "ἱλασμόν."
[5] "Placatio."

man he suffered for unrighteous men—then he acquired salvation for us by his righteousness, which is tantamount to deserving it. But, as Paul says, "We were reconciled, and received reconciliation through his death" [Rom. 5:10–11 p.]. But reconciliation has no place except where an offense precedes it. The meaning therefore is: God, to whom we were hateful because of sin, was appeased by the death of his Son to become favorable toward us. And we must diligently note the antithesis that follows shortly thereafter. "As by one man's disobedience many were made sinners, so by one man's obedience many are made righteous." [Rom. 5:19.] This is the meaning: as by the sin of Adam we were estranged from God and destined to perish, so by Christ's obedience we are[5a] received into favor as righteous. The future tense of the verb does not exclude present righteousness, as is apparent from the context. For, as Paul had said previously, "the free gift[6] following many trespasses is unto justification" [Rom. 5:16].

4. The substitution of Christ

^eBut when we say that grace was imparted to us by the merit of Christ, we mean this: by his blood we were cleansed, and his death was an expiation for our sins. "His blood cleanses us from all sin." [I John 1:7.] "This is my blood . . . which is shed . . . for the forgiveness of sins." [Matt. 26:28; cf. Luke 22:20.] If the effect of his shedding of blood is that our sins are not imputed to us, it follows that God's judgment was satisfied by that price. On this point John the Baptist's words apply: "Behold, the Lamb of God, who takes away the sin of the world" [John 1:29]. For he sets Christ over against all the sacrifices of the law, to teach that what those figures showed was fulfilled in him alone. We know what Moses often says: "Iniquity will be atoned for, sin will be blotted out and forgiven" [cf. Ex. 34:7; Lev. 16:34]. In short, the old figures well teach us the force and power of Christ's death. And in The Letter to the Hebrews the apostle skillfully using this principle explains this point: "Without the shedding of blood there is no forgiveness of sins" [Heb. 9:22]. From this he concludes that "Christ has appeared once for all . . . to wipe out sin by the sacrifice of himself" [Heb. 9:26]. Again, "Christ was offered . . . to bear the sins of many" [Heb. 9:28]. He had previously said: "He entered once for all into the Holy Place not through the blood of goats and calves but through his own blood, thus securing an eternal redemption" [Heb. 9:12]. He now reasons on this wise: "If the blood of a heifer sanctifies unto the cleanness of the flesh, much more does the blood of Christ . . .

5a κατασταθήσονται [Rom. 5:19].

6 "χάρισμα."

cleanse your consciences from dead works" [Heb. 9:13–14 p.]. This readily shows that Christ's grace is too much weakened unless we grant to his sacrifice the power of expiating, appeasing, and making satisfaction. As he adds a little later: "He is the mediator of a new covenant, so that those who are called may receive the promised eternal inheritance, since a death has occurred meanwhile which redeems them from the preceding transgressions that remained under the law" [Heb. 9:15 p.].

It is especially worth-while to ponder the analogy set forth by Paul: "Christ . . . became a curse for us," etc. [Gal. 3:13]. It was superfluous, even absurd, for Christ to be burdened with a curse, unless it was to acquire righteousness for others by paying what they owed. Isaiah's testimony is also clear: "The chastisement of our peace was laid upon Christ, and with his stripes healing has come to us" [Isa. 53:5 p.]. For unless Christ had made satisfaction for our sins, it would not have been said that he appeased God by taking upon himself the penalty to which we were subject. The words that follow in the same passage agree with this: "I have stricken him for the transgression of my people" [Isa. 53:8 p.]. Let us add the interpretation of Peter, which will remove all uncertainty: "He . . . bore our sins . . . on the tree" [I Peter 2:24]. He is saying that the burden of condemnation, from which we were freed, was laid upon Christ.

5. Christ's death the price of our redemption

ᵉThe apostles clearly state that he paid the price to redeem us from the penalty of death, "being justified . . . by his grace through the redemption that is in Christ . . . , whom God put forward as a propitiation[7] through faith which is in his blood" [Rom. 3:24–25 p.]. Paul commends God's grace in this respect: for God has given the price of redemption in the death of Christ [Rom. 3:24]; then he bids us take refuge in Christ's blood, that having acquired righteousness we may stand secure before God's judgment [Rom. 3:25]. Peter's statement means the same thing: "You were ransomed . . . not with . . . silver and gold, but with the precious blood . . . of a lamb without blemish" [I Peter 1:18–19]. This comparison would not apply unless satisfaction had been made for our sins with this price. This is why Paul says that we "were bought with a price" [I Cor. 6:20]. His other statement also would not stand, "One mediator . . . who gave himself as a ransom"[8] [I Tim. 2:5–6], unless the penalty that we deserved had been cast upon him. For this reason the apostle defines the re-

7 "ἱλαστήριον."
8 "ἀντίλυτρον."

demption in Christ's blood as "the forgiveness of sins" [Col. 1:14]. It is as if he were saying, "We are justified or acquitted before God, because that blood corresponds to satisfaction for us." Another passage agrees with this: "In the cross he canceled the written bond which stood against us" [Col. 2:14 p.]. He notes there the payment or compensation that absolves us of guilt. And these words of Paul's are very weighty: "If we are justified through the works of the law, then Christ died for nothing" [Gal. 2:21 p.]. From this we infer that we must seek from Christ what the law would give if anyone could fulfill it; or, what is the same thing, that we obtain through Christ's grace what God promised in the law for our works: "He who will do these things, will live in them" [Lev. 18:5, cf. Comm.]. This is no less clearly confirmed in the sermon delivered at Antioch, which asserts that by believing in Christ "we are justified from everything from which we could not be justified by the law of Moses" [Acts 13:39; cf. Vg., ch. 13:38]. For if righteousness consists in the observance of the law, who will deny that Christ merited favor for us when, by taking that burden upon himself, he reconciled us to God as if we had kept the law? What he afterward taught the Galatians has the same purpose: "God sent forth his Son . . . subject to the law, to redeem those who were under the law" [Gal. 4:4–5 p.]. What was the purpose of this subjection of Christ to the law but to acquire righteousness for us, undertaking to pay what we could not pay? Hence, that imputation of righteousness without works which Paul discusses [Rom., ch. 4]. For the righteousness found in Christ alone is reckoned as ours. Surely the only reason why Christ's flesh is called "our food" [John 6:55] is that we find in him the substance of life. Now that power arises solely from the fact that the Son of God was crucified as the price of our righteousness. As Paul says, "Christ . . . gave himself up for us, a fragrant offering and sacrifice." [Eph. 5:2.] And in another place: "He was put to death for our sins and rose for our justification" [Rom. 4:25]. From this we conclude: not only was salvation given to us through Christ, but, by his grace the Father is now favorable to us. For there is no doubt that there is perfectly fulfilled in him what God declared through Isaiah in a figure: "I shall do this for my own sake and for the sake of my servant David" [Isa. 37:35 p.]. The apostle is the best witness of this when he says, "Your sins are forgiven for his name's sake" [I John 2:12]. For even though the name "Christ" is not mentioned, John designates him, as is his custom, by the pronoun αὐτός. The Lord also speaks in this sense: "As I live because of the Father, so . . . you too will live because of me" [John 6:57 p.]. Paul's statement accords with this: "It has been granted to you that for the sake of Christ[9] you should not only believe in him but also suffer for his sake" [Phil. 1:29].

6. Christ acquired no merit for himself

cBut to ask whether Christ merited anything for himself, as Lombard and the Schoolmen[10] do, is no less stupid curiosity than their temerity in making such a definition. What need was there for God's only Son to come down in order to acquire something new for himself? God, in setting forth his own plan, banishes all doubt. For it is said not that the Father provided, in his Son's merits, for the needs of the Son; but that he delivered him over to death, and "did not spare him" [Rom. 8:32] because he "loved the world" [John 3:16 p.; cf. Rom. 8:35, 37]. And we should note the prophets' expressions: "To us a child is born" [Isa. 9:6]. "Rejoice, . . . O daughter of Zion! . . . Lo, your king comes to you" [Zech. 9:9, cf. Comm.]. Also, that confirmation of love which Paul commends would otherwise be barren: that Christ suffered death for his enemies [cf. Rom. 5:10]. From this we conclude that he had no regard for himself; as he clearly affirms, "For their sake I sanctify myself" [John 17:19]. For he who gave away the fruit of his holiness to others testifies that he acquired nothing for himself. And this is indeed worth noting: to devote himself completely to saving us, Christ in a way forgot himself. But they absurdly apply Paul's testimony to this: "Therefore the Father has highly exalted him and bestowed on him the name," etc. [Phil. 2:9 p.].[11] By what merits, they ask, could a man become judge of the world and head of the angels, acquire God's supreme dominion, and have abiding in himself that majesty, when all the power and virtue of men and angels cannot attain even a thousandth part of it? But there is a ready and full answer: Paul is not there discussing the reason why Christ was exalted, but, for our example, is merely showing how Christ's exaltation follows his humiliation. And this means nothing else than what is said elsewhere: "It was necessary that the Christ should suffer . . . and so enter into the glory of the Father" [Luke 24:26 p.].

[9] "ὑπὲρ χριστοῦ."
[10] Lombard, *Sentences* III. xviii. 1 (MPL 192. 792 ff.); Aquinas, *Summa Theol.* III. lix. 3 (tr. English Dominican Fathers, *Summa Theol.* III. second number, pp. 455 f.). Bonaventura, *In sententias* III. xviii. 1, 2 (*Opera omnia,* ed. College of St. Bonaventura, III. 379 f.). Cf. Augustine, *John's Gospel* civ. 3 (MPL 35. 1903; tr. NPNF VII. 395).
[11] In the French text the misrepresentation is charged against the Sorbonnists.

BOOK THREE

THE WAY IN WHICH WE RECEIVE THE GRACE OF CHRIST: WHAT BENEFITS COME TO US FROM IT, AND WHAT EFFECTS FOLLOW

The Way in Which We Receive the Grace of Christ: What Benefits Come to Us from It, and What Effects Follow

ᶜCHAPTER I

THE THINGS SPOKEN CONCERNING CHRIST PROFIT US BY THE SECRET WORKING OF THE SPIRIT

1. The Holy Spirit as the bond that unites us to Christ

ᶜ⁽ᵃ⁾We must now examine this question. How do we receive those benefits which the Father bestowed on his only-begotten Son—not for Christ's own private use, but that he might enrich poor and needy men? First, we must understand that as long as Christ remains outside of us, and we are separated from him, all that he has suffered and done for the salvation of the human race remains useless and of no value for us. Therefore, to share with us what he has received from the Father, he had to become ours and to dwell within us. For this reason, he is called "our Head" [Eph. 4:15], and "the first-born among many brethren" [Rom. 8:29]. We also, in turn, are said to be "engrafted into him" [Rom. 11:17], and to "put on Christ" [Gal. 3:27]; for, as I have said, all that he possesses is nothing to us until we grow into one body with him. It is true that we obtain this by faith. Yet since we see that not all indiscriminately embrace that communion with Christ which is offered through the gospel, reason itself teaches us to climb higher and to examine into the secret energy of the Spirit, by which we come to enjoy Christ and all his benefits.

Earlier I discussed the eternal deity and essence of the Spirit.[1] Now let us be content with this particular point: that Christ so "came by water and blood" in order that the Spirit may witness concerning him [I John 5:6–7], lest the salvation imparted through him escape us. For, as three witnesses in heaven are named—the Father, the Word, and the Spirit—so there are three on earth: the water, the blood, and the Spirit [I John 5:7–8]. There is good reason for the repeated mention of the "testimony of the Spirit," a testimony we feel engraved like a seal upon our hearts, with the result that it seals the cleansing and sacrifice of Christ. For this reason, also, Peter says that believers have been "chosen in the sanctification of the Spirit unto obedience and sprinkling of the blood of Christ" [I Peter 1:2 p.]. By these words he explains that, in order that the shedding of his sacred blood may not be nullified, our souls are cleansed by the secret watering of the Spirit. For the same reason, also, Paul, in speaking of cleansing and justification, says that we come to possess both, "in the name of . . . Jesus Christ and in the Spirit of our God" [I Cor. 6:11]. To sum up, the Holy Spirit is the bond by which Christ effectually unites us to himself. To this, also, pertains what we taught in the previous book concerning his anointing.[2]

2. *How and why Christ was endowed with the Holy Spirit**

e(a)But, in order to get a clearer notion of this matter, so well worth investigating, we must bear in mind that Christ came endowed with the Holy Spirit in a special way: that is, to separate us from the world and to gather us unto the hope of the eternal inheritance. Hence he is called the "Spirit of sanctification" [cf. II Thess. 2:13; I Peter 1:2; Rom. 1:4] because he not only quickens and nourishes us by a general power that is visible both in the human race and in the rest of the living creatures, but he is also the root and seed of heavenly life in us. To the Kingdom of Christ, then, the prophets give the lofty title of the time when there will be a richer outpouring of the Spirit. There is a passage in Joel notable above all others: "And in that day I shall pour forth of my spirit upon all flesh" [ch. 2:28 p.]. For even if the prophet seems to restrict the gifts of the Spirit to the prophetic office, under this figure he signifies that, in manifesting his Spirit, God will make disciples of those who were previously destitute and empty of heavenly doctrine.

Further, God the Father gives us the Holy Spirit for his Son's sake, and yet has bestowed the whole fullness of the Spirit upon the Son to be minister and steward of his liberality. For this

[1] I. xiii. 14–15.
[2] II. xv. 2.

reason, the Spirit is sometimes called the "Spirit of the Father," sometimes the "Spirit of the Son."[3] Paul says: "You are not in the flesh, but in the spirit, if indeed the Spirit of God dwells in you. But if anyone does not have the Spirit of Christ, he is not his" [Rom. 8:9, cf. Vg.]. Hence, he arouses hope of a full renewal "because he who raised Christ from the dead will quicken our mortal bodies, because of his Spirit that dwells in us" [Rom. 8: 11 p.]. For there is nothing absurd in ascribing to the Father praise for those gifts of which he is the Author, and yet in ascribing the same powers to Christ, with whom were laid up the gifts of the Spirit to bestow upon his people. For this reason he invites unto himself all who thirst, that they may drink [John 7:37]. And Paul teaches that the Spirit is given to each "according to the measure of Christ's gift" [Eph. 4:7]. Also, we ought to know that he is called the "Spirit of Christ" not only because Christ, as eternal Word of God, is joined in the same Spirit with the Father, but also from his character as the Mediator. For he would have come to us in vain if he had not been furnished with this power. In this sense he is called the "Second Adam," given from heaven as "a life-giving spirit" [I Cor. 15:45]. This unique life which the Son of God inspires in his own[4] so that they become one with him, Paul here contrasts with that natural life which is common also to the wicked. Likewise, he asks "the grace of . . . Christ and the love of God" for believers, at the same time coupling with it "participation in the . . . Spirit" [II Cor. 13:14], without which no one can taste either the fatherly favor of God or the beneficence of Christ; just as he also says in another passage, "The love of God has been poured into our hearts through the Holy Spirit, who has been given to us" [Rom. 5:5, cf. Vg.].

---

[3] Cf. the language used in Comm. John 1:13: "Faith flows from regeneration" and is followed by "newness of life and other gifts of the Holy Spirit." Calvin does not differentiate "Spirit of God" and "Holy Spirit," as some contemporary theologians have done. Cf. N. Ferré, *The Christian Understanding of God*, pp. 250 f.; N. Bulgakov, *Le Paraclet*, pp. 145 ff. G. S. Hendry argues that in the New Testament the Holy Spirit is, "in an exclusive sense, the Spirit of Christ": *The Holy Spirit in Christian Theology*, p. 26; cf. pp. 44 ff., 119. H. P. Van Dusen remarks on Paul's "alternative use, as though interchangeable, of the variant terms 'Spirit,' 'Spirit of God,' 'Spirit of Christ,' 'Holy Spirit,' " while the basic concept of the Spirit is of the agency of "transformation . . . into the likeness of Christ": *Spirit, Son, and Father*, pp. 66 f.

[4] "*Singularem quam suis vitam inspirat filius Dei.*" For "*suis*" the French has "*à ses fidèles.*" Cadier explains that Calvin sometimes uses *fidèles* to translate not only the Latin *fideles* and *pii* but also *sui*, where the pronoun designates those who belong to Christ, and sometimes in a strong sense, *electi*. Cadier, *Institution* III. 11, note 2.

3. *Titles of the Holy Spirit in Scripture*

e(a)And here it is useful to note what titles are applied to the Holy Spirit in Scripture, when the beginning and the whole renewal of our salvation are under discussion.

First, he is called the "spirit of adoption" because he is the witness to us of the free benevolence of God with which God the Father has embraced us in his beloved only-begotten Son to become a Father to us; and he encourages us to have trust in prayer. In fact, he supplies the very words so that we may fearlessly cry, "Abba, Father!" [Rom. 8:15; Gal. 4:6].

e(b)For the same reason he is called "the guarantee and seal" of our inheritance [II Cor. 1:22; cf. Eph. 1:14] ebecause from heaven he so gives life to us, on pilgrimage in the world and resembling dead men, as to assure us that our salvation is safe in God's unfailing care. He is also called "life" because of righteousness [cf. Rom. 8:10].

e(b)By his secret watering the Spirit makes us fruitful to bring forth the buds of righteousness. Accordingly, he is frequently called "water," as in Isaiah: b"Come, all ye who thirst, to the waters" [ch. 55:1]. Also, "I shall pour out my Spirit upon him who thirsts, and rivers upon the dry land." [Isa. 44:3.] e(b)To these verses Christ's statement, quoted above,[5] corresponds: "If anyone thirst, let him come to me" [John 7:37]. bAlthough sometimes he is so called because of his power to cleanse and purify, as in Ezekiel, where the Lord promises "clean water" in which he will "wash away the filth" of his people [ch. 36:25].

From the fact that he restores and nourishes unto vigor of life those on whom he has poured the stream of his grace, he gets the names "oil" and "anointing" [I John 2:20, 27].

b(a)On the other hand, persistently boiling away and burning up our vicious and inordinate desires, he enflames our hearts with the love of God[6] and with zealous devotion. bFrom this effect upon us he is also justly called "fire" [Luke 3:16].

eIn short, he is described as the "spring" [John 4:14] whence all heavenly riches flow forth to us; or as the "hand of God" [Acts

---

[5] Sec. 2, above.

[6] *"Corda nostra incendit amore Dei et studio pietatis."* Calvin's emblem of the flaming heart on an outstretched hand bore the motto: *"Cor meum quasi immolatum tibi offero, Domine."* Cf. Luther's language in *Preface to Romans* (1522), where he says that faith "sets the heart aflame [*cor inflammat*]," and the reflection of this in John Wesley's experience as recorded in his *Journal* May 24, 1738: "As one was reading Luther's Preface to Romans . . . I felt my heart strangely warmed." Countless passages from the Mystics, and some from Aquinas, offer parallels to Calvin's language here, but the parallels are often more verbal than substantial. Cf., for example, R. C. Petry's remarks on the *Incendium amoris* of Richard Rolle (d. 1349) in LCC XIII. 210–213, and the studies there cited.

11:21], by which he exercises his might. ᵇFor by the inspiration of his power he so breathes divine life into us that we are no longer actuated by ourselves, but are ruled by his action and prompting. ᵃAccordingly, whatever good things are in us are the fruits of his grace; and without him our gifts are darkness of mind and perversity of heart [cf. Gal. 5:19–21].

ᵉ⁽ᵇ⁾As has already been clearly explained, until our minds become intent upon the Spirit, Christ, so to speak, lies idle because we coldly contemplate him as outside ourselves—indeed, far from us.[7] We know, moreover, that he benefits only those whose "Head" he is [Eph. 4:15], for whom he is "the first-born among brethren" [Rom. 8:29], and who, finally, "have put on him" [Gal. 3:27]. This union alone ensures that, as far as we are concerned, he has not unprofitably come with the name of Savior. The same purpose is served by that sacred wedlock through which we are made flesh of his flesh and bone of his bone [Eph. 5:30], and thus one with him. But he unites himself to us by the Spirit alone. By the grace and power of the same Spirit we are made his members, to keep us under himself and in turn to possess him.

4. Faith as the work of the Spirit

ᵉBut faith is the principal work of the Holy Spirit. Consequently, the terms commonly employed to express his power and working are, in large measure, referred to it because by faith alone he leads us into the light of the gospel, as John teaches: to believers in Christ is given the privilege of becoming children of God, who are born not of flesh and blood, but of God [John 1:12–13]. Contrasting God with flesh and blood, he declares it to be a supernatural gift that those who would otherwise remain in unbelief receive Christ by faith. Similar to this is that reply of Christ's: "Flesh and blood have not revealed it to you, but my Father, who is in heaven" [Matt. 16:17]. I am now touching briefly upon these things because I have already treated them at length elsewhere.[8] Like this, too, is the saying of Paul's that the Ephesians had been "sealed with the Holy Spirit of promise" [Eph. 1:13]. Paul shows the Spirit to be the inner teacher by whose effort the promise of salvation penetrates into our minds, a promise that would otherwise only strike the air or beat upon our ears. Similarly, where he says that the Thessalonians have been chosen by God "in sanctification of the Spirit and belief in the truth" [II Thess. 2:13], he is briefly warning us that faith itself has no other source than the Spirit. John explains this more

---

[7] Sec. 1, above.
[8] II. ii. 18–21, on the limitations of human reason.

clearly: "We know that he abides in us from the Spirit whom he has given us" [I John 3:24]. Likewise, "From this we know that we abide in him and he in us, because he has given us of his Spirit." [I John 4:13.] Therefore, Christ promised to his disciples "the Spirit of truth that the world cannot receive" [John 14:17] that they might be capable of receiving heavenly wisdom. And, as the proper office of the Spirit, he assigned the task of bringing to mind what he had taught by mouth. For light would be given the sightless in vain had that Spirit of discernment [Job 20:3] not opened the eyes of the mind. ᵇConsequently, he may rightly be called the key that unlocks for us the treasures of the Kingdom of Heaven [cf. Rev. 3:7]; and his illumination, the keenness of our insight. ᵉ⁽ᵇ⁾Paul so highly commends the "ministry of the Spirit" [II Cor. 3:6] for the reason that teachers would shout to no effect if Christ himself, inner Schoolmaster,⁹ did not by his Spirit draw to himself those given to him by the Father [cf. John 6:44; 12:32; 17:6]. We have said that perfect salvation is found in the person of Christ. Accordingly, that we may become partakers of it "he baptizes us in the Holy Spirit and fire" [Luke 3:16], bringing us into the light of faith in his gospel and so regenerating us that we become new creatures [cf. II Cor. 5:17]; and he consecrates us, purged of worldly uncleanness, as temples holy to God [cf. I Cor. 3:16–17; 6:19; II Cor. 6:16; Eph. 2:21].

ᶜCHAPTER II

Faith: Its Definition Set Forth, and Its Properties Explained

(The object of faith is Christ, 1)

1. ᶜBut it will be easy to understand all these matters after a clearer definition of faith has been presented,¹ to enable our readers to grasp its force and nature. ᵉ⁽ᵃ⁾We may well recall here what was explained before:² First, God lays down for us through the law what we should do; if we then fail in any part of it, that dreadful sentence of eternal death which it pronounces will rest upon us. ᵃSecondly, it is not only hard, but above our strength

---

⁹ Note that a similar phrase is used above of the Holy Spirit. Calvin frequently dwells on the thought of Christ as Teacher. In Comm. Harmony of the Evangelists, Matt. 17:5, he observes that the words "Hear ye him" recall the church to its unique Teacher, Christ, *"ad unicum doctorem Christum."* Cf. Comm. John 15:14: *"Ordinatus est ecclesiae magister et doctor unicus,"* and similar expressions in Comm. John 15:20; 20:30; *Sermons on Daniel* xlvi (on Dan. 12:5–7), CR XLII. 150. The concept of Christ, the Logos, as Tutor, or Teacher, was developed by Clement of Alexandria in his Ὁ Παιδαγωγός.

¹ The definition of faith begins with sec. 7, below.

² II. viii. 3.

and beyond all our abilities, to fulfill the law to the letter; thus, if we look to ourselves only, e(a)and ponder what condition we deserve, no trace of good hope will remain; but cast away by God, we shall lie under eternal death. Thirdly, it has been explained that there is but one means of liberation that can rescue us from such miserable calamity: the appearance of Christ the Redeemer, through whose hand the Heavenly Father, pitying us out of his infinite goodness and mercy, willed to help us; b(a)if, indeed, with firm faith we embrace this mercy and rest in it with steadfast hope.

But now we ought to examine what this faith ought to be like, e(b)through which those adopted by God as his children come to possess the Heavenly Kingdom, bsince it is certain that no mere opinion or even persuasion is capable of bringing so great a thing to pass. And we must scrutinize and investigate the true character of faith with greater care and zeal because many are dangerously deluded today in this respect. Indeed, most people, when they hear this term, understand nothing deeper than a common assent to the gospel history.[3] e(b)In fact, when faith is discussed in the schools, they call God simply the object of faith, and by fleeting speculations, as we have elsewhere stated,[4] lead miserable souls astray rather than direct them to a definite goal. For, since "God dwells in inaccessible light" [I Tim. 6:16], Christ must become our intermediary. Hence, he calls himself "the light of the world" [John 8:12], and elsewhere, "the way, the truth, and the life"; for no one comes to the Father, who is "the fountain of life" [Ps. 36:9], except through him [John 14:6] because he alone knows the Father, and afterward the believers to whom he wishes to reveal him [Luke 10:22]. On this ground, Paul declares that he considers nothing worth knowing save Christ [I Cor. 2:2]. In the twentieth chapter of Acts he relates that he has preached "faith in . . . Christ" [v. 21]. And in another passage he has Christ speak as follows: "I shall send you among the Gentiles . . . , that they may receive forgiveness of sins and a place among the saints through faith that is in me" [Acts 26:17–18]. And Paul testifies that the glory of God is visible to us in His person, or—what amounts to the same thing—that the enlightening knowledge of the glory of God shines in His face [II Cor. 4:6].

Indeed, it is true that faith looks to one God. But this must

---

[3] Melanchthon, *Loci communes*, 1521, in the section "On Justification and Faith," charges the "Sophists" with this *opinio vulgaris* of the sufficiency of a historical faith that is vacant of spiritual force. (Ed. H. Engelland, in the series *Melanchthons Werke in Auswahl*, ed. R. Stupperich, II. i. 99; tr. C. L. Hill [from Th. Kolde's 1910 edition], *The Loci Communes of Philip Melanchthon*, p. 185.)

[4] I. ii. 2; I. x. 1; II. vi. 4.

also be added, "To know Jesus Christ whom he has sent" [John 17:3]. For God would have remained hidden afar off if Christ's splendor had not beamed upon us.[5] For this purpose the Father laid up with his only-begotten Son all that he had to reveal himself in Christ so that Christ, by communicating his Father's benefits, might express the true image of his glory [cf. Heb. 1:3]. bIt has been said[6] that we must be drawn by the Spirit to be aroused to seek Christ; so, in turn, we must be warned that the invisible Father is to be sought solely in this image. dAugustine has finely spoken of this matter: in discussing the goal of faith, he teaches that we must know our destination and the way to it. Then, immediately after, he infers that the way that is most fortified against all errors is he who was both God and man: namely, as God he is the destination to which we move; as man, the path by which we go. Both are found in Christ alone.[7] eBut, while Paul proclaims faith in God, he does not have in mind to overturn what he so often emphasizes concerning faith: namely, that all its stability rests in Christ. Peter, indeed, most effectively connects both, saying that through him we believe in God [I Peter 1:21].

(Faith involves knowledge; the true doctrine obscured by the Scholastic notion of implicit faith, 2–5)

2. *Faith rests upon knowledge, not upon pious ignorance*

bThis evil, then, like innumerable others, must be attributed to the Schoolmen, who have, eas it were, drawn a veil over Christ to hide him. Unless we look straight toward him, we shall wander through endless labyrinths.

bBut besides wearing down the whole force of faith e(b)and almost annihilating it by their obscure definition, they have fabricated the fiction of "implicit faith." Bedecking the grossest ignorance with this term, they ruinously delude poor, miserable folk.[8]

---

[5] Cf. IV. viii. 5. It is Calvin's constant teaching that apart from Christ we have no real knowledge of God. Cf. II. vi. 2, where he presents Christ, the Mediator, as the object of faith for the "holy fathers" of the Old Testament. Cf. E. A. Dowey, *The Knowledge of God in Calvin's Theology,* p. 164; W. Niesel, *The Theology of Calvin,* p. 33.

[6] III. i. 4.

[7] Augustine, *City of God* XI. ii (MPL 41. 318; tr. NPNF II. 227).

[8] Lombard, *Sentences* III. xxv. 1–4 (MPL 192. 809 f.); Aquinas, *Summa Theol.* II IIae. ii. 5–8. Aquinas teaches implicit faith with the caution that "the simple-minded have faith implicit in the faith of the wiser only to the extent to which the wiser adhere to the divine teaching" (art. 6) (tr. LCC XI. 250 f.). Cf. III. ii. 5, where Calvin uses the term "implicit faith" in an acceptable sense, referring to John 4:53 and Acts 8:27, 31. Cf. also Augustine, *The Usefulness of Belief* xi. 25–xiii. 29 (MPL 42. 82–86; tr. LCC VI. 311–315); Bonaventura, *Commentary on the Sentences (In libros sententiarum)* III. xxv. 1. qu. 3 *(Opera omnia* III. 582 ff.).

[b]Furthermore, to state truly and frankly the real fact of the matter, this fiction not only buries but utterly destroys true faith. Is this what believing means—to understand nothing, provided only that you submit your feeling obediently to the church? Faith rests not on ignorance, but on knowledge. And this is, indeed, knowledge not only of God but of the divine will. We do not obtain salvation either because we are prepared to embrace as true whatever the church has prescribed, or because we turn over to it the task of inquiring and knowing. But we do so when we know that God is our merciful Father, because of reconciliation effected through Christ [II Cor. 5:18–19], and that Christ has been given to us as righteousness, sanctification, and life. By this knowledge, I say, not by submission of our feeling, do we obtain entry into the Kingdom of Heaven. For when the apostle says, "With the heart a man believes unto righteousness, with the mouth makes confession unto salvation" [Rom. 10:10, cf. Vg.], he indicates that it is not enough for a man implicitly to believe what he does not understand or even investigate. But he requires explicit recognition of the divine goodness upon which our righteousness rests.

3. The Roman doctrine of "implicit" faith is basically false
   [b]Indeed, I do not deny—such is the ignorance with which we are surrounded—that most things are now implicit for us, and will be so until, laying aside the weight of the flesh, we come nearer to the presence of God. In these matters we can do nothing better than suspend judgment, and hearten ourselves to hold unity with the church. But on this pretext it would be the height of absurdity to label ignorance tempered by humility "faith"! For faith consists in the knowledge of God and Christ [John 17:3], not in reverence for the church. We see the sort of labyrinth they have constructed with this "implication" of theirs! Anything at all, provided it be palmed off on them under the label "church" —sometimes even the most frightful errors—the untutored indiscriminately seize upon as an oracle. This heedless gullibility, although it is the very brink of ruin, yet is excused by them; only on condition that "such is the faith of the church" does it definitely believe anything.[9] Thus they fancy that in error they possess truth; in darkness, light; in ignorance, right knowledge.

---

[9] Ockham, *De sacramento altaris*, ch. i: "For whatever the Roman Church explicitly believes, this and nothing else either explicitly or implicitly I believe." (The *De sacramento altaris of William of Ockham*, edited and translated by T. B. Birch, I. 164 f.) Cf. Biel, *Epythoma pariter et collectorium circa quatuor sententiarum libros* (1510) III. xxv. qu. unica, note 2.

But let us not tarry longer over refuting them; we merely admonish the reader to compare these doctrines with ours. The very clarity of truth itself will of itself provide a sufficiently ready refutation. ᵉFor they do not ask whether faith is wrapped[10] in many remnants of ignorance, but define right believers as those who go numb in their own ignorance, and even brag about it, provided they give assent to the authority and judgment of the church in things unknown to them. As if Scripture does not regularly teach that understanding is joined with faith!

4. Even right faith is always surrounded by error and unbelief

ᵉWe certainly admit that so long as we dwell as strangers in the world there is such a thing as implicit faith; not only because many things are as yet hidden from us, but because surrounded by many clouds of errors we do not comprehend everything. The height of wisdom for the most perfect is to go forward and, quietly and humbly, to strive still further.[11] Therefore Paul exhorts believers that, if some disagree with others in any matter, they should wait for revelation [Phil. 3:15]. Experience obviously teaches that until we put off the flesh we attain less than we should like. And in our daily reading of Scripture we come upon many obscure passages that convict us of ignorance. With this bridle God keeps us within bounds, assigning to each his "measure of faith" [Rom. 12:3] so that even the best teacher may be ready to learn.

Remarkable examples of this implicit faith may be noted in Christ's disciples before they attained full enlightenment. We see how with difficulty they taste even the first rudiments, halting over the slightest matters, and though hanging on their Master's words, making but little progress. Indeed, when, warned by the women, they rush to the tomb, the resurrection of their Master seems to them like a dream [Luke 24:11–12; cf. John 20:8]. Since Christ previously bore witness to their faith, it is wrong to say that they were completely devoid of it. No, unless they had been persuaded that Christ would rise again, all zeal would have failed them. Nor was it superstition that prompted the women to anoint with spices the corpse of a dead man for whose life there could be no hope. But although they had faith in the words of him

---

10 *"Implicita."* Calvin is playing on the word.
11 Vincent of Lérins, *Commonitorium* I. xxiii. 28 f., calls for *"progress, not alteration of the faith . . . a great increase and a vigorous progress, in individuals and in the whole group, in the single man as well as in the entire church, as the ages and centuries march on,"* but with retention of "the same doctrine." (MPL 50. 667 f.; tr. LCC IX. 69; cf. p. 31.) Cf. III. ii. 19.

whom they knew to be truthful, the ignorance that as yet occupied their minds so enveloped their faith in darkness that they were almost dumfounded. Hence, also, it said that they finally believed after they themselves had discovered the truth of Christ's words through the very fact of his resurrection. Not that they then began to believe, but because the seed of hidden faith—which had been dead, as it were, in their hearts—at that time burst through with renewed vigor! For there was in them a true but implicit faith because they had reverently embraced Christ as their sole teacher. Then, taught by him, they were convinced he was the author of their salvation. And finally, they believed he came from heaven that, through the Father's grace, he might gather his disciples thither. We ought not to seek any more intimate proof of this than that unbelief is, in all men, always mixed with faith.

5. "Implicit" faith as prerequisite of faith

ᵉWe may also call that faith implicit which is still strictly nothing but the preparation of faith. The Evangelists relate that very many believed who, caught up into wonderment by the miracles only, did not advance farther than to believe Christ the Messiah who had been promised, although they had not been imbued with even a trace of the gospel teaching. Such reverent attention, which disposed them to submit themselves willingly to Christ, is graced with the title "faith"; yet it was only the beginning of faith. Thus, the court official[12] who believed Christ's promise concerning the healing of his son [John 4:50], having returned to his house, as the Evangelist testifies, believed anew [John 4:53] because he first received as an oracle what he had heard from the mouth of Christ, and then submitted to Christ's authority to receive the teaching. Yet we must know that he was so teachable and ready to learn that in the first passage his admission of belief signifies a particular faith, while in the second passage he is counted among the disciples who had enlisted with Christ. John sets forth a like example in the Samaritans who so believed the word of a woman that they eagerly rushed to Christ, but spoke to her, when they heard him, as follows: "Now we do not believe on account of your speaking, but we have heard him and we know that it is the Savior of the world" [John 4:42]. From these instances it is clear that even those who are not yet imbued with the first elements but are still inclined to hearken are called "believers"; not in an exact sense, indeed, but in so far as God in his kindness deigns to grace that pious affec-

[12] "*Aulicus*" instead of Vg. "*regulus*," John 4:49.

tion with such great honor. But this teachableness, with the desire to learn, is far different from sheer ignorance in which those sluggishly rest who are content with the sort of "implicit faith" the papists invent. For if Paul severely condemns those who "are always learning but never arrive at a knowledge of the truth" [II Tim. 3:7], how much greater ignominy do those merit who deliberately affect complete ignorance!

(*Relation of faith to the Word and brief definition of faith, 6–7*)

6. Faith rests upon God's Word

ᵇThis, then, is the true knowledge of Christ, if we receive him as he is offered by the Father: namely, ᶜ⁽ᵇ⁾clothed with his gospel. For just as he has been appointed as the goal of our faith, so we cannot take the right road to him unless the gospel goes before us. And there, surely, the treasures of grace are opened to us; for if they had been closed, Christ would have benefited us little. ᵉThus Paul yokes faith to teaching, as an inseparable companion, with these words: "You did not so learn Christ if indeed you were taught what is the truth in Christ" [Eph. 4:20–21 p.].

Yet I do not so restrict faith to the gospel without confessing that what sufficed for building it up had been handed down by Moses and the prophets. But because a fuller manifestation of Christ has been revealed in the gospel, Paul justly calls it the "doctrine of faith" [cf. I Tim. 4:6]. For this reason, he says in another passage that by the coming of faith the law was abolished [Rom. 10:4; cf. Gal. 3:25]. He understands by this term the new and extraordinary kind of teaching by which Christ, after he became our teacher, has more clearly set forth the mercy of the Father, and has more surely testified to our salvation.

Yet it will be an easier and more suitable method if we descend by degrees from general to particular. ᵉ⁽ᵇ⁾First, we must be reminded that there is a permanent relationship between faith and the Word. He could not separate one from the other any more than we could separate the rays from the sun from which they come. ᵉFor this reason, God exclaims in The Book of Isaiah: "Hear me and your soul shall live" [ch. 55:3]. And John shows this same wellspring of faith in these words: "These things have been written that you may believe" [John 20:31]. The prophet, also, desiring to exhort the people to faith, says: "Today if you will hear his voice" [Ps. 95:7; 94:8, Vg.]. "To hear" is generally understood as meaning to believe. In short, it is not without reason that in The Book of Isaiah, God distinguishes the children of the church from outsiders by this mark: he will teach all his children [Isa. 54:13; John 6:45] that they may learn of him [cf. John 6:45]. For if benefits were indiscriminately given, why would he have directed his Word to a few? To this corresponds the fact that the Evangelists commonly use the words "believers" and "disciples" as synonyms. This is especially Luke's usage in The Acts of the Apostles: indeed he extends this title even to a woman in Acts 9:36 [Acts 6:1–2,7; 9:1, 10, 19, 25–26, 38; 11:26, 29; 13:52; 14:20, 28; 15:10; also chs. 16 to 21].

e(b/a)Therefore if faith turns away even in the slightest degree from this goal toward which it should aim, it does not keep its own nature, b(a)but becomes uncertain credulity and vague error of mind. The same Word is the basis whereby faith is supported and sustained; if it turns away from the Word, it falls. bTherefore, take away the Word and no faith will then remain.

We are not here discussing whether a human ministry is necessary for the sowing of God's Word, from which faith may be conceived. This we shall discuss in another place.[13] But we say that the Word itself, however it be imparted to us, is like a mirror in which faith may contemplate God. Whether, therefore, God makes use of man's help in this or works by his own power alone, he always represents himself through his Word to those whom he wills to draw to himself. eAnd for this reason, Paul defines faith as that obedience which is given to the gospel [Rom. 1:5], and elsewhere praises allegiance to faith in Philippians [Phil. 1:3–5; cf. I Thess. 2:13]. b(a)In understanding faith it is not merely a question of knowing that God exists, but also—and this especially—of knowing what is his will toward us.[14] bFor it is not so much our concern to know who he is in himself, as what he wills to be toward us.

Now, therefore, we hold faith to be a knowledge of God's will toward us, perceived from his Word. b(a)But the foundation of this is a preconceived conviction of God's truth. As for its certainty, so long as your mind is at war with itself, the Word will be of doubtful and weak authority, or rather of none. And it is not even enough to believe that God is trustworthy [cf. Rom. 3:3], who can neither deceive nor lie [cf. Titus 1:2], unless you hold to be beyond doubt that whatever proceeds from him is sacred and inviolable truth.[15]

7. *Faith arises from God's promise of grace in Christ*

bBut since man's heart is not aroused to faith at every word

---

[13] IV. i. 5.
[14] Cf. I. ii. 2; I. x. 2, note 6.
[15] Cf. Luther, *Enchiridion piarum precationum* (*Werke* WA X. ii. 389).

of God, we must find out at this point what, strictly speaking, faith looks to in the Word. God's word to Adam was, "You shall surely die" [Gen. 2:17]. God's word to Cain was, "The blood of your brother cries out to me from the earth" [Gen. 4:10]. But these words are so far from being capable of establishing faith that they can of themselves do nothing but shake it. In the meantime, we do not deny that it is the function of faith to subscribe to God's truth whenever and whatever and however it speaks. But we ask only what faith finds in the Word of the Lord upon which to lean and rest.[16] Where our conscience sees only indignation and vengeance, how can it fail to tremble and be afraid? or to shun the God whom it dreads? Yet faith ought to seek God, not to shun him.

It is plain, then, that we do not yet have a full definition of faith, inasmuch as merely to know something of God's will is not to be accounted faith. But what if we were to substitute his benevolence or his mercy in place of his will, ᵉthe tidings of which are often sad and the proclamation frightening? ᵇThus, surely, we shall more closely approach the nature of faith; for it is after we have learned that our salvation rests with God that we are attracted to seek him. This fact is confirmed for us when he declares that our salvation is his care and concern. Accordingly, we need the promise of grace, which can testify to us that the Father is merciful; since we can approach him in no other way, and upon grace alone the heart of man can rest.

ᵉOn this basis the psalms commonly yoke these two, mercy and truth, as if they were mutually connected [Ps. 89:14, 24; 92:2; 98:3; 100:5; 108:4; 115:1; etc.]; for it would not help us at all to know that God is true unless he mercifully attracted us to himself. Nor would it have been in our power to embrace his mercy if he had not offered it with his word: "I have declared thy truth and thy salvation; I have not concealed thy goodness and thy truth. . . . Let thy goodness and thy truth . . . preserve me" [Ps. 40:10–11, Comm.]. Another passage: "Thy mercy . . . extends to the heavens, thy truth to the clouds." [Ps. 36:5, Comm.] Likewise: "All the ways of Jehovah are kindness and truth to those who keep his covenant." [Ps. 25:10, Comm.] "For his mercy is multiplied upon us, and the truth of the Lord endures forever." [Ps. 117:2; 116:2, Vg.; cf. Comm.] Again, "I will sing thy name for thy mercy and thy truth." [Ps. 138:2.] I pass over what we read in the Prophets along the same line, that God is kind and steadfast in his promises. For it will be rash for us to decide that God

16 Cf. II. ii. 15, note 58.

is well disposed toward us unless he give witness of himself, and anticipate us by his call, that his will may not be doubtful or obscure. But we have already seen that the sole pledge of his love is Christ, without whom the signs of hatred and wrath are everywhere evident.

ᵇNow, the knowledge of God's goodness will not be held very important unless it makes us rely on that goodness. Consequently, understanding mixed with doubt is to be excluded, as it is not in firm agreement, but in conflict, with itself. Yet far indeed is the mind of man, blind and darkened as it is, from penetrating and attaining even to perception of the will of God! And the heart, too, wavering as it is in perpetual hesitation, is far from resting secure in that conviction! Therefore our mind must be otherwise illumined and our heart strengthened, that the Word of God may obtain full faith among us. Now we shall possess a right definition of faith if we call it a firm and certain knowledge of God's benevolence toward us, founded upon the truth of the freely given promise in Christ, both revealed to our minds and sealed upon our hearts through the Holy Spirit.

(Various unacceptable significations of the term "faith," 8–13)
8. "Formed" and "unformed" faith
ᵉBut before we proceed farther, some preliminary remarks will be necessary to explain difficulties that could otherwise offer a stumbling block to our readers. First, we must refute ᵉ⁽ᵇ⁾that worthless distinction between formed and unformed faith which is tossed about the schools.[17] ᵉFor they imagine that people who are touched by no fear of God, no sense of piety, nevertheless believe whatever it is necessary to know for salvation. As if the Holy Spirit, by illumining our hearts unto faith, were not the witness to us of our adoption! And yet they presumptuously ᵉ⁽ᵇ⁾dignify that persuasion, devoid of the fear of God, with the name "faith" even though all Scripture cries out against it. ᵇWe need no longer contend with their definition; our task is simply to explain the nature of faith as it is set forth in the Word of God. From this it will be very clear how ignorantly and foolishly they shout rather than speak about it.

ᵉ⁽ᵇ⁾I have already touched upon part;[18] I shall later insert the rest in its proper place. I now say that nothing more absurd than

---

[17] Lombard, *Sentences* III. xxiii. 4 f. (MPL 192. 805 f.); Aquinas. *Summa Theol.* II IIae. iv. 3, 4 (tr. LCC XI. 268 f.).
[18] Sec. 2, above

their fiction can be imagined. They would have faith to be an assent by which any despiser of God may receive what is offered from Scripture.[19] But first they ought to have seen whether every man attains faith by his own effort, or whether through it the Holy Spirit is witness of his adoption. Therefore they babble childishly in asking whether faith is the same faith when it has been formed by a superadded quality; or whether it be a new and different thing. From such chatter it certainly looks as if they never thought about the unique gift of the Spirit. For the beginning of believing already contains within itself the reconciliation whereby man approaches God. But if they weighed Paul's saying, "With the heart a man believes unto righteousness" [Rom. 10:10], they would cease to invent that cold quality of faith.

If we possessed only this one reason, it would have been sufficient to end the dispute: that very assent itself—as I have already partially suggested, and will reiterate more fully—is more of the heart than of the brain, and more of the disposition than of the understanding.[20] bFor this reason, it is called "obedience of faith" [Rom. 1:5], and the Lord prefers no other obedience to it —and justly, since nothing is more precious to him than his truth. To this truth believers set their seal as if they have affixed their signatures, as John the Baptist testifies [John 3:33]. Since there is no doubt about the matter, we establish in one word that they are speaking foolishly when they say that faith is "formed" when pious inclination is added to assent.[21] For even assent rests upon such pious inclination—at least such assent as is revealed in the Scriptures!

But another much clearer argument now offers itself. aSince faith embraces Christ, as offered to us by the Father [cf. John 6:29]—that is, since he is offered not b(a)only for righteousness, forgiveness of sins, and peace, but also for sanctification [cf. I Cor. 1:30] and the fountain of the water of life [John 7:38; cf. ch. 4: 14]—without a doubt, no one can duly know him without at the same time apprehending the sanctification of the Spirit. bOr, if anyone desires some plainer statement, faith rests upon the knowledge of Christ. And Christ cannot be known apart from

---

[19] Augustine, *Predestination of the Saints* ii. 5 (MPL 44. 963; tr. NPNF V. 499 f.); Lombard, *Sentences* III. xxiii. 5 (MPL 192. 805 f.); Bonaventura, *Commentary on the Sentences* III. xxiii. art. 3. qu. 4, 5. (*Opera omnia* IV. 505–511); Aquinas, *Summa Theol.* II IIae. iv. 4 (tr. LCC XI. 269 f.).

[20] For Calvin's view that the knowledge of God is primarily a matter of the heart rather than of the intellect, see also I. v. 9, note 29; III. ii. 33, 36.

[21] Cf. sec. 10, below.

the sanctification of his Spirit. It follows that faith can in no wise be separated from a devout disposition.

9. I Corinthians 13:2—a proof of the difference between "formed" and "unformed" faith

ᵃThey are accustomed to urge Paul's words: "If anyone has all faith so as to remove mountains, but has not love, he is nothing" [I Cor. 13:2 p.]. By this they would de-form faith by depriving it of love. They do not consider what the apostle means by "faith" in this passage.[22] For after he has discussed in the preceding chapter the various gifts of the Spirit—including the divers kinds of tongues, powers, and prophecy [I Cor. 12:4–10]—and has exhorted the Corinthians to "seek after the better of these gifts," thereby to render greater benefit and advantage to the whole body of the church, he adds that he will show "a still more excellent way" [I Cor. 12:31]. All such gifts, however excellent they may be in themselves, are still to be considered as nothing unless they serve love. For they were given for the edification of the church, and unless they contribute to this they lose their grace. To prove this, Paul elaborates by repeating those same gifts which he had enumerated before, but under other names. Moreover, he uses the terms "powers" and "faith" for the same thing, that is, for the ability to work miracles. This power or faith, therefore, is a special gift of God, which any impious man can brag about and abuse, as the gift of tongues, as prophecy, as the other graces. No wonder, then, if it be separated from love! ᵇBut the whole error of these men lies in that, although the meanings of "faith" are diverse,[23] they do not observe the diversity of the thing signified therein, but dispute as if the acceptation of the word were everywhere the same. The passage of James [James 2:21] that they bring forward in support of the same error will be discussed elsewhere.

ᵇ⁽ᵃ⁾Although we concede, for the purpose of instruction, that there are divers forms of faith. But, while we wish to show what kind of knowledge of God can exist among the impious—we nevertheless recognize and proclaim that there is only one kind of faith among the pious—as Scripture teaches. Of course, most people believe that there is a God, and they consider that the gospel history and the remaining parts of the Scripture are true. Such a judgment is on a par with the judgments we ordinarily make concerning those things which are either narrated as having once taken place, or which we have seen as eyewitnesses. ᵇThere

---

[22] Cf. Augustine, *On Baptism* I. ix. 12 (MPL 43. 116; tr. NPNF IV. 417).
[23] "πολύσαμον." For the treatment of James 2:21, see III. xvii. 11.

are, also, those who go beyond this, holding the Word of God to be an indisputable oracle; they do not utterly neglect his precepts, and are somewhat moved by his threats and promises. To such persons an ascription of faith is made, but by misapplication,[24] because they do not impugn the Word of God with open impiety, or refuse or despise it, but rather pretend a certain show of obedience.

10. What is called "unformed" faith is only an illusion of faith

[a]But this shadow or image of faith, as it is of no importance, does not deserve to be called faith. [b]It will soon be seen more fully how far removed from the solid reality of faith it is, yet nothing prevents this from being briefly indicated now. It is said that even Simon Magus believed [Acts 8:13], who a little later nevertheless betrayed his unbelief [Acts 8:18]. When he is said to have had faith attributed to him, we do not understand the statement as do some, who hold that he pretended in words a faith that he did not have in his heart. Rather, we consider that, conquered by the majesty of the gospel, he showed a certain sort of faith, and thus recognized Christ to be the author of life and salvation, so that he willingly enlisted under him. In the same way, in the Gospel of Luke they are said to believe for a while [Luke 8:13], in whom the seed of the Word is choked before it bears fruit, or immediately withers and dies even before it takes any root [Luke 8:6–7].

We do not doubt that such persons, prompted by some taste of the Word, greedily seize upon it, and begin to feel its divine power; so that they impose a false show of faith not only upon the eyes of men but even upon their own minds. For they persuade themselves that the reverence that they show to the Word of God is very piety itself, because they count it no impiety unless there is open and admitted reproach or contempt of his Word. Whatever sort of assent that is, it does not at all penetrate to the heart itself, there to remain fixed. And although it seems sometimes to put down roots, they are not living roots. The human heart has so many crannies where vanity hides, so many holes where falsehood lurks, is so decked out with deceiving hypocrisy, that it often dupes itself. [b(a)]Yet let those who boast of such shadow-shapes of faith understand that in this respect they are no better than the devils! Surely those of the former class are far inferior to the devils, for they stupidly listen to and understand things the knowledge of which makes even the devils shudder

---

[24] "*Per* κατάχρησιν."

[James 2:19]. The others are like the devils in this respect, that whatever feeling touches them ends in dread and dismay.

11. "Faith" even among the reprobate?

ᵉI know that to attribute faith to the reprobate seems hard to some, when Paul declares it the result of election [cf. I Thess. 1:4–5]. Yet this difficulty is easily solved. For though only those predestined to salvation receive the light of faith and truly feel the power of the gospel, yet experience shows that the reprobate are sometimes affected by almost the same feeling as the elect, so that even in their own judgment they do not in any way differ from the elect [cf. Acts 13:48]. Therefore it is not at all absurd that the apostle should attribute to them a taste of the heavenly gifts [Heb. 6:4–6]—and Christ, faith for a time [Luke 8:13]; not because they firmly grasp the force of spiritual grace and the sure light of faith, but because the Lord, to render them more convicted and inexcusable, steals into their minds to the extent that his goodness may be tasted without the Spirit of adoption.[25]

Suppose someone objects that then nothing more remains to believers to assure themselves of their adoption. I reply: although there is a great likeness and affinity between God's elect and those who are given a transitory faith, yet only in the elect does that confidence flourish which Paul extols, that they loudly proclaim Abba, Father [Gal. 4:6; cf. Rom. 8:15]. Therefore, as God regenerates only the elect with incorruptible seed forever [I Peter 1:23] so that the seed of life sown in their hearts may never perish, thus he firmly seals the gift of his adoption in them that it may be steady and sure.

But this does not at all hinder that lower working of the Spirit from taking its course even in the reprobate. In the meantime, believers are taught to examine themselves carefully and humbly, lest the confidence of the flesh creep in and replace assurance of faith. Besides this, the reprobate never receive anything but a confused awareness of grace, so that they grasp a shadow rather than the firm body of it. For the Spirit, strictly speaking, seals forgiveness of sins in the elect alone, so that they apply it by special faith to their own use. Yet the reprobate are justly said to believe that God is merciful toward them, for they

---

[25] Calvin's use of the Pauline concept of "adoption" as sons of God (Rom. 8:15, 23; Rom. 9:4; Gal. 4:5; Eph. 1:5; cf. John 1:12) is frequent in the *Institutes*. The principal references are: II. vi. 1; II. vii. 15; II. xi. 9; II. xii. 2; III. i. 3; III. ii. 22; III. xi. 6; III. xiv. 18; III. xvii. 6; III. xviii. 2; III. xx. 36 f.; III. xxi. 7; III. xxii. 1, 4.

receive the gift of reconciliation, although confusedly and not distinctly enough. Not that they are partakers of the same faith or regeneration with the children of God, but because they seem, under a cloak of hypocrisy, to have a beginning of faith in common with the latter. And I do not deny that God illumines their minds enough for them to recognize his grace; but he so distinguishes that awareness from the exclusive testimony he gives to his elect that they do not attain the full effect and fruition thereof. He does not show himself merciful to them, to the extent of truly snatching them from death and receiving them into his keeping, but only manifests to them his mercy for the time being. Only his elect does he account worthy of receiving the living root of faith so that they may endure to the end [Matt. 24:13]. Thus is that objection answered: if God truly shows his grace, this fact is forever established. For nothing prevents God from illumining some with a momentary awareness of his grace, which afterward vanishes.

12. True and false faith

ᶜAlso, although faith is a knowledge of the divine benevolence toward us and a sure persuasion of its truth, there is no wonder that the awareness of divine love vanishes in temporary things. Even if it is close to faith, it differs much from it. The will of God is unchangeable, I admit, and his truth ever remains in agreement with itself. Yet I deny that the reprobate proceed so far as to penetrate into that secret revelation which Scripture vouchsafes only to the elect. I deny, therefore, that they either grasp the will of God as it is immutable, or steadfastly embrace its truth, for they tarry in but a fleeting awareness. They are like a tree not planted deep enough to put down living roots. For some years it may put forth not only blossoms and leaves, but even fruits; nevertheless, it withers after the passage of time. To sum up, just as by the rebellion of the first man the image of God could be wiped out from his mind and soul, no wonder he illumines wicked persons with some rays of his grace, which he later allows to be quenched. Nor does anything prevent him from lightly touching some with a knowledge of his gospel, while deeply imbuing others. In the meantime we ought to grasp this: however deficient or weak faith may be in the elect, still, because the Spirit of God is for them the sure guarantee and seal of their adoption [Eph. 1:14; cf. II Cor. 1:22], the mark he has engraved can never be erased from their hearts; but on the wicked such light is shed as may afterward pass away. Yet, because he does not give life to the seed that lies in their hearts to keep it ever incorruptible as in the elect, it must not be supposed that the Holy Spirit is false.

Furthermore, although it is evident from the teaching of Scripture and daily experience that the wicked are sometimes touched by the awareness of divine grace, a desire to love one another must be aroused in their hearts. Thus, for a time in Saul there flourished a pious impulse to love God. For he knew God was as a father to him, and he was attracted by something delightful about His goodness [I Sam., chs. 9 to 11]. But as a persuasion of God's fatherly love is not deeply rooted in the reprobate, so do they not perfectly reciprocate his love as sons, but behave like hirelings. For that Spirit of love was given to Christ alone on the condition that he instill it in his members. And surely that saying of Paul's is confined to the elect: "The love of God has been shed abroad in our hearts through the Holy Spirit, who has been given to us" [Rom. 5:5, cf. Vg.], that is, the love that generates the above-mentioned confidence that we can call upon him [cf. Gal. 4:6].[26]

From the other side we see that God, while not ceasing to love his children, is wondrously angry toward them; not because he is disposed of himself to hate them, but because he would frighten them by the feeling of his wrath in order to humble their fleshly pride, shake off their sluggishness, and arouse them to repentance. Therefore, at the same time they conceive him to be at once angry and merciful toward them, or toward their sins. For they unfeignedly pray that his wrath be averted, while with tranquil confidence they nevertheless flee to him for refuge. Indeed, this evidence discloses that some are not pretending a faith, who nevertheless lack true faith; but while they are carried away with a sudden impulse of zeal, they deceive themselves in a false opinion. There is no doubt that indolence so fills them that they do not rightly examine their hearts as they should. It is likely that such are those to whom, according to John, Christ "did not trust himself," although they believed in him, "because he knew all men and . . . knew what was in man" [John 2:24–25]. If many did not fall from the common faith (I call it "common" because there is a great likeness and affinity between transitory faith and living and permanent faith), Christ would not have said to his disciples, "If you continue in my word, you are truly my disciples, and you will know the truth, and the truth will make you free" [John 8:31–32]. For he is addressing those who had embraced his teaching and is urging them to advance in

[26] Apparently the reference is to the opening sentences of this section. Cf. also sec. 15, below, and III. xx. 11, 12, 28.

faith, lest by their sluggishness they extinguish the light given them. Therefore, Paul attributes faith exclusively to the elect [Titus 1:1], meaning that many vanish because they have not taken living root. Christ says the same thing in the Gospel of Matthew: "Every tree that my Heavenly Father has not planted will be uprooted" [Matt. 15:13].

There is a grosser kind of lying in others, who are not ashamed to mock God and men. James inveighs against this type of men, who impiously profane faith on this deceitful pretext [James 2:14–26]. And Paul would not require "a faith unfeigned" from the children of God [I Tim. 1:5], except that many boldly boast of what they do not have, and deceive others or even sometimes themselves with vain pretense. Therefore, he compares a good conscience to a chest in which faith is kept. For many in falling from good conscience "have made shipwreck of their faith" [I Tim. 1:19; cf. ch. 3:9].

13. Different meanings of the word "faith" in Scripture

eWe must understand that the meaning of the word "faith" is ambiguous. Often faith means only sound doctrine of godliness,[27] as in the passage we have just cited; and in the same letter where Paul desires that deacons keep "the mystery of faith in a pure conscience" [I Tim. 3:9]. Likewise, when he declares that some will fall away from faith [I Tim. 4:1]. But on the other hand, he says that Timothy had been "nourished on the words of the faith" [I Tim. 4:6]. Likewise, when he terms "godless chatter and contradictions of what is falsely called knowledge," the cause why many fall from faith [I Tim. 6:20–21; cf. II Tim. 2:16]; elsewhere he calls these "reprobate" in regard to faith [II Tim. 3:8]. Again, where he enjoins Titus, "Bid them" [Titus 2:2] "be sound in the faith" [Titus 1:13], by the word "soundness" Paul means simply purity of doctrine, easily rendered corrupt and degenerate by men's fickleness. That is, because in Christ whom faith possesses "are hidden all the treasures of knowledge and wisdom" [Col. 2:3], faith is rightly extended to the whole sum of heavenly doctrine, from which it cannot be separated.

On the other hand, it is sometimes confined to a particular object, as when Matthew says that Christ saw the faith of those who let the paralytic down through the tile roof [Matt. 9:2]. And he exclaimed that even in Israel he had not found so great faith as the centurion manifested [Matt. 8:10]. Yet it is probable that the centurion was wholly intent upon the healing of his son [cf. John 4:47 ff.], whose cure occupied his entire mind, because,

[27] "Sana pietatis doctrina." Cf. Introduction, pp. li f.

content with only the nod and answer of Christ, he does not demand his bodily presence. On account of this circumstance his faith is greatly commended.

A little while ago[28] we taught that Paul takes "faith" as the gift of performing miracles, a gift that certain ones possess who have neither been regenerated by the Spirit of God nor zealously worship him. Also, in another passage, he identifies faith with the teaching whereby we are established in faith. For when he writes that faith will pass away [I Cor. 13:10; cf. Rom. 4:14], he doubtless is referring to the ministry of the church, which today is useful for our weakness. Now, in these forms of speech there appears an analogy. When the term "faith" is improperly transferred to a false profession or a lying label, this misapplication of the term[29] should seem no harsher than when vicious and perverted worship is termed "fear of God." For example, it is often stated in the Sacred History that the foreign tribes that had been transplanted to Samaria and neighboring districts feared false gods and the God of Israel [II Kings 17:24–41]. This means, in so many words, that they mixed heaven and earth.

But now we ask, of what sort is that faith which distinguishes the children of God from the unbelievers, by which we call upon God as Father, by which we cross over from death into life, and by which Christ, eternal salvation and life, dwells in us? I believe that I have briefly and clearly explained the force and nature of faith.

(Detailed examination of what the definition of faith in paragraph 7 implies: the element of knowledge, 14–15)
14. Faith as higher knowledge
bNow let us examine anew the individual parts of the definition of faith. After we have diligently examined it no doubt, I believe, will remain. When we call faith "knowledge" we do not mean comprehension of the sort that is commonly concerned with those things which fall under human sense perception. For faith is so far above sense that man's mind has to go beyond and rise above itself in order to attain it. Even where the mind has attained, it does not comprehend what it feels. But while it is persuaded of what it does not grasp, by the very certainty of its persuasion it understands more than if it perceived anything human by its own capacity. Paul, therefore, beautifully describes it as the power "to comprehend . . . what is the breadth and length and depth and height, and to know the love of Christ, which surpasses

[28] III. ii. 9.
[29] "κατάχρησις."

knowledge" [Eph. 3:18–19]. He means that what our mind embraces by faith is in every way infinite, and that this kind of knowledge is far more lofty than all understanding. Nevertheless, the Lord has "made manifest to his saints" the secret of his will, which had been "hidden for ages and generations" [Col. 1:26; cf. ch. 2:2]. For very good reason, then, faith is frequently called "recognition"[30] [see Eph. 1:17; 4:13; Col. 1:9; 3:10; I Tim. 2:4; Titus 1:1; Philemon 6; II Peter 2:21], but by John, "knowledge."[31] For he declares that believers know themselves to be God's children [I John 3:2]. And obviously they surely know this. But they are more strengthened by the persuasion of divine truth than instructed by rational proof. Paul's words also point this out· "While dwelling in this body, we wander from the Lord, for we walk by faith, not by sight" [II Cor. 5:6–7]. By these words he shows that those things which we know through faith are nonetheless absent from us and go unseen. From this we conclude that the knowledge of faith consists in assurance rather than in comprehension.

15. Faith implies certainty*

ᵇWe add the words "sure and firm" in order to express a more solid constancy of persuasion. For, as faith is not content with a doubtful and changeable opinion, so is it not content with an obscure and confused conception; but requires full and fixed certainty, such as men are wont to have from things experienced and proved. ᶜFor unbelief is so deeply rooted in our hearts, and we are so inclined to it, that not without hard struggle is each one able to persuade himself of what all confess with the mouth: namely, that God is faithful. Especially when it comes to reality itself, every man's wavering uncovers hidden weakness. And not without cause the Holy Spirit with such notable titles ascribes authority to the Word of God. He wishes to cure the disease I have mentioned so that among us God may obtain full faith in his promises. "The words of Jehovah are pure words," says David, "silver melted in an excellent crucible of earth, purified seven times." [Ps. 12:6, cf. Comm. and Ps. 11:7, Vg.] Likewise, "The Word of Jehovah is purified; it is a shield to all those who trust in him." [Ps. 18:30, cf. Comm.] Solomon, moreover, confirms this very idea in almost identical words, "Every word of God is purified" [Prov. 30:5]. But because almost the entire 119th Psalm is taken up with this proof, it would be superfluous to list more. Surely, as often as God commends his Word to us, he indirectly

---

30 *"Agnitio."* Cf. I. i, note 1.
31 *"Scientia."*

rebukes us for our unbelief, for he has no other intention than to uproot perverse doubts from our hearts.

ᵇAlso, there are very many who so conceive God's mercy that they receive almost no consolation from it. They are constrained with miserable anxiety at the same time as they are in doubt whether he will be merciful to them because they confine that very kindness of which they seem utterly persuaded within too narrow limits. For among themselves they ponder that it is indeed great and abundant, shed upon many, available and ready for all; but that it is uncertain whether it will even come to them, or rather, whether they will come to it. This reasoning, when it stops in mid-course, is only half. Therefore, it does not so much strengthen the spirit in secure tranquillity as trouble it with uneasy doubting. But there is a far different feeling of full assurance[32] that in the Scriptures is always attributed to faith. It is this which puts beyond doubt God's goodness clearly manifested for us [Col. 2:2; I Thess. 1:5; cf. Heb. 6:11 and 10:22]. But that cannot happen without our truly feeling its sweetness and experiencing it in ourselves. For this reason, the apostle derives confidence[33] from faith, and from confidence, in turn, boldness.[34] For he states: "Through Christ we have boldness and access with confidence which is through faith in him" [Eph. 3:12 p., cf. Vg.]. ᶜBy these words he obviously shows that there is no right faith except when we dare with tranquil hearts to stand in God's sight. This boldness arises only out of a sure confidence in divine benevolence and salvation. ᵇThis is so true that the word "faith" is very often used for confidence.

(Certainty of faith in relation to fear, 16–28)
16. Certainty of faith

ᵇHere, indeed, is the chief hinge on which faith turns: that we do not regard the promises of mercy that God offers as true only outside ourselves, but not at all in us; rather that we make them ours by inwardly embracing them. Hence, at last is born that confidence which Paul elsewhere calls "peace" [Rom. 5:1], unless someone may prefer to derive peace from it. Now it is an assurance that renders the conscience calm and peaceful before God's judgment. Without it the conscience must be harried by disturbed alarm, and almost torn to pieces; unless perhaps, forgetting God and self, it for the moment sleeps. And truly for

---

32 "πληροφορίας."
33 "Fiduciam."
34 "Audaciam."

the moment, for it does not long enjoy that miserable forgetfulness without the memory of divine judgment repeatedly coming back and very violently rending it. Briefly, he alone is truly a believer who, convinced by a firm conviction that God is a kindly and well-disposed Father toward him, promises himself all things on the basis of his generosity; who, relying upon the promises of divine benevolence toward him, lays hold on an undoubted expectation of salvation. As the apostle points out in these words: "If we hold our confidence and glorying in hope, firm even to the end" [Heb. 3:7, cf. Vg.]. Thus, he considers that no one hopes well in the Lord except him who confidently glories in the inheritance of the Heavenly Kingdom. No man is a believer, I say, except him who, leaning upon the assurance of his salvation, confidently triumphs over the devil and death; as we are taught from that masterly summation of Paul: I have confessed that "neither death nor life, nor angels, nor principalities, nor powers, nor things present, nor things to come . . . can separate us from the love of God which embraces us in Christ Jesus" [Rom. 8:38–39 p.]. Thus, in the same manner, the apostle does not consider the eyes of our minds well illumined, except as we discern what the hope of the eternal inheritance is to which we have been called [Eph. 1:18]. And everywhere he so teaches as to intimate that we cannot otherwise well comprehend the goodness of God unless we gather from it the fruit of great assurance.

17. Faith in the struggle against temptation
ᵇStill, someone will say: "Believers experience something far different: In recognizing the grace of God toward themselves they are not only tried by disquiet, which often comes upon them, but they are repeatedly shaken by gravest terrors. For so violent are the temptations that trouble their minds as not to seem quite compatible with that certainty of faith." Accordingly, we shall have to solve this difficulty if we wish the above-stated doctrine to stand. Surely, while we teach that faith ought to be certain and assured, we cannot imagine any certainty that is not tinged with doubt, or any assurance that is not assailed by some anxiety. On the other hand, we say that believers are in perpetual conflict with their own unbelief. Far, indeed, are we from putting their consciences in any peaceful repose, undisturbed by any tumult at all. Yet, once again, we deny that, in whatever way they are afflicted, they fall away and depart from the certain assurance received from God's mercy.

ᵉScripture sets forth no more illustrious or memorable example of faith than in David, especially if you look at the whole course of his life. Yet with innumerable complaints he declares how unquiet his mind always was. From these plaints it will be enough to choose a few examples. When he reproaches his own soul for its disturbed emotions, with what else is he angry than with his own unbelief? "Why do you tremble," he says, "my soul, and why are you disquieted within me? Hope in God." [Ps. 42:5, 11; 43:5.] Surely, that very dismay was an open sign of unbelief, as if he thought himself forsaken by God. Elsewhere we read an even fuller confession: "I have said in my alarm, I am cast away from the sight of thine eyes" [Ps. 31:22, cf. Comm.]. In another passage he also argues with himself in anxious and miserable perplexity; indeed, he starts a quarrel concerning the very nature of God: "Has God forgotten to be merciful? . . . Will he turn away forever?" [Ps. 77:9, 7; cf. Comm.]. Even harsher is what follows: "And I said, to slay is mine, the changes of the right hand of the Most High" [Ps. 77:10, Comm.]. In despair he condemns himself to death, and not only confesses himself to be troubled with doubt, but, as if he had fallen in the struggle, he feels that there is nothing left to him. For God has forsaken him, and has turned his hand, which was once his help, to his destruction. So, he justifiably urges his soul to return to its repose [Ps. 116:7] because he had experienced what it was to be tossed among stormy waves.

And yet—and this is something marvelous—amidst all these assaults faith sustains the hearts of the godly and truly in its effect resembles a palm tree [cf. Ps. 92:12, Vg.]: for it strives against every burden and raises itself upward. So David, even when he might have seemed overwhelmed, in rebuking himself did not cease to rise up to God. He who, struggling with his own weakness, presses toward faith in his moments of anxiety is already in large part victorious. Thus we may infer from this statement and ones like it: "Wait for Jehovah, be strong; he will strengthen your heart. Wait for Jehovah!" [Ps. 27:14, cf. Comm.]. David shows himself guilty of timidity, and, in repeating the same thought twice, confesses himself to be repeatedly subject to many troublesome emotions. In the meantime, he is not only displeased with himself for these weaknesses, but earnestly strives to correct them.

Surely, if we would duly weigh him in a fair balance with Ahaz, we shall find a great difference. Isaiah is sent to bring a remedy for the anxiety of the wicked and hypocritical king. He addresses him in these words: "Be on your guard, be still, fear not" [Isa. 7:4], etc. What does Ahaz do? It had previously been said that his heart was moved even as the trees of the forest are shaken by the wind [Isa. 7:2]; thus though he has heard the promise, he does not cease to tremble. Here, then, is the proper reward and penalty of unbelief: so to tremble as to turn aside from God when one does not open the door for himself by faith. But, on the other hand, believers whom the weight of temptation bends down and almost crushes constantly rise up, although not without difficulty and trouble. And because they are aware of their own weak-mindedness, they pray with the prophet, "Take not the word of truth utterly out of my mouth" [Ps. 119: 43, cf. Comm., and Ps. 118:43, Vg.]. By these words we are taught that they sometimes become dumb as if their faith had been laid low; yet they do not fail or turn their backs, but persevere in their struggle. And by prayer they spur on their sluggishness, lest, at least, out of self-indulgence they become benumbed.

18. The conflict in the heart of the believer

ᵇIn order to understand this, it is necessary to return to that division of flesh and spirit which we have mentioned elsewhere.[35] It most clearly reveals itself at this point. Therefore the godly heart feels in itself a division because it is partly imbued with sweetness from its recognition of the divine goodness, partly grieves in bitterness from an awareness of its calamity; partly rests upon the promise of the gospel, partly trembles at the evidence of its own iniquity; partly rejoices at the expectation of life, partly shudders at death. This variation arises from imperfection of faith, since in the course of the present life it never goes so well with us that we are wholly cured of the disease of unbelief and entirely filled and possessed by faith. Hence arise those conflicts; when unbelief, which reposes in the remains of the flesh, rises up to attack the faith that has been inwardly conceived.

But if in the believing mind certainty is mixed with doubt, do we not always come back to this, that faith does not rest in a certain and clear knowledge, but only in an obscure and confused knowledge of the divine will toward us? Not at all. For even if we are distracted by various thoughts, we are not on that account completely divorced from faith. Nor if we are troubled on all sides by the agitation of unbelief, are we for that reason immersed in its abyss. If we are struck, we are not for that reason cast down from our position. For the end of the conflict is always this: that faith ultimately triumphs over those difficulties which besiege and seem to imperil it.

[35] II. i. 9; II. ii. 27; II. iii. 1.

19. Even weak faith is real faith

ᵇTo sum up: When first even the least drop of faith is instilled in our minds, we begin to contemplate God's face, peaceful and calm and gracious toward us. We see him afar off, but so clearly as to know we are not at all deceived. Then, the more we advance as we ought continually to advance,³⁶ with steady progress, as it were, the nearer and thus surer sight of him we obtain; and by the very continuance he is made even more familiar to us. So we see that the mind, illumined by the knowledge of God, is at first wrapped up in much ignorance, which is gradually dispelled. Yet, by being ignorant of certain things, or by rather obscurely discerning what it does discern, the mind is not hindered from enjoying a clear knowledge of the divine will toward itself. For what it discerns comprises the first and principal parts in faith. It is like a man who, shut up in a prison into which the sun's rays shine obliquely and half obscured through a rather narrow window, is indeed deprived of the full sight of the sun. Yet his eyes dwell on its steadfast brightness, and he receives its benefits. Thus, bound with the fetters of an earthly body, however much we are shadowed on every side with great darkness, we are nevertheless illumined as much as need be for firm assurance when, to show forth his mercy, the light of God sheds even a little of its radiance.

20. The weakness and strength of faith

ᵇThe apostle finely teaches both points in various passages. For when he teaches that "we know in part and prophesy in part" [I Cor. 13:9, 12], and "see in a mirror dimly" [I Cor. 13:12], he indicates what a tiny portion of that truly divine wisdom is given us in the present life. ᵉThese words do not simply indicate that faith is imperfect so long as we groan under the burden of the flesh, but that, because of our own imperfection, we must constantly keep at learning. Nevertheless, he implies that the immeasurable cannot be comprehended by our inadequate measure and with our narrow capacities. Paul declares this also of the whole church: to each one of us his own ignorance is an obstacle and a hindrance, preventing him from coming as near as was to be desired.

ᵇBut in another passage the same apostle shows what a sure

---

³⁶ Cf. II. ii. 22–25; III. ii. 4, note 11. C. Trinkhaus, citing this section, remarks, "While for Plato men sinned out of ignorance, for Calvin men were ignorant out of sin": "Renaissance Problems in Calvin's Theology," *Studies in the Renaissance* III, ed. W. Peery, p. 61.

and genuine taste of itself even a small drop of faith gives us when he declares that through the gospel, with uncovered face and no veil intervening, we behold God's glory with such effect that we are transformed into his very likeness [II Cor. 3:18]. The greatest doubt and trepidation must be mixed up with such wrappings of ignorance, since our heart especially inclines by its own natural instinct toward unbelief. Besides this, there are innumerable and varied temptations that constantly assail us with great violence. But it is especially our conscience itself that, weighed down by a mass of sins, now complains and groans, now accuses itself, now murmurs secretly, now breaks out in open tumult. And so, whether adversities reveal God's wrath, or the conscience finds in itself the proof and ground thereof, thence unbelief obtains weapons and devices to overthrow faith. Yet these are always directed to this objective: that, thinking God to be against us and hostile to us, we should not hope for any help from him, and should fear him as if he were our deadly enemy.

21. The Word of God as the shield of faith

ᵇTo bear these attacks faith arms and fortifies itself with the Word of the Lord. And when any sort of temptation assails us— suggesting that God is our enemy because he is unfavorable toward us—faith, on the other hand, replies that while he afflicts us he is also merciful because his chastisement arises out of love rather than wrath. When one is stricken by the thought that God is Avenger of iniquities, faith sets over against this the fact that his pardon is ready for all iniquities whenever the sinner betakes himself to the Lord's mercy. Thus the godly mind, however strange the ways in which it is vexed and troubled, finally surmounts all difficulties, and never allows itself to be deprived of assurance of divine mercy. Rather, all the contentions that try and weary it result in the certainty of this assurance. A proof of this is that while the saints seem to be very greatly pressed by God's vengeance, yet they lay their complaints before him; and when it seems that they will not at all be heard, they nonetheless call upon him. What point would there be in crying out to him if they hoped for no solace from him? Indeed, it would never enter their minds to call upon him if they did not believe that he had prepared help for them. Thus the disciples whom Christ rebuked for the smallness of their faith complained that they were perishing, and yet were imploring his help [Matt. 8:25–26]. ᵉIndeed, while he reproves them for their little faith, he does not cast them out from the ranks of his disciples or count them among unbelievers, but urges them to shake off that fault. ᵇTherefore, we repeat what we have already stated: that the root of faith can never be torn from the godly breast, but clings so fast to the inmost parts that, however faith seems to be shaken or to bend this way or that, its light is never so extinguished or snuffed out that it does not at least lurk as it were beneath the ashes. ᵉAnd this example shows that the Word, which is an incorruptible seed, brings forth fruit like itself, whose fertility never wholly dries up and dies. ᵇThe ultimate cause of despair for the saints is to feel God's hand in their ruin, taking into account things present. And yet Job declares that his hope will extend so far that even if God should slay him he will not for that reason cease to hope in him [Job 13:15]. ᶜThe matter stands thus: Unbelief does not hold sway within believers' hearts, but assails them from without. It does not mortally wound them with its weapons, but merely harasses them, or at most so injures them that the wound is curable. Faith, then, as Paul teaches, serves as our shield [Eph. 6:16]. When held up against weapons it so receives their force that it either completely turns them aside or at least weakens their thrust, so that they cannot penetrate to our vitals. When, therefore, faith is shaken it is like a strong soldier forced by the violent blow of a spear to move his foot and to give ground a little. When faith itself is wounded it is as if the soldier's shield were broken at some point from the thrust of the spear, but not in such a manner as to be pierced. For the godly mind will always rise up so as to say with David, "If I walk in the midst of the shadow of death, I shall fear no evils, for thou art with me" [Ps. 22:4, Vg.; 23:4, EV]. Surely it is terrifying to walk in the darkness of death; and believers, whatever their strength may be, cannot but be frightened by it. But since the thought prevails that they have God beside them, caring for their safety, fear at once yields to assurance. However great are the devices, as Augustine says, that the devil throws up against us, while he holds no lodgment in the heart, where faith dwells, he is cast out.[37] ᵉThus, if we may judge from the outcome, believers not only emerge safely from every battle, so that, having received fresh strength, they are shortly after ready to descend again into the arena; but besides, what John says in his canonical letter is also fulfilled: "This is the victory that overcomes the world, your faith" [I John 5:4 p.]. And he affirms that our faith will be victor not only in one battle, or a few, or against any particular assault; but that, though it be assailed a thousand times, it will prevail over the entire world.

[37] Augustine, *John's Gospel* lii. 9 (on John 12:31) (MPL 35. 1772; tr. NPNF VII. 289).

22. *Right fear*

ᵇThere is another kind of "fear and trembling" [Phil. 2:12], one that, so far from diminishing the assurance of faith, the more firmly establishes it. This happens when believers, considering that the examples of divine wrath executed upon the ungodly as warnings to them, take special care not to provoke God's wrath against them by the same offenses; or, when inwardly contemplating their own misery, learn to depend wholly upon the Lord, without whom they see themselves more unstable and fleeting than any wind. For the apostle, by describing the chastisement with which the Lord of old punished the people of Israel, strikes terror into the Corinthians so that they should avoid entangling themselves in like misdeeds [I Cor. 10:11]. In that way he does not weaken their confidence, but only shakes the sluggishness of their flesh, by which faith is commonly more destroyed than strengthened. And while he takes from the fall of the Jews the basis for his exhortation that "he who stands take heed lest he fall" [I Cor. 10:12 p.; Rom. 11:20], he is not bidding us to waver, as if we were unsure of our steadfastness. Rather, he is merely taking away arrogance and rash overconfidence in our own strength so that after the Jews have been rejected, the Gentiles, received into their place, may not exult more wildly. ᶜYet, he there not only addresses believers but in his prayer includes also the hypocrites, who gloried only in outward show. And he does not admonish individual men, but makes a comparison between Jews and Gentiles; and he shows that the Jews in being rejected underwent the just punishments of their unbelief and ingratitude. He then also exhorts the Gentiles not to lose, through pride and self-display, the grace of adoption, recently transferred to them. Just as in that rejection of the Jews some of them remained who had not fallen away from the covenant of adoption, so from the Gentiles some might arise who, without true faith, would only be puffed up with stupid confidence of the flesh, and thus, to their own destruction, would abuse God's generosity. But even if you take this statement to apply to the elect and believers, this will cause no discomfiture. For it is one thing to restrain presumption, which sometimes creeps upon the saints from the vestiges of the flesh, in order that it may not play the wanton in vain confidence. It is another thing so to dishearten the conscience with fear that it cannot rest with full assurance in God's mercy.

23. *"Fear and trembling"*

ᵇThen, when the apostle teaches that we should "work out our own salvation in fear and trembling" [Phil. 2:12], he demands only that we become accustomed to honor the Lord's power, while greatly abasing ourselves. For nothing so moves us to repose our assurance and certainty of mind in the Lord as distrust of ourselves, and the anxiety occasioned by the awareness of our ruin. In this sense we must understand what is said by the prophet: "I, through the abundance of thy goodness, will enter thy temple; I will worship . . . in fear" [Ps. 5:7 p.]. Here he fitly joins the boldness of faith that rests upon God's mercy with the reverent fear that we must experience whenever we come into the presence of God's majesty, and by its splendor understand how great is our own filthiness. Solomon, also, speaks truly when he declares that man blessed who is always afraid in his own heart, since by hardening it falls into evil [Prov. 28:14]. But he means that fear which renders us more cautious—not the kind that afflicts us and causes us to fall—while the mind confused in itself recovers itself in God, cast down in itself is raised up in him, despairing of itself is quickened anew through trust in him.

Accordingly, nothing prevents believers from being afraid and at the same time possessing the surest consolation; according as they turn their eyes now upon their own vanity, and then bring the thought of their minds to bear upon the truth of God. ᵉHow, someone will ask, can fear and faith dwell in the same mind? Indeed, in the same way that, conversely, sluggishness and worry so dwell. For while the impious seek freedom from pain for themselves that no fear of God may trouble them, yet the judgment of God so presses them that they cannot attain what they desire. Thus, nothing hinders God from training his own people in humility, that while fighting stoutly they may restrain themselves under the bridle of self-control. And from the context it is clear that this was the intention of the apostle where he assigns the cause of fear and trembling to God's good pleasure, whereby He gives to His people the capacity to will aright and to carry through valiantly [Phil. 2:12–13]. In this sense we may rightly understand the prophet's saying: "The children of Israel shall fear the Lord and his goodness" [Hos. 3:5]. For not only does piety beget reverence toward God, but the very sweetness and delightfulness of grace so fills a man who is cast down in himself with fear, and at the same time with admiration, that he depends upon God and humbly submits himself to his power.

24. The indestructible certainty of faith rests upon Christ's oneness with us

ᶜYet we do not thus accept that most pestilent philosophy which certain half-papists are furtively beginning to fashion today. For because they cannot defend that rude doubt which has been handed down in the schools, they take refuge in another fiction: that they may make an assurance mingled with unbelief. Whenever we look upon Christ, they confess that we find full occasion for good hope in him. But because we are always unworthy of all those benefits which are offered to us in Christ, they would have us waver and hesitate at the sight of our unworthiness. In brief, they so set conscience between hope and fear that it alternates from one to the other intermittently and by turns. They so relate hope and fear that when the former is rising up the latter is oppressed; when the latter rises again, the former falls once more. Thus, when Satan once sees that those open devices with which he formerly had been wont to destroy the certainty of faith are now of no avail, he tries to sap it by covert devices. But what kind of confidence will that be, which now and again yields to despair? If, they say, you contemplate Christ, there is sure salvation: if you turn back to yourself, there is sure damnation. Therefore unbelief and good hope must alternately reign in your mind. As if we ought to think of Christ, standing afar off and not rather dwelling in us! For we await salvation from him not because he appears to us afar off, but because he makes us, ingrafted into his body, participants not only in all his benefits but also in himself. So I turn this argument of theirs back against them: if you contemplate yourself, that is sure damnation. But since Christ has been so imparted to you with all his benefits that all his things are made yours, that you are made a member of him, indeed one with him, his righteousness overwhelms your sins; his salvation wipes out your condemnation; with his worthiness he intercedes that your unworthiness may not come before God's sight. Surely this is so: We ought not to separate Christ from ourselves or ourselves from him. Rather we ought to hold fast bravely with both hands to that fellowship by which he has bound himself to us. So the apostle teaches us: "Now your body is dead because of sin; but the Spirit of Christ which dwells in you is life because of righteousness" [Rom. 8: 10 p.]. According to these men's trifles, he ought to have said: "Christ indeed has life in himself; but you, as you are sinners, remain subject to death and condemnation." But he speaks far otherwise, for he teaches that that condemnation which we of ourselves deserve has been swallowed up by the salvation that is in Christ. And to confirm this he uses the same reason I have brought forward: that Christ is not outside us but dwells within us. Not only does he cleave to us by an indivisible bond of fellowship, but with a wonderful communion, day by day, he grows more and more into one body with us, until he becomes completely one with us. ᵉYet I do not deny what I stated above:[38] that certain interruptions of faith occasionally occur, according as its weakness is violently buffeted hither and thither; so in the thick darkness of temptations its light is snuffed out. Yet whatever happens, it ceases not its earnest quest for God.

25. Bernard of Clairvaux on the two aspects of faith
ᶜBernard of Clairvaux reasons similarly when he expressly discusses this question in his Fifth Sermon on the Dedication of a Church. "Now when I reflect upon my soul—which by the grace of God I sometimes do—it seems to me that I discover in it, so to speak, two opposite aspects. If I consider it in and of itself, I can say nothing more truly of it than that it is reduced to nothing [Ps. 72:22, Vg.]. What need is there now to enumerate the individual miseries of the soul; how it is burdened with sins, enveloped in darkness, enslaved to pleasure, itching with lusts, subject to passions, filled with delusions, always prone to evil, bent to every sort of vice—in a word, full of shame and confusion? To be sure, if all our acts of righteousness, scrutinized in the light of truth, are found to be like 'the rag of a menstruous woman' [Isa. 64:6, Vg.], then to what will our unrighteous acts be compared? 'If then the light in us is darkness, how great will be the darkness!' [Matt. 6:23.] What then? Without doubt . . . 'Man has been made like unto vanity' [Ps. 143:4, Vg.; 144:4, EV]. Man 'has been reduced to nothing' [Ps. 72:22, Vg.]. Man is nought. Yet how can he whom God magnifies be utterly nothing? How can he upon whom God has set his heart be nothing?

"Brethren, let us take heart again. Even if we are nothing in our own hearts, perchance something of us may be hidden in the heart of God. O 'Father of mercies' [II Cor. 1:3]! O Father of the miserable! How canst thou set thy heart upon us. . . . 'For where thy treasure is, thine heart is also.' [Matt. 6:21.] But how are we thy treasure if we are nothing? 'All the nations are as nothing before thee, they will be accounted by thee as nothing.' [Isa. 40:17 p.] So, indeed, *before* thee, not *within* thee: so in the judgment of thy truth, but not so in the intention of thy faithfulness. So, indeed, thou 'callest those things which are not as though they were' [Rom. 4:17]. And they *are not,* therefore, because it is the things that are not that thou callest, and they *are* at the same time because thou callest them. For although, as regards themselves, they are not, nevertheless with thee they are; but, as the apostle says, 'Not of their works' of righteousness, 'but of him

³⁸ Cf. II. i. 1; III. ii. 17.

who calls' [Rom. 9:11]. Then he says that this connection between the two considerations is wonderful. Surely those things which are connected do not destroy one another!"

Also, in conclusion, he more openly declares this in these words: "Now if we diligently examine what we are, under these two considerations, or rather, if we examine how from the one point of view we are nothing, and from the other how magnified, . . . I believe our glorying will appear moderate, yet will perchance be greater and better founded than before, so that we glory not in ourselves but in the Lord [II Cor. 10:17]. Surely if we think, 'If he has decreed to save us, we shall be immediately freed' [cf. Jer. 17:14]; in this, then, we may take heart.

"But climbing up to a higher watchtower, let us seek the City of God, let us seek his temple, let us seek his house, let us seek his bride. I have not forgotten . . . , but with fear and reverence . . . I say: 'We, I say, are, but in the heart of God. We are, but by his dignifying us, not by our own dignity.' "[39]

26. Fear of God and honor of God

[b]Now, "the fear of the Lord"—to which all the saints give witness—and which is in some places called "the beginning of wisdom" [Ps. 111:10; Prov. 1:7], in other places "wisdom itself" [Prov. 15:33; Job 28:28]—although one, yet derives from a double meaning. For God has in his own right the reverence of a father and of a lord. Therefore, he who would duly worship him will try to show himself both an obedient son to him and a dutiful servant. The Lord, through the prophet, calls "honor" that obedience which is rendered to him as Father. He calls "fear" the service that is done to him as Lord. "A son," he says, "honors his father; a servant, his lord. If, then, I am a father, where is my honor? If I am a lord, where is my fear?" [Mal. 1:6]. However he may distinguish them, you see how he fuses together the two terms. Therefore, let the fear of the Lord be for us a reverence compounded of honor and fear. No wonder if the same mind embraces both dispositions! For he who ponders within himself what God the Father is like toward us[40] has cause enough, even if there be no hell, to dread offending him more gravely than any death. But also—such is the wanton desire of our flesh to sin without restraint—in order to check it by every means we must at once seize upon this thought: that the Lord, under whose

Bernard of Clairvaux, *In dedicatione ecclesiae,* sermon v (MPL 183. 531–534; tr. *St. Bernard's Sermons for the Seasons,* by a priest of Mount Melleray II. 419–426).
[40] Cf. I. ii. 2; I. x. 1; II. vi. 4.

power we live, abhors all iniquity. And they who, by living wickedly, provoke his wrath against themselves will not escape his vengeance.

27. *Childlike and servile fear*

ᵇJohn, moreover, says: "There is no fear in love, but perfect love casts out fear, for fear has to do with punishment" [I John 4:18]. This does not clash with what we have said. For he is speaking of the dread arising from unbelief, far different from believers' fear. For the wicked fear God not because they are afraid of incurring his displeasure, if only they could do so with impunity; but because they know him to be armed with the power to take vengeance, they shake with fright on hearing of his wrath. And they so fear his wrath because they think it hangs over them, because they expect that at any moment it will fall upon their heads. But believers, as has been said, both fear offending God more than punishment, and are not troubled by fear of punishment, as if it hung over their necks. But they are rendered more cautious not to incur it. So speaks the apostle when he addresses believers: "Let no one deceive you, . . . for it is because of this that the wrath of God comes upon the sons of unbelief"⁴¹ [Eph. 5:6, Vg.; cf. Col. 3:6]. He does not threaten that God's wrath will descend upon them, but he warns them to think on the wrath of the Lord, prepared for the impious, on account of those wicked deeds which he had recounted, lest they themselves also should wish to experience it. ᶜYet it rarely happens that the wicked are aroused by simple threats alone. Rather, whenever God thunders with words from heaven, slow and sluggish in their hardness they persist in their stubbornness. But once struck by his hand, they are compelled, whether they will or not, to fear. This fear men commonly call "servile" and contrast to it the free and voluntary fear that befits children. Others subtly interpolate an intermediate kind of fear because that servile and constrained feeling sometimes so subdues men's minds that they accede willingly to a proper fear of God.⁴²

28. *Faith assures us not of earthly prosperity but of God's favor**

ᵇNow, in the divine benevolence, which faith is said to look to, we understand the possession of salvation and eternal life is obtained. For if, while God is favorable, no good can be lacking,

---

⁴¹ *"In filios diffidentiae"*: So Vg., Eph. 5:6.
⁴² Augustine, *John's Gospel* lxxxv. 3 (MPL 35. 1849; tr. NPNF VII. 352); *Epistle of John* ix. 4 (MPL 35. 2047 f.; tr. NPNF VII. 515); Lombard, *Sentences* III. xxxiv. 5–8 (MPL 192. 825 f.); Aquinas, *Summa Theol.* II IIae. xix. 2, 8.

when he assures us of his love we are abundantly and sufficiently assured of salvation. "Let him show his face," says the prophet, "and we will be saved." [Ps. 80:3 p.; cf. Ps. 79:4, Vg.] Hence Scripture establishes this as the sum of our salvation, that he has abolished all enmities and received us into grace [Eph. 2:14]. By this they intimate that when God is reconciled to us no danger remains to prevent all things from prospering for us. Faith, therefore, having grasped the love of God, has promises of the present life and of that to come [I Tim. 4:8], and firm assurance of all good things, but of such sort as can be perceived from the Word. For faith does not certainly promise itself either length of years or honor or riches in this life, since the Lord willed that none of these things be appointed for us. But it is content with this certainty: that, however many things fail us that have to do with the maintenance of this life, God will never fail. Rather, the chief assurance of faith rests in the expectation of the life to come, which has been placed beyond doubt through the Word of God. Yet whatever earthly miseries and calamities await those whom God has embraced in his love, these cannot hinder his benevolence from being their full happiness. Accordingly, when we would express the sum of blessedness, we have mentioned the grace of God; for from this fountain every sort of good thing flows unto us. And we may commonly observe in the Scriptures that we are recalled to the love of the Lord whenever mention is made not only of eternal salvation but of any good we may have. For this reason, David sings of that divine goodness which, when felt in the godly heart, is sweeter and more desirable than life itself [Ps. 63:3].

ᶜIn short, if all things flow unto us according to our wish, but we are uncertain of God's love or hatred, our happiness will be accursed and therefore miserable. But if in fatherly fashion God's countenance beams upon us, even our miseries will be blessed. For they will be turned into aids to salvation. So Paul heaps up all adverse things, but glories that we are not separated from God's love through them [Rom. 8:35, cf. v. 39], and always begins his prayers with God's grace, whence flows all prosperity; in like manner, against all terrors that disturb us David sets God's favor alone: "If I walk in the midst of the shadow of death, I shall fear no evils, for thou art with me" [Ps. 22:4, Vg.; 23:4, EV]. And we always feel our minds wavering unless, content with God's grace, they seek their peace in it, and hold fixed deep within what is said in the psalm: "Blessed is the people whose God is Jehovah, and the nation he has chosen as his inheritance" [Ps. 33:12, cf. Comm.].

(Basis of faith the free promise, given in the Word, of grace in Christ, 29-32)

29. God's promise the support of faith[t]

bWe make the freely given promise of God the foundation of faith because upon it faith properly rests. Faith is certain that God is true in all things whether he command or forbid, whether he promise or threaten; and it also obediently receives his commandments, observes his prohibitions, heeds his threats. Nevertheless, faith properly begins with the promise, rests in it, and ends in it. For in God faith seeks life: a life that is not found in commandments or declarations of penalties, but in the promise of mercy, and only in a freely given promise. For a conditional promise that sends us back to our own works does not promise life unless we discern its presence in ourselves. Therefore, if we would not have our faith tremble and waver, we must buttress it with the promise of salvation, which is willingly and freely offered to us by the Lord in consideration of our misery rather than our deserts. The apostle, therefore, bears this witness to the gospel: that it is the word of faith [Rom. 10:8]. He distinguishes the gospel both from the precepts of the law and from the promises, since there is nothing that can establish faith except that generous embassy by which God reconciles the world to himself [cf. II Cor. 5:19-20]. Thence, also, arises that frequent correlation of faith and gospel in the apostle, when he teaches that the ministry of the gospel is committed to him to further "obedience to the faith" [Rom. 1:5], that "it is the power of God for salvation to every believer; . . . in it the righteousness of God is revealed through faith for faith" [Rom. 1:16-17]. And no wonder! Indeed, since the gospel is the "ministry of reconciliation" [II Cor. 5:18], no other sufficiently firm testimony of God's benevolence to us exists, the knowledge of which faith seeks.[43]

Therefore, when we say that faith must rest upon a freely given promise, we do not deny that believers embrace and grasp the Word of God in every respect: but we point out the promise of mercy as the proper goal of faith. As on the one hand believers ought to recognize God to be Judge and Avenger of wicked deeds, yet on the other hand they properly contemplate his kindness, since he is so described to them as to be considered "one who is kind" [cf. Ps. 86:5, Comm.], "and merciful" [cf. Ps. 103:8, Comm.; 102:8, Vg.], "far from anger and of great goodness" [cf.

---

[43] *"Cuius agnitionem fides requirit."* Cf. Anselm, *Proslogion*, Preface (MPL 158; tr. LCC X. 70, and the literature cited by E. R. Fairweather, *ibid.*, pp. 65 ff.).

Ps. 103:8, Comm.], "sweet to all" [Ps. 144:9, Vg.], "pouring out his mercy upon all his works" [cf. Ps. 145:9, Comm.].

30. Why faith depends solely on the promise of grace

dAnd I do not tarry over the barkings of Pighius and dogs like him, when they attack this restriction, as if by tearing faith to pieces they might grab up a single piece.[44] I admit, as I have already said, that God's truth is, as they call it, the common object of faith, whether he threaten or hold out hope of grace. Therefore, the apostle attributes to faith the fact that Noah feared the world's destruction when it was not as yet visible [Heb. 11:7]. If fear of imminent punishment was the product of faith, then threats ought not to be excluded from the definition of it. This is indeed true. But our slanderers unjustly charge us with denying, as it were, that faith has regard to all parts of the Word of God. It is our intention to make only these two points: first, that faith does not stand firm until a man attains to the freely given promise; second, that it does not reconcile us to God at all unless it joins us to Christ. Both points are worth noting. We seek a faith that distinguishes the children of God from the wicked, and believers from unbelievers. If someone believes that God both justly commands all that he commands and truly threatens, shall he therefore be called a believer? By no means! Therefore, there can be no firm condition of faith unless it rests upon God's mercy. Now, what is our purpose in discussing faith? Is it not that we may grasp the way of salvation? But how can there be saving faith except in so far as it engrafts us in the body of Christ? Accordingly, when we define it there is no absurdity in our thus emphasizing its particular effect and, as a distinction, subordinating to the class that special mark which separates believers from unbelievers. In short, in this doctrine the malicious have nothing to carp at without implicating Paul in the same censure with us, who rightly calls the gospel "the word of faith" [Rom. 10:8].

31. The significance of the Word for faith

eHence, we again infer what had been explained before:[45] that faith needs the Word as much as fruit needs the living root of a tree. For no others, as David witnesses, can hope in God but

---

[44] Calvin's definition of faith (in the 1539 *Institutio*, ch. iv) was assailed by Albert Pighius, archdeacon of Utrecht, as "indefinite," "confused," and tending to "a false security": *Controversiarum praecipuarum . . . explicatio* (1542), ch. ii, fo. 58a–60a.
[45] Sec. 6, above.

those who know his name [Ps. 9:10]. But this knowledge does not arise out of anyone's imagination, but only so far as God himself is witness to his goodness. This the prophet confirms in another place: "Thy salvation according to thy word" [Ps. 119: 41]. Likewise, "I have hoped in thy word; make me safe." [Ps. 119:42, 40, 94.] Here we must first note the relation of faith to the Word, then its consequence, salvation.

Yet in the meantime we do not exclude God's power in respect to which, unless faith sustains itself, it can never render to God the honor due him. Paul seems to apply to Abraham a barren commonplace: that he believed God, who had promised him blessed offspring, to be mighty [Rom. 4:21]. Likewise, he says elsewhere concerning himself: "I know whom I have believed, and I am sure that he is mighty to guard until that day what has been entrusted to me" [II Tim. 1:12]. But if anyone considers in himself how many doubts concerning the power of God often creep in, he will sufficiently recognize that they who magnify it as it deserves have made no slight progress in faith. All of us will confess that God is able to do whatever he wills; but when the slightest temptation strikes us down in fear and stuns us with fright, from this it is plain that we detract from God's might, preferring to it the threatening of Satan against His promises. This is the reason why Isaiah, when he wishes to impress the certainty of salvation upon the hearts of the people, so grandly discusses God's boundless power [Isa. 40:25 ff., and often in Isa., chs. 40 to 45]. It often seems that, when he begins to speak concerning the hope of pardon and reconciliation, he turns to something else and wanders through long and superfluous mazes, recalling how wonderfully God governs the frame of heaven and earth together with the whole order of nature. Yet there is nothing here that does not serve the present circumstance. For unless the power of God, by which he can do all things, confronts our eyes, our ears will barely receive the Word or not esteem it at its true value.

Besides this, his effectual might is here declared, since piety— as has appeared elsewhere[46]—always adapts God's might to use and need; and especially sets before itself the works of God by which he has testified that he is the Father. Hence comes the very frequent mention of redemption in the Scriptures, from which the Israelites could learn that God, who had once for all been the Author of salvation, was to be its eternal guardian. By his example David, also, reminds us that those benefits which God bestows individually upon each man serve to confirm faith in him

[46] I. xvi. 3.

for the future. Indeed, when it seems that he has deserted us we must stretch our thoughts farther, that his former benefits may revive us, as is said in another psalm: "I remember the days of old, I have meditated on all thy deeds . . . " [Ps. 143:5; 142:5, Vg.]. Likewise, "I will remember the works of the Lord . . . and his wonders from the beginning." [Ps. 77:11, Comm.]

But because whatever we conceive concerning God's might and works is fleeting without the Word, we declare with good reason that there is no faith until God illumines it by the testimony of his grace.

Yet here it would be possible to raise the question What should we think of Sarah and Rebecca? both of whom, it seems, were fired with a zealous faith and went beyond the limits of the Word. Sarah, passionately desiring the promised offspring, yielded her maidservant to her husband [Gen. 16:2, 5]. We must not deny that she sinned in many ways; but I am now dealing with her failure, when carried away with zeal, to confine herself within the limits of God's Word. Yet it is certain that that desire arose out of faith. Rebecca, assured by divine oracle of the choice of her son Jacob, obtains the blessing for him by a wicked subterfuge [Gen. 27:9]: She deceives her husband, the witness and minister of God's grace. She compels her son to lie. She corrupts God's truth by various guiles and deceits. In short, in scorning his promise, she destroys it as far as she can [Gen., ch. 27].

Yet this act, although a failing and deserving of rebuke, was not devoid of faith. For it was necessary that she overcome many little obstacles that she might stoutly strive after something that offered no hope of earthly benefit, and was teeming with huge troubles and dangers. In the same way, we do not regard the patriarch Isaac as entirely devoid of faith for the reason that, admonished by the same oracle concerning the honor transferred to his younger son, he still did not cease to be inclined to his first-born son, Esau. These examples surely teach that errors are often mingled with faith, yet in such a way that when it is a true faith it always holds the upper hand. For just as Rebecca's particular error did not render void the effect of the blessing, so it did not render void her faith, which generally held mastery in her mind and was the beginning and cause of that action. Nonetheless, Rebecca betrayed in this how slippery are the turnings of the human mind, as soon as it relaxes its control in the slightest degree. But even though man's default and weakness obscure faith, they do not extinguish it. In the meantime, they warn us how carefully we ought to wait upon God's voice; and at the same time they confirm what we have taught: that faith vanishes unless it is supported by the Word. The minds of Sarah and Isaac and Rebecca would have vanished in their devious shiftings if they had not been kept in obedience to the Word by God's secret bridle.

32. The promise of faith fulfilled in Christ

ᵇAgain, it is not without cause that we include all the promises in Christ, since the apostle includes the whole gospel under the knowledge of him [cf. Rom. 1:17], and elsewhere teaches that "however many are the promises of God, in him they find their yea and amen" [II Cor. 1:20 p.]. The reason for this fact is at hand; for if God promises anything, by it he witnesses his benevolence, so that there is no promise of his which is not a testimony of his love. Nor does it make any difference that, while the wicked are plied with the huge and repeated benefits of God's bounty, they bring upon themselves a heavier judgment. For they neither think nor recognize that these benefits come to them from the Lord's hand; or if they do recognize it, they do not within themselves ponder his goodness. Hence, they cannot be apprised of his mercy any more than brute animals can, which, according to their condition, receive the same fruit of God's liberality, yet perceive it not. Nothing prevents them, in habitually rejecting the promises intended for them, from thereby bringing upon themselves a greater vengeance. For although the effectiveness of the promises only appears when they have aroused faith in us, yet the force and peculiar nature of the promises are never extinguished by our unfaithfulness and ingratitude. Therefore, since the Lord, by his promises, invites man not only to receive the fruits of his kindness but also to think about them, he at the same time declares his love to man. Hence we must return to the point: that any promise whatsoever is a testimony of God's love toward us.

But it is indisputable that no one is loved by God apart from Christ:⁴⁷ "This is the beloved Son" [Matt. 3:17; 17:5 p.], ᶜin whom dwells and rests the Father's love. And from him it then pours itself upon us, just as Paul teaches: "We receive grace in the beloved" [Eph. 1:6 p.]. ᵇIt must therefore derive and reach us when he himself intercedes. Consequently, the apostle in one passage calls him "our peace" [Eph. 2:14]; in another, Paul puts him forward as the bond whereby God may be found to us in fatherly faithfulness [cf. Rom. 8:3 ff.]. It follows that we should turn our eyes to him as often as any promise is offered to us. And

⁴⁷ Calvin often asserts this, with various forms of expression. Cf. esp. Comm. John 3:16.

Paul rightly teaches us that all God's promises are confirmed and fulfilled in him [Rom. 15:8].

eSome instances disagree with this. When, for example, Naaman the Syrian inquired of the prophet as to the proper way of worshiping God, it is not likely that he was instructed concerning the Mediator. Still, his piety is praised [II Kings 5:1–14; Luke 4:27]. Cornelius, a Gentile and a Roman, could scarcely grasp what was known only obscurely to the Jews, and not to all of them. Yet his alms and his prayers were acceptable to God [Acts 10:31]. And Naaman's sacrifice was approved by the prophet's response [II Kings 5:17–19]. Neither could have occurred except by faith. The same reasoning applies to the eunuch to whom Philip was brought: unless he had been endowed with some faith, he would not have undertaken the labor and expense of a difficult journey in order to worship [Acts 8:27]. Yet we see that when asked by Philip, he showed his ignorance of the Mediator [Acts 8:31]. And I even confess that their faith was in some part implicit, not only with respect to the person of Christ, but also with respect to the power and office enjoined upon him by the Father. In the meantime, it is certain that they were instructed in principles such as might give them some taste, however small, of Christ. This ought not to seem strange, for the eunuch would not have hastened to Jerusalem from a far-off region to worship an unknown God; and certainly Cornelius, having once embraced the Jewish religion, did not spend much time without becoming acquainted with the rudiments of true doctrine. As far as Naaman was concerned, it would have been too absurd, when Elisha instructed him concerning small things, to have been silent on the principal point. Therefore, although the knowledge of Christ was obscure among them, it is inconceivable to suppose that there was none at all; because they practiced the sacrifices of the law, which by their very end—that is, Christ—should be distinguished from the false sacrifices of the Gentiles.

(Faith revealed in our hearts by the Spirit, 33–37)

33. The Word becomes efficacious for our faith through the Holy Spirit

bAnd this bare and external proof of the Word of God should have been amply sufficient to engender faith, did not our blindness and perversity prevent it. But our mind has such an inclination to vanity that it can never cleave fast to the truth of God; and it has such a dullness that it is always blind to the light of God's truth. Accordingly, without the illumination of the Holy Spirit, the Word can do nothing. From this, also, it is clear that faith is much higher than human understanding. And it will not be enough for the mind to be illumined by the Spirit of God unless the heart is also strengthened and supported by his power. In this matter the Schoolmen go completely astray, who in considering faith identify it with a bare and simple assent arising out of knowledge, and leave out confidence and assurance of heart.[48] In both ways, therefore, faith is a singular gift of God, both in that the mind of man is purged so as to be able to taste the truth of God and in that his heart is established therein. ᵉFor the Spirit is not only the initiator of faith, but increases it by degrees, until by it he leads us to the Kingdom of Heaven. "Let each one," says Paul, "guard the precious truth . . . entrusted by the Holy Spirit who dwells in us." [II Tim. 1:14 p.] We can with no trouble explain how Paul teaches that the Spirit is given by the hearing of faith [Gal. 3:2]. If there had been only one gift of the Spirit, it would have been absurd of Paul to call the Spirit the "effect of faith," since he is its Author and cause. But because he proclaims the gifts with which God adorns his church and brings it to perfection by continual increase of faith, it is no wonder if he ascribes to faith those things which prepare us to receive them! ᵇThis, indeed, is considered most paradoxical: when it is said that no one, unless faith be granted to him, can believe in Christ [John 6:65]. But this is partly because men do not consider either how secret and lofty the heavenly wisdom is, or how very dull men are to perceive the mysteries of God; partly because they do not have regard to that firm and steadfast constancy of heart which is the chief part of faith.

34. Only the Holy Spirit leads us to Christ

ᵇBut if, as Paul preaches, no one "except the spirit of man which is in him" [I Cor. 2:11] witnesses the human will, what man would be sure of God's will? And if the truth of God be untrustworthy among us also in those things which we at present behold with our eyes, how could it be firm and steadfast when the Lord promises such things as neither eye can see nor understanding can grasp [cf. I Cor. 2:9]? But here man's discernment is so overwhelmed and so fails that the first degree of advancement in the school of the Lord is to renounce it. For, like a veil cast over us, it hinders us from attaining the mysteries of God, "revealed to babes alone" [Matt. 11:25; Luke 10:21]. "For flesh and blood does not reveal this" [Matt. 16:17], "but the natural man

---

[48] Cf. I. v. 9; III. ii. 1, 8, 36; Augustine, *Predestination of the Saints* ii. 5 (MPL 44. 963; tr. NPNF V. 499); Cadier, *Institution* III. 56, note 1.

does not perceive the things that are of the Spirit"; rather, God's teaching is "foolishness to him . . . because it must be spiritually discerned" [I Cor. 2:14, cf. Vg.]. Therefore, the support of the Holy Spirit is necessary, or rather, his power alone thrives here. "There is no man who has known the mind of God, or has been his counselor." [Rom. 11:34 p.] But "the Spirit searches everything, even the depths of God." [I Cor. 2:10.] It is through the Spirit that we come to grasp "the mind of Christ" [I Cor. 2:16]. "No one can come to me," he says, "unless the Father who has sent me draw him." [John 6:44.] "Everyone who has heard from the Father and has learned, comes." [John 6:45.] Not that anyone has ever seen the Father but him who was sent by God [John 1:18 and 5:37, conflated]. Therefore, as we cannot come to Christ unless we be drawn by the Spirit of God, so when we are drawn we are lifted up in mind and heart above our understanding. For the soul, illumined by him, takes on a new keenness, as it were, to contemplate the heavenly mysteries, whose splendor had previously blinded it. And man's understanding, thus beamed by the light of the Holy Spirit, then at last truly begins to taste those things which belong to the Kingdom of God, having formerly been quite foolish and dull in tasting them. For this reason, Christ, in clearly interpreting the mysteries of his Kingdom to two disciples [Luke 24:27], still makes no headway until "he opens their minds to understand the Scriptures" [Luke 24:45]. Although the apostles were so taught by his divine mouth, the Spirit of truth must nevertheless be sent to pour into their minds the same doctrine that they had perceived with their ears [John 16:13]. Indeed, the Word of God is like the sun, shining upon all those to whom it is proclaimed, but with no effect among the blind. Now, all of us are blind by nature in this respect. Accordingly, it cannot penetrate into our minds unless the Spirit, as the inner teacher, through his illumination makes entry for it.

35. Without the Spirit man is incapable of faith

ᵉIn another place, when we had to discuss the corruption of nature, we showed more fully how unfit men are to believe.[49] Accordingly, I shall not weary my readers with repeating the same thing. Let it suffice that Paul calls faith itself, which the Spirit gives us but which we do not have by nature, "the spirit of faith" [II Cor. 4:13]. He therefore prays that in the Thessalonians "God . . . may fulfill with power all his good pleasure . . . and work of faith" [II Thess. 1:11, cf. Vg.]. Here Paul calls

[49] II. ii. 18–25.

faith "the work of God," and instead of distinguishing it by an adjective, appropriately calls it "good pleasure."[50] Thus he denies that man himself initiates faith, and not satisfied with this, he adds that it is a manifestation of God's power. In the letter to the Corinthians he states that faith does not depend upon men's wisdom, but is founded upon the might of the Spirit [I Cor. 2:4–5]. He is speaking, indeed, of outward miracles; but because the wicked, being blind, cannot see these, he includes also that inner seal which he mentions elsewhere [Eph. 1:13; 4:30]. And God, to show forth his liberality more fully in such a glorious gift, does not bestow it upon all indiscriminately, but by a singular privilege gives it to those to whom he will. We have above cited testimonies of this. Augustine, the faithful interpreter of them, exclaims: "Our Savior, to teach us that belief comes as a gift and not from merit, says: 'No one comes to me, unless my Father . . . draw him' [John 6:44 p.], and ' . . . it be granted him by my Father' [John 6:65 p.]. It is strange that two hear: one despises, the other rises up! Let him who despises impute it to himself; let him who rises up not arrogate it to himself." In another passage he says: "Why is it given to one and not to another? I am not ashamed to say: 'This is the depth of the cross.' Out of some depth or other of God's judgments, which we cannot fathom, . . . comes forth all that we can do. . . . I see what I can do; I do not see whence I can do it—except that I see this far: that . . . it is of God. But why one and not the other? This means much to me. It is an abyss, the depth of the cross. I can exclaim in wonder; I cannot demonstrate it through disputation."[51] To sum up: Christ, when he illumines us into faith by the power of his Spirit, at the same time so engrafts us into his body that we become partakers of every good.

36. Faith as a matter of the heart

ᵇIt now remains to pour into the heart itself what the mind has absorbed. For the Word of God is not received by faith if it flits about in the top of the brain, but when it takes root in the depth of the heart that it may be an invincible defense to withstand and drive off all the stratagems of temptation. But if it is true that the mind's real understanding is illumination by the Spirit of God, then in such confirmation of the heart his power is much more clearly manifested, to the extent that the

---

50 "Motu."
51 Augustine, Sermons cxxxi. 2, 3; clxv. 5 (MPL 38. 730, 905; tr. LF Sermons II. 586 f., 839 f.).

heart's distrust is greater than the mind's blindness.[52] It is harder for the heart to be furnished with assurance than for the mind to be endowed with thought. The Spirit accordingly serves as a seal, to seal up in our hearts those very promises the certainty of which it has previously impressed upon our minds; and takes the place of a guarantee to confirm and establish them. After "you believed" (the apostle declares), "you were sealed with the Holy Spirit of promise, who is the guarantee of our inheritance" [Eph. 1:13–14, Comm.]. Do you see how Paul teaches that the hearts of believers have, so to speak, been sealed with the Spirit; how, for this reason, Paul calls him the "Spirit of promise," because he makes firm the gospel among us? In like manner, he says in the letter to the Corinthians: "He who . . . has anointed us, is God; who has also sealed us, and given the guarantee of the Spirit in our hearts" [II Cor. 1:21–22, KJV]. And, in another passage, when Paul speaks of confidence and boldness of hope, he lays as its foundation the guarantee of the Spirit [II Cor. 5:5].

37. Doubt cannot smother faith

ᵉAnd I have not forgotten what I have previously said,[53] the memory of which is repeatedly renewed by experience: faith is tossed about by various doubts, so that the minds of the godly are rarely at peace—at least they do not always enjoy a peaceful state. But whatever siege engines may shake them, they either rise up out of the very gulf of temptations, or stand fast upon their watch. Indeed, this assurance alone nourishes and protects faith—when we hold fast to what is said in the psalm: "The Lord is our protection, our help in tribulation. Therefore we will not fear while the earth shakes, and the mountains leap into the heart of the sea" [Ps. 46:2–3, cf. Comm.]. Another psalm, also, extols this very sweet repose: "I lay down and slept; I awoke again, for the Lord sustained me" [Ps. 3:5]. Not that David always dwelt in a tranquil and happy state! But to the extent that he tasted God's grace, according to the measure of faith, he boasts that he fearlessly despises everything that could trouble his peace of mind. For this reason, Scripture, meaning to urge us to faith, bids us be quiet. In Isaiah: "In hope and in silence shall your strength be" [ch. 30:15, Vg.]. In the psalm: "Be still before Jehovah and wait . . . for him" [Ps. 37:7, Comm.]. To these verses corresponds the apostle's statement in The Letter to the Hebrews: "For you have need of patience," etc. [ch. 10:36].

[52] Cf. I. v. 9; III. ii. 8, 33; III. vi. 4.
[53] Sec. 17, above.

(Refutation of Scholastic objections to this, 38–40)
38. Scholastic error concerning the assurance of faith*

ᵇHence we may judge how dangerous is the Scholastic dogma that we can discern the grace of God toward us only by moral conjecture, according as every man regards himself as not unworthy of it.⁵⁴ Indeed, if we should have to judge from our works how the Lord feels toward us, for my part, I grant that we can in no way attain it by conjecture. But since faith ought to correspond to a simple and free promise, no place for doubting is left. For with what sort of confidence will we be armed, I pray, if we reason that God is favorable to us provided our purity of life so merit it? But because I have reserved a suitable place to treat these matters,⁵⁵ I will not for the present pursue them any longer; especially since it is abundantly clear that there is nothing more averse to faith than either conjecture or anything else akin to doubt.

The Schoolmen most wickedly twist the testimony of Ecclesiastes, which they have continually on their lips: "No one knows whether he deserves hate or love" [Eccl. 9:1, Vg.]. For, to pass over how this passage is erroneously translated in the Vulgate, even children cannot miss what Solomon means by these words. That is, if anyone would judge by the present state of things, which men God pursues with hatred and which ones he embraces in love, he labors in vain and troubles himself to no profit, "since all things happen alike to righteous and impious, . . . to those who sacrifice victims and to those who do not sacrifice" [Eccl. 9:2, cf. Vg.].⁵⁶ From this it follows that God does not everlastingly witness his love to those for whom he causes all things to prosper, nor does he always manifest his hate to those whom he afflicts. And he does this to prove the innate folly of humanity, since among things so necessary to know it is grasped with such great stupidity. As Solomon had written a little before, one cannot discern how the soul of a man differs from the soul of a beast because both seem to die in the same way [Eccl. 3:19]. If any man would infer from this that the opinion that we hold concerning the immortality of souls rests upon conjecture alone, should we not justly consider him insane? Are they sane men

---

⁵⁴ Bonaventura so teaches in his *Commentary on the Sentences* IV. xx. 1. dubium 1 (*Opera theologica selecta* IV. 514). He cites Augustine, *Sermons* cccxciii (MPL 39. 1713). Cf. Aquinas, *Summa Theol.* I IIae. cxii. 5 ("Whether a Man Can Know that He Has Grace") (tr. LCC XI. 180 ff.).

⁵⁵ III. xv.

⁵⁶ Bonaventura and Aquinas, as cited in note 54, above; De Castro, *Adversus omnes haereses* VII (1543, fo. 133). Vg. reads: "*Nescit homo utrum amore an odio dignus est.*" See the widely different RSV.

who infer—since we can comprehend nothing by the physical beholding of present things—that there is no certainty of God's grace?

39. The Christian rejoices in the indwelling of the Spirit*

bBut they contend that it is a matter of rash presumption for us to claim an undoubted knowledge of God's will. Now I would concede that point to them only if we took upon ourselves to subject God's incomprehensible plan to our slender understanding. But when we simply say with Paul: "We have received not the spirit of this world, but the Spirit that is from God . . . ," by whose teaching "we know the gifts bestowed on us by God" [I Cor. 2:12], how can they yelp against us without abusively assaulting the Holy Spirit? But if it is a dreadful sacrilege to accuse the revelation given by the Spirit either of falsehood or uncertainty or ambiguity, how do we transgress in declaring its certainty?

But they cry aloud that it is also great temerity on our part that we thus dare to glory in the Spirit of Christ. Who would credit such stupidity to those who wish to be regarded as the schoolmasters of the world, that they so shamefully trip over the first rudiments of Christianity? Surely, it would not have been credible to me, if their extant writings did not attest it. Paul declares that those very ones "who are led by the Spirit of God are sons of God . . . " [Rom. 8:14]. And these men would have it that those who are the children of God are moved by their own spirit, but empty of God's Spirit. Paul teaches that God is called "Father" by us at the bidding of the Spirit, who alone can "witness to our spirit that we are children of God" [Rom. 8:16]. Even though these men do not keep us from calling upon God, they withdraw the Spirit, by whose leading he ought to have been duly called upon. Paul denies that those who are not moved by the Spirit of Christ are servants of Christ [cf. Rom. 8:9]. These men devise a Christianity that does not require the Spirit of Christ. He holds out no hope of blessed resurrection unless we feel the Spirit dwelling in us [Rom. 8:11]. These men invent a hope devoid of such a feeling.

Yet perchance they will answer that they do not deny we ought to be endowed with the Spirit; but that it is a matter of modesty and humility not to be sure of it.[57] What, then, does he mean

---

[57] Cf. Cochlaeus, *Philippicae in apologiam Philippi Melanchthon* (1534) III. 42; J. Latomus, *De fide et operibus* (*Opera adversus haereses* [1550], fo. 141b f.); A. Pighius, *Controversiarum praecipuarum . . . explicatio*, fo. 50b ff., assailing Luther's teaching on *fiducia*, "confident faith."

when he bids the Corinthians examine themselves whether they
are in the faith, to prove themselves whether they have Christ?
Unless one knows that Christ dwells in him, he is reprobate [II
Cor. 13:5]. "Now we know," says John, "that he abides in us
from the Spirit whom he has given us." [I John 3:24; 4:13.] And
what else do we do but call Christ's promises into question when
we wish to be accounted God's servants apart from his Spirit, whom
he has declared he would pour out upon all his own people? [Isa.
44:3; cf. Joel 2:28.] What else is it, then, than to do injury to
the Holy Spirit if we separate faith, which is his peculiar work,
from him? Since these are the first beginnings of piety, it is a
token of the most miserable blindness to charge with arrogance
Christians who dare to glory in the presence of the Holy Spirit,
without which glorying Christianity itself does not stand! But,
actually, they declare by their own example how truly Christ
spoke: "My Spirit was unknown to the world; he is recognized
only by those among whom he abides" [John 14:17].

*40. The alleged uncertainty as to whether we will persevere to
the end*

   ᵇNot content with trying to undermine firmness of faith in
one way alone, they assail it from another quarter. Thus, they
say that even though according to our present state of righteousness we can judge concerning our possession of the grace of God,
the knowledge of final perseverance remains in suspense.[58] A fine
confidence of salvation is left to us, if by moral conjecture we
judge that at the present moment we are in grace, but we know
not what will become of us tomorrow! The apostle speaks far
otherwise: "I am surely convinced that neither angels, nor powers,
nor principalities, nor death, nor life, nor things present, nor
things to come . . . will separate us from the love by which the
Lord embraces us in Christ" [Rom. 8:38–39 p.]. They try to escape with a trifling solution, prating that the apostle had his assurance from a special revelation.[59] But they are held too tightly
to escape. For there he is discussing those benefits which come
to all believers in common from faith, not those things which
he exclusively experiences. Now the same apostle, in another
place, puts us in fear by speaking of our weak-mindedness and inconstancy: "Let him who stands well," Paul says, "take heed lest
he fall" [I Cor. 10:12 p.]. It is true; but not such a fear as to put
us to confusion, but such that we may learn to humble ourselves
under God's mighty hand, as Peter explains it [I Peter 5:6].

[58] Latomus, *op. cit., loc. cit.*
[59] Aquinas, *Summa Theol.* I IIae. cxii. 5 (tr. LCC XI. 181).

Then, how absurd it is that the certainty of faith be limited to some point of time, when by its very nature it looks to a future immortality after this life is over! Since, therefore, believers ascribe to God's grace the fact that, illumined by his Spirit, they enjoy through faith the contemplation of heavenly life, such glorying is so far from arrogance that if any man is ashamed to confess it, in that very act he betrays his extreme ungratefulness by wickedly suppressing God's goodness, more than he testifies to his modesty or submission.

(Relation of faith to hope and love, 41–43)
41. Faith according to Heb. 11:1

ʰThe nature of faith could, seemingly, not be better or more plainly declared than by the substance of the promise upon which it rests as its proper foundation. Consequently, when that promise is removed, it will utterly fall, or rather vanish. Therefore, we have taken our definition from this fact. ᵇ⁽ᵃ⁾Yet this does not at all differ from the apostle's definition, or rather the description he applies to his discourse, where he teaches that "faith is the substance of things to be hoped for, the indication of things not appearing" [Heb. 11:1, cf. Vg.]. Now, by the word "hypostasis," which he uses, he means a sort of support upon which the godly mind may lean and rest. ᵃIt is as if he were to say that faith itself is a sure and secure possession of those things which God has promised us, ᵈunless someone prefers to understand "hypostasis" as confidence![60] This does not displease me, although I accept what is more commonly received. ᵃOn the other hand, Paul intended to signify that even to the last day, when "the books shall be opened" [Dan. 7:10], the things pertaining to our salvation[60a] are too high to be perceived by our senses, or seen by our eyes, or handled by our hands; and that in the meantime we do not possess these things in any other way than if we transcend all the limits of our senses and direct our perception beyond all things of this world and, in short, surpass ourselves. Therefore he adds that this assurance of possession is of those things which lie in hope, and are therefore not seen. "Whatsoever," as Paul writes, "is visible, is not hope; nor do we hope for what we see." [Rom. 8:24 p.] When he calls it an "indication" or "proof"—ᶜ⁽ᵃ⁾or, as Augustine has often translated it,[61] "a conviction of things not

---

[60] *"Nisi quis ὑπόστασιν pro fiducia accipere malit."*
[60a] VG 1560.
[61] Augustine, *John's Gospel* lxxix. 1; xcv. 2 (MPL 35. 1837, 1872; tr. NPNF VII. 342, 369); *On the Merits and Remission of Sins* II. xxxi. 50 (MPL 44. 181; tr. NPNF V. 43).

present" (the word for "conviction" is ἔλεγχος in Greek [Heb. 11:1])— ᵃPaul speaks as if to say that faith is an evidence of things not appearing, a seeing of things not seen, a clearness of things obscure, a presence of things absent, a showing forth of things hidden. The mysteries of God, and especially those which pertain to our salvation, cannot be discerned in themselves, or as it is said, in their own nature. But we contemplate them only in his Word, of the truth of which we ought to be so persuaded that we should count whatever he speaks as already done and fulfilled.

(Faith and love)
ᵇBut how can the mind be aroused to taste the divine goodness without at the same time being wholly kindled to love God in return? For truly, that abundant sweetness which God has stored up for those who fear him cannot be known without at the same time powerfully moving us. And once anyone has been moved by it, it utterly ravishes him and draws him to itself. Therefore, it is no wonder if a perverse and wicked heart never experiences that emotion by which, borne up to heaven itself, we are admitted to the most hidden treasures of God and to the most hallowed precincts of his Kingdom, which should not be defiled by the entrance of an impure heart.

For the teaching of the Schoolmen, ᵇ⁽ᵃ⁾that love is prior to faith and hope,⁶² is mere madness; for it is faith alone that first engenders love in us.⁶³ ᶜHow much more rightly Bernard states: "I believe that the testimony of the conscience, which Paul calls 'the glory of the pious,' [II Cor. 1:12] consists of three things. First of all, it is necessary to believe that you cannot have forgiveness of sins apart from God's mercy. Second, you can have no good work at all unless he gives it. Finally, you cannot merit eternal life by any works unless that is also given free." Shortly thereafter he adds that these things are not enough, but are a beginning of faith; because in believing that sins cannot be forgiven except by God, we ought at the same time to believe that they are forgiven, so long as we are persuaded also by the testimony of the Holy Spirit that salvation is stored up for us. And because God himself forgives sins, gives merits, and gives back

---

⁶² Lombard, *Sentences* III. xxiii. 9; xxv. 5 (MPL 192. 807, 811). Bonaventura, *Commentary on the Sentences* III. xxxvi. 6 (*Opera selecta* III. 813).
⁶³ Cf. Luther, *On Christian Liberty* (1520): "*Fluit ex fide charitas*" (*Werke* WA VII. 66; tr. *Works of Martin Luther* II. 338); Melanchthon, *Loci communes* (1521), ed. H. Engelland, *Melanchthons Werke in Auswahl* II. i. 114 (tr. C. L. Hill, *The Loci Communes of Philip Melanchthon,* p. 204).

rewards, we must also believe that we cannot take a firm stand in this beginning.[64] [b]But these and other matters will have to be discussed in their place.[65] Now, let us be content merely to grasp what faith itself is.

42. Faith and hope belong together

[b(a)]Yet, wherever this faith is alive, it must have along with it the hope of eternal salvation as its inseparable companion. Or rather, it engenders and brings forth hope from itself. When this hope is taken away, however eloquently or elegantly we discourse concerning faith, we are convicted of having none. For [a]if faith, as has been said above,[66] is a sure persuasion of the truth of God—that it can neither lie to us, nor deceive us, nor become void—then those who have grasped this certainty assuredly expect the time to come when God will fulfill his promises, which they are persuaded cannot but be true. Accordingly, in brief, hope is nothing else than the expectation of those things which faith has believed to have been truly promised by God. Thus, faith believes God to be true, hope awaits the time when his truth shall be manifested; faith believes that he is our Father, hope anticipates that he will ever show himself to be a Father toward us; faith believes that eternal life has been given to us, hope anticipates that it will some time be revealed; faith is the foundation upon which hope rests, hope nourishes and sustains faith. For as no one except him who already believes His promises can look for anything from God, so again the weakness of our faith must be sustained and nourished by patient hope and expectation, lest it fail and grow faint. [b]For this reason, Paul rightly sets our salvation in hope [Rom. 8:24]. [b(a)]For hope, while it awaits the Lord in silence, restrains faith that it may not fall headlong from too much haste. Hope strengthens faith, that it may not waver in God's promises, or begin to doubt concerning their truth. [b]Hope refreshes faith, that it may not become weary. It sustains faith to the final goal, that it may not fail in midcourse, or even at the starting gate. In short, by unremitting renewing and restoring, it invigorates faith again and again with perseverance.

And we shall better see in how many ways the support of hope is necessary to establish faith if we ponder how many

---

[64] Bernard, *On the Feast of the Annunciation of the Blessed Virgin* i. 1, 3 (MPL 183. 383 f.; tr. *St. Bernard's Sermons for the Seasons*, by a priest of Mount Melleray III. 137).

[65] III. xviii. 8.

[66] III. ii. 6.

forms of temptation assail and strike those who have embraced the Word of God. First, the Lord by deferring his promises often holds our minds in suspense longer than we would wish. Here it is the function of hope to carry out what the prophet bids: "That, if they should tarry, we wait for them" [Hab. 2:3 p.]. Occasionally he not only allows us to faint but exhibits open indignation toward us. Here it is much more necessary for hope to help us, that, according to another prophet's statement, we may "wait for the Lord who hid his face from . . . Jacob" [Isa. 8:17]. Scoffers also rise up, as Peter says [II Peter 3:3], asking: "Where is the promise of his coming? Since the fathers fell asleep, all things continue as they were from the beginning of creation" [II Peter 3:4, Vg.]. Indeed, the flesh and the world whisper these same things to us. Here we must keep our faith buttressed by patient hope, so fixed upon the contemplation of eternity as to reckon a thousand years as one day [Ps. 90:4; II Peter 3:8].

43. Faith and hope have the same foundation: God's mercy

ᵇBecause of this connection and kinship, Scripture sometimes uses the words "faith" and "hope" interchangeably. For when Peter teaches that we are "guarded by God's power through faith until salvation is revealed" [I Peter 1:5 p.], he attributes to faith something that corresponds to hope. And not unjustly, since we have already taught that hope is nothing but the nourishment and strength of faith.

ᶜSometimes they are joined together, as in the same letter: "So that your faith and hope are in God" [I Peter 1:21]. But in the letter to the Philippians, Paul derives expectation from hope because by hoping patiently we suspend our own desires until God's appointed time is revealed [Phil. 1:20]. This whole matter can be better understood from the eleventh chapter of Hebrews, which I have already cited [v. 1].⁶⁷ In another passage, although speaking inexactly, Paul means the same thing by these words: "Through the Spirit, by faith, we wait for the hope of righteousness" [Gal. 5:5]. That is, because, embracing the testimony of the gospel concerning freely given love, we look for the time when God will openly show that which is now hidden under hope.

ᵇIt is now clear how foolishly Peter Lombard lays two foundations of hope: grace of God and merit of works.⁶⁸ Hope can have no other goal than faith has. But we have already explained very

⁶⁷ Calvin writes "the tenth chapter," but the citation is of Heb. 11:1; cf. sec. 41, above.
⁶⁸ Lombard, *Sentences* III. xxvi. 1 (MPL 192. 811)

clearly that the single goal of faith is the mercy of God[69]—to
which it ought, so to speak, to look with both eyes. But it behooves us to hear what a cogent reason Lombard brings forward:
"If," he says, "you dare to hope for anything without merit, that
ought not to be called 'hope' but rather 'presumption.' "[70] Who,
dear reader, will not justly despise such beasts, who declare that
a man is acting rashly and presumptuously if he trust that God is
true? For, though the Lord wills that we await all things from
his goodness, they say that it is presumption to lean and rest upon
it. A master indeed—worthy of such pupils as he found in the
mad schools of wranglers![71] But for our part, when we as sinners
see that we are commanded by the oracles of God to conceive of
hope of salvation, let us so willingly presume upon his truth
that, relying upon his mercy alone, abandoning reliance upon
works, we dare to have good hope. ᵉHe will not deceive, who
said, "According to your faith be it done to you" [Matt. 9:29].

ᵉCHAPTER III

OUR REGENERATION BY FAITH: REPENTANCE[1]

(*Repentance the fruit of faith: review of some errors connected
with this point, 1–4*)
1. Repentance as a consequence of faith
    ᵉEven though we have taught in part how faith possesses Christ,
and how through it we enjoy his benefits, this would still remain
obscure if we did not add an explanation of the effects we feel.
With good reason, the sum of the gospel is held to consist in repentance and forgiveness of sins [Luke 24:47; Acts 5:31]. Any discussion of faith, therefore, that omitted these two topics would
be barren and mutilated and well-nigh useless. Now, both repentance and forgiveness of sins—that is, newness of life and free
reconciliation—are conferred on us by Christ, and both are attained by us through faith. As a consequence, reason and the
order of teaching demand that I begin to discuss both at this
point. ᵉ⁽ᵇ⁾However, our immediate transition will be from faith

---

[69] III. ii. 7.
[70] Lombard, *Sentences, loc. cit.*
[71] Cf. Bonaventura's criticism of this opinion, *Commentary on the Sentences*
III. xxvi. 1. qu. 4 (*Opera selecta* III. 571).
[1] "*Poenitentia*" is used by Calvin, as by his medieval predecessors, for both repentance and penance. Cf. the treatment of ecclesiastical penance in III. iv,
v; IV. xix. 14–17; and of church discipline in IV. xii. The present chapter
treats repentance in its relation to faith. In sec. 9 it is identified with regeneration.

to repentance.[2] [c]For when this topic is rightly understood it will better appear how man is justified by faith alone, and simple pardon; nevertheless actual holiness of life, so to speak, is not separated from free imputation of righteousness. [c(b)]Now it ought to be a fact beyond controversy that repentance not only constantly follows faith, but is also born of faith.[3] [b]For since pardon and forgiveness are offered through the preaching of the gospel [c(b)]in order that the sinner, freed from the tryanny of Satan, the yoke of sin, and the miserable bondage of vices, may cross over into the Kingdom of God, surely [b]no one can embrace the grace of the gospel without betaking himself from the errors of his past life into the right way, and applying his whole effort to the practice of repentance. There are some, however, who suppose that repentance precedes faith,[4] rather than flows from it, [c]or is produced by it as fruit from a tree. Such persons have never known the power of repentance, [b]and are moved to feel this way by an unduly slight argument.

2. Repentance has its foundation in the gospel, which faith embraces

[b]Christ, they say, and John in their preaching first urge the people to repentance,[5] then add that the Kingdom of Heaven has come near [Matt. 3:2; 4:17]. Such was the command the apostles received to preach; such was the order Paul followed, as Luke reports [Acts 20:21]. Yet while they superstitiously cling to the joining together of syllables, they disregard the meaning that binds these words together. For while Christ the Lord and John preach in this manner: "Repent, for the Kingdom of

[2] The high importance given to repentance here corresponds to the statement, and reflects the language, of Bucer in his *In sacra quatuor Evangelia enarrationes* (edition of Geneva, 1543, fo. 97b). The surprising order in which the treatment of repentance precedes that of justification is chosen, as Calvin indicates, to give emphasis to the doctrine of salvation by faith alone through first calling attention to its effect on holiness. Niesel remarks that this served to forestall Romanist objections, but indicates that it had a more positive theological purpose as well: *The Theology of Calvin*, p. 130.

[3] The Reformation doctrine that regeneration follows faith as an effect of it is stressed also in Comm. John 1:13. Cf. III. ii. 1, note 3. Melanchthon, *Loci communes* (1521), ed. Engelland, *Melanchthons Werke in Auswahl* II. i. 112–114, 149 f.; tr. C. H. Hill, *The Loci Communes of Philip Melanchthon*, pp. 202 ff., 249 f.

[4] Cf. the closing words of sec. 2; also Luther, *Ninety-five Theses* (1517) 1: "*Christus . . . omnem vitam fidelium poenitentiam esse voluit*" (*Werke* WA I. 233); Augsburg Confession, art. xii.

[5] "*Ad resipiscentiam.*" Cf. sec. 5, below, where (following Bucer: see note 15) the verb *resipiscere*, "to come back to one's senses," is joined with the *poenitentiam agere* of Matt. 3:2.

Heaven is at hand" [Matt. 3:2], do they not derive the reason for repenting from grace itself and the promise of salvation? Accordingly, therefore, their words mean the same thing as if they said, "Since the Kingdom of Heaven has come near, repent." For Matthew, when he has related that John so preached, teaches that the prophecy of Isaiah had been fulfilled in him: "The voice of one crying in the wilderness: prepare the way of the Lord, make straight the paths of our God" [Matt. 3:3; Isa. 40:3]. But in the prophet that voice is bidden to begin with comfort and glad tidings [Isa. 40:1–2]. Yet, when we refer the origin of repentance to faith we do not imagine some space of time during which it brings it to birth; but we mean to show that a man cannot apply himself seriously to repentance without knowing himself to belong to God. But no one is truly persuaded that he belongs to God unless he has first recognized God's grace. These matters will be more clearly discussed in what follows. ᵉPerhaps some have been deceived by the fact that many are overwhelmed by qualms of conscience or compelled to obedience before they are imbued with the knowledge of grace, nay, even taste it. And this is the initial fear that certain people reckon among the virtues, for they discern that it is close to true and just obedience.⁶ But here it is not a question of how variously Christ draws us to himself, or prepares us for the pursuit of godliness. I say only that no uprightness can be found except where that Spirit reigns that Christ received to communicate to his members. Secondly, I say that, according to the statement of the psalm: "There is propitiation with thee . . . that thou mayest be feared" [Ps. 130:4, Comm.], no one will ever reverence God but him who trusts that God is propitious to him. No one will gird himself willingly to observe the law but him who will be persuaded that God is pleased by his obedience. This tenderness in overlooking and tolerating vices is a sign of God's fatherly favor. Hosea's exhortation also shows this: "Come, let us return to Jehovah; for he has torn, and he will heal us; he has stricken, and he will cure us" [Hos. 6:1, cf. Vg.]. For the hope of pardon is added like a goad, that men may not sluggishly lie in their sins. ᵇBut lacking any semblance of reason is the madness of those who, that they may begin from repentance, prescribe to their new converts certain days during which they must practice penance, and when these at length are over, admit them into communion of the grace of the gospel. I am speaking of very many

---

⁶ Aquinas, *Summa Theol.* II IIae. xix. 2, 8, discussing "initial fear" in relation to "filial," "servile," and "worldly fear"; tr. LCC XI. 311 ff., 321 f.

of the Anabaptists, especially those who marvelously exult in being considered spiritual;[7] [c]and of their companions, the Jesuits,[8] and like dregs. [b]Obviously, that giddy spirit brings forth such fruits that it limits to a paltry few days a repentance that for the Christian man ought to extend throughout his life.

3. Mortification and vivification

[b]But [a]certain men well versed in penance, even long before these times, meaning to speak simply and sincerely according to the rule of Scripture, said that it consists of two parts: mortification and vivification.[9] Mortification they explain as sorrow of soul and dread conceived from the recognition of sin and the awareness of divine judgment. For when anyone has been brought into a true knowledge of sin, he then begins truly to hate and abhor sin; then he is heartily displeased with himself, he confesses himself miserable and lost and wishes to be another man. Furthermore, when he is touched by any sense of the judgment of God (for the one straightway follows the other) he then lies stricken and overthrown; humbled and cast down he trembles; he becomes discouraged and despairs. This is the first part of repentance, commonly called "contrition." "Vivification" they understand as the consolation that arises out of faith. That is, when a man is laid low by the consciousness of sin and stricken by the fear of God, and afterward looks to the goodness of God—to his mercy, grace, salvation, which is through Christ—he raises himself up, he takes heart, he recovers courage, and as it were, returns from death to life. [c]Now these words, if only they have a right interpretation, express well enough the force of repentance; but when they understand vivification as the happiness that the mind receives after its perturbation and fear have been quieted,[10] I do not agree. It means, rather, the desire to live in a holy and devoted manner, a desire arising from rebirth; as if it were said that man dies to himself that he may begin to live to God.

---

[7] Cf. CR VII. 56, and Zwingli, *Opera*, ed. M. Schuler and J. Schulthess, III. 388 (tr. *Selected Works of Huldreich Zwingli*, ed. S. M. Jackson, p. 178).

[8] Loyola, *Spiritual Exercises*, sections on penance, e.g., First Week, sec. 82, on exterior and interior penance (*The Spiritual Exercises of St. Ignatius;* tr. L. J. Puhl, p. 370).

[9] These terms are employed by Melanchthon, *Loci communes* (1521), section on penance (ed. Engelland, *op. cit.*, p. 149; tr. Hill, *op. cit.*, pp. 249 f.). Cf. *Apology of the Augsburg Confession* XII. 26 (*Bekenntnisschriften der Evangelisch-Lutherischen Kirche*), p. 257, note 2.

[10] Calvin's use of the word "joy" (*laetitia*) here reflects a passage of Bucer, *In sacra quatuor Evangelia enarrationes:* "*Certe longe plus mellis quam fellis, laetitiae quam tristitiae obtinens*" (1543 edition, fo. 33b).

4. Penance under law and under gospel

ᵃOthers, because they saw the various meanings of this word in Scripture, posited two forms of repentance. To distinguish them by some mark, they called one "repentance of the law." Through it the sinner, wounded by the branding of sin and stricken by dread of God's wrath, remains caught in that disturbed state and cannot extricate himself from it. The other they call "repentance of the gospel." Through it the sinner is indeed sorely afflicted, but rises above it and lays hold of Christ as medicine for his wound, comfort for his dread, the haven of his misery.[11] They offer as examples of "repentance of the law" Cain [Gen. 4:13], Saul [I Sam. 15:30], and Judas [Matt. 27:4]. While Scripture recounts their repentance to us, it represents them as acknowledging the gravity of their sin, and afraid of God's wrath; but since they conceived of God only as Avenger and Judge, that very thought overwhelmed them. Therefore their repentance was nothing but a sort of entryway of hell, which they had already entered in this life, and had begun to undergo punishment before the wrath of God's majesty.[12] We see "gospel repentance" in all those who, made sore by the sting of sin but aroused and refreshed by trust in God's mercy, have turned to the Lord. When Hezekiah received the message of death, he was stricken with fear. But he wept and prayed, and looking to God's goodness, he recovered confidence [II Kings 20:2; Isa. 38:2]. The Ninevites were troubled by a horrible threat of destruction; but putting on sackcloth and ashes, they prayed, hoping that the Lord might be turned toward them and be turned away from the fury of his wrath [Jonah 3:5, 9]. David confessed that he sinned greatly in taking a census of the people, but he added, "O Lord, . . . take away the iniquity of thy servant" [II Sam. 24:10]. When he was rebuked by Nathan, David acknowledged his sin of adultery, and he fell down before the Lord, but at the same time he awaited pardon [II Sam. 12:13, 16]. Such was the repentance of those who felt remorse of heart at Peter's preaching; but, trusting in God's goodness, they added: "Brethren, what shall we do?" [Acts 2:37]. Such, also, was Peter's own

---

[11] Bucer (op. cit., loc. cit.) employs this distinction of legal and evangelical penance. Melanchthon uses the illustrations of Saul and Judas here introduced, and observes that "faith marks the distinction between the contrition of Judas and of Peter." Cf. Apology of the Augsburg Confession XII. 8 (Bekenntnisschriften der Evangelisch-Lutherischen Kirche, p. 254; cf. p. 258; Concordia Triglotta, pp. 254 f.).

[12] Melanchthon, Apology, loc. cit. See also Calvin, Comm. Acts 2:37–38.

repentance; he wept bitterly indeed [Matt. 26:75; Luke 22:62], but he did not cease to hope.[13]

(Repentance defined: explanation of its elements, mortification of the flesh and vivification of the spirit, 5–9)
5. Definition
ᵃAlthough all these things are true, yet the word "repentance" itself, so far as I can learn from Scripture, is to be understood otherwise. For their inclusion of faith under repentance disagrees with what Paul says in Acts: "Testifying both to Jews and Gentiles of repentance to God, and of faith . . . in Jesus Christ" [Acts 20:21]. There he reckons repentance and faith as two different things. What then? Can true repentance stand, apart from faith? Not at all. But even though they cannot be separated, they ought to be distinguished. As faith is not without hope, yet faith and hope are different things, so repentance and faith, although they are held together by a permanent bond, require to be joined rather than confused.

ᵇIndeed, I am aware of the fact that the whole of conversion to God is understood under the term "repentance," and faith is not the least part of conversion; but in what sense this is so will very readily appear when its force and nature are explained. The Hebrew word for "repentance" is derived from conversion ᶜor return; ᵇthe Greek word, from change of mind or of intention. And the thing itself corresponds closely to the etymology of both words. The meaning is that, departing from ourselves, we turn to God, and having taken off our former mind, we put on a new. ᵇ⁽ᵃ⁾On this account, in my judgment, repentance can thus be well defined: it is the true turning of our life to God, a turning that arises from a pure and earnest fear of him;[14] and it consists in the mortification of our flesh and of the old man, and in the vivification of the Spirit.

ᵃIn that sense we must understand all those preachings by which either the prophets of old or the apostles later exhorted men of their time to repentance. For they were striving for this ᵇ⁽ᵃ⁾one thing: that, confused by their sins and pierced by the fear of divine judgment, they should fall down and humble them-

---

13 Melanchthon, *Apology, loc. cit.*, citing Saul, Judas, and Peter; Bucer, *op. cit., loc. cit.*, citing the prodigal son and Acts 2:37.
14 Calvin, in Preface to Comm. Psalms, impressively recalled that his own conversion, though delayed, had been "sudden." (Cf. LCC XXIII. 52.) Here he uses the word "conversion" to describe repentance, which is thought of as lifelong.

selves before him whom they had offended, and with true repentance return into the right path. Therefore these words are used interchangeably in the same sense: "Turn or return to the Lord," "repent," and "do penance"[15] [Matt. 3:2]. ᵉWhence even the Sacred History says that "penance is done after God," where men who had lived wantonly in their own lusts, neglecting him, begin to obey his Word [I Sam. 7:2–3] and are ready to go where their leader calls them. ᵇ⁽ᵃ⁾And John and Paul use the expression "Producing fruits worthy of repentance" [Luke 3:8; Acts 26:20; cf. Rom. 6:4] for leading a life that demonstrates and testifies in all its actions repentance of this sort.

6. Repentance as turning to God

ᵇBut before we go farther, it will be useful to explain more clearly the definition that we have laid down. We must examine repentance mainly under three heads. First, when we call it a "turning of life to God," we require a transformation, not only in outward works, but in the soul itself. Only when it puts off its old nature does it bring forth the fruits of works in harmony with its renewal. The prophet, wishing to express this change, bids whom he calls to repentance to get themselves a new heart [Ezek. 18:31]. Moses, therefore, intending to show how the Israelites might repent and be duly turned to the Lord, often teaches that it be done with "all the heart" and "all the soul" [Deut. 6:5; 10:12; 30:2, 6, 10]. This expression we see frequently repeated by the prophets [Jer. 24:7]. ᵉMoses also, in calling it "circumcision of heart," searches the inmost emotions [Deut. 10:16; 30:6]. ᵇNo passage, however, better reveals the true character of repentance than Jer., ch. 4: "If you return, O Israel," says the Lord, "return to me. . . . Plow up your arable land and do not sow among thorns. Circumcise yourselves to the Lord, and remove the foreskin of your hearts" [vs. 1, 3–4]. See how he declares that they will achieve nothing in taking up the pursuit of righteousness unless wickedness be first of all cast out from their inmost heart. ᵉAnd to move them thoroughly he warns them that it is with God that they have to deal,[16] with whom shifts avail nothing, for He hates a double heart [cf. James 1:8]. ᵇIsaiah for this reason satirizes the gauche efforts of hypocrites who were actively striving after outward repentance in ceremonies while they made no effort to undo the burden of injustice with which they bound

---

[15] Cf. Bucer, op. cit., 1536 edition, p. 85; 1543 edition, fo. 33b.
[16] "Monet cum Deo esse negotium." Cf. Introduction, pp li ff.; III. iii. 16; III. vii. 2; III. xx. 29; IV. xi. 2.

the poor [Isa. 58:6]. There he also beautifully shows in what duties unfeigned repentance properly consists.

7. Repentance as induced by the fear of God?

bThe second point was our statement that repentance proceeds from an earnest fear of God. For, before the mind of the sinner inclines to repentance, it must be aroused by thinking upon divine judgment. When this thought is deeply and thoroughly fixed in mind—that God will someday mount his judgment seat to demand a reckoning of all words and deeds—it will not permit the miserable man to rest nor to breathe freely even for a moment without stirring him continually to reflect upon another mode of life whereby he may be able to stand firm in that judgment. For this reason, Scripture often mentions judgment when it urges to repentance, as in the prophecy of Jeremiah: "Lest perchance my wrath go forth like fire . . . , and there be no one to quench it, because of the evil of your doings" [Jer. 4:4 p.]. In Paul's sermon to the Athenians: "Although God has hitherto overlooked the times of this ignorance, he now calls upon all men everywhere to repent because he has fixed a day on which he will judge the world in equity" [Acts 17:30–31, cf. Vg.]. And in many other passages.

Sometimes by punishments already inflicted Scripture declares God to be judge in order that sinners may reflect on the greater punishments that threaten if they do not repent in time. You have an example of this in Deut., ch. 29 [vs. 19 ff.]. Inasmuch as conversion begins with dread and hatred of sin, the apostle makes "the sorrow . . . according to God" the cause of repentance [II Cor. 7:10, cf. Vg.]. He calls it "sorrow . . . according to God" when we not only abhor punishment but hate and abominate sin itself, because we know that it displeases God. eAnd no wonder! For if we were not sharply pricked, the slothfulness of our flesh could not be corrected. Indeed, these prickings would not have sufficed against its dullness and blockishness had God not penetrated more deeply in unsheathing his rods. There is, besides, an obstinacy that must be beaten down as if with hammers. Therefore, the depravity of our nature compels God to use severity in threatening us. For it would be vain for him gently to allure those who are asleep. I do not list the texts that we repeatedly come upon. There is also another reason why fear of God is the beginning of repentance. For even though the life of man be replete with all the virtues, if it is not directed to the worship of God, it can indeed be praised by the world; but in heaven it will be sheer abomination, since the chief part of righteousness is to render to

God his right and honor, of which he is impiously defrauded when we do not intend to subject ourselves to his control.

8. Mortification and vivification as component parts of repentance

ᵇIn the third place it remains for us to explain our statement that repentance consists of two parts: namely, mortification of the flesh and vivification of the spirit. The prophets express it clearly—although simply and rudely, in accordance with the capacity of the carnal folk—when they say: "Cease to do evil, and do good" [Ps. 36:8, 3, 27, conflated, Vg.]. Likewise, "Wash yourselves; make yourselves clean; remove the evil of your doings from before my eyes; cease to do evil; learn to do good; seek judgment; help the oppressed." [Isa. 1:16–17, cf. Vg., etc.] For when they recall man from evil, they demand the destruction of the whole flesh, which is full of evil and of perversity. It is a very hard and difficult thing to put off ourselves and to depart from our inborn disposition. Nor can we think of the flesh as completely destroyed unless we have wiped out whatever we have from ourselves. But since all emotions of the flesh are hostility against God [cf. Rom. 8:7], the first step toward obeying his law is to deny our own nature. Afterward, they designate the renewal by the fruits that follow from it—namely, righteousness, judgment, and mercy. It would not be enough duly to discharge such duties unless the mind itself and the heart first put on the inclination to righteousness, judgment, and mercy. That comes to pass when the Spirit of God so imbues our souls, steeped in his holiness, with both new thoughts and feelings, that they can be rightly considered new. ᶜSurely, as we are naturally turned away from God, unless self-denial precedes, we shall never approach that which is right. Therefore, we are very often enjoined to put off the old man, to renounce the world and the flesh, to bid our evil desires farewell, to be renewed in the spirit of our mind [Eph. 4:22–23]. Indeed, the very word "mortification" warns us how difficult it is to forget our previous nature. For from "mortification" we infer that we are not conformed to the fear of God and do not learn the rudiments of piety, unless we are violently slain by the sword of the Spirit and brought to nought. As if God had declared that for us to be reckoned among his children our common nature must die!

9. Rebirth in Christ!

ᵇ⁽ᵃ⁾Both things happen to us by participation in Christ. For if we truly partake in his death, "our old man is crucified by his power, and the body of sin perishes" [Rom. 6:6 p.], that the corruption of original nature may no longer thrive. ᵇIf we share in his resurrection, through it we are raised up into newness of life to correspond with the righteousness of God. Therefore, in a word, I interpret repentance as regeneration, whose sole end is to restore in us the image of God that had been disfigured and all but obliterated through Adam's transgression.[17] So the apostle teaches when he says: "Now we, with unveiled face, beholding the glory of the Lord, are being changed into his likeness from glory to glory even as from the Spirit of the Lord" [II Cor. 3:18]. Likewise, another passage: "Be ye renewed in the spirit of your mind, and put on the new man which is after God created in righteousness and holiness of truth" [Eph. 4:23, Vg.]. "Putting on the new man . . . who is being renewed into the knowledge and the image of him who created him." [Col. 3:10, cf. Vg.] Accordingly, we are restored by this regeneration through the benefit of Christ into the righteousness of God; from which we had fallen through Adam. In this way it pleases the Lord fully to restore whomsoever he adopts into the inheritance of life. ᵉAnd indeed, this restoration does not take place in one moment or one day or one year; but through continual and sometimes even slow advances God wipes out in his elect the corruptions of the flesh, cleanses them of guilt, consecrates them to himself as temples renewing all their minds to true purity that they may practice repentance throughout their lives and know that this warfare will end only at death. All the greater is the depravity of that foul wrangler and apostate Staphylus, who babbles that I confuse the state of present life with heavenly glory when from Paul I interpret the image of God [II Cor. 4:4] as "true holiness and righteousness" [cf. Eph. 4:24].[18] As if when anything is defined we should not seek its very integrity and perfection. Now this is not to deny a place for growth; rather I say, the closer any man comes to the likeness of God, the more the image of God shines in him. In order that believers may reach this goal, God assigns

---

[17] Cf. note 1, above. Calvin thinks here of regeneration as a restoration of the original but ruined image of God in man. The expansion of the passage in the 1539 edition stressing the conflict of flesh and spirit and the distinction between the natural and the regenerate man appears in OS IV. 63. Cf. W. Niesel, *The Theology of Calvin*, pp. 128 f.

[18] Frederick Staphylus (1512–1564) was a Wittenberg alumnus who turned against Lutheranism and his former teacher Melanchthon (1553) and wrote an attack on the Reformation, *Theologiae Martini Lutheri trimembris epitome* (1558). The reference is to a passage in this (then very recent) work found in the collected writings of Staphylus: *In causa religionis sparsim editi libri, in unum volumen digesti* (Ingolstadt, 1613), Part II, col. 35.

to them a race of repentance, which they are to run throughout their lives.

(Believers experience sanctification, but not sinless perfection in this life, 10–15)
10. Believers are still sinners
ᶜThus, then, are the children of God freed through regeneration from bondage to sin. Yet they do not obtain full possession of freedom so as to feel no more annoyance from their flesh, but there still remains in them a continuing occasion for struggle whereby they may be exercised; and not only be exercised, but also better learn their own weakness. In this matter all writers of sounder judgment agree that there remains in a regenerate man a smoldering cinder of evil,[19] from which desires continually leap forth to allure and spur him to commit sin. They also admit that the saints are as yet so bound by that disease of concupiscence that they cannot withstand being at times tickled and incited either to lust or to avarice or to ambition, or to other vices. And we do not need to labor much over investigating what ancient writers thought about this; Augustine alone will suffice for this purpose, since he faithfully and diligently collected the opinions of all.[20] Let my readers, therefore, obtain from him whatever certainty they desire concerning the opinion of antiquity.

But between Augustine and us we can see that there is this difference of opinion: while he concedes that believers, as long as they dwell in mortal bodies, are so bound by inordinate desires[21] that they are unable not to desire inordinately, yet he dare not call this disease "sin." Content to designate it with the term "weakness," he teaches that it becomes sin only when either act or con-

---

[19] Calvin here uses the word *"fomes,"* originally "tinder" or "kindling wood," but employed in Gen. 37:8, Vg., and by Tertullian, Augustine, and other church fathers in the sense of incitement to sin. In Scholastic theology it was a well-understood term for the irrepressible inner motion of sin, never completely destroyed in this life. Lombard, *Sentences* II. xxx. 7 f.; II. xxii. 1 (MPL 192. 722, 726 f.); Aquinas, *Summa Theol.* I IIae. lxxiv. 3, reply to obj. 2.

[20] Augustine, *Against Two Letters of the Pelagians* IV. x. 27; IV. xi. 31 (MPL 44. 629–632, 634–636; tr. NPNF V. 429, 432 f.); *Against Julian the Pelagian* I. i. 3; II. iii. 5–v. 14; II. viii. 23; II. ix. 32 (MPL 44. 642, 673–675, 688 ff., 695 f.; tr. FC 35. 56 f., 59 ff., 68 ff., 82–92). Barth and Niesel give citations of the passages adduced by Augustine in this connection from earlier fathers to which Calvin alludes. See also Cadier, *Institution* III. 77, note 4.

[21] *"Concupiscentiis."* Cf. Augustine, *John's Gospel* xli. 8, 10 (MPL 35. 1698; tr. NPNF VII. 232 f.); *On the Merits and Remission of Sins* II. vii. 9 (MPL 44. 156; tr. NPNF V. 47 f.); *Against Julian* II. i. 3; II. v. 12 (MPL 44. 673, 682; tr. FC 35. 57, 70 f.); *Against Two Letters of the Pelagians* III. iii. 5 (MPL 44. 590 f.; tr. NPNF V. 404). The ensuing quotation is from Augustine, *Sermons* clv. 1 (MPL 38. 841; tr. LF *Sermons* II. 747 f.).

sent follows the conceiving or apprehension of it, that is, when the will yields to the first strong inclination. We, on the other hand, deem it sin when man is tickled by any desire at all against the law of God. Indeed, we label "sin" that very depravity which begets in us desires of this sort. We accordingly teach that in the saints, until they are divested of mortal bodies, there is always sin; for in their flesh there resides that depravity of inordinate desiring which contends against righteousness. ᶜAnd Augustine does not always refrain from using the term "sin," as when he says: "Paul calls by the name 'sin,' the source from which all sins rise up into carnal desire. As far as this pertains to the saints, it loses its dominion on earth and perishes in heaven." By these words he admits that in so far as believers are subject to the inordinate desires of the flesh they are guilty of sin.

11. In believers sin has lost its dominion; but it still dwells in them

ᶜGod is said to purge his church of all sin, in that through baptism he promises that grace of deliverance, and fulfills it in his elect [Eph. 5:26–27]. This statement we refer to the guilt of sin, rather than to the very substance of sin. God truly carries this out by regenerating his own people, so that the sway of sin is abolished in them. For the Spirit dispenses a power whereby they may gain the upper hand and become victors in the struggle. But sin ceases only to reign; it does not also cease to dwell in them. Accordingly, we say that the old man was so crucified [Rom. 6:6], and the law of sin [cf. Rom. 8:2] so abolished in the children of God, that some vestiges remain; not to rule over them, but to humble them by the consciousness of their own weakness. And we, indeed, admit that these traces are not imputed, as if they did not exist; but at the same time we contend that this comes to pass through the mercy of God, so that the saints—otherwise deservedly sinners and guilty before God—are freed from this guilt. And it will not be difficult for us to confirm this opinion, since there are clear testimonies to the fact in Scripture. What clearer testimony do we wish than what Paul exclaims in the seventh chapter of Romans? First, Paul speaks there as a man reborn [Rom. 7:6]. This we have shown in another place,[22] and Augustine proves it with unassailable reasoning.[23] I have nothing to say about the fact that he uses the words "evil" and "sin," so that they who wish to cry out against us can

[22] II. ii. 27.
[23] Augustine, *John's Gospel* xli. 11 (MPL 35. 1698; tr. NPNF VII. 234); *Sermons* cliv. 1 (MPL 38. 833 f.; tr. LF *Sermons* II. 735); *Against Julian* III. xxvi. 61 f. (MPL 44. 733 f.; tr. FC 35. 160 ff.). Cf. IV. xv. 12, note 20.

cavil at those words; yet who will deny that opposition to God's law is evil? Who will deny that hindrance to righteousness is sin? Who, in short, will not grant that guilt is involved wherever there is spiritual misery? But Paul proclaims all these facts concerning this disease.

Then we have a reliable indication from the law by which we can briefly deal with this whole question. For we are bidden to "love God with all our heart, with all our soul, and with all our faculties" [Deut. 6:5; Matt. 22:37]. Since all the capacities of our soul ought to be so filled with the love of God, it is certain that this precept is not fulfilled by those who can either retain in the heart a slight inclination or admit to the mind any thought at all that would lead them away from the love of God into vanity. What then? To be stirred by sudden emotions, to grasp in sense perception, to conceive in the mind—are not these powers of the soul? Therefore, when these lay themselves open to vain and depraved thoughts, do they not show themselves to be in such degree empty of the love of God? For this reason, he who does not admit that all desires of the flesh are sins, but that that disease of inordinately desiring which they call "tinder" is a wellspring of sin,[24] must of necessity deny that the transgression of the law is sin.

12. What does "natural corruption" mean?

ᶜIt may seem absurd to some that all desires by which man is by nature affected are so completely condemned—although they have been bestowed by God himself, the author of nature.[25] To this I reply that we do not condemn those inclinations which God so engraved upon the character of man at his first creation, that they were eradicable only with humanity itself, but only those bold and unbridled impulses which contend against God's control. Now, all man's faculties are, on account of the depravity of nature, so vitiated and corrupted that in all his actions persistent disorder[26] and intemperance threaten because these inclinations cannot be separated from such lack of restraint. Accordingly, we contend that they are vicious. Or, if you would have the matter summed up in fewer words, we teach that all human desires are evil, and charge them with sin—not in that they are natural, but because they are inordinate. Moreover, we hold that they are inordinate because nothing pure or sincere can come forth from a corrupt and polluted nature.

Nor does this teaching disagree as much with that of Augustine

---

[24] "Quem fomitem appellant." Cf. note 19, above.
[25] Cf. J. Fisher, Assertionis Lutheranae confutatio (1523), p. 150.
[26] "ἀταξία."

as appears on the surface. While he is too much afraid of the odium that the Pelagians endeavored to saddle upon him, he sometimes refrains from using the word "sin." Yet when he writes that, while the law of sin still remains in the saints, guilt alone is removed, he indicates clearly enough that he does not disagree very much with our meaning.[27]

13. Augustine as witness to the sinfulness of believers

ᶜWe shall bring forward some other statements from which it will better appear what he thought. In the second book of his treatise Against Julian, he says: "This law of sin is both remitted by spiritual regeneration and remains in mortal flesh. Remitted, namely, because guilt has been removed in the sacrament by which believers are regenerated. But it remains because it prompts the desires against which believers contend." Another passage: "Therefore, the law of sin which was also in the members of the great apostle himself is remitted in baptism, not ended." Another passage: "Ambrose called the law of sin 'iniquity,' the guilt of which was removed in baptism although it itself remains. For it is iniquitous that 'the flesh inordinately desires against the Spirit'" [Gal. 5:17]. Another passage: "Sin is dead in that guilt with which it held us; and until it be cured by the perfection of burial, though dead, it still rebels." The passage in Book V is even clearer: "Blindness of heart is at once sin, punishment of sin, and the cause of sin—sin because by it a man does not believe in God; punishment of sin because by it a proud heart is punished with due punishment; the cause of sin when something is committed through the error of the blind heart. In the same way, inordinate desire of the flesh, against which the good spirit yearns, is at once sin, the punishment of sin, and the cause of sin: it is sin because there inheres in it disobedience against the mind's dominion; the punishment of sin because it is in payment for the deserts of him who is disobedient; the cause of sin in him who consents by rebellion, or in him born by contagion."[28] Here he calls it sin without any ambiguity because when error is laid low and truth strengthened he fears slanders less. In like manner, in Homily 41 on John, where without contention he speaks according to his very own understanding: If you

---

[27] Augustine, *Against Two Letters of the Pelagians* I. xiii. 27; III. iii. 5 (MPL 44. 563, 590 f.; tr. NPNF V. 385 f., 404). Cf. also his *On the Merits and Remission of Sins* I. xxxix. 70 (MPL 44. 150 f.; tr. NPNF V. 43); *Against Julian* II. i. 3; II. iv. 8; II. v. 12; VI. xix. 61 (MPL 44. 673, 678 f., 682, 860; tr. FC 35. 57, 65 f., 70 f., 372).

[28] Ambrose, *On Isaac or the Soul* viii. 65 (MPL 14. 553; CSEL 32. 688); Augustine, *Against Julian* II. ix. 32; V. iii. 8 (MPL 44. 696, 787; tr. FC 35. 95, 247 ff.).

serve the law of sin with your flesh, do what the apostle himself says: "Let not sin . . . reign in your mortal body to obey its lusts" [Rom. 6:12]. He does not say: "Let it not be," but "Let it not reign." So long as you live, sin must needs be in your members. At least let it be deprived of mastery. Let not what it bids be done. Those who claim that inordinate desire is no sin commonly quote James' saying by way of objection: "Desire after it has conceived, gives birth to sin" [James 1:15].[29] But this can be refuted without trouble. For unless we understand that he is speaking solely concerning evil works or actual sins, not even evil intention will be considered sin. But from the fact that he calls shameful acts and evil deeds the "offspring of inordinate desire" and applies the name "sin" to them, it straightway follows that inordinately desiring is an evil thing and damnable before God.

14. Against the illusion of perfection

[b]Certain Anabaptists of our day conjure up some sort of frenzied excess instead of spiritual regeneration. The children of God, they assert, restored to the state of innocence, now need not take care to bridle the lust of the flesh, but should rather follow the Spirit as their guide, under whose impulsion they can never go astray. It would be incredible that a man's mind should fall into such madness, if they did not openly and haughtily blab this dogma of theirs. The thing is indeed monstrous! But it is fitting that those who have persuaded their minds to turn God's truth into falsehood should suffer such punishments for their sacrilegious boldness. Shall all choice between dishonest and honest, righteous and unrighteous, good and evil, virtue and vice, be thus taken away? "Such difference arises," they say, "from the curse of old Adam, from which we have been freed through Christ." Therefore, there will now be no difference between fornication and chastity, integrity and cunning, truth and falsehood, fair dealing and extortion. "Take away," say the Anabaptists, "vain fear—the Spirit will command no evil of you if you but yield yourself, confidently and boldly, to his prompting."[30] Who would not be astonished at these monstrosities? Yet it is a popular philosophy among those who are blinded by the madness of lusts and have put off common sense.

But what sort of Christ, I beseech you, do they devise for us? And what sort of Spirit do they belch forth? For we recognize one

---

[29] Augustine, *John's Gospel* xli. 12 (MPL 35. 1698; tr. NPNF VII. 234). Cf. Fisher as cited in note 25, above.
[30] Cf. Calvin's description of outrageous perversions of the doctrine of regeneration by the Quintinists, who were among the more extreme of the Libertine sectarians: *Contre la secte des Libertins* xviii (CR VII. 200 ff.).

Christ and one Spirit of Christ, whom the prophets have commended, the gospel proclaims as revealed to us, and of whom we hear no such thing. That Spirit is no patron of murder, fornication, drunkenness, pride, contention, avarice, or fraud; but the author of love, modesty, sobriety, moderation, peace, temperance, truth. The Spirit is not giddy—to run headlong, thoughtless, through right and wrong—but is full of wisdom and understanding rightly to discern between just and unjust. The Spirit does not stir up man to dissolute and unbridled license; but, according as it distinguishes between lawful and unlawful, it teaches man to keep measure and temperance. Yet why should we spend more effort in refuting this brutish madness? For Christians the Spirit of the Lord is not a disturbing apparition, which they have either brought forth in a dream or have received as fashioned by others. Rather, they earnestly seek a knowledge of him from the Scriptures, where these two things are taught concerning him.

First, he has been given to us for sanctification in order that he may bring us, purged of uncleanness and defilement, into obedience to God's righteousness. This obedience cannot stand except when the inordinate desires to which these men would slacken the reins have been tamed and subjugated. Second, we are purged by his sanctification in such a way that we are besieged by many vices and much weakness so long as we are encumbered with our body. Thus it comes about that, far removed from perfection, we must move steadily forward, and though entangled in vices, daily fight against them. From this it also follows that we must shake off sloth and carelessness, and watch with intent minds lest, unaware, we be overwhelmed by the stratagems of our flesh. Unless, perchance, we are confident that we have made greater progress than the apostle, who was still harassed by an angel of Satan [II Cor. 12:7] "whereby his power was made perfect in weakness" [II Cor. 12:9], and who in his own flesh unfeignedly represented that division between flesh and spirit [cf. Rom. 7:6 ff.].

15. Repentance according to II Cor. 7:11

cIt is for a very good reason that the apostle enumerates seven causes, effects, or parts in his description of repentance. They are earnestness or carefulness, excuse, indignation, fear, longing, zeal, and avenging [II Cor. 7:11]. It should not seem absurd that I dare not determine whether they ought to be accounted causes or effects, for either is debatable. And they can also be called inclinations joined with repentance. But because, leaving out those questions, we can understand what Paul means, we shall be content with a simple exposition.

Therefore, he says that from "sorrow . . . according to God" [II Cor. 7:10] carefulness arises. For he who is touched with a lively feeling of dissatisfaction with self because he has sinned against his God is at the same time aroused to diligence and attention that he may escape from the devil's snares, that he may better take precaution against his wiles, and that he may not afterward fall away from the governance of the Holy Spirit, nor be lulled into a sense of security.

Next is "excuse," which in this passage does not signify a defense whereby the sinner, in order to escape God's judgment, either denies that he has offended or extenuates his fault; but rather purification, which relies more on asking pardon than on confidence in one's own cause. Just as children who are not froward, while they recognize and confess their errors, plead for pardon, and to obtain it, testify in whatever way they can that they have not at all abandoned that reverence which they owe their parents. In short, they so excuse themselves not to prove themselves righteous and innocent, but only to obtain pardon. There follows indignation, when the sinner moans inwardly with himself, finds fault with himself, and is angry with himself, while recognizing his own perversity and his own ungratefulness toward God.

By the word "fear" Paul means that trembling which is produced in our minds as often as we consider both what we deserve and how dreadful is the severity of God's wrath toward sinners. We must then be troubled with an extraordinary disquiet, which both teaches us humility and renders us more cautious thereafter. But if that carefulness of which we have previously spoken arises from fear, we see the bond by which these two are joined together.

It seems to me that he has used the word "longing" to express that diligence in doing our duty and that readiness to obey to which recognition of our sins ought especially to summon us. To this also pertains the "zeal" that he joins directly to it, for it signifies an ardor by which we are aroused when those spurs are applied to us. What have I done? Whither had I plunged if God's mercy had not succored me?

Lastly, there is "avenging." For the more severe we are toward ourselves, and the more sharply we examine our own sins, the more we ought to hope that God is favorable and merciful toward us. And truly, it could not happen otherwise than that the soul itself, stricken by dread of divine judgment, should act the part of an avenger in carrying out its own punishment. Those who are really religious experience what sort of punishments are shame, confusion, groaning, displeasure with self, and other emotions that arise out of a lively recognition of sin. Yet we must remember to exercise restraint, lest sorrow engulf us. For nothing more readily happens to fearful consciences than falling into despair. And also by this stratagem, whomever Satan sees overwhelmed by the fear of God he more and more submerges in that deep whirlpool of sorrow that they may never rise again. That fear cannot, indeed, be too great which ends in humility, and does not depart from the hope of pardon. Nevertheless, in accordance with the apostle's injunction the sinner ought always to beware lest, while he worries himself into dissatisfaction weighed down by excessive fear, he become faint [Heb. 12:3]. For in this way we flee from God, who calls us to himself through repentance. On this matter Bernard's admonition is also useful: "Sorrow for sins is necessary if it be not unremitting. I beg you to turn your steps back sometimes from troubled and anxious remembering of your ways, and to go forth to the tableland of serene remembrance of God's benefits. Let us mingle honey with wormwood that its wholesome bitterness may bring health when it is drunk tempered with sweetness. If you take thought upon yourselves in your humility, take thought likewise upon the Lord in his goodness."[31]

(The fruits of repentance: holiness of life, confession and remission of sins; repentance is lifelong, 16–20)
16. Outward and inward repentance
    bNow we can understand the nature of the fruits of repentance: cthe duties of piety toward God, of charity toward men, and in the whole of life, holiness and purity. eBriefly, the more earnestly any man measures his life by the standard of God's law, the surer are the signs of repentance that he shows. Therefore, the Spirit, while he urges us to repentance, often recalls us now to the individual precepts of the law, now to the duties of the Second Table. Yet in other passages the Spirit has first condemned uncleanness in the very wellspring of the heart, and then proceeded to the external evidences that mark sincere repentance. I will soon set before my readers' eyes a table of this matter in a description of the life of the Christian.[32] I will not gather evidences from the prophets, wherein they sometimes scorn the follies of those who strive to appease God with ceremonies and show them to be mere laughingstocks, and at other times teach that outward uprightness of life is not the chief point of repentance, for God looks into men's hearts. Whoever is moderately versed in Scripture will understand by himself, without the admonition of another, that when we have

31 Bernard, *Sermons on the Song of Songs* xi. 2 (MPL 183. 824 f.; tr. Eales, *Life and Works of St. Bernard* IV. 55).
32 III. vi–x.

to deal with God[33] nothing is achieved unless we begin from the inner disposition of the heart. And the passage from Joel will contribute no little to the understanding of the rest: "Rend your hearts and not your garments" [ch. 2:13]. Both of these exhortations also are briefly expressed in these words of James, "Cleanse your hands, you sinners, and purify your hearts, you men of double mind" [James 4:8], where there is indeed an addition in the first clause; yet the source and origin is then shown: namely, that men must cleanse away secret filth in order that an altar may be erected to God in the heart itself.

cBesides, there are certain outward exercises that we use privately as remedies, either to humble ourselves or to tame our flesh, but publicly as testimony of repentance [II Cor. 7:11]. Moreover, they arise from that "avenging" of which Paul speaks [II Cor. 7:11]. For these are the characteristics of an afflicted mind: to be in squalor, groaning, and tears; to flee splendor and any sort of trappings; to depart from all delights. Then he who feels what a great evil rebellion of the flesh is seeks every remedy to restrain it. Moreover, he who well considers how serious it is to have run counter to God's justice cannot rest until, in his humility, he has given glory to God.

The old writers often mention exercises of this sort when they discuss the fruits of repentance.[34] But although they do not place the force of repentance in them—my readers will pardon me if I say what I think—it seems to me that they depend too much upon such exercises. And if any man will wisely weigh this matter, he will agree with me, I trust, that they have in two respects gone beyond measure. For when they urged so much and commended with such immoderate praises that bodily discipline, they succeeded in making the people embrace it with greater zeal; but they somewhat obscured what ought to have been of far greater importance. Secondly, in inflicting punishments they were somewhat more rigid than the gentleness of the church would call for, as we shall have occasion to show in another place.[35]

17. The outward practice of penance must not become the chief thing

bSome persons, when they hear weeping, fasting, and ashes

---

[33] Cf. sec. 6, note 16, above.
[34] Calvin's "vetusti scriptores" here may include not only church fathers but also the authors of medieval handbooks of penance, the libri poenitentiales, in which severe physical penalties were sometimes prescribed. Cf. J. T. McNeill and H. M. Gamer, Medieval Handbooks of Penance, pp. 5, 30 ff., 142 ff., 258 ff., 348.
[35] IV. xii. 8–13.

spoken of in various passages, and especially in Joel [ch. 2:12], consider that repentance consists chiefly of fasting and weeping.[36] This delusion of theirs must be removed. What is there said concerning the conversion of the entire heart to the Lord, and concerning the rending not of garments but of the heart, belongs properly to repentance. But weeping and fasting are not subjoined as perpetual or necessary effects of this, but have their special occasion. Because he had prophesied that the Jews were threatened with a very great disaster, he counseled them to forestall the wrath of God; not only by repenting, but also by manifesting their sorrow. For just as an accused man is wont to present himself as a suppliant with long beard, uncombed hair, and mourner's clothing to move the judge to mercy; so it behooved them when arraigned before the judgment seat of God to beg, in their miserable condition, that his severity be averted. But although perhaps sackcloth and ashes better fitted those times, it is certain that there will be a very suitable use among us for weeping and fasting whenever the Lord seems to threaten us with any ruin or calamity. When he causes some danger to appear, he announces that he is ready and, after a manner, armed for revenge. Therefore, the prophet does well to exhort his people to weeping and fasting—that is, to the sorrow of accused persons, for he had just stated that their evil deeds were brought to trial.

In like manner, the pastors of the church would not be doing ill today if, when they see ruin hanging over the necks of their people, they were to cry out to them to hasten to fasting and weeping; provided—and this is the principal point—they always urge with greater and more intent care and effort that "they should rend their hearts and not their garments" [Joel 2:13]. There is no doubt whatsoever that fasting is not always closely connected with repentance, but is especially intended for times of calamity. Accordingly, Christ links it with mourning when he releases the apostles from need of it, until, deprived of his presence, they should be overwhelmed with grief [Matt. 9:15]. I am speaking concerning a public fast, for the life of the godly ought to be tempered with frugality and sobriety that throughout its course a sort of perpetual fasting may appear. ᶜBut because that whole matter is to be investigated again where we discuss the discipline of the church,[37] I now touch upon it rather sparingly.

18. Confession of sin before God and before men

ᶜNevertheless, I shall insert this point here: when the term

[36] Jerome, *Commentary on Joel* 2:12 (MPL 25. 967).
[37] IV. xii. 14–21.

"repentance" is applied to this external profession, it is improperly diverted from its true meaning, which I have set forth. For it is not so much a turning to God as a confession of guilt, together with a beseeching of God to avert punishment and accusation. Thus, to "repent in sackcloth and ashes" [Matt. 11:21; Luke 10: 13] is only to evidence our self-displeasure when God is angry with us because of our grave offenses. Public, indeed, is this kind of confession, by which we, condemning ourselves before the angels and the world, anticipate the judgment of God. For Paul, rebuking the slothfulness of those who are indulgent toward their own sins, says: "If we judged ourselves . . . we should not be judged" by God [I Cor. 11:31]. Now, while it is not always necessary to make men open and conscious witnesses of our repentance, yet to confess to God privately is a part of true repentance that cannot be omitted. For there is nothing less reasonable than that God should forgive those sins in which we flatter ourselves, and which we hypocritically disguise lest he bring them to light.

Not only is it fitting to confess those sins which we commit daily, but graver offenses ought to draw us further and recall to our minds those which seem long since buried. David teaches us this by his example. For, touched with shame for his recent crime, he examines himself even to the time when he was in his mother's womb, and acknowledges that even then he was corrupted and infected with the filthiness of the flesh [Ps. 51:3–5]. And he does not do this to extenuate his guilt, as many hide themselves in a crowd and seek to go unpunished by involving others with them. David does far otherwise. He openly magnifies his guilt, confessing that, corrupted from his very infancy, he has not ceased to heap misdeeds upon misdeeds. Also, in another passage, he undertakes such an investigation of his past life as to implore God's mercy for the sins of his youth [Ps. 25:7]. Surely then, at last, we shall prove that our drowsiness has been shaken from us, if we seek from God a release by groaning under our burden, by bewailing our evil deeds.

Moreover, we ought to note that the repentance which we are enjoined constantly to practice differs from that repentance which, as it were, arouses from death those who have either shamefully fallen or with unbridled vices cast themselves into sinning, or have thrown off God's yoke by some sort of rebellion. For often Scripture, in exhorting to repentance, means by it a kind of passage and resurrection from death to life. And in referring to a people as having "repented," it means that they have been converted from idol worship and other gross offenses. For this reason, Paul declares that he will mourn for those sinners who "have not repented of lewdness, fornication, and licentiousness" [II Cor. 12:21 p.]. We ought carefully to observe this distinction, lest when we hear that few are called to repentance we become careless, as if mortification of the flesh no longer concerned us. For the base desires that always pester us, and the vices that repeatedly sprout in us, do not allow us to slacken our concern for mortification. Therefore, the special repentance that is required only of certain ones whom the devil has wrenched from fear of God and entangled in deadly snares does not do away with the ordinary repentance to which corruption of nature compels us to give attention throughout our lives.

19. Repentance and forgiveness are interrelated
ᵇNow if it is true—a fact abundantly clear—ᵇ⁽ᵃ⁾that the whole of the gospel is contained under these two headings, repentance and forgiveness of sins, do we not see that the Lord freely justifies his own in order that he may at the same time restore them to true righteousness by sanctification of his Spirit? ᵃJohn, a messenger sent before the face of Christ to prepare his ways [Matt. 11:10], proclaimed: "Repent, for the Kingdom of Heaven has come near" [Matt. 3:2; 4:17, Vg.]. By inviting them to repentance, he admonished them to recognize that they were sinners,[38] and their all was condemned before the Lord, that they might with all their hearts desire the mortification of their flesh, and a new rebirth in the Spirit. By proclaiming the Kingdom of God, he was calling them to faith, for by the Kingdom of God, which he taught was at hand, he meant the forgiveness of sins, salvation, life, and utterly everything that we obtain in Christ. Hence we read in the other Evangelists: "John came preaching a baptism of repentance for the remission of sins" [Mark 1:4; Luke 3:3]. What else is this than that they, weighed down and wearied by the burden of sins, should turn to the Lord and conceive a hope of forgiveness and salvation? So, also, Christ entered upon his preaching: "The Kingdom of God has come near; repent, and believe in the gospel" [Mark 1:15 p.]. First he declares that the treasures of God's mercy have been opened in himself; then he requires repentance; finally, trust in God's promises. Therefore, when he meant to summarize the whole gospel in brief, he said that he "should suffer, . . . rise from the dead, and that repentance and forgiveness of sins should be preached in his name" [Luke 24:26, 46–47]. And after his resurrection the apostles preached this: "God raised Jesus . . . to give repentance to Israel

[38] Bucer, *In sacra quatuor Evangelia enarrationes* (1536 edition, pp. 35, 85, 259).

and forgiveness of sins" [Acts 5:30–31]. Repentance is preached in the name of Christ when, through the teaching of the gospel, men hear that all their thoughts, all their inclinations, all their efforts, are corrupt and vicious. Accordingly, they must be reborn if they would enter the Kingdom of Heaven. Forgiveness of sins is preached when men are taught that for them Christ became redemption, righteousness, b(a)salvation, and life [I Cor. 1:30], by whose name they are freely accounted righteous and innocent in God's sight. bSince both kinds of grace are received by faith, as I have elsewhere proved,[39] still, because the proper object of faith is God's goodness, by which sins are forgiven, it was expedient that it should be carefully distinguished from repentance.

20. In what sense is repentance the prior condition of forgiveness?

aNow the hatred of sin, which is the beginning of repentance, first gives us access to the knowledge of Christ, who reveals himself to none but poor and afflicted sinners, who groan, toil, are heavy-laden, hunger, thirst, and pine away with sorrow and misery b(a)[Isa. 61:1–3; Matt. 11:5, 28; Luke 4:18]. Accordingly, we must strive toward repentance itself, devote ourselves to it throughout life, and pursue it to the very end if we would abide in Christ. bFor he came to call sinners, but it was to repentance [cf. Matt. 9:13]. He was sent to bless the unworthy, but in order that every one may turn from his wickedness [Acts 3:26; cf. ch. 5:31]. Scripture is full of such testimonies. For this reason, when God offers forgiveness of sins, he usually requires repentance of us in turn, implying that his mercy ought to be a cause for men to repent. He says, "Do judgment and righteousness, for salvation has come near." [Isa. 56:1 p.] Again, "A redeemer will come to Zion, and to those in Jacob who repent of their sins." [Isa. 59: 20.] Again, "Seek the Lord while he can be found, call upon him while he is near; let the wicked man forsake his way and the unrighteousness of his thoughts; let him return to the Lord, and he will have mercy upon him." [Isa. 55:6–7 p.] Likewise, "Turn again, and repent, that your sins may be blotted out." [Acts 3:19.] Yet we must note that this condition is not so laid down as if our repentance were the basis of our deserving pardon, but rather, because the Lord has determined to have pity on men to the end that they may repent, he indicates in what direction men should proceed if they wish to obtain grace. Accordingly, so long as we dwell in the prison house of our body we must continually contend with the defects of our corrupt nature, indeed with our own natural soul. aPlato sometimes says that the

[39] III. iii. 1.

life of a philosopher is a meditation upon death;[40] but we may more truly say that the life of a Christian man is a continual effort and exercise in the mortification of the flesh, till it is utterly slain, and God's Spirit reigns in us. Therefore, I think he has profited greatly who has learned to be very much displeased with himself, not so as to stick fast in this mire and progress no farther, but rather to hasten to God and yearn for him in order that, having been engrafted into the life and death of Christ, he may give attention to continual repentance. bTruly, they who are held by a real loathing of sin cannot do otherwise. For no one ever hates sin unless he has previously been seized with a love of righteousness.[41] aThis thought, as it was the simplest of all, so has it seemed to me to agree best with the truth of Scripture.

(Sins for which there is no repentance or pardon, 21–25)
21. Repentance as God's free gift
cFurther, that repentance is a singular gift of God I believe to be so clear from the above teaching that there is no need of a long discourse to explain it. Accordingly, the church praises God's benefit, and marvels that he "granted repentance to the Gentiles unto salvation" [Acts 11:18, cf. II Cor. 7:10]. And Paul bids Timothy be forbearing and gentle toward unbelievers: If at any time, he says, God may give them repentance to recover from the snares of the devil [II Tim. 2:25–26]. Indeed, God declares that he wills the conversion of all, and he directs exhortations to all in common. Yet the efficacy of this depends upon the Spirit of regeneration. For it would be easier for us to create men than for us of our own power to put on a more excellent nature. Accordingly, in the whole course of regeneration, we are with good reason called "God's handiwork, created . . . for good works, which God prepared beforehand, that we should walk in them" [Eph. 2:10, cf. Vg.]. Whomsoever God wills to snatch from death, he quickens by the Spirit of regeneration. Not that repentance, properly speaking, is the cause of salvation, but because it is already seen to be inseparable from faith and from God's mercy, when, as Isaiah testifies, "a redeemer will come to

---

[40] Plato, *Apology of Socrates* 29 A, B; 41 C, D; *Phaedo* 64 A, B; 67 A–E; 81 A (LCL Plato I. 106 f., 142 ff., 222 f., 232–235, 280 ff.).
[41] *"Nisi prius iustitiae amore captus."* Cf. Luther, Letter to J. Staupitz, May 30, 1518: *"Quod penitentia vera non est, nisi quae ab amore iustitiae et Dei incipit"* (*Werke* WA I. 525; O. Scheel, *Dokumente zu Luthers Entwicklung,* 2d ed., p. 10; tr. *Works of Martin Luther* I. 40); Luther, *Sermon on Repentance* (*Werke* WA I. 320).

Zion, and to those in Jacob who turn back from iniquity" [Isa. 59:20].

This fact indeed stands firm: wherever the fear of God flourishes, the Spirit has worked toward the salvation of man. Therefore believers, according to Isaiah, while they complain and grieve that they have been forsaken by God, set this as a sort of sign of reprobation, that their hearts have been hardened by him [Isa. 63:17]. The apostle, also wishing to exclude apostates from the hope of salvation, gives the reason that "it is impossible to restore them to repentance" [Heb. 6:4–6 p.]. For obviously God, renewing those he wills not to perish, shows the sign of his fatherly favor and, so to speak, draws them to himself with the rays of his calm and joyous countenance. On the other hand, he hardens and he thunders against the reprobate, whose impiety is unforgivable.

With this sort of vengeance the apostle threatens willful apostates who, while they fall away from faith in the gospel, mock God, scornfully despise his grace, profane and trample Christ's blood [Heb. 10:29], yea, as much as it lies in their power, crucify him again [Heb. 6:6]. For Paul does not, as certain austere folk would preposterously have it, cut off hope of pardon from all voluntary sins.[42] But he teaches that apostasy deserves no excuse, so that it is no wonder God avenges such sacrilegious contempt of himself with inexorable rigor. b"For," he teaches, "it is impossible to restore again to repentance those who have once been enlightened, who have tasted the heavenly gift, have become partakers of the Holy Spirit, and have tasted the goodness of the word of God and the powers of the age to come, if they fall away, since they crucify the Son of God on their own account and hold him up to contempt." [Heb. 6:4–6.] Another passage: "If we sin willfully," he says, "after receiving the knowledge of the truth, there remains no longer a sacrifice for sins, but a certain dreadful expectation of judgment," etc. [Heb. 10:26].

These are, also, the passages from the wrong understanding of which the Novatianists long ago found occasion for their ravings. Offended by the harshness in these passages, certain good men believed this to be a spurious letter,[43] even though in every

---

[42] Cf. I Clement ii. 3. This view is attributed by Calvin to the Anabaptists: *Brief Instruction Against the Anabaptists* (CR VII. 73 f.). Cf. the Anabaptist articles of Schleitheim, quoted and answered by Zwingli (Zwingli, *Opera*, ed. M. Schuler and J. Schulthess, III. 390; tr. S. M. Jackson, *Selected Works of Huldreich Zwingli*, pp. 180 f.; tr. J. C. Wenger from the German text, "The Schleitheim Confession of Faith," *Mennonite Quarterly Review* XIX [1945], 248). Cf. IV. xvi. 1, note 2.

[43] Both the Montanists of Tertullian's time and the Novatianists later argued

part it breathes an apostolic spirit. But since we are contending only against those who accept this letter, it is easy to show how these statements do not at all support their error. First, it is necessary for the apostle to agree with his Master, who declares that "every sin and blasphemy shall be forgiven . . . but the sin against the Holy Spirit," which is forgiven "neither in this age nor in the age to come" [Matt. 12:31–32; Mark 3:28–29; Luke 12:10]. It is certain, I say, that the apostle was content with this exception, unless we would make him an opponent of the grace of Christ. From this it follows e(b)that pardon is not denied to any individual sins except one, which, arising out of desperate madness, cannot be ascribed to weakness, and clearly demonstrates that a man is possessed by the devil.

22. Unpardonable sin

bBut in order to settle this point it behooves us to inquire into the nature of this abominable crime which is never to be forgiven. Augustine somewhere defines it as persistent stubbornness even to death, with distrust of pardon;[44] but this does not sufficiently agree with the very words of Christ, that it is not to be forgiven in this age [Matt. 12:31–32, etc.]. For either this is said in vain, or the unpardonable sin can be committed within the compass of this life. But if Augustine's definition is true, it is not committed unless it continue even to death. Others say that he who envies the grace bestowed upon his brother sins against the Holy Spirit.[45] I do not see where they get this idea.

But let us set forth the true definition, which, when it is buttressed by firm testimonies, will of itself easily overcome all others. I say, therefore, that they sin against the Holy Spirit who, with evil intention, resist God's truth, although by its brightness they are so touched that they cannot claim ignorance. Such resistance alone constitutes this sin. For Christ, to explain what he had said, immediately adds: "He who speaks against the Son of man will have his sin forgiven; but he who blasphemes against

---

from Heb. 6:4–6 in support of their rigorism in excluding the lapsed from penance. This was one of the reasons (as Filaster of Brescia [d. ca. 397] affirms in De heresibus lxi [margin lxxxix]; MPL 12. 1202) for the delay in according canonical status to Hebrews. Cf. J. Moffatt, International Critical Commentary: Hebrews, pp. xviii, xx. When Tertullian became a Montanist, he so interpreted the passage as to hold apostates incapable of repentance and ineligible for admission to penance.

44 Augustine, Unfinished Exposition of the Epistle to the Romans xxii (MPL 35. 2104); Letters clxxxv. 11. 49 (MPL 33. 814; tr. FC 12. 188 f.).

45 Augustine, Sermon on the Mount I. xxii. 73 (MPL 34. 1266; tr. NPNF VI. 30 f.); Bede, Exposition of Matthew's Gospel II. 12 (MPL 92. 63).

the Spirit will not be forgiven" [Matt. 12:32, 31, Vg.; cf. Luke 12:10; Mark 3:29]. And Matthew writes in place of "blasphemy against the Spirit," the "spirit of blasphemy."[46]

But how can anyone hurl a reproach against the Son without its being at the same time trained against the Spirit? Those can who unconsciously attack God's truth, it being unknown to them. Those can who ignorantly curse Christ, yet who would not consciously will to extinguish the truth of God if it were revealed to them, who would not wound with a single word him whom they know to be the Anointed of the Lord. Such men it is who sin against the Father and the Son. Thus, there are many today who most wickedly curse the gospel teaching, which, if they knew it to be of the gospel, they would be ready to revere whole-heartedly.

But they whose consciences, though convinced that what they repudiate and impugn is the Word of God, yet cease not to impugn it—these are said to blaspheme against the Spirit, since they strive against the illumination that is the work of the Holy Spirit. Such were certain of the Jews, who, even though they could not withstand the Spirit speaking through Stephen, yet strove to resist [Acts 6:10]. There is no doubt that many of them were impelled to it by zeal for the law, but it appears that there were others who raged against God himself with malicious impiety; that is to say, against the doctrine that they well knew came from God. Such, also, are the Pharisees themselves, against whom the Lord inveighs, who in order to enfeeble the power of the Holy Spirit slander him with the name "Beelzebub" [Matt. 9:34; 12:24]. This, therefore, is the spirit of blasphemy, when man's boldness deliberately leaps into reproach of the divine name. Paul hints at this when he asserts that he obtained mercy because he had committed those things ignorantly in unbelief [I Tim. 1:13], by virtue of which he would otherwise have been unworthy of the Lord's favor. If ignorance joined with unbelief caused him to obtain pardon, it follows that there is no place for pardon where knowledge is linked with unbelief.

23. How the impossibility of "second repentance" is to be understood

e(b)Now if you pay close attention, you will understand that the apostle is speaking not concerning one particular lapse or

---

[46] *"Ponit Spiritum blasphemiae"* (VG, *"esprit de blaspheme"*), in agreement with Froben's text of Matt. 12:31, Basel, 1538. The Greek is τοῦ πνεύματος βλασφημία (lit., "blasphemy of the Spirit"; RSV, "blasphemy against the Spirit").

another, but concerning the universal rebellion by which the reprobate forsake salvation. ᶜNo wonder, then, God is implacable toward those of whom John, in his canonical letter, asserts that they were not of the elect, from whom they went out [I John 2:19]! ᵇFor he is directing his discourse against those who imagine that they can return to the Christian religion even though they had once departed from it. Calling them away from this false and pernicious opinion, he says something very true, that a return to the communion of Christ is not open to those who knowingly and willingly have rejected it. But those who reject it are not those who with dissolute and uncontrolled life simply transgress the Word of the Lord, but those who deliberately reject its entire teaching. Therefore the fallacy lies in the words "lapsing" and "sinning" [Heb. 6:6; 10:26], since the Novatianists interpret "lapsing" to mean the act of a man who, taught by the law of the Lord not to steal or fornicate, does not abstain from theft or fornication.[47] On the contrary, I affirm that here is an underlying tacit antithesis in which all things ought to be recapitulated that are contrary to those which had been stated before; ᵈso that it is not any particular failing that is here expressed, but complete turning away from God and, so to speak, apostasy of the whole man. ᵇWhen, therefore, he speaks of those who have lapsed after they have once been illumined, have tasted the heavenly gift, have been made sharers in the Holy Spirit, and also have tasted God's good Word and the powers of the age to come [Heb. 6:4–5], it must be understood that they who choke the light of the Spirit with deliberate impiety, and spew out the taste of the heavenly gift, will cut themselves off from the sanctification of the Spirit, and trample upon God's Word and the powers of the age to come. And the better to express an impiety deliberately intended, in another passage he afterward expressly adds the word "willfully."[48] For when he says that they who, willing, sin after having received knowledge of the truth have no sacrifice left for them [Heb. 10:26], he does not deny that Christ is a continual sacrifice to atone for the iniquities of the saints. Almost the whole letter eloquently proclaims this, in explaining Christ's priesthood. But he says that no other sacrifice remains when His has been rejected. Moreover, it is rejected when the truth of the gospel is expressly denied.

---

[47] This phraseology has not been located in the literature of the Novatianist controversy, but Cyprian charges Novatianus with identifying apostasy (or lapsing) with the sin against the Holy Ghost (MPL 35. 2304). Cf. O. D. Watkins, *A History of Penance* I. 17, 132–221.
[48] *"Voluntarie."*

24. Those who cannot be forgiven are those who cannot repent*

ᵇTo some it seems too hard and alien to the mercy of God that any who flee for refuge in calling upon the Lord's mercy are wholly deprived of forgiveness. This is easily answered. For the author of Hebrews does not say that pardon is refused if they turn to the Lord, but he utterly denies that they can rise to repentance, because they have been stricken by God's just judgment with eternal blindness on account of their ungratefulness.

There is nothing that opposes this in the example of Esau, which he later applies to this point: Esau vainly tried to retrieve his lost birthright by tears and wailing [Heb. 12:16–17]. This is no less true of that warning of the prophet: "When they cry, I shall not hear" [Zech. 7:13]. For such expressions do not designate either true conversion or calling upon God, but that anxiety by which in extremity impious men are bound and compelled to have regard for what previously they complacently neglected, the fact that their every good depends upon the Lord's help. But they do not so much implore it as groan that it has been taken from them. By "cry" the prophet [Zech. 7:13], and by "tears" the apostle [Heb. 12:17], signifies nothing but that dreadful torment which burns and tortures the wicked in their despair.

ᵉThis fact deserves careful note: that otherwise God, who by the prophet proclaims he will be merciful as soon as the sinner repents, would be at war with himself [Ezek. 18:21–22]. And, as I have already said,[49] it is certain that the mind of man is not changed for the better except by God's prevenient grace. Also, his promise to those who call upon him will never deceive. But it is improper to designate as "conversion" and "prayer" the blind torment that distracts the reprobate when they see that they must seek God in order to find a remedy for their misfortunes and yet flee at his approach.

25. Sham repentance and honest repentance

ᵉThe question arises, however, inasmuch as the apostle denies that sham repentance appeases God, how Ahab obtained pardon and turned aside the punishment imposed upon him; since he appears, from the later conduct of his life, to have been stricken only by some sudden fear [I Kings 21:28–29]. He, indeed, put on sackcloth, cast ashes over himself, lay upon the ground [I Kings 21:27], and as is testified concerning him, humbled himself before God; but it meant little to rend his garments while his heart remained obstinate and swollen with malice. Yet we see how God is turned to mercy.

⁴⁹ Sec. 21, above.

I reply: Hypocrites are sometimes spared thus for a while, yet the wrath of God ever lies upon them, and this is done not so much for their own sake as for an example to all. For even though Ahab had his punishment mitigated, what profit was this to him, but that while alive upon earth he should not feel it? Therefore God's curse, although secret, had a fixed seat in his house, and he went to eternal destruction.

The same is to be seen in Esau; for, even though he suffered a repulse, a temporal blessing was granted to his tears [Gen. 27: 40]. But because the spiritual inheritance from the oracle of God could rest in the possession of only one of the brothers, when Esau was passed over and Jacob chosen, the disinheriting of Esau excluded God's mercy; yet this solace remained to him as an animal man: to become fat with the fatness of the earth and the dew of heaven [Gen. 27:28].[50]

And this which I have just said ought to be applied as an example for the others in order that we may learn more readily to apply our minds and our efforts to sincere repentance, because there must be no doubt that when we are truly and heartily converted, God, who extends his mercy even to the unworthy when they show any dissatisfaction with self, will readily forgive us. By this means, also, we are taught what dread judgment is in store for all the obstinate, who with shameless forehead no less than iron heart now make it a sport to spurn and set at nought the threats of God. In this way he often stretched out his hand to the sons of Israel to relieve their calamity, even though their cries were feigned and their hearts were deceitful and false [cf. Ps. 78:36–37], as he complains in the psalm, that they forthwith reverted to their own character [v. 57]. And thus by such kindly gentleness he willed to bring them to earnest conversion or render them inexcusable. Yet in remitting punishments for a time, he does not bind himself by perpetual law, but rather sometimes rises up more severely against the hypocrites and doubles their punishment to show how much their pretense displeases him. But as I have said, he sets forth some examples of his readiness to give pardon, by which the godly may be encouraged to amend their lives, and the pride of those who stubbornly kick against the pricks may be more severely condemned.

[50] Following LXX and Vg. here (as in his Comm. Gen. 27:38, 39), Calvin has interchanged the blessing of Esau with that of Jacob in Gen., ch. 27. Cf., however, Heb. 11:20.

^cCHAPTER IV

How Far from the Purity of the Gospel Is All That the Sophists in Their Schools Prate About Repentance; Discussion of Confession and Satisfaction

(The Scholastic doctrine of confession and contrition, with its alleged Scriptural basis, examined, 1–6)
1. The Scholastic doctrine of penance

^aNow I come to discuss what the Scholastic Sophists have taught concerning repentance. This I will run through in as few words as possible because it is not my intention to pursue everything, lest this book which I am anxious to prepare as a short textbook burst all bounds. They have involved this matter, otherwise not very complicated, in so many volumes that there would be no easy way out if you were to immerse yourself even slightly in their slime.

First, in their definition, they clearly disclose that they have never understood what repentance is. For they take certain clichés from the books of the ancient writers, which do not express the force of repentance at all. For example: to repent is to weep over former sins, and not to commit sins to be wept over; again, it is to bewail past evil deeds and not again to commit deeds to be bewailed; again, it is a certain sorrowing vengeance that punishes in oneself what one is sorry to have committed; again, it is sorrow of heart and bitterness of soul for the evil deeds that one has committed, or to which one has consented.[1]

Let us grant that these things have been well said by the fathers, although a contentious man could without difficulty deny this. Yet they were not spoken with the intent to define repentance, but only to urge their hearers not to fall again into the same transgressions from which they had been rescued. ^bBut if they would turn all statements of this sort into definitions, others also ought with equal right to have been patched on. Such a one is this statement of Chrysostom: "Repentance is a medicine

---

[1] Cf. Gregory the Great, *Homilies on the Gospels* II. hom. xiv. 15 (MPL 76. 1256); Columbanus, *Penitential* [ca. 600] A. 1 (MPL 80. 223; tr. J. T. McNeill, *Medieval Handbooks of Penance*, p. 250); Pseudo-Ambrose, *Sermons* xxv. 1 (MPL 17. 655); Lombard, *Sentences* IV. xiv. 1 (MPL 192. 869); Pseudo-Augustine, *De vera et falsa poenitentia* viii. 22 (MPL 40. 1120). The last-named work appeared only about 1100 but was held genuine and authoritative by the Schoolmen and was first declared spurious by Trithemius of Spannheim, ca. 1495. The present chapter has all the 17 references to it in the *Institutes* cited by Smits (II. 263), with four exceptions, which are from the 1536 edition. Cf. III. iv. 39, note 83; Smits I. 184, 190.

that wipes out sin, a gift given from heaven, a wondrous power, a grace surpassing the might of laws."[2]

ᶜBesides, the doctrine taught by the Scholastics in later times is somewhat worse than these patristic definitions. For they are so doggedly set in outward exercises that you gather nothing else from their huge volumes than that repentance is a discipline and austerity that serves partly to tame the flesh, partly to chastise and punish faults. They are wonderfully silent concerning the inward renewal of the mind, which bears with it true correction of life. ᵇAmong them there is, indeed, much talk concerning contrition and attrition. They torture souls with many misgivings, and immerse them in a sea of trouble and anxiety. But where they seem to have wounded hearts deeply, they heal all the bitterness with a light sprinkling of ceremonies.

ᵃThey divide repentance, thus subtly defined, into contrition of heart, confession of mouth, and satisfaction of works.[3] This division is no more logical than the definition—even though they wish to appear to have spent their whole life in framing syllogisms. Suppose someone reasons from their definition—a kind of argument prevalent among dialecticians—that anyone can weep for previously committed sins and not commit sins that ought to be wept over, can bewail past evil deeds and not commit evil deeds that ought to be bewailed, can punish what he is sorry to have committed, etc., even though he does not confess with his

---

[2] Chrysostom, *Homilies on Repentance,* hom. vii. 1 (MPG 49. 338). The conception of penance as medicine for sin is a commonplace of the early fathers and of the medieval penitential handbooks. Cf. A. Harnack, *Medizinisches aus der ältesten Kirchengeschichte* (Texte und Untersuchungen zur Geschichte der altchristlichen Literatur VIII [1892]), pp. 137 ff.; McNeill and Gamer, *Medieval Handbooks of Penance,* pp. 44 f., 182; McNeill, *A History of the Cure of Souls,* pp. 44 f., 114, 119, 134, 179, 315. Calvin's *Ecclesiastical Ordinances* (1541) command "that there be no rigour by which anyone may be injured; for even the corrections are only medicines" (CR X i. 30; tr. LCC XXII. 71).

[3] The "three parts of penance"—contrition, confession, and satisfaction—were formally treated in innumerable medieval works. This scheme is followed in Lombard's *Sentences* IV. xvi. 1 (MPL 192. 877) and in the *Decretum* of Gratian II. i. 40 (Friedberg I. 1168), where it is supported by a work on repentance wrongly ascribed to Chrysostom (*Opera,* edited by Erasmus, 1530, II. 347; 1547 edition, V. 904). Cf. Melanchthon, *Loci communes* (1521), section *"vis peccati et fructus"* (ed. Engelland, *op. cit.,* p. 35; tr. Hill, *op. cit.,* p. 103: both editors have useful notes on attrition, the prelude to contrition). The "immense volumes" to which Calvin here refers may include such elaborate treatises as those generally called *summae confessorum:* see A. M. Walz, *Compendium historiae ordinis praedicatorum,* p. 145. Luther several times attacked this threefold conception of penance: see, for example, *Werke* WA VI. 610; VII. 112. Fisher, in replying to Luther, defends it at length in *Assertionis Lutheranae confutatio* (1523), pp. 156–178.

mouth. How, then, will they maintain their division? For if he does not confess though truly penitent, there can be repentance without confession. But if they reply that this division applies to penance only in so far as it is a sacrament, or is understood concerning the whole perfection of repentance, which they do not include in their definitions, there is no reason to accuse me; let them blame themselves for not defining it more precisely and clearly. Now, for my part, when there is a dispute concerning anything, I am stupid enough to refer everything back to the definition itself, which is the hinge and foundation of the whole debate.

But let that be the teachers' license. Now let us survey in order the various parts themselves. ᵉI negligently leap over the trifles that they, with grave mien, hawk as mysteries, and I am not doing this unwittingly. For it would not be very toilsome for me to investigate all that they think they are skillfully and subtly disputing. But it would be mere meticulousness for me to tire my readers with such trifles to no avail. Surely, it is easy to recognize from the questions that move and excite them, and which miserably encumber them, that they are chattering about unknown things. For example: whether repenting of one sin is pleasing to God when in others obstinacy remains. Or: whether divinely inflicted punishments are able to make satisfaction. Or: whether repentance may be frequently repeated for mortal sins, when they foully and impiously define that men daily practice penance for venial sins only. Similarly, on the basis of a saying of Jerome, they torment themselves greatly with a gross error, that repentance is the "second plank after shipwreck."[4] By this they show themselves never to have awakened from their brute stupor, to feel a thousandth part, or even less, of their faults.

2. The Scholastic doctrine of penance torments the conscience

ᵃBut I would have my readers note that this is no contention over the shadow of an ass,[5] but that the most serious matter of

---

[4] On daily repentance for venial sins, cf. Augustine, *Enchiridion* xix. 71 (MPL 40. 265; tr. LCC VII. 381); Caesarius of Arles (d. 542) in MPL 39. 2220; and Columbanus, *Regula coenobialis,* ed. O. Seebass in *Zeitschrift für Kirchengeschichte* XV (1895), 366–386, sec. 1 (tr. McNeill and Gamer, *op. cit.,* p. 258); Aquinas, *Summa Theol.* III. lxxxvii. 1. The description of penance as "the second plank after shipwreck" is called by Luther "that dangerous saying of St. Jerome's" (*Babylonish Captivity,* section on Baptism, *Werke* WA VI; tr. *Works of Martin Luther* II. 219, 222). See Jerome, *Letters* lxxxiv. 6; cxxx. 9 (MPL 22. 748, 1115; tr. NPNF 2 ser. VI. 178, 266). Cf. Lombard, *Sentences* IV. xiv. 1 (MPL 192. 869; tr. LCC X. 348). Jerome's phrase is approved in the Council of Trent, session 6, ch. xiv. Schaff, *Creeds* II. 105.

[5] *"De asini umbra rixam esse."* In a fable of Aesop (ca. 570 B.C.), the owner

all is under discussion: namely, forgiveness of sins. For while they require three things for repentance—compunction of heart, confession of mouth, and satisfaction of works—at the same time they teach that these things are necessary to attain forgiveness of sins. But if there is anything in the whole of religion that we should most certainly know, we ought most closely to grasp by what reason, with what law, under what condition, with what ease or difficulty, forgiveness of sins may be obtained! Unless this knowledge remains clear and sure, the conscience can have no rest at all, no peace with God, no assurance or security; but it continuously trembles, wavers, tosses, is tormented and vexed, shakes, hates, and flees the sight of God.

But if forgiveness of sins depends upon these conditions which they attach to it, nothing is more miserable or deplorable for us. They make contrition the first step in obtaining pardon, and they require it to be a due contrition, that is, just and full.[6] But at the same time they do not determine when a man can have assurance that he has in just measure carried out his contrition.

[e]We must, I admit, carefully and sharply urge every man, by weeping bitterly for his sins, to what his displeasure and hatred toward them, for we ought not to repent this sorrow which begets repentance unto salvation [II Cor. 7:10]. But when a bitterness of sorrow is demanded that corresponds to the magnitude of the offense, and which may balance in the scales with assurance of pardon, [a]here truly miserable consciences are tormented in strange ways, and troubled when they see due contrition for sins imposed upon them. And they do not grasp the measure of the debt so that they are able to discern within themselves that they have paid what they owed. If they say that we must do what is in us, we are always brought back to the same point. For when will anyone dare assure himself that he has applied all of his powers to lament his sins? Therefore, when consciences have for a long time wrestled with themselves, and exercised themselves in long struggles, they still do not find a haven in which to rest. Consequently, to calm themselves, at least in part, they wrest

who hired out his ass and accompanied the rider on foot disputed the latter's right to rest at noonday under the ass's shadow. "To dispute about the shadow of an ass" became a commonplace of Greek writers. Erasmus (*Adagia* [1523] I. iii. 52) associates the expression with Demosthenes; cf. Plutarch, *Lives of the Orators* (*Moralia* 848 A, B), where Demosthenes makes dramatic use of the fable (LCL Plutarch, *Moralia* X. 434 f.).

[6] Biel, *Epythoma pariter et collectorium circa quatuor sententiarum libros* IV. ix. On contrition in obtaining pardon, cf. C. R. Meyer, *The Thomistic Concept of Justifying Contrition*, pp. 60 f., 190 ff. Cf. II. ii. 4, note 15; III. iv. 17, note 36.

sorrow from themselves and squeeze out tears that they may thereby accomplish their contrition.

3. Not the sinner's contrition, but the Lord's mercy awaits*

ªBut if they say that I accuse them falsely, let them actually bring forward and exhibit anyone who, by a doctrine of contrition of this sort, either is not driven to desperation or has not met God's judgment with pretended rather than true sorrow. And we have said in some place that forgiveness of sins can never come to anyone without repentance, because only those afflicted and wounded by the awareness of sins can sincerely invoke God's mercy. But we added at the same time that repentance is not the cause of forgiveness of sins. Moreover, we have done away with those torments of souls which they would have us perform as a duty. We have taught that the sinner does not dwell upon his own compunction or tears, but fixes both eyes upon the Lord's mercy alone.[7] We have merely reminded him that Christ called those who "labor and are heavy-laden" [Matt. 11:28], when he was sent to publish good news to the poor, to heal the brokenhearted, to proclaim release to the captives, to free the prisoners, to comfort the mourners [Isa. 61:1; Luke 4:18, conflated]. Hence are to be excluded both the Pharisees, who, sated with their own righteousness, do not recognize their poverty; and despisers, who, oblivious of God's wrath, do not seek a remedy for their own evil. For such do not labor, are not heavy-laden, are not brokenhearted, nor prisoners or captives. But it makes a great difference whether you teach forgiveness of sins as deserved by just and full contrition, which the sinner can never perform; or whether you enjoin him to hunger and thirst after God's mercy to show him— through the recognition of his misery, his vacillation, his weariness, and his captivity—where he ought to seek refreshment, rest, and freedom; in fine, to teach him in his humility to give glory to God.

4. Confession not enjoined: refutation of Scholastic allegorical argument from the lepers that were cleansed*

ªThere has always been great strife between the canon lawyers and the Scholastic theologians concerning confession. The latter contend that confession is enjoined by divine precept; the former claim that it is commanded only by ecclesiastical constitutions.[8]

---

[7] III. iii. 20. Cf. Melanchthon, *Loci communes*, ed. Engelland, *op. cit.*, pp. 92, 96, 119; tr. Hill, pp. 117, 181 f., 211.
[8] Numerous divergent opinions of medieval theologians and canonists on confession are cited by H. C. Lea, *History of Confession and Indulgences* I.

Now in that quarrel the marked shamelessness of the theologians is evident, who corrupted and forcibly twisted all the passages of Scripture they cited for their purpose. And when they saw that what they wanted could not even in this way be obtained, those who wished to appear more astute than others resorted to the evasion that confession is derived from divine law with respect to its substance, but later took its form from positive law. Of course, the most incompetent among pettifogging lawyers thus relate the citation to the divine law because it is said: "Adam, where are you?" [Gen. 3:9]. The exception,[9] too, because Adam answered as if taking exception: "The wife that thou gavest me," etc. [Gen. 3:12]. In both cases, however, the form is derived from the civil law. But let us see by what proofs they demonstrate this confession—formed or unformed—to be a command of God.

The Lord, they say, sent the lepers to the priests [Matt. 8:4; Mark 1:44; Luke 5:14; 17:14]. What? Did he send them to confession? Who ever heard it said that the Levitical priests were appointed to hear confessions [Deut. 17:8–9]? They therefore take refuge in allegories: it was laid down by the Mosaic law that priests should distinguish between stages of leprosy [Lev. 14:2–3]. Sin is spiritual leprosy; it is the duty of priests to pronounce concerning this.

Before I answer, I ask in passing why, if this passage makes them judges of spiritual leprosy, do they assume cognizance of natural and carnal leprosy? As if this reasoning were not to mock Scripture: the law entrusts the recognition of leprosy to the Levitical priests, let us take this over for ourselves; sin is spiritual leprosy, let us also be judicial examiners of sin!

Now I reply: "When the priesthood is transferred, there is necessarily a transference of the law as well" [Heb. 7:12]. All priestly offices have been transferred to Christ and are fulfilled and completed in him. The whole right and honor of the priesthood has therefore been transferred to him. If they are so fond of chasing after allegories, let them set before themselves Christ as their sole priest, and in his judgment seat concentrate unlimited jurisdiction over all things. We shall readily allow that. Moreover, their allegory, which reckons the merely civil law among the ceremonies, is unsuitable.

Why then does Christ send lepers to the priests? That the priests may not charge him with breaking the law, which bade

168 ff. Lombard, in *Sentences* IV. xvii. 1–4 (MPL 192. 880 ff.), is not in agreement with Gratian, *Decretum* II. i. 30–37 (Friedberg I. 1165–1167).

9 *"Exceptionem item, quia responderit Adam quasi excipiens."* Calvin is using terms of law: *exceptio* is a plea or objection formally entered.

that one cured of leprosy be shown to the priest, and atoned for by offering sacrifice. He bids cleansed lepers do what the law enjoins. "Go," he says, "show yourselves to the priests" [Luke 17:14]; "and offer the gift that Moses prescribes in the law, for a proof to the people" [Matt. 8:4 p.]. Truly, this miracle was to be a proof for them. They had declared them lepers; now they declare them cured. Are they not, even against their will, compelled to become witnesses of Christ's miracles? Christ permits them to investigate his miracles. They cannot deny it. But because they still try to evade, this work serves for them as a testimony. Thus, in another passage: "This gospel will be preached throughout the whole world, as a testimony to all nations" [Matt. 24:14 p.]. Likewise, "You will be dragged before kings and governors . . . to bear testimony before them." [Matt. 10:18.] That is, that they may be more strongly convicted by God's judgment. ᵇBut if they prefer to agree with Chrysostom, he also teaches that this was done by Christ on account of the Jews, that He might not be regarded as a transgressor of the law.[10] ᶜHowever, in such a clear matter one should be ashamed to seek the support of any man, when Christ declares that he relinquishes the whole legal right to the priests, even to professed enemies of the gospel who had always been intent upon shouting against it if their mouths were not stopped. Therefore, that the papal sacrificers may retain this possession, let them openly side with those whom it is necessary forcibly to restrain from cursing Christ. For this has nothing to do with his true ministers.

5. The unbinding of Lazarus misapplied*

ᵃThey derive a second argument from the same source, that is from an allegory—as if allegories were of great value in confirming any dogma! But, let them be of value, unless I show that I can apply those very allegories more plausibly than they. Now they say that the Lord bade the disciples unbind the risen Lazarus and let him go [John 11:44].[11] First, they falsely declare this, for nowhere does one read that the Lord said this to his disciples. It is much more probable that he said this to the Jews (who were present in order that his miracle might be demonstrated beyond any suspicion of fraud, and might display his greater power), in that he raised the dead by his voice alone, and not by his touch. So do I interpret the fact that the Lord, in order to relieve the Jews of all perverse suspicion, willed that they roll away the

---

[10] Chrysostom, *Homilies on the Canaanite Woman,* hom. ix (MPG 52. 456 f.).
[11] Pseudo-Augustine, *De vera et falsa poenitentia* x. 25 (MPL 40. 1122); Gratian, *Decretum* II. i. 88 (Friedberg I. 1188).

stone, smell the stench, look upon the sure signs of death, see him rising up by the power of his Word alone, and be the first to touch him, alive. eAnd this is the opinion of Chrysostom.[12]

bBut suppose we regard this statement as made to the disciples, what then will our opponents maintain? That the Lord gave the apostles the power of loosing? How much more aptly and skillfully this could be treated as allegory if we should say that by this figure God willed to instruct his believers; to loose those raised up by him, that is, so that they should not recall to memory their sins, which he himself had forgotten, nor damn as sinners those whom he himself had absolved, nor still upbraid them for those things that he himself had condoned, nor be harsh and captious to punish where he himself was merciful and ready to spare! cCertainly, nothing ought to incline us more to pardon than the example of the judge, who warns that he will be implacable to those who are too severe and inhuman. aNow let them go and peddle their allegories.

6. Scriptural confession*

aNow they come into closer combat when, as they suppose, they fight, armed with the plain testimonies of Scripture: those who came to the baptism of John confessed their sins [Matt. 3:6]; and James would have us "confess our sins to one another" [James 5:16].[13]

No wonder if those who wished to be baptized confessed their sins! For, as it was said before, "John . . . preached a baptism of repentance" [Mark 1:4]. He baptized with water unto repentance. Whom, therefore, would he have baptized except those who had confessed themselves sinners? Baptism is the symbol of forgiveness of sins. Who would have been admitted to this symbol but sinners and those who recognize themselves as such? Therefore, they confess their sins in order to be baptized.

It is with good reason that James enjoins us to "confess . . . to one another" [James 5:16]. But if they had paid attention to what follows immediately, they would have understood that this also gives them little support. "Confess," he says, "your sins to one another, and pray for one another." [James 5:16.] He combines mutual confession and mutual prayer. If we must confess to priestlings alone, then we must pray for them alone. What? Suppose it followed from the words of James that only priests could confess? Indeed, while he wants us to confess to one an-

[12] Pseudo-Chrysostom, Contra Judaeos, Gentiles et haereticos (MPG 48. 1078).
[13] These were stock proof texts employed by innumerable medieval writers to justify auricular confession.

other, he addresses those alone who could hear one another's confession; 'αλλήλοις is his word, "mutually," "in turn," "interchangeably," or, if they prefer, "reciprocally." ᵇBut only those qualified to hear confessions can confess to one another reciprocally. Since they assign this prerogative to priests alone, we also relegate the function of confessing to them alone.

ᵃAway, then, with trifles of this sort! Let us take the apostle's view, which is simple and open: namely, that we should lay our infirmities on one another's breasts, to receive among ourselves mutual counsel, mutual compassion, and mutual consolation. Then, as we are aware of our brothers' infirmities, let us pray to God for these. Why, then, do they quote James against us though we so strongly urge the confession of God's mercy? But no one can confess the mercy of God until he has previously confessed his own misery. Rather, we pronounce anathema upon everyone who has not confessed himself a sinner before God, before his angels, before the church, and in short, before all men. For the Lord has "shut up all things under sin" [Gal. 3:22] "that every mouth may be stopped" [Rom. 3:19] and all flesh be humbled before God [cf. Rom. 3:20; I Cor. 1:29]. But let him alone be justified [cf. Rom. 3:4] and exalted.

(Evidence for late origin of auricular confession, 7–8)
7. Compulsory confession unknown in the ancient church

ᵃBut I marvel how shamelessly our opponents dare contend that the confession of which they speak is divinely ordained. Of course we admit its practice to have been very ancient, but we can easily prove that it was formerly free. Surely, even their records declare that no law or constitution concerning it had been set up before the time of Innocent III. ᶜSurely, if they had had a more ancient law than those, they would have seized upon it rather than, content with the decree of the Lateran Council, made themselves ridiculous even to children. In other matters they do not hesitate to invent fictitious decretals, which they ascribe to the most ancient councils, that by a veneration for antiquity they may hoodwink the simpleminded. On this point, it did not enter their heads to introduce such a falsehood. Therefore, as they themselves witness, not yet three hundred years have passed since Innocent III set that trap and imposed the necessity of confession.[14]

---

[14] A reference to the Forged Decretals (ascribed to early popes), which appeared about 850 in France. See P. Hinschius, *Decretales Pseudo-Isidorianae et Capitula Angilramni;* E. H. Davenport, *The Forged Decretals;* J. Haller, *Nikolaus I und Pseudoisidor;* P. Fournier and G. Le Bras, *Histoire des collections*

But, to say nothing of the time, the barbarism of the words alone discredits that law! These good fathers enjoin everyone of both sexes[15] once a year to confess all their sins before their own priest. Facetious men humorously take exception that this precept refers only to hermaphrodites, but applies to no one who is either male or female. Then, a grosser absurdity arises in their pupils when they are unable to explain what the expression "their own priests" means.[16]

Whatever all these hired wranglers of the pope may prate, we maintain that Christ was not the author of this law which compels men to list their sins—indeed, that twelve hundred years went by after the resurrection of Christ before any such law was brought forth. And so this tyranny was at length introduced when, after piety and doctrine were extinguished, mere ghosts of pastors had taken all license, without distinction, upon themselves.

[a]Then, there are clear testimonies, both in histories and among other ancient writers, that teach that this was a discipline of polity, instituted by bishops, not a law laid down by Christ or the apostles. I shall bring forward only one of these many testimonies, which will provide clear proof of this matter. Sozomen relates that this constitution of the bishops was diligently observed in the Western churches, especially at Rome. This means that it was not a universal practice of all the churches. Moreover, he says that one of the presbyters was especially designated for this office. This thoroughly refutes what the papists falsely state concerning the keys given in common to the whole priestly order for this use. Indeed, it was not a function common to all priests, but the exclusive function of one priest who had been chosen for

canoniques en Occident depuis les fausses décrétales jusqu'au décret de Gratien I. 196 f. (arguing for origin in Brittany); W. Ullmann, The Growth of Papal Government in the Middle Ages, pp. 167–189.

[15] Fourth Lateran Council (1215) canon xxi. Text in Mansi XXII. 1007 ff.; Hefele-Leclercq V. 1350. Calvin's chuckle over "both sexes" is an example of his familiarity with the jests of the learned in the Middle Ages. Cf. H. C. Lea (op. cit., I. 230) citing William of Ware (ca. 1300): "The ponderous jocularity of the Schoolmen explained that the phrase omnis utriusque sexus was not intended to mean hermaphrodites exclusively and was to be construed distributively and not conjunctively." About 1379 one Richard Hemslay in a sermon at Newcastle on Tyne facetiously alluded to this. He was cited to Rome for his impertinence and was dubbed "Friar Richard of both sexes." See W. A. Pantin, The English Church in the Fourteenth Century, pp. 164 f.

[16] "Proprius sacerdos." Each person was commanded, in the Lateran canon, to confess to "his own priest." The term was discussed with animation where jurisdiction was disputed, especially after the friars became active in the confessional.

it by the bishop. ᵉIt is he whom even today they call in individual cathedral churches the "penitentiarius," the examiner of serious crimes and of those to be censured as an example. ᵃThen he adds that this also had been the custom at Constantinople until a certain matron, pretending to confess, was found to have hidden under the guise of confession an affair which she was having with a certain deacon. On account of this crime, Nectarius, a man renowned for his holiness and learning, bishop of that church, abolished the rite of confession.[17] Here, here, let these asses prick up their ears! If auricular confession were the law of God, why would Nectarius have dared to set it aside and uproot it? Will they accuse Nectarius—a holy man of God, approved by the consent of all the fathers—of heresy and schism? But with this same sentence they will condemn the Church of Constantinople in which, Sozomen declares, the practice of confession was not only neglected for a time, but allowed to fall into disuse within his memory. Indeed, let them accuse of defection not only the Church of Constantinople but all the Eastern churches—if they speak the truth—that neglected an inviolable law enjoined upon all Christians.

8. Chrysostom does not enjoin confession to men*

ᵇNow in very many passages Chrysostom clearly attests this abolition of confession; and he was bishop of the Church of Constantinople, so that it is a wonder they dare mutter to the contrary. "Tell your sins," he says, "that you may wipe them away. If you are embarrassed to tell anyone what sins you have committed, recite them daily to your own soul. I do not tell you to confess them to your fellow servant, who may upbraid you. Recite them to God who heals them. Confess your sins upon your bed that there your conscience may daily acknowledge its misdeeds." Again: "Now, moreover, it is not necessary to confess in the presence of witnesses. Examine your sins in your own thought. Let this judgment be without witness: let God alone see you confessing." Again: "I do not lead you onto the stage before your fellow servants. I do not compel you to uncover your sins to men. Betake your conscience to God's presence and lay it open before him. Show your wounds to the Lord, the most excellent physician, and seek remedy from him. Show them to him, who does not reproach but most gently heals." Again: "Surely, you

---

[17] Sozomen, *Ecclesiastical History* vii. 16 (ed. R. Hussey [Oxford, 1860], II. 724 ff.); Cassiodorus, *Tripartite History* IX. 85 (MPL 69. 1151; tr. NPNF 2 ser. II. 386 f.). The account in Socrates, *Ecclesiastical History* v. 19, differs from this in some details. Cf. McNeill, *A History of the Cure of Souls*, p. 98.

should tell no man, lest he upbraid you; for you should confess nothing to a fellow servant, who may make it public. But show your wounds to the Lord, who takes care of you and is your kind physician." Afterward he has God say: "I do not compel you to come on mid-stage before many witnesses. Tell your sin privately to me only that I may heal your sore."[18] Shall we say that Chrysostom acted rashly when he wrote these and like things to free the consciences of men from those bonds by which they were constrained by divine law? Not at all. But he dare not require as necessary what he understands never to have been prescribed by the Word of God.

(Scriptural confession of sins, public and private, 9–13)
9. Confession before God
[a]But, to make the whole matter plainer and easier, we will first faithfully relate what kind of confession we are taught in the Word of God. Then we will add an account of their inventions —not indeed all, for who could empty such an immense sea—but only those with which they embrace the sum of their secret confession.
[e(a)]Here I am ashamed to recall how frequently the old translator renders the word "to praise" as "to confess" [Ps. 7:18; 9:2; 94(95, Heb.):2; 99(100, Heb.):4; 117(118, Heb.):1, all Vg.],[19] a commonplace to the most unlettered laymen. Still, it is well to lay bare their boldness, transferring as they do to their tyrannical law what had been written concerning the praises of God. To prove that confession has the power to cheer the mind, they drag in that statement of the psalm, "in the voice of rejoicing and confession" [Ps. 42:4; 41:5, Vg.]. Now if such a transformation be valid, we can derive anything from anything. But since they have become so shameless, let pious readers recall that they have been cast into a reprobate mind by God's just vengeance in order that their boldness might be the more detestable. But

---

[18] The four statements here ascribed to Chrysostom were all assumed to be his in Calvin's time, and were printed in his *Opera* edited by Erasmus, 1530. The first is from homily ii on Ps. 50, sec. 5, and is given as spurious in MPG 55. 580 ff. The second, from *Sermon on Penance and Confession*, is in the 1530 edition, V. 512 (1547 edition, V. 906) and is not in MPG. The other passages are genuine and are as follows: *Incomprehensible Nature of God, Against the Anomeans*, hom. v. 7 (MPG 48. 746); *Discourses on Lazarus* iv. 4 (MPG 48. 1012).
[19] In Ps. 7:17, the Hebrew word אוֹדָה (from יָדָה , "to praise aloud") is rendered in LXX ἐξομολογησάμεναι; in Vg., *confiteri* (to confess). Cf. Ps. 9:1; Ps. 42:4.

if we are willing to rest upon simple Scriptural teaching, there will be no danger of anyone's deceiving us with such false colors

For in Scripture, one way of confession is prescribed to this effect: [a]since it is the Lord who forgives, forgets, and wipes out, sins, let us confess our sins to him in order to obtain pardon. He is the physician; therefore, let us lay bare our wounds to him. It is he who is hurt and offended; from him let us seek peace. He is the discerner of hearts, the one cognizant of all thoughts [cf. Heb. 4:12];[20] let us hasten to pour out our hearts before him. He it is, finally, who calls sinners: let us not delay to come to God himself. "I acknowledged my sin to thee," says David, "and I did not hide my iniquity; I said, 'I will confess my transgression to the Lord'; and thou forgavest the iniquity of my heart." [Ps 32:5; 31:5, Vg.] Of similar nature is another confession of David himself: "Have mercy upon me, O God, according to thy great loving-kindness" [Ps. 51:1; 50:3, Vg.]. Such, too, is Daniel's statement: "We have sinned and done wrong and acted wickedly and rebelled, O Lord, in turning aside from thy commandments" [Dan. 9:5]. And there are other confessions that often occur in Scripture, [c]the recital of which would almost fill a volume. [a]"If we confess our sins," says John, "the Lord is faithful . . . to forgive our sins." [I John 1:9, cf. Vg.] To whom should we confess? Surely to him, that is, if we fall down before him with troubled and humbled heart; if wholeheartedly accusing and condemning ourselves before him, we seek to be acquitted by his goodness and mercy.

10. Confession of sins before men

[a]He who will embrace this confession in his heart and before God will without doubt also have a tongue prepared for confession, whenever there is need to proclaim God's mercy among men; and not only to whisper the secret of his heart to one man and at one time, and in the ear, but often, publicly, with all the world hearing, unfeignedly to recount both his own disgrace and God's magnificence and honor. In this way, when David was rebuked by Nathan he was pricked by the sting of conscience, and confessed his sin before both God and men. "I have sinned," he said, "against the Lord." [II Sam. 12:13.] That is, I now make no excuse; I do not try to avoid being judged by all to be a sinner, nor to prevent what I tried to hide from the Lord being revealed also even to men. [c]Therefore, a willing confession among men follows that secret confession which is made to God, as often as either divine glory or our humiliation demands it. For this reason,

[20] "Cognitor." In this phrase (Heb. 4:1) Vg. has "discretor."

the Lord ordained of old among the people of Israel that, after the priest recited the words, the people should confess their iniquities publicly in the temple [cf. Lev. 16:21]. For he foresaw that this help was necessary for them in order that each one might better be led to a just estimation of himself. And it is fitting that, by the confession of our own wretchedness, we show forth the goodness and mercy of our God, among ourselves and before the whole world.

11. General confession of sin

ᶜNow this sort of confession ought to be ordinary in the church and be used extraordinarily in a special way, whenever it happens that the people are guilty of some transgression in common. ᶜ⁽ᵇ⁾We have an example of this second sort in that public confession ᵇwhich all the people performed under the guidance and direction of Ezra and Nehemiah [Neh. 1:7; 9:1–2]. ᶜFor since the punishment for the common rebellion of all the people consisted in that long exile, that destruction of the city and the Temple, and that overthrow of religion, they could not rightly recognize the benefit of liberation, had they not previously accused themselves. Nor does it matter if sometimes a few in one congregation be innocent, for when they are members of a feeble and diseased body they ought not to boast of health. ᶜNay, they cannot but contract some contagion and also bear some part of the guilt.

ᶜTherefore, every time we are afflicted either by pestilence or war, or barrenness, or any other sort of calamity, if it is our duty to take refuge in mourning, fasting, and other signs of our guilt, we must least of all neglect this very confession upon which all the rest depends.

Besides the fact that ordinary confession has been commended by the Lord's mouth, no one of sound mind, who weighs its usefulness, can dare disapprove it. For since in every sacred assembly we stand before the sight of God and the angels, what other beginning of our action will there be than the recognition of our own unworthiness? But that, you say, is done through every prayer; for whenever we pray for pardon, we confess our sin. Granted. But if you consider how great is our complacency, our drowsiness, or our sluggishness, you will agree with me that it would be a salutary regulation if the Christian people were to practice humbling themselves through some public rite of confession. For even though the ceremony that the Lord laid down for the Israelites was a part of the tutelage of the law,[21] still the reality underlying it in some manner pertains also to us. ᶜ⁽ᵇ⁾And

[21] "Paedagogia."

indeed, we see this custom observed with good result in well-regulated churches: that every Lord's Day the minister frames the formula of confession in his own and the people's name, and by it he accuses all of wickedness and implores pardon from the Lord.[22] ᶜIn short, with this key a gate to prayer is opened both to individuals in private and to all in public.

12. Private confession in the cure of souls

ᵃScripture, moreover, approves two forms of private confession: one made for our own sake, to which the statement of James refers that we should confess our sins to one another [James 5:16]. For he means that, disclosing our weaknesses to one another, we help one another with mutual counsel and consolation. The other form we are to use for our neighbor's sake, to appease him and to reconcile him to us if through fault of ours he has been in any way injured. ᵇAnd in the first kind of confession, even though James, by not expressly determining on whose bosom we should unburden ourselves, leaves us free choice to confess to that one of the flock of the church who seems most suitable. Yet we must also preferably choose pastors inasmuch as they should be judged especially qualified above the rest. Now I say that they are better fitted than the others because the Lord has appointed them by the very calling of the ministry to instruct us by word of mouth to overcome and correct our sins, and also to give us consolation through assurance of pardon [Matt. 16:19; 18:18; John 20:23]. ᶜFor, while the duty of mutual admonition and rebuke is entrusted to all Christians, it is especially enjoined upon ministers. Thus, although all of us ought to console one another and confirm one another in assurance of divine mercy, we see that the ministers themselves have been ordained witnesses and sponsors of it to assure our consciences of forgiveness of sins, to the extent that they are said to forgive sins and to loose souls. When you hear that this is attributed to them, recognize that it is for your benefit.[23]

ᵇTherefore, let every believer remember that, if he be privately

---

[22] Calvin, in his Strasbourg Liturgy (1539), and in that of Geneva (1542), used a form of confession of sins that had been employed by Bucer. Text with variants of different editions CR VI. 173 ff.; tr. B. Thompson, "Reformed Liturgies in Translation iii. Calvin": *Bulletin of the Theological Seminary of the Evangelical and Reformed Church* XXVIII (1957), 52 f. Cf. W. D. Maxwell, *Outline of Christian Worship*, pp. 112–119.

[23] Calvin's high doctrine of the authority of ministers in confession and absolution, subject to the authority of the Word of God, comes to expression here. Cf. J.-D. Benoit, *Calvin, directeur d'âmes*, pp. 245 f.; McNeill, *A History of the Cure of Souls*, pp. 197, 209.

troubled and afflicted with a sense of sins, so that without outside help he is unable to free himself from them, it is a part of his duty not to neglect what the Lord has offered to him by way of remedy. Namely, that, for his relief, he should use private confession to his own pastor; and for his solace, he should beg the private help of him whose duty it is, both publicly and privately, to comfort the people of God by the gospel teaching. But he should always observe this rule: that where God prescribes nothing definite, consciences be not bound with a definite yoke. ᶜHence, it follows that confession of this sort ought to be free so as not to be required of all, but to be commended only to those who know that they have need of it. Then, that those who use it according to their need neither be forced by any rule nor be induced by any trick to recount all their sins. But let them do this so far as they consider it expedient, that they may receive the perfect fruit of consolation. Faithful pastors ought not only to leave this freedom to the churches but also to protect it and stoutly defend it if they want to avoid tyranny in their ministry and superstition in the people.

13. Private confession for the removal of an offense

ᵃNow Christ speaks of the other sort of confession in the Gospel of Matthew: "If you are offering your gift at the altar, and there remember that your brother has something against you, leave your gift there . . . and go; first be reconciled to your brother, and then come and offer your gift" [Matt. 5:23–24]. For the love, which was broken by our offense, is thus repaired by our acknowledging the wrong we have committed, and asking pardon for it.

ᶜIn this class is included the confession of those who have sinned even to the point of offending against the whole church. For if Christ considers the private offense of one man so serious that he bars from the sacred rites all those who sin in any respect against their brothers until they become reconciled by a just satisfaction, how much greater is the reason that he who offends the church by any evil example should be reconciled to it by the acknowledgment of his offense.[24] Thus was the Corinthian received again into communion when he had obediently yielded to correction [II Cor. 2:6].

This was also the form of confession in the early church as Cyprian also recalls it. He says: "They do penance for a certain period; then they come to confession, and through the imposition

---

[24] Calvin's *Ecclesiastical Ordinances* (1541) provided for procedures in such cases. (CR X i. 29 f.; tr. LCC XXII. 70 f.)

of the hands of bishop and clergy receive the privilege of communion."[25] [a]Scripture does not know any other manner or form of confession at all, [c]and it is not our task to bind with new bonds consciences that Christ most sternly forbids to enslave.

In the meantime, I do not so much object to sheep presenting themselves to their shepherd as often as they wish to partake of the Sacred Supper; rather, I ardently wish this to be observed everywhere. For both those who have an encumbered conscience can thence receive a remarkable benefit and those who should be admonished may thus be prepared for admonitions, provided tyranny and superstition be always excluded!

(The power of the keys, and absolution, 14–15)
14. Nature and value of the power of the keys
[c]The power of the keys has a place in these three kinds of confession: either when the entire church with solemn recognition of its faults implores pardon or when an individual, who has by some notable transgression committed a common offense, declares his repentance, or when one who needs a minister's help on account of a troubled conscience discloses his weakness to him. [e]Where an offense is to be removed the method is different; for even though in that case peace of conscience is also provided for, the chief end is to remove hatred and to unite men's minds with one another in the bond of peace [cf. Eph. 4:3].

But the benefit of which I have spoken is not at all to be spurned, that we may more willingly confess our sins. [c]For when the whole church stands, as it were, before God's judgment seat, confesses itself guilty, and has its sole refuge in God's mercy, it is no common or light solace to have present there the ambassador of Christ, armed with the mandate of reconciliation, by whom it hears proclaimed its absolution [cf. II Cor. 5:20]. Here the usefulness of the keys is deservedly commended, when this embassy is carried out justly, in due order, and in reverence. Similarly, when one who in some degree had estranged himself from the church receives pardon and is restored into brotherly unity, how great a benefit it is that he recognizes himself forgiven by those to whom Christ said, "To whomsoever you shall remit sins on earth, they shall be remitted in heaven" [John 20:23; conflated with Matt. 18:18]! And private absolution is of no less efficacy or benefit, when it is sought by those who need to remove their weakness by a singular remedy. For it often happens that one who hears general promises that are intended for the whole congregation of believers remains nonetheless in some doubt, and as if he

[25] Cyprian, *Letters* xvi. 2 (CSEL 3. ii. 518; tr. ANF [letter ix. 2] IV. 290).

had not yet attained forgiveness, still has a troubled mind. Likewise, if he lays open his heart's secret to his pastor, and from his pastor hears that message of the gospel specially directed to himself, "Your sins are forgiven, take heart" [Matt. 9:2 p.], he will be reassured in mind and be set free from the anxiety that formerly tormented him.

But when it is a question of the keys, we must always beware lest we dream up some power separate from the preaching of the gospel. e(c)I shall explain this matter again more fully in another place, where I shall deal with the government of the church. There we shall see that any right of binding or loosing which Christ conferred upon his church is bound to the Word.[26] cThis is especially true in the ministry of the keys, whose entire power rests in the fact that, through those whom the Lord had ordained, the grace of the gospel is publicly and privately sealed in the hearts of the believers. This can come about only through preaching.

15. Summary of the Roman doctrine of confession

aWhat do the Roman theologians say? They decree that all persons of "both sexes," as soon as they attain the age of discretion, should confess all their sins to their own priest at least once a year, and that their sin is not forgiven unless they have a firmly conceived intent to confess it. And if they do not carry out this intent when occasion is offered, the entrance to paradise is no longer open to them. Now, the theologians assert, the priest has the power of the keys with which to bind and loose the sinner because Christ's word is not void: "Whatever you bind," etc. [Matt. 18:18].[27]

Yet they quarrel fiercely among themselves over this power. Some say that there is essentially only one key—namely, the power to bind and loose—that knowledge is indeed required for good use, but it is only like an accessory, not joined to the other in essence.[28] Others, because they saw that this was excessively unbridled license, posited two keys: discretion and power. Still others, since they saw the depravity of the priests restrained by such moderation, forged other keys: the authority to discern, which they should use in passing sentence, and the power they

---

[26] IV. xi, xii.

[27] Cf. sec. 7, above. Lombard affirms the opinions here reported: *Sentences* IV. xvii. 2, 4; IV. xviii. 1 (MPL 192. 881, 883, 885). This section has numerous reminiscences of works of Augustine; cf. Smits II. 39.

[28] This view is mentioned and rejected by Alexander of Hales, *Summa theologiae* IV. qu. lxxix. memb. 3. art. 1.

should exercise in the execution of their sentence; and they add knowledge as counselor.

But they dare not interpret binding and loosing simply as remitting and blotting out sins, for they hear the Lord proclaiming through the prophet: "I am, and no other but me; I am, I am he who blots out your transgressions, O Israel" [Isa. 43:11, 25 p.]. But they say that it is the priest's task to declare who are to be bound or loosed, and to state whose sins are to be remitted or retained; to declare this, moreover, either through confession when he absolves and retains sins or through sentence when he excommunicates or receives into the partaking of the sacraments.[29]

Finally, suppose they understand that they have not yet removed this difficulty, but that the objection can always be raised against them, that unworthy persons are often bound and loosed by their priests, who will not therefore be bound or loosed in heaven. Their last refuge is then to reply that the conferring of the keys is to be understood with this one limitation: Christ promised that the sentence of the priests would be approved before his judgment seat, provided it was justly pronounced according as the deserts of the one bound or loosed required.[30] Now, they say that these keys have been given by Christ to all priests and are conferred upon them by the bishops at the time of promotion, but their free use remains only in the possession of those who perform ecclesiastical functions; that the keys indeed remain in the possession of the excommunicated and suspended clergy, but rusted and bound. And those who say these things may rightly seem modest and sober in comparison with those who have forged

[29] Lombard, *Sentences* IV. xviii. 4, 6, 7, 8; IV. xix. 1 (MPL 192. 886–889).

[30] The doctrine of the *thesaurus ecclesiae* was formulated by Alexander of Hales (*Summa theologiae* IV. qu. lxxxiii. memb. 1. art. 1; memb. 3. art. 5) and revised by Aquinas and others. With respect to its bearing on jurisdiction (the power of the keys), it was discussed with wide divergence of opinion. The doctrine is succinctly defined in Clement VI's constitution *Unigenitus* (1343) (Friedberg II. 1304; tr. Bettenson, *Documents of the Christian Church,* pp. 259 f.; J. F. Clarkson, *et al., The Church Teaches,* p. 31). It is explained as inexhaustible, being derived from the free outpouring of Christ's blood and from the merits of the Mother of God and of all the elect. Cf. Bonaventura, *Commentary on the Sentences* IV. xx. part 2. art. 1. qu. 3, 4 (*Opera omnia* IV. 521–525); Lea, *op. cit.,* I, ch. vii; I. 506; R. Seeberg. *History of Doctrines;* tr. C. E. Hay, II. 139. It should be acknowledged that conceptions of vicarious merit in penance were a commonplace of the penitential booklets centuries before Hales (McNeill and Gamer, *Medieval Handbooks of Penance,* p. 48, and index, *s.v.* "composition"). The doctrine of the treasury was assailed by Luther from 1517 and was spiritedly defended by his early opponents: see, for example, Fisher, *Assertionis Lutheranae confutatio* (1523), ch. xviii (pp. 298–313).

new keys on a new anvil and who teach that the treasury of the church is locked under these keys. cWe shall discuss these matters afterward in their place.[31]

(*Criticism of Romanist errors and injurious practices related to confession and satisfaction, 16–25*)

16. The enumeration of all sins is impossible

aI shall now reply to each point in a few words. But I shall remain silent for the present as to what right or lack of right they have to bind the souls of believers with their laws, since this will be dealt with in its place.[32] But it is utterly unbearable that they lay down a law on the recounting of all sins, that they deny that sin is forgiven except upon the condition that an intent to confess has been firmly conceived, and that they prate that no entrance to paradise would remain if the office of confession were neglected.

Are all sins to be recounted? Now David, who in himself had, I believe, rightly pondered confession of sins, exclaimed: "Who will understand errors? Cleanse thou me from my secret errors, O Lord" [Ps. 19:12 p.]. And in another place: "My iniquities have gone over my head, and like a heavy burden they burden me beyond my strength" [Ps. 38:4; cf. Ps. 37:5, Vg.]. He understood only too well how deep is the pit of our sins, how many are the faces of crime, how many heads this hydra bore, and what a long tail it dragged along. Therefore, he did not catalogue them. But from the depths of his evil deeds he cried out to the Lord: I am overwhelmed, I am buried, I am choked, "the gates of hell have encompassed me" [Ps. 18:6; cf. Ps. 17:6, Vg.], I am sunk down into the deep pit [Ps. 69:2–3, 15–16], may thy hand draw me out, weak and dying. Who would now think of reckoning up his sins when he sees that David cannot begin to number his?

17. The requirement of complete confession is a measureless torment

aThe souls of those who have been affected with some awareness of God are most cruelly torn by this butchery.[33] First they called themselves to account, and divided sins into arms, branches,

[31] III. v. 2.
[32] IV. x.
[33] *"Carnificina."* Luther, Melanchthon, and Calvin habitually protested against the old practice of the confessional on the ground that it left consciences in torment. See esp. Luther's *Explanations of the Ninety-five Theses,* 7th thesis (*Werke* WA I. 542 f.; tr. *Luther's Works,* American Edition, ed. H. Grimm; general ed., H. T. Lehmann, 31. 100, 103); McNeill, *A History of the Cure of Souls,* pp. 166 f.

twigs, and leaves, according to their formulas. They then weighed the qualities, quantities, and circumstances; and so the matter pressed forward a bit. But when they had progressed farther, and sky and sea were on every side,[34] there was no port or anchorage. The more they had crossed over, the greater was the mass ever looming before their eyes, indeed, it rose up like high mountains; nor did any hope of escape appear, even after long detours. And so they were stuck between the victim and the knife.[35] And at last no other outcome but despair was found.

There these cruel butchers, to relieve the wounds that they had inflicted, applied certain remedies, asserting that each man should do what lay in his power.[36] But again new anxieties crept in. Indeed, new tortures flayed helpless souls: "I have not spent enough time"; "I have not duly devoted myself to it"; "I have overlooked many things out of negligence, and the forgetfulness that has come about from my carelessness is inexcusable!"

Still, other medicines that alleviated this sort of pain were applied. Repent of your negligence; provided it is not utterly careless, it will be forgiven. But all these things cannot cover the wound, and are less an alleviation of the evil than poisons disguised with honey in order not to cause offense at the first taste because of their harshness, but to penetrate deep within before they are felt. Therefore, that dreadful voice always presses and resounds in the ears: "Confess all your sins." And this terror cannot be allayed except by a sure consolation.

eHere let my readers consider how it is possible to reckon up all the acts of an entire year and to gather up what sins they have committed each day. For experience convinces each one that, when we have at evening to examine the transgressions of only a single day, the memory is confused; so great is the multitude and variety of them that press upon us! And I am not speaking of brutish and stupid hypocrites who, paying attention to three or four of their more serious offenses, think they have fulfilled their obligation. But I speak of the true worshipers of God who, after they see themselves overwhelmed by the examination they have undergone, also add that saying of John's: "If our heart

---

[34] "*Caelum undique et undique pontus*": Vergil, *Aeneid* III. 193 (LCL Vergil I. 360). On the elaborate tabulation of sins, cf. McNeill and Gamer, *op. cit.,* pp. 19 f., 341 f. See also Pseudo-Augustine, *De vera et falsa poenitentia* xiv. 29 (MPL 40. 1122).

[35] An apt phrase of Plautus to suggest the plight of one who has no resource left: "*Nunc ego inter sacrum saxumque sto, nec quid faciam scio:*" *The Captives* 617 (LCL Plautus I. 522 f.).

[36] Cf. III. iv. 2, note 6; Alexander of Hales, *Summa theologiae* IV. qu. lxix. memb. 8.

condemns us, God is greater than our heart" [I John 3:20]; thus they tremble at the sight of the Judge, whose knowledge is far beyond our understanding.

18. The pernicious effect of demanding complete confession

[a]Moreover, the lulling of a good many people by the flatteries with which such deadly poison was tempered did not cause them to believe that these blandishments would satisfy God or even truly satisfy themselves. Rather, the effect was that of an anchor put down on the high seas, providing a brief respite from sailing, or the wayside rest of a traveler drooping with exhaustion. I do not labor to prove this point. Every man can be his own witness of this.

I shall sum up what sort of law this is. First, it is simply impossible; therefore it can only destroy, condemn, confound, and cast into ruin and despair. Then, depriving sinners of a true awareness of their sins, it makes them hypocrites, ignorant of God and of themselves. Indeed, while wholly occupied with the cataloguing of sins, they in the meantime forget that hidden slough of vices, their own secret transgressions and inner filth, the knowledge of which ought particularly to have brought home to them their own misery. But a very sure rule for making confession was to recognize and confess that the abyss of our evil is beyond our comprehension. We see that the publican's confession was composed according to this rule: "Lord, be merciful to me a sinner" [Luke 18:13]. It is as if he had said: "How great, how great a sinner I am; I am wholly a sinner, nor can my mind grasp or my tongue utter the very magnitude of my sins! May the abyss of thy mercy swallow up this abyss of sin."

What? you will ask. Is, then, not each single sin to be confessed? Is, then, no confession accepted by God unless it consists of these simple words: "I am a sinner"? Nay, we must rather take care as much as we are able to pour out our whole heart in the Lord's presence, not only to confess ourselves sinners in one word, but to acknowledge ourselves as such, truly and sincerely; to recognize with all our thought how great and how varied is the stain of our sin; to acknowledge not only that we are unclean, but of what sort and how great and how manifold our uncleanness is; to recognize not only that we are debtors, but with what great debts we are burdened and with how many obligations we are bound; not only wounded, but with how many and how deadly stripes we are wounded. Yet when, with this acknowledgment, the sinner has poured out himself entirely before God, let him earnestly and sincerely consider that still more sins remain, and that the recesses of their evils are deep beyond fathoming. Consequently, let him exclaim with David: "Who can understand errors? Cleanse thou me from my secret errors, O Lord" [Ps. 19:12].

Let us by no means concede to them their assertion that sins are forgiven only when there is a firmly conceived will to confess, and that the gate to paradise is closed to one who has neglected an opportunity offered him to confess. For there is now no other forgiveness of sins than there always has been. Whenever we read that men have obtained forgiveness of sins from Christ, we do not read that they confessed into the ear of some priestling. Apparently, then they could not confess, where there was not a priestling confessor, nor even confession itself. And for many ages after, this confession was unheard of, yet all the while sins were being forgiven without this condition. But, that we may not too long dispute, as it were, over something doubtful, the word of God is clear and abides forever: "Whenever the sinner bewails his sins, I shall not recall all his iniquities" [Ezek. 18:21–22 p.]. He who ventures to add anything to this word binds not sins but the Lord's mercy.

ᵉFor there is a ready solution for their contention that judgment cannot be rendered unless the cause is heard, namely, that those who have made themselves judges have rashly taken this upon themselves. And it is wonderful how unconcernedly they fabricate principles that no one of sound mind will admit! They boast that the office of binding and loosing has been committed to them as though it were a certain jurisdiction, joined with investigation! Furthermore, their whole doctrine proclaims that this right was unknown to the apostles. And to know for certain whether the sinner is absolved does not pertain to the priest but to him from whom absolution is sought, since he who hears can never know whether the list is exact and integral.[37] Thus, there would be no absolution unless it were restricted to the words of him who is to be judged. Besides, the whole reckoning of absolution depends upon faith and repentance. And these two things elude the knowledge of a man when he has to pass sentence upon another man. Therefore, it follows that certainty of binding and loosing does not lie within the competence of earthly judgment

---

[37] "*Iusta et integra enumeratio.*" Cf. sec. 22, below. The requirement that confession of sins should be "integral," i.e., complete and without any reservation or concealment, is frequently stressed in *libri poenitentiales* from the eighth century down. Long series of questions were often provided to secure this end. Cf. McNeill and Gamer, *op. cit.*, pp. 154, 214, 281, 315 ff., 324 ff., 380, 396, 403.

because the minister of the word, when he duly performs his functions, can absolve only conditionally. But this is said for the sake of sinners, "If you forgive the sins of any," etc. [John 20:23], lest they should doubt whether the pardon promised in God's commandment and Word will be ratified in heaven.

19. Against auricular confession

ᵃNo wonder, then, that we condemn this auricular confession and desire it to be banished from our midst—a thing so pestilent and in so many ways harmful to the church! Even if of itself this were something indifferent, still, since it is useless and fruitless, but has occasioned so many impieties, sacrileges, and errors, who would not consider that it should be abolished forthwith? They do, indeed, count on some uses that they peddle as very fruitful, but those are either false or utterly worthless. They especially esteem only one of these: that the confessant's blush of shame is a heavy punishment by which the sinner both becomes more cautious afterward and, by punishing himself, turns aside God's vengeance. As if we did not humble a man enough, with great shame, when we call him, I say, to that supreme heavenly judgment seat to be examined by God! What a remarkable gain it is if we cease to sin on account of the shame of one man, and are not ashamed to have God as witness of our evil conscience![38]

Nonetheless, that itself is also utterly false, for we can see that nothing gives us greater confidence or license to sin than when, having made confession to a priest, men think themselves able to wipe their mouths and say, "I have not done it" [Prov. 30:20]. And not only are they emboldened throughout the year to sin; but, freed from the necessity of confession for the rest of the year, they never sigh unto God, they never return to their senses, but heap up sins upon sins until they vomit all of them up at once, as they suppose. When, moreover, they have disgorged them, they seem to themselves unburdened of their load, and feel that they have transferred judgment from God and bestowed it upon the priest, and have made God forgetful when they have made the priest their confidant. Indeed, who happily looks forward to the day of confession? Who hastens to confession with an eager mind and does not, rather, come to it against his will, reluctantly, as one is dragged by the neck to prison? Except, perhaps, priestlings themselves, who delight in exchanging anecdotes of their misdeeds as if they were amusing stories. I will not defile many sheets

---

[38] Cf. Tertullian, *On Repentance* x: "If we conceal something from men's notice, shall we conceal it from God? . . . Is it better to be damned in secret than to be absolved in public?" (CCL Tertullianus I. 337; tr. ANF III. 664).

of paper by relating those horrible abominations with which auricular confession swarms! I only say, if that holy man did not act unwisely who on account of one rumor of fornication removed confession from his church, or rather from the memory of his people,[39] we are warned what must be done when, as today, there are infinite whoredoms, adulteries, incests, and panderings.

20. Baseless appeal to the power of the keys

[a]The confessioners allege the power of the keys for this purpose, and in it place the whole ship of their kingdom—"prow and poop," as the saying goes.[40] We ought to see what all this adds up to. Were the keys, then, given to no purpose? they ask. Was this, then, groundlessly said, they ask: "Whatever you loose on earth will be loosed in heaven also" [Matt. 18:18]?[41] Do we, then, render void the word of Christ? I reply: It was for a weighty reason that the keys were given, [e(c)]as I have recently explained, and I shall treat it more specifically again when I deal with excommunication.[42] [a]But what if I cut off the handle of their every demand of this kind, with one sword: their priestlings are not vicars or successors of the apostles? But this, also, will have to be treated in another place.[43] Now, out of wishing to fortify themselves, they erect a siege engine, only to cast down thereby all their contrivances. For Christ did not give the power of binding and loosing to the apostles before he gave them the Holy Spirit. Therefore, I deny that the power of the keys belongs to any persons who have not first received the Holy Spirit. I deny that anyone can use the keys unless the Holy Spirit has first come to teach him and tell him what to do. They babble that they have the Holy Spirit, but in reality they deny it, unless perchance they fancy, as they surely do, that the Holy Spirit is something vain and of no account; but they will not be believed. And by this device, indeed, they are utterly overthrown; so that, of whatever door they boast that they have the key, they must always be asked whether they have the Holy Spirit, who is the judge and keeper of the keys. If they reply that they have him, they must, on the other hand, be asked whether the Holy Spirit can err. This they will not dare to say forthrightly, even though they hint at it obliquely in their teaching. We must therefore infer that no

---

[39] I.e., Nectarius: cf. sec. 7, above.
[40] *"Proram (ut aiunt) et puppim."* Cicero calls this a Greek proverb: *Letters to His Friends* XVI. xxiv. 1 (LCL edition, III. 374). Cf. IV. xvii. 33; IV. xviii. 18.
[41] Lombard, *Sentences* IV. xvii. 1 (MPL 192. 880).
[42] References are to sec. 14, above, and IV. xii, below.
[43] IV. v. 1–4; IV. vi.

priestlings have the power of the keys who without discrimination repeatedly loose what the Lord had willed to be bound, and bind what he had bidden to be loosed.

21. The uncertainty of priestly binding and loosing

ᵃWhen they see themselves convicted by very clear proofs of loosing and binding the worthy and the unworthy indiscriminately, they usurp power without knowledge. They dare not deny that knowledge is required for the good use of power, but they write that the power itself has been entrusted to evil ministrants. Yet this is the power: "Whatever you bind or loose on earth will be bound or loosed in heaven" [Matt. 16:19 or 18:18 p.]. Either Christ's promise must be a lie, or those who have been endowed with this power bind and loose rightly.

Nor can they evade the issue by saying that Christ's statement is limited according to the merits of him who is bound or loosed. And we also admit that only those worthy of being bound or loosed can be bound or loosed; but the messengers of the gospel and the church have the Word to measure this worthiness. In this Word, the messengers of the gospel can through faith promise forgiveness of sins to all in Christ; they can proclaim damnation against all and upon all who do not embrace Christ. In this Word the church proclaims, "Neither whoremongers, . . . adulterers, . . . thieves, murderers, greedy, nor wicked will partake of the Kingdom of God" [I Cor. 6:9–10 p.]. The church binds such persons with no uncertain bonds. And with the same Word the church looses and comforts those who are penitent. But what power will this be—not to know what is to be bound or loosed, yet not to be able to bind or loose unless you know? Why, then, do they say that they absolve by the authority given them, when their absolution is uncertain? What is this imaginary power to us if it is useless? Now I hold that it is either nothing or so uncertain that it ought to be considered as nothing. For since they admit that a good many priests do not use the keys rightly, and that the power is ineffective without lawful use,⁴⁴ who will convince me that he by whom I am loosed is a good dispenser of the keys? But if he is evil, what else does he have but this empty dispensing of them! "I do not know what ought to be bound or loosed in you, since I lack a just use of the keys; but if you deserve it, I absolve you." I do not say, "A lay person," since they cannot bear to hear this, but a Turk or the devil could do as much. For that is to say: I do not have the Word of God, the sure rule of loosing, but authority has been given to me to absolve you, provided your

⁴⁴ Lombard, *Sentences* IV. xix. 1, 5 (MPL 192. 889, 892).

merits are such. We therefore see what they were aiming at when they explained that the keys are the authority to discern and the power to carry out; that knowledge is added as counselor, and like a counselor, for good use.[45] That is to say, they wished to rule lustfully, licentiously, without God and his Word.

22. The difference between perverted and right use of the power of the keys

ᵉIf anyone objects that lawful ministers of Christ will be no less perplexed in their duties because that absolution which depends upon faith will always remain ambiguous, and further, that there will be no comfort, or cold comfort, for sinners because the minister himself who is not qualified to judge of their faith is not sure about their absolution—then there is a ready answer. For they say that sins are not remitted by the priest unless he is informed of them. Thus, according to them, forgiveness depends upon the judgment of the priest, and unless he wisely discerns who deserve pardon, his whole action is null and void. In a word, the power of which they speak is a jurisdiction connected with examination, to which pardon and absolution are confined. On this point one finds no firm ground. Indeed, there is a bottomless pit. For where confession is not complete,[46] the hope of pardon is also impaired. Secondly, the priest must suspend judgment so long as he does not know whether the sinner recounts his transgressions in good faith. Finally, such is the consummate ignorance of priests that the greater part of them are no more fitted to exercise this office than a shoemaker to till fields. And almost all the others ought, by rights, to suspect themselves. Hence, therefore, the perplexity and hesitation concerning papal absolution, because they would have it founded upon the person of the priest; and not that only, but also upon his knowledge, that he may judge solely concerning matters reported, investigated, and proved.

Now if anyone asks these good doctors whether, after some sins have been forgiven, the sinner will be reconciled to God, I do not see what they can answer, unless they are obliged to confess that whatever the priest may pronounce concerning sins forgiven, the recital of which he has heard, is unfruitful so long as other sins remain open to accusation. On the part of the one confessing, the pernicious anxiety that holds his conscience bound is evident from the fact that while he depends upon the discretion of the priest, as they say, he can determine nothing from the Word of God.

[45] Cf. sec. 15, note 28, above.
[46] *"Ubi integra non est confessio."* Cf. sec. 18, note 37, above.

The doctrine we teach is free and clear of all these absurdities. For absolution is conditional upon the sinner's trust that God is merciful to him, provided he sincerely seek expiation in Christ's sacrifice and be satisfied with the grace offered him. Thus, he who, functioning as a herald, publishes what has been dictated to him from the Word of God cannot err. The sinner can, indeed, embrace true and clear absolution when that simple condition is applied of embracing the grace of Christ according to the general rule of the Master himself, a rule wickedly spurned in the papacy: "According to your faith be it done to you" [Matt. 9:29; cf. ch. 8:13].

23. Perverse claims exposed*

eI have promised to discuss in another place how absurdly they mix up what Scripture teaches about the power of the keys. A more appropriate occasion will be under the section dealing with the government of the church.[47] Yet let my readers recall that Christ's utterances made partly concerning the preaching of the gospel, partly concerning excommunication, are preposterously twisted about to auricular and secret confession [Matt. 16:19; 18:15–18; John 20:23]. Therefore, while they object that the right of loosing exercised by the priests in forgiving sins recognized by them was given to the apostles, it is plain that this principle is to be considered false and foolish because the absolution that serves faith is nothing else than the testimony of a pardon taken from the freely given promise of the gospel. But the other kind of confession, which depends upon the discipline of the church, has nothing to do with secret sins, but rather with example, that it may remove public offense to the church.

But they rake together from here and there testimonies by which to prove that it is not enough to confess sins either to God alone or to the laity, unless a priest be examiner. Their diligence is loathsome and shameful. For if ever the ancient fathers advise sinners to unburden themselves before their pastors, this cannot be understood of a recital that was then not in use. Then, so per- verse were Lombard and his like that they seem to have been willfully addicted to spurious books in order to deceive the sim- ple-minded by their pretense. Indeed, they rightly admit that inasmuch as loosing always accompanies repentance, no bond really remains where a man has been touched by repentance, al- though he may not yet have confessed. And for this reason, the priest does not so much forgive sins as pronounce and declare

47 IV. xii. 1–13.

them forgiven. Still, in the word "declare" they slyly introduce a crass error, supplanting doctrine by ceremonies. But they add that he who has already obtained pardon before God is absolved in the eyes of the church. Thus they unseasonably draw away to the private use of each what we have already said was intended for the common discipline, where the offense of a serious and known fault is to be removed. Shortly after, they pervert and corrupt their moderation, adding another way of forgiveness: namely, one enjoining penalty and satisfaction.[48] In this they claim for their sacrifices the right to divide in half what God has everywhere promised to us undivided. Since he simply requires repentance and faith, this division or exception is an utter sacrilege. For this has the same force as though the priest, taking on the role of tribune,[49] should make intercession to God, and should not suffer God of his mere generosity to receive into grace anyone who has not lain prostrate before the tribune's seat, and been beaten there.

24. Summary

ᵉThe whole matter adds up to this: if they want to make God the author of this fictitious confession, their vanity is refuted, just as I have shown them falsifiers in the few passages that they cite. But since it is clear that the law has been imposed by men, I say that it is both a tyrannous law and one promulgated in contempt of God, who, binding consciences to his Word, would have them loosed from the power of men. Now when that thing which God wished to be free is prescribed as necessary to obtain pardon, I call it an utterly intolerable sacrilege, because there is no function more proper to God than the forgiveness of sins, wherein our salvation rests. Moreover, I have shown that this tyranny was introduced at the time when the world was oppressed by foul barbarity. Furthermore, I have taught that it is a pestilential law, which either, where the fear of God flourishes, dashes miserable souls into despair or, where there is unconcern, soothes them with empty blandishments and renders them more sluggish. Lastly, I have explained that whatever mitigations they bring forward tend only to entangle, obscure, and corrupt, pure doctrine, camouflaging their impious actions.

[48] Lombard, *Sentences* IV. xvii. 4, 5; IV. xviii. 6, 7 (MPL 192. 882 f., 887 f.). Lombard, in dist. xvii, here employs numerous citations of Pseudo-Augustine, *De vera et falsa poenitentia* viii. 22 (MPL 40. 1120 f.; Smits II. 263). Cf. III. iv. 1, note 1.

[49] *"Tribuni personam sustinens, Deo intercederet."* The reference is to the right of *intercessio*, or veto, exercised at discretion by Roman tribunes on measures proposed in the Senate and Comitia, ca. 400 B.C.

25. General presentation and refutation of the Roman doctrine

ᵃThey assign the third place in penance to satisfaction. With one word we can overthrow all their empty talk about this. They say that it is not enough for the penitent to abstain from past evils, and change his behavior for the better, unless he make satisfaction to God for those things which he has committed. But they say that there are many helps by which we may redeem sins: tears, fasting, offerings, and works of charity. With these we must propitiate the Lord. With these we must pay our debts to God's righteousness. With these we must compensate for our transgressions. With these we must merit his pardon. For although he has forgiven the guilt through the largeness of his mercy, yet by the discipline of his justice he retains punishment. It is this punishment which must be redeemed by satisfaction.[50] ᵇIt all comes down to this: we indeed obtain pardon for our transgressions from God's kindness, but only through the intervening merit of works, by which the offense of our sins may be paid for, in order that due satisfaction may be made to God's justice.

ᵃOver against such lies I put freely given remission of sins; nothing is more clearly set forth in Scripture [Isa. 52:3; Rom. 3:24–25; 5:8; Col. 2:13–14; II Tim. 1:9; Titus 3:5]! First, what is forgiveness but a gift of sheer liberality? For the creditor who gives a receipt for money paid is not the one who is said to forgive, but he who, without any payment, willingly cancels the debt out of his own kindness. Why, then, is the word "freely" added but to take away all thought of satisfaction? With what confidence, then, do they still set up their satisfactions, which are laid low by so mighty a thunderbolt? ᵇWhat then? When the Lord proclaims through Isaiah: "I, I am he who blots out your transgressions for my sake, and I will not remember your sins" [Isa. 43:25], does he not openly declare that the cause and foundation of forgiveness are to be sought in his goodness alone? ᵃMoreover, since all Scripture bears witness to Christ—that through his name we are to receive forgiveness of sins [Acts 10:43]—does it not exclude all other names? How, then, do they teach that forgiveness is to be understood under the term "satisfactions"? Nor can they deny that they ascribe this to satisfactions, even if they seem to introduce them as helps. When Scripture says, "by the name of Christ," it means that we bring nothing, we claim nothing of

---

[50] Following a long development of composition in penance (redemption of penalties by payments), Lombard and Gratian authorized the requirement of satisfactions in accordance with Calvin's statement here: Lombard, *Sentences* IV. xvi. 4 (MPL 192. 879); Gratian, *Decretum* II. xxxiii. 3. 1. 42, 63 (MPL 187. 1532, 1544; Friedberg I. 1168, 1177).

our own, but rely solely upon the commendation of Christ, as Paul declares: "God was in Christ reconciling the world to himself, not counting their trespasses against men on his account" [II Cor. 5:19 p.]. ᶜAnd he immediately adds the how and the why: "For our sake he made him to be sin who was without sin" [II Cor. 5:21 p.].

(The grace of Christ alone provides true satisfaction for sin and peace to the conscience, 26–27)
26. Christ has provided full satisfaction

ᵃBut such is their perversity, they say that both forgiveness of sins and reconciliation take place once for all when in Baptism we are received through Christ into the grace of God; that after Baptism we must rise up again through satisfactions; that the blood of Christ is of no avail, except in so far as it is dispensed through the keys of the church. ᵇAnd I am not speaking of a doubtful matter, since not one or another, but all the Schoolmen, have, in very clear writings, betrayed their own taint. For their master,[51] after he confessed that Christ on the tree paid the penalty of our sins, according to Peter's teaching [I Peter 2:24], corrected that statement by adding the exception that in Baptism all temporal penalties of sins are relaxed, but after Baptism they are lessened by the help of penance, so that the cross of Christ and our penance may work together.[52] ᵃBut John speaks far differently: "If anyone has sinned, we have an advocate with the Father, Jesus Christ . . . ; and he is the propitiation for our sins" [I John 2:1–2]. "I am writing to you, little children, because your sins are forgiven in his name." [I John 2:12 p.] Surely he is addressing believers, to whom, while he sets forth Christ as the propitiation of sins, he shows that there is no other satisfaction whereby offended God can be propitiated or appeased. He does not say: "God was once for all reconciled to you through Christ; now seek for yourselves another means." But he makes him a perpetual advocate in order that by his intercession he may always restore us to the Father's favor; an everlasting propitiation by which sins may be expiated. For what the other John said is ever true: "Behold the Lamb of God, who takes away the sins of the world!" [John 1:29; cf. ch. 1:36]. He, I say, not another, takes them away; that is, since he alone is the Lamb of God, he also is the sole offering for sins, the sole expiation, the sole satisfaction. ᵉFor while the right and power of forgiving sins properly belong to the Father, in

[51] Cf. Comm. II Cor. 5:19–20.
[52] A summary of Lombard, *Sentences* III. xix. 4 (MPL 192. 797). Cf. Aquinas, *Summa Theol.* III. Suppl. xiv. 5: Works diminish the pains of hell.

which respect he is distinguished from the Son, as we have already seen,[53] Christ is here placed on another level because, taking upon himself the penalty that we owe, he has wiped out our guilt before God's judgment. From this it follows that we shall share in the expiation made by Christ only if that honor rest with him which those who try to appease God by their own recompense seize for themselves.

27. The Roman doctrine deprives Christ of honor, and the conscience of every assurance

[a]And here we ought to consider two things: that Christ's honor be kept whole and undiminished; that consciences assured of pardon for sin may have peace with God.[54]

Isaiah says that the Father laid upon the Son the iniquity of us all [Isa. 53:6] to heal us by his stripes [Isa. 53:6, 5]. Peter repeats this in other words: Christ in his body bore our sins upon the tree [I Peter 2:24]. Paul writes that sin was condemned in his flesh when he was made sin for us [Gal. 3:13 and Rom. 8:3, conflated]; that is, the force and the curse of sin were slain in his flesh when he was given as a victim, upon whom the whole burden of our sins—with their curse and execration, with the dreadful judgment of God and the damnation of death—should be cast. [b]Here we never hear such falsehoods: as that after the initial purgation each one of us feels the efficacy of Christ's suffering solely in proportion to the measure of satisfying penance; but as often as we lapse we are recalled solely to the satisfaction of Christ.

Now set before yourself their pestilent absurdities: that in the first forgiveness of sins only the grace of God operates, but if we have fallen afterward, our works co-operate in obtaining the second pardon.[55] [b(a)]If these principles have a place, do those functions which have previously been attributed to Christ remain intact with him? [a]What a vast difference there is between saying that our iniquities have been lodged with Christ in order that they be expiated in him and saying that they are expiated by our works; that Christ is the propitiation for our sins, and that God must be propitiated by works!

But if it is a question of quieting the conscience, what will this quieting be if a man hears that sins are redeemed by satisfactions? When can he at length be certain of the measure of that satisfac

---

[53] II. xvi. 3–5.
[54] Cf. III. xiii. 3.
[55] Aquinas holds that sin cannot be taken away without the sacrament of penance: Summa Theol. III. lxxxvi. 4, reply to obj. 3. Cf. Council of Trent, session 6, canon xxix. Schaff, Creeds II. 116 f.

tion? Then he will always doubt whether he has a merciful God; he will always be troubled, and always tremble. For those who rely upon trifling satisfactions hold the judgment of God in contempt, and reckon of little account the great burden of sin, as we shall state elsewhere.[56] But even though we should grant that they redeem some sins by appropriate satisfaction, still, what will they do when they are overwhelmed by so many sins for the satisfaction of which a hundred lives, even if they were wholly devoted to this purpose, could not suffice? *Besides, all those passages which declare forgiveness of sins do not pertain to catechumens, but to the reborn children of God, who have long been nourished in the bosom of the church. That embassy which Paul so glowingly extols—"I beseech you in Christ's name, be reconciled to God" [II Cor. 5:20 p.]—is directed not to outsiders, but to those who have already been reborn. But having bidden farewell to satisfactions, he relegates them to the cross of Christ. So where Paul writes to the Colossians that Christ has "reconciled all things that are on heaven or earth . . . by the blood of the cross" [Col. 1:20 p.], he does not confine this to the moment we are received into the church, but extends it throughout life. This is readily apparent from the context, where he says that believers have redemption through the blood of Christ, that is, the forgiveness of sins [Col. 1:14]. Now it is superfluous to heap up more such passages, which repeatedly occur.

(Various distinctions and objections critically examined, 28–39)
28. Venial and mortal sins
ªAt this point they take refuge in the foolish distinction that certain sins are venial, others mortal; for mortal sins a heavy satisfaction is required; venial sins can be purged by easier remedies—by the Lord's Prayer, by the sprinkling of holy water, by the absolution afforded by the Mass. Thus they dally and play with God. Though they are always talking about venial and mortal sins, they still cannot distinguish one from the other,[57] except that they make impiety and uncleanness of heart a venial sin. But we declare, as Scripture, the rule of righteous and unrighteous, teaches, "the wages of sin is death" [Rom. 6:23]; and "the soul that sins is worthy of death" [Ezek. 18:20 p.]; but that the sins of believers are venial, not because they do not deserve death, but because by God's mercy "there is no condemnation for those who are in

---

[56] III. xii. 1, 5.
[57] Cf. Lombard, *Sentences* IV. xvi. 4 (MPL 192. 879); Aquinas, *Summa Theol.* III. lxxxvii. 3; I IIae. lxxxviii.

Christ Jesus" [Rom. 8:1], because they are not imputed, because they are wiped away by pardon [cf. Ps. 32:1–2].

I know how unjustly they slander this doctrine of ours, for they call it the paradox of the Stoics, concerning the equality of sins,[58] but they will be easily refuted by their own mouth. For I ask whether among those very sins which they confess as mortal they recognize one as less than another. It does not therefore immediately follow that sins that are mortal are at the same time equal. Since the Scripture precisely states that "the wages of sin is death" [Rom. 6:23], but obedience to the law is the way of life [cf. Lev. 18:5; Ezek. 18:9; 20:11,13; Gal. 3:12; Rom. 10:5; Luke 10:28]—transgression of the law, death [cf. Rom. 6:23; Ezek. 18:4, 20]—they cannot evade this verdict. Amid such a great heap of sins, what outcome of satisfaction will they find? If it takes one day to make satisfaction for one sin, while they are contemplating it they implicate themselves in more. [b(a)]For not a day passes when the most righteous of men does not fall time and again [cf. Prov. 24:16]. While they gird themselves to make satisfaction for their sins, they will heap up numerous—or rather, innumerable—others. [a]Now that the assurance of being able to make satisfaction for their sins is cut off, why do they tarry? How dare they still think of making satisfaction?

29. Forgiveness of sins involves remission of penalty

[a]Indeed, they try to extricate themselves, but "the water," as the proverb goes, "clings to them."[59] They fashion a distinction between penalty and guilt. They admit that guilt is remitted by God's mercy, but after guilt has been remitted there remains the penalty that God's justice demands to be paid. Therefore, they hold that satisfactions properly are concerned with the remission of the penalty.[60]

[b(a)]Good God, what flitting levity is this! They admit that forgiveness of guilt is freely available, yet repeatedly teach men to deserve it through prayers and tears, and all sorts of other preparations. [a]And yet all that we are taught in Scripture concerning

---

[58] Cf. Comm. Zech. 5:4. Lactantius, *Divine Institutes* III. xxiii. 8 (CSEL 19. 253; MPL 6. 427; tr. ANF VII. 93), attributes this teaching to Zeno. Cf. Cicero, *Pro Murena* xxix. 6: "*Omnia peccata esse paria*" (LCL edition, p. 222); Fisher, *Assertionis Lutheranae confutatio,* p. 158; Melanchthon, *Loci communes,* ed. Engelland, pp. 138 f.; tr. Hill, pp. 237 ff.

[59] The expression is Cicero's: *On Duties* III. xxxiii. 117 (LCL edition, p. 398).

[60] Aquinas, *Summa Theol.* III. lxxxvi. 4; III. Suppl. xv. 1. Cf. I IIae. lxxxvii. 4; Bonaventura, *Commentary on the Sentences* IV. xviii. part 1. art. 2. qu. 2: "*Poena inseparabilis est a culpa. . . . Dominus dum remittat culpam, remittat poenam totam*" (*Opera selecta* IV. 460).

forgiveness of sins directly opposes this distinction. ᵇBut even though I believe I have already more than fully confirmed this, I shall add certain other testimonies by which these wriggling snakes may be so held fast that after this they will be unable to coil up even the tip of their tail. ᵃThis is the new covenant that God in Christ has made with us, that he will remember our sins no more [Jer. 31:31, 34]. What he meant by these words we learn from another prophet, where the Lord says: "If a righteous man turns away from his righteousness, . . . I will not remember his righteous deeds" [Ezek. 18:24 p.]; "if a wicked man turns away from his impiety, I will not remember all his sins" [Ezek. 18:21–22 p.; cf. v.27]. His statement that he will not remember their righteous acts means virtually this: he will not keep an account of them to reward them. The statement that he will not remember their sins therefore means that he will not demand the penalty for them. The same thing is said elsewhere: ᵇ"Cast . . . behind my back" [Isa. 38:17]; "swept away like a cloud" [Isa. 44:22]; "cast . . . into the depths of the sea" [Micah 7:19]; ᵃ"not to reckon it to his account and to keep it hidden" [cf. Ps. 32:1–2]. By such expressions the Holy Spirit clearly would have explained his meaning to us, if we had listened to them attentively. Surely, if God punishes sins, he charges them to our account; if he takes vengeance, he remembers them; if he calls to judgment, he does not hide them; ᵇif he weighs them, he has not cast them behind his back; if he scrutinizes them, he has not blotted them out like a cloud; if he airs them, he has not cast them into the depths of the sea. ᶜAnd Augustine explains it in clear words as follows: "If God has covered sins, he has willed not to look upon them; if he has willed not to pay attention to them, he has willed not to punish them; he has willed not to recognize them, and he has preferred to overlook them. Why, then, does he say, 'Sins are covered'? That they may not be seen. Why was it that God saw sins, except to punish them?"[61]

ᵃBut let us hear from another passage of the prophet by what laws the Lord forgives sins: "Though your sins," he says, "are as scarlet, they shall be as white as snow; though they are red like crimson, they shall be as wool" [Isa. 1:18]. ᵇIn Jeremiah we read as follows: "In that day iniquity shall be sought in Jacob, and it shall not be found; sin in Judah, and there shall be none; for I shall be propitiated by those whom I leave as a remnant" [ch. 50:20 p.]. Would you like briefly to understand what these words mean? Ponder what, on the other hand, he means by these expres-

---

[61] Augustine, *Psalms*, Ps. 32 (Latin, Ps. 31). ii. 9 (MPL 36. 264; tr. LF *Psalms* I. 288).

sions: the Lord "gathers up my iniquities in a bag" [Job 14:17 p.];
"binds them up and stores them in a bundle" [Hos. 13:12 p.];
"with a pen of iron engraves them upon a diamond" [cf. Jer. 17:1].
Now if these passages mean that vengeance shall be repaid—
which is beyond doubt—we also must not doubt that by contrary
statements the Lord affirms that he remits all penalty of vengeance. ᵃHere I must adjure my readers not to heed my glosses,
but only to yield some place to the Word of God.⁶²

*30. Christ's unique sacrifice can alone remove both penalty and
guilt**
ᵃWhat, I ask you, would Christ have bestowed upon us if the
penalty for our sins were still required? For when we say that he
bore all our sins in his body upon the tree [I Peter 2:24], we
mean only that he bore the punishment and vengeance due for
our sins. Isaiah has stated this more meaningfully when he says:
"The chastisement (or correction) of our peace was upon him"
[Isa. 53:5]. What is this "correction of our peace" but the penalty
due sins that we would have had to pay before we could become
reconciled to God—if he had not taken our place? Lo, you see
plainly that Christ bore the penalty of sins to deliver his own
people from them, ᵃand whenever Paul mentions that redemption was accomplished through Christ, he customarily calls it
ἀπολύτρωσις⁶³ [Rom. 3:24; see also I Cor. 1:30; Eph. 1:7; Col. 1:14].
By this he does not simply signify redemption as it is commonly
understood, but the very price and satisfaction of redemption.
This is why Paul writes that Christ gave himself as a ransom⁶⁴
for us [I Tim. 2:6]. ᶜ"What is propitiation before the Lord," asks
Augustine, "but sacrifice? What is the sacrifice, but what has
been offered for us in the death of Christ?"⁶⁵
ᵇBut what is prescribed in the law of Moses for the expiation
of the harmful effects of sins furnishes us, first of all, with a stout
battering-ram. For the Lord does not there establish this or that
manner of making satisfaction, but he requires a complete payment in sacrifices. Yet in other respects he sets forth most mi-
nutely and in most rigid order all rites of atonement [Ex. 30:10;

---

⁶² This striking sentence remained unchanged from the 1536 edition (OS I. 119)
although in an altered context. Such a statement should be given due weight
in any estimate of Calvin's judgment of his function as an exegete. Cf. CR
VII. 248: "I do not ask anyone to tarry with me [s'arreste à moi] or with my
opinion except on the condition that he has first recognized that my teaching
is useful."
⁶³ "ἀπολύτρωσιν."
⁶⁴ "ἀντίλυτρον."
⁶⁵ Augustine, *Psalms*, Ps. 129. 3 (MPL 37. 1697; tr. NPNF VIII. 13).

Lev., chs. 4 to 7:16; Num. 15:22 ff.]. How does it happen that he bids committed transgressions to be recompensed by no works at all, but requires sacrifices alone in expiation, unless he wills to testify that there is only one kind of satisfaction by which his judgment is appeased? For such sacrifices as the Israelites offered were not accounted works of men but were judged in their very reality, that is, by the unique sacrifice of Christ. Hosea has eloquently expressed in few words what sort of recompense the Lord requires of us: "Thou shalt take away," O God, "all iniquity." See, there is forgiveness of sins. "And we will render the calves of our lips." [Hos. 14:2.] See, indeed, there is satisfaction.

dI know, indeed, that they are still more subtly evasive when they distinguish between eternal and temporal penalties. But when they teach that temporal penalty is any sort of punishment that God inflicts either upon the body or upon the soul—apart from eternal death—this limitation helps them little. For the above passages that we have cited mean this explicitly: we are received by God into grace on the condition that whatever penalties we deserve he remits by pardoning our guilt. And whenever David or the other prophets seek pardon for sin, at the same time they pray the penalty be taken away. Indeed, awareness of divine judgment drives them to this. On the other hand, when they promise mercy from the Lord, they almost always avowedly preach about the penalties and their remission. Surely, when the Lord declares through Ezekiel that he will bring the Babylonian exile to an end, and not for the Jews' sake, but for his own [Ezek. 36: 22, 32], he shows sufficiently that both are free. Finally, if we are delivered from guilt through Christ, the penalties that arise from it must cease.

31. Misinterpretations exposed: God's judgments, penal and corrective

aBut inasmuch as they arm themselves with testimonies from Scripture, let us see what sort of arguments they put forward. David, they say, rebuked by the prophet Nathan for adultery and murder, received pardon for his sin, and yet he was afterward punished by the death of his son born of adultery [II Sam. 12:13– 14]. We are taught to recompense with satisfaction such punishments as had to be inflicted even after remission of guilt. For Daniel enjoined Nebuchadnezzar to make recompense for his sins with alms [Dan. 4:27]. And Solomon writes: "On account of equity and godliness iniquities are remitted" [Prov. 16:6 p.]. In another place, also: "Love covers a multitude of sins" [Prov. 10:12]. bPeter, also, confirms this opinion [I Peter 4:8]. aIn Luke the Lord says the same thing about the sinning woman: that "her many sins are forgiven, for she loved much" [Luke 7:47 p.].[66]

How perversely and wrongheadedly do they always judge God's deeds! Yet if they had observed—and it is something they ought not at all to have overlooked—that there are two kinds of divine judgment, they would have seen a far different form of penalty in this rebuke of David than one that is to be thought of as directed to vengeance.

ᵇBut all of us are not a little concerned to understand the purpose of the chastisements by which God reproves our sins, and how different they are from the examples in which he pursues the impious and the reprobate with his indignation. Consequently, I think we can, with good reason, sum up the whole matter.

ᵃOne judgment we call, for the sake of teaching, that of vengeance; the other, of chastisement.

ᵇ⁽ᵃ⁾Now, by the judgment of vengeance, God should be understood as taking vengeance upon his enemies; so that he exercises his wrath against them, he confounds them, he scatters them, he brings them to nought. Therefore, let us consider this to be God's vengeance, properly speaking: when punishment is joined with his indignation.

In the judgment of chastisement he is not so harsh as to be angry, nor does he take vengeance so as to blast with destruction. Consequently, it is not, properly speaking, punishment ᵃor vengeance, but correction and admonition.

The one is the act of a judge; the other, of a father. For when a judge punishes an evildoer, he weighs his transgression and applies the penalty to the crime itself. But when a father quite severely corrects his son, he does not do this to take vengeance on him or to maltreat him, but rather to teach him and to render him more cautious therefore. ᵇChrysostom somewhere uses a slightly different comparison, but it amounts to the same thing. "The son," he says, "is flogged; the slave is also flogged. But the latter, as a slave, is punished because he sins; the former is chastised as a freeman and son in need of discipline. Correction for the son serves as trial and amendment; for the slave, as scourge and punishment."[67]

---

[66] Aquinas, *Summa Theol.* III. lxxxvi. 1, 4, reply to obj. 3; III. xlix. 1; De Castro, *Adversus omnes haereses* (1543, fo. 147 D); Fisher, *Assertionis Lutheranae confutatio* (on I Peter 4:8), p. 302; Eck, *Enchiridion*, ch. ix.

[67] Pseudo-Chrysostom, *De fide et lege naturae* iii (MPG 48. 1085). The punishment of a son as contrasted with that of a slave is introduced again in III. viii. 6.

*32. God's judgment in vengeance has a wholly different purpose
from that of his judgment in chastisement: the distinction*

b(a)In order that we may quickly summarize the whole matter,
let this stand as the first of two distinctions: wherever punishment is for vengeance, there the curse and wrath of God manifest
themselves, and these he always withholds from believers. On the
other hand, chastisement is a blessing of God and also bears witness to his love, as Scripture teaches [Job 5:17; Prov. 3:11–12;
Heb. 12:5–6].

bThis distinction is sufficiently pointed out through all God's
Word. For all the afflictions that the impious bear in the present life depict for us, as it were, a sort of entry way of hell, from
which they already see afar off their eternal damnation. And yet
they are so far from changing themselves on this account, or
profiting by it at all, that by such preliminaries they are rather
prepared for the dire Gehenna that at last awaits them.

The Lord chastens his servants sorely, but he does not give
them over to death [Ps. 118:18 p.]. Therefore, they confess that
to be beaten with his rod has been good for them and has
furthered their true instruction [Ps. 119:71]. b(a)Just as we read
everywhere that the saints took such punishments with a calm
mind, so they have always prayed fervently to escape scourgings
of the first sort. a"Correct me, O Lord," says Jeremiah, "but in
judgment, not in thine anger, lest perchance thou bring me to
nothing. Pour out thy wrath bupon the nations that know thee
not, and upon the kingdoms that call not on thy name" [Jer.
10:24–25]. Moreover, David says: "O Lord, rebuke me not in
thine anger, nor chasten me in thy wrath." [Ps. 6:1 or 38:2; 6:2
or 37:2, Vg.]

And there is no contradiction in the fact that the Lord is said
quite often to be angry toward his saints, when he chastens them
for their sins. As in Isaiah: "I shall confess unto thee, O Lord,
although thou wert angry with me; thine anger turned away,
and thou didst comfort me." [Isa. 12:1 p.] Likewise, Habakkuk:
"When you are angry, you will remember mercy." [Hab. 3:2 p.]
eAnd Micah, too: "I will bear God's wrath, for I have sinned
against him." [Micah 7:9 p.] There he teaches that he who is
justly punished gains nothing by loudly complaining, but also
that believers get relief from their sorrow by considering God's
purpose. bFor the same reason, he is said to profane his heritage
[Isa. 47:6; cf. ch. 42:24], yet, as we know, he will not profane it
forever. But that refers not to the purpose or disposition of God
as one who punishes but to the acute sense of pain, which those
experience who bear any of its rigors. Nevertheless, he not only

pricks his believers with slight severity, but sometimes so wounds them that they seem to themselves to be not far distant from the damnation of hell. Thus, he testifies that they deserve his wrath, ᵉand so it is fitting for them to be displeased with their own evil acts, and be touched with a greater care to appease God, and anxiously hasten to seek pardon. ᵇBut, in the meantime, in this very fact he shows a clearer testimony of his mercy than of his wrath.[68] There is a covenant still in force that God made with us in our true Solomon [II Sam. 7:12–13]. He who cannot deceive has declared that its force will never be voided. "If his children forsake my law and do not walk according to my ordinances, if they violate my statutes and do not keep my commandments, . . . I will punish their iniquities with the rod and their sins with scourges, but I will not remove from him my mercy." [Ps. 89:30–33; 88:31–34, Vg.; but cf. Comm.] To render us more certain of his mercy, he says that the rod, whereby he will prove Solomon's posterity, will be of man; the stripes, of the sons of man [II Sam. 7:14]. While by these phrases he signifies moderation and gentleness, at the same time he hints that those who feel the hand of God against them cannot but be confounded by extreme and deadly terror. In the prophet he shows how great a regard he has for this leniency in chastising his people Israel: "In fire I have refined you," he says, "but not as silver" [Isa. 48:10]. For then you would have been totally consumed [cf. Isa. 43:2]. Although the Lord teaches that chastisements serve to cleanse his people, he adds that he tempers those chastisements so as not to wear down his people unduly. ᵉAnd that is quite necessary. For the more any man reveres God and devotes himself to the cultivation of godliness, the more tender he is to bear God's wrath. For although the wicked groan under his scourges, yet because they do not weigh the case, but rather turn their backs on both their own sins and the judgment of God, from this negligence they become hardened. Or because they murmur and kick against him and rant against their Judge, their violent fury stupefies them with madness and rage. But believers, admonished by God's scourges, immediately descend into themselves to consider their sins, and struck with fear and dread, flee to prayer as suppliants for pardon. Unless God assuaged these sorrows with which miserable souls torture themselves, they would faint a hundred times even at slight signs of his wrath.

---

[68] Similarly, Augustine contrasts "the anger of God" with "the far more striking evidence of his mercy": *Enchiridion* viii. 27 (MPL 40. 245; ed. O. Scheel, p. 18; tr. LCC VII. 355).

33. Judgment of vengeance serves to punish; judgment of chastisement to improve

ᵇThen let us note a second distinction, that while the wicked are beaten with God's scourges they already begin, in a manner, to suffer punishments according to his judgment. And although they shall not escape unpunished because they have not heeded such evidences of God's wrath, they nevertheless are not punished that they may come to a better mind; but only that in their great distress they may find God to be a Judge and Avenger. But the children are beaten with rods, not to pay the penalty for their sins to God, but in order thereby to be led to repentance. Accordingly, we understand that these things have to do rather with the future than with the past. I would prefer to express this thought in the words of Chrysostom rather than my own: "On this account," he says, "he imposes a penalty upon us—not to punish us for past sins, but to correct us against future ones."⁶⁹ ᶜSo also Augustine: "What you suffer, what you complain about, is your medicine, not your penalty; your chastisement, not your condemnation. Do not put away the scourge if you do not want to be put away from the inheritance," etc. "Know, brethren, that all this misery of humankind in which the world groans is medicinal pain and not a penal sentence,"⁷⁰ etc. I decided to quote these passages in order that the expression I have used may not seem new or unusual to anyone.

ᵉAnd this is the purport of the complaints, charged with indignation, in which God often expostulates concerning the ungratefulness of his people, because they perversely hold all penalties in contempt. In Isaiah: "Why should I smite you further? ... From the sole of the foot even to the head, there is no health" [Ch. 1:5–6 p.]. But, because the prophets abound in such statements, it will be sufficient to have indicated briefly that the sole purpose of God in punishing his church is that the church may be brought low and repent. ᵃTherefore, when He deprived Saul of the kingdom. He was punishing for vengeance [I Sam. 15:23]. When he took away David's little son from him [II Sam. 12:18] he was rebuking for amendment. Paul's statement is to be understood in this sense: "When we are judged by the Lord, we are chastened so that we may not be condemned along with the world" [I Cor. 11:32]. That is, while we as children of God are

---

⁶⁹ Pseudo-Chrysostom, *Sermo de poenitentia et confessione,* in the edition of Chrysostom edited by Erasmus (Basel, 1530), V. 514 (1547 edition, V. 907).
⁷⁰ Augustine, *Psalms,* Ps. 102 (Latin, Ps. 101). 20 (MPL 37. 1332; tr. NPNF VIII. 500); Ps. 139 (Latin, Ps. 138). 15 (MPL 37. 1793; tr. LF *Psalms* VI. 204).

afflicted by the hand of the Heavenly Father, this is not a penalty to confound us, but only a chastisement to instruct us.

ᵇIn this matter, Augustine is plainly on our side, for he teaches that the penalties by which men are equally chastised by God ought to be variously considered. For the saints these are, after forgiveness of sins, struggles and exercises; for the wicked, without forgiveness of sins, the punishments of iniquity. There he lists the penalties inflicted upon David and other godly persons and says that they are concerned with exercising or testing their godliness by this sort of humbling experience.⁷¹ And Isaiah's statement that iniquity is forgiven the Jewish people because they have suffered a full chastisement at the Lord's hand [Isa. 40:2] does not prove that pardon for our transgressions depends upon the payment of the penalty. But it is as if he had said: "You have already suffered enough punishments; on account of their weight and multitude,. because you have already been consumed by long grief and sorrow, it is time for you to receive the tidings of full mercy that your hearts may rejoice and feel me as your Father." ᵉFor there God takes upon himself the person of Father, and repents even of his just severity when compelled to mete out a rather harsh punishment to his child.

34. The believer undergoing God's chastisement is not to lose heart

ᵃIn the bitterness of afflictions, the believer must be fortified by these thoughts. "The time has come for judgment to begin with the household of God" [I Peter 4:17], . . . in which his name is called upon [cf. Jer. 25:29]. What would the children of God do if they believed the severity they feel is his vengeance? For he who, struck by the hand of God, thinks God a punishing Judge cannot conceive of him as other than wrathful and hostile; cannot but detest the very scourge of God as curse and damnation. In short, he who feels that God still intends to punish him can never be persuaded that he is loved by God. ᵇBut he who in the end profits by God's scourges is the man who considers God angry at his vices, but merciful and kindly toward himself. ᶜFor otherwise there must come to pass what the prophet complains of having experienced: "Thy furies have swept over me [Ps. 88:16, cf. Comm.], thy terrors have oppressed me" [cf. Ps. 87:17, Vg.]. Also,

---

⁷¹ Augustine, *On the Merits and Remission of Sins* II. xxxiii. 53–xxxiv. 56 (MPL 44. 182 ff.; tr. NPNF V. 65–67). For numerous other examples of Calvin's claim that "Augustine is with us," see Smits I. 271. Cf. the statement in *De aeterna Dei praedestinatione: "Totus noster est"* (CR VIII. 266).

what Moses writes: "For we have fainted in thine anger; in thine indignation we have been troubled. Thou hast set our iniquities before thy sight, our secret sins in the light of thy countenance. For all our days have passed away in thy wrath. Our years have been consumed as a word uttered by the mouth" [Ps. 90:7–9; cf. Ps. 89:7–9, Vg. and Comm.]. On the contrary, David, to teach that believers are more helped by God's fatherly chastisements than oppressed by them, sings of them thus: "Blessed is the man whom thou shalt chasten, O Lord, and shalt instruct in thy law; to give him rest from evil days, until a pit is dug for the sinful one" [Ps. 94:12–13; cf. LXX Ps. 93:12–13]. ᵉSurely, this is a hard trial when God, sparing the unbelievers and disregarding their crimes, appears more rigid against his own people. On this account, he adds a reason for comfort: the admonition of the law, by which they may learn that there is concern for their salvation when they are called back to the way; but that the impious are borne headlong into their own errors, the end of which is the pit. ᵃWhether the penalty is everlasting or temporal makes no difference. For wars, famines, pestilence, diseases, are just as much curses of God as the very judgment of eternal death, ᵇwhen they are inflicted to the end that they may be the instruments of the Lord's wrath and vengeance against the wicked.

35. *The punishment of David*

ᵃNow all see, unless I am deceived, the purpose of the Lord's punishment against David. It is that it might be a proof that murder and adultery gravely displease God. He had declared himself so greatly offended against this in his beloved and faithful servant that David himself might be taught not to dare commit such a crime thereafter; but not that it might be a penalty by which he should make certain payment to God. So also should we judge concerning the other correction, whereby the Lord afflicted his people with a violent plague [II Sam. 24:15], on account of David's disobedience, into which he had fallen in taking a census of his people. For he freely forgave David the guilt of his sin, but because it was appropriate both for the public example of all ages and also for the humiliation of David that such a crime should not go unpunished, he very harshly chastised him with his scourge.

ᵇThis end we ought to hold in view with regard to the universal curse of the human race [cf. Gen. 3:16–19]. For when, after we have obtained grace, we nevertheless put up with all the miseries that were inflicted upon our first parent as a penalty for sin, we feel that we are warned by such trials how gravely God is displeased with our transgression of his law. Thus, dejected and humbled by the consciousness of our miserable lot, we aspire more eagerly to true blessedness. Anyone would be utterly foolish to think that calamities of the present life have been imposed upon us for the punishment of our sin. This is what Chrysostom seems to me to have meant when he wrote as follows: "If God inflict punishments on this account—that he may call those who persevere in evil-doing to repentance—after penitence has been shown, penalties will already be superfluous."[72] Therefore, according as he knows it to be expedient for the nature of each man, he treats this one with greater harshness, that one with more kindly indulgence. ᶜConsequently, when he would teach that he is not immoderate in meting out punishments, he reproaches a hard and stubborn people because, when smitten, they do not cease to sin [Jer. 5:3]. In this sense he complains that Ephraim is like a cake scorched on one side, uncooked on the other [Hos. 7:8], obviously because the corrections did not reach the hearts, so that, with vices cooked out, the people might become capable of pardon. Surely, he who speaks thus shows that, as soon as anyone repents, he will soon be placable; and that it is our stubbornness toward him that causes him to exercise rigor in chastising our transgressions—a rigor that voluntary correction may counteract. ᵇSince all of us, however, have such hardness and ignorance as to need chastisement, our most wise Father saw fit to exercise all of us without exception throughout life with a common scourge.

ᵃBut it is strange why they thus cast their eyes upon the one example of David, and are not moved by so many other examples in which they could have contemplated the free forgiveness of sins. We read that the publican went down from the Temple justified; no punishment ensues [Luke 18:14]. Peter obtained pardon for transgression [Luke 22:61]; we read of his tears, says Ambrose, we do not read of satisfaction.[73] And the paralytic heard: "Rise up, your sins are forgiven" [Matt. 9:2]; no punishment is imposed. All the absolutions that are mentioned in Scripture are described as free. The rule ought to have been sought from these frequent examples rather than from a single one that contained some special feature.

---

[72] Chrysostom, *Homilies on Providence, to Stagirius* III. xiv (Basel edition, 1547, V. 666; MPG 47. 493 f.).
[73] Ambrose, *Exposition of the Gospel of Luke* X. 88: "I do not find what he said; I find that he wept" (CSEL 32. iv. 489. 8; MPL 15. 1918). Cf. Gratian, *Decretum* III. xxxiii. 3. 1. 1 (MPL 187. 1520; Friedberg I. 1159).

36. Good works as redemption of punishment

[a]Daniel, by the exhortation with which he persuaded Nebuchadnezzar to make recompense for his sins by righteousness and his iniquities by pity for the poor [Dan. 4:27], did not mean to imply that righteousness and mercy were the propitiation of God and the recompense of punishment. Banish the thought that there should be any other ransom[74] than the blood of Christ! But in the phrase "to make recompense," he referred to men rather than to God. It was as if he said: "O King, you have exercised unjust and violent mastery, you have oppressed the humble, you have despoiled the poor, you have treated your people harshly and unjustly; now replace with mercy and righteousness your unjust exactions, your violence and oppression."

Similarly, Solomon says that "love covers a multitude of sins" [Prov. 10:12], not before God, but among men. The whole verse reads: "Hatred stirs up strife, but love covers all offenses" [Prov. 10:12]. In this verse, as his habit is, through antithesis, he contrasts the evil things that arise out of hatreds with the fruits of love. His meaning is that those who hate one another bite, harry, reproach, injure, one another and make a fault of everything; but that those who love one another conceal many things among themselves, wink at many things, condone many things in one another —not that one man approves of another's faults, but that he tolerates them, and heals them by admonishing instead of aggravating them by reproaches. Undoubtedly, Peter quotes this passage in the same sense, unless we would accuse him of debasing and craftily twisting Scripture [cf. I Peter 4:8].

[b]Where Solomon teaches that "by mercy and kindliness sins are atoned for" [Prov. 16:6 p.], he does not mean that they are paid for in the Lord's sight, that God, appeased by such satisfaction, may remit the punishment that he otherwise was about to mete out. Rather, in the familiar manner of Scripture, he indicates that he will be found merciful to those who, having bidden farewell to past vices and evils, are in piety and truth turned to him. It is as if he said that the Lord's wrath subsides and his judgment rests when our transgressions rest. [c]And he is not describing the cause of pardon, but rather the means of true conversion. Just as the prophets frequently denounce hypocrites for vainly forcing upon God false rites instead of repentance, when God is pleased, rather, with uprightness and the duties of love. In like manner the author of The Letter to the Hebrews, praising kindliness and humaneness, reminds us that such sacrifices are pleasing to God [Heb. 13:16]. When Christ, deriding the Pharisees for

[74] "ἀπολύτρωσις."

paying attention only to cleansing dishes but neglecting cleanness of heart, bids them give alms to make all things pure [Luke
11:39–41; cf. Matt. 23:25], he surely does not urge them to make
satisfaction. Rather, he teaches only what sort of purity is approved of God. [b]We have discussed this expression in another
place.[75]

37. The woman who was a sinner

[a]As far as the passage in Luke is concerned [Luke 7:36–50], no
one, who has read with sound judgment, the parable set forth
there by the Lord will pick a quarrel with us over it. The Pharisee
thought to himself that the Lord did not know the woman whom
he had so readily received. For he felt that Christ would not have
received her if he had known what sort of sinner she was. And
he inferred from this that Christ was not a prophet, since he could
be deceived to this extent. The Lord, to show that she was not a
sinner whose sins he had already forgiven, set forth a parable. "A
certain moneylender had two debtors. One owed fifty denarii,
the other five hundred. The debt of each was forgiven. Which
one has the greater gratitude? The Pharisee answered, 'The one,
I suppose, to whom he forgave more.' The Lord said: 'From this
know that this woman's sins are forgiven, for she loved much'"
[Luke 7:41–43, 47 p.]. By these words, you see, he does not make
her love the cause, but the proof, of forgiveness of sins. For they
are taken from the comparison of that debtor who was forgiven
five hundred denarii; to him he did not say that they were forgiven because he loved much, but that he loved much because
they were forgiven. Hence, this comparison ought to be applied
in this form: You think that this woman is a sinner, yet you ought
to have recognized that she is not such, since her sins have been
forgiven her. Her love, by which she gives thanks for his benefit,
ought to have convinced you of the forgiveness of her sins. Now
this is an argument a posteriori, by which something is proved
from the evidences that follow. The Lord clearly testifies in what
way she obtained forgiveness of sins: "Your faith," he says, "has
saved you" [Luke 7:50]. By faith, therefore, we gain forgiveness;
by love we give thanks and testify to the Lord's kindness.

38. The Roman doctrine cannot claim the authority of the church fathers[†]

[a]The opinions widely expressed in the books of the ancient
writers concerning satisfaction move me little. I see, indeed, that
some of them—I will simply say almost all whose books are extant

[75] III. xiv. 21; Comm. Harmony of the Evangelists, Matt. 23:25; Luke 11:34–41.

—have either fallen down in this respect or have spoken too sharply and harshly. But I do not admit that they were so rude and untutored as to write those things in the sense in which they are understood by our new exponents of satisfaction. ᵇChrysostom in one place writes as follows: "Where mercy is importuned, investigation ceases; where mercy is implored, judgment does not rage; where mercy is sought, there is no place for penalty; where there is mercy, there is no inquisition; where there is mercy, the answer is pardoned."⁷⁶ However these words may be twisted, they cannot ever be made to agree with the tenets of the Schoolmen. But in a book, *The Dogmas of the Church,* ascribed to Augustine, one reads as follows: "The satisfaction of repentance is to cut off the causes of sin, not to grant entry to their suggestions."⁷⁷ From this it is clear that even in those times the doctrine of satisfaction, which was said to be in recompense for sins committed, was commonly laughed at, since they associated all satisfaction with caution in abstaining from sins thereafter. I shall not quote what the same Chrysostom teaches, that God requires nothing of us beyond our confessing our transgressions before him with tears,⁷⁸ since statements of this sort occur frequently in his and others' writings. It is true, Augustine somewhere calls the works of mercy "remedies to obtain forgiveness of sin"; but, lest anyone stumble over this word, he meets this objection in another place. "The flesh of Christ," he says, "is the true and only sacrifice for sins, not only for those sins which are wholly blotted out in baptism, but for those which creep in afterward through weakness. For this reason, the whole church daily cries: 'Forgive us our debts' [Matt. 6:12]; and they are forgiven through that unique sacrifice."⁷⁹

39. The Schoolmen corrupt the teaching of the fathers*

ᵃNow they have largely called satisfaction not a payment that was rendered to God but a public testimony whereby those who had been sentenced with excommunication, when they wish to be received back into communion, assure the church of their repentance. For there were imposed upon those repentant ones certain fastings and other duties by which they might prove that they truly and heartily loathed their former life, or rather, that they

---

⁷⁶ Pseudo-Chrysostom, *Homily on Ps. 50,* hom. ii. 2 (MPG 55. 577).

⁷⁷ Pseudo-Augustine, *De dogmatibus ecclesiasticis* xxiv (MPL 58. 994).

⁷⁸ Chrysostom, *Homilies on Genesis,* hom. x. 2 (MPG 53. 83 ff.).

⁷⁹ Augustine, *Enchiridion* xix. 72 (MPL 40. 266; ed. O. Scheel, p. 46; tr. LCC VII. 382); *Against Two Letters of the Pelagians* III. vi. 16 (MPL 44. 600; tr. NPNF V. 409 f.).

would wipe out the memory of their previous actions, and thus were said to have made satisfaction not to God but to the church. ᶜAugustine has expressed this in these very words in his *Enchiridion* to Laurentius.[80] ᵃFrom that ancient rite, the confessions and satisfactions that today are in use took their origin. Truly viperous offspring [cf. Matt. 3:7; 12:34], these, by which it comes to pass that not even a shadow of that better form remains!

I know that the old writers sometimes speak rather harshly; and, as I have just said,[81] I do not deny that they perhaps erred; but those of their writings that were marred with a few spots here and there become utterly defiled when they are handled by these men's unwashed hands. And if we must contend by the authority of the fathers, what fathers, good God, do these men thrust upon us? A good part of those authors from whom Lombard, their leader,[82] has sewn together his patchworks, were collected from the senseless ravings of certain monks, which pass under the names Ambrose, Jerome, Augustine, and Chrysostom; as in the present argument almost all his evidence is taken from Augustine's book *On Repentance*, which was bunglingly patched together by some rhapsodist from good and bad authors indiscriminately. Indeed, it bears the name of Augustine, but nobody of even mediocre learning would deign to acknowledge it as his.[83] ᶜLet my readers pardon me if I do not expressly examine the Schoolmen's follies, for I would lighten their burden. It would surely not be very difficult for me, and a praiseworthy thing, to expose to ridicule, to their great shame, what they have heretofore boasted of as mysteries; but because my purpose is to teach profitably, I pass them over.

[80] Augustine, *Enchiridion* xvii. 65 (MPL 40. 262 f.; tr. LCC VII. 377); Gratian, *Decretum* II. xxxiii. 3. 84 (Friedberg I. 1183; MPL 187. 1533).

[81] Sec. 38, above.

[82] *"Coryphaeus."*

[83] Calvin has quoted without suspicion a number of Pseudo-Augustine texts, but again rejects with contempt the obviously late *De vera et falsa poenitentia.* Cf. III. iv. 1, note 1; III. iv. 23, note 48. In III. xiv. 8, however, a particular statement from this work is approved.

^cCHAPTER V

THE SUPPLEMENTS THAT THEY ADD TO SATISFACTIONS, NAMELY,
INDULGENCES AND PURGATORY

*(The erroneous doctrine of indulgences and its evil conse-
quences, 1–5)*
*1. Indulgences according to Romanist doctrine, and the mischief
caused by them*

^cNow indulgences flow from this doctrine of satisfaction. For
our opponents pretend that to make satisfaction those indulgences
supply what our powers lack. ^{e(a)}And they go to the mad extreme
of defining them as the distribution of the merits of Christ and
the martyrs, which the pope distributes by his bulls.[1] These men
are fit to be treated by drugs for insanity[2] rather than to be argued
with. ^aFor it is hardly worth-while to undertake to refute errors
so foolish, which under the onslaught of many battering-rams are
of themselves beginning to grow old and to show deterioration.
^cBut because a brief refutation will be useful for certain unin-
structed persons, I shall not omit it.

^aThe fact that indulgences have so long stood untouched, and
in such unrestrained and furious license have retained such lasting impunity, can truly serve as a proof of how deeply men were
immersed for centuries in a deep night of errors. Men saw themselves openly and undisguisedly held up to ridicule by the pope
and his bull-bearers, their souls' salvation the object of lucrative
trafficking, the price of salvation reckoned at a few coins, nothing
offered free of charge. By this subterfuge they saw themselves
cheated of their offerings, which were filthily spent on whores,
pimps, and drunken revelries. But they also saw that the greatest
trumpeters of indulgences hold them in most contempt; that this
monster daily runs more riotously and lecherously abroad, and
that there is no end; that new lead is daily put forward and new
money taken away.[3] Yet with the highest veneration they received

---

[1] Cf. N. Paulus, *Geschichte des Ablasses am Ausgange des Mittelalters;* W. E.
Lunt, *Papal Revenues in the Middle Ages:* I. 111–125, documents in II.
148–485; B. J. Kidd, *Documents Illustrative of the Continental Reformation,* pp. 1–20. Aquinas, *Summa Theol.* III. Suppl. xxv. 1, states that "indulgences hold good both in the church's court and in the judgment of God"
because of "the oneness of the mystical body in which many have performed
works of satisfaction beyond the requirements."

[2] *"Helleboro."*

[3] *"Plumbum semper novum afferri, novos nummos elici."* Cf. *Grievances of
the German Nation Against the Roman Curia* (1521), ed. C. G. F. Walch,
Monimenta medii aevi (Göttingen, 1757), I. i. 109; Kidd, *Documents,* pp.
113 f. The clerks whose function it was to affix the leaden seals to papal bulls

indulgences, worshiped them as pious frauds by which men could with some profit be deceived. Finally, when the world has ventured to become a little wise, indulgences grow cold and gradually freeze up, until they will altogether vanish.

2. *Indulgences contrary to Scripture*

[a]Now very many persons see the base tricks, deceits, thefts, and greediness with which the indulgence traffickers have heretofore mocked and beguiled us, and yet they do not see the very fountain of the impiety itself. As a consequence, it behooves us to indicate not only the nature of indulgences but also what in general they would be, wiped clean of all spots. [a]The merits of Christ and the holy apostles and martyrs our opponents call the "treasury of the church." They pretend that the prime custody of this storehouse, as I have already hinted,[4] has been entrusted to the Bishop of Rome, who controls the dispensing of these very great benefits, so that he can both distribute them by himself and delegate to others the management of their distribution. Consequently, plenary indulgences, as well as indulgences for certain years, stem from the pope; indulgences for a hundred days, from the cardinals; and of forty days, from the bishops![5]

Now these, to describe them rightly, are a profanation of the blood of Christ, a Satanic mockery, to lead the Christian people away from God's grace, away from the life that is in Christ, and turn them aside from the true way of salvation. For how could the blood of Christ be more foully profaned than when they deny that it is sufficient for the forgiveness of sins, for reconciliation, for satisfaction—unless the lack of it, as of something dried up and exhausted, be otherwise supplied and filled? "To Christ, the Law and all the Prophets bear witness," says Peter, that "through him we are to receive forgiveness of sins." [Acts 10:43 p.] Indulgences bestow forgiveness of sins through Peter, Paul, and the martyrs. "The blood of Christ cleanses us from sin," says John [I John 1:7 p.]. Indulgences make the blood of martyrs the cleansing of

---

were known as *plumbatores*. W. E. Lunt, *Papal Revenues in the Middle Ages* II. 298.

[4] Sec. 1, above. Cf. III. iv. 15, note 30. From Aquinas down, the Scholastics accorded to the pope the primary authority to dispense the treasury of merits (*Summa Theol.* III. Suppl. xxvi. 3). This was defended by opponents of the Reformation. Leo X's bull, *Exsurge Domine*, June 15, 1520, reciting the errors of Luther, includes his rejection of "the treasury of the church from which the pope grants indulgences": *"Thesaurus Ecclesiae, unde Papa dat indulgentias, non sunt merita Christi et sanctorum"* (17th error). (Kidd, *Documents,* no. 38, p. 77.)

[5] *Decretals* V. xxviii. 14 (Friedberg II. 889); Aquinas, *Summa Theol.* III. Suppl. xxvi. 3; Fisher, *Assertionis Lutheranae confutatio,* art. xvii, p. 305.

sins. "Christ," says Paul, "who knew no sin, was made sin for us" (that is, satisfaction of sin) "so that we might be made the righteousness of God in him" [II Cor. 5:21 p., cf. Vg.]. Indulgences lodge satisfaction of sins in the blood of martyrs. Paul proclaimed and testified to the Corinthians that Christ alone was crucified and died for them [cf. I Cor. 1:13]. Indulgences declare: "Paul and others died for us." Elsewhere Paul says, "Christ acquired the church with his own blood." [Acts 20:28 p.] Indulgences establish another purchase price in the blood of martyrs. "By a single offering Christ has perfected for all time those who are sanctified." [Heb. 10:14.] Indulgences proclaim: Sanctification, otherwise insufficient, is perfected by the martyrs. John says that "all the saints have washed their robes . . . in the blood of the Lamb." [Rev. 7:14.] Indulgences teach that they wash their robes in the blood of the saints.

*3. Authorities against indulgences and merits of martyrs**

ᶜTo the Palestinians, Leo, Bishop of Rome, writes very clearly against this sacrilege: "Although," he says, " 'Precious in the sight of the Lord was the death of many saints' [Ps. 116:15; cf. Ps. 115: 15, Vg.], yet the slaying of no innocent person has been the propitiation of the world. The righteous have received, not given, crowns; and from believers' fortitude have come examples of patience, not gifts of righteousness. Each one surely died his own death, not paying by his end the debt of another, since one Lord Christ exists, in whom all are crucified, all are dead, buried, raised." As this idea was worth remembering, he repeated it in another place.[6] Surely, nothing clearer could be desired to puncture this impious dogma. And Augustine, no less appropriately, expresses the same judgment: "Even though we as brethren," he says, "die for our brethren, no martyr's blood is shed for the forgiveness of sins. This Christ has done for us, and he has bestowed this upon us not for us to imitate him, but for us to rejoice." The same idea occurs in another place: "Just as the only Son of God became the Son of Man that he might make us sons of God with him, so on our behalf he alone underwent punishment without deserving ill that we through him, without deserving good, might attain a grace not due us."[7]

ᵃAssuredly, while all their doctrine is patched together out of

[6] Leo I, Letters cxxiv. 4; clxv. 5 (MPL 54. 1064 f.; tr. NPNF 2 ser. XII. 107); clxv. 5 (MPL 54. 1163); Leo I, Sermons lxv. 3 (MPL 54. 359 f.).
[7] Augustine, John's Gospel lxxxiv. 2 (MPL 35. 1847; tr. NPNF VII. 350); Against Two Letters of the Pelagians IV. iv. 6 (MPL 44. 613; tr. NPNF V. 419).

terrible sacrileges and blasphemies, this is a more astounding blasphemy than the rest. Let them recognize whether or not these are their judgments: that martyrs by their death have given more to God and deserved more than they needed for themselves, and that they had a great surplus of merits to overflow to others. In order, therefore, that this great good should not be superfluous, they mingle their blood with the blood of Christ; and out of the blood of both, the treasury of the church is fabricated for the forgiveness and satisfaction of sins. And Paul's statement, "In my body I complete what is lacking in Christ's afflictions for the sake of his body, that is, the church" [Col. 1:24], is to be understood in this sense.[8]

What is this but to leave Christ only a name, to make him another common saintlet who can scarcely be distinguished in the throng? He, he alone, deserved to be preached; he alone set forth; he alone named; he alone looked to when there was a question of obtaining forgiveness of sins, expiation, sanctification. But let us listen to their notions. Lest the martyrs' blood be fruitlessly poured out, let it be conferred upon the common good of the church. Is this so? Was it unprofitable for them to glorify God through their death? to attest his truth by their blood? to bear witness by their contempt of the present life that they are seeking a better life? by their constancy, to strengthen the faith of the church but to break the stubbornness of its enemies? But the fact is that they recognize no fruit if Christ alone is the propitiator, if he alone has died for the sake of our sins, if he alone has been offered for our redemption. ᵉPeter and Paul, nonetheless, they say, would have received the crown of victory if they had died in their beds. But since they strove even unto death, it would not have squared with God's justice for their sacrifice to go barren and unfruitful. It is as if God did not know how to increase his glory in his servants according to the measure of his gifts. But the church in general receives benefit great enough, when by their triumphs it is kindled with a zeal to fight.

4. Refutation of opposing Scriptural proofs

ᵃHow maliciously they twist the passage in Paul wherein he says that in his own body he supplies what was lacking in Christ's sufferings [Col. 1:24]![9] For he refers that lack or that supplement not to the work of redemption, satisfaction, and expiation but to those afflictions with which the members of Christ—namely, all

---

[8] Cf. III. v. 2, note 4; Aquinas, *Summa Theol.* III. Suppl. xxv. 1. 2; Eck, *Enchiridion,* ch. xxiv (1533); Fisher, *Confutatio,* pp. 304 ff.

[9] Sec. 3, above, and passages cited in note 8.

believers—must be exercised so long as they live in this flesh. Therefore, Paul says that of the sufferings of Christ this remains: what once for all he suffered in himself he daily suffers in his members. And Christ distinguishes us by this honor, that he accounts and makes our afflictions his own. Now, when Paul adds "for the church," he does not mean for redemption, for reconciliation, or for satisfaction of the church, but for its upbuilding and advancement. As he says in another place: He endures everything for the sake of the elect, that they may obtain the salvation that is in Christ Jesus [II Tim. 2:10]. And he wrote to the Corinthians that it was for their comfort and salvation that he endured whatever tribulations he was suffering [II Cor. 1:6].

ᶜHe immediately explains himself by adding that he became a minister of the church not for redemption, but "according to the dispensation that had been given to him, to preach the gospel of Christ" [Col. 1:25 p., cf. Rom. 15:19].

But if my opponents require still another interpreter, let them hear Augustine: "The sufferings," he said, "of Christ are in Christ alone, as in the head; in Christ and the church, as in the whole body. Consequently Paul, as one member, says: 'I supply in my body what is lacking in the sufferings of Christ.' If, then, you—whoever you are who hear this—are among Christ's members, whatever you suffer from those who are not members of Christ was lacking in the sufferings of Christ." But he explains elsewhere to what end the sufferings of the apostles, undergone for the church, tended. "Christ is for me the door [cf. John 10:7] unto you, because you are the sheep of Christ, made ready by his blood. Acknowledge your price, which is not paid by me but preached through me." Then he adds, "As he has laid down his life, so also ought we to lay down our lives for our brethren, for the upbuilding of peace and the strengthening of faith."[10] These are Augustine's words. ᵃAway with the notion that Paul thought anything was lacking in Christ's sufferings with regard to the whole fullness of righteousness, salvation, and life; or that he meant to add anything. For Paul clearly and grandly preaches that Christ so bountifully poured out the richness of grace that it far surpassed the whole power of sin [cf. Rom. 5:15]. By this alone, not by the merit of their life or death, have all the saints been saved, as Peter eloquently witnesses [cf. Acts 15:11]. So, then, one who would rest the worthiness of any saint anywhere save in God's mercy would be contemptuous of God and his Anointed. But why do I tarry here any longer, as if this were still some-

---

[10] Augustine, *Psalms*, Ps. 61. 4 (MPL 36. 730; tr. LF [Ps. 62] *Psalms* III. 187); *John's Gospel* xlvii. 2 (MPL 35. 1733; tr. NPNF VII. 260).

thing obscure, when to lay bare such monstrous errors is to vanquish them?

5. Indulgences oppose the unity and the comprehensive activity of the grace of Christ

ªNow—to pass over such abominations—who taught the pope to inclose in lead and parchment the grace of Jesus Christ, which the Lord willed to be distributed by the word of the gospel? Obviously, either the gospel of God or indulgences must be false. ᵇPaul testifies ªthat Christ is offered to us through the gospel, with every abundance of heavenly benefits, with all his merits, all his righteousness, wisdom, and grace, without exception. ᵇHe states that the message of reconciliation was entrusted to ministers to act as ambassadors with Christ, as it were, appealing through them [II Cor. 5:18–21]. "We beseech you, be reconciled to God. For our sake he made him to be sin who knew no sin, so that in him we might become the righteousness of God" [II Cor. 5:20–21]. ᶜAnd believers know the value of the fellowship[11] of Christ, which, as the same apostle testifies, is in the gospel offered us to enjoy. ªOn the other hand, indulgences draw from the pope's storehouse some modicum of grace. They attach it to lead, parchment, and a certain place—and tear it away from the Word of God!

ᶜIf anyone would ask its origin, this abuse seems to have arisen from the fact that when satisfactions severer than all could bear were formerly enjoined upon the penitents, who felt weighed down beyond all measure by the penance imposed upon them, they sought relaxation from the church. The remission made to such persons was called "indulgence." But when they transferred satisfactions to God and said that they were compensations by which men redeemed themselves from God's judgment, at the same time also they converted those indulgences into expiatory remedies that were to free us from our deserved punishments.[12] They have with such great shamelessness fashioned those blasphemies to which we have referred that they can have no excuse.

(Refutation of the doctrine of purgatory by an exposition of the Scriptural passages adduced to support it, 6–10)
6. Refutation of the doctrine of purgatory is necessary
ªNow let them no longer trouble us with their "purgatory," because with this ax it has already been broken, hewn down, and overturned from its very foundations. And I do not agree with

---

[11] κοινωνία.
[12] Luther, *Disputatio pro declaratione virtutis indulgentiarum*, positio 33 (*Werke* WA I. 235).

certain persons who think that one ought to dissemble on this point, and make no mention of purgatory, from which, as they say, fierce conflicts arise but little edification can be obtained.[13] Certainly, I myself would advise that such trifles be neglected if they did not have their serious consequences. But, since purgatory is constructed out of many blasphemies and is daily propped up with new ones, and since it incites to many grave offenses, it is certainly not to be winked at. One could for a time perhaps in a way conceal the fact that it was devised apart from God's Word in curious and bold rashness; that men believed in it by some sort of "revelations" forged by Satan's craft; and that some passages of Scripture were ignorantly distorted to confirm it. Still, the Lord does not allow man's effrontery so to break in upon the secret places of his judgments; and he sternly forbade that men, to the neglect of his Word, should inquire after truth from the dead [Deut. 18:11]. Neither does he allow his Word to be so irreligiously corrupted.

Let us, however, grant that all those things could have been tolerated for a time as something of no great importance; but when expiation of sins is sought elsewhere than in the blood of Christ, when satisfaction is transferred elsewhere, silence is very dangerous. Therefore, we must cry out with the shouting not only of our voices but of our throats and lungs that purgatory is a deadly fiction of Satan, which nullifies the cross of Christ, [b]inflicts unbearable contempt upon God's mercy, [a]and overturns and destroys our faith. For what means this purgatory of theirs but that satisfaction for sins is paid by the souls of the dead after their death? [b]Hence, when the notion of satisfaction is destroyed, purgatory itself is straightway torn up by the very roots. [a]But if it is perfectly clear from our preceding discourse that the blood of Christ is the sole satisfaction for the sins of believers, the sole expiation, the sole purgation,[14] what remains but to say that purgatory is simply a dreadful blasphemy against Christ? I pass over the sacrileges by which it is daily defended, the minor offenses that it breeds in religion, and innumerable other things that we see have come forth from such a fountain of impiety.

7. *Alleged proofs of purgatory from the Gospels**
  [b]But it behooves us to wrest from their hands those passages of

---

[13] A reference to Melanchthon's omission of the topic of purgatory in the Augsburg Confession (1530) and the *Apology of the Augsburg Confession* (1532).
[14]   sec. 2, above, and Aquinas on purgatory, *Summa Theol.* III. Suppl., Appendix II.

Scripture which they falsely and wrongly are accustomed to seize upon.

When the Lord, they say, makes known that the "sin against the Holy Spirit is not to be forgiven either in this age or in the age to come" [Matt. 12:32; Mark 3:28–29; Luke 12:10], he hints at the same time that there is forgiveness of certain sins in the world to come.[15] But who cannot see that the Lord is there speaking of the guilt of sin? But if this is so, what has it to do with their purgatory? Since, in their opinion, punishment of sins is undergone in purgatory, why do they not deny that their guilt is remitted in the present life? But to stop their railing against us, they shall have an even plainer refutation. When the Lord willed to cut off all hope of pardon for such shameful wickedness, he did not consider it enough to say that it would never be forgiven; but in order to emphasize it even more, he used a division by which he embraced the judgment that the conscience of every man experiences in this life and the final judgment that will be given openly at the resurrection. It is as if he said: "Beware of malicious rebellion as of present ruin. For he who would purposely try to extinguish the proffered light of the Spirit will attain pardon neither in this life, which is given to sinners for their conversion, nor in the Last Day, on which the lambs will be separated from the goats by the angels of God and the Kingdom of Heaven will be cleansed of all offenses" [cf. Matt. 25: 32–33].

Then they bring forward that parable from Matthew: "Make friends with your adversary . . . lest sometime he hand you over to the judge, and the judge to the constable, and the constable to the prison . . . whence you cannot get out until you have paid the last penny" [Matt. 5:25–26 p.]. If in this passage the judge signifies God, the accuser the devil, the guard the angel, the prison purgatory, I shall willingly yield to them. But suppose it be clear to all that Christ, in order to urge his followers more cogently to equity and concord, meant to show the many dangers and evils to which men expose themselves who obstinately prefer to demand the letter of the law[16] rather than to act out of equity and goodness. Where, then, I ask, will purgatory be found?

---

[15] Lombard, *Sentences* IV. xxi. 1 (MPL 192. 895); Eck, *Enchiridion* (1526), ch. xxv; Bernard, *Sermons on the Song of Songs* lxvi. 11, citing Matt. 12:32 for purgatory (MPL 183. 1100; tr. S. J. Eales, *Life and Works of St. Bernard* IV. 405 f.).

[16] "*Summum ius*," the full demand of the letter of the law as distinct from equity or discerning justice. Calvin evidently has in mind the maxim *summum ius, summa iniuria* (Cicero, *On Duties* I. x), which was then familiar and was employed by Luther. Cf. McNeill, "Natural Law in the Thought of Luther," *Church History* X (1941), 220.

8. From Philippians, Revelation, and Second Maccabees*

ᵇThey seek proof from Paul's statement wherein he declares that the knees of those in heaven, in earth, and in the nether regions[17] bow to Christ [Phil. 2:10]. For they take it to be generally acknowledged that "nether regions" cannot be understood to mean those who have been bound over to eternal damnation; accordingly, it remains to apply the term to souls agonizing in purgatory. They would not be reasoning badly if by the bowing of the knee the apostle designated true and godly worship. But since he is simply teaching that dominion has been given to Christ with which to subject all creatures, what hinders us from understanding by the expression "nether regions" the devils, who will obviously be brought before God's judgment seat and who will recognize their judge with fear and trembling [cf. James 2:19; II Cor. 7:15]? So Paul himself elsewhere explains the same prophecy: "We shall all stand before Christ's judgment seat. For it is written: 'As I live . . . every knee shall bow to me,' " etc. [Rom. 14:10–11, Vg.; Isa. 45:23].

Yet what is said in Revelation must not be interpreted in that way: "I heard every creature in heaven and on earth and under the earth and in the sea, and all therein, saying: 'To him who sits upon the throne and to the Lamb be blessing and honor and glory and power forever and ever!' " [Rev. 5:13]. That, indeed, I readily concede, but what sorts of creatures do they think are here spoken of? For surely it is quite certain here that both creatures lacking in reason and inanimate ones are comprehended. This merely declares the fact that individual parts of the world, from the very peak of heaven even to the center of the earth, in their own way declare the glory of their Creator [cf. Ps. 19:1].

What they bring forward from the history of the Maccabees [II Macc. 12:43] I deem unworthy of reply, lest I seem to include that work in the canon of the sacred books. ᶜBut Augustine, they say, takes it as canonical. First, with what assurance? "The Jews," he says, "do not consider the writing of the Maccabees as the Law, Prophets, and Psalms, to which the Lord attests as to his witnesses, saying: 'Everything written about me in the Law . . . and the Prophets and the Psalms must be fulfilled' [Luke 24:44]. But it is not unprofitably received by the church if it be soberly read or hearkened to."[18] But Jerome teaches without hesitation that its

---

[17] "*Infernorum.*" The opinions here controverted are expressed in Eck, *Enchiridion* (1526), ch. xxv; cf. Herborn, *Enchiridion* xlviii (CC 12. 162).
[18] Augustine, *Against Gaudentius* I. xxxi. 38 (MPL 43. 729).

authority is of no value for the proving of doctrine.[19] From that ancient work attributed to Cyprian, *On the Exposition of the Creed*, it is perfectly clear that this book had no place in the ancient church.[20] And why do I here carry on this vain argument? As if the author himself does not well enough show what deference is due him, when at the end he implores pardon if he has said anything amiss [II Macc. 15:39]! Surely, he who admits that his writings are in need of pardon does not claim to be the oracle of the Holy Spirit. ᵉBesides this, the piety of Judas is praised for no other distinction than that he had a firm hope of the final resurrection when he sent an offering for the dead to Jerusalem [II Macc. 12:43]. Nor did the writer of that history set down Judas' act to the price of redemption, but regarded it as done in order that they might share in eternal life with the remaining believers who had died for country and religion. This deed was not without superstition and wrongheaded zeal, but utterly foolish are those who extend the sacrifice of the law even down to us, when we know that by the advent of Christ what was then in use ceased.

9. The crucial passage in I Cor., ch. 3*

ᵇBut in Paul they claim to have an invincible phalanx, that cannot be so easily overwhelmed. "If anyone builds on this foundation with gold, silver, precious stones, wood, hay, stubble —each man's work, such as it is, will become manifest; for the Day of the Lord will disclose it, because it will be revealed with fire, and the fire will test what sort of work each one has done. . . . If any man's work is burned up, he will suffer loss, though he himself will be saved, but only as through fire" [I Cor. 3:12–13, 15]. What fire, they ask, can this be but that of purgatory, by which the filth of sins is cleansed away that we may enter into the Kingdom of God as pure men? Yet very many of the ancient writers understood this in another way, namely, as tribulation, or the cross, through which the Lord tests his own that they may not linger in the filth of the flesh.[21] And that is much more probable than any fictitious purgatory. Notwithstanding, I do not

---

[19] Jerome, *Preface to the Books of Samuel and Malachi* (MPL 28. 556 f.).

[20] Rufinus, *Commentary on the Apostles' Creed* xxviii (MPL 21. 374). This treatise was published as a work of Cyprian in Erasmus' edition of Cyprian (1530–1540). Calvin does not so regard it. Cf. IV. i. 2, note 5.

[21] Chrysostom, *Homilies on Repentance,* hom. vi. 3 (MPG 49. 317 f.); Augustine, *Enchiridion* viii. 68 (MPL 40. 864 f.; tr. LCC VII. 379 f.); *City of God* XXI. xxvi. 1, 2 (MPL 41. 743 f.; tr. NPNF II. 473 f.). Cf. Lombard, *Sentences* IV. xxi. 1–3, where I Cor. 3:15 is made to refer to purgatory.

agree with these men, for it seems to me that I have attained a much surer and clearer understanding of this passage.

^cYet before I set it forth, I should like my opponents to answer me whether they think that all the apostles and the saints had to go through this purgatorial fire. They will deny it, I know, for it would be utterly absurd that purgation should be required of those whose merits they imagine to redound beyond measure to all the members of the church. But the apostle declares this, and he does not say that the works of certain ones will be proved, but of all. And this is not my argument but Augustine's, who thus opposes that interpretation. And, what is more absurd, he says not that they shall pass through the fire on account of any works whatsoever, but that if they have built up the church with the highest faithfulness, they will receive a reward when their work has been tested by fire.[22]

^bFirst, we see that the apostle used a metaphor when he called the doctrines devised by men's own brains "wood, hay, and stubble." Besides, the metaphor is readily explained: namely, that just as wood when put on fire is at once consumed and lost, so those things cannot last when the hour comes for them to be tested. Now everyone knows that such a trial proceeds from the Spirit of God. Therefore, to follow the thread of his metaphor and put the parts in their proper relationships to one another, he calls the trial of the Holy Spirit "fire." For the nearer gold and silver are placed to the fire, the more certain proofs do they give of their genuineness and purity. So, too, the more carefully the truth of the Lord is tested in a spiritual examination, the more completely its authority is confirmed. As "hay, wood, and stubble" are set on fire, they are suddenly consumed. Thus the inventions of men, not grounded in the Word of the Lord, cannot bear testing by the Holy Spirit, but immediately fall and perish. In short, if forged doctrines are compared to "wood, hay, and stubble" because like "wood, hay, and stubble" they are burned in the fire and destroyed, it is, however, by the Spirit of the Lord only that they are destroyed and dissipated. It follows that the Spirit is that fire whereby they will be tested, whose test Paul calls "the Day of the Lord" [I Cor. 3:13, Vg.], according to the common usage of Scripture. For it is called "the Day of the Lord" whenever he reveals his presence to men in any way; then, indeed, does his face most of all shine, when his truth gleams forth. Now we have proved that Paul means by "the fire" nothing else but the testing by the Holy Spirit.

[22] Augustine, *Enchiridion, loc. cit.*

But how are those saved through that fire who suffer the loss of their works? [I Cor. 3:15.] This will not be difficult to understand if we consider what kind of men he is speaking of. For he is referring to those builders of the church who, keeping a lawful foundation, build upon it with unsuitable materials. That is, those who do not fall away from the principal and necessary doctrines of the faith go astray in less important and less dangerous ones, mingling their own invention with the Word of God. Such persons, I say, must undergo the loss of their work with the annihilation of their inventions. "Yet they are saved, but as through fire." [I Cor. 3:15.] That is, not that their ignorance and delusion are acceptable to the Lord, but because they are cleansed from these by the grace and power of the Holy Spirit. Accordingly, anyone who fouls the golden purity of God's Word with this filth of purgatory must undergo the loss of his work.

10. The appeal to the early church cannot help the Romanists
ᶜBut, they say, this was a most ancient observance of the church. Paul answers this objection, while also embracing his own age in his judgment, when he declares that all must undergo loss of their work who in building the church lay any foundation unsuitable to it [I Cor. 3:11–15].

When my adversaries, therefore, raise against me the objection that prayers for the dead have been a custom for thirteen hundred years,[23] I ask them, in turn, by what word of God, by what revelation, by what example, is this done? Not only are testimonies of Scripture lacking on this point, but all examples of the saints that one may there read of show no such thing. Concerning mourning and the office of burial, one there finds many and sometimes detailed accounts; but concerning such prayers, you can see not one tittle. Yet, the more important the matter is, the more it ought to have been expressly mentioned. And also, those ancient writers who poured out prayers for the dead saw that in this point they lacked both the command of God and lawful example.[24] Why, then, did they dare do it? On this ground, I say,

---

[23] Aquinas, in *Summa Theol.* III. Suppl. lxxi. 2–8, treats at length prayers for the dead: they benefit souls in purgatory, but not the unbaptized children in limbo or the souls in heaven. Qu. lxxi. 10 is on indulgences for the dead. Cf. J. Latomus, *De quibusdam articulis in ecclesia controversis* (*Opera* [1550], fo. 199a); J. Cochlaeus, *Confutatio ccccc articulorum M. Lutheri ex xxvi sermonibus eius*, xviii (art. 305); Augustine, *Enchiridion* xxix. 109 f. (MPL 40. 283; tr. LCC VII. 405).
[24] Tertullian, *Exhortation to Chastity* xi; *On Monogamy* x (CCL Tertullianus II. 1031, 1243; tr. ANF IV. 56, 66 f.).

that they yielded something to human nature; and for that reason, I contend that what they did ought not to be made an example to imitate. For since believers ought to undertake no task, except with an assured conscience, as Paul teaches [Rom. 14:23], this certainty is especially needed in prayer. Yet it is likely that they were impelled for another reason: namely, they were seeking comfort to relieve their sorrow, and it seemed inhuman to them not to show before God some evidence of their love toward the dead. All men know by experience how man's nature is inclined to this feeling.

eThere was, also, an accepted custom that, like a brand, set men's minds on fire. We know that among all the Gentiles and in all times rites have been held for the dead, and each year cleansing rites were held for their souls. But even though Satan deluded stupid mortals with these tricks, he took occasion to deceive them from a correct principle: that death is not destruction but a crossing over from this life to another. There is no doubt that this very superstition holds the Gentiles convicted before God's judgment seat because they neglected to give thought to the life to come in which they professed to believe. Now Christians, in order not to be worse than profane men, were ashamed not to devote some rite to the dead, as if they had quite ceased to be. From this arose that ill-advised diligence. For if they had hesitated to attend to funeral rites, banquets, and offerings, they thought they would be exposed to great reproach. But that which derived from perverse emulation was so constantly increased by new additions that to help the dead in distress became the papacy's principal mark of holiness. cBut Scripture supplies another far better and more perfect solace when it testifies: "Blessed are the dead who die in the Lord" [Rev. 14:13]. And it adds the reason: "Henceforth they rest from their labors." Moreover, we ought not to indulge our affection to the extent of setting up a perverse mode of prayer in the church.

eSurely, any man endowed with a modicum of wisdom easily recognizes that whatever he reads among the ancient writers concerning this matter was allowed because of public custom and common ignorance. I admit that the fathers themselves were also carried off into error. For heedless credulity commonly deprives men's minds of judgment. And yet, the reading of those authors shows how hesitantly they commended prayers for the dead. Augustine relates in his *Confessions* that his mother, Monica, emphatically requested that she be remembered in the celebration of rites at the altar. This was obviously an old woman's request, which the son did not test by the norm of Scripture; but he wished to be approved by others for his natural affection.[25] Moreover, the book *The Care to Be Taken for the Dead,* composed by him, contains so many doubts that by its coldness it ought rightly to extinguish the heat of foolish zeal on the part of anyone who desires to be an intercessor for the dead; with its cold conjectures, to be sure, this treatise will render careless those who previously were careful.[26] Its only support for the practice is that this office of prayers for the dead is not to be despised, for the custom has been prevalent.

But, though I concede to the ancient writers of the church that it seemed a pious act to help the dead, we ought ever to keep the rule that cannot deceive: that it is not lawful to interject anything of our own in our prayers. But our requests ought to be subjected to the Word of God; for it is within his decision to prescribe what he wills to be asked. Now, since the entire law and gospel do not furnish so much as a single syllable of leave to pray for the dead, it is to profane the invocation of God to attempt more than he has bidden us.

cBut, lest our adversaries boast that the ancient church is, as it were, their partner in error, I say that there is a wide difference. The ancients did it in memory of the dead, lest they should seem to have cast away all concern for them. But at the same time they confessed that they were in doubt regarding the state of the dead. About purgatory they were so noncommittal that they considered it as a thing uncertain. Our present adversaries demand that what they have dreamed up concerning purgatory be held without question as an article of faith. The ancients rarely and only perfunctorily commended their dead to God in the communion of the Sacred Supper. The moderns zealously press the care of the dead, and with importunate preaching cause it to be preferred to all works of love.[27]

dIndeed, it would be not at all difficult for us to bring forth some testimonies of the ancient writers that clearly overthrow all those prayers for the dead then in use. Such a one is the statement of Augustine when he teaches that the resurrection of the flesh

---

[25] Augustine, *Confessions* IX. xi. 27; IX. xiii. 37 (MPL 32. 775, 779 f.; tr. LCC VII. 195, 200).

[26] Augustine, *On Care for the Dead* (MPL 40. 591–610; tr. NPNF III. 539–551). Augustine is negative on benefits to the dead by the living.

[27] Augustine, *Enchiridion* xviii. 69; xxix. 110 (MPL 40. 265, 283 f.; tr. LCC VII. 381, 405); Tertullian, *Exhortation to Chastity* and *On Monogamy,* as cited in note 24, above; Aquinas, *Summa Theol.* III. Suppl. lxxi; Latomus, as cited in note 23, above; Paris Faculty of Theology, *Instruction on the Articles of Melanchthon* (1535), art. 12, in Daniel Gerdesius, *Historia reformationis sive annales evangelii seculo XVI* IV. 86.

and everlasting glory are awaited by all, but that every man when he dies receives the rest that follows death if he is worthy of it. Therefore, he bears witness that all godly men, no less than prophets, apostles, and martyrs, immediately after death enjoy blessed repose.[28] If such is their condition, what, I beg of you, will our prayers confer upon them?

ᶜI pass over those grosser superstitions with which they have bewitched the simple-minded; although these are innumerable, and for the most part so monstrous that no color of decency can be given to them. I am also silent upon those utterly base traffickings which, in view of the world's great ignorance, they have in their lust carried on. For there would never be an end; and without an enumeration of them my good readers will have enough to steady their consciences.

ᶜCHAPTER VI

THE LIFE OF THE CHRISTIAN MAN; AND FIRST, BY WHAT ARGUMENTS SCRIPTURE URGES US TO IT

1. Plan of the treatise

The object of regeneration, as we have said,[1] is to manifest in the life of believers a harmony and agreement between God's righteousness and their obedience, and thus to confirm the adoption that they have received as sons [Gal. 4:5; cf. II Peter 1:10].

The law of God contains in itself that newness by which his image can be restored in us. But because our slowness needs many goads and helps, it will be profitable to assemble from various passages of Scripture a pattern for the conduct of life[2] in order that those who heartily repent may not err in their zeal.

Now, ʰin setting forth how the life of a Christian man is to be ordered, I am not unaware that I am entering into a varied and diverse subject, which in magnitude would occupy a large volume, were I to try to treat it in full detail. In composing exhortations on but a single virtue, the ancient doctors, as we see, became very prolix. Yet in this they waste no words. For when a man sets out to commend any one virtue in his discourse, abundance of material drives him to a style of such fullness that he seems not to

---

[28] Augustine, *John's Gospel* xlix. 10 (MPL 35. 1751; tr. NPNF VII. 273 f.). Cf. Calvin's treatment of the topic in *Psychopannychia* (written 1534; published 1542) (CR V. 177–231; tr. Calvin, *Tracts* I. 419–490).

[1] III. iii. 9. On III. vi–x, see Introduction, pp. xlii, n. 19, and lx, n. 65. Ch. vi is introductory to the four ensuing chapters.

[2] "*Rationem vitae formandae.*"

treat it properly unless he speaks at length. But I do not intend to develop, here, the instruction in living that I am now about to offer to the point of describing individual virtues at length, and of digressing into exhortations. Such may be sought from others' writings, especially from the homilies of the fathers. To show the godly man how he may be directed to a rightly ordered life, and briefly to set down some universal rule with which to determine his duties—this will be quite enough for me. Perhaps there will be opportunity for declamations, ᶜor I may turn over to others the tasks for which I am not so well suited. By nature I love brevity;³ and perhaps if I wished to speak more amply it would not be successful. But though a more extended form of teaching were highly acceptable, I would nevertheless scarcely care to undertake it. ᵇMoreover, the plan of the present work demands that we give a simple outline of doctrine as briefly as possible.

As philosophers have fixed limits of the right and the honorable, whence they derive individual duties and the whole company of virtues, so Scripture is not without its own order in this matter, but holds to a most beautiful dispensation, and one much more certain than all the philosophical ones. The only difference is that they, as they were ambitious men, diligently strove to attain an exquisite clarity of order to show the nimbleness of their wit. But the Spirit of God, because he taught without affectation, did not adhere so exactly or continuously to a methodical plan; yet when he lays one down anywhere he hints enough that it is not to be neglected by us.

2. Motives for the Christian life

ᵇNow this Scriptural instruction of which we speak has two main aspects. The first is that the love of righteousness, to which we are otherwise not at all inclined by nature, may be instilled and established in our hearts; the second, that a rule be set forth for us that does not let us wander about in our zeal for righteousness.

There are in Scripture very many and excellent reasons for commending righteousness, not a few of which we have already noted in various places. And we shall briefly touch upon still others here. From what foundation may righteousness better arise than from the Scriptural warning that we must be made holy because our God is holy? [Lev. 19:2; I Peter 1:15–16]. Indeed, though we had been dispersed like stray sheep and scattered through the labyrinth of the world,⁴ he has gathered us together

---

³ See the discussion of this point in the Introduction, pp. lxx f.

⁴ "Per mundi labyrinthum." Cf. I. v. 12, note 36.

again to join us with himself. When we hear mention of our union with God, let us remember that holiness must be its bond; not because we come into communion with him by virtue of our holiness! Rather, we ought first to cleave unto him so that, infused with his holiness, we may follow whither he calls. But since it is especially characteristic of his glory that he have no fellowship with wickedness and uncleanness, Scripture accordingly teaches that this is the goal of our calling to which we must ever look if we would answer God when he calls [Isa. 35:8, etc.]. For to what purpose are we rescued from the wickedness and pollution of the world in which we were submerged if we allow ourselves throughout life to wallow in these? Moreover, at the same time Scripture admonishes us that to be reckoned among the people of the Lord we must dwell in the holy city of Jerusalem [cf. Ps. 116:19; 122:2–9]. As he has consecrated this city to himself, it is unlawful to profane it with the impurity of its inhabitants. Whence these declarations: there will be a place in God's Tabernacle for those who walk without blemish and strive after righteousness [Ps. 15:1–2; cf. Ps. 14:1–2, Vg.; cf. also Ps. 24:3–4]. ᵉFor it is highly unfitting that the sanctuary in which he dwells should like a stable be crammed with filth.

3. The Christian life receives its strongest motive to God's work through the person and redemptive act of Christ
ᵇAnd to wake us more effectively, Scripture shows that God the Father, as he has reconciled us to himself in his Christ [cf. II Cor. 5:18], has in him stamped for us the likeness [cf. Heb. 1:3] to which he would have us conform. Now, let these persons who think that moral philosophy is duly and systematically set forth solely among philosophers find me among the philosophers a more excellent dispensation. They, while they wish particularly to exhort us to virtue, announce merely that we should live in accordance with nature.[5] But Scripture draws its exhortation from the true fountain. It not only enjoins us to refer our life to God, its author, to whom it is bound; but after it has taught that we have degenerated from the true origin and condition of our creation, it also adds that Christ, through whom we return into favor with God, has been set before us as an example, whose pattern we ought to express in our life. What more effective thing can you require than this one thing? Nay, what can you require

---

[5] Cicero, *On Duties* III. iii. 13 (LCL edition, pp. 280 f.); *De finibus* II. xi. 34; III. vii. 26; IV. xv. 41 (LCL edition, pp. 120 f., 245 f., 344 ff.); Seneca, *On the Happy Life* viii. 2 (LCL Seneca, *Moral Essays* II. 116 f.): "To live happily is to live according to nature."

beyond this one thing? For we have been adopted as sons by the Lord with this one condition: that our life express Christ, the bond of our adoption. Accordingly, unless we give and devote ourselves to righteousness, we not only revolt from our Creator with wicked perfidy but we also abjure our Savior himself.

Then the Scripture finds occasion for exhortation in all the benefits of God that it lists for us, and in the individual parts of our salvation. Ever since God revealed himself Father to us, we must prove our ungratefulness to him if we did not in turn show ourselves his sons [Mal. 1:6; Eph. 5:1; I John 3:1]. Ever since Christ cleansed us with the washing of his blood, and imparted this cleansing through baptism, it would be unfitting to befoul ourselves with new pollutions [Eph. 5:26; Heb. 10:10; I Cor. 6:11; I Peter 1:15,19]. Ever since he engrafted us into his body, we must take especial care not to disfigure ourselves, who are his members, with any spot or blemish [Eph. 5:23–33; I Cor. 6:15; John 15:3–6]. Ever since Christ himself, who is our Head, ascended into heaven, it behooves us, having laid aside love of earthly things, wholeheartedly to aspire heavenward [Col. 3:1 ff.]. Ever since the Holy Spirit dedicated us as temples to God, we must take care that God's glory shine through us, and must not commit anything to defile ourselves with the filthiness of sin [I Cor. 3:16; 6:19; II Cor. 6:16]. Ever since both our souls and bodies were destined for heavenly incorruption and an unfading crown [I Peter 5:4], we ought to strive manfully to keep them pure and uncorrupted until the Day of the Lord [I Thess. 5:23; cf. Phil. 1:10]. These, I say, are the most auspicious foundations upon which to establish one's life. One would look in vain for the like of these among the philosophers, who, in their commendation of virtue, never rise above the natural dignity of man.[6]

*4. The Christian life is not a matter of the tongue but of the inmost heart**

ᵇAnd this is the place to upbraid those who, having nothing but the name and badge of Christ, yet wish to call themselves "Christians." Yet, how shamelessly do they boast of his sacred name? Indeed, there is no intercourse with Christ save for those who have perceived the right understanding of Christ from the word of the gospel. Yet the apostle says that all those who were not taught that they must put on him have not rightly learned Christ, as they have not put off the old man, who is corrupt through deceptive desires [Eph. 4:22,24]. Therefore, it is proved that they

---

[6] Cicero, *De finibus* II. xxi. 68; II. xxiii. 76 (LCL edition, pp. 156 f., 164 ff.); Seneca, *Moral Epistles* lxxxiv. 13 (LCL Seneca, III. 284 f.).

have falsely, and also unjustly, pretended the knowledge of Christ, whatever they meanwhile learnedly and volubly prate about the gospel. For it is a doctrine not of the tongue but of life. It is not apprehended by the understanding and memory alone, as other disciplines are, but it is received only when it possesses the whole soul, and finds a seat and resting place in the inmost affection of the heart.[7] Accordingly, either let them cease to boast of what they are not, in contempt of God; or let them show themselves disciples not unworthy of Christ their teacher. We have given the first place to the doctrine in which our religion is contained, since our salvation begins with it. But it must enter our heart and pass into our daily living, and so transform us into itself that it may not be unfruitful for us. The philosophers rightly burn with anger against, and reproachfully drive from their flock, those who when they profess an art that ought to be the mistress of life, turn it into sophistical chatter.[8] With how much better reason, then, shall we detest these trifling Sophists who are content to roll the gospel on the tips of their tongues when its efficacy ought to penetrate the inmost affections of the heart, take its seat in the soul, and affect the whole man a hundred times more deeply than the cold exhortations of the philosophers!

5. Imperfection and endeavor of the Christian life

[b]I do not insist that the moral life of a Christian man breathe nothing but the very gospel, yet this ought to be desired, and we must strive toward it. But I do not so strictly demand evangelical perfection that I would not acknowledge as a Christian one who has not yet attained it. For thus all would be excluded from the church, since no one is found who is not far removed from it, while many have advanced a little toward it whom it would nevertheless be unjust to cast away.

What then? Let that target be set before our eyes at which we are earnestly to aim. Let that goal be appointed toward which we should strive and struggle. For it is not lawful for you to divide things with God in such a manner that you undertake part of those things which are enjoined upon you by his Word but omit part, according to your own judgment. For in the first place, he everywhere commends integrity as the chief part of worshiping him [Gen. 17:1; Ps. 41:12; etc.]. By this word he means a sincere simplicity of mind, free from guile and feigning, the opposite of a double heart. [e]It is as if it were said that the beginning of

[7] Cf. III. ii. 36, note 52.
[8] Seneca, *Moral Epistles* cviii. 23; xlviii. 4, 12 (LCL Seneca, III. 244; I. 316 f., 320 f.).

right living is spiritual, where the inner feeling of the mind is unfeignedly dedicated to God for the cultivation of holiness and righteousness.

ᵇBut no one in this earthly prison of the body⁹ has sufficient strength to press on with due eagerness, and weakness so weighs down the greater number that, with wavering and limping and even creeping along the ground, they move at a feeble rate. Let each one of us, then, proceed according to the measure of his puny capacity and set out upon the journey we have begun. No one shall set out so inauspiciously as not daily to make some headway, though it be slight. Therefore, let us not cease so to act that we may make some unceasing progress in the way of the Lord. And let us not despair at the slightness of our success; for even though attainment may not correspond to desire, when today outstrips yesterday the effort is not lost. Only let us look toward our mark with sincere simplicity and aspire to our goal; not fondly flattering ourselves, nor excusing our own evil deeds, but with continuous effort striving toward this end: that we may surpass ourselves in goodness until we attain to goodness itself. It is this, indeed, which through the whole course of life we seek and follow. But we shall attain it only when we have cast off the weakness of the body, and are received into full fellowship with him.

ᶜCHAPTER VII

THE SUM OF THE CHRISTIAN LIFE: THE DENIAL OF OURSELVES

(*The Christian philosophy of unworldliness and self-denial; we are not our own, we are God's, 1–3*)

1. We are not our own masters, but belong to God

ᵇEven though the law of the Lord provides the finest and best-disposed method of ordering a man's life, it seemed good to the Heavenly Teacher to shape his people by an even more explicit plan to that rule which he had set forth in the law. Here, then, is the beginning of this plan: the duty of believers is "to present their bodies to God as a living sacrifice, holy and acceptable to him," and in this consists the lawful worship of him [Rom. 12:1]. From this is derived the basis of the exhortation that "they be not conformed to the fashion of this world, but be transformed by the renewal of their minds, so that they may prove what is the

---

⁹ "*In terreno hoc corporis carcere.*" Cf. III. ix. 4, note 7, and III. xxv. 1, "*carnis ergastulo inclusi.*" The notion of the body as prison of the soul is from Plato: cf. *Phaedo* 62 B, 81 E, 82 E, 83 A; *Cratylus* 400 (LCL Plato I. 216 f., 284 f., 288 ff.; Plato VI. 62 f.).

will of God" [Rom. 12:2]. Now the great thing is this: we are consecrated and dedicated to God in order that we may thereafter think, speak, meditate, and do, nothing except to his glory. For a sacred thing may not be applied to profane uses without marked injury to him.

If we, then, are not our own [cf. I Cor. 6:19] but the Lord's, it is clear what error we must flee, and whither we must direct all the acts of our life.

We are not our own: let not our reason nor our will, therefore, sway our plans and deeds. We are not our own: let us therefore not set it as our goal to seek what is expedient for us according to the flesh. We are not our own: in so far as we can, let us therefore forget ourselves and all that is ours.

Conversely, we are God's: let us therefore live for him and die for him. We are God's: let his wisdom and will therefore rule all our actions. We are God's: let all the parts of our life accordingly strive toward him as our only lawful goal [Rom. 14:8; cf. I Cor. 6:19]. O, how much has that man profited who, having been taught that he is not his own, has taken away dominion and rule from his own reason that he may yield it to God! For, as consulting our self-interest is the pestilence that most effectively leads to our destruction, so the sole haven of salvation is to be wise in nothing and to will nothing through ourselves but to follow the leading of the Lord alone.

Let this therefore be the first step, that a man depart from himself in order that he may apply the whole force of his ability in the service of the Lord. I call "service" not only what lies in obedience to God's Word but what turns the mind of man, empty of its own carnal sense, wholly to the bidding of God's Spirit. While it is the first entrance to life, all philosophers were ignorant of this transformation, which Paul calls "renewal of the mind" [Eph. 4:23]. For they set up reason alone as the ruling principle in man, and think that it alone should be listened to; to it alone, in short, they entrust the conduct of life. But the Christian philosophy[1] bids reason give way to, submit and subject itself to, the Holy Spirit so that the man himself may no longer live but hear Christ living and reigning within him [Gal. 2:20].

2. Self-denial through devotion to God

[b]From this also follows this second point: that we seek not the things that are ours but those which are of the Lord's will and

---

[1] The impressive sentences above, beginning, "We are not our own," add substance to Calvin's concept of "the Christian philosophy." Cf. p. 6, note 8; III. viii. 9, note 7.

will serve to advance his glory. This is also evidence of great progress: that, almost forgetful of ourselves, surely subordinating our self-concern, we try faithfully to devote our zeal to God and his commandments. For when Scripture bids us leave off self-concern, it not only erases from our minds the yearning to possess, the desire for power, and the favor of men, but it also uproots ambition and all craving for human glory and other more secret plagues. Accordingly, the Christian must surely be so disposed and minded that he feels within himself it is with God he has to deal throughout his life.[2] In this way, as he will refer all he has to God's decision and judgment, so will he refer his whole intention of mind scrupulously to Him. For he who has learned to look to God in all things that he must do, at the same time avoids all vain thoughts. This, then, is that denial of self which Christ enjoins with such great earnestness upon his disciples at the outset of their service [cf. Matt. 16:24]. When it has once taken possession of their hearts, it leaves no place at all first either to pride, or arrogance, or ostentation; then either to avarice, or desire, or lasciviousness, or effeminacy, or to other evils that our self-love spawns [cf. II Tim. 3:2–5]. On the other hand, wherever denial of ourselves does not reign, there either the foulest vices rage without shame or if there is any semblance of virtue, it is vitiated by depraved lusting after glory. Show me a man, if you can, who, unless he has according to the commandment of the Lord renounced himself, would freely exercise goodness among men. For all who have not been possessed with this feeling have at least followed virtue for the sake of praise. Now those of the philosophers who at any time most strongly contended that virtue should be pursued for its own sake[3] were puffed up with such great arrogance as to show they sought after virtue for no other reason than to have occasion for pride. Yet God is so displeased, both with those who court the popular breeze[4] and with such swollen souls, as to declare that they have received their reward in this world [Matt. 6:2,5,16], and to make harlots and publicans nearer to the Kingdom of Heaven than are they [Matt. 21:31]. Yet we

---

[2] Cf. I. xvii. 2, note 2.

[3] Cicero, *De finibus* III. xi. 36: "Nothing else than moral worth is to be counted as a good" (LCL edition, pp. 254 f.); *De legibus* I. xiv. 40 (LCL edition, *Laws, and Republic*, pp. 340 f.); Seneca, *Dialogues* VII. ix. 4 (LCL Seneca, *Moral Essays* II. 122 f.); Diogenes Laertius, *Lives and Opinions of the Philosophers* VII. lxxxix. 127 (LCL edition, II. 196 f.). Cf. Lactantius, *Divine Institutes* V. xvii. 16 (CSEL 19. 454; MPL 6 [ch. xviii]. 606; tr. ANF VII. 153).

[4] From Livy, *History* III. xxxiii. 7 (LCL Livy, II. 110). Among numerous references to man's vainglory and pride, see I. i. 2; I. iii. 1 (end); II. i. 4; III. xiii. 1.

have still not clearly explained how many and how great are the obstacles that hinder man from a right course so long as he has not denied himself. For it was once truly said: "A world of vices is hidden in the soul of man."[5] And you can find no other remedy than in denying yourself and giving up concern for yourself, and in turning your mind wholly to seek after those things which the Lord requires of you, and to seek them only because they are pleasing to him.

3. Self-renunciation according to Titus, ch. 2

ᵉIn another place, Paul more clearly, although briefly, delineates the individual parts of a well-ordered life. "The grace of God has appeared, bringing salvation to all men, training us to renounce irreligion and worldly passions and to live sober, upright, and godly lives, in the present age; awaiting our blessed hope, and the appearing of the glory of our great God and of our Savior Jesus Christ, who gave himself for us to redeem us from all iniquity and to purify for himself a people of his own who are zealous for good deeds." [Titus 2:11–14.] For, after he proffered the grace of God to hearten us, in order to pave the way for us to worship God truly he removed the two obstacles that chiefly hinder us: namely, ungodliness, to which by nature we are too much inclined; and second, worldly desires, which extend more widely. And by ungodliness, indeed, he not only means superstition but includes also whatever contends against the earnest fear of God. Worldly lusts are also equivalent to the passions of the flesh [cf. I John 2:16; Eph. 2:3; II Peter 2:18; Gal. 5:16; etc.]. Thus, with reference to both Tables of the Law, he commands us to put off our own nature and to deny whatever our reason and will dictate. Now he limits all actions of life to three parts: soberness, righteousness, and godliness. Of these, soberness doubtless denotes chastity and temperance as well as a pure and frugal use of temporal goods, and patience in poverty. Now righteousness embraces all the duties of equity in order that to each one be rendered what is his own [cf. Rom. 13:7].[6] There follows godliness, which joins us in true holiness with God when we are separated from the iniquities of the world. When these things are joined together by an inseparable bond, they bring about complete perfection. But, nothing is more difficult than, having

---

[5] "Mundum vitiorum esse reconditum in hominis anima."

[6] "Ut reddatur unicuique quod suum est." Cf. Rom. 13:7; III. v. 7, note 16; IV. xx. 3, note 9; Comm. Titus 2:11–14; and Aristotle's fundamental treatment of the relation of justice and equity (ἐπιείκεια), Nicomachean Ethics V. 10 (LCL edition, pp. 312 f.).

bidden farewell to the reason of the flesh and having bridled our desires—nay, having put them away—to devote ourselves to God and our brethren, and to meditate, amid earth's filth, upon the life of the angels. Consequently, Paul, in order to extricate our minds from all snares, recalls us to the hope of blessed immortality, reminding us that we strive not in vain [cf. I Thess. 3:5]. For, as Christ our Redeemer once appeared, so in his final coming he will show the fruit of the salvation brought forth by him. In this way he scatters all the allurements that becloud us and prevent us from aspiring as we ought to heavenly glory. Nay, he teaches us to travel as pilgrims in this world[7] that our celestial heritage may not perish or pass away.

(The principle of self-denial in our relations with our fellow men, 4–7)
4. Self-denial gives us the right attitude toward our fellow men
      ^bNow in these words we perceive that denial of self has regard partly to men, partly, and chiefly, to God.

For when Scripture bids us act toward men so as to esteem them above ourselves [Phil. 2:3], and in good faith to apply ourselves wholly to doing them good [cf. Rom. 12:10], it gives us commandments of which our mind is quite incapable unless our mind be previously emptied of its natural feeling. For, such is the blindness with which we all rush into self-love that each one of us seems to himself to have just cause to be proud of himself and to despise all others in comparison. If God has conferred upon us anything of which we need not repent, relying upon it we immediately lift up our minds, and are not only puffed up but almost burst with pride. The very vices that infest us we take pains to hide from others, while we flatter ourselves with the pretense that they are slight and insignificant, and even sometimes embrace them as virtues. If others manifest the same endowments we admire in ourselves, or even superior ones, we spitefully belittle and revile these gifts in order to avoid yielding place to such persons. If there are any faults in others, not content with noting them with severe and sharp reproach, we hatefully exaggerate them. Hence arises such insolence that each one of us, as if exempt from the common lot, wishes to tower above the rest, and loftily and savagely abuses every mortal man, or at least looks

---

⁷ *"Docet perigrinandum esse in mundo."* Calvin here adopts, without developing in detail, the familiar pilgrimage metaphor as appropriate to the Christian and the church in the world, in preparation for the glory that shall be. Cf. III. ix. 4–5; III. x. 1; Augustine, *City of God* XV. vi (MPL 41. 442; tr. NPNF II. 287).

down upon him as an inferior. The poor yield to the rich; the common folk, to the nobles; the servants, to their masters; the unlearned, to the educated. But there is no one who does not cherish within himself some opinion of his own pre-eminence.

Thus, each individual, by flattering himself, bears a kind of kingdom in his breast.[8] For claiming as his own what pleases him, he censures the character and morals of others. But if this comes to the point of conflict, his venom bursts forth. For many obviously display some gentleness so long as they find everything sweet and pleasant. But just how many are there who will preserve this even tenor of modesty when they are pricked and irritated? There is no other remedy than to tear out from our inward parts this most deadly pestilence of love of strife and love of self,[9] even as it is plucked out by Scriptural teaching. For thus we are instructed to remember that those talents which God has bestowed upon us are not our own goods but the free gifts of God; and any persons who become proud of them show their ungratefulness. e"Who causes you to excel?" Paul asks. "If you have received all things, why do you boast as if they were not given to you?" [I Cor. 4:7].

bLet us, then, unremittingly examining our faults, call ourselves back to humility. Thus nothing will remain in us to puff us up; but there will be much occasion to be cast down. On the other hand, we are bidden so to esteem and regard whatever gifts of God we see in other men that we may honor those men in whom they reside. For it would be great depravity on our part to deprive them of that honor which the Lord has bestowed upon them. But we are taught to overlook their faults, certainly not flatteringly to cherish them; but not on account of such faults to revile men whom we ought to cherish with good will and honor. Thus it will come about that, whatever man we deal with, we shall treat him not only moderately and modestly but also cordially and as a friend. You will never attain true gentleness except by one path: a heart imbued with lowliness and with reverence for others.

---

[8] Cf. sec. 2, above. Calvin adopts the traditional view that pride is the mother of the deadly sins. Cf. I. i. 2: *"ingenita est omnibus nobis superbia"*; II. i. 1 He here rebukes a superiority-conscious and self-sufficient intellectualism, and places under divine judgment such humanist gratification over intellectual gifts as we find in Sir Edward Dyer's well-loved verse (1588):

> My minde to me a kingdom is,
> Such perfect joy therein I finde
> As farre exceeds all earthly blisse
> That God or nature hath assignde.

[9] "τῆς φιλονεικίας καὶ φιλαυτίας."

5. Self-renunciation leads to proper helpfulness toward our neighbors

[b]Now, in seeking to benefit one's neighbor, how difficult it is to do one's duty! Unless you give up all thought of self and, so to speak, get out of yourself, you will accomplish nothing here. For how can you perform those works which Paul teaches to be the works of love, unless you renounce yourself, and give yourself wholly to others? "Love," he says, "is patient and kind, not jealous or boastful, is not envious or puffed up, does not seek its own, is not irritable," etc. [I Cor. 13: 4–5 p.] If this is the one thing required—that we seek not what is our own—still we shall do no little violence to nature, which so inclines us to love of ourselves alone that it does not easily allow us to neglect ourselves and our possessions in order to look after another's good, nay, to yield willingly what is ours by right and resign it to another. But Scripture, to lead us by the hand to this, warns that whatever benefits we obtain from the Lord have been entrusted to us on this condition: that they be applied to the common good of the church. And therefore the lawful use of all benefits consists in a liberal and kindly sharing of them with others. No surer rule and no more valid exhortation to keep it could be devised than when we are taught that all the gifts we possess have been bestowed by God and entrusted to us on condition that they be distributed for our neighbors' benefit [cf. I Peter 4:10].

But Scripture goes even farther by comparing them to the powers with which the members of the human body are endowed [I Cor. 12:12 ff.]. No member has this power for itself nor applies it to its own private use; but each pours it out to the fellow members. Nor does it take any profit from its power except what proceeds from the common advantage of the whole body. So, too, whatever a godly man can do he ought to be able to do for his brothers, providing for himself in no way other than to have his mind intent upon the common upbuilding of the church. Let this, therefore, be our rule for generosity and beneficence: We are the stewards of everything God has conferred on us by which we are able to help our neighbor, and are required to render account of our stewardship. Moreover, the only right stewardship is that which is tested by the rule of love. Thus it will come about that we shall not only join zeal for another's benefit with care for our own advantage, but shall subordinate the latter to the former.

And lest perhaps we should not realize that this is the rule for the proper management of all gifts we have received from God, he also in early times applied it to the least gifts of his generosity. For he commanded that the first fruits be brought to him by which the people were to testify that it was unlawful to accept for themselves any enjoyment of benefits not previously consecrated to him [Ex. 23:19; cf. ch. 22:29, Vg.]. But if the gifts of God are only thus sanctified to us when we have dedicated them by our hand to the Author himself, that which does not savor of such dedication is clearly a corrupt abuse. Yet you wish to strive in vain to enrich the Lord by sharing your possessions; since, then, your generosity cannot extend to him, you must, as the prophet says, practice it toward the saints on earth [Ps. 16:2–3]. ᵉAnd alms are compared to holy sacrifices so as to correspond now to those requirements of the law [Heb. 13:16].

6. Love of neighbor is not dependent upon manner of men but looks to God

ᵇFurthermore, not to grow weary in well-doing [Gal. 6:9], which otherwise must happen immediately, we ought to add that other idea which the apostle mentions: "Love is patient . . . and is not irritable" [I Cor. 13:4–5]. The Lord commands all men without exception "to do good" [Heb. 13:16]. Yet the great part of them are most unworthy if they be judged by their own merit. But here Scripture helps in the best way when it teaches that we are not to consider that men merit of themselves but to look upon the image of God in all men, to which we owe all honor and love. However, it is among members of the household of faith that this same image is more carefully to be noted [Gal. 6:10], in so far as it has been renewed and restored through the Spirit of Christ. Therefore, whatever man you meet who needs your aid, you have no reason to refuse to help him. Say, "He is a stranger"; but the Lord has given him a mark that ought to be familiar to you, ᵉby virtue of the fact that he forbids you to despise your own flesh [Isa. 58:7, Vg.]. ᵇSay, "He is contemptible and worthless"; but the Lord shows him to be one to whom he has deigned to give the beauty of his image. Say that you owe nothing for any service of his; but God, as it were, has put him in his own place in order that you may recognize toward him the many and great benefits with which God has bound you to himself. Say that he does not deserve even your least effort for his sake; but the image of God, which recommends him to you, is worthy of your giving yourself and all your possessions. Now if he has not only deserved no good at your hand, but has also provoked you by unjust acts and curses, not even this is just reason why you should cease to embrace him in love and to perform the duties of love on his behalf [Matt. 6:14; 18:35; Luke 17:3]. You will say, "He has deserved something far different of me." Yet what has the

Lord deserved? While he bids you forgive this man for all sins he has committed against you, he would truly have them charged against himself. Assuredly there is but one way in which to achieve what is not merely difficult but utterly against human nature: to love those who hate us, to repay their evil deeds with benefits, to return blessings for reproaches [Matt. 5:44]. It is that we remember not to consider men's evil intention but to look upon the image of God in them,[10] which cancels and effaces their transgressions, and with its beauty and dignity allures us to love and embrace them.

7. *The outward work of love is not sufficient, but it is intention that counts!*[†]

ᵇThis mortification, then, will take place in us only if we fulfill the duties of love. Now he who merely performs all the duties of love does not fulfill them, even though he overlooks none; but he, rather, fulfills them who does this from a sincere feeling of love. For it can happen that one who indeed discharges to the full all his obligations as far as outward duties are concerned is still all the while far away from the true way of discharging them. For you may see some who wish to seem very liberal and yet bestow nothing that they do not make reprehensible with a proud countenance or even insolent words. And in this tragic and unhappy age it has come to this pass, that most men give their alms contemptuously. Such depravity ought not to have been tolerable even among the pagans; of Christians something even more is required than to show a cheerful countenance and to render their duties pleasing with friendly words. First, they must put themselves in the place of him whom they see in need of their assistance, and pity his ill fortune as if they themselves experienced and bore it, so that they may be impelled by a feeling of mercy and humaneness to go to his aid just as to their own.

He who, thus disposed, proceeds to give help to his brethren will not corrupt his own duties by either arrogance or upbraiding. Furthermore, in giving benefits he will not despise his needy brother or enslave him as one indebted to himself. This would no

10 Cf. "the image of God in all men," above, and I. xv. 3–4, where (sec. 3) the image of God in man includes all things in which man excels other animals and (sec. 4) has not been utterly destroyed through Adam's sin. Cf. II. viii. 45. Further illustration from Calvin's writings of the obligation to others involved in their participation in the image of God may be found in W. Kolfhaus, *Vom christlichen Leben nach Johannes Calvin*, pp. 328 ff.; R. S. Wallace, *Calvin's Doctrine of the Christian Life*, pp. 150 ff. Bucer had argued similarly in *Das ihm selbs niemant sonder anderen leben soll . . .* (1523); tr. P. T. Fuhrmann, *Instruction in Christian Love*, p. 29.

more be reasonable than that we should either chide a sick member that the rest of the body labors to revive or consider it especially obligated to the remaining members because it has drawn more help to itself than it can repay. Now the sharing of tasks among members is believed to have nothing gratuitous about it but, rather, to be a payment of that which, due by the law of nature,[11] it would be monstrous to refuse. Also, in this way it will come about that he who has discharged one kind of task will not think himself free, as commonly happens when a rich man, after he has given up something of his own, delegates to other men other burdens as having nothing at all to do with him. Rather, each man will so consider with himself that in all his greatness he is a debtor to his neighbors, and that he ought in exercising kindness toward them to set no other limit than the end of his resources; these, as widely as they are extended, ought to have their limits set according to the rule of love.

(*The principle of self-denial in our relation to God, 8–10*)
8. *Self-denial toward God: devotion to his will!*
    ᵇLet us reiterate in fuller form the chief part of self-denial, which, as we have said, looks to God. And indeed, many things have been said about this already that it would be superfluous to repeat. It will be enough to show how it forms us to fair-mindedness and tolerance.

To begin with, then, in seeking either the convenience or the tranquillity of the present life, Scripture calls us to resign ourselves and all our possessions to the Lord's will, and to yield to him the desires of our hearts to be tamed and subjugated. To covet wealth and honors, to strive for authority, to heap up riches, to gather together all those follies which seem to make for magnificence and pomp, our lust is mad, our desire boundless. On the other hand, wonderful is our fear, wonderful our hatred, of poverty, lowly birth, and humble condition! And we are spurred to rid ourselves of them by every means. Hence we can see how uneasy in mind all those persons are who order their lives according to their own plan. We can see how artfully they strive—to the point of weariness—to obtain the goal of their ambition or avarice, while, on the other hand, avoiding poverty and a lowly condition.

In order not to be caught in such snares, godly men must hold

---

[11] *"Naturae lege."* In this section, Calvin brings together Christian charity and natural law. Cf. Seneca's recognition that we are born to help each other: *"Homo in adiutorum mutuum genitus est." De ira* I. v. 2 (LCL Seneca, *Moral Essays* I. 118 f.).

to this path. First of all, let them neither desire nor hope for, nor contemplate, any other way of prospering than by the Lord's blessing.[12] Upon this, then, let them safely and confidently throw themselves and rest. For however beautifully the flesh may seem to suffice unto itself, while it either strives by its own effort for honors and riches or relies upon its diligence, or is aided by the favor of men, yet it is certain that all these things are nothing; nor will we benefit at all, either by skill or by labor, except in so far as the Lord prospers them both. On the contrary, however, his blessing alone finds a way, even through all hindrances, to bring all things to a happy and favorable outcome for us; again, though entirely without it, to enable us to obtain some glory and opulence for ourselves (as we daily see impious men amassing great honors and riches),[13] yet, inasmuch as those upon whom the curse of God rests taste not even the least particle of happiness, without this blessing we shall obtain nothing but what turns to our misfortune. For we ought by no means to desire what makes men more miserable.

9. Trust in God's blessing only

ᵇTherefore, suppose we believe that every means toward a prosperous and desirable outcome rests upon the blessing of God alone; and that, when this is absent, all sorts of misery and calamity dog us. It remains for us not greedily to strive after riches and honors—whether relying upon our own dexterity of wit or our own diligence, or depending upon the favor of men, or having confidence in vainly imagined fortune—but for us always to look to the Lord so that by his guidance we may be led to whatever lot he has provided for us. Thus it will first come to pass that we shall not dash out to seize upon riches and usurp honors through wickedness and by stratagems and evil arts, or greed, to the injury of our neighbors; but pursue only those enterprises which do not lead us away from innocence.

Who can hope for the help of a divine blessing amidst frauds, robberies, and other wicked arts? For as that blessing follows only him who thinks purely and acts rightly, thus it calls back from crooked thoughts and wicked actions all those who seek it. Then will a bridle be put on us that we may not burn with an immoderate desire to grow rich or ambitiously pant after honors. For with what shamelessness does a man trust that he will be

[12] Sections 8 and 9 present what is a frequent theme in Calvin. A worldly prosperity may be attained in forgetfulness of God, but it is accursed. Poverty with piety is an incomparably happier state. Cf. II. x. 12, note 11; III. xx. 46.
[13] Cf. I. xvii. 10; III. ix. 6; III. x. 5.

helped by God to obtain those things which he desires contrary to God's Word? Away with the thought that God would abet with his blessing what he curses with his mouth! Lastly, if things do not go according to our wish and hope, we will still be restrained from impatience and loathing of our condition, whatever it may be. For we shall know that this is to murmur against God, by whose will riches and poverty, contempt and honor, are dispensed. To sum up, he who rests solely upon the blessing of God, as it has been here expressed, will neither strive with evil arts after those things which men customarily madly seek after, which he realizes will not profit him, nor will he, if things go well, give credit to himself or even to his diligence, or industry, or fortune. Rather, he will give God the credit as its Author. But if, while other men's affairs flourish, he makes but slight advancement, or even slips back, he will still bear his low estate with greater equanimity and moderation of mind than some profane person would bear a moderate success which merely does not correspond with his wish. For he indeed possesses a solace in which he may repose more peacefully than in the highest degree of wealth or power. Since this leads to his salvation, he considers that his affairs are ordained by the Lord. ᵉWe see that David was so minded; while he follows God and gives himself over to his leading, he attests that he is like a child weaned from his mother's breast, and that he does not occupy himself with things too deep and wonderful for him [Ps. 131:1–2].

10. Self-denial helps us bear adversity
ᵇAnd for godly minds the peace and forbearance we have spoken of ought not to rest solely in this point; but it must also be extended to every occurrence to which the present life is subject. Therefore, he alone has duly denied himself who has so totally resigned himself to the Lord that he permits every part of his life to be governed by God's will. He who will be thus composed in mind, whatever happens, will not consider himself miserable nor complain of his lot with ill will toward God. How necessary this disposition is will appear if you weigh the many chance happenings to which we are subject. Various diseases repeatedly trouble us: now plague rages; now we are cruelly beset by the calamities of war; now ice and hail, consuming the year's expectation, lead to barrenness, which reduces us to poverty; wife, parents, children, neighbors, are snatched away by death; our house is burned by fire. It is on account of these occurrences that men curse their life, loathe the day of their birth, abominate heaven and the light of day, rail against God, and as they are eloquent in

blasphemy, accuse him of injustice and cruelty. But in these matters the believer must also look to God's kindness and truly fatherly indulgence. Accordingly, if he sees his house reduced to solitude by the removal of his kinsfolk, he will not indeed even then cease to bless the Lord, but rather will turn his attention to this thought: nevertheless, the grace of the Lord, which dwells in my house, will not leave it desolate. Or, if his crops are blasted by frost, or destroyed by ice, or beaten down with hail, and he sees famine threatening, yet he will not despair or bear a grudge against God, but will remain firm in this trust [cf. Ps. 78:47]: "Nevertheless we are in the Lord's protection, sheep brought up in his pastures" [Ps. 79:13]. The Lord will therefore supply food to us even in extreme barrenness. If he shall be afflicted by disease, he will not even then be so unmanned by the harshness of pain as to break forth into impatience and expostulate with God; but, by considering the righteousness and gentleness of God's chastening, he will recall himself to forbearance. In short, whatever happens, because he will know it ordained of God, he will undergo it with a peaceful and grateful mind so as not obstinately to resist the command of him into whose power he once for all surrendered himself and his every possession.

Especially let that foolish and most miserable consolation of the pagans be far away from the breast of the Christian man; to strengthen their minds against adversities, they charged these to fortune.[14] Against fortune they considered it foolish to be angry because she was blind[15] and unthinking, with unseeing eyes wounding the deserving and the undeserving at the same time.[16] On the contrary, the rule of piety is that God's hand alone is the judge and governor of fortune, good or bad, and that it does not rush about with heedless force, but with most orderly justice deals out good as well as ill to us.

[14] Cf. I. v. 4

[15] "ἄσκοπος."

[16] In his essay, On Tranquillity of Mind viii–xi, Seneca, without introducing religion, recommends fortitude in response to the mutability of fortune. In Moral Epistles cvii. 7, he writes: "Fortiter fortuita patiemur." However, in Epistles lxxvi. 23 he speaks similarly of what has happened "by divine law" (LCL Seneca, Moral Essays II. 240–262; Epistulae morales III. 226; II. 160 f.).

ᵉCHAPTER VIII

BEARING THE CROSS, A PART OF SELF-DENIAL

(*We are to take up our cross, as followers of Christ, 1–2*)
1. Christ's cross and ours

ᵇBut it behooves the godly mind to climb still higher, to the height to which Christ calls his disciples: that each must bear his own cross [Matt. 16:24]. For whomever the Lord has adopted and deemed worthy of his fellowship ought to prepare themselves for a hard, toilsome, and unquiet life, crammed with very many and various kinds of evil. It is the Heavenly Father's will thus to exercise them so as to put his own children to a definite test. Beginning with Christ, his first-born, he follows this plan with all his children. For even though that Son was beloved above the rest, and in him the Father's mind was well pleased [Matt. 3:17 and 17:5], yet we see that far from being treated indulgently or softly, to speak the truth, while he dwelt on earth he was not only tried by a perpetual cross but his whole life was nothing but a sort of perpetual cross. ᵉThe apostle notes the reason: that it behooved him to "learn obedience through what he suffered" [Heb. 5:8].

ᵇWhy should we exempt ourselves, therefore, from the condition to which Christ our Head had to submit, especially since he submitted to it for our sake to show us an example of patience in himself? Therefore, the apostle teaches that God has destined all his children to the end that they be conformed to Christ [Rom. 8:29]. Hence also in harsh and difficult conditions, regarded as adverse and evil, a great comfort comes to us: we share Christ's sufferings in order that as he has passed from a labyrinth of all evils into heavenly glory, we may in like manner be led through various tribulations to the same glory [Acts 14:22]. So Paul himself elsewhere states: when we come to know the sharing of his sufferings, we at the same time grasp the power of his resurrection; and when we become like him in his death, we are thus made ready to share his glorious resurrection [Phil. 3:10–11]. How much can it do to soften all the bitterness of the cross, that the more we are afflicted with adversities, the more surely our fellowship with Christ is confirmed! By communion with him the very sufferings themselves not only become blessed to us but also help much in promoting our salvation.

2. *The cross leads us to perfect trust in God's power*

[b]Besides this, our Lord had no need to undertake the bearing of the cross except to attest and prove his obedience to the Father. But as for us, there are many reasons why we must pass our lives under a continual cross. First, as we are by nature too inclined to attribute everything to our flesh—unless our feebleness be shown, as it were, to our eyes—we readily esteem our virtue above its due measure. And we do not doubt, whatever happens, that against all difficulties it will remain unbroken and unconquered. Hence we are lifted up into stupid and empty confidence in the flesh; and relying on it, we are then insolently proud against God himself, as if our own powers were sufficient without his grace.

He can best restrain this arrogance when he proves to us by experience not only the great incapacity but also the frailty under which we labor. Therefore, he afflicts us either with disgrace or poverty, or bereavement, or disease, or other calamities. Utterly unequal to bearing these, in so far as they touch us, we soon succumb to them. Thus humbled, we learn to call upon his power, which alone makes us stand fast under the weight of afflictions. But even the most holy persons, however much they may recognize that they stand not through their own strength but through God's grace, are too sure of their own fortitude and constancy unless by the testing of the cross he bring them into a deeper knowledge of himself. [e]This complacency even stole upon David: "In my tranquillity I said, 'I shall never be moved.' O Jehovah, by thy favor thou hadst established strength for my mountain; thou didst hide thy face, I was dismayed" [Ps. 30:6–7].[1] For he confesses that in prosperity his senses had been so benumbed with sluggishness that, neglecting God's grace, upon which he ought to have depended, he so relied upon himself as to promise himself he could ever stand fast. If this happened to so great a prophet, what one of us should not be afraid and take care?

[b]In peaceful times, then, they preened themselves on their great constancy and patience, only to learn when humbled by adversity that all this was hypocrisy. Believers, warned, I say, by such proofs of their diseases, advance toward humility and so, sloughing off perverse confidence in the flesh, betake themselves to God's grace. Now when they have betaken themselves there they experience the presence of a divine power in which they have protection enough and to spare.

[1] Cf. Comm. Ps. 30:5, 7.

(This is needful to teach us patience and obedience, 3–6)

3. The cross permits us to experience God's faithfulness and gives us hope for the future

bAnd this is what Paul teaches: "Tribulations produce patience; and patience, tried character" [Rom. 5:3–4, cf. Vg.]. That God has promised to be with believers in tribulation [cf. II Cor. 1:4] they experience to be true, while, supported by his hand, they patiently endure—an endurance quite unattainable by their own effort. The saints, therefore, through forbearance experience the fact that God, when there is need, provides the assistance that he has promised. Thence, also, is their hope strengthened, inasmuch as it would be the height of ingratitude not to expect that in time to come God's truthfulness will be as constant and firm as they have already experienced it to be. Now we see how many good things, interwoven, spring from the cross. For, overturning that good opinion which we falsely entertain concerning our own strength, and unmasking our hypocrisy, which affords us delight, the cross strikes at our perilous confidence in the flesh. It teaches us, thus humbled, to rest upon God alone, with the result that we do not faint or yield. Hope, moreover, follows victory in so far as the Lord, by performing what he has promised, establishes his truth for the time to come. Even if these were the only reasons, it plainly appears how much we need the practice of bearing the cross.[2]

And it is of no slight importance for you to be cleansed of your blind love of self that you may be made more nearly aware of your incapacity; to feel your own incapacity that you may learn to distrust yourself; to distrust yourself that you may transfer your trust to God; to rest with a trustful heart in God that, relying upon his help, you may persevere unconquered to the end; to take your stand in his grace that you may comprehend the truth of his promises; to have unquestioned certainty of his promises that your hope may thereby be strengthened.

4. The cross trains us to patience and obedience

bThe Lord also has another purpose for afflicting his people: to test their patience and to instruct them to obedience. Not that they can manifest any other obedience to him save what he has given them. But it so pleases him by unmistakable proofs to make manifest and clear the graces which he has conferred upon the saints, that these may not lie idle, hidden within. Therefore, by bringing into the open the power and constancy to forbear, with

---

[2] Cf. Luther, *Fourteen Comforts* (1520) i. 7 (*Werke* WA VI. 110; tr. B. L. Woolf, *Reformation Writings of Martin Luther* II. 43).

which he has endowed his servants, he is said to test their patience. From this arise those expressions: that God tried Abraham, and proved his piety from the fact that he did not refuse to sacrifice his one and only son [Gen. 22:1,12]. Therefore, Peter likewise teaches that our faith is proved by tribulations as gold is tested in a fiery furnace [I Peter 1:7]. For who would say it is not expedient that the most excellent gift of patience, which the believer has received from his God, be put to use that it may be certain and manifest? Nor will men otherwise ever esteem it as it deserves.

But if God himself does right in providing occasion to stir up those virtues which he has conferred upon his believers in order that they may not be hidden in obscurity—nay, lie useless and pass away—the afflictions of the saints, without which they would have no forbearance, are amply justified. They are also, I assert, instructed by the cross to obey, because thus they are taught to live not according to their own whim but according to God's will. Obviously, if everything went according to their own liking, they would not know what it is to follow God. And Seneca recalls that it was an old proverb, in exhorting any man to endure adversities, to say, "Follow God."[3] By this the ancients hinted, obviously, that a man truly submitted to God's yoke only when he yielded his hand and back to His rod. But if it is most proper that we should prove ourselves obedient to our Heavenly Father in all things, we must surely not refuse to have him accustom us in every way to render obedience to him.

5. The cross as medicine

[b]Still we do not see how necessary this obedience is to us unless we consider at the same time how great is the wanton impulse of our flesh to shake off God's yoke if we even for a moment softly and indulgently treat that impulse. For the same thing happens to it that happens to mettlesome horses. If they are fattened in idleness for some days, they cannot afterward be tamed for their high spirits; nor do they recognize their rider, whose command they previously obeyed. And what God complains of in the Israelites is continually in us: fattened and made flabby, we kick against him who has fed and nourished us [Deut. 32:15]. Indeed, God's beneficence ought to have allured us to esteem and love his goodness. But inasmuch as our ill will is such that we are, instead, repeatedly corrupted by his indulgence, it is most neces-

---

[3] Both Cicero and Seneca introduce the injunction, "Follow God," as an old precept. Cicero, *De finibus* III. xxii. 73 (LCL edition, pp. 292 f.); Seneca, *On the Happy Life* xv. 5 (LCL Seneca, *Moral Essays* II. 138).

sary that we be restrained by some discipline in order that we
may not jump into such wantonness. Thus, lest in the unmeasured abundance of our riches we go wild; lest, puffed up with
honors, we become proud; lest, swollen with other good things—
either of the soul or of the body, or of fortune—we grow haughty,
the Lord himself, according as he sees it expedient, confronts us
and subjects and restrains our unrestrained flesh with the remedy
of the cross. And this he does in various ways in accordance with
what is healthful for each man. For not all of us suffer in equal
degree from the same diseases or, on that account, need the same
harsh cure. From this it is to be seen that some are tried by one
kind of cross, others by another. But since the heavenly physician
treats some more gently but cleanses others by harsher remedies,
while he wills to provide for the health of all, he yet leaves no one
free and untouched, because he knows that all, to a man, are
diseased.

6. The cross as fatherly chastisement

ᵇBesides this, it is needful that our most merciful Father should
not only anticipate our weakness but also often correct past transgressions so that he may keep us in lawful obedience to himself.
Accordingly, whenever we are afflicted, remembrance of our past
life ought immediately to come to mind; so we shall doubtless
find that we have committed something deserving this sort of
chastisement. And yet, exhortation to forbearance is not to be
based principally upon the recognition of sin. For Scripture furnishes a far better conception when it says that the Lord chastens
us by adversities "so that we may not be condemned along with
the world" [I Cor. 11:32]. Therefore, also, in the very harshness
of tribulations we must recognize the kindness and generosity of
our Father toward us, since he does not even then cease to promote
our salvation. For he afflicts us not to ruin or destroy us but,
rather, to free us from the condemnation of the world. That
thought will lead us to what Scripture teaches in another place:
"My son, do not despise the Lord's discipline, or grow weary
when he reproves you. For whom God loves, he rebukes, and embraces as a father his son" [Prov. 3:11–12 p.]. When we recognize
the Father's rod, is it not our duty to show ourselves obedient and
teachable children rather than, in arrogance, to imitate desperate
men who have become hardened in their evil deeds? When we
have fallen away from him, God destroys us unless by reproof he
recalls us. Thus he rightly says that if we are without discipline
we are illegitimate children, not sons [Heb. 12:8]. We are, then,
most perverse if when he declares his benevolence to us and the

care that he takes for our salvation, we cannot bear him. Scripture teaches that this is the difference between unbelievers and believers: the former, like slaves of inveterate and double-dyed wickedness, with chastisement become only worse and more obstinate. But the latter, like freeborn sons, attain repentance. Now you must choose in which group you would prefer to be numbered. But since we have spoken concerning this matter elsewhere,[4] content with a brief reference, I shall stop here.

(Bearing the cross in persecution and other calamities, 7–8)
7. Suffering for righteousness' sake
bNow, to suffer persecution for righteousness' sake is a singular comfort. For it ought to occur to us how much honor God bestows upon us in thus furnishing us with the special badge of his soldiery. I say that not only they who labor for the defense of the gospel but they who in any way maintain the cause of righteousness suffer persecution for righteousness. Therefore, whether in declaring God's truth against Satan's falsehoods or in taking up the protection of the good and the innocent against the wrongs of the wicked, we must undergo the offenses and hatred of the world, which may imperil either our life, our fortunes, or our honor. Let us not grieve or be troubled in thus far devoting our efforts to God, or count ourselves miserable in those matters in which he has with his own lips declared us blessed [Matt. 5:10]. Even poverty, if it be judged in itself, is misery; likewise exile, contempt, prison, disgrace; finally, death itself is the ultimate of all calamities. But when the favor of our God breathes upon us, every one of these things turns into happiness for us. We ought accordingly to be content with the testimony of Christ rather than with the false estimation of the flesh. So it will come about that we shall rejoice after the apostle's example, "whenever he will count us worthy to suffer dishonor for his name" [Acts 5:41 p.]. What then? If, being innocent and of good conscience, we are stripped of our possessions by the wickedness of impious folk, we are indeed reduced to penury among men. But in God's presence in heaven our true riches are thus increased. If we are cast out of our own house,[5] then we will be the more intimately received into God's family. If we are vexed and despised, we but

---

[4] I. xvii. 8; III. iv. 31, 35.
[5] This section appeared first in the 1539 edition, after Calvin's flight from France (1535) and from Geneva (1538). But it resembles a passage in his Preface to Olivétan's French New Testament, written in 1534. (CR IX. 809.) (See J. Haroutunian's translation, LCC XXIII. 67 f.)

take all the firmer root in Christ. If we are branded with disgrace and ignominy, we but have a fuller place in the Kingdom of God. If we are slain, entrance into the blessed life will thus be open to us. Let us be ashamed to esteem less than the shadowy and fleeting allurements of the present life, those things on which the Lord has set so great a value.

8. Suffering under the cross, the Christian finds consolation in God*

ᵇScripture, then, by these and like warnings gives us abundant comfort in either the disgrace or the calamity we bear for the sake of defending righteousness. Consequently, we are too ungrateful if we do not willingly and cheerfully undergo these things at the Lord's hand; especially since this sort of cross most properly belongs to believers, and by it Christ wills to be glorified in us, just as Peter teaches [I Peter 4:12 ff.]. ᶜBut since for honorable natures to suffer disgrace is harsher than a hundred deaths, Paul specifically warns us we shall suffer not only persecutions but also reproaches because we hope in the living God [I Tim. 4:10]. Thus, in another passage he bids us walk after his example through ill repute and good repute [II Cor. 6:8].

ᵇYet such a cheerfulness is not required of us as to remove all feeling of bitterness and pain. Otherwise, in the cross there would be no forbearance of the saints unless they were tormented by pain and anguished by trouble. If there were no harshness in poverty, no torment in diseases, no sting in disgrace, no dread in death—what fortitude or moderation would there be in bearing them with indifference? But since each of these, with an inborn bitterness, by its very nature bites the hearts of us all, the fortitude of the believing man is brought to light if—tried by the feeling of such bitterness—however grievously he is troubled with it, yet valiantly resisting, he surmounts it. Here his forbearance reveals itself: if sharply pricked he is still restrained by the fear of God from breaking into any intemperate act. Here his cheerfulness shines if, wounded by sorrow and grief, he rests in the spiritual consolation of God.

(*The Christian meets suffering as sent by God, but with no Stoic insensibility, 9–11*)

9. The Christian, unlike the Stoic, gives expression to his pain and sorrow*

ᵇThis struggle which believers when they strive for patience and moderation maintain against the natural feeling of sorrow is fittingly described by Paul in these words: "We are pressed in every way but not rendered anxious; we are afflicted but not left destitute; we endure persecution but in it are not deserted; we are cast down but do not perish" [II Cor. 4:8–9 p.]. You see that patiently to bear the cross is not to be utterly stupefied and to be deprived of all feeling of pain. It is not as the Stoics of old foolishly described "the great-souled man": one who, having cast off all human qualities, was affected equally by adversity and prosperity, by sad times and happy ones—nay, who like a stone was not affected at all.[6] And what did this sublime wisdom profit them? They painted a likeness of forbearance that has never been found among men, and can never be realized. Rather, while they want to possess a forbearance too exact and precise, they have banished its power from human life.

Now, among the Christians there are also new Stoics,[7] who count it depraved not only to groan and weep but also to be sad and care ridden. These paradoxes proceed, for the most part, from idle men who, exercising themselves more in speculation than in action, can do nothing but invent such paradoxes for us. Yet we have nothing to do with this iron philosophy which our Lord and Master has condemned not only by his word, but also by his example. For he groaned and wept both over his own and others' misfortunes. And he taught his disciples in the same way: "The world," he says, "will rejoice; but you will be sorrowful and will weep" [John 16:20 p.]. And that no one might turn it into a vice, he openly proclaimed, "Blessed are those who mourn" [Matt. 5:4]. No wonder! For if all weeping is condemned, what shall we judge concerning the Lord himself, from whose body tears of blood trickled down [Luke 22:44]? If all fear is branded as unbelief, how shall we account for that dread with which, we read, he was heavily stricken [Matt. 26:37; Mark 14:33]? If all sadness displeases us, how will it please us that he confesses his soul "sorrowful even to death" [Matt. 26:38]?

---

[6] The ancient literature of consolation has many examples of this. Cicero illustrates the teaching of the Stoics, who "construct foolish syllogisms to prove that pain is not an evil." *Tusculan Disputations* II. xii. 20 (LCL edition, pp. 176 f.). Cf. McNeill, *A History of the Cure of Souls*, pp. 26–36. On Calvin's admission of tears and anxiety here, cf. Wallace, *Calvin's Doctrine of the Christian Life*, p. 191.

[7] Calvin owed much to the ancient Stoics, but he frequently condemns features of their writings incompatible with Christian faith, including their principle of ἀπάθεια, the rejection of feeling, and their related doctrine of fate. Cf. I. xvi. 8; III. iv. 28; III. vii. 15, and appended notes; Comm. Ezek. 1:4; 17:10; Matt. 10.29; L. Zanta, *La Renaissance du Stoïcisme au seizième siècle*, chs. i, ii; Q. Breen, *John Calvin: A Study in French Humanism*, ch. iv.

10. Real sorrow and real patience in conflict with each other

ᵇI decided to say this in order to recall godly minds from despair, lest, because they cannot cast off the natural feeling of sorrow, they forthwith renounce the pursuit of patience. This must necessarily happen to those who make patience into insensibility, and a valiant and constant man into a stock. For Scripture praises the saints for their forbearance when, so afflicted with harsh misfortune, they do not break or fall; so stabbed with bitterness, they are at the same time flooded with spiritual joy; so pressed by apprehension, they recover their breath, revived by God's consolation. In the meantime, their hearts still harbor a contradiction between their natural sense, which flees and dreads what it feels adverse to itself, and their disposition to godliness, which even through these difficulties presses toward obedience to the divine will. The Lord expresses this contradiction when he speaks to Peter as follows: "When you were young, you girded yourself and walked where you would. But when you become old . . . another will gird you and lead you where you do not wish to go" [John 21:18 p.]. It is unlikely that Peter, when it became necessary to glorify God through death, was drawn to it, unwilling and resisting. Otherwise, there would have been little praise for his martyrdom. But, even though he obeyed the divine command with the utmost fervor of heart, yet, because he had not put off his human nature, he was pulled apart by a double will. For while he contemplated that bloody death which he was to die, stricken with dread of it, he would gladly have escaped. On the other hand, when it came to his mind that he was called to it by God's command, having overcome and trampled his fear, he willingly and even cheerfully undertook it. This, therefore, we must try to do if we would be disciples of Christ, in order that our minds may be steeped in such reverence and obedience toward God as to be able to tame and subjugate to his command all contrary affections. Thus it will come to pass that, by whatever kind of cross we may be troubled, even in the greatest tribulations of mind, we shall firmly keep our patience. For the adversities themselves will have their own bitterness to gnaw at us; thus afflicted by disease, we shall both groan and be uneasy and pant after health; thus pressed by poverty, we shall be pricked by the arrows of care and sorrow; thus we shall be smitten by the pain of disgrace, contempt, injustice; thus at the funerals of our dear ones we shall weep the tears that are owed to our nature. But the conclusion will always be: the Lord so willed, therefore let us follow his will. Indeed, amid the very pricks of pain, amid groaning and tears, this thought must intervene: to incline our heart to bear cheerfully those things which have so moved it.

11. Patience according to philosophic and Christian understanding

ᵇNow, since we have taken the prime reason for bearing the cross from the contemplation of the divine will, we must define in a few words the difference between philosophic and Christian patience. Certainly, very few philosophers have climbed to such a height of reason as to understand that through afflictions we are tested by the hand of God, and to reckon that in this respect we must obey God. But they also advance no other reason than that it must be so.[8] What else is this but to say that you must yield to God because it is vain for you to try to resist him? For if we obey God only because it is necessary, if we should be allowed to escape, we will cease to obey him. But Scripture bids us contemplate in the will of God something far different: namely, first righteousness and equity, then concern for our own salvation. Of this sort, then, are Christian exhortations to patience. Whether poverty or exile, or prison, or insult, or disease, or bereavement, or anything like them torture us, we must think that none of these things happens except by the will and providence of God, that he does nothing except with a well-ordered justice.[9] What then? Do not our innumerable and daily offenses deserve to be chastised more severely and with heavier rods than the afflictions he lays upon us out of his kindness? Is it not perfectly fair that our flesh be tamed and made accustomed, as it were, to the yoke, lest it lustfully rage according to its own inward nature? Are not God's right and truth worth our trouble? But if God's undoubted equity appears in afflictions, we cannot either murmur or wrestle against it without iniquity. Now we do not hear that barren incantation, "We must yield because it is necessary," but a living and fully effective precept, "We must obey because it is unlawful to resist; we must bear patiently, since impatience would be insolence against God's righteousness."

Now, because that only is pleasing to us which we recognize to be for our salvation and good, our most merciful Father consoles us also in this respect when he asserts that in the very act of afflicting us with the cross he is providing for our salvation.

---

[8] Cf. Seneca: "[*Creator*] *scripsit quidem fata, sed sequitur.*" *On Providence* v. 8 (LCL Seneca, *Moral Essays* I. 38).

[9] The translation is influenced by VG: "*Qu'il ne fait rien sinon d'une justice bien ordonné.*"

But if it be clear that our afflictions are for our benefit, why should we not undergo them with a thankful and quiet mind? Therefore, in patiently suffering these tribulations, we do not yield to necessity but we consent for our own good. These thoughts, I say, bring it to pass that, however much in bearing the cross our minds are constrained by the natural feeling of bitterness, they are as much diffused with spiritual joy. From this, thanksgiving also follows, which cannot exist without joy; but if the praise of the Lord and thanksgiving can come forth only from a cheerful and happy heart—and there is nothing that ought to interrupt this in us—it thus is clear how necessary it is that the bitterness of the cross be tempered with spiritual joy.

ᵉCHAPTER IX

MEDITATION ON THE FUTURE LIFE[1]

(By our tribulations God weans us from excessive love of this present life, 1–2)
1. The vanity of this life
ᵇWhatever kind of tribulation presses upon us, we must ever look to this end: to accustom ourselves to contempt for the present life and to be aroused thereby to meditate upon the future life. For since God knows best how much we are inclined by nature to a brutish love of this world, he uses the fittest means to draw us back and to shake off our sluggishness, lest we cleave too tenaciously to that love. There is not one of us, indeed, who does not wish to seem throughout his life to aspire and strive after heavenly immortality. For it is a shame for us to be no better than brute beasts, whose condition would be no whit inferior to our own if there were not left to us hope of eternity after death. But if you examine the plans, the efforts, the deeds, of anyone, there you will find nothing else but earth. Now our blockishness arises from the fact that our minds, stunned by the empty dazzlement of riches, power, and honors, become so deadened that they can see no farther. The heart also, occupied with avarice, ambition, and lust, is so weighed down that it cannot rise up higher. In fine, the whole soul, enmeshed in the allurements of the flesh, seeks its happiness on earth. To counter this evil the Lord instructs his followers in the vanity of the present life by continual

[1] Cf. J. Bohatec, *Budé und Calvin*, pp. 416–420; H. Quistorp, *Calvin's Doctrine of the Last Things*, tr. H. Knight, pp. 41–54; W. Kolfhaus, *Vom christlichen Leben nach Johannes Calvin*, pp. 539–565; R. S. Wallace, *Calvin's Doctrine of the Christian Life*, Part II, ch. iv.

proof of its miseries. Therefore, that they may not promise themselves a deep and secure peace in it, he permits them often to be troubled and plagued either with wars or tumults, or robberies, or other injuries. That they may not pant with too great eagerness after fleeting and transient riches, or repose in those which they possess, he sometimes by exile, sometimes by barrenness of the earth, sometimes by fire, sometimes by other means, reduces them to poverty, or at least confines them to a moderate station. That they may not too complacently take delight in the goods of marriage,[2] he either causes them to be troubled by the depravity of their wives or humbles them by evil offspring, or afflicts them with bereavement. But if, in all these matters, he is more indulgent toward them, yet, that they may not either be puffed up with vainglory or exult in self-assurance, he sets before their eyes, through diseases and perils, how unstable and fleeting are all the goods that are subject to mortality.

Then only do we rightly advance by the discipline of the cross,[3] when we learn that this life, judged in itself, is troubled, turbulent, unhappy in countless ways, and in no respect clearly happy; that all those things which are judged to be its goods are uncertain, fleeting, vain, and vitiated by many intermingled evils. From this, at the same time, we conclude that in this life we are to seek and hope for nothing but struggle; when we think of our crown, we are to raise our eyes to heaven. For this we must believe: that the mind is never seriously aroused to desire and ponder the life to come unless it be previously imbued with contempt for the present life.

2. Our tendency to leave unnoticed the vanity of this life

ᵇIndeed, there is no middle ground between these two: either the world must become worthless to us or hold us bound by intemperate love of it. Accordingly, if we have any concern for eternity, we must strive diligently to strike off these evil fetters. Now, since the present life has very many allurements with which to entice us, and much show of pleasantness, grace, and sweetness wherewith to wheedle us, it is very much in our interest to be called away now and again so as not to be captivated by such panderings. What, then, I beg of you, would happen if we enjoyed here an enduring round of wealth and happiness, since we cannot, even with evil continually goading us, be sufficiently awakened to weigh the misery of this life?

[2] Cf. Augustine, *On the Good of Marriage* (MPL 40. 373–391; tr. NPNF III. 399–413).
[3] Cf. III. viii. 3.

That human life is like smoke [cf. Ps. 102:3] or shadow [cf. Ps. 102:11] is not only obvious to the learned, but even ordinary folk have no proverb more commonplace than this. And since they counted this something very profitable to know, they have couched it in many striking sayings. But there is almost nothing that we regard more negligently or remember less. For we undertake all things as if we were establishing immortality for ourselves on earth. If some corpse is being buried, or we walk among graves, because the likeness of death then meets our eyes, we, I confess, philosophize brilliantly concerning the vanity of this life. Yet even this we do not do consistently, for often all these things affect us not one bit. But when it happens, our philosophy is for the moment; it vanishes as soon as we turn our backs, and leaves not a trace of remembrance behind it. ᵉIn the end, like applause in the theater for some pleasing spectacle, it evaporates. ᵇForgetful not only of death but also of mortality itself, as if no inkling of it had ever reached us, we return to our thoughtless assurance of earthly immortality. If anyone in the meantime croaks the proverb: "Man is the creature of a day,"⁴ we indeed admit it; but with no attention, so that the thought of perpetuity nonetheless remains fixed in our minds. Who, then, can deny that it is very much worth-while for all of us, I do not say to be admonished with words, but by all the experiences that can happen, to be convinced of the miserable condition of earthly life; inasmuch as, even when convinced, we scarcely cease to be stunned with a base and foolish admiration of it, as if it contained in itself the ultimate goal of good things. But if God has to instruct us, it is our duty, in turn, to listen to him calling us, shaking us out of our sluggishness, that, holding the world in contempt, we may strive with all our heart to meditate upon the life to come.

(A right estimate of the present life, which is transient and unsatisfying, leads us to meditate on the life to come, 3–6)
3. Gratitude for earthly life!
ᵇBut let believers accustom themselves to a contempt of the present life that engenders no hatred of it or ingratitude against God. Indeed, this life, however crammed with infinite miseries it may be, is still rightly to be counted among those blessings of God which are not to be spurned. Therefore, if we recognize in it no divine benefit, we are already guilty of grave ingratitude toward God himself. For believers especially, this ought to be a tes-

⁴ *"Hominem animal esse ἐφήμερον."* Cf. Plato, *Laws* XI. 923 (LCL Plato, *Laws* II. 420); *Republic* X. 617 D *("ψυχαὶ ἐφήμεραι")* (LCL Plato, *Republic* II. 506).

timony of divine benevolence, wholly destined, as it is, to promote their salvation. For before he shows us openly the inheritance of eternal glory, God wills by lesser proofs to show himself to be our Father. These are the benefits that are daily conferred on us by him. Since, therefore, this life serves us in understanding God's goodness, should we despise it as if it had no grain of good in itself? We must, then, become so disposed and minded that we count it among those gifts of divine generosity which are not at all to be rejected. For if testimonies of Scripture were lacking, and they are very many and very clear, nature itself also exhorts us to give thanks to the Lord because he has brought us into its light, granted us the use of it, and provided all the necessary means to preserve it.

And this is a much greater reason if in it we reflect that we are in preparation, so to speak, for the glory of the Heavenly Kingdom. For the Lord has ordained that those who are one day to be crowned in heaven should first undergo struggles on earth in order that they may not triumph until they have overcome the difficulties of war, and attained victory.

Then there is another reason: we begin in the present life, through various benefits, to taste the sweetness of the divine generosity in order to whet our hope and desire to seek after the full revelation of this. When we are certain that the earthly life we live is a gift of God's kindness, as we are beholden to him for it we ought to remember it and be thankful. Then we shall come in good time to consider its most unhappy condition in order that we may, indeed, be freed from too much desire of it, to which, as has been said, we are of ourselves inclined by nature.

4. The right longing for eternal life

ᵇNow whatever is taken away from the perverse love of this life ought to be added to the desire for a better one. I confess that those showed a very sound judgment who thought it the best thing not to be born, and the next best thing to die as quickly as possible [cf. Eccl. 4:2–3].⁵ Since they were deprived of the light of God and true religion, what could they see in it that was not unhappy and repulsive? And they did not act without reason who celebrated the birthdays of their kindred with sorrow and tears, but their funeral rites with solemn joy.⁶ But they did this with-

---

⁵ Theognis, *Elegies* 425–428 (LCL *Greek Elegy* I. 280 f.); Cicero, *Tusculan Disputations* I. xlviii. 113 f. (LCL edition, pp. 136 f.); Herodotus, *History* I. 31 (self-immolation of Cleobis and Biton) (LCL Herodotus I. 34 ff.).
⁶ Euripides on Cresphontes, quoted in Latin by Cicero, *Tusculan Disputations* I. xlviii. 115 (LCL edition, pp. 138 f.).

out profit because, bereft of the right teaching of faith, they did not see how something that is neither blessed nor desirable of itself can turn into something good for the devout. Thus in despair they brought their judgment to a close.

Let the aim of believers in judging mortal life, then, be that while they understand it to be of itself nothing but misery, they may with greater eagerness and dispatch betake themselves wholly to meditate upon that eternal life to come. When it comes to a comparison with the life to come, the present life can not only be safely neglected but, compared to the former, must be utterly despised and loathed. For, if heaven is our homeland, what else is the earth but our place of exile? If departure from the world is entry into life, what else is the world but a sepulcher? And what else is it for us to remain in life but to be immersed in death? If to be freed from the body is to be released into perfect freedom, what else is the body but a prison?[7] If to enjoy the presence of God is the summit of happiness, is not to be without this, misery? But until we leave the world "we are away from the Lord" [II Cor. 5:6]. Therefore, if the earthly life be compared with the heavenly, it is doubtless to be at once despised and trampled under foot. Of course it is never to be hated except in so far as it holds us subject to sin; although not even hatred of that condition may ever properly be turned against life itself. In any case, it is still fitting for us to be so affected either by weariness or hatred of it that, desiring its end, we may also be prepared to abide in it at the Lord's pleasure, so that our weariness may be far from all murmuring and impatience. For it is like a sentry post[8] at which the Lord has posted us, which we must hold until he recalls us. Paul, indeed, held too long in the bonds of the body, laments his lot and sighs with fervent desire for redemption [Rom. 7:24]. Nonetheless, that he may obey God's command he professes himself ready for either [Phil. 1:23–24]. For he acknowledges that he owes it to God to glorify his name whether through death or through life [Rom. 14:8]. But it is for God to determine what best conduces to his glory. Therefore, if it befits us to live and die to the Lord, let us leave to his decision the hour of our death and life, but in such a way that we may both burn with the zeal for death and be constant in meditation. But in comparison with the immortality to come, let us despise this life and long to

[7] Plato, *Phaedo* 64 A, 80 E (LCL *Plato* I. 222 f., 280 f.; Cicero, *Tusculan Disputations* I. xlix. 118 (LCL edition, pp. 142 ff.). Cf. Melanchthon: "*Neque vero Christiana est vita, nisi assiduo moreamur.*" *Loci communes*, ed. Engelland, p. 156; tr. Hill, p. 259. On the body as prison, cf. III. vi. 5, note 9.

[8] Cf. III. x. 6, note 9.

renounce it, on account of bondage of sin, whenever it shall please the Lord.

5. Against the fear of death!

ᵇBut monstrous it is that many who boast themselves Christians are gripped by such a great fear of death, rather than a desire for it, that they tremble at the least mention of it, as of something utterly dire and disastrous. Surely, it is no wonder if the natural awareness in us bristles with dread at the mention of our dissolution. But it is wholly unbearable that there is not in Christian hearts any light of piety to overcome and suppress that fear, whatever it is, by a greater consolation. For if we deem this unstable, defective, corruptible, fleeting, wasting, rotting tabernacle of our body to be so dissolved that it is soon renewed unto a firm, perfect, incorruptible, and finally, heavenly glory, will not faith compel us ardently to seek what nature dreads? If we should think that through death we are recalled from exile to dwell in the fatherland, in the heavenly fatherland, would we get no comfort from this fact?

But, someone will object, there is nothing that does not crave to endure.⁹ To be sure, I agree; and so I maintain that we must have regard for the immortality to come, where a firm condition will be ours which nowhere appears on earth. ᵉFor Paul very well teaches that believers eagerly hasten to death not because they want to be unclothed but because they long to be more fully clothed [II Cor. 5:2–3]. ᵇShall the brute animals, and even inanimate creatures—even trees and stones—conscious of the emptiness of their present existence, long for the final day of resurrection, to be released from emptiness with the children of God [Rom 8:19 ff.]; and shall we, endowed with the light of understanding, and above understanding illumined with the Spirit of God, when our very being is at stake, not lift our minds beyond this earthly decay?

But it is not my present purpose, nor is it the proper place, to dispute against this very great perversity. At the very beginning I stated that I had no intention of undertaking a detailed treatment of commonplaces. I would advise such timid minds to read Cyprian's treatise *On the Mortality*,¹⁰ unless they deserved to be sent off to the philosophers, that they may begin to blush when they see the contempt of death that the latter display.

---

⁹ The corresponding sentence in VG may be translated: "But someone will object that all things crave to persist in their being."

¹⁰ Cyprian, *On the Mortality* (i.e., on the plague of A.D. 252) iii. 1 (CSEL 3. 294 ff.; tr. ANF V. 470).

Let us, however, consider this settled: that no one has made progress in the school of Christ who does not joyfully await the day of death and final resurrection. Paul, too, distinguishes all believers by this mark [Titus 2:13; cf. II Tim. 4:8], and Scripture habitually recalls us to it whenever it would set forth proof of perfect happiness. "Rejoice," says the Lord, "and raise your heads; for your redemption is drawing near." [Luke 21:28 p.] Is it reasonable, I ask you, that what our Lord meant to be sufficient to arouse us to rejoicing and good cheer should engender nothing but sorrow and dismay? If this is so, why do we still boast of him as our Master? Let us, then, take hold of a sounder view, and even though the blind and stupid desire of the flesh resists, let us not hesitate to await the Lord's coming, not only with longing, but also with groaning and sighs, as the happiest thing of all. He will come to us as Redeemer, and rescuing us from this boundless abyss of all evils and miseries, he will lead us into that blessed inheritance of his life and glory.

6. The comfort prepared for believers by aspiration for the life to come

ᵇThis is obvious: the entire company of believers, so long as they dwell on earth, must be "as sheep destined for the slaughter" [Rom. 8:36] to be conformed to Christ their Head. They would therefore have been desperately unhappy unless, with mind intent upon heaven, they had surmounted whatever is in this world, and passed beyond the present aspect of affairs [cf. I Cor. 15:19]. On the contrary, when they have once lifted their heads above everything earthly, even though they may see wicked men flourishing in wealth and honors, even though they may observe the latter enjoying deep peace, taking pride in the splendor and luxury of all their possessions, abounding with every delight[11]—if, moreover, believers are troubled by the wickedness of these men, bear their arrogant insults, are robbed through their greed, or harried by any other sort of inordinate desire on their part—they will without difficulty bear up under such evils also. For before their eyes will be that day when the Lord will receive his faithful people into the peace of his Kingdom, "will wipe away every tear from their eyes" [Rev. 7:17; cf. Isa. 25:8], will clothe them with "a robe of glory . . . and rejoicing" [Ecclus. 6:31, EV], will feed them with the unspeakable sweetness of his delights, will elevate them to his sublime fellowship—in fine, will deign to make them sharers in his happiness. But those impious ones who have flourished on earth he will cast into utter disgrace; he will turn

[11] Cf. I. x. 2; III. vii. 8.

their delights into tortures, their laughter and mirth into weeping and gnashing of teeth; he will trouble their peace with the dire torment of conscience; he will punish their wantonness with unquenchable fire [cf. Isa. 66:24; Matt. 25:41; Mark 9:43, 46; Rev. 21:8];[12] he will also make them bow their heads in subjection to the godly, whose patience they have abused. ᵉFor, as Paul testifies, this is righteousness: to grant rest to the unhappy and unjustly afflicted, to repay with affliction the wicked who afflict the godly, when the Lord Jesus is revealed from heaven [II Thess. 1:6–7].

ᵇThis truly is our sole comfort. If it be taken away, either our minds must become despondent or, to our destruction, be captivated with the empty solace of this world. Even the prophet confesses that his steps had well-nigh wavered when he stopped too long to dwell upon the present prosperity of the wicked [Ps. 73:2–3], and he could not understand it until he entered God's sanctuary and gazed upon the ultimate end of the pious and the wicked [Ps. 73:17]. To conclude in a word: if believers' eyes are turned to the power of the resurrection, in their hearts the cross of Christ will at last triumph over the devil, flesh, sin, and wicked men.

ᶜCHAPTER X

How We Must Use the Present Life and Its Helps

(*The good things of this life are to be enjoyed as gifts of God, 1–2*)

1. Double danger: mistaken strictness and mistaken laxity

ᵇBy such elementary instruction, Scripture at the same time duly informs us what is the right use of earthly benefits—a matter not to be neglected in the ordering of our life. For if we are to live, we have also to use those helps necessary for living. And we also cannot avoid those things which seem to serve delight more than necessity. Therefore we must hold to a measure so as to use them with a clear conscience, whether for necessity or for delight. By his word the Lord lays down this measure when he teaches that the present life is for his people as a pilgrimage[1] on which they are hastening toward the Heavenly Kingdom [Lev. 25:23; I Chron. 29:15; Ps. 39:13; 119:19; Heb. 11:8–10, 13–16; 13:14; I Peter 2:11]. If we must simply pass through this world, there is no doubt we ought to use its good things in so far as they help rather

---

[12] See III. xxv. 12, where Calvin interprets the corporeal images that figuratively represent the state of the damned.

[1] Cf. III. vii. 3, note 7.

than hinder our course. ᵉThus Paul rightly persuades us to use this world as if not using it; and to buy goods with the same attitude as one sells them [I Cor. 7:31–30].

ᵇBut because this topic is a slippery one and slopes on both sides into error, let us try to plant our feet where we may safely stand. There were some otherwise good and holy men who when they saw intemperance and wantonness, when not severely restrained, ever raging with unbridled excess, desired to correct this dangerous evil. This one plan occurred to them: they allowed man to use physical goods in so far as necessity required.² A godly counsel indeed, but they were far too severe. For they would fetter consciences more tightly than does the Word of the Lord— a very dangerous thing. ᶜNow, to them necessity means to abstain from all things that they could do without; thus, according to them, it would scarcely be permitted to add any food at all to plain bread and water. And others are even more severe. We are told of Crates the Theban, that he cast all his goods into the sea; for he thought that unless they were destroyed, they would destroy him.³

ᵇBut many today, while they seek an excuse for the intemperance of the flesh in its use of external things, and while they would meanwhile pave the road to licentious indulgence, take for granted what I do not at all concede to them: that this freedom is not to be restrained by any limitation but to be left to every man's conscience to use as far as seems lawful to him. Certainly I admit that consciences neither ought to nor can be bound here to definite and precise legal formulas; but inasmuch as Scripture gives general rules for lawful use, we ought surely to limit our use in accordance with them.

2. The main principle

ᵇLet this be our principle: that the use of God's gifts is not wrongly directed when it is referred to that end to which the Author himself created and destined them for us, since he created them for our good, not for our ruin. Accordingly, no one will hold to a straighter path than he who diligently looks to this end. Now if we ponder to what end God created food, we shall find that he meant not only to provide for necessity but also for delight and good cheer. Thus the purpose of clothing, apart from necessity, was comeliness and decency. In grasses, trees, and fruits, apart

---

² Cf. Augustine, *On the Good of Marriage* ix. 9 (MPL 40. 380; tr. NPNF III. 403); *Psalms*, Ps. 4. 8 (MPL 36. 81; tr. LF *Psalms* I. 21).

³ Diogenes Laertius, *Lives and Opinions of the Philosophers* VI. v. 4 (LCL edition, II. 90 f.).

from their various uses, there is beauty of appearance and pleasantness of odor [cf. Gen. 2:9]. For if this were not true, the
prophet would not have reckoned them among the benefits of
God, "that wine gladdens the heart of man, that oil makes his
face shine" [Ps. 104:15 p.]. Scripture would not have reminded
us repeatedly, in commending his kindness, that he gave all such
things to men. And the natural qualities themselves of things
demonstrate sufficiently to what end and extent we may enjoy
them. Has the Lord clothed the flowers with the great beauty that
greets our eyes, the sweetness of smell that is wafted upon our
nostrils, and yet will it be unlawful for our eyes to be affected by
that beauty, or our sense of smell by the sweetness of that odor?
What? Did he not so distinguish colors as to make some more
lovely than others? What? Did he not endow gold and silver, ivory
and marble, with a loveliness that renders them more precious
than other metals or stones? Did he not, in short, render many
things attractive to us, apart from their necessary use?[4]

(*We are not to use these blessings indulgently, or to seek wealth
greedily, but to serve dutifully in our calling, 3–6*)
*3. A look at the Giver of the gift prevents narrow-mindedness and
immoderation*
    bAway, then, with that inhuman philosophy which, while con-
ceding only a necessary use of creatures, not only malignantly
deprives us of the lawful fruit of God's beneficence but cannot be
practiced unless it robs a man of all his senses and degrades him
to a block.
    But no less diligently, on the other hand, we must resist the lust
of the flesh, which, unless it is kept in order, overflows without
measure. And it has, as I have said,[5] its own advocates, who, under
the pretext of the freedom conceded, permit everything to it.
First, one bridle is put upon it if it be determined that all things
were created for us that we might recognize the Author and give
thanks for his kindness toward us. Where is your thanksgiving if
you so gorge yourself with banqueting or wine that you either
become stupid or are rendered useless for the duties of piety and
of your calling? Where is your recognition of God if your flesh

---

[4] A passage significant for Calvin's recognition of beauty as possessing value
beyond mere utility. Cf. Comm. Gen. 4:20: Although music serves our enjoyment rather than our need, "it ought not on that account to be judged of no
value; still less should it be condemned" (J. Haroutunian's translation, LCC
XXIII. 355). For further illustration, see R. S. Wallace, *Calvin's Doctrine of
the Christian Life*, pp. 137 ff.; L. Wencelius, *L'Esthétique de Calvin*, pp.
112 f., 134.
[5] End of sec. 1, above.

boiling over with excessive abundance into vile lust infects the mind with its impurity so that you cannot discern anything that is right and honorable? Where is our gratefulness toward God for our clothing if in the sumptuousness of our apparel we both admire ourselves and despise others, if with its elegance and glitter we prepare ourselves for shameless conduct? Where is our recognition of God if our minds be fixed upon the splendor of our apparel? ᵉFor many so enslave all their senses to delights that the mind lies overwhelmed. Many are so delighted with marble, gold, and pictures that they become marble, they turn, as it were, into metals and are like painted figures. The smell of the kitchen or the sweetness of its odors so stupefies others that they are unable to smell anything spiritual. ᵇThe same thing is also to be seen in other matters. Therefore, clearly, leave to abuse God's gifts⁵ᵃ must be somewhat curbed, ᶜand Paul's rule is confirmed: that we should "make no provision for the flesh, to gratify its desires" [Rom. 13:14], for if we yield too much to these, they boil up without measure or control.

4. Aspiration to eternal life also determines aright our outward conduct of life

ᵇBut there is no surer or more direct course than that which we receive from contempt of the present life and meditation upon heavenly immortality. For from this two rules follow: those who use this world should be so affected as if they did not use it; those who marry, as if they did not marry; those who buy, as if they did not buy, just as Paul enjoins [I Cor. 7:29–31]. The other rule is that they should know how to bear poverty peaceably and patiently, as well as to bear abundance moderately. He who bids you use this world as if you used it not destroys not only the intemperance of gluttony in food and drink, and excessive indulgence at table, in buildings and clothing, ambition, pride, arrogance, and overfastidiousness, but also all care and inclination that either diverts or hinders you from thought of the heavenly life and zeal to cultivate the soul. Long ago Cato truly said: "There is great care about dress, but great carelessness about virtue." To use the old proverb: those who are much occupied with the care of the body are for the most part careless about their own souls.⁶

Therefore, even though the freedom of believers in external

⁵ᵃ Cf. VG.

⁶ The expression *"Magna cura cibi, magna virtutis incuria"* is attributed to Cato by Ammianus Marcellinus: *De rebus gestis* (ca. 390) XVI. v. 2 (LCL edition, I. 214).

matters is not to be restricted to a fixed formula, yet it is surely subject to this law: to indulge oneself as little as possible; but, on the contrary, with unflagging effort of mind to insist upon cutting off all show of superfluous wealth, not to mention licentiousness, and diligently to guard against turning helps into hindrances.

5. Frugality, earthly possessions held in trust[t]

[b]The second rule will be: they who have narrow and slender resources should know how to go without things patiently, lest they be troubled by an immoderate desire for them. If they keep this rule of moderation, they will make considerable progress in the Lord's school. So, too, they who have not progressed, in some degree at least, in this respect have scarcely anything to prove them disciples of Christ. For besides the fact that most other vices accompany the desire for earthly things, he who bears poverty impatiently also when in prosperity commonly betrays the contrary disease. This is my point: he who is ashamed of mean clothing will boast of costly clothing; he who, not content with a slender meal, is troubled by the desire for a more elegant one, will also intemperately abuse those elegances if they fall to his lot. He who will bear reluctantly, and with a troubled mind, his deprivation and humble condition if he be advanced to honors will by no means abstain from arrogance. To this end, then, let all those for whom the pursuit of piety is not a pretense strive to learn, by the Apostle's example, how to be filled and to hunger, to abound and to suffer want [Phil. 4:12].

Besides, Scripture has a third rule with which to regulate the use of earthly things. Of it we said something when we discussed the precepts of love.[7] It decrees that all those things were so given to us by the kindness of God, and so destined for our benefit, that they are, as it were, entrusted to us, and we must one day render account of them. Thus, therefore, we must so arrange it that this saying may continually resound in our ears: "Render account of your stewardship" [Luke 16:2]. At the same time let us remember by whom such reckoning is required: namely, him who has greatly commended abstinence, sobriety, frugality, and moderation, and has also abominated excess, pride, ostentation, and vanity; who approves no other distribution of good things than one joined with love; who has already condemned with his own lips all delights that draw man's spirit away from chastity and purity, or befog his mind.

[7] III. vii. 5.

6. The Lord's calling a basis of our way of life*

[b]Finally, this point is to be noted: the Lord bids each one of us in all life's actions to look to his calling.[8] For he knows with what great restlessness human nature flames, with what fickleness it is borne hither and thither, how its ambition longs to embrace various things at once. Therefore, lest through our stupidity and rashness everything be turned topsy-turvy, he has appointed duties for every man in his particular way of life. And that no one may thoughtlessly transgress his limits, he has named these various kinds of living "callings." Therefore each individual has his own kind of living assigned to him by the Lord as a sort of sentry post[9] so that he may not heedlessly wander about throughout life. Now, so necessary is this distinction that all our actions are judged in his sight by it, often indeed far otherwise than in the judgment of human and philosophical reason. No deed is considered more noble, even among philosophers, than to free one's country from tyranny. Yet a private citizen who lays his hand upon a tyrant is openly condemned by the heavenly judge [I Sam. 24:7, 11; 26:9].[10]

But I will not delay to list examples. It is enough if we know that the Lord's calling is in everything the beginning and foundation of well-doing. And if there is anyone who will not direct himself to it, he will never hold to the straight path in his duties.

[8] On Calvin's conception of vocation, see Karl Holl, "Die Geschichte des Worts Beruf," *Gesammelte Aufsätze* III, no. 9, 189–219; H. Hauser, "L'Économie Calvinienne," *Étude sur Calvin et le Calvinisme*, pp. 227–242; G. Harkness, *John Calvin: The Man and His Ethics*, chs. viii–x; on this section, see esp. p. 211. Miss Harkness has, perhaps too gently, criticized the exaggerated opinions of M. Weber, *The Protestant Ethic and the Spirit of Capitalism*, tr. T. Parsons, to which R. H. Tawney largely subscribes in *Religion and the Rise of Capitalism*. Despite the brilliance of Weber's essay, Calvin's statements on vocation were very inadequately brought to notice in it. Some other studies bearing on this point are briefly described in J. T. McNeill, "Thirty Years of Calvin Study," *Church History* XVII (1948), 232–235. R. S. Wallace, in *Calvin's Doctrine of the Christian Life* (a significant independent examination of Calvin's entire ethical teaching in its religious setting), sheds light on the conception of occupational calling, esp. in Part III, chs. iii–vi. Cf. Kolfhaus, *op. cit.*, pp. 420–433. A. Biéler, in a more recent work, *La Pensée économique et sociale de Calvin*, brings a basic knowledge of Calvin to the examination of the various theories, and offers an adverse view of Weber's interpretation. See especially Part II, ch. vi, pp. 477–514, and, on vocation, Part II, ch. v, pp. 391–414. Valuable also is *Protestantism and Capitalism: The Weber Thesis and Its Critics*, ed. R. W. Green, with critical appraisals by W. S. Hudson, H. Sée, H. M. Robertson, A. Fanfani, and A. Hyma. Cf. II. x. 12, note 11.

[9] Cf. Cicero, *On Old Age* xx. 73: "Pythagoras forbids us to desert our fort and station in life unbidden by God, our commander."

[10] Cf. IV. xx. 25–30; Seneca, *On Benefits* VII. xv. 2; xx. 3 (LCL Seneca, *Moral Essays* III. 490 f., 504 f.).

Perhaps, sometimes, he could contrive something laudable in appearance; but whatever it may be in the eyes of men, it will be rejected before God's throne. Besides, there will be no harmony among the several parts of his life. Accordingly, your life will then be best ordered when it is directed to this goal. ᵉFor no one, impelled by his own rashness, will attempt more than his calling will permit, because he will know that it is not lawful to exceed its bounds. A man of obscure station will lead a private life ungrudgingly so as not to leave the rank in which he has been placed by God. Again, it will be no slight relief from cares, labors, troubles, and other burdens for a man to know that God is his guide in all these things. The magistrate will discharge his functions more willingly; the head of the household will confine himself to his duty; each man will bear and swallow the discomforts, vexations, weariness, and anxieties in his way of life, when he has been persuaded that the burden was laid upon him by God. ᵇFrom this will arise also a singular consolation: that no task will be so sordid and base, provided you obey your calling in it, that it will not shine and be reckoned very precious in God's sight.[11]

ᵉCHAPTER XI

JUSTIFICATION BY FAITH: FIRST THE DEFINITION OF THE WORD AND OF THE MATTER

(Justification and regeneration, the terms defined, 1–4)
1. Place and meaning of the doctrine of "justification"
ᵇI believe I have already explained above, with sufficient care, how for men cursed under the law there remains, in faith, one sole means of recovering salvation. I believe I have also explained what faith itself is, and those benefits of God which it confers upon man, and the fruits it brings forth in him.[1] Let us sum these up. Christ was given to us by God's generosity, to be grasped and possessed by us in faith. By partaking of him, we principally receive a double grace: namely, that being reconciled to God through Christ's blamelessness, we may have in heaven instead of a Judge a gracious Father; and secondly, that sanctified by Christ's spirit we may cultivate blamelessness and purity of life. Of regeneration, indeed, the second of these gifts, I have said what seemed sufficient. The theme of justification was therefore more lightly touched upon because it was more to the point to under-

---

[11] Here we have Calvin's far-reaching observation on the splendor of God brightening even the lowliest daily task that is done in his service. Cf. Wallace, *op. cit.*, p. 155.
[1] The reference is to II. xii. 1; III. ii; III. iii, *passim*.

stand first how little devoid of good works is the faith, through which alone we obtain free righteousness by the mercy of God; and what is the nature of the good works of the saints, with which part of this question is concerned.[2] Therefore we must now discuss these matters thoroughly. And we must so discuss them as to bear in mind that this is the main hinge on which religion turns,[3] so that we devote the greater attention and care to it. For unless you first of all grasp what your relationship to God is, and the nature of his judgment concerning you, you have neither a foundation on which to establish your salvation nor one on which to build piety toward God. But the need to know this will better appear from the knowledge itself.

2. The concept of justification

ᵇBut that we may not stumble on the very threshold—and this would happen if we should enter upon a discussion of a thing unknown—first let us explain what these expressions mean: that man is justified in God's sight, and that he is justified by faith or works. He is said to be justified in God's sight who is both reckoned righteous in God's judgment and has been accepted on account of his righteousness. Indeed, as iniquity is abominable to God, so no sinner can find favor in his eyes ᶜin so far as he is a sinner and so long as he is reckoned as such. ᵇAccordingly, wherever there is sin, there also the wrath and vengeance of God show themselves. Now he is justified who is reckoned in the condition not of a sinner, but of a righteous man; and for that reason, he stands firm before God's judgment seat while all sinners fall. If an innocent accused person be summoned before the judgment seat of a fair judge, where he will be judged according to his innocence, he is said to be "justified" before the judge. Thus, justified before God is the man who, freed from the company of sinners, has God to witness and affirm his righteousness. In the same way, therefore, he in whose life that purity and holiness will be found which deserves a testimony of righteousness before God's throne will be said to be justified by works, or else he who, by the wholeness of his works, can meet and satisfy God's judgment. On the contrary, justified by faith is he who, excluded from the righteousness of works, grasps the righteousness of Christ through

---

[2] III. iii. 1; III. iii. 6–10.

[3] On the primary importance of the doctrine of justification by faith, see Melanchthon, *Loci communes* (1535) (CR Melanchthon XXI. 420); *Apology of the Augsburg Confession* IV. 2 (*Bekenntnisschriften der Evangelisch-Lutherischen Kirche*, pp. 158 f., 415: "*praecipuus locus doctrinae Christianae*"; *Concordia Triglotta*, pp. 120 f.); Doumergue, *Calvin* IV. 267–271; J. S. Whale, *The Protestant Tradition*, pp. 43 f.

faith, and clothed in it, appears in God's sight not as a sinner but as a righteous man.

ᶜTherefore, we explain justification simply as the acceptance with which God receives us into his favor as righteous men. And we say that it consists in the remission of sins and the imputation of Christ's righteousness.

3. Scriptural usage

ᶜThere are many clear testimonies of Scripture to confirm this fact. First, it cannot be denied that this is a proper and most customary meaning of the word. But because it would take too long to collect all the passages and to compare them, let it suffice to have called them to our readers' attention, for they will readily observe such of themselves. I shall bring forward only a few, where this justification of which we are speaking is expressly treated.

ᵉFirst, when Luke relates that the people, having heard Christ, justified God [Luke 7:29], and when Christ declares that "wisdom is justified by . . . her children" [Luke 7:35], Luke in the former passage (v. 29) does not mean that they confer righteousness. For righteousness always remains undivided with God, although the whole world tries to snatch it away from him. Nor does he, in v. 35, intend to justify the doctrine of salvation, which is righteous of itself. Rather, both expressions have the same force —to render to God and his teaching the praise they deserve. On the other hand, when Christ upbraids the Pharisees for justifying themselves [Luke 16:15], he does not mean that they acquire righteousness by well-doing but that they ambitiously seize upon a reputation for righteousness of which they are devoid. Those skilled in the Hebrew language better understand this sense: where not only those who are conscious of their crime but those who undergo the judgment of damnation are called "wicked." For when Bathsheba says that she and Solomon will be wicked [I Kings 1:21], she does not acknowledge any offense. But she complains that she and her son are going to be put to shame, to be counted among the wicked and condemned. Yet from the context it readily appears that this word, even when it is read in Latin, cannot otherwise be understood than relatively, but not so as to signify any quality.[3a]

But, because it pertains to the present case, ᶜwhen Paul says that Scripture foresaw that God would justify the Gentiles by faith [Gal. 3:8], what else may you understand but that God imputes righteousness by faith? Again, when he says that God justifies the impious person who has faith in Christ [Rom. 3:26 p.],

---

[3a] The word to which Calvin alludes is רָשָׁע . The plural form is used in I Kings 1:21.

what can his meaning be except that men are freed by the benefit of faith from that condemnation which their impiety deserved? This appears even more clearly in his conclusion, when he exclaims: "Who will accuse God's elect? It is God who justifies. Who will condemn? It is Christ who died, yes, who rose again . . . and now intercedes for us" [Rom. 8:33–34 p.]. For it is as if he had said: "Who will accuse those whom God has absolved? Who will condemn those whom Christ defends with his protection?" Therefore, "to justify" means nothing else than to acquit of guilt him who was accused, as if his innocence were confirmed. Therefore, since God justifies us by the intercession of Christ, he absolves us not by the confirmation of our own innocence but by the imputation of righteousness, so that we who are not righteous in ourselves may be reckoned as such in Christ. Thus it is said in Paul's sermon in the thirteenth chapter of The Acts: Through Christ is forgiveness of sins announced to you, and everyone who believes in him is justified of all things from which the law of Moses could not justify him [Acts 13:38–39]. You see that, after forgiveness of sins, this justification is set down, as it were, by way of interpretation. You see that it is plainly understood as absolution, you see that it is separated from the works of the law. You see it as the mere benefit of Christ, and you see that it is received by faith. ᵉYou see finally that a satisfaction is introduced where he says that we are justified from our sins through Christ. ᶜThus, when the publican is said to have gone down from the Temple justified [Luke 18:14], we cannot say that he achieved righteousness by any merit of works. This, therefore, is what is said: after pardon of sins has been obtained, the sinner is considered as a just man in God's sight. Therefore, he was righteous not by approval of works but by God's free absolution. Ambrose has, accordingly, fitly expressed it when he calls the confession of sins a lawful justification.[4]

4. Justification as gracious acceptance by God and as forgiveness of sins

ᶜAnd to avoid contention over a word, if we look upon the thing itself as described to us, no misgiving will remain. For Paul surely refers to justification by the word "acceptance" when in Eph. 1:5–6 he says: "We are destined for adoption through Christ according to God's good pleasure, to the praise of his glorious grace by which he has accounted us acceptable and beloved" [Eph. 1:5–6 p.]. That means the very thing that he commonly says elsewhere, that "God justifies us freely" [Rom. 3:24].

[4] Ambrose, *Exposition of Psalm 118* x. 47 (CSEL 62. 231; MPL 15. 1418).

Moreover, in the fourth chapter of Romans he first calls justification "imputation of righteousness." And he does not hesitate to include it within forgiveness of sins. Paul says: "That man is declared blessed by David whom God renders acceptable or to whom he imputes righteousness apart from works, as it is written: 'Blessed are they whose transgressions have been forgiven' " [Rom. 4:6–7 p.; Ps. 32:1]. ᵈThere he is obviously discussing not a part of justification but the whole of it. Further, he approves the definition of it set forth by David when he declares those men blessed to whom free pardon of sins is given [Ps. 32:1–2]. From this it is clear that the righteousness of which he speaks is simply set in opposition to guilt. ᶜBut the best passage of all on this matter is the one in which he teaches that the sum of the gospel embassy is to reconcile us to God, since God is willing to receive us into grace through Christ, not counting our sins against us [II Cor. 5:18–20]. ᶜLet my readers carefully ponder the whole passage. For a little later Paul adds by way of explanation: "Christ, who was without sin, was made sin for us" [II Cor. 5:21], to designate the means of reconciliation [cf. vs. 18–19]. Doubtless, he means by the word "reconciled" nothing but "justified." And surely, what he teaches elsewhere—that "we are made righteous by Christ's obedience" [Rom. 5:19 p.]—could not stand unless we are reckoned righteous before God in Christ and apart from ourselves.

(*Refutation of Osiander's doctrine of "essential righteousness,"* *5–12*)
5. *Osiander's doctrine of essential righteousness*
ᶜBut Osiander has introduced some strange monster of "essential" righteousness⁵ by which, although not intending to abolish freely given righteousness, he has still enveloped it in such a fog as to darken pious minds and deprive them of a lively experience

---

⁵ Calvin here assails Osiander's radical view of justification. See W. Niesel's brief treatment of the issues between Osiander and Calvin, *The Theology of Calvin*, pp. 133 ff., and his study "Calvin wider Osianders Rechtfertigungslehre," *Zeitschrift für Kirchengeschichte* XLVI (1927), 410–430. Osiander's doctrine was set forth in his *Disputation on Justification* (1550), containing 81 propositions, and in his *Confession of the Only Mediator and of Justification by Faith* (1551). A brief, clear account of the controversy within Lutheranism, which arose from these treatises and from his *An filius Dei fuerit incarnandus* (cf. I. xv. 3, note 8), is found in *Concordia Triglotta*, pp. 152–159. His view that Christ is our righteousness solely by his divine nature, whereby he imparts to us "essential righteousness," was regarded as invalidating the Reformation doctrine of Christ's sacrifice in the agony of the cross. Cf. sec. 8, below.

of Christ's grace. Consequently, before I pass on to other matters, it behooves me to refute this wild dream.

First, this speculation arises out of mere feeble curiosity. Indeed, he accumulates many testimonies of Scripture by which to prove that Christ is one with us, and we, in turn, with him[6]—a fact that needs no proof. But because he does not observe the bond of this unity, he deceives himself. Now it is easy for us to resolve all his difficulties. For we hold ourselves to be united with Christ by the secret power of his Spirit.

That gentleman had conceived something bordering on Manichaeism, in his desire to transfuse the essence of God into men.[7] From this arises another fiction of his, that Adam was formed to the image of God because Christ had already been destined as the prototype of human nature before the Fall.[8] But because I am striving after brevity, I must concentrate on the present matter.

He says that we are one with Christ. We agree. But we deny that Christ's essence is mixed with our own. Then we say that this principle is wrongly applied to these deceptions of his: that Christ is our righteousness because he is God eternal, the source of righteousness, and the very righteousness of God. My readers will pardon me if I now only touch upon what my teaching plan demands that I defer to another place. Although he may make the excuse that by the term "essential righteousness" he means nothing else but to meet the opinion that we are considered righteous for Christ's sake, yet he has clearly expressed himself as not content with that righteousness which has been acquired for us by Christ's obedience and sacrificial death, but pretends that we are substantially righteous in God by the infusion both of his essence and of his quality. For this is the reason why he contends so vehemently that not only Christ but also the Father and the Holy Spirit, dwell in us. Although I admit this to be true, yet I say that it has been perversely twisted by Osiander; for he ought to have considered the manner of the indwelling—namely, that the Father

---

[6] Osiander challenged Augustine's view (*De Trinitate* X. xii. 19) that the image of God is in the mind of man, with its three parts, memory, intellect, and will: *An filius Dei* (appended essay, *De imagine Dei*) B 3a; Satan too has these (B 4a). The image of God was shut up (*inclusa*) in Christ's human nature (C 2a), which was from eternity in God (D 1b). Adam's original righteousness is defined as the righteousness of God dwelling in Adam (F 4a).

[7] Cf. Augustine, *Sermons* clxxxii. 4 (MPL 38. 986; tr. LF *Sermons* II. 956 f.); *On Christ's Agony* x. 11 (MPL 40. 297); *City of God* XI. xxii (MPL 41. 336; tr. NPNF II. 217); *Against Two Letters of the Pelagians* II. ii. 2 (MPL 44. 572; tr. NPNF V. 392); *Unfinished Treatise Against Julian* III. clxxxvi; II. clxxviii (MPL 45. 1325, 1218 f.); *On Genesis, Against the Manichees* II. viii. 11 (MPL 34. 202).

[8] Osiander, *An filius Dei* E 3b–4a; D 1b–2a. Cf. I. xv. 3, note 8; II. xii. 4–7.

and Spirit are in Christ, and even as the fullness of deity dwells in him [Col. 2:9], so in him we possess the whole of deity. Therefore, all that he has put forward separately concerning the Father and the Spirit tends solely to seduce the simple-minded from Christ.

Then he throws in a mixture of substances by which God—transfusing himself into us, as it were—makes us part of himself. For the fact that it comes about through the power of the Holy Spirit that we grow together with Christ, and he becomes our Head and we his members, he reckons of almost no importance unless Christ's essence be mingled with ours. But in his treatment of the Father and the Holy Spirit he more openly, as I have said, brings out what he means: namely, that we are not justified by the grace of the Mediator alone, nor is righteousness simply or completely offered to us in his person, but that we are made partakers in God's righteousness when God is united to us in essence.[9]

6. Osiander erroneously mixes forgiveness of sins with rebirth

ᵉSuppose he had only said that Christ, in justifying us, by conjunction of essence becomes ours, not only in that in so far as he is man is he our Head, but also in that the essence of the divine nature is poured into us. Then he would have fed on these delights with less harm, and perhaps such a great quarrel on account of this delusion would not have had to arise. But inasmuch as this principle is like the cuttlefish,[10] which by voiding its black and turbid blood hides its many tails, unless we would knowingly and willingly allow that righteousness to be snatched from us which alone gives us the confidence to glory in our salvation, we must bitterly resist. For in this whole disputation the noun "righteousness" and the verb "to justify"[10a] are extended in two directions; so that to be justified is not only to be reconciled to God through free pardon but also to be made righteous, and righteousness is not a free imputation but the holiness and uprightness that the essence of God, dwelling in us, inspires. Secondly, he sharply states that Christ is himself our righteousness, not

---

[9] The points challenged above are advanced in Osiander's *Confession* A 4b; G 1a. Calvin is anxious to refute the doctrine of essential righteousness in order to guard that of righteousness imparted solely through Christ's sacrifice. Cf. secs. 8 and 10, below.

[10] *"Sepiae."* The cuttlefish is described by Aristotle, *Parts of Animals* IV. v (LCL edition, pp. 318 f.), and by Pliny, *Natural History* IX. xxix. 45 (tr. J. Bostock and C. H. Riley II. 417). The illustration is used by Tertullian, *Against Marcion* II. xx. 1 (CCL Tertullianus I. 497; tr. ANF III. 312 f.).

[10a] *"Nomen iustitiae et verbum iustificandi."*

in so far as he, by expiating sins as Priest, appeased the Father on our behalf, but as he is eternal God and life.

To prove the first point—that God justifies not only by pardoning but by regenerating—he asks whether God leaves as they were by nature those whom he justifies, changing none of their vices. This is exceedingly easy to answer: as Christ cannot be torn into parts, so these two which we perceive in him together and conjointly are inseparable—namely, righteousness and sanctification. Whomever, therefore, God receives into grace, on them he at the same time bestows the spirit of adoption [Rom. 8:15], by whose power he remakes them to his own image. But if the brightness of the sun cannot be separated from its heat, shall we therefore say that the earth is warmed by its light, or lighted by its heat? Is there anything more applicable to the present matter than this comparison? The sun, by its heat, quickens and fructifies the earth, by its beams brightens and illumines it. Here is a mutual and indivisible connection. Yet reason itself forbids us to transfer the peculiar qualities of the one to the other. In this confusion of the two kinds of grace that Osiander forces upon us there is a like absurdity. For since God, for the preservation of righteousness, renews those whom he freely reckons as righteous, Osiander mixes that gift of regeneration with this free acceptance and contends that they are one and the same. Yet Scripture, even though it joins them, still lists them separately in order that God's manifold grace may better appear to us. For Paul's statement is not redundant: that Christ was given to us for our righteousness and sanctification [I Cor. 1:30].[11] And whenever he reasons—from the salvation purchased for us, from God's fatherly love, and from Christ's grace—that we are called to holiness and cleanness, he clearly indicates that to be justified means something different from being made new creatures.

When it comes to Scripture, Osiander completely corrupts every passage he cites. In Paul's statement that "faith is reckoned as righteousness" not for the "one who works" but for the "one who believes in him who justifies the ungodly" [Rom. 4:4–5 p.], Osiander explains "justify" as "to make righteous." With the same rashness he corrupts that whole fourth chapter of Romans. And he does not hesitate to tinge with the same deceit a passage that we have recently cited:[12] "Who will accuse God's elect? It is God who justifies" [Rom. 8:33]. There it is plain that the question is simply one of guilt and acquittal, and the meaning of the

[11] In the preceding sentences Calvin has reference to statements in Osiander's *Confession*, between E 3a and M 3b of that treatise.
[12] Sec. 3, above.

apostle depends on this antithesis. Therefore, both in that reason and in citing Scriptural evidence, Osiander proves himself an incompetent interpreter.

Also, he discusses the term "righteousness" no more correctly, holding that the faith of Abraham was imputed to him as righteousness after he, having embraced Christ—who is the righteousness of God and God himself—had excelled in singular virtues.[13] From this it appears that he has incorrectly made one corrupt statement out of two sound ones. For righteousness, of which mention is there made, does not extend throughout the whole course of Abraham's calling. Rather, the Spirit testifies—although the excellence of the virtues of Abraham was outstanding, and by persevering in them for a long time he at length increased them—that he pleased God only when he received in faith the grace offered in the promise. From this it follows that, as Paul skillfully contends, there is in justification no place for works.

7. The significance of faith for justification

eI willingly concede Osiander's objection that faith of itself does not possess the power of justifying, but only in so far as it receives Christ. For if faith justified of itself or through some intrinsic power, so to speak, as it is always weak and imperfect it would effect this only in part; thus the righteousness that conferred a fragment of salvation upon us would be defective. Now we imagine no such thing, but we say that, properly speaking, God alone justifies; then we transfer this same function to Christ because he was given to us for righteousness. We compare faith to a kind of vessel; for unless we come empty and with the mouth of our soul open to seek Christ's grace, we are not capable of receiving Christ. From this it is to be inferred that, in teaching that before his righteousness is received Christ is received in faith, we do not take the power of justifying away from Christ.

Yet, in the meantime, I do not admit the distorted figures of this Sophist when he says that "faith is Christ"[14]—as if an earthen pot were a treasure because gold is hidden in it. For the reasoning is similar: namely, that faith, even though of itself it is of no worth or price, can justify us by bringing Christ, just as a pot crammed with money makes a man rich. Therefore, I say that

---

[13] Osiander, op. cit., E 3ab; G 1a–3a; O 4a–P 3a.

[14] Osiander, op. cit., G 1b–2a. Various references to the same work can be traced in this section. See Cadier, Institution III. 200, note 4; 201, note 9. In secs. 8–12, Calvin is vigorously combatting a view that would confine the redemptive work of Christ to his divine nature, thus rendering meaningless his cross and resurrection.

faith, which is only the instrument for receiving righteousness, is ignorantly confused with Christ, who is the material cause and at the same time the Author and Minister of this great benefit. Now we have disposed of the problem as to how the term "faith" ought to be understood when justification is under consideration.

8. Osiander's doctrine that Christ is, according to his divine nature, our righteousness

ᵉIn the receiving of Christ, Osiander goes farther: that the inner word is received by the ministry of the outer word. By this he would lead us away from the priesthood of Christ and the person of the Mediator to his outward deity. Now we do not divide Christ but confess that he, who, reconciling us to the Father in his flesh, gave us righteousness, is the eternal Word of God, and that the duties of the Mediator could not otherwise have been discharged by him, or righteousness acquired for us, had he not been eternal God. But Osiander's opinion is that, since Christ is God and man, he is made righteousness for us with respect to his divine nature, not his human nature. Yet if this properly applies to divinity, it will not be peculiar to Christ but common with the Father and the Spirit, inasmuch as the righteousness of one differs not from the righteousness of the other. Then, because he was by nature from eternity, it would not be consistent to say that he was "made for us." But even though we should grant that God was made righteousness for us, how will this harmonize with what Paul interposes: that Christ was made righteousness by God [I Cor. 1:30]? This is surely peculiar to the person of the Mediator, which, even though it contains in it the divine nature, still has its own proper designation by which the Mediator is distinguished from the Father and the Spirit.

Osiander absurdly gloats over one word of Jeremiah, where he promises that Jehovah will be our righteousness [Jer. 51:10; cf. chs. 23:6; 33:16]. But from this he shall deduce nothing but the fact that Christ, who is our righteousness, is God manifested in flesh [cf. I Tim. 3:16]. Elsewhere we have quoted from Paul's sermon:[15] "With his blood God purchased the church for himself" [Acts 20:28 p.]. If anyone should infer from this that the blood whereby sins have been expiated is divine and of the divine nature, who could bear such a foul error? Yet Osiander thinks that he has obtained all things by this very childish cavil; he swells up, exults, stuffs many pages with his bombast[16]—while

---

[15] II. xiv. 2.

[16] In VG the text varies from this and may be rendered: "He raises his crest [like a crowing cock] and fills many pages with boasts."

there is a simple and ready explanation of the words that Jehovah, when he should become the offspring of David, would be the righteousness of the godly. But Isaiah teaches in what sense this is so: "By knowledge of himself shall the righteous one, my servant, make many to be accounted righteous" [Isa. 53:11].

Let us note that it is the Father who is speaking; that he assigns to the Son the office of justifying; that he adds the reason—that he is righteous; and that he has lodged the mode and means, as they say, in the teaching whereby Christ becomes known. For it is more fitting to take the word צדק as a passive.[17] Hence I gather that Christ was made righteousness when "he took upon him the form of a servant" [Phil. 2:7]; secondly, that he justifies us in that he has shown himself obedient to the Father [Phil. 2:8]. Therefore he does this for us not according to his divine nature but in accordance with the dispensation enjoined upon him. For even though God alone is the source of righteousness, and we are righteous only by participation in him, yet, because we have been estranged from his righteousness by unhappy disagreement, we must have recourse to this lower remedy that Christ may justify us by the power of his death and resurrection.

9. Justification as the work of the Mediator

ᵉIf Osiander should object that this work, by its very excellence, surpasses human nature; and for this reason can be ascribed only to divine nature, I grant the first point; in the second I say that he is grossly deluded. For even though Christ if he had not been true God could not cleanse our souls by his blood, nor appease his Father by his sacrifice, nor absolve us from guilt, nor, in sum, fulfill the office of priest, because the power of the flesh is unequal to so great a burden, yet it is certain that he carried out all these acts according to his human nature. For if we ask how we have been justified, Paul answers, "By Christ's obedience" [Rom. 5:19 p.]. But did he obey in any other way than when he took upon himself the form of a servant [Phil. 2:7]? From this we conclude that in his flesh, righteousness has been manifested to us. Similarly in other words—I am surprised that Osiander is not ashamed to cite that so often—Paul has established the source of righteousness in the flesh of Christ alone. "Him who knew no sin he made to be sin for us that we might be the righteousness of God in him." [II Cor. 5:21 p.] At the top of his lungs Osiander extols God's righteousness, and sings a song of triumph as if he had confirmed that ghost of his of "essential righteousness." Yet the words express something far different, that we are made righteous through the atone-

17 Cf. Comm. Isa. 53:11.

ment wrought by Christ. Every schoolboy should know that God's righteousness is to be understood as that righteousness which is approved of God, as in the Gospel of John where God's glory is compared with men's glory [John 12:43, RV; 5:44].[18] I know that it is sometimes called the righteousness of God because God is its author and bestows it upon us. But discerning readers will recognize without my saying anything that this expression means only that we stand, supported by the sacrifice of Christ's death, before God's judgment seat.

And the word is not very important, provided Osiander agrees with us, that we are justified in Christ, in so far as he was made an atoning sacrifice for us: something that does not comport with his divine nature. For this reason also, when Christ would seal the righteousness and salvation that he has brought us, he sets forth a sure pledge of it in his own flesh. Now he calls himself "the bread of life" [John 6:48], but, in explaining how, he adds that "his flesh is truly meat, and his blood truly drink" [John 6:55]. This method of teaching is perceived in the sacraments;[19] even though they direct our faith to the whole Christ and not to a half-Christ, they teach that the matter both of righteousness and of salvation resides in his flesh; not that as mere man he justifies or quickens by himself, but because it pleased God to reveal in the Mediator what was hidden and incomprehensible in himself. Accordingly, I usually say that Christ is, as it were, a fountain, open to us, from which we may draw what otherwise would lie unprofitably hidden in that deep and secret spring, which comes forth to us in the person of the Mediator. In this way and sense, I do not deny that Christ, as he is God and man, justifies us; and also that this work is the common task of the Father and the Holy Spirit; finally, that righteousness of which Christ makes us partakers with himself is the eternal righteousness of the eternal God —provided Osiander accept the firm and clear reasons that I have brought forward.

10. What is the nature of our union with Christ?
   eNow, lest Osiander deceive the unlearned by his cavils, I con-

---

[18] At several points in this section the French text somewhat expands the Latin, evidently for clarification and simplification of the thought. Here the explanation is inserted: "meaning that those of whom he speaks have been swimming between two waters, for they love rather to keep their good reputation in the world than to be prized in God's sight."

[19] Cf. IV. xvii. 4. See also Cadier, *Institution* III. 201, note 4; R. S. Wallace, *Calvin's Doctrine of the Word and Sacrament,* pp. 167 ff. The relation of the divine and the human in the Eucharist corresponds to the work of Christ as God *and* man in justification.

fess that we are deprived of this utterly incomparable good until Christ is made ours. Therefore, that joining together of Head and members, that indwelling of Christ in our hearts—in short, that mystical union[20]—are accorded by us the highest degree of importance, so that Christ, having been made ours, makes us sharers with him in the gifts with which he has been endowed. We do not, therefore, contemplate him outside ourselves from afar in order that his righteousness may be imputed to us but because we put on Christ and are engrafted into his body—in short, because he deigns to make us one with him. For this reason, we glory that we have fellowship of righteousness with him. Thus is Osiander's slander refuted, that by us faith is reckoned righteousness. As if we were to deprive Christ of his right when we say that by faith we come empty to him to make room for his grace in order that he alone may fill us! But Osiander, by spurning this spiritual bond, forces a gross mingling of Christ with believers. And for this reason, he maliciously calls "Zwinglian" all those who do not subscribe to his mad error of "essential righteousness" because they do not hold the view that Christ is eaten in substance in the Lord's Supper. I consider it the highest glory to be thus insulted by a proud man, and one entangled in his own deceits; albeit he attacks not only me but world-renowned writers whom he ought modestly to have respected. It makes no difference to me, for I am not pleading my own private cause. I am the more sincerely pleading this case for the reason that I am free from all perverted motives.

The fact, then, that he insists so violently upon essential righteousness and essential indwelling of Christ in us has this result: first, he holds that God pours himself into us as a gross mixture, just as he fancies a physical eating in the Lord's Supper; secondly, that he breathes his righteousness upon us, by which we may be really righteous with him, since according to Osiander this righteousness is both God himself and the goodness or holiness or integrity of God.

I shall not labor much in refuting the Scriptural proofs that he brings forward, which he wrongly twists from the heavenly life to the present state. "Through Christ," says Peter, "were granted to us precious and very great promises . . . that we might become partakers of the divine nature." [II Peter 1:4 p.] As if we now

---

[20] *"Mystica . . . unio"; VG: "union sacrée."* Cf. "fellowship of righteousness" and "spiritual bond [*conjunctio*]," below. Cf. III. ii. 24; IV. xvii. 8–12. Niesel notes that Calvin nowhere teaches "the absorption of the pious mystic into the sphere of the divine being": *The Theology of Calvin*, p. 126; cf. pp. 144, 222.

were what the gospel promises that we shall be at the final coming of Christ! Indeed, John then reminds us we are going to see God as he is because we shall be like him [I John 3:2].[21] I only wanted to give a small sample to my readers. Consequently, I purposely pass over these trifles. Not that it would be difficult to refute them, but I do not want to elaborate tediously and superfluously.

11. Osiander's doctrine of the essential righteousness nullifies the certainty of salvation

ᵉBut more poison lurks in the second phase, where Osiander teaches that we are righteous together with God. I have already sufficiently proved, I think, that this doctrine even though it were not so pestilent, yet because it is cold and barren and is dissipated in its own vanity—ought rightly to be unsavory for intelligent and pious readers. To enfeeble our assurance of salvation, to waft us above the clouds in order to prevent our calling upon God with quiet hearts after we, assured of expiation, have laid hold upon grace—to do all this under pretense of a twofold righteousness[22] is an utterly intolerable impiety.

Osiander laughs at those men who teach that "to be justified" is a legal term; because we must actually be righteous. Also, he despises nothing more than that we are justified by free imputation. Well then, if God does not justify us by acquittal and pardon, what does Paul's statement mean: "God was in Christ, reconciling the world to himself, not imputing men's trespasses against them" [II Cor. 5:19]? "For our sake he made him to be sin who had done no sin so that we might be the righteousness of God in him." [V. 21 p.] First, I conclude that they are accounted righteous who are reconciled to God. Included is the means: that God justifies by pardoning, just as in another passage justification is contrasted with accusation. This antithesis clearly shows that the expression was taken from legal usage. Anyone moderately versed in the Hebrew language, provided he has a sober brain,[23] is not ignorant of the fact that the phrase arose from this source, and drew from it its tendency and implication. Where

---

[21] Osiander, *Confession* R 1a, T 1b. VG inserts here: *"Osiander tire de là que Dieu a meslé son essence avec la nostre."*

[22] Cf. sec. 6, above; sec. 11, below. Osiander's Lutheran opponents commonly said, as Calvin does, that he confused justification with regeneration. Niesel has discussed the *duplex iustitia* in his article "Calvin wider Osianders Rechtfertigungslehre" (cited above, sec. 5, note 5), pp. 418 f. Cf. "two kinds of grace" in sec. 6, above.

[23] By the parenthetic phrase Calvin impugns Osiander's judgment while disparaging his competence to interpret the Hebrew words he freely employs.

Paul says that righteousness without works is described by David in these words, "Blessed are they whose transgressions are forgiven" [Ps. 32:1; 31:1, Vg.; Rom. 4:7], let Osiander answer me whether this be a full or half definition. Surely, Paul does not make the prophet bear witness to the doctrine that pardon of sins is part of righteousness, or merely a concomitant toward the justifying of man; on the contrary, he includes the whole of righteousness in free remission, declaring that man blessed whose sins are covered, whose iniquities God has forgiven, and whose transgressions God does not charge to his account. Thence, he judges and reckons his happiness because in this way he is righteous, not intrinsically but by imputation.

Osiander objects that it would be insulting to God and contrary to his nature that he should justify those who actually remain wicked. Yet we must bear in mind what I have already said, that the grace of justification is not separated from regeneration, although they are things distinct. But because it is very well known by experience that the traces of sin always remain in the righteous, their justification must be very different from reformation into newness of life [cf. Rom. 6:4]. For God so begins this second point in his elect, and progresses in it gradually, and sometimes slowly, throughout life, that they are always liable to the judgment of death before his tribunal. But he does not justify in part but liberally, so that they may appear in heaven as if endowed with the purity of Christ. No portion of righteousness sets our consciences at peace until it has been determined that we are pleasing to God, because we are entirely righteous before him. From this it follows that the doctrine of justification is perverted and utterly overthrown when doubt is thrust into men's minds, when the assurance of salvation is shaken and the free and fearless calling upon God suffers hindrance—nay, when peace and tranquillity with spiritual joy are not established. Thence Paul argues from contraries that the inheritance does not come from the law [Gal. 3:18], for in this way "faith would be nullified" [Rom. 4:14, cf. Vg.]. For faith totters if it pays attention to works, since no one, even of the most holy, will find there anything on which to rely.

This distinction between justification and regeneration, which two things Osiander confuses under the term "double righteousness," is beautifully expressed by Paul. Speaking of his own real righteousness, or of the uprighteous that had been given him, which Osiander labels "essential righteousness," he mournfully exclaims: "Wretched man that I am! Who will deliver me from the body of this death?" [Rom. 7:24]. But fleeing to that righteousness which is founded solely upon God's mercy he gloriously triumphs over both life and death, reproaches and hunger, the sword and all other adverse things. "Who will make accusation against God's elect," whom he justifies [Rom. 8:33 p.]? For I am surely convinced that nothing "will separate us from his love in Christ" [Rom. 8:38–39 p.]. He clearly proclaims that he has a righteousness which alone entirely suffices for salvation before God, so that he does not diminish his confidence in glorying, and no hindrance arises from the miserable bondage, consciousness of which had a moment before caused him to bemoan his lot. This diversity is sufficiently known, and so familiar to all the saints who groan under the burden of iniquities and yet with victorious confidence surmount all fears.

But Osiander's objection that this is out of accord with God's nature topples back upon him. For, even though he clothed the saints with this "double righteousness," like a furred garment, he is still compelled to confess that no one can please God without forgiveness of sins. But if this is true, let him at least grant that those who are not intrinsically righteous are reckoned righteous according to the fixed proportion[24] of imputation, as they say. But how far will a sinner parcel out this free acceptance which stands in place of righteousness? By the pound or by the ounce? Assuredly, he will hang uncertainly, wavering to this side and to that, for he will not be allowed to assume in himself as much righteousness as he needs for assurance. It is well that he who would lay down a law for God is not the judge of this case. But this saying will stand fast: "So that thou mayest be justified in thy words and mayest overcome when thou art judged" [Ps. 50:6, Vg.; cf. Ps. 51:4, EV].

How great presumption is it to condemn the supreme Judge when he freely absolves, so that this answer may not have full force: "I will show mercy on whom I will show mercy"? [Ex. 33:19.] And yet Moses' intercession, which God restrains in these words, was not to the effect that he should spare no one but that he should wipe away the charge against them even though they were guilty, and absolve them all equally. And on this account, indeed, we say that those who were lost have their sins buried and are justified before God because, as he hates sin, he can love only those whom he has justified. This is a wonderful plan of justification that, covered by the righteousness of Christ, they should not tremble at the judgment they deserve, and

---

[24] *"Secundum ratam partem,"* a variation of the commercial law phrase *pro rata parte,* whence English "prorate."

that while they rightly condemn themselves, they should be accounted righteous outside themselves.

12. Refutation of Osiander

^eYet my readers ought to be warned to pay careful attention to that mystery which Osiander boasts he does not wish to hide from them. For first he contends long and verbosely that we attain favor with God not by imputation of Christ's righteousness alone, because it would be impossible (I use his words) for him to regard as just those who are not just. In the end, he concludes that Christ has been given to us as righteousness, not in respect to his human but to his divine nature. And although this can be found only in the person of the Mediator, still it is not a righteousness of man but of God. Now he does not weave his rope from the two kinds of righteousness but obviously deprives Christ's human nature of the office of justifying. Moreover, it behooves us to understand how he fights. In the same place it is said that Christ has become wisdom for us [I Cor. 1:30], but this applies only to the eternal word. Therefore Christ the man is not righteousness. I reply: the only-begotten Son of God was indeed his eternal wisdom, but in a different way this name is applied to him in Paul's letters, for in him "are hid all the treasures of wisdom and knowledge" [Col. 2:3]. What he had with the Father [cf. John 17:5] he revealed to us. Hence what Paul says applies not to the essence of the Son of God but to our use, and rightly fits Christ's human nature. For even though the light shone in the darkness before he assumed flesh [John 1:5], yet the light was hidden until Christ came forth in the nature of man, the Sun of Righteousness, and he therefore calls himself "the light of the world" [John 8:12].

Osiander also stupidly objects that the power of justifying is far above both angels and men, inasmuch as this depends not upon the dignity of any creature but upon God's appointment. If the angels should wish to make satisfaction to God, they would achieve nothing, for they are not destined for this end. But this especially belonged to the man Christ, as he submitted to the law to redeem us from its curse [Gal. 3:13; cf. ch. 4:4].

Also, those who deny that Christ is our righteousness according to his divine nature are by Osiander very basely accused of leaving only one part of Christ and—what is worse—making two Gods. For even though they confess that God dwells in us, they still claim that we are not righteous by the righteousness of God. For if we call Christ the author of life, seeing that he underwent death "that . . . he might destroy him who had the power of death" [Heb. 2:14 p.], we do not thereby deprive the whole Christ of this honor, as he is God manifested in the flesh. Rather, we are only making clear how God's righteousness comes to us that we may enjoy it. On this point Osiander has fallen into abominable error. We do not deny that what has been plainly revealed to us in Christ derives from God's secret grace and power, nor do we contend over the fact that the righteousness Christ bestows upon us is the righteousness of God, which proceeds from him. But we steadfastly hold that in Christ's death and resurrection there is righteousness and life for us. I leave out that shameful heap of passages with which, without discrimination and even without common sense, he burdened his readers, to the effect that whenever righteousness is mentioned one ought to understand it as "essential righteousness." For example, when David calls upon God's righteousness to help him, even though he does so more than a hundred times, Osiander does not hesitate to corrupt as many passages.

The other objection is not a whit stronger: that righteousness is properly and correctly defined as that by which we are moved to act rightly, but that "God alone is at work in us both to will and to perfect" [Phil. 2:13 p.]. I do not deny that God reforms us by his Spirit into holiness and righteousness of life. First, however, it must be seen whether he does this of himself and directly or through the hand of his Son, to whom he has entrusted the whole fullness of the Holy Spirit in order that by his abundance he may supply what is lacking in his members. Then, although righteousness comes forth to us from the secret wellspring of his divinity, it does not follow that Christ, who in the flesh sanctified himself for our sake [John 17:19], is righteousness for us according to his divine nature.

What he adds is no less absurd: that Christ himself was righteous by divine righteousness; for unless the will of the Father had impelled him not even he would have fulfilled the tasks enjoined upon him.[25] For even though it was elsewhere said that all the merits of Christ himself flow solely from God's good pleasure,[26] this adds nothing to the fantasy wherewith Osiander bewitches his own eyes and those of the simple-minded. For who allows anyone to infer that because God is the source and beginning of our righteousness we are righteous in essence, and the essence of God's righteousness dwells in us? In redeeming the church, says Isaiah, God "put on his own righteousness as a breastplate" [Isa. 59:17]. Did he do this to deprive Christ of the armor

[25] Osiander, Confession N 4b–O 3a.
[26] II. xvii. 1.

that he had given him so that Christ might not be the perfect Redeemer? But the prophet only meant that God borrowed nothing outside himself, nor had he any help to redeem us. Paul has briefly indicated this in other words, saying, that he gave us salvation to show his righteousness [Rom. 3:25]. But this in no way contradicts what he teaches elsewhere: that "we are righteous by the obedience of one man" [Rom. 5:19 p.]. In short, whoever wraps up two kinds of righteousness in order that miserable souls may not repose wholly in God's mere mercy, crowns Christ in mockery with a wreath of thorns [Mark 15:17, etc.].

(*Refutation of Scholastic doctrines of good works as effective for justification, 13–20*)

13. Righteousness by faith and righteousness by works

ᵇBut a great part of mankind[27] imagine that righteousness is composed of faith and works.[28] Let us also, to begin with, show that faith righteousness so differs from works righteousness that when one is established the other has to be overthrown. The apostle says that he "counts everything as dross" that he "may gain Christ and be found in him, . . . not having a righteousness of [his] own, based on law, but one that is through faith in Jesus Christ, the righteousness from God through faith" [Phil. 3:8–9 p.]. You see here both a comparison of opposites and an indication that a man who wishes to obtain Christ's righteousness must abandon his own righteousness. Therefore, he states elsewhere that this was the cause of the Jews' downfall: "Wishing to establish their own righteousness, they did not submit to God's righteousness" [Rom. 10:3 p.]. If by establishing our own righteousness we shake off the righteousness of God, to attain the latter we must indeed completely do away with the former. He also shows this very thing when he states that our boasting is not excluded by law but by faith [Rom. 3:27]. From this it follows that so long as any particle of works righteousness remains some occasion for boasting remains with us. Now, if faith excludes all boasting, works righteousness can in no way be associated with faith righteousness. ᶜIn this sense he speaks so clearly in the fourth chapter of Romans that no place is left for cavils or shifts: "If Abraham," says Paul, "was justified by works, he has something to boast about." He adds, "Yet he has no reason to boast before God"

---

[27] Cf. Horace, *Satires* I. i. 61: "*At bona pars hominum decepta cupidine falso*" (LCL edition, p. 8).

[28] Fisher, *Confutatio*, pp. 65 ff.; Cochlaeus, *Confutatio ccccc articulorum M. Lutheri*, articles 26, 462; Cochlaeus, *Philippicae in apologiam Philippi Melanchthonis* (1534) III. 10, fo. H 2b, 3a.

[Rom. 4:2]. It follows, therefore, that he was not justified by works. Then Paul sets forth another argument from contraries. When reward is made for works it is done out of debt, not of grace [Rom. 4:4]. But righteousness according to grace is owed to faith. Therefore it does not arise from the merits of works. Farewell, then, to the dream of those who think up a righteousness flowing together out of faith and works.

14. Likewise, the works of the regenerated can procure no justification

ᵉThe Sophists, who make game and sport in their corrupting of Scripture and their empty caviling, think they have a subtle evasion. For they explain "works" as meaning those which men not yet reborn do only according to the letter by the effort of their own free will, apart from Christ's grace. But they deny that these refer to spiritual works. For, according to them, man is justified by both faith and works provided they are not his own works but the gifts of Christ and the fruit of regeneration. For they say that Paul so spoke for no other reason than to convince the Jews, who were relying upon their own strength, that they were foolish to arrogate righteousness to themselves, since the Spirit of Christ alone bestows it upon us not through any effort arising from our own nature. Still they do not observe that in the contrast between the righteousness of the law and of the gospel, which Paul elsewhere introduces, all works are excluded, whatever title may grace them [Gal. 3:11–12]. For he teaches that this is the righteousness of the law, that he who has fulfilled what the law commands should obtain salvation; but this is the righteousness of faith, to believe that Christ died and rose again [Rom. 10:5, 9].

Moreover, we shall see afterward, in its proper place, that the benefits of Christ—sanctification and righteousness—²⁹ are different. From this it follows that not even spiritual works come into account when the power of justifying is ascribed to faith. The statement of Paul where he denies that Abraham had any reason to boast before God—a passage that we have just cited³⁰—because he was not righteous by his works, ought not to be restricted to a literal and outward appearance of virtues or to the effort of free will. But even though the life of the patriarch was spiritual and well-nigh angelic, he did not have sufficient merit of works to acquire righteousness before God.

²⁹ Cf. III. xiv. 9.
³⁰ Referring to the quotation of Rom. 4:2 in sec. 13.

15. The Roman doctrine of grace and good works

e(b)Somewhat too gross are the Schoolmen, who mingle their concoctions. Yet these men infect the simple-minded and unwary with a doctrine no less depraved, cloaking under the disguise of "spirit" and "grace" even the mercy of God, which alone can set fearful souls at rest.[31] Now we confess with Paul that the doers of the law are justified before God; but, because we are all far from observing the law, we infer from this that those works which ought especially to avail for righteousness give us no help because we are destitute of them.

bAs regards the rank and file of the papists or Schoolmen, they are doubly deceived here both because they call faith an assurance of conscience in awaiting from God their reward for merits and because they interpret the grace of God not as the imputation of free righteousness but as the Spirit helping in the pursuit of holiness. They read in the apostle: "Whoever would draw near to God must first believe that he exists and then that he rewards those who seek him" [Heb. 11:6]. But they pay no attention to the way in which he is to be sought. It is clear from their own writings that in using the term "grace" they are deluded. For Lombard explains that justification is given to us through Christ in two ways. First, he says, Christ's death justifies us, while love is aroused through it in our hearts and makes us righteous. Second, because through the same love, sin is extinguished by which the devil held us captive, so that he no longer has the wherewithal to condemn us.[32] You see how he views God's grace especially in justification, in so far as we are directed through the grace of the Holy Spirit to good works. Obviously, he intended to follow Augustine's opinion, but he follows it at a distance and even departs considerably from the right imitation of it. For when Augustine says anything clearly, Lombard obscures it, and if there was anything slightly contaminated in Augustine, he corrupts it. The schools have gone continually from bad to worse until, in headlong ruin, they have plunged into a sort of Pelagian-

---

31 "These men" are sixteenth-century defenders of the medieval system who have gone beyond the Scholastics in their perverse treatment of justification and grace, concealing the divine mercy. See the references in OS IV. 198 f. to Faber, Cochlaeus, Schatzgeyer, Fisher, and Latomus. The important decree on justification of the Council of Trent, session 6 (Jan. 13, 1547), with 33 canons anathematizing those who deviate from the doctrine, closed the debate from the Roman side. (Schaff, Creeds II. 89–118.) Cf. Melanchthon, Acta Concilii Tridentini anno MDXLVI celebrati (dated by Old Style calendar), especially his spirited reply to canon ix of the series, which condemns justification by faith alone, n 7b ff.

32 Lombard, Sentences III. xix. 1 (MPL 192. 795 f.).

ism. For that matter, Augustine's view, or at any rate his manner of stating it, we must not entirely accept. For even though he admirably deprives man of all credit for righteousness and transfers it to God's grace, he still subsumes grace under sanctification, by which we are reborn in newness of life through the Spirit.[33]

16. Our justification according to the judgment of Scripture

ᵇBut Scripture, when it speaks of faith righteousness, leads us to something far different: namely, to turn aside from the contemplation of our own works and look solely upon God's mercy and Christ's perfection. Indeed, it presents this order of justification: to begin with, God deigns to embrace the sinner with his pure and freely given goodness, finding nothing in him except his miserable condition to prompt Him to mercy, since he sees man utterly void and bare of good works; and so he seeks in himself the reason to benefit man. Then God touches the sinner with a sense of his goodness in order that he, despairing of his own works, may ground the whole of his salvation in God's mercy. This is the experience of faith through which the sinner comes into possession of his salvation when from the teaching of the gospel he acknowledges that he has been reconciled to God: that with Christ's righteousness interceding and forgiveness of sins accomplished he is justified. And although regenerated by the Spirit of God, he ponders the everlasting righteousness laid up for him not in the good works to which he inclines but in the sole righteousness of Christ. When these things are pondered one by one, they will give a clear explanation of our opinion. However, they might be arranged in another order, better than the one in which they have been set forth. But it makes little difference, provided they so agree among themselves that we may have the whole matter rightly explained and surely confirmed.

17. Faith righteousness and law righteousness according to Paul

ᵇHere we should recall to mind the relation that we have previously established between faith and the gospel. For faith is said to justify because it receives and embraces the righteousness offered in the gospel. Moreover, because righteousness is said to be offered through the gospel, all consideration of works is excluded. Paul often shows this elsewhere but most clearly in two passages. For in comparing the law and the gospel in the letter to the Romans he says: "the righteousness that is of the law" is

---

[33] Cf. Augustine, *Sermons* cxxx. 2 (MPL 38. 726 f.; tr. LF *Sermons* II. 581 f.); *On the Spirit and the Letter* xiii. 21 (MPL 44. 214; tr. NPNF V. 92), *et passim*. Other citations in Smits II. 41.

such that "the man who practices these things will live by them" [Rom. 10:5]. But the "righteousness that is of faith" [Rom. 10:6] announces salvation "if you believe in your heart and confess with your mouth that Jesus is Lord and that the Father raised him from the dead" [Rom. 10:9 p.]. Do you see how he makes this the distinction between law and gospel: that the former attributes righteousness to works, the latter bestows free righteousness apart from the help of works? This is an important passage, and one that can extricate us from many difficulties if we understand that that righteousness which is given us through the gospel has been freed of all conditions of the law. Here is the reason why he so often opposes the promise to the law, as things mutually contradictory: "If the inheritance is by the law, it is no longer by promise" [Gal. 3:18]; and passages in the same chapter that express this idea.

Now, to be sure, the law itself has its own promises. Therefore, in the promises of the gospel there must be something distinct and different unless we would admit that the comparison is inept. But what sort of difference will this be, other than that the gospel promises are free and dependent solely upon God's mercy, while the promises of the law depend upon the condition of works? ^eAnd let no one here snarl at me that it is the righteousness which men, of their own strength and free will, would obtrude upon God that is rejected—[34] inasmuch as Paul unequivocally teaches that the law, in commanding, profits nothing [cf. Rom. 8:3]. For there is no one, not only of the common folk, but of the most perfect persons, who can fulfill it. To be sure, love is the capstone of the law. When the Spirit of God forms us to such love, why is it not for us a cause of righteousness, except that even in the saints it is imperfect, and for that reason merits no reward of itself?

18. Justification not the wages of works, but a free gift*

^bThe second passage is this: "It is evident that no man is justified before God by the law. For the righteous shall live by faith [cf. Hab. 2:4]. But the law is not of faith; rather, the man who does these things shall live in them" [Gal. 3:11–12, Comm., cf. Vg.]. How would this argument be maintained otherwise than by agreeing that works do not enter the account of faith but must be utterly separated? The law, he says, is different from faith. Why? Because works are required for law righteousness. Therefore it follows that they are not required for faith righteousness.

[34] Eck, *Enchiridion,* ch. v; Council of Trent, session 6, canon i (Schaff, *Creeds* II. 110).

From this relation it is clear that those who are justified by faith are justified apart from the merit of works—in fact, without the merit of works. For faith receives that righteousness which the gospel bestows. Now the gospel differs from the law in that it does not link righteousness to works but lodges it solely in God's mercy. Paul's contention in Romans is similar to this: that Abraham had no occasion to boast, for faith was reckoned as righteousness for him [Rom. 4:2–3]; and he adds as confirmation that the righteousness of faith has a place in circumstances where there are no works for which a reward is due. "Where," he says, "there are works, wages are paid as a debt; what is given to faith is free." [Rom. 4:4–5 p.] Indeed, the meaning of the words he uses there applies also to this passage. He adds a little later that we on this account obtain the inheritance from faith, as according to grace. Hence he infers that this inheritance is free, for it is received by faith [cf. Rom. 4:16]. How is this so except that faith rests entirely upon God's mercy without the assistance of works? eAnd in another passage he teaches, doubtless in the same sense, that "the righteousness of God has been manifested apart from law, although it is attested by the Law and the Prophets" [Rom. 3:21 p.]. For, excluding the law, he denies that we are aided by works and that we attain righteousness by working; instead, we come empty to receive it.

19. Through "faith alone"

bNow the reader sees how fairly the Sophists today cavil against our doctrine when we say that man is justified by faith alone [Rom. 3:28].[35] They dare not deny that man is justified by faith because it recurs so often in Scripture. But since the word "alone" is nowhere expressed, they do not allow this addition to be made. Is it so? But what will they reply to these words of Paul where he contends that righteousness cannot be of faith unless it be free [Rom. 4:2 ff.]? How will a free gift agree with works? With what chicaneries will they elude what he says in another passage, that God's righteousness is revealed in the gospel [Rom. 1:17]? If righteousness is revealed in the gospel, surely no mutilated or half righteousness but a full and perfect righteousness is contained

---

[35] Luther, in translating the New Testament, used the expression "by faith alone" in Rom. 3:28. This is defended by Melanchthon, *Apology of the Augsburg Confession* IV. 73 (*Bekenntnisschriften der Evangelisch-Lutherischen Kirche* I. 174; *Concordia Triglotta*, p. 141). Calvin, in defending *sola fide*, is aware that numerous attacks have been made on it, and that it has been roundly condemned by the Council of Trent (see note 31). Cf. Fisher, *Confutatio*, p. 60; Herborn, *Enchiridion* iv (CC 12. 27).

there. The law therefore has no place in it. Not only by a false but by an obviously ridiculous shift they insist upon excluding this adjective. Does not he who takes everything from works firmly enough ascribe everything to faith alone? What, I pray, do these expressions mean: "His righteousness has been manifested apart from the law" [Rom. 3:21 p.]; and, "Man is freely justified" [Rom. 3:24 p.]; and, "Apart from the works of the law" [Rom. 3:28]?

Here they have an ingenious subterfuge: even though they have not devised it themselves but have borrowed it from Origen and certain other ancient writers, it is still utterly silly. They prate that the ceremonial works of the law are excluded, not the moral works.[36] They become so proficient by continual wrangling that they do not even grasp the first elements of logic. Do they think that the apostle was raving when he brought forward these passages to prove his opinion? "The man who does these things will live in them" [Gal. 3:12], and, "Cursed be every one who does not fulfill all things written in the book of the law" [Gal. 3:10 p.]. Unless they have gone mad they will not say that life was promised to keepers of ceremonies or the curse announced only to those who transgress the ceremonies. If these passages are to be understood of the moral law, there is no doubt that moral works are also excluded from the power of justifying. These arguments which Paul uses look to the same end: "Since through the law comes knowledge of sin" [Rom. 3:20], therefore not righteousness. Because "the law works wrath" [Rom. 4:15], hence not righteousness. Because the law does not make conscience certain, it cannot confer righteousness either. Because faith is imputed as righteousness, righteousness is therefore not the reward of works but is given unearned [Rom. 4:4–5]. Because we are justified by faith, our boasting is cut off [Rom. 3:27 p.]. "If a law had been given that could make alive, then righteousness would indeed be by the law. But God consigned all things to sin that the promise might be given to those who believe." [Gal. 3:21–22 p.] Let them now babble, if they dare, that these statements apply to ceremonies, not to morals. Even schoolboys would hoot at such impudence. Therefore, let us hold as certain that when the ability to justify is denied to the law, these words refer to the whole law.

---

[36] Apparently the reference to Origen is in error. It has been traced (OS IV. 203) to a quotation of Pelagius by Jerome, *Commentary on Romans*, ch. 3 (MPL 30. 66), and is found also in Pseudo-Ambrose, *Commentary on Romans* 3 (MPL 17. 79). It is employed by Herborn, *Enchiridion* iv (CC 12. 30), and other disputants.

20. "Works of the law"

ᵇIf anyone should wonder why the apostle, not content with naming works, uses such a qualification, there is a ready explanation. Though works are highly esteemed, they have their value from God's approval rather than from their own worth. For who would dare recommend works righteousness to God unless God himself approved? Who would dare demand a reward due unless he promised it? Therefore, it is from God's beneficence that they are considered worthy both of the name of righteousness and of the reward thereof. And so, for this one reason, works have value, because through them man intends to show obedience to God. Therefore, to prove that Abraham could not be justified by works, the apostle declares in another place that the law was given fully four hundred and thirty years after the covenant was made [Gal. 3:17]. The ignorant would laugh at this sort of argument, on the ground that before the promulgation of the law there could have been righteous works. But because he knew that works could have such great value only by the testimony and vouchsafing of God, he took as a fact that previous to the law they had no power to justify. We have the reason why he expressly mentions the works of the law when he wants to take justification away from them, for it is clearly because a controversy can be raised only over them.

Yet he sometimes excepts all works without any qualification, as when on David's testimony he states that blessedness is imparted to that man to whom God reckons righteousness apart from works [Rom. 4:6; Ps. 32:1–2]. Therefore no cavils of theirs can prevent us from holding to the exclusive expression[37] as a general principle.

Also, they pointlessly strive after the foolish subtlety that we are justified by faith alone, which acts through love, so that righteousness depends upon love.[38] Indeed, we confess with Paul that no other faith justifies "but faith working through love" [Gal. 5:6]. But it does not take its power to justify from that working of love. Indeed, it justifies in no other way but in that it leads us into fellowship with the righteousness of Christ. Otherwise, everything that the apostle insists upon so vigorously would fall. "Now to him who works the pay is not considered a gift but his due," says he. [Rom. 4:4.] "But to one who does not work but believes in him who justifies the ungodly, his faith is reckoned as righteousness." [Rom. 4:5.] Could he have spoken more clearly

---

[37] *"Quin generalem exclusivam obtineamus."*
[38] Fisher, *Confutatio*, pp. 65 f., 80; Herborn, *Enchiridion* iv (CC 12. 27 ff.); Cochlaeus, *Philippicae* III. 10; De Castro, *Adversus haereses* VII, art. *"fides"* (1543, fo. 24 K–105 D).

than in contending thus: that there is no righteousness of faith
except where there are no works for which a reward is due? And
then that faith is reckoned as righteousness only where righteousness is bestowed through a grace not owed?

(*Sins are remitted only through the righteousness of Christ,
21–23*)

21. Justification, reconciliation, forgiveness of sins

ᵇNow let us examine how true that statement is which is spoken
in the definition, that the righteousness of faith is reconciliation
with God, which consists solely in the forgiveness of sins.³⁹ We
must always return to this axiom: the wrath of God rests upon
all so long as they continue to be sinners. Isaiah has very well
expressed it in these words: "The Lord's hand is not shortened,
that it cannot save, or his ear dull, that it cannot hear; but your
iniquities have made a separation between you and your God,
and your sins have hid his face from you lest he hear" [Isa. 59:
1–2]. We are told that sin is division between man and God, the
turning of God's face away from the sinner; and it cannot happen
otherwise, seeing that it is foreign to his righteousness to have any
dealings with sin. For this reason, the apostle teaches that man
is God's enemy until he is restored to grace through Christ [Rom.
5:8–10]. Thus, him whom he receives into union with himself
the Lord is said to justify, because he cannot receive him into
grace nor join him to himself unless he turns him from a sinner
into a righteous man. We add that this is done through forgiveness of sins; for if those whom the Lord has reconciled to himself
be judged by works, they will indeed still be found sinners,
though they ought, nevertheless, to be freed and cleansed from
sin. It is obvious, therefore, that those whom God embraces are
made righteous solely by the fact that they are purified when
their spots are washed away by forgiveness of sins. Consequently,
such righteousness can be called, in a word, "remission of sins."

*22. Scriptural proof for the close relation between justification
and forgiveness of sins*

ᵇPaul's words, which I have already quoted,⁴⁰ express both of
these points very beautifully: "God was in Christ reconciling the
world to himself, not counting men's trespasses against them, and
has entrusted to us the word of reconciliation" [II Cor. 5:19, cf.
Comm. and Vg.]. Then Paul adds the summation of Christ's

³⁹ Secs. 2 and 4, above.
⁴⁰ Sec. 4.

embassy: "Him who knew not sin he made to be sin for us so that we might be made the righteousness of God in him" [II Cor. 5:21]. Here he mentions righteousness and reconciliation indiscriminately, to have us understand that each one is reciprocally contained in the other. Moreover, he teaches the way in which this righteousness is to be obtained: namely, when our sins are not counted against us. Therefore, doubt no longer how God may justify us when you hear that he reconciles us to himself by not counting our sins against us. Thus, by David's testimony Paul proves to the Romans that righteousness is imputed to man apart from works, for David declares that man "blessed whose transgressions are forgiven, whose sins are covered, to whom the Lord has not imputed iniquity" [Rom. 4:6–8; Ps. 32:1 2]. Undoubtedly, he there substitutes blessedness for righteousness; since he declares that it consists in forgiveness of sins, there is no reason to define it differently. Accordingly, Zechariah, the father of John the Baptist, sings that the knowledge of salvation rests in the forgiveness of sins [Luke 1:77]. Paul followed this rule in the sermon on the sum of salvation that he delivered to the people of Antioch. As Luke reports it, he concluded in this way: "Through this man forgiveness of sins is proclaimed to you, and every one that believes in him is justified from all things from which you could not be justified by the law of Moses" [Acts 13:38–39 p.]. The apostle so connects forgiveness of sins with righteousness that he shows them to be exactly the same. From this he duly reasons that the righteousness that we obtain through God's kindness is free to us.

ᶜAnd this ought not to seem an unusual expression, that believers are made righteous before God not by works but by free acceptance, since it occurs so often in Scripture, and ancient writers also sometimes speak thus. So says Augustine in one place: "The righteousness of the saints in this world consists more in the forgiveness of sins than in perfection of virtues."[41] ᵉBernard's famous sentences correspond to this: "Not to sin is the righteousness of God; but the righteousness of man is the grace of God."[42] And he had previously declared: "Christ is our righteousness in absolution, and therefore those alone are righteous who obtain pardon from his mercy."[43]

---

[41] Augustine, *City of God* XIX. xxvii (MPL 41. 657; tr. NPNF II. 419).
[42] Bernard, *Sermons on the Song of Songs* xxiii. 15 (MPL 183. 892; tr. S. J. Eales, *Life and Works of St. Bernard* IV. 141).
[43] Bernard, *op. cit.,* xxii. 6, 11 (MPL 183. 880, 884; tr. Eales, *op. cit.,* IV. 126, 130).

23. Righteous—not in ourselves but in Christ

ᵇFrom this it is also evident that we are justified before God solely by the intercession of Christ's righteousness. This is equivalent to saying that man is not righteous in himself but because the righteousness of Christ is communicated to him by imputation —something worth carefully noting. Indeed, that frivolous notion disappears, that man is justified by faith because by Christ's righteousness he shares the Spirit of God, by whom he is rendered righteous.[44] This is too contrary to the above doctrine ever to be reconciled to it. And there is no doubt that he who is taught to seek righteousness outside himself is destitute of righteousness in himself. Moreover, the apostle most clearly asserts this when he writes: "He who knew not sin was made the atoning sacrifice of sin for us so that we might be made the righteousness of God in him" [II Cor. 5:21 p.].[45]

You see that our righteousness is not in us but in Christ, that we possess it only because we are partakers in Christ; indeed, with him we possess all its riches. And this does not contradict what he teaches elsewhere, that sin has been condemned for sin in Christ's flesh that the righteousness of the law might be fulfilled in us [Rom. 8:3–4]. The only fulfillment he alludes to is that which we obtain through imputation. For in such a way does the Lord Christ share his righteousness with us that, in some wonderful manner, he pours into us enough of his power to meet the judgment of God. It is quite clear that Paul means exactly the same thing in another statement, which he had put a little before: "As we were made sinners by one man's disobedience, so we have been justified by one man's obedience" [Rom. 5:19 p.]. To declare that by him alone we are accounted righteous,[46] what else is this but to lodge our righteousness in Christ's obedience, because the obedience of Christ is reckoned to us as if it were our own?

For this reason, it seems to me that Ambrose beautifully stated an example of this righteousness in the blessing of Jacob: noting that, as he did not of himself deserve the right of the first-born, concealed in his brother's clothing and wearing his brother's coat, which gave out an agreeable odor [Gen. 27:27], he ingratiated himself with his father, so that to his own benefit he received the blessing while impersonating another. And we in like manner hide under the precious purity of our first-born brother,

---

[44] Lombard, *Sentences* II. xxvii. 6 (MPL 192. 715); Duns Scotus, *On the Sentences* II. xxvii. 1. 3 (*Opera omnia* XIII. 249).

[45] Cf. Comm. II Cor. 5:21, where Calvin discusses Christ's "expiatory sacrifice."

[46] *"Nos haberi iustos."*

Christ, so that we may be attested righteous in God's sight. [46x]Here are the words of Ambrose: "That Isaac smelled the odor of the garments perhaps means that we are justified not by works but by faith, since the weakness of the flesh is a hindrance to works, but the brightness of faith, which merits the pardon of sins, overshadows the error of deeds."[47]

[b]And this is indeed the truth, for in order that we may appear before God's face unto salvation we must smell sweetly with his odor, and our vices must be covered and buried by his perfection.

[c]CHAPTER XII

WE MUST LIFT UP OUR MINDS TO GOD'S JUDGMENT SEAT THAT WE MAY BE FIRMLY CONVINCED OF HIS FREE JUSTIFICATION

(Justification in the light of the majesty and perfection of God, 1–3)

1. No one is righteous before God's judgment seat

[b]Even though all these things are by shining testimonies shown to be perfectly true, still, how necessary they are will not be clear to us until we set before our eyes what ought to be the basis of this whole discussion. First, therefore, this fact should occur to us: that our discourse is concerned with the justice not of a human court but of a heavenly tribunal, lest we measure by our own small measure the integrity of works needed to satisfy the divine judgment. Yet it is amazing with what great rashness and boldness this is commonly defined. Indeed, one can see how there are none who more confidently, and as people say, boisterously chatter over the righteousness of works than they who are monstrously plagued with manifest diseases, or creak with defects beneath the skin. That happens because they do not think about God's justice, which they would never hold in such derision if they were affected even by the slightest feeling of it. [b(a)]Yet surely it is held of precious little value if it is not recognized as God's justice and so perfect that nothing can be admitted except what is in every part whole and complete and undefiled by any corruption. [b]Such was never found in man and never will be. [b(a)]In the shady cloisters of the schools anyone can easily and readily prattle about the value of works in justifying men. [b]But when we come before the presence of God we must put away such amusements! For there we deal with a serious matter, and do not engage in

[46x] "Here are the words . . . error of deeds." Addition of 1553.
[47] Ambrose, *On Jacob and the Happy Life* II. ii. 9 (CSEL 32. ii. 36 f.).

frivolous word battles.[1] To this question, I insist, we must apply our mind if we would profitably inquire concerning true righteousness: How shall we reply to the Heavenly Judge when he calls us to account?[2] Let us envisage for ourselves that Judge, not as our minds naturally imagine him, but as he is depicted for us in Scripture: by whose brightness the stars are darkened [Job 3:9]; by whose strength the mountains are melted; by whose wrath the earth is shaken [cf. Job 9:5–6]; whose wisdom catches the wise in their craftiness [Job 5:13]; beside whose purity all things are defiled [cf. Job 25:5]; whose righteousness not even the angels can bear [cf. Job 4:18]; who makes not the guilty man innocent [cf. Job 9:20]; whose vengeance when once kindled penetrates to the depths of hell [Deut. 32:22; cf. Job 26:6]. Let us behold him, I say, sitting in judgment to examine the deeds of men: Who will stand confident before his throne? "Who . . . can dwell with the devouring fire?" asks the prophet. "Who . . . can dwell with everlasting burnings? He who walks righteously and speaks the truth" [Isa. 33:14–15 p.], etc. But let such a one, whoever he is, come forward. Nay, that response causes no one to come forward. For, on the contrary, a terrible voice resounds: "If thou, O Lord, shouldst mark iniquities, Lord, who shall stand?" [Ps. 130:3; 129:3, Vg.]. Indeed, all must soon perish, as it is written in another place: "Shall a man be justified in comparison with God, or shall he be purer than his maker? Behold, they that serve him are not faithful, and in his angels he found wickedness. How much more shall those who dwell in houses of clay, who have an earthly foundation, be consumed before the moth. From morn to eve they shall be cut down" [Job 4:17–20]. Likewise: "Behold, among his saints none is faithful, and the heavens are not pure in his sight. How much more abominable and unprofitable is man, who drinks iniquity like water?" [Job 15:15–16, cf. Vg.].

ᵉIndeed, I admit that in The Book of Job mention is made of a righteousness higher than the observance of the law, and it is worth-while to maintain this distinction. For even if someone satisfied the law, not even then could he stand the test of that righteousness which surpasses all understanding. Therefore, even though Job has a good conscience, he is stricken dumb with astonishment, for he sees that not even the holiness of angels can please

---

[1] "λογομαχία."

[2] This sentence first appears in the Latin *Institutio* published in August, 1539. It is related to the letter of Sadoleto to the magistrats of Geneva, March 18, and Calvin's reply to this, September 1, 1539. Sadoleto asked how a convert to the Reformation would answer "before the dread tribunal of the sovereign Judge," and to this Calvin cogently replied. See OS I. 451, 480-486; tr. Calvin, *Tracts* I. 16, 55 ff.; LCC XXII. 246-250.

God if he should weigh their works in his heavenly scales. Therefore, I now pass over that righteousness which I have mentioned, for it is incomprehensible. I only say that if our life is examined according to the standard of the written law, we are sluggish indeed if we are not tormented with horrid fear at those many maledictions with which God willed to cleanse us—among others this general curse: "Cursed be everyone who does not abide by everything written in this book" [Gal. 3:10, Vg.; cf. Deut. 27:26]. In short, this whole discussion will be foolish and weak unless every man admit his guilt before the Heavenly Judge, and concerned about his own acquittal, willingly cast himself down and confess his nothingness.

2. Righteousness before men and righteousness before God

ᵇHither, hither we ought to have raised up our eyes to learn how to tremble rather than vainly to exult. Indeed, it is easy, so long as the comparison stops with men, for anyone to think of himself as having something that his fellows ought not to despise. But when we rise up toward God, that assurance of ours vanishes in a flash and dies. And exactly the same thing happens to our souls with respect to God as happens to our bodies with respect to the visible heavens. For keenness of sight, so long as it confines itself to examining nearby objects, is convinced of its discernment. But directed toward the sun, stricken and numbed by excessive brightness, our vision feels as weak as it did strong in gazing at objects below.[3] Let us, then, not be deceived by empty confidence. Even though we consider ourselves either equal or superior to other men, that is nothing to God, to whose judgment the decision of the matter must be brought. But if our wildness cannot be tamed by these warnings, he will answer us as he spoke to the Pharisees: "Ye are they that justify yourselves before men; but . . . what is exalted among men is an abomination to God" [Luke 16:15, cf. Vg.]. Go now and haughtily boast of your righteousness among men, while God from heaven abominates it!

But what say God's servants, truly instructed by his Spirit? "Enter not into judgment with thy servant, for no man living is righteous in thy sight." [Ps. 143:2; cf. Comm. and Ps. 142:2, Vg.] Another servant speaks, although in a slightly different sense: "A man cannot be righteous before God. If he wished to contend with him, he could not answer him once in a thousand times" [Job 9:2–3; cf. v. 3, Vg.]. Here, then, we are clearly told the nature of God's righteousness, which will indeed not be satisfied by any works of man. When it examines our thousand sins,

---

[3] Cf. I. i. 2.

we cannot be cleansed of even one. Surely that chosen instrument of God, Paul, had sincerely conceived such a righteousness when he confessed that he was not aware of anything against himself but that he was not thereby justified [I Cor. 4:4].

3. Augustine and Bernard of Clairvaux as witnesses of true righteousness

ᶜSuch examples are found not only in Holy Scripture but all devout writers show that this was their view. So Augustine says: "All the pious who groan under this burden of corruptible flesh and in this weakness of life have one hope: that we have one Mediator, Jesus Christ the righteous one, and he is the appeasement for our sins" [cf. I Tim. 2:5–6].[4] What do we hear? If this is their only hope, where is confidence in works? For when he says "only," he leaves no other hope. Now Bernard says: "Where, in fact, are safe and firm rest and security for the weak but in the Savior's wounds? The mightier he is to save, the more securely I dwell there. The world menaces, the body weighs us down, the devil sets his snares. I fall not, for I am grounded upon firm rock. I have sinned a grave sin. My conscience is disturbed, but it will not be perturbed[5] because I shall remember the Lord's wounds." From these thoughts he afterward concludes: "Accordingly, the Lord's compassion is my merit. Obviously, I am not devoid of merit so long as he is not devoid of compassion. But if the mercies of the Lord abound, then equally do I abound in merits. Shall I sing my own righteous acts? O Lord, I shall remember thy righteousness only, for it is also mine. Namely, he was made righteousness for me by God." Also, in another place, "This is man's whole merit if he put his whole hope in him who makes safe the whole man." ᶜSimilarly, where keeping peace to himself, he leaves the glory to God. "To Thee," he says, "may glory remain undiminished. It will go well with me if I shall have peace. I utterly abjure glory, lest, if I usurp what is not mine, I shall also lose what has been offered to me." He speaks even more openly in another passage: "Why should the church be concerned about merits, since it has in God's purpose a surer reason for glorying? Thus there is no reason why you should ask by what merits we may hope for benefits, especially since you hear in the prophet: 'It is not for your sake . . . that I am about to act, but for mine . . . says the Lord' [Ezek. 36:22, 32 p.]. Merit enough it is to know that merits are not enough; but as it is merit enough not to presume

---

[4] Augustine, *Against Two Letters of the Pelagians* III. v. 15 (MPL 44. 599; tr. NPNF V. 409).

[5] "*Turbatur . . . non perturbabitur.*"

upon merits, so to be without merits is enough for judgment."
The fact that he uses the term "merits" freely for good works,
we must excuse as the custom of the time. But essentially his intention was to strike fear in hypocrites, who in their unbridled
sinning act shamelessly against God's grace. This he presently
explains: "Happy is the church that lacks neither merits without
presumption nor presumption without merits. It has cause for
presumption but not merits. It has merits, but to make it deserving, not to make it presumptuous. Is not to refrain from presum-
ing really to merit? It then presumes the more boldly in that it
presumes not, having ample occasion to glory in the Lord's abundant mercies."[6]

(*Conscience and self-criticism before God deprive us of all
claim to good works and lead us to embrace God's mercy, 4–8*)
4. The gravity of God's judgment puts an end to all self-deception
ᶜThis is the truth. Awakened consciences, when they have to do
with God's judgment, recognize this as the only safe haven in
which they can securely breathe. ᵇFor if the stars, which seem so
very bright at night, lose their brilliance in the sight of the sun,
what do we think will happen even to the rarest innocence of man
when it is compared with God's purity? For it will be a very severe
test, which will penetrate to the most hidden thoughts of the
heart; and, as Paul says, "he will bring to light the things hidden
in darkness, and will uncover the hidden purposes of hearts" [I
Cor. 4:5 p.]. This will compel the lurking and lagging conscience
to utter all things that have now even been forgotten. Our accuser
the devil, mindful of all the transgressions that he has impelled
us to perpetrate, will press us. Outward parade of good works,
which alone we now esteem, will be of no benefit there; purity
of will alone will be demanded of us. And therefore hypocrisy
shall fall down confounded, even as it now vaunts itself with
drunken boldness. This applies not only to that hypocrisy by
which a man, knowing himself guilty before God, strives to show
himself off among men but also to that by which every man
deceives himself before God, prone as we are to pamper and
flatter ourselves. They who do not direct their attention to such
a spectacle can, indeed, for the moment pleasantly and peacefully
construct a righteousness for themselves, but one that will soon
in God's judgment be shaken from them, just as great riches

---

[6] Bernard, *On the Psalm, He That Dwelleth* (Ps. 91) xv. 5 (MPL 183. 246); *Sermons on the Song of Songs* lxi. 3; xiii. 4; lxviii. 6 (MPL 183. 1072, 836, 1111;
tr. Eales, *Life and Works of St. Bernard* IV. 367, 69, 424 f.).

heaped up in a dream vanish upon awakening. But they who seriously, and as in God's sight, will seek after the true rule of righteousness, will certainly find ᵇ⁽ᵃ⁾that all human works, if judged according to their own worth, are nothing but filth and defilement. And what is commonly reckoned righteousness is before God sheer iniquity; what is adjudged uprightness, pollution; what is accounted glory, ignominy.

5. Away with all self-admiration!

ᵇLet us not be ashamed to descend from this contemplation of divine perfection to look upon ourselves,⁷ without flattery and without being affected by blind self-love. For it is no wonder if we be so blind in this respect, since none of us guards against that pestilent self-indulgence which, as Scripture proclaims, inheres in all of us by nature. "To every man," says Solomon, "his way is right in his own eyes." [Prov. 21:2 p.] Again, "All the ways of a man seem pure in his own eyes." [Prov. 16:2.] What then? Is he acquitted by this delusion? No indeed, but, as is added in the same passage, "the Lord weighs men's hearts" [Prov. 16:2 p.]. That is, while man flatters himself on account of the outward mask of righteousness that he wears, the Lord meanwhile weighs in his scales the secret impurity of the heart. Since, therefore, a man is far from being benefited by such flatteries, let us not, to our ruin, willingly delude ourselves. In order that we may rightly examine ourselves, our consciences must necessarily be called before God's judgment seat. For there is need to strip entirely bare in its light the secret places of our depravity, which otherwise are too deeply hidden. Then only will we clearly see the value of these words: "Man is far from being justified before God, man who is rottenness and a worm" [Job 25:6, cf. Vg.], "abominable and empty, who drinks iniquity like water" [Job 15:16]. "For who could make clean what has been conceived of unclean seed? Not one." [Job 14:4, cf. Vg.] Then we shall also experience what Job said of himself: "If I would show myself innocent, my own mouth will condemn me; if righteous, it will prove me perverse" [Job 9:20, cf. Vg.]. For the complaint that the prophet of old made concerning Israel does not apply to one age but to all ages: "All . . . like sheep have gone astray; everyone has turned to his own way" [Isa. 53:6 p.]. Indeed, he there includes all those to whom the grace of redemption was to come. And the rigor of this examination ought to proceed to the extent of casting us down into complete consternation, and in this way preparing us

⁷ Cf. I. i. 2; I. v. 3, 10; II. viii. 1; III. xiii. 3.

to receive Christ's grace. For he who considers himself capable of enjoying it is deceived unless he has first humbled all haughtiness of mind. This is a well-known passage: "God confounds the proud, but gives grace to the humble" [I Peter 5:5; James 4:6; cf. Prov. 3:34].

6. What humility before God is

ᵇBut what way do we have to humble ourselves except that, wholly poor and destitute, we yield to God's mercy? ᵃFor if we think that we have anything left to ourselves, I do not call it humility. And those who have hitherto joined these two things together—namely, that we must think humbly concerning ourselves before God and must reckon our righteousness to be of some value—have taught a pernicious hypocrisy.[8] For if we confess before God contrary to what we feel, we wickedly lie to him. ᵇBut we cannot feel as we ought without immediately trampling upon whatever seems glorious in us. Therefore, when you hear in the prophet that salvation has been prepared for the humble people, and abasement for the eyes of the proud [Ps. 18:27; cf. Ps. 17:28, Vg.], first consider that the gateway to salvation does not lie open unless we have laid aside all pride and taken upon ourselves perfect humility; secondly, that this humility is not some seemly behavior whereby you yield a hair of your right to the Lord, as those who do not act haughtily or insult others are called humble in the sight of men, although they rely upon some consciousness of excellence. Rather, this humility is an unfeigned submission of our heart, stricken down in earnest with an awareness of its own misery and want. For so it is everywhere described by the Word of God.

When the Lord speaks thus in Zephaniah, "I will remove from you the proudly exultant . . . and leave in the midst of your people the afflicted and poor, and they shall hope in the Lord," does he not clearly point out who the humble are? [ch. 3:11–12]. They are those who lie afflicted with the knowledge of their own poverty. On the other hand, Scripture calls the proud ones "exultant" because men happy in their prosperity usually leap for joy. But to the humble, whom he plans to save, he leaves nothing but to hope in the Lord. So also in Isaiah: "But to whom will I look, save to him who is lowly and contrite in spirit, and trembles at my words" [Isa. 66:2, Vg.]? Likewise: "The high and lofty one

---

[8] Cf. Cochlaeus, *De libero arbitrio hominis* (1525), fo. O 7a: *"Non sumus natura impii."* (It is not sin for us to be bipeds, or to walk with countenance uplifted toward the stars . . .; vice is against nature.)

who inhabits eternity, whose name is Holy, dwelling in the high and holy place, and with a contrite and humble spirit, to quicken the spirit of the humble and . . . the heart of the contrite." [Isa. 57:15, Vg.]

Whenever you hear the word "contrition," understand a wound of the heart that does not permit a man cast to the ground to be raised up. If you would, according to God's judgment, be exalted with the humble,[9] your heart ought to be wounded with such contrition. If that does not happen, you will be humbled by God's powerful hand to your shame and disgrace.

7. *Christus calls sinners, not the righteous*

[b]And our most excellent Master, not content with words, in a parable represents to us, as in a picture, the image of proper humility. For he brings forward a "publican, standing afar off, and not daring to lift his eyes to heaven, who prays with much weeping, 'Lord, be merciful to me a sinner'" [Luke 18:13 p.]. Let us not think these signs of feigned modesty: that he does not dare to look up to heaven or to come nearer, and that, beating his breast, he confesses himself a sinner. But let us know these to be testimonies of an inner feeling. On the other side he puts the Pharisee, who thanks God because he is not a common man, either an extortioner or unjust, or an adulterer, and since he fasts twice in the week and gives tithes of all that he has [Luke 18:11–12]. In his open confession he acknowledges that the righteousness he has is a gift of God; but because he is confident that he is righteous, unpleasing and hateful, he departs from God's face. The publican is justified by the acknowledgment of his iniquity [Luke 18:14]. Hence, we may see how much favor our abasement has before the Lord, so that the heart cannot be opened to receive his mercy unless it be utterly empty of all opinion of its own worth. When it has been occupied with these things it closes the entry to him. That no one should doubt concerning this, Christ was sent to the earth by the Father with this commission: "To publish good tidings to the poor, to heal the contrite of heart, to preach liberty to the captives, deliverance to the imprisoned, . . . to console the sorrowing . . . , to give them glory instead of ashes, oil . . . instead of mourning, the mantle of praise instead of a spirit of grief" [Isa. 61:1–3 p.]. According to this commandment, he invites to share his beneficence only those who labor and are heavy-laden [Matt. 11:28]. [e]And in another passage: "I have come not to call the righteous but sinners" [Matt. 9:13].

---

[9] Cf. II. i. 2; II. ii. 11, note 49.

8. Arrogance and complacency before God block our way to Christ

ᵉTherefore, if we would give ear to Christ's call, away with all arrogance and complacency! Arrogance arises from a foolish persuasion of our own righteousness, when man thinks that he has something meritorious to commend him before God. Complacency can exist even without any belief in works. For many sinners are so drunk with the sweetness of their vices that they think not upon God's judgment but lie dazed, as it were, in a sort of drowsiness, and do not aspire to the mercy offered to them. Such sloth is no less to be shaken off than any confidence in ourselves is to be cast away in order that we may without hindrance hasten to Christ, and empty and hungering, may be filled with his good things. ᵃFor we will never have enough confidence in him unless we become deeply distrustful of ourselves; we will never lift up our hearts enough in him unless they be previously cast down in us; we will never have consolation enough in him unless we have already experienced desolation in ourselves.

ᵇ⁽ᵃ⁾Therefore we are ready to seize and grasp God's grace when we have utterly cast out confidence in ourselves and rely only on the assurance of his goodness—"when," as Augustine says, "forgetting our own merits, we embrace Christ's gifts."¹⁰ ᶜFor if he sought merits in us, we would not come to his gifts. Bernard is in agreement with this when he neatly compares to faithless servants the proud, who claim even the slightest thing for their own merits because they wrongfully retain the credit for grace that passes through them, as if a wall should say that it gave birth to a sunbeam that it received through a window.¹¹ ᵇNot to halt any longer with this, let us hold it as a brief but general and sure rule that prepared to share the fruit of God's mercy is he who has emptied himself, I do not say of righteousness, which exists not, but of a vain and airy semblance of righteousness. For to the extent that a man rests satisfied with himself, he impedes the beneficence of God.

¹⁰ Augustine, *Sermons* clxxiv. 2 (MPL 38. 941; tr. LF *Sermons* II. 891 f.).
¹¹ Bernard, *Sermons on the Song of Songs* xiii. 5 (MPL 183. 836; tr. Eales, *op. cit.*, IV. 70).

ᶜCHAPTER XIII

Two Things to Be Noted in Free Justification

1. Justification serves God's honor; and revelation, his justice

ᵇHere, indeed, we are especially to note two things: namely, that the Lord's glory should stand undiminished and, so to speak, in good repair,[1] and that our consciences in the presence of his judgment should have peaceful rest and serene tranquillity.

We see how often and how earnestly Scripture urges us, wherever righteousness is concerned, to give thanks[2] to God alone. And the apostle even testifies that the Lord's purpose in bestowing righteousness upon us in Christ was "to show us his own righteousness" [Rom. 3:25]. But he immediately adds what the nature of this showing of his righteousness is, in the words: "If he alone is recognized as righteous, and justifying him who has faith in Jesus Christ" [Rom. 3:26 p., cf. Vg.]. Do you see that the righteousness of God is not sufficiently set forth unless he alone be esteemed righteous, and communicate the free gift of righteousness to the undeserving? For this reason he wills that "every mouth be stopped and all the world be rendered accountable to him" [Rom. 3:19 p.]. For, so long as man has anything to say in his own defense, he detracts somewhat from God's glory. Thus in Ezekiel, God teaches how much we glorify his name by recognizing our iniquity. "You shall remember," he says, "your ways and all the crimes with which you have polluted yourselves, and you shall loathe yourselves in your own sight for all the evils you have committed." [Ezek. 20:43, Vg.] "And you shall know that I am the Lord when I shall have bestowed benefits upon you for my name's sake, and not . . . according to your wicked offenses." [Ezek. 20:44, Vg.]

If these things are parts of the true knowledge of God—to be stricken by the awareness of our own iniquity and to reflect that he benefits us, unworthy as we are—why do we attempt, to our great harm, to filch from the Lord even a particle of the thanks we owe his free kindness? Likewise, when Jeremiah proclaims, "Let not the wise man glory in his wisdom, or the rich man in his riches, or the mighty man in his might" [Jer. 9:23, order changed, cf. Vg.], but "let him who glories, glory in the Lord" [I Cor. 1:31, Vg.; cf. Jer. 9:24], does he not imply that God's glory is somewhat diminished if man glories in himself? ᶜSurely

---

[1] *"Sarta tecta,"* lit., "mended and covered," is used by Plautus in this sense: *Trinummus* 317 (LCL Plautus V. 126).

[2] Cf. III. iv. 9, note 19.

Paul accommodates those words to this use when he teaches that every part of our salvation rests with Christ that we may glory in the Lord alone [I Cor. 1:30–31]. His meaning is this: whoever thinks that he has anything at all of his own rises up against God and casts a shadow upon his glory.

2. *He who glories in his own righteousness robs God of his honor*
ᵇThus the matter stands: we never truly glory in him unless we have utterly put off our own glory. On the other hand, ᵃwe must hold this as a universal principle: whoever glories in himself, glories against God. Indeed, ᵇ⁽ᵃ⁾Paul considers that the world only becomes subject to God [cf. Rom. 3:19] when men are utterly deprived of any occasion for glorying. ʰAccordingly, Isaiah, when he announces that the justification of Israel will rest in God, adds at the same time "and praise" [Isa. 45:26, Vg.; cf. ch. 45:25, EV]. It is as if he were to say that the elect are justified by the Lord to the end that they may glory in him and in no other. But he had taught in the preceding verse how we ought to glory in the Lord: namely, that we should swear that our righteous acts and our strength are in the Lord [Isa. 45:24]. Note that not a simple confession is required but one confirmed by an oath, lest you should think it something to be discharged by any kind of feigned humility. And let no man here allege that he does not glory in himself at all when without arrogance he recognizes his own righteousness. For there can be no such estimation without engendering confidence, and no confidence without giving birth to glorying.

Therefore, let us remember in all discussion of righteousness to keep this end in view: that the praise of righteousness remain perfect and whole in the Lord's possession, since it was to manifest his own righteousness that—as the apostle attests—he poured out his grace upon us "so that he himself may be righteous, and the justifier of him who has faith in Christ" [Rom. 3:26, Vg.]. Accordingly, in another passage, having stated that the Lord conferred salvation upon us in order to show forth the glory of his name [Eph. 1:6], so to speak, repeating the same thing, he afterward adds: "By grace you have been saved . . . and . . . by the gift of God, not by works, lest any man should boast" [Eph. 2:8–9 p.]. ᶜAnd Peter, when he points out that we have been called to the hope of salvation so "that we may declare the excellences of him who called us out of darkness into his marvelous light" [I Peter 2:9 p.], doubtless intends that the sole praises of God may so resound in the ears of believers as to overwhelm in deep silence all arrogance of the flesh. ᵇTo sum up, man cannot without sacrilege claim for himself even a crumb of righteousness, for just so much is plucked and taken away from the glory of God's righteousness.

3. A glance at one's own righteousness provides no peace for the conscience

bNow if we ask in what way the conscience can be made quiet before God, we shall find the only way to be that unmerited righteousness be conferred upon us as a gift of God. Let us ever bear in mind Solomon's question: "Who will say, 'I have made my heart clean; I am pure from my sin'?" [Prov. 20:9]. Surely there is no one who is not sunken in infinite filth! Let even the most perfect man descend into his conscience[3] and call his deeds to account, what then will be the outcome for him? Will he sweetly rest as if all things were well composed between him and God and not, rather, be torn by dire torments, since if he be judged by works, he will feel grounds for condemnation within himself? The conscience, if it looks to God, must either have sure peace with his judgment or be besieged by the terrors of hell. Therefore we profit nothing in discussing righteousness unless we establish a righteousness so steadfast that it can support our soul in the judgment of God. When our souls possess that by which they may present themselves fearless before God's face and receive his judgment undismayed, then only may we know that we have found no counterfeit righteousness. b(a)The apostle, then, with good reason strongly insists on this point. I prefer to express it in his words rather than mine. a"If the promise of the inheritance comes from the law, faith is nullified and the promise is void." [Rom. 4:14, cf. Vg.] He first infers that faith has been nullified and canceled if the promise of righteousness looks to the merits of our works, or depends upon the observance of the law. For no one can ever confidently trust in it because no one will ever come to be really convinced in his own mind that he has satisfied the law, as surely no one ever fully satisfies it through works. Not to seek the proof of this too far afield, every man willing to look upon himself with an honest eye can be his own witness.

eAnd this shows in what deep and gloomy recesses hypocrisy buries men's minds when they so confidently coddle themselves that they do not hesitate to set their self-flatteries against God's judgment as if to compel the suspension of his legal proceedings. But a far different concern troubles and torments believers who sincerely examine themselves. aFirst, then, doubt would enter

---

[3] Cf. III. iv. 27; III. xii. 5, note 7.

the minds of all men, and at length despair, while each one reckoned for himself how great a weight of debt still pressed upon
him, and how far away he was from the condition laid down for
him. See faith already oppressed and extinguished! For to have
faith is not to waver, to vary, to be borne up and down, to hesitate, to be held in suspense, to vacillate— finally, to despair!
Rather, to have faith is to strengthen the mind with constant assurance and perfect confidence, to have a place to rest and plant
your foot [cf. I Cor. 2:5; II Cor. 13:4].

4. Attention to one's own righteousness also nullifies the promises
    b(a)Paul also adds another point: that the promise will be void
and without force. bFor if the fulfillment of it depends upon our
merit, when will we at last have reached a place to deserve God's
blessing? b(a)Of a truth, this second point follows from the first:
the promise will be fulfilled only to those who have faith in him.
When, therefore, faith fails, the promise will not remain in force.
b(a)Consequently, the inheritance arises from faith in order to establish the promise according to grace. For it is abundantly confirmed when it rests solely upon God's mercy, since mercy and
truth are joined together by an everlasting bond. aThat is, whatever God mercifully promises, he also faithfully performs. eThus
David, before he asks salvation for himself according to God's
word, first states that its cause lies in God's mercy. "Let thy
mercies come," he says, "to me, thy salvation according to thy
word." [Ps. 119:76; cf. Ps. 118:76, Vg.] And rightly, because it is
by his mere mercy alone that God is led to promise. aTherefore,
on this point we must establish, and as it were, deeply fix all our
hope, paying no regard to our works, to seek any help from them.
    cAugustine also teaches us to act thus—lest you suppose we are
saying something new. "Christ," he says, "will reign forever in
his servants. God has promised this; God has said this; if that is
not enough, God has sworn it. Therefore, since the promise is
firm not according to our merits but according to his mercy, no
one ought to proclaim with misgiving what he cannot doubt."[4]
Also Bernard: " 'Who . . . can be saved?' the disciples of Christ
ask. But Jesus replies: 'With men this is impossible, but not with
God' [Matt. 19:25–26 p.]. This is our whole confidence; this, our
sole comfort; this, the whole reason for our hope. But, sure of
Christ's ability, what do we say of his will? 'Who knows whether
he deserves hate or love?' [Eccl. 9:1, Vg.] 'Who knows the mind of
the Lord, or who has been his counselor?' [Rom. 11:34; cf. Isa.
40:13.] Here, now, plainly there is need of faith to help us; here

Augustine, *Psalms*, Ps. 88. i. 5 (MPL 37. 1123; tr. LF *Psalms* IV. 243 f.).

truth must succor us, that what is hidden from us in the Fat.er's heart may be revealed through the Spirit, and his Spirit testifying may persuade our hearts that we are the children of God [Rom. 8:16]. It is needful, moreover, that he persuade by freely calling and justifying us through faith. In these things, surely, there is a certain intermediate passage from eternal predestination to future glory."[5]

[b]Let us conclude briefly as follows: Scripture shows that God's promises are not established unless they are grasped with the full assurance of conscience. Wherever there is doubt or uncertainty, it pronounces them void. Again, it declares that these promises do nothing but vacillate and waver if they rest upon our own works. Therefore, righteousness must either depart from us or works must not be brought into account, [b(a)]but faith alone must have place, whose nature it is to prick up the ears and close the eyes—that is, to be intent upon the promise alone and to turn thought away from all worth or merit of man. [b]Thus Zechariah's famous prophecy is fulfilled: when the iniquity of this land will be removed, each man "will invite his friend under his vine and under his fig tree" [Zech. 3:9–10]. There the prophet implies that believers will not enjoy true peace until they have obtained forgiveness of sins. [e]For we must grasp this analogy in the prophets: when they discuss Christ's Kingdom, they set forth God's outward blessings as figures of spiritual goods. Hence Christ is called "King of peace" [Isa. 9:6] and "our peace" [Eph. 2:14] because he quiets all agitations of conscience. If we ask the means, we must come to the sacrifice by which God has been appeased. For anyone unconvinced that God is appeased by that one atonement in which Christ endured his wrath will never cease to tremble. In short, we must seek peace for ourselves solely in the anguish of Christ our Redeemer.[6]

5. *Faith in God's free grace alone gives us peace of conscience and gladness in prayer*

[e]But why do I use a rather obscure testimony? Paul consistently denies that peace or quiet joy are retained in consciences unless we are convinced that we are "justified by faith" [Rom. 5:1]. At the same time he declares the source of this assurance: it is when "God's love has been poured into our hearts through the Holy Spirit" [Rom. 5:5]. It is as if he had said that our souls cannot be

---

[5] Bernard, *Sermon on the Dedication of a Church* v. 6 (MPL 183. 523; tr. *St. Bernard's Sermons for the Seasons,* by a priest of Mount Melleray, II. 424).

[6] An adverse reference to Osiander's view of justification is implied here. Cf. III. xi. 5, note 5.

quieted unless we are surely persuaded that we are pleasing to God. Hence also in another passage he exclaims on behalf of all the godly, "Who will separate us from the love of God which is in Christ?" [Rom. 8:35, 39, conflated]. For we shall tremble even at the slightest breath until we arrive at that haven, but we shall be secure even in the darkness of death so long as the Lord shows himself our shepherd [cf. Ps. 23:1, 4]. Therefore, those who prate that we are justified by faith because, being reborn, we are righteous by living spiritually[7] have never tasted the sweetness of grace,[8] so as to consider that God will be favorable to them. Hence, it also follows that they no more know the right way to pray than do the Turks and other profane nations. For, as Paul attests, faith is not true unless it asserts and brings to mind that sweetest name of Father[9]—nay, unless it opens our mouth freely to cry, "Abba, Father" [Gal. 4:6; Rom. 8:15]. He expresses this more clearly elsewhere: "In Christ we have boldness and access with confidence through . . . faith in him" [Eph. 3:12 p.]. This surely does not take place through the gift of regeneration, which, as it is always imperfect in this flesh, so contains in itself manifold grounds for doubt. Therefore, we must come to this remedy: that believers should be convinced that their only ground of hope for the inheritance of a Heavenly Kingdom lies in the fact that, being engrafted in the body of Christ, they are freely accounted righteous. For, as regards justification, faith is something merely passive, bringing nothing of ours to the recovering of God's favor but receiving from Christ that which we lack.

^cCHAPTER XIV

THE BEGINNING OF JUSTIFICATION AND ITS CONTINUAL PROGRESS

(*Man in his natural state dead in sins and in need of redemption, 1–6*)
1. Four classes of men with regard to justification[†]
  ^bTo make this matter clearer, let us examine what kind of righteousness is possible to man through the whole course of his life; let us, indeed, make a fourfold classification of it. For men are either (1) endowed with no knowledge of God and immersed in idolatry, or (2) initiated into the sacraments, yet by impurity of life denying God in their actions while they confess him with their lips, they belong to Christ only in name; or (3) they are

---

[7] Again alluding to Osiander; cf. III. xi. 6, note 13.
[8] "*Gratiae dulcedinem.*"
[9] "*Suavissimum illud patris nomen.*" Cf. I. xiv. 2, 22; III. xx. 36–38.

hypocrites who conceal with empty pretenses their wickedness of heart, or (4) regenerated by God's Spirit, they make true holiness their concern.

ªIn the first instance, when they are to be judged according to their natural gifts, not one spark of good will be found in them from the top of their heads to the soles of their feet, ᵇ⁽ᵃ⁾unless perhaps we would accuse Scripture of falsehood when it sets off all the sons of Adam with these titles: that they are wicked and inflexible of heart [Jer. 17:9]; that the whole imagination of men's hearts is evil from their first years [Gen. 8:21]; "that their thoughts are vain" [Ps. 94:11, cf. Comm.]; that they have not the fear of God before their eyes [cf. Ex. 20:20]; that "no one of them understands or seeks after God" [Ps. 14:2]. ªIn short, that they are flesh [Gen. 6:3]. By this word are meant all those works which Paul lists: "fornication, impurity, immodesty, licentiousness, idolatry, sorcery, enmity, strife, jealousy, anger, quarreling, dissension, party spirit, envy, murder," and everything foul and abominable that can be imagined [Gal. 5:19–21, cf. Vg.]. This, then, is the worth on which they should be proud to rely!

ᵇBut if anyone among them excels in that decency of morals which has some appearance of holiness among men, still, because we know that God cares nothing for outward splendor, we must penetrate to the very source of the works if we should wish these to have any value for righteousness. We must investigate deeply, I say, from what disposition of the heart these works come forth. Now, although here a vast field for discussion lies open, still, because the matter can be disposed of in a very few words, I will be as brief as possible in what I teach.

2. The virtues of unbelievers are God-given*

ᵇTo begin with, I do not deny that all the notable endowments that manifest themselves among unbelievers are gifts of God.[1] And I do not so dissent from the common judgment as to contend that there is no difference between the justice, moderation, and equity of Titus and Trajan and the madness, intemperance, and savagery of Caligula or Nero or Domitian, or between the obscene lusts of Tiberius and the continence of Vespasian, in this respect, and—not to tarry over individual virtues and vices—between observance and contempt of right and of laws. For there is such a great difference between the righteous and the unrighteous that it appears even in the dead image thereof. For if we confuse these things, what order will remain in the world? Therefore, the Lord has not only engraved such a distinction between

[1] Cf. I. v. 3, 5; I. xv. 2–4.

honorable and wicked deeds in the minds of individual men but often confirms it also, by the dispensation of his providence. For we see that he bestows many blessings of the present life upon those who cultivate virtue among men. Not because that outward image of virtue deserves the least benefit of him; but it pleases him so to prove how much he esteems true righteousness, when he does not allow even external and feigned righteousness to go without a temporal reward. Hence, there follows what we just now acknowledged: that all these virtues—or rather, images of virtues—are gifts of God, since nothing is in any way praiseworthy that does not come from him.

3. No true virtue without true faith*

ᵇYet what Augustine writes is nonetheless true: that all who are estranged from the religion of the one God, however admirable they may be regarded on account of their reputation for virtue, not only deserve no reward but rather punishment, because by the pollution of their hearts they defile God's good works. For even though they are God's instruments for the preservation of human society in righteousness, continence, friendship, temperance, fortitude, and prudence, yet they carry out these good works of God very badly. For they are restrained from evil-doing not by genuine zeal for good but either by mere ambition or by self-love, or some other perverse motive. Therefore, since by the very impurity of men's hearts these good works have been corrupted as from their source, they ought no more to be reckoned among virtues than the vices that commonly deceive on account of their affinity and likeness to virtue. In short, when we remember the constant end of that which is right—namely, to serve God—whatever strives to another end already deservedly loses the name "right." Therefore, because they do not look to the goal that God's wisdom prescribes, what they do, though it seems good in the doing, yet by its perverse intention is sin. ᶜHe therefore concludes that all Fabriciuses, Scipios, and Catos in their excellent deeds have sinned in that, since they lacked the light of faith, they did not apply their deeds to the end to which they ought to have applied them. Therefore, true righteousness was not in them, because duties are weighed not by deeds but by ends.[2]

4. Without Christ there is no true holiness

ᵇMoreover, if what John says is true, that there is no life apart from the Son of God [I John 5:12], ᵃthose who have no part in

---

[2] Augustine, *Against Julian* IV. iii. 16 ff., 21, 25–26 (MPL 44. 744 ff., 749 ff.; tr. FC 35. 179 ff., 186 f., 189 f.).

Christ, whatever they may be, whatever they may do or undertake, yet hasten all their lives to destruction and to the judgment of eternal death. ᶜIn agreement with this idea is the statement of Augustine's: "Our religion distinguishes the just from the unjust not by the law of works but by that of faith, without which what seemed good works are turned into sins."³ ᵇHe also beautifully expresses the same thought in another passage when he compares the zeal of such men to a runner off his course. For the more strenuously anyone runs who is off the path, the farther he gets from his goal, and the more pitiable he therefore becomes. Consequently, Augustine contends that it is better to limp on the path than to run outside it.⁴ Finally, since there is no sanctification apart from communion with Christ, it is evident that they are evil trees; they can bear fruits beautiful and comely to the sight, and even sweet to the taste, but not at all good. From this we easily discern that whatever a man thinks, plans, or carries out before he is reconciled to God through faith is accursed, not only of no value for righteousness, but surely deserving condemnation. Yet why do we argue over this as if it were something doubtful, when it has already been proved by the apostle's testimony that "without faith it is impossible for anyone to please God" [Heb. 11:6]?

5. Righteousness before God comes not from works, though ever so good, but from grace
ᵇBut the proof will shine even clearer if we set the grace of God directly against the natural condition of man. For Scripture everywhere proclaims that God finds nothing in man to arouse him to do good to him but that he comes first to man in his free generosity. For what can a dead man do to attain life? Yet when he illumines us with knowledge of himself, he is said to revive us from death [John 5:25], to make us a new creature [II Cor. 5:17]. In this metaphor we see that God's generosity toward us is often commended, especially by the apostle. "God," he says, "who is rich in mercy, out of the great love with which he loved us, even when we were dead through our sins, made us alive together with Christ," etc. [Eph. 2:4–5.] Elsewhere, in discussing under Abraham as type the general calling of believers, he says: "It is God who brings the dead to life and calls things that are not as though they were" [Rom. 4:17, cf. Vg.]. If we are nothing, what, I ask, can we do? In the history of Job, therefore, the Lord strongly

³ Augustine, *Against Two Letters of the Pelagians* III. v. 14 (MPL 44. 597 f.; tr. NPNF V. 404).
⁴ Augustine, *Psalms,* Ps. 31. ii. 4 (MPL 36. 259 f.; tr. LF *Psalms* I. 253 f.).

restrains this arrogance, in the words: "Who anticipates me, that I should repay him? For all things are mine" [Job 41:11 p.; cf. ch. 41:2, Vg.]. Paul, explaining this statement [Rom. 11:35], draws the inference: let us not suppose that we bring anything to the Lord but the sheer disgrace of need and emptiness.

Therefore, in the passage cited above,[5] to prove that we have attained the hope of salvation by his grace alone, not by works [cf. Eph. 2:8–9], he states that "we are his creatures, since we have been reborn in Christ Jesus for good works, which God prepared beforehand that we should walk in them" [Eph. 2:10, cf. Vg.]. It is as if he said: Who of us can boast that he has appealed to God by his own righteousness when our first capacity for well-doing flows from regeneration? For, as we have by nature been created, oil will sooner be pressed from a stone than any good work from us. It is truly wonderful that man, condemned to such disgrace, dares still assume that he has anything left. Let us therefore admit, with this very great instrument of God, that the Lord "called us with a holy calling, not according to our works, but according to his purpose and . . . grace" [II Tim. 1:9 p.], and that "the generosity and love of God our Savior was manifested toward us, for he saved us, not because of deeds done by us in righteousness, but on account of his own mercy, . . . that we might be justified by his grace and be made heirs of eternal life" [Titus 3:4–5, 7 p.]. By this confession we deprive man of all righteousness, even to the slightest particle, until, by mercy alone, he is reborn into the hope of eternal life, since if the righteousness of works brings anything to justify us, we are falsely said to be justified by grace. Obviously, the apostle was not forgetful when he declared justification free, since he proves in another passage that grace would no longer be grace if works availed [Rom. 11:6]. And what else does the Lord mean when he says that he "came not to call the righteous but sinners" [Matt. 9:13]? If only sinners are admitted, why do we seek entry through feigned righteousness?

6. Man can contribute nothing to his own righteousness
^bThe thought repeatedly returns to my mind that there is danger of my being unjust to God's mercy when I labor with such great concern to assert it, as if it were doubtful or obscure. But since our ill will is such that it never yields to God that which is his, unless it is powerfully compelled, I am obliged to dwell on this a little longer. Now as Scripture is sufficiently clear on this matter, I shall contend by means of its words rather than my own. Isaiah, when he has described the universal destruction of

---

[5] III. xiii. 2.

mankind, beautifully adds the order of restoration: "The Lord saw it, and it appeared evil in his sight. . . . He saw that there was no man, and wondered that there was no one to intervene; and he entrusted salvation to his own arm, and with his own righteousness strengthened himself" [Isa. 59:15–16 p.]. Where are our righteous acts if what the prophet says is true: that there is no one who helps the Lord to recover his salvation? Thus another prophet, when he represents the Lord as acting to reconcile sinners to himself, says: "I will betroth you to me forever . . . in righteousness, judgment, grace, and mercy. . . . I will say to her who has not obtained mercy, you have attained mercy" [Hos. 2:19, 23 p.]. If a covenant[6] of this sort, which is clearly the first union of us with God, depends upon God's mercy, no basis is left for our righteousness.

And I should like to learn from those who pretend that man goes to meet God with some work righteousness whether they think there can be any other righteousness at all than that which is accepted by God. If it is mad to think so, what acceptable thing can come to God from his enemies, all of whom he spurns with all their doings? Truth testifies that all of us, I say, are mortal and open enemies of our God [cf. Rom. 5:10; Col. 1:21] until we are justified and received into friendship. If justification is the beginning of love, what righteousness of works will precede it? To turn aside that pestilent arrogance, John faithfully reminds us how we did not first love Him [I John 4:10]. And the Lord had at an earlier time taught this very thing through his prophet. "I will love them with a willing love," he says, "for my anger has turned from them." [Hos. 14:4 p.] If his love has willingly inclined itself to us, surely it is not aroused by works.

But the ignorant mass of men suppose this to mean only that no one has deserved Christ's completion of our redemption but that in entering into possession of redemption we are aided by our own works.[7] Nay, rather, however we may have been redeemed by Christ, until we are engrafted into his fellowship by the calling of the Father, we are both the heirs of darkness and death and the enemies of God. For Paul teaches that we are not cleansed and washed of our uncleanness by Christ's blood except when the Spirit works that cleansing in us [I Cor. 6:11]. Peter,

---

[6] *"Foedus."* Cf. II. x. 1–5; III. xvii. 2; III. xxi. 5–7, where Calvin outlines his version of the "federal theology," which had earlier beginnings. Typical observations on the covenant of grace are also found in I. vi. 1; II. viii. 21; II. x. 7; II. xi. 4, 7, 11; IV. xiv. 6.

[7] Aquinas, *Summa Theol.* I IIae. cxii. 2; Duns Scotus, *On the Sentences* III. xix. qu. unica. 8 (*Opera omnia* XIV. 719).

meaning to say the same thing, asserts that the sanctification of the Spirit is effectual "for obedience and for sprinkling with the blood of Christ" [I Peter 1:2]. If we are sprinkled through the Spirit with the blood of Christ for purification, let us not think that before this cleansing we were anything other than is a sinner without Christ. Therefore let this be regarded as a fact: the beginning of our salvation is a sort of resurrection from death into life, ᵉbecause when it has been granted to us to believe in Christ for his sake [Phil. 1:29], then at last we begin to pass over from death into life.

(Hypocrites and nominal Christians, under condemnation, 7–8)
7. *Righteousness is a thing of the heart!*ᵗ
ᵇUnder this condition are included those who are listed as the second and third classes in the above-mentioned division.[8] For impurity of conscience proves that both classes have not yet been regenerated by the Spirit of God. On the other hand, the absence of regeneration in them shows their lack of faith. From this it is clear that they have not yet been reconciled to God, not yet been justified in his sight, inasmuch as men attain these benefits only by faith. What can sinners, estranged from God, bring forth except what is hateful to his judgment? All ungodly men, and especially all hypocrites, are puffed up with this stupid assurance because, however much they recognize that their hearts teem with impurities, still if they bring forth any well-seeming works, they think these worthy not to be despised by God. Hence arises the pernicious error that, convicted of a wicked and evil mind, they still cannot be compelled to confess themselves empty of righteousness. Even when they acknowledge themselves unrighteous because they cannot deny it, they still claim for themselves some righteousness.

The Lord eloquently refutes this vanity through the prophet: "Ask," he says, "the priests to decide this question, 'If one carries holy flesh in the skirt of his garment . . . and touches . . . bread . . . or any other food, does it become holy?' The priests answered, 'No.' Then Haggai said, 'If one polluted in soul touches anything of these, does it not become unclean?' The priests replied, 'It will become unclean.' Haggai said, 'So it is with this people . . . before me, says the Lord, and so with every work of their hands, and everything that they offer me will be unclean' " [Hag. 2:11–14 p.]. Would that this utterance could obtain credit with us, or duly lodge in our memory! For there is no one, howsoever wicked in his whole life, who can let himself be persuaded of what the Lord

[8] Sec. 1, above.

here clearly declares. As soon as any very wicked person has performed one or another of the duties of the law, he does not doubt that it will be accounted to him as righteousness; but the Lord proclaims that no sanctification can be acquired from this action unless the heart has first been well cleansed. And not content with this, he declares that all the works that come forth from sinners are contaminated with impurity of heart. Take, then, the name of righteousness from those works which are condemned as works of pollution by the Lord's mouth! And with what a fitting comparison does he demonstrate this! For the objection could have been raised that what the Lord had commanded is inviolably holy. But he takes the opposite position, that it is no wonder things sanctified in the law of the Lord are contaminated by the filth of the wicked. For by handling something sacred, the unclean hand profanes it.

8. Person and work

ᵇHe beautifully treats the same matter also in Isaiah, saying: "Bring no more vain offering; incense is an abomination to me. . . . My soul hates your new moons and solemn feasts; they have become a burden to me, I am weary of bearing them. When you spread forth your hands, I will hide my eyes from you; even though you multiply prayer, I will not listen; for your hands are full of blood. Wash yourselves, make yourselves clean, remove the evil of your thoughts . . ." [Isa. 1:13–16 p.; cf. ch. 58:1–5]. What does this mean, that the Lord abominates the observance of his law? Surely, he despises nothing that is of the genuine observance of the law, the beginning of which he everywhere teaches to be a true fear of his name. Once that is taken away not only are all the things offered to him trifles but loathsome and abominable filth.

Now let the hypocrites go, and keeping wickedness wrapped up in their hearts, let them try to win God's favor by works! In this way they will more and more anger him. For "the sacrifices of the wicked are an abomination to him, but the prayer of the upright is acceptable to him" [Prov. 15:8 p.]. We therefore hold to be beyond doubt what ought to be a mere commonplace even to one indifferently versed in the Scriptures, that in men not yet truly sanctified works manifesting even the highest splendor are so far away from righteousness before the Lord that they are reckoned sins.

Accordingly, they have spoken very truly who have taught that favor with God is not obtained by anyone through works, but on the contrary works please him only when the person has previously found favor in his sight.[9] And here we must faithfully keep the order to which Scripture leads us by the hand. Moses writes: "The Lord had regard for Abel and his works" [Gen. 4: 4 p.]. Do you see that he points out how the Lord is favorable to men before he has regard for their works? Therefore, purification of heart must precede, in order that those works which come forth from us may be favorably received by God. ᵉFor the statement of Jeremiah is always in force, that the eyes of God have regard for truth [Jer. 5:3]. ᵇThat it is faith alone, moreover, by which men's hearts are purified, the Holy Spirit has declared through the mouth of Peter [Acts 15:9]. From this it is evident that the first foundation lies in true and living faith.

(*Those who are regenerated, justified by faith alone, 9–11*)
9. *Also, true believers do no good works of themselves*
ᵇNow let us examine what righteousness is possessed by those whom we have placed in the fourth class. We confess that while through the intercession of Christ's righteousness God reconciles us to himself, and by free remission of sins accounts us righteous, his beneficence is at the same time joined with such a mercy ᵃthat through his Holy Spirit he dwells in us and by his power the lusts of our flesh are each day more and more mortified; we are indeed sanctified,[10] that is, consecrated to the Lord in true purity of life, with our hearts formed to obedience to the law. The end is that our especial will may be to serve his will and by every means to advance his glory alone.[11]

But even while by the leading of the Holy Spirit we walk in the ways of the Lord, to keep us from forgetting ourselves and becoming puffed up, traces of our imperfection remain to give us occasion for humility. ᵇScripture says: There is no righteous man, no man who will do good and not sin [Eccl. 7:21, Vg.; cf. I Kings 8:46]. What sort of righteousness will they obtain, then, from their works? First, I say ᵃthat the best work that can be brought forward from them is still always spotted and corrupted with some impurity of the flesh, and has, so to speak, some dregs mixed with it. ᵇLet a holy servant of God, I say, choose from the whole course of his life what of an especially noteworthy character

---

[9] Pseudo-Augustine, *De vera et falsa poenitentia* xv. 30 (MPL 40. 1125); Gregory the Great, *Letters* IX. 122, as quoted in Gratian, *Decretum* II. iii. 7. 5 (Friedberg I. 527).
[10] Cf. Melanchthon, *Loci communes*, ed. Engelland, *Melanchthons Werke in Auswahl* II. i. 145; tr. Hill, p. 245.
[11] Cf. Bucer, *In quatuor Evangelia enarrationes* (1536, p. 122; 1553, fo. 75a).

he thinks he has done. Let him well turn over in his mind its several parts. Undoubtedly he will somewhere perceive that it savors of the rottenness of the flesh, since our eagerness for well-doing is never what it ought to be but our great weakness slows down our running in the race. Although we see that the stains that bespatter the works of the saints are plainly visible, though we admit that they are only the slightest spots, will they not offend God's eyes, before which not even the stars are pure [Job 25:5]? We have not a single work going forth from the saints that if it be judged in itself deserves not shame as its just reward.

10. He who thinks he has his own righteousness misunderstands the severity of the law
aNext, even if it were possible for us to have some wholly pure and perfect works, yet, as the prophet says, one sin is enough to wipe out and extinguish every memory of that previous righteousness [Ezek. 18:24]. James agrees with him: "Whoever," he says, "fails in one point, has become guilty of all" [James 2:10 p.]. Now since this mortal life is never pure or devoid of sin, whatever righteousness we might attain, when it is corrupted, oppressed, and destroyed, by the sins that repeatedly follow, could not come into God's sight or be reckoned to us as righteousness.

In short, when it is a question of the righteousness of works, we must have regard not for the work of the law but for the commandment. Therefore, if righteousness is sought from the law we will in vain bring forward one work or another, but unceasing obedience to the law is necessary. Therefore, God does not, as many stupidly believe, once for all reckon to us as righteousness that forgiveness of sins concerning which we have spoken in order that, having obtained pardon for our past life, we may afterward seek righteousness in the law;[12] this would be only to lead us into false hope, to laugh at us, and mock us. For since no perfection can come to us so long as we are clothed in this flesh, and the law moreover announces death and judgment to all who do not maintain perfect righteousness in works, it will always have grounds for accusing and condemning us unless, on the contrary, God's mercy counters it, and by continual forgiveness of sins repeatedly acquits us. Therefore, what I said at the beginning always holds good:[13] if we are judged by our own worth, whatever we plan or undertake, with all our efforts and labors we still deserve death and destruction.

[12] Cf. Latomus, *De fide et operibus* (*Opera* [1550], fo. 135a ff.).
[13] Sec. 1, above.

11. Believers' righteousness is always faith righteousness

ᵇWe must strongly insist upon these two points: first, that there never existed any work of a godly man which, if examined by God's stern judgment, would not deserve condemnation; secondly, if such a work were found (something not possible for man), it would still lose favor—weakened and stained as it is by the sins with which its author himself is surely burdened.

ᶜThis is the pivotal point of our disputation.[14] For on the beginning of justification there is no quarrel between us and the sounder Schoolmen:[15] that a sinner freely liberated from condemnation may obtain righteousness, and that through the forgiveness of sins; except that they include under the term "justification" a renewal, by which through the Spirit of God we are remade to obedience to the law. Indeed, they so describe the righteousness of the regenerated man that a man once for all reconciled to God through faith in Christ may be reckoned righteous before God by good works and be accepted by the merit of them.[16] But on the contrary, the Lord declares that for Abraham he reckoned faith as righteousness [Rom. 4:3], not at the time when Abraham was as yet serving idols but after he had for many years excelled in holiness of life. Therefore, Abraham had long worshiped God with a pure heart, and kept such obedience to the law as can be kept by mortal man. Yet he still had a righteousness set in faith. From this we infer, according to Paul's reasoning, that it was not of works [Eph. 2:9]. Similarly, when a prophet says, "The just shall live by faith" [Hab. 2:4], the statement does not apply to impious and profane persons, whom the Lord by turning them to faith may justify, but the utterance is directed to believers, and to them life is promised by faith. Paul also removes all doubt when, to confirm that idea, he takes this verse of David's: "Blessed are they whose transgressions are forgiven" [Ps. 32:1; 31:1, Vg.; cf. Rom. 4:7]. It is certain that David is not speaking concerning the ungodly but of believers, such as he himself was. For he spoke from the prompting of his own conscience. Therefore, we must have this blessedness not just once but must hold to it throughout life. Finally, he testifies that the

---

[14] VG: *"le principal poinct de la dispute, que nous avons avec les papists."*

[15] Cf. II. ii. 6, note 35; III. xiii. 3; III. xvii. 7. VG is here expanded to this effect: "It is quite true that the poor world has been seduced until now to think that man could of himself prepare to be justified by God, and that this blasphemy has commonly reigned both in preaching and in the schools, as it is today upheld by those who would maintain all the abominations of the papacy. But those who have possessed any reason have always agreed with us, as I have said."

[16] Aquinas, *Summa Theol.* I IIae. cxiii. 1; cxiv. 3.

embassy of free reconciliation with God is published not for one day or another but is attested as perpetual in the church [cf. II Cor. 5:18–19]. Accordingly, to the very end of life, believers have no other righteousness than that which is there described. For Christ ever remains the Mediator to reconcile the Father to us; and his death has everlasting efficacy: namely, cleansing, satisfaction, atonement, and finally perfect obedience, with which all our iniquities are covered. And Paul does not say to the Ephesians that we have the beginning of salvation from grace but that we have been saved through grace, "not by works, lest any man should boast" [Eph. 2:8–9].

(*Scholastic objections to justification by faith, and doctrine of the supererogatory merits of the saints examined and refuted, 12–21*)

12. Evasions of opponents

[b]The evasions that the Schoolmen seek here in order to escape do not help them out. They say: [c(b)]Good works are not as important in their intrinsic worth as to be sufficient to obtain righteousness, but their great value lies in "accepting grace."[17] Accordingly, because they are compelled to admit that here works righteousness is always imperfect, they concede that as long as we live we need forgiveness of sins to supply the defect of works; but that the transgressions [b]committed are compensated by works of supererogation.[18]

I reply that "accepting grace," as they call it, is nothing else than his free goodness, with which the Father embraces us in Christ when he clothes us with the innocence of Christ and accepts it as ours that by the benefit of it he may hold us as holy, pure, and innocent. [a]For Christ's righteousness, which as it alone is perfect alone can bear the sight of God, must appear in court on our behalf, and stand surety in judgment. [b(a)]Furnished with this righteousness, we obtain continual forgiveness of sins in faith. Covered with this purity, the sordidness and uncleanness of our imperfections are not ascribed to us but [a]are hidden as if buried that they may not come into God's judgment, until the hour arrives when, the old man slain and clearly destroyed in us, the divine goodness will receive us into blessed peace with the new Adam. There let us await the Day of the Lord in which, having

---

[17] Duns Scotus, *On the Sentences* I. xvii. 3. 25 f. (*Opera omnia* X. 84a); Jean Gerson (d. 1429), *De vita spirituali,* corollary x (*Opera omnia,* ed. L. E. Du Pin, III. 13).

[18] Bonaventura, *On the Sentences* IV. xx. part 2. art. 1. qu. 3 (*Opera selecta* IV. 507); Aquinas, *Summa Theol.* III. Suppl. xxv. 1.

received incorruptible bodies, we will be carried into the glory of the Heavenly Kingdom [cf. I Cor. 15:45 ff.].

13. One who speaks of "supererogatory" works misunderstands the sharpness of God's demand and the gravity of sin
ᵇIf these things are true, surely no works of ours can of themselves render us acceptable and pleasing to God; nor can even the works themselves please him, except to the extent that a man, covered by the righteousness of Christ, pleases God and obtains forgiveness of his sins. ᶜFor God has not promised the reward of life for particular works but he only declares that the man who does them shall live [Lev. 18:5], leveling that well-known curse against all those who do not persevere in all things [Deut. 27:26; Gal. 3:10]. The fiction of partial righteousness is abundantly refuted by these statements, where no other righteousness than the complete observance of the law is allowed in heaven.

ᵇ⁽ᵃ⁾Their usual loose talk about "works of supererogation" providing sufficient compensation is no sounder.[19] Why? Do they not always return to the position from which they have already been driven, that he who partly keeps the law is to that extent righteous by works? What no one of sound judgment will concede to them they too shamelessly assume as a fact. The Lord often testifies that he recognizes no righteousness of works except in the perfect observance of his law. What perversity is it for us, when we lack righteousness, in order not to seem deprived of all glory —that is, utterly to have yielded to God—to boast of some little bits of a few works and try through other satisfactions to pay for what is lacking?

ᵇSatisfactions have already been effectively demolished,[20] so that they ought not even to come to our minds in a dream. ᵇ⁽ᵃ⁾I say that those who talk such nonsense do not realize what an execrable thing sin is in God's sight. Truly, they should have understood that men's whole righteousness, gathered together in one heap, could not make compensation for a single sin. ᵃFor we see that man was so cast away and abandoned by God for one transgression that he lost at the same time all capacity to recover his salvation [Gen. 3:17]. Therefore, the capacity to make satisfaction was taken away. Those who preen themselves on it surely will never satisfy God, to whom nothing is pleasing or acceptable that comes forth from his enemies. Now God's enemies are all those to whom he determines to impute sins. Therefore, our sins must be covered and forgiven before the Lord recognizes any

[19] The reference is to the opinion condemned in sec. 12; cf. note 18.
[20] III. iv. 25–39.

work of ours. From this it follows that forgiveness of sins is free, and those who thrust in any satisfactions wickedly blaspheme it. Let us therefore, after the apostle's example, "forgetting what lies behind and straining forward to what lies before us," run our race, pressing "on toward . . . the prize of the upward call" [Phil. 3:13–14 p.].

14. Even the perfect fulfillment of our obligation would bring us no glory; but this also is not at all possible!

[a]To boast about works of supererogation—how does this square with the injunction laid upon us that, when we have done whatever is commanded us, we call ourselves "unworthy servants," and say that "we have done no more than we ought to have done" [Luke 17:10 p.]? To speak before God is not to pretend or lie but to determine within yourself what you hold for certain. Therefore, the Lord bids us sincerely perceive and consider within ourselves that we perform no unrequired duties for him but render him our due service. [b(a)]And rightly! For we are servants obligated to render so many services that we cannot perform them, even though all our thoughts and all our members were turned to the duties of the law. Consequently, his statement, "When you have done whatever is commanded you," is as much as to say that all the righteous acts of men—and more—belonged to one alone. How dare we, then, since we, every one, are very far away from this goal, boast that we have accumulated something beyond the measure due?

[b]Now there is no reason for any man to object that, though he partly fails in the necessary duties, nothing prevents him from extending his endeavor beyond them.[21] This fact we must accept completely: that there is nothing that can come to mind which contributes to the honoring of God or the love of neighbor[22] that is not comprised within God's law. But if it is a part of the law, let us not boast of voluntary liberality when we are constrained by necessity.

15. God is entitled to all that we are and have; hence there can be no supererogatory works

[b]Now they improperly apply to this matter Paul's boasting that among the Corinthians he voluntarily yielded his right, which he could otherwise have used if he had wished; and he devoted to them not only what he owed out of duty but bestowed a free service beyond the bounds of duty [I Cor. 9:1 ff.]. But they should

[21] Aquinas, *Summa Theol.* I IIae. cix. 4.
[22] "*Ad dilectionem.*" Cf. II. viii. 54, note 61; III. xviii. 8, note 11.

have paid attention to the reason there indicated, that his action might not become an offense to the weak [I Cor. 9:12]. For evil and deceitful workmen recommended themselves by this false show of kindness in order to gain favor for their dangerous doctrines and to breathe hatred upon the gospel, so that it was necessary for Paul either to imperil the doctrine of Christ or to oppose such devices. Well then, if for a Christian man it is a matter of indifference to give offense when he can abstain from it, I admit the apostle performed some work of supererogation for the Lord. But if this was duly required of a prudent steward of the gospel, I say that he did what he ought. Finally, even if such a reason is not apparent, this statement of Chrysostom is always true: all our belongings have the same status as the possessions of slaves, which by right belong to their master himself.[23] And Christ did not conceal this in his parable, for he asks what thanks we shall give our servant when after a whole day of various tasks he returns to us at evening [Luke 17:7–9]. Yet it can happen that he labored with greater industry than we would have dared demand. Granted. Still, he did nothing that was not required of the condition of servitude. For he with his whole capacity is ours.

aI am not speaking of the sort of supererogations that such persons wish to display before God, for they are trifles that he never either commanded or approves, nor will he accept them when account of them is to be rendered before him. In this sense only, we agree that there are works of supererogation—namely, those of which it is said in the prophet: "Who has required this of your hands?" [Isa. 1:12, cf. Vg.]. bBut let them remember what is said of them in another place: "Why do you spend your money, and not for bread; why do you use up your labor, and not for repletion?" [Isa. 55:2 p.]. b(a)Indeed, it is not very laborious for these leisured rabbis to dispute these matters under the shade in easy chairs. But when that supreme Judge sits in his judgment seat such windy opinions will have to vanish. aIt is this that we had to seek: what confidence we can bring to his judgment seat in our defense, not what we can talk about in the schools and corners.[24]

16. No trust in works and no glory in works!

bIn this respect there are two plagues that we must especially banish from our minds: we must not put any confidence in the

---

[23] Chrysostom, *Homilies on Philemon* ii. 4 (MPG 62. 713 f.).
[24] Cf. III. xii. 1.

righteousness of works, and we must not ascribe to works any glory.

In teaching that all our righteous deeds are foul in God's sight unless these derive a good odor from Christ's innocence, Scripture consistently dissuades us from confidence. Works can only arouse God's vengeance unless they be sustained by his merciful pardon. Thus they leave us nothing but to implore our Judge for mercy with that confession of David's: that no one will be justified before him if he demands a reckoning from his servants [Ps. 143:2 p.]. But when Job says: "If I have acted wickedly, woe to me! but if justly, I will not lift up my head" [Job 10:15 p.], ^calthough he is concerned with that highest righteousness of God, to which not even the angels answer, he at the same time shows that when it comes to God's judgment, nothing remains to all mortals but to keep silence. ^bFor it not only concerns the fact that Job prefers to yield willingly rather than to struggle perilously against God's severity but signifies that he did not experience any other righteousness in himself than what at the first moment would wither before God's face.

When confidence is banished, all glorying also must necessarily depart. For who would accord credit for righteousness to works, trust in which trembles at God's sight? ^cWe must therefore come whither Isaiah calls us: "In God all the seed of Israel shall triumph and glory" [Isa. 45:25 p.]; for what he says elsewhere is very true, that we are "the planting of the glory of God" [Isa. 61:3 p.]. ^bThe mind will then be duly cleansed when it does not in any respect settle back in the confidence, or exult in the glory, of works. But this error disposes stupid men to be puffed up with false and lying confidence because they always lodge in works the cause of their salvation.

17. In no respect can works serve as the cause of our holiness

^bThe philosophers postulate four kinds of causes to be observed in the outworking of things. If we look at these, however, we will find that, as far as the establishment of our salvation is concerned, none of them has anything to do with works. For Scripture everywhere proclaims that the efficient cause[25] of our obtaining eternal life is the mercy of the Heavenly Father

[25] Cf. Aristotle, *Physics* ii. 3, 7 (LCL Aristotle, *Physics* I. 128 ff., 166 f.); *Metaphysics* I. iii (LCL *Metaphysics* I. 16 f.); Aquinas, *Summa Theol.* I. xix. 8; II IIae. xv. 1, 2. Louis Goumaz utilizes the series of causes for the structure of his searching treatise, *La Doctrine du salut d'après les commentaires de Jean Calvin sur le Nouveau Testament*. See esp. pp. 93 ff., 130 ff., 184 ff., 225 ff., 249 ff. The four "causes" of salvation are respectively identified with God the Father, Christ, the Holy Spirit, and the glory of God.

and his freely given love toward us. Surely the material cause is Christ, with his obedience, through which he acquired righteousness for us. What shall we say is the formal or instrumental cause but faith? And John includes these three in one sentence when he says: "God so loved the world that he gave his only-begotten Son that everyone who believes in him may not perish but have eternal life" [John 3:16]. As for the final cause, the apostle testifies that it consists both in the proof of divine justice and in the praise of God's goodness, ᶜand in the same place he expressly mentions three others. For so he speaks to the Romans: "All have sinned and lack the glory of God; moreover, they are justified freely by his grace" [Rom. 3:23–24; cf. Eph. 1:6, cf. Vg.]. Here you have the head and primal source: that God embraced us with his free mercy. There follows: "Through the redemption which is in Christ Jesus" [Rom. 3:24]. Here you have, as it were, the material cause by which righteousness is brought about for us. In the words "through faith in his blood" [Rom. 3:25 p.], is shown the instrumental cause whereby the righteousness of Christ is applied to us. Lastly, he adds the final cause when, to demonstrate his righteousness, he says, "In order that he himself may be righteous, and the justifier of him who has faith in Christ" [Rom. 3:26, Vg.]. And to note also, by the way, that this righteousness stands upon reconciliation, he expressly states that Christ was given as reconciliation. Thus also in the first chapter of Ephesians he teaches that we are received into grace by God out of sheer mercy, that this comes about by Christ's intercession and is apprehended by faith, and that all things exist to the end that the glory of divine goodness may fully shine forth [Eph. 1:3–14]. ᵇSince we see that every particle of our salvation stands thus outside of us, why is it that we still trust or glory in works? The most avowed enemies of divine grace cannot stir up any controversy with us concerning either the efficient or the final cause, unless they would deny the whole of Scripture. They falsely represent the material and the formal cause, as if our works held half the place along with faith and Christ's righteousness.[26] But Scripture cries out against this also, simply affirming that Christ is for us both righteousness and life, and that this benefit of righteousness is possessed by faith alone.

18. The sight of good works, however, can strengthen faith
ᵇNow the saints quite often strengthen themselves and are comforted by remembering their own innocence and upright-

---

[26] Herborn, *Enchiridion* xliv (CC 12. 154 ff.); Latomus, *De fide et operibus* (*Opera* [1550], fo. 138a).

ness, and they do not even refrain at times from proclaiming it. This is done in two ways: either comparing their good cause with the evil cause of the wicked, they thence derive confidence of victory, not so much by the commendation of their own righteousness as by the just and deserved condemnation of their adversaries. Or, without comparison with others, while they examine themselves before God, the purity of their own conscience brings them some comfort and confidence.

We shall look at the first reason later.[27] Now concerning the second, let us briefly explain how what we said above[28] agrees with it: that under God's judgment we must not put any trust in works, or glory in any esteem of them. The agreement lies in this: that the saints, when it is a question of the founding and establishing of their own salvation, without regard for works turn their eyes solely to God's goodness. Not only do they betake themselves to it before all things as to the beginning of blessedness but they repose in it as in the fulfillment of this. A conscience so founded, erected, and established is established also in the consideration of works, so far, that is, as these are testimonies of God dwelling and ruling in us. Inasmuch, therefore, as this reliance upon works has no place unless you first cast the whole confidence of your mind upon God's mercy, it ought not to seem contrary to that upon which it depends. Therefore, when we rule out reliance upon works, we mean only this: that the Christian mind may not be turned back to the merit of works as to a help toward salvation but should rely wholly on the free promise of righteousness. But we do not forbid him from undergirding and strengthening this faith by signs of the divine benevolence toward him. For if, when all the gifts God has bestowed upon us are called to mind, they are like rays of the divine countenance by which we are illumined to contemplate that supreme light of goodness; much more is this true of the grace of good works, which shows that the Spirit of adoption has been given to us [cf. Rom. 8:15].

19. Works as fruits of the call
ᵇWhen, therefore, the saints by innocence of conscience strengthen their faith and take from it occasion to exult, from the fruits of their calling they merely regard themselves as having been chosen as sons by the Lord. Accordingly, the statement of Solomon: "In the fear of the Lord one has strong confidence" [Prov. 14:26], and the fact that in order to be heard by him the saints sometimes use this calling of God to witness that they

27 III. xvii. 14.
28 III. xii. 2.

have walked before him in uprightness and simplicity [cf. Gen. 24:40; II Kings 20:3] are matters that have no place in laying a foundation to strengthen the conscience but are of value only when taken a posteriori. For there is nowhere that fear which is able to establish full assurance. And the saints are conscious of possessing only such an integrity as intermingled with many vestiges of the flesh. But since they take the fruits of regeneration as proof of the indwelling of the Holy Spirit, from this they are greatly strengthened to wait for God's help in all their necessities, seeing that in this very great matter they experience him as Father. And they cannot do even this unless they first apprehend God's goodness, sealed by nothing else than the certainty of the promise. For if they begin to judge it by good works, nothing will be more uncertain or more feeble; for indeed, if works be judged of themselves, by their imperfection they will no less declare God's wrath than by their incomplete purity they testify to his benevolence.

eIn sum, they so proclaim God's benefits as not to turn away from God's freely given favor, in which, as Paul testifies, there is set "length, breadth, depth, and height" [Eph. 3:18]. It is as if he said: "Wherever the minds of the godly turn, however high they mount up, however far and wide they extend, still they ought not to depart from the love of Christ but should apply themselves wholly to meditating upon it. For in itself it embraces all dimensions." Therefore, he says that it excels and overtops all knowledge, and that when we acknowledge how much Christ loved us we are "filled with all the fullness of God" [Eph. 3:19]. As elsewhere, while Paul boasts that the godly are victors in every contest, he soon adds the reason: "on account of him who loved us" [Rom. 8:37 p.].

20. Works are God's gift and cannot become the foundation of self-confidence for believers

bWe now see that the saints have not a confidence in works that either attributes anything to their merit, since they regard them solely as gifts of God from which they may recognize his goodness and as signs of the calling by which they realize their election,[29] or in any degree diminishes the free righteousness that we attain in Christ, since it depends upon this and does not subsist without it. cAugustine expresses this idea in few words but elegantly when he writes: "I do not say to the Lord, 'Despise not the works of my hands.' [Ps. 138:8; cf. Ps. 137:8, Vg.] 'I have

---

[29] Cf. III. xxiv. 4; W. Niesel, *The Theology of Calvin*, 178 f.; F. Wendel, *Calvin*, pp. 209 f.

sought the Lord with my hands and am not deceived.' [Ps. 77:2; cf. Ps. 76:3, Vg.] But I do not commend the works of my hands, for I fear lest, when Thou lookest upon them, thou mayest find more sins than merits. This only I say, this I ask, this I desire: despise not the works of thy hands; see in me thy work, not mine. For if thou seest mine, thou wilt condemn it. If thou seest thine own, thou wilt crown it. For whatever good works are mine are from thee."[30] He gives two reasons why he dared not vaunt his works before God: because if he has anything of good works, he sees in them nothing of his own; and secondly, because these are also overwhelmed by a multitude of sins. From this it comes about that his conscience feels more fear and consternation than assurance. Therefore, he would like God to look upon his good deeds only that, recognizing the grace of his own call in them, he may finish the work he has begun.

*21. Sense in which good works are sometimes spoken of as a reason for divine benefits**

[b]The fact that Scripture shows that the good works of believers are reasons why the Lord benefits them is to be so understood as to allow what we have set forth before to stand unshaken:[31] that the efficient cause of our salvation consists in God the Father's love; the material cause in God the Son's obedience; the instrumental cause in the Spirit's illumination, that is, faith; the final cause, in the glory of God's great generosity.[32] These do not prevent the Lord from embracing works as inferior causes. But how does this come about? Those whom the Lord has destined by his mercy for the inheritance of eternal life he leads into possession of it, according to his ordinary dispensation, by means of good works. What goes before in the order of dispensation he calls the cause of what comes after. In this way he sometimes derives eternal life from works, not intending it to be ascribed to them; but because he justifies those whom he has chosen in order at last to glorify them [Rom. 8:30], he makes the prior grace, which is a step to that which follows, as it were the cause. But whenever the true cause is to be assigned, he does not enjoin us to take refuge in works but keeps us solely to the contemplation of his mercy. What sort of thing is this teaching of the apostle: "The wages of sin is death; the grace of the Lord, eternal life" [Rom. 6:23]? Why does he not contrast righteousness with sin, as he con-

---

[30] Augustine, *Psalms,* Ps. 137. 18 (MPL 37. 1783 f.; tr. NPNF [Ps. 138, sec. 13] VIII. 635).
[31] Sec. 17, above, and note 25.
[32] *"Tantae Dei benignitatis gloriam."*

trasts life with death? Why does he not make righteousness the cause of life, as he does sin that of death? For thus an antithesis would duly have been set up that is somewhat broken by this variation. But the apostle intended by this comparison to express what was true: namely, that death is owing to men's deserts but life rests solely upon God's mercy.

ᵉIn short, by these expressions sequence more than cause is denoted. For God, by heaping grace upon grace, from the former grace takes the cause for adding those which follow that he may overlook nothing for the enrichment of his servants. And he so extends his liberality as to have us always look to his freely given election, which is the source and beginning. For, although he loves the gifts which he daily confers upon us, seeing that they proceed from that source, still it is our part to hold to that free acceptance, which alone can support our souls; and so to subordinate to the first cause the gifts of the Holy Spirit he then bestows, that they may nowise detract from it.

ᶜCHAPTER XV

BOASTING ABOUT THE MERITS OF WORKS DESTROYS OUR PRAISE OF GOD FOR HAVING BESTOWED RIGHTEOUSNESS, AS WELL AS OUR ASSURANCE OF SALVATION

(*Doctrine of human merit in justification opposed by Augustine and Bernard as well as by Scripture, 1–4*)

1. False and true questioning

ᵇNow we have disposed of the main issue in this discussion: If righteousness is supported by works, in God's sight it must entirely collapse; and it is confined solely to God's mercy, solely to communion with Christ, and therefore solely to faith. But let us carefully note that this is the chief turning point[1] of the matter in order to avoid becoming entangled in the common delusion, not of the common folk only, but also of the learned. For as soon as there is a question concerning justification of faith or of works, they rush off to those passages which seem to attribute to works some merit in God's sight. As if justification of works would be fully proved by showing that they have some value with God!

To be sure, we have clearly shown above[2] that works righteousness consists solely in perfect and complete observance of the law. From this it follows that no man is justified by works unless, hav-

---

[1] *"Praecipuum . . . causae cardinem."* The phrasing is intentionally similar to that used in III. xi. 1 at note 3.

[2] II. vii. 3.

ing been raised to the highest peak of perfection, he cannot be accused even of the least transgression. There is consequently another separate question: Though works may by no means suffice for justification, should they not yet deserve favor with God?

2. *"Merit," an unscriptural and dangerous word!*

ᵇI must first make these prefatory remarks concerning the term "merit": whoever first applied it to men's works over against God's judgment[3] provided very badly for sincere faith. Of course, I would like to avoid verbal battles, but I wish that Christian writers had always exercised such restraint as not to take it into their heads needlessly to use terms foreign to Scripture that would produce great offense and very little fruit. Why, I ask, was there need to drag in the term "merit" when the value of good works could without offense have been meaningfully explained by another term? How much offense this term contains is clear from the great damage it has done to the world. Surely, as it is a most prideful term, it can do nothing but obscure God's favor and imbue men with perverse haughtiness.

I admit that the ancient writers of the church commonly used it, and would that they had not given posterity occasion for error by their misuse of one little word! Nevertheless, in some passages they also testify that they did not intend to prejudice the truth. For in one place Augustine speaks thus: "Let human merits, which perished through Adam, here keep silence, and let God's grace reign through Jesus Christ." ᶜAgain: "The saints attribute nothing to their merits; they will attribute all to thy mercy alone, O God." Again: "And when man sees that all the good that he has, he has not from himself but from his God, he sees that all that is praiseworthy in himself arises not from his own merits but from God's mercy."[4] You see that Augustine, when he has denied to man the power of well-doing, also overthrows any worth of merit. ᵇMoreover, Chrysostom says: "Our works, if there are any that follow the freely given call of God, are repayment and debt, but God's gifts are grace and beneficence and great generosity."[5]

But laying aside the term, let us rather look at the thing itself. ᶜPreviously, indeed, I cited a statement from Bernard: "As it is

---

[3] The objection is against Tertullian's use of the word "merit" in this sense. Cf. Tertullian, *Apology* I. xxi. 16; *On Repentance* ii (CCL Tertullianus I. 125, 322; tr. NPNF III. 35, 657 f.).

[4] Augustine, *On the Predestination of the Saints* xv. 31 (MPL 44. 983; tr. NPNF V. 513); *Psalms,* Ps. 139. 18 (MPL 37. 1814; tr. NPNF [Ps. 140, sec. 16] VIII. 644); Ps. 84. 9 (MPL 37. 1073; tr. NPNF [Ps. 85, sec. 6] VIII. 406).

[5] Chrysostom, *Homilies on Genesis,* hom. xxxiv. 6 (MPG 53. 321).

sufficient for merit not to presume concerning merit, so to lack merits is sufficient for judgment." But he immediately adds his interpretation, in which he sufficiently softens the harshness of the utterance by saying: "Accordingly, take care to have merits. When you have them, know that they have been given. Hope for fruit, the mercy of God, and you have escaped all peril of poverty, ungratefulness, and presumption. Happy is the church that lacks neither merits without presumption nor presumption without merits." And a little before, he had abundantly shown the godly sense in which he had used the word. "For why," he asks, "should the church concern itself with merits when it has a firmer and more secure reason to glory in God's purpose? God cannot deny himself; he will do what he has promised [cf. II Tim. 2:13]. Thus you have no reason to ask, 'By what merits may we hope for benefits?' Especially since you hear: 'It is not for your sake . . . but for mine' [Ezek. 36:22, 32 p.]. For merit, it suffices to know that merits do not suffice."[6]

3. The whole value of good works comes from God's grace

[b]Scripture shows what all our works deserve when it states that they cannot bear God's gaze because they are full of uncleanness. What, then, will the perfect observance of the law deserve, if any such can be found, when Scripture enjoins us to consider ourselves unprofitable servants even when we do everything required of us [Luke 17:10]? For to the Lord we have given nothing unrequired but have only carried out services owed, for which no thanks are due.

Yet those good works which he has bestowed upon us the Lord calls "ours," and testifies they not only are acceptable to him but also will have their reward. It is our duty in return to be aroused by so great a promise, to take courage not to weary in well-doing [cf. Gal. 6:9; II Thess. 3:13], and to receive God's great kindness with true gratefulness. There is no doubt that whatever is praiseworthy in works is God's grace; there is not a drop that we ought by rights to ascribe to ourselves. [b(a)]If we truly and earnestly recognize this, not only will all confidence in merit vanish, but the very notion. [a]We are not dividing the credit for good works between God and man, as the Sophists do,[7] but we are preserving it whole, complete, and unimpaired for the Lord. To man we assign only this: that he pollutes and contami-

[6] Bernard, *Sermons on the Song of Songs* lxviii. 6 (MPL 183. 1111; tr. Eales, *Life and Works of St. Bernard* IV. 419).
[7] Lombard, *Sentences* II. xxvii. 5 (MPL 192. 715); Aquinas, *Quodlibetal Questions* IV. vii.

nates by his impurity those very things which were good. For nothing proceeds from a man, however perfect he be, that is not defiled by some spot. Let the Lord, then, call to judgment the best in human works: he will indeed recognize in them his own righteousness but man's dishonor and shame! ᵇGood works, then, are pleasing to God and are not unfruitful for their doers. But they receive by way of reward the most ample benefits of God, not because they so deserve but because God's kindness has of itself set this value on them. What unkindness it is that men are not content with that generosity of God which bestows unearned rewards upon works that merit no such thing, and with profane ambition strive that what comes entirely from God's munificence may seem to be credited to the merit of works!

Here I appeal to every man's common sense. If anyone who holds the usufruct of a field by another's liberality also claims the title to the property for himself, does he not by such ungratefulness deserve to lose the very possession that he has held? Similarly, if a slave, liberated by his master, hides his base freedman's condition and claims to be freeborn, does he not deserve to be reduced to his former servitude? For the only lawful way of enjoying a benefit is neither to claim for ourselves more than was given nor to defraud of his praise the author of the good, but so to behave that what he has transferred to us may still seem in a way to reside with him. If we must maintain such restraint toward men, let each of us see and ponder what sort of restraint God requires.

4. Defense against counterevidence

ᵇI know that these sophisters misuse certain passages to prove that the term "merit toward God" is found in Scripture. They cite a sentence from Ecclesiasticus: "Mercy will make room for every man according to the merit of his works" [Ecclus. 16:15, Vg.]. And another from The Letter to the Hebrews: "Do not forget to do good and to share, for such sacrifices are pleasing to God" [Heb. 13:16 p.].⁸

I now forgo my right to reject the authority of Ecclesiasticus. Nevertheless, I say that they do not faithfully quote what Ecclesiasticus has written, whoever that writer was, for the original Greek text has the following: πάσῃ ἐλεημοσύνῃ ποιήσει τόπον. ἕκαστος

---

⁸ It is argued by Eck, *Enchiridion*, ch. v (1533 edition, fo. 28a–32b), Herborn, *Enchiridion* v (CC 12. 32), and other opponents of the Reformation, that faith is insufficient for eternal life, and that good works are meritorious thereto.

γὰρ κατὰ τὰ ἔργα αὐτοῦ εὑρήσει. "He will make room for every work of mercy; each man shall find according to his works." [Ecclus. 16:14, tr. RV.] And that this is the genuine reading, which is corrupted in the Latin version, appears both from the construction of these words alone and from the larger context of the previous sentence.

There is no reason why, in The Letter to the Hebrews, they should try to ensnare us in one little word when in the Greek words of the apostle nothing else is meant than that such sacrifices are pleasing and acceptable to God.

To restrain and check the insolence of our pride it ought to be quite enough that we attribute no importance to works beyond the measure of Scripture. Now it is the teaching of Scripture that our good works are always spattered with much uncleanness, by which God is rightly offended and is angry against us. So far are they from being able to appease him or arouse his kindness toward us! Yet because he examines our works according to his tenderness, not his supreme right, he therefore accepts them as if they were perfectly pure; and for that reason, although unmerited, they are rewarded with infinite benefits, both of the present life and also of the life to come. For I do not accept the distinction made by learned and otherwise godly men that good works deserve the graces that are conferred upon us in this life, while everlasting salvation is the reward of faith alone.[9] For the Lord almost always lodges in heaven the reward of toil and the crown of battle. On the other hand, so to attribute to the merit of works the fact that we are showered with grace upon grace as to take it away from grace is contrary to the teaching of Scripture. For even though Christ says, "To him who has will be given" [Matt. 25:29; Luke 8:18], and the faithful and upright servant who has been faithful over a few things will be set over many things [Matt. 25:21], at the same time he shows elsewhere that the increases of the believers are the gifts of his freely given kindness [cf. John 1:16]. "All who thirst," he says, "come ye to the waters; and ye who have no money, come, buy without money, and buy wine and milk without price." [Isa. 55:1 p.] Whatever, therefore, is now given to the godly as an aid to salvation, even blessedness itself, is purely God's beneficence. Yet both in this blessedness and in those godly persons, he testifies that he takes works into account. For in order to testify to the greatness of his love toward us, he makes not only us but the gift that he has given us worthy of such honor.

⁹ "Solius fidei praemium." Cf. III. xi. 19, note 35; III. xvii. 7, 8, 10.

(Rejection of the substitution of man's merit for Christ's, 5–8)

5. Christ as the sole foundation, as beginner and perfecter

^aIf these matters had in bygone ages been treated and dealt with in proper order, so many tumults and dissensions would never have arisen. Paul says that in the upbuilding of Christian teaching we must keep ^{b(a)}the foundation that he had laid among the Corinthians [cf. I Cor. 3:10], "beside which no other can be laid, which is Jesus Christ" [I Cor. 3:11]. What sort of foundation have we in Christ? Was he the beginning of our salvation in order that its fulfillment might follow from ourselves? Did he only open the way by which we might proceed under our own power? Certainly not. But, ^bas Paul had set forth a little before, Christ, when we acknowledge him, is given us to be our righteousness [I Cor. 1:30]. He alone is well founded in Christ who has perfect righteousness in himself: since the apostle does not say that He was sent to help us attain righteousness but himself to be our righteousness [I Cor. 1:30]. Indeed, he states that ^{b(a)}"he has chosen us in him" from eternity "before the foundation of the world," through no merit of our own "but according to the purpose of divine good pleasure" [Eph. 1:4–5, cf. Vg.]; that by his death we are redeemed from the condemnation of death and freed from ruin [cf. Col. 1:14, 20]; that we have been adopted unto him as sons and heirs by our Heavenly Father [cf. Rom. 8:17; Gal. 4:5–7]; that we have been reconciled through his blood [Rom. 5:9–10]; that, given into his protection, we are released from the danger of perishing and falling [John 10:28]; that thus ingrafted into him [cf. Rom. 11:19] we are already, in a manner, partakers of eternal life, having entered in the Kingdom of God through hope. Yet more: we experience such participation in him that, although we are still foolish in ourselves, he is our wisdom before God; while we are sinners, he is our righteousness; while we are unclean, he is our purity; while we are weak, while we are unarmed and exposed to Satan, yet ours is that power which has been given him in heaven and on earth [Matt. 28:18], by which to crush Satan for us and shatter the gates of hell; while we still bear about with us the body of death, he is yet our life. In brief, because all his things are ours and we have all things in him, in us there is nothing. Upon this foundation, I say, we must be built if we would grow into a holy temple to the Lord [cf. Eph. 2:21].

6. Roman theology curtails Christ's might and honor

^bBut for a long time the world has been taught otherwise. So all sorts of "moral" good works have been discovered whereby men are rendered pleasing to God before they are engrafted into

Christ. As if Scripture were lying when it says that all who have not the Son are in death [I John 5:12]! If they are in death, how can they beget the substance of life? As if it were meaningless that "whatsoever is done outside faith is sin" [Rom. 14:23]! As if good fruits could come from an evil tree! [Cf. Matt. 7:18; Luke 6:43.] What place have these most pestilent Sophists left to Christ to exert his power? They say that he deserved for us the first grace, that is, the occasion of deserving, but that it is now our part not to fail the occasion offered.[10] O overweening and shameless impiety! Who would have thought that those who professed the name of Christ would dare so strip him of his power and virtually trample him underfoot? The testimony commonly rendered to him is that whoever believes in him has been justified These Sophists teach that no other benefit comes from him except that the way has been opened for individuals to justify themselves. Would that they had tasted what these sentences mean: "Whoever have the Son of God have life" [I John 5:12 p.]; "Whoever believes . . . has passed out of death into life" [John 5:24; cf. ch. 6:40]; We have been justified by his grace that we might be made heirs of eternal life [Titus 3:7; cf. Rom. 5:1–2]; dBelievers ehave Christ abiding in them [I John 3:24], through whom they may cleave to God; Sharers in his life, they sit with him in the heavenly places [Eph. 2:6]; "They are translated into the Kingdom of God" [Col. 1:13 p.], and attain salvation—and innumerable like passages. For they do not mean that by faith in Christ there comes to us the capacity either to procure righteousness or only to acquire salvation, but that both are given to us. Therefore, as soon as you become engrafted into Christ through faith, you are made a son of God, an heir of heaven, a partaker in righteousness, a possessor of life; and (by this their falsehood may be better refuted) you obtain not the opportunity to gain merit but all the merits of Christ, for they are communicated to you.

7. *Roman theology understands neither Augustine nor Scripture*
    bThus the schools of the Sorbonne, mothers of all errors, have taken away from us justification by faith, which is the sum of all piety. Indeed, they confess by word that man is justified by "formed faith," but this they afterward explain on the ground that good works derive from faith the capacity to justify;[11] they

---

[10] Duns Scotus, *On the Sentences* III. xix. qu. unica. 8 (*Opera omnia* XIV. 719).
[11] According to Aquinas, unformed faith (*fides informata*) is faith without works of charity; formed faith (*fides formata*) is faith that works by charity: *Summa Theol.* I IIae. cxiii. 4; cxiv. 3, 4, 8; II IIae. v. 3 (tr. LCC XI. 189 f., 206–209, 214 f., 282–284).

seem to mention faith almost in mockery, because it could not be passed over in silence without great embarrassment, since 't is frequently repeated by Scripture.

Still not content, in praise of good works they filch something from God and turn it over to man. Because they see that good works are of little avail to exalt man and that these are not even called merits, properly speaking, if they be accounted fruits of God's grace, they derive them from the power of free will, as oil from a stone. And they do not deny that the principal cause, indeed, lies in grace. But they still contend that in this, free will is not ruled out, through which all merit exists.[12] Not only the later Sophists teach this, but their Pythagoras, Peter Lombard, whom, if you were to compare him with them, you would call sane and sober. It was truly remarkable blindness, when he had Augustine constantly on his lips,[13] not to see how much care that father took not to convey to man even the least particle of glory arising from good works. Above, when we were discussing free will, we related some of his testimonies on this matter,[14] and similar ones repeatedly occur in his writings; for example: ᶜwhen he forbids us ever to boast of our own merits, for even they are gifts of God; and ᵇwhen he writes that all our merit is but of grace and not obtained through our sufficiency but wholly comes to be through grace, etc.[15]

Little wonder that Lombard was blind to the light of Scripture, in which it appears that he was not so happily trained. Yet nothing clearer against him and his disciples could be desired than this word of the apostle, for having forbidden all glorying to Christians, he adds why glorying is wrong: "We are God's workmanship, created for good works, which he prepared beforehand that we should walk in them" [Eph. 2:10, cf. Vg.]. Since, therefore, no good comes forth from us except in so far as we have been regenerated, but our regeneration is entirely and without

[12] Aquinas, *Summa Theol.* I IIae. ciii. 3; civ. 3, 4; cix. 2 (tr. LCC XI. 140 f.). In *Contra gentes* iii. 149, Aquinas points out that "the divine help is the influence of the first cause upon secondary causes. . . . God does not destroy our acts of will; indeed he causes them" (tr. A. T. Gilby, *St. Thomas Aquinas: Philosophical Texts,* p. 158).

[13] Lombard, *Sentences* II. xxvi–xxviii (MPL 192. 709–719). Smits finds in Augustine no less than twenty-six passages bearing on the argument here: these characteristically assert the unaided grace of God in salvation: e.g., *Psalms,* Ps. 68 (Vg., Ps. 67). 41 (MPL 36. 838; tr. LF *Psalms* III. 351); *Enchiridion* ix. 32; xxviii. 106; xxxi. 117 (MPL 40. 248, 282, 287; tr. LCC VII. 358 f., 403 f., 409).

[14] II. ii. 8.

[15] Augustine, *Psalms,* Ps. 144. 11 (MPL 37. 1876; tr. LF [Ps. 145] *Psalms* VI. 325); *Letters* cxciv. 4. 16–19 (MPL 33. 879 ff.; tr. FC 30. 311–313).

exception from God, there is no reason why we should claim an ounce of good works for ourselves.

b(a)Finally, while they repeatedly inculcate good works, they in the meantime so instruct consciences as to discourage all their confidence that God remains kindly disposed and favorable to their works.[16] But we, on the other hand, without reference to merit, still remarkably cheer and comfort the hearts of believers by our teaching, when we tell them that they please God in their works and are without doubt acceptable to him. But here too ᵃwe require that no man attempt or go about any work without faith, that is, unless with firm assurance of mind he first determines that it will please God.

8. Admonition and comfort on the basis of right doctrine

b(a)Therefore, let us not allow ourselves to be drawn even a finger's breadth from this sole foundation. For once it is laid, wise master builders build rightly and in order upon it.

ᵃFor if there is need of teaching and exhortation, they inform us that "the Son of God manifested himself in order to destroy the works of the devil"; that those who are of God may not sin [I John 3:8–9]; that the time past suffices for carrying out the Gentiles' wishes [I Peter 4:3]; that God's elect are vessels of mercy chosen to honor and ought to be purged of uncleanness [II Tim. 2:20–21]. But everything is said once for all when it is shown that Christ wants disciples who deny themselves, take up their cross, and follow him [Matt. 16:24; Luke 9:23]. He who has denied himself has cut off the root of all evils so as to seek no longer the things that are his own. He who has taken up his cross has readied himself for all patience and gentleness. But the example of Christ embraces both this and all other duties of piety and holiness. He presented himself to the Father as obedient even to death. [Phil. 2:8.] He entered completely into the accomplishing of God's works. [Cf. John 4:34; also Luke 2:49.] He breathed heart and soul the glory of the Father. [Cf. John 8:50; also John 7:16–18.] He laid down his life for his brothers. [John 10:15; cf. John 15:13.] He did good to his enemies and prayed for them. [Cf. Luke 6:27, 35; also Luke 23:34.]

But if there is need of consolation, the following passages will bring a wonderful consolation: "We are afflicted yet not made anxious, we fail but are not deserted, are humbled but not confounded, we are cast down but have not perished, ever bearing

---

[16] Aquinas, Summa Theol. I IIae. cxii. 5 (tr. LCC XI. 180 f.), quoting Job 36:26 and I Cor. 4:3. He says that "a man cannot judge with certainty whether he has grace."

the mortification of Jesus Christ about in our bodies that Jesus' life may be manifested in us" [II Cor. 4:8–10 p.]; "If we died with him, we shall also live with him; if we endure, we shall also reign with him" [II Tim. 2:11–12]; thus we are conformed to his sufferings, until we attain to the likeness of his resurrection [Phil. 3:10–11], since "the Father has predestined those whom he has chosen in himself to conform to the image of his Son that Christ may be the first-born among all the brethren" [Rom. 8:29 p.]. Therefore, "neither death, . . . nor things present, nor things to come, . . . will separate us from the love of God which is in Christ" [Rom. 8:38–39 p.]; bbut rather all things will turn to our good and salvation [cf. Rom. 8:28]. aTake note that we do not justify man by works before God, but all who are of God we speak of as being "reborn" [cf. I Peter 1:3], and as becoming "a new creation" [II Cor. 5:17], so that they pass from the realm of sin into the realm of righteousness; and we say that by this testimony they confirm their calling [II Peter 1:10], and, like trees, are judged by their fruits [Matt. 7:20; 12:33; Luke 6:44].[17]

cCHAPTER XVI

REFUTATION OF THE FALSE ACCUSATIONS BY WHICH THE PAPISTS TRY TO CAST ODIUM UPON THIS DOCTRINE

1. Does the doctrine of justification do away with good works?
aThis, in one word, is enough to refute the shamelessness of certain impious persons who slanderously charge us with abolishing good works, b(a)and with seducing men from the pursuit of them, when we say that men are not justified by works and do not merit salvation by them; and again, charge us with making the path to righteousness too easy when we teach that justification lies in free remission of sins; and, by this enticement, with luring into sin men who are already too much inclined to it of their own accord.[1] These false charges, I say, are sufficiently refuted by that simple statement. Still, I shall briefly reply to each. bThey contend that through the justification of faith, good works are destroyed.
cI forbear to say what sort of zealots for good works they are who thus carp at us. Let them rail with impunity even as they

---

[17] Cf. Melanchthon, *Loci communes* (1521), ed. H. Engelland, *Melanchthons Werke in Auswahl* II. i. 112; tr. C. L. Hill, *The Loci Communes of Philip Melanchthon*, p. 212.

[1] Eck, *Enchiridion*, ch. v (1533 edition, fo. 24b f.); Erasmus, *De libero arbitrio*, ed. J. von Walter, pp. 9 f. ("opening a door to impiety of all sorts"); Cochlaeus, *Philippicae* III. 15, 20, 21–62; fo. I 2b, fo. K 1b–2a ("spread of irreligion"), fo. N 2a.

wantonly infect the whole world with their own foul lives! They pretend to be grieved that, when faith is so gloriously extolled, works are degraded. ᵇWhat if, rather, these were encouraged and strengthened? For we dream neither of a faith devoid of good works nor of a justification that stands without them. This alone is of importance: having admitted that faith and good works must cleave together, we still lodge justification in faith, not in works. We have a ready explanation for doing this, provided we turn to Christ to whom our faith is directed and from whom it receives its full strength.

Why, then, are we justified by faith? Because by faith we grasp Christ's righteousness, by which alone we are reconciled to God. Yet you could not grasp this without at the same time grasping sanctification also.[2] ᵇ⁽ᵃ⁾For he "is given unto us for righteousness, wisdom, sanctification, and redemption" [I Cor. 1:30]. ᵇTherefore Christ justifies no one whom he does not at the same time sanctify. These benefits are joined together by an everlasting and indissoluble bond, so that those whom he illumines by his wisdom, he redeems; those whom he redeems, he justifies; those whom he justifies, he sanctifies.

But, since the question concerns only righteousness and sanctification, let us dwell upon these. Although we may distinguish them, Christ contains both of them inseparably in himself. Do you wish, then, to attain righteousness in Christ? You must first possess Christ; but you cannot possess him without being made partaker in his sanctification, because he cannot be divided into pieces [I Cor. 1:13]. Since, therefore, it is solely by expending himself that the Lord gives us these benefits to enjoy, he bestows both of them at the same time, the one never without the other. Thus it is clear how true it is that we are justified not without works yet not through works, since in our sharing in Christ, which justifies us, sanctification is just as much included as righteousness.

2. Does the doctrine of justification stifle zeal for good works?

ᵃThis charge is also very false: that men's hearts are seduced from desiring to do good when we take from them their regard for merit. ᵇHere, in passing, my readers must be warned that our opponents stupidly reason from reward to merit, as I shall after-

---

[2] This statement seems on the surface out of accord with parts of Calvin's argument against Osiander in III. xi. But there also (sec. 6), while distinguishing justification from sanctification, he strongly asserts that they are "inseparable," citing, as here, I Cor. 1:30. Cf. also III. xx. 45.

ward explain more clearly.[3] For they obviously do not know the principle that God is no less generous when he assigns a reward for works than when he bestows the capacity to act rightly. But I prefer to postpone this to its proper place.

Now it will be enough to touch upon how weak their objection is. This will be done in two ways. [a]For first, in saying men will take no care to regulate their lives aright unless hope of reward is held out to them, they are completely in error.[4] For if it is only a matter of men looking for reward when they serve God, and hiring or selling their labor to him, it is of little profit. God wills to be freely worshiped, freely loved. That worshiper, I say, he approves who, when all hope of receiving reward has been cut off, still ceases not to serve him.

Indeed, if men have to be aroused, no one can put sharper spurs to them than [b]those derived from the end of our redemption and calling. Such spurs the Word of the Lord employs when it teaches [c]that it would bespeak our too impious ingratitude for us not to reciprocate the love of him "who first loved us" [I John 4:19; cf. v. 10]; [b]that by Christ's blood our consciences are cleansed from dead works, that we should serve the living God [Heb. 9:14]; [c]that it is an unworthy, unholy act for us, once cleansed, to contaminate ourselves with new filth, and to profane that sacred blood [Heb. 10:29]; [b]that "we have been delivered from the hand of our enemies in order that we may serve him without fear in holiness and righteousness before him all our days" [Luke 1:74–75 p.]; [c]that we have been freed from sin to cultivate righteousness with a free spirit [Rom. 6:18]; that "our old man was crucified" [Rom. 6:6], that "we . . . may arise to newness of life" [Rom. 6:4 p.]. Likewise, if we be dead with Christ, as befits his members, we must seek the things that are above, and be pilgrims on earth, so that we may aspire to heaven where our treasure is [cf. Col. 3:1–3; also Matt. 6:20]. [b]In this "the grace of the Lord has appeared, that, having renounced all irreligion and worldly desires, we may live sober, holy, and godly lives in this age, awaiting our blessed hope and the appearing of the glory of our great God and Savior." [Titus 2:11–13 p.] Therefore we were not appointed to rouse wrath against ourselves but to obtain salvation through Christ [I Thess. 5:9]. [b(a)]We are temples of the Holy

---

[3] III. xviii. Cf. Erasmus, *De libero arbitrio*, ed. von Walter, p. 78; De Castro, *Adversus haereses* XII (1543, fo. 150). The passage from Erasmus is translated by M. M. McLaughlin in *The Portable Renaissance Reader*, ed. J. B. Ross and M. M. McLaughlin, p. 684. See also L. Goumaz, *La Doctrine du salut*, pp. 259 ff.

J. Faber, *De fide et operibus* xxiii, xxv (*Opera* [1550], fo. 103b f.).

Spirit, which it is unlawful to profane [I Cor. 3:16–17; II Cor. 6:16; Eph. 2:21]. We are not darkness but light in the Lord, and must walk as children of light [Eph. 5:8–9; cf. I Thess. 5:4–5]. We have not been called to uncleanness but to holiness [I Thess. 4:7], for this is the will of God, our sanctification, that we abstain from unlawful desires [I Thess. 4:3]. Ours is a holy calling [II Tim. 1:9]. It demands purity of life and nothing less; we have been freed from sin to this end, that we may obey righteousness [Rom. 6:18]. Could we be aroused to love by any livelier argument than that of John's: that "we love one another as God has loved us" [I John 4:11; cf. John 13:34]? that herein his children differ from the devil's children as children of light from children of darkness, because they abide in love [I John 3:10; 2:10–11]? Again, with that argument of Paul's: that we, if we cleave to Christ, are members of one body [I Cor. 6:15, 17; 12:12], who must help one another in our mutual tasks [cf. I Cor. 12:25]? ªCan we be more forcefully summoned to holiness than when we hear again from John that "all who have this hope . . . sanctify themselves" because their God is holy [I John 3:3]? ᵉLikewise, from Paul's lips: since we rely on the promise of adoption, "let us cleanse ourselves of all defilement of flesh and spirit" [II Cor. 7:1, Vg.]? ªOr again, than when we hear Christ putting himself forward as our example in order that we may follow his footsteps [I Peter 2:21; cf. John 15:10; 13:15]?

3. God's honor and God's mercy as motives for action: subordination of works[t]

ªThese few Scriptural proofs, indeed, I have set forth as a mere taste. For if it were my purpose to go through every one, a large volume would have to be compiled. All the apostles are full of exhortations, urgings, and reproofs with which to instruct the man of God in every good work [cf. II Tim. 3:16–17], and that without mention of merit. ᵇRather, they derive their most powerful exhortations from the thought that our salvation stands upon no merit of ours but solely upon God's mercy. Accordingly, Paul, when he devoted an entire letter to showing that we have no hope of life save in Christ's righteousness, when he gets down to exhortations, implores us by that mercy of God which He has deigned to give us [Rom. 12:1]. ªAnd surely this one reason ought to have been enough: that God may be glorified in us [Matt. 5:16]. But if anyone is still not so forcibly affected by the glory of God, the remembrance of his benefits will, nevertheless, amply suffice to arouse such persons to well-doing.[5] But

[5] Chrysostom, *Homilies on Genesis,* hom. xxvi. 5, 6 (MPG 53. 235–239).

these men, since, by stressing merits, they perchance force out some slavish and coerced observances of the law, say falsely that we have no basis for exhorting men to good works because we do not enter upon the same road.[6] As if such obedience were highly pleasing to God, who declares that he "loves a cheerful giver" and forbids anything to be given as if "grudgingly or of necessity" [II Cor. 9:7]!

[b(a)]And I do not say this because I either despise or neglect the kind of exhortation that Scripture very often uses in order not to overlook any means of arousing us. For it recalls how "God will render to every man according to his works" [Rom. 2:6–7; Matt. 16:27; I Cor. 3:8, 14–15; II Cor. 5:10; etc.]. [b]But I deny that this is the only thing, and even the principal thing among many. Again, I do not concede that we should take our beginning from that point. Furthermore, I contend that it does nothing to support the kind of merits they preach, as we shall afterward see.[7] Finally, I say that it is of no use unless we give prior place to the doctrine that we are justified by Christ's merit alone, which is grasped through faith, but by no merits of our own works, because no men can be fit for the pursuit of holiness save those who have first imbibed this doctrine.

And the prophet beautifully suggests this when he addresses God thus: "There is propitiation with thee, O Lord, that thou mayest be feared" [Ps. 130:4, cf. Comm.]. For he shows that there is no honoring of God unless his mercy be acknowledged, upon which alone it is founded and established. [e]This is especially worthy of note: that we may know not only that the beginning of honoring God aright is trust in his mercy but that the fear of God, which the papists would have meritorious,[8] cannot be reckoned under the term "merit" because that fear is founded upon the pardon and forgiveness of sins.

4. The doctrine of justification as incitement to the sinful

[b(a)]But it is the most worthless of slanders to say men are invited to sin, when we affirm the free forgiveness of sins in which we assert righteousness consists.[9] For we say that it is of such great value that it cannot be paid for by any good of ours. Therefore, it can never be obtained except as a free gift. Now for us

---

[6] Sec. 2, above.

[7] III. xviii. 3.

[8] E.g., Latomus, *De fide et operibus* (*Opera* [1550], fo. 141ab).

[9] Cf. Erasmus, *De libero arbitrio*, ed. J. von Walter, p. 10; Cochlaeus, *Philippicae* III. 21 (fo. K 1b–2a) on the Saxon Visitations (1528). The latter document is translated by C. Bergendoff in *Luther's Works*, American Edition, 40. 269–320.

indeed it is free, ᵃbut not so for Christ, who dearly bought it at the cost of his most sacred blood, apart from which there was no ransom of sufficient worth to satisfy God's judgment. When men are taught this, they are made aware that they cannot do anything to prevent the shedding of his most sacred blood as often as they sin. Furthermore, we say that our foulness is such that it can never be cleansed except by the fountain of this purest blood. ᵇOught not they ᵃwho hear these things ᵇto conceive a greater dread of sin than if it were said that they are cleansed by the sprinkling of good works? And ᵃif they have any sense of God, how can they but dread, once purified, to wallow once more in the mire, so as to disturb and poison, as much as they can, the purity of this fountain? "I have washed my feet," says the believing soul according to Solomon, "how shall I defile them anew?" [Cant. 5:3].

Now it is plain which persons prefer to cheapen the forgiveness of sins, and which ones to prostitute the dignity of righteousness. They make believe that God is appeased by their wretched satisfactions, which are but dung [Phil. 3:8].¹⁰ We affirm that the guilt of sin is too heavy to be atoned for by such light trifles, that it is too grave an offense against God to be remitted by these worthless satisfactions, that this, then, is the prerogative of Christ's blood alone. ᵇThey say that righteousness, if ever it fails, is restored and repaired by works of satisfaction.¹¹ We count it too precious to be matched by any compensation of works; and therefore, to recover it, we must take refuge in God's mercy alone. The remaining matters that pertain to forgiveness of sins belong in the next chapter.¹²

ᶜCHAPTER XVII

THE AGREEMENT OF THE PROMISES OF THE LAW AND OF THE GOSPEL

(Works as related to the law: the instance of Cornelius, 1–5)
1. Scholastic arguments stated and confuted*

ᵇNow let us pursue the other arguments with which Satan, through his minions, tries to overthrow or weaken justification of faith. This, I think, we have already hammered out for the slanderers, so they may not charge us with being hostile to good

---

¹⁰ Cf. Bonaventura, *Commentary on the Sentences* IV. part 2. art. 1. qu. 4 (*Opera selecta* IV. 350 ff.).
¹¹ Aquinas, *Summa Theol.* III. Suppl. xii. 3; xv. 1.
¹² "*Ex capite proximo.*" For "*proximo,*" here erroneous, the 1539 edition has "*quinto,*" "fifth"; the editions 1543–1554 have "*nono,*" "ninth." The passages to be consulted are, in fact, III. iii. 19; III. iv. 25, 27, 30.

works. For justification is withdrawn from works, not that no good works may be done, or that what is done may be denied to be good, but that we may not rely upon them, glory in them, or ascribe salvation to them. For our assurance, our glory, and the sole anchor of our salvation are that Christ the Son of God is ours, and we in turn are in him sons of God and heirs of the Kingdom of Heaven, called to the hope of eternal blessedness by God's grace, not by our worth.

But because, as we said, they assail us with still other devices, come, let us keep beating them back! First, they return to the promises of the law that the Lord has made to the keepers of his law, and they ask us whether we wish them completely nullified or effective. Since it would be ridiculous and absurd to say "nullified," they take it as a fact that they are effective. From this they reason that it is not by faith alone that we are justified.[1] For the Lord speaks as follows: "And it shall come to pass, if you hearken to these precepts and judgments, and keep and do them, the Lord shall keep with you the covenant and the mercy that he swore unto your fathers; and he will love you and increase you and bless you," etc. [Deut. 7:12–13 p.]. Likewise: "If you direct your ways and your efforts aright, . . . not walk after strange gods, execute judgment between man and man, and not slip back into wickedness" [Jer. 7:5–7, cf. Vg.; cf. also Jer. 7:23], I shall walk in your midst. I do not wish to recite a thousand passages of the same type, which, since they do not differ in meaning, will be explained by the exposition of those I have cited. To sum up, Moses testifies that in the law a blessing and a curse [Deut. 11:26], death and life [Deut. 30:15], are set before us. So, then, they maintain either that this blessing becomes idle and unfruitful or that justification is not of faith alone.

We have already shown above[2] how, if we cleave to the law, we are bereft of all blessing and a curse hangs over us, one ordained for all transgressors [cf. Deut. 27:26]. For the Lord promises nothing except to perfect keepers of his law, and no one of the kind is to be found. ªThe fact, then, remains that through the law the whole human race is proved subject to God's curse and wrath, and in order to be freed from these, it is necessary to depart from the power of the law and, as it were, to be released from its bondage into freedom. This is no carnal freedom, which would draw us away from the observance of the law, incite us to license

---

[1] Such arguments were advanced by many of Luther's opponents, including Erasmus, *De libero arbitrio*, ed. J. von Walter, pp. 23 ff., 33; Latomus, *De fide et operibus* (*Opera* [1550], fo. 141ab).

[2] II. vii. 3.

in all things, and let our concupiscence play the wanton as if locks were broken or reins slackened. Rather, it is spiritual freedom, which would comfort and raise up the stricken and prostrate conscience, showing it to be free from the curse and condemnation with which the law pressed it down, bound and fettered. When through faith we lay hold on the mercy of God in Christ, we attain this liberation and, so to speak, manumission from subjection to the law, for it is by faith we are made sure and certain of forgiveness of sins, the law having pricked and stung our conscience to the awareness of them.

2. We cannot bring the promises of the law to fulfillment through our works

ªIn this way, the promises also that are offered us in the law would all be ineffectual and void, had God's goodness not helped us through the gospel. For this condition, that we should carry out the law—upon which the promises depend and by which alone they are to be performed—will never be fulfilled. ᵇThus the Lord helps us, not by leaving us a part of righteousness in our works, and by supplying part out of his loving-kindness, but by appointing Christ alone as the fulfillment of righteousness. For the apostle, having previously said that he and the other Jews, "knowing that man is not justified by the works of the law . . . have believed in Jesus Christ," adds the reason: not that they might be helped to perfect righteousness by faith in Christ but that they might be justified by that faith and not by works of the law [Gal. 2:16]. If believers pass from the law to faith in order to find righteousness in faith, which they see to be far from the law, surely they renounce the righteousness of the law. Let him, therefore, who so wishes enlarge upon the recompense said to await the keeper of the law, provided he at the same time ponder that our depravity makes us experience no benefit therefrom until we have obtained another righteousness from faith. So David, when he recalls the recompense that the Lord has prepared for his servants, immediately descends to the recognition of sins, which nullify it. Also, in Ps. 19:12, he nobly extols the benefits of the law but immediately exclaims: "Who can understand his faults? Cleanse thou me from my secret faults, O Lord" [Ps. 18:13, Vg.; 19:12, EV]. This passage completely agrees with a preceding one, where, after he had said, "All the ways of the Lord are goodness and truth" [Ps. 25:10] to those who fear him [cf. Ps. 25:12], he adds, "For thy name's sake, O Lord, thou wilt pardon my depravity, for it is great" [Ps. 25:11; cf. 24:11, Vg.]. So also ought we to recognize that God's benevolence has been set forth for us in the law, if we could merit it by works, but that it never comes to us by this merit.

3. The promises of the law are put into effect through the gospel
ᵇWhat then? Have the promises been given only to vanish without bearing fruit? I declared just above that this was not my meaning. I say, indeed, that the promises have no beneficent effect upon us so long as they have reference to the merits of works, and consequently, if considered in themselves, they are in a sense abolished. Thus that renowned promise: "I have given you good precepts" [cf. Ezek. 20:11], and he who does them, shall live in them [Lev. 18:5]. The apostle teaches that this promise is of no importance [cf. Rom. 10:5; Gal. 3:12]; if we stop there, it will benefit not a whit more than if it had not been given. For it does not apply even to God's most holy servants, who are far from fulfilling the law, hemmed in as they are by many transgressions. But when the promises of the gospel are substituted, which proclaim the free forgiveness of sins, these not only make us acceptable to God but also render our works pleasing to him. And not only does the Lord adjudge them pleasing; he also extends to them the blessings which under the covenant were owed to the observance of his law. I therefore admit that what the Lord has promised in his law to the keepers of righteousness and holiness is paid to the works of believers, but in this repayment we must always consider the reason that wins favor for these works.

Now we see that there are three reasons. The first is: God, having turned his gaze from his servants' works, which always deserve reproof rather than praise, embraces his servants in Christ, and with faith alone intervening, reconciles them to himself without the help of works. The second is: of his own fatherly generosity and loving-kindness, and without considering their worth, he raises works to this place of honor, so that he attributes some value to them. The third is: He receives these very works with pardon, not imputing the imperfection with which they are all so corrupted that they would otherwise be reckoned as sins rather than virtues.

And this shows how deluded the Sophists are, who thought they had neatly got around all these absurdities by saying that works of their own intrinsic goodness are of no avail for meriting salvation but by reason of the covenant,³ because the Lord of his own liberality esteemed them so highly. Meanwhile they did not

---

³ *"Ex pacti ratione."* Cf. Bonaventura, *On the Sentences* II. xxvii. 2. qu. 3 (*Opera selecta* II. 659); De Castro, *Adversus haereses* X: *"ex pacto . . . ex conventione"* (1543, fo. 160 B, C).

observe how far those works, which they meant to be meritorious, were from fulfilling the condition of the promises unless preceded by justification resting on faith alone, and by forgiveness of sins, through which even good works must be cleansed of spots. Of the three causes of God's liberality, then, which make the works of believers acceptable, they noted only one, and suppressed two—and the chief ones at that!

4. The twofold acceptance of man before God

ᵇThey cite Peter's statement, which Luke quotes in The Acts: "In truth I find that God accepts no one person over another" [Acts 10:34–35, Comm.].⁴ But in every nation he who does righteousness is acceptable to him. And from this passage, which seems quite clear, they infer that if by right efforts a man may gain God's favor for himself, it is not the gift of God alone that gains him salvation; nay, rather that God of his own mercy so helps the sinner that by works He is inclined to mercy.

But you can in no way make the Scriptural passages agree unless you recognize a double acceptance of man before God.

For God finds nothing in man's nature but his miserable condition to dispose Him to mercy. If, therefore, when he is first received by God, it is certain that man is naked and bereft of all good, and on the other hand, stuffed and laden with all kinds of evils—on the basis of what endowment, I ask, shall we say he is worthy of a heavenly calling [cf. Heb. 3:1]? Away, then, with this empty dreaming about merits, where God so clearly sets off his free mercy! For they most wickedly twist what the angel's voice said to Cornelius—that his prayers and alms mounted up unto God's presence [Acts 10:31]—to mean that by zeal for good works man is prepared to receive God's grace.⁵ Indeed, Cornelius must have been already illumined by the Spirit of wisdom, for he was endowed with true wisdom, that is, the fear of God; and he was sanctified by the same Spirit, for he was a keeper of righteousness, which the apostle taught to be the Spirit's surest fruit [Gal. 5:5]. All those things in him which are said to have pleased God he received from God's grace—so far is he from preparing himself to receive grace by means of them through his own effort. Truly, not one syllable of Scripture can be cited contrary to this doctrine: God's sole reason to receive man unto himself is that he sees him

---

⁴ Cf. III. xxiii. 10; Cochlaeus, *Philippicae* III. 13, fo. H 4a; Lombard, *Sentences* III. xxv. 4 (MPL 192. 810).

⁵ Aquinas, *Summa Theol.* I IIae. cix. 6 (tr. LCC XI. 146 ff.); III. Suppl. x. 4, reply to obj. 3; lix. 4, reply to obj. 2. Cf. Eck, *Enchiridion*, ch. v; Herborn, *Enchiridion* xxxviii (CC 12. 128–132).

utterly lost if left to himself, but because he does not will him to be lost, he exercises his mercy in freeing him. Now we see how it is that this acceptance has nothing to do with man's righteousness but is pure proof of divine goodness toward miserable sinners, utterly unworthy of so great a benefit.

*5. In what sense the Lord is pleased with the good works of the regenerate**

ᵇThe Lord, having rescued man from the pit of perdition, has through the grace of adoption set him apart for his own. Thereupon, because he has begotten him anew and conformed him to a new life, he now embraces him as a new creature [cf. II Cor. 5:17] endowed with the gifts of his Spirit. This is that "acceptance" which Peter mentions [Acts 10:34; cf. I Peter 1:17] whereby believers are, after their call, approved of God also in respect of works [cf. I Peter 2:5]. For the Lord cannot fail to love and embrace the good things that he works in them through his Spirit. But we must always remember that God "accepts" believers by reason of works only because he is their source ᵉ⁽ᵇ⁾and graciously, by way of adding to his liberality, ᵇdeigns ᵉ⁽ᵇ⁾also ᵇto show "acceptance" ᵉ⁽ᵇ⁾toward the good works he has himself bestowed. ᵇFor whence come their good works, save that the Lord, having chosen them as vessels unto honor [Rom. 9:21], thus is pleased to adorn them with true purity? Whence, also, are these works reckoned good as if they lacked nothing, save that the kindly Father grants pardon for those blemishes and spots which cleave to them? To sum up, by this passage he means nothing else but that God's children are pleasing and lovable to him, since he sees in them the marks and features of his own countenance. For we have elsewhere taught that regeneration is a renewal of the divine image in us.⁶ Since, therefore, wherever God contemplates his own face, he both rightly loves it and holds it in honor, it is said with good reason that the lives of believers, framed to holiness and righteousness, are pleasing to him.

But because the godly, encompassed with mortal flesh, are still sinners, and their good works are as yet incomplete and redolent of the vices of the flesh, he can be propitious neither to the former nor to the latter unless he embrace them in Christ rather than in themselves. In this sense we are to understand those passages which attest that God is kind and merciful to the keepers of righteousness. Moses said to the Israelites, "The Lord your God, keeping covenant and mercy with those who love him and keep his commandments to a thousand generations" [Deut. 7:9 p.]. This

⁶ I. xv. 4.

sentence was afterward used as a common expression by the people. Thus Solomon solemnly prays, "O Lord God of Israel, . . . who keepest covenant and mercy with thy servants who walk before thee with all their heart" [I Kings 8:23]. And Nehemiah repeats the same words [Neh. 1:5].

Indeed, in all covenants of his mercy the Lord requires of his servants in return uprightness and sanctity of life, lest his goodness be mocked or someone, puffed up with empty exultation on that account, bless his own soul, walking meanwhile in the wickedness of his own heart [Deut. 29:19]. Consequently, in this way he wills to keep in their duty those admitted to the fellowship of the covenant; nonetheless the covenant is at the outset drawn up as a free agreement, and perpetually remains such. ᵉAccording to this reason, David, although he proclaims that he had been rewarded for the cleanness of his hands [II Sam. 22:21; cf. Ps. 18:20], still did not omit that source to which I referred: that he was drawn from the womb "because God loved him" [II Sam. 22:20 p.]. There he commends the goodness of his cause in such a way that he withdraws nothing of the free mercy that anticipates all gifts whose source it is.

(Passages that relate justification to works examined, 6–15)
6. *The promises of grace of the Old Covenant as distinct from the promises of the law*
ᵇAnd here it is useful to note in passing how these expressions differ from the promises of the law. I call "promises of the law" not those sprinkled everywhere in the books of Moses, since in them many evangelical promises also occur, but those properly pertaining to the ministry of the law. Promises of this sort, by whatever name you wish to call them, declare that there is recompense ready for you if you do what they enjoin.

But when it is said that "the Lord keeps covenant of mercy with those who love him" [cf. Deut. 7:9; I Kings 8:23; Neh. 1:5], this indicates what kind of servants they are who have undertaken his covenant[7] in good faith rather than expresses the reason why the Lord benefits them. Now this is the way it is indicated: as God deigns to give us the grace of eternal life to the end that he may be loved, feared, and honored by us, so whatever promises of mercy are contained in Scripture are justly directed to the end that we may reverence and honor the Author of these benefits. Whenever, therefore, we hear that he does good to those who keep his law, let us remember that the children of God are there designated by the duty that ought in them to be perpetual, and that

⁷ *"Foedus."* Cf. III. xiv. 6, note 6; III. xxi. 5–7.

we have been adopted for this reason: to reverence him as our Father. Accordingly, not to renounce our right of adoption, we must ever strive in the direction of our call.

But again, let us keep in mind that the fulfillment of the Lord's mercy does not depend upon believers' works but that he fulfills the promise of salvation for those who respond to his call with upright life, because in those who are directed to the good by his Spirit he recognizes the only genuine insignia of his children. What is said in Ps. 15:1 concerning citizens of the church should be referred to this: "O Lord, who shall sojourn in thy Tabernacle? Who shall dwell on thy holy hill?" [Ps. 14:1, Vg.; 15:1, EV]. "The innocent of hands and clean of heart," etc. [Ps. 23:4, Vg.; 24:4, EV.] Likewise, in Isaiah: "Who . . . shall dwell with the devouring fire?" [Isa. 33:14.] He who does righteousness, who speaks uprightly [Isa. 33:15], etc. It is not the foundation by which believers stand firm before God that is described but the means whereby our most merciful Father introduces them into his fellowship, and protects and strengthens them therein. For because he abhors sin, and loves righteousness, in order to conform them to himself and to his Kingdom he purifies by his Spirit those whom he has joined to himself. Therefore if one seeks the first cause that opens for the saints the door to God's Kingdom, and hence gives them a permanent standing-ground in it, at once we answer: Because the Lord by his own mercy has adopted them once for all, and keeps them continually. But if the question is of the manner, we must proceed to regeneration and its fruits as recounted in this psalm [cf. Ps. 15:2 ff.].

7. Does not Scripture speak of the "righteousness" of the works of the law?
ᵇBut there seems to be far greater difficulty in those passages which grace good works with the title of "righteousness," and declare that man is justified by them. Most are of the former type, where ᵇ⁽ᵃ⁾observances of commandments are called "justifications" or "righteousnesses." ᵇAn example of the latter type is what we find in Moses: "It shall be our righteousness if we . . . keep all these precepts" [Deut. 6:25 p.]. And if you raise the objection that this is a legal promise, which, joined to an impossible condition, proves nothing, there are other objections to which you cannot make the same answer, such as this: "And it will be righteousness to you before the Lord to return to the poor man his pledge," etc. [Deut. 24:13 p.]. What the prophet says is the same thing: the zeal in revenging the shame of Israel was imputed to Phinehas as righteousness [Ps. 106:30–31].

Therefore the Pharisees of our day think that they have here ample ground for exultation. For when we say that after faith righteousness has been established justification of works ceases, they argue on this same basis: if righteousness is of works, then it is untrue that we are justified by faith alone.

My admission that the precepts of the law are called "righteousnesses" is nothing strange, for they are truly such. ᵉStill I must warn my readers that the Greeks inadequately rendered the Hebrew word "HUCIM," substituting for "edicts," "righteousnesses."[8] Yet on this word I readily yield the point at issue.

ᵇIndeed, we do not deny that the law of God contains perfect righteousness. For even though, because we are bound to perform everything it requires, we should have yielded full obedience to it, still "we are unprofitable servants" [Luke 17:10]. Yet because the Lord deigns to accord to it the honor of righteousness, we do not take away what he has given. We therefore willingly confess that perfect obedience to the law is righteousness, and that the keeping of each commandment is a part of righteousness; provided that in the remaining parts the whole sum of righteousness is contained. But we deny that such a form of righteousness exists anywhere. And we cast off law righteousness, not because it is defective and mutilated of itself, but because, due to the weakness of our flesh, it is nowhere visible.

Still, not only does Scripture call the Lord's precepts simply "righteousnesses" but it also applies this term to the works of the saints. For example, when it reports that Zechariah and his wife "walked in the righteousnesses of the Lord" [Luke 1:6], obviously in so speaking it estimates the works more from the nature of the law than from their own character. ᵉYet here again what I have just said must be noted, that a rule is not to be established upon the carelessness of the Greek translator. But because Luke had no wish to change anything in the received version [cf. Luke 1:3], I shall not contend over it. ᵇFor those things which are contained in the law, God commended as righteousness; but we do not attain that righteousness save by observing the whole law, and it is broken by every transgression. Since the law enjoins only righteousness, therefore, if we have regard to it, all its commandments are righteousnesses; if we have in view the men by whom they are kept, they win no praise for righteousness from one work, as they are transgressors in many—that one work being always in some part faulty because of its imperfection.

---

8 "δικαιώματα," the LXX rendering of חֻקִּים , which Calvin would prefer to render "edicts." VG has *"edits ou statuts."*

8. Twofold value of work before God

ᵇBut I now come to the second type, in which there is especial difficulty. Paul advances no firmer proof of faith righteousness than what he writes of Abraham, that "his faith was reckoned to him for righteousness" [Rom. 4:3; Gal. 3:6]. Since, therefore, it is said that the deed committed by Phinehas "was reckoned to him as righteousness" [Ps. 106:31], Paul's contention concerning faith permits us to infer the same concerning works. Accordingly, our opponents, as if having victory in hand, decide that without faith we are indeed not justified but that we are also not justified by it alone—that it is works that complete our righteousness.⁹ Here I beseech the godly, if they know the true rule of righteousness is to be sought from Scripture alone, religiously and earnestly to ponder with me how Scripture may, without quibbling, be duly brought into agreement with itself.

Since Paul knew that justification of faith is a refuge for those who lack righteousness of their own [cf. Rom., ch. 5], he boldly infers that all who are justified by faith are excluded from works righteousness. But since it is certain that this is common to all believers, from this fact Paul with equal assurance determines that no one is justified by works [cf. Rom. 3:20]—on the contrary, that men are justified without any help from our works. But it is one thing to discuss what value works have of themselves, another, to weigh in what place they are to be held after faith righteousness has been established.

If we are to determine a price for works according to their worth, we say that they are unworthy to come before God's sight; that man, accordingly, has no works in which to glory before God; that hence, stripped of all help from works, he is justified by faith alone. But we define justification as follows: the sinner, received into communion with Christ, is reconciled to God by his grace, while, cleansed by Christ's blood, he obtains forgiveness of sins, and clothed with Christ's righteousness as if it were his own, he stands confident before the heavenly judgment seat.

After forgiveness of sins is set forth, the good works that now follow are appraised otherwise than on their own merit. For everything imperfect in them is covered by Christ's perfection, every blemish or spot is cleansed away by his purity in order not to be brought in question at the divine judgment. Therefore, after the guilt of all transgressions that hinder man from bringing forth

⁹ Note the insistence on "faith alone" in secs. 7, 8, 10. The view that works complete justification was frequently put forth in controversy against Luther, and was concisely affirmed by the Council of Trent in canon xxiv of the Decree on Justification (Schaff, *Creeds* II. 115).

anything pleasing to God has been blotted out, and after the fault of imperfection, which habitually defiles even good works, is buried, the good works done by believers are accounted righteous, or, what is the same thing, are reckoned as righteousness [Rom. 4:22].

9. Justification by faith is the basis of works righteousness

bNow if anyone raises this objection against me to impugn faith righteousness, I shall first ask whether a man is reckoned righteous because of one or two holy works, while he is a transgressor in the remaining works of his life. This is indeed more than absurd. Then I shall inquire whether he is reckoned righteous even on account of many good works if he is in some part indeed found guilty of transgression. He will not dare put forward this contention when the sanction of the law cries out and proclaims accursed all who have not completely fulfilled all the commandments of the law [Deut. 27:26]. I shall inquire still further—whether there be any work that does not deserve to be censured for some impurity or imperfection. And how could there be such work before those eyes, to which not even the stars are clean enough [Job 25:5], nor the angels righteous enough [Job 4:18]? Thus he shall be compelled to admit that no good work exists which is not so defiled both with attendant transgressions and with its own corruption that it cannot bear the honorable name of righteousness. But if, of a certainty, it follows from justification of faith that works otherwise impure, unclean, half done, unworthy of God's sight, not to mention his love, are accounted righteousness, why do they by boasting of works righteousness try to destroy justification of faith, without whose existence they would boast of such righteousness in vain?

Do they wish to spawn a viper's brood?[10] The statements of the impious tend in this direction. They cannot deny that justification of faith is the beginning, foundation, cause, proof, and substance of works righteousness. Nevertheless, they conclude that man is not justified by faith, because good works are also accounted righteousness.

Let us, then, pass over these absurdities and confess the fact of the matter: if works righteousness, whatever its character be finally reckoned, depends upon the justification of faith, the latter is by this not only not diminished but actually strengthened, while thereby its power shines forth even stronger. And also let us not consider works to be so commended after free justification that they afterward take over the function of justifying

10 Clarified in VG by the addition: *"que les enfans meurtrissent leur mère."*

man, or share this office with faith. For unless the justification of faith remains whole and unbroken, the uncleanness of works will be uncovered. Moreover, it is no absurdity that man is so justified by faith that not only is he himself righteous but his works are also accounted righteous above their worth.

10. Works acceptable only when sins have been pardoned*

ᶜIn this sense we shall concede not only a partial righteousness in works, as our adversaries themselves hold,[11] but also that it is approved by God as if it were whole and perfect. But if we recall the foundation that supports it, every difficulty will be solved. A work begins to be acceptable only when it is undertaken with pardon. Now whence does this pardon arise, save that God contemplates us and our all in Christ? Therefore, as we ourselves, when we have been engrafted in Christ, are righteous in God's sight because our iniquities are covered by Christ's sinlessness, so our works are righteous and are thus regarded because whatever fault is otherwise in them is buried in Christ's purity, and is not charged to our account. Accordingly, we can deservedly say that by faith alone not only we ourselves but our works as well are justified. Now if this works righteousness—whatever its character—depends upon faith and free justification, and is effected by this, it ought to be included under faith and be subordinated to it, so to speak, as effect to cause, so far is it from having any right to be raised up either to destroy or becloud justification of faith.

ᵇThus Paul, to convince us that our blessedness consists in God's mercy, not in our works, particularly presses David's statement upon us: "Blessed are they whose iniquities are forgiven, whose sins are covered. Blessed is the man to whom the Lord has not imputed sin" [Ps. 32:1–2; 31:2, Vg.; cf. Rom. 4:7–8]. Suppose someone thrusts in countless sayings in which blessedness seems to be attributed to works, such as: "Blessed is the man who fears the Lord" [Ps. 112:1; 111:1, Vg.], "who has pity on the poor" [Prov. 14:21], "who walks not in the counsel of the ungodly" [Ps. 1:1], "who endures temptation" [James 1:12]; "Blessed are they who keep judgment" [Ps. 106:3, KJV], "the unstained" [Ps. 119:1; cf. Vg. 118:1, Knox tr.], "the poor in spirit," "the meek," "the merciful" [Matt. 5:3, 5, 7]—these statements do not gainsay the truth of what Paul says. For inasmuch as all those qualities there commended never so exist in man that he should therefore be approved by God, it follows that man ever remains miserable unless he is released from misery by the pardon of his sins. Since, therefore, all the kinds of blessedness extolled in Scripture become

[11] Fisher, *Confutatio,* p. 492.

void, so that man receives no profit from any of them until by forgiveness of sins he acquires blessedness, which may then make a place for them, it follows that this is not only the highest and chief, but also the only, blessedness; unless perhaps you insist that it is sapped by those very kinds of blessedness which are grounded in it alone.

Now there is much less reason why we should be troubled by the title "righteous," which is customarily applied to believers. Of course, I admit that the righteous are so called from holiness of life; but since they rather lean to the pursuit of righteousness than actually fulfill righteousness itself, it is meet that this righteousness, such as it is, should yield to the justification of faith, whence it has what it is.

11. James against Paul?

ᵇBut they say that we still have trouble with James, as one who forthrightly contends against us.¹² For he teaches that even "Abraham was justified by works" [James 2:21], and that all of us also are "justified . . . by works, not by faith alone" [James 2:24]. What then? Will they drag Paul into conflict with James? If they consider James a minister of Christ, his statement must be so understood as not to disagree with Christ speaking through Paul's lips. The Spirit declares through Paul's mouth that Abraham attained righteousness through faith, not through works [Rom. 4:3; Gal. 3:6]. We also teach that by faith all are justified apart from the works of the law. The same Spirit teaches through James that the faith both of Abraham and of ourselves consists in works, not only in faith. It is sure that the Spirit is not in conflict with himself. What, then, will be the agreement of these passages?

Our adversaries would be content if they could uproot faith righteousness, which we wish to see established with the deepest of roots, but they do not much care about imparting their peace to consciences. From this you may see that they indeed gnaw at justification of faith but meantime set no standard of righteousness upon which consciences may rely. Let them triumph, then, as they please, provided they could boast of no other victory than to have taken away all certainty of righteousness. And they will

---

¹² This passage from James was naturally a favorite among opponents of the doctrine of justification by faith, especially since Luther called James "truly an epistle of straw" ("*ein recht strohern Epistel*") (1522) as compared with the writings of John and Paul. Cf. Kaspar Schatzgeyer, *Scrutinium divinae Scripturae pro conciliatione dissidentium dogmatum* (1522) ii (CC 5. 27); De Castro, *Adversus haereses* X (1543, fo. 128 E); Fisher, *Confutatio*, p. 76; Aquinas, *Summa Theol.* II IIae. iv. 4 (tr. LCC XI. 269).

indeed obtain this miserable victory when they have snuffed out the light of truth, and the Lord permits them to shed the darkness of their falsehoods. But wherever the truth of God stands firm, they will achieve nothing.

I therefore deny that the statement of James, which they persistently thrust at us like Achilles' shield,[13] affords them the slightest support. To make that plain, we shall first have to look at the apostle's intention, and then note wherein they are deluded.

At that time there were many—and this tends to be a perpetual evil in the church—who openly disclosed their unbelief by neglecting and overlooking all the proper works of believers, yet did not cease to boast of the false name of faith. James here makes fun of the stupid assurance of such men. It is not therefore his intention to weaken in any respect the force of true faith, but rather to show how ineptly these triflers arrogated so much to the empty image of it that, content therewith, they unconcernedly abandoned themselves to a wholly licentious life.

Understanding this condition, it will be easy to note where our opponents are at fault. For they fall into a double fallacy: one in the word "faith," the other in the word "justify."

When the apostle labels "faith" an empty opinion far removed from true faith, he is making a concession that in no way detracts from the argument. This he sets forth at the outset in these words: "What does it profit, my brethren, if a man say he has faith but have not works?" [James 2:14]. He does not say "if anyone have faith without works" but "if he boast." He states it even more clearly a little later where in derision he makes it worse than devils' knowledge [James 2:19], and finally, where he calls it "dead" [James 2:20]. But from the definition you may understand sufficiently what he means. "You believe," he says, "that there is a God." [James 2:19.] Obviously, if this faith contains nothing but a belief that there is a God, it is not strange if it does not justify! And when this is taken away from it, let us not think that anything is removed from Christian faith, whose nature is far otherwise. For in what way does true faith justify save when it binds us to Christ so that, made one with him, we may enjoy participation in his righteousness? It therefore justifies not because it grasps a knowledge of God's essence but because it rests upon the assurance of his mercy.

---

[13] Referring to the post-Homeric legend of the Aethiopsis in which Achilles is mortally wounded in the one vulnerable spot in his body, the heel that had been grasped in the hand of his mother Thetis when in infancy he was immersed.

12. The word "justify" used by James in a sense different from Paul's*

ᵇWe have not yet reached the end unless we discuss the other fallacy as well: namely, that James puts part of justification in works.¹⁴ If you would make James agree with the rest of Scripture and with himself, you must understand the word "justify" in another sense than Paul takes it. For we are said by Paul to be justified when the memory of our unrighteousness has been wiped out and we are accounted righteous. If James had taken that view, it would have been preposterous for him to quote Moses' statement: "Abraham believed God" [Gen. 15:6; James 2:23], etc. For this is the context: Abraham attained righteousness by works because at God's command he did not hesitate to sacrifice his son [James 2:21]. Thus is the Scripture fulfilled that says: "He believed God, and it was reckoned to him as righteousness" [James 2:23]. If it is absurd that an effect precedes its cause, either Moses testifies falsely in that place that faith was reckoned to Abraham as righteousness or, from that obedience which he manifested by offering Isaac, he did not merit righteousness. Abraham had been justified by his faith when Ishmael was as yet not conceived, who had already reached adolescence before Isaac was born. How, then, shall we say that he obtained righteousness by an obedience that followed long after? Therefore, either James wrongly inverted the order—unlawful even to imagine!—or he did not mean to call him justified, as if he deserved to be reckoned righteous. What then? Surely it is clear that he himself is speaking of the declaration, not the imputation, of righteousness. It is as if he said: "Those who by true faith are righteous prove their righteousness by obedience and good works, not by a bare and imaginary mask of faith." To sum up, he is not discussing in what manner we are justified but demanding of believers a righteousness fruitful in good works. And as Paul contends that we are justified apart from the help of works, so James does not allow those who lack good works to be reckoned righteous.

The consideration of this intention will free us from all difficulty. For our opponents are chiefly deceived in thinking that

¹⁴ Paul and James differ not in doctrine, but by their use of the word "justify" in different senses. Cf. Cadier, *Institution* III. 282, note 1. Calvin, in *Sermons on Various Passages of Genesis,* third sermon on Abraham's justification, speaks of a double justification—first, a general pardon of those who are called, and thereafter "justification even in our works by pure faith" (CR XXIII. 718–719). Cf. Comm. Rom. 8:30, where election and calling are distinguished from the other aspect of justification, which is the continuance of God's favor through the course of life. Paul, says Cadier, treats of justification in the first sense; James, in the second.

James is defining the manner of justification when he is attempting only to shatter the evil confidence of those who vainly pretended faith as an excuse for their contempt of good works. Therefore, in whatever ways they may twist James's words, they will express but two ideas: an empty show of faith does not justify, and a believer, not content with such an image, declares his righteousness by good works.

13. Romans 2:13

ᵇThat they indeed quote Paul in the same sense does them very little good: "The doers of the law, not the hearers, are justified" [Rom. 2:13 p.]. I do not intend to evade the question through Ambrose's solution: that this was said because fulfillment of the law is faith in Christ.[15] For I see this as a mere evasion, quite needless where the way lies open. Here the apostle is casting down the foolish confidence of the Jews, who claimed for themselves the sole knowledge of the law, even while they were its greatest despisers. Lest, then, mere skill in the law should please them so much, he warns that if righteousness be sought from the law, not knowledge but observance of it is sought. We assuredly do not question that the righteousness of the law consists in works, and not even that righteousness consists in the worth and merits of works. But it has not yet been proved that we are justified by works unless they produce some one man who has fulfilled the law.

That Paul meant precisely this is sufficiently attested by the context of his utterance. After having condemned Gentiles and Jews together for their unrighteousness, he then gets down to details and says: "Those who have sinned without law will perish without law," which has reference to the Gentiles; and "those who have sinned in the law will be judged by the law" [Rom. 2:12], which concerns the Jews. Now, since they, winking at their own shortcomings, plumed themselves on the law alone, Paul adds something especially fitting: the law was not laid down merely that men might be made righteous by hearing its voice; but only if and when they obeyed it. It is as if he said: "Do you seek righteousness in the law? Do not claim to have heard it, something of little weight in itself, but bring works whereby you may declare that the law was not laid down for you in vain." Since

---

[15] Romans 2:13 is cited in this sense by Eck, *Enchiridion,* ch. v (1533 edition, fo. 23a), and by others on the papal side. For "Ambrose" read "Ambrosiaster," the writer so designated by Erasmus, a contemporary of Ambrose and the author of a *Commentary on Paul's Epistles* long ascribed to that father. See his Commentary on Rom. 2:13 (MPL 17. 67).

they were all lacking in these works, it followed that they were bereft of boasting about the law. Paul's meaning, then, requires us, rather, to frame the opposite argument: the righteousness of the law lies in perfection of works; no one can boast that he has fulfilled the law through works; consequently, there is no righteousness arising from the law.

14. What does it mean when before God believers appeal to their works?

ᵇNow they make their contention from these passages in which believers boldly offer their righteousness to be examined by God's judgment; and they wish to be judged on that basis. Such passages are these: "Judge me, O Lord, according to my righteousness and according to my innocence that are in me" [Ps. 7:8 p.]. Likewise: "Hear, O God, my righteousness" [Ps. 17:1]. "Thou hast tried my heart and hast visited me by night, . . . thou hast found no wickedness in me." [Ps. 17:3; cf. 16:3, Vg.] Likewise: "The Lord will recompense me according to my righteousness, according to the cleanness of my hands he will repay me. For I have kept the ways of the Lord, and have not wickedly departed from my God. . . . And I shall be spotless . . . and shall keep myself from my iniquity." [Ps. 18:20, 21, 23; 17:21, 22, 24, Vg.] Again: "Judge me, O Lord, for I have walked in my innocence" [Ps. 26:1; 25:1, Vg.]. "I have not sat with lying men, and I will not consort with evildoers." [Ps. 26:4; 25:4, Vg.] Also: "Lose not my soul, O God, with the wicked, nor my life with bloodthirsty men" [Ps. 26:9; 25:9, Vg.]. "In their hands are iniquities; their right hand is filled with gifts. But as for me, I have walked innocently." [Ps. 26:10–11; cf. 25:10–11, Vg.]

I spoke above concerning the assurance the saints seem to derive simply from works.[16] As for the testimonies we have adduced at this point, they will not hinder us much if they are understood according to their context [περίστασιν, *complexum*], or, in common parlance, circumstances. Now this is twofold. For neither would they have a full investigation of themselves so as to be either condemned or acquitted according to the character of their entire lives—rather they bring to judgment a special cause to be decided—nor do they claim righteousness for themselves with reference to divine perfection but in comparison with evil and wicked men.

First, when it is a question of justifying man, it is not only required that he have a good cause in some particular matter but a certain harmony of righteousness, lasting throughout life. Yet

[16] III. xiv. 18–20.

the saints, while they appeal to God's judgment to approve their innocence, do not present themselves as free from all guilt and faultless in every respect; but while they have fixed their assurance of salvation in his goodness alone, they still, trusting in him as avenger of the poor afflicted beyond right and equity, assuredly commend to him the cause in which the innocent are oppressed.

On the other hand, when they hale their opponents with them before God's judgment seat, they do not boast of an innocence that under strict test would correspond to God's own purity; but because, in comparison with their adversaries' malice, dishonesty, craft, and wickedness, they know that their sincerity, righteousness, simplicity, and purity are known and pleasing to God, they are not afraid to call upon him to act as judge between themselves and their adversaries. Thus, when David said to Saul: "May the Lord render to every man according to his righteousness and truthfulness" [I Sam. 26:23 p.], he did not mean that the Lord should by himself examine and reward each according to his merits, but he declared to the Lord how great his innocence was compared to Saul's wickedness. And even Paul, when he in this glorying that he has a good testimony of conscience boasts he has behaved with sincerity and uprightness in the church of God [II Cor. 1:12; cf. Acts 23:1], does not propose to rely upon such boasting before God. Rather, compelled by ungodly men's slanders, he defends his faithfulness and probity, which he knew to be acceptable to divine compassion, against the evilspeaking of the wicked. For we see what he says in another place, that he is not aware of anything evil against himself but is not thereby justified [I Cor. 4:4]. For he obviously knew God's judgment far transcends men's bleared vision. However, therefore, the godly may, with God as witness and judge, defend their innocence against the hypocrisy of the ungodly, still, when they are dealing with God alone, all cry out with one voice: e"If thou, O Lord, shouldst mark iniquity, Lord, who shall stand?" [Ps. 130:3; 129:3, Vg.]. Again: b"Enter not into judgment with thy servants, for no man living is righteous before thee" [Ps. 143:2 p.]; and, distrusting their own works, they gladly sing: "Thy goodness is better than life" [Ps. 63:3 p.].

15. Perfection of believers?
bThere are also other passages not unlike those above, upon which someone may still take a stand. Solomon says that he who walks in his own uprightness is righteous [Prov. 20:7]. Likewise: "In the path of righteousness is life, and in that indeed . . . is no death." [Prov. 12:28.] In this manner, Ezekiel asserts that "he

shall surely live who has kept judgment and done justice" [Ezek. 18:9, 21; cf. ch. 33:15]. We neither deny nor obscure anything of these. But let one of Adam's children come forward with such uprightness. If there is no one, they must either perish out of God's sight or flee to the shelter of his mercy.

Moreover, we do not deny that for believers uprightness, albeit partial and imperfect, is a step toward immortality. But what is its source except that the Lord does not examine for merits the works of those whom he has received into the covenant of grace but embraces them with fatherly affection? By this we understand not only what the Schoolmen teach—that works have their value from "accepting grace." For they mean that works, otherwise insufficient to obtain salvation in accordance with the covenant of the law, still, by God's acceptance of them, are advanced to a value adequate for this.[17] But I say that those works, defiled as well with other transgressions as with their own spots, have no other value except that the Lord extends pardon to both, that is, to bestow free righteousness upon man.

And not here untimely thrust upon us are those prayers of the apostle in which he desires so much perfection of believers that they may be blameless and irreproachable [Col. 1:22; cf. Eph. 1:4] in the Day of the Lord [I Cor. 1:8; cf. I Thess. 3:13; 5:23]. In the past the followers of Coelestius indeed vigorously urged these words in order to assert perfection of righteousness in this life.[18] But we briefly reply according to Augustine what we consider sufficient: all the godly ought to aspire to this goal, that they may one day appear spotless and blameless before God's face [cf. Col. 1:22, cf. Vg.]. But because even the best and most excellent plan of the present life is only a progression, we shall arrive at that goal only when, having put off this sinful flesh, we cleave wholly to the Lord.[19] cAnd yet I shall not stubbornly contend with him who would apply the label "perfection" to the saints, provided he also defines it in the words of Augustine himself. "When we," he says, "call the virtue of the saints perfect, to this very perfection also belongs the recognition of imperfection, both in truth and in humility."[20]

---

[17] The doctrine of *gratia acceptans,* accepting grace, was developed by the Franciscan Scholastics Duns Scotus and Ockham, and was asserted by Eck (*Enchiridion,* ch. v.) and others of the period.

[18] Augustine, *On Man's Perfection in Righteousness* i (MPL 44. 292 f.); tr. NPNF V. 159 f.). Coelestius was the associate of Pelagius: cf. II. i. 5, note 8.

[19] Augustine, *On Man's Perfection in Righteousness* ix. 20 (MPL 44. 301 f.; tr. NPNF V. 165 f.).

[20] Augustine, *Against Two Epistles of the Pelagians* III. vii. 19 (MPL 44. 602; tr. NPNF V. 411).

ᶜCHAPTER XVIII

WORKS RIGHTEOUSNESS IS WRONGLY INFERRED FROM REWARD

(Passages referring to reward do not make works the cause of salvation, 1–4)

1. What does "recompense according to works" mean?

ᵇLet us now proceed to those statements which affirm that God will repay every man according to his works [Matt. 16:27].[1] Of this sort are these: "Everyone will receive the things done in his body . . . whether . . . good or bad" [II Cor. 5:10]. "Glory and honor . . . to the doer of good; hardship and tribulation upon every evildoer's soul" [Rom. 2:10, 9]. And: "They who have done good shall come forth into the resurrection of life; they who have done ill, into the resurrection of judgment" [John 5:29, order changed]. "Come, blessed of my Father, . . . I was hungry and you gave me food; I was thirsty and you gave me drink," etc. [Matt. 25:34–35, conflated with v. 42, cf. Comm. and Vg.].

Let us join to them those statements which call eternal life the reward of works. Of this sort are these: "The recompense of a man's hands will be paid to him" [Prov. 12:14, conflated with Isa. 3:11, Vg.]. "He who fears the commandment . . . shall be rewarded" [Prov. 13:13]. "Rejoice and be exceeding glad" [Matt. 5:12]; "behold your reward is great in heaven" [Luke 6:23]. "Each shall receive a reward according to his labor" [I Cor. 3:8].

The statement that "God will render to every man according to his works" [Rom. 2:6] is explained with little difficulty. For the expression indicates an order of sequence rather than the cause. But, beyond any doubt, it is by these stages of his mercy that the Lord completes our salvation when "he calls those chosen to himself; those called he justifies; those justified he glorifies" [Rom. 8:30 p.]. That is to say, he receives his own into life by his mercy alone. Yet, since he leads them into possession of it through the race of good works in order to fulfill his own work in them according to the order that he has laid down, it is no wonder if they are said to be crowned according to their own works, by which they are doubtless prepared to receive the crown of immortality. But they are fitly said to "work out their own salvation" [Phil. 2:12 p.], for the reason that, while devoting

---

[1] This beginning is related to the opening sentence of III. xiv. 14. Cf. III. xvi. 2, note 3. The argument associating merit with reward ("*ubi merces ibi merita,*" Cochlaeus, *Philippicae* III. 65, fo. N 2b) was a commonplace of Roman theology. Cf. De Castro, *Adversus omnes haereses* IX (1543, fo. 150): "*Quomodo toties auditur praemium, ubi prorsus nullum est meritum?*"

themselves to good works, they meditate upon eternal life. ^cThis corresponds to another passage in which they are enjoined to "work for the food that does not perish" [John 6:27], while by believing in Christ they receive life for themselves. And yet the clause is immediately added: "which the Son of Man will give to you" [John 6:27]. From this it appears that the word "to work" is not opposed to grace but refers to endeavor. ^bAccordingly, it does not follow that believers are themselves the authors of their own salvation, or that salvation stems from their own works. What then? Once they are, by knowledge of the gospel and illumination of the Holy Spirit, called into the fellowship of Christ, eternal life begins in them. Now that God has begun a good work in them, it must also be made perfect until the Day of the Lord Jesus [Phil. 1:6]. It is, however, made perfect when, resembling their Heavenly Father in righteousness and holiness, they prove themselves sons true to their nature.

2. Reward as "inheritance"

^{b(a)}The use of the term "reward" is no reason for us to suppose that our works are the cause of our salvation. First, let us be heartily convinced ^athat the Kingdom of Heaven is not servants' wages but sons' inheritance [Eph. 1:18], which only they who have been adopted as sons by the Lord shall enjoy [cf. Gal. 4:7], and that for no other reason than this adoption [cf. Eph. 1:5–6]. ^b"For the son of the bondwoman shall not be the heir, but the son of the free woman." [Gal. 4:30 p.] Even in these very passages where the Holy Spirit promises everlasting glory as a reward for works, by expressly terming it an "inheritance" he is showing that it comes to us from another source. So Christ enumerates the works, which he repays with the reward of heaven [Matt. 25:35–37], in calling the elect into possession of it; but at the same time he adds that they must possess it by right of inheritance [Matt. 25:34]. Thus Paul enjoins servants, faithfully doing what is of their duty, to hope for recompense from the Lord, but he adds "of the inheritance" [Col. 3:24]. We see how, as it were, in prescribed terms, they carefully warn us not to credit everlasting blessedness to works but to our adoption by God.

Why, then, do they make mention of works at the same time? This question is cleared up by one example of Scripture. Before the birth of Isaac, Abraham was promised seed in whom all the nations of the earth would be blessed. The increase of his seed was to equal the stars of heaven, the sands of the sea, and other things like these [Gen. 15:5; 17:1 ff.; cf. ch. 18:18]. Many years later, as he had been commanded by the oracle, Abraham girds himself to sacrifice his son [Gen. 22:3]. Having performed this act of obedience, he receives the promise. "By myself have I sworn, says the Lord, because you have done this thing, and have not spared . . . your only son, I will bless you, . . . and I will multiply your seed as the stars of heaven and the sands of the sea, and your seed shall possess the gates of his enemies, and in your seed shall all the nations of the earth be blessed, because you have obeyed my voice." [Gen. 22:16–18 p.] What is it that we hear? Did Abraham merit by his obedience the blessing whose promise he had received before the commandment was given? Here, surely, we have shown without ambiguity that the Lord rewards the works of believers with the same benefits as he had given them before they contemplated any works, as he does not yet have any reason to benefit them except his own mercy.

3. Reward as grace

ᵇStill, the Lord does not trick or mock us when he says that he will reward works with what he had given free before works. He wills that we be trained through good works to meditate upon the presentation or fruition, so to speak, of those things which he has promised, and to hasten through them to seek the blessed hope held out to us in heaven. Hence the fruit of the promises is duly assigned to works, which bring us to the ripeness of that fruit. The apostle beautifully expressed both thoughts when he said that the Colossians occupied themselves with the duties of love, for the sake of the hope laid up for them in heaven, of which they had previously heard through the word of the truth-telling gospel [Col. 1:4–5]. For in saying that they knew from the gospel that their hope was laid up in heaven, he declares that it was supported by Christ alone, not by works. ᵉWith this, Peter's statement agrees, that the godly are "guarded by God's power through faith, unto the salvation that has been prepared to be manifested in" its "time" [I Peter 1:5 p.]. ᵇIn saying that they labor on this account, Paul means that to attain it believers are to run the whole course of their life.

But lest we should think that the reward the Lord promises us is reduced to a matter of merit, he has set forth a parable, in which he has made himself a householder who sends whomever he meets to cultivate his vineyard. Some are sent, indeed, at the first hour, others at the second, still others at the third, and some even at the eleventh; and at evening he pays them all equally [Matt. 20:1 ff.]. That ancient writer—whoever he was—whose book *The Call of the Gentiles* goes under the name of Ambrose, briefly and truly interprets this parable. I shall use his words rather than my own. "The Lord has by this comparison illustrated the diversity of his manifold calling, pertaining to the one and only grace . . . where it is clear that those sent to the vineyard at the eleventh hour and put on an equal footing with those who had labored the whole day represent the destiny of those . . . whom God's mercy rewards at the decline of the day, that is, at the end of their lives, in order to reveal the excellence of his grace. For he does not pay the price of their labor but showers the riches of his goodness upon those whom he has chosen apart from works. Thus they also, . . . who sweated in much labor, and did not receive more than the latecomers, should understand that they received a gift of grace, not the reward for their works."[2]

cFinally, this also is worth noting: in those passages where eternal life is called the reward of works, it is not understood simply as that communion we have with God until the blessed immortality when his fatherly benevolence embraces us in Christ but as the possession or "fruition," as they call it, of blessedness. So also Christ's very own words declare: "In the world to come eternal life" [Mark 10:30]. And in another passage: "Come . . . take possession . . . of the Kingdom," etc. [Matt. 25:34, Vg.]. For this reason, Paul terms "adoption" the revealing of adoption that will be made at the resurrection [cf. Rom. 8:18 ff.]; and afterward he interprets it as the "redemption of our body" [Rom. 8:23]. But otherwise, just as estrangement from God is eternal death,[3] so when man is received into grace by God to enjoy communion with him and be made one with him, he is transported from death to life—something done by the benefit of adoption alone. eAnd if, as is their wont, they stubbornly urge the reward of works, we can throw back at them that statement of Peter that the reward of faith is eternal life [I Peter 1:9].

4. The purpose of the promise of reward

aTherefore, let us not consider that the Holy Spirit approves the worthiness of our works by this sort of promise, as if they merited such a reward. For Scripture leaves us no reason to be exalted in God's sight. Rather, its whole end is to restrain our pride, to humble us, cast us down, and utterly crush us. But our weakness, which would immediately collapse and fall if it did not sustain itself by this expectation and allay its own weariness by this comfort, is relieved in this way.

First, let everyone consider with himself how hard it would be

---

[2] Pseudo-Ambrose, *The Call of the Gentiles* I. v (MPL 17. 1091). The text of Prosper in MPL 51 does not contain these sentences. Cf. II. ii. 5, note 27.
[3] Cf. III. xxv. 12. For related passages in Augustine, see Smits II. 43.

for him to leave and renounce not only all his possessions but himself as well. Still, it is with this first lesson that Christ initiates his pupils, that is, all the godly. Then he so trains them throughout life under the discipline of the cross that they may not set their hearts upon desire of, or reliance on, present benefits. In short, he usually so deals with them that wherever they turn their eyes, as far as this world extends, they are confronted solely with despair. Thus Paul says, "We are of all men most to be pitied if we hope only in this world." [I Cor. 15:19 p.] Lest they fail amidst these great tribulations, the Lord is with them, warning them to hold their heads higher, to direct their eyes farther so as to find in him that blessedness which they do not see in the world. He calls this blessedness "prize," "reward," "recompense" [cf. Matt. 5:12; 6:1 ff., etc.], not weighing the merit of works, but signifying that it is a compensation for their miseries, tribulations, slanders, etc. For this reason, nothing prevents us, with Scriptural precedent (cf. II Cor. 6:13; Heb. 10:35; 11:26], from calling eternal life a "recompense," because in it the Lord receives his own people from toil into repose, from affliction into a prosperous and desirable state, from sorrow into joy, from poverty into affluence, from disgrace into glory. To sum up, he changes into greater goods all the evil things that they have suffered. Thus also it will be nothing amiss if we regard holiness of life to be the way, not indeed that gives access to the glory of the Heavenly Kingdom, but by which those chosen by their God are led to its disclosure. For it is God's good pleasure to glorify those whom he has sanctified [Rom. 8:30].

ᵇOnly let us not imagine the correlation between merit and reward on which the Sophists rudely insist because they do not consider the end that we have set forth.[4] How absurd is it, when God calls us to one end, for us to look in the other direction? Nothing is clearer than that a reward is promised for good works to relieve the weakness of our flesh by some comfort but not to puff up our hearts with vainglory. Whoever, then, deduces merit of works from this, ᶜor weighs works and reward together, ᵇwanders very far from God's own plan.

(Answers to objections against this view, 5–10)
5. *Reward rests upon forgiveness*
ᵇAccordingly, when Scripture says, "The Lord, the righteous Judge, will one day give to his own the crown of righteousness" [II Tim. 4:8 p.], I begin by replying with Augustine: "To whom

⁴ Aquinas, *Summa Theol.* I IIae. cxiv. 1 (tr. LCC XI. 203 f.); Cochlaeus, *Philippicae* III. 65.

should the righteous Judge have awarded the crown if the merciful Father had not bestowed grace? And how could there be righteousness unless the grace that 'justifies the ungodly' had gone before? And how could these things now be awarded as due unless things not due had previously been given?"[5] But I also add something else: How could he impute righteousness to our works unless his compassion covered over whatever unrighteousness was in them? And how could he judge them worthy of reward save that he wiped out by his boundless kindness what in them deserves punishment? For Augustine is accustomed to call eternal life "grace," because, while it is rendered to works, it is given for God's free gifts. But Scripture humbles us more and at the same time lifts us up. For besides forbidding us to glory in works, because they are God's free gifts, it teaches us at the same time that they are ever defiled with some foul dregs so that if they are weighed according to the standard of his judgment they cannot satisfy God; ᵉbut lest we become discouraged, Scripture teaches that our works are pleasing only through pardon. ᶜBut even though Augustine elsewhere speaks somewhat differently from us, his words in the Third Book to Boniface will show that he does not substantially disagree with these words. There he has compared two men: the one of marvelously holy and perfect life; the other upright indeed and of wholesome habits, but still so imperfect as to leave much to be desired. Finally he concludes: "Certainly the latter man, who seems so inferior in morals to the former, on account of the right faith that he has in God, by which he lives, and according to which in all his wrongdoings he accuses himself and in all his good works praises God, giving shame to himself, glory to God, and receiving from him both forgiveness of sins and love of right deeds—this man shall be delivered from this life and depart . . . into the fellowship . . . of Christ. Why does he so live if not on account of faith? Although without works it saves no man, for it is not a reprobate faith, since it works through love [cf. Gal. 5:6], yet through it sins are also remitted, for 'the just lives by faith' [Hab. 2:4]; for without it what seem to be good works are turned into sins." ⁶Here, surely, he clearly con-

---

5 Augustine, *On Grace and Free Will* vi. 14 (MPL 44. 890; tr. NPNF V. 449). The passage, II Tim. 4:8, is cited by Eck, *Enchiridion*, ch. v (1533 edition, fo. 26a). J. Clichtove, in *Improbatio quorundam articulorum Martini Lutheri* (1533), citing this text, asks: "Works of righteousness: what are they but merits? [*Quid sunt nisi merita?*]" Cf. Fisher, *Confutatio*, art. i, p. 66; Herborn, *Enchiridion* v (CC 12. 33).
6 Augustine, *Against Two Letters of the Pelagians* III. v. 14 (MPL 44. 598; tr. NPNF V. 409).

fesses what we strongly contend: that the righteousness of good works depends upon the fact that God by pardon approves them.

6. On "treasures in heaven"

ᵇThe following passages are close in meaning to those cited above: "Make yourselves friends of the Mammon of unrighteousness that when you fail, they may receive you into the eternal tabernacles" [Luke 16:9]. "Admonish the rich of this world not to be proudly wise, nor to set their hopes on uncertain riches but on the living God . . . that they do good, that they be rich in good works . . . and treasure for themselves a good foundation for the coming age, that they may lay hold on eternal life" [I Tim. 6:17–19].[7] For good works are likened to the riches we shall enjoy in the blessedness of eternal life. I reply, we shall never gain access to a true understanding of them unless we turn our eyes to the purpose to which the Spirit addresses his words. If what Christ says is true—"Where our treasure is, there resides our heart" [Matt. 6:21 p.]—as the children of this age are wont to be intent upon getting things that make for delight in the present life, so believers ought to see to it that, after they have learned that this life will soon vanish like a dream, they transfer the things they want truly to enjoy to a place where they will have life unceasing.

We ought, then, to imitate what people do who determine to migrate to another place, where they have chosen a lasting abode. They send before them all their resources and do not grieve over lacking them for a time, for they deem themselves the happier the more goods they have where they will be for a long time. But if we believe heaven is our country, it is better to transmit our possessions thither than to keep them here where upon our sudden migration they would be lost to us. But how shall we transmit them? Surely, by providing for the needs of the poor; whatever is paid out to them, the Lord reckons as given to himself [cf. Matt. 25:40]. From this comes that notable promise: "He who gives to the poor lends to the Lord" [Prov. 19.17]. Likewise, "He who sows bountifully shall reap bountifully." [II Cor. 9:6.] For what is devoted to our brothers out of the duty of love is deposited in the Lord's hand. He, as he is a faithful custodian, will one day repay it with plentiful interest. Are our duties, then, of such importance in God's sight that they are like riches hidden for us in his hand? And who would shrink from saying this, when Scripture so often and so openly attests it?

[7] De Castro, *Adversus haereses, s.v. "opera,"* XI (1543, fo. 140 A); Latomus, *De fide et operibus (Opera* [1550], fo. 133a), on Luke 16:9 and I Tim. 6:17–19.

But if anyone wishes to jump from God's pure kindness to the value of works, by these testimonies he will not be helped to build up his error. For from these you can duly infer nothing except the pure inclining of God's mercy toward us. To quicken us to well-doing, although the services we offer him are unworthy even of his glance, he permits none of them to be lost.

7. Reward for tribulation endured?

ᵇBut the apostle's words press us all the more. While comforting the Thessalonians in their tribulations, he teaches that such tribulations are sent to them in order that they may be counted worthy of God's Kingdom, for which they suffer [II Thess. 1:5]. Indeed, he says, "God deems it just to repay with affliction those who afflict you, . . . and to grant rest with us to you . . . when the Lord Jesus is revealed from heaven." [II Thess. 1:6–7.] And the author of The Letter to the Hebrews says: "God is not so unjust as to forget your work and the love that you showed in his name, in that you ministered to the saints." [Heb. 6:10.]⁸

To the first passage I reply: "No worth of merit is there meant, but because God the Father wills that we, whom he has chosen as sons, be conformed to Christ, his first-born [Rom. 8:29], as he had first to suffer, and then at last enter into his appointed glory [Luke 24:26], so also "through many tribulations we must enter the Kingdom of Heaven" [Acts 14:22 p.]. Therefore, while we suffer tribulations for Christ's name, certain marks, as it were, are branded upon us by which God commonly designates the sheep of his flock. In this way, then, we are accounted worthy of God's Kingdom, for "we bear in our body the marks of our Lord and Master" [Gal. 6:17 p.], which are the signs of God's children. The following statements also belong here: We carry about the mortification of Jesus Christ in our bodies so that his life may be manifested in us [II Cor. 4:10]. We are conformed to his sufferings to attain to the likeness of resurrection from the dead [Phil. 3:10–11].

And the reason appended by Paul is not to prove that works have any worth but to strengthen hope in God's Kingdom. It is as if he said, "As it agrees with God's righteous judgment to take vengeance upon your enemies for those troubles which they have inflicted upon you, it also agrees with his judgment for you to be granted rest and peace from your troubles." The second passage

---

⁸ Hebrews 6:10 is so cited by Herborn, *Enchiridion* v (CC 12. 33), and in the Tridentine decree on justification, ch. xvi (Schaff, *Creeds* II. 107): "Life eternal . . . a reward [*merces*] . . . to be faithfully rendered to their good works and merits."

[Heb. 6:10] teaches that it so befits God's justice not to relegate to oblivion his children's service so as to hint that it would be well-nigh unjust for him to forget. This means that God, to prick our sloth, has given us the assurance that the trouble we have borne to the glory of his name will not be in vain. Let us always remember that this promise, like all others, would not bear fruit for us if the free covenant of his mercy had not gone before, upon which the whole assurance of our salvation depended. Now, relying on this, we ought to have firm confidence that, however unworthy our services, a reward will not be lacking from God's generosity. To confirm us in this expectation the apostle declares that God is not unjust but that he will keep his pledge once given. This justice, then, refers more to the truth of the divine promise than to the equity of rendering what is due. In this sense, Augustine's saying is well known, and as this holy man did not hesitate to repeat it often as worth remembering, I judge it not unworthy of being constantly impressed upon our memory. "The Lord," he says, "is faithful, who made himself our debtor—not by accepting anything from us, but by promising us all things."[9]

8. Justification through love

[b]They also bring up the following statements of Paul in their own support: "If I have all faith, so as to remove mountains, but have not love, I am nothing" [I Cor. 13:2]. Again, "Now hope, faith, love abide, . . . but the greatest of these is love" [I Cor. 13:13 p.]. Likewise, "Above all these put on love, which is the bond of perfection" [Col. 3:14 p.]. [b(a)]From these two passages our Pharisees contend that we are justified by love rather than faith, doubtless by a stronger power, as they say.[10] Yet this subtlety is refuted without difficulty. For we have elsewhere explained [a]that what is said in the first passage has nothing to do with true faith.[11] The second we also explain in terms of true faith. Paul says love is greater than faith, not as being more meritorious, but because it is more fruitful, because it extends farther, because it serves more, because it flourishes forever, while the use of faith continues only for a time [cf. I Cor. 13:2 ff.]. [b]If we regard excellence, love of God should rightly take first place, but with this Paul's

[9] Augustine, *Psalms*, Ps. 32. ii. 1. 9; Ps. 83. 16; Ps. 109. 1 (MPL 36. 284; 37. 1068; 37. 1445; tr. LF [Ps. 33] *Psalms* I. 317 f.; [Ps. 34] IV. 164; [Ps. 110] V. 229 f.); *Sermons* clviii. 2. 2 (MPL 38. 863; tr. LF *Sermons* II. 779).

[10] Fisher, *Confutatio*, p. 63; De Castro, *Adversus haereses* VII, *s.v.* "gratia" (1543, fo. 128ab, 132b); Lombard, *Sentences* III. xxiii. 5 (MPL 192. 811); Aquinas, *Summa Theol.* I IIae. cxiii. 4, reply to obj. 1; II IIae. xxiii, xxvii (tr. LCC XI. 342–368). Cf. Augustine, *Enchiridion* xxxi. 117 (MPL 40. 287; tr. LCC VII. 409).

[11] III. ii. 9–13.

statement is not concerned. Indeed, he stresses this one point: that we should edify one another in the Lord with mutual love. But let us imagine that love excels faith in all respects: ᵃwhat man of sound judgment—indeed, what man of wholly sound mind—would reason from this that it justifies more? The power of justifying, which faith possesses, does not lie in any worth of works. Our justification rests upon God's mercy alone and Christ's merit, and faith, when it lays hold of justification, is said to justify.

ᵇNow if you ask our adversaries in what sense they attribute justification to love, they will answer: Because the duty is pleasing to God, by its merit from the acceptance by divine goodness, righteousness is imputed to us. From this point you see how beautifully their argument proceeds. We say that faith justifies, not because it merits righteousness for us by its own worth, but because it is an instrument whereby we obtain free the righteousness of Christ. They, overlooking God's mercy and passing over Christ, in whom lies the sum of righteousness, contend that we are justified by the benefit of love because it excels faith. It is as if someone argued that a king is more capable of making a shoe than a shoemaker is because he is infinitely more eminent. This one syllogism gives us ample proof that none of the schools of the Sorbonne has even slightly tasted what justification of faith is.

ᵃBut if at this point some wrangler should interrupt and ask why in such a short space we variously understand the term "faith" as used by Paul, I have very good and sound reason for this interpretation. For inasmuch as these gifts which Paul enumerates are in a way subsumed under faith and hope, because they have to do with the knowledge of God, he includes them all by way of recapitulation[12] under the terms "faith" and "hope." It is as if he said: "Prophecy and tongues, the gift of interpretation, and knowledge alike have the purpose of leading us to know God, but in this life we know God only through hope and faith. When, therefore, I mention faith and hope, I at the same time include all these." "So faith, hope, love abide, these three" [I Cor. 13:13a]—that is, however great the variety of gifts, all are referred thereto—"the chief among these is love" [I Cor. 13:13b p.], etc.

ᵇFrom the third passage they infer: If love is the "bond of perfection" [Col. 3:14], it is therefore that of righteousness, which is nothing else but perfection.[13] First, to pass over the fact that Paul calls it perfection when the members of a duly constituted church

---

[12] "κατ' ἀνακεφαλαίωσιν."

[13] Cf. III. xvii. 15; Duns Scotus, *On the Sentences* I. xvii. 3. 22 (*Opera omnia* X. 82); Cochlaeus, *Philippicae* III. 10.

cleave together well, and to admit that love perfects us in God's sight, still, what new notion do they bring forward? For I shall always reply to the contrary: we shall never attain this perfection unless we fulfill all the duties of love. From this I shall conclude that, since all men are very far away from fulfilling love, all hope of perfection is cut off from them.

9. Matthew 19:17

ᵇI do not want to pursue the individual testimonies that the stupid Sorbonnists of today have groundlessly torn from Scripture —whatever first came to hand—to fling at us. For some are so ridiculous that I could not mention them unless I wished to be justly accounted foolish. I shall terminate this matter after I have explained a statement of Christ's, in which they take marvelous pleasure. For he answers the lawyer who asks him what is needed for salvation, "If you would enter into life, keep the commandments" [Matt. 19:17]. What more do we want, they ask, when we are bidden by the Author of grace to attain God's Kingdom by observing the commandments?[14] As if it were not evident that Christ did not accommodate his replies to those with whom he saw that he had to deal! Here a doctor of law asks about the manner of obtaining blessedness—and not simply that but by what deeds men may arrive at it. And the person of the speaker and the question itself prompted the Lord to answer thus. The lawyer, accustomed to the persuasion of law righteousness, blinded himself with confidence in works. Then he sought only what were works of righteousness whereby salvation is acquired. Therefore he is rightly sent back to the law wherein there is a perfect mirror of righteousness.

With a clear voice we too proclaim that these commandments are to be kept if one seeks life in works. And Christians must know this doctrine, for how could they flee to Christ unless they recognized that they had plunged from the way of life over the brink of death? How could they realize how far they had wandered from the way of life unless they first understood what that way is like? Only, therefore, when they distinguish how great is the difference between their life and divine righteousness that consists in accepting the law are they made aware that, in order to recover salvation, their refuge is in Christ.

To sum up, if we seek salvation in works, we must keep the

---

[14] De Castro, *Adversus haereses* VII (1543, fo. 128 C B; K. Schatzgeyer, *Scrutinium divinae Scripturae pro conciliatione dissidentium dogmatum* (1522) ii (CC 5. 26); Cochlaeus, *Philippicae* III. 55, fo. M 3b; Clichtove, *Improbatio*, fo. 14a (on Matt. 19:12).

commandments by which we are instructed unto perfect righteousness. But we must not stop here unless we wish to fail in midcourse, for none of us is capable of keeping the commandments. Therefore, since we are barred from law righteousness, we must betake ourselves to another help, that is, to faith in Christ. For this reason, as the Lord in this passage recalls to the law a teacher of the law whom he knew to be puffed up with empty confidence in works, in order that he may learn he is a sinner, subject to the dreadful judgment of eternal death, so elsewhere he comforts with the promise of grace without any mention of the law others who have already been humbled by this sort of knowledge: "Come to me all who labor and are heavy-laden, and I will refresh you . . . and you will find rest for your souls" [Matt. 11:28–29].[14x]

10. Righteousness and unrighteousness are not comparable with each other by the same rule
ᵇAt last, after they tire of misapplying Scripture, they resort to subtleties and sophistries. They cavil over the fact that faith is in some places called a "work" [John 6:29]. From this they infer that we wrongly oppose faith to works.[15] As if faith, in so far as it is obedience to the divine will, obtains righteousness for us on its own merits—and not, rather, in embracing God's mercy, seals upon our hearts Christ's righteousness, by that mercy offered to us in the preaching of the gospel. My readers will pardon me if I do not tarry to demolish such fooleries, for by their own weakness they are, without outside force, sufficiently shattered.

I should like, however, in passing to dispose of one objection that has some semblance of truth, lest it trouble some who are inexperienced. Since common sense teaches that the same rule applies to contraries, and each sin is imputed to us as unrighteousness, they say that it is appropriate also that each good work be credited as righteousness. Those who answer that men's condemnation properly arises from unbelief alone, not from particular sins,[16] do not satisfy me. I certainly agree with them that unbelief is the wellspring and root of all evils. For it is the first defection from God, and it is followed by individual transgressions against the law. But because in weighing righteousness and unrighteousness, they seem to apply the same reckoning to good and

[14x] These words are from the 1545 edition.
[15] Eck, *Enchiridion*, ch. v: "*Fides opus vocatur*" (1533 edition, fo. 25b), quoting John 6:29. Cf. Calvin, Comm. John 6:29.
[16] Calvin here records dissent from Luther's position. Cf. Luther, sermons on Mark 16:14, May 29, 1522, and Mark 8:1, July 19, 1523 (*Werke* WA X. iii. 14 1f.; XII. 637; cf. XXI. i. 360).

evil works, in this I am constrained to disagree with them. For works righteousness is perfect obedience to the law. Therefore, you cannot be righteous according to works unless you unfailingly follow this straight line, so to speak, throughout life. The minute you turn aside from it, you slip into unrighteousness. From this it is apparent that righteousness does not come about from one or a few works but from an unwavering and unwearying observance of the divine will. But very different is the rule for judging unrighteousness. For a fornicator or thief is by one offense guilty of death because he has offended against God's majesty. These Sophists of ours stumble because they do not pay attention to James's statement, "Whoever sins in one point is already made guilty of all, for he who forbade killing also forbade stealing" [James 2:10-11 p.], etc. Accordingly, it ought not to seem absurd when we say that death is the just payment for each several sin, for each one deserves God's just wrath and vengeance. But you would be a foolish reasoner if you concluded, on the contrary, that man can be reconciled to God by a single good work when by his many sins he deserves God's wrath.

eCHAPTER XIX

CHRISTIAN FREEDOM

(Necessity of a doctrine of Christian freedom, which has three parts, the first seen in Gal., chs. 1 to 3)
*1. Need for a right understanding of the Christian doctrine of freedom**

aWe must now discuss Christian freedom. He who proposes to summarize gospel teaching ought by no means to omit an explanation of this topic. For it is a thing of prime necessity, and apart from a knowledge of it consciences dare undertake almost nothing without doubting; they hesitate and recoil from many things; they constantly waver and are afraid. eBut freedom is especially an appendage of justification and is of no little avail in understanding its power. Indeed, those who seriously fear God will enjoy the incomparable benefit of this doctrine, one that impious and Lucianic men[1] humorously satirize with their witticisms. For in the spiritual drunkenness that has laid hold upon them every sort of impudence is lawful. Accordingly, here is the right place to introduce this topic. aIt was profitable to put off a

---

[1] *"Lucianici homines,"* i.e., men of the spirit of Lucian of Samosata (d. ca. 200), who satirized Christian belief and practice in his *De morte Peregrini.*

fuller discussion of it to this place, although we have lightly touched upon it several times before.[2]

For, as soon as Christian freedom is mentioned, either passions boil or wild tumults rise unless these wanton spirits are opposed in time, who otherwise most wickedly corrupt the best things. Some, on the pretext of this freedom, shake off all obedience toward God and break out into unbridled license. Others disdain it, thinking that it takes away all moderation, order, and choice of things. What should we do here, hedged about with such perplexities? Shall we say good-by to Christian freedom, thus cutting off occasion for such dangers? But, as we have said, unless this freedom be comprehended, neither Christ nor gospel truth, nor inner peace of soul, can be rightly known. Rather, we must take care that so necessary a part of doctrine be not suppressed, yet at the same time that those absurd objections which are wont to arise be met.

2. Freedom from the law

[a]Christian freedom, in my opinion, consists of three parts.[3] The first: that the consciences of believers, in seeking assurance of their justification before God, should rise above and advance beyond the law, forgetting all law righteousness. For since, as we have elsewhere shown, the law leaves no one righteous, either it excludes us from all hope of justification or we ought to be freed from it, and in such a way, indeed, that no account is taken of works. For he who thinks that in order to obtain righteousness he ought to bring some trifle of works is incapable of determining their measure and limit but makes himself debtor to the whole law. Removing, then, mention of law, and laying aside all consideration of works, we should, when justification is being discussed, embrace God's mercy alone, turn our attention from ourselves, and look only to Christ. For there the question is not how we may become righteous but how, being unrighteous and unworthy, we may be reckoned righteous. If consciences wish to attain any certainty in this matter, they ought to give no place to the law.

Nor can any man rightly infer from this that the law is super-

---

[2] II. vii. 14, 15; III. xi. 17, 18.
[3] Melanchthon, *Loci communes* (1521), ed. H. Engelland, *Melanchthons Werke in Auswahl* II. i. 129; tr. C. S. Hill, pp. 214 f. The 1559 edition (*Loci praecipui*) distinguishes four stages (*gradus*) of Christian liberty: the remission of sins, the illumination of the spirit, political life not subject to the Mosaic law, and freedom of conscience in things indifferent (ed. Engelland, *op. cit.*, II. ii. 764–772).

fluous for believers,[4] since it does not stop teaching and exhorting and urging them to good, even though before God's judgment seat it has no place in their consciences. For, inasmuch as these two things are very different, we must rightly and conscientiously distinguish them. The whole life of Christians ought to be a sort of practice of godliness, for we have been called to sanctification [I Thess. 4:7; cf. Eph. 1:4; I Thess. 4:3]. Here it is the function of the law, by warning men of their duty, to arouse them to a zeal for holiness and innocence. But where consciences are worried how to render God favorable, what they will reply, and with what assurance they will stand should they be called to his judgment, there we are not to reckon what the law requires, but Christ alone, who surpasses all perfection of the law, must be set forth as righteousness.

3. The argument of Galatians*

ªAlmost the entire argument of the letter to the Galatians hinges upon this point. For those who teach that Paul in this contends for freedom of ceremonies alone are absurd interpreters, as can be proved from the passages adduced in the argument. Such passages are these: That Christ "became a curse for us" to "redeem us from the curse of the law" [Gal. 3:13]. Likewise: "Stand fast in the freedom wherewith Christ has set you free, and do not submit again to the yoke of slavery. Now I, Paul, say . . . that if you receive circumcision, Christ will become of no advantage to you. . . . And every man who receives circumcision is a debtor to the whole law. For any of you who are justified by the law, Christ has become of no advantage; you have fallen away from grace" [Gal. 5:1–4 p.]. These passages surely contain something loftier than freedom of ceremonies! ᶜOf course I admit that Paul is there discussing ceremonies, for his quarrel is with false apostles who were trying to reintroduce into the Christian church the old shadows of the law that had been abolished by Christ's coming. But for the discussion of this question, the higher topics upon which the whole controversy rested had to be considered. First, because the clarity of the gospel was obscured by those Jewish shadows, Paul showed that we have in Christ a perfect disclosure of all those things which were foreshadowed in the Mosaic ceremonies. Further, because those impostors imbued the common people with the very wicked notion that this obedience obviously availed to deserve God's grace, Paul here strongly in-

---

[4] Cf. Servetus, *On the Righteousness of Christ's Kingdom* (1532) iii, "a comparison of the law and the gospel," D 7a–8b (tr. Wilbur, *Two Treatises of Servetus*, pp. 239–241).

sists that believers should not suppose they can obtain righteousness before God by any works of the law, still less by those paltry rudiments! And at the same time he teaches that through the cross of Christ they are free from the condemnation of the law, which otherwise hangs over all men [Gal. 4:5], so that they may rest with full assurance in Christ alone. This topic properly pertains to our argument. Finally, he claims for the consciences of believers their freedom, that they may not be obligated in things unnecessary.[5]

(*The second, freedom of conscience willingly obeying without compulsion of the law, 4–6*)
4. *Freedom from the constraint of the law establishes the true obedience of believers*

[a]The second part, dependent upon the first, is that consciences observe the law, not as if constrained by the necessity of the law, but that freed from the law's yoke they willingly obey God's will.[6] For since they dwell in perpetual dread so long as they remain under the sway of the law, they will never be disposed with eager readiness to obey God unless they have already been given this sort of freedom. By an example we shall more briefly and clearly arrive at the meaning of this. The precept of the law is that "we love our God with all our heart, with all our soul, and with all our strength" [Deut. 6:5]. To bring this about, our soul must first be emptied of all other feeling and thought, our heart cleansed of all desires, and our powers gathered and concentrated upon this one point. They who have progressed farther than all others on the Lord's way are yet far distant from that goal. For even though they love God deeply and with sincere affection of heart, they have a great part of their heart and soul still occupied with fleshly desires, by which they are drawn back and prevented from hastening forward to God. Indeed, they struggle with much effort, but the flesh partly weakens their powers, partly draws them to itself. What are they to do here, while they feel that there is nothing they are less able to do than to fulfill the law? They will, they aspire, they try, but they do nothing with the required perfection. If they look upon the law, whatever work they attempt or intend they see to be accursed. And there is no reason for any

---

[5] Calvin asserts liberty of conscience "*in rebus non necessariis.*" Cf. Rupert Meldenius (Peter Meiderlin), *Paraenesis votiva pro pace ecclesiae* (1626), motto at end: "*In necessariis unitas, in non necessariis libertas, in omnibus caritas.*" (McNeill, *Unitive Protestantism*, pp. 267 f., note 12; 311.)

[6] Cf. Melanchthon, *Loci communes*, ed. Engelland, p. 137; tr. Hill, p. 224: "They who are in Christ as driven by the Spirit to do the law . . ."

man to deceive himself by concluding that his work is not entirely evil because it is imperfect, and that God nonetheless finds acceptable what is good in it.[7] For unless its rigor be mitigated, the law in requiring perfect love condemns all imperfection. Let him therefore ponder his own work, which he wished to be adjudged in part good, and by that very act he will find it, just because it is imperfect, to be a transgression of the law.

5. Freedom from constraint makes us capable of joyous obedience
ᵃSee how all our works are under the curse of the law if they are measured by the standard of the law! But how, then, would unhappy souls gird themselves eagerly for a work for which they might expect to receive only a curse? But if, freed from this severe requirement of the law, or rather from the entire rigor of the law, they hear themselves called with fatherly gentleness by God, they will cheerfully and with great eagerness answer, and follow his leading. To sum up: Those bound by the yoke of the law are like servants assigned certain tasks for each day by their masters. These servants think they have accomplished nothing, and dare not appear before their masters unless they have fulfilled the exact measure of their tasks. But sons, who are more generously and candidly treated by their fathers, do not hesitate to offer them incomplete and half-done and even defective works, trusting that their obedience and readiness of mind will be accepted by their fathers, even though they have not quite achieved what their fathers intended. Such children ought we to be, firmly trusting that our services will be approved by our most merciful Father, however small, rude, and imperfect these may be. ᵇThus also he assures us through the prophet: "I will spare them as a man spares his son who serves him" [Mal. 3:17]. The word "spare" is clearly here used in the sense of "to be indulgent or compassionately to overlook faults,"[8] while also mention is made of "service." ᵃAnd we need this assurance in no slight degree, for without it we attempt everything in vain. For God considers that he is revered by no work of ours unless we truly do it in reverence toward him. But how can this be done amidst all this dread, where one doubts whether God is offended or honored by our works?

---

[7] Fisher, *Confutatio*, art. xxxi, p. 492.

[8] *"Parcere pro indulgere vel humaniter ad vitia connivere"* (VG: *"dissimulant les vices"*). For Calvin's explanation of the Hebrew word חָמַל as "to overlook or spare" and hence "to pardon or take pity on," see Comm. Jer. 15:5; Comm. Joel 2:18.

*6. Emancipated by grace, believers need not fear the remnants of sin**

ᵃAnd this is the reason why the author of The Letter to the Hebrews refers to faith all the good works of which we read as being done among the holy fathers, and judges them by faith alone [Heb. 11:2 ff.; 11:17; etc.]. In the letter to the Romans, there is a famous passage on this freedom, wherein Paul reasons that sin ought not to rule us [Rom. 6:12 and 6:14, conflated], for we are not under the law but under grace [Rom. 6:14]. For he had exhorted believers not to let "sin reign in" their "mortal bodies" [Rom. 6:12], nor to "yield" their "members to sin as weapons of iniquity," but to "give" themselves "to God as those who have come to life from the dead, and" their "members to God as weapons of righteousness" [Rom. 6:13]. On the other hand, they might object that they still bore with them their flesh, full of lusts, and that sin dwelt in them. Paul adds this consolation, in freedom from the law. It is as if he said: "Even though they do not yet clearly feel that sin has been destroyed or that righteousness dwells in them, there is still no reason to be afraid and cast down in mind as if God were continually offended by the remnants of sin, seeing that they have been emancipated from the law by grace, so that their works are not to be measured according to its rules. Let those who infer that we ought to sin because we are not under the law understand that this freedom has nothing to do with them. For its purpose is to encourage us to good.

Freedom in "things indifferent" with proofs from Romans, 7–9

7. ᵃThe third part of Christian freedom lies in this: regarding outward things that are of themselves "indifferent,"⁹ we are not bound before God by any religious obligation preventing us from sometimes using them and other times not using them, indifferently. And the knowledge of this freedom is very necessary for us, for if it is lacking, our consciences will have no repose and there will be no end to superstitions. Today we seem to many to be unreasonable because we stir up discussion over the unrestricted

---

⁹ "ἀδιάφοροι," things indifferent, a topic discussed in many contexts in Calvin's time. Cf. Melanchthon's *Apology of the Augsburg Confession* XV. 52 (*Concordia Triglotta*, pp. 328 f.: "For love's sake we do not refuse to observe adiaphora with others"). For Calvin, the subject has been examined by T. W. Street, *John Calvin on Adiaphora, an Exposition* (doctoral dissertation, Union Theological Seminary, New York, 1954). Referring to this section, Dr. Street stresses the high importance for Calvin of liberty in adiaphora (pp. 66 f.). Cf. IV. x. 22. See also R. S. Wallace, *Calvin's Doctrine of the Christian Life,* pp. 309 f.

eating of meat, use of holidays and of vestments, and such things, which seem to them vain frivolities.

But these matters are more important than is commonly believed. For when consciences once ensnare themselves, they enter a long and inextricable maze, not easy to get out of. If a man begins to doubt whether he may use linen for sheets, shirts, handkerchiefs, and napkins, he will afterward be uncertain also about hemp; finally, doubt will even arise over tow. For he will turn over in his mind whether he can sup without napkins, or go without a handkerchief. If any man should consider daintier food unlawful, in the end he will not be at peace before God, when he eats either black bread or common victuals, while it occurs to him that he could sustain his body on even coarser foods. If he boggles at sweet wine, he will not with clear conscience drink even flat wine, and finally he will not dare touch water if sweeter and cleaner than other water. To sum up, he will come to the point of considering it wrong to step upon a straw across his path, as the saying goes.[10]

Here begins a weighty controversy, for what is in debate is whether God, whose will ought to precede all our plans and actions, wishes us to use these things or those. As a consequence, some, in despair, are of necessity cast into a pit of confusion; others, despising God and abandoning fear of him, must make their own way in destruction, where they have none ready-made. For all those entangled in such doubts, wherever they turn, see offense of conscience everywhere present.

8. Freedom in the use of God's gifts for his purposes*

[a]"I know," says Paul, "that nothing is common" (taking "common" in the sense of "profane"), "but it is common for anyone who thinks it common" [Rom. 14:14 p.]. With these words Paul subjects all outward things to our freedom,[11] provided our minds are assured that the basis for such freedom stands before God.

---

[10] Calvin's discerning comment here on the conscience entrapped in a compulsive and progressively severe austerity may be compared with his counsels of moderation in the enjoyment of God's temporal gifts in III. x. 1–4. Some early monastic texts contain warnings against such extremes, especially with reference to fasting. See, for example, Cassian, *Conferences* xxi. 13, 14 (MPL 41. 1187–1190; CSEL 13. 587–590; tr. NPNF 2 ser. XI. 508 f.); *Sayings of the Fathers* X. 1 (LCC XII. 105). However, in the instance of Dioscorus of Namisias, a protracted resolute reduction of food and drink is held exemplary: *Sayings of the Fathers* IV. 13 (LCC XII. 50).

[11] *"Res omnes externas libertati nostrae subiicit."* Cf. III. x. 4: *"in rebus externis libertas."* In this and the following section Calvin's Christian view of the adiaphora finds expression. This is not to deny his debt to the Stoics in clarification of the concept. Cf. E. F. Meylan, "The Stoic Doctrine of Indiffer-

But if any superstitious opinion poses a stumbling block for us, things of their own nature pure are for us corrupt. For this reason, he adds: "Happy is he who does not judge himself in what he approves. But he who judges, if he eats, is condemned, because he does not eat of faith. For whatever is not of faith is sin" [Rom. 14:22–23 p.].

Amidst such perplexities, do not those who show themselves rather bold by daring all things confidently, nonetheless to this extent turn away from God? But they who are deeply moved in any fear of God, when they are compelled to commit many things against their conscience, are overwhelmed and fall down with fright. All such persons receive none of God's gifts with thanksgiving, yet Paul testifies that by this alone all things are sanctified for our use [I Tim. 4:4–5]. Now I mean that thanksgiving which proceeds from a mind that recognizes in his gifts the kindness and goodness of God. For many of them, indeed, understand them as good things of God which they use, and praise God in his works; but inasmuch as they have not been persuaded that these good things have been given to them, how can they thank God as the giver?

To sum up, we see whither this freedom tends: namely, that we should use God's gifts for the purpose for which he gave them to us, with no scruple of conscience, no trouble of mind. With such confidence our minds will be at peace with him, and will recognize his liberality toward us. cFor here are included all ceremonies whose observance is optional, that our consciences may not be constrained by any necessity to observe them but may remember that by God's beneficence their use is for edification made subject to him.

9. Against the abuse of Christian freedom for gluttony and luxury!

aBut we must carefully note that Christian freedom is, in all its parts, a spiritual thing. Its whole force consists in quieting frightened consciences before God—that are perhaps disturbed and troubled over forgiveness of sins, or anxious whether unfinished works, corrupted by the faults of our flesh, are pleasing to God, or tormented about the use of things indifferent. Accordingly, it is perversely interpreted both by those who allege it as an excuse for their desires that they may abuse God's good gifts to their own lust and by those who think that freedom does not

ent Things and the Conception of Christian Liberty in Calvin's *Institutio Christianae Religionis*" (*Romanic Review* VIII [1937], 135–145).

exist unless it is used before men, and consequently, in using it have no regard for weaker brethren.

Today men sin to a greater degree in the first way. There is almost no one whose resources permit him to be extravagant who does not delight in lavish and ostentatious banquets, bodily apparel, and domestic architecture; who does not wish to outstrip his neighbors in all sorts of elegance; who does not wonderfully flatter himself in his opulence. And all these things are defended under the pretext of Christian freedom. They say that these are things indifferent. I admit it, provided they are used indifferently. But when they are coveted too greedily, when they are proudly boasted of, when they are lavishly squandered, things that were of themselves otherwise lawful are certainly defiled by these vices.

Paul's statement best distinguishes among things indifferent: "To the clean all things are clean, but to the corrupt and unbelieving nothing is clean, inasmuch as their minds and consciences are corrupted" [Titus 1:15, cf. Vg.]. For why are the rich cursed, who have their consolation, who are full, who laugh now [Luke 6:24–25], who sleep on ivory couches [Amos 6:4], "who join field to field" [Isa. 5:8], whose feasts have harp, lyre, timbrel, and wine [Isa. 5:12]? Surely ivory and gold and riches are good creations of God, permitted, indeed appointed, for men's use by God's providence. And we have never been forbidden to laugh, or to be filled, or to join new possessions to old or ancestral ones, or to delight in musical harmony, or to drink wine. True indeed. But where there is plenty, to wallow in delights, to gorge oneself, to intoxicate mind and heart with present pleasures and be always panting after new ones—such are very far removed from a lawful use of God's gifts.

Away, then, with uncontrolled desire, away with immoderate prodigality, away with vanity and arrogance—in order that men may with a clean conscience cleanly use God's gifts. Where the heart is tempered to this soberness they will have a rule for lawful use of such blessings. But should this moderation be lacking, even base and common pleasures are too much. It is a true saying that under coarse and rude attire there often dwells a heart of purple,[12] while sometimes under silk and purple is hid a simple humility. Thus let every man live in his station, whether slenderly, or moderately, or plentifully, so that all may remember God nourishes them to live, not to luxuriate. And let them regard this as the law of Christian freedom; to have learned with Paul, in whatever state they are, to be content; to know how to be humble and exalted; to have been taught, in any and all circum-

12 The source of this saying has not been identified.

stances, to be filled and to hunger, to abound and to suffer want [Phil. 4:11–12].

(Relation of Christian freedom to the weak and to the question of offenses, 10–13)
10. Against the abuse of Christian freedom to the injury of the weak!
ᵃIn this respect also many err; they use their freedom indiscriminately and unwisely, as though it were not sound and safe if men did not witness it. By this heedless use, they very often offend weak brothers. You can see some persons today who reckon their freedom does not exist unless they take possession of it by eating meat on Fridays.¹³ I do not blame them for eating meat, but this false notion must be driven from their minds. For they ought to think that from their freedom they obtain nothing new in men's sight but before God, and that it consists as much in abstaining as in using. If they understand that it makes no difference in God's sight whether they eat meat or eggs, wear red or black clothes, this is enough and more. The conscience, to which the benefit of such freedom was due, is now set free. Consequently, even if men thereafter abstain from meat throughout life, and ever wear clothes of one color, they are not less free. Indeed, because they are free, they abstain with a free conscience. But in having no regard for their brothers' weakness they slip most disastrously, for we ought so to bear with it that we do not heedlessly allow what would do them the slightest harm.

But it is sometimes important for our freedom to be declared before men. This I admit. Yet we must with the greatest caution hold to this limitation, that we do not abandon the care of the weak, whom the Lord has so strongly commended to us.

11. On offenses
ᵃHere, then, I shall say something about offenses¹⁴—how they are to be distinguished, which ones avoided, which overlooked. From this we may afterward be able to determine what place

¹³ In 1522 some Zurich citizens, to celebrate their Scriptural liberty, held meat dinners on Fridays, and on Ash Wednesday the printer Christopher Froschauer and others, in Zwingli's presence, ate "two dried sausages." (Kidd, *Documents*, p. 390.) These, or similar, incidents may have been remembered here.
¹⁴ "*De scandalis.*" The topic of giving offense in religious practices is treated by Calvin in his treatise *De scandalis* (1550) (OS II. 162–240; CR VIII. 1–84; tr. A. Golding, *A Little Booke Concernyng Offences*, 1567). Cf. Melanchthon, *Loci communes* (1521) at end; ed. Engelland, *op. cit.*, pp. 161 ff.; tr. Hill, *op. cit.*, pp. 265 ff.

there is for our freedom among men. Now I like that common distinction between an offense given and one received, inasmuch as it has the clear support of Scripture and properly expresses what is meant.

If you do anything with unseemly levity, or wantonness, or rashness, out of its proper order or place, so as to cause the ignorant and the simple to stumble, such will be called an offense given by you, since by your fault it came about that this sort of offense arose. And, to be sure, one speaks of an offense as given in some matter when its fault arises from the doer of the thing itself.

An offense is spoken of as received when something, otherwise not wickedly or unseasonably committed, is by ill will or malicious intent of mind wrenched into occasion for offense.[15] Here is no "given" offense, but those wicked interpreters baselessly so understand it. None but the weak is made to stumble by the first kind of offense, but the second gives offense to persons of bitter disposition and pharisaical pride. Accordingly, we shall call the one the offense of the weak, the other that of the Pharisees. Thus we shall so temper the use of our freedom as to allow for the ignorance of our weak brothers, but for the rigor of the Pharisees, not at all!

For Paul fully shows us in many passages what must be yielded to weakness. "Receive," he says, "those weak in faith." [Rom. 14:1 p.] Also: "Let us no more pass judgment upon one another, but rather not put a stumbling block or occasion to fall in the way of our brother" [Rom. 14:13 p.], and many passages with the same meaning, which are more suitably sought in their place than referred to here. The sum is: "We who are strong ought to bear with the infirmities of the weak, and not to please ourselves; but let each of us please his neighbor for his good, to edify him" [Rom. 15:1–2 p.; for v. 2, cf. Vg.]. In another place: "But take care lest your freedom in any way cause offense to those who are weak." [I Cor. 8:9 p.] Likewise: "Eat whatever is sold in the meat market without raising any question on the ground of conscience." [I Cor. 10:25.] "Now I say your conscience, not another's.[16] . . . In short, be so that you may give no offense to Jews or to Greeks or to the church of God." [I Cor. 10:29, 32 p.] Also, in another passage: "You were called to freedom, brothers, only do not use your

---

[15] In this section, Calvin varies his language by using without distinction *"offensio"* and *"offendiculum"* as well as *"scandalum."* Cf. Melanchthon: "A scandal is an offense by which either faith or charity is injured in a neighbor" (ed. Engelland, *op. cit.*, p. 161; tr. Hill, *op. cit.*, p. 265 f.).

[16] An inversion of I Cor. 10:29: it is given correctly in sec. 16, near the end.

freedom as an opportunity for the flesh but through love be servants of one another." [Gal. 5:13.] So indeed it is. Our freedom is not given against our feeble neighbors, for love makes us their servants in all things; rather it is given that, having peace with God in our hearts, we may also live at peace with men.

We learn from the Lord's words how much we ought to regard the offense of the Pharisees: He bids us let them alone because they are blind leaders of the blind. [Matt. 15:14.] His disciples had warned him that the Pharisees had been offended by his talk. [Matt. 15:12.] He answered that they were to be ignored and their offense disregarded.

12. On the right use of Christian freedom and the right renunciation of it

ªStill the matter will remain in doubt unless we grasp whom we are to consider weak, whom Pharisees. If this distinction is removed, I do not see what use for freedom really remains in relation to offenses, for it will always be in the greatest danger. But Paul seems to me most clearly to have defined, both by teaching and by example, how far our freedom must either be moderated or purchased at the cost of offenses.[17] When Paul took Timothy into his company, he circumcised him. [Acts 16:3.] But he could not be brought to circumcise Titus. [Gal. 2:3.] Here was a diversity of acts but no change of purpose or mind. That is, in circumcising Timothy, although he was "free from all," he made himself "a slave to all"; and "to the Jews" he "became as a Jew" in order to win Jews; to those under the law he "became as one under the law . . . that" he "might win those under the law" [I Cor. 9:19–20 p.]; "all things to all men that" he "might save many" [I Cor. 9:22 p.], as he elsewhere writes. We have due control over our freedom if it makes no difference to us to restrict it when it is fruitful to do so.

What he had in view when he strongly refused to circumcise Titus he testifies when he thus writes: "But even Titus, who was with me, was not compelled to be circumcised, though he was a Greek, but because of false brethren surreptitiously brought in, who slipped in to spy out our freedom, which we have in Christ Jesus, that they might bring us into bondage—to them we did not yield submission, even for a moment, that the truth of the gospel might be preserved among you" [Gal. 2:3–5 p.]. We have

---

[17] "*Vel moderanda . . . vel offendiculis redimenda.*" The answer lies in care for charity and the neighbor's good, but this principle is to be guarded from hypocritical pretense (sec. 13).

need also to assert our freedom if through the unjust demands of false apostles it be endangered in weak consciences.

We must at all times seek after love and look toward the edification of our neighbor. "All things," he says elsewhere, "are lawful to me, but not all things are helpful. All things are lawful, but not all things build up. Let no one seek his own good but another's." [I Cor. 10:23–24 p.] Nothing is plainer than this rule: that we should use our freedom if it results in the edification of our neighbor, but if it does not help our neighbor, then we should forgo it. There are those who pretend a Pauline prudence in abstaining from freedom, while there is nothing to which they apply it less than to the duties of love. To protect their own repose, they wish all mention of freedom to be buried; when it is no less important sometimes to use our neighbors' freedom for their good and edification than on occasion to restrain it for their own benefit. ᶜBut it is the part of a godly man to realize that free power in outward matters has been given him in order that he may be the more ready for all the duties of love.

*13. We must not on pretext of love of neighbor offend against God**

ᵃAll that I have taught about avoiding offenses I mean to be referred to things intermediate and indifferent. For the things necessary to be done must not be omitted for fear of any offense. ᵇFor as our freedom must be subordinated to love, so in turn ought love itself to abide under purity of faith. ᵃSurely, it is fitting here also to take love into consideration, even as far as to the altar [cf. Matt. 5:23–24]; that is, that for our neighbor's sake we may not offend God. We must not approve the intemperance of those who do nothing without raising a tumult and who prefer to tear into everything rather than open a matter gently. But those people also are not to be listened to who, after making themselves leaders in a thousand sorts of wickedness, pretend that they must act so as not to cause offense to their neighbors [cf. I Cor. 8:9]; as if they were not in the meantime building up their neighbors' consciences into evil, especially when they ever stick fast in the same mud without hope of getting out. And suave fellows are they who, whether their neighbor is to be instructed in doctrine or in example of life, say he must be fed with milk while they steep him in the worst and deadliest opinions. Paul recalls that he fed the Corinthians with milk. [I Cor. 3:2.] But if the papal Mass had then been among them, would he have performed sacrifice to furnish them with milk? No, for milk is not poison. They are therefore lying when they claim to be feeding those whom they are cruelly killing under the guise of blandishments. Granted that this sort of dissimulation is to be approved for the moment—how long will they feed their children with this same milk? For if these never grow up sufficiently to be able to bear even some light food at least, it is certain that they were never brought up on milk.

ᵉTwo reasons prevent me from contending with them more sharply: first, their banalities are scarcely worth refuting, since they are deservedly despised among all sane men; secondly, I do not want to do again what I have already abundantly demonstrated in special treatises.[18] Only let my readers remember this: with whatever obstacles Satan and the world strive to turn us away from God's commands or delay us from following what he appoints, we must nonetheless vigorously go forward. Then, whatever dangers threaten, we are not free to turn aside even a finger-nail's breadth from this same God's authority, and it is not lawful under any pretext for us to attempt anything but what he allows.

(*Freedom and conscience in relation to traditions, and to civil government, 14–16*)

14. Freedom of conscience from all human law

ªNow, since believers' consciences, having received the privilege of their freedom, which we previously described, have, by Christ's gift, attained to this, that they should not be entangled with any snares of observances in those matters in which the Lord has willed them to be free, we conclude that they are released from the power of all men. For Christ does not deserve to forfeit our gratitude for his great generosity—nor consciences, their profit. And we should not put a light value upon something that we see cost Christ so dear, since he valued it not with gold or silver but with his own blood [I Peter 1:18–19]. Paul does not hesitate to say that Christ's death is nullified if we put our souls under men's subjection [cf. Gal. 2:21]. For in certain chapters of the letter to the Galatians, Paul is solely trying to show how to us Christ is obscured, or rather extinguished, unless our consciences stand firm in their freedom. They have surely fallen away from it if they can, at men's good pleasure, be ensnared by the bonds of

---

[18] These writings include: *Epistolae duae de rebus hoc saeculo cognitu apprime necessariis* (Basel, 1537) (OS I. 287–362; Epistle i tr. in Calvin, *Tracts* III. 360–411: *On Shunning the Unlawful Rites of the Ungodly*); *What a Believer Ought to Do . . . Among the Papists* (1543) (CR VI. 537–578; tr. R. G. [1548]: *The Mynde of John Calvyne, What a Faithful Man Ought to Do, Dwelling Among the Papists*); *Excuse of John Calvin to the Nicodemites* (1544) (CR VI. 589–614); *On Avoiding Superstition* (1549) (CR VI. 617–640); *De scandalis* (1550) (OS II. 162–240).

laws and constitutions[19] [cf. Gal. 5:1, 4]. But as this is something very much worth knowing, so it needs a longer and clearer explanation. For immediately a word is uttered concerning the abrogating of human constitutions, huge troubles are stirred up, partly by the seditious, partly by slanderers—as if all human obedience were at the same time removed and cast down.

15. The two kingdoms

ᵃTherefore, in order that none of us may stumble on that stone, let us first consider that there is a twofold government in man: one aspect is spiritual, whereby the conscience is instructed in piety and in reverencing God; the second is political, whereby man is educated for the duties of humanity and citizenship that must be maintained among men. These are usually called the "spiritual" and the "temporal" jurisdiction[20] (not improper terms) by which is meant that the former sort of government pertains to the life of the soul, while the latter has to do with the concerns of the present life—not only with food and clothing but with laying down laws whereby a man may live his life among other men holily, honorably, and temperately. For the former resides in the inner mind, while the latter regulates only outward behavior. The one we may call the spiritual kingdom, the other, the political kingdom. Now these two, as we have divided them, must always be examined separately; and while one is being considered, we must call away and turn aside the mind from thinking about the other. There are in man, so to speak, two worlds, over which different kings and different laws have authority.

ᶜThrough this distinction it comes about that we are not to misapply to the political order the gospel teaching on spiritual freedom, as if Christians were less subject, as concerns outward government, to human laws, because their consciences have been set free in God's sight; as if they were released from all bodily servitude because they are free according to the spirit.

Then, because there can be some delusion in the constitutions that seem to apply to the spiritual kingdom, among these also we should discern what must be considered lawful, as consonant with God's word, and on the other hand what ought to have no place among the godly. Of civil government we shall speak in another

---

[19] By "constitutions" Calvin has reference to the papal constitutions mentioned in IV. x. 8, 9.

[20] Cf. the thirteenth-century papal claim of *"plenitudo potestatis in temporalibus et in spiritualibus,"* combatted by Marsiglio of Padua and William of Ockham. See esp. Ockham, *De imperatorum et pontificum potestate,* ed. C. K. Brampton, chs. i–iv, pp. 5–10; ch. xi, p. 24.

place.[21] Concerning e(c)church claws e(c)also I forbear to speak for the present, for a fuller treatment will more appropriately come in the fourth book, where the power of the church will be discussed.[22]

Let this be the conclusion of the present discussion. dThe question, as I have said, is not of itself very obscure or involved. However, it troubles many because they do not sharply enough distinguish the outer forum, as it is called, and the forum of conscience.[23] Moreover, the difficulty is increased by the fact that Paul enjoins obedience toward the magistrate, not only for fear of punishment, but for conscience' sake [Rom. 13:1, 5]. From this it follows that consciences are also bound by civil laws. But if this were so, all that we said a little while ago and are now going to say about spiritual government would fall.

To resolve this difficulty it first behooves us to comprehend what conscience is; we must seek the definition from the derivation of the word. For just as when through the mind and understanding men grasp a knowledge of things, and from this are said "to know," this is the source of the word "knowledge," so also when they have a sense of divine judgment, as a witness joined to them, which does not allow them to hide their sins from being accused before the Judge's tribunal, this sense is called "conscience."[24] For it is a certain mean between God and man, because it does not allow man to suppress within himself what he knows, but pursues him to the point of convicting him. This is what Paul understands when he teaches that conscience also testifies to men, where their thought either accuses or excuses them in God's judgment [Rom. 2:15–16]. A simple knowledge could reside, so to speak, closed up in man. Therefore this awareness which hales man before God's judgment is a sort of guardian appointed for man to note and spy out all his secrets that nothing may remain buried in darkness. Whence that ancient proverb: "Conscience is a thousand witnesses."[25] For the same reason, Peter

[21] IV. xx.

[22] IV. x, xi.

[23] "Conscientiae forum." Cf. IV. x. 3. See R. J. Deferrari and others, A Lexicon of St. Thomas Aquinas, s.v. "forum," p. 443; Catholic Encyclopedia, art. "forum."

[24] See HDRE IV, art. "conscience," opening paragraph, and section "Greek and Roman," esp. pp. 39 ff.; Cicero, Nature of the Gods III. xxxv. 85 (LCL edition, pp. 370 f.); Plutarch, Moralia 476 (LCL Plutarch, Moralia VI. 234 f.); Aquinas, Summa Theol. I. lxxix. 13; I IIae. xix. 5; De veritate xvii. 5 (A. T. Gilby, St. Thomas Aquinas: Philosophical Texts, p. 115); and literature cited in W. F. Arndt and F. W. Gingrich, A Greek-English Lexicon of the New Testament, s.v. "συνείδησις."

[25] Quintilian, Institutes of Oratory V. xi. 41 (LCL Quintilian II. 294 f.). Cf. Comm. Seneca, On Clemency I. xiii: "magis vis conscientiae" (CR V. 102).

also put "the response of a good conscience to God" [I Peter 3:21] as equivalent to peace of mind, when, convinced of Christ's grace, we fearlessly present ourselves before God. And when the author of The Letter to the Hebrews states that we "no longer have any consciousness of sin" [Heb. 10:2], he means that we are held to be freed or acquitted, so that sin may no longer accuse us.

16. Bondage and freedom of conscience

ᵈTherefore, as works have regard to men, so conscience refers to God. A good conscience, then, is nothing but inward integrity of heart. In this sense, Paul writes that the fulfillment of the law is love from a clear conscience and sincere faith [cf. I Tim. 1:5]. Afterward, also, in the same chapter, he shows how much it differs from understanding, stating that "certain persons made shipwreck of their faith" [I Tim. 1:19] because they had forsaken good conscience. By these words he signifies a lively inclination to serve God and a sincere effort to live piously and holily.

Sometimes, indeed, it is also extended to men, as when the same Paul, according to Luke, declares that he "took pains" to walk "with a clear conscience toward God and men" [Acts 24:16]. But this was said because the fruit of a good conscience flows forth and comes even to men. But properly speaking, as I have already said, it has respect to God alone.

Hence it comes about that a law is said to bind the conscience when it simply binds a man without regard to other men, or without taking them into account. For example: God not only bids us keep our minds pure and undefiled from all lust but also forbids all obscenity of speech and outward licentiousness. My conscience is subject to the observance of this law, even if no man lived on earth. So he who conducts himself intemperately not only sins because he gives a bad example to his brothers but has a conscience bound by guilt before God.

In things of themselves indifferent there is another consideration. For we ought to abstain from anything that might cause offense, but with a free conscience. Thus Paul speaks concerning meat consecrated to idols. "If anyone," he says, "raises a scruple, do not touch it, for conscience' sake. Now I mean the other man's conscience—not yours." [I Cor. 10:28–29 p.][26] A believer who, though previously warned, nonetheless ate meat of this sort would sin. But however necessary it may be with respect to his brother for him to abstain from it, as God enjoins, he still does not cease to keep freedom of conscience. We see how this law, while binding outward actions, leaves the conscience free.

[26] Cf. sec. 11, note 16.